NEW YORK STATE

CHRISTIANE BIRD

NEW YORK

CANADA

16

401

Ogdensburg

Canton

37

11

Peterborough

401

Kingston

Alexandria
Bay

Cape
Vincent

Watertown

81

12

Toronto

Lake Ontario

104

Oswego

Rome

Oneida Lake

90

Syracuse

Eric Canal

104

Rochester

Auburn

Skaneateles
Lake

Batavia

Canandaigua

Seneca
Falls

Owasco
Lake

405

90

20

Geneva

Finger Lakes

Cayuga
Lake

Cortland

13

Niagara Falls

Buffalo

Canandaigua
Lake

81

3

20A

Letchworth
State Park

390

21

Keuka
Lake

Seneca
Lake

Ithaca

Binghamton

Watkins
Glen

219

17

Corning

Elmira

6

Dunkirk

90

Salamanca

417

Wellsville

Olean

Troy

Chautauqua
Lake

Chautauqua

Allegany
State Park

Bradford

15

14

Jamestown

Allegany
Reservoir

6

62

PENNSYLVANIA

Williamsport

80

Oil City

Ridgway

219

0   25 mi

0   25 km

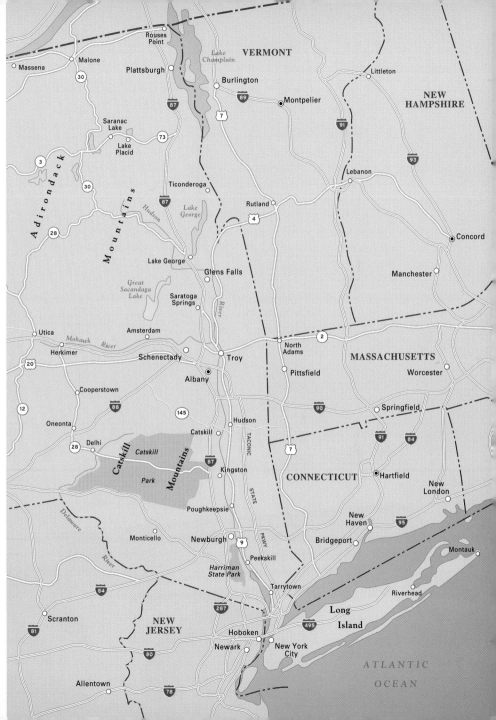

DISCOVER NEW YORK STATE

New York is not an easy state to get to know
or understand. Home to both the largest city in the United States and
the largest semi-wilderness area east of the Mississippi, vast acres of
farmland and an enormous number of industries, some of the most
sophisticated attractions in the world and a fair number of homespun
spots, New York defies most, if not all, generalizations.

Most discussions of New York State focus on New York City.
No matter what the hour of day or night, New York City teems with
activity, offering visitors a sumptuous smorgasbord of neighborhoods, museums, historic sites, shops, restaurants, hotels, theaters,
nightclubs, parks, and events to sample. There's never enough time
to do everything you want to do in the Big Apple, whether you're a
first-time visitor, a 100th-time visitor, or a resident.

Washington Square Arch, New York City

And yet, the Big Apple is but a smudged dot on the New York State map, occupying far less than one percent of the state's total land mass. Upstate sprawls above the city reaching as far north as Canada and almost as far west as Ohio. In it, you'll find another sumptuous smorgasbord of delights, most of these more rural in nature. Among them are the fine white-sand beaches of Long Island, the great river estates of the Hudson Valley, the enigmatic peaks and valleys of the Catskills, the world-class museums of Leatherstocking Country, the vast hiking and canoeing network of the Adirondacks, the Thousand Islands, the Finger Lakes, Niagara Falls, and the historic cities of Albany, Ithaca, Rochester, and Buffalo.

What New York City and New York State have in common are sheer size and diversity. New York City alone is home to approximately

East Hampton Beach, Long Island

eight million people, while upstate holds another 12 million inhabitants scattered across approximately 47,370 square miles. Though it seldom gets credit as such, New York is one of the oldest states in the union, with landmarks that date back to the 1600s.

New York's first European settlers were the Dutch, followed by the English, French, German Protestants, and Scots. African slaves were first brought to the colony in 1626, and the first Jews – fleeing persecution in Spain and Brazil – arrived in Manhattan in the 1650s. By the time of the Revolutionary War, half of the colony's population claimed English descent. Today, the state is home to more than 200 ethnic groups, most living in New York City.

Historically, New Yorkers have also shared a love for making money. Though this is especially true for New York City, it also applies to the whole state. The Dutch first came to Fort Orange – today's Albany – not to start a new settlement, but to engage in the prosperous fur trade. They were followed first by frugal New Englanders, seeking more fertile farmland, and then by hardworking immigrants, all deeply intent on getting ahead. Nearly a third of the country's top

canoeing on the Cheumung River, The Finger Lakes

500 corporations got their starts in metropolitan New York, while upstate served as the spawning grounds for Eastman Kodak, Bausch & Lomb, Xerox, General Electric, IBM, Endicott-Johnson, and Corning Glass Works, to name but a few.

A counterpoint to New York's many business tycoons has been its many farmers. Up until 1860, agriculture was the state's most important industry, and even today, it plays a major economic role. Farmland represents about 25 percent of the state's total acreage, and New York ranks third in the nation, behind California and Wisconsin, in dairy production.

Yet despite New York's healthy commercial appetite, often bordering on the greedy and the crass, it is also a state of dreamers. Something in the land's silken fields and dark blue twilights seems to bring out all-but-impossible hopes and longings, most destined to go unfulfilled.

From the late 1700s to mid-1800s especially, New York supported an extraordinary number of idealists, reformers, and religious leaders. Mother Ann Lee founded the first Shaker community near Albany. Joseph Smith founded the Mormon religion in Palmyra. John

Macy's Herald Square, New York City

Humphrey Noyes established the Perfectionist utopian society in Oneida. The Fox Sisters founded the Spiritualist movement near Rochester. Elizabeth Cady Stanton and Susan B. Anthony spearheaded the women's rights movement from Auburn and Rochester. Frederick Douglass, William Seward, and Gerrit Smith helped lead the abolitionist movement from the Finger Lakes.

Some of this idealistic spirit continues into the modern era. As one of the most progressive states in the union, New York has been the first to institute everything from the first seat belt law and the first acid rain law to the first state-assisted housing program and the first Council on the Arts. New York consistently spends more than nearly every other state in nearly every social category, from education to hospitals. Following the tragic events of September 11, 2001, when more than 2,700 people died in terrorist attacks on the World Trade Center, ordinary New Yorkers poured out by the thousands to give what they could, in time and money, to ease the crisis.

New York has something to offer everyone. Come once, and you're sure to come again.

Heron Hill Winery, The Finger Lakes

Contents

MAP CONTENTS

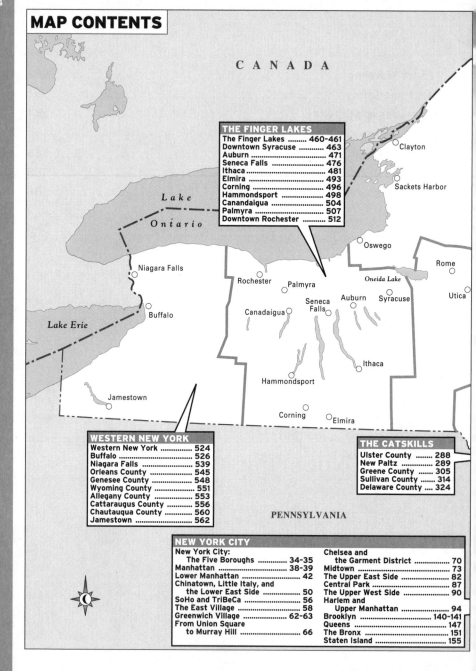

CANADA

Lake Ontario

Lake Erie

PENNSYLVANIA

Niagara Falls
Buffalo
Jamestown
Rochester
Palmyra
Canadaigua
Seneca Falls
Auburn
Syracuse
Oneida Lake
Oswego
Rome
Utica
Ithaca
Hammondsport
Corning
Elmira
Clayton
Sackets Harbor

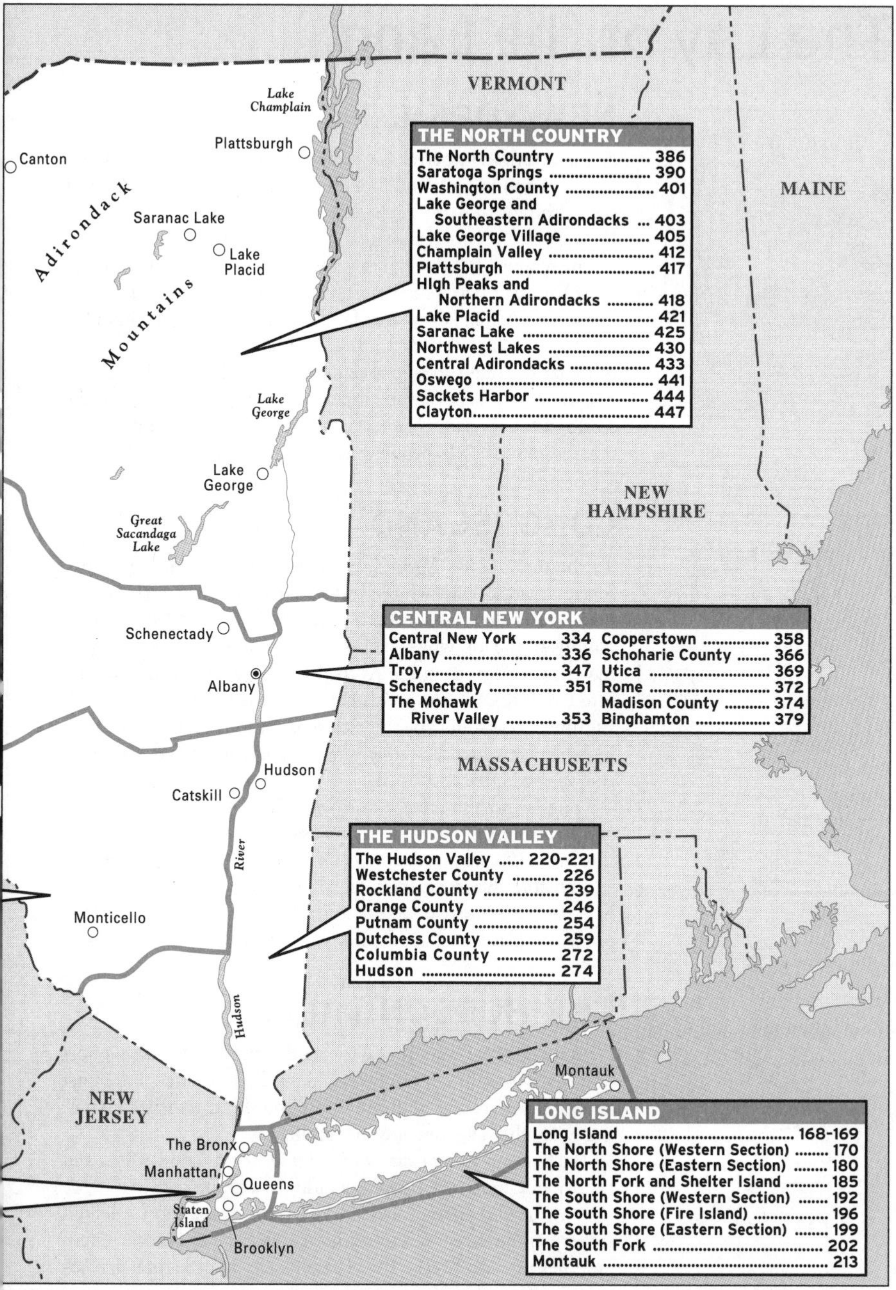
VERMONT
Lake Champlain
Plattsburgh
Canton
Adirondack Mountains
Saranac Lake
Lake Placid
MAINE
THE NORTH COUNTRY
The North Country 386
Saratoga Springs 390
Washington County 401
Lake George and Southeastern Adirondacks ... 403
Lake George Village 405
Champlain Valley 412
Plattsburgh 417
High Peaks and Northern Adirondacks 418
Lake Placid 421
Saranac Lake 425
Northwest Lakes 430
Central Adirondacks 433
Oswego 441
Sackets Harbor 444
Clayton.. 447
Lake George
Great Sacandaga Lake
NEW HAMPSHIRE
Schenectady
Albany
CENTRAL NEW YORK
Central New York 334
Albany 336
Troy 347
Schenectady 351
The Mohawk River Valley 353
Cooperstown 358
Schoharie County 366
Utica 369
Rome 372
Madison County 374
Binghamton 379
MASSACHUSETTS
Hudson
Catskill
Hudson River
Monticello
THE HUDSON VALLEY
The Hudson Valley 220-221
Westchester County 226
Rockland County 239
Orange County 246
Putnam County 254
Dutchess County 259
Columbia County 272
Hudson 274
NEW JERSEY
Montauk
The Bronx
Manhattan
Queens
Staten Island
Brooklyn
LONG ISLAND
Long Island 168-169
The North Shore (Western Section) 170
The North Shore (Eastern Section) 180
The North Fork and Shelter Island 185
The South Shore (Western Section) 192
The South Shore (Fire Island) 196
The South Shore (Eastern Section) 199
The South Fork 202
Montauk 213

The Lay of the Land

NEW YORK CITY

At New York's southern base, wedged between New Jersey, Connecticut, and Long Island, lies the famed Big Apple, spread over five boroughs (Manhattan, Brooklyn, Queens, the Bronx, Staten Island) covering a total of 301 miles. Only the Bronx sits on the mainland; the rest of the city occupies a group of islands in New York Bay, where the Hudson River meets the Atlantic. Manhattan and Staten Island are islands in their own right. Brooklyn and Queens are on the western tip of Long Island.

By far the state's most popular destination, New York City is a vast, dazzling, shape-shifting metropolis that belongs more to the world than it does to the state. Great art, theater, restaurants, nightlife, shopping, hotels, people-watching, and people—it's all here.

LONG ISLAND

To the east of New York City extends long, thin Long Island, home to world-class white-sand beaches, which stretch out for many miles along its southern coast. Jones Beach is the most famous of the lot, while the Fire Island National Seashore may be the most unusual. At the island's eastern end, it divides into two forks. On the South Fork, find the fabled Hamptons, summer playground of the rich and famous. The towns here look like New England–style villages, albeit ones filled with posh restaurants, inns, and B&Bs.

Long Island also offers a northern "Gold Coast," lined with grand turn-of-the-19th-century mansions, many of which are now museums. On the North Fork beckon dozens of inviting vineyards and pristine villages centered on white-steeple churches and town halls. Between the two forks lies Shelter Island, one of the least populated places on Long Island, accessible only by ferry.

THE HUDSON VALLEY

Directly north of New York City lies the Hudson Valley, extraordinarily rich with historic, cultural, and scenic sites. Foremost among them are several dozen sumptuous Hudson River estates, many of which are open to the public.

The Hudson Valley is also known for its world-renowned art and history museums, eye-popping outdoor sculpture gardens, West Point, Revolutionary War sites, and some of the most splendid scenery in the state—not to mention a plethora of upscale restaurants, resorts, and B&Bs. The Hudson Valley may be rural in character, but its ambience is most decidedly sophisticated.

THE CATSKILLS

Across from the Hudson Valley rise the romantic and strangely evocative **Catskill Mountains.** Albeit run-down in more than a few spots, the Catskills—once a popular resort area—are now in the midst of being "rediscovered." Here you'll find striking scenic vistas, the fabled villages of **Woodstock and Saugerties,** Max Yasgur's former farm (where the 1968 Woodstock festival took place), excellent hiking and fishing, and many one-of-a-kind, offbeat sights.

The region's **Ulster County** is home to the **Shawangunk Mountains,** a rock-climber's paradise dotted with glacial lakes, and **New Paltz,** home to the "the oldest street in America with its original buildings." Sullivan County holds the Upper Delaware River, a favorite haunt among inner tube enthusiasts, and some of the best trout fishing sites in the world.

CENTRAL NEW YORK

In Central New York lie **Albany,** the state capital, founded by the Dutch; and **Cooperstown,** home to the National Baseball Hall of Fame and Museum. Albany and its environs are rich with historic sites, including the New York State Capitol Building, handsome house museums, and the Stockade in nearby **Schenectady,** first settled in 1690. Cooperstown contains two other world-class museums while all around spread the lush, forested, lake-speckled hills of **"Leatherstocking Country."**

Not far from Cooperstown is Howe Caverns, the site of an extensive labyrinth of cathedral-like caves and the superb Iroquois Indian Museum. Through the region runs the Mohawk River Valley, once a teeming industrial belt that's still home to a handful of factories and many historic sites.

NORTH COUNTRY

The North Country begins north of Albany in Victorian-era **Saratoga Springs**—host to the country's finest horse racing meet every summer—and extends north to the isolated **Thousand Islands,** scattered over the St. Lawrence River between New York and Canada. In between sprawls Adirondack Park, the East's greatest wilderness. In it, you'll find 42 peaks over 4,000 feet and an intricate maze of navigable lakes and rivers, along with towns, resorts, and commercial attractions. At the park's southern end is **Lake George,** anchored by a village of the same name. Near the park's center is **Lake Placid,** the site of the 1932 and 1980 Olympics. To the park's east is magnificent **Lake Champlain,** which borders Vermont.

THE FINGER LAKES

West of Central New York laze the long, narrow Finger Lakes, where the Iroquois flourished before the coming of the white man. There are six major Finger Lakes, of which Skaneateles is the most beautiful, and four minor ones.

The Finger Lakes are flanked by vineyards, stately 19th-century towns, and a surprising number of historic landmarks, many of which have to do with civil rights and women's history. **Auburn** was once home to abolitionists Harriet Tubman and William Seward; **Seneca Falls** was the site of the first women's rights convention, held in 1848. In the region's southern tier lie **Ithaca,** a progressive college town surrounded by gorges and waterfalls, and **Corning,** home to the popular Corning Museum of Glass. To the region's far west lies Letchworth Park and its "Grand Canyon of the East," while to the north are **Lake Ontario,** a Great Lake, and the friendly, cultured city of **Rochester.**

WESTERN NEW YORK

Far Western New York is home to **Buffalo,** the state's second largest city, once known for its steel industry and many theaters; and **Niagara Falls,** New York's second most popular tourist attraction (after New York City), bordering Canada.

To the region's south are the dark, mysterious foothills of the **Allegheny Mountains,** which extend deep into Pennsylvania. Highlights of a visit here include the all-but-undiscovered Allegany State Park and the Chautauqua Institution, a self-contained Victorian village-cum-learning camp for families and adults.

Planning Your Trip

New York is a large and extraordinarily diverse state, so to get the most out of your trip, it's best to plan your itinerary carefully.

Most visitors will probably want to start their trip in New York City, and then head out to Long Island, the Hudson Valley, the Catskills, Central New York, and/or the North Country. Visitors who wish to concentrate their time in the Finger Lakes or Western New York could choose to start their trip in Rochester or Buffalo instead.

Many visitors come to New York City for its cultural, historical, and commercial attractions. Many come to upstate New York for its outdoors—beaches, forests, mountains, rivers, and lakes—as well as historic sites, relaxing hostelries, and picturesque villages. A trip that combines a visit to both provides the best of two very different worlds.

WHEN TO GO

New York City has plenty to offer year-round, but the best times to visit are spring, early summer, and fall, when temperatures are moderate and conducive to exploring on foot. Autumns are often especially wonderful, with deep cobalt blue skies and the excitement of a new season in the air. Winter in New York can be bitterly cold (in the 20s, with bone-chilling winds), mid-summers stiflingly hot (in the 90s, with high humidity).

The climate upstate varies considerably from region to region. Long Island is lovely in the spring and fall, but if you're a beach lover, you'll probably want to come in summer, when the beaches are in full swing; bear in mind, however, that between Memorial Day and Labor Day, traffic on the island is horrendous. The Hudson Valley is a terrific destination at any time of year, though some attractions close down in winter and mid-summers are often hot and humid. The Catskills and Central New York are best visited in the summer, when they provide a welcome retreat from the heat, and in the fall, when fall foliage is a major draw.

Unless you're a skier, summer and early fall are really the only times to visit the Adirondacks and Thousand Islands. Winters are frigid up here, and many attractions are only open in July and August. Fall foliage is usually magnificent, especially in the Adirondacks.

The Finger Lakes and Western New York are best visited in the summer and fall as well. In the winter, temperatures near Lake Ontario (including Rochester) and Lake Erie (including Buffalo) drop precipitously.

WHAT TO TAKE

Visitors to New York City will want to bring comfortable walking shoes, casual clothes, and a few items of more sophisticated attire—including a sports jacket for men and nicer pants or skirts for women. During the day, most anything goes, but in the evening, many restaurants, theaters, and nightspots are filled with well-dressed fashionable folk. Black is the hip New Yorker's color of choice. Upstate New York is casual at almost all times, though cities such as Rochester and Albany also have their more sophisticated spots.

Since much of New York State is quite humid during the summer, with temperatures in the 80s and 90s, bring plenty of short-sleeved cotton shirts and tees. In the fall and spring, you'll need a jacket, long-sleeved shirts and pants, and rain gear. In the winter, dress for cold winds, icy rains, and snow.

Even if you don't plan to do any serious hiking while upstate, bring along a pair of sturdy shoes or sneakers—they'll come in handy for casual exploring. Insect repellent is a must, and sunscreen is essential in summer.

Although most places in New York State take credit cards, you can't count on small restaurants, shops, and museums doing so—especially upstate. Be sure to have enough cash on you to cover such expenditures.

Explore New York State

TWO WEEKS IN NEW YORK STATE

An excellent way to get a taste of both urban and rural New York is to spend a few days in the Big Apple and then head north to the historic Hudson Valley, Catskills, and Adirondacks.

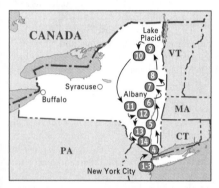

DAY 1: NEW YORK CITY

Start your day early with a visit to the Statue of Liberty and Ellis Island. Eat a simple lunch from a vendor's cart in Battery Park, which offers glorious views of New York Harbor. In the afternoon, visit the Empire State Building. At night, take in a Broadway show and dinner in the theater district.

DAY 2: NEW YORK CITY

Spend the morning at the Metropolitan Museum of Art, where you'll also find a pleasant café and restaurant. Afterward, head south through Central Park. When the park ends at 59th Street, continue south on Fifth Avenue, shopping or window-shopping along the way.

DAY 3: NEW YORK CITY

In the morning, take in the Museum of Modern Art and Rockefeller Center in Midtown, or the Guggenheim Museum or Frick Collection on the Upper East Side. In the early evening, take a walk over the Brooklyn Bridge.

DAY 4: TARRYTOWN

Head north on Route 9 about 30 minutes to Tarrytown in the Hudson Valley, where you can tour the historic homes of Washington Irving (Sunnyside), John D. Rockefeller Sr. (Kykuit) and/or Jay Gould (Lyndhurst). If time permits, take a late afternoon stroll in the Rockefeller State Park Preserve. At night, dine in one of the town's many excellent restaurants; if your budget permits, overnight in one of its two "castles."

DAY 5: BEACON, HYDE PARK, AND RHINEBECK

Head north on Route 9 for about an hour to reach Beacon, home to the Dia:Beacon, a huge contemporary art museum. Then continue on for about a half-hour to reach Hyde Park, where the Culinary Institute of America offers a tasty lunch at its Apple Pie Bakery Café. In Hyde Park, you'll find Franklin Delano Roosevelt's Home, Library, and Museum; Valkill, which was Eleanor Roosevelt's retreat, and the Vanderbilt Mansion.

DAY 6: HUDSON AND ALBANY

Continue north another 40 miles or so into Columbia County, stopping in the historic town of Hudson, home to a Persian-style castle, **Olana, the American Museum of Firefighting,** lots of antique shops, and plenty of restaurants for lunch. Afterward, head on to Albany, about a half hour further north on I-87. Stop at the Albany Heritage Area Visitor Center for a good introduction to this historic region or go straight to the **New York State Museum** at the Empire State Plaza.

DAY 7: SARATOGA SPRINGS

Continue another 40 minutes north on I-87 to Saratoga Springs. In the morning, visit the **Heritage Area Visitors Center, Congress Park,** and **Canfield Casino,** and shop and eat lunch along Broadway. In the afternoon, take in the **National Museum of Racing** and/or indulge in a spa treatment at the **Saratoga Spa State Park.**

DAY 8: SARATOGA SPRINGS AND GLENS FALLS

Before leaving the Saratoga area, make a stop at the **Saratoga National Historic Park,** where the battles that turned the course of the American Revolution were fought. Then continue on Route 9 another half hour to Glens Falls, home to the **Hyde Collection,** a mansion filled with Old Masters paintings.

DAY 9: LAKE PLACID

Take Route 9N north along the shores of Lake George and Lake Champlain. In picturesque Westport, continue on Route 9N (which turns west), past the mountain villages of Elizabethtown and Keene, to Route 73, which leads to Lake Placid. Spend the rest of the day exploring Lake Placid and, if time permits, the **Olympic Ski Jump Complex** and/or **John Brown Farm State Historic Site.**

DAY 10: THE ADIRONDACKS

Drive eight miles south of Lake Placid and visit the Adirondak Loj on the shores of Heart Lake. Set out from the lodge and spend the day hiking, snowshoeing, or cross-country skiing on trails in the Adirondacks.

DAY 11: COOPERSTOWN

Take Routes 73 and 9N east to the New York Throughway (I-87) and head south to the Albany area, where you can pick up I-88, which leads to the Cooperstown area. Have a late lunch in the pretty village and then explore its shops and lakefront or visit one of its three first-class museums **(the National Baseball Hall of Fame, Farmers' Museum, Fenimore Art Museum).** Have a cocktail at the Otesaga Hotel, a delicious grande dame of a 1902 hostelry.

DAY 12: WOODSTOCK AND SAUGERTIES

Spend the morning exploring more of Cooperstown's attractions. After lunch, take Route 28 south, which leads into the heart of the Catskills. Pass the pretty mountain towns of Andes and Margaretville before arriving in **Woodstock** and **Saugerties,** both home to numerous restaurants, shops, and B&Bs.

DAY 13: NEW PALTZ AND ORANGE COUNTY

From the Woodstock/Saugerties area, head south to New Paltz and historic **Huguenot Street.** After lunch in town, continue on to Orange County, where, depending on your interests, you can visit **Washington's Headquarters, the Storm King Art Center,** or **West Point.**

DAY 14: BEAR MOUNTAIN STATE PARK

Take Route 9W south to Bear Mountain State Park, where you can take a short hike or drive to the top of Bear Mountain. Continue on to the pretty villages of **Piermont** and **Nyack,** good places for lunch and antique shopping. Then head back to New York City.

CULTURE OUTSIDE NEW YORK CITY

Yes, all you New York City–philes and New York State–phobes, there *is* culture outside the Big Apple and its immediate environs (meaning Long Island and the Hudson Valley).

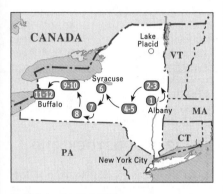

the general public, or the **Saratoga Spa State Park,** a pristine European-like retreat complete with mineral baths. At night, dine in one of the city's many first-class restaurants and take in some music at one of its many music clubs; among them is **Caffe Lena,** the oldest continuously running coffee house in America. If you visit during the summer, when the outdoor **Saratoga Performing Arts Center** is in session, you can also take in a performance by the New York City Ballet, the New York City Opera, the Philadelphia Orchestra, or a variety of rock, pop, and jazz stars.

DAY 1: ALBANY

One especially good place to find it is in the region where Central New York and the North Country meet. Begin your tour in Albany, whose downtown is home to the **Albany Institute of History and Art,** the **New York State Museum,** and a variety of unique historic house-museums. At night, check to see what's playing at the **Egg** (the capital's premier arts venue), in the city's various theaters, or in its jazz clubs.

DAY 2: SARATOGA SPRINGS

The next morning, take I-87 north for about 40 minutes to reach Victorian-era Saratoga Springs. Here you'll find several more interesting museums, including the **Tang Teaching Museum and Art Gallery at Skidmore College,** the **National Museum of Dance,** and the **National Museum of Racing and Hall of Fame.** Spend the morning at one and have lunch in one of the many casual restaurants along Broadway. In the afternoon, make a stop at **Yaddo,** a famed artists' retreat whose gardens are open to

DAY 3: EAGLE BRIDGE, GLENS FALLS, AND SARATOGA SPRINGS

From Saratoga Springs, meander northeast on Route 67 for about an hour to reach Eagle Bridge, where the **homestead of the painter Grandma Moses** is now a gallery operated by her descendants; even more interesting than the gallery itself is the surrounding picturesque countryside, which more than resembles a Grandma Moses painting. Head back to the northwest for about an hour to reach Glens Falls (or drive directly north from Saratoga Springs to Glens Falls on I-87 for about 30 miles), home to the remarkable **Hyde Collection.** Also in Glens Falls is the **Chapman Historical Museum,** and another half hour north, on the shores of Lake George, is Bolton Landing, home to the **Marcella Sembrich Opera Museum,** open during the summer only. Return to Saratoga Springs for another evening of nightlife.

DAY 4: SCHENECTADY, CANAJOHARIE, AND COOPERSTOWN

Head south on I-87 and then west on Route 146 for about a half hour to reach Schenectady, home to the **Stockade.** Have a simple lunch in the historic district or a more elaborate one in the nearby **Glen Sanders Mansion,** partially housed in a Dutch stone home. Continue west on I-90 for about 40 minutes to reach the **Canajoharie Art Gallery** in the small town of the same name; it's said to be the "finest private gallery of any municipality of its size." About a half hour west of Canajoharie is Herkimer, which doesn't have much in the way of culture but is a must-stop for fans of Theodore Dreiser's *An American Tragedy*. The novel was based on the sensational Gillette murder trial of 1906 and it was in the striking red-brick Herkimer County Courthouse that the case was tried. Travel on Route 28 south for about 45 minutes to spend the night in Cooperstown, home to many fine inns and restaurants.

DAY 5: COOPERSTOWN

Spend the day exploring Cooperstown, which likes to think of itself as the most famous small town in America. Built on the shores of Otsego Lake, the town is best known for its **National Baseball Hall of Fame,** which will take a full morning to explore. Have lunch in one of the casual restaurants on or just off Main Street and then head to the world-class **Fenimore Art Museum,** which houses the state's premier collection of folk art, fine art, and Native American art. Explore these in the late afternoon/early evening or have a cocktail at the grand 1902 Otesaga Hotel. Dine here as well, or try one of the town's many excellent restaurants. In summer, Cooperstown is host to the renowned **Glimmerglass Opera Festival,** which takes place in an amphitheater overlooking Otsego Lake.

DAY 6: UTICA, SYRACUSE, AND SKANEATELES

From Cooperstown, head north on Route 28 and west on I-90 to reach Utica – about an hour's drive away. Here, you'll find the **Munson-Williams-Proctor Institute** – partially designed by architect Philip Johnson – which contains more than 5,000 works by the likes of Picasso, Dali, and Pollock, and the "Voyage of Life" series by Hudson River School artist Thomas Cole. Have lunch in cheery, bustling **Grimaldi's,** one of the oldest and biggest Italian restaurants in town, and then travel another hour west on I-90 to reach Syracuse. Spend the afternoon at the I. M. Pei-designed **Everson Museum of Art,** which contains one of the world's largest collections of ceramics. Overnight in one of the city's luxurious B&Bs, or travel west another 40 minutes to reach the village and lake of Skaneateles. The furthest village east of the Finger Lakes, Skaneateles is also the most beautiful.

DAY 7: ITHACA

Take a scenic drive down the east or west shore of Skaneateles Lake and then pick up Route 13, which will bring you to Ithaca – about an hour's drive away. Home to Cornell University and Ithaca College, the scenic, progressive town is all but surrounded by waterfalls and gorges, and offers much in the way of cultural attractions. Start your visit with a stop at Cornell's **Herbert Johnson Museum of Art,** which houses an especially strong collection of Asian and contemporary art. Have a late lunch at the Moosewood Restaurant, a famed health-foods eatery, and take a stroll down the pedestrian-only Commons, where you'll find lots of shops and art galleries. For dinner, you can choose between many first-rate restaurants. Take in a play, concert, or dance performance, and then retire to one of Ithaca's many luxurious B&Bs.

DAY 8: ELMIRA AND CORNING

Continue south on Route 13 for about 45 minutes to reach Elmira, once the summer home of Mark Twain. His restored study, a freestanding building modeled after a Mississippi steamboat pilot house, now stands on the Elmira College campus, where it is open to visitors during the summer. Also in Elmira is the **Arnot Museum,** a neoclassical mansion holding a fine collection of 17th- to 19th-century European paintings, including works by Breughel, Daubigny, Rousseau, and Millet. From Elmira, travel about 45 minutes southwest on Route 17 to reach Corning, whose famed **Corning Museum of Glass** is the third-most popular tourist destination in the state. The museum's collection includes everything from a Glass Sculpture Garden to objects that date back to 1400 B.C. Have a late lunch and dinner in Corning, home to many excellent restaurants, and overnight in one of its attractive B&Bs.

DAY 9: ROCHESTER

Take Route 17 west and I-395 north about 100 miles to reach Rochester, New York's third-largest city, long known for its cultural scene. A good first stop here is the **Memorial Art Gallery** in southeast Rochester. Connected with the University of Rochester, this small gem contains a little bit of everything, from ancient Chinese ceramics to American folk art. Have a late lunch in one of the many ethnic restaurants along nearby Monroe Avenue, and spend the afternoon at the **George Eastman House** and adjacent **International Museum of Photography,** which hosts superb photography exhibits. At night, dine in one of the city's many excellent restaurants and take in a performance of the renowned **Rochester Philharmonic Orchestra,** if possible, or attend an event at the **Eastman School of Music.**

DAY 10: ROCHESTER

On your second day in Rochester, make a stop at the **Rochester Museum and Science Center** to view "At the Western Door." This powerful permanent exhibit about the Seneca Nation examines Seneca life from pre-European contact in the 1550s to the present. Afterward, visit the **Strong Museum.** In the afternoon, travel about 20 miles southwest of the city to the **Genesee Country Village and Museum.** Return to Rochester for the night.

DAY 11: BUFFALO

Travel west on I-490 and I-90 about 80 miles to visit Buffalo, a city of striking architectural landmarks and unique cultural institutions. On your first morning, visit the **Albright-Knox Art Gallery,** the centerpiece of the city's art scene. Have lunch in the museum's airy Garden Restaurant or in one of the trendy restaurants along nearby Elmwood Avenue. In the afternoon, make a stop at the **Burchfield-Penney Art Center.** At night, have dinner in the **Theater District** downtown and take in a play; the opulent 1926 **Shea's Performing Arts Center** is an especially interesting venue. Buffalo has an impressive theater history dating back to the mid-1800s, and still offers much in the way of live theater.

DAY 12: BUFFALO

Spend the morning touring the **Darwin Martin House,** one of Frank Lloyd Wright's most important works (call ahead to verify hours and make reservations). Afterward, have lunch at the Anchor Bar, where Buffalo wings were invented. In the afternoon, visit the renowned **HallWalls Contemporary Arts Center** and/or the **CEPA Gallery;** Buffalo has an active alternative-arts scene. In the evening, catch some jazz at **Nietzche's,** the city's best-known jazz club, or the Colored Musicians Club, once the union local for black musicians.

DAY TRIPS FROM NEW YORK CITY

LONG ISLAND

Jones Beach

During the summer, join the hordes of New Yorkers making a day trip to Long Island's Jones Beach; the Long Island Railroad, leaving from Pennsylvania Station, offers packages. The six-mile-long beach and adjoining park, envisioned and planned by New York's master builder Robert Moses, is one of the most popular destinations on Long Island. Facilities include two pools, bathhouses, piers, picnic areas, basketball courts, and a 1.5-mile-long boardwalk where special events are often featured. Lifeguards are on duty May–September, while the Tommy Hilfiger at Jones Beach Theater hosts big-name popular entertainers on summer nights. If you opt to drive to Jones Beach rather than take the train, nine miles to the north is the town of Freeport, where you can take a stroll along the Nautical Mile, home to numerous seafood restaurants and gift shops.

Sailors Haven, Fire Island

If you prefer a less-hectic summer scene, you can also take the Long Island Railroad, followed by a ride on a ferry, to Fire Island's Sailors Haven. Here, you'll find a much wilder and emptier beach, dunes and grasses, and the unusual Sunken Forest – a scrappy, 300-year-old maritime forest located below sea level between two lines of sand dunes. A boardwalk leads from the ferry dock through the 40-acre forest and to the beach. Facilities include bathhouses, a snack bar, and interpretive center. Lifeguards are on duty May–September, when guided tours of the forest are also offered.

Oyster Bay

A popular day trip on the North Shore is Oyster Bay, home to Sagamore Hill, Theodore Roosevelt's former summer home. After touring the estate and its adjoining visitors center, have lunch in the Canterbury Ales Oyster Bar & Grill in the village or head east another six miles to Cold Spring Harbor. Here you'll find a number of other good lunch spots, along with attractive shops and art galleries, a fish hatchery, the Dolan DNA Learning Center (an arm of the Cold Spring Harbor Laboratory), and the Cold Spring Harbor Whaling Museum – all interesting places in which to while away the afternoon.

THE HUDSON VALLEY

Tarrytown

One of the best day trips in the Hudson Valley is Tarrytown, home to a plethora of mansions that once belonged to famous men. Among these are the former homes of Washington Irving (Sunnyside), John D. Rockefeller (Kykuit), and Jay Gould (Lyndhurst). Visit one of the mansion-museums in the morning and another in the afternoon, and have lunch in one of the village's many good restaurants. If time permits, make a stop in the Old Dutch Burying Ground, where Washington Irving found inspiration for The Legend of Sleepy Hollow, or the Union Church of Pocantico Hills, holding nine stunning stained-glass windows by artist Marc Chagall. During the summer, an especially enjoyable way to get to Tarrytown is via the NY Waterway ferryboats.

West Point and Storm King

Another good choice for a day trip in the Hudson Valley is West Point, perched on a cliff at a bend in the Hudson River, and the nearby Storm King Arts Center. Spend the morning at the United States Military Academy, where you'll find a fascinating museum of military history, a visitors center, and bus tours of the campus. Have lunch at the academy's **Thayer Hotel.** In the afternoon, take in the Storm King Arts Center, a stunning mountainside sculpture park featuring the work of world-famous artists spread out over 500 acres with great views. The center is only open from late spring to early fall.

THE CATSKILLS
New Paltz and Environs

Fall is an especially good time to make a day trip to the Catskills; the foliage there is often spectacular. On your way north, make a stop in New Paltz, founded by French Huguenots in the late 1600s. The main sight here is **Huguenot Street,** "the oldest street in America with its original buildings"; official walking tours are offered May–October. New Paltz also holds many good lunch spots. After lunch, continue north on Routes 213 and 209, past the scenic villages of High Falls, Stone Ridge, and Hurley. A bit further north, pick up Route 28, which will bring you into **Catskill Park.** Take a scenic drive on Route 28A around **Ashokan Reservoir,** if time allows, and then head east to the artsy village of **Woodstock,** home to numerous shops, galleries, and good restaurants.

EXPLORING THE OUTDOORS

THE ADIRONDACKS

Adirondack Park is New York's premier wilderness preserve, a six-million-acre refuge that contains an unusual mixture of public and private lands. In the park's center tower the **46 High Peaks,** most over 4,000 feet high.

The Adirondacks also hold the 2,000-acre **St. Regis Canoe Area** and over 100 miles of other canoe routes that run throughout the region. Canoe trips ranging in length from a day to a week or more can be set up on your own or through regional outfitters.

Nonoutdoors-types can also enjoy the region's magnificent beauty by swimming in or boating on one of its many lakes, or by simply driving along its many scenic highways and byways. **Blue Mountain Lake,** the northern part of **Lake George,** much of the western shores of **Lake Champlain,** and the routes and lakes of the High Peaks region are especially scenic.

THE CATSKILLS

New York's other premier outdoors area is **Catskill State Park,** a 900-square-mile preserve that, like Adirondack Park, includes both public and private lands. Day hikes of varying difficulty are especially plentiful here, especially in **Greene County,** which contains many of the park's highest peaks. One very popular hike is the historic **Escarpment Trail,** which stretches for 24 miles between Haines Falls and East Windham; parts of the trail have been in use for more than 150 years.

In the Ulster County section of the Catskill region, but not part of the Catskill mountain range, are the considerably more ancient **Shawangunk Mountains,** a mecca for rock-climbing enthusiasts. In the heart of the Shawangunks lie **Minnewaska State Park,** which holds two stunning glacier lakes, accessible by foot only; and the mountain-top **Mohonk Preserve,** laced with 28 miles of trails.

THE HUDSON VALLEY

The Hudson Valley region contains some stunning state parks. Nearest New York City, find the 5,000-acre **Bear Mountain State Park** and the 46,000-acre **Harriman State Park.** Bear Mountain is often thick with New York City folk on the weekends; Harriman, much less so. Both offer excellent hiking. Bear Mountain also holds the Bear Mountain Inn and a Wildlife Center, while Harriman offers the scenic Seven Lakes Drive and 200 miles of marked trails.

Putnam County is home to the **Constitution Marsh Sanctuary,** a 207-acre tidal marsh managed by the National Audubon Society, which operates a visitors center, and the 12,000-acre **Clarence Fahnestock State Park,** crisscrossed with hiking trails. Further north, in Columbia County, are **Taconic State Park** and **Lake Taghkanic State Park.** The former spreads over 5,000 acres and offers two separate recreation areas, complete with hiking trails and waterfalls; the latter is considerably smaller, but holds the lovely Lake Taghkanic.

CENTRAL NEW YORK

Near Albany lies **John Boyd Thatcher State Park,** where you'll find the unusual Indian Ladder Geological Trail, one of the richest fossil-bearing formations in the world. **Glimmerglass State Park,** on the shore of Otsego Lake in Cooperstown, features a swimming beach, hiking trails, and a grand neoclassical mansion now in the midst of being restored. The highly commercial **Howe Caverns** and much less commercial **Secret Caverns,** both in the town of Howe Caverns, offer glimpses of an underground New York filled with stalactites and stalagmites.

THE APPALACHIAN TRAIL

The famous Appalachian Trail, the 2,158-mile route that stretches from Georgia to Maine, cuts through only a small section of New York in the Hudson Valley region for about 90 miles. The trail, which travels through Orange, Putnam, and Dutchess Counties, can most easily be picked up at Bear Mountain, Harriman, and Clarence Fahnestock State Parks.

THE FINGER LAKES

Between Cayuga and Seneca Lakes lies the **Finger Lakes National Forest,** a 16,000-acre preserve laced with 25 miles of easy-to-moderate hiking trails. Though the region's terrain is largely flat, the forest does contain some high hills with excellent vistas.

The **Finger Lakes Trail** is a 557-mile route that begins at the Pennsylvania border and runs to the Catskills; six branch trails and two loop trails extend the system another 278 miles. Maps are available through the Finger Lakes Trail Conference.

The town of Ithaca is surrounded by deep gorges and thundering waterfalls, several of which run through the heart of the downtown. Some of the most stunning of these gorges and waterfalls can be found at the wild and rugged **Robert Treman State Park,** spread over 1,025 acres.

At the Finger Lakes' western edge lies the 17-mile-long **Letchworth Gorge,** dubbed the "Grand Canyon of the East." All around grows a dense, thicketed forest laced with about 20 miles of hiking trails. The park also contains various historic buildings and a museum.

WESTERN NEW YORK

At the westernmost end of the state you'll find the world-famous **Niagara Reservation State Park** and the all-but-unknown **Allegany State Park.** The former is home to the famed Niagara Falls and offers plenty of excellent vista points, along with a superb visitors center, geological museum, guided tours, and boat rides. The latter is one of the largest and wildest state parks in New York. Situated in the foothills of the Allegheny Mountains, it features 90 miles of hiking trails and two cobalt-blue lakes.

LONG ISLAND

Long Island contains excellent beach parks, including the Fire Island, Orient Beach, Hither Hills, and Montauk Point state parks. Most of 32-mile-long Fire Island belongs to the **Fire Island National Seashore** and is accessible by ferryboat and boat taxi only. The exceptions are **Robert Moses State**

Park and **Smith Point County Park,** located at either end of the island; at the end of the former is the striking 1858 Fire Island Lighthouse, accessible via a half-mile trail only. Fire Island is also home to the unique **Sunken Forest.**

Orient Beach State Park is a favorite among bird-watchers. **Hither Hills State Park** is known for its so-called Walking Dunes, which move three or more feet a year due to strong winds; trails here travel through cranberry bogs, beach terrain, and pine forests. **Montauk Point State Park,** at the very tip of the island, is an excellent fishing and bird-watching spot. Adjoining the park is another striking lighthouse, the Montauk Lighthouse, which is the oldest lighthouse still in operation in the state, commissioned by George Washington in 1792.

Long Island is also home to the state's third forest preserve: the 53,000-acre **Pine Barrens,** located near the island's eastern end. A five-mile trail leading through the park can be accessed near Riverhead.

AFRICAN AMERICAN HISTORIC SITES

It goes without saying that you'll find innumerable important African American historic sites in New York City, especially Harlem. Elsewhere in the state, historic African American sites are few and far between. Those that do exist, however, honor figures of enormous importance.

NEW YORK CITY

Begin your tour in Harlem with the **Studio Museum,** a world-class institution with changing exhibits by such masters as Romare Bearden and Jacob Lawrence. Then head to **The Apollo,** perhaps the single most important landmark in the history of African American music. The **Malcolm Shabazz Mosque** is where civil rights leader Malcolm X taught in the 1960s, and the **Schomburg Center** is a renowned institution for research in black culture, and includes a spacious art gallery and gift shop. While you're in Harlem, stop to see the **Abyssinian Baptist Church.** This is the former church of Adam Clayton Powell and has one of largest black congregations in the United States. Then there's **Striver's Row,** designed by architects McKim, Mead & White. It was once home to W. C. Handy and Eubie Blake, among numerous others.

In Lower Manhattan, stop by **Fraunces Tavern.** Many historians believe that the original Revolutionary War-era Fraunces Tavern, of which this is a replica, was owned by a black French West Indian. The former slave market in Lower Manhattan was one of the busiest slave markets of the 1700s and once stood on Wall Street. Only rediscovered in 1991, the **African Burial Grounds** may once have covered nearly six acres and held the remains of 20,000 African Americans. In the outer boroughs visit the **Louis Armstrong house** in Corona, Queens. The legendary trumpeter's home from the early 1940s until his death in 1971 is now a museum.

LONG ISLAND

In Hempstead, visit the **African American Museum.** It's one of the only African American museums in the state and has changing historical and cultural exhibits. The **Joseph Lloyd Manor House** on Lloyd Harbor Peninsula in Huntington was once home to Jupiter Hammon, a slave who became the first published black poet in America. **Sag**

Harbor was once the home port of many African American whaling-ship captains, some of whose mansions still stand along Main Street.

THE CATSKILLS

In Kingston, the Ulster County Courthouse has a plaque out front honoring abolitionist and evangelist Sojourner Truth, who won a lawsuit here in 1797 that saved her son from slavery. The Hardenberg House in Hurley is where Sojourner Truth spent the first nine years of her life, as a slave.

NORTH COUNTRY

In the North Country, the John Brown Farm State Historic Site in Lake Placid is the site of a farming community for escaped slaves established in 1849 by abolitionists Gerrit Smith and John Brown. You can find related exhibits in the Lake Placid–North Elba Historical Society Museum.

THE FINGER LAKES

Farther north in Syracuse visit the Jerry Rescue Monument. The monument honors William "Jerry" McHenry, who escaped from slavery in North Carolina to Syracuse. McHenry's subsequent recapture and rescue in 1851 was one of the early precipitating events leading up to the Civil War. In Auburn, save time for the Harriet Tubman Home. The escaped slave and abolitionist who made 19 trips south, rescuing more than 300 slaves, settled here after the Civil War. Then head up to the Frederick Douglass Statue and Grave in Rochester. The escaped slave, abolitionist, and writer settled in Rochester in 1847, and published his newspaper here for 17 years. His statue, erected in 1898, was the first in the United States to honor an African American.

WESTERN NEW YORK

In Western New York, visit Stations of the Underground Railroad in the Niagara Frontier. Seven "Stations," marked with sculptures, honor those who helped the many slaves who escaped through this region to Canada.

NATIVE AMERICAN HISTORIC SITES

Though it's seldom thought of in such terms, New York has a rich Native American history. Before the arrival of the Europeans, the area was home to two major tribal groups: the Algonquin and the Iroquois. The Algonquin lived in the south and along the Hudson River Valley, while the Iroquois spread out across the north. Today, the state is home to a number of major Native American museums and collections, along with a smattering of historic monuments.

NEW YORK CITY

In the Big Apple, visit the National Museum of the American Indian. A branch of the Smithsonian, it exhibits some of the finest Native American art and artifacts around.

LONG ISLAND

In Southold, check out the Indian Museum, a small museum housing one of the country's largest collections of Native American pottery. Also on Long Island is the Shinnecock Nation Cultural Center and Museum in Southampton. The museum shows artifacts of the past and present and is located on the Shinnecock Reservation, where a large powwow is held on Labor Day weekend. Indian Field in Montauk is a burial ground whose permanent residents were buried according to ancient custom, in a circle, sitting up.

CENTRAL NEW YORK

The Fenimore Art Museum in Cooperstown contains the Eugene and Clare Thaw Collection of American Indian Art, perhaps the most important privately owned collection of its kind. Another of the finest Native American museums in the state is the Iroquois Indian Museum in Howe Caverns, which holds a remarkable collection of contemporary Iroquois art.

Iroquois artifacts and modern art are on display at the Mohawk-Caughnawaga Museum and Kateri Tekakwitha Memorial Shrine in Fonda. Here, you'll also find an excavated Native American village and a shrine devoted to the first laywoman in North America to be declared "Blessed" by Pope John Paul II. Housed in a snug historic house, the Noteworthy Indian Museum in Amsterdam contains over 60,000 artifacts tracing the history of Native Americans in the Mohawk Valley. The Shako:Wi Cultural Center in Oneida is a modern center housing classrooms, a small gift shop, and a small museum dedicated to the Oneida Nation.

NORTH COUNTRY

At the Six Nations Indian Museum in Onchiota, you'll find a fantastic, delirious array of pictographs, paintings, basketwork, beadwork, quillwork, pottery, canoes, masks, drums, and lacrosse sticks – all collected by one man, Ray Fadden. Then there's the Akwesasne Museum in Hogansburg, featuring Mohawk medicine masks, wampum belts, carved cradle boards, water drums, modern artwork, basketry, and stunning historic photographs.

THE FINGER LAKES

Begin your tour in Syracuse with Saint Marie Among the Iroquois, which recreates the 17th-century world of the French Jesuits and Iroquois who once lived near Onondaga Lake. Then visit the Logan Monument at the Fort Hill Cemetery in nearby Auburn; the 57-foot-high obelisk honors the famed Cayuga orator who was born nearby.

At the other end of the Finger Lakes, the Ganondagan State Historic Site in Victor is the former site of an important Seneca village and granary, now equipped with historic walking trails and a visitors center. The Ontario County Courthouse in Canandaigua is where the Pickering Treaty, which granted whites the right to settle the Great Lakes Basin, was signed. A plaque outside the courthouse commemorates the event; an original copy of the treaty is in the Ontario County Historical Society Museum. The Mary Jemison Grave and Council House in Letchworth State Park is the grave of the "White Woman of the Genesee" and the site of the region's last Iroquois council meeting. In Rochester, the Rochester Museum contains "At the Western Door," a powerful permanent exhibit on the Seneca Nation.

WESTERN NEW YORK

The Forest Lawn Cemetery in Buffalo is the final resting place of the famed Seneca orator Red Jacket. Further south, in Salamanca, you'll find the Seneca-Iroquois National Museum, a thoughtful, well-laid-out museum covering the history of the Seneca Nation from its pre-history to the present day.

NEW YORK CITY

New York is a city people love to hate. It's dirty, it's crowded, it's crass, and it's loud. It's cynical, corrupt, cold, and uncomfortable. Worst of all, say some out-of-towners, there's something un-American about it. All that pushiness, all that traffic, all those people actually choosing to live in ugly apartment buildings with no green front lawns or white picket fences in sight. This can't be the American Dream, or the United States as our forefathers meant it to be. No, New York may be a fine place to visit, but it's no place to live.

New Yorkers don't disagree. In fact, they'll enthusiastically endorse any negative a visitor comes up with, and add a few of their own: New York's transportation system sucks, its taxes are too high, its real estate prices are exorbitant, and everything is way too expensive. The school system is falling apart, the middle class is being forced out, the job market is impossible, and everyone is only out for himself. No, New Yorkers sigh, wearily shaking their heads, New York is no place to live. …

But then again—they arch their eyebrows—it is the *only* place to live.

Imagine New York in the early morning, when a pink light bathes the buildings, and the sky turns from black to a shimmering blue. Imagine New York at rush hour when hundreds of thousands of workers whoosh energetically through the subways and streets. Imagine New York at midday, when the air crackles and pops with imagination and ideas and deals in the making. Imagine New York in the evening, when a quiet calm briefly descends and secrets are exchanged in shadow-filled bars and restaurants. And most of all, imagine New York at night, when the brilliant

TABITHA LAHR

HIGHLIGHTS

Statue of Liberty and Ellis Island: The country's most famous statue stands 151 feet tall, with a three-foot mouth and 25-foot waist. Between 1882 and 1924, 12 million immigrants beheld the sight of the statue while passing through the red-and-white Byzantine-style castle at Ellis Island (page 37).

Chinatown's Mott Street: The bustling heart of Chinatown is lined with restaurants, bakeries, tiny food stores, and cheery souvenir shops (page 51).

A Stroll Through SoHo: Wander down the main shopping drags of Broadway, West Broadway, Prince, and Spring, where you'll find everything from street vendors to chic boutiques (page 55).

Empire State Building: The quintessential skyscraper was erected during the Depression in an astonishing 14 months (page 72).

Times Square: Top talent is always hard at work in the extravagant theaters around neon-splashed Times Square (page 75).

Museum of Modern Art (MoMA): Newly renovated, with twice the exhibition space, MoMA is one of the world's foremost museums of modern art (page 79).

The Metropolitan Museum of Art: The largest museum in the Western Hemisphere houses nearly three million works of art from all over the world (page 83).

Central Park: The 843-acre "lungs of New York" is entirely human constructed, with every bush, tree, and rock planted by someone (page 86).

Coney Island and Brighton Beach: A magnificent boardwalk, old-fashioned amusement rides, tawdry snack stands, and a buoyant Russian community, Coney Island is quintessential old-time New York (page 143).

The Bronx Zoo and Botanical Garden: One of the world's largest and most important zoos, housing over 4,000 animals, many of which roam relatively freely in large landscaped habitats (page 150).

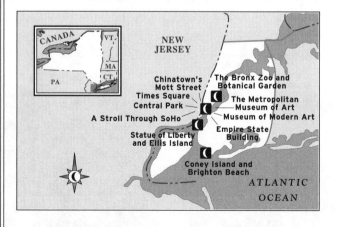

LOOK FOR **[** TO FIND RECOMMENDED SIGHTS, ACTIVITIES, DINING, AND LODGING.

lights beckon, warding off the darkness, and everything seems possible.

There's no other place in the United States quite like New York City. Where else can you find teeming sidewalks at most any hour of the day and night? Where else can you meet people of a dozen nationalities in just a few blocks? Where else can you choose from more than 18,000 eating establishments, 150 museums, 400 art galleries, 240 theaters, 50 dance spots, 60 live music spots, 90 institutions of higher learning, and 10,000 shops and boutiques?

John Steinbeck may have said it best. New York "is an ugly city," he wrote, "a dirty city. Its climate is a scandal. Its politics are used to frighten children. Its traffic is madness. Its competition is murderous. But there is one thing about it—once you have lived in New York and it has become your home, no other place is good enough."

PLANNING YOUR TIME

There's never enough time to explore New York City. That said, you can also see a lot in a few days, as Manhattan, where most of the city's most famous attractions are located, is a compact place with an excellent pub-lic transportation system. First-time visitors will probably want to spend a day visiting the **Empire State Building** and **Metropolitan Museum of Art,** perhaps taking a stroll in **Central Park** afterward. The next day could be devoted to the **Statue of Liberty, Ellis Island,** and a short walking tour of lower Manhattan, where highlights include **Wall Street** and the **South Street Seaport.** On your third day, explore the **streets of Chinatown, SoHo, and Greenwich Village.** At night, take in a **Broadway play,** visit a **jazz club,** and eat in one of the city's many **ethnic restaurants.**

If you have more time, spend a day at the **Museum of Modern Art** and take a stroll down Fifth Avenue and across East 42nd Street, visiting **Rockefeller Center, St. Patrick's Cathedral, the New York Public Library, Grand Central Station,** and the **United Nations** along the way. Or, explore the **American Museum of Natural History** and take the A Train up to revitalized **125th Street** in Harlem. A fifth day could be spent shopping, visiting another museum, and taking a closer look at Central Park. On your sixth day, walk over the **Brooklyn Bridge** to **Brooklyn Heights** or visit **Coney Island.**

Manhattan

To many people, Manhattan *is* New York. On this small island, just 12 miles long by three miles wide, are crowded most of the city's sky-scrapers, businesses, museums, theaters, hotels, restaurants, and famous sites. Though by far the smallest of the five boroughs in area, Man-hattan is by far the largest in reputation.

Manhattan was settled from south to north, with the first Dutchmen arriving near what is now known as Battery Park in 1500. By 1650, the city had spread northward to include to-day's Financial District, and by 1800, Green-wich Village was a thriving community. The wealthy began moving to the Upper East Side in the late 1800s, and the Dakota—New York's first grand apartment building—went up on the Upper West Side in 1884. Harlem existed as an independent farming community until 1873, when it was annexed to the borough.

LOWER MANHATTAN SIGHTS

New York City began down here, on this tip of an island where the Hudson and East Rivers meet. This is where the Dutch West India Com-pany established its first New World outpost, and where Peter Minuit "bought" Manhattan from the Algonquins for the grand sum of $24. This is where George Washington bade farewell to his troops at the end of the Revolutionary War, and where he was inaugurated as the first president of the United States. Here the New York Stock Exchange was born beneath a buttonwood tree,

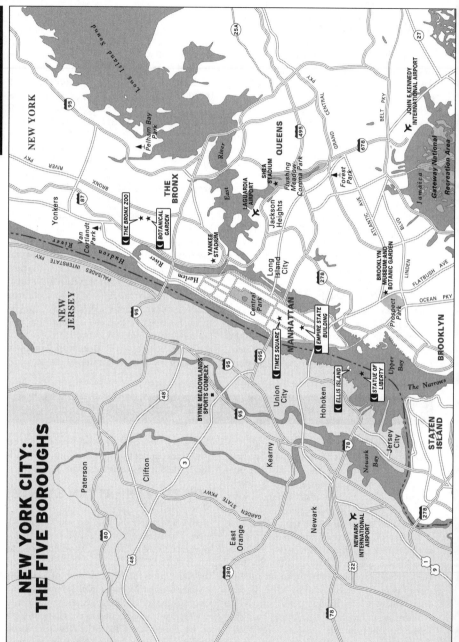

NEW YORK CITY:
THE FIVE BOROUGHS

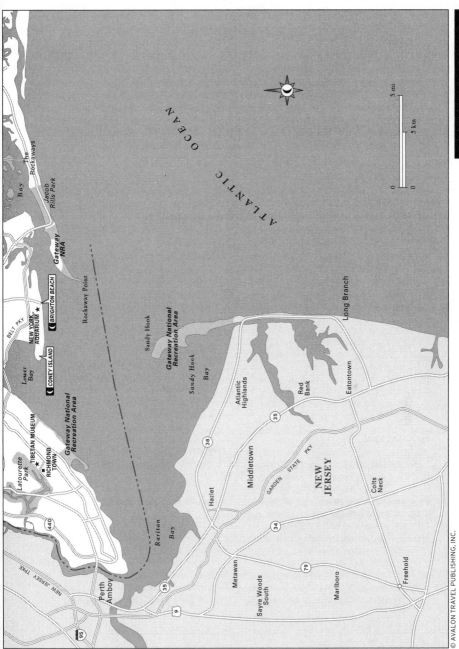

ATLANTIC OCEAN

The Rockaways

Bay

Jacob Riis Park

Gateway NRA

Rockaway Point

Rockaway Point

Sandy Hook

Gateway National Recreation Area

Sandy Hook Bay

Long Branch

Atlantic Highlands

Red Bank

Eatontown

BELT PKY

NEW YORK AQUARIUM ★

★ BRIGHTON BEACH

◄ CONEY ISLAND

Lower Bay

Gateway National Recreation Area

TIBETAN MUSEUM ★

■ RICHMOND TOWN

Latourette Park

38

35

Middletown

GARDEN STATE PKY

NEW JERSEY

Hazlet

Colts Neck

440

Raritan Bay

34

Metawan

Sayre Woods South

79

Marlboro

Freehold

NEW JERSEY TPKE

Perth Amboy

35

9

95

5 mi

5 km

0

0

© AVALON TRAVEL PUBLISHING, INC.

THE BOROUGHS: AN OVERVIEW

New York City, official population eight million, is made up of five boroughs – Manhattan, Brooklyn, Queens, the Bronx, and Staten Island – covering a total of 301 square miles. Only the northernmost borough, the Bronx, sits on the mainland; the rest of the city is spread out over a group of islands in New York Bay, where the Hudson River meets the Atlantic Ocean. Manhattan and Staten Island are islands in their own right. Brooklyn and Queens are on the western tip of Long Island.

Queens is the largest borough in area (118 square miles), followed by Brooklyn (78.5 square miles), Staten Island (61 square miles), the Bronx (43 square miles,) and Manhattan (23 square miles). By population, Brooklyn takes top spot with 2.5 million residents, followed by Queens (2.2 million), Manhattan (1.5 million), the Bronx (1.3 million), and Staten Island (just 443,000).

Between Staten Island and Brooklyn runs the Verrazano Narrows, a strait separating the upper and lower parts of New York Bay. Manhattan lies in upper New York Bay and is separated from the mainland by the East River to the east, the Hudson River to the west, and the Harlem River and Spuyten Duyvil to the northeast. Technically, the East River isn't a river at all, but a strait running between Long Island Sound and New York Bay.

MANHATTAN

Manhattan is the epicenter of New York City. Its preeminent status is evidenced by the fact that when people speak of "the boroughs," they're usually referring to the *other* boroughs, outside Manhattan.

The island is 12 miles long and three miles wide, and scored by a grid of streets (running east-west) and avenues (running north-south). "Downtown" generally refers to anything south of 14th Street, "Midtown" to addresses between 34th and 59th Streets, and "Uptown" to areas above 59th Street. "Downtown" also translates as hip, bohemian, and avant-garde;

"Midtown" as high-rise offices and the corporate world; and "Uptown" as either the sophisticated and the well-heeled, or the ethnic worlds of the Harlems, depending on whom you're talking to. These shorthand definitions hardly do justice to the island's complexities, but they're true enough to be part of every New Yorker's lexicon.

The East Side encompasses everything east of Fifth Avenue; the West Side, everything to the west. The East Side has the reputation of being stuffier, wealthier, and less interesting than the West, but again, this is a generalization of limited utility.

BROOKLYN

A separate city until 1898, Brooklyn boasts its own civic center, cultural institutions, downtown shopping district, and residential neighborhoods. Among its many visitor attractions are the Brooklyn Museum, Brooklyn Botanic Gardens, Brooklyn Academy of Music, New York Aquarium, and Coney Island boardwalk.

QUEENS

A largely residential borough that many Manhattanites once dismissed as a snore, Queens is now one of the most ethnically diverse sections of the city. Flushing Meadows–Corona Park and Shea Stadium are among the borough's biggest attractions.

THE BRONX

The Bronx holds some of the city's worst pockets of urban decay, but also the city's biggest parks. The Bronx Zoo, New York Botanical Garden, and Yankee Stadium are here, too.

STATEN ISLAND

Largely residential, Staten Island is the most rural and isolated of the boroughs, and the only one whose residents speak longingly of seceding from New York City. Its major visitor attractions include the Jacques Marchais Museum of Tibetan Art and the Staten Island ferry.

and here more than 20 million immigrants entered the country on their way to new and often difficult lives as Americans.

Whispers of this early history still echo throughout Lower Manhattan, in sites tucked away among the glistening towers and stone fortresses of corporate and financial America. In this most compressed of cities, this is the most compressed of neighborhoods. Everything here—the old and the new, the glitzy and the drab—is squeezed together on narrow, crooked streets that seem to belong more to the past than to the present.

Tragically, lower Manhattan is also the site of the former World Trade Center, destroyed in the September 11, 2001 terrorist attacks. The ghost of the twin towers still lingers over everything, yet the area is also on its way back. Many businesses are thriving again; new buildings and a memorial for the site are in the works.

Battery Park

At Manhattan's tip is Battery Park—a gentle, crescent-shaped park filled with curved pathways, statues, and sculptures. Built on landfill, it's lined by the wide **Admiral George Dewey Promenade.** Wooden benches along the promenade make great places to relax in the sun and enjoy superb harbor views.

Battery Park is part of "the Battery," the term used for the whole downtown tip of Manhattan. The name comes from the battery of cannons that once stood along Battery Place, on the park's north side. The Dutch erected the cannons to protect Fort Amsterdam, their original settlement, established in 1624. The fort was located where the former U.S. Custom House is today.

Castle Clinton

Though not much to look at now, this roofless red sandstone ring (north end of Battery Park, 8:30 A.M.–5 P.M. daily, 212/344-7220, free admission) was once an American fort protecting the city against the British. When it was built in 1807, it stood on an outcropping of land some 200 feet out in the harbor and could only be reached by drawbridge.

WEIRD, WONDERFUL, OFF-THE-BEATEN PATH NEW YORK CITY

New York City Police Museum, Financial District: Antique guns, Al Capone's marriage certificate, and "recently acquired contraband weapons."

Sideshows by the Sea, Coney Island, Brooklyn: Snake ladies, fire eaters, escape artists, and the Torture King.

New York Panorama, Queens Museum of Art: A scale model of the city, showing virtually every single building in the five boroughs – some 895,000 of them.

After the War of 1812, the fort was converted into the Castle Garden theater. In 1850, P. T. Barnum made a fortune there by presenting Swedish singer Jenny Lind. Barnum was New York's original impresario and the man who coined the phrase "there's a sucker born every minute." He created such a fervor over Lind—hitherto unknown in America—that six thousand people paid three dollars each (a lot of money at the time) for the privilege of hearing her sing.

From 1855 to 1890, before the establishment of Ellis Island, Castle Clinton served as the Immigrant Landing Depot. In 1896, it was remodeled into the New York Aquarium. Today, the edifice houses a small bookstore, tourist information center, and the **ticket booth for the Statue of Liberty and Ellis Island ferries.** On the monument's east side, a small National Park Service museum chronicles the castle's history.

◖ Statue of Liberty and Ellis Island

Visible from Battery Park is New York's most famous symbol, the Statue of Liberty (www.nps.gov/stli), accessible only by ferry. Despite all the clichés, sentimentalities, and ironies attached to the statue, it's still a powerful sight. If nothing else, there's something strangely eloquent about an enormous statue of a woman standing alone above a choppy blue-gray sea.

The Statue of Liberty Enlightening the

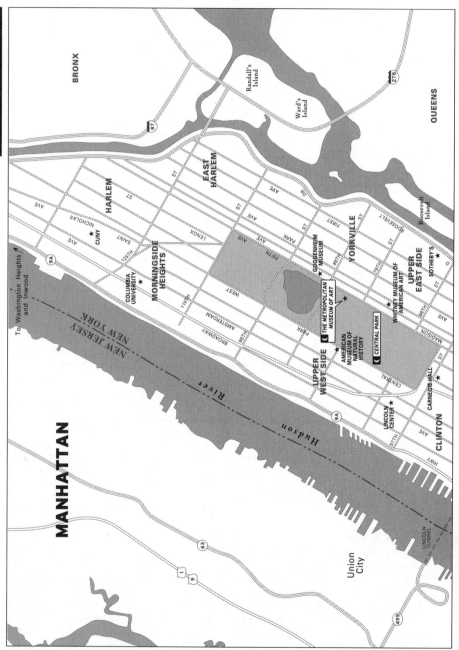

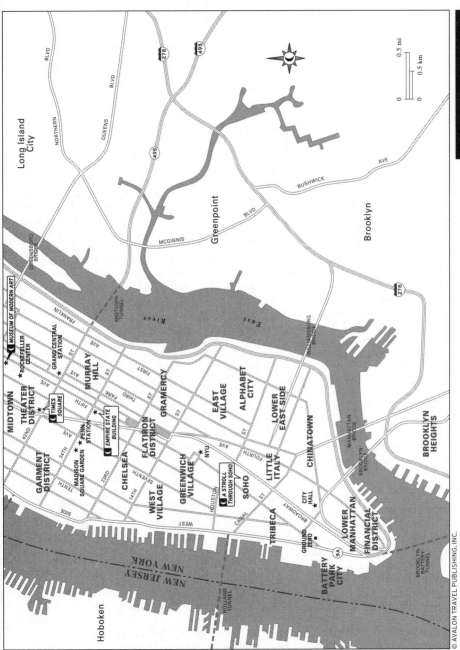

NEW YORK CITY

MANHATTAN

Long Island
City

Greenpoint

Brooklyn

Hoboken

NEW JERSEY
NEW YORK

GARMENT
DISTRICT

MIDTOWN

THEATER
DISTRICT

MUSEUM OF MODERN ART
ROCKEFELLER
CENTER

GRAND CENTRAL
STATION

MURRAY
HILL

TIMES
SQUARE

PENN
STATION

EMPIRE STATE
BUILDING

MADISON
SQUARE GARDEN

CHELSEA

FLATIRON
DISTRICT

GRAMERCY

WEST
VILLAGE

GREENWICH
VILLAGE

NYU

A STROLL
THROUGH SOHO

SOHO

EAST
VILLAGE

ALPHABET
CITY

LOWER
EAST SIDE

LITTLE
ITALY

CHINATOWN

TRIBECA

GROUND
ZERO

CITY
HALL

LOWER
MANHATTAN

FINANCIAL
DISTRICT

BATTERY
PARK
CITY

HOLLAND
TUNNEL

BROOKLYN
BATTERY
TUNNEL

MANHATTAN
BRIDGE

BROOKLYN
BRIDGE

BROOKLYN
HEIGHTS

East River

WILLIAMSBURG
BRIDGE

MIDTOWN
TUNNEL

QUEENSBORO
BRIDGE

FRANKLIN

MCGINNIS

BUSHWICK

NORTHERN

QUEENS

BLVD

BLVD

BLVD

BLVD

AVE

AVE

278
495
495
278
9A

FIFTH AVE
AVE
AVE
AVE
42ND ST
34TH
23RD
14TH
THIRD AVE
PARK AVE
FIRST AVE
SEVENTH AVE
TENTH
SIDE
WEST ST
HOUSTON ST
CANAL ST
BROADWAY
FOURTH AVE

0   0.5 mi
0   0.5 km

© AVALON TRAVEL PUBLISHING, INC.

World, created by sculptor Frédéric-Auguste Bartholdi, was given to the United States by France in the late 1800s. The French people paid for the sculpture largely because they believed in the American cause and wanted to show support. The statue was made in France and shipped to New York in 214 crates. But once here, getting the statue erected proved difficult. In 1876, its right arm, carrying the torch, was set up in Madison Square Park in what was supposed to be a temporary exhibit. The arm sat there for over seven years, while its American supporters tried to raise money for the statue's base. Finally, journalist Joseph Pulitzer, himself an immigrant from Hungary, ran a major campaign in the *New York World* and raised the necessary $100,000. Eighty percent of that money came from contributions of less than a dollar.

The statue stands 151 feet tall and has a three-foot mouth, an eight-foot index finger, and a 25-foot waist. Post 9/11, the only way to view her insides is via guided tour; reservations are a must (866/782-8834, www.statuereservations.com).

A half mile north of Liberty Island is Ellis Island (www.ellisisland.com), the primary point of entry for immigrants to the United States from 1892 to 1924. From a distance, the main building looks like a Byzantine castle, with red-brick towers topped with white domes. Inside, the cavernous halls still seem to echo with the voices of the 12 million immigrants who passed through here. Powerful black-and-white photographs, films, taped oral histories, and other exhibits re-create the immigrant experience.

Ferries (212/269-5755; www.circleline-ferry.com, 9:30 A.M.–3:15 P.M., with extended hours in summer, adults $10, seniors $8, children 3–17 $4) serve both the Statue of Liberty and Ellis Island, which have no entrance fees, on the same trip. The boats leave from the dock near Castle Clinton every half-hour 9 A.M.–3:50 P.M. during peak season, and every 45 minutes the rest of the year. Tickets go on sale at 8:30 A.M.; arrive early to avoid the inevitable long lines, and allow time for security checks.

Staten Island Ferry

Few people—New Yorkers or tourists—ever get around to exploring Staten Island, but nearly everyone rides the Staten Island ferry (southern tip of Manhattan, 718/727-2508, www.siferry.com, 24 hours/day, no fee), one of the best deals in the city. The views of Manhattan from the harbor are spectacular, especially at twilight when the sunset reflects off a hundred thousand windows, or at night, when the skyline lights up like a carnival midway.

On your right, as you head toward Staten Island, are Ellis Island and the Statue of Liberty. On your left are Governors Island and the Verrazano-Narrows Bridge. Governors Island, where 1,500 Confederate soldiers were imprisoned during the Civil War, became a U.S. Coast Guard Station in 1966. The Coast Guard left in 1998, and the city is currently considering various development projects, including public parks and luxury housing.

The Staten Island ferries leave every 15 minutes during rush hour, every half hour during much of the day, and every hour at night.

National Museum of the American Indian

At State Street and Battery Place is the stunning former U.S. Custom House, a 1907 beaux arts masterpiece designed by Cass Gilbert. Standing on the site of New York's first European settlement, the Custom House now houses the New York branch of the Smithsonian's National Museum of the American Indian (1 Bowling Green, between Broadway and Whitehall St., 212/514-3700, www.american-indian.si.edu, 10 A.M.–5 P.M. daily, 5–8 P.M. Thurs., free admission). Inside the center are displays holding some of the country's finest Native American art and artifacts, ranging in date of origin from 3200 B.C. to the 20th century. The maze of galleries surrounds a gorgeous elliptical rotunda lined with Reginald Marsh murals.

Don't leave the museum without noticing the anthropomorphized sculptures of the four continents standing out front; under the circumstances, they're more than a little ironic. Designed by Daniel Chester French, who's best known for his Lincoln Monument in Wash-

TABITHA LAHR

National Museum of the American Indian

ington, D.C., the sculptures show a personi-fied young "America" of European ancestry holding a sheath of corn in her lap while an American Indian hovers uncertainly behind her. The area in front of the Custom House was where Peter Minuit closed his $24 deal with the Algonquins.

Bowling Green

The Custom House sits on the southern edge of small, circular Bowling Green, the city's first park. Used initially as a cattle market and then as a parade ground, the park was leased out as a bowling green in 1733 for the fee of one pepper-corn per year. A statue of King George III once stood in the park, but irate patriots tore it down on July 9, 1776. Parts of the statue were then melted down "to make musket balls so that his troops will have melted Majesty fired at them."

Broadway, the city's central and most id-iosyncratic avenue, begins at the north end of Bowling Green. Once an Algonquin trail, it runs diagonally the entire length of Manhat-tan and on up into upstate, where it's known

as Albany Post Road. A street of commerce, entertainment, and public ceremony, it's wit-nessed everything from Washington's first public reading of the Declaration of Indepen-dence, to Malcolm X's assassination 189 years later (at the Audubon Ballroom, Broadway and 166th St.).

Broad Street Area

About two blocks southeast of Bowling Green, off Broad Street, is **Stone Street,** a narrow, nondescript lane that in 1658 became the first paved street in Manhattan. Legend has it that the street's resident brewer, Oloff Stephensen Van Cortlandt, had the street paved at the urg-ing of his wife and her friends, who hated the dust raised by the brewery's horses and carts. The job was completed in three years, with most of the work done by African slaves.

Run by New York's Police Academy, the **New York City Police Museum** (100 Old Slip, between South and Water Sts., 212/480-3100, www.nycpolicemuseum.org, 10 A.M.–5 P.M. Tues.–Sat., free admission) is a fascinating

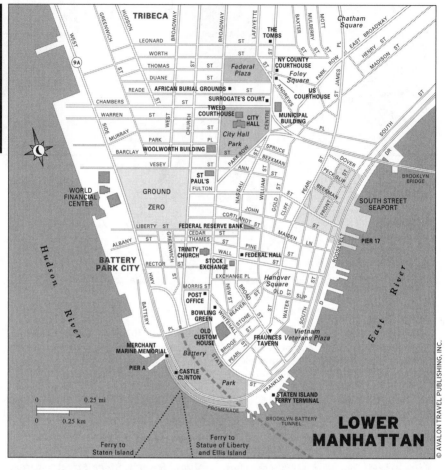

TRIBECA

LOWER MANHATTAN

place. One exhibit is devoted to antique fire-arms, including a palm-size pistol, a long-bar-reled "game getter," and a .410-caliber cane, circa 1895. Another explains how fingerprints are used in crime detection, and another chronicles New York's mobsters. Al Capone's baptism and marriage certificates are on dis-play, along with his machine guns. Most in-triguing of all is an exhibit entitled "Recently Acquired Contraband Weapons: Youth Gang Weapons." Here you'll see a concrete-filled blackjack, a dagger disguised as a fountain pen, and a baseball bat with horseshoes attached.

The bat's wielder apparently wanted the police to believe that his victim had been kicked to death by a horse.

At the corner of Broad and Pearl Streets is the red-brick, yellow-shuttered **Fraunces Tavern** (54 Pearl St.), a 1907 reconstruction of the historic pub where George Washington bade good-bye to his troops in 1783. During the late 1700s, the tavern was owned by one Samuel Fraunces, who many historians be-lieve was a black French West Indian. If so, Fraunces would have been one of the most im-portant African Americans of his day. Following Washington's election to the presidency, Fraunces was appointed steward of the presidential mansion.

The reconstructed site offers a **taproom/restaurant** (212/968-1776, lunch Mon.–Fri., dinner Sat.) and a small **museum** (212/425-1778, www.frauncestavernmuseum.org, 10 A.M.–5 P.M. Tues.–Fri., 11 A.M.–4 P.M. Sat., adults $3, students and seniors $2) with exhibits on early American history.

A few blocks north and west of Fraunces Tavern is **Delmonico's** (56 Beaver St.), perched on a triangular plot of land between two narrow streets. New York's premier restaurant for generations, Delmonico's almost single-handedly changed America's eating habits. Before Delmonico's, the city's only eateries were grimy boardinghouses and rough-and-ready taverns, serving what Charles Dickens called "piles of indigestible matter." Then, in 1827, a family of Swiss restaurateurs introduced to America the idea of fresh food served in a clean environment. It was a welcome innovation and Delmonico's took off. For 96 years, nearly everyone who was anyone ate here or at other locations later established farther uptown. Boss Tweed, Lillian Russell, Diamond Jim Brady, Jenny Lind, and Oscar Wilde—all were among the restaurant's patrons. The original Delmonico's restaurants shut down in 1923; the current version opened in 1998.

Wall Street

One block north of Hanover Square, Pearl Street bumps into that most famous of New York thoroughfares: Wall Street. Before heading west toward the canyon of financial buildings, look right, toward the East River, where the city's slave market once stood. Established by the British in the late 1600s to accommodate the Royal African Company's growing human cargo, this was once the busiest slave market outside of Charleston, South Carolina. In the early 1700s, nearly 20 percent of New York City's inhabitants were slaves, and it was here they were examined and sold to the highest bidder.

The wall for which Wall Street was named was erected by the Dutch in 1653 to defend

the city against an expected attack by the British (Britain and the Netherlands were at war at that time). All able-bodied men were called upon to dig a ditch from river to river and "prepare jointly the stakes and rails." The attack never did come, and the British tore down the wall in 1699.

If you've never seen it before, Wall Street will seem surprisingly narrow, dark, and short. Surrounded by towering edifices that block out the sun most of the day, the street stretches only about a third of a mile before bumping into the lacy, Gothic spires of Trinity Church. At **55 Wall Street** is a landmark building with double tiers of Ionic and Corinthian columns; the Ionic ones were hauled here from Quincy, Massachusetts, by 40 teams of oxen. At **23 Wall Street** is the Morgan Guarantee Trust building, erected by J. P. Morgan in 1913.

Near the western end of Wall Street stands the **Federal Hall Memorial** (26 Wall St., at Broad St., 212/825-6888), a fine Greek Revival building with a wide set of stairs that make a perfect perch for watching financial wizs

Trinity Church

and fellow tourists go by. Beside the stairs is a bronze statue of George Washington, who took his inaugural oath of office here in 1789. Back then, the English City Hall stood on this site, and Washington, dressed in a plain brown suit, spoke to the crowds from the building's second-story balcony.

The English City Hall also witnessed the 1735 libel trial of John Pete Zenger, publisher of the *Weekly Journal*. Zenger's acquittal established a precedent for freedom of the press, a concept later incorporated into the Bill of Rights.

In 1842, the English City Hall was replaced with the present structure. Inside is a small museum commemorating the English City Hall events; at the time of this writing, the building was closed for renovations.

Just south of Federal Hall Memorial is an enormous building resembling a Roman temple—the **New York Stock Exchange** (20 Broad St., 212/656-5168, www.nyse.com). As a plaque on the building reads, the exchange was founded in 1792 when a group of 24 brokers drew up a trading agreement beneath a buttonwood tree on Wall Street. Ever since 9/11, the Stock Exchange has been closed to visitors; barricades and security personnel guard its entrance.

Trinity Church (Wall St. and Broadway, 212/602-0872, 7 A.M.–6 P.M. Mon.–Fri., 7 A.M.–4 P.M. Sat.–Sun.) is one of the oldest and wealthiest churches in Manhattan. The present building—the third Trinity Church to be built on the site—was designed by architect Richard Upjohn in 1846. For almost fifty years, it stood as the city's tallest building, thanks to its 264-foot tower from which visitors could view the sea.

Inside is a small museum (9–11:45 A.M. and 1–3:45 P.M. Mon.–Fri., 10 A.M.–3:45 P.M. Sat., 1–3:45 P.M. Sun., free admission) documenting Trinity's history. Surrounding the church is a pretty cemetery where some of New York's most illustrious early residents, among them Alexander Hamilton, are buried.

The **Federal Reserve Bank of New York** is a massive, fortresslike structure of dark lime-stone (33 Liberty St., between Nassau and Liberty Sts., 212/720-6130, www.nyfed.org) that fills an entire city block and safeguards a huge pile of gold—over 10,000 tons, worth about $140 billion. Built in the style of an Italian Renaissance palace, the Federal Reserve is a "bank for banks," where cash reserves are stored. Nearly 80 foreign countries also keep gold bullion here, in vaults five stories underground. As international fortunes change, the bars are simply moved from one country's pile to the next.

Free tours (9:30 A.M.–2:30 P.M. Mon.–Fri., make reservations at least one week in advance, frbnytours@ny.frb.org) include an informative video and a look at the vaults. No one has ever attempted to rob the Fed, but if someone should, the entire building shuts down in 31 seconds.

World Trade Center Site and Environs

Though no longer extant, the twin, 110-story towers of Minoru Yamasaki's World Trade Center—once bounded by Church, West, Vesey, and Liberty Streets—still seem to hover over downtown Manhattan, and all of New York. Erected between 1966 and 1970 by the New York and New Jersey Port Authority, the 1,350-foot-high towers were among the first modern skyscrapers built with weight-bearing walls instead of the steel frame construction popular since the late 1800s.

Entering the World Trade Center complex from the east, visitors would climb a wide set of steps onto Tobin Plaza, where it was hard not to feel overwhelmed. The plaza was so stark, and the towers so tall. Human beings seemed insignificant—which was just one of the many complaints about the complex initially voiced by everyone from architectural critics to office workers.

In the end, the World Trade Center stood for just 28 years, during which time New Yorkers grew accustomed to them. Their sleek self-containment, their shimmering prosperity, their constant reassuring presence. ... New York didn't know what it had until it was gone.

The cleanup of Ground Zero, as the former World Trade Center site has become known, was completed in June 2002. Proposals for an overall design of the 16-acre area were unveiled the following month. As of this writing, however, the rebuilding of the site has yet to begin, as its final design has been embroiled in controversy. In the meantime, simple plaques honoring those who died in the attacks hang along the fence of the site's Church and Liberty Street sides.

To the immediate west of the World Trade Center Site is the **World Financial Center,** designed by Cesar Pelli and Associates. Though badly damaged during the September 11 attacks, it has since been restored to its former self: a glittering complex of ultramodern office towers, complete with shops and restaurants, an outdoor plaza, and the **Winter Garden**—a splendid glass-domed public space with enormous palm trees imported from the Mojave Desert. Both the plaza and the Winter Garden overlook the Hudson River, and the Winter Garden is the site of frequent free concerts.

Stretching south and north of the World Financial Center is a breezy **esplanade and park** offering great river views. Along the way are playful sculptures, inviting benches, and playgrounds. At the southern end of the esplanade is **Battery Park City,** largely built on landfill excavated during the construction of the World Trade Center.

The **Museum of Jewish Heritage** (36 Battery Pl., at First Pl., Battery Park City, 212/968-1800, www.mjhnyc.org, 10 A.M.–5:45 P.M. Sun.–Thurs., 10 A.M.–5 P.M. Fri., adults $10, seniors $7, students $5; last tickets sold one hour before closing) overlooking the Hudson River is a freestanding hexagonal building symbolic of the Star of David. Opened in 1997, the museum features thousands of moving photographs, cultural artifacts, and archival films documenting both the inconceivable inhumanity of the Holocaust and the resilience of the Jewish community.

Extending east from Ground Zero is **Fulton Street,** a narrow street filled with discount clothing stores and cheap eateries. The street is named after Robert Fulton, who invented the steamship in 1807 and started a ferry service between Manhattan and Brooklyn in 1814. Each of Fulton's ferries could accommodate 200 passengers and numerous horses and wagons, and could cross the river in eight minutes. At the east end of Fulton Street, where it meets the East River, is the site of the old ferry terminal, which until recently housed the Fulton Fish Market. The market relocated to Hunts Point, Queens, in 2005.

Dedicated in 1766, **St. Paul's Chapel** (Broadway and Fulton St., 212/233-4164, 9 A.M.–3 P.M. Mon.–Sat., 7 A.M.–3 P.M. Sun.) is one of Manhattan's oldest buildings and the only one built by the British. Designed by Thomas McBean, the Georgian church is surprisingly light inside, with pale pink and blue walls, white trim, and cut-glass chandeliers.

George Washington worshipped at St. Paul's, in a pew on the north aisle now marked with an oil painting of the Great Seal of the United States. The church was also a central place of solace for emergency workers toiling at the World Trade Center site following the September 11 attacks.

South Street Seaport

Fulton Street meets the East River at South Street Seaport, one of the city's oldest and most historic areas. A thriving port during the 19th century, the seaport went into a steep decline in the 20th. In the early 1980s, the Rouse Company took over the place and filled it with commercial enterprises, restaurants, and shops.

The Seaport's historic sites are scattered throughout the 12-block district. Many of the sites are free, but to get into the Seaport's galleries and 19th-century sailing ships—or to join a walking tour—you'll need to purchase a ticket at the **Seaport Museum's Visitor Center** (12 Fulton St., at South St. and Pier 16, 212/748-8600, www.southstseaport.org, 10 A.M.–5 P.M. daily in summer, Fri.–Sun. in winter, adults $8, students and seniors $6, children 5–12 $4).

Schermerhorn Row is the heart of the Seaport. Built in 1812, it's made up of pretty,

Federal-style buildings that once housed warehouses and accounting offices. Docked at Piers 15 and 16 are a half-dozen sailing ships, including the **Pioneer,** an 1885 schooner that cruises the harbor in summer, and the **Peking,** a 1911 four-masted ship now housing exhibits on maritime life and a fascinating documentary about the ship's early journeys around Cape Horn.

Around City Hall

At the edge of City Hall Park stands the **Woolworth Building** (233 Broadway, between Barclay and Park Pl.). Its glistening white walls and green copper roofs are best seen from a distance, where they can be appreciated in all their glory, but up close, the 1913 Cass Gilbert extravaganza is also a visual feast. Craggy-faced gargoyles peer down from a detailed Gothic exterior, while mosaic-covered ceilings grace the lobby. One lobby caricature shows Frank Woolworth, king of the discount stores, counting out his nickels and dimes.

A farmer's son, Woolworth began as a salesman earning $8 a week. By the time he built his $13.5 million headquarters, however, he was able to pay for it in cash.

The diagonal street across from the Woolworth Building is **Park Row,** once the center of New York's newspaper industry. From the 1850s well into the 1920s, as many as 12 papers were published here, including Joseph Pulitzer's *New York World,* Horace Greeley's *New York Tribune,* Charles Anderson Dana's *New York Sun,* and the *New York Times* (once at 41 Park Row).

The busy **City Hall Park** was first a cow pasture, then a gathering place for Revolutionary-era political meetings. Now it's the site of City Hall (212/788-3000, www.nyc.gov), one of the finest Federal-style buildings in New York. Inside the surprisingly small building is an unusual circular staircase that hangs with no visible signs of support. Open to the public on a limited basis (call 212/788-2170 for an appointment, must be arranged well in advance) are the Rotunda and the Governor's Room, which is lined with portraits by John Trumbull.

Near the park's southern end is the new **NYC Heritage Tourism Center** (Broadway and Barclay St., 9 A.M.–6 P.M. Mon.–Fri., 10 A.M.–6 P.M. Sat.–Sun.), a joint venture between the city and The History Channel. The kiosk provides information on history-themed tours, activities, and events in downtown New York.

Behind City Hall is **Tweed Courthouse** (52 Chambers St.). The building was named for William Marcy "Boss" Tweed, the corrupt Tammany Hall official who embezzled millions of dollars from the city. The courthouse was Tweed's most notorious project. It was projected to cost the city $250,000, but ultimately cost over $13 million thanks to exorbitant bills submitted by Tweed-controlled contractors. For just three tables and 40 chairs, the city paid $179,729. For carpets, $350,000. For brooms, $41,190. And then there were the gaudy courthouse thermometers—11 of them, each five feet long and one foot wide, with cheap paper fronts. Their cost: $7,500.

The Tweed Ring was exposed in 1871, the same year the building was completed. The "Boss" was tried in his own courthouse and sentenced to 12 years in prison for fraud, but the Court of Appeals reduced that sentence to one year on a legal technicality. In 1875, Tweed was arrested again on other charges of theft. While in prison awaiting trial, he escaped to Spain. There he had the bad luck to be recognized from a Thomas Nast caricature, and soon was returned to the Ludlow Street jail. He died there on April 12, 1878, at the age of 55.

The courthouse is now home to the city's Board of Education. In the building's lobby is a notable WPA mural.

At the north end of City Hall Park is the **Surrogate's Court and Hall of Records** (31 Chambers St.), a glorious, ostentatious building in the traditional beaux arts style. To its east is the skyscraping 1913 **Municipal Building,** designed by McKim, Mead & White. The building houses many city offices, including those of the justice of the peace, where as many as 14,000 couples are married every year.

Brooklyn Bridge

Near the northern edge of Lower Manhattan, across from City Hall Park, is the entrance ramp to the spectacular Brooklyn Bridge. Nothing can compare to walking over this soaring span—intricate as a spider's web—with the roar of the traffic below you, the lights of Manhattan behind, and the mysteries of Brooklyn ahead. The best time to cross is at sunset, when the rays of the sun reflect off the steel cables and wires.

Design of the bridge was begun by John A. Roebling and completed by his son, Washington. Construction took 14 years, and the bridge finally opened in 1883. The world's first steel suspension bridge, it was built largely by Irish immigrants working for 12 cents an hour.

From the beginning, the bridge's construction was plagued with tragedy. Only three weeks after the city approved the elder Roebling's plans, his foot was crushed by the Fulton Ferry. He died of gangrene a few weeks later. His son, then age 32, took over the project, but soon fell prey to caisson disease—known today as the bends. At the time, the dangers of rapid decompression were not yet understood, and Roebling and his employees spent hours working in the caissons (huge up-

side-down boxes filled with compressed air) far beneath the river. In the end, as many as 110 workers may have suffered or died from the disease.

When Roebling became too sick to work on site, he supervised the project from his Brooklyn Heights apartment, watching via telescope. His wife Emily became his emissary, carrying messages between Roebling and his foremen. By the time the bridge was finished, Emily was an engineer in her own right. A plaque in her honor can be found on the bridge, near the Brooklyn side.

African Burial Grounds

On the east side of Broadway, about one block north of City Hall Park, is an enclosed field of green and plaque marking the African Burial Grounds (near the corner of Duane and Elk Sts.). The grounds were only discovered in 1991, during the construction of a new skyscraper.

The centuries-old boneyard dates to about 1755. At that time, blacks were not allowed to join the city's churches and so were buried outside the city limits. Scholars studying old

TABITHA LAHR

a view of the Brooklyn Bridge from the South Street Seaport

THE "GREAT NEGRO PLOT"

The tragic "Great Negro Plot" of 1741, which resulted in 33 needless deaths, was supposedly hatched in a seedy Irish pub in Lower Manhattan. Hughson's Tavern, once located on Broadway near today's City Hall Park, had an unsavory reputation as a gathering place for sailors and prostitutes. After several mysterious fires erupted in the city, Mary Burton – an indentured servant working at the tavern – testified in court that the fires had been set by slaves who met with her employers at the bar. They were plotting to burn the entire city, she said, free all slaves, declare Hughson king, and divide the white women among the black men. On the basis of Burton's testimony alone, the Hughsons, their daughter, a prostitute, and four slaves were found guilty and hanged or burned at the stake.

But Burton's conspiracy charges didn't end there. Over the next few months, she began to point her finger wildly in all directions. Hysteria gripped the city as she accused first one slave and then another, then identified a white schoolteacher as the mastermind behind the plot. Only after she had accused several other white men in even more prominent positions did the judge declare it time to have "a little relaxation from this intricate pursuit." But by then, for many, it was far too late. Sixteen blacks and four whites had been hung, 13 blacks had been burned at the stake, and 70 blacks had been deported.

city maps believe that the graveyard may once have covered nearly six acres and held the remains of 20,000 free and enslaved African Americans.

Excavating the site, archaeologists discovered about 390 bodies, all buried east to west, with their heads toward Africa. Many were buried with seashells, and some in the remnants of British uniforms. During the Revolutionary War, the British offered freedom to slaves who joined their cause.

Foley Square

Just northeast of City Hall Park is another government hub, this one dominated by two imposing courthouses. The neoclassical **U.S. Courthouse,** designed by Cass Gilbert in 1936, is the building with the incongruous 32-story tower on top. Facing it is the 1926 **New York County Courthouse,** the inside rotunda of which is covered with worn WPA murals depicting "Law Through the Ages." Both buildings are open to the public, and if you've a hankering to see a trial, ask the guards at the doors which rooms are in session.

The Tombs

One block north of Foley Square is the forbidding New York Criminal Courts Building (100 Centre St.), an imposing gray hulk that makes even the innocent feel guilty. On one side of its columns are inscribed the stern words, "Where Law Ends There Tyranny Begins"; on the other, the daunting "Only the Just Man Enjoys Peace of Mind."

Both prison and courthouse, the Criminal Courts Building works around the clock in its disheartening, seemingly futile attempt to cope with the city's staggeringly high arrest load. Inside, Room 130 is the site of **Night Court,** a depressing yet eerily fascinating place where arraignments take place after hours. Night court is open to the public.

LOWER EAST SIDE SIGHTS

No region of New York has been home to more immigrants than the East Side between the Brooklyn Bridge and Houston Street. Various ethnic groups have lived here over the years, including the Irish, Germans, and freed blacks in the mid-1800s; and the Italians and especially the Jews in the late 1800s and early 1900s. Around the turn of the 20th century, more than 700 people per acre lived on the Lower East Side, making it the second-most-crowded place in the world, after Bombay.

Today, the district is still home to small enclaves of Jews and Italians, but it is the Chinese population that has exploded. On an island quickly becoming homogenized by white-col-

LOCATING CROSS STREETS

To find the nearest cross street of an avenue address, drop the last digit of the address number and divide by two. Then, add or subtract the number shown below. (For example, to find the cross street of 666 Fifth Avenue, drop the last 6, divide 66 by 2 which is 33, and add 18 to get 51.)

Ave. A, B, C, D: add 3
First Ave.: add 3
Second Ave.: add 3
Third Ave.: add 10
Fourth Ave.: add 8
Fifth Ave.–
   up to #200: add 13
   up to #400: add 16
   up to #600: add 18
   up to #775: add 20
   #775 to #1286: do not divide by 2, subtract 18
   up to #1500: add 45
   up to #2000: add 24

Sixth Ave.: subtract 12
Seventh Ave.–
   below 110th St.: add 12
   above 110th St.: add 20
Eighth Ave.: add 10
Ninth Ave.: add 13
Tenth Ave.: add 14
Amsterdam Ave.: add 60
Audubon Ave.: add 165
Broadway above 23rd St.: subtract 30
Central Park West: divide full address by 10, add 60
Columbus Ave.: add 60
Convent Ave.: add 127
Lenox Ave.: add 110
Lexington Ave.: add 22
Madison Ave.: add 26
Park Ave.: add 35
Riverside Dr.: divide full address by 10, add 72
St. Nicholas Ave.: add 110
West End Ave.: add 60
York Ave.: add 4

lar professionals, this is one of the few districts left where you can see and feel the immigrant vibrancy that once characterized much of Manhattan.

Chinatown, Little Italy, and parts of the Lower East Side are the sorts of neighborhoods where you can have a great time wandering haphazardly about, going nowhere in particular. Especially in Chinatown, the streets teem with jostling crowds and exotic markets. Chinatown's central street is Mott, just below Canal. What's left of Little Italy is centered on Mulberry Street just north of Canal. Orchard Street was once the heart of the Lower East Side.

Many New Yorkers visit Chinatown for lunch or dinner, and then head to Little Italy for dessert in one of its pastry shops. Orchard Street is at its liveliest on Sunday afternoons.

Chinatown History

The Chinese began arriving in New York in the late 1870s. Many were former transconti-

nental railroad workers who came to escape the violent persecution they were encountering on the West Coast. But they weren't exactly welcomed on the East Coast either. Pushed out of a wide variety of occupations, they were forced to enter low-status service work—part of the reason they established so many laundries.

Then came the Exclusion Acts of 1882, 1888, 1902, and 1924. Those acts prohibited further Chinese immigration—including the families of those who were already here—and denied Chinese the right to become American citizens. Chinatown became a "bachelor society" almost devoid of women and children. The Exclusion Acts were repealed in 1943, but even then only 105 Chinese per year were allowed to enter the country.

As a result, Chinatown was for many years just a small enclave contained in the six blocks between the Bowery and Mulberry, Canal and Worth Streets (now known as "traditional Chinatown"). Not until 1965, when racial quotas

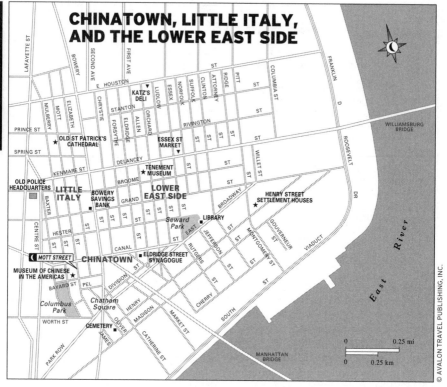

CHINATOWN, LITTLE ITALY, AND THE LOWER EAST SIDE

© AVALON TRAVEL PUBLISHING, INC.

for immigration were abolished, could the Chinese establish a true community here. Since then, Manhattan's Chinese population has grown to an estimated 100,000.

Chatham Square/Kim Lau Square

At the southeastern entrance to traditional Chinatown, where 10 streets meet, is Chatham Square, also known as Kim Lau Square. The first name comes from the Earl of Chatham, William Pitt, an Englishman who supported American opposition to the Stamp Act. The second comes from the Kim Lau Memorial Arch in the middle of the square. Erected in 1962 in memory of the Chinese-Americans who died in WW II, the arch is named after Lt. Kim Lau. Lieutenant Lau was flying a training mission over a residential district when his

plane developed engine trouble. He ordered the rest of the crew to bail safely out while he stayed with the plane, guiding it away from city streets and crashing to his death in the ocean.

To the east side of the square at Division Street is Confucius Plaza, where a statue of the philosopher is dwarfed by a high-rise apartment building—one of the few new buildings in Chinatown.

Slightly south of Chatham Square along St. James Place is **First Shearith Israel Cemetery,** a small cemetery dating back to 1683—the oldest artifact in New York City. Buried here in the "Jew Burying Ground" are 18 Revolutionary War–era soldiers and patriots, and the first American-born rabbi.

By the time the 23 Jews who later established this cemetery arrived in Manhattan in 1654, they had already been thrown out of Spain and Brazil. Dutch governor Peter Stuyvesant didn't want them here either, but when he wrote to the Dutch West India Company, asking permission to throw them out, he was firmly reprimanded. First of all, his employers replied, we're a corporation, and these Jewish merchants and traders can help us make money; secondly, we have a number of important Jewish stockholders.

Doyers Street

From Chatham Square, cross over to the odd elbow-shaped street just to the north. Some say that more people have died at this "Bloody Angle"—a *New York Post*–coined nickname—than at any other intersection in America.

For much of the 1900s, Doyers Street was the battleground of the Hip Sing and On Leong tongs. Similar to criminal gangs, the tongs fought for control of the opium trade and gambling racket. The On Leongs were the more powerful of the two tongs at first. But then, around 1900, a man named Mock Duck appeared. A loner who wore chain mail and a silver-dollar belt buckle, he liked to psych out his enemies by squatting in the middle of the street, closing his eyes, and firing his guns in all directions. With Mock Duck as their leader, the Hip Sings took over Pell and Doyers Streets, and the On Leongs retreated to Mott.

The tong wars continued off and on through at least the 1940s, with vestiges continuing into the modern day. Nearby **Pell Street** is still the headquarters of the Hip Sing Business Association, housed in a red-and-gold building with a green awning (No. 16). As recently as 1992, members of the Flying Dragons—a youth gang said to be controlled by the Hip Sing—could be found loitering on the street. Crackdowns from police have since changed that, although as far as the visitor is concerned, it hardly matters. Chinatown has long been one of the city's safest neighborhoods.

◖ Chinatown's Mott Street

Crowded with restaurants and shops, Mott is the oldest Chinese-inhabited street in the city.

A man named Ah Ken moved in here in 1858, and New York's first Chinese grocery store, Wo Kee, opened here in 1878.

Chu Shing (12 Mott St., 212/227-0079) is an antique shop that was once the office of the Chinese Revolutionary Dr. Sun Yat-sen (1866–1925). Dr. Yat-sen is sometimes referred to as the "father of modern China."

The **Chinese Community Centre** (62 Mott St.) is run by the Chinese Consolidated Benevolent Association (CCBA). The CCBA was established in 1883 by wealthy merchants who spoke English and served as unofficial "mayors" for the neighborhood. These merchants were exempt from the Exclusion Acts and were allowed to bring their families into the country. Today, the CCBA is closely aligned with the Taiwan government.

The **Eastern States Buddhist Temple of America** (64 Mott St., 212/966-6229) is aimed primarily at tourists, with $1 fortunes for sale near the front. Yet here you'll also find many Chinese, resting on the wooden pews after a hard afternoon's shopping. Some buy joss (incense) sticks, which they place at a pretty altar covered with golden Buddhas and offerings of fresh fruit.

Museum of Chinese in the Americas

This small but fascinating museum (70 Mulberry St., at Bayard, 2nd Fl., 212/619-4785, www.moca-nyc.org, noon–6 P.M. Tues.–Sun., adults $3, students and seniors $1) centers on a permanent exhibit entitled "Where Is Home?" Encased in a large structure reminiscent of a glowing lantern, the exhibit features personal stories, photographs, mementos, and poetry culled from 16 years of research in the Chinese community; among the topics explored are women's roles, religion, the Chinese laundry, and the bachelor society. Another permanent exhibit focuses on "Chinatowns in North America."

On sale in the museum's bookstore is an excellent "Chinatown Historical Map & Guide," which provides insights into the neighborhood's history, as well as tips on what to order in Chinese restaurants, where to shop, and what to buy. The bookstore also carries many other titles by or about Asian Americans.

Canal Street

You'll find it all on this remarkable street— fruits and vegetables, plastic toys, burglar alarms, car stereos, art supplies, Asian banks, and hordes and hordes of people. It's easy to spend hours here just meandering about, soaking it all in.

Most overwhelming at first are the fish stores near Baxter Street, where huge piles of fish seem to stare balefully at you as you pass by. Next you'll notice the large number of banks. Some say that banks in Chinatown now outnumber restaurants, and although that seems hard to believe, the banks' presence is indicative of the enormous investments from Hong

Kong, Taiwan, and China that have flooded New York in recent years.

On Canal near West Broadway, runs a stretch of stores selling hardware, industrial ware, machine parts, etc.; boxes of *stuff* line the sidewalks. On the south side of Canal, near Mercer, is the venerable, five-story **Pearl Paint Company** (308 Canal St., 212/431-7932), the world's largest art and graphics discount center, with more than 100 clerks on duty at all times. **Kam Man Food Products** (200 Canal St., at Walker, 212/571-0330) stocks a large selection of Oriental foods, along with cooking utensils.

Once located in the heart of Canal Street but now relocated a few blocks further north is **Pearl River Mart** (477 Broadway, at Broome, 212/431-4770), Chinatown's largest department store. On sale are Chinese musical in-

FROM POND TO SLUM

Collect Pond – early Manhattan's largest body of water – once covered a large chunk of Chinatown between present-day Franklin and Worth, and Lafayette and Baxter Streets. Though full of fish when the Dutch arrived, the pond was nearly exhausted by the mid-1700s. Then, around 1800, the city began filling it in with mounds of dirt and garbage; by 1807, a 15-foot-high pile of nasty-smelling refuse towered in its middle. Finally, in 1808, the city built a canal to drain the pond into the sea. That paved-over canal later became Canal Street.

Though advised against it, developers started building on the newly drained land without waiting for it to settle. The new homes were no sooner completed than they began to crack and tilt. No one with money would move in, and the area quickly evolved into Manhattan's first and arguably most notorious slum ever – Five Points. Named after the five streets that once intersected where Columbus Park is today, the neighborhood housed more than 40,000 people in less than half a square mile. Most of its residents were desperate immigrants earning $1 a day and freed blacks earning even less. Local lore had it that

policemen were afraid to enter the area except in squads of 10, and some said that at least one murder a day was committed there.

Wrote Charles Dickens in 1842, after his ill-fated trip to New York (he hated everything about it): "What place is this, to which the squalid street conducts us? A kind of square of leprous houses... reeking everywhere with dirt and filth. ... See how the rotten beams are tumbling down, and how the patched and broken windows seem to scowl dimly, like eyes that have been hurt in drunken frays."

Desperate living conditions gave rise to dangerous gangs, among them the Forty Thieves, the Dead Rabbits ("dead" meant "best," "rabbit" meant "tough guy"), the Plug Uglies, and the Shirt Tails. The latter, as might be expected, wore their shirts outside their pants, while the Plug Uglies wore big plug hats stuffed with leather and wool. The gangs' weapons of choice were clubs, bats, and hobnail boots.

Recent scholarship indicates, however, that Five Points had another side to it. In 1996, archaeologists examining remnants concluded that the neighborhood had also been home to a large, family-oriented population.

struments, paper lanterns, kites, dried herbs, and clothing.

Little Italy

In contrast to Chinatown, Little Italy—at its zenith between 1890 and 1924—is but a shadow of its former self. Only about 10 percent of the neighborhood's residents are of Italian ancestry, and the heart of its dining and shopping district has shrunk to just three short blocks. Even on those blocks, the buildings tend to be owned by Asian Americans, who—knowing a good thing when they see it—rent to Italian-Americans on the understanding that the buildings be used to perpetuate the tourist trade.

Most of what is left of Little Italy is along **Mulberry Street** just above Canal Street. Here, Italian restaurants and cafés line the street, with tables and striped umbrellas set out in warm weather. It's all very touristy, but it's also a lot of fun, with mustachioed waiters gesticulating wildly like caricatures of themselves, and lots and lots of bright, garish colors.

At 109 Mulberry Street stands the **Church of the Most Precious Blood,** its pretty courtyard often filled with birds. Though usually shuttered and empty, the church is the center of the feast of San Gennaro, held for 10 days around September 19. San Gennaro is the patron saint of Naples, and his blood—kept in a church in his home city—is said to turn to liquid on his feast day. During the festival, the streets of Little Italy are filled with bright lights, tacky games of chance, and food stands, very few of which sell Italian food.

At the intersection of Mulberry and Grand Streets is a mother lode of great Italian food stores, including the **Italian Food Center** (186 Grand St., 212/925-2954), stocked with a wide variety of wares; **Alleva Dairy** (188 Grand St., 212/226-7990), said to sell two tons of cheese a week; and **Piemonte Homemade Ravioli** (190 Grand St., 212/226-0475). **Rossi & Co.** (191 Grand St., 212/966-6640) is a variety store where you can buy everything from a Mussolini T-shirt to opera CDs.

On the fringes of SoHo is **Old St. Patrick's Cathedral** (233 Mott St., near Prince, 212/226-8075, 8 a.m.–12:30 p.m. and 3:30–6 p.m. Mon.–Tues. and Thurs.–Sat., 8 a.m.–4 p.m. Sun.). The predecessor to the famous St. Patrick's Cathedral on Fifth Avenue, this 1809 Gothic structure was once the cathedral of the see of New York.

The Bowery

Heading east, you'll bump into one of the city's most famous thoroughfares—the Bowery. Though long associated with alcoholism and abject poverty, the Bowery has a long and singular history that predates New York.

Named after the Dutch word for farm *(bouwerie)*, the street was first an Indian path, then a trail leading to Peter Stuyvesant's farm in what is now the East Village. In the 18th century, the Bowery became part of the Boston Post Road and was lined with fine homes and estates, and roadside taverns.

By the mid-1800s, the Bowery had become a glittering strip of lowbrow theaters where rowdy audiences roared out their laughter or jeers. Extravagant productions were the order of the day, with dozens of horses or full-rigged ships often appearing on stage.

Around 1880, the Bowery began changing again. Cheap boardinghouses, gin mills, missions, and brothels began replacing the theaters. Crime became rampant, and the street slowly slid into poverty and despair. By 1907, an estimated 25,000 homeless men were living in the flophouses and missions here.

The Bowery continued to be known as a haven for the down-and-out until well into the 1960s, but today, the area is rapidly becoming gentrified.

East of the Bowery

East of the Bowery is the sprawling Lower East Side, where a once-thriving Jewish community has dwindled away, to be replaced by other ethnicities and, in the last few years, urban professionals looking for real estate deals. In 1892, some 75 percent of New York's Jews lived here; by 1916, that figure had dropped to 23 percent;

today, the figure is less than one percent. Nonetheless, many older Jews in other parts of the city still regard the neighborhood as a sort of spiritual center, coming here to shop for religious articles or to eat a kosher meal in the few remaining traditional establishments.

The Jewish people began arriving on the Lower East Side in the late 1800s, many finding work either as peddlers or in the garment industry. Sweatshops—so named because their stoves had to be kept on at all times to heat the flatirons—sprang up throughout the neighborhood, employing both on-premises laborers and outside workers who took enormous piles of piecework home with them to sew by candlelight. Children were often employed along with adults, the pay was extremely low, and suicide was not uncommon.

Nonetheless, the Lower East Side possessed extraordinary vitality and intellectual life. Many actors, artists, and writers came out of the neighborhood, including Eddie Cantor, Fannie Bryce, Al Jolson, Jacob Epstein, and Abraham Cahan.

Orchard Street

The heart of the Jewish Lower East Side was Orchard Street, a major shopping strip once jammed with pushcarts selling fruits, vegetables, knishes, bagels, hardware, and work clothes. Often the first stop for an immigrant after Ellis Island, the street was known for cutrate bargains. Many of the city's most successful retailers, including Brooks Brothers, got their starts here.

Today, Orchard Street is still known for bargains, although a new generation of upscale boutiques is also moving in. Most of the old bargain stores sell clothing—both designer goods and casual wear—and linens. One of the oldest and most popular of these shops is **Forman's** (82 Orchard St., with branches at 78 Orchard and 94 Orchard, 212/228-2500), selling discounted women's designer clothes. For more information on shopping in the area, stop by the **Orchard Street Shopping District Center** (261 Broome St., between Orchard and Allen Sts., 212/226-9010,

10 A.M.–4 P.M. daily). Note: Most Orchard Street stores are closed on Saturday, the Jewish Sabbath.

Houston Street

Orchard Street ends at Houston (HOW-ston) Street, the dividing line between the Lower East Side and the East Village. Houston is home to the famous **Katz's Delicatessen** (205 E. Houston, at Ludlow, 212/254-2246), as well as to several traditional Jewish food shops. **Russ & Daughters** (179 E. Houston, between Allen and Orchard, 212/475-4880) is a bustling place filled with smoked fish and dried fruits, all arranged in neat rows. **Yonah Schimmel's** (137 E. Houston St., at Chrystie, 212/477-2858) is a rickety old storefront selling some of the best knishes in New York.

Lower East Side Tenement Museum

To get a taste of what Jewish immigrant life was like in the mid-to-late 1800s, visit this museum,

Take a tour of the historical Lower East Side Tenement Museum.

housed in an 1863 building (97 Orchard St., between Delancey and Broome, 212/431-0233, www.tenement.org, tours Tues.–Sat., call for details, advance purchase recommended, adults $13, seniors and students $11). It's a deliberately dark and oppressive place; the building originally had no windows, except in front, and no indoor plumbing. Declared illegal in 1935, it was sealed up and forgotten about until 1988, when historians looking for a structurally unaltered tenement building stumbled upon it.

The museum's ground floor is devoted to temporary exhibits, while the upstairs rooms have been left as they were when the house was occupied. Still eerily visible on one wall are the scribblings of a garment worker, listing the numbers of skirts, dresses, and "jackets #2" he or she had cut or sewn.

Across from the museum is **Gallery 90** (90 Orchard St., 11 A.M.–5:30 P.M. Mon.–Fri., 11 A.M.–6 P.M. Sat.–Sun.), which serves as a visitors center. It holds a wonderful miniature model of an inhabited tenement building. On weekends in spring, summer, and fall, the center conducts 90-minute walking tours of the Lower East Side (adults $12, students and seniors $10).

Eldridge Street Synagogue

About four blocks south of the Tenement Museum is the 1886 Eldridge Street Synagogue (12 Eldridge St., between Division and Canal). The first synagogue in New York built by Eastern European Jews, it's a large and startlingly elaborate building with beautifully carved wooden doors. Due to a dwindling congregation, the main sanctuary was sealed in the 1930s and not entered again for 40 years. In the early 1990s, restoration work began, and the synagogue now houses the **Eldridge Street Project** (212/219-0903, www.eldridgestreet.org), an exhibition space. **Tours** of the synagogue are offered on the hour 11 A.M.–4 P.M., last tour at 3 P.M., Sunday and Tuesday–Thursday (adults $5, seniors and students $3).

SOHO SIGHTS

Once known for its art galleries, SoHo—short for **So**uth of **Ho**uston—is now primarily an upscale shopping and dining center. Within its 25 glittering blocks, bounded by Houston and Canal Streets, Lafayette Street and West Broadway, beckon dozens of restaurants, bars, hotels, and, especially, shops.

◖ A Stroll Through SoHo

Early in New York City history, SoHo was a quiet residential suburb. By the 1870s, however, it had metamorphosed into an industrial center, home to foundries, factories, warehouses, and sweatshops. Frequent fires started by machinery sparks garnered the district the nickname, "Hell's Hundred Acres."

By the 1960s, most of the factories were gone and artists began moving in. Attracted to the area by its low rents and high-ceilinged spaces—perfect for studios—they illegally converted the commercial buildings into living spaces. Soon thereafter, the art galleries arrived, and then the shops and restaurants. Almost overnight, SoHo became fashionable, so much so that the artists could no longer afford the high rents. The gallery owners held on until the mid-1990s, but more recently, they, too, have largely moved on. Many have resettled in Chelsea.

In the end, SoHo's cast-iron buildings remain its greatest treasure. Originally envisioned as a cheap way to imitate elaborate stone buildings, the cast-iron facades were prefabricated in a variety of styles—including Italian Renaissance, French Second Empire, and Classical Greek—and bolted onto iron-frame structures. An American invention, the cast-iron building was erected primarily in New York, with SoHo boasting the largest collection.

SoHo is a compact neighborhood, perfect for just wandering about. **Broadway and West Broadway** are the main thoroughfares; **Prince and Spring Streets** hold an enormous array of shops. The intersections of Prince and Spring Streets with West Broadway is the heart of the district.

Broadway Architectural Gems

Many of SoHo's finest cast-iron gems can be found along Broadway. Foremost among

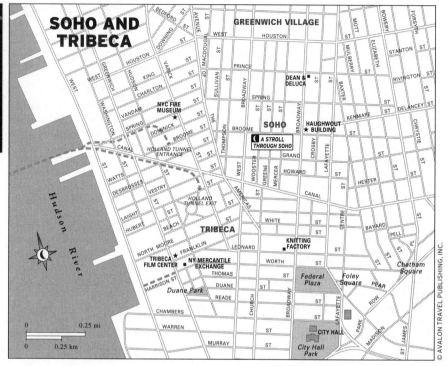

SOHO AND TRIBECA

GREENWICH VILLAGE

NYC FIRE MUSEUM ★

DEAN & DELUCA

SOHO

HAUGHWOUT ★ BUILDING

A STROLL THROUGH SOHO

HOLLAND TUNNEL ENTRANCE

HOLLAND TUNNEL EXIT

TRIBECA

KNITTING ★ FACTORY

TRIBECA FILM CENTER ★

NY MERCANTILE ★ EXCHANGE

Duane Park

Federal Plaza

Foley Square

Chatham Square

Hudson River

CITY HALL

City Hall Park

0   0.25 mi

0   0.25 km

© AVALON TRAVEL PUBLISHING, INC.

them is the Italianate **Haughwout Building** (488 Broadway, at Broome). The magnificent edifice is five stories tall and nine bays wide on the Broadway side, and sports 92 windows all flanked by Corinthian columns. Built for a merchant who once provided china to the White House, the store was the first in the city to install a passenger elevator.

Farther north is the **Singer Building** (561 Broadway), designed by the innovative architect Ernest Flagg in 1904. It's decked out with red terra-cotta panels, delicate wrought-iron detailing, and large plate-glass windows. Also be sure to note the maroon-and-white facade of **575 Broadway.**

Farther south, below Grand Street, is the so-called **"Queen of Greene Street,"** (28 and 30 Greene St.), built in ornate Second Empire style.

New York City Fire Museum

Technically outside of SoHo to the west is the New York City Fire Museum (278 Spring St., between Varick and Hudson, 212/691-1303, www.nycfiremuseum.org, 10 A.M.–5 P.M. Tues.–Sat., 10 A.M.–4 P.M. Sun., adults $5, children under 12, $2). Housed in an actual firehouse that was active up until 1959, the museum is staffed by ex-firefighters. It's filled with intriguing items, including a 1790 hand pump, a life-saving net (which "caught you 75 percent of the time"), gorgeous 19th-century fire carriages, and evocative photographs. Another exhibit honors the fire department's courageous work following the World Trade Center attacks. The ex-firefighters will give you a personalized tour filled with anecdotes if they're not too busy.

© LAURIE STALTER

typical SoHo architecture

Art Spaces

Not all of SoHo's art galleries have left the neighborhood. **Ronald Feldman Fine Arts** (31 Mercer St., between Houston and Prince Sts., 212/925-6190), for one, has long been a mainstay in SoHo, with a focus on avant-garde installations. For a complete list of who's still around, pick up a copy of the *Art Now Gallery Guide,* available at many bookstores. *Time Out New York* also has good listings.

The **Children's Museum of the Arts** (182 Lafayette St., between Broome and Grand Sts., 212/274-0986, noon–5 P.M. Wed.–Sun., admission $5, seniors and children under one free) is an experimental museum designed to expose kids to the visual and performing arts. In the "Artist's Studio," youngsters can try their hand at sand painting, origami, and sculpture.

TriBeCa

Heading south out of SoHo and crossing over Canal Street, you'll enter TriBeCa, short for **Tri**angle **Be**low **Ca**nal. Encompassing about 40 blocks between Canal, Chambers, West, and Church Streets, the district is often referred to as another SoHo. Yet large sections of TriBeCa remain quiet and residential, with a 19th-century feel. Like SoHo, TriBeCa's main thoroughfares are Broadway and West Broadway, though some of its best cast-iron buildings are on side streets, especially White Street.

EAST VILLAGE SIGHTS

For much of its existence, the East Village was simply an extension of the Lower East Side. At the turn of the 20th century, most of its residents were German Lutheran immigrants. By World War I, most were Poles, Ukrainians, Greeks, Jews, and Russians—some of whom still live in the neighborhood. Not long thereafter, a sizeable Latino population moved in, settling in the easternmost stretches. They, too, are still here.

Then, in the 1950s, artists, writers, radicals, and counterculturists began arriving. Many

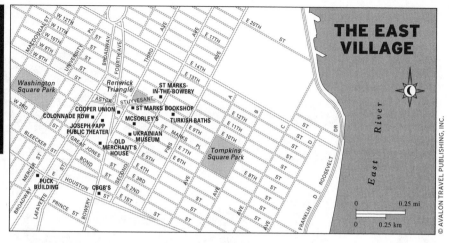

THE EAST VILLAGE

East River

0   0.25 mi

0   0.25 km

were fleeing the rising rents in Greenwich Village, and they transformed the East Village into a distinct neighborhood with a character all its own. First on the scene were artists such as Willem de Kooning, Paul Georges, and Joan Mitchell, followed quickly by writers such as Norman Mailer, W. H. Auden, and Allen Ginsberg. Next came the beatniks, and then the hippies and yippies, rock groups and punk musicians, artists and fashion designers.

Only in the 1980s did the East Village begin to gentrify. Young professionals moved in, bringing with them upscale restaurants and shops. Still, the East Village has not completely succumbed and offers a thriving mix of artists and careerists, students and tourists. Owners of hip boutiques share sidewalk space with the homeless. Drug dealers skulk outside trendy restaurants.

Nightlife is a key component of East Village character. The neighborhood is home to scores of restaurants and bars, along with fly-by-night clubs, which in recent years have pushed as far east as Avenue D in the once notorious Alphabet City (Avenues A, B, C, and D).

St. Mark's-in-the-Bowery

Historic **St. Mark's Church** (131 E. 10th St., at Second Ave., 9 A.M.–4 P.M. Mon.–Fri., 9 A.M.–1 P.M. Sun., 212/674-6377) stands near the for-

mer site of Peter Stuyvesant's farm. The church is a hodgepodge of architectural styles, made up of a 1799 base, an 1828 Greek Revival steeple, and an 1854 cast-iron Italianate porch.

Buried in the bricked-in graveyard surrounding the church is "Petrus Stuyvesant" himself, the last and most colorful of the Dutch governors. By all accounts a crusty, often forbidding man, Stuyvesant spent the last of his years stomping around his farm on his wooden leg. Some say Stuyvesant's ghost still haunts the graveyard. A tapping noise, like that made by the famous leg, has allegedly been heard from deep inside his tomb.

Also once buried in St. Mark's cemetery was Alexander Stewart, the founder of the modern department store. But in 1878, body snatchers dug up his body—buried 12 feet down under three heavy slabs—and held it for ransom. Two years went by before Stewart's widow, worth millions, finally coughed up $20,000 for her husband's remains. The corpse was reburied in Garden City, an early planned suburb on Long Island that Stewart had financed. His new tomb was equipped with a burglar alarm.

Today St. Mark's is known primarily for its **poetry readings** (212/674-0910), **dance presentations** (212/674-8112), and leftist politics. An annual poetry fest is held on New Year's Day.

St. Mark's Place

Raucous and run-down in spots, outrageously entertaining in others, St. Mark's is the heart of the East Village. Artists and musicians, students and tourists, drug dealers and the down-and-out, all jostle each other, while the stores on either side sell everything from gourmet pretzels to frightening-looking leather goods. To get the full effect of the craziness, come after 10 P.M. on a weekend night.

Between First and Second Avenues, St. Mark's becomes residential. Poet W. H. Auden lived in a fourth-floor apartment at 77 St. Mark's Place from 1953 to 1972. A plaque by the door commemorates the man and quotes the line: "If total affection cannot be, let the more loving one be me." In contrast to those noble sentiments, Auden lived in considerable filth, amidst piles of dirty plates and a cockroach population reputedly so large that the walls of his apartment appeared to be moving.

Ukrainian Museum

Begun in an East Village brownstone in 1976, the Ukrainian Museum (222 E. 6th St., between Second and Third Aves., 212/228-0110, www.ukrainianmuseum.org, 11:30 A.M.–5 P.M. Wed.–Sun., adults $8, seniors and students $6, children under 12 free) relocated into a handsome, three-story, glass-and-brick building in 2005. Built with money raised from Ukrainians in New York and nationwide, the museum presents the work of major Ukrainian artists, along with exhibits on history and culture. The inaugural show focused on Alexander Archipenko, an avant-garde sculptor; on permanent display is a rich folk-art collection.

McSorley's Old Ale House

Established in 1854, famed McSorley's (15 E. 7th St., 212/473-9148) was once a hangout of *New Yorker* writer Joseph Mitchell, who wrote of the place in his book, *McSorley's Wonderful Saloon.* Inside, find a potbellied stove, old gas lamps, a carved mahogany bar, and pressed tin ceilings. Memorabilia collected by old John McSorley hangs everywhere, but the old neighborhood drinking crowd is gone, replaced

© CHRISTIANE BIRD

McSorley's Old Ale House was a male-only preserve clear up until the early 1970s.

primarily by boisterous twenty-something males (McSorley's only opened its doors to women in the early 1970s, and then only under court order). The best time to come is at lunch, when you can take a look around while munching on a plowman's lunch of bread and cheese. Ale is the only beverage served, and it comes two glasses at a time, light or dark.

Merchant's House Museum

This classic Greek Revival home (29 E. 4th St., between Bowery and Lafayette, 212/777-1089, www.merchantshouse.com, noon–5 P.M. Thurs.–Mon., adults $6, students and seniors $4) is furnished exactly as it was in 1835 when merchant Seabury Tredwell and his family lived here. On display are the family's entire belongings, including the framed diplomas of the Tredwell daughters and trunks filled with sumptuous satin clothes. On the second floor is a secret trapdoor that may once have led to an underground tunnel.

The Public Theater

Two blocks further north stands an imposing, columned building with colorful banners beckoning out front. Once the Astor Library, this is now the Public Theater (425 Lafayette St., 212/260-2400, www.publictheater.org), founded by Joseph Papp.

Until his death in 1991, Papp was one of America's most important theater producers. Best known as founder of the New York Shakespeare Festival, he was also the man who first produced *Hair, A Chorus Line,* and 15 other plays that later moved to Broadway. Today, the Public is home to five stages, a coffee bar, and a cabaret space called Joe's Pub.

Astor Place and Cooper Union

Adjoining the Public Theater is a windy, disjointed plaza centering on the "Alamo," a big black cube by artist Bernard Rosenthal. Precariously balanced on one corner, the cube is supposed to rotate when pushed, but that's easier said than done. The plaza also holds a cast-iron reproduction of one of the original subway kiosks that once stood all over the city.

The largest brownstone in New York City is Cooper Union, located in the triangle between Astor Place and Third and Fourth Avenues. The 1859 building was financed by Peter Cooper, a remarkable engineer who—among many other things—made a fortune in the iron industry, designed the first American locomotive, invented gelatin and a self-rocking cradle, and helped develop Morse's telegraph. The son of a poor storekeeper, Cooper built his Union to house a free school of practical arts and sciences. Still in operation today, Cooper Union was also the first coeducational, racially integrated school in the country.

Downstairs inside Cooper Union is the Great Hall, where Abraham Lincoln made his famous "Right makes might" speech that won him the Republican presidential nomination in 1860. Abolitionists Henry Ward Beecher, Frederick Douglass, and William Cullen Bryant also spoke here, as did every president following Lincoln up through Woodrow Wilson, and Bill Clinton.

GREENWICH VILLAGE SIGHTS

It's easy to knock Greenwich Village. Once a hotbed of radical and artistic activity, its narrow winding streets now sometimes seem too tame, its restored buildings too cute, its shops and boutiques too artsy and out of sync with sleek, modern times. Only the well-to-do can afford to live here now, and nearly all the dingy old dives have gone safely commercial and mainstream. Worst of all, the streets are always filled with busloads of tourists and bands of roving teenagers looking for wild, sinful times.

And yet—Greenwich Village cannot be dismissed that easily. For all its patina of tourism and well-fed complacency, it still has a bohemian soul lurking somewhere underneath. You can feel it sometimes in the old jazz clubs, or in Washington Square on a windy afternoon, or in the faces of some of the older residents, who saw it all happen, not so long ago.

Once an Algonquin village, Greenwich Village was settled by Dutch tobacco farmers in the late 1600s and by English landowners in the early 1700s. By the 1790s, however, the large estates were breaking up as New Yorkers fled north to escape the yellow-fever epidemics in Lower Manhattan. During the epidemics, the city erected barricades along Chambers Street to prevent people from returning to the infected areas, and Greenwich Village started filling up with stores, banks, and other businesses.

Over the next few decades, Greenwich Village turned into a low-rent backwater that attracted immigrants. First came the Irish in the 1850s, then the African Americans after the Civil War, and the Italians in the 1890s.

Around 1910, artists and writers also discovered the low rents, and soon the area was teeming with artistic and political activity. Max Eastman founded his radical paper, *The Masses;* tea rooms, literary bars, and basement poetry clubs sprouted up; and theater groups flourished. Among the Village residents during this period were Eugene O'Neill, Edna St. Vincent Millay, Bette Davis, Sherwood Anderson, Theodore Dreiser, John Dos Passos, and e. e. cummings. Greenwich Village's tolerance of "the Third Sex," as gays and lesbians were discreetly called, also dates from this period.

In the 1960s, folk clubs, antiwar rallies, and the civil rights movement brought to the Village another wave of new settlers, including Bob Dylan and Jimi Hendrix, Abbie Hoffman and Jerry Rubin. In 1969, the Village's Stonewall Riots marked the beginning of the national gay-rights movement.

Nearly every street in Greenwich Village has something interesting to offer, and you can't go wrong just wandering about. But be sure to bring a map—there's no grid system here and even the locals get confused.

Washington Square

Washington Square Park is the heart of the Village. On a sunny day you'll find everyone here, from kids hotdogging on skateboards and students strumming guitars, to die-hard Hare Krishnas spreading the word and old men taking in the sun. At the park's southwest corner are stone chess tables where the click-clack of

TABITHA LAHR

Washington Square Arch

the pieces never seems to stop; near the center is the dog run, where dogs of every conceivable shape and size dash madly to and fro.

Once marshland, the eight-acre park was purchased by the city near the end of the 18th century to be used as a potter's field. During the yellow fever epidemic of 1797, at least 660 people were buried here. In the late 1700s, the park was used as a public hanging ground, with many of the doomed coming from the state penitentiary that once stood above Christopher Street at the Hudson River. Physical evidence of those days still exists: in the park's extreme northwest corner is an enormous tree bearing the sign, The Hangman's Elm.

In the late 1820s, the square was turned into a park. Elegant townhouses went up all around, and by the 1830s, Washington Square was considered to be the city's most fashionable residential neighborhood.

New York University (NYU) erected its first building on the park in 1837, and now occupies much of the park's periphery. Most of the old townhouses have been replaced by institutional buildings; the genteel old families, by students.

The park's biggest landmark is the marble **Washington Square Arch** marking the north entrance. Eighty-six feet tall, the arch replaces a temporary wooden one erected in 1889 to commemorate the centennial of George Washington's inauguration. Citizens liked the wooden arch so much that they decided to have it remade in marble. The designer was architect Stanford White, and the sculptor was A. Stirling Calder (father of famous mobile sculptor Alexander Calder).

The beautiful red-brick Greek Revival townhouses on the north side of Washington Square date back to the early 1830s. The house at 1 Washington Square North was home, at different times, to novelists Edith Wharton and Henry James, who once described the neighborhood as "the ideal of quiet and of genteel retirement." James was born in 1843 just off Washington Square at 21 Washington Place, and he set his novel *Washington Square* at his grandmother's house, 19 Washington Square

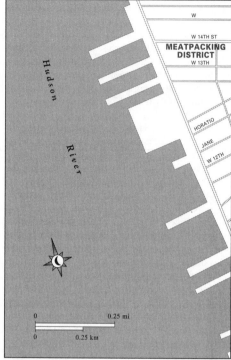

North. Neither of these two buildings still stands.

The painter Edward Hopper lived at 3 Washington Square North—once known as the "Studio Building"—from 1913 until his death in 1967. Other notables claiming this address at one time or another include painter Rockwell Kent, literary critic Edmund Wilson, and writer John Dos Passos, who started his novel *Manhattan Transfer* in this building in 1922.

8th Street

To the immediate north of Washington Park runs 8th Street. Once a highlight of Greenwich Village, 8th Street is now best known for its impossible number of shoe stores, grungy boutiques, and food joints.

Eighth Street has been a tourist attraction since the late 1940s, when straight couples came to dance at the Bon Soir or the Vil-

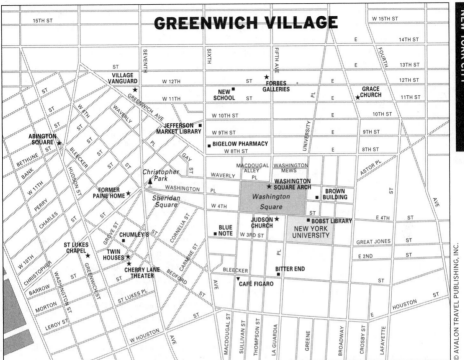

GREENWICH VILLAGE

© AVALON TRAVEL PUBLISHING, INC.

lage Barn, and gay men hung out at a bar called Mary's. In 1970, Jimi Hendrix built his **Electric Lady Studios,** shaped like a giant guitar (since removed), into a row of brownstones at 52 West 8th. Hendrix recorded some 600 hours of tapes at his studio, but he died the following September—from inhalation of vomit following barbiturate intoxication—before anything was released.

The building at 5 West 8th Street was once the **Marlton Hotel,** where nightclub comedian Lenny Bruce stayed during his highly publicized obscenity trial in 1964. Arrested for an "obscene" performance at the Cafe Au Go Go on Bleecker Street, he was eventually found innocent.

Across from the old Marlton, in what is now the New York Studio School, was the first home of the **Whitney Museum of American Art.** Gertrude Vanderbilt Whitney founded the museum in 1931, with her own collection of over 500 works by artists such as Edward Hopper, Joseph Stella, and Isamu Noguchi.

If you continue east on 8th Street to the shopping mecca of Lower Broadway, then look north, you'll see that Broadway takes a wide swerve to the left at 11th Street. That's because in 1847, a stubborn old farmer named Hendrick Brevoort refused to let the city's new grid street system cut through his property. It would have meant the death of his beloved gardens and his favorite elm tree.

At the curve today stands **Grace Church** (802 Broadway), a lovely, lacy, Gothic Revival cathedral built by Brevoort's son-in-law James Renwick. Then a young construction engineer who had never studied architecture, Renwick entered a contest for the church's design, and won.

On February 10, 1863, Gen. Tom Thumb and Lavinia Warren Bumpus were married at the church, much to the chagrin of many of its parishioners who regarded the P. T. Barnum–

planned stunt as beneath the church's dignity. Nonetheless, when the wedding took place, over 1,200 of these same parishioners pushed and shoved and climbed up on the pews to get a better view of the little people.

Lower Fifth Avenue

Fifth Avenue begins at Washington Square Park. One block north, at the southwest corner of Fifth Avenue and 8th Street, stands the lovely, art deco **1 Fifth.**

The streets between Fifth and Sixth Avenues in this part of town are among the prettiest in the city; 9th, 10th, and 11th Streets in particular are lined with one gorgeous brownstone after another, many with colorful window boxes.

Poet Marianne Moore lived at 35 West 9th Street from 1966 until her death in 1971 at the age of 84. Mark Twain lived at 14 West 10th Street from 1900 to 1901. Dashiell Hammett was living at 28 West 10th Street in 1951 when he was sent to prison for 22 weeks for refusing to testify about the Civil Rights Congress, a leftist organization of which he was a member.

On the ground floor of the Forbes Building are the **Forbes Magazine Galleries** (62 Fifth Ave., near 12th St., 212/206-5548, 10 A.M.–4 P.M. Tues.–Sat., free admission). The museum is best known for its fabulous collection of Fabergé eggs—perfect in their miniature beauty—but you'll also find much else of interest. Highlights include over 500 toy boats, 12,000 toy soldiers, lots of historical documents, and a weird and wacky trophy section called the "Mortality of Immortality." Everything was collected by idiosyncratic media tycoon Malcolm Forbes, and the whole place feels like the giant playhouse of a precocious kid.

One block west of the Forbes Building is the **New School for Social Research** (66 W. 12th St., near Sixth Ave., 212/229-5600), especially known for its excellent social sciences department and adult education classes. Worth a quick look is the school's lobby mural, *The Coming Together of the Races,* by Mexican artist José Clemente Orozco.

Reigning over Sixth Avenue and 10th Street

are the Gothic turrets and towers of **Jefferson Market Library.** Designed by Frederick Clarke Withers and Calvert Vaux in 1876, the stunning maroon and white building was originally a courthouse and part of a complex that also included a jail, firehouse, and market. The jail was later replaced by the Women's House of Detention, where jazz great Billie Holiday was once imprisoned for the possession of marijuana. The market's former site is now a community garden bursting with color in the spring.

Christopher Park/ Sheridan Square

At Christopher Street and Seventh Avenue South is Christopher Park, often mistaken for Sheridan Square. The latter is just southeast of Christopher Park at the triangle where Washington Place, Barrow, Grove, and West 4th Streets meet. The confusion is understandable—in Christopher Park stands a statue of Gen. Philip Sheridan. Sheridan was a Union general best remembered for the unfortunate, often misquoted, line, "The only good Indians I saw were dead."

Next to the general is a George Segal sculpture depicting two gay couples—one male, the other female. Erected in 1991, the statue commemorates the Stonewall Riots, which took place across the street at the Stonewall Inn on June 27, 1969. (The original Stonewall was at 51 Christopher St. and is now gone; the bar called Stonewall at 53 Christopher is a namesake.)

The night began with what cops later said was a routine raid of a bar serving alcohol without a liquor license. But the gay men inside the Stonewall didn't see it that way. All too used to being unfairly harassed by the police, they resisted arrest. Friends in neighboring bars called out their support, and beer bottles began to fly. Eventually, 13 protestors were arrested. More significantly, the riots marked the first time that gays had collectively engaged in civil disobedience. The next night, an even bigger group of protestors gathered; the modern gay-rights movement had begun.

Across the street from Christopher Park is

the former **home of Thomas Paine** (59 Grove St.), the Revolutionary War–era author of *Common Sense, The Crisis*, and *The Rights of Man*. It was Paine who wrote the famous words, "These are the times that try men's souls."

Born to Quaker parents in England, Paine immigrated to the United States in 1774 and served in the Revolutionary army. He moved into this house in 1808, at the age of 71. By then Paine was a difficult and crusty man, and also an atheist—a fact his straight-laced neighbors could not forgive. Upon his death in 1809, only six mourners attended his funeral and his request to be buried in a Quaker graveyard was denied.

Paine's house, marked with a plaque, is now the venerable gay piano bar **Marie's Crisis Cafe** (212/243-9323), named partly as a tribute to Paine.

Christopher Street

Built along a path that the Algonquins once used to carry lobsters and oysters inland from a cove on the Hudson, Christopher Street was a working-class address for most of its modern existence. For years, longshoremen working the nearby Hudson River piers lived here with their families. But long before Stonewall, the street also had a thriving, underground gay nightlife. Gay bars such as the Colony operated as early as the 1940s. And by the early 1970s, the street's gay nightlife had become known around the world.

Christopher Street is still one center of gay New York, but because gay men and women no longer feel as shunned by the rest of the city as they once did, they've moved into other neighborhoods as well—most notably Chelsea.

Bedford Street

One of the prettiest and oldest areas in the Village is centered on Bedford Street, just south of Christopher. Much of the property around here once belonged to Aaron Burr; his former coach house is now a restaurant, **One If By Land, Two If By Sea** (17 Barrow St., near Seventh Ave., 212/228-0822).

At 102 Bedford is a small building known as **Twin Peaks** because of its two odd, very steep roofs, added to the 1830 house in 1926. At 77 Bedford, at Commerce Street, is the oldest existing house in the Village, the 1799 **Isaacs-Hendricks House**. At 75 Bedford is the so-called **Narrowest House in New York**. Though not much to look at, it was poet Edna St. Vincent Millay's home in the 1920s.

Commerce Street

One of the shortest streets in the city is Commerce, which runs a graceful arch from Seventh Avenue South to Barrow Street. At the curve is the **Cherry Lane Theater** (38 Commerce St., 212/989-2020), founded by Edna St. Vincent Millay and others in 1924. Experimental in nature at first, the Cherry Lane is now an off-Broadway theater with an excellent reputation.

At 39 and 41 Commerce Street, where Commerce meets Barrow, are two delightful **Twin Houses,** separated by a shared garden. Legend has it they were built by a sea captain for his two feuding daughters; the more mundane land records say they were built by a local milk merchant.

St. Luke's Place

This picturesque 1850s block is lined with 15 Italianate row houses on one side, St. Luke's Park on the other. The charming but corrupt Jimmy Walker, mayor of New York City from 1926 to 1933, once lived at 6 St. Luke's Place; two "lamps of honor" mark the spot. Other former residents of the street include Sherwood Anderson, who lived at No. 12 in 1923; Theodore Dreiser, who began *An American Tragedy* while living at No. 16 in 1922–23; and Marianne Moore, who lived at No. 14 with her mother in the earliest years of her career, 1918–29.

UNION SQUARE/ MURRAY HILL SIGHTS

The East Side between 14th and 42nd Streets is mostly residential, and lacks both the history of Lower Manhattan and the energy of the Villages. But it does have a considerable quiet charm and a number of quirky

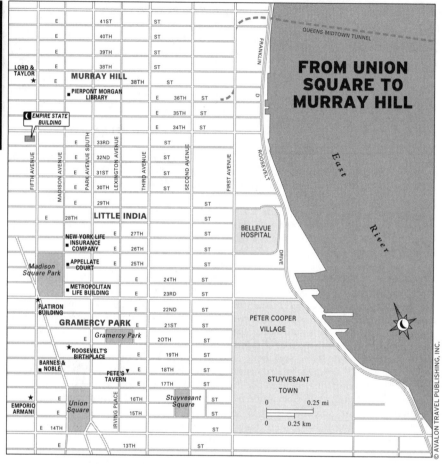

FROM UNION SQUARE TO MURRAY HILL

LORD & TAYLOR

MURRAY HILL

PIERPONT MORGAN LIBRARY

EMPIRE STATE BUILDING

LITTLE INDIA

NEW YORK LIFE INSURANCE COMPANY

APPELLATE COURT

Madison Square Park

METROPOLITAN LIFE BUILDING

FLATIRON BUILDING

GRAMERCY PARK

Gramercy Park

ROOSEVELT'S BIRTHPLACE

BARNES & NOBLE

PETE'S TAVERN

EMPORIO ARMANI

Union Square

Stuyvesant Square

BELLEVUE HOSPITAL

PETER COOPER VILLAGE

STUYVESANT TOWN

East River

QUEENS MIDTOWN TUNNEL

FRANKLIN   D   ROOSEVELT   DRIVE

FIFTH AVENUE, MADISON AVENUE, PARK AVENUE SOUTH, LEXINGTON AVENUE, THIRD AVENUE, SECOND AVENUE, FIRST AVENUE, IRVING PLACE

0   0.25 mi
0   0.25 km

© AVALON TRAVEL PUBLISHING, INC.

attractions sandwiched between brownstones and apartment buildings.

Various neighborhoods make up this section of the East Side. **Union Square** begins at 14th Street and Broadway. **Madison Square** begins at 23rd Street and Broadway. Further east is **Gramercy Park,** a residential square centered at 20th Street and Irving Place. **Murray Hill,** between Madison and Third Avenues, 34th and 42nd Streets, is named for Quaker Robert Murray, who owned all the land in the area in the Revolutionary War era. Legend has it that Murray's wife, Mary Lindley, helped George Washington win the war by detaining the British officers for tea while the Americans escaped up the West Side to Harlem Heights.

Union Square

Built over a central subway station, Union Square is a bustling urban center complete with sleek megastores, upscale restaurants, fashionable bars, and a farmers **Greenmarket** (212/477-3220), operating on Monday, Wednesday, Friday, and Saturday mornings.

Laid out as a park in 1815, Union Square was originally the province of prominent local families such as the Roosevelts, who lived nearby. Then, in the mid-1800s, the city's entertainment and commercial industries moved in. The famous Academy of Music started up on 14th Street, and department stores went up all along Broadway from 8th to 23rd Streets. This commercialism was short lived, however. By 1900 the theaters and the shops had moved uptown, to Madison Square at 23rd Street, and Union Square was home to garment factories and immigrants.

From the 1910s until after WWII, Union Square was a center for political demonstrations. Socialists, communists, and the Wobblies (members of the Industrial Workers of the World) protested here, while many left-wing organizations had headquarters on or near the square. One of the most dramatic protests took place on August 22, 1927, the night anarchists Nicola Sacco and Bartolomeo Vanzetti were executed. The police had machine guns mounted on a roof overlooking the square, but the demonstration remained peaceful.

The sixth floor of the narrow Moorish-accented building at 33 Union Square West (between 16th and 17th Sts.) was once home to **Andy Warhol's Factory,** frequented by the likes of Lou Reed, John Cale, Nico of the Velvet Underground, Truman Capote, and John Lennon. Here Warhol made many of his underground films, including *Blow Job, Flesh,* and *I, Man.*

Founded in 1864, **Pete's Tavern** (129 E. 18th St., at Irving Pl., 212/473-7676) bills itself as the city's oldest bar. The creaky joint was once a favorite hangout of short-story writer O. Henry, who lived across the street at 55 Irving Place. Henry—whose real name was William Sydney Porter—had previously served time in Texas for embezzlement. Apparently, he wrote his famous short story, "The Gift of the Magi," in a booth at the back. Pete's is open for lunch and dinner, but go for the atmosphere and drink, not the food.

Gramercy Park

Between Park Avenue South and Third Avenue, 20th and 21st Streets, is Gramercy Park, bought and laid out in 1831 by lawyer and real estate developer Samuel Ruggles. As fashionable today as it was back then, the park consists

© SEAN WATTERS

Only residents can access this beautiful park within Gramercy Park, but it's worth a look.

of both stately buildings and an enclosed green to which only residents have access. Outsiders have to content themselves with peering in through an eight-foot-high iron fence.

John Steinbeck lived in a small, dingy room on the sixth floor of 38 Gramercy Park North in 1925. He'd been working as a reporter for the *New York World,* but got fired. After that he holed up in his room, living on sardines and crackers and writing around the clock. Also on the north side is the **Gramercy Park Hotel** (2 Lexington Ave.). Humphrey Bogart lived in the hotel in 1926, just after marrying his first wife, and critic Edmund Wilson lived here with novelist Mary McCarthy in the early 1940s.

Gramercy Park South

The square's most impressive buildings stand on the south side. The **National Arts Club** (15 Gramercy Park S.) is a formidable Gothic Revival brownstone that was once home to New York governor Samuel Tilden. Tilden is best remembered as the man who lost the 1876 presidency to Rutherford Hayes by only one electoral vote. But he was also responsible for Boss Tweed's downfall. After Tweed was arrested, Tilden had steel doors installed in his windows and an escape tunnel dug to 19th Street in case of repercussions.

Across the street is the **Players Club** (16 Gramercy Park S.), an extravagant, columned building with large flags out front. The building was purchased by the great thespian Edwin Booth in 1888, who turned it into a home for a group of actors. The brother of Lincoln-assassin John Wilkes Booth, Edwin Booth ironically was the president's favorite actor. After the assassination, Edwin holed himself up in the club and refused to come out. A crowd of thousands gathered in Gramercy Park to show him their support. Today, a statue of Booth playing Hamlet stands in the park, facing his former home.

Broadway and Lower Fifth Avenue

During the late 1800s, Broadway between 8th and 23rd Streets was known as **Ladies Mile** because of the many fashionable department

stores located there. The original stores themselves are long gone, but their elaborate cast-iron building facades remain. Two of the finest examples stand opposite each other on Broadway just south of 20th Street. On the east side, at 900 Broadway, is an 1887 McKim, Mead & White creation notable for its lovely brickwork; on the west side, at 901 Broadway, is the former home of Lord & Taylor, cast in deluxe French Second Empire style.

Theodore Roosevelt's Birthplace National Historic Site (28 E. 20th St., near Broadway, 212/260-1616, 9 A.M.–5 P.M. Tues.–Sat., admission $3, children under 16 free) is a handsome four-story brownstone and an exact replica of Theodore Roosevelt's birthplace. It was rebuilt by Roosevelt's family and friends just after his death in 1919 and only a few years after the original building was torn down. The museum is filled with thousands of engrossing photographs and the world's largest collection of Roosevelt memorabilia, including TR's christening dress and his parents' wedding clothes.

Born in 1858, Theodore grew up a sickly, asthmatic child—a fact he more than made up for later in life. In addition to his political achievements, he also spent years in North Dakota raising cattle, served as New York's first police commissioner, led the Rough Riders at San Juan Hill, wrote over 50 books, shot game in Africa for the Smithsonian, and raised a large family. "No president has ever enjoyed himself as much as I," he once said.

Where Fifth Avenue and the Ladies Mile meet 23rd Street is one of Manhattan's most famous and idiosyncratic landmarks. The **Flatiron Building,** more formally known as the Fuller Building, was designed by Chicago architect Daniel H. Burnham in 1902. Its nickname comes from its narrow triangular shape, only six feet wide at the northern end. H. G. Wells once described it as a "prow... ploughing up through the traffic of Broadway and Fifth Avenue in the afternoon light."

Madison Square

Between 23rd and 26th Streets, and Fifth and Madison Avenues, is **Madison Square.** Once a marsh, potter's field, and parade ground, the square became fashionable in the mid-1800s. In those days, expensive hotels stood along its west side, the old Madison Square Garden stood to the north, and the Statue of Liberty's torch-bearing right arm stood in the center of the square, awaiting funding for the monument's base. Today all those buildings—and the arm—are gone, but other graceful structures have taken their place.

On the park's east side between 23rd and 25th Streets is the 1932 **Metropolitan Life Insurance Company,** an enormous art deco building made of limestone that seems to change color with the day. On the north corner of 25th Street is the 1900 **Appellate Division of the New York State Supreme Court,** covered with an impossible number of marble sculptures. Taking up the whole block between 26th and 27th Streets is the **New York Life Insurance Company,** an 1898 wedding-cake extravaganza designed by Cass Gilbert.

Morgan Library

An elegant neoclassic gem, the Morgan Library (Madison Ave. and 36th St., 212/685-0610, www.morganlibrary.org) was designed by McKim, Mead & White in 1906 as John Pierpont Morgan's personal library and art gallery. Now a museum, it retains its original elaborately carved wooden ceilings, medieval tapestries, renaissance paintings, and domed rotunda. At the heart of the museum's collection are Morgan's priceless illuminated manuscripts and Old Master drawings.

The Morgan is closed until summer 2006 for a $102 million expansion and renovation. When it reopens, it will include a crisp new building that will increase its exhibition space by 75 percent, a central plaza, and an underground concert and lecture hall.

CHELSEA AND THE GARMENT DISTRICT SIGHTS

Part residential, part industrial, this section of the city has no major public spaces. But it does have a solid, gritty feel and its share of one-of-a-kind attractions, including cutting-edge arts organizations, New York's newest center for art galleries, and the Empire State Building.

Roughly stretching between 14th and 28th Streets, Sixth Avenue and the Hudson River, Chelsea is made up of dozens of brownstones, row houses, tenements, and apartment buildings. Most of the area was once owned by Capt. Thomas Clarke, whose grandson, Clement Charles Clarke, laid out the district in the early 1800s. Clement Charles was also a scholar who wrote the *Compendious Lexicon of the Hebrew Language* and the famous poem beginning, "'Twas the night before Christmas."

Chelsea ends and the historic Garment District begins somewhere around 28th Street, where the area changes from residential to commercial. The heart of today's Garment District is farther north, however, around Seventh Avenue and 35th Street.

Dia Center for the Arts

Founded in 1974 to support a select group of artists working outside the mainstream, the Dia Center (548 W. 22nd St., between Tenth and Eleventh Aves., 212/989-5566, www.diaarts .org) has since grown into a prominent New York institution. Its permanent collection is now housed upstate at the Dia:Beacon in Beacon, New York. The Chelsea center is closed for renovation until sometime in 2006.

West Chelsea Galleries

Over the last decade, West Chelsea has metamorphosed into the new SoHo. Dozens of galleries have moved into the neighborhood, turning it from a rather nondescript area into one of New York's most exciting places. Even if you have little interest in contemporary art, it's worth visiting some of the exhibition spaces for their architectural exuberance alone.

Most of the galleries are in the West 20s between Tenth and Eleventh Avenues, with an especially large collection located along West 22nd, 25th, 26th and 29th Streets. Among them are such major names in the New York art world as **PaceWildenstein** (534 W. 25th St., between 10th and 11th Aves., 212/929-7000;

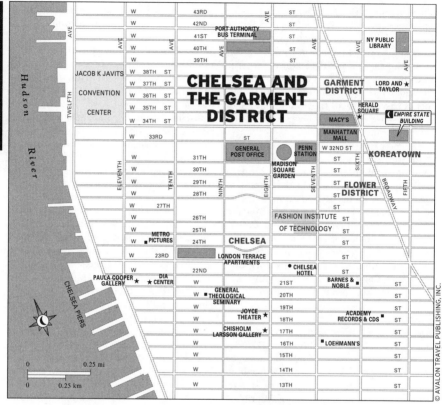

also uptown), exhibiting works by the likes of Sol LeWitt and Julian Schnabel; the **Paula Cooper Gallery** (534 W. 21st St., between 10th and 11th Aves., 212/255-1105), representing such heavyweights as Jonathan Borofsky, Carl Andre, and Elizabeth Murray; and **Barbara Gladstone** (515 W. 24th St., 212/239-1181) specializing in painting, sculpture, and photography by established artists. The enormous **Gagosian Chelsea** (555 W. 24th St., between 10th and 11th Aves., 212/741-1111; also uptown) is dedicated to artists such as Andy Warhol, Richard Serra, and David Salle, while British expatriate **Sean Kelly** (528 W. 29th St., between 10th and 11th Aves., 212/239-1181) focuses on conceptual art.

To find out more about the galleries, or about who's exhibiting where, pick up a copy of *Art Now Gallery Guide,* available in many bookstores and galleries. Or, check the listings in *Time Out New York.*

Chelsea Hotel

With its deep maroon paint job, black gables, chimneys, and ornate cast-iron balconies, the Chelsea Hotel (222 W. 23rd St., between Seventh and Eighth Aves., 212/243-3700) is a West Side landmark. One of the city's first cooperative apartment buildings when it opened in 1884, the Chelsea became a hotel in 1905 and almost immediately began attracting writers, many of whom took up residence. Plaques at the door honor Dylan Thomas, Thomas Wolfe, Brendan Behan, Ar-

© CHRISTIANE BIRD

Chelsea Hotel

girlfriend Nancy Spungen. The two were living here in 1978 when Nancy was found in her negligee beneath the bathroom sink, stabbed to death with a hunting knife. Vicious was indicted for the murder but died of a heroin overdose before he could stand trial. The hotel has since gotten rid of Room 100, where the murder was committed.

Artists, tourists, and well-heeled pseudo bohemians still live and stay at the Chelsea, whose lobby is hung floor-to-ceiling with artwork by present and former tenants. The rooms are relatively big and reasonably priced, but the place is well worn and without amenities.

Sixth Avenue

A continuation of the Ladies Mile, Sixth Avenue between 17th and 23rd Streets is flanked by impressive cast-iron buildings, considerably larger than the ones on Broadway. Dirty and underused until the early 1990s, the buildings now house a variety of megastores. At night, their brightly lit facades cast mysterious shadows onto the street.

The relatively new **Center for Jewish History** (15 W. 16th St., between Fifth and Sixth Aves., 212/294-8301, www.cjh.org) brings the American Jewish Historical Society, the American Sephardic Federation, the Leo Baeck Institute, the Yeshiva University Museum, and the YIVO Institute for Jewish Research together under one roof. Of special interest to visitors is the **Yeshiva University Museum** (www.yu.edu/museum, 11 A.M.– 5 P.M. Mon.–Thurs. and 11 A.M.–3 P.M. Sun.), formerly located on the Yeshiva University campus at 155th Street. Now considerably more accessible to the general public, the museum houses an impressive collection of art and religious objects, including detailed models of 10 historic synagogues from around the world.

thur Miller, and Mark Twain. Others who've lived here include Tennessee Williams, Vladimir Nabokov, Mary McCarthy, and Nelson Algren. Arthur C. Clarke wrote *2001: A Space Odyssey* here. William S. Burroughs wrote *Naked Lunch* here.

The hotel has also attracted an extraordinary number of actors, painters, photographers, musicians, and film producers over the years, among them Sarah Bernhardt, Jackson Pollock, Willem de Kooning, Jane Fonda, Robert Mapplethorpe, and Milos Forman. Andy Warhol filmed part of his movie *Chelsea Girls* here. Musician Virgil Thompson lived on the ninth floor for over 40 years.

In the late 1960s, the Chelsea became a favorite stopover for rock stars passing through town, including Janis Joplin, Jimi Hendrix, the Grateful Dead, the Mamas and the Papas, Leonard Cohen, and Patti Smith. Bob Dylan wrote "Sad-Eyed Lady of the Lowlands" while staying at the Chelsea.

The hotel's most notorious residents were Sid Vicious, lead singer for the Sex Pistols, and his

One of the newest museums in town is the **Rubin Museum of Art** (150 W. 17th St., near Seventh Ave., 212/620-5000, 11 A.M.–7 P.M. Tues. and Sat., 11 A.M.–9 P.M. Thurs.–Fri., 11 A.M.–5 P.M. Wed. and Sun., adults $7, students and seniors $5, children under 11 free), the only museum in the world dedicated to the art of the Himalayas. Opened in 2004, the Rubin was founded by private collectors reluctant to donate their work to a larger institution that might bury it in their basement. In the museum's stunning permanent collection are paintings, sculpture, textiles, and prints ranging in age from the 2nd to the 19th centuries, and in origin from Nepal to southern Siberia. Housed in the former Barney's department store, the museum also offers films, lectures, concerts, and dance events in its state-of-the-art auditorium.

The Garment District

Centering on Seventh Avenue in the mid-30s is the Garment District, now sporting the more tony "Fashion Center" label (www.fashioncenter.com). Once stretching roughly between Fifth and Ninth Avenues, 25th and 42nd Streets, the district—like the American garment industry itself—has shrunk considerably in recent years. Now it reaches only between 34th and 42nd Streets, and is currently being threatened by real estate developers and rising rents. Nonetheless, for now, this is still the country's largest clothing-manufacturing district and constitutes an important part of New York's economy. About $10 billion a year in clothing is designed, cut, and sewn here.

Visiting the Garment District on a weekday morning you'll see long lines of double-parked trucks, brawny men wheeling clothing racks, and young fashion assistants hustling to and fro with large boxes and bags. The industry's showrooms are closed to the public, but you can get a good sense of the place just by wandering the streets. Especially interesting are the many millinery, trimming, and fabric outlets—most catering to the trade only—along 37th and 38th Streets.

◖ Empire State Building

One of the world's most famous buildings, this art deco landmark (350 Fifth Ave., at 34th St., 212/736-3100, www.esbnyc.com, 8 A.M.–midnight daily, tickets sold until 11:15 P.M., adults $14, seniors and youth 12–17 $13, children

© BARBARA GRIFFITH

The Empire State Building is the world's quintessential skyscraper.

6–11 $9) was built during the Depression in an astonishing 14 months, at the rate of four stories a week. For years, it stood as the world's tallest building. That's no longer true, yet the Empire State remains the quintessential skyscraper, holding 73 elevators, 6,500 windows, 3,500 miles of telephone and telegraph wire, 1,860 steps, and two observation decks, one on the 86th floor, the other on the 102nd.

In 1933, Irma Eberhardt became the first person to commit suicide by jumping off the Empire State. That same year, the original classic film *King Kong* was made, showing a giant ape climbing up the skyscraper. In 1945, a B-25 bomber smacked into the building's 79th floor, killing 14 people. And in 1986, two parachutists jumped from the 86th floor to land safely on Fifth Avenue. Also, in case you're wondering, pennies thrown off the Empire State *cannot* kill passersby walking below, but they can cause severe burns.

In the Empire State Building is **Skyride** (212/279-9777, 10 A.M.–10 P.M. daily, adults $21.50, seniors and youth 12–17 $18.50, children 6–11 $16.50; combination tickets with observation deck available), a virtual-reality flight that takes viewers over, under, and through New York. The 7.5-minute journey takes place in a theater built with a hydraulic floor that rises, falls, and banks left and right to match the on-screen action.

MIDTOWN SIGHTS

Rush, rush, rush. Sometimes all the people in the world seem to be elbowing their way through here. Most of Manhattan's skyscrapers are in Midtown, along with most of its offices, major hotels, theaters, famous shops and restaurants, and many visitor attractions.

Fifth Avenue is the heart of Midtown, the artery to which all other addresses relate. Though nothing more than a line on a map as late as 1811, Fifth Avenue was the city's most fashionable address by the time of the Civil War. The Astors, Vanderbilts, and many other wealthy families all had homes along it.

Fifth Avenue began to turn commercial in the early 1900s. Today, its Midtown stretch is almost entirely lined with shops and office buildings. In the lower 40s and upper 30s, these shops tend to be tourist traps selling discounted electronic gadgetry and souvenirs; in the upper 40s and 50s stand the upscale boutiques and department stores for which the avenue is famous.

To see Midtown at its frenzied best, come on a weekday. However, most of the visitor attractions are also open on weekends. With the exception of Times Square, much of Midtown shuts up tight after business hours.

Grand Central Station

Grand Central Station (42nd St., between Vanderbilt and Lexington) is one of New York's most glorious buildings. To step inside its vast 125-foot-high concourse—with glassed-in catwalks, grand staircases, and a vaulted, star-studded, aquamarine ceiling—is to be transported back to a more romantic era when women wore hoop skirts and men wore top hats.

Completed in 1913 by the design firms of Reed & Stem and Warren & Wetmore, Grand Central Station is a city within a city. Beaux arts eclectic on the outside, early 20th-century

ROBERT MOSES, MASTER BUILDER

City Parks Commissioner Robert Moses – part civil servant, part evil genius – was one of the most unusual and controversial figures in New York's history. Though a nonelected official, he wielded enormous political power extending far beyond his office, the city, and even the state.

In power for 44 years (1924-68), Moses conceived of and executed public works costing $27 billion, thereby shaping virtually the entire modern landscape of New York. He was responsible for all but one of the city's major expressways, most of Long Island's parkways and beaches, thousands of public housing units, and more than 600 playgrounds and parks. Literally hundreds of major construction projects were completed during his tenure, among them the Henry Hudson, Bronx-Whitestone, Cross Bay, Throgs Neck, Verrazano Narrows, Marine Parkway, and Triborough Bridges; the Brooklyn-Battery Tunnel; Lincoln Center; the New York Coliseum; Shea Stadium; Co-Op City; the United Nations; the giant dams at the St. Lawrence and Niagara Rivers; and both the 1939 and 1964 World's Fairs.

According to biographer Robert Caro, Moses began his career as a visionary idealist yearning to bring about social change but ended it as a power-hungry tyrant who would stop at nothing to achieve his goals. To build his highways, he evicted over 250,000 people and destroyed scores of neighborhoods; the housing he designed for the poor was "bleak, sterile, cheap"; his World's Fairs cost the city hundreds of thousands of dollars; his highways sapped funding for the subways and created the mess of a transportation system New York suffers from today.

Writes Caro in *The Power Broker,* "Robert Moses was America's greatest builder. He was the shaper of the greatest city in the New World. But what did he build? What was the shape into which he pounded the city?... It is impossible to say that New York would have been a better city if Robert Moses had never lived. It is possible to say only that it would have been a different city."

Moses died in 1981 at the age of 92.

modern on the inside, it houses innumerable new shops and newsstands, several bars and restaurants, and a library devoted to railroading (open by appointment only). Adjoining the station are 27 miles of track that loop and stretch beneath Park Avenue as far north as 50th Street, and seven stories of tunnels containing electric power facilities, water and gas mains, sewage pipes, steam, and rats.

In its heyday, Grand Central was the terminus for two major railroads: the New York Central, and the New York, New Haven, and Hartford lines. Trains with romantic names such as the Empire State Express and Super Chief rolled in daily. A theater in the station screened newsreels, and CBS broadcast from the roof. Today, Grand Central Station is but a shadow of its former self. Only about 500 commuter trains arrive and depart daily (long-distance trains use Penn Station).

To get the best view of Grand Central, take the escalators up to the balconies on the north side. From here, you can watch the foot traffic crisscrossing below in seemingly choreographed style. Adjoining Grand Central to the north, via the escalators, is the wide, 59-story Met Life Building.

Fascinating one-hour tours of the terminal are conducted every Wednesday by the Municipal Art Society (212/935-3960, www.mas.org, $10 per person). Groups meet at 12:30 P.M. at the information booth in the center of the concourse.

The Chrysler Building

At the northeast corner of 42nd Street and Lexington Avenue stands the stunning Chrysler Building, a 1930 art-deco masterpiece. Financed by Walter Chrysler, the towering building is a tribute to the automobile age. Winged gargoyles shaped like hood ornaments, and brick designs taken from wheels and hubcaps lead the eye up to a gleaming, stainless-steel spire. At night, the concentric circles of the spire light up, tripping the city with a touch of the light fantastic.

United Nations Plaza

Extending from 42nd to 48th Streets and from First Avenue to FDR Drive is the windswept United Nations Plaza, where the flags of the nearly 200 member nations flap noisily in the breeze. Legally, the United Nations isn't part of New York at all but is international territory. The U.N. has its own post office, postage stamps, and uniformed security force.

Built in 1948, on 18 acres bought and donated by J. D. Rockefeller, Jr., the United Nations complex is made up of three buildings. The vertical greenish glass slab is the Secretariat Building, housing many offices. The low-slung horizontal edifice is the Conference Building, and the dramatic white building with concave sides is the General Assembly.

Only the General Assembly Building is open to the public; to see it, you must join one of the scheduled 45-minute tours, which leave from the visitor entrance at 46th Street and First Avenue (212/963-8687, www.un.org, 9:30 A.M.–4:45 P.M. Mon.–Fri., 10 A.M.–4:30 P.M. Sat.–Sun., adults $11.50, seniors $8.50, high school and college students $7.50, children 6–14 $6.50, children under six not permitted).

◖ Times Square

Simultaneously New York's glitziest and seediest symbol, Times Square centers on the intersection of Broadway and Seventh Avenue between 42nd and 48th Streets. Not really a square at all, but rather two elongated triangles, it is named after the *New York Times,* which was once located in the white Times Tower building where Broadway, Seventh Avenue, and 42nd Street meet. (The *Times* is now nearby at 229 W. 43rd St.) It is from Times Tower that the illuminated ball drops every December 31, ushering in the New Year.

Before 1904, when the *New York Times* moved in, Times Square was known as Lon-

gacre Square. The center of the horse business in a city then largely dependent upon four-footed transportation, the square was lined with horse exchanges, carriage factories, stables, and blacksmith shops. Not until the 1910s did Times Square become a bona fide theater district; not until the 1960s did it become known for its thriving sex industry.

Times Square has been much cleaned up in recent years, thanks largely to the efforts of the Times Square Business Improvement District—a nonprofit organization formed of the area's business and community leaders. Almost all of the old porn shops have been closed down and the three-card-monte games broken up. Police and private security officers patrol the streets 24 hours a day.

Times Square is best visited after sundown. That's when the street performers—each one more inventive than the next—come out in droves and the neon signs start to burn. By night, the streets are ablaze with huge panels of red, green, yellow, blue, and white. Except for the Las Vegas Strip, no other place in America boasts more neon lights.

A **Times Square Information Center** is situated in the landmark Embassy Movie Theater (Seventh Ave. between 46th and 47th Sts., 212/869-1890, www.timessquarenyc.org, 8 A.M.–8 P.M. daily). Free walking tours of Times Square, led by actors, leave from the center Fridays at noon.

Theater District

Most of the Broadway theaters are not on Broadway at all, but on the side streets surrounding Times Square. The area is home to 37 legitimate theaters, 22 of which are city landmarks. West 44th and 45th Streets between Seventh and Eighth Avenues are especially rich blocks; here you'll find the **Shubert, Helen Hayes, Booth, Majestic,** and **Minskoff** theaters, among others.

Next to the Shubert, connecting 44th and 45th Streets, is **Shubert Alley,** where unemployed performers once waited, hoping for a part. Today, a souvenir shop selling theater memorabilia is located here. Across from the Shubert is the legendary **Sardi's** restaurant (234 W. 44th St., 212/221-8440), its walls lined with caricatures. Once frequented by theater folks, Sardi's now attracts mostly tourists, but is still a fun and lively spot serving a varied international cuisine.

West 42nd Street

During the last decade, big changes have come to West 42nd Street, especially between Seventh and Eighth Avenues. For years a center for porn movies, this most historic of theatrical streets has regained some of its former glory.

Most of the block's nine historic theaters have been restored. The Victory (207 W. 42nd St.), opened by Oscar Hammerstein in 1900, is now the **New Victory,** specializing in programming for young people. The **New Amsterdam** (214 W. 42nd), once home to the Ziegfeld Follies, is now owned by Disney. On its docket are both movies and plays.

Also on 42nd Street is **Madame Tussaud's New York** (234 W. 42nd St., between Seventh and Eighth Aves., 800/246-8872, www.nyc-wax.com, 10 A.M.–8 P.M. daily, adults $29, seniors $26, children 4–12 $23), where you'll find waxy renditions of famous New Yorkers, past and present.

Hell's Kitchen

Until the 1990s, the whole area west of Eighth Avenue between 23rd and 59th Streets was usually referred to as Hell's Kitchen. During the late 1800s and much of the 1900s, this seedy part of town was gangland territory, home to such rival groups as the Gophers, the Gorillas, the Hudson Dusters, and more recently, the Westies. The Westies were still in business up until 1987 when former gang member Mickey Featherstone, arrested for murder, testified against his former colleagues in exchange for immunity.

Today, many civic-improvement types prefer to call the northern part of Hell's Kitchen "Clinton," in recognition of the extensive cleanup efforts made here in recent years. Though still home to plenty of crumbling tenements and shady characters, Clinton is rapidly becoming gentrified.

Intrepid Sea-Air-Space Museum

Docked at Pier 86 is the *Intrepid* (W. 46th St., at 12 Ave., 212/245-0072, www.intrepidmuseum.org, 10 A.M.–5 P.M. daily, with extended weekend hours in summer, closed Mondays in winter, adults $16.50, veterans and seniors $12.50, college students $12.50, students 6–17 $11.50, children 2–5 $4.50). A former World War II aircraft carrier now devoted to military history, the museum houses lots of hands-on exhibits, most designed to appeal to kids. The decks are strewn with small aircraft and space capsules; permanent exhibits explore the mysteries of satellite communication and ship design; special exhibits focus on such subjects as women pilots and Charles Lindbergh.

New York Public Library

This lavish, 1911 beaux arts building (Fifth Ave., between 40th and 42nd Sts.), designed by Carrere & Hastings, houses one of the world's top five research libraries. The library's collection of over nine million books and 21 million other objects occupies some 88 miles of shelves above ground and 84 miles below.

The library's grand entrance hall is flanked by sweeping staircases, while just beyond lies **Gottesman Hall** (212/869-8089), where exhibits on such subjects as illustrator Charles Addams or photographer Berenice Abbott are displayed. On the third floor is the **Main Reading Room,** big as a football field and sumptuous as the lobby of a luxury hotel. Books are ordered via a pneumatic tube system that sucks call slips down into the bowels of the stacks. It was in the library's Map Room that the U.S. Army planned the invasion of North Africa during World War II, and in the library's Science and Technology Room that Chester Carlson invented Xerox and Edwin Land invented the Polaroid camera.

The stone lions lounging outside the library were originally named "Leo Astor" and "Leo Lenox," after the library's founders John Jacob Astor and James Lenox. In the 1930s, Mayor La Guardia dubbed the felines "Patience" and "Fortitude"—qualities he felt New York would

© SEAN WATTERS

New York Public Library

need to survive the Depression. A popular saying of that time had it that the lions roared whenever a virgin passed by, but no one's mentioned that bit of folklore in years.

Free **tours** of the library are given Tuesday–Saturday at 11 A.M. and 2 P.M.

Bryant Park

Just behind the library is Bryant Park, filled with pretty flower beds, gravel paths, a stylish indoor-outdoor restaurant, and lots of benches that are usually packed with office workers at lunchtime. The park is named after poet and journalist William Cullen Bryant, a great proponent of parks and one of the people most responsible for the creation of Central Park.

International Center of Photography

Heading north one block, you'll find the largely subterranean International Center of Photography (1133 Sixth Ave., at 43rd St., 212/857-0000, www.icp.org, 10 A.M.–5 P.M.

Tues.–Thurs., 10 A.M.–8 P.M. Fri., 10 A.M.–6 P.M. Sat.–Sun., adults $10, students and seniors $7, children under 12 free). Once an offshoot of its parent institution on East 94th Street, the Sixth Avenue location now houses the center's entire operations, including spacious exhibit areas, a school, library, and bookshop. Founded in 1974 by Cornell Capa, Robert Capa's brother (Robert Capa was a photojournalist killed in Vietnam), the center presents many of the city's most important contemporary photography exhibits.

Diamond District

Continuing north, you'll come to the Diamond District, West 47th Street between Fifth and Sixth Avenues, where an estimated $400 million in gems is exchanged daily. Many—but far from all—of the dealers and cutters of the 2,500 companies crammed into this block are Hasidic Jews, identifiable by their long beards, earlocks, and black frock coats. As has long been their tradition, the Hasidim often negotiate their biggest deals in back rooms or out on the sidewalks.

Dahesh Museum of Art

One block north of the Diamond District is the compact Dahesh Museum (580 Madison Ave., between 56th and 57th St., 212/759-0606, www.daheshmuseum.org, 11 A.M.–6 P.M. Tues.–Sun., adults $9, students and seniors $4, children under 12 free), dedicated to 19th- and early-20th-century European academic art. The museum is named after a Lebanese writer and philosopher who acquired many of the works in the museum's collection. The changing exhibits cover a wide range, from Middle Eastern drawings to French landscapes.

Rockefeller Center

The area between 48th and 51st Streets, Fifth and Sixth Avenues, was once a notorious red-light district. Today it's occupied by New York's most famous city within a city, Rockefeller Center. Built by John D. Rockefeller during the height of the Depression, the magnificent art deco complex is comprised of 19 buildings, connected by plazas and underground passageways.

At the heart of the complex is the sunken **Lower Plaza,** home to an outdoor restaurant in summer, an ice-skating rink in winter, and great people-watching year-round. All around the plaza are towering flagpoles bearing colorful banners flapping in the wind, while at one end lounges an ungainly gilded Prometheus. At Christmastime, the famous Rockefeller tree is erected directly behind him.

Just west of Lower Plaza is **30 Rockefeller Plaza,** a 70-story art deco skyscraper designed by Raymond Hood. In its lobby is a rather bland mural, *American Progress,* painted by Jose Maria Sert to replace a much more controversial one by Diego Rivera. Commissioned by Rockefeller to create the original artwork, Rivera chose to depict Lenin and the proletariat taking over industry while important plutocrats were being eaten away by syphilis. Not surprisingly, that was too much for Rockefeller, and he had it replaced.

© SEAN WATTERS

Rockefeller Center

In 30 Rockefeller Plaza are the **NBC Studios** (49th St. between Fifth and Sixth Aves., 212/664-3700, www.shopnbc.com), where you can peer into the *Today* show studio window or take a tour. The one-hour tours leave from the **New York Experience Store** every 15 minutes 8:30 A.M.–5:30 P.M. Mon.–Sat. and 9:30 A.M.–4:30 P.M. Sunday (adults $17.95, children 6–16 and seniors $15.50, children under six not permitted, reservations recommended). Tours of Rockefeller Center also leave from here (adults $12, children 6–16 and seniors $10, children under six not permitted).

Radio City Music Hall

Despite, or perhaps because of, its dated feel, this art deco landmark (Sixth Ave. and 50th St., www.radiocity.com) has been bringing them back for generations. An over-the-top creation with a stage as wide as a city block, it's the world's largest indoor theater.

Part of Rockefeller Center, the Music Hall was largely created by impresario Samuel Lionel Rothafel, nicknamed Roxy. Born in a Lower East Side tenement, Roxy began his career by showing movies in the back room of a bar. From that humble beginning, he soon rose to become a major power in show business, producing radio shows and plays, and managing a string of theaters.

Though the Music Hall has hosted many unusual performers over the years—including elephants and horses—its most famous are the Rockettes. Chorus girls all between five feet four inches and five feet seven inches in height, the Rockettes once appeared nightly. Now they kick and strut their stuff only during the Music Hall's two-month-long Christmas show.

One-hour **backstage tours** (212/247-4777) are offered 10 A.M.–3 P.M. daily in summer; call for winter hours (adults $17, seniors $14, children under 12 $11).

◖ Museum of Modern Art (MoMA)

After a two-year stint in Queens, during which time its home was renovated and enlarged by architect Yoshio Taniguchi, the famed Museum of Modern Art (11 W. 53rd St., between Fifth and Sixth Aves., 212/708-9400, www.moma.org, 10:30 A.M.–5:30 P.M. Wed.–Mon. and 5:30–8 P.M. Fri., adults $20, seniors $16, students $12, children under 16 free) is back in Manhattan, bigger and better than ever. The museum's exhibit space has nearly doubled, to 620,000 square feet, and a bustling promenade, 110-foot atrium, sky-lit galleries, and a fine-dining restaurant, The Modern, have been added.

One of the world's foremost museums of modern art, MoMA opened in 1929, shortly after the crash of the stock market. The museum's collection includes over 150,000 paintings, sculptures, drawings, prints, photographs, and architectural models, and some 22,000 films, videos, and media works. Among its many famous holdings are Cezanne's *The Bather,* van Gogh's **Starry Night,** Rousseau's *The Sleeping Gypsy,* Magritte's *The Empire of Light,* Hopper's *Gas,* Rothko's *Red, Brown and Black,* de Chirico's *The Song of Love,* Picasso's *Les Demoiselles d'Avignon,* and Monet's *Water Lilies.*

MoMA screens films from its superb collection in two downstairs theaters. Ticket price is included in museum admission.

Other Museums

The shiny **Museum of Television and Radio** (25 W. 52nd St., between Fifth and Sixth Aves., 212/621-6800, www.mtr.org, noon–6 P.M. Tues.–Sun. and 6–8 P.M. Thurs., adults $10, students and seniors $8, children under 14 $5) was founded by William Paley and designed by Philip Johnson. Here you can watch your favorite old TV shows, listen to a classic radio broadcast, or research pop-culture subjects such as '50s sitcoms or beer commercials. The museum offers 96 semiprivate radio and television consoles, two large theaters, and two screening rooms, as well as more traditional exhibits on such topics as animation and costume design. If you'd like to use one of the consoles on the weekend, come early.

Formerly known as the American Crafts Museum, the **Museum of Arts & Design** is a sleek, modern institution (40 W. 53rd St., 212/956-3535, www.americancrafts-museum.org, 10 A.M.–6 P.M. Tues.–Sun. and 6–8 P.M. Thurs., adults $10, students and seniors $6, children under 12 free) engaged in an ambitious decade-long exhibit series tracing the history of American crafts and design. Exquisite textiles, ceramics, glasswork, and other crafts are on display. Also on site is a unique gift shop.

Recently relocated to 53rd Street from its old digs directly across from Lincoln Center is the **American Folk Art Museum** (45 W. 53rd St., between Fifth and Sixth Aves., 212/977-7170, www.folkartmuseum.org, 10:30 A.M.–5:30 P.M. Tues.–Sun., 5:30–7:30 P.M. Fri., adults $9, seniors and students $7, under 12 free). Now housed in an airy eight-story building—complete with a striking central atrium/staircase—the museum exhibits a wide range of folk art, including quilts, toys, weather vanes, paintings, sculpture, handmade furniture, and the like. Temporary exhibits often focus on the work of individual self-taught artists.

Fifth Avenue Churches

On Fifth Avenue between 50th and 51st Streets is **St. Patrick's Cathedral,** the largest Roman Catholic cathedral in the United States. Designed by James Renwick, this elaborate Gothic creation with its soaring towers and lovely rose window took 21 years to build, replacing the old St. Pat's in Little Italy in 1879. Its grandeur attests to the success of New York's Irish Catholics who, at that time, were largely shunned by the city's predominantly Protestant upper classes. Back then, some snooty upper crusts even went out of their way not to cross in front of the cathedral.

Kitty-corner to St. Pat's, at the corner of 53rd Street, is another famous New York church, the Protestant Episcopal **St. Thomas Church,** completed in 1914. A French Gothic gem known for its lovely stonework and stained glass, the church has long been a favorite site for society weddings. St. Thomas has a wonderful choir that can be heard on Sunday mornings or daily at evensong.

Villard Houses/ New York Palace Hotel

On Madison Avenue between 49th and 50th Streets are the 1886 Villard Houses, a group of six Italianate brownstones now incorporated into the New York Palace Hotel. Built for railroad magnate Henry Villard by McKim, Mead & White, the houses center on a courtyard, with the glass hotel tower rising behind. It's incongruous, but it works. Especially wonderful are two sweeping staircases and the Gold Room, built to resemble the music room of an Italian Renaissance palace.

Appropriately, the north wing of the Villard Houses serves as the **Urban Center** of the Municipal Art Society (457 Madison Ave., 212/935-3960, www.mas.org, 11 A.M.–5 P.M. Mon.–Wed. and Fri.–Sat., free admission), dedicated to historic preservation and urban planning. The center holds an excellent bookstore and exhibition halls; the society sponsors some of the city's best walking tours.

Trump Tower

At Fifth Avenue and 56th Street stands Trump Tower, a glittering rose-and-gilt edifice with its own nexus of shops. Open daily (8 A.M.–10 P.M.; shop hours vary), Trump Tower boasts a skinny cascading waterfall, far too much brass, and a multitude of glitzy escalators.

57th Street

Like 42nd Street, 57th Street is one of the city's major east-west thoroughfares and one that changes character as it heads crosstown. To the east, 57th is the poshest of areas, with some of the city's most expensive boutiques and art galleries. To the west, the street becomes sort of an outdoor theme park for adults.

Among the street's most famous galleries is the uptown branch of **PaceWildenstein** (32 E. 57th St., 212/421-3292), representing such heavyweights as Picasso, Louise Nevelson, and Julian Schnabel. **Marian Goodman** (24 W. 57th, 212/977-7160) specializes in contemporary European artists. **Greenberg Van Doren** (730 Fifth Ave., at 57th St., 212/445-0444) represents primarily American artists, both established and up-and-coming.

As for that theme park, the fun begins at Sixth Avenue, where you'll find the **Jekyll and Hyde Club** (1409 Sixth Ave., 212/541-9517, www.jekyllandhydeclub.com), decked out with sinking bar stools and talking corpses. On 57th Street proper are the **Brooklyn Diner USA** (212 W. 57th St., 212/977-2280, www.brooklyn-diner.com), serving enormous platters of home-style cooking; and the **Hard Rock Cafe** (221 W. 57th St., between Broadway and Seventh Ave., 212/489-6565, www.hardrock.com), bejeweled with shiny guitars and gold records.

The Plaza

Just west of Fifth Avenue between 58th and 59th Streets stands the famed Plaza Hotel, still one of New York's loveliest buildings. Designed by Henry Hardenbergh in 1907, it's built in a French Renaissance style, with lots of dormers, high roofs, and rounded corners. In early 2005, it appeared as if the Plaza would soon be closed to the general public, to be completely converted into condominiums. However, a last minute deal between the hotel's new owners and its workers union, brokered by Major Bloomberg, led to a compromise. About 350 of the Plaza's 800 rooms will remain hotel rooms; the rest will be converted into 150 apartments. The hotel's famed public spaces, including the Palm Court and the Oak Bar, will remain just that.

The hotel closed in April 2005 for renovations, and is scheduled to reopen in late 2006 or early 2007.

Central Park South (59th Street) on the Plaza's north side is a gathering place for the **horse-drawn hansoms** that clip-clop their way throughout this part of town ($34 for 20 minutes). For more information, call the Manhattan Carriage Company (212/664-1149).

UPPER EAST SIDE SIGHTS

Since the turn of the century, the Upper East Side has been associated with wealth. Everyone from Andrew Carnegie to Gloria Vanderbilt has resided in this hushed, exclusive neighborhood. Here you'll find so many mansions and brownstones, clubs and penthouses, that at times the neighborhood resembles an open-air museum.

The wealthy began arriving on the Upper East Side in the late 1800s as an ever-encroaching business tide forced them off the Midtown stretches of Fifth Avenue. But the real turning point came in 1905, when steel magnate Andrew Carnegie built his mansion on Fifth Avenue at 91st Street. Soon thereafter, one industrialist after another followed suit, until the stretch of Fifth Avenue facing Central Park became known as "Millionaire's Row." Many of these mansions have since been converted into museums and cultural institutions.

But the Upper East Side is not only about the wealthy. It's also about more ordinary folk, who—as elsewhere in Manhattan—settled closer to the river. At one time, Madison, Park, and Lexington Avenues were basically middle-class, while the area east of Lexington was working-class and home to recent immigrants. Yorkville, a hamlet established in the 1790s between what are now 83rd and 88th Streets, had an especially large German population.

Stretching roughly from 59th to 100th Street, Fifth Avenue to the East River, the Upper East Side's long residential blocks are pleasant for strolling. Most of the sights and shops are along the north-south avenues rather than the east-west side streets. Madison Avenue is famed for its upscale shops.

The Frick Collection

Now a museum, the former home of industrialist Henry Clay Frick (1 E. 70th St., 212/288-0700, www.frick.org, 10 A.M.–6 P.M. Tues.–Sat., 1–6 P.M. Sun., adults $12, students and seniors $8, children under 10 not admitted) is one of the city's most beautiful residences. It's a classic 1914 mansion built around a courtyard and an exquisite European art collection. Every room is hung with masterpieces—by Breughel, El Greco, Hogarth, Vermeer, Rembrandt, Turner, and others—yet the place maintains a private, homey feel.

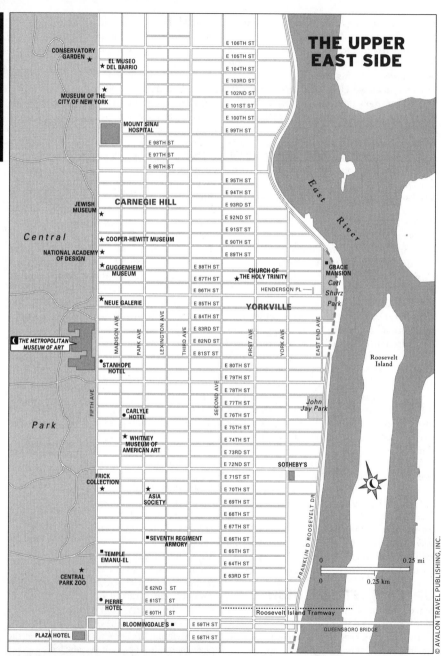

THE UPPER EAST SIDE

CONSERVATORY GARDEN ★

★ EL MUSEO DEL BARRIO

★ MUSEUM OF THE CITY OF NEW YORK

MOUNT SINAI HOSPITAL

JEWISH MUSEUM ★

CARNEGIE HILL

★ COOPER-HEWITT MUSEUM

NATIONAL ACADEMY OF DESIGN ★

★ GUGGENHEIM MUSEUM

★ NEUE GALERIE

Central

☾ THE METROPOLITAN MUSEUM OF ART

● STANHOPE HOTEL

● CARLYLE HOTEL

★ WHITNEY MUSEUM OF AMERICAN ART

FRICK COLLECTION ★

★ ASIA SOCIETY

■ SEVENTH REGIMENT ARMORY

■ TEMPLE EMANU-EL

★ CENTRAL PARK ZOO

Park

● PIERRE HOTEL

■ BLOOMINGDALE'S

PLAZA HOTEL

East River

CHURCH OF ★ THE HOLY TRINITY

HENDERSON PL —

YORKVILLE

■ GRACIE MANSION

Carl Shurz Park

Roosevelt Island

John Jay Park

SOTHEBY'S

E 106TH ST
E 105TH ST
E 104TH ST
E 103RD ST
E 102ND ST
E 101ST ST
E 100TH ST
E 99TH ST
E 98TH ST
E 97TH ST
E 96TH ST
E 95TH ST
E 94TH ST
E 93RD ST
E 92ND ST
E 91ST ST
E 90TH ST
E 89TH ST
E 88TH ST
E 87TH ST
E 86TH ST
E 85TH ST
E 84TH ST
E 83RD ST
E 82ND ST
E 81ST ST
E 80TH ST
E 79TH ST
E 78TH ST
E 77TH ST
E 76TH ST
E 75TH ST
E 74TH ST
E 73RD ST
E 72ND ST
E 71ST ST
E 70TH ST
E 69TH ST
E 68TH ST
E 67TH ST
E 66TH ST
E 65TH ST
E 64TH ST
E 63RD ST
E 62ND ST
E 61ST ST
E 60TH ST
E 59TH ST
E 58TH ST

MADISON AVE
PARK AVE
LEXINGTON AVE
THIRD AVE
SECOND AVE
FIRST AVE
YORK AVE
EAST END AVE
FIFTH AVE
FRANKLIN D ROOSEVELT DR

Roosevelt Island Tramway

QUEENSBORO BRIDGE

0   0.25 mi
0   0.25 km

The Frick's most famous room is the Fragonard Room, where all four walls are covered with *The Progress of Love,* painted by French artist Jean-Honoré Fragonard. The panels were originally commissioned by Louis XV for his lover, Mme. du Barry.

Despite his impeccable taste, Frick was reputedly one of the nastiest of the early American capitalists. A pioneer in the coke and steel industries, he repeatedly used violence to break up labor unions, at one time sending in 300 thugs who provoked a riot in which 14 people were killed.

Whitney Museum of American Art

The boxy gray building with the wedge-shaped front at the corner of Madison Avenue and 75th Street is the Whitney Museum of American Art (945 Madison Ave., 212/570-3676, www.whitney.org, 11 A.M.–6 P.M. Wed.–Sun., 6–9 P.M. Fri., adults $12, students and seniors $9.50, children under 12 free). Designed by Marcel Breuer in 1966, the museum offers plenty to see but not enough to overwhelm.

Many of the museum's changing exhibits feature the work of one 20th-century American artist. Past shows have focused on Edward Hopper, Maurice Prendergast, Jasper Johns, Isamu Noguchi, and Jacques Basquiat, to name just a few. Founded in Greenwich Village by Gertrude Vanderbilt Whitney in 1930 (see *Greenwich Village,* above), the museum is also known for its superb permanent collection and its controversial "Biennial" show, presented every two years to showcase the latest works of contemporary American artists. The next biennial will be held in the year 2006.

◖ The Metropolitan Museum of Art

One of the world's greatest museums is the Metropolitan Museum of Art (1000 Fifth Ave., at 82nd St., 212/535-7710, www.metmuseum.org, 9:30 A.M.–5:30 P.M. Tues.–Sun., 5:30–9 P.M. Fri.–Sat., recommended admission adults $15, seniors $10, students $7), on the east side of Central Park at Fifth Avenue

and 82nd Street. Housed behind an imposing beaux arts facade designed by Robert Morris Hunt, the museum boasts collections of almost everything from Egyptian sarcophagi to modern American paintings.

Equally important, the museum's exhibitions are well edited and well viewed. This is not an elite or stuffy institution. On weekends, the place takes on a carnival air as jugglers, acrobats, and vendors hawk their talents and wares on the museum's wide staircase out front.

Founded in 1870, the Met centers on the Great Hall, a vast entrance room with an imposing staircase. From the hall, the Met spreads out over about 1.5 million square feet holding nearly three million works of art.

Directly up the staircase from the Great Hall is one of the Met's most stunning collections—the **European paintings,** filling some 20-odd galleries. One room is filled with Rembrandts only; others house Vermeer, Van Dyck, Breughel, Rubens, Botticelli, El Greco, Goya, and many others.

To the right of the Great Hall is its famed

the peerless Met – to be visited time and again

Egyptian collection, displaying items as old as 4,000 years. The Met houses the largest collection of Egyptian art outside Egypt.

Three sides of the Met's original building are flanked by modern glass wings. At the back is the Robert Lehman Collection, housing an impressive collection of Old Masters and 19th-century French painters. On the south side are the Rockefeller and Acheson Wings. The Rockefeller Wing is named after Michael C. Rockefeller, who disappeared while on a research expedition in New Guinea. Many of the items on display were collected during Rockefeller's earlier expeditions, and they're mind-boggling works ranging from intricately carved 100-foot-long canoes to towering musical instruments made of hollowed logs. The Lila Acheson Wing is devoted to 20th-century art; on its roof is a sculpture garden with great views of Central Park.

On the Met's north side are the Sackler and American Wings. The Sackler Wing houses the 15th-century-B.C. Temple of Dendur, carved in faded hieroglyphics. The American Wing contains exhaustive galleries of decorative arts, and many fine paintings by the likes of Gilbert Stuart, Thomas Eakins, John Singer Sargent, and Mary Cassatt.

If possible, avoid the Met on weekends, when it can get exceedingly crowded. Come on a weekday morning instead, or on a Friday or Saturday evening when the candlelit Great Hall Balcony Bar is open and a jazz or classical quintet performs.

Neue Galerie

One of the newer museums in town is the Neue Galerie (1048 Fifth Ave., at 86th St., 212/628-6200, www.neuegalerie.org, 11 A.M.–6 P.M. Sat.–Mon., 11 A.M.–9 P.M., adults $10, seniors and students $7, children under 12 not admitted), devoted solely to the fine and decorative arts of Germany and Austria from the first half of the 20th century. Housed in a renovated beaux arts mansion, the museum holds a large permanent collection of works by Gustav Klimt and Egon Schiele, a bookstore, design shop, and the smart Cafe Sabarsky, where you can indulge in Viennese coffee and a piece of Sacher torte.

Guggenheim Museum

The Solomon R. Guggenheim Museum (1071 Fifth Ave., at 89th St., 212/423-3500, www.guggenheim.org, 10 A.M.–6 P.M. Sat.–Wed., 10 A.M.–8 P.M. Fri., adults $15, students and seniors $10, children under 12 free) first opened its doors in 1959, and immediately met with considerable controversy. The city's only Frank Lloyd Wright–designed building, it was compared to everything from a snail to a toilet bowl. Nowadays it's hard to see what the fuss was about. From the outside, the circular building seems as permanent a part of Fifth Avenue as the neoclassic buildings that surround it, while from the inside, the multi-leveled spirals of the main galleries seem almost staid. To show how times have changed, the museum was even declared a New York City landmark in 1989—the youngest building ever to be so honored.

The main galleries of the Guggenheim are usually devoted to a temporary exhibition of a major modern artist or group of artists. Abutting the main galleries is a small rotunda housing the Justin K. Thannhauser Collection. Works by Picasso, Rousseau, van Gogh, Modigliani, and Seurat, to name but a few, are on permanent display, and they're a stunning group, not to be missed. Also abutting the main galleries is a 10-story tower with lots more exhibition space, lit by skylights, and an outdoor sculpture garden.

Cooper-Hewitt National Design Museum

A branch of the Smithsonian Institution dedicated to design and the decorative arts, the Cooper-Hewitt (2 E. 91st St., 212/849-8400, www.si.edu/ndm, 10 A.M.–5 P.M. Tues.–Sat., 5–9 P.M. Fri., noon–6 P.M. Sun., adults $10, students and seniors $7, free to children under 12) focuses on such areas as textiles, metal-work, wallpaper, ceramics, furniture, and architectural design. But half the story is the building itself; the museum occupies a 64-

room mansion built by industrialist Andrew Carnegie.

Carnegie was a Scottish immigrant who began his career as a bobbin boy in a cotton factory. By the time he built this mansion, he was one of the world's richest men, head of an empire that included steamship and railroad lines, and iron, coal, and steel companies.

The magnificent 1901 building is a delight to wander through. Built by Babb, Cook & Willard in a heavy Georgian style, the mansion boasts dark wood paneling, an imposing carved staircase, and what was once the first passenger elevator in a private home. Out back is a romantic garden, where concerts are sometimes presented.

The Jewish Museum

Housed in a magnificent French Gothic mansion once belonging to businessman Felix Warburg, the Jewish Museum (1109 Fifth Ave., at 92nd St., 212/423-3200, www.thejewishmuseum.org, 11 A.M.–5:45 P.M. Sun.–Wed., 11 A.M.–8 P.M. Thurs., 11 A.M.–3 P.M. Fri., adults $10, students and seniors $7.50, free to children under 12) is the nation's largest Jewish-culture museum. Spread over three floors and a basement are top-notch, changing exhibits on such subjects as "The Dreyfus Affair," or "Jews and African Americans," as well as an outstanding permanent collection of ceremonial objects and cultural artifacts.

Museum of the City of New York

The renovated, neo-Georgian building on Fifth Avenue between 103rd and 104th Streets houses the one-of-a-kind Museum of the City of New York (1220 Fifth Ave., 212/534-1672, www.mcny.com, 10 A.M.–5 P.M. Tues.–Sat., suggested donation adults $7; students, seniors and children $5; families $15). Inside this eclectic establishment, find a vast collection of paintings and photographs, maps and prints, furniture and clothing, Broadway memorabilia and old model ships—all telling the story of New York City. The museum also features imaginative temporary exhibits, on such subjects as Duke Ellington, New York

City mayors, photographer Jessie Tarbox Beals, and stickball.

El Museo del Barrio

Dedicated to the art and culture of Puerto Rico and Latin America, El Museo del Barrio (1230 Fifth Ave., between 104th and 105th Sts., 212/831-7272, www.elmuseo.org, 11 A.M.–5 P.M. Wed.–Sun., 5–8 P.M. Thurs., adults $8, students and seniors $5, children under 12 free) presents both contemporary and historical exhibits. Just a few blocks from Spanish Harlem, it was founded in an elementary school classroom over 25 years ago, and continues to work closely with local residents. Most of its exhibits are temporary; on permanent display is a superb collection of *santos de palo,* or carved wooden saints.

Note: One block north of El Museo at 105th Street is Central Park's lovely **Conservatory Garden,** most easily entered from Fifth Avenue (see *Central Park,* below).

The Asia Society

First-rate temporary exhibits, concerts, films, and lectures on various aspects of Asian culture and history are always on the docket at the Asia Society (725 Park Ave., at 70th St., 212/288-6400, www.asiasociety.org, 11 A.M.–6 P.M. Tues.–Sun., 6–9 P.M. Fri., adults $7, students and seniors $5, children under 16 free). Inside the modern red-granite building, centered on a striking undulating staircase, you'll also find a permanent collection containing everything from Nepalese sculpture to Chinese paintings.

Roosevelt Island

Swinging high above the east end of 60th Street is one of Manhattan's more incongruous sights—the Roosevelt Island cable car (tram station at Second Ave. and 60th St., 212/832-4540, maps of island available at ticket booth). The ride lasts four minutes, costs $2 one way, and sets you down in one of New York's stranger neighborhoods, Roosevelt Island.

Eerily quiet after the hubbub of Manhattan, Roosevelt Island is a planned residential

Roosevelt Island cable car

community where no private cars are allowed. Designed by Philip Johnson and John Burgee, it was built in the 1970s as an "Instant City." In addition to about 3,200 units of mixed-income housing, the community has its own schools, stores, and hospitals, and a promenade with good views of Manhattan.

Roosevelt Island was once known as Blackwell's Island, named after its original owner, Robert Blackwell. In 1828, the city bought the island and turned it into a penal institution for petty criminals. A grim and nasty place, it was notorious for frequent riots and innovative tortures, including "cooler" rooms and the "water drop cure." Politician Boss Tweed served time there in 1873, and actress Mae West spent 10 days behind bars in 1927 for her notorious play *Sex*. Others incarcerated on the island included anarchist Emma Goldman and birth control advocate Ethel Byrne.

During the 1800s, a poorhouse, pavilion for the insane, and several hospitals were added to the island, which in 1921 was renamed Welfare Island. These institutions were also notori-ous for their inhumane conditions—eventually exposed by Charles Dickens and Nellie Bly. Today, the remains of the insane pavilion—a haunting octagonal structure of gray stone—still stand near the island's north end.

◖ CENTRAL PARK

Between the Upper East and the Upper West Sides lies that most glorious of New York institutions, Central Park (between Fifth and Eighth Aves., 59th and 110th Sts., 212/794-6564, www.centralpark.org). Without this vast, rolling estate of green—the lungs of the city—life in New York would become unbearable. Central Park is where New Yorkers go to escape cramped apartments, roaring traffic, and an endless cityscape of concrete and steel.

The Central Park, as it was once known, was the brainchild of poet turned newspaper editor William Cullen Bryant. Worried that the city was being smothered by block after block of relentless building, Bryant first called for the park's creation in the July 3, 1844, edition of his *Evening Post*. Landscape architect Andrew Jackson Downing and a number of politicians soon added their voices to Bryant's plea. Together, they hammered away at city government for 12 years until finally, in 1856, the city bought most of what is now the park for $5 million.

Frederick Law Olmsted and Calvert Vaux were the visionary landscape architects who turned Bryant's Central Park dream into reality. As Olmsted saw it, the park had two functions. One was to provide a place for the contemplation of nature. The other was to create a social mixing bowl where the haves and have-nots could pass each other every day, providing an opportunity for the poor to become inspired by the rich.

Entirely manufactured—with every bush, tree, and rock planned—the park took 20 years to complete. By the time it was finished, workers had shifted 10 million cartloads of dirt, imported a half-million cubic yards of topsoil, and planted four to five million trees. Central Park was such an immediate success that it led to a park movement across the United States and the world.

Central Park is 2.5 miles long and a half mile wide, covers 843 acres, and hosts 15–20 million visitors annually. Walking through it is like walking through some gigantic carnival site. You'll see scantily clad in-line skaters, svelte bicyclists, oblivious lovers, sports-crazed kids, cough-racked beggars, cashmere-clad matrons, professional dog-walkers, and musicians playing everything from rock to rap. Every size, shape, color, and make of humanity is here.

Generally speaking, the park is safe, but it's always advisable to stick to well-populated areas, especially during the week, when fewer people use the park. Avoid the park completely at night.

South of 65th Street

Entering Central Park at Fifth Avenue and 59th Street, you'll soon come to the **Central Park Wildlife Center** (830 Fifth Ave., 212/439-6500, 10 A.M.–5:30 P.M. daily in summer, reduced hours in winter, adults $6, seniors $1.25, children 3–12 $1). This small gem groups its animals by climatic zones; especially fun is Polar Circle, where polar bears prowl and penguins promenade in a snowy clime behind thick glass. At the zoo's northeast end is **Delacorte Clock,** where every hour a parade of bronze animals marches around playing nursery tunes.

Across from the wildlife center is **Wollman Rink** (212/439-6900, www.wollmanskatingrink.com), packed in winter with exuberant ice-skaters. North of the rink is the octagonal **Chess and Checkers House,** complete with 24 concrete game boards outside and 10 inside.

The nearby **Dairy** building houses a **Visitors' Information Center** (212/794-6564, 10 A.M.–5 P.M. Tues.–Sun.; events hotline, 212/360-3456). West of the Dairy is the 1908 **Carousel** (10 A.M.–4:30 P.M. daily, extended hours in summer, weather permitting, $1), where 58 carved horses go 'round. Other amusement rides are here as well.

The sunken transverse road running from East 65th Street to West 66th Street is one of four such roads in the park (others at 79th, 85th, and 97th Streets). These roads were one

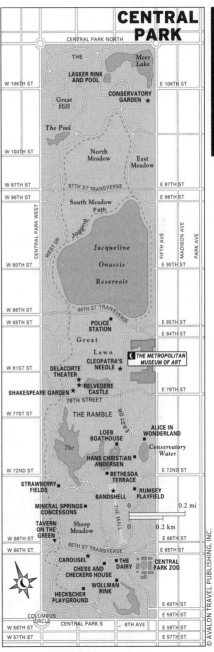

of Olmsted's most brilliant innovations. Dynamited out of bedrock, they allow cars and buses to pass below the level of the park, while pedestrians pass on bridges above.

65th Street to 72nd Street

Heading a bit farther north and west, you'll come to **Tavern-on-the-Green** (67th St. and Central Park West, 212/873-3200), a glittering extravaganza of a restaurant. Built to resemble a deluxe Victorian cottage, the over-the-top Tavern is packed to the bursting point with brass, glass, mirrors, chandeliers, and thousands upon thousands of tiny lights. In the late afternoons, the place takes on a fairy-tale air.

Next door is **Sheep Meadow,** a huge expanse of lawn covered with thousands of semiclad sun-worshippers in warm weather. Real sheep grazed here until 1934. By then, the sheep were so inbred that many were malformed.

East of Sheep's Meadow is the **Mall,** a promenade lined with trees and busts of famous men. This quarter-mile avenue was once a parade ground for the elite, who cruised up and down in the late afternoons, courting and showing

off their fancy carriages. Today, the Mall is frequented by in-line skaters; on the weekends, dozens of lithe, muscular skaters dressed in tight, bright spandex, twist and turn, jump and flex as music blasts from a big black box.

North of the Mall is the bandshell at **Rumsey Playfield,** where a first-rate series of free outdoor concerts is presented every summer by **SummerStage** (212/360-2777, www.summerstage.org). Past performers have ranged from blueswoman Ruth Brown to the Erick Hawkins Dance Company.

72nd Street to 79th Street

Bethesda Terrace, just north of the bandshell and the 72nd Street Transverse, is one of the park's grandest sights. The wide, brick-paved plaza centers on an ornate fountain; a semicircle of tiered steps cups the plaza's southern side. Lapping at the north end is **The Lake,** usually crowded with splish-splashing rowboats. These boats can be rented at the nearby **Loeb Boathouse** (212/517-4723, 10 A.M.–6 P.M. daily, $10 per hour, with a $20 cash deposit). Also at the boathouse is a bike-rental shop.

© SEAN WATTERS

Loeb Boathouse in Central Park

West of Bethesda Terrace is **Strawberry Fields,** which Yoko Ono had landscaped into a Garden of Peace as a memorial to her husband John Lennon, who was murdered outside The Dakota apartment building (see *Upper West Side Sights* in this chapter) in 1980. Just inside the garden's wall at 72nd Street is a circular marble mosaic spelling out the word *Imagine.*

East of Bethesda Terrace is **Conservatory Water,** a.k.a., the "model-boat pond." The pond is often dotted with miniature boats, most radio-controlled. During warm weather, model-boat regattas are held Saturday mornings.

Near the pond are two of the park's most famous statues. *Alice in Wonderland,* by Jose de Creefts, perches on a mushroom to the north, while *Hans Christian Andersen,* by Georg Lober, sits with his *Ugly Duckling* to the west. Both statues are usually covered with adoring children.

West of the pond and north of The Lake is the 38-acre **Ramble,** a near wild place crisscrossed with meandering paths. Far removed from city life, the Ramble is a favorite spot among bird-watchers; on a typical morning, about 15 kinds of warblers and 35 other species can be seen. It's also a prime haunt for gay men on the make. It's best not to visit the Ramble alone.

79th Street to 97th Street

North of the Ramble reigns the Gothic Revival **Belvedere Castle,** designed in 1858 by Calvert Vaux. Situated atop Vista Rock, one of the park's highest spots, the castle offers bird's-eye views. Downstairs is the **Central Park Learning Center** (9 A.M.–dusk, free admission).

Near the castle is the **Shakespeare Garden,** filled with plants and flowers mentioned in the playwright's work, and the **Delacorte Theater,** where a free **New York Shakespeare Festival** (212/539-8750 or 212/539-8500) is produced every summer. Two plays are usually featured, each running about a month. The free tickets for each day's show are handed out beginning at 6:15 P.M. the same day; people start lining up in the early afternoon.

Abutting the Delacorte Theater is the often dusty **Great Lawn.** Tens of thousands of New Yorkers spread out their blankets and picnic baskets on the lawn when the New York Philharmonic and the Metropolitan Opera Company perform here.

North of the Great Lawn is Central Park Reservoir, now known as **Jacqueline Onassis Reservoir** because the former first lady used to jog around its 1.58-mile perimeter. This is the city's most popular jogging course; the reservoir holds about a billion gallons of water, most of which comes via aqueduct from the Catskills.

North of 97th Street

As Frederick Law Olmsted originally intended, the northernmost section of Central Park, between 97th and 110th Streets, becomes more rugged and wild, filled with secret waterfalls and craggy cliffs. But at 105th Street near Fifth Avenue is the lovely, formal **Conservatory Garden.** Actually three gardens in one, the Conservatory blooms from late spring through early fall. Its most popular spot is the Secret Garden, named after Frances Hodgson Burnett's classic book.

Just above the Conservatory is 11-acre **Meer Lake.** Up until the mid 1990s, this lake—like much of the park above 97th Street—was avoided by New Yorkers fearful of crime. But since then, the Central Park Conservancy has poured millions of dollars into the area, and it's been vastly improved. Meer Lake is now stocked with some 50,000 bluegill, largemouth bass, and catfish, and is a favorite fishing grounds for youngsters who are given free poles.

On the edge of Meer Lake is the **Charles A. Dana Discovery Center** (10 A.M.–5 P.M. daily, free admission). The center houses natural-history exhibits and offers hands-on science programs.

UPPER WEST SIDE SIGHTS

The Upper West Side is a mix of ornate 19th-century landmarks, solid pre–WWII apartment buildings, well-worn tenements, and some outstanding cultural institutions, including Lincoln Center and the American Museum of Natural

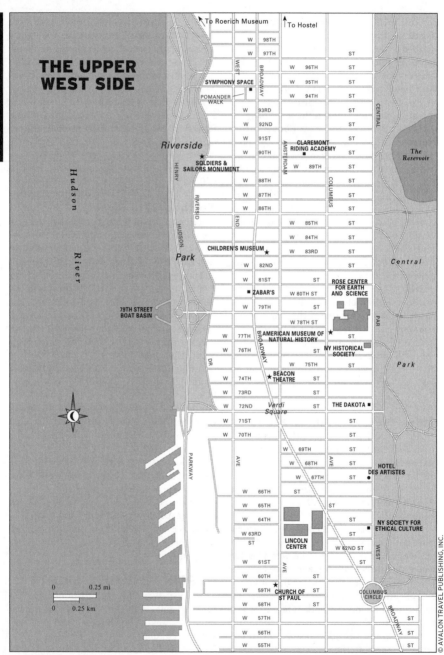

THE UPPER WEST SIDE

To Roerich Museum

To Hostel

SYMPHONY SPACE

POMANDER WALK

Riverside

SOLDIERS & SAILORS MONUMENT

CLAREMONT RIDING ACADEMY

The Reservoir

H u d s o n

R i v e r

HENRY HUDSON

RIVERSID

END

Park

CHILDREN'S MUSEUM

ZABAR'S

ROSE CENTER FOR EARTH AND SCIENCE

Central

79TH STREET BOAT BASIN

AMERICAN MUSEUM OF NATURAL HISTORY

NY HISTORICAL SOCIETY

Park

BEACON THEATRE

Verdi Square

THE DAKOTA

HOTEL DES ARTISTES

NY SOCIETY FOR ETHICAL CULTURE

LINCOLN CENTER

CHURCH OF ST PAUL

COLUMBUS CIRCLE

PARKWAY

DR

BROADWAY

WEST

AMSTERDAM

COLUMBUS

CENTRAL

AVE

PAR

WEST

BROADWAY

W 98TH
W 97TH ST
W 96TH ST
W 95TH
W 94TH
W 93RD ST
W 92ND
W 91ST
W 90TH ST
W 89TH ST
W 88TH ST
W 87TH ST
W 86TH
W 85TH
W 84TH
W 83RD
W 82ND
W 81ST ST
W 80TH ST
W 79TH
W 78TH ST
W 77TH ST
W 76TH ST
W 75TH ST
W 74TH ST
W 73RD ST
W 72ND ST
W 71ST
W 70TH ST
W 69TH ST
W 68TH ST
W 67TH ST
W 66TH ST
W 65TH ST
W 64TH ST
W 63RD ST
W 62ND ST
W 61ST
W 60TH ST
W 59TH ST
W 58TH
W 57TH
W 56TH ST
W 55TH ST

0   0.25 mi

0   0.25 km

History. The neighborhood is also known for its feisty liberal politics, love of culture, and upper-middle class, including an especially large quotient of doctors, lawyers, writers, actors, musicians, dancers, and intellectuals.

Throughout the 19th century, the Upper West Side was called the Bloomingdale district, named after the Dutch word for "vale of flowers." The area only began developing in the late 1800s with the building of the Dakota, a grand apartment house. Prior to the Dakota, most middle-class and wealthy Americans regarded the apartment-house concept as too "French"—i.e., risqué and common. All those strangers rubbing shoulders together in communal hallways! The lavish appointments of the Dakota quickly changed that attitude.

Today, the best streets for wandering are Broadway and Columbus Avenue, both lined with a multitude of shops. In comparison, the streets running from east to west tend to be quiet and almost exclusively residential.

Lincoln Center

On Broadway between 62nd and 66th Streets is the famed Lincoln Center for the Performing Arts (212/LINCOLN, www.lincolncenter.org), presenting about 3,000 performances each year. The center is built around a wide marble plaza with a circular fountain in the middle.

Lincoln Center consists of three major theaters and an assortment of related buildings. **Avery Fisher Hall,** on the plaza's north side, is where the New York Philharmonic performs. The **Metropolitan Opera House,** on the plaza's west side, is the center's most ornate building, graced with sparkling multistoried windows and two vivid murals by Marc Chagall. The **New York State Theater,** on the plaza's south side, is home to the New York City Opera and the New York City Ballet.

Lincoln Center tours (212/875-5350) leave daily from the concourse level. Metropolitan Opera House tours (212/769-7020) are also offered. In July and August, the Lincoln Center Festival takes place in and around the arts complex; in late July and early August, **Midsummer Night Swing** offers dancing to live bands on the plaza beneath the stars. For more information on Lincoln Center festivals, call 212/875-5766.

In 2004, Lincoln Center opened **Jazz at Lincoln Center's Frederick P. Rose Hall,** the first large facility in the world designed specifically for jazz.

The Dakota

Impressive buildings stand sentinel along Central Park West (CPW), the extension of Eighth Avenue that borders Central Park. Most famous among them is the Dakota (northwest corner of 72nd St. and CPW). Built in 1884, the Dakota was financed by Edward Clark, heir to the Singer Sewing Machine fortune. At that time, the building stood so far north of the rest of Manhattan that it was said to be as remote as Dakota. Clark liked that idea, and had the architect, Henry Hardenburgh, add ears of corn and an Indian's head above the entrance.

the grand Dakota apartment building

© CHRISTIANE BIRD

Built of light-colored brick, the Dakota resembles a European chateau. A dry moat topped with a cast-iron fence surrounds the building, and a porter in a sentry box guards the front door.

The Dakota's roster of famous tenants is exceptionally long; on it are Lauren Bacall, Judy Holliday, Jack Palance, Roberta Flack, Fannie Hurst, Jose Ferrer, Rosemary Clooney, John Lennon, Yoko Ono, Gilda Radner, and William Henry Pratt, a.k.a. Boris Karloff. Legend has it that on Halloween, the kids in the building were too afraid of Karloff to take any of the trick-or-treat candy he left outside his door.

John Lennon was murdered outside the Dakota on December 8, 1980. His assassin, Mark David Chapman (whose *Double Fantasy* album Lennon had autographed only six hours earlier), jumped out of the shadows as the star returned home and shot him four times in the back and chest. By the time the cops arrived, Chapman was leaning against the side of the Dakota reading *Catcher in the Rye.* "Please don't hurt me," he said as he was arrested.

New-York Historical Society

After a few shaky financial years in the 1990s, the New-York Historical Society (2 W. 77th St., at CPW, 212/873-3400, www.nyhistory.org, 10 A.M.–6 P.M. Tues.–Sun., adults $10, children and seniors $5, children under 12 free) is back with a roar. Founded in 1806, it was one of the country's first cultural institutions, and now boasts a brand new 17,000-square-foot gallery space. On permanent display are such artifacts as George Washington's Valley Forge cot and an exhibit about New York circa 1901 for kids. Temporary exhibits focus all aspects of the city's history, from immigrants to board games.

American Museum of Natural History

One of the city's greatest museums, the huge, sprawling American Museum of Natural History (CPW at 79th St., 212/769-5100, www.amnh.org, 10 A.M.–5:45 P.M. Sun.–Thurs., 10 A.M.–8:45 P.M. Fri.–Sat., adults $13, students and seniors $10, children under 12 $7.50) is es-

pecially famous for its breathtaking dioramas of animals in their natural habitats and state-of-the-art dinosaur exhibitions. Housed beneath soaring windows, the dinosaurs are mounted in dramatic poses, just as they might have appeared millions of years ago. The most amazing skeleton of all is that of a skinny, 50-foot-high barosaurus arching its angry neck high into a dome as it protects its young from the much smaller allosaurus.

Other highlights of the museum include the African Mammals wing, featuring seven furious stampeding elephants, and the Hall of Human Biology and Evolution, where a holographic "Visible Woman" struts her circulatory stuff. In total, the museum owns close to 40 million specimens.

Adjoining the museum is the **Rose Center for Earth and Space.** Here, you'll find the Hayden Planetarium, equipped with a state-of-the-art Zeiss sky projector capable of projecting 9,100 stars as viewed from earth.

Children's Museum of Manhattan

The bright and cheery Children's Museum (212 W. 83rd St., between Broadway and Amsterdam Ave., 212/721-1223, www.cmom.org, 10 A.M.–5 P.M. Wed.–Sun., also Tues. in summer, admission $8, free to children up to age one) is full of hands-on exhibits for kids ages 2–10. Here, children can draw and paint, learn crafts, play at being newscasters, listen to stories, or just explore one of the always-changing play areas.

Riverside Park and the Boat Basin

Riverside Drive abuts Riverside Park, a long and narrow sloping slice of green that stretches from 72nd to 153rd Street along the Hudson River. Designed in the 1870s by Frederick Law Olmsted and Calvert Vaux, the park is a pleasant place with glorious views of the Hudson. Near the park's south end is the **79th Street Boat Basin,** where houseboats dock.

HARLEM AND UPPER MANHATTAN SIGHTS

Stretching roughly from 110th to 168th Streets, between the Harlem and Hudson Rivers, Harlem is one of the city's most historic and least understood neighborhoods. Once written off as a crime-infested no-man's-land, it's actually always been quite a diverse place, with many streets that are well-worn rather than raw, and a landscape studded with an impressive number of elegant brownstones and churches.

Harlem is currently in the midst of what some are calling the Second Harlem Renaissance. Middle-class New Yorkers—black and white—have moved back in, new businesses have opened up, and property values have risen, much to the lament of many locals. Former president Bill Clinton brought much attention to Harlem when he opened his post–White House office here (at 55 W. 125th St.). A **Harlem USA Mall,** complete with the area's first Disney Store and The Gap, now stands on 125th Street.

The area is divided into West/Central Harlem—composed mostly of African Americans—and East Harlem, home to many Latinos and some Italians. To the north of 155th Street is **Washington Heights,** home to the Cloisters.

Much of Harlem can safely be explored on foot. The areas around 116th Street, 125th Street, and the Schomburg Center, especially, are always crowded with people. It's still best to stick to the main streets, however, and avoid the parks.

In Harlem, many numbered avenues take on proper names. Sixth Avenue is Lenox Avenue or Malcolm X Boulevard; Seventh Avenue is Adam Clayton Powell Jr. Boulevard (ACP Blvd.); and Eighth Avenue is Frederick Douglass Boulevard.

Established as Niew Haarlem in 1658, Harlem remained a quiet farming community until 1837. Then the Harlem Railroad arrived, bringing with it hundreds of new settlers. In 1873, the village was annexed to the city, and by the early 1900s, it was an affluent white suburb.

In 1901, the IRT subway was extended along Lenox Avenue and wealthy speculators, seeing the chance to make millions, built row after row of attractive townhouses. But they overextended themselves, and sales were slow.

When a black realtor offered to fill the empty buildings with black tenants, the developers jumped at the chance. Fearing racial changes, the neighborhood's white residents fled.

During the 1920s and '30s, Harlem was the country's African American cultural center. The Harlem Renaissance bloomed, attracting writers and intellectuals such as Langston Hughes and W. E. B. DuBois, while the streets were jammed with jazz clubs, theaters, dance halls, and speakeasies. Duke Ellington played at the Cotton Club, Chick Webb at the Savoy.

Harlem lost much of this vibrancy during and after the Depression, when poverty began taking a stronger hold. In the '60s, civil rights leaders Malcolm X, Stokely Carmichael, and others turned the neighborhood into a mecca for black consciousness.

Columbia University Area

The world's largest Gothic cathedral, the **Cathedral of St. John the Divine** (Amsterdam Ave. at W. 112th St., 212/316-7540, www.stjohndivine.org, 7 A.M.–6 P.M. daily) is said to be large enough to fit both Notre Dame and Chartres inside. The church can accommodate some 10,000 people and is still under construction. Scheduled completion date, *if* enough money becomes available: 2050.

Begun in 1892, the cathedral's imposing facade is covered with stone carvings and bronze sculptures. Inside, it's a vast and cavernous space with endless rows of seats and many floor inscriptions ("Live all you can; it's a mistake not to."—Henry James; "Out of space—out of time."—Edgar Allan Poe). Several chapels house changing exhibits, while out back is a workshop where you can watch stonemasons at work. Immediately south of the cathedral is its Peace Fountain, lined with an odd and whimsical mix of figures and animals, many of them sculpted by schoolchildren. **Cathedral tours** (212/932-7347) are given Tues.–Sat. at 11 A.M., Sun. at 1 P.M.

Columbia University (www.columbia.edu) stretches from West 114th Street to West 120th Street, between Amsterdam Avenue

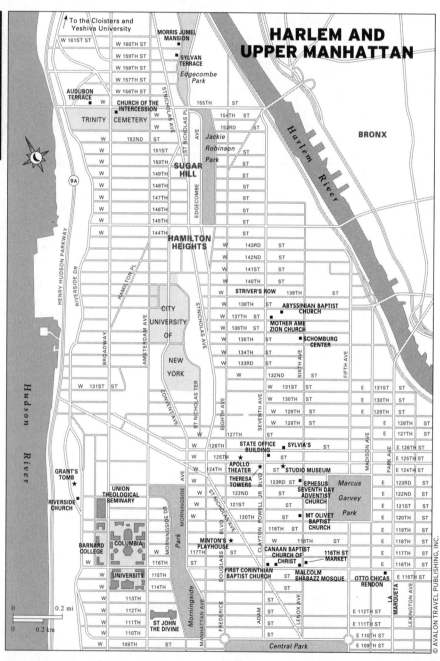

HARLEM AND UPPER MANHATTAN

To the Cloisters and
Yeshiva University

W 161ST ST
W 160TH ST
MORRIS JUMEL
MANSION
W 159TH ST
W 158TH ST
SYLVAN
TERRACE
W 157TH ST
Edgecombe
Park
W 156TH ST
AUDUBON
TERRACE
CHURCH OF THE
INTERCESSION
155TH   ST

BRONX

TRINITY   CEMETERY
154TH   ST
153RD   ST
W 152ND   ST
151ST   ST
Jackie
Robinson
Park
150TH   ST
149TH   ST
SUGAR
HILL
148TH   ST
147TH   ST
146TH   ST
145TH   ST
144TH   ST
HAMILTON
HEIGHTS
W 143RD   ST
W 142ND   ST
W 141ST   ST
W 140TH   ST
STRIVER'S ROW   139TH   ST
W 138TH   ST
ABYSSINIAN BAPTIST
CHURCH
W 137TH   ST
MOTHER AME
ZION CHURCH
W 136TH   ST
W 135TH   ST
SCHOMBURG
CENTER
W 134TH   ST
W 133RD   ST
W 132ND   ST

Harlem River

CITY
UNIVERSITY
OF
NEW
YORK

W 131ST   ST   W 131ST   ST   E 131ST   ST
W 130TH   ST   E 130TH   ST
W 129TH   ST   E 129TH   ST
W 128TH   ST   E 128TH   ST
127TH   ST   E 127TH   ST
W 126TH   ST
STATE OFFICE
BUILDING
SYLVIA'S   E 126TH   ST
W 125TH   ST   E 125TH   ST
APOLLO
THEATER
W 124TH   ST
STUDIO MUSEUM   E 124TH   ST
THERESA
TOWERS
123RD   ST
EPHESUS
SEVENTH DAY
ADVENTIST
CHURCH
Marcus   E 123RD   ST
W 122ND   ST   Garvey   E 122ND   ST
W 121ST   ST   Park   E 121ST   ST
MT OLIVET
BAPTIST
CHURCH
W 120TH   ST   E 120TH   ST
W 119TH   ST   E 119TH   ST
W 118TH   ST   E 118TH   ST
MINTON'S
PLAYHOUSE
CANAAN BAPTIST
CHURCH OF
CHRIST
116TH ST
MARKET
W 117TH   ST   E 117TH   ST
W 116TH   ST   E 116TH   ST
FIRST CORINTHIAN
BAPTIST CHURCH
MALCOLM
SHABAZZ MOSQUE
OTTO CHICAS
RENDON
E 115TH ST
W 115TH   ST
W 114TH   ST

GRANT'S
TOMB

RIVERSIDE
CHURCH

UNION
THEOLOGICAL
SEMINARY

BARNARD
COLLEGE

COLUMBIA

UNIVERSITY

LA
MARQUETA
LEXINGTON AVE
W 113TH   ST   E 112TH ST
W 112TH   ST   E 111TH ST
W 111TH   ST   E 110TH ST
ST JOHN
THE DIVINE
W 110TH   ST
109TH   ST   E 109TH ST
Central Park

Hudson
River

HENRY HUDSON PARKWAY
RIVERSIDE DR
9A
BROADWAY
HAMILTON PL
AMSTERDAM AVE
CONVENT AVE
ST NICHOLAS TER
ST NICHOLAS AVE
EIGHTH AVE
SEVENTH AVE
SIXTH AVE
FIFTH AVE
ST NICHOLAS PL
EDGECOMBE
AVE
MORNINGSIDE AVE
MORNINGSIDE DR
Morningside   Park
ST NICHOLAS AVE
DOUGLAS BLVD
CLAYTON POWELL JR BLVD
MANHATTAN AVE
FREDERICK
ADAM
LENOX AVE
MADISON AVE
PARK AVE

0   0.2 mi
0   0.2 km

© AVALON TRAVEL PUBLISHING, INC.

© SEAN WATTERS

The Cathedral of St. John the Divine will not be completed before the year 2050.

and Broadway. Founded as King's College in 1754, it educated some of the country's earliest leaders, including Alexander Hamilton and John Jay (first chief justice of the U.S. Supreme Court). Free **tours** (212/854-4900) are given year-round.

Across Broadway from Columbia is **Barnard College,** founded in 1899 by Frederick A. P. Barnard, a former president of Columbia and a champion of higher education for women. Among the college's alumni are anthropologists Margaret Mead and Zora Neale Hurston.

High on a bluff overlooking the Hudson is **General Grant's National Memorial** (122nd St. and Riverside Dr., 212/666-1668, 9 A.M.–5 P.M. daily, free admission), an imposing mausoleum where the former president and his wife are buried. The site is run by the National Park Service.

Randolph Square Area

One of the greatest revolutions in jazz was spawned in a neighborhood club, **Minton's Playhouse,** run by one-time bandleader Teddy

Hill in the Cecil Hotel (210 W. 118th St., just west of St. Nicholas Ave.), now elderly housing. Hill hired a house band that included pianist Thelonious Monk and drummer Kenny Clarke, and soon the small, dark place was packed every night with talent eager to jam. Dizzy Gillespie, Charlie Parker, Charlie Christian, and Max Roach were among the regulars who came here to experiment with a brand-new style of jazz that came to be called bebop. Still hanging in the back of the club is a striking mural depicting four musicians, two of whom have been identified as Tony Scott and Charlie Christian.

For years, plans were in the works to restore Minton's—now on the National Register of Historic Places. But the project, once backed by Robert DeNiro and his restaurateur partner Drew Nieporent, has stalled, due to investors are wary of signing onto this $3.1 million project.

At Adam Clayton Powell Jr. Boulevard and 116th Street is **First Corinthian Baptist Church,** a playful building covered with a multitude of colored tiles. The building was once the Regent Theater, completed in 1913 as the city's first deluxe movie palace. Before that, movies had been shown in storefronts or tiny vaudeville theaters. In its heyday, the Regent had its own eight-piece orchestra, pipe organ, uniformed ushers, and printed programs.

Just east of the First Corinthian is **Canaan Baptist Church of Christ** (132 W. 116th St., 212/866-0301), known for its high-spirited gospel choirs. Call ahead for service times.

The silver-domed mosque topped with a star and a crescent is the **Malcolm Shabazz Mosque** (102 W. 116th St., at Lenox Ave., 212/662-2200), named after civil-rights leader Malcolm X, who taught here in the 1960s just before his break with the Black Muslims. After his death, the mosque was firebombed. Surrounding the mosque is busy **Malcolm Shabazz Harlem Market,** a hodgepodge of small Muslim-run businesses.

El Barrio

Heading farther east on 116th Street, you'll

come to Spanish Harlem, filled with discount clothing stores, toy shops, beauty and wig salons, storefront churches, bakeries selling towering wedding cakes, pet stores selling homing pigeons, botanicas, and the sounds of salsa. Most of the residents here are of Puerto Rican, Cuban, and Dominican ancestry.

At Park Avenue between 116th and 111th Streets is **La Marqueta,** a large indoor market selling fruits and vegetables, meats and poultry. **Otto Chicas Rendon** (60 E. 116th St., between Madison and Park Aves., 212/289-0378) is the city's oldest and best-known botanica, selling everything from crystal balls to herbs and love potions. Founded in 1945, the store has been so successful that it now sells wholesale to botanicas around the country.

125th Street

The heart of Harlem is 125th Street, always alive with vibrant colors, sights, and sounds. As the neighborhood's main commercial drag for decades, 125th Street has had many ups and downs. Today, it's riding an optimistic wave, with more businesses in operation now than at any other time in recent history. The street is also home to two major Harlem landmarks—the Studio Museum in Harlem and the Apollo. Just south of 125th Street, on Fifth Avenue, is **Marcus Garvey Park,** lined with elegant brownstones.

The **Studio Museum** (144 W. 125th St., between Malcolm X Blvd. and ACP Blvd., 212/864-4500, www.studiomuseuminharlem.org, noon–6 P.M. Wed.–Fri. and Sun., 10 A.M.–6 P.M. Sat., suggested admission adults $7, students and seniors $3, children under 12 $1) was founded in 1968 in a small factory loft. Today, it's a first-class institution spread over several well-lit floors of a turn-of-the-century building. The "principal center for the study of Black art in America," the museum offers a permanent display of works by such masters as Romare Bearden, James VanDerZee, and Jacob Lawrence. Some of the temporary exhibits focus on world-renowned figures, others on emerging artists.

The glistening white-brick **Theresa Hotel**

(2090 ACP Blvd., at 125th St.) was once Harlem's largest and most famous hotel. Among the notables who stayed here were musicians Lena Horne, Jimi Hendrix, Dizzy Gillespie, Lester Young, Milt Hinton, and Andy Kirk (who managed the place in the late 1950s).

In 1960, Cuban leader Fidel Castro and his 85-member entourage checked into the Theresa after checking out of a downtown hotel due to what Castro considered to be poor treatment. Castro was in town to deliver an address to the United Nations, and while he was at the Theresa, thousands of demonstrators and Soviet leader Nikita Khrushchev stopped by to show their support.

The Theresa is now an office building. In 1990, Nelson Mandela, then the leader of the South African antiapartheid movement, held a huge rally outside the hotel's doors to celebrate his release from prison.

Perhaps the single most important landmark in the history of African American music, the **Apollo** (253 W. 125th St., between ACP and Frederick Douglass Blvds., 212/531-5305) has hosted nearly every major jazz, blues, R&B, and soul artist to come along since the 1930s. Bessie Smith, Ella Fitzgerald, Billie Holiday, Duke Ellington, Louis Armstrong, Count Basie, Ray Charles, James Brown, Aretha Franklin, Diana Ross, and Michael Jackson all played the Apollo, and the list could go on and on. It is said that when a teenage Elvis Presley first came to New York, the one place he wanted to see was the Apollo. The same was later said of the Beatles.

Originally built in 1913, the Apollo was once Hurtig & Seamon's New Burlesque Theatre, which presented vaudeville to a Harlem that was then predominantly white. But by 1935, the neighborhood's racial mix had shifted, and the two-balconied theater, capable of seating 2,000, became famous for its Amateur Nights.

Now a nonprofit enterprise, the Apollo continues to present a variety of entertainment, including a Wednesday amateur night. In the lobby is a small exhibit on the theater's early history (212/531-5337).

© CHRISTIANE BIRD

the Apollo

Central Harlem

The Schomburg Center for Research in Black Culture

(515 Malcolm X Blvd. [Lenox Ave.], at 135th St., 212/491-2200) is a world-renowned institution founded by Arthur A. Schomburg, a Puerto Rican of African descent who as a child was told that the Negro had no history. Scholars come from all over the world to consult the extensive collections of this branch of the New York Public Library, housed in a modern brick and glass building.

For the sightseer, the center's most interesting attraction is its adjacent **gallery** (10 A.M.–6 P.M. Tues.–Sat., 1–5 P.M. Sunday, free admission), where a wide array of changing exhibits is presented. In the back is an excellent book and gift shop.

The **Mother A.M.E. Zion Church,** a neo-Gothic building (140 W. 137th St., between Lenox Ave. and ACP Blvd.), was New York City's first church organized by and for blacks. It was founded in 1796—originally downtown at 156 Church Street—with money donated by a former slave. The current church was

designed by the noted African American architect George Washington Foster, Jr.

Also known as the "Freedom Church" because of its connection to the Underground Railroad, the church has had many famous members, including Harriet Tubman, Frederick Douglass, Paul Robeson, and a woman named Isabella. One Sunday morning, Isabella, already highly respected by her community, announced during the service that she wanted to be called Sojourner Truth—"Sojourner because I am a wanderer, Truth because God is truth."

One of Harlem's most famous addresses is the impressive **Abyssinian Baptist Church** (132 W. 138th St., near ACP Blvd., 212/862-7474, 9 A.M.–5 P.M.). It was founded in 1801 when a few members of the First Baptist Church refused to accept that church's racially segregated seating policy. The Abyssinian now has one of the country's largest black congregations.

Two of the church's most famous leaders were the Adam Clayton Powells—Sr. and Jr. The flamboyant Powell Jr. was also the first black U.S. congressman from an Eastern state, and he did much to empower the black community before being charged with misconduct and failing to win reelection. The church houses a small memorial room honoring both Powells.

The Reverend Dr. Calvin Butts is the Abyssinian's current pastor, and he continues the church's activist tradition. Sunday services, complete with gospel music, are held at 9 A.M. and 11 A.M. Visitors are welcome; arrive early to get a seat.

Striver's Row

Just down the street from the Abyssinian church are two famous blocks, located on 138th and 139th Streets between Adam Clayton Powell Jr. and Frederick Douglass Boulevards. Built in 1891 by developer David King, the blocks—lined with 158 four-story buildings—were designed by three sets of architects, with McKim, Mead & White designing the most impressive, northernmost row. The blocks acquired their nickname when they became the preferred address of early ambitious blacks. They continue to be immaculately kept, with service alleys running behind and flower boxes out front. Among the rich and famous who've lived here are W. C. Handy, Eubie Blake, and Stepin Fetchit.

Morris-Jumel Mansion

This big white gem of a mansion (W. 160th St. and Edgecombe Ave., 212/923-8008, www.morrisjumel.org, 10 A.M.–4 P.M. Wed.–Sun., adults $3, students and seniors $2, children under 12 free) sits in a small, lush park. Manhattan's last remaining Colonial residence, it was built in 1765 as a country home for British colonel Roger Morris. It served as a temporary headquarters for George Washington during the Revolutionary War.

Several decades following the war, the house was purchased by Stephen Jumel, a wealthy French wine merchant. His wife, Mme. Jumel, was said to have been a manipulative, scheming ex-prostitute who let her husband die of neglect after he was seriously wounded in a

carriage accident. His death made her one of America's richest women, and she then married Aaron Burr. She continued to live in the mansion until her death in 1865 at the age of 93, and her ghost is said to haunt the place.

Audubon Terrace

This monumental marble terrace is lined with impressive beaux arts buildings to the south and friezes and statuary to the north. All of the land once belonged to ornithologist John James Audubon; the terrace was built later, in 1904.

One of the beaux arts buildings houses the **Hispanic Society of America** (212/926-2234, 10 A.M.–4:30 P.M. Tues.–Sat., 1–4 P.M. Sun., free admission), one of the city's hidden treasures. Dark, somber, and mansionlike in feel, it houses exquisite paintings by Goya, Velasquez, and El Greco, along with heavy Spanish furnishings, porcelain, and mosaics.

To reach Audubon Terrace, take the No. 1 train to 157th Street and Broadway, or the B train to 155th Street near Amsterdam Avenue and walk two blocks west.

serenity in a Cloisters courtyard

The Cloisters and Fort Tyron Park

High on a hill at the northern tip of Manhattan reigns the Cloisters (212/923-3700, www.metmuseum.org, 9:30 A.M.–5:15 P.M. Tues.–Sun., closes at 4:45 P.M. Nov.–Feb., suggested admission adults $15, seniors $10, students $7, children under 12 free), a magical "medieval monastery" with wonderful views of the Hudson. Financed in 1938 by John D. Rockefeller, the Cloisters house the Metropolitan Museum of Art's medieval collections. Incorporated into the building are the actual remains of four medieval cloisters, transported here from Europe.

The museum's most prized possessions are its 16th-century Unicorn Tapestries, hung in a darkened room all their own. Six of the seven priceless tapestries are complete, and they tell the story of the "Hunt of the Unicorn" in rich, astonishing detail.

Surrounding the museum are the flowering plants, walkways, and benches of Fort Tyron Park. Near the park's south end is a plaque marking the site of the fort where the Americans were defeated by the British on November 16, 1776.

To reach the Cloisters, take the A train to 190th St.–Overlook Terrace. Exit by elevator, then catch the M4 bus or walk 15 minutes through Fort Tyron Park to the museum.

ENTERTAINMENT

Excellent entertainment listings can be found in *The New Yorker, New York, New York Free Press,* the *Village Voice,* the Friday and Sunday editions of the *New York Times,* and—especially—*Time Out New York,* which includes hundreds upon hundreds of listings. The *Voice, Time Out,* and *Free Press* do a very good job of covering downtown, while *The New Yorker* is the best source for capsule theater reviews. The most complete daily movie schedules are published by the *Daily News, New York Post,* and *New York Free Press.* For information on the volatile club scene, pick up *Time Out,* the *Free Press,* or the monthly *Paper.*

The venues below are listed from downtown to uptown under each heading.

Popular Music Venues

New York's largest venue is the 19,000-seat **Madison Square Garden** (Seventh Ave. between 31st and 33rd Sts., 212/465-6741), also home to the city's basketball and hockey teams. The 5,600-seat **Paramount** is a separate venue inside the Garden.

The grand, art deco **Radio City Music Hall** (1260 Sixth Ave., at 50th St., 212/247-4777) sometimes presents popular music acts. The historic **Beacon Theater** (2124 Broadway, at 74th St., 212/496-7070) is a convivial spot with an eclectic booking policy. Ditto **The Town Hall** (123 W. 43rd St., between Sixth and Seventh Aves., 212/840-2824), which presents a variety of jazz, world, and traditional music.

The atmospheric **Apollo** (253 W. 125th St., near Adam Clayton Powell Jr. Blvd., 212/531-5305) offers mostly R&B, soul, and rap, while on Wednesdays, the famed amateur-night tradition continues. Don't hesitate to venture up here at night—125th Street is always bustling.

© SEAN WATTERS

Radio City Music Hall

THE STANFORD WHITE SCANDAL

New York's first Madison Square Garden, built in 1890 and demolished in 1925, once stood where the New York Life Insurance Company stands today. Designed by architect Stanford White, the sports arena was a sumptuous affair, complete with turrets, towers, and a revolving golden statue of Diana on top. In addition, the building housed an upscale restaurant, theater, and roof garden, and it was in the roof garden that Stanford White was murdered by the husband of his former mistress, Evelyn Nesbit.

A pretty chorus girl from Pittsburgh, Nesbit was only 16 when White fell in love with her and took her to his studio. Already well known for his philandering, he had love nests all over town, including one at 22 West 24th Street (the building still stands), which he had lined with mirrors and hung with a red velvet swing. He liked his girlfriends to swing in the nude above him while he watched from the bed.

Nesbit, intent on finding a rich husband, soon left White, and in 1905 married millionaire Harry Kendall Thaw. But Thaw seemed obsessed with White, asking her about him again and again, until the evening of June 25, 1906, when they were all in the roof garden together. Then he pulled out a gun and shot White three times in the back of the head.

Thaw was found unfit to stand trial, due to what his lawyer called "dementia Americana," a mental disease supposedly afflicting husbands trying to defend their wives' honor. Thaw was sent to an insane asylum instead, where he stayed until 1915. Nesbit, divorced, starred in a silent film about the scandal (called *The Girl in the Red Velvet Swing*) and joined a traveling cabaret show. Later, she became a heroin addict and worked in a Panamanian brothel. She died in 1966.

Rock, Blues, Soul, World

S.O.B., short for "Sounds of Brazil," (204 Varick St., at Houston, 212/243-4940) is a stylish, multiethnic place emphasizing "tropical music," including African, Caribbean, reggae, Latin, and some jazz; cover $8–20. Most of the bands are dance-oriented, and the small dance floor stays packed with beautiful bodies. Tasty Caribbean food is served.

Long, dark **Mercury Lounge** (217 E. Houston, near Essex, 212/260-4700), features an antique wooden bar, exposed brick walls, heavy red drapes, and an excellent sound system. Some hip rock and jazz acts play here; cover, $8–25. Owned by the same people who own Mercury Lounge, **Bowery Ballroom** (Delancey St., between the Bowery and Chrystie St., 212/533-2111) is one of the city's few midsize venues. Complete with a balcony, it presents a wide variety of music acts; cover $8–25.

The granddaddy of New York rock clubs is the ratty, hole-in-the-wall **CBGB & OMFUG** (315 Bowery, at Bleecker, 212/982-4052), still in operation as of this writing despite serious rent woes. During the 1970s, the battle-scarred CBGBs—short for "Country, Bluegrass, Blues, and Other Music for Uplifting Gormandizers"—was America's cradle of punk rock, home to such later legends as the Talking Heads, Television, and Patti Smith. Nowadays, a half-dozen fledgling bands are booked nightly; cover, $5–12. Next door is **CB's 313 Gallery** (212/677-0455), concentrating primarily on singer-songwriters.

At the dark, black, down-and-dirty **Continental** (25 Third Ave., at St. Mark's Pl., 212/529-6924) you'll hear local bands playing alternative, roots rock, punk, or metal; cover, $3–10. Another good place to catch up-and-coming or favorite local bands is **Arlene's Grocery** (95 Stanton St., between Ludlow and Orchard Sts., 212/995-1652), housed in a former bodega; cover $3–10.

Lakeside Lounge (162 Ave. B, between 10th and 11th Sts., 212/529-8463) often hosts young rock bands and boasts a great blues jukebox.

The laid-back **C-Note** (157 Ave. C, at 10th St., 212/677-8142) features mostly singer-songwriters, along with the occasional jazz musician; $5–8. **Sidewalk** (94 Ave. A, at 6th St., 212/473-7373), bills itself as an "anti-folk" club but nonetheless features plenty of acoustic types; no cover, one-drink minimum.

Joe's Pub (425 Lafayette St., between Astor Pl. and W. 4th St., 212/539-8770) is a snug cabaret housed inside the Public Theater. Named in honor of the theater's founder, Joseph Papp, the upscale spot offers an eclectic line-up ranging from country to world and jazz; cover $12–35.

In Greenwich Village, the **Lion's Den** (214 Sullivan St., between Bleecker and W. 3rd St., 212/477-2782), hosts rock, reggae, and funk acts; cover at both, $3–10. The low-ceilinged, dark, and intimate **Cafe Wha?** (115 MacDougal St., near W. 3rd St., 212/254-3706), usually presents rock, R&B, and soul, but on Monday nights, Brazilian big bands play, attracting crowds of enthused Brazilian ex-pats. **Terra Blues** (149 Bleecker St., near Thompson, 212/777-7776) is a small upstairs club with picture windows; here, you'll hear local and regional blues bands; cover, $5–10.

Just north of the East Village is **Irving Plaza** (17 Irving Pl., at 15th St., 212/777-6800), an unusual venue with a wide balcony, large dance floor, and elaborate ornamentation left over from its days as a Polish dance hall. Many bigger-name rock and new-music groups play here, along with some reggae, blues, rap, and world bands; cover, $12–35.

Midtown, the rustic, peanut-shell-strewn **Rodeo Bar,** attached to the Albuquerque Eats restaurant (375 Third Ave., at 27th St., 212/683-6500), presents local rock, blues, and country; no cover. One of the city's newest clubs is **Satalla** (37 W. 26th St., between Broadway and Sixth Ave., 212/576-1155), presenting a wide range of world music, along with singer-songwriters and blues; cover $7–15.

Posh, state-of-the-art **B.B. King Blues Club & Grill** (237 W. 42nd St., between Seventh and Eighth Aves., 212/997-4144) sits smack in the heart of heavy-duty tourist territory. Nonetheless, it's an enjoyable venue, with a superb sound system, intimate stage, and good menu.

Despite its namesake, blues acts are the exception here; most nights feature rock or pop acts; cover $15–45.

Jazz and Experimental

New York is an international center for jazz, and top-caliber musicians can be heard in dozens of top-caliber clubs every night of the week. One of the most exciting new additions to the city in recent years is **Jazz at Lincoln Center's** $128 million home in the Time Warner Center at 10 Columbus Circle.

The three-story **Knitting Factory** (74 Leonard St., between Church St. and Broadway, 212/219-3055) features four snug rooms, all equipped with state-of-the-art sound systems. Once best known for its avant-garde jazz, the club now books everything from alternative rock to pop; cover $5–20. Hip, cavernous, bare-boned **Tonic** (107 Norfolk St., between Delancey and Rivington Sts., 212/358-7501), presents everything from outsider jazz to klezmer music; cover $5–12.

The dark **Zinc Bar** (90 Houston St., between La Guardia Pl. and Thompson St., 212/477-8337) is a tiny cellar joint showcasing jazz and Latin acts. Superb jazz guitarist Ron Affif is a regular here; cover $7–12.

One of the more unusual venues in town is the second-story **Jazz Gallery** (290 Hudson St., near Spring St., 212/242-1063). Long and thin, this intimate space features an imaginative array of concert series with titles such as "Jazz Cubano" and "Strings that Swing" (guitar duos); cover $12–20.

The oldest and arguably best jazz club in the city is the **Village Vanguard** (178 Seventh Ave. S, at 11th St., 212/255-4037), a dark, wedge-shaped basement room filled with rickety tables and fading photographs. Established in 1934, the Vanguard has booked all the greats, from Miles Davis and Dinah Washington to Wynton Marsalis and Terence Blanchard; cover, $15–25, plus a two-drink minimum. On Mondays, the 17-piece Vanguard Jazz Orchestra jams.

One avenue over is the pricey **Blue Note** (131 W. 3rd St., near Sixth Ave., 212/475-8592),

JAZZ AT LINCOLN CENTER

Up until 2004, Jazz at Lincoln Center (JALC) was just one of the several superb music programs offered by the famed performing arts center on Broadway and 66th Street. But since then, JALC has moved, into a dramatic new home: the multilevel, 100,000-square-foot **Frederick P. Rose Hall** (Broadway at 60th St., 212/258-9800, www.jazzatlincolncenter.com, tickets $30-150) in the Time Warner Center (10 Columbus Circle). The glitzy new center, built on the site of the old New York Coliseum, also houses upscale shops, restaurants, and the Mandarin Oriental Hotel.

The first large facility in the world specifically designed for jazz, Rose Hall holds an education center, recording studio, and three state-of-the-art music venues: the 1,200-seat Rose Theater, the 500-seat Allen Room, and Dizzy's Club Coca-Cola, an intimate nightclub. The Allen Room is the most spectacular of the three, as it boasts a two-story-high glass window with unobstructed views straight down 59th Street.

JALC is run by musical director, trumpet player, and composer Wynton Marsalis. With the Lincoln Center Jazz Orchestra, the Afro-Latin Jazz Orchestra, and a large roster of guest artists, the center runs a year-round schedule of performances, radio broadcasts, and special events.

the city's premier jazz supper club, all done up in glitzy blues. The club is at its best during late weeknight sets, when the crowds are small and the intimacy level is high; cover $25–65, with $5 minimum.

Also in Greenwich Village is **55 Bar** (55 Christopher St., near Seventh Ave., 212/929-9883), a convivial hole-in-the-wall with live jazz as well as a great jazz jukebox; cover $5, with a one-drink minimum. The dark, sardine-can **Arthur's Tavern** (57 Grove St., near Seventh Ave., 212/675-6879) is another traditional jazz venue; no cover.

Further uptown, find the **Jazz Standard** (116 E. 27th St., between Park and Lexington Aves., 212/576-2232), a sleek and upscale basement spot with a friendly wait staff, tasty menu, and excellent sight lines and acoustics. Top names such as David Newman and Greg Osby play here; cover $15–25.

Spiffy **Birdland** (315 W. 44th St., between Eighth and Ninth Aves., 212/581-3080) offers excellent sight lines, a good dinner menu, and a regular line-up of some of the best big bands in the city, along with top-name individual acts; cover $15–25, with a $10 minimum.

Recently relocated to just north of Times Square, **Iridium** (1650 Broadway, at 51st St., 212/582-2121) is a posh basement spot that features many of the top names in jazz. Guitar legend Les Paul performs Mondays; cover $15–30.

Woody Allen blows clarinet with the **Eddy Davis New Orleans Jazz Band** every Wednesday at the posh Cafe Carlyle in the Carlyle Hotel (Madison Ave. at 76th St., 212/744-1600). Tickets cost $50.

Small, cozy, and easy-going elegant, **Smoke** (2751 Broadway, between 105th and 106th Sts., 212/864-6662) is largely a haven for bebop, although avant-garde types play here, too; cover $10–12.

After years of inactivity, jazz is hot in Harlem again. One not-to-be-missed spot is the vintage art deco **Lenox Lounge** (88 Lenox Ave., between 124th and 125th Sts., 212/427-0253), now known for its smoking Monday-night jam sessions led by Patience Higgins; cover $10, two-drink minimum. **Showman's** (375 W. 125th St., at Eighth Ave., 212/864-8941) is a convivial club presenting local jazz favorites; no cover, two-drink minimum.

Classical Music

Classical music thrives in New York City, especially at the **Lincoln Center for the Performing Arts** (Broadway between 62nd and 66th Sts., 212/546-2656). The center presents an astonishing 3,000 performances a year. On its north side is the 2,700-seat **Avery Fisher Hall** (212/875-5030), home to the New

York Philharmonic (Sept.–May), the Great Performers Series (Oct.–May), and the Mostly Mozart Festival (July–Aug.). Ticket prices run $20–90, depending on the event.

Just north of Avery Fisher, above 66th Street, is the 1,096-seat **Alice Tully Hall** (212/875-5050), where the Chamber Music Society of Lincoln Center performs. Tickets run $15–50.

A dozen or so blocks from Lincoln Center is Manhattan's other major classical-music venue, **Carnegie Hall** (Seventh Ave. and 57th St., 212/247-7800). Saved from demolition by Isaac Stern and others in the early 1960s, this legendary hall was once home to the New York Philharmonic and remains a favorite spot among musicians of all persuasions. Tickets run $15–90.

Opera

On the west side of Lincoln Center is the grand **Metropolitan Opera House** (212/362-6000), home of the Metropolitan Opera Company. A good seat here costs over $100, but under-$20 seats and standing-room tickets are often available in the upper balcony (bring binoculars).

On the south side of the center is the **New York State Theater** (212/870-5570), where the less exalted New York City Opera performs. Regular tickets run $25–100; standing-room tickets and cheap seats also available.

The tiny **Amato Opera Theater** (319 Bowery, at Bleecker, 212/228-8200) puts on splendid weekend productions in a creaky turn-of-the-century vaudeville house. Tickets cost under $30; reserve well in advance.

Clubs

Since the mid-1990s, night life in New York has been under siege, due in part to a "quality-of-life" campaign begun by former mayor Rudolph Giuliani and in part to skyrocketing rents. Some long-established clubs have been shuttered; others have been toned down considerably. In their wake has come a new, more modest generation of clubs.

Part live-music venue and part dance club, **Don Hill's** (511 Greenwich St., at Spring St., 212/334-1390) hosts top DJs spinning ev-

erything from jump-blues to hip hop. Lesbians, gays, and straights frequent the scene, with the crowd changing nightly, according to the music.

Sapphire (249 Eldridge St., between Houston and Stanton Sts., 212/777-5153) is a tiny Lower East Side lounge, offering hip-hop, house, R&B, reggae, and disco classics. Five-storied **Webster Hall** (125 E. 11th St., near Third Ave., 212/353-1600) is often packed with out-of-towners. Each room has a different sound—disco, Latin, hip hop, house, and soul.

In the meatpacking district, the hard-to-find basement **APT** (419 W. 13th St. between Ninth Ave. and Washington St., 212/414-4245) spins funk, hip hop, and soul. Rotating DJs host the parties.

The **Roxy** (515 W. 18th St., between 10th and 11th Aves., 212/645-5156), once solely a roller-skating rink, is now part roller-disco, part straight dance club. Some nights are gays only, other nights are mixed.

For Latin dance music, the huge, three-story **Copacabana** (560 W. 34th St., between 9th and 10th Aves., 212/239-2672) is the place to go.

One of the best dance clubs in town, **Club Shelter** (20 W. 39th St., between Fifth and Sixth Aves., 212/719-4479) offers a mix of DJs spinning everything from house to techno, along with live performances.

Theater and Performance Art

Theater productions in New York are listed as "Broadway," "Off-Broadway," and "Off-Off Broadway." The terms do not refer to geographic location, but to theater size and cost of production. "Broadway" shows are the big, expensive kind, playing to audiences of over 500; "Off-Broadway" are smaller shows, playing to audiences of 100–499; and "Off-Off Broadway" are the smallest of all, with audiences of fewer than 100. Broadway productions lean toward the mainstream, and Off-Broadway productions—which began in the 1930s as a rebellion against Broadway values—almost equally so. Off-Off Broadway theater was a 1960s rebellion against the rebellion; its shows are often quirky and experimental.

© CHRISTIANE BIRD

The TKTS booth in Times Square is the place for discount tickets.

For information on major shows and ticket availability, call the **NYC/ON STAGE hotline** (212/768-1818).

Attending a Broadway show is a quintessential New York experience. No matter whether the play you see turns out to be a dazzler or a dud, there's nothing quite like hurrying down the neon-splashed streets of Times Square along with thousands of other theatergoers, most of whom always seem to be running late. Among Broadway's many gorgeous, historic venues—most located just off Times Square—are the **Shubert, Booth, Nederlander, Majestic, Belasco,** and **Lyceum.**

Tickets: Full-price tickets to Broadway plays usually run $65–100, although some of the larger theaters offer $25 seats far in the back. Half-price orchestra-seat tickets to same-day performances are sold daily at the **TKTS** booth (47th St. and Broadway, 212/221-0013, 3–8 P.M. Mon.–Sat. for evening performances, 10 A.M.–2 P.M. Wed. and Sat. for matinees, 11 A.M.–2 P.M. Sun. for matinees, 11 A.M.–7 P.M. Sun. for evening performances).

The lines are often very long, but they move quickly. If you don't want to wait, come early, or—surprisingly enough—come late. Your selection will be more limited then, but there's often no wait at all after about 7 P.M.

TKTS also operates a booth in Lower Manhattan at the South Street Seaport (John and Front Sts., 11 A.M.–5:30 P.M. Mon.–Fri. for evening performances, 11 A.M.–3:30 P.M. Sat., closed Sun.). Here, tickets to matinee performances are sold 11 A.M.–closing the day *before* the performance.

Many Off-Broadway theaters are in the East Village or in Greenwich Village, or along Theater Row on 42nd Street between 9th and 10th Avenues. Off-Broadway tickets generally run $25–60, with discounted tickets also available through TKTS. Off-Off Broadway shows, which can cost as little as $7, tend to be produced in theaters below 14th Street. A number of these theaters consistently produce fine theater.

Foremost among Off-Broadway companies is the **Public Theater** (425 Lafayette St., near

Astor Pl., 212/260-2400), founded by the late Joseph Papp, who also fought long and hard to bring the free **New York Shakespeare Festival** to the city. The Public still puts on two free Shakespeare plays—featuring top actors—every summer in Central Park's Delacorte Theater (near Central Park West and 81st St., 212/539-8750).

Not far from the Public Theater is a bastion of the avant-garde: **La MaMa E.T.C.** (74A E. 4th St., near Second Ave., 212/475-7710). It's a sprawling three-theater complex run by the innovative Ellen Stewart, one of the founders of the Off-Off Broadway movement. **Theatre for the New City** (155 First Ave., near 11th St., 212/254-1109) presents new and experimental drama, often at very low prices.

For performance art, **P.S. 122** (150 First Ave., at 9th St., 212/477-5288), housed in a former school, is a mecca. The **Nuyorican Poets Cafe** (236 E. 3rd St., between Aves. B and C, 212/505-8183) is best known for its weekly poetry slams, in which poets compete with one another in front of an opinionated audience. The rest of the week, performance art and literary readings are frequently featured.

The **Performing Garage** (33 Wooster St., between Grand and Broome, 212/966-3651), is home to the Wooster Group, one of the country's oldest experimental theater companies. The **Cherry Lane Theater** (38 Commerce St., near Barrow St., 212/989-6200) is a small, appealing venue founded by Edna St. Vincent Millay and others in 1924.

The **Atlantic Theater Company** (336 W. 20th St., between Eighth and Ninth Aves., 212/239-6200), housed in a converted church, is an acting ensemble that grew out of a series of workshops taught by David Mamet and William H. Macy in the mid 1980s. The **Vineyard Theatre** (108 15th St., just off Union Square, 212/353-3366) is a nonprofit theater company that focuses on new voices for the New York stage; writers such as Nicky Silver, Brian Friel, and Paula Vogel have premiered works here. **Playwrights Horizons** (416 W. 42nd St., near Ninth Ave., 212/279-4200) produces many plays that eventually move on to Broadway.

Symphony Space (2537 Broadway, at 95th St., 212/864-1414), complete with a spiffy bar/café and cinema, features a wide diversity of cultural offerings ranging from live theater to jazz concerts to French cinema.

Dance

New York is home to two major ballet companies, several smaller ones, and numerous modern-dance troupes. The **American Ballet Theater,** once directed by Mikhail Baryshnikov, performs at the Metropolitan Opera House in Lincoln Center (212/362-6000), May–July; tickets cost $25–130. The **New York City Ballet,** founded by George Balanchine, performs at the New York State Theater in Lincoln Center (212/870-5570) during the winter and spring; tickets cost $16–85.

Many of the city's other companies perform in three major venues. The gorgeous, Moorish-style **City Center** (131 W. 55th St., between Sixth and Seventh Aves., 212/581-7907) annually hosts the Dance Theater of Harlem, the Alvin Ailey Dance Company, the Paul Taylor Dance Company, and the Merce Cunningham Dance Company, among others; tickets cost $25–75. The more intimate **Joyce Theater** (175 Eighth Ave., at 19th St., 212/242-0800) hosts the Eliot Feld Ballet and numerous touring dance troupes.

Comedy Clubs

Carolines (1626 Broadway, at 49th St., 212/757-4100, www.carolines.com) is the glitziest and most expensive club around, booking big-name acts on a regular basis; cover is $15–35, with a two-drink minimum. A good, alternative club, where the comics work less-traditional material, is **Laugh Lounge NYC** (151 Essex St., between Rivington and Stanton Sts., 212/614-2500); cover $15–25, plus two-drink minimum.

Cinema

For independent and foreign films, and retrospectives, the best place in town is the **Film Forum** (209 W. Houston St., near Sixth Ave., 212/727-8110), equipped with three screens and a small coffee bar. Lincoln Center's **Walter Reade Theater** (70 Lincoln Center Plaza on 65th St., above Alice Tully Hall, between Broadway and Amsterdam, 212/875-5600) is another excellent venue for foreign films and retrospectives.

The **Museum of Modern Art** (11 W. 53rd St., between Fifth and Sixth Aves., 212/708-9480) features many classic films that are free with museum admission. In Astoria, Queens, the **American Museum of the Moving Image** (35th Ave. at 36th St., 718/784-0077) has three full-size theaters presenting film in all its forms. Two smaller venues for avant-garde films are **Anthology Film Archives** (32 Second Ave., at 2nd St., 212/505-5181) and **Millennium Film Workshop** (66 E. 4th St., near Second Ave., 212/673-0090).

The only magnificent historic movie theater left in Manhattan is the **Clearview Ziegfeld** (141 W. 54th St., between Sixth and Seventh Aves., 212/777-FILM), which has one of the largest screens in America and a deliciously ornate red-and-gold decor. Disneyfied **Loews**

© SEAN WATTERS

Museum of Modern Art

Cineplex Lincoln Square & IMAX Theatre (1992 Broadway, at 68th St., 212/50-LOEWS) offers an eight-story-high IMAX screen, along with 12 feature screens and a movie memorabilia shop.

EVENTS

New York is a city of parades and festivals, the larger of which are usually announced in the daily papers. Or you can call NYC & Company, New York's tourism marketing organization (212/484-1222 or 212/397-8222, www.nycvisit.com). Telephone numbers for smaller or more site-specific events are listed below.

January

On New Year's Day, the intrepid **Arctic Ice Bears** take a dip in the icy waters off Coney Island. Between mid-January and early February, the streets of Chinatown come alive with dragon dances, lion dances, and fireworks celebrating **Chinese New Year.** The two-day **Winter Antiques Show,** in the Seventh Regiment Armory (Park Ave. and 67th St.) is a great excuse to see the building's grand, cavernous interior, designed by Stanford White and Louis Tiffany.

February

Black History Month is celebrated throughout the city with a variety of events, including concerts, films, exhibits, and lectures. For two days mid-month, dogs of every imaginable breed strut their stuff at the **Westminster Kennel Club Dog Show,** Madison Square Garden (Seventh Ave. and 33rd St., 212/465-6741). For one week mid-month, the **National Antiques Show** comes to Madison Square Garden.

March

Felines from around the world primp and preen at the two-day **International Cat Show,** also at Madison Square Garden. The 17th marks the date of one of the city's biggest events and the oldest parade in the United States—the **St. Patrick's Day Parade,** first marched in 1752.

TABITHA LAHR

Madison Square Garden is a major location for Manhattan events.

A bright green stripe runs up Fifth Avenue from 44th to 86th Streets, and Midtown swells with thousands upon thousands of spectators and party animals. Meanwhile, throughout the city, Irish taverns celebrate St. Pat's with party favors and green beer, and many New Yorkers—Irish or not—don something green. Smaller St. Patrick's parades are held on Staten Island and in Brooklyn on the weekends before and after the 17th, respectively.

Greek Independence Day is celebrated on the 25th with a more sedate parade on Fifth Avenue. Madison Square Garden blooms with the **New York Flower Show.** At the end of the month, the **Ringling Brothers and Barnum & Bailey Circus** comes to Madison Square Garden for its annual two-month stint; the animals parade into town around midnight through the Queens Midtown Tunnel.

April

On Easter Sunday, citizens show off their spring finery in the **Easter Parade** on Fifth Avenue near St. Patrick's Cathedral (49th Street). This is not an organized event but a sort of free-for-all in which participants dress to the hilt. At the Brooklyn Botanic Garden (718/623-7200), the two-day **Cherry Blossom Festival** celebrates both the flower and Asian culture through performances and traditional crafts demonstrations.

May

In mid-May, the colorful three-day **Ukrainian Festival** on 7th Street in the East Village (212/228-0110) commemorates Ukraine's conversion to Christianity. The enormously popular two-day **Ninth Avenue Food Festival,** between 36th and 59th Streets, features delectable edibles from around the world. The **Martin Luther King Jr. Day Parade** is held on Fifth Avenue on or around May 17.

Also mid-month, the city's Norwegian population celebrates its heritage by marching down Brooklyn's Fifth Avenue from 90th to 67th Streets in a **Norwegian Day Parade.** Other ethnic festivals celebrated during the month include the **Czechoslovak Festival,** held in the city's last beer garden, Bohemian Hall in Astoria, Queens (718/274-4925), and the **Salute to Israel Parade,** down Fifth Avenue.

Over Memorial Day weekend, artists of varying talents pack the streets around Washington Square, selling their wares during the **Washington Square Outdoor Art Exhibition** (212/982-6255). The same exhibition also takes place in the fall.

June

The city's enormous smorgasbord of free, and mostly outdoor, summer festivities begins in June. Events include dance, drama, opera, jazz, pop, and folk music. Among the top series are performances by the **Metropolitan Opera** (212/362-6000) and the **New York Philharmonic** (212/875-5709), held in parks throughout the city; the **Central Park SummerStage** series at the bandstand in Central Park, which features everything from dance and poetry to salsa and rock (212/360-2777); the **Lincoln Center Out-of-Doors** performing-arts festival (212/875-5928); and the **New York Shakespeare Festival** at the Delacorte Theater in Central Park (212/539-8750).

During the day-long **Museum Mile Festival,** all of the museums on Fifth Avenue from 82nd to 102nd Streets are free to the public (212/606-2296). The fabulistic **Mermaid Parade,** displaying eye-popping costumes down the boardwalk in Coney Island, is an event not to be missed (718/372-5159). In mid-June, Puerto Ricans celebrate their heritage with the boisterous **Puerto Rican Day Parade** on Fifth Avenue. In late June and early July, the 10-day **JVC Jazz Festival** takes place at various concert halls around the city and also offers a few free outdoor events (212/501-1390). Accompanying it is the eclectic, multi-faceted **New York Jazz Festival,** presenting hundreds of imaginative, less-traditional events; its sponsor, and hence its name, changes from year to year. Late in the month, the **Gay and Lesbian Pride March** (212/807-7433) heads down Fifth Avenue to Greenwich Village.

July

On the Fourth of July, Macy's lights up the skies with spectacular **fireworks** over either the Hudson or the East River. One of the city's favorite concert series, the **Mostly Mozart Festival** at Lincoln Center, begins mid-month and lasts through August (212/875-5400). Also at Lincoln Center in July and August is the **Serious Fun Festival,** a series that celebrates the avant-garde performing arts.

Mid-month, the four-day **African Street Festival** offers sports, art, music, and food on Fulton Street in Brooklyn between Schenectady and Utica Avenues. On the second Saturday, during the **Feast of Our Lady of Mt. Carmel** in East Harlem, a statue of Our Lady of Mt. Carmel is carried through the streets as churches ring their bells and street vendors hawk their wares (212/534-0681). The highlight of the mid-month, week-long **Feast of the Giglio** in Williamsburg, Brooklyn, comes when a platform weighing thousands of pounds and carrying an enormous tower is "danced" through the streets on the shoulders of 250 men (718/384-0223). On the Saturday closest to the full moon, the **Obon Festival** comes to Riverside Park; featured is a ritual dance with drummers and kimono-clad dancers.

August

Harlem Week, which began as Harlem Day back in 1975, now lasts almost the entire month, and festivities run the gamut from fashion shows, open houses, and sports competitions to concerts, films, and food. Mid-month, Ecuador's independence from Spain is celebrated with an **Ecuadorian Festival** in Flushing Meadows-Corona Park, Queens. Also mid-month is the **India Day Parade,** when floats depicting landmark events in India's history parade down Madison Avenue between 34th and 21st Streets. Late in the month, the **U.S. Open Tennis Tournament** comes to Flushing, Queens. The **Fringe Festival,** held at various locations in downtown Manhattan, showcases up-and-coming talent in theater and performing arts; nearly 200 productions are offered in a two-week period.

September

Over a million spectators gather along Brooklyn's Eastern Parkway every Labor Day to watch the most fantastic of fantastic parades—the **West Indian American Day Carnival.** Steel bands ring out with calypso music, feathered dancers balance on stilts, and West Indians of all ages strut their stuff, many wearing costumes that have taken months to construct (718/625-1515). Also on Labor Day is **Wigstock,** a take-off on Woodstock performed in drag, which takes place in Tompkins Square Park.

The first Saturday of the month marks the **Brazilian Carnival,** when West 46th Street rocks with the samba, bossa nova, and dancing in the street. Also early in the month is the 10-day **Feast of San Gennaro,** the best-known Italian festival in the city. An effigy of the saint is paraded through the streets, but otherwise the celebration—complete with a small Ferris wheel—is a commercial affair with over 300 vendors.

A second **Washington Square Outdoor Art Exhibit** (see May) takes place early in September. Mid-month is the **"New York Is Book Country"** fest, when over 150 publishers and booksellers set up booths along Fifth Avenue in Midtown. The three-week **New York Film Festival,** previewing some of the ensuing year's finest films, starts mid-September at Alice Tully Hall, Lincoln Center (212/875-5610); tickets should be ordered well in advance.

Other special events in September include the **African American Day Parade,** featuring hundreds of bands. On the last Sunday of September, Koreans celebrate the autumn moon during the splendid **Korean Harvest and Folklore Festival** in Flushing Meadows-Corona Park, Queens.

October

On or about October 5, the **Pulaski Parade** on Fifth Avenue salutes Polish heritage. On or about October 9, the **Hispanic Day Parade**

celebrates the city's Latinos. And on or about October 12, the popular **Columbus Day Parade** salutes the explorer and his Italian heritage.

The **Blessing of the Animals** is a singular event held at the Cathedral of St. John the Divine (Amsterdam Ave., at 112th St., 212/316-7540) on the feast day of Saint Francis of Assisi. Thousands of New Yorkers bring their animals in for a special mass.

October 31 marks the night of the grand-daddy of the city's outrageous parades, the **Greenwich Village Halloween Parade.** Each costume seems more fantastic than the next as the procession wends its way downtown, ending with a party in Washington Square.

November

On the first Sunday of the month, the **New York Marathon** is run through all five boroughs. Early in November, the week-long **National Horse Show** comes to Madison Square Garden. On Thanksgiving, the traditional **Macy's Thanksgiving Day Parade** makes its way down Broadway. From just after Thanksgiving well into the New Year, many of the stores in the city deck out their windows for the holidays. Fifth Avenue is especially well decorated; check out Lord & Taylor, between 38th and 39th Streets, and Saks Fifth Avenue, between 49th and 50th Streets.

December

One afternoon in early December, a huge Christmas tree is raised and lighted at Rockefeller Center, behind the skating rink. The **tree-lighting ceremony** is one of the city's signature events, drawing celebrities and dignitaries, tourists and, yes, even cynical native New Yorkers. Also during the month is the lighting of the **Chanukah Menorah** at Grand Army Plaza, Fifth Avenue and 59th Street, and the **Kwanzaa Holiday Expo,** at the Javits Convention Center. **New Year's Eve** is celebrated with events including the traditional dropping of the Big Apple ball from the top of Times Tower, Times Square; a **midnight run** in Central Park; and family-oriented **First Night** events held at various locations.

SHOPPING

Sometimes it seems as if all of New York City is one enormous shopping center, with new stores opening up and older ones closing down daily. Nevertheless, certain areas of town are particularly well known for their shops.

Fifth Avenue, between 49th and 59th Streets, has long been home to many of the city's most famous and expensive stores, including Saks Fifth Avenue, Bergdorf Goodman's, and Tiffany's. In recent years, tourist meccas such as the Warner Brothers Studio store have also set up shop here. **Madison Avenue** between 59th and 82nd Streets has many exclusive

antique and designer shops. **Herald Square** at 34th Street and Sixth Avenue, and **34th Street** between Fifth and Sixth Avenues feature more moderately priced stores such as Macy's, The Gap, and The Limited, as well as bargain shops. **Columbus Avenue** between 66th and 86th Streets and **Lower Fifth Avenue** between 14th and 23rd Streets offer a large number of stylish clothing stores, most upscale chains (Banana Republic, Club Monaco).

SoHo is known for trendy clothing stores, many very expensive, and gift and home furnishings shops, while the **East Village** has a smattering of some of the most imaginative and reasonably priced stores in town. On the **Lower East Side,** Ludlow Street south of Houston is home to some of the town's hippest young designers, while Orchard Street is known for its old-fashioned bargain clothing shops.

Antiques and Furnishings

In SoHo, **Portico Home** (72 Spring St., between Broadway and Lafayette St., 212/941-7800) is the place to go for country chic, while **Moss** (146–150 Greene St., at Houston, 212/226-2190) is a spacious emporium devoted to modern design. **Wyeth** (315 Spring St., at Greenwich St., 212/243-3661) sells fine vintage furniture from the 20th century. **Urban Archaeology** (143 Franklin St., between Hudson and Varick Sts., 212/431-4646) specializes in artifacts from demolished buildings.

Bleecker Street is known for antique stores. Among them are old stand-bys such as **Old Japan, Inc.** (382 Bleecker St., 212/633-0922) and **Susan Parrish** (390 Bleecker St., 212/645-5020), selling American country and folk. At 506 Hudson St., near Christopher, is **Uplift Lighting** (212/929-3632), specializing in art deco fixtures.

The beguiling **ABC Carpet and Home** (888 Broadway, at 19th St., 212/473-3000), arranged more like a luxurious living room than a shop, sells everything from painted country furniture to French antiques.

The **Manhattan Art & Antiques Center** (1050 Second Ave., near 57th St., 212/355-4400) houses about 100 small antique shops.

SIDEWALK FORTUNES

"Mrs. Crystal will read your entire life without asking a single question." "Mrs. Lisa tells past–present–future." "Thousands of people who have been CROSSED, HAVE SPELLS, CAN'T HOLD MONEY, WANT LUCK, WANT THEIR LOVED ONES BACK, WANT TO STOP NATURE PROBLEMS or WANT TO GET RID OF STRANGE SICKNESS... are amazed at the results gotten by MRS. STELLA."

Walk the streets of Manhattan for any length of time and chances are good a silent dark-haired man or woman will hand you a flyer printed with promises similar to these. Follow the flyer's advice, and you'll probably find yourself in a small storefront where a woman dressed in long flowing garments sits next to a crystal ball. In the back, children and cats hover.

Though not as plentiful as they once were, unlicensed and unregulated fortune-tellers dot the streets of Manhattan. Many are Roma (Gypsies) who've immigrated here from Eastern Europe. Others are "professional" astrologers, psychics, and New Age spiritualists. The former usually charge around $10 to read your palm or the tarot cards; the latter charge $20-50 and up, and advertise in the Yellow Pages.

Things Japanese (127 E. 60th St., 2nd Fl., between Lexington and Park Aves., 212/371-4661) offers antiques, kimonos, and folk art.

Books and Magazines

One of the city's best bookstores, **St. Mark's Bookshop** is no longer on its namesake street but just around the corner at 31 Third Ave. (at Stuyvesant St., 212/260-7853). Open daily until midnight, the store has an especially fine selection of fiction and alternative publications.

In Greenwich Village, the **Oscar Wilde Memorial Bookshop** (15 Christopher St., near Sixth Ave., 212/255-8097), established in 1967, is said to be the world's oldest gay bookstore. **Three Lives & Co.** (154 W. 10th St., between Sixth and Seventh Aves., 212/741-2069) is one of the city's top literary bookstores, and hosts frequent readings by well-known authors.

Other independent Village bookstores of note include **Biography Bookshop** (400 Bleecker St., at 11th St., 212/807-8655), specializing in biographies, memoirs, and letters; the literary **Shakespeare & Co.** (716 Broadway, 212/529-1330); and **East West Books** (78 Fifth Ave., at 14th St., 212/243-5994), specializing in Eastern and New Age philosophy books.

Two blocks south of Union Square is **Strand Book Store** (828 Broadway, at 12th St., 212/473-1452). By far the city's largest secondhand bookstore, it claims to stock some two million books on eight miles of shelves. Some New Yorkers seem to spend their entire lives here, browsing, browsing, browsing. The store is open until 10 P.M. every evening. Across the street is **Forbidden Planet** (840 Broadway, 212/473-1576), a gold mine for science fiction lovers, selling books, comic books, and games.

Manhattan's oldest **Barnes & Noble** store, in operation decades before the current crop of megastores, is at 105 Fifth Ave. (at 18th St., 212/807-0099). The **Barnes & Noble** flagship is now at 33 East 17th Street (between Broadway and Park Ave. S., 212/253-0810). About a half-dozen megastores, complete with cafés and reading series, are scattered throughout the city.

Revolution Books (9 W. 19th St., 212/691-3345), the country's largest radical bookstore, harks back to Union Square's inflammatory Sacco-and-Vanzetti days. **Books of Wonder** (16 W. 18th St., 212/989-3270), is a great children's bookstore.

Travel lovers should stop by the **Complete Traveller Bookstore** (199 Madison Ave., at 35th St., 212/685-9007). **Hagstrom Map and Travel Center** (57 W. 43rd St., between Fifth and Sixth Aves., 212/398-1222) stocks an impossible number of maps.

Tucked in between the glittering jewelry stores in the Diamond District is one of the city's most historic bookstores, the **Gotham Book Mart** (41 W. 47th St., between Fifth and Sixth Aves., 212/719-4448). The store was established in 1920 by Frances Steloff, who was an early supporter of such writers as James Joyce, Henry Miller, and T. S. Eliot.

The classy, wood-paneled **Rizzoli** (31 W. 57th St., 212/759-2424) stocks an especially fine collection of art and photography books. **Mysterious Book Shop** (129 W. 56th St., between Sixth and Seventh Aves., 212/765-0900), sells hardcover, paperback, new, and used books. The **Argosy** (116 E. 59th St., between Park and Lexington Aves., 212/753-4455) carries an excellent selection of used books.

On the Upper West Side, **Applause Theatre Books** (211 W. 71st St., just west of Broadway, 212/496-7511) specializes in drama. **Gryphon Bookshop** (2246 Broadway, at 80th St., 212/362-0706) is a good shop for secondhand books and records. **Murder Ink** (2486 Broadway, between 92nd and 93rd Sts., 212/362-8905) sells mysteries new and old.

Clothing: New

SoHo abounds with chic designer stores. Among them are **Agnes B.** (76 Greene St., between Prince and Spring St., 212/925-4649), **Anna Sui** (113 Greene St., between Prince and Spring Sts., 212/941-8406), **Marc Jacobs** (163 Mercer St., between Houston and Prince Sts., 212/343-1490), and **Prada** (575 Broadway at Prince St., 212/334-8888). Some more affordable shops include **French Connection** (435 W. Broadway, at Prince, 212/219-1197) and **Phat Farm** (129 Prince St., 212/533-7428), selling the hip-hop couture of impresario Richard Simmons.

Along **Fifth Avenue between 23rd and 14th Streets,** you'll find **Anthropologie** (85 Fifth Ave., 212/627-5885), offering an interesting mix of ethnic-influenced urban wear, and **Bebe** (100 Fifth Ave., at 15th St., 212/675-2323), offering hip urban styles, some sleek, some frilly. **Emporio Armani** (110 Fifth Ave., at 16th St., 212/727-3240) is an expensive designer showroom, while **Daffy's** (111 Fifth Ave., at 18th St., 212/529-4477) sells discounted designer fashions. **Reminiscence** (50 W. 23rd St., near Sixth Ave., 212/243-2292) is the place to go for reasonably priced retrowear.

Along 34th Street between Fifth and Sixth Avenues are shops, shops, and more shops, most selling clothing and shoes. Some are branches of national stores such as **The Gap, The Limited,** and **Benetton.** Others are discount emporiums.

Among the many upscale clothing stores you'll find on Madison Avenue are **Polo Ralph Lauren** (650 Madison, at 60th St., 212/318-7000), **Yves St. Laurent** (855 Madison, near 71st St., 212/988-3821), and **Issey Miyake** (992 Madison, near 78th St., 212/439-7822).

Columbus Avenue is home to various upscale chain stores including **J. Crew, Banana Republic,** and **The Gap.** Designer **Laura Ashley** has a store at 398 Columbus Avenue (at 79th St., 212/496-5110).

Clothing: Vintage

In SoHo, **Alice Underground** (481 Broadway, between Broome and Grand, 212/431-9067) sells vintage clothing at relatively reasonable prices; styles range from Victorian to funk. **What Comes Around Goes Around** (351 W. Broadway, near Broome, 212/343-9303) houses over 60,000 vintage designer items, as well as denim and military threads. **Stella Dallas** (218 Thompson St., between Prince and Houston, 212/674-0447) specializes in the '40s look.

In the East Village, **Love Saves the Day** (119 Second Ave., at 7th St., 212/228-3802) is

Love Saves the Day

the stuffed-to-the-rafters secondhand clothing (etc.) store where Rosanna Arquette bought her jacket in the movie *Desperately Seeking Susan*. **Screaming Mimi's** (382 Lafayette St., near E. 4th St., 212/677-6464) is known for '50s-, '60s-, and '70s-era duds.

The **Antique Boutique** (712 Broadway, near Astor, 212/460-8830) is a creaky emporium selling everything from vintage cocktail dresses to leather jackets. Greenwich Village's **Star Struck** (43 Greenwich Ave., near W. 10th St., 212/691-5357) carries a good selection of old coats.

Clothing: Discount

One of the city's largest and oldest discount clothing stores is **Century 21** (22 Cortlandt St., near Broadway, 212/227-9092). Located directly across the street from Ground Zero, the store was shuttered for months after the attacks, but is thriving once again.

Another famed discount institution is **Loehmann's**, once a Bronx institution, but now located in Chelsea (101 Seventh Ave., at 16th St., 212/352-0856). Smaller stores featuring both discounted designer and casual wear include **Daffy's, Bolton's**, and **Hit or Miss;** all have multiple outlets in the city.

The **Second Chance Consignment Shop** (1109 Lexington Ave., 2nd Fl., 212/744-6041) is the place to go for secondhand couture. **Off Broadway** (139 W. 72nd St., off Broadway, 212/724-6713) sells secondhand clothes once worn by stars.

Department Stores

King of the department stores is **Macy's** (151 34th St., at Sixth Ave., 212/695-4400). Ten stories high and a full block wide, the store was founded in 1858 by Rowland Hussey Macy, a Quaker from Nantucket. Macy went to sea at the age of 15 and returned four years later with $500 and, legend has it, a red star tattooed on his hand—now Macy's logo. Six times Macy tried to establish a shop, and six times he failed. Then he started Macy's.

A few blocks farther northeast, find **Lord & Taylor** (424 Fifth Ave., at 38th St., 212/391-

3344), a comfortable midsize store that may not be as glamorous as some, but still carries a first-rate selection. One of the store's most gracious touches is the free coffee, served in a silver pot, that it offers to shoppers who arrive before the place opens at 10 A.M.

Lots of fun for both shopping and browsing is **Saks Fifth Avenue** (611 Fifth Ave., between 49th and 50th Sts., 212/753-4000), a wonderfully plush store with high-quality merchandise. **Henri Bendel** (712 Fifth Ave., between 55th and 56th Sts., 212/247-1100) is frequented by the very rich and very thin. **Bergdorf Goodman** (754 Fifth Ave., 212/753-7300, between 57th and 58th Sts.), is a favorite among wealthy socialites.

Cheap, cheerful, and trendy, the Swedish department store **H&M** (640 Fifth Ave., at 51st St., 212/489-0390) opened in 2000 to a rave reception. Other branches are located at 558 Broadway at Prince Street (212/343-2722) and 1328 Broadway at 34th Street (646/473-1165).

Once a bargain basement, **Bloomingdale's** (1000 Third Ave., at 60th St., 212/705-2000) is now one of New York's most glamorous department stores. It's well worth a browse, even if you're not planning to buy. **Barney's New York** (660 Madison Ave., at 61st St., 212/826-8900) carries fashionable and expensive clothing for men and women.

Hats

New York's largest and oldest hat store is the **J.J. Hat Center** (310 Fifth Ave., at 32nd St., 212/239-4368). Established in 1911, J.J.'s stocks over 15,000 men's hats, including fedoras, Stetsons, homburgs, and caps. For imaginative handmade women's hats, check out the **Hat Shop** (120 Thompson St., between Prince and Spring Sts., 212/219-1445).

Cameras, Etc.

Once just a record store, **J&R** (23 Park Row and adjoining buildings, between Ann and Beekman Sts., near City Hall, 212/238-9000) has branched out over the years to become a long row of shops selling every conceivable electronic device, including audio equipment, TVs, computers, and appliances. And, oh yes, they still sell recordings, too.

Run by Hasidic Jews, **B&H Photo-Video** (420 Ninth Ave., between 33rd and 34th Sts., 212/444-6615) is worth visiting just to see its efficient staff and Red Grooms–esque check-out system at work. Good bargains can be found, too.

Food and Gourmet Treats

In Greenwich Village, **Murray's Cheese Shop** (257 Bleecker St., 212/243-3289) is a neighborhood institution, selling cheeses from around the world. **McNulty's Tea and Coffee** (109 Christopher, near Bedford, 212/242-5351) is an aromatic haven over 100 years old. **Li-Lac Chocolates** (120 Christopher, 212/242-7374) sells luscious homemade sweets.

In Little India, a number of food stores waft their luscious smells out onto the street. Foremost among them is the venerable **Kalustyan's** (123 Lexington Ave., 212/685-3451). The first store to import Indian foodstuffs into the city, the bustling shop sells everything from homemade *labne* yogurt to Afghan naan bread to stuffed pita pockets to go. On the opposite side of town, **Poseidon Bakery** (629 Ninth Ave., 212/757-6173) is a Greek shop that has been hand-rolling phyllo dough for about 75 years.

On the Upper East Side, the German-run **Elk Candy Company** (1628 Second Ave., near 86th St., 212/585-2303) is best-known for old-fashioned marzipan. **Schaller & Weber** (1654 Second Ave., 212/879-3047) is a 1937 German butcher shop that will mail sausages anywhere in the world.

On the Upper West Side, **Zabar's** (2245 Broadway, at 80th St., 212/787-2000) is the city's most beloved food store. Dating back to the 1930s, when it moved to Broadway from Brooklyn, Zabar's sells over 10,000 pounds of coffee, 10 tons of cheese, and 1,000 pounds of salmon a week, not to mention pots and pans, microwave ovens, vacuum cleaners, and the like. Some 10,000 customers are said to pass through its friendly portals on a Saturday afternoon. The best time to come is weekdays

before 5 P.M. Not far away is **Citarella's** (2135 Broadway, at 75th St., 212/874-0383), a fish market with elaborate window displays.

Games and Toys

One of the city's most wonderful toy stores is SoHo's **Enchanted Forest** (85 Mercer St., just south of Spring, 212/925-6677). Made up to look like a magical rain forest, the store attracts as many adults as children. **After the Rain,** a long-time SoHo store specializing in kaleidoscopes, has recently merged with the Enchanted Forest.

In Greenwich Village, the famed **Chess Shop** (230 Thompson St., just south of W. 3rd St., 212/475-9580), may sell all sorts of chessboards and pieces, but more importantly, endless chess games are always in session. Players of all levels are welcome. **Classic Toys** (218 Sullivan St., 212/674-4434) is a fun and unusual spot, specializing in old and new toys and miniature figures; children, sophisticate collectors, and the general public are all welcome.

Across the street from the Plaza Hotel is **F.A.O. Schwarz** (767 Fifth Ave., at 58th St., 212/759-5851), a vast and imaginative toy emporium that's as much fun for adults as it is for kids. The new **Toys "R" Us** (1514 Broadway, at 44th St., 800/869-7787) in Times Square is said to be the largest toy store in the world. Inside, find a 60-foot-tall Ferris wheel, along with three floors of toys and games. **A Bear's Place** (789 Lexington Ave., at 61st St., 212/826-6465) sells a whole menagerie of stuffed animals.

Gifts

In SoHo, the irrepressible **Pop Shop** (292 Lafayette St., between Houston and Prince Sts., 212/219-2784) sells T-shirts, posters, hats, refrigerator magnets, inflatable baby dolls, jigsaw puzzles, and more, all designed by the late artist Keith Haring. **Evolution Nature Store** (120 Spring St., between Greene and Mercer, 212/343-1114) is an odd natural history store where you can pick up a giraffe skull or wild boar tusk.

A long-time East Village favorite is **Surma**

(11 E. 7th St., between Second and Third Aves., 212/477-0729), a one-of-a-kind shop selling Ukrainian crafts, books, and records. Two other unusual shops, selling exactly what their names imply, are **Howdy Do Toy Collectibles** (72 E. 7th St., 212/979-1618) and **Dinosaur Hill** (306 E. 9th St., 212/473-5850). For offbeat souvenirs and postcards, step into **Alphabets** (115 Ave. A., between St. Mark's Pl. and 7th St., 212/475-7250).

Hammacher-Schlemmer (147 E. 57th St., near Lexington, 212/421-9000), and at other Midtown locations) features the world's most imaginative and expensive high-tech gadgets. **Star Magic** (1256 Lexington Ave., between 84th and 85th Sts., 212/988-0300) sells a fascinating selection of space-age gifts, including science kits, mobiles, prisms, kaleidoscopes, and books.

Health and Beauty

In the East Village, the traditional **Tenth Street Russian and Turkish Baths** (268 E. 10th St., between First Ave. and Ave. A, 212/674-9250) is filled with saunas, steam rooms, and massage rooms. At one time, many such establishments existed in the East Village, but this is the last one left. Some days are coed, others for men or women only. The 1851 **Kiehl's** (109 Third Ave., near 13th St., 212/677-3171) is an old-fashioned chemist's where you can buy a full line of natural, handmade beauty products.

Bigelow Pharmacy (414 Sixth Ave., 212/533-2700) in Greenwich Village is New York's oldest continuously operating pharmacy; the official historic landmark was established in 1838, and still sports its original oak fittings and gaslight fixtures. **Caswell-Massey** (518 Lexington Ave., at 48th St., 212/755-2254) is Manhattan's oldest apothecary. The wood-paneled den dates back to 1752 and claims to have sold George Washington his shaving cream.

Jewelry

Fifth Avenue is home to two famed jewelry stores, **Cartier's** (2 E. 52nd St., at Fifth Ave., 212/753-0111) and **Tiffany's** (727 Fifth Ave.,

Tiffany's

© SEAN WATTERS

at 56th St., 212/755-8000). In Truman Capote's *Breakfast at Tiffany's,* character Holly Golightly opines, "Nothing bad can ever happen to you at Tiffany's," and she may be right. The store is as classy as Cartier's, but much friendlier.

Music and Musical Instruments

In the East Village, **Sounds** (20 St. Mark's Pl., between Second and Third Aves., 212/677-3444) is stocked with a good selection of alternative music and used CDs. **Fat Beats** (406 Sixth Ave., 212/673-3883) carries a mix of new hip hop, reggae, and break-beat vinyl. **Footlight Records** (113 E. 12th St., between Third and Fourth Aves., 212/533-1572) carries a good selection of show tunes, jazz, and used CDs. **Finyl Vinyl** (204 E. 6th St., near Second Ave., 212/533-8007) features records from the '30s to the '70s.

Tower Records (692 Broadway, at E. 4th St., 212/505-1500) offers an overwhelming array of recordings from rock to classical to everything in between. The store opened in

1983 and was largely responsible for transforming this one-time no-man's-land between the two villages into a distinct shopping strip. Another, equally large **Tower Records** is located on the Upper West Side (1961 Broadway, at 66th St., 212/799-2500).

In Greenwich Village, **Bleecker Bob's** (118 W. Third St., near MacDougal, 212/475-9677) is a neighborhood institution, as is the nationally renowned **Matt Umanov Guitar Store** (273 Bleecker St., between Sixth and Seventh Aves., 212/675-2157). Farther north, **Academy Records and CDs** (12 W. 18th St., between Fifth and Sixth Aves., 212/242-3000) sells used classical and jazz recordings. **Skyline Books and Records** (13 W. 18th St., 212/759-5463) specializes in used books. J&R Music World operates the **Jazz Record Center** (236 W. 26th St., Eighth Fl., 212/675-4480).

Just east of Broadway on West 48th Street is a row of top-notch musical-instrument stores, including **Sam Ash** (160 W. 48th St., 212/719-2299), **Manny's** (156 W. 48th St., 212/819-0576), and the **International Woodwind & Brass Center** (174 W. 48th St., 212/840-7165). **Colony Records** (1619 Broadway, at 49th St., 212/265-2050) is the largest provider of sheet music in New York City. **Steinway & Sons** (109 W. 57th St., between Sixth and Seventh Aves., 212/246-1100) is a lovely, old-fashioned piano showroom.

The three-tiered **Virgin Mega Store** (1540 Broadway, between 45th and 46th Sts., 212/921-1020), with branches elsewhere in the city) bills itself as "the largest music and entertainment store in the world." Inside find more than a million CDs, 7,400 film titles on laserdisc, and 20,000 videotapes and DVDs. Also on site are a bookstore and a café.

Shoes and Sneakers

Manhattan's two main thoroughfares for shoes are **West 8th Street** between Fifth and Sixth Avenues in Greenwich Village and **West 34th Street** between Fifth and Sixth Avenues near Herald Square. The former caters to young fashion mavens with money, the latter to office workers looking for bargains.

Homage to the almighty sneaker is paid at **Niketown** (6 E. 57th St., at Fifth Ave., 212/891-6453), a sleek gray emporium built in neo-art deco style. As many as 30,000 people a day are said to pass through this five-story shrine, which sits on prime Manhattan real estate. Inside, you'll find not only Nike sneakers and clothing, but also multiple aquariums, a recreated Town Square, a short film, and museum-style cases displaying Nike sneakers once worn by such stars as Michael Jordan.

Stationery and Cards

Kate's Paperie (561 Broadway, at Prince, 212/941-9816) is an upscale stationery shop filled with handmade paper products. A good selection of art postcards are available at **Untitled** (159 Prince St., near W. Broadway, 212/982-2088). **Jam Paper and Envelope** (111 Third Ave., near 13th St., 212/473-6666), stocks a wide array of budget-priced stationery.

Other

Paragon Sporting Goods (867 Broadway, at 18th, 212/255-8036) is the city's top sporting-goods department store. **Chisholm Larsson Gallery** (145 Eighth Ave., at 17th St., 212/741-1703) specializes in European travel and product posters. **Abracadabra** (19 W. 21st St., near Fifth Ave., 212/627-5194) features an enormous number of rubber Halloween masks and wacky gag gifts.

Most of the Garment District shops are wholesale only. Some of the stores that sell retail are **Margola** (48 W. 37th St., between Fifth and Sixth Aves., 212/695-1115), offering glass beads, rhinestones, and trinkets; **Manny's Millinery Supply** (26 W. 38th St., 212/840-2235), selling hats and notions; and **M&J Trimming** (1008 Sixth Ave., 212/391-6200), offering beads, buttons, lace, and feathers.

On the Upper West Side, **La Belle Époque** (280 Columbus Ave., near 73rd St., 212/362-1770) specializes in French posters of the 1890s and 1900s. **Maxilla & Mandible** (451 Columbus Ave., near 81st St., 212/724-6173) offers a most unusual assortment of skulls, skeletons, bones, teeth, beetles, butterflies, seashells, and fossils.

Flea and Vendor Markets

Though much smaller now than it once was, thanks to real estate development, the empty lot along Sixth Avenue between 25th and 26th Streets still hosts the enormous outdoor **Annex Antique Fair and Flea Market** (212/243-5343) every weekend, as it has for over 30 years ago. The market is open Saturday–Sunday, sunrise to sunset.

The Annex's success led to the establishment of several nearby indoor markets. Run by the same people who run the Annex is the **Garage** (112 W. 25th St.), a former parking garage with about 125 vendors. Next door is the 12-floor **Chelsea Antiques Building** (110 W. 25th St., 212/929-0909, open daily).

On 116th Street between Lenox and Fifth Avenues is the **Malcolm Shabazz Harlem Market** (212/987-8131), where dozens of vendors sell T-shirts, Kente cloth, African art, wool skullcaps, Gambian drums, women's hair twists, down coats, and CDs. Prices range from about $5 for the skullcaps to about $100 for the down coats, and many of the shoppers are European.

SPORTS AND RECREATION
Baseball

New Yorkers take their baseball seriously, and even if you're not much of a fan, it's worth riding the subway out to Shea or Yankee Stadium just to take in the scene. The season starts in April and runs into October. Tickets are usually available at the box office for $12–55.

The **New York Yankees** play at Yankee Stadium in the Bronx (161st St. and River Ave., 718/293-6000 [box office] or 718/293-4300, www.yankees.com); take the No. 4 train to 161st Street and follow the crowd. Built by a brewery magnate in 1923, the stadium is sometimes called "the house that Ruth built," in honor of the man who hit 60 home runs here in 1927 alone. The **New York Mets** play at Shea Stadium (126th St. at Roosevelt Ave. in Queens, 718/507-METS or 718/507-8499, www.mets.com); take the No. 7 train to Willets Point-Shea Stadium and follow the crowd.

Basketball

The **New York Knicks** play out of Madison Square Garden (Seventh Ave. and 33rd St., 212/465-6741 or 212/465-JUMP [fan line], www.nba.com/knicks) from late fall to late spring. Theoretically, ticket prices start around $30, but that doesn't mean much as the games are usually sold out well in advance.

Football

Both New York teams, the **Giants** (www.giants.com) and the **Jets,** play across the river in Giants Stadium, New Jersey Meadowlands Sports Complex (East Rutherford, New Jersey, 201/935-3900). Buses to the complex operate out of the Port Authority (212/564-8484), but since tickets to Giants games are nearly impossible to get (there's a 10-year waiting list) and to Jets games nearly as bad, you'll probably end up staying in the city and watching them on TV.

Hockey

The **New York Rangers** (www.newyorkrangers.com) play out of Madison Square Garden (Seventh Ave. and 33rd St., 212/465-6741) from late fall to late spring. The **New York Islanders** (www.newyorkislanders.com) play out of Nassau Veterans Memorial Coliseum (off Hempstead Turnpike, Uniondale, Long Island, 516/794-9300). Train service to and from the stadium is available on the Long Island Rail Road (718/217-5477). Tickets to both teams' games run $20–60 and are generally available.

Horse Racing

The city's two racetracks run alternately. **Belmont Park** (Hempstead Tnpk. and Plainfield Ave., Belmont, Long Island, 718/641-4700) is by far the more attractive of the two, with a large grandstand and pond, and red and white geraniums. Races run May–July and September–mid-October, Wednesday–Sunday. (In August, the entire industry migrates up to Saratoga Springs; see the *North Country* chapter.) To reach Belmont, take the Long Island Rail Road from Pennsylvania Station.

The **Aqueduct Racetrack** (108th St. and Rockaway Blvd., Jamaica, Queens, 718/641-4700) is a considerably smaller and seedier affair. Built in 1894, it's named for an aqueduct that once ran nearby. Races run late October–early May, Wednesday–Sunday. To reach Aqueduct, take the A or C train to the Aqueduct station.

Grandstand admission at both tracks costs $2, and bets start at $1. Daily programs include explicit instructions on how to place a bet.

Tennis

The **U.S. Open** is held in late August and early September at the U.S. Tennis Association's Tennis Center (Flushing Meadows Park, Queens, 718/760-6200). Tickets, which cost $35–75, go on sale May 31st and sell out quickly.

Bicycling

Although very crowded on nice weekends, one of the best places to ride bikes in New York is Central Park, where bikes can be rented at the **Loeb Boathouse** (near the Fifth Ave. and E. 72nd St. entrance, 212/517-4723). Other rental shops near Central Park include **Metro Bicycles** (1311 Lexington Ave., at 88th St., 212/427-4450) and the **Pedal Pusher Bicycle Shop** (1306 Second Ave., between 68th and 69th Sts., 212/288-5592). Rates usually run $8–10 an hour, $28–35 a day, and security deposits are required.

Boating

Paddling about on The Lake in Central Park is a popular pastime. Rowboats can be rented at the **Loeb Boathouse** (near the Fifth Ave. and E. 72nd St. entrance, 212/517-4723). Rates are $10 an hour, with a $20 cash deposit.

Fitness Classes

New York has a plethora of well-equipped health clubs offering a wide variety of fitness classes, but most are closed to visitors. One of the few exceptions is **Crunch,** where you can take a single aerobics or yoga class for about $20. Crunch has branches at various locations, including 54 East 13th Street (212/475-2018),

162 West 83rd Street (212/875-1902), 404 Lafayette Street (212/614-0120), and 1109 Second Avenue (212/758-3434).

Single classes are also offered by **Steps** (2121 Broadway, 212/874-2410). The **Integral Yoga Institute** (227 W. 13th St., 212/929-0585) offers single yoga classes for about $15.

Day passes are available at the enormous **Sports Center at Chelsea Piers** (Pier 60, 23rd St. at the Hudson River, 212/336-6000, www.chelseapiers.com), where you'll find a quarter-mile indoor track, an Olympic-sized swimming pool, basketball and volleyball courts, a weight room, multiple fitness classes, and an indoor climbing wall. Passes cost $50.

Horseback Riding

Manhattan's oldest and largest riding center is **Claremont Riding Academy** (173–177 W. 89th St., at Amsterdam, 212/724-5100), which rents horses with English-style saddles to ride in Central Park. The horses are well taken care of, and some are quite spirited. Rates run $50 an hour, and lessons are also available.

Ice-Skating

The city's most famous rink, often surrounded by spectators, is the sunken **Rockefeller Center Ice Rink** (Fifth Ave. and 50th St., 212/332-7654). The wonderful **Wollman Memorial Rink,** in Central Park near 64th St., 212/439-6900, offers great views of the city skyline. The **Chelsea Piers Sky Rink** (23rd St. at the Hudson River, 212/336-6100) belongs to the Chelsea Piers sports complex. Skates can be rented at all three locations for under $10, and admission prices are adults $10–15, children $7–10.

Indoor Games

Indoor batting cages, basketball courts, in-line skating rinks, a gymnastics center, driving range, rock-climbing wall, health club, and spa are just some of the many attractions at the **Chelsea Piers Sports & Entertainment Complex** (23rd St. at the Hudson River, 212/336-6666, $50/day pass).

© SEAN WATTERS

Chelsea Piers

Many spiffy **pool halls** can be found in Manhattan. Among them are **Soho Billiards** (298 Mulberry St., at Mott, 212/925-3753), and the **Amsterdam Billiards Club** (344 Amsterdam, near 77th St., 212/496-8180).

For bowling fans, the **Leisure Time Bowling and Recreation Centre** at the Port Authority (Eighth Ave. and 42nd St., 212/268-6909) is a well-kept place with 30 lanes and a bar. In Greenwich Village, the 44-lane **Bowlmor Lanes and Pressure** (110 University Pl., at 12th St., 212/255-8188) is an old-fashioned bowling spot by day and a hip downtown club by night.

Jogging
New Yorkers jog in all sorts of places in all sorts of weather, but one especially popular route is the track around the **Jacqueline Onassis Reservoir,** in Central Park, where the late former first lady herself often ran. The main entrance is at Fifth Avenue and East 90th Street; one lap is about a mile and a half.

Kayaking
To get an unusual view of Manhattan, explore the Hudson River and New York Harbor by kayak. Because navigating the currents and water traffic is tricky, kayaks cannot be rented for individual use, but you can take a class or tour. **New York Kayak** (Houston St. at West Side Hwy., 212/924-1327, www.nykayak.com) offers beginner to advanced classes, as well as short tours. The **Manhattan Kayak Company** (23rd St. at West Side Hwy., Pier 63, 212/924-1788, www.manhattankayak.com) also offers beginner to advanced classes, and tours ranging from 90 minutes to eight hours.

ACCOMMODATIONS
With real estate values continually spiraling upward, cheap sleeps are not readily available in New York City. An "inexpensive" room costs $80–100 per night, while a moderately priced one, with "nothing special" rooms, costs $100–200. The average hotel room now runs over $200 per night.

Areas in which to look for relatively inexpensive rooms include: lower Midtown between 23rd and 34th Streets near Fifth Avenue, the Theater District in Midtown, and the Upper West Side. B&Bs and hostels can also be a good option.

At the other end of the economic scale, New York is a glittering wonderland, home to some of the world's grandest hotels. The Plaza, Pierre, Four Seasons, and St. Regis are among the reigning monarchs. Even if you can't afford to stay in these elegant hostelries—and at $400–600 a night, who can?—they're well worth stepping into for afternoon tea, a drink, or just a look-see.

NYC & Company (800/NYC-VISIT or www.nycvisit.com), the city's official convention and visitors' bureau, publishes free booklets listing about 150 hotels. NYC & Co. also sponsors a **Visitors Hotel Hotline** (212/582-3352), which matches visitors with hotels of all price ranges during the summer and Christmas seasons.

Another option is to use a booking service. These companies buy large blocks of rooms at a discount and pass on the savings to consumers. Among the best of these companies are **Quikbook** (800/789-9887), **Express Hotel Reservations** (800/407-3351), **Accommodations Express** (800/444-7666), and **Central Reservation Service** (800/555-7555).

Another option is to book through the Internet, where you'll find some of the cheapest rates around. Among the most ubiquitous sites are www.hoteldiscounts.com, www.hotels.com, and www.hotwire.com.

The hostelries below are listed by neighborhood, with the less expensive places listed first. Prices quoted are generally for the high season. Keep in mind that in addition to the room rate, you'll also have to pay a hefty hotel tax of 13.25 percent, plus two dollars.

Lower Manhattan

$100-200: At the **Cosmopolitan Hotel** (95 West Broadway, at Chambers St., 212/566-1900 or 888/895-9400, www.cosmohotel.com,

$119–169 s or d), you'll find simple but very clean rooms furnished with comfortable beds and ceiling fans. Though nothing special, the hotel does offer both an excellent location (within easy walking distance of TriBeCa, Chinatown, SoHo, and the Financial District) and reasonable rates.

Over $350: The ultra-luxurious ◖ **Ritz-Carlton New York, Battery Park** (2 West St., at Battery Pl., 212/344-0800 or 800/241-3333, www.ritz-carlton.com, $370–550 s or d) provides spectacular views of New York Harbor and the Statue of Liberty. Everything in this gracious hostelry is in impeccable taste, from its goose-down pillows to its original artwork to its "water sommelier," who'll serve you a choice of mineral waters.

Chinatown, Little Italy, and the Lower East Side

Under $50: Popular with students and backpackers, the **Bowery's Whitehouse Hotel of New York** (340 Bowery, between Second and Third Aves., 212/477-5623, $37 s, $67 d) is part flophouse, part hostel. Built in 1917 for railroad workers, it still houses permanent residents. Rooms are basic but clean and safe.

$100-200: A five-minute walk east of SoHo is **Off-SoHo Suites** (11 Rivington St., between Chrystie and the Bowery, 212/979-9808 or 800/OFF-SOHO, www.offsoho.com, $99–109 s or d with shared bath, $139–159 s or d with private bath, suites for four $159–209), a clean and friendly budget hotel featuring large, homey suites with kitchenettes and marble bathtubs. Adjoining the narrow, mirror-lined lobby is a spartan café and self-service laundry room.

$200-350: All of the 110 rooms at the new, sleekly minimalist, 20-story **Hotel on Rivington** (107 Rivington St., between Essex and Ludlow Sts., 212/475-2600, www.hotelonrivington.com, $250–325 s or d) are wrapped in glass, offering stunning views of Manhattan. Velvet couches, heated-tile bathroom floors, private terraces, and in-room spa services are among the hotel's attractions.

SoHo and TriBeCa

$100-200: A banal HoJo's in the heart of trendy SoHo? It seems like a contradiction in concepts, but the **Howard Johnson Express Inn-SoHo** (135 E. Houston St., at Forsyth St., 212/358-8844, $139–189 s or d) is a welcome reasonably-priced hostelry in this hyper-expensive neighborhood.

$200-350: When it opened in 1996, the 370-room **☾ SoHo Grand** (310 W. Broadway, at Grand, 212/965-3000 or 800/965-3000, www.sohogrand.com, $250–570 s or d) was SoHo's first hotel since the 1800s. Sleekly done up in industrial metals, oversized lamps, columns, and sofas in its lobby, the hotel has become a chic, minimalist haven for well-heeled fashionables and Europeans. The custom-designed guest rooms feature muted grays, while adjoining the lobby is a classy, high-ceilinged bar.

The SoHo Grand's sister hotel, the **TriBeCa Grand** (2 Sixth Ave., between Church and White Sts., 212/519-6600 or 800/965-3000, www.tribecagrand.com, $250–459 s or d) was the first hotel to open in the triangle below Canal Street. Noisier, less stylish, and less spacious than its big sister, the TriBeCa features a large and trendy bar lobby area that's always mobbed. Getting a good night's sleep seems like an afterthought here.

Over $350: The Mercer (147 Mercer St., at Prince, 212/966-6060 or 888/918-6060, $345–395 s, $375–625 d) is a stylish spot, located smack in the middle of SoHo. Each of its 75 understated rooms is done up in furniture made of exotic African woods and features a large bathroom with tubs made for two. Downstairs is the Mercer Kitchen restaurant.

Greenwich Village

Under $100: Stepping into the beaux arts **Larchmont Hotel** (27 W. 11th St., between Fifth and Sixth Aves., 212/989-9333, www.larchmonthotel.com, $75–95 s, $90–115 d, with breakfast) is like stepping into a private home. Umbrellas are standing in the tiled foyer; someone is asleep on the loveseat in the tiny lobby. Well situated in the heart of the Village, the Larchmont offers 77 attractive rooms with rattan furnishings, good lighting, and clean, shared bathrooms down the hall.

$100-200: Though small, the lobby of the family-owned **☾ Washington Square Hotel** (103 Waverly Pl., between MacDougal St. and Sixth Ave., 212/777-9515 or 800/222-0418, www.washingtonsquarehotel.com, $145–185 s or d, includes continental breakfast) is stunning—all black and white tiles, lacy iron grillwork, gilded adornments, and Audubon prints. The recently renovated rooms feature art deco touches, and you can't beat the location, just off Washington Square.

Union Square and Murray Hill

Under $100: A bunk in a dorm-style room at the irrepressible **Gershwin** (see $100–200, below) goes for $40–55 a night. Some dorm rooms accommodate four people, others eight. Shared bathrooms are reasonably clean.

At the cheap and cheerful **Carlton Arms** (160 E. 25th St., at Third Ave., 212/679-0680, $70 s and $80 d with shared bath, $85 s and $95 d with private one), artists' murals cover most of the walls. The decor and furnishings are minimal, but this can be a fun place to stay for the exuberant and the young.

$100-200: More hostel than hotel, the **Murray Hill Inn** (143 E. 30th St., between Lexington and Third Ave., 212/683-6900 or 888/996-6376, www.murrayhillinn.com, $80–95 s or d with shared bath, $99–149 s or d with private bath), located on a quiet residential street, offers 50 small but clean rooms at budget rates. All rooms have cable TV and daily maid service. The inn has a second location, the **Union Square Inn** (209 E. 14th St., between Second and Third Aves., 212/614-0500), where rates are somewhat higher.

The high-spirited **Gershwin Hotel** (7 E. 27th St., between Fifth and Madison, 212/545-8000, $99–200 s or d), awhirl with artwork and young budget travelers from around the world, is a sort of cheaper, more modern version of the classic Chelsea Hotel. Here you'll find a lobby brimming with color, no-frills rooms of all shapes and sizes, an art gallery, and a rooftop bar in summer.

$200-350: The intimate **Park South Hotel** (122 E. 28th St., between Lexington and Park Ave., 212/448-0811 or 800/315-4642, $189–339 d), housed in a 1906 building, offers 143 tidy rooms complete with art deco furnishings, an open-air lounge, business center, and excellent restaurant, the Black Duck. A mezzanine library focuses on local history. Some of the rooms have great views of the Chrysler building.

At the stylish **W Union Square** (201 Park Ave. S, at 17th St., 212/253-9119, $250–450 d), you'll find well-appointed rooms filled with ultra-comfortable furnishings and a lively lobby-bar filled with beautiful people. This is one of five W hotels in the city.

Downstairs at the charming ◖ **Shelburne Murray Hill** (303 Lexington Ave., at 37th St., 212/689-5200 or 800/ME-SUITE, suites from $280) is an attractive lobby filled with baroque antiques, and an especially helpful staff. Upstairs are very spacious suites with two double beds and well-equipped kitchens, making this good value for the money. The blue and gold furnishings are plush, yet comfortable.

Chelsea

Under $50: The **Chelsea Center** (313 W. 29th St., between Eighth and Ninth Aves., 212/643-0214, www.chelseacenterhostel.com, $30–33 per person) is a small, friendly hostel with dorm-style accommodations and a garden out back. All rooms share bathrooms.

$100-200: Once the home of *Life* magazine, the friendly, beaux arts ◖ **Herald Square Hotel** (19 W. 31st St., between Fifth and Sixth Aves., 212/279-4017 or 800/727-1888, www.heraldsquarehotel.com, $70 s or d with shared bath, $130–170 s or d with private bath) boasts a lovely facade complete with lacy iron fretwork and a plump, gilded cherub reading the magazine. Rooms are small, but adequate and very clean.

Just east of the Herald Square is another beaux arts hostelry—the **Hotel Wolcott** (4 W. 31st St., near Fifth Ave., 212/268-2900,

www.wolcott.com, $109–179 s or d). Its elaborate but well-worn lobby is packed with marble columns, enormous mirrors, and shiny chandeliers—all contrasting strangely with the room's utilitarian furnishings. Rooms are small but adequate.

A European-style hostelry for budget travelers, the **Chelsea Lodge** (318 W. 20th St., between Eighth and Ninth Aves., 212/243-4499, www.chelsealodge.com, $95 s, $110 d) is housed in a historic brownstone. All of the 22 rooms have a shower and sink; toilets are down the hall.

Good value accommodations can be found at the **Red Roof Inn** (6 W. 32nd St., between Fifth Ave. and Broadway, 212/643-7100 or 800/RED-ROOF, $140–210 s or d). Surprisingly stylish, the inn offers small but clean rooms and a 24-hour fitness center.

Built in 1901, the spiffy, neo–art deco ◖ **Metro** (45 W. 35th St., between Fifth and Sixth Aves., 212/947-2500 or 800/356-3870, $155–295 s or d, includes continental breakfast) offers 175 comfortable guest rooms and a large, comfortable lobby. On the top floor is an exercise room and lively rooftop terrace, where drinks are served in summer.

One of the city's most historic hostelries is the **Chelsea Hotel** (222 W. 23rd St., between Seventh and Eighth Aves., 212/243-3700, www.chelseahotel.com, $170–290 s or d), once home to everyone from Dylan Thomas to Sid Vicious. Nowadays, the Chelsea is neither particularly clean nor particularly cheap, but it does have atmosphere. Offbeat, bohemian, and chic in its own faded way, it offers thick walls, many rooms with kitchenettes, a friendly staff, and excellent people-watching. In the basement is a trendy cocktail lounge, Serena.

Midtown East

Under $100: The centrally located **Vanderbilt YWCA** (224 E. 47th St., between Third and Second Aves., 212/756-9600, www.ymcanyc.org, $79 s, $89 d) is a good bet for budget travelers. Open to both men and women, it offers small, clean rooms with shared baths. Reserve well in advance.

$100-200: One of the better deals in the city is **Pickwick Arms** (230 E. 51st St., between Third and Second Aves., 212/355-0300 or 800/742-5945, www.pickwickarms.com, $79–119 s, $139–199 d), on a quiet block that's nonetheless near everything. The Pickwick's rooms are small but comfortable, and there's a sundeck on the roof. Some of the single rooms share baths.

The bustling 1920s lobby of the historic **Roosevelt Hotel** (45 E. 45th St., at Madison, 212/661-9600 or 888/TEDDY-NY, www.theroosevelthotel.com, $159–289 s or d) features tall fluted columns, lots of marble, and fresh flowers. The rooms are quite comfortable as well.

$200-350: No two rooms are alike at the **Roger Smith** (501 Lexington Ave., at 47th St., 212/755-1400 or 800/445-0277, www.rogersmith.com, $265–295 s or d), a jazzy retreat complete with several art galleries, a gift shop selling arts and crafts, and a long, narrow restaurant painted with floor-to-ceiling murals. The rooms are quite spacious and tastefully furnished.

The ◖ **Drake Swissôtel** (440 Park Ave., at 56th St., 212/421-0900 or 800/372-5369, $285–325 s, $295–365 d) is a lovely hostelry, managed to perfection in impeccable Swiss style. The lobby gleams with marble and polished glass; the rooms are spacious and airy, with separate sitting areas and oversized desks. In back of the lobby is the Drake Bar and Cafe, serving Swiss, European, and American specialties.

The European-styled ◖ **Hotel Elysée** (60 E. 54th St., between Madison and Park Aves., 212/753-1066 or 800/535-9733, $285–325 s or d, continental breakfast included) is furnished in dark woods, plush carpets, and Oriental antiques. Most of the rooms have Italian marble bathrooms, and adjoining the lobby is the classy Monkey Bar, its walls covered with murals. Among the famous residents who once lived in the Elysée were Joe DiMaggio, Tallulah Bankhead, and Tennessee Williams.

Over $350: Built in 1931, the famed **Waldorf-Astoria** (301 Park Ave., between 49th and 50th Sts., 212/355-3000 or 800/WALDORF, www.waldorf.com, $275–400 s, $325–450 d) continues to beckon with opulence and romance. Surrounding the art deco lobby are glittering stores selling jewelry, antiques, and rare books. Downstairs is Peacock Alley, an elegant café with a piano that once belonged to Cole Porter. Upstairs are 1,120 rooms in varying shapes and sizes.

Step into the lobby of the minimalist I. M. Pei–designed **Four Seasons New York** (57 E. 57th St., between Madison and Park Aves., 212/758-5700 or 800/332-3442, www.fourseasons.com, $475–625 s or d) and you feel as if you're about to request an audience with the king. The reception desk is just so big and far away—up two flights of stairs—and you're so small. Once you get used to it, however, the place feels grand. Designed with earth tones, a muted skylight, and octagonal columns, it offers an understated restaurant to one side, a lounge to the other. The guest rooms are the largest in New York (600 square feet), and come equipped with all things state-of-the-art, including bathtubs that fill in 60 seconds.

One of the city's most opulent and atmospheric hostelries is the **St. Regis Hotel** (2 E. 55th St., at Fifth Ave., 212/753-4500 or 800/759-7550, $675–825 s or d), built by John Jacob Astor in 1904. Filled with marble, crystal, and gold leaf, the St. Regis is home to the fabulous King Cole Bar, backed with a Maxfield Parrish mural. Guest rooms feature high ceilings, Louis XVI antiques, marble bathrooms with double sinks, and every conceivable amenity.

Midtown West

$100-200: A good option in the Theater District is the attractive, spanking clean, friendly and reasonably priced ◖ **Broadway Inn** (264 W. 46 St., at Eighth Ave., 212/997-9200 or 800/826-6300, www.broadwayinn.com, $99–199 s or d, continental breakfast included). The inn offers 45 basic rooms appointed in greens and grays and an airy, second-floor lobby filled with potted plants, inviting chairs, and well-stocked bookshelves.

© SEAN WATTERS

the St. Regis Hotel

One of the largest hotels in New York is the 1,000-room **Hotel Edison** (228 W. 47th St., near Eighth Ave., 212/840-5000 or 800/637-7070, www.edisonhotelnyc.com, $150 s, $170 d). Most notable for its striking art deco lobby lined with murals of the 1920s Yankees, the Cotton Club, construction workers, and more, the hotel also offers clean, good-sized rooms. Adjoining the lobby is a hair salon, two restaurants, and a café popular among young actors.

$200-350: Filled with eclectic touches, the sleek **Paramount** (235 W. 46th St., near Eighth Ave., 212/764-5500 or 800/225-7474, www.paramount-hotel.net, $190–285 d) is a fun place to stay. Created by Ian Schrager of Studio 54 fame, it features a darkened lobby filled with lollipop-colored chairs and a big-checked rug, and, in the rooms, beds slung close to the floor and stainless-steel sinks shaped like ice-cream cones. A second-story restaurant wraps around the lobby, and the hotel's Whiskey Bar is a popular late-night spot.

Adding a little downtown glamour to Times Square is the sleek, trendy **W Times Square** (1567 Broadway, at 47th St., 212/930-7400 or 877/976-8357, www.whotels.com, $270–350 s or d). In the entrance hall is a cascading waterfall behind glass, while the futuristic, seventh-floor lobby is all adorned in white on white. All rooms have ceiling-high mirror headboards and spiffy space-age bathrooms. Superb sushi is offered by the bi-level Blue Fin restaurant.

Still deliciously old-fashioned, with lots of wood paneling and brocaded chairs, is the 1902 **Algonquin** (59 W. 44th St., between Fifth and Sixth Aves., 212/840-6800 or 800/555-8000, www.thealgonquin.net, $195–299 s or d). Each floor has a different color scheme, and the inviting rooms offer plump beds, comfy armchairs, and bathrooms equipped with plenty of amenities. Downstairs, where Dorothy Parker and friends once met, are several snug lounges perfect for afternoon tea, cocktails, or aperitifs.

The **Mansfield** (12 W. 44th St., between Fifth and Sixth Aves., 212/944-6050 or 877/847-4444, www.mansfieldhotel.com, $265 s, 295 d) was built in 1904 as a residence for well-to-do bachelors. Now a gleaming 123-room hotel, it features gorgeous woodwork, a

12-story oval staircase, and rooms equipped with everything from Victorian sleigh beds to etched-glass French doors. Many of the rooms are quite small, however.

The **Plaza** (768 Fifth Ave., at 59th St., 212/759-3000 or 800/759-3000, www.fairmont.com, $275–575 s or d), one of New York's best-known hotels, was nicely restored by the Trumps in the late 1980s. The rooms come in all shapes and sizes and are furnished with both period antiques and reproductions. Some rooms offer grand four-poster beds, others marble fireplaces and crystal chandeliers.

Upper East Side
$200-350: Downstairs at the small and stylish **Franklin** (164 E. 87th St., between Lexington and Third Aves., 212/369-1000, www.franklinhotel.com, $229–269 s or d, includes continental breakfast) is a tiny streamlined lobby done up in black and burnished steel with mirrors and fresh flowers. Upstairs are 53 cozy guest rooms featuring beds with billowing canopies, cherrywood furnishings, and a fresh rose at each bedside.

Over $350: A magnificent slice of the Old World can be found at the ❰ **Pierre Hotel** (Fifth Ave. at 61st St., 212/838-8000 or 800/PIERRE4, www.fourseasons.com/pierre, $425–590 s, $475–630 d). The stunning lobby is adorned with chandeliers, fresh flowers, silks, and damasks, while the guest rooms are lavishly furnished with antiques. A good way to sample the Pierre, even if you can't afford to stay, is to stop in at the baroque-styled Rotunda for an elegant afternoon tea.

First-class service and unerring good taste have made the **Carlyle Hotel** (35 E. 76th St., at Madison Ave., 212/744-1600 or 800/227-5737, www.thecarlyle.com, $550–800 s or d) one of the city's top hotels ever since it opened in 1930. The airy, spacious rooms are equipped with every conceivable amenity, while downstairs is the Cafe Carlyle, a superb cabaret.

The Mark (25 E. 77th St., near Madison Ave., 212/744-4300 or 800/843-6275, www.themarkhotel.com, $550–600 s, $600–650 d, continental breakfast included) is small,

stylish, and very elegant, with a neoclassical Italian look. In the lobby, gleaming marble floors reflect sumptuous vases overflowing with fresh flowers. The Mark's Bar offers plenty of cozy nooks and crannies; the guest rooms are large and comfortably furnished.

Upper West Side
Under $100: One of the cheapest places to stay in New York is **Hosteling International New York** (891 Amsterdam Ave., between 103rd and 104th Sts., 212/932-2300. www.hinewyork.org). Occupying a block-long landmark building, this hostel is the nation's largest, with 90 clean, dorm-style rooms, each sleeping four to eight in bunk beds, as well as some family rooms. Also on the premises are kitchens, coin-operated laundry machines, and a garden.

You must be a member of Hosteling International-American Youth Hostel (202/783-6161, www.hiayh.org, adults $28, seniors $18, youths under 18 free) to stay in the hostel, and reservations should be made two to three months in advance. Rates are $29–40 per person for dorm rooms, $120 for a family room, and $135 for a private room with bath.

Jazz on the Park (36 W. 106th St., between Central Park West and Manhattan Ave., 212/932-1600, www.jazzhostel.com) offers small basic rooms and a basement lounge that features live jazz and hip hop on the weekends. Rates are $25–38 per person for dorm rooms, $110 d for private room.

$100-200: Country Inn the City (W. 77th St., between Broadway and West End Ave., 212/580-4183, www.countryinnthecity.com, $150–200 s or d) is a lovely landmark townhouse with four bed-and-breakfast units, all equipped with a large bedroom, sitting area, and antiques.

The friendly ❰ **Hotel Beacon** (2130 Broadway, at 75th St., 212/787-1100 or 800/572-4969, $180–235 s or d) offers good value for the money. Its rooms are large and attractive and equipped with two double beds and kitchenettes. The lobby gleams with black-and-white marble and brass.

$200-350: The stylish **On the Ave Hotel** (2178 Broadway, at 77th St., 212/362-1100 or 800/509-7598, www.ontheave-nyc.com, $225–325 s or d) is a welcome new addition to the Upper West Side. Rooms feature canopied beds, original artwork, and industrial-style bathrooms.

Harlem

Under $100: The **Sugar Hill International House** (722 St. Nicholas Ave., at 146th St., 212/283-1490) offers both dorm-style ($25 per person) and private rooms ($60 per person). A passport is required of all guests, including U.S. citizens. At the **New York Uptown International Hostel** (239 Lenox Ave., at 122nd St., 212/666-0559), beds are available in small, clean dorm rooms sleeping four to six for $25 a night.

The **International House of New York** (500 Riverside Dr., at W. 122nd St., 212/316-8473, $120 s, $135 d) is primarily in the business of renting rooms to Columbia University graduate students and visiting scholars. In the summer, however, when occupancy rates are low, rooms are available to the general public.

$100–200: In the late 1990s, the **Efuru Guesthouse** (106 W. 120th St., at Malcolm X Blvd. [Lenox Ave.], 212/961-9855, www.efuruguesthouse.com, $95–125 s or d) was an abandoned building. Enter Lydia Smith, who bought the house through a lottery system, put in five years of hard renovation work, and transformed the property into a serene four-room B&B. All rooms have private baths and refrigerators, the living room features a fireplace, and there's a small garden out back.

Bed-and-Breakfasts

Though not necessarily cheaper than an inexpensive or moderately priced hotel, a B&B can be a good, friendly alternative. Some New York City B&Bs are the traditional kind—a room or two in a host's home. Others are entire apartments that you'll have completely to yourself. Rooms usually run $90–150/night, apartments $135–250/night, and minimum stays of two or three nights are often required. Among the B&B registries operating in New York City are:

Bed and Breakfast Network of New York (212/645-8134, www.bedandbreakfastnetny.com), in operation since 1986.

CitySonnet (212/614-3034, www.citysonnet.com), run by artists and specializing mostly in downtown Manhattan.

City Lights Bed & Breakfast (212/737-7049, www.citylightsbandb.com), matching artists and professionals with like-minded hosts.

For longer stays, check out **New York Habitat** (212/352-8018, www.nyhabitat.com), which offers furnished apartment sublets in all prices and locations throughout the city.

FOOD

New York boasts about 18,000 eating establishments. Some come and go almost overnight, while others have been around for decades. A few rules of thumb: The East Village is an excellent neighborhood for cheap eats and ethnic restaurants; SoHo, TriBeCa, and Columbus Avenue boast lots of trendy spots; and Midtown and the Upper East Side are home to some of the city's most venerable and expensive restaurants.

Lower Manhattan

At the foot of Brooklyn Bridge is Manhattan's oldest restaurant building, said to date back to 1794. It's now home to the casual, atmospheric **Bridge Cafe** (279 Water St., near Dover, 212/227-3344), serving lots of seafood and a popular brunch; average entrée $19.

A downtown branch of the acclaimed midtown bistro run by chef-turned-writer Anthony Bourdain (author of *Kitchen Confidential,*), **Les Halles Downtown** (15 John St., between Broadway and Nassau, 212/285-8585) is heralded for its "American beef, French style" and lively atmosphere; average entrée $20.

Once a hole-in-the-wall waterside bar, **Jeremy's Ale House** (254 Front St., near Dover, 212/964-3537) is still best known for its pints, but it also offers simple fish dishes, burgers, and its trademark—fish and chips; average entrée $9.

For scrumptious Argentine take-out, including more than a dozen types of empanadas, stop by **Ruben's Empanadas** (15 Bridge St., between Broad and Whitehead, 212/509-3825).

Chinatown

Chinatown is home to over 300 restaurants serving various cuisines including Hunan, Szechuan, Shanghai, Cantonese, Vietnamese, and Thai. You can't go wrong with most of the restaurants here, especially those catering to a large Asian clientele. All are inexpensive to moderately priced, with the average entrée less than $12.

Chinese: A good choice on Mott Street is **Tai Hong Lau** (70 Mott, near Bayard, 212/219-1431), offering unusual Hong Kong–style cuisine and cheap dim sum. Bustling **(Joe's Shanghai** (9 Pell St., between Bowery and Mott St., 212/233-8888) features some of the freshest food in Chinatown (with another branch in Flushing, Queens) and is especially famous for its "soup dumplings"—a mouthful of soup *inside* the dough.

Despite its name, the tri-level **(Sweet-n-Tart Café** (76 Mott St., 212/334-8088) serves some of the most authentic Chinese food in town.

The modern **Nice Restaurant** (35 E. Broadway, near Catherine, 212/406-9510) offers fresh Hong Kong–style Chinese cuisine and dim sum.

A half-dozen or so cavernous, gaily decorated restaurants serve dim sum from mid-morning until late afternoon, and fixed-price banquets thereafter. One of the largest and best of these eateries is **Golden Unicorn** (18 E. Broadway, at Catherine, 212/941-0911), where waiters use walkie-talkies to communicate—arrive early, as there's often a long wait.

Other Asian Fare: Fresh and healthy Vietnamese fare is the specialty at the unassuming **Nha Trang** (87 Baxter St., between Bayard and Canal, 212/233-5948). Some of the city's best Thai food can be found at **Thailand Restaurant** (106 Bayard St., at Baxter, 212/349-3132); average entrée $15.

Treats: Chinatown is also filled with bakeries. Near where Pell meets Mott is the cheery **May May Bakery** (35 Pell St., 212/267-0733). Try the moon cakes, almond cookies, "cow ears" (chips of fried dough), or pork buns. Also, don't miss the **Chinatown Ice Cream Factory** (65 Bayard St., near Mott, 212/608-4170), where you can buy every flavor of ice cream from ginger to mango.

Watering Holes: On the northern edge of Chinatown you'll find **Double Happiness** (173 Mott St., between Broome and Grande Sts., 212/941-1282), a hip basement bar that's always packed with young urbanites.

Little Italy

Though Little Italy is generally *not* the place to go for good Italian food, it does hold some bargain-priced eateries, cheery cafés, and a few noteworthy dinner houses.

The friendly, old-fashioned **Da Nico** (164 Mulberry St., between Grand and Broome, 212/343-1212), with a garden out back, specializes in excellent coal-oven pizza and savory roasted meats and fish; average entrée $13. Homey **Benito I** (174 Mulberry St., between Grand and Broome, 212/226-9171)

GOT LUNCH?

During the 1992 Democratic Convention, some of the city's top restaurants—including the "21" Club, Lutece, and Four Seasons – celebrated the extravaganza by offering a $19.92 prix fixe luncheon. The program proved so popular that it's been repeated every summer since, with the luncheon's cost increasing one cent each year. In 2005, for example, about 200 top restaurants offered the $20.05 prix fixe lunch during the last week in June, with some extending the program throughout the summer. It's a great way to sample the city's poshest eateries. For details, contact NYC & Company, the city's convention and visitors bureau (212/397-9222, www.nycvisit.com).

serves good, traditional Sicilian food; average entrée $12.

One of Little Italy's best restaurants is **Il Cortile** (125 Mulberry St., near Hester, 212/226-6060), a multi-roomed spot with brick walls and an indoor garden, specializing in Northern Italian cuisine; average entrée $20. Also very good is **Taormina** (147 Mulberry St., between Hester and Grand, 212/219-1007), once former mobster John Gotti's favorite spot; average entrée $19.

Cafés: For an afternoon snack, try the cozy, tile-floored **Cafe Roma** (385 Broome St., at Mulberry, 212/226-8413), a wonderful espresso-and-pastry café that was once a hangout for opera singers. Another good choice is the flashy **Ferrara's** (195 Grand St., near Mulberry, 212/226-6150).

Watering Holes: In the 1940s, *Daily News* photographer Arthur Felig, better known as Weegee, hung out at **Onieal's Grand Street Bar** (174 Grand St., between Mulberry and Court St., 212/941-9119) while waiting to follow police sirens to nasty crime scenes. Nowadays, the clientele tends to be younger, trendier, and more upscale.

Lower East Side

The granddaddy of New York delicatessens is **Katz's** (205 Houston St., at Ludlow, 212/254-2246), a huge, cafeteria-style place where you take a number at the door. Overhead hang WWII–era signs reading "Send a salami to your boy in the Army"; average sandwich $9.

Among the neighborhood's more modern eateries is **Oliva** (161 E. Houston St., at Allen St., 212/228-4143), specializing in tasty Basque fare. Pitchers of sangria are set up on the bar and a wide range of seafood tapas are on the menu; average entrée $16. **Paladar** (161 Ludlow St., between Houston and Stanton Sts., 212/473-3535) is a funky Cuban joint serving spicy sea bass and other favorite dishes; average entrée $13.

Schiller's (131 Rivington St., at Norfolk St., 212/260-4555) is the newest Keith McNally (Balthazar, Pastis) hotspot, done up in casual bistro style. On the menu is everything from Cuban sandwiches to pasta; average entrée $16.

Watering Holes: Ludlow, Stanton, and Clinton Streets are the hub of the hip Lower East Side nightlife, where you'll find lots of laid-back bars and lounges, some holes-in-the-wall, others more upscale. One of the oldest is **Max Fish** (178 Ludlow St., between Houston and Stanton Sts., 212/529-3959), a long, comfortable watering hole drawing an artsy crowd.

SoHo

Though now a bit worn, the **Moondance Diner** (80 Sixth Ave., at Grand, 212/226-1191) is a classic New York spot, offering gourmet sandwiches and the like; average entrée $9. **Jerry's** (101 Prince St., between Mercer and Greene, 212/966-9464) is an upscale diner with red leather booths and an eclectic menu; average entrée $15. The light and airy **Spring Street Natural** (62 Spring St., at Lafayette, 212/966-0290) features lots of plants, big windows, and solid vegetarian fare; average entrée $14.

Lucky Strike (59 Grand St., between Wooster and W. Broadway, 212/941-0479) is a casual bistro that turns into a lively bar at night, when the young, the beautiful, and the hopeful gather to exchange glances; average entrée $14. **Ideya** (349 W. Broadway, between Broome and Grand Sts., 212/625-1441) specializes in Caribbean fare, served to a Brazilian beat; average entrée $18.

Once too hot for its own good, **⬛ Balthazar** (80 Spring St., between Crosby and Broadway, 212/965-1414), a large and bustling brasserie, still draws a sleek, celebrity-studded crowd; average entrée $24. **Zoe** (90 Prince St., between Broadway and Mercer, 212/966-6722) is a handsome spot known for its open kitchen and California-style cuisine; average entrée $21.

The dark and stylish **⬛ Raoul's** (180 Prince St., between Sullivan and Thompson, 212/966-3518), a French bistro, is a downtown mecca and with good reason; the food and ambience are top-notch; average entrée $24. Tiny, cozy **Le Pescadou** (16 King St., at Sixth Ave.,

212/924-3434) specializes in fresh fish, and attracts a loyal following; average entrée $19.

Treats: At the south end of SoHo is the cozy **Cupping Room Cafe** (359 W. Broadway, near Broome, 212/925-2898), especially good for afternoon snacks. Many New Yorkers go out of their way to visit **Eileen's Special Cheesecake** (15 Cleveland Pl., near Lafayette St., just below Spring, 212/966-5585); takeout only. For some of the best crepes in town, check out snug, tin-tabled **Palacinka** (28 Grand St., between Sixth Ave. and Thompson St., 212/625-0362).

Watering Holes: The classic bar in SoHo is **Fanelli's** (94 Prince St., at Mercer, 212/226-9412), an 1876 pub complete with beveled glass doors, tiled floors, and heavy dark wood. In the back are worn wooden tables where passable bar food is served.

The **Merc Bar** (151 Mercer St., near Houston, 212/966-2727), done up in sleek, modernized Adirondackiana, attracts a lively crowd. **Milano's** (51 Houston St., between Mulberry and Mott, 212/226-8632) is a long, narrow dive with a good jukebox.

TriBeCa

The simple **Thai House Cafe** (151 Hudson St., at Hubert, 212/334-1085) is especially good for weekday lunch, when specials are served; average entrée $11. A longtime favorite among night-crawlers is the chic, art deco **Odeon** (145 W. Broadway, at Thomas, 212/233-0507), serving consistently good food in a lively, downtown setting; average entrée $19.

Still going strong is Robert DeNiro's brick-walled **TriBeCa Grill** (375 Greenwich St., at Franklin, 212/941-3900). The place draws hordes of celebrity watchers, and very few celebrities, but the food and service are nonetheless surprisingly good; average entrée $25.

Reserve months in advance to get a seat at **Nobu** (105 Hudson St., at Franklin St., 212/219-0500), arguably the most famous Japanese restaurant (with Peruvian touches) in America. Partly owned by Robert DeNiro, and a favorite among celebrities, the sleek eatery offers lots of innovative fare created by acclaimed chef Nobu Matsuhisa; average small dish $16. If you have no reservation, check out **Next Door Nobu** (212/334-4445), where you may have to wait (they accept no reservations), but the food and ambience are similar, and the prices not quite so high.

Watering Holes: Once an artists' hangout, **Puffy's Tavern** (81 Hudson St., at Harrison, 212/766-9159) now attracts everyone from bankers and bikers to police and firefighters. **Walker's** (16 N. Moore St., at Varick, 212/941-0142) is an 1890s saloon that serves tasty pub grub and Guinness on tap. The **Church Lounge** in the trendy TriBeCa Grand Hotel (2 Sixth Ave., between Church and White Sts., 212/519-6677) is an enormous bar-lobby that is always filled with downtown revelers.

East Village

The East Village has traditionally been known for its cheap, Eastern European eateries, where the average main course costs $7–9. Two legendary Second Avenue spots are **Second Avenue Deli** (156 Second Ave., at 10th St., 212/677-0606), a classic Jewish delicatessen serving great pastrami and corned beef sandwiches, and **Veselka** (144 Second Ave., at 9th St., 212/228-9682), the place to go for borscht, pierogi, and scrumptious poppy-seed cake. Another classic is **Odessa** (119 Ave. A, between 7th and 8th Sts., 212/253-1470), serving heaping platters of Ukrainian food.

The East Village is also known for its inexpensive Indian restaurants, most of which lie along 6th Street between First and Second Avenues. One of the best of the group is the **Sonar Goan Indian Restaurant** (328 E. 6th St., 212/677-8876), where the chicken and lamb dishes are especially good.

A long-time neighborhood stand-by is the **Miracle Grill** (112 First Ave., at 7th St., 212/254-2353), offering tasty Southwestern cuisine and a scruffy but romantic garden; average entrée $14. Also still going strong after many years is **Angelika Kitchen** (300 E. 12th St., between First and Second Aves.,

212/228-2909), serving the city's best vegan fare; average entrée $11.

Two Boots (37 Ave. A, between 2nd and 3rd Sts., 212/505-2276), is known for its first-rate pizza and other spicy fare from the lands shaped like "Two Boots"—Italy and Louisiana; average main dish $11. Cheery, old-fashioned **Lanza** (168 First Ave., between 10th and 11th Sts., 212/674-7014) sports bright oil paintings of Italy. Out back is a pleasant garden; average entrée $14. **Cyclo** (203 First Ave., between 12th and 13th Sts., 212/673-3957) serves fresh, tasty Vietnamese fare in an airy setting; average entrée $13. **Time Cafe** (380 Lafayette St., at Great Jones St., 212/533-7000) attracts a sleek neighborhood clientele with its varied menu and Moroccan-style bar; average entrée $14.

Among more upscale spots, cozy **(Jules** (65 St. Mark's Pl., between First and Second Aves., 212/477-5560) is a lively French bistro with live jazz most weekends; average entrée $17. **First** (87 First Ave., at 5th St., 212/674-3823), lined with burnished steel and comfy gray booths, serves an eclectic international fare that's part Asian, part Mexican, part Italian, and part French; average entrée $18. Creative American food with a Mediterranean flair is the specialty at **(Five Points** (31 Great Jones St., between the Bowery and Lafayette St., 212/253-5700), where the menu changes nightly; average entrée $21.

Cafés: One of the oldest pastry shops in the East Village is the century-old **Veniero's** (342 E. 11th St., near First Ave., 212/674-7070), featuring classic Italian treats. Across First Avenue is **De Robertis** (176 First Ave., at 11th St., 212/674-7137), a cheery Italian shop with a handful of tables and wonderful window displays.

Watering Holes: The large and friendly **Telephone Bar & Grill** (149 Second Ave., between 9th and 10th Sts., 212/529-5000) sports bright red English-style phone booths out front. **KGB** (85 E. 4th St., between Second and Third Aves., 212/505-3360) is a former speakeasy now filled with eclectic Soviet souvenirs. Especially popular among writers and

editors, it hosts frequent readings and literary get-togethers.

McSorley's Old Ale House (15 E. 7th St., between Second and Third Aves., 212/473-9148) is one of New York's oldest bars (see description in East Village chapter). The elegant **Temple Bar** (332 Lafayette St., between Bleecker and Houston, 212/925-4242) is a lush hideaway with Oriental rugs and expensive drinks.

Greenwich Village

One of the best places for a burger is the **Corner Bistro** (331 W. 4th St., at Jane and Eighth Ave., 212/242-9502), a dark pub with creaky wooden booths and an excellent jazz jukebox. A burger here costs $7. The city's best pizzeria is **(John's** (278 Bleecker St., near Seventh Ave., 212/243-1680), where the New York–style pies are thin, crispy, and low on grease; sold by the whole pie only, no slices. Expect long lines unless you come during the off-hours; medium pizza $12.

The cheery, upscale **Mi Cocina** (57 Jane St., at Hudson, 212/627-8273) serves authentic Mexican food in a simple, brick-walled setting; average entrée $17. Stylish **Tangerine** (228 W. 10th St., between Bleecker and Hudson, 212/463-8585) serves up first-rate Thai food—try the purple-blossom appetizers; average entrée $16. For some of the freshest sushi in town, step into **Japonica** (100 University Pl., at 12th St., 212/243-7752), a longtime Village favorite; average entrée $18.

Low-key, low-ceilinged **(Cafe Loup** (105 W. 13th St., near Sixth Ave., 212/255-4746) is a Village institution serving a wide range of excellent French fare; average entrée $19. A longtime favorite among connoisseurs of Italian food is comfortable, brick-walled **Il Mulino** (86 W. 3rd St., between Thompson and Sullivan, 212/673-3783), serving traditional Abruzzese fare; average entrée $25.

The sleek and fashionable **Gotham Bar and Grill** (12 E. 12th St., near Fifth Ave., 212/620-4020) has won numerous top awards for both its design and food; average entrée $30.

In the meatpacking district, find **Pastis** (9

TABITHA LAHR

John's Pizzeria is the perfect place to experience true New York-style pizza.

Ninth Ave., at Little 12th St., 212/929-4844), an airy, ultra-hip bistro complete with excellent food, beautiful people, and reasonable prices; average entrée $16. Not far away is ▐ **Spice Market** (403 13th St., at Ninth Ave., 212/675-2322), a neighborhood hotspot that's as acclaimed for its lush Eastern décor as it is for its Southeast Asian fare; average entrée $18. The 24-hour bistro/diner **Florent** (69 Gansevoort St., between Greenwich and Washington, 212/989-5779), a pioneering eatery in the district, is a longstanding hipster fave; average main dish, $14.

Cafés: Bleecker and MacDougal Streets are known for their many Italian coffee and pastry shops. Among the best are **Cafe Dante** (79 MacDougal St., 212/982-5275) and **Caffé Reggio** (119 MacDougal St., 212/475-9557). **Tea and Sympathy** (108 Greenwich Ave., at 13th St., 212/807-8329) features a British-style afternoon tea.

Watering Holes: Sturdy old **White Horse Tavern** (567 Hudson St., at 11th St., 212/243-9260) was once a writer's hangout; Dylan

Thomas drank himself to death here. Now the tavern caters mostly to a collegiate crowd. Outdoor picnic tables are set up in summer.

Chumley's (86 Bedford St., between Barrow and Grove, 212/675-4449) is an old speakeasy/restaurant where writers John Dos Passos and Theodore Dreiser once drank. It's unmarked, but not hard to find. The big, worn **Cedar Tavern** (82 University Pl., between 11th and 12th Sts., 212/741-9754) was once frequented by Jackson Pollock and other abstract expressionists. It's still a good place for a beer, but avoid the food.

In the meatpacking district, find the raucous, testosterone-filled **Hogs & Heifers** (859 Washington St., near Gansevoort St., 212/929-0655), its crowds spilling out onto the streets.

Among gay bars, the low-key **Stonewall** (53 Christopher St., near Seventh Ave. S, 212/463-0950) is named after the landmark riots. Across the street sprawls the **Monster** (80 Grove St., 212/924-3558), featuring a drag cabaret. **Henrietta Hudson** (438 Hudson St., at Morton, 212/924-3347) is a popular lesbian bar, drawing largely professional crowds.

Union Square and Murray Hill

Sam's Noodles (411 Third Ave., at 29th St., 212/213-2288) offers a wide array of noodle dishes from various parts of Asia. **Sarge's** (548 Third Ave., near 36th St., 212/679-0442) is a classic old–New York deli.

The **Galaxy** (15 Irving Pl., at 15th St., 212/777-3631) is an intimate spot bestrewn with tiny ceiling lights. On the menu, find a wide variety of tasty Asian-influenced fare; average entrée $11.

In Little India, Indian fast food can be picked up at **Curry in a Hurry** (119 Lexington Ave., at 28th St., 212/683-0900), housed in a bright turquoise building. Another good choice is **Joy of India** (127 E. 28th St., 212/685-0808), a spic-and-span cafeteria-style eatery always crowded with Indians. **Muriya** (129 E. 27th St., near Lexington Ave., 212/689-7925) specializes in Mughali fare; average entrée $14.

The city's best Turkish restaurant, serving fare made with the freshest of ingredients, is the red-and-gilt **Turkish Kitchen** (386 Third Ave., between 27th and 28th Sts., 212/679-6633); average entrée $16. Well-lit, blond wood **Tatany** (380 Third Ave., between 27th and 28th Sts., 212/686-1871), serves excellent sushi, reasonably priced; average entrée $15.

Housed in a stunning former bank building with lots of white marble and red lamps is the popular **Blue Water Grill** (31 Union Square W., at 16th St., 212/675-9500), serving fresh seafood; average entrée $19.

America (9 E. 18th St., between Fifth Ave. and Broadway, 212/505-2110) is a huge, cheery hangar of a place serving an astonishing array of foods from the 50 states; average main dish $16.

Lola (30 W. 22nd St., between Fifth and Sixth Aves., 212/675-6700) offers spicy Caribbean food in a colorful, sophisticated setting, along with a popular gospel brunch on Sunday;

average entrée $19. Chef/author Anthony Bourdain's **Les Halles** (411 Park Ave. S., between 28th and 29th Sts., 212/679-4111) is a boisterous French bistro and butcher shop with meats hanging in the windows.

A longtime favorite among restaurant critics and New Yorkers alike is Danny Meyer's **☾ Union Square Cafe** (21 E. 16th St., near Fifth Ave., 212/243-4020), a gracious and hospitable place serving an imaginative mix of Italian, French, and American cuisine; average entrée $26.

The café's youngest and most casual sibling is the big, high-ceilinged **Blue Smoke** (116 E. 27th St., between Park Ave. S. and Lexington Ave., 212/447-7733), the ultimate take on an urban barbecue joint. There's a spiffy jukebox to one side, a bar stocked with 30 varieties of bourbon to the other, and one of the best jazz clubs in town downstairs (the Jazz Standard).

Cafés: City Bakery (3 W. 18th St., near Fifth Ave., 212/366-1414) is a good place for simple gourmet lunches and baked goods. Farther uptown, find **Chez Laurence** (245 Madison Ave., at 38th St., 212/683-0284), also serving baked goods, coffees, and sandwiches.

Watering Holes: Old Town (45 E. 18th St., between Broadway and Park Ave. S., 212/529-6732) is a stunning, historic bar complete with high ceilings, mosaic floors, and a gorgeous back bar. Upstairs is a casual dining room serving passable food. Open in the summer only is **Luna Park,** a lively bar-café on the northern end of Union Square Park.

Near Union Square is **119** (119 E. 15th St., near Irving Pl., 212/995-5904), a comfortable dive with a pool table in front, dart boards in back, and a handful of creaky booths in between. Historic **Pete's Tavern** (129 E. 18th St., at Irving Pl., 212/473-7676) is touristy, but nicely soaked in the ale of time.

Chelsea

The **Empire Diner** (210 10th Ave., at 22nd St., 212/243-2736) is an art deco original well worth visiting. Tiny **La Taza De Oro** (96 Eighth

Ave., between 14th and 15th Sts., 212/243-9946) serves authentic Puerto Rican food; average main dish $8. For hearty Cuban-Chinese fare, try hole-in-the-wall **La Chinita Linda** (166 Eighth Ave., between 18th and 19th Sts., 212/633-1791); average main dish $7.

Numerous restaurants, many with outdoor tables in summer, line Seventh and Eighth Avenues between 14th and 23rd Streets. Among them is **Cafeteria** (119 Seventh Ave., at 17th St., 212/414-1717), serving excellent brunches and a wide range of American fare; average entreé $15. **Le Singe Vert** (160 Seventh Ave., between 18th and 19th Sts., 212/366-4100) is a popular French bistro; average entreé $18.

Tiny, cheerful **Bright Food Shop** (216 Eighth Ave., at 21st St., 212/243-4433) offers highly unusual and delicious Mexican-Asian cuisine; average entrée $15. Gourmet-style Mexican fare can be found at the bustling **Rocking Horse Mexican Cafe** (182 Eighth Ave., between 19th and 20th Sts., 212/463-9511); average entrée $17. **Gascogne** (158 Eighth Ave., near 18th St., 212/675-6564), specializes in the hearty foods of southern France. In summer, a backyard garden opens; average entrée $20.

Colorful, festive **Negril** (362 W. 23rd St. between Eighth and Ninth Aves., 212/807-6411) serves spicy Caribbean fare in a lively setting; average entrée $15. **Da Umberto** (107 W. 17th St., near Sixth Ave., 212/989-0303) is a classy, albeit noisy, spot acclaimed for its Northern Italian fare, wines, and well-dressed crowd; average entrée $24.

Farther north in Koreatown, find the spotless, narrow **Gam Mee Ok** (43 W. 32nd St., between Fifth and Sixth Aves., 212/695-4113) filled with artwork and Korean clients; average entrée $12. The tranquil **Hangawi** (12 E. 23rd St., 212/213-0077) is the place to go for vegetarian dishes, including pancakes and "porridges" (warm sweetened vegetable purees); average dish $18.

For a taste of late-19th-century New York, visit **Keens Steakhouse** (72 W. 36th St., between Fifth and Sixth Aves., 212/947-3636), an atmospheric multi-roomed pub with a crackling fireplace in winter; average entrée $20.

Watering Holes: Merchants (112 Seventh Ave., at 17th St., 212/366-7267) is a comfortable modern bar with a sidewalk café in summer and a crackling fireplace in winter; on the menu are gourmet sandwiches, salads, and desserts. Martinis are the specialty of the house at **Serena,** a subterranean club located in the basement of the Chelsea Hotel (222 W. 23rd St., between Seventh and Eighth Aves., 212/255-4646). The well-worn **Peter McManus** (152 Seventh Ave., at 19th St., 212/929-9691) attracts both longtime regulars and young professionals; juicy burgers are served at the big, rickety booths in back.

Midtown West

Note: If you're planning to eat in the Theater District before a show, make reservations or give yourself plenty of time. Many restaurants are packed between 6:30 and 8 P.M.

In the Theater District, inexpensive eats can be found at bustling **Ollie's Noodle Shop** (200B W. 44th St., near Broadway, 212/921-5988), offering a wide variety of noodle and dumpling dishes. Popular **Virgil's Real BBQ** (152 W. 44th St., between Broadway and Sixth Ave., 212/921-9494) serves up enormous portions of spare ribs, smoked brisket, and the like in a lively, two-story setting; average main course $13.

West 46th Street between Eighth and Ninth Avenues is known as "Restaurant Row." Here you'll find **Joe Allen** (326 W. 46th St., near Eighth Ave., 212/581-6464), a classic, well-known pub with a celebrity-studded clientele; average entrée $17. Not far away is the **Firebird** (365 W. 46th St., between Eighth and Ninth Aves., 212/586-0244). Housed in two posh brownstones, the Firebird resembles a prerevolutionary St. Petersburg mansion, complete with paintings, objets d'art, antiques, crystal, and authentic cuisine; average entrée $26.

On West 42nd Street is the upscale **West Bank Cafe** (407 W. 42nd St., near Ninth

Ave., 212/695-6909), an airy, friendly spot that attracts many actors; average entrée $17. **Chez Josephine** (414 W. 42nd St., near Ninth Ave., 212/594-1925) is a charming, low-lit French/Southern bistro run by one of Josephine Baker's adopted French children; average entrée $18.

During warm weather, both Bryant Park (between 40th and 42nd Streets, Fifth and Sixth Avenues) and the steps of the New York Public Library are good spots for lunch. Nearby vendors sell everything from hot dogs to gourmet fare.

Overlooking Bryant Park behind the New York Public Library are the **Bryant Park Grill** and the **Bryant Park Cafe** (25 W. 42nd St., 212/840-6500). Both serve imaginative American fare in a handsome setting, but the grill is somewhat more formal. In summer, a rooftop terrace opens up; average entrée $19.

Farther north, **Rock Center Cafe** (20 W. 50th St., 212/332-7620) serves American-style food in a superb setting overlooking the skating rink at Rockefeller Center. Be sure to make reservations; average entrée $20.

The **Carnegie Deli** (854 Seventh Ave., near 54th St., 212/757-2245) is a New York City landmark, famous for enormous overstuffed deli sandwiches. Similar in style is **Stage Deli** (834 Seventh Ave., between 53rd and 54th Sts., 212/245-7850), the Carnegie's major competitor. Average sandwich at both, $12. The stylish **Trattoria dell'Arte** (900 Seventh Ave., between 56th and 57th Sts., 212/245-9800) features tasty pastas and thin-crust pizzas; average main course $20.

Ninth Avenue between 42nd and 59th Streets is lined with one ethnic restaurant after another. Among them is the **Afghan Kebab House** (764 Ninth Ave., between 51st and 52nd Sts., 212/307-1612), serving succulent kebabs in exotic surroundings (average entrée $11), and airy, well-lit **Uncle Nick's** (747 Ninth Ave., between 50th and 51st Sts., 212/245-7992), one of Manhattan's few Greek restaurants (average entrée $13).

Watering Holes: For a drink in the city's only revolving bar, overlooking Times Square, take an elevator to the top of the glitzy

Marriott Marquis (1535 Broadway, at 45th St., 212/398-1900).

Back on ground level, near the Theater District is the elegant, wood-paneled **Algonquin Hotel** (59 W. 44th St., between Fifth and Sixth Aves., 212/840-6800), offering several bars and lounges. The Plaza Hotel's famed **Oak Bar** (Fifth Ave. and 59th St., 212/546-5200) is a plush and pricey one-of-a-kind spot, usually filled with tourists.

Nearby, find **Mickey Mantle's** (42 Central Park S, between Fifth and Sixth Aves., 212/688-7777), the city's best-known sports bar. However, many sports fans regard **ESPN Zone** (4 Times Square Plaza, 212/921-3776) as the best sports bar in town.

Midtown East

Just north of Grand Central in the Met Life Building (200 Park Ave.) is **Cucina & Co.** (212/682-2700), an Italian-accented eatery serving gourmet sandwiches, salads, pastas, and baked goods. **Mangia** (16 E. 48th St., between Fifth and Sixth Aves., and various other Midtown locations, 212/754-0637) offers excellent gourmet sandwiches and salad bars.

For a classic New York lunch, eat at Grand Central Station's 🦪 **Oyster Bar** (42nd St. and Park Ave., lower level, 212/490-6650), complete with red-checked tablecloths and a vaulted ceiling. On the menu is a wide variety of fish dishes, priced at about $25. Adjoining the main restaurant is a cheaper counter area, where dishes average $12. Closed weekends.

Overlooking Grand Central Terminal reigns **Michael Jordan's–The Steak House NYC** (23 Vanderbilt Ave., at 43rd St., 212/655-2300). The popular spot serves humongous portions and some of the best French fries in the city; average entrée $30.

A top-tier Chinese restaurant is the **Shun Lee Palace** (155 E. 55th St., between Lexington and Third Aves., 212/371-8844), featuring gourmet fare in an elegant setting; average entrée $23. The sophisticated **Dawat** (210 E. 58th St., near Third Ave., 212/355-7555) is considered to be one of the city's best Indian restaurants; average entrée $20.

Watering Holes: For a bird's-eye view of New York at night, Midtown is the neighborhood. The cozy **Top of the Tower** at the Beekman Tower Hotel (3 Mitchell Pl., off First Ave. at 49th St., 212/355-7300) offers an art deco lounge and an outdoor terrace open in summer.

Reopened in restored Grand Central Terminal is the **Campbell Apartment** (15 Vanderbilt Ave., at 43rd St., 212/953-0409), once the private office of railroad trustee John Campbell. Designed to resemble a 13th-century Florentine palazzo, the bar offers expensive drinks in an intimate setting.

P.J. Clarke's (915 Third Ave., at 55th St., 212/759-1616) is an out-of-time saloon sporting brass railings, worn wood, and sawdust on the floor. Featured in the 1945 movie *The Lost Weekend,* P.J.'s also serves pricey burgers and sandwiches.

In the post-modern Four Seasons Hotel is the **Fifty Seven Fifty Seven Bar** (57 E. 57th St., between Madison and Park Aves., 212/758-5700), serving 15 different kinds of oversized martinis. Drinks at the posh St. Regis Hotel's **King Cole Bar and Lounge** (2 E. 55th St., at Fifth Ave., 212/753-4500) don't come cheap, but the room's stunning historic mural makes it all worthwhile.

Upper East Side

The **Barking Dog Luncheonette** (1678 Third Ave., at 94th St., 212/831-1800) is a cheery place with good soups, sandwiches, and simple entrées. The **Lexington Candy Shop** (1226 Lexington Ave., at 83rd St., 212/288-0057) is an old-fashioned luncheonette founded in 1925. **Pig Heaven** (1540 Second Ave., between 80th and 81st Sts., 212/744-4333) specializes in all things porcine—including spicy pigs' ears; average entrée $15.

Good Persian food can be found at **Persepolis** (1423 Second Ave., between 74th and 75th Sts., 212/535-1100), offering succulent kabobs, unusual stews, and sour cherry rice; average entrée $14. **Baluchi's** (1565 Second Ave., at 81st St., 212/288-4810) is named after Baluchistan, the region that stretches from Iran to Pakistan. On the menu are lots of lamb, eggplant, and

spicy dishes; average entrée $13. A good, reliable Thai restaurant is the unpretentious **Sala Thai** (1718 Second Ave., between 89th and 90th Sts., 212/410-5557); average entrée $13.

◖ **Rosa Mexicano** (1063 First Ave., at 58th St., 212/753-7407) is a haute-Mexican restaurant serving fresh, flavorful food that draws large crowds; average entrée $20. At languorous, tropical **Le Colonial** (149 E. 57th St., between Lexington and Third Ave., 212/752-0808), it's easy to imagine yourself in pre-war Saigon. Downstairs is a main dining room serving French-Vietnamese fare, upstairs is a sexy lounge; average entrée $20.

Chic **Paper Moon Milano** (39 E. 58th St., between Madison and Park Aves., 212/758-8600) is a stylish bistro serving beautifully presented Northern Italian fare; average entrée $20. **Daniel** (60 E. 65th St., between Madison and Park Aves., 212/288-0033) wins kudos from food critics all over Manhattan for its superb French cuisine, discerning wine list, and impeccable decor; prix fixe dinner $85–150.

Watering Holes: An institution in this part of town is **J.G. Melon** (1291 Third Ave., at 74th St., 212/744-0585), a friendly saloon that also serves great burgers. The famed **Elaine's** (1703 Second Ave., between 88th and 89th Sts., 212/534-8103), celebrity hangout and Italian restaurant, sports a crowded bar that's especially worth a visit if you've just got to spot *someone.* For class, stop into the dark and gracious **Bemelmans Bar** in the posh Hotel Carlyle (35 E. 76th St., at Madison Ave., 212/744-1600).

The Upper East Side is also home to many singles bars that come and go with the seasons. One that's been around for a while is **Merchants NY** (1125 First Ave., at 62nd St., 212/832-1551), complete with a polished semicircular bar, small tables with flickering candles, and a good bar menu.

Upper West Side

For good people-watching during the summer, stake out an outdoor table in one of the many eateries located directly across from Lincoln Center.

Funky **Gray's Papaya** (2090 Broadway, at 72nd St., 212/799-0243) sells some of the city's best cheap hot dogs—to be eaten standing up. The hole-in-the-wall **La Caridad** (199 Broadway, at 78th St., 212/874-2780) is the best of the Cuban-Chinese restaurants in this part of town—just look at the long line of cab drivers out front; average main dish $8. The no-frills **Cafe con Leche** (24 Amsterdam Ave., at 80th St., 212/595-7000) is a modern Latin diner with first-rate beans and rice; average main dish $9.

Housed in the turn-of-the-19th-century Hotel des Artistes is **Cafe des Artistes** (1 W. 67th St., at CPW, 212/877-3500), a plush and romantic belle époque spot known for its superb French food and naked nymphs cavorting on the walls; average entrée $32. The art deco **Cafe Luxembourg** (200 W. 70th St., near Amsterdam Ave., 212/873-7411) is sister restaurant to the Odeon downtown. Still a hot spot after all these years, it offers an excellent menu, zinc bar, rattan chairs, and a lively late-night scene; average entrée $22.

In Central Park, the sleek, upscale **Boat House** (on East Dr., near 72nd St., 212/517-2233) serves grilled meats and fish, salads, and sandwiches on a patio overlooking the lake; average dinner entrée $20. A traditional New York favorite for celebrating graduations and the like is the festive **Tavern-on-the-Green** (CPW and 67th St., 212/873-3200), ablaze with mirrors, chandeliers, and 350,000 lightbulbs. The menu features imaginative American and continental cuisine; average entrée $29.

Farther north, tasty homemade soups and breads are the specialties at **Popover Cafe** (551 Amsterdam Ave., between 86th and 87th Sts., 212/595-8550); average main dish $10. **Good Enough to Eat** (483 Amsterdam Ave., near 80th St., 212/496-0163) serves hearty brunches; average main dish $12. The longtime, no-frills, neighborhood institution **Barney Greengrass** (541 Amsterdam Ave., between 86th and 87th Sts., 212/724-4707) is best-known for its traditional bagels and lox; average main dish $9.

Elegant yet laid-back **Calle Ocho** (446 Columbus Ave., between 81st and 82nd Sts., 212/873-5025) offers Nuevo Latino cuisine to an enthusiastic following; average entrée $20. The streamlined **Isola** (485 Columbus Ave., between 83rd and 84th Sts., 212/362-7400) serves tasty Northern Italian fare cooked in a wood-burning oven; average entrée $17. **Gabriela's** (685 Amsterdam Ave., at 93rd St., 212/961-0574) offers authentic Mexican cooking in an inviting spot accented with desert murals. The cheese- and spinach-stuffed eggplant and *posole* (traditional Mexican stew) are especially good; average entrée $12.

For Middle Eastern fare, along with live jazz and a circular bar, try **Cleopatra's Needle** (2485 Broadway, between 92nd and 93rd Sts., 212/769-6969); average entrée $12. The popular **Empire Szechuan Gourmet** (2574 Broadway, at 97th St., 212/663-6004), is one of a reliable chain; average entrée $11. Tiny **Awash** (947 Amsterdam Ave., between 106th and 107th Sts., 212/961-1416) is one of the best of the Ethiopian restaurants that dot the Upper West Side; average entrée $10.

Cafés: During warm weather, an outdoor café operates near Lincoln Center's fountain. **Cafe Mozart** (154 W. 70th St., near Broadway, 212/595-9797) serves especially good desserts and other light bites.

Watering Holes: Time Out (349 Amsterdam Ave., between 76th and 77th Sts., 212/362-5400) is a popular sports bar. The friendly **Dive Bar** (732 Amsterdam Ave., at 96th St., 212/749-4358) and **Dive 75** (101 W. 75th St., at Columbus, 212/362-7518) are all decked out in aquatic themes. Two popular Irish pubs are the rowdy **Dublin House** (225 W. 79th St., between Broadway and Amsterdam Ave., 212/874-9528) which boasts a good jukebox, and the more low-key **Emerald Inn** (205 Columbus Ave., near 70th St., 212/874-8840).

Harlem

M&G Soul Food Diner (383 W. 125th St., between St. Nicholas and Morningside Aves., 212/864-7326) is an excellent spot for fried chicken; average main dish, $9. **Miss Maude's Spoonbread Too** (547 Lenox Ave., between 137th and 138th Sts., 212/690-3100) serves up heaping portions of tasty Southern dishes, as does its sister restaurant, **Miss Mamie's Spoonbread Too** (366 W. 110th St., between Manhattan and Columbus Aves., 212/865-6744); average main dish at both, $12.

The legendary **Sylvia's** (328 Lenox Ave., between 126th and 127th Sts., 212/996-0660) has been expanding over the years, and attracting tourists by the busload. The food's still fine but the atmosphere is not what it once was; average entrée $13. **Copeland's** (549 W. 145th St., between Broadway and Amsterdam, 212/234-2357) is the soul food restaurant of choice among politicians and businesspeople, and a popular gospel brunch is offered on Sundays; average entrée $13.

Some of the best fried chicken and grits to be found anywhere in the city are on the menu at **Charles' Southern Style Kitchen** (2837 Eighth Ave., near 152nd St., 212/926-4313); average entrée $10. The **Jamaican Hot Pot** (2260 Seventh Ave., at 133rd St., 212/491-5270) offers mouthwatering curried goat stews, oxtail soups, and the like; average main dish $9.

On Harlem's east side, **Patsy's Pizzeria** (2287 First Ave., between 117th and 118th Sts., 212/534-9783) was the country's first coal-stoked brick-oven pizzeria. A Frank Sinatra favorite, it was established in 1932, and now has branches elsewhere in the city; average small pizza $12. To get into tiny **Rao's** (455 E. 114th St., near Pleasant, 212/722-6709), you have to book about three months in advance. The Rao family has been serving fine home cooking in this former Dutch saloon since 1896; average entrée $27.

Pastries: The traditional **Hungarian Pastry Shop** (1030 Amsterdam Ave., near 111th St., 212/866-4230), sells mouthwatering strudel and other sweet treats. **Wimp's Bakery** (29 W. 125th, between Fifth and Lenox Aves., 212/410-2296) is a modern spot also serving excellent sweet-potato pies, banana puddings, and the like.

Watering Holes: Near Columbia University, the sprawling **West End** (2911 Broadway, between 113th and 114th Sts., 212/662-8830) was once a favorite haunt of Jack Kerouac and Allen Ginsberg. It still offers cheap pitchers of beer and a standard bar menu.

© SEAN WATTERS
Sylvia's

Brooklyn

The largest borough in population (2.5 million) and the second largest in area (78.5 square miles), Brooklyn was a city in its own right, separate from New York, up until 1898. It had its own city hall, central park, downtown shops, museums, theaters, beaches, botanical garden, and zoo—all of which helps account for its fierce sense of identity and pride. Of all the boroughs, Brooklyn is the most individualistic, the most mythic, and the most complex.

Brooklyn is: Walt Whitman, Coney Island, the Brooklyn Dodgers, the Brooklyn Bridge, Mae West, Nathan's Famous, Bazooka bubble gum, Lena Horne, John Travolta, Jackie Gleason, the Brooklyn Navy Yards, Mickey Rooney, Topps baseball cards, Pete Hamill, Barbra Streisand, Prospect Park, Chock Full o' Nuts, Junior's cheesecake, Spike Lee. Brooklyn is also "the borough of churches" and the borough of ethnic neighborhoods. In total, more than 90 ethnic groups call Brooklyn home, among them Hasidic Jews, West Indians, Latin Americans, Russians, Poles, Scandinavians, Asians, Italians, Middle Easterners, and Irish.

For information on special events, or to obtain a visitors guide, contact **Brooklyn Information & Culture Inc.** (718/855-7882, www.brooklynx.org).

BROOKLYN HEIGHTS AND VICINITY

Quiet, tree-lined streets; dignified, perfectly preserved brownstones; well-dressed parents out playing with their apple-cheeked kids—such is the refined atmosphere of Brooklyn Heights, one of New York City's prettiest neighborhoods. Manhattanites even deign to visit, largely because of the **Promenade** that runs along the district's western edge, offering magnificent, bluff-high views of the skyline, the harbor, and the Brooklyn Bridge.

Used as a refuge by Gen. Washington and his troops after an early defeat in the Revolutionary War, Brooklyn Heights became the country's first suburb when Robert Fulton started up his ferry service in the early 1800s. Soon thereafter, wealthy Brooklyn Heights landowners—many of them bankers commuting to Wall Street—divided their property into standard building lots, and the neighborhood filled up with brownstones and churches.

Much of the pleasure of visiting Brooklyn Heights lies in simply wandering its idyllic streets. Orange, Pineapple, Clark, Pierrepont, and Montague Street will all take you down to the Promenade, which blooms profusely with flowers during warm weather. Montague Street is Brooklyn Heights' main commercial thoroughfare, where you'll find most of the neighborhood's restaurants, bars, and shops. During warm weather, many of these establishments set up tables on the street, giving it a vaguely European air.

From Manhattan, the best way to get to Brooklyn is to walk over the Brooklyn Bridge, then cross through Cadman Plaza Park to the Heights. By subway, take the A train to High Street, or the No. 2 or 3 to Clark Street. You can also take the No. 4 to Borough Hall and walk west.

Brooklyn Historical Society

The pretty, terra cotta building at Pierrepont and Clinton Streets is home to the **Brooklyn Historical Society** (128 Pierrepont St., 718/222-4111, www.brooklynhistory.org, noon–5 P.M. Fri.–Sun.), which recently completed a four-year, $23 million renovation. Both library and museum, the museum (adults $6, seniors and students $4) showcases exhibits on such Brooklyn subjects as the Brooklyn Navy Yard, the Dodgers, Coney Island, and the borough's many ethnic communities. The society also sponsors occasional walking tours.

D.U.M.B.O.

Short for "Down Under the Manhattan Bridge Overpass," DUMBO is a former warehouse district now becoming rapidly gentrified by artists, galleries, boutiques, and restaurants. Located along the water beneath the Brooklyn Bridge, happening DUMBO also offers a riverside park with great views of Manhattan. The **d.u.m.b.o arts center** (30 Washington St., between Plymouth and Water Sts. 718/694-0831) sponsors a neighborhood-wide arts festival every October.

Along Old Fulton Street leading down to the water stand a clutch of historic buildings. Among them is the medieval-looking **Eagle Warehouse** (28 Old Fulton St.), now a residential co-op. Near the entrance, a plaque honors Walt Whitman and the *Brooklyn Eagle,* which was published on this site from 1841 to 1892. Whitman served as the newspaper's editor until he was fired for his stand against slavery.

Atlantic Avenue

Brooklyn Heights ends at Atlantic Avenue, a wide, gray boulevard known for its Arab restaurants and shops. The Middle Eastern community began settling here back in the days when Brooklyn was a bustling seaport. While the thoroughfare is not as lively as it once was, the block between Court and Clinton Street still has a number of Arab-run businesses, including the well-stocked **Sahadi Importing Company** (187–189 Atlantic Ave., 718/624-4550), selling dried fruits and grains, olives, feta cheese, stuffed grape leaves, and the like.

Food

For tasty blintzes, pierogi, and thick French toast, head to **Teresa's** (80 Montague St., 718/797-3996), a neighborhood institution for over a decade. Also still going strong for many years is cozy **Henry's End** (44 Henry St., 718/834-1776); on the menu are such exotic dishes as antelope and elk. Average entrée $20.

Down at the waterfront is the famed **River Cafe** (1 Water St., 718/522-5200), offering creative American cuisine and marvelous views of Manhattan; prix fixe dinner, $78. It's also possible to come just for a drink.

For Middle Eastern fare, try **Tripoli** (154 Atlantic Ave., 718/596-5800); average entrée $15. The **Waterfront Ale House** (136 Atlantic Ave., 718/522-3794) is a favorite local watering hole known for its happy hours and burgers.

DOWNTOWN BROOKLYN

Adjacent to genteel Brooklyn Heights is scrappy downtown Brooklyn, home to a number of imposing government buildings that hark back to the days when Brooklyn was a city in its own right. The Greek Revival **Borough Hall,** at the intersection of Joralemon, Fulton, and Court Streets, was once Brooklyn's City Hall and still houses government offices. The Romanesque Revival **Brooklyn General Post Office** (271 Cadman Pl. E.) once handled all of the city's mail. To reach downtown Brooklyn from Manhattan, take the No. 2, 3, or 4 train to Borough Hall.

New York Transit Museum

Two blocks southwest of Borough Hall is the New York Transit Museum (northwest corner of Schermerhorn St. and Boerum Pl., 718/243-3060, www.mta.info, 10 A.M.–4 P.M. Tues.–Fri., noon–5 P.M. Sat.–Sun., adults $5, seniors and children 3–17 $3), run by the Metropolitan Transit Authority (MTA). Appropriately housed in a former subway station, the museum sports well-lit tiled walls that seem to stretch out forever into the darkness. Some wonderful old restored subway cars are housed here, along with fascinating exhibits on such subjects as the building of the subway, the history of the "Els" ("elevated" subways lines), trolleys, and buses.

Junior's Cheesecake

Just east of Borough Hall along Fulton Street is the pedestrians-only **Fulton Mall,** a lively place crowded with discount stores and multiethnic crowds. For visitors, the main reason to come here is to make a stop at Junior's (386 Flatbush Ave., at DeKalb, 718/852-5257), a

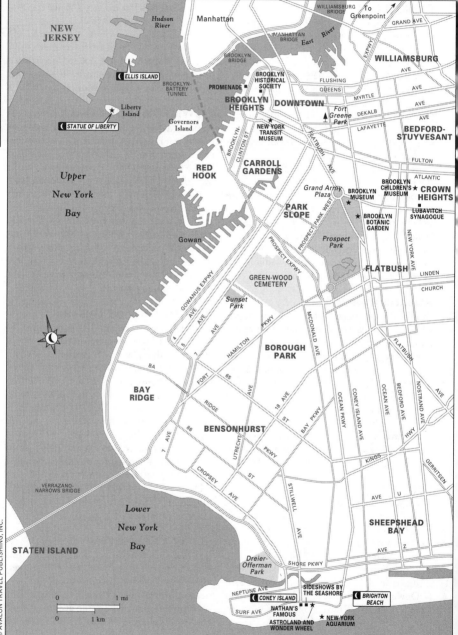

NEW JERSEY

Hudson River

Manhattan

WILLIAMSBURG BRIDGE

To Greenpoint

GRAND AVE

EXPWY

MANHATTAN BRIDGE

East River

WILLIAMSBURG

BROOKLYN BRIDGE

AVE

ELLIS ISLAND

BROOKLYN-BATTERY TUNNEL

FLUSHING

AVE

PROMENADE

BROOKLYN HISTORICAL SOCIETY

QUEENS

MYRTLE

AVE

Liberty Island

BROOKLYN HEIGHTS

DOWNTOWN

Fort Greene Park

DEKALB

AVE

STATUE OF LIBERTY

Governors Island

CLINTON ST

NEW YORK TRANSIT MUSEUM

LAFAYETTE

BEDFORD-STUYVESANT

FULTON

Upper New York Bay

RED HOOK

CARROLL GARDENS

BROOKLYN

Grand Army Plaza

BROOKLYN MUSEUM

BROOKLYN CHILDREN'S MUSEUM

ATLANTIC

CROWN HEIGHTS

PARK SLOPE

PROSPECT PARK WEST

BROOKLYN BOTANIC GARDEN

LUBAVITCH SYNAGOGUE

Gowan

Prospect Park

NEW YORK AVE

FLATBUSH

PROSPECT EXPWY

LINDEN

CHURCH

GREEN-WOOD CEMETERY

GOWANUS EXPWY

Sunset Park

PKWY

McDONALD AVE

FLATBUSH

AVE

AVE

HAMILTON

BOROUGH PARK

CONEY ISLAND AVE

OCEAN AVE

BEDFORD AVE

NOSTRAND AVE

BAY RIDGE

BA

FORT

65

RIDGE

86

18 AVE

ST

BAY PKWY

OCEAN PKWY

AVE

HWY

BENSONHURST

UTRECHT

PKWY

KINGS

7 AVE

ST

CROPSEY

AVE

STILLWELL

AVE

GERRITSEN

VERRAZANO-NARROWS BRIDGE

Lower New York Bay

AVE U

SHEEPSHEAD BAY

STATEN ISLAND

AVE

AVE Z

Dreier-Offerman Park

SHORE PKWY

NEPTUNE AVE

CONEY ISLAND

SIDESHOWS BY THE SEASHORE

BRIGHTON BEACH

SURF AVE

NATHAN'S FAMOUS

ASTROLAND AND WONDER WHEEL

NEW YORK AQUARIUM

0   1 mi

0   1 km

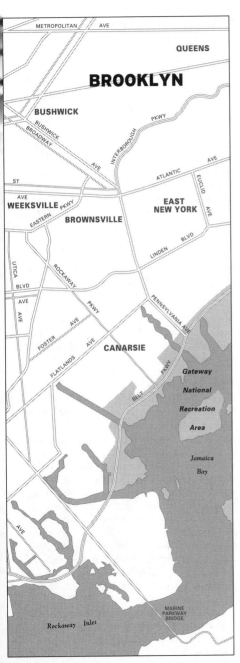

sprawling mega-diner famed for its smooth, rich cheesecake.

Brooklyn Academy of Music (BAM)

In nearby Fort Greene reigns BAM (30 Lafayette Ave., at Atlantic and Flatbush, 718/636-4100, www.bam.org), a world-famous institution that's especially known for its avant-garde productions. BAM also holds several small movie theaters presenting mostly foreign and art films, and the inviting BAM-café, serving everything from gourmet sandwiches to simple entrées.

WILLIAMSBURG

For decades, Williamsburg was best known for its community of Satmarer Hasidim, a strict orthodox Jewish sect originally from Hungary. Since the mid-1990s, however, the area has been home to a steadily growing enclave of young artists and professionals, attracted to the area by its low (but rapidly rising) rents and abandoned industrial spaces. Most of the newcomers live near **Bedford Avenue,** lined with a clutch of moderately priced restaurants, shops, bars, and clubs.

Neighborhood galleries include **Momenta Art** (72 Berry St., at N. 10th St., 718/218-8058) and **Pierogi** (167 N. 9th St., near Bedford, 718/599-2144). Tiny **Pete's Candy Store** (709 Lorimer St., between Frost and Richardson Sts., 718/302-3770) presents lots of local singer-songwriters and the occasional jazz band. **Galapagos Art Space** (70 N. 6th St., between Kent and Wythe Ave., 718/782-5188) is two clubs in one. The back room presents live music ranging from hip-hop to a "house string quartet," while the front room is a popular hangout filled with tall tables and stools.

To reach the area from Manhattan, take the L train to Bedford Avenue.

Food

Try **Vera Cruz** (195 Bedford Ave., near N. 6th St., 718/599-7914) for cheap and tasty Mexican food, a lively bar scene, Latin music, and an outdoor garden in summer; average entrée $11. Across the street is popular **Planet Thailand** (133 N. Bedford Ave., near Berry St., 718/599-5758), serving cheap and tasty Thai; average entrée $11.

PROSPECT PARK AND VICINITY

Three of Brooklyn's finest attractions—the Brooklyn Museum of Art, the Brooklyn Botanic Garden, and Prospect Park—are all within a few minutes' walk of each other, while next door is one of the borough's most historic residential districts, Park Slope. Here you'll find many young professionals strolling about with dogs and kids, along with a decreasing number of older families who've lived in the area for generations. From Manhattan, take the No. 2 or 3 train to Eastern Parkway.

Brooklyn Museum of Art

The lovely beaux arts Brooklyn Museum (200 Eastern Pkwy., at Washington, 718/638-5000, www.brooklynart.org, 10 A.M.–5 P.M. Wed.–Fri., 11 A.M.–6 P.M. Sat.–Sun., suggested admission adults $8, students and seniors $4, children under 12 free) was designed by McKim, Mead & White in 1897. Though one of the world's largest museums, it's always lived in the shadow of its mighty cousin across the river, the Metropolitan Museum of Art. But the Brooklyn Museum is very different from the Met or any other Manhattan art museum. It's usually quieter and less crowded. And more importantly, it stages some of the more unusual shows in town, among them major retrospectives by African American artists such as Romare Bearden and Jacob Lawrence, and women artists such as Elizabeth Murray and Louise Bourgeois.

Like the Metropolitan, the Brooklyn Museum's collections span virtually the entire history of art. Highlights include extensive Egyptian holdings, an excellent Native American collection, and a permanent collection of contemporary art. The museum also has one of the city's most eclectic gift shops, filled with handicrafts from around the world. On the first Saturday of every month, the museum is open until 11 P.M. for an evening of special events.

Brooklyn Botanic Garden

Next door to the Brooklyn Museum is the Brooklyn Botanic Garden (1000 Washington Ave., 718/623-7200, www.bbg.org, 8 A.M.–6 P.M. Tues.–Fri. and 10 A.M.–6 P.M. Sat.–Sun. Apr.–Sept., 8 A.M.–4:30 P.M. Tues.–Fri. and 10 A.M.–4:30 P.M. Sat.–Sun. Oct.–Mar., adults $5, students and seniors $3, children under 16 free), another unusual and much beloved Brooklyn institution. Though considerably smaller than the world-famous botanical gardens in the Bronx, the Brooklyn gardens are in many ways more conducive to a visit, as they're more manageable in size. Spread out over 50 carefully designed acres are a rose garden, a children's garden, a Japanese scholar's garden, and a garden for the blind, complete with Braille signs. The Steinhardt Conservatory houses tropical and desert plants, along with the country's largest collection of bonsai. The best time to visit is May, when the cherry blossoms burst forth, all pink and white froth.

Prospect Park

Behind the Brooklyn Museum and the Brooklyn Botanic Garden is enormous Prospect Park (718/965-8999, www.prospectpark.org)—525 acres of forests and meadows, lakes and streams. Prospect Park was designed by Frederick Law Olmsted and Calvert Vaux, who also designed Central Park. The two men considered this park, which is considerably wilder than Central Park, to be their masterpiece.

The main entrance is at **Grand Army Plaza,** just up from the Brooklyn Museum at the intersection of Eastern Parkway, Flatbush Avenue, and Prospect Park West. In the center of the plaza, surrounded by an ever-present rush of traffic, is a towering triumphal arch honoring the Union soldiers of the Civil War.

Immediately inside the main entrance is the park's most glorious sight—Long Meadow. Stretching over a mile, this gently rolling lawn is lined with lush trees that completely hide the cityscape. During warm weather, the meadow attracts West Indian cricket players; in winter, cross-country skiers come out.

East of Long Meadow are an 18th-century **carousel;** the wooden Dutch farmhouse **Lefferts Homestead;** and the **Prospect Park Wildlife Center** (450 Flatbush Ave., 718/399-7339, 10 A.M.–4:30 P.M. daily, adults $5, seniors $1.25, children 3–12 $1). At the park's south end shimmers **Prospect Lake.**

Like Central Park, Prospect Park is generally safe, but it's not advisable to explore isolated areas alone or to enter the park after dark.

Park Slope

West of Prospect Park and south of Grand Army Plaza is Park Slope. Once known as the "Gold Coast," the area is home to one of the country's largest concentrations of Victorian brownstones. Park Slope fell on hard times after World War II, but has been on the upswing since the 1970s.

The main commercial thoroughfares are **Seventh and Fifth Avenues,** while most of the neighborhood's prettiest brownstones are on the side streets between Prospect Park and Sixth Avenue. **Carroll Street** and **Montgomery Place** are especially worth a gander. The **Montauk Club** (25 Eighth Ave., at Lincoln), is one of Park Slope's finest buildings. It's an eclectic Venetian palace with a frieze depicting the history of Long Island's Montauk Indians.

Food

Cousin John's (70 Seventh Ave., between Berkeley and Lincoln, 718/622-7333) offers light fare and tasty baked goods. **Red Hot Szechuan** (347 Seventh Ave., at 10th St., 718/369-0700) is a neighborhood favorite, serving especially good vegetarian dishes; average entrée $9.

On Fifth Avenue, you'll find some of the neighborhood's best restaurants, including **Al Di Lá** (248 Fifth Ave., at Carroll St., 718/783-4565), which specializes in Northern Italian fare; average entrée $17. **◖ Long Tan** (196 Fifth Ave., 718/622-8444) is a convivial Thai restaurant, with a long bar to one side, red banquettes to another, and a patio out back. On the menu are such creative dishes as mango and shrimp rolls; average main dish $14.

◖ CONEY ISLAND AND BRIGHTON BEACH

If you've only got time to make one stop in Brooklyn, Coney Island/Brighton Beach should probably be it. Though no longer the amusement center it once was, there's something about this windy, run-down place—with its magnificent boardwalk, rusting rides, tawdry snack stands, buoyant Russian community, and hordes of summertime sunbathers—that's quintessential New York.

From Manhattan, take the D, F, or Q train to Coney Island/Stillwell Avenue. It's a long subway ride out, and you'll wind up on the elevated tracks above scrappy Surf Avenue. One block west are the beach and boardwalk—crowded to the bursting point on hot summer days, pleasantly empty the rest of the year. Old Russian women sit gossiping beneath big black umbrellas, young boys run fishing lines off the piers, joggers kick up sand on the wide expanse of beach.

History

Coney Island was uninhabited until the early 1800s, when several genteel resorts for the rich were built. After the Civil War, the railroad opened the area up to the masses, and the island's honky-tonk days and nights began. Saloons, gambling dens, boxing rings, and racetracks soon packed the place, to be followed by three enclosed parks, or "small cities of pleasure," called Steeplechase, Luna Park, and Dreamland.

But it was the building of the subway in 1920 that really transformed Coney Island; for just a five-cent fare, almost everyone could escape the oppression of the city for a day, and Coney Island grew and grew. New technologies led to the invention of the Ferris wheel and the roller coaster, and in 1923, the 80-foot-wide boardwalk was built.

Coney Island was magical. It seemed nothing could dull its shine. But Dreamland

© BARBARA GRIFFITH

the famous Cyclone roller coaster on Coney Island

burned down in 1911, and Luna Park went up in flames in the 1940s. Next came the rise of the automobile, the flight to the suburbs, and the invention of a new kind of midway—a tamed, sanitized place known as Disneyland. Steeplechase Park closed in 1966, leaving only a remnant of itself behind.

Astroland and Wonder Wheel

That remnant is today called the Astroland Amusement Park (on the boardwalk at 1000 Surf Ave., around W. 10th St., 718/372-0275, www.astroland.com, weekends in spring, noon–midnight daily in summer). Inside find the **Cyclone,** a classic 1920s roller coaster built on an old wooden frame that shakes and clatters as the cars shoot by. Enthusiasts consider the 60-mile-an-hour Cyclone—declared a city landmark in 1988—to be one of the country's best roller coasters. Also in the park are about 20 modern rides and plenty of honky-tonk video arcades and game booths.

Adjoining Astroland is the **Wonder Wheel,** a regal 1920s Ferris wheel offering fairy-tale views of Manhattan, especially at night (weekends in spring, noon–midnight daily in summer).

Nathan's Famous

On the island side of the amusement park, find Nathan's Famous (Surf and Stillwell Aves., 718/946-2202). Nathan's was started in 1916 by Nathan Handwerker, a sometime employee of Charles Feltman. Feltman is said to have "invented" the hot dog by his simple act of putting a wiener inside a bun. Handwerker undersold his boss's fare by a nickel, and so secured his place in entrepreneurial history. Nowadays, on a busy summer weekend, the stand-up eatery sells as many as 50,000 hot dogs, 20,000 orders of French fries, and 500 gallons of lemonade.

Sideshows by the Seashore

Heading east on the boardwalk from the amusement park, you'll soon come to the brightly painted storefront (1208 Surf Ave., at W. 12th St., 718/372-5159, www.coneyisland.com, noon–5 P.M. Fri.–Sun. in summer, call for off-season hours, admission 99 cents). A fierce-looking tattooed man lounges by the door, while inside is a madcap scene crowded with Snake Ladies, the Fire Eater, Human Blockheads, the Elastic Lady, Escape Artists, and the Torture King. It's all a sort of shrine to the way Coney Island used to be, run by a group of actors and performance artists, many from the East Village.

Started in 1985 by a Yale Drama School graduate Dick Zigun, the nonprofit Sideshows also presents a whimsical, not-to-be-missed Mermaid Parade every June, a Tattoo Festival in late summer, and alternative rock-and-roll bands on summer nights. Next door to the theater you'll find a small museum of Coney Island memorabilia and a souvenir shop.

New York Aquarium for Wildlife Conservation

Between the boardwalk and Surf Avenue at West 8th Street is the delightful New York Aquarium (718/265-FISH, www.nyaquarium.com, 10 A.M.–4:30 P.M. daily, with extended hours in summer, adults $11, seniors and children 2–12 $7). The thoroughly up-to-date place contains close to 4,000 residents, including walruses, beluga whales, sharks, stingrays, sea otters, and electric eels. In summer, dolphin and sea lion shows are featured daily.

Brighton Beach

Next door to Coney Island, and spilling over into it, is Brighton Beach. For many years home to a small and aging Russian Jewish community, Brighton Beach has been exploding with new life ever since the end of the Cold War. More than 100,000 Russians have settled in New York since 1989—some with green cards, others without—and about 75 percent of them have moved to Brooklyn. Stroll the streets and boardwalk here and you'll see old women in babushkas, middle-aged men and women in drab socialist dress, and teenagers courting a hipness that is half East, half West. Many of the store signs speak of Russia—Vladimir's Unisex, Rasputin, the Stolichny Deli—as do the smells and the music.

Brighton Beach Avenue is lined with

Nathan's Famous

© BARBARA GRIFFITH

dozens of Russian shops, restaurants, and nightclubs (see below). Of the many food shops, bright and modern **M&I International** (249 Brighton Beach Ave., 718/615-1011) is the best. It's stocked with an enormous array of cheeses, sausages, smoked fish, and—of course—caviar and borscht.

Entertainment

Brighton Beach is famous for its over-the-top, Las Vegas–style Russian nightclubs where the music is fast and loud and the vodka flows nonstop. The oldest and best-known of these spots is **The National** (273 Brighton Beach Ave., at 2nd St., 718/646-1225, www.come-2national.com), immortalized in the 1984 film *Moscow on the Hudson,* starring Robin Williams. Also popular is the glamorous **Rasputin** (2670 Coney Island Ave., at Ave. X, 718/332-8333), complete with a balcony and oft-packed dance floor, and the more intimate **Primorski** (282-B Brighton Beach Ave., 718/891-3111). Plan on spending about $50 per person for dinner and a show; reservations are a must.

Accommodations

In downtown Brooklyn is the **Awesome Bed & Breakfast** (136 Lawrence St., between Fulton and Willougby Sts., 718/858-4859, www.awesome-bed-and-breakfast.com, $75–150 s or d), where you'll find cheery theme rooms with names such as Ancient Madagascar. All share baths. The B&B is one stop from Manhattan on the No. 4 or 5 train.

Also in downtown Brooklyn is the **New York Marriot at the Brooklyn Bridge** (333 Adams St., 718/246-7000, www.marriott.com, $175–240 s or d). With 360 rooms, all priced about 20 percent less than they would be in Manhattan, the hostelry is a good value.

In Park Slope, find **Bed & Breakfast on the Park** (113 Prospect Park West, between Sixth and Seventh Sts., 718/499-6115, www.bbnyc.com, $150–225 s or d), a spacious 1895 brownstone overlooking Prospect Park. All seven guestrooms are furnished with oriental rugs and comfortable canopied beds.

In Bedford-Stuyvesant, not far from Park Slope, is the **Akwaaba Mansion** (347 MacDonough St., between Stuyvesant and Lewis Aves., 718/455-5968, www.akwaaba.com, $120–150 s or d). This grand stone edifice, sitting on a peaceful tree-lined street, offers four luxurious guestrooms, each with a different theme. African artifacts decorate the home.

Queens

Until recently, Queens was widely regarded as a snore. This was where the complacent everyman lived, in a row house exactly like his neighbor's. Queens was home to Archie Bunker and hundreds of thousands of others like him. Queens was mediocrity. Queens was suburbia. Queens was boring, boring, boring.

Whether or not this was ever really true, it certainly isn't so today. New York's largest borough now boasts some of the city's biggest and most vibrant ethnic neighborhoods, as well as some architectural and cultural gems that are just beginning to be appreciated. Queens is also where Louis Armstrong, Will Rogers, Jackie Robinson, and Jack Kerouac all once lived; where the early movie industry was headquartered; and where the wealthy once summered, on grand estates in Bayside or on the then-pristine beaches of the Rockaways.

Named for Queen Catherine of Braganza, the wife of England's Charles II, Queens was annexed to New York City in 1898. Western Queens began developing in the mid-1800s, but it wasn't until the building of the Long Island Rail Road in 1910 that the borough really boomed. Then, apartment houses and private homes sprang up all over, and thousands of New Yorkers moved out into the "country."

A Note on Addresses and Events

Theoretically, Queens is laid out according to a grid system. The streets run north-south, from 1st Street, paralleling the East River, to 250th Street, at the borough's eastern end. Similarly, the avenues run east-west, with the lowest numbered addresses to the north and the highest numbered addresses to the south. Addresses are supposedly coded with their nearest cross-street or avenue: 28-13 23rd Ave., for example, should mean that the building is at No. 13 23rd Avenue near 28th Street. But things don't always work out that neatly. When in doubt, it's best to call ahead.

The **Queens Council on the Arts** operates a hotline (718/647-3377) that lists community cultural events.

LONG ISLAND CITY

Directly east of the Queensboro Bridge lies Long Island City. Though largely a dreary industrial area filled with windowless factory buildings, Long Island City has in the last decade or so become home to a growing artistic community. That fact went largely unnoticed by the general public until June 2002, when the Museum of Modern Art, undergoing extensive renovation, was temporarily located here. MoMA has since

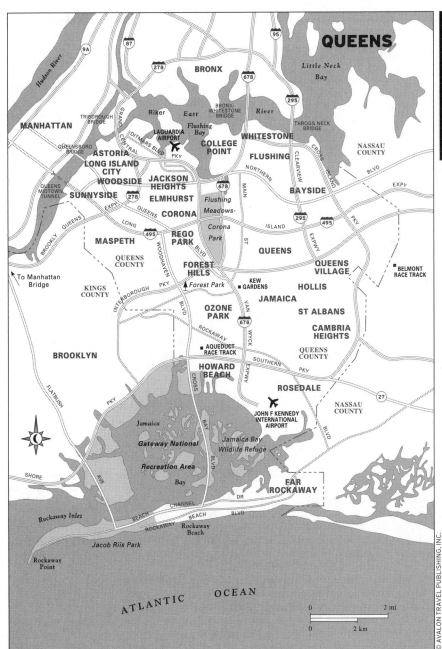

QUEENS

Little Neck Bay

BRONX

Hudson River

MANHATTAN

Riker

East

River

Flushing Bay

WHITESTONE

NASSAU COUNTY

TRIBOROUGH BRIDGE

BRONX-WHITESTONE BRIDGE

THROGS NECK BRIDGE

QUEENSBORO BRIDGE

LAGUARDIA AIRPORT

COLLEGE POINT

FLUSHING

QUEENS MIDTOWN TUNNEL

ASTORIA

LONG ISLAND CITY

WOODSIDE

JACKSON HEIGHTS

BAYSIDE

SUNNYSIDE

ELMHURST

CORONA

Flushing Meadows-Corona Park

To Manhattan Bridge

MASPETH

REGO PARK

QUEENS

QUEENS VILLAGE

BELMONT RACE TRACK

QUEENS COUNTY

FOREST HILLS

KINGS COUNTY

KEW GARDENS

Forest Park

HOLLIS

JAMAICA

ST ALBANS

OZONE PARK

CAMBRIA HEIGHTS

BROOKLYN

AQUEDUCT RACE TRACK

QUEENS COUNTY

HOWARD BEACH

ROSEDALE

NASSAU COUNTY

JOHN F KENNEDY INTERNATIONAL AIRPORT

Jamaica

Gateway National Recreation Area

Jamaica Bay Wildlife Refuge

Bay

SHORE AVE

FAR ROCKAWAY

Rockaway Inlet

Rockaway Beach

Jacob Riis Park

Rockaway Point

ATLANTIC OCEAN

0   2 mi

0   2 km

WHERE THE WILD THINGS ARE

At the far southern end of Queens is the Jamaica Bay Wildlife Refuge (718/318-4340, 8:30 A.M.-5 P.M. daily), where over 300 species of birds, 80 types of fish, and dozens of kinds of reptiles and amphibians live. It seems amazing that wildlife can flourish here. JFK Airport is directly across the bay, and all around the refuge, traffic – both ground and air – drones on incessantly. Still, the refuge is on the Atlantic flyway, and well worth a visit during the autumn and spring. Call for directions by public transportation or car.

moved back to Manhattan, but Long Island City's other museums and galleries flourish.

Noguchi Museum and Socrates Sculpture Park

The austere Isamu Noguchi Garden Museum (32-37 Vernon Blvd., at 33rd Rd., 718/204-7088, www.noguchi.org, 10 A.M.–5 P.M. Wed.–Fri., 11 A.M.–6 P.M. Sat.–Sun., adults $5, seniors and students $2.50) is housed in the late sculptor's former studio. Its many rooms are filled with stone, metal, and wood sculptures, along with models of many large-scale environments designed by Noguchi. A side yard holds a peaceful sculpture garden.

A few blocks north of the Noguchi Museum is the delightful Socrates Sculpture Park (31-29 Vernon Blvd., at Broadway, 718/956-1819, 9 A.M.–sunset daily, free). Dotted with huge outdoor sculptures, the park is the brainchild of artist Mark di Suvero. For 10 years, di Suvero and other area artists worked to turn the once-garbage-strewn lot into a bona fide park. The city officially recognized their efforts in 1994, and the site is now part of New York's park system. The park offers great views of Manhattan.

To reach the museum and park from Manhattan, take the N train to the Broadway station in Queens. On weekends, a shuttle bus to the museum leaves from the Asia Society in Manhattan (70th St. and Park Ave., roundtrip $10).

P.S. 1 Contemporary Art Center

New York's premier center for art on the cutting edge, acquired by the Museum of Modern Art in 1999, P.S. 1 (22-25 Jackson Ave., at 46th St., 718/784-2084, www.ps1.org, noon–6 P.M. Thurs.–Mon., suggested admission adults $5, seniors and students $2.50) specializes in the avant-garde, conceptual, and experimental. Housed in a four-story building that was once a public school, it offers artwork in all sorts of nooks and crannies—stairwells, basements, holes in the floor—as well as in large galleries. Two or three shows are usually featured at once, and traveling international shows are showcased as well.

To reach P.S. 1 from Manhattan, take the No. 7 train to 45th Road/Court House Square, or the E or F train to 23rd Street.

ASTORIA

Not far from Long Island City is Astoria, one of the oldest settlements in Queens. It was developed in 1839 by John Jacob Astor, who built it up into a thriving shipping port. Later, in the 1920s and 1930s, the neighborhood was the center of the movie-making business on the East Coast; Astoria Movie Studios produced such legendary stars as Rudolf Valentino and Gloria Swanson.

Astoria today is a stable and well-kept working- and middle-class community with the largest concentration of Greeks outside of Greece. Greek shops can be found along 30th Avenue between 31st and Steinway Streets, while Broadway is home to numerous Greek bakeries and butcher shops, the latter advertising baby pigs, baby lambs, and baby goats for sale. **Titan Supermarket** (25-56 31st St., between 25th and 30th Aves., 718/626-7771) is an especially popular stop for Greek groceries. To reach the Greek community directly from Manhattan, take the N train to 30th Avenue.

American Museum of the Moving Image

This museum (36-01 35th Ave., 718/784-0077, www.ammi.org, 11 A.M.–5 P.M. Wed.–Fri., 11 A.M.–6:30 P.M. Sat.–Sun., adults $10, seniors $7.50, students and children 5–18 $5) houses over 70,000 artifacts covering all aspects of the film industry—from make-up to fan magazines. Featured are hands-on exhibits in which visitors can create their own animated films, design soundtracks, and the like. The museum also boasts an excellent screening program; call for schedule.

In the fall of 2005, the museum began a $25 million expansion that will double its exhibition space. Plans include a new outdoor theater and garden, more gallery space, and a new virtual space, the VR room, where computer programs will simulate three-dimensional alternative realities.

The museum is housed in a section of the old Astoria Movie Studios (34-12 36th St.), other parts of which were reopened as the **Kaufman-Astoria Studios** in the late 1970s. Among the many movies and television shows that have been completely or partially produced here are *The Wiz, The Verdict, The World According to Garp,* and *The Cosby Show.*

To reach the American Museum of the Moving Image directly from Manhattan, take the R or G train to Steinway Street and walk south to 35th Avenue.

Food
Among Astoria's many Greek restaurants, bright, 24-hour **Uncle George's** (33-19 Broadway, at 34th St., 718/626-0593) is an inexpensive neighborhood favorite; average entrée $9. Informal **Telly's Taverna** (28-13 23rd Ave., between 28th and 29th Sts., 718/728-9056) offers especially delicious grilled lamb dishes and an outdoor garden in summer; average entrée $16. Glitzy **Taverna Vraka** (23-15 31st St., between 23rd and 24th Aves., 718/721-3007) has been attracting Greek celebrities for over 20 years. Greek music and dancing are often featured on weekends; average entrée $17.

FLUSHING MEADOWS CORONA PARK
Today, Flushing Meadows Corona Park is a peaceful green oasis attracting families, couples, and kids. But back in the early 1900s, it was a towering, reeking garbage dump that smoldered by day and glowed at night. More than a hundred railroad carloads of Brooklyn's refuse were dumped here daily, providing succulent meals for hordes of rats "big enough to wear saddles," as one observer put it. F. Scott Fitzgerald, writing in *The Great Gatsby,* described the place as "a valley of ashes—a fantastic farm where ashes grow like wheat into ridges and hills and grotesque gardens. ..."

Enter Robert Moses, city parks commissioner. Looking at the noxious heap, Moses saw not an irredeemable wasteland but a potential park. In 1934, he directed the removal of some 50 million cubic tons of garbage. Thereafter began the construction of the 1939 World's Fair, followed 25 years later by the construction of the 1964 World's Fair. Both extravaganzas were largely created through Moses' sheer force of will, and both ended up costing the city and its backers millions of dollars.

Remains of the fairs still dot the 1,225-acre park. Most conspicuous is the 1964 **Unisphere,** a shining 140-foot-high, 380-ton hollow globe sitting in the middle of a pretty fountain. Other park attractions include a miniature golf course, playgrounds, a botanical garden, zoo, two lakes, and an old-fashioned carousel. Across the street is the huge, 55,000-seat **Shea Stadium,** home to the New York Mets.

From Manhattan, take the No. 7 train to Willets Point/Shea Stadium and follow the signs.

Queens Museum of Art
Next to the Unisphere is the Queens Museum (718/592-9700, www.queens-museum.org, 10 A.M.–5 P.M. Wed.–Fri., noon–5 P.M. Sat.–Sun., with extended hours in summer, suggested admission adults $5, seniors and students $2.50, children under five free), housed in what was the New York City pavilion at both the 1939 and the 1964 World's Fairs. Renovated in the late 1990s to the tune of $15 million, the museum presents first-rate temporary exhibitions and houses an unusual permanent exhibit—the New York Panorama. First showcased at the 1964 fair, the panorama is a scale model of the city, showing every single building and

house in the five boroughs—some 895,000 of them, built of plastic and wood. One of Moses' pet projects, the panorama was originally intended to be a serious tool for urban planners but now feels more like a nostalgic work of art.

New York Hall of Science

Ranked as one of the country's top 10 science museums, the New York Hall of Science (47-01 111th St., 718/699-0005, www.ny-hallsci.org, 9:30 A.M.–2 P.M. Mon.–Thurs., 9:30 A.M.–5 P.M. Fri., 10:30 A.M.–6 P.M. Sat.–Sun., with extended hours July–Aug., adults $11, seniors and children 2–17 $8) is housed in a dramatic, undulating building—another leftover from the 1964 World's Fair. Inside, you'll find lots of hands-on exhibits, including a distorted room that makes people appear to shrink or grow and an enlarged drop of water showing microscopic organisms going about their daily lives. Out back is a large Science Playground, where kids can learn about the laws of physics.

Louis Armstrong Home

To the south of Flushing Meadows is Corona, a solid, middle-class black community that was home to many jazz musicians in the early-to-mid 20th century. Foremost among them was Louis Armstrong, who lived in a red-brick building here from the early 1940s until his death in 1971. Tales are often told of how the jazz giant used to sit on his front steps with his trumpet and entertain the neighborhood kids, some of whom came by with horns of their own.

Now owned by Queens College, the Louis Armstrong Home (34-56 107th St., 718/997-36780, www.satchmo.net, 10 A.M.–5 P.M. Tues.–Fri., noon–5 P.M. Sat–Sun., adults $8, seniors and children $6) can be viewed via 40-minute tours. To reach the home directly from Manhattan, take the No. 7 subway to 103rd Street-Corona Plaza.

The Bronx

The Bronx is New York City's second smallest borough both in size and population, and it's the only one attached to the mainland. Purchased from the Algonquins by the Dutch West India Company in 1639, it was first settled in 1644 by a Scandinavian named Jonas Bronck. The area soon became known as "The Broncks," and remained a peaceful rural community up until the late 1800s. Then the 3rd Avenue Elevated Railway arrived, bringing with it thousands of European immigrants. By 1900, the borough's population had soared to over 200,000.

Many consider the 1920s through the early 1950s to be the golden era of the Bronx. That's when the borough was filled with many tightly knit ethnic neighborhoods, each with its own vibrant community life. The arrival of the affordable automobile, however, soon allowed many of the Bronx's more affluent residents to move to Long Island or Westchester. And in 1950, Robert Moses' six-lane Cross-Bronx Expressway was constructed, destroying a number of the borough's most stable neighborhoods.

Today, the Bronx is best known as the home of such great New York institutions as the Bronx Zoo, the New York Botanical Garden, and Yankee Stadium. For more information on the borough, contact the **Bronx Tourism Council** (198 E. 161st St., 718/590-3518, www.ilovethebronx.com).

◖ THE BRONX ZOO AND BOTANICAL GARDEN

Though the zoo and botanical garden are next door to each other, to visit both in one day would require much fortitude, as both are very large. It's smarter to opt for one, and combine it with a meal or coffee and dessert on Arthur Avenue. The botanical garden is at its best in May and June.

One of the most beloved of New York

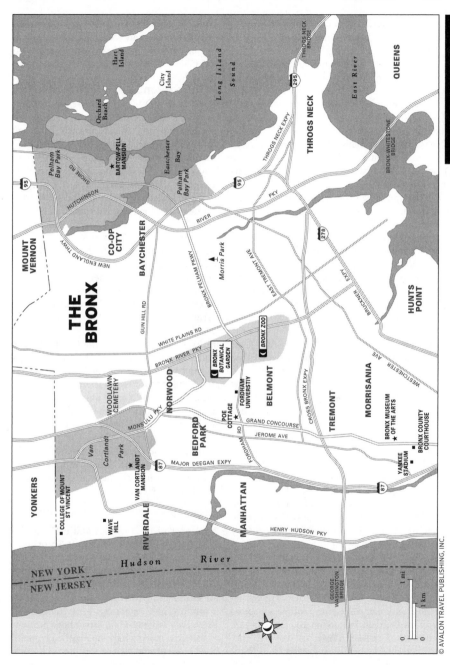

QUEENS

THROGS NECK BRIDGE

BRONX-WHITESTONE BRIDGE

East River

Long Island Sound

Hart Island

City Island

Orchard Beach

THROGS NECK

295

Eastchester Bay

Pelham Bay Park

BARTOW-PELL MANSION

SHORE RD

Pelham Bay Park

HUTCHINSON

95

HUNTS POINT

278

THROGS NECK EXPY

EAST TREMONT AVE

BRUCKNER EXPY

PKY

RIVER

95

BRONX PELHAM PKWY

Morris Park

MOUNT VERNON

NEW ENGLAND THWY

CO-OP CITY

BAYCHESTER

THE BRONX

GUN HILL RD

WHITE PLAINS RD

BRONX RIVER PKY

WESTCHESTER AVE

MORRISANIA

TREMONT

CROSS BRONX EXPY

BRONX ZOO

BRONX BOTANICAL GARDEN

NORWOOD

WOODLAWN CEMETERY

MONSULU PKY

BEDFORD PARK

POE COTTAGE

FORDHAM UNIVERSITY

BELMONT

GRAND CONCOURSE

FORDHAM RD

JEROME AVE

BRONX MUSEUM OF THE ARTS

BRONX COUNTY COURTHOUSE

YANKEE STADIUM

87

MAJOR DEEGAN EXPY

87

YONKERS

COLLEGE OF MOUNT ST VINCENT

Van Cortlandt Park

VAN CORTLANDT MANSION

WAVE HILL

RIVERDALE

MANHATTAN

HENRY HUDSON PKY

GEORGE WASHINGTON BRIDGE

NEW YORK
NEW JERSEY

Hudson River

1 mi

1 km

0

0

institutions is the enormous **Bronx Zoo** (Fordham Rd. and Bronx River Pkwy., 718/367-1010, www.bronxzoo.org, 10 A.M.–5 P.M. daily Apr.–Oct., adults $11, seniors and children 2–12 $8, reduced hours and admission prices in winter), where New Yorkers have been spending weekends with their families for generations. It's among the world's largest and most important zoos, housing over 4,000 animals, many of which roam relatively freely in large landscaped habitats. The Bronx Zoo was one of the world's first wildlife centers to adopt this technique.

Among the 250-acre zoo's most popular attractions is its Wild Asia Express, a monorail ride above a 38-acre savanna inhabited by elephants, Siberian tigers, rhinos, and many different kinds of deer. In the World of Birds, centered on a towering waterfall, about 100 species flit from tree to tree. In the World of Darkness, low lights make it possible to see nocturnal animals at their most active; included here is the world's largest collection of captive bats.

To reach the zoo from Manhattan, take the No. 2 or 5 train to East Tremont Ave.-West Farm Square. Or, take the BMX11 Express Bus (718/652-8400).

Just north of the zoo is the 250-acre **New York Botanical Garden** (Southern Blvd. and 200th St., 718/817-8700, www.nybg.org, 10 A.M.–6 P.M. Tues.–Sun., reduced hours in winter, grounds admission adults $6, seniors and students $3, children 2–12 $1). Made up of both the cultivated and the wild, the park contains dozens of constituent gardens such as a rose garden and an herb garden, an arboretum, a hemlock forest, a children's garden, and—best of all—the enormous, shimmering, Victorian-style **Enid Haupt Conservatory** (separate admission; adults $7, seniors and students $5, children $3). Here, you'll find over 100 varieties of palms, tropical plants, desert flora, and ferns, and changing seasonal exhibits. The 1902 conservatory, with its 11 glass pavilions and many reflecting pools, was inspired by Kew Gardens in London and is the largest building of its type in America.

To reach the botanical garden from Manhattan, take the No. 4 or D train to Bedford Park Boulevard and walk a half-dozen or so long blocks east. Or, take a Metro North train (212/532-4900).

Arthur Avenue and Belmont

Just west of Bronx Zoo is the Italian community of Belmont. A stable, middle-class haven of spick-and-span streets and small backyard shrines, Belmont is chock-a-block with Italian restaurants, pastry shops, butcher shops, and food markets. Most are located along Arthur Avenue or **187th Street.**

At the heart of things is the indoor **Arthur Avenue Retail Market** (2344 Arthur Ave., at 187th St., 718/295-5033), where some of the city's freshest and cheapest fruits and vegetables can be found, along with fresh mozzarella, ravioli cutters, and espresso machines. Just up the street are **Madonia Brothers Bakery** (2348 Arthur Ave., 718/295-5573), selling mouthwatering crusty bread, and **Biancardi's** (2350 Arthur Ave., 718/733-4058), selling whole baby lambs and goats (no place for the squeamish). Down the street is the **Calabria Pork Store** (2338 Arthur Ave., 718/367-5145), its ceiling densely hung with meats and sausages, and **Randazzo's Fish Market** (2327 Arthur Ave., 718/367-4139), piled high with crab, sole, scrod, and the like. In warm weather, Randazzo's operates a raw seafood bar out front.

To reach Belmont from the zoo, walk west seven long blocks, or catch the Bx22 bus on East Fordham Road. From the garden, walk south through the campus of Fordham University.

Food

A number of pastry shops and cafés are on 187th Street. **DeLillo's Pastry Shop** (606 187th St., 718/367-8198) serves both pastries and homemade gelato and spumoni. **Egidio** (622 187th St., 718/295-6077) is renowned for its miniature pastries.

Mario's (2342 Arthur Ave., between 184th and 185th Sts., 718/584-1188) serves huge portions of Southern Italian food, and may be Belmont's best-known restaurant; it was featured in the film

The Godfather; average entrée $16. **Dominick's** (2335 Arthur Ave., at 187th St., 718/733-2807) has some of the neighborhood's best food, served family style at long tables covered with red tablecloths; average entrée $12. Good pizza joints can also be found along Arthur Avenue.

POE COTTAGE AND THE GRAND CONCOURSE

Today, it seems inconceivable that this tiny white cottage (Grand Concourse and East Kingsbridge Rd., 718/881-8900, www.bronxhistoricalsociety.org, 10 A.M.–4 P.M. Sat., 1–5 P.M. Sun., adults $3, seniors and students $2) surrounded by well-worn buildings and pothole-filled streets was once an isolated farmhouse. But in 1846, writer Edgar Allan Poe moved in here with his wife, Virginia, in hopes that the country air would cure her tuberculosis. When Poe wrote his famous poem "Annabel Lee," beginning "It was many and many a year ago/In a kingdom by the sea/That a maiden there lived whom you may know/By the name of Annabel Lee," it was his wife and the Bronx that he was talking about.

The cottage is a simple place with a large kitchen and sitting room downstairs and Poe's old cramped office and bedroom upstairs. A short video covers the highlights of Poe's life, leaving out many of the more controversial aspects (such as his serious drinking problem) and focusing on what the couple's lives were like while they were here. At that time, they were suffering from extreme poverty and often survived by foraging in the fields for dandelions and other edible plants. They had no money for fuel, and spent many winter days as well as nights bundled up in blankets.

Outside Poe Cottage runs the Grand Concourse, once one of the city's most glamorous boulevards. During the 1920s and 1930s, the avenue was known as the "Jewish Fifth Avenue." One of the country's first controlled-access parkways, it featured separate lanes for carriages, cyclists, and pedestrians, and was lined with one stunning art deco building after another—many of which still stand.

To reach the Poe Cottage from Manhattan, take the No. 4 train to Kingsbridge Road/Jerome Avenue and walk three blocks east to the Grand Concourse, or take the D train to Kingsbridge Road.

CITY ISLAND

City Island is one of New York City's oddest communities, a sailors' haven that fancies itself part of New England. "Welcome to New York City's Nautical Community, 1645," reads the sign arching over the bridge leading from the mainland. And then you're there, on a narrow strip of land lined with boatyards, tiny clapboard houses, and bustling seafood restaurants.

Back in the 1700s, the inhabitants of City Island hoped to develop a port that would rival New York's. Obviously their plan failed, but the community has been home to a number of thriving industries, including a shipbuilding industry that continues to this day. Several America's Cup yachts were built here.

City Island has only one real street—City Island Avenue. But some of its side roads, which are only a few blocks long, are pretty and worth a gander. To reach the island from Manhattan, take the No. 6 train to Pelham Bay Park, the last stop, and catch the Bx12 (summer only) or Bx29 bus to City Island.

Food

City Island restaurants run the gamut from simple diners to elaborate (and expensive) old-fashioned affairs with nautical themes and plush booths. The rambling **Johnny's Reef Restaurant** (2 City Island Ave., 718/885-2086) is a local favorite, offering huge portions of fried fish cafeteria-style, along with great views of the Sound; average main dish, $11. More sedate and also very good is the **Crab Shanty** (361 City Island Ave., 718/885-1810).

Staten Island

Sometimes dubbed "the forgotten borough," Staten Island is different from the rest of New York City. Significantly more rural and suburban than the other boroughs, it's also predominantly white, politically conservative, and working- to middle-class.

All of which means that Staten Island frequently feels estranged from the rest of the city—and periodically threatens to secede. The last time was in 1993 when the issue was put to a public vote; the referendum was enthusiastically passed, but its implementation remains doubtful.

Fourteen miles long by seven miles wide, Staten Island is a hilly place made up largely of bedrock. A military camp for the British during the Revolutionary War, the borough remained predominantly agricultural until the early 1900s and was still largely undeveloped when the Verrazano-Narrows Bridge opened in 1964. The bridge connected the island to the rest of the city for the first time, bringing with it new industry, residents, and crime. Many Staten Islanders still blame the bridge for many of the island's current problems, and divide life into "Before the Bridge" and "After the Bridge."

To reach Staten Island from Manhattan, take the Staten Island ferry (718/727-2508) from Battery Park to St. George, where buses fan out to cover the island. For more information and help with travel directions, contact the **Staten Island Chamber of Commerce** (718/727-1900, www.sichamber.com).

STATEN ISLAND INSTITUTE OF ARTS & SCIENCES

Two blocks from the ferry terminal in St. George is the Staten Island Institute of Arts & Sciences (75 Staten Island Pl., 718/727-1135, 9 A.M.– 5 P.M. Mon.–Sat., 1–5 P.M. Sun., suggested

STATEN ISLAND NATURE PRESERVE

Smack in the middle of Staten Island is the Greenbelt, a 2,500-acre nature preserve made up of contiguous woodlands, wetlands, and open fields, along with a golf course and a few historic sites. Though surrounded by development, the Greenbelt is a favorite stop for migratory birds on the Atlantic flyway. It also supports one of the most diverse floras in the northeast, thanks to a wide variety of soils deposited by the Wisconsin glacier about 10,000 years ago. In the Greenbelt's upland hills, the soil covers an uncommon serpentinite bedrock found only a few places in the world. When exposed to the elements, the bedrock weathers to a light gray-green.

Two major hiking trails traverse the Greenbelt. One is the 8.5-mile Blue Trail (17 miles round-trip), marked with blue dots, which runs east-west from the College of Staten Island to the William Davis Wildlife Refuge. Highlights along the way include Deer Park, which lies on the slopes of the highest point along the Atlantic coastline between Maine and Florida;

Reed's Basket Willow Swamp, often filled with blooming wildflowers; and High Rock Park, where outcroppings of the serpentinite bedrock can be seen. To reach the College of Staten Island from the ferry terminal, take the S66 bus. The trail begins on Milford Drive and is marked by a sign.

The other trail is the four-mile White Trail (eight miles roundtrip), marked with white dots, which begins at High Rock Park and runs north to Willowbrook Park. Highlights along the way include Bucks Hollow, notable for its wetlands, and the steep Egbertville Ravine. To reach the trail, take the S74 bus to the corner of Richmond Road and Rockland Avenue. Walk two blocks on Rockland to Nevada Avenue and turn right up the hill to the park's entrance and **visitors center.** Maps are available at the visitors center on weekends; on weekdays, stop by the Greenbelt's administration office (200 Nevada Ave., 718/667-2165). Other, shorter trails also traverse the Greenbelt.

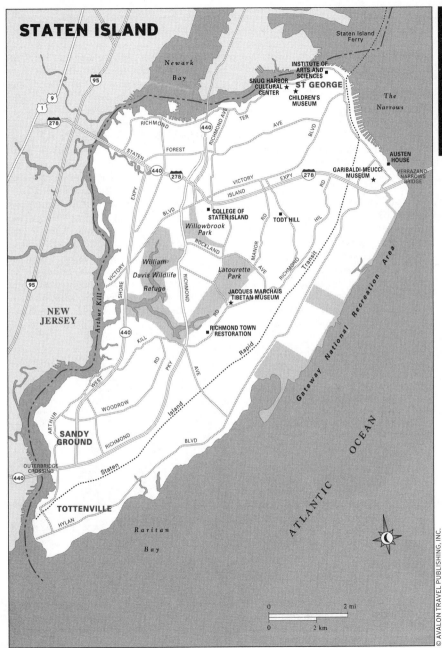

STATEN ISLAND

Newark Bay

Staten Island Ferry

INSTITUTE OF ARTS AND SCIENCES

SNUG HARBOR CULTURAL CENTER

ST GEORGE

CHILDREN'S MUSEUM

The Narrows

AUSTEN HOUSE

GARIBALDI-MEUCCI MUSEUM

VERRAZANO NARROWS BRIDGE

COLLEGE OF STATEN ISLAND

TODT HILL

Willowbrook Park

William Davis Wildlife Refuge

Latourette Park

JACQUES MARCHAIS TIBETAN MUSEUM

RICHMOND TOWN RESTORATION

NEW JERSEY

Gateway National Recreation Area

Arthur Kill

SANDY GROUND

OUTERBRIDGE CROSSING

TOTTENVILLE

Raritan Bay

ATLANTIC OCEAN

0   2 mi

0   2 km

RICHMOND, FOREST, RICHMOND AVE, TER, AVE, BLVD, STATEN, VICTORY, ISLAND, EXPY, RD, EXPY, BLVD, ROCKLAND, MANOR, AVE, RICHMOND, Transit, RICHMOND, RD, SHORE, VICTORY, KILL, WEST, RD, PKY, AVE, ARTHUR, WOODROW, RICHMOND, BLVD, Island, Rapid, Staten, HYLAN

© AVALON TRAVEL PUBLISHING, INC.

admission adults $2.50, students and seniors $1.50). Founded in 1881, the institute features small but well-done changing exhibits on the arts, natural sciences, and culture of the borough.

ALICE AUSTEN HOUSE

Several miles southwest of St. George is a pretty gabled house (2 Hylan Blvd., 718/816-4506, noon–5 P.M. Thurs.–Sun., closed Jan.–Feb., suggested admission $3) that was once home to photographer Alice Austen. A contemporary of Jacob Riis, Austen never worked professionally but took photographs just "for fun." Between 1884 and 1932 she produced more than 8,000 photos, which comprise one of the finest extant pictorial records of turn-of-the-century American life.

Austen lived in her 17th-century cottage from the age of two until she was 70, when she was forced out due to poverty. Crippled with arthritis, she moved into the poorhouse. There she was "discovered" by an editor of *Life* magazine, and lived to see her photographs published to much acclaim.

The house has been restored to the way it was in Austen's day and is full of Victoriana clutter. One room houses a gallery which mounts changing photography exhibits. Outside is a wonderful view of the harbor.

From the ferry terminal, take the S51 bus; the ride takes 15 minutes.

JACQUES MARCHAIS MUSEUM OF TIBETAN ART

Perched on a steep hill midway down the island is the Tibetan Museum (338 Lighthouse Ave., at Windsor, off Richmond Hill Rd., 718/987-3500, www.tibetanmuseum.com, 1–5 P.M. Wed.–Sun., adults $5, seniors and students $3, children $2). The museum was created by Jacqueline Norman Klauber, who adopted the alias Jacques Marchais to promote her career as a New York art dealer. Fascinated with Tibetan figurines from childhood (her great-grandfather had brought some home from his travels), she spent her adult years collecting Asian art. In the 1940s, she built this personalized museum, which was designed to resemble a Buddhist temple.

a historic Richmond Town building

The Marchais Center houses the biggest collection of Tibetan art in the Western world, but is still quite small, contained in just one high-ceilinged room and a rectangular garden. Highlights include a series of brightly colored masks, and a large collection of golden *thangkas,* or religious images, lined up at a red-and-gold altar.

From the ferry terminal, take the S74 bus; the ride takes 30–40 minutes.

HISTORIC RICHMOND TOWN

Just a few minutes' walk from the Tibetan Museum is Richmond Town (441 Clarke Ave., at Patrick's Pl., 718/351-1611, www.historicrichmondtown.org, 10 A.M.–5 P.M. Wed.–Sat. and 1–5 P.M. Sun. July–Aug., Wed.–Sun. 1–5 P.M.

Feb.–June, adults $5, seniors $4, children 5–17 $3.50), a 30-acre complex filled with 29 historic buildings, seven of which are open to the public. Most have been moved here from elsewhere on the island, and they line up neatly along several streets that come alive in summer with craftspeople and guides in period dress.

Richmond Town sits on the site of an early Dutch settlement and interprets three centuries of daily life. The oldest building is the 1695 Voorlezer's House (a *voorlezer* was a lay minister); one of the newest is the New Dorp Railroad Station. Other interesting buildings include a two-story jail, tinsmith shop, general store, and carriage "manufactory."

From the ferry terminal, take the S74 bus; the ride takes 30–40 minutes.

Information and Services

New York City's Official Visitor Information Center (810 Seventh Ave., at 53rd St., 212/484-1222, www.nycvisit.com), run by NYC & Company, New York's tourism marketing organization is open 365 days a year, Mon.–Fri. 8:30 A.M.–6 P.M., Sat.–Sun. 8:30 A.M.–5:30 P.M., with shorter hours on major holidays. Maps, hundreds of brochures, and calendars of events are available, while kiosks provide up-to-date information. The center also rungs a visitor information kiosk in Harlem (163 W. 125th St., just east of Adam Clayton Powell Jr. Blvd., 10 A.M.–6 P.M. daily) and the **NYC Heritage Tourism Center,** focusing on history, near City Hall Park (Broadway and Barclay St., 9 A.M.–6 P.M. Mon.–Fri., 10 A.M.–6 P.M. Sat.–Sun.).

When out of town, written information can be ordered by calling **NYC & Company** at 800/NYC-VISIT or 212/397-8222.

The **Downtown Alliance** (212/566-6700, www.downtownny.com) can provide you with information about Lower Manhattan. Vari-ous business partnerships operate carts stocked with tourist brochures near such visitor-heavy sites as Grand Central Station and the Empire State Building.

TIPS FOR TRAVELERS
Publications

New York City has three major daily newspapers—the *New York Times,* the *Daily News,* and the *New York Post.* The *Times* is the country's unofficial paper of record, exhaustively covering the national and international scene. But it also contains good information on happenings around town, especially in its Friday Weekend sections.

You'd be coming away with a skewed view of New York, however, if you didn't also pick up occasional copies of the *Daily News* and the *New York Post.* Both tabloids, with their in-your-face headlines, do a much better job of covering local news than does the *Times.* The *Daily News* is also a good source for crisp, pithy features and reviews of local events. The

NEW YORK RADIO STATIONS

FM
WBAI/99.5 Pacifica radio, diverse programming.
WBGO/88.3 Jazz, broadcast from Newark.
WBLS/107.5 Urban contemporary.
WCBS/101.1 All-era music.
WFMU/91.1 Eclectic programming, listener-supported station.
WKCR/89.9 Columbia University's station has first-rate jazz.
WNEW/102.7 Music and entertainment.
WNYC/93.9 News and culture.
WPLJ/95.5 Top 40.
WQXR/96.3 Commercial classical music station.
WRKS/98.7 Urban contemporary.
WXRK/92.3 Alternative rock.

AM
WINS/1010 News around the clock.
WNYC/820 Excellent talk station; NPR's New York outlet.
WOR/710 Interviews and talk programs.

New York Post's Page Six gossip column is must reading for many New Yorkers, and many of its reviews are excellent. Both papers also feature a daily movie schedule, which the *Times* does not.

When it comes to "alternative" papers, the weekly **Village Voice** is the granddaddy. Though best known for its leftist politics, the *Voice*'s strongest suit is its cultural coverage and events listings—among the city's most comprehensive. The *Voice* is free of charge and can be found in red boxes on street corners, or in bookstores, music stores, clubs, and delis.

Free neighborhood newspapers containing good listings and reviews are also plentiful. The best of these papers, giving the *Voice* a run for its money, is the **New York Press.**

Among magazines, **New York, The New** **Yorker,** and **Time Out New York** cover the city extensively. *New York* is mostly lightweight mainstream patter, with entertaining articles, good reviews, and a solid events listing. *The New Yorker* is renowned for its acerbic, and usually deadly accurate, listings and reviews. *Time Out New York* features excellent round-up articles and a phenomenal listings section—the most comprehensive in the city. More consciously hip is the monthly **Paper,** which covers the ever-changing downtown nightlife scene.

Budget Tips
New York is an expensive city, but there are ways to keep costs down:

Stay in hotels a bit off the beaten track. Take advantage of hotel packages.

Avoid routine purchases in Midtown. You'll get much better values in other parts of the city. Avoid those Midtown restaurants and stores that obviously cater to tourists—their prices are always inflated.

Eat in ethnic restaurants. They're ubiquitous and often amazingly cheap; the East Village has an especially large supply.

Watch the papers for free events. Top performers in many artistic disciplines often appear in public plazas or parks, especially in summer.

Take advantage of free regularly scheduled activities, such as the tours offered by the Federal Reserve and the exhibits presented by the New York Public Library and Harlem's Schomburg Center. Many museums also offer free admission one night a week.

Walk or take public transportation. New York is a great walking city, and public transportation is excellent.

Take advantage of discount services. The TKTS booth in Times Square sells half-price orchestra tickets to many Broadway shows.

Explore the small music clubs that feature unknown performers. In New York, the "unknowns" are often well-known performers in their hometowns, and many small clubs charge little or no cover.

Citypass (707/256-0490) is a discount pass (adults $53, youths 6–17 $41) to six famous New York City attractions: the Empire State Building, Guggenheim Museum, American Museum of Natural History, Museum of Modern Art, *Intrepid* Sea-Air-Space Museum, and the Circle Line (which offers cruises around Manhattan). The passes can be purchased at any of the six sites and are good for nine days from first use.

Tipping

A 15–20 percent tip is customary for waiters and taxi drivers. Hotel bellhops expect $1 a bag, porters $1 for hailing a cab, and room attendants $1 per person per night.

Safety

As in most big cities, crime in New York can be a serious problem. But according to the FBI, New York is one of America's safest large cities. It doesn't even make the top-25 list of cities with the highest homicide rates. Statistically, your chances of being mugged are less than 30,000 to 1. To avoid being that one:

Act as if you know where you're going, especially when passing through empty neighborhoods. New Yorkers—forever blasé—keep up a brisk, disinterested pace at all times. If you spend too long ogling the sites or looking nervously about, you'll be targeted as an easy mark.

Don't carry large quantities of cash or large bills, but do carry something; $20 is recommended.

Ignore hustlers and con artists, especially the three-card-monte players and anyone who approaches you with an elaborate sob story.

Avoid the parks at night, and be extra careful around transportation centers such as the Port Authority and Penn Station.

Don't carry valuables in lightweight backpacks that can easily be slashed open. Carry handbags close to your body.

When in rougher neighborhoods, stick to blocks where other people are in sight or at least where cars are passing by. At night, on empty streets, walk near the curb, away from dark overhangs.

If you're mugged, hand over your valuables immediately—they're not worth dying for.

Gay and Lesbian Travelers

Founded in 1983, the **Lesbian, Gay, Bisexual & Transgender Community Center** (208 W. 13th St., between Seventh and Eighth Aves., 212/620-7310, www.gaycenter.org) works with hundreds of organizations, including Act-Up and GLAAD, and houses the National Museum and Archive of Lesbian and Gay History. Everything from dances to movies is presented here, and free information "Welcome Packets" about the city are available for travelers. The **Gay and Lesbian Hotline** (212/989-0999, 4 P.M.–midnight Mon.–Fri., noon–5 P.M. Sat., www.glnh.org) offers peer counseling and information on accommodations, restaurants, and clubs.

Travelers with Disabilities

New York is a difficult city for visitors with disabilities to navigate, but help is available. One source is the **Mayor's Office for People with Disabilities** (212/788-2830), which puts out a free Access Guide. Another is **Hospital Audiences, Inc.** (212/575-7676), which publishes a guide to the city's cultural institutions that includes information on elevators, ramps, Braille signage, services for the hearing impaired, and restroom facilities. For more general information, contact the **Society for Accessible Travel and Hospitality** (212/447-7284), a nationwide, nonprofit membership organization that collects data on travel facilities around the country.

Two hundred of the 500 volunteer "Big Apple Greeters" are specifically trained to help the handicapped enjoy the city. The Big Apple Greeter program (212/669-8159), available free to all visitors, matches out-of-towners with New Yorkers eager to share their hometown.

All of New York's buses are wheelchair accessible, but only a handful of subway stations are. **New York City Transit** (718/596-8585) publishes the free brochures *Accessible Travel* and *Accessible Transfer Points within the NYC Subway.*

TOURS

No matter where your interests lie—in architecture, ethnic foods, or social history—chances are good you'll find a tour tailor-made for you. Walking tours abound all over the city, especially in the spring and fall, with each one more imaginative than the next ("Famous Murder Sites," "Edith Wharton's New York") and most priced under $15.

City Tours

One of the best ways to get an overview of the city is to take a **Circle Line** cruise (Pier 83, West 42nd Street and the Hudson River, 212/563-3200, www.circleline.com). The boats leave daily April–December. Standard daytime cruises last three hours; "express" and evening cruises last two (adults $23–28, seniors $19–23, children under 12 $12–15).

World Yacht (Pier 81, West 41st St. and the Hudson, 212/630-8100) offers three-hour luxury dinner cruises with live entertainment and dancing ($80 per person).

Gray Line Sightseeing (900 8th Ave., near 53rd St., 212/397-2600, www.graylinenewyork.com) offers over a dozen bus tours lasting anywhere from two hours to a full day. Tours are offered year-round ($30–80 per person).

For a spectacular bird's-eye view of the city, try **Liberty Helicopter Tours,** 212/967-4550. Flights leave from the VIP heliport at Twelfth Avenue and West 30th Street. ($60 per person, reservations required).

Walking Tours

The **Municipal Art Society** (457 Madison Ave., near 51st St., 212/935-3960, www.mas.org) runs an extensive series of walking tours almost daily year-round. Most focus on architecture and history.

Big Onion Walking Tours (212/439-1090, www.bigonion.com), founded by two Columbia University graduate students, offers some

of the city's most fun and well-researched tours. Many concentrate on New York's immigrant history and on neighborhoods below 14th Street.

The 92nd Street Y (1395 Lexington Ave., at 92nd St., 212/415-5500, www.92ndsty.org), a leading cultural institution, offers many excellent walking and bus tours. They're very popular and must be signed up for weeks in advance.

Harlem Spirituals (212/391-0900, www.harlemspirituals.com) specializes in visits to gospel services and soul-food restaurants, as well as historic sites. **Harlem Heritage Tours** (212/280-7888, www.harlemheritage.com) offers about 30 different tours, ranging from "jazz nights in Harlem" to gospel walking tours.

Downtown, the **Lower East Side Tenement Museum** (90 Orchard St., between Delancey and Broome, 212/431-0233, www.tenement.org) sponsors walking tours of old immigrant neighborhoods. For a hip tour of the East Village and environs, check out **Rock Junket Tours** (212/696-6578). "Rocker guides" lead participants past legendary rock, punk, and glam sites from the '60s to the present.

Radical Walking Tours (718/492-0069) specializes in revolutionary and labor history. **Foods of New York Walking and Tasting Tours** (212/334-5070, www.foodsofny.com) explores some of the most famous restaurants and food shops in Greenwich Village and Chelsea ($38 per person, tastings included).

Worth watching out for are the free nature walks offered in all five boroughs by the **Urban Park Rangers** (212/360-2774 or 866/NYC-HAWK, www.nyc.gov/parks).

The **Big Apple Greeter** (212/669-8159, www.bigapplegreeter.org) matches visitors up with enthusiastic volunteers eager to introduce the city to out-of-towners. The service is completely free and especially helpful to the disabled and tourists interested in visiting off-the-beaten-track spots.

During the summer, the **Alliance for Downtown New York** (212/566-6700) offers free 90-minute Wall Street Walking Tours every Thursday and Saturday at noon. The tours leave from One Bowling Green (in front of the National Museum of the American Indian).

EMERGENCIES

Dial 911 for emergency **police, ambulance,** or **fire-department** response. For the location of the nearest police precinct, dial 646/610-5000.

Private hospitals with 24-hour emergency rooms include **St. Vincent's Hospital** (Seventh Ave. at 11th St., 212/604-7000), **Beth Israel Medical Center** (First Ave. at 16th St., 212/420-2000), **New York University Medical Center** (First Ave. at 34th St., 212/263-7300), **St. Luke's-Roosevelt Hospital** (Ninth Ave. at 58th St., 212/523-4000), **New York Hospital** (York Ave. at 68th St., 212/746-5454), and **Mount Sinai Hospital** (Fifth Ave. at 100th St., 212/241-6500).

POST OFFICES

Many post offices are open weekdays 8 A.M.– 6 P.M., and Saturday 8 A.M.–1 P.M., but hours vary from branch to branch. The city's main post office on Eighth Avenue at 33rd Street is open 24 hours a day, seven days a week.

TELEPHONES

The area code in Manhattan has historically been 212, while the other boroughs use 718. Since July 1999, however, Manhattan now has a second area code—646—while the boroughs now also use 347. It is necessary to dial all 10 numbers when placing a call.

For **directory assistance** in Manhattan, call 411. For directory assistance in the other boroughs, call 718/555-1212.

Other useful numbers include **time** (212/976-2828), **weather** (212/976-1212), and **wake-up calls** (212/540-WAKE).

RESTROOMS

Some of the most accessible public restrooms in Manhattan are at Cooper Union (41 Cooper Square, near Third Ave. and 8th St., downstairs), Penn Station (Seventh Ave., between 30th and 32nd Sts.), Grand Central Station (42nd St. and Park Ave.), the New York Public Library (Fifth Ave. and 42nd St., ground and third floors), the GE Building (30 Rockefeller Plaza, concourse level), Citicorp Center (153 Lexington Ave., at 53rd St., lower level), Trump Tower (725 Fifth Ave., at 56th St., downstairs), and the 92nd Street Y (1395 Lexington Ave., at 92nd St., ground level).

COCKROACHES

Much to its residents' dismay, New York is home to four kinds of cockroaches – the brown German, the one- to two-inch-long American, the striped brown-banded, and the stocky Oriental. All are much despised, but it is the German who elicits the foulest expletives, inhabiting dark crevices in kitchens and bathrooms from the dingiest East Village dive to the most luxurious Upper East Side condo.

New Yorkers have sense enough to know that it's impossible to eradicate *Blatella germanica*. The bugs have been around for about 350 million years, after all, and can survive on next to nothing, including salts from tennis shoes, grease spots on a wall from cooking, and starch on postage stamps. In one laboratory experiment, a cockroach colony lived two and a half years without any protein at all. Then, too, a female cockroach needs but one sex act a year to store enough sperm to produce 35,000 more cockroaches.

So instead of eradication, New Yorkers have to content themselves with pest control. In the past, this has meant chemical sprays and fumigations. In today's more environmentally aware times, the most popular methods are bait traps, boric acid, and – the Tokay gecko. This small blue-skinned lizard with orange spots measures between six inches and two feet long, and loves to eat cockroaches. A nocturnal creature, it's rarely seen during the day, but has an odd, distinctive bark that's sometimes heard at night.

Getting There

BY AIR

New York is serviced by three airports. **John F. Kennedy International Airport** is about 15 miles from Manhattan in Queens. It's the largest of the three and handles primarily international flights. **La Guardia Airport,** also in Queens, is about eight miles from Manhattan and handles primarily domestic flights. **Newark Airport,** across the Hudson River in New Jersey, handles domestic and some international flights. Kennedy is generally the most congested of the three airports, Newark the least.

Public transportation from the airports into Manhattan and the other boroughs is excellent; call 800/AIR-RIDE for general information.

A **taxi ride** into Manhattan from La Guardia takes 20–30 minutes and costs about $25, including tolls and tip. The ride from Kennedy to Manhattan takes 30–45 minutes and costs a flat fare of $45, plus tolls and tip (when going the other way, from Manhattan to Kennedy, the trip is metered, but usually costs about the same). The 45-minute ride from Newark usually runs about $50. Cabs leave from well-marked stands staffed by dispatchers, just outside the flight-arrival areas at all airports. Avoid the gypsy cabs near baggage-claim areas.

New York Airport Service (212/875-8200, www.nyairportservice.com) offers frequent bus service to and from La Guardia ($12 one-way; $21 round-trip) and Kennedy ($15 one-way; $27 round-trip). Stops are made near Grand Central Terminal (Park Ave. between 41st and 42nd Sts.), inside the Port Authority Bus Terminal (42nd St. and Eighth Ave.), near Pennsylvania Station (33rd St. and Seventh Ave.), and outside several hotels (call for details).

Olympia Trails of Coach USA (212/964-6233 or 877/894-9155, www.olympiabus.com) offers frequent bus service between Newark Airport and Manhattan ($12 one-way; $19 round-trip). Buses leave every 15–20 min-

utes, and make three stops in Manhattan: near Grand Central Station (41st St. and Park Ave.), outside Pennsylvania Station (34th St. and Eighth Ave.), and inside the Port Authority (42nd St. and Eighth Ave.).

SuperShuttle (212/209-7000, www.supershuttle.com) offers door-to-door pick-up van service from homes and hotels to any of the three area airports. Fares are $17–23.

BY TRAIN

Manhattan has two main railroad stations: **Pennsylvania Station** (33rd St. and Seventh Ave.) and **Grand Central Station** (42nd St. and Park Avenue). All **Amtrak** trains (800/872-7245) arrive and depart from Pennsylvania Station. **New Jersey Transit** (973/762-5100) and **Long Island Rail Road** (718/217-5477) also offer passenger-train service out of Pennsylvania Station. **Metro-North** (212/532-4900) runs commuter trains to suburban New York and Connecticut from Grand Central. Both stations are well serviced by buses, subways, and taxis.

BY BUS

The **Port Authority** (Eighth Ave. between 40th and 42nd Sts., 212/564-8484) is the world's largest bus terminal, serving both commuter and long-distance travelers. Major bus lines departing from the terminal include **Greyhound** (800/231-2222), **Peter Pan** (800/343-9999), and **New Jersey Transit** (973/762-5100 or 800/772-2222).

BY CAR

If you must drive into Manhattan, be prepared to pay a steep price for parking at a garage (often $8–12/hour) or to spend 20 minutes or so looking for street parking. In contrast, street parking in most sections of the boroughs is generally available. When parking on the street, never leave *anything* on the seats; cars are broken into frequently.

Getting Around

Most of Manhattan is laid out in a grid pattern, which makes it easy to find your way around. Avenues run north-south, streets east-west, and most are one way. Fifth Avenue, which marks the center of the city, separates the East and West Sides. Street addresses are labeled accordingly (1 E. 50th Street, 1 W. 50th Street), with the numbers increasing as you head away from Fifth. Broadway, following an old Algonquin trail, cuts through the city on a diagonal.

Streets with ordinals are spelled with numerals (1st Street, 2nd Street, etc.) and Avenues with ordinals are spelled with letters (First Avenue, Second Avenue, etc.) throughout this book, including on maps.

Those neighborhoods not laid out in a numbered grid pattern—essentially everything south of 14th Street—are much more difficult to navigate, and it helps to have a good map. The same applies in the other boroughs, where it's also a good idea to get exact directions to your destination before you set out.

If you don't know how to get where you're going, call the New York City Transit Authority (718/330-1234) between 6 A.M. and 9 P.M., and they'll tell you the best route via subway or bus.

BY SUBWAY

Despite their reputation and the constant complaints of commuting New Yorkers, the subways are the easiest and quickest way to get around town. Service is frequent—at least in Manhattan—and the trains run all night.

To ride the subways, you'll need an electronic fare card, known as a **MetroCard.** The basic fare is $2, though you get a free ride when you purchase a $20 card. Unlimited-ride cards are also available and can be an excellent bargain for those making many stops in a short period: the one-day pass costs $7; the 7-day pass, $21; and the 30-day pass, $70.

Subway maps are usually posted in each station, and free copies are sometimes available at the token booths. You can also pick up a copy at New York City's Official Visitor Information Center (810 Seventh Ave., between 52nd and 53rd Sts., 212/484-1222).

Three subway lines service the city: The IRT runs north-south on either side of Manhattan; the IND runs along Sixth and Eighth Avenues; and the BMT runs from lower Manhattan to Brooklyn and Queens. The subway lines used most frequently by visitors are the IRT No. 6

HORSEPOWERED POLLUTION IN THE 1800S

New York today may not seem like the cleanest of cities, but before you voice a complaint, consider the way it was back in the late 1800s. Back then, the 120,000-some horses in the city left about 1,300 tons of manure a day on the streets. The city employed only a handful of street cleaners, and "that foul aliment" was allowed to accumulate in huge piles, breeding "pestilential vapours" and millions of flies. In addition, whenever one of the poor, overworked horses expired, it was simply left to rot by the side of the road. In 1880 alone, New York City removed 15,000 dead horses from its streets.

Reported *Harper's Weekly* on February 26, 1881: "The condition of the streets of New York during the present winter has been frightful beyond all precedent even for the dirtiest city in the U.S. ... The thaw that followed aggravated the evil, and today the city lies ankle-deep in liquid filth through which the pedestrians are obliged to wade and flounder. There is no such thing as picking one's way, for with a few exceptions, one spot is as bad as another and everybody plunges in and ploughs through it without regard to the consequences."

train, which makes local stops along the East Side of Manhattan, and the IRT No. 1/9 train, which makes local stops along the West Side. There's also a Grand Central—Times Square Shuttle connecting the east and west sides of the IRT at 42nd Street.

New Yorkers will delight in telling you stories about how dangerous their city's subway system is, but in reality, over 3.5 million passengers travel the 700 miles of track every day without mishap. Still, crime can be a problem and you should take certain precautions. Keep a close eye on your belongings, especially during rush hours when the crush of the crowd makes pickpocketing easy. Don't wear expensive jewelry. Avoid empty or near-empty cars, even during the day when the subways are theoretically the safest. During off hours, wait for your train in the well-lit "Off-Hour" waiting areas near the token booths. When your train comes, sit in the center car, which has a conductor and is usually the most crowded car on the train. Finally, although many New Yorkers ride the subways at all hours, it's not especially advisable to take them after midnight.

BY BUS

Buses run 24 hours a day uptown along Tenth, Eighth, Sixth, Madison, Third, and First Avenues, and downtown along Ninth, Seventh, Fifth, and Second Avenues. East-west crosstown service can be found along 14th, 23rd, 34th, 42nd, 57th, 65th/66th, 79th, 86th, and 96th Streets. Bus stops are usually located every two blocks, and signs or shelters mark the spots.

The fare is $2, payable with either exact change or the electronic MetroCard. Free transfers are available between uptown-downtown buses and crosstown buses, enabling you to make any one-way trip in Manhattan on a single fare. Good bus service is also available in the outer boroughs.

BY TAXI AND CAR SERVICE

Another notorious mode of New York City transportation that's nonetheless quite good are taxi cabs, all painted yellow with lighted signs on their roofs. When the sign is lit, the cab is available and may be hailed anywhere. Fares begin at $2.50 for the first quarter-mile, then jump 40 cents for each additional quarter-mile and 40 cents for every two minutes of waiting time. A $1 surcharge is added to rides begun between 4 P.M. and 8 P.M.; a 50-cent surcharge is added to rides begun between 8 P.M. and 6 A.M. A 15–20 percent tip is the norm.

In the boroughs, where licensed cabs are few and far between, your best bet is to call one of the many private car services. Ask for recommendations at the place you're visiting or check the Yellow Pages. The services charge a flat rate that's usually reasonable, and pick you up wherever you wish.

BY FOOT

Walking is by far the best way to see Manhattan and many parts of the boroughs. In Manhattan, figure on needing about a minute for each north-south block, two minutes for each east-west one.

LONG ISLAND

Long, thin Long Island stretches east from Manhattan for about 120 miles. The largest island on the East Coast, Long Island is a jumbled mix of ugly suburbs, magnificent estates, congested highways, pristine nature preserves, sanitized shopping malls, one-stoplight villages, glitzy corporate headquarters, and some of the finest white-sand beaches in the world.

At the westernmost end of the island are the New York City boroughs of Brooklyn and Queens, so in common parlance, Long Island begins at the Queens-Nassau County border. East of there, the island is divided into two counties: Nassau and Suffolk. At 252 square miles, Nassau is about one-fourth the size of Suffolk but is considerably more populated, holding half of Long Island's 2.6 million

people. Nassau is quintessential suburbia, the birthplace of the single-family-home bedroom community.

Suffolk County has its share of suburbanization as well. Remarkably though, given its proximity to New York City, much of it is still farmland, dunes, and beach. The farther east you travel, the more the island resembles its Algonquin name, *Paumanok,* said to mean "the island with its breast long drawn out and laid against the sea."

For many visitors, Long Island's beaches are its biggest attraction. The most spectacular shores are along the southern coast, where white sands and dunes stretch out for an incredible, all-but-unbroken 123 miles. Most of the beaches along the northern coast front

© CHRISTIANE BIRD

LONG ISLAND

HIGHLIGHTS

☾ Old Westbury Gardens: The sumptuous mansion sits surrounded by what are considered the finest English gardens in the United States (page 173).

☾ Sagamore Hill: The former summer home of Theodore Roosevelt is packed with fascinating memorabilia (page 174).

☾ Walt Whitman Birthplace State Historic Site: The poet's serene and sunny home, built by his father, is filled with exhibits chronicling Whitman's life (page 177).

☾ Stony Brook: The restored 18th-century village is home to a historic inn and the Long Island Museum of American Art, History, and Carriages (page 180).

☾ Jones Beach: Just 25 miles from midtown Manhattan is New York's most famous (and crowded) beach: six miles of white sands lined with a wide, weathered boardwalk and art-deco facilities (page 192).

☾ Sag Harbor: The lively old whaling port holds a fascinating whaling museum, 19th-century sea captains' homes, and a wharf with great views of a busy harbor (page 207).

☾ Montauk Lighthouse: Commissioned by George Washington in 1792, the beacon stands sentinel on a lonely bluff at Long Island's easternmost tip (page 214).

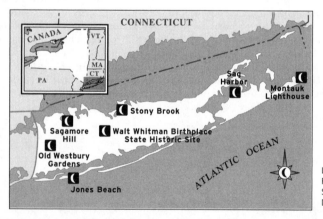

LOOK FOR ☾ TO FIND RECOMMENDED SIGHTS, ACTIVITIES, DINING, AND LODGING.

the gentle waters of Long Island Sound, and are small and pebbly. One glorious exception is Orient Beach State Park, located at the far eastern tip of North Fork.

Beaches aside, both shores and forks have much to offer the visitor. The North Shore is home to many of Long Island's 75 museums, as well as private mansions and nature preserves. The jet-setting South Fork boasts the fashionable Hamptons, interesting historic sites, and a glittering social scene. The more rural North Fork holds yet more historic sites, picturesque harbors and bays, and a flourishing wine industry.

PLANNING YOUR TIME

Each of Long Island's four sections—the North Shore, North Fork, South Shore, and South Fork—can easily be done in a day or two, depending on how many stops you make, or can be combined into one long loop that begins and ends in New York City. If you do make the 120-mile trip from Manhattan to either the busy **South Fork** or the quieter **North**

Fork, you'll want to overnight there at least two nights. A five-day trip would give you time to explore both forks and make stops at the North Shore's **Oyster Bay** and **Cold Spring Harbor** on the way back. Good day trips from Manhattan include Oyster Bay and Cold Spring Harbor, as well as **Jones Beach, Fire Island, Northport,** and **Port Jefferson.**

THE LAND

Long Island's shape has often been compared to a whale. Its western bulk, never much more than 20 miles wide, splits at the 80-mile point into two curving spits of land, or "flukes," most commonly referred to as the North and South Forks.

The island was once an extension of a barren plain that stretched east from the Alleghenies. But about 15 million years ago, two glaciers moving southward dug out the deep valley that is now Long Island Sound and severed the island from the mainland. The glacier also cut hundreds of notches into the north shore, forming the coves, bays, and peninsulas seen there today. Furthermore, as the glacier

melted, its waters ran south, flooding a huge meadow—now the Great South Bay and its neighboring waters—and creating low sand bars that became the foundation of today's miles-long barrier beach.

HISTORY
The Algonquins

Before the arrival of the whites, 13 Algonquin Indian tribes inhabited Long Island, including the Canarsees, Rockaways, Merricks, Massapeaques, Shinnecocks, Montauks, and Setaukets. Today, many of the island's villages, harbors, and bays are named for these early peoples.

The Algonquins fished in coastal waters, harvested quahog clams (producing much of the wampum used by the Northeastern Indians from the shells), and grew such crops as corn, pumpkin, melon, and tobacco. According to one settler's journal, "they were a tall proud and handsome people with grace of walk, active of body carried straight as arrows."

The Montauk chief, Wyandanch, was the grand sachem of the Long Island tribes, and

© CHRISTIANE BIRD

one of Long Island's numerous roadside farm stands

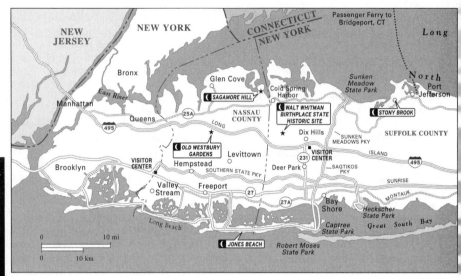

he befriended the white settlers who began arriving in the 1640s. Ninicraft, the chief of the Narragansetts who lived across the Sound, tried to enlist Wyandanch's help in killing off the whites in 1652. When Wyandanch refused, the Narragansetts opened war on the Montauks and nearly destroyed them.

Within a century after the arrival of the Dutch and English, only about 400 Indians remained on Long Island. Most had died of diseases introduced by the Europeans, and those who survived were subject to innumerable indignities. In 1759, for example, the Indians had to beg for the right to cut firewood.

Today, a small Algonquin community of about 400 Shinnecocks still lives on the Shinnecock Reservation near Southampton. Each Labor Day weekend, they celebrate their heritage with a three-day pow-wow that attracts Native Americans from across the country.

Farming and Fishing

The Dutch were the first to arrive on Long Island and were quickly followed by the English, who began settling the North and South Forks in 1640. Unlike many Colonial settlers elsewhere, the new Long Islanders had it easy.

The land around them was flat, rich, and easy to cultivate; the sea was brimming with seafood and shellfish. Soon dozens of small communities were flourishing.

During the Revolutionary War, Long Island was occupied by the British, and many settlers chose to flee rather than remain under the king's rule. But post-war, the island prospered once again. Cattle ranching (in Montauk) and whaling (in Cold Spring Harbor, Sag Harbor, and Greenport) joined farming and fishing as important industries. In the mid-1800s, the Long Island Rail Road was built and agriculture became big business. To this day, Suffolk County remains one of New York's most productive farming regions.

Long Island's fishing industry has not fared as well. As Long Island native Peter Matthiessen writes in *Men's Lives,* "In recent decades, most fishing families have been forced to sell off land that had been in the family for generations. Those who are left subsist in the last poor corner of a community in which they were once the leading citizens." Much of this decline, not surprisingly, is due to suburbanization and pollution. But powerful sportsmen's organizations with much political clout

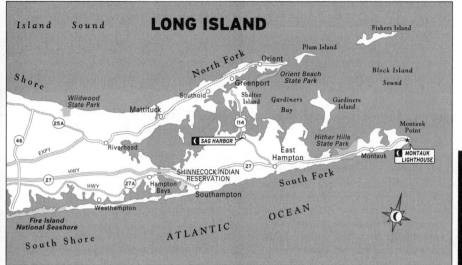

© AVALON TRAVEL PUBLISHING, INC.

have also been instrumental in limiting the commercial fisherman's harvest of certain game fish.

Long Island's dwindling number of fisherfolk live much the way their ancestors did. Writes Matthiessen: "Moving at daybreak on back roads, the fishermen go their traditional way down to the sea. They are tough, resourceful, self-respecting, and also (some say) hidebound and cranky, too independent to organize for their own survival. Yet even their critics must acknowledge a gritty spirit that was once more highly valued in this country than it is today."

Suburbanization and Modern Woes

If few people connect Long Island with fishing or even farming any more, almost everyone connects it with suburbia. Long Island is the archetypal American suburb.

Early suburbs began springing up in western Nassau County in the 1920s. But the island's real transformation came with World War II, when factories producing aircraft and specialized weapons systems turned Long Island into an important manufacturing center. After the war, large housing tracts were built to accommodate the returning GIs. The most famous of these tracts was Levittown. Between 1950 and 1960, Long Island's population doubled from 670,000 to 1.3 million, and between 1960 and 1980 it doubled again.

The island's suburban explosion has not been without its negative consequences, including poverty, homelessness, and high infant mortality rates. Local governments originally set up to serve a suburban middle class are ill-equipped to deal with such urban-style malaise.

Fortunately, none of this affects the tourists much. And despite its problems, Long Island is a unique and complex place that becomes more and more interesting the closer you look. The North Shore boasts a number of impressive museum-mansions and untouched nature preserves; the South Shore is lined with unparalleled white-sand beaches. Both the North and South Forks, with their historic villages and windswept shores, are astonishingly beautiful, and remind you of a central fact that's curiously easy to forget: This really is an island, with an idiosyncratic culture very different from that of the mainland.

The North Shore

In its stretch nearest New York City, the North Shore is a densely packed suburbia, stuffed to the bursting point with single-family homes, shopping malls, and highways and byways so thick with traffic you'll want to scream. Yet even here, once you get off the main roads up into the peninsulas, you'll find a number of wonderful historic sites and nature preserves.

The farther east you travel along the North Shore, the more rural it gets. Around Oyster Bay, the traffic thins out considerably, and by the time you reach Centerport—located less than 20 miles from the Queens-Nassau border—you've left the city far behind.

Route 25A, also known as Northern Boulevard and North Hempstead Turnpike in Nassau County, is the northernmost major route that traverses Long Island, and the best one to use for unhurried exploring. Running parallel

to it to the south is the Long Island Expressway (LIE), or I-495, which is the quicker route (except during rush hour) and therefore good to use when driving directly to a specific site.

GREAT NECK AND PORT WASHINGTON PENINSULAS

Heading into Long Island on congested Route 25A, you'll immediately cut across the bases of two large peninsulas, Great Neck and Port Washington. F. Scott Fitzgerald and his wife Zelda once lived at 6 Gateway Drive, Great Neck, and it was on these two thick thumbs of land that he modeled his West and East Eggs of *The Great Gatsby.*

Many opulent estates such as the ones Fitzgerald describes are still scattered along the so-called **Gold Coast,** which stretches 30 miles between Great Neck and Eatons Neck.

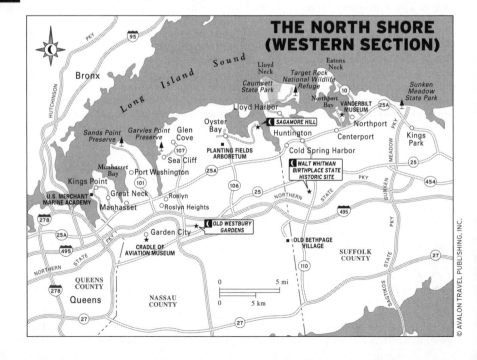

THE NORTH SHORE (WESTERN SECTION)

© AVALON TRAVEL PUBLISHING, INC.

Most were built in the early 20th century by captains of industry and commerce such as J. P. Morgan, F. W. Woolworth, and Louis Tiffany. At one time, there were some 600–700 mansions here; today—due to fire, demolition, and subdivision—only about 200 remain. About half of these are still privately owned, and most of the others have been converted into schools, religious retreats, and country clubs. Only a handful of the mansions are open to the public.

American Merchant Marine Museum

Turning off onto the Great Neck peninsula on Bay View Avenue, you'll soon come to Kings Point and the American Merchant Marine Museum (foot of Steamboat Rd., off West Shore Rd., 516/773-5515, www.usmma.edu, 10 A.M.–3 P.M. Tues.–Fri., 1–4:30 P.M. Sat.–Sun., closed July and during semester breaks, suggested donation $2) on the campus of the U.S. Merchant Marine Academy. The academy's grounds offer good views of Throgs Neck Bridge, City Island, and the Bronx. The museum showcases such odd treasures as models of well known passenger liners, the wooden wheel of the USS *Constitution,* and a life-size model of a cargo ship, used to train students during World War II.

Port Washington

The attractive town of Port Washington, on its namesake peninsula, overlooks Manhasset Bay. Here you'll find the **Polish-American Museum** (16 Bellview Ave., at Main St., 516/883-6542, call for hours). Small and informal, the museum focuses on well-known Poles and Polish-Americans, including Copernicus, Frédéric Chopin, Marie Curie, Pope John Paul II, and Gen. Thaddeus Kosciuszko, whose namesake bridge straddles Brooklyn and Queens.

For a town its size, Port Washington holds a large number of restaurants. **Louie's Oyster Bar & Grill** (395 Main St., next to the town dock, 516/883-4242) is a local institution, offering classic seafood dishes and great views

of Manhasset Bay; average entrée $16. **Chez Noelle** (34 Willowdale Ave., 516/883-3191) is an upscale French restaurant serving both classic and modern dishes that draws raves from the locals. Entrées are $26–30; a $25 prix-fixe dinner is offered Sunday–Friday.

Sands Point Preserve

Just beyond Port Washington at the tip of the peninsula is the 216-acre Sands Point Preserve (95 Middleneck Rd. [Rte. 101], 516/571-7900, 10 A.M.–5 P.M. Tues.–Sun., admission $2 in summer), filled with woods, shoreline, ball fields, nature trails, and several castle-like buildings. One of these, **Castlegould,** now houses a visitors center and natural history museum.

Sands Point was originally developed by railroad heir Howard Gould, and later purchased by the Guggenheims. Between the two families, they built three mansions: the immense Tudor-style **Hempstead House,** the much smaller **Mille Fleures,** and the Norman-style chateau, **Falaise** (guided tours of Falaise offered noon–3 P.M. Wed.–Sun. May–Oct., adults and children over 10 $6, seniors $5, children under 10 not admitted). At Falaise—perched on a cliff overlooking the Sound—you'll find Guggenheim's purple Cadillac, parked next to the station wagon that once belonged to his good friend Charles Lindbergh.

WEIRD, WONDERFUL, OFF-THE-BEATEN-PATH LONG ISLAND

Wicks Farm and Garden, St. James: Guarded by a looming 25-foot-high witch complete with hooked nose and broomstick.

Sunken Forest, Fire Island: A 300-year-old maritime forest growing below sea level between two lines of dunes.

The Big Duck, Flanders: A 20-foot-high pure white duck with a bright orange bill and eyes made from red Model T headlights.

LONG ISLAND

THE GOLD COAST AT A GLANCE

Stretching between Great Neck and Eatons Neck, the so-called Gold Coast was once home to hundreds of opulent estates: French chateaus, English castles, Italian palazzos, and the like. Most were built in the early 20th century by such prominent families as the Vanderbilts, Astors, Morgans, Woolworths, Tiffanys, and Chryslers.

Today, only about 200 of these mansions still exist. Most were killed off by the Great Depression, fire, demolition, and subdivision. And of the mansions that do remain, only a handful are easily accessible to the general public. Among them are:

Wiley Hall at the U.S. Merchant Museum Academy, Kings Point

Castlegould and **Falaise** at Sands Point Preserve, near Port Washington

Nassau County Museum of Art, Roslyn

Westbury House at Old Westbury Gardens, Old Westbury

Coe Hall at Planting Fields Arboretum, Oyster Bay

Eagle's Nest at the Suffolk County Vanderbilt Museum, Centerport

To find out more about the history of the Gold Coast, visit the fledgling **Museum of Long Island's Gold Coast,** Coindre Hall, Huntington. Housed in what was once the estate of George McKesson Brown, heir to a pharmaceutical fortune, the museum is very much a project in the making, as the mansion—originally known as West Neck Farm—is gradually being restored. Free tours of Coindre Hall can be arranged by calling Splashes of Hope (631/424-8230), a nonprofit group housed in the mansion.

ROSLYN

Though now surrounded by congested highways and upscale shops, Roslyn still lays claim to a small, historic, and attractive downtown. Many of the buildings along its short but friendly Main Street predate the Civil War, giving the place a low-key, old-fashioned feel. To learn more about the historic town, contact the Roslyn Landmark Society (516/625-4363, www.historicroslyn.org).

Nassau County Museum of Art

At the northern end of Roslyn is the Nassau County Museum of Art (Museum Dr., off Rte 25A [Northern Blvd.] between Roslyn Rd. and Glen Cove Rd., 516/484-9337, www.nassaumuseum.com, 11 A.M.–5 P.M. Tues.–Sun., adults $7, seniors $6, students and children over 5 $4; admission to grounds free), Long Island's largest art museum. Occupying the 145-acre former Frick estate, the museum grounds boast about 30 outdoor sculptures by the likes of Roy Lichtenstein and Richard Serra, and formal gardens. Inside the mansion house are first-rate temporary exhibits, while an adjacent annex holds 100 miniature rooms depicting living environments from the 18th century to the present.

Cedarmere

The prominent New York City newspaper editor William Cullen Bryant bought this former Quaker farmhouse (225 Bryant Ave., 516/571-8130, 10 A.M.–5 P.M. Saturday, 1–5 P.M. Sun. May–Nov., free admission) in 1843 to use as a retreat. A poet and lover of nature, Bryant planted a large garden filled with exotic plants and flowers, and continued to live here until his death in 1878. A civic leader, Bryant was largely responsible for the creation of Central Park. His papers are housed in Roslyn's Bryant Library (2 Paper Mill Rd., 516/621-2240).

Accommodations and Food

Rooms at the plain but comfortable **Gold Coast Inn** (1053 Northern Blvd., 516/627-2460, $75–110 d) are adequate and clean.

Within walking distance of historic Main Street is the plush and elegant **◖ Roslyn Claremont** (1221 Old Northern Blvd., 516/625-2700 or 800/626-9005, www.roslynclaremonthotel.com, $215–290 d), a European-style hotel offering 77 well-appointed guest rooms done in deep roses and greens, and a small health club. Adjoining the lobby is **⟨ Cristina's,** an intimate spot s erving global cuisine; average entrée $25.

The old-fashioned **George Washington Manor** (1305 Old Northern Blvd., 516/621-1200) is housed in a Colonial-era mansion where George Washington once ate breakfast. Specialties include Yankee pot roast, chicken pot pie, and seafood; entrées run $16–27.

The plain and simple **Chicken Shish Kebab** (92 Mineola Ave., 516/621-6828), one block from the post office in Roslyn Heights, is a local favorite, serving Greek and Middle Eastern specialties; average entrée $9.

SEA CLIFF AND GARVIES POINT

Perched high on bluffs overlooking Hempstead Harbor is Sea Cliff, a charming, off-the-beaten-path village filled with wooden Victorian homes. Some are in dire need of a facelift, but most are well kept and well adorned with fanciful turrets, wide front porches, and gingerbread eaves. Many of the best of these houses are located along Sea Cliff Avenue, Central Avenue, and Glen Avenue.

Near Sea Cliff Avenue is the **Sea Cliff Village Museum** (95 10th St., 516/671-0090, www.seacliff.org, 2–5 P.M. Sat.–Sun., closed Aug.), filled with early-20th-century photographs of village life. Back then, Sea Cliff was a popular resort, and the photographs show marvelous old hotels and dressed-to-the-hilt summer vacationers.

On Carpenter Avenue near Eighth Avenue is **St. Seraphim Russian Orthodox Church,** a small white sanctuary with an onion dome. Russians began settling in Sea Cliff in 1917.

Just north of Sea Cliff in Glen Cove is the 62-acre **Garvies Point Preserve** (50 Barry Dr., 516/571-8010, 8:30 A.M.–dusk daily, free admission), overlooking Long Island Sound. Five miles of nature trails meander through the preserve, and a small museum (10 A.M.–4 P.M. Tues.–Sun., adults $2, children $1) focuses on local archaeology and geology.

To reach Sea Cliff from Route 25A, take Glen Cove Road or Route 107 north, and turn left onto Sea Cliff Avenue. To reach Garvies Point from Sea Cliff, continue on Glen Cove Road north and look for Barry Drive or signs.

Food

A long-time favorite lunch spot in Sea Cliff is the cozy **⟨ Once Upon a Moose** (304 Sea Cliff Ave., 516/676-9304), across the street from the Village Complex. Sandwiches start at $9; regulars recommend the "purple moose float."

⟨ OLD WESTBURY GARDENS

A few miles beyond Roslyn, near the Long Island Expressway, stands one of Long Island's most sumptuous mansions, now known as Old Westbury (71 Old Westbury Rd., Exit 39 S off the LIE, 516/333-0048, www.oldwestburygardens.org, 10 A.M.–5 P.M. Wed.–Mon. May–Oct., no admission after 4:15 P.M., adults $10, seniors $8, children $5). Built in 1906 in a palatial Charles II style, this grand edifice was once home to John S. Phipps and his wife Margarita Grace, heirs to steel and shipping fortunes.

The mansion is magnificently furnished with 18th-century antiques, but it's the 88 acres of formal gardens out front and back that draw the crowds. Considered to be the finest English gardens in the United States, Old Westbury's grounds are filled with tree-lined walks, grand allées, ponds, statuary, architectural "follies," and hundreds of species of plants, including historic varieties and new hybrids.

OYSTER BAY

In the mid-1700s, both the English and the Dutch inhabited picturesque Oyster Bay, which accounts for the fact that the place has two main streets just a block apart. East Main Street was once controlled by the Dutch, West Main Street by the English. To reach Oyster Bay from Route 25A, head north on Route 106.

Raynham Hall

Raynham Hall (20 W. Main St., 516/922-6808, www.raynhamhallmuseum.com,

1–5 P.M. Tues.–Sun., adults $3, students and seniors $2, children under six free) was once the home of prosperous Revolutionary War–era merchant Samuel Townsend. Townsend was a suspected Tory, but his son was George Washington's chief spy in New York City. When the war broke out, Raynham Hall was confiscated by the British, but Townsend's daughter Sally remained in the house. There she overheard the British discussing Benedict Arnold's planned betrayal of West Point and conveyed that information to the colonists.

Sagamore Hill

On the outskirts of Oyster Bay is the Sagamore Hill National Historic Site (20 Sagamore Rd., off Cove Rd., 516/922-4788, www.nps.gov/sahi, 10 A.M.–4 P.M. daily June–Sept., 10 A.M.–4 P.M. Wed.–Sun. Oct.–May, adults $5, children under 16 free), a rambling hilltop estate that was once the summer home of Theodore Roosevelt. The former president of the United States, assistant secretary of the Navy, governor of New York State, police chief of New York City, and author of 30-odd books came here with his wife and six children to indulge in the "strenuous life"—i.e., hiking, swimming, playing tennis, and horseback riding. Roosevelt never forgot his public duties while living here, however; out front is a wide porch with its railing removed so that he could more easily address the crowds who often assembled to hear him speak.

Sagamore is now operated by the National Park Service, and rangers conduct tours through the dark, creaky house, filled with antiques—and an enormous number of preserved animal parts. There's a rhinoceros-foot inkwell, elephant-foot wastepaper basket, a chair made of moose antlers, chimes made out of elephant tusks, and, of course, scores and scores of mounted animal heads, most shot by Roosevelt. Upstairs there's even a taxidermy room where the former president taught his son how to stuff animals at the tender age of seven.

Sagamore's grounds are sleepy and serene,

hilltop estate Sagamore Hill, former residence of Theodore Roosevelt overhung with the boughs of huge trees. Near the entrance is a windmill, while out back are stables, an icehouse, and the Old Orchard House, showcasing exhibits and a film on Roosevelt's life.

To reach Sagamore from downtown Oyster Bay, head east on East Main Street to Cove Road and follow the signs; to avoid congestion in summer, arrive early and/or check the park's website for time-saving detour directions.

Theodore Roosevelt Sanctuary

Across the street from Sagamore is the 12-acre Theodore Roosevelt Sanctuary (134 Cove Rd., 516/922-3200, http://ny.audubon.org/trsac, 9 A.M.–4:30 P.M. daily, free admission). Now owned by the National Audubon Society, the refuge is planted with trees, shrubs, and vines specifically chosen to attract birds. A small visitors center (9 A.M.–4:30 P.M. Mon.–Fri., 1–4:30 P.M. Sat.–Sun.) features exhibits on the area's wildlife and on Roosevelt's extensive involvement in the then-new conservation movement.

Planting Fields Arboretum

West of Oyster Bay is Planting Fields Arboretum State Historic Park (Planting Fields Rd., 516/922-9200, www.plantingfields.org, 9 A.M.–5 P.M. daily, $6–8 parking), a lush affair on the former estate of insurance executive William Robertson Coe. Some 160 acres here are planted with ornamental trees and shrubs, while about 200 other acres are preserved in their natural state. One large greenhouse is devoted to orchids, ferns, cacti, begonias, bromeliads, and "economic plants" (bananas, citrus trees, etc.), while a second greenhouse is devoted exclusively to camellias.

At the heart of Planting Fields is **Coe Hall** (516/922-9210, 12–3:30 P.M. daily Apr.–Sept., adults $5, seniors $3.50, children 7–12 $1), a Tudor Revival stone mansion. The 1918 house is furnished with European antiques to give it the feel of an old English country manor.

Accommodations and Food

The **East Norwich Inn** (6321 Northern Blvd. [Rte. 25A] at Rte. 106, 516/922-1500, $122 s, $137 d) is a pleasant, upscale motel offering comfortable rooms with double beds.

In downtown Oyster Bay, you'll find the **Canterbury Ales Oyster Bar & Grill** (46 Audrey Ave., 516/922-3614), specializing in its namesake—direct from Oyster Bay, of course. Also on the menu are various fish entrées, lobster, pasta, and wild game; dinner entrées range $14–28.

In Bayville, 10 miles north of Oyster Bay, **Pier 1** (33 Bayville Ave., 516/628-2153) serves fresh seafood in a beautiful setting overlooking the Sound. In summer, an outside deck opens up; average entrée $22.

COLD SPRING HARBOR

Cold Spring Harbor is now a small, tourist-oriented village holding shops and galleries, historic buildings, and two museums. But during the mid-1800s, the village was a busy whaling port. Its main street—now Route 25A—was called Bedlam Street for the cacophony of foreign languages heard there. The village's taverns were full of exotic objects that sailors had brought back from all ends of the earth. And on the village's outskirts was Bungtown, a small settlement where barrels for whale oil were made. Today, only the boats bobbing in the harbor recall the port's rich and adventurous past.

Whaling Museum

The Whaling Museum (25 Main St., 631/367-3418, www.cshwhalingmuseum.org, 11 A.M.–5 P.M. Tues.–Sun., also open Mon. in summer, adults $4, seniors $3, students 5–18 $3) is a small and friendly institution founded in 1936. Exhibits in the trim, whitewashed building include a large collection of scrimshaw (the folk art of whalers), a fully rigged whale boat, huge iron caldrons used to process whale blubber, thousands of journals and letters, and a great collection of historical photographs.

In the museum you'll learn that Cold Spring Harbor was once the 27th largest whaling port in the world, and that whaling was the first racially integrated American industry. As early as the 1810s and 1820s, white and black seamen, captains, shipbuilders, and ship owners were working alongside each other. One boat, the *Industry,* out of Nantucket, Massachusetts, was captained and crewed entirely by African Americans.

Dolan DNA Learning Center

Down the street from the Whaling Museum is a large red-brick building that houses the DNA Learning Center (334 Main St., 516/367-5170, www.dnalc.org, 10 A.M.–4 P.M. Mon.–Fri., noon–4 P.M. Sat., free admission), "the world's first biotechnology museum." As the educational arm of the Cold Spring Harbor Laboratory, the museum presents changing exhibits on such subjects as the use of DNA testing in criminal cases. Though the exhibits are aimed at children, the subject is new and complex enough to interest adults as well. The center also presents frequent screenings of *Long Island Discovery,* a 28-minute video show that's a good introduction to the island's history.

SPLIA Gallery

At the intersection of Main St. and Shore Rd. is a small but excellent gallery (631/692-4664, 11 A.M.–5 P.M. Tues.–Sun. May–Dec., call for winter hours) operated by the Society for the Preservation of Long Island Antiquities (www.splia.org). Changing exhibits trace the island's social and cultural history, while next door is a bookstore stocked with books about Long Island.

Cold Spring Harbor Fish Hatchery and Aquarium

A few miles south of the village center is New York's oldest fish hatchery (Rte. 25A, 516/692-6768, www.cshfha.org, 10 A.M.–5 P.M. daily, adults $4, children 3–17 $2), established in 1883. As recently as the early 1970s, this small plant produced about 100,000 brook trout a year, to be shipped upstate to stock the waters of the Adirondacks and the Catskills.

The hatchery suspended such mammoth

operations in 1979, following the construction of larger facilities upstate, but it still operates as an educational institution. A half-dozen pools teem with hundreds of thousands of growing trout—all swimming together in one direction at one moment, switching to another the next. You'll also see a hatch house where the eggs are incubated; a warm-water pond stocked with bass, bowfin, catfish, carp, bluegill, and the like; a turtle pond; and aquariums holding about 30 species of freshwater fish native to New York State.

Food

New and upscale, with a retro tin ceiling and friendly bar, the **Bedlam Street Fish & Clam Co.** (55 Main St., 631/692-5655) is the place to go for fresh seafood and new American cuisine; average entrée $17. Recently revamped, the **Inn on the Harbor** (105 Harbor Rd. [Rte. 25A], 631/367-3166) is housed in a romantic 17th-century building with great views of the harbor. On the menu is contemporary American fare and there's live entertainment on the weekends; average entrée $18.

OLD BETHPAGE VILLAGE RESTORATION

About 10 miles south of Cold Spring Harbor is Old Bethpage Village (Round Swamp Rd., Exit 48 S off the LIE, 516/572-8400, www.old-bethpage.org, 10 A.M.–4 or 5 P.M. Wed.–Sun. Mar.–Dec., closed Jan.–Feb., adults $7, seniors and children 5–12 $5), a restored 19th-century village filled with craftspeople and interpreters in period dress. Spread out over the restoration's 200-odd acres are a blacksmith shop, general store, hat shop, tavern, working farm, and about 20 other pre–Civil War buildings, most moved here from other locations on the island.

Each time you visit Old Bethpage, you'll see something different. Come in December and you'll witness a 19th-century Christmas. Come in May and you'll spot Union soldiers training in the fields. Come in August, and baseball games, played according to 1860 rules, will be in progress.

Camping is available nearby at the 64-site **Battle Row Campground,** 1 Claremont Rd. (516/572-8690). A recreation center is on site.

HUNTINGTON

Though Huntington is now principally a tidy suburban community with an especially large contingency of restaurants and shops, evidence of its vibrant Colonial past can still be spotted here and there. The 1750 **Conklin Farmhouse** (2 High St.) once housed four generations of Conklins, and is now a historic museum furnished in a mix of Colonial, Federal, and Victorian styles. The 1795 Federal-style **Kissam House** (434 Park Ave.), also open to the public, was once home to an early family of physicians. Both houses are run by the **Huntington Historical Society** (631/427-7045; call for museum hours).

One of the state's largest independent bookstores is the **Book Revue** (313 New York Ave., 631/271-1442).

Heckscher Museum of Art

Huntington is also home to the lovely Heckscher Museum (2 Prime Ave. at Rte. 25A, 631/351-3250, www.heckscher.org, 10 A.M.–5 P.M. Tues.–Fri., 1–5 P.M. Sat.–Sun., extended hours in summer, suggested donation adults $5, seniors and students $3, children 5–12 $1). Surrounded by a small park, the museum houses a small but excellent collection of American and European art. The museum's array of 19th-century American landscapes is especially noteworthy.

◖ Walt Whitman Birthplace State Historic Site

A few miles south of Huntington proper stands the clapboard farmhouse where Walt Whitman was born (246 Old Walt Whitman Rd., Huntington Station, 631/427-5240, 11 A.M.–4 P.M. Mon.–Fri. and noon–5 P.M. Sat.–Sun. June–Aug.; 1–4 P.M. Wed.–Fri. and 11 A.M.–4 P.M. Sat.–Sun. Sept.–May, adults $3, seniors and students $2, children 7–12 $1). Driving here on multi-lane highways, past an enormous

shopping mall named in his honor, it's hard not to shudder at what's become of the bard's beloved Long Island.

For all the congestion surrounding it, the Walt Whitman House sits in serene isolation behind a tall hedge. Stepping into its snug, sunny hall is like stepping into a well-crafted poem. Whitman's father built this house, and everything within it is meticulously designed and constructed—from hand-hewn beams held together with wooden pegs, to innovative storage closets built into the fireplace walls.

Whitman only lived here until he was five, when his family moved to Brooklyn. But he came back to Long Island as a young man to teach school, and the museum does a good job of chronicling his entire life. A short movie covers the highlights of his career, while upstairs and in an interpretive center next door are exhibit rooms filled with his papers, early editions of *Leaves of Grass,* and his schoolmaster's desk.

To reach the Whitman House from Huntington, take Route 110 south and watch for Old Walt Whitman Road (not to be confused with Walt Whitman Road, which is another name for Route 110 south of Jericho Turnpike)—it's on the right about a half mile south of Jericho Turnpike.

Other Whitman Sites

Other sites connected with Walt Whitman are located throughout the West Hills region. Some are buildings, others are hills or hollows through which the poet liked to meander on his frequent trips back to the village of his birth. Ask at the Walt Whitman Birthplace for a copy of the booklet and trail map outlining these sites.

Accommodations and Food

The large, full-service **Melville Marriott** (1350 Old Walt Whitman Rd., Melville, 631/423-1600, $79–219 d) offers a glass-enclosed lobby, 370 rooms, indoor pool, fitness center, business center, and restaurant.

For Greek food or fresh fish, try the bustling

Mediterranean Snack Bar (360 New York Ave., 631/423-8982), where everything from the souvlaki dishes to soft-shell crabs are served with a Greek salad; average entrée $13. **Jonathan's Ristorante** (15 Wall St., 631/549-0055) is a bistro serving eclectic Italian fare, including a wide range of pastas; average entrées $17.

LLOYD NECK PENINSULA

The drive north of Huntington to the Lloyd Neck peninsula is exquisite, especially on a late spring day when the trees and grasslands are a pale lime green and the bay is a biting cobalt blue. The narrow, winding roads are flanked by low wooden-rail fences that suddenly give way to vistas of choppy seas specked with sailboats.

Joseph Lloyd Manor House

Nearing the peninsula on West Neck and Lloyd Harbor Roads, you'll pass by the Joseph Lloyd Manor House (1 Lloyd Lane Rd., at Lloyd Harbor Rd., 631/692-4664, www.splia.org, 1–5 P.M. Sat.–Sun. June–Oct., adults $3, seniors and children under 12 $1.50), an imposing white Colonial home overlooking Lloyd Harbor. Built in 1766 to replace an earlier Lloyd manor, the house is filled with antiques and hand-carved woodwork, while out back is a formal garden.

Now run by the Society for the Preservation of Long Island Antiquities, the house was once home to Jupiter Hammon, a slave who became the first published black poet in America. Hammon was taught to read in the manor's school and was allowed to use his master's library. His owners encouraged him to learn, and he published his first poem in 1760 at the age of 49. Later, at age 75, he wrote "An Address to the Negroes in the State of New York," in which he pointed out the irony of the American Revolution. That address may have been the impetus for New York State's 1799 law freeing slaves born after July 4, 1799, after they reached the age of 25 (females) or 28 (males).

Caumsett State Historic Park

Occupying most of the Lloyd Neck peninsula is wild Caumsett State Historic Park (37 Lloyd Harbor Rd., off West Neck Rd., 631/423-1770, dawn–dusk, $6–8 parking). No motor vehicles are allowed here, and no visitor facilities are available. To explore, you park your car in a wide grassy lot and then hike through meadows filled with wildflowers or along paths and dirt roads shrouded by tall, leafy trees.

One side of the 1,500-acre park abuts Long Island Sound and sports a pebbly beach from which anglers cast their lines. The beach—one of the few wild public beaches on the North Shore—is an easy, two-mile walk from the parking lot. Near the beach is a salt marsh that's excellent for bird-watching.

On another side of the park is a complex of buildings constructed in the 1920s by Marshall Field III, the grandson of the founder of the department store. Caumsett State Historic Park was once Field's estate. He built it to be self-sufficient, complete with its own electricity, dairy, and vegetable farm. The buildings are not open to the public; some fields are still being cultivated.

Target Rock National Wildlife Refuge

Just east of Caumsett, on Target Rock Road off Lloyd Harbor Road, is Target Rock National Wildlife Refuge (631/271-2409, dawn–dusk, $5 parking in summer). The refuge is laced with nature trails, and is especially interesting in May when an enormous number of warblers stop over during their spring migration. The refuge is also known for its rhododendron and azalea gardens.

NORTHPORT AND VICINITY

One of the prettiest undiscovered towns along the North Shore is Northport, just off Route 10. The downtown centers on a picturesque marina with a shoreside park and bandstand, and an old-fashioned Main Street lined with shops and 19th-century homes. Recreational boaters frequent Northport, but it is still blessedly free of commercialism and tourist kitsch.

Once known as Cowharbor, Northport was purchased by the English from the

Matinecock Indians in 1656. By the early 1800s, the village had become an important shipbuilding center; 170 vessels were constructed here between 1820 and 1884. In the early 1900s, Northport was a summer resort "known as one of the most healthful in the State," according to one guidebook of the day.

The town's history is chronicled in the surprisingly large **Northport Historical Society Museum** (215 Main St., 631/757-9859, www.northporthistorical.org, 1–4:30 P.M. Tues.–Sat, admission by donation).

Suffolk County Vanderbilt Museum and Planetarium

In Centerport, just west of Northport, is the Vanderbilt Museum (180 Little Neck Rd., off Rte. 25A, 631/854-5555, www.vanderbiltmuseum.org, noon–4 or 5 P.M. Tues.–Sun, also Mon. in summer, adults $7, seniors and students $6, children under 12 $3), a storybook Spanish Baroque mansion built in the 1910s by William K. Vanderbilt II, the great-grandson of Commodore Vanderbilt. Two huge black eagles that once sat atop Grand Central Station mark the estate's entrance, while inside the 24-room mansion are such odd treasures as suits of armor and Napoleon's bed and desk.

Vanderbilt was an eccentric who liked to disguise himself and go into town to drink with the locals. A man of many interests, he was especially fascinated with marinelife and collected hundreds of specimens which he housed in his own enormous **Marine Museum.** Still located on the estate's grounds, the museum is now a musty affair stuffed with fishes, Egyptian mummies, and shrunken heads.

Also on the estate's grounds is the **Vanderbilt Planetarium.** One of the country's largest planetariums, the facility puts on sky shows (admission $3) filled with more than 11,000 stars.

Eatons Neck

North of town on Route 10 is a long, skinny spit leading to windswept Eatons Neck. Along one side is a pebbly beach frequented by fisherfolk; along the other is Northport Bay, often filled with pleasure craft. All around are the blue, blue waters of the sea. Though it can get crowded during the summer, Eatons Neck is more often a lonely spot good for strolling or bird-watching.

Food

Show Win (325 Fort Salonga Rd., Northport, 631/261-6622) offers some of the best sushi rolls on Long Island; on the menu are almost 50 different kinds. For traditional German cuisine, try **Pumpernickel's** (640 Main St., 631/757-7959), a Northport institution. Live music is often featured on the weekends; average entrée $16.

EAST TO ST. JAMES
Sunken Meadow State Park

The main attraction at the popular, 1,266-acre Sunken Meadow State Park (intersection of Rte. 25A and Sunken Meadow Pkwy., near Kings Park, 631/269-4333, dawn–dusk, $6–8 parking) is a mile-long beach, often packed in summer with thousands of sun-worshippers baking, swimming, napping, and playing. Also within the park are three golf courses, lots of hiking trails, a salt marsh, and a small natural history museum.

The Long Island Greenbelt Trail runs the 34-mile width of Long Island from Heckscher State Park to Sunken Meadow (see *Long Island Greenbelt Trail* under *Bay Shore and Vicinity* for more information).

St. James

Continuing east on Route 25A, through the large, traffic-clogged town of Smithtown, you'll soon come to tiny St. James, whose biggest claim to fame is the **St. James General Store** (516 Moriches Rd., at Harbor Hill Rd., 631/854-3740, 10 A.M.–5 P.M. daily Mar.–Dec., 10 A.M.–5 P.M. Wed.–Sun. Jan.–Feb.). Listed with the National Register of Historic Places and used continuously since 1857, the store is a creaky, hodgepodge affair stuffed to the bursting point with old-fashioned candy,

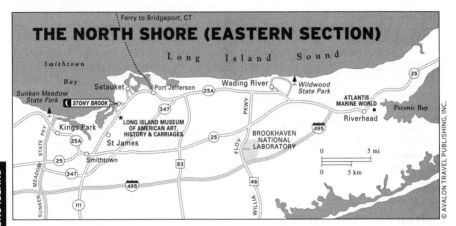

scented soaps, historic postcards, and the like. Out front is a wooden cigar-store Indian.

Also in St. James is the family-owned **Wicks Farm and Garden** (445 North Country Rd. [Rte. 25A], 631/584-5727). At 200 acres, Wicks is one of the larger produce farms dotting Suffolk County, and is unique in one respect—looming over its greenhouses is a black-caped 25-foot-high witch, her crooked nose and broomstick outlined against the sky. It's not to be missed by lovers of roadside architecture.

◖ STONY BROOK

Built on a hill sloping down to the water is the restored 18th-century village of Stony Brook. Though a popular tourist destination, complete with shopping malls and an ultraclean feel, Stony Brook has managed to retain a rural character and is an enjoyable town in which to meander.

Much of Stony Brook's charm is due to a man named Ward Melville, owner of the Thom McAn shoe company. Back in the 1940s, Melville—concerned about encroaching suburbia—had the village rebuilt along historical lines while at the same time successfully fighting for strict zoning codes. He paid for much of the rebuilding himself.

Along Main Street are the harbor and Village Center, where well-marked signs point the way to shops and historic sites. To one side is an old **U.S. post office,** equipped with a mechanical eagle that flaps its wings every hour on the hour. To the other side is the **Three Village Inn** (150 Main St.), built in 1751. Once the

the post office on Main Street in Stony Brook

home of Capt. Jonas Smith—Long Island's first millionaire—the rambling white house is now a historic inn.

Beyond the post office is the **All Souls' Episcopal Church,** built by architect Stanford White in 1889. Pitched on the steep slope of a small hill, the tiny church—complete with zigzagging steps and a narrow steeple—has a fairy-tale quality, as if it were built for elves.

Continue walking a few blocks past the church to wide, dark Mill Pond and the gray-shingled **Grist Mill** (Harbor Rd. off Main St., 631/751-2244, noon–4:30 P.M. Wed.–Sun. June–Aug., noon–4:30 P.M. Sat.–Sun. Apr.– May and Sept.–Dec., adults $2, children $1). Built in 1751, the mill has been restored and still grinds corn.

Walking-tour maps of Stony Brook are available in the Three Village Inn, in many of the stores, and at the Ward Melville Heritage Center (111 Main St., 631/751-2244, www.stony-brookvillage.com), a few doors down from the post office.

Long Island Museum of American Art, History, and Carriages

Formerly known as the Museums at Stony Brook, this nine-acre complex (1208 Rte. 25A, 631/751-0066, www.longislandmuseum.org, 10 A.M.–5 P.M. Wed.–Sat., noon–5 P.M. Sun., adults $7, seniors $6, students and children 6–17 $3) on the outskirts of town focuses on American history and art. Foremost among its museum buildings is the renowned Carriage House, which contains about 90 horse-drawn vehicles ranging from hand-painted coaches and fire-fighting equipment to elaborate sleighs and a very rare Roma wagon. Roma wagons seldom survive because of the Roma custom of burying all of a person's possessions after his or her death—even wagons.

The Art Museum holds both changing exhibits and a large collection of works by William Sidney Mount, a 19th-century African-American painter from Stony Brook who depicted rural Long Island life. The Bayman's Art Gallery of history features hand-carved an-

tique decoys and 15 miniature period rooms. Also on site are a blacksmith's shop, barn, one-room schoolhouse, and other 19th-century buildings.

Accommodations and Food

The lovely **❰ Three Village Inn** (150 Main St., 631/751-0555, www.threevillageinn.com, $129–209 d) offers period antiques, fireplaces, ceiling beams, and plenty of Colonial atmosphere in a setting overlooking the water. Some of the rooms are housed in the historic, white-clapboard main building; others in an attractive modern wing. An adjoining restaurant specializes in old-fashioned American dishes such as New England lobster pie and clam chowder, served by waiters in Colonial garb; dinner entrées, $17–36.

A good restaurant choice for families is the **Brook House** (in the Village Center, off Main St., 631/751-4617), serving everything from burgers and sandwiches ($6–8) to dinner entrées such as steak and chicken ($13–15).

SETAUKET

Along with St. James and Stony Brook, Setauket is one of the communities historically referred to as the "Three Villages." All are filled with shady winding roads, historic homes, meadows dusted with wildflowers, and peaceful ponds.

During the Revolutionary War, the Three Villages served as a center of espionage for George Washington. Members of the Setauket Spy Ring, as it later became known, were recruited by a friend of Nathan Hale's who was from Setauket. The ring's function was to warn Washington of enemy ships entering the Sound. One of the patriot spies was a housewife named Anna Strong, whose clothesline was used to send messages.

Strong's house no longer stands, but you can get a sense of early Long Island life at the **Thompson House** (93 N. Country Rd., 631/692-4664, www.splia.org, 1–5 P.M. Sat.– Sun. June–Oct., 1–5 P.M. Fri. July–Aug., adults $3, seniors and children $1.50), now owned by

LONG ISLAND

COURTESY OF EAGLE REALTY HOLDINGS, INC.

Three Village Inn

the Society for the Preservation of Long Island Antiquities. Built circa 1770, the gray-shingled saltbox contains a fine collection of early island furniture. Out back is a Colonial herb garden and the Thompson family cemetery.

PORT JEFFERSON

Another harbor town, located just beyond Stony Brook, is Port Jefferson. Once a thriving shipbuilding community, and then home to several lace factories and gravel pits, Port Jefferson today caters mostly to the tourist trade. It has a rawer and more windswept feel than does Stony Brook. Witness the town's many visiting Harleys—Port Jeff has long been a favorite stop among touring motorcyclists.

Downtown offers several small tourist-oriented malls as well as some one-of-a-kind shops, including **Good Times Bookshop** (150 E. Main St., 631/928-2664), carrying about 20,000 scarce and out-of-print titles, and **Village Chairs & Wares** (402 Main St., 631/331-5791), which specializes in handmade reproduction chairs and tables.

Also downtown are a number of historic homes. Most are privately owned, but one that is open to the public is the **Mather House Museum** (115 Prospect St., at High St., 631/473-2665, 1–4 P.M. Tues.–Wed. and Sat.–Sun. June–Sept., suggested donation $4), once owned by a shipbuilder. Inside, find an eclectic collection of 19th-century garments, Native American artifacts, and model boats, while out back are herb gardens, a marine barn, and a crafts house.

The ferry to Bridgeport, Connecticut (631/473-0286) leaves from the Port Jefferson docks. For brochures and a map of the village, stop into the **Port Jefferson Chamber of Commerce** (118 W. Broadway [Rte. 25A], 631/473-1414, www.portjeffchamber.com, 10 A.M.–4 P.M. Mon.–Fri. year-round, noon–4 P.M. Sat.–Sun. June–Sept.).

Accommodations and Food

The large and always bustling **(** **Danford's on the Sound** (25 E. Broadway, 631/928-5200,

THE PINE BARRENS

Much of the eastern end of Long Island, from just east of Port Jefferson to Hampton Bays, is covered by a 100,000-acre pine-barren wilderness. Five times larger than Manhattan, it sits over what is said to be the purest underground drinking-water supply in the state. In its scruffy wooded growth, dominated by pitch pine and scrub oak, are several rare plant and animal species, including unusual stands of dwarf pine.

For many years, the pine barrens were at the center of an intense environmental debate that pitted conservationists against builders and local government officials. In 1989, an environmental group, the Long Island Pine Barrens Society, sued Suffolk County for approving building projects in the wilderness area without studying the environmental impact. The New York State Court ruled that no study was required but said that the state needed to draw up a plan to protect the area. A Central Pine Barrens Joint Policy and Planning Commission was created, and in 1994, they proposed establishing a 53,000-acre core area where building would be banned, surrounded by a 47,000-acre area open to controlled development.

The plan became law in July 1995—a major environmental victory. The Pine Barrens are now New York's third forest preserve, following the Adirondacks and the Catskills.

To access a five-mile trail that leads through the pine barrens, head south of the Riverhead Traffic Circle on Route 104 for about two miles and watch for signs. The trail should be avoided during the hunting season, October–February. For more information, contact the Long Island Pine Barrens Society (P.O. Box 5636, Hauppauge 11799, 631/369-0753). Or, stop by the Pine Barrens Trail Information Center (631/369-9768, 9 A.M.–5 P.M. Fri.-Mon. June-Oct.), a quarter-mile north of the Long Island Expressway Exit 70 in Manorville.

www.danfords.com) serves as a de facto anchor for downtown Port Jefferson. Most of the rooms have balconies and views of the water ($159–389 d). The inn's restaurant, American Bistro, also overlooking the water, serves seafood and contemporary American fare. During warm weather, an outside deck is opened up; average dinner entrée $22.

The casual, laid-back **Village Way** (106 Main St., 631/928-3395) is a Port Jefferson institution. On the menu are seafood and pasta entrées, sandwiches, and burgers.

EAST TO WADING RIVER

East of Port Jefferson, the North Shore becomes flatter and more rural. Fruit and vegetable farms replace suburban lawns, small empty roads replace congested highways. Pale green fields and lumbering farm vehicles are everywhere.

Wildwood State Park

Just northeast of Wading River, off Route 25A along Hulse Landing Road, is Wildwood State Park (631/929-4314, dawn–dusk, $6–8 parking). Surrounded by farm country, Wildwood is blissfully empty during the off-season, but crowded during the summer. Within its 737 acres are nearly a mile and a half of beach, 10 miles of hiking trails, bathhouses, picnic areas, ball fields, refreshment stands, and a 322-site campground. For campground reservations, call 800/456-CAMP.

RIVERHEAD

Riverhead lies on the shores of Peconic Bay, right between the North and South Forks. The Suffolk County seat since 1727, Riverhead was once a thriving commercial center that benefited from the area's many farms. In more recent years, it has suffered its share of economic depression, but is now experiencing something of a renaissance, thanks in large part to its spiffy new aquarium, the Atlantis Marine World. The downtown is also home to a number of lovely old brick buildings, while its revitalized waterfront is a good place for a summer stroll.

Atlantis Marine World

This large, state-of-the-art aquarium (431 E. Main St., 631/208-9200, www.atlantismarineworld.com, 10 A.M.–5 P.M. daily, adults $15.50, seniors and children 3–11 $13.50) houses everything from native Long Island fishes to moray eels, Pacific octopuses, piranhas, stingrays, and seals. Near the entrance reigns a figure of Poseidon, king of the sea, while further on is a large live coral reef, awhirl with colorful tropical fish; an underwater cavern that's home to more than a dozen sharks, and about 80 other exhibits. Visitors can also embark on a simulated submarine dive and take in a seal show.

The aquarium was built around the **Riverhead Foundation for Marine Research** (467 E. Main St., 631/369-9840, www.riverheadfoundation.org), which maintains several exhibits on site. Among them are a center for rehabilitating injured seals, sea turtles, and other marinelife; and a touch-tank where children can handle starfish, crabs, snails, and small fish. The Riverhead Foundation also offers seal-watching cruises that depart from Point Lookout on the South Shore (see *Freeport*) and naturalist cruises down the Peconic River.

Suffolk County Historical Society

At the other end of Main Street is the Suffolk County Historical Society (300 W. Main St. [Rte. 25], 631/727-2881, www.riverheadli.com/museum, 12:30–4:30 P.M. Tues.–Sat., admission by donation). An excellent place in which to get a sense of Suffolk County's past, this large, rambling museum is filled with eclectic treasures. Among them are a good-size collection of Indian artifacts, Colonial furniture and ceramics, and some nice examples of early crafts. Also on site is an excellent bookstore.

Recreation

West of town is **Splish Splash** (2549 Middle Country Rd., 631/727-3600), a 40-acre water theme park with a wave pool, 16 water slides, four kiddie pools, a kiddie car wash, and tube rides. The park is open weekends and holidays mid-May–mid-June, and daily mid-June–Labor Day (adults $27, children under 48 inches $20, children under 3 free, parking $7). To reach Splish Splash directly from the LIE, take Exit 72 and watch for signs.

The North Fork and Shelter Island

The North Fork is: fertile farms, rolling vineyards, pebble-strewn beaches, one-stoplight towns, white-steepled churches, Colonial saltboxes, village greens. Like the better-known South Fork across Great Peconic Bay, the North Fork was first settled in 1640 by colonists from New England, and that heritage flavors everything, from the look of the villages to the independent mindset of the people. Unlike the South Fork, the North Fork is still predominantly rural, with a correspondingly smaller number of tourist hotels and "attractions." This is changing, but for the moment at least, the North Fork is still sleepy, friendly, and unpretentious.

You can easily explore the North Fork in a day, although the area is so achingly beautiful—

especially near the windswept beaches of Orient Point—that it's well worth lingering a while longer. Highlights include the historic villages of Cutchogue, Southold, and Orient, the bustling harbor town of Greenport, and four-mile-long Orient Beach. The region is also known for its many vineyards, most located in the vicinity of Cutchogue.

Accommodation options on the North Fork are largely limited to simple beachfront resort motels and B&Bs. Shelter Island has several historic inns. As in other shore areas, rates tend to be on the high side in season (Memorial Day–Labor Day), reasonable the rest of the year. Two- or three-night minimum stays are often required in summer, especially on weekends.

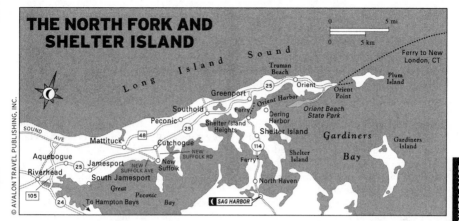

THE NORTH FORK AND SHELTER ISLAND

© AVALON TRAVEL PUBLISHING, INC.

LONG ISLAND

SOUND AVENUE SIGHTS

Heading east onto the North Fork via the northern route of Sound Avenue (which turns into Route 48), you'll soon come to **Briermere Farms** (4414 Sound Ave., at Rte. 105, 631/722-3931, www.briermere.com). Especially well known for its homemade pies, Briermere features about 15 different varieties on any given day, ranging from the standard blueberry and peach to the more unusual blackberry-apple and strawberry-rhubarb.

Entering Wine Country reads a sign, and almost immediately you'll spy **Palmer Vineyards** (108 Sound Ave., 631/722-WINE, www.palmervineyards.com, 11 A.M.–5 P.M. daily). One of Long Island's largest vineyards, it attracts close to 500 visitors on a summer's day. Palmer offers self-guided tours, a tasting room made up to look like an English pub, and an outdoor deck overlooking its vineyards.

Near the intersection of Sound Avenue and Herricks Lane is the **Hallockville Museum Farm and Folklife Center** (6038 Sound Ave. [Rte. 48], 631/298-5292, www.hallockville.com, 11 A.M.–4 P.M. Tues.–Sat., adults $7, seniors and children 6–12 $4), a 102-acre farm that was owned by the Hallock family for over 200 years. Now a museum listed on the National Register of Historic Places, Hallockville centers on a 1765 homestead, a large barn, a smokehouse, and a shoemaker's shop

(in which one Capt. Zachariah Hallock made over 1,700 pairs of shoes between the years 1771 and 1820). The museum also stages frequent crafts demonstrations, festivals, and workshops.

ROUTE 25 TO CUTCHOGUE

Heading onto the North Fork via the southern route—Route 25, also known as Main Road in many spots—you'll pass one pretty little town after another. **Aquebogue** and **Jamesport** are dotted with small stores and a number of good lunch spots. The **Modern Snack Bar** (628 Main Rd. [Rte. 25], Aquebogue, 631/722-3655) is a family-style roadside diner that has been offering home cooking since 1950; average main dish $9. The ◖ **Jamesport Country Kitchen** (1601 Main Rd. [Rte. 25], Jamesport, 631/722-3537) specializes in North Fork produce and wine. Everything is fresh, with entrées ranging from burgers to grilled salmon. The place can get packed in summer, and reservations are recommended; average dinner entrée $15.

New Suffolk

Worth the short detour is New Suffolk Avenue, leading south off Route 25 at Mattituck to New Suffolk. To the left are lime-green wetlands, specked with osprey nests; to the right, the shimmering blue and white waters of Great

Peconic Bay. New Suffolk itself is a sleepy place equipped with a tiny post office and a wide beach. Back in the 1800s, however, New Suffolk—then known as Robin's Island Neck—was a busy port. In 1899–1900, the U.S. Navy tested its first commissioned submarine here.

Cutchogue

One of the prettiest of the North Fork hamlets is Cutchogue, filled with white churches, leafy trees, and weathered, shingled homes. The town—named after the Indian word for "principal place"—centers on the village green, in the middle of which are clustered a group of historic wooden buildings (631/734-7122, 1–4 P.M. Sat.–Mon. July–Aug., call for off-season hours, adults $2, children $1) operated by the Cutchogue–New Suffolk Historical Council.

By far the most interesting of the group is the **Old House,** which dates back to 1649. Dark and very cozy inside, it's outfitted with all the luxuries of its day, including wooden paneling, leaded glass windows, and a fluted chimney. The house was "lost" for close to 100 years, but was rediscovered in the 1930s by a WPA worker who noticed its unusual chimney.

Next to the Old House is the 1840 **Old Schoolhouse Museum** and the **Wickham Farmhouse,** equipped with furniture and farm implements from the early 1700s. Across the street is the **Village Library,** Main Rd. (Rte. 25), housed in a lovely New England–style church. The church was built in 1862 because of a schism within its congregation. The Presbyterian minister was an ardent abolitionist who preached against slavery week after week until the church elders got tired of it and threw him out. The minister then gathered his followers together and built the new church.

Near the village green is the vintage, chrome-laden **Cutchogue Diner** (Main Rd. [Rte. 25], 631/734-9056). Especially good are the pancakes and meatloaf; average main meal $7. Also nearby is **Braun's Seafood** (Main Rd. [Rte. 25], 631/734-6700), where you can purchase clam pies, an East End specialty (these can't be eaten on the spot; they must be cooked).

WINE COUNTRY

Cutchogue—along with Peconic, just down the road—is the center of Long Island's wine-producing country. In general, the wineries are open for tastings daily 11 A.M.–5 P.M., but during the off-season, it's best to call in advance. Tours can usually be arranged by appointment.

Off Route 25 east of Cutchogue are **Peconic Bay Vineyard** (631/734-7361, www.peconicbaywinery.com), which produces an especially fine chardonnay; **Bedell Cellars** (631/734-7537, www.bedellcellars.com), a small but highly regarded winery that has won a number of awards; and **Pugliese Vineyards** (631/734-4057, www.puglisevineyards.com), which features a lovely collection of hand-painted bottles containing a chardonnay, blanc de blanc champagne, cabernet sauvignon, and merlot.

Along Route 25 closer to Peconic is the 300-acre **Pindar Vineyards** (631/734-6200, www.pindar.net), the largest vineyard on the island. Over 20 different wines are produced here annually, and tours run continuously throughout the day. Also popular is the nearby **Lenz Winery** (Rte. 25, 631/734-6010, www.lenzwine.com), a 60-acre vineyard with a striking modern main building.

To the north, along Route 48 in Cutchogue, are **Castello di Borghese-Hargrave Vineyard** (631/734-5111, www.castellodiborghese.com), the oldest vineyard on the island, founded in 1973; and **Bidwell Vineyards** (631/734-5200).

SOUTHHOLD AND VICINITY

Settled in 1640, Southold is one of the oldest communities in New York State. The earliest white settlers to arrive here came from New Haven, Connecticut.

Southold Historical Society Museums

Standing testimony to the town's long past is a sleepy museum complex smack in the middle of the low-key downtown. Among many historic buildings here are the weathered 1750 **Thomas Moore House,** the lavishly furnished

Victorian **Currie-Bell House,** and the lovely, hand-hewn **Pine Neck Barn.** Also on the museum grounds are a working blacksmith shop, a buttery, and a millinery filled with an assortment of 19th- and early 20th-century hats.

A map and more information about the museum complex can be picked up in the 19th-century **Prince Building** (Main Rd. [Rte. 25], where the Southold Historical Society (631/765-5500) is headquartered. Also in the building is the **Museum Shop,** selling gifts and antiques. The complex is open July–Labor Day, Wednesday, Saturday, and Sunday 1–4 P.M.; suggested donation $2. The museum shop is open weekdays 9:30 A.M.–2:30 P.M.

Horton Point Lighthouse

Just north of downtown is the striking Horton Point Lighthouse (631/765-5500 or 631/765-2101, 11:30 A.M.–4 P.M. Sat.–Sun. June–Oct., adults $2), which stands high on a bluff at the end of Lighthouse Road. The first lighthouse on this site was commissioned by George Washington in 1790. The current

lighthouse was built in 1857 and is still operational. Painted in stark white and surrounded by rhododendrons, the building overlooks a lonely stretch of beach.

Tours of the lighthouse take visitors through the keeper's quarters and the working light tower. Downstairs is a small museum filled with artifacts, paintings, and "treasures" from sunken ships.

Southold Indian Museum

Run by the Long Island chapter of the New York State Archeological Association, this museum (1080 Main Bayview Rd., 631/765-5577, 1:30–4:30 P.M. Sat.–Sun. July–Aug., 1:30–4:30 P.M. Sun. off season, adults $2, children 50 cents) houses an extensive array of Algonquin artifacts. Here you'll find the country's largest collection of Native American pottery (from 3000 B.C. to Colonial times).

Accommodations and Food

Housed in a Victorian farmhouse with several fireplaces, four guest rooms (all with private

Horton Point Lighthouse

baths), and lots of antiques is the **(Home Port Bed & Breakfast** (2500 Peconic Ln., Peconic, 631/765-1435, www.homeport-bandb.com, $200–225 d May–Oct.; $150–175 d Nov.–Apr.). The guesthouse is surrounded by woods; next door is a park equipped with tennis courts and a running track.

Offering great views of Peconic Bay, along with creative seafood dishes prepared with fresh local ingredients, is the popular **Seafood Barge** (Port of Egypt Marina, 62980 Main Rd., 631/765-3010); average entrée $20.

GREENPORT

The principal commercial center on the North Fork is the bustling town of Greenport, laid out in neat squares that slope down to the harbor. The main streets are lined with restaurants and shops—some tourist-oriented, some not—while the harbor is always full of fishing boats and pleasure craft. **Mitchell Park** on the waterfront is a great place from which to watch all the maritime activity. Children will enjoy a ride on the 1920s **Mitchell Park Carousel** (10 A.M.–10 P.M. daily June–Sept., ride $1).

Greenport has been a boating community since before the Revolutionary War. In the 1700s, cargo ships from the West Indies docked here to unload molasses and rum. Later, the port became a center for whaling and the oyster trade. Even today, an estimated two-thirds of Greenport's population earns its living from boats and related industries.

At the end of Main Street is Claudio's Restaurant (see *Food,* below) and **Preston's Outfitters** (Main St. Wharf, 631/477-1990), a not-to-be-missed barn of a store where you can buy everything from rope and paint to paintings and Top-Sider shoes. Preston's was established in 1883.

Docked just outside Preston's is the **Mary E.** (631/477-8966 or 631/369-0468), a historic 53-foot schooner that offers two-and-a-half-hour cruises of the bay May–Oct. (adults $30, children under 12 $12).

Museums

The **East End Seaport Maritime Museum** (end of 3rd St., 631/477-2100, www.eastendsea-port.org, 11 A.M.–5 P.M. Wed.–Mon. June–Sept., weekends in May, free admission) is loaded with artifacts from the fishing and boatbuilding industries. Changing exhibits focus on such subjects as women and the sea, and yacht racing.

Railroad buffs will want to visit the **Railroad Museum of Long Island** (440 4th St., 631/477-0439 or 631/727-7920, 11 A.M.–4 P.M. Sat.–Sun. June–Oct., adults $1, children 50 cents). Housed in what was once a freight station, the museum traces the history of railroading on the island and holds a 20-foot model of the Greenport freight yard as it looked in 1955.

Camping and Accommodations

Camping is available at the 150-site **Eastern Long Island Kampground** (690 Queen St., 631/477-0022). On site are a camp store, laundry facility, and children's playground.

The main building at the **(Townsend Manor Inn** (714 Main St., 631/477-2000, www.townsendmanorinn.com, $125–250 d in summer, $80–185 d off-season) is a historic 1835 Greek Revival house complete with a restaurant, old-fashioned cocktail lounge, and cozy living room. Guest rooms are located in several modern additions, and in between is a pool.

Along the beach in the Greenport area, you'll find the popular '50s-era **Silver Sands Motel** (Rte. 25 at Silvermere Rd., 631/477-0011, www.silversands-motel.com, $175 d in summer, when week-long reservations are usually required), painted bright pink and blue. Set on a quarter-mile of private beach, it offers a variety of accommodations ranging from motel rooms to apartments and beach cottages. Also a good choice, with a variety of accommodation options, is the smaller **Sunset Motel** (62005 Rte. 48, 631/477-1776, www.sunset-greenport.com, $145–185 d in season, $100–145 d off season). At the very, very long **(Sound View Inn** (57185 North Rd. [Rte. 48], 631/477-1910, www.soundviewinn.com, $195–225 d in mid-summer, $125–175 d in March–early June and Sept.–Oct.), also on the beach, all the rooms have balconies, and some have kitchenettes. On the grounds are tennis courts and a pool. All three motels are closed in winter.

Food

Dominating the harbor area is 🄲 **Claudio's** (111 Main St., 631/477-0715), a huge, rambling seafood restaurant; average entrée $22. First established by a Portuguese sailor in 1870, Claudio's bills itself as the "oldest same family owned restaurant in the United States." Inside is much heavy carved wood, stained glass, and an enormous bar brought to the restaurant by barge from a New York City hotel in 1885. Claudio's also runs the less expensive **Claudio's Clam Bar and Wharf** (631/477-1889), which features live bands on summer weekends; average main dish $12.

In the Brewer Yacht Yard, find **Antares Cafe** (2530 Manhasset Ave., 631/477-8839), serving New American cuisine; average entrée $19. **Aldo's** (103-5 Front St., 631/477-1699) is a casual bistro serving breakfast, lunch, and dinner. Fresh breads are featured for breakfast; French/Mediterranean peasant food for lunch and dinner. Average dinner entrée $15.

For a light bite, step into the high-ceilinged 🄲 **Greenport Tea Company** (119A Main St., 631/477-8744), where tea is served in china cups from vintage tea pots. On the menu are clam pie, scones, and finger sandwiches.

ORIENT

At the far, far end of the North Fork is Orient, one of the most glorious spots on the island. Only a few buildings dot this narrow windswept piece of land. Instead you'll find osprey nests, gentle beaches, and a tiny historical town.

In the 1930s, the WPA guide described the village of Orient in terms that still apply today: "The little weathered shingle houses, few more than one-and-a-half stories high, sit primly behind picket fences. In sun or storm the Atlantic winds roll in. ..."

To reach Orient proper, you cross a narrow isthmus. To the left are crescent-shaped Truman Beach and Long Island Sound; to the right, Orient Harbor and Gardiners Bay.

The town centers around an old-fashioned post office and the **Orient Country Store.** The former is still equipped with turn-of-the-century stamp windows, while the latter sells sandwiches at bargain prices.

Historical Sites

At the end of Village Lane is the **Oysterponds Historical Society** (1555 Village Ln., 631/323-2480, 2–5 P.M. Thurs. and Sat.–Sun. July–Sept., adults $5), a group of seven well-preserved historic buildings. The **Webb House** is a pre–Revolutionary War inn, while the **Village House** is a 19th-century home containing memorabilia from the 1800s. Back then, Orient was a popular resort with two big hotels. Temporary exhibits are showcased in the **Schoolhouse Building,** the only building open year-round.

If you continue down Village Lane to King Street and turn onto Narrow Avenue, you'll come to an early slaves' burial ground, where 20 slaves are buried along with Dr. Seth Tuthill and his wife Maria. "It was [the Tuthills'] wish that they be buried with their former slaves" reads a plaque near the cemetery, which occupies a pretty spot overlooking the sea.

Orient Point and Beach

A few miles beyond Orient, at the very tip of the North Fork, is Orient Point, where ferries dock on their way to and from New London, Connecticut. Abutting the point is Orient Beach State Park (N. County Rd., off Rte. 25, 631/323-2440, dawn–dusk, $6–8 parking), one of the finest beaches on Long Island. Stretching west over a long finger of land, the 357-acre park features endless miles of white, ocean-washed sands. It's especially popular among bird-watchers and nature-lovers. Facilities include a bathhouse, refreshment stand, horseshoe court, and hiking trails.

From Orient Point and the park, you have a good view of **Gardiners Island.** Privately owned by the Gardiner family for over three centuries, the island was given to Lion Gardiner by King Charles I of England in 1639. Lion Gardiner was an engineer, diplomat, and statesman whose daughter, Elizabeth, was the first English child born in New York State.

Today Gardiners Island is the only known English land grant of its kind in the United States that remains in the hands of its original family. On its premises—which are strictly off-limits to the public—stand a manor house, windmill, and farm.

SHELTER ISLAND

In the middle of the bay between the North and South Forks is Shelter Island, a quiet retreat of wooded hills, uncrowded beaches, and expensive vacation homes, some of which date back to the Victorian era. Shelter Island has an exclusive air about it, due partly to its moneyed population, partly to the fact that it can be reached only by ferry. The high cost of the very short ferry rides—$9–10 one-way—also helps keep out the hoi polloi.

The island's first European resident was Nathaniel Sylvester, one of four businessmen who bought the island in 1651. Thanks to Sylvester, the island subsequently became a haven for Quakers fleeing persecution in Massachusetts. Sylvester gave the Quakers shelter—hence the island's name—and allowed them to practice their religion.

Sights

For the day visitor, Shelter Island has few especially compelling attractions, but it is the sort of place that's fun to explore without any particular destination in mind. Many of the roads wander past sun-splashed meadows and bays, dark woods and historic homes. Near the North Ferry dock is **Shelter Island Heights,** filled with steep streets and Victorian-era gingerbread cottages. Across the bay from the Heights is **Dering Harbor,** boasting a number of impressive mansions along Shore Road. Dering Harbor is the smallest incorporated village in New York State, holding just 32 houses and less than 30 year-round residents (some homes are occupied only in the summer, when the population swells to about 90).

History buffs might also want to stop at

Havens House (16 South Ferry Rd. [Rte. 114], 631/749-0025, 1–5 P.M. Fri.–Sun. June–Sept., admission by donation), a 1743 home on the National Register of Historic Places. The five-room house, run by the Shelter Island Historical Society, is outfitted with period furnishings and features a nice collection of antique dolls and toys.

Mashomack Preserve

Shelter Island does have one major treasure—Mashomack Preserve (79 S. Ferry Rd., 631/749-1001, 9 A.M.–4 or 5 P.M. daily, adults $2, children $1), operated by the Nature Conservancy. Occupying nearly a third of the island, the preserve spreads out over 2,000-plus acres of oak woodlands, marshes, freshwater ponds, tidal creeks, and shoreline. Within its confines is one of the East Coast's largest concentrations of nesting osprey, along with everything from ibis and hummingbirds to harbor seals and terrapins. Nature trails and hikes 1.5–11 miles in length meander through the preserve. The entrance to the preserve is located about a mile from the South Ferry dock.

Accommodations and Food

Built on bluffs overlooking Coecles Inlet is the 1929 **Ram's Head Inn** (Ram Island Dr., 631/749-0811, www.shelterislandinns.com/ramshead, $175–315 d in summer, with breakfast, about a third less off-season), boasting its own private beach, small boats, tennis courts, restaurant, and wide porch complete with wicker furniture. Most of the 17 rooms are filled with lots of light and simple antiques. Lunch and dinner is served in a high-ceilinged room hung with paintings; average dinner entrée $20.

In Shelter Island Heights is the friendly, turn-of-the-century **House on Chase Creek** (3 Locust Ave., 631/749-4379, www.chase-creek.com, $110–215 d summer; $65–175 d off-season), offering three comfortable guest rooms. Also in town find the **Dory** (Bridge St., 631/749-8871), serving simple seafood dishes on a outdoors deck during the summer.

INFORMATION AND SERVICES

The **North Fork Tourist Information Center** (www.northfork.org) operates two separate branches. One is just east of Mattituck (Main Road [Rte. 25], 631/298-5757, 10 A.M.–4 P.M. daily July–Aug., 10 A.M.–4 P.M. Thurs.–Sun. Apr.–June and Sept.–Nov.). The other is about one mile west of Greenport (Main Road, 631/477-1383, 10 A.M.–4 P.M. daily July–Aug., 10 A.M.–4 P.M. Fri.–Mon. Apr.–June and Sept.–Nov.).

GETTING THERE AND AROUND

Two major roads traverse the North Fork. Route 25 to the south is the more popular route and can get congested on summer weekends. Sound Avenue/Route 48 to the north offers a good alternative.

To reach Shelter Island from the North Fork, take the North Ferry (631/749-0139, www.northferry.com), which leaves from Route 114 at the foot of 3rd Street in Greenport. From the South Fork, take the South Ferry (631/749-1200, www.southferry.com), which leaves from Route 114 in North Haven, about three miles north of Sag Harbor. Both ferries operate every 10–15 minutes from about 6 A.M. to midnight, and cost $9–10 one-way for a car and driver, plus $1 for each additional passenger. Less expensive round-trip tickets to and from Greenport or to and from North Haven are available ($12–13) but cannot be applied to a trip that combines the two ferry services.

LONG ISLAND

The South Shore

Like the North Shore, the South Shore is unbearably congested near New York City. Unlike the North Shore, the South Shore has few isolated peninsulas or moneyed ex-estates to escape to. Much of the South Shore is composed of bumper-to-bumper working- and middle-class communities.

What the South Shore does have, however, just off its coast, is a long line of barrier islands lined with beaches, beaches, beaches. The South Shore is home to some of the longest, widest, whitest beaches in the world, stretching out for miles and miles against the pounding surf of the Atlantic. Nearest the city are Lido Beach, Long Beach, and the famed Jones Beach, followed by the beaches of Fire Island, and the beaches of the South Fork.

FREEPORT

Heading into Nassau County on the Sunrise Highway (Route 27), you'll soon come to Freeport, a bustling fishing and boating community that's the largest town on the South Shore. Freeport's most famous native son was Guy Lombardo, and a long avenue named in his honor runs through downtown.

Freeport's main visitor attraction is its "Nautical Mile," located along the **Woodcleft Canal,** bordered by a street of the same name. Much of Freeport was built on landfill, and Woodcleft is one of seven or eight canals in town. Along it, you'll find lots of shops, many selling arts and crafts, and a plethora of seafood restaurants, as well as fishing boats sporting signs advertising "Halfday Flounder" and "Blues AM." On summer evenings, music beckons from outdoor bars while party boats set sail for dinner and moonlight cruises.

For more information on Freeport, contact the **Freeport Chamber of Commerce** (300 Woodcleft Ave., 516/223-8840, www.freeportny.com). For more information on sportfishing, call the **Freeport Boatmen's Association** (540 Guy Lombardo Ave., 516/378-4838).

Seal-Watching Cruises

In the fall, the **Riverhead Foundation for Marine Research** (631/369-9840, www.riverheadfoundation.org), offers seal-watching cruises that leave from Point Lookout, south

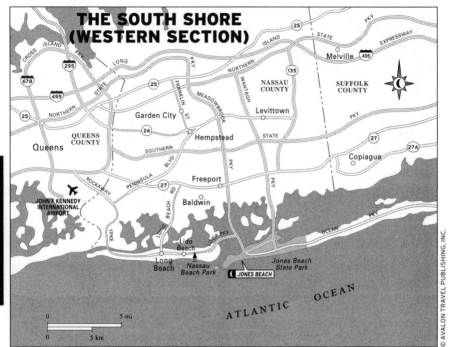

THE SOUTH SHORE
(WESTERN SECTION)

© AVALON TRAVEL PUBLISHING, INC.

of Freeport near Jones and Lido Beaches. Rates are adults $20, children and seniors $17.

Accommodations and Food

Just north of Jones Beach is **Freeport Motor Inn and Boatel** (445 S. Main St., 516/623-9100, www.freeportmotorinn.com, $90–105 d), a good, clean choice popular with boaters and landlubbers alike.

One of the best restaurants along the Nautical Mile is the boisterous **Hudson & McCoy** (340 Woodcleft Ave., 516/868-3411), serving both seafood and steaks; average entrée $18. The clientele here tends to be young and trendy; in summer, bands play on a crowded outdoor deck.

In Baldwin, a few miles west of Freeport, is **Raay-Nor's Cabin** (550 Sunrise Hwy., 516/223-4886), a local institution, serving up fried chicken, yams, and corn fritters since 1932. Housed in a block-long log cabin, Raay-

Nor's is decked out with wooden tables, red booths, and chicken-shaped lamps; average entrée $13.

◖ JONES BEACH

The most famous beach in the New York City metropolitan region is Jones Beach, just 25 miles from midtown Manhattan. Though packed cheek-to-jowl on a hot summer's day, the beach is so magnificent—its white sands stretching out for well over five miles—that it still manages to impress. And talk about good people-watching. ...

Jones Beach is also more than just a beach. Another one of Robert Moses' many creations, his goal here was to transform a sandbar off a windswept reef into the finest public beach in America. He largely succeeded, in an engineering feat that took two years to complete. Finished in 1929, the beach boasts an enormous number of well-worn but first-class facilities, including two lovely art deco bathhouses, wading and Olympic-size pools, ball fields, pitch-and-putt golf, shuffleboard courts, basketball courts, picnic areas, refreshment stands, a restaurant, a wide weathered boardwalk, and a 200-foot-high water tower shaped like an obelisk. Also at the beach is the **Tommy Hilfiger at Jones Beach Theater** (516/221-1000), which presents big-name acts in summer.

Jones Beach (Ocean State Pkwy., south of Wantagh, 516/785-1600) is open year-round, sunrise–sunset, but lifeguards are on duty only Memorial Day–Labor Day. Parking is $6–8, but there's no fee to use the beach.

To reach Jones Beach, take the Wantagh State or Meadowbrook State Parkways south off the Sunrise Highway (Route 27), and watch for signs. Traffic can be horrendous in summer, so if you're coming from New York City, consider taking the Long Island Rail Road (718/217-5477). The train travels to Freeport, where shuttlebuses operate to and from the beach.

West of Jones Beach are several smaller beaches—including Long Beach and Lido Beach—that are fun to explore. To reach these often less-crowded locales, take the Meadowbrook State Parkway to the Loop Parkway. In Lido Beach is the 74-site **Nassau Beach Park Campground** (Lido Blvd., 516/571-7724), where reservations are highly recommended.

CENTRAL NASSAU COUNTY

Heading into Long Island on Southern State Parkway, you'll pass one of the state's only African American museums and two historic residential communities. Neither of the latter are tourist attractions in the traditional sense, but both have played an interesting role in America's suburban development.

BAY HOUSES

If you pay close attention while driving along the Wantagh, Meadowbrook, or Loop Parkways linking Jones Beach and Point Lookout to the mainland, you'll spot small cottages perched on platforms and surrounded by marshland and water. At one time, there were hundreds of such bay houses, as they are called, in the Town of Hempstead. Now there are only 32.

The building of the bay houses began back in the early 1700s when the island's farmers, needing hay for their cattle, hired their neighbors the baymen to row out to remote marshlands and bring back hay for their animals. The journey often took several hours each way, so it wasn't long before the baymen began building shacks in which to overnight. At first, these shacks were crude affairs. But as the years went by, the baymen developed them into cozy cabins that they could also use for recreation and for the planting and harvesting of oysters and clams.

In the early 1900s, recreational fishermen discovered the South Shore and the bay houses developed yet another purpose: bait stations. Then, a decade or two later, Prohibition arrived. Some baymen, writes folklorist Nancy Solomon in her book *On the Bay*, "played an indispensable role in rum running, smuggling, via their bay houses, illegal booze from large cargo ships offshore to hotels. ..."

All this history was almost lost in 1993, when the baymen's lease on their bay houses—last renewed by the Town of Hempstead in 1965—ran out. The town government had voted to have the houses destroyed, but Solomon's book, together with the efforts of the South Shore Bayhouse Owners' Association, convinced the town board of the homes' historic value. Their leases have since been extended virtually indefinitely.

Although the bay houses can be seen from the parkways, the best way to view them is by boat. The charter fishing boats that run out of Freeport pass close by.

Approximately 50 other bay houses are located in Suffolk County opposite Captree State Park near Captree Island, Sexton Island, and Havermeyer Island.

African American Museum

On a scruffy main drag in sprawling downtown Hempstead is the African American Museum (110 N. Franklin St., 516/572-0730, 10 A.M.–5 P.M. Tues.–Sat., 5–9 P.M. Thurs., free admission), a small but very active institution where the exhibits change every 8–10 weeks. Most of the exhibits are arts or history oriented, and range in style from locally produced shows to traveling Smithsonian productions. Subjects covered in the past have included the role of African Americans in the Civil War, and contemporary black Long Island artists.

Garden City

Just north of Hempstead is Garden City, a ritzy residential enclave that was one of America's first planned communities. Filled with broad avenues, elegant homes, and a plethora of parks, Garden City was developed by Alexander Stewart, a Scottish immigrant who'd made a fortune by opening the world's first department store—Stewart's—in 1846 in New York City.

Stewart died in 1876 and was originally buried in New York City, in the cemetery of St. Mark's-in-the-Bowery. In one of the odder incidents in New York City history, his corpse was stolen for ransom. After his widow bought it back, she had it reburied beneath Garden City's imposing **Cathedral of the Incarnation,** which still stands on Cathedral Avenue at 6th Street. Stewart's new grave was equipped with a burglar alarm.

The poshest hotel in Long Island is the **Garden City Hotel** (45 7th St., 516/747-3000, www.gardencityhotel.com, $250–375 d), featuring a gleaming, marble-filled lobby, luxurious rooms with all the amenities, health spa, piano lounge, several restaurants, shopping arcade, and impeccable service. Established in 1874, the hotel has hosted many famous guests, including Charles Lindberg, who slept here before his transatlantic flight.

Museum Row

The hangars of Mitchel Field, a former airfield just outside Garden City, are slowly being transformed into a Museum Row. At the heart the project is the impressive **Cradle of Aviation Museum** (1 Davis Ave., off

Cradle of Aviation Museum

Charles Lindbergh Blvd., 516/572-0411, www.cradleofaviation.org, 9:30 A.M.–5 P.M. Tues.–Sun., adults $9, children 2–12 $8). In the atrium here, biplanes and fighter planes seem to soar up above, while all around are dozens of rare aircraft documenting the history of flight. Many major aviation events took place on Long Island, including Charles Lindbergh's 1927 nonstop transatlantic flight, which departed from nearby Roosevelt Field (now a shopping mall). Also in the museum are Long Island's first IMAX theater and the Red Planet Cafe, designed to look like a 21st century Mars space base.

The long-established **Long Island Children's Museum** (11 Davis Ave., off Charles Lindbergh Blvd., 516/222-5800, www.licm.org, 10 A.M.–5 P.M. Wed.–Sun., adults and children over age one $8, seniors $7) has also relocated to Mitchel Center. Here, find numerous hands-on exhibits for kids of all ages. Build a skyscraper, be a musician, or climb a two-story play tower.

To reach Mitchel Center from the Northern State Parkway, take Exit 31A south to the Meadowbrook Parkway. Take Exit M4 to Charles Lindbergh Boulevard. From the Southern State Parkway, take Exit 22 and head north on Meadowbrook Parkway to Exit M4 and Charles Lindbergh Boulevard.

Levittown

Another important landmark in American suburban history is Levittown, transformed from potato fields into 17,447 inexpensive ranch homes by developer William Levitt in 1949. The largest housing development ever created by a single builder, Levittown was the American Dream come true for the working class, as well as the butt of countless jokes about "ticky-tacky houses" all looking just the same.

Levittown was originally built exclusively for GIs returning from World War II, but was later opened up to the general public. Each pre-assembled house was built in 27 steps in five days, and each had a living room, two bedrooms, a kitchen and bath, an attic, washing machine, barbecue grill, and television set. The

cost to young families was $60 a month, no money down.

In the end, the individuality and imagination of Levittown's residents foiled many of the community's detractors. Drive down the streets here today and you'd be hard-pressed to find any house that closely resembles another. Some owners have added rooms and second floors, others have changed the facades or added driveways.

To reach Levittown from Hempstead, head east on Hempstead Turnpike (Route 24).

FIRE ISLAND

Fire Island is a long skinny stick of land stretching 32 miles parallel to Long Island's south shore. It's a near-mythic place known for both its party atmosphere and its wilderness. Four distinct visitor areas and 17 resort communities make up the island, but it's all part of the National Seashore system. No cars are allowed on most of Fire Island, where park rangers administer a number of the magnificent white sand beaches.

One note of caution: Fire Island has abundant poison ivy and a large deer-tick population. A tick bite can cause Lyme disease; small posters describing precautions and symptoms are posted all over the island. As long as you stick to the beaches and boardwalks, however, or wear long pants when exploring the grasses and woodlands, you shouldn't have a problem.

Free and excellent maps of Fire Island are available at the various interpretive centers mentioned below, or from the **Fire Island National Seashore Headquarters** (120 Laurel St., Patchogue, 631/289-4810, www.nps.gov/fiis). Other helpful websites are www.fireisland.com, www.fireislandbeaches.com, and www.barrierbeaches.com.

Robert Moses State Park

At Fire Island's westernmost end is the 1,000-acre Robert Moses State Park (off Robert Moses Causeway, 631/669-0449, dawn–dusk, $6–8 parking), one of only two sections of the island that you can drive to. A public beach since 1898, the park feels like a smaller, less

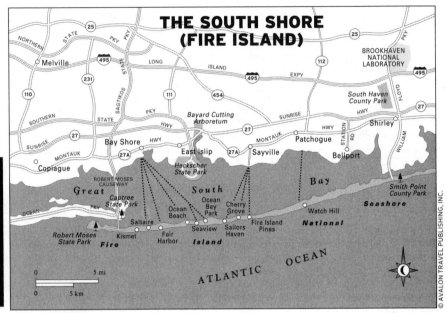

THE SOUTH SHORE
(FIRE ISLAND)

BROOKHAVEN
NATIONAL
LABORATORY

South Haven
County Park

Bayard Cutting
Arboretum

Shirley

Bay Shore

East Islip   Sayville   Patchogue   Bellport

Copiague

Heckscher
State Park

ROBERT MOSES
CAUSEWAY

Great   *South*   Smith Point
County Park

Captree
State Park

Ocean
Beach

Ocean
Bay
Park

Cherry
Grove

Watch Hill

Seashore

Saltaire

Bay

Robert Moses
State Park   Kismet   Fair
Harbor   Seaview   Sailors
Haven   Fire Island
Pines   *National*

Fire   *Island*

ATLANTIC   *OCEAN*

0   5 mi

0   5 km

© AVALON TRAVEL PUBLISHING, INC.

crowded version of Jones Beach. Run by the National Seashore, it's equipped with bathhouses, shops, and snack bars.

At the park's western end is the black-and-white-striped **Fire Island Lighthouse,** first built in 1827 to help put an end to the many shipwrecks that had occurred here. The current lighthouse dates back to 1858, and at its base is a visitors center (631/661-4876, 9:30 A.M.–5:30 P.M. daily July–Sept., call for off-season hours). Tower tours (adults $5, seniors $4, children 5–11 $3.50) should be reserved in advance.

To reach the park, take the Robert Moses Causeway off the Sunrise Highway (Route 27) or the Southern State Parkway.

Sailors Haven

For the day visitor, one of the island's most interesting beaches is Sailors Haven, reached via ferry from Sayville. Sailors Haven is part wild beach and boardwalk, part dunes and grasses, and part **Sunken Forest**—a scrappy 300-year-old maritime forest located below

sea level between two lines of sand dunes. A weathered gray boardwalk leads from the ferry dock through the 40-acre forest lush with oak, maple, red cedar and sour gum trees, as well as sassafras, bayberry, inkberry, and cattail. Due to the island's strong winds and salty air, none of the trees can grow taller than the dunes, even though beneath their roots fresh water extends as deep as 40 yards. Essential to the forest's existence, this fresh water occurs because the island's annual rainfall exceeds its annual evaporation.

Run by the National Seashore, Sailors Haven is well equipped with bathhouses, a snack bar, and an interpretive center. Ferries operated by the Sayville Ferry Service (River Rd., Sayville, 631/589-8980, www.sayvilleferry.com, adults round-trip $12, children round-trip $6) run May–November.

Watch Hill

Another National Seashore visitors center, similar to but larger than the one at Sailors Haven, is located at Watch Hill, at the eastern end of Fire Island. Remote and lonely in feel, Watch Hill is filled with windswept dunes and an often unpopulated beach, while adjacent to it is a national wilderness area that visitors are welcome to explore. Fall and spring are especially good times to come, as Fire Island is on the Atlantic flyway, a major avian migratory route. At the center of Watch Hill are bathhouses, a snack bar, nature trails, and an interpretive center.

Ferries operated by the Davis Park Ferry Co. (West and Division Sts., Pachogue, 631/475-1665, www.davisparkferry.com, adults round-trip $12, children round-trip $7) run May–November.

Smith Point County Park

East of Watch Hill and its adjacent National Wilderness Area is another beach park accessible by car. Like Robert Moses Park, Smith Point Park has plenty of bathhouses and concession stands, and attracts large crowds on summer weekends. Technically speaking, the park is not part of the National Seashore, but since it's located next to **Smith Point West,** which *is,* and both are lined with the same wide and wonderful beach, it all feels the same. Smith Point West also has a National Seashore visitors center and self-guiding nature trail.

Smith Point County Park (631/852-1313) and Smith Point West (631/281-3010) are at the southern end of the William Floyd Pkwy., off the Sunrise Highway (Route 27). Parking in summer is $10.

William Floyd Estate

As you drive down William Floyd Parkway to and from Smith Point, you'll pass by signs for the William Floyd Estate (245 Park Dr., 631/399-2030, 11 A.M.–4:30 P.M. Fri.–Sun. June–Oct., free admission), now part of the National Seashore. Floyd was one of the signers of the Declaration of Independence. After his death, his family's estate grew to include over 600 acres of forests and meadows, along with a grand 25-room mansion and 12 outbuildings. The estate remained in the Floyd family's hands until 1977, when Cornelia Floyd Nichols

signed it over to the National Park Service one year before her death.

Resort Communities

Fire Island wasn't declared a National Seashore until 1964, by which time 17 resort communities had already been established. These communities were allowed to remain, as long as they didn't grow beyond their designated boundaries. Today they are popular vacation spots, especially among Manhattanites.

Each Fire Island community has its own distinct character. **Cherry Grove** and **Fire Island Pines** are the island's two gay retreats; **Kismet** and **Fair Harbor** attract a large singles crowd; **Saltaire** and **Seaview** cater primarily to well-heeled families.

Most of these communities are not designed for the casual visitor. Their vacationers tend to rent or share houses—usually for the entire summer—and often arrive via hired water taxi. Most of these communities also do not offer bathhouses or other public facilities.

Two communities that *do* welcome day-trippers and overnight visitors are **Ocean Beach** and **Ocean Bay Park.** Ocean Beach attracts many families, Ocean Bay Park many singles. Both are friendly, middle-class communities equipped with public facilities and serviced by Fire Island Ferries in Bay Shore (631/665-3600, www.fireislandferries.com, adults round-trip $14, children round-trip $6.50).

Cherry Grove also welcomes the casual visitor. Older, smaller, less expensive, and more exuberant than its sister community, the Pines, it centers around the **Cherry Grove Beach Hotel,** which always teems with a gay crowd—talking, drinking, and partying. Cherry Grove is serviced by the Sayville Ferry Co. (River Rd., Sayville, 631/589-8980, www.sayvilleferry.com, adults round-trip $12, children round-trip $6).

Accommodations

One of the few hotels on Fire Island is the simple but comfortable **《 Fire Island Hotel and Resort** (25 Cayuga Park, Ocean Bay Park, 631/583-8000, www.fireislandhotel .com), housed in converted U.S. Coast Guard buildings. The hotel caters primarily to families, but rooms go very fast—reserve well in advance. Rates in summer range from $140 d midweek to $1,100 d for a three-night weekend stay; rates drop 25–50 percent in June and September. Another good choice for families is the comfortable, air-conditioned, 1940s-era **Cleggs Hotel** (478 Bayberry Walk, Ocean Beach, 631/583-5399, $110 d midweek, $320 d for the weekend).

The **Grove Hotel** (Ocean Walk, Cherry Grove, 631/597-6600, www.grovehotel.com) caters to the gay community. Summer rates for a clean, basic room are $60–160 d midweek and $470–750 d for a two-night weekend stay; rates drop significantly in the off-season.

BAY SHORE AND VICINITY

Several of the Fire Island ferries leave from the town of Bay Shore. Once a popular resort community—and still surrounded by some very wealthy estates—Bay Shore has more recently been stricken with urban blight, and feels tired and run-down.

The ferry docks at the foot of Maple Avenue, and on summer days, beachgoers stream down the thoroughfare, armed with coolers, beach chairs, and umbrellas. Few stop at the **Gibson/Mack/Holt House** (22 Maple Ave., 631/665-7003, 2–4 P.M. Tues. and Sat., free admission), but the very attractive historical home is well worth a look. Several rooms have been restored to their original 1820 condition, while others house memorabilia from the town's turn-of-the-century heyday. The house is run by the Bay Shore Historical Society and was restored almost entirely by volunteers.

Day Cruises

Hour-and-a-half sightseeing cruises around Great South Bay offered by **South Bay Cruises** (631/321-9005, July–Sept., adults $10, seniors and children $8). The cruises leave from the Bayshore Marina at the foot of Clinton Avenue. Lunch and dinner cruises are also available.

Heckscher State Park

East of Bay Shore is 1,500-acre Heckscher State Park (off Heckscher State Pkwy., East Islip, 631/581-2100, dawn–dusk, $6–8 parking), the protected bay waters of which make it an especially good place for families. Facilities include three beaches, a pool, bathhouses, nature trails, and a 69-site campground. For camping reservations, call 800/456-CAMP.

Bayard Cutting Arboretum

One of the greatest estates along the South Shore is the Bayard Cutting Arboretum (466 Montauk Hwy., Oakdale, 631/581-1002, 10 A.M.-sunset Tues.–Sun., $6–8 parking), once owned by railroad magnate William Bayard Cutting. The 690-acre estate was designed by Frederick Law Olmsted, the famed landscape architect who also designed New York City's Central Park.

The arboretum centers on a dark baronial Tudor mansion. Inside are a few natural history exhibits and a snack bar, but the place feels oddly empty. Perhaps that's because compared to the estate's glorious grounds, the mansion seems almost an afterthought.

Just outside the mansion is a verdant lawn, stretching 600 feet down to the Connetquot River. On either side stand huge old black oak trees, spreading out their leafy boughs, while all around are various gardens—the azalea garden, the rhododendron garden, the lilac garden, the holly garden.

Parts of the arboretum were badly hit by Hurricane Gloria in 1985. An estimated 1,000 trees were lost during that storm, including about 20 of Long Island's oldest trees and 80 of the 120 species originally planted by Mr. Cutting. Younger trees have since been planted in their stead, but it will be many years before they reach their predecessors' 70–90-foot heights.

Long Island Maritime Museum

The laid-back Long Island Maritime Museum (86 West Ave., off Montauk Hwy., West Sayville, 631/854-4974, 10 A.M.–4 P.M. Mon.–Sat., noon–4 P.M. Sun., adults $4, seniors and children $2) occupies an idyllic spot overlooking Great South Bay. Housed in shipshape buildings, the museum holds the largest collection of small craft in Long Island. On display is everything from oyster vessels and sailboats to ice scooters and clam boats.

Also at the museum are a historic oyster house and an 1890s' bayman's cottage, both of which were moved here from elsewhere on the island. The oyster house holds an extensive exhibit on the harvesting of shellfish, while next door is a working boat shop where volunteers build new boats and restore old ones.

Food

The **Bay Shack** (end of Maple Ave., Bay Shore, no phone, serves great clam chowder, lobster rolls, and other seafood to ferry passengers. Opposite the train station is tiny **Siam Lotus** (1664 Union Blvd., 631/968-8196), serving first-rate Thai food in a cramped but friendly setting; average entrée $11.

EAST TO HAMPTON BAYS

Turning south off Sunrise Highway onto Montauk Highway around Sayville or Patchogue will save you time and take you past a number of pretty villages, including Bellport, the Moriches, Westhampton, Quogue, East Quogue, and Hampton Bays.

Quogue

One of the prettiest villages along Montauk Highway is Quogue, a tiny place filled with big old shingled homes and wide empty streets. In the center of things reigns the **Inn at Quogue** (52 Quogue St., 631-653-6560, www.innat-quogue.com), housed in both a 200-year-old inn and several modern buildings. The inn's 70 rooms, many of which were renovated by a consultant for Ralph Lauren, vary considerably in style (from historic to upscale motel) and in price ($175–450 d in summer; $135–300 d off-season). The **Inn at Quogue Restaurant** (52 Quogue St., 631/653-6800) serves a New World cuisine; average entrée $28, with a less expensive menu available at the bar.

Dockers (94 Dune Rd., 631/653-0653) is a bustling restaurant on the waterfront, serving everything from steak to seafood. Live music is often featured on the weekends.

The Big Duck

Before heading onto the South Fork, take a short detour north for a look at the Big Duck (Rte. 24, Flanders, at the entrance to Sears Bellows County Park, 631/852-8292 or 631/854-4970, 10 A.M.–5 P.M. Tues.–Sat. and

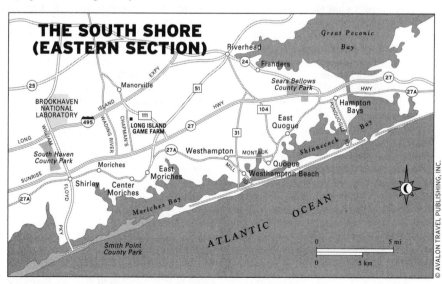

THE SOUTH SHORE (EASTERN SECTION)

© AVALON TRAVEL PUBLISHING, INC.

LONG ISLAND

© CHRISTIANE BIRD

The Big Duck houses a nonprofit shop whose proceeds support the preservation of Long Island history.

12:30–5 P.M. Sun. June–Sept.; call for off-season hours). Sitting all by itself by the side of the road, the pure white bird—with its orange bill and bright red eyes made from Model-T taillights—looks like a simple child's drawing come to life. The only giveaway that something else is afoot is the dark outline of a door just beneath the duck's throat.

The 20-foot-high Big Duck was built in 1931 by an ambitious duck-raising farmer who hoped to attract more customers. Ducks were big business on Long Island at that time; in 1939 there were 90 duck farms in Quogue alone.

Today the Big Duck is a shop run by Friends for Long Island's Heritage, a nonprofit group working to preserve Long Island's past. On sale are lots of duck collectibles—duck books, duck T-shirts, duck coffee mugs, and the like—along with postcards and books.

The South Fork

The South Fork is New York City's playground. The rich and the influential, the middle-class and the obscure—all flock here during the summer to rent weathered cottages, poke around in picture-perfect towns, indulge in fast-paced nightlife, and, most of all, explore the beaches. Like the South Shore, the South Fork is home to some of the world's most magnificent beaches, and they're considerably less crowded here than they are near the city.

But the South Fork also has a culture all its own that has nothing to do with tourists. Farmers and, to a lesser extent, fisherfolk continue to practice their livelihoods here just as they have for hundreds of years. Humble potato fields butt up against multi-million-dollar second homes, fishing boats share harbors with pleasure craft.

The South Fork is also often referred to as the Hamptons. Several of the Hamptons (Westhampton Beach, Quogue, Hampton Bays) are actually west of the South Fork, but when people speak of the "Hamptons," they're generally referring to those towns east of Shinnecock Canal.

History

The English first arrived in Southampton from Lynn, Massachusetts, in 1640—the same year settlers from New Haven arrived on the North Fork. Much of their reason for coming was the fact that the Algonquin Indians made wampum on the island. Wampum could be exchanged for valuable beaver and other furs, and the English wanted to get access to the beads before the Dutch.

The Algonquins welcomed the English and in a matter of decades, English villages were flourishing. Most featured New England-style village greens, white-steepled churches, and Colonial saltboxes. Many of these early buildings still stand today.

Tourists started arriving in the 1800s. Residents opened up their homes to the visitors and by the 1850s, the local press was reporting that all rooms in East Hampton were fully booked, at $7 a night. Shortly thereafter, Southampton started building hotels, and in 1895, the railroad arrived, marking the beginning of the end of sleepy village life.

LODGING

As in many other resort areas, peak-season accommodations in the Hamptons don't come cheap. Peak season rates usually apply from mid-June through Labor Day, and minimum two- or three-night stays are often required, especially on weekends. Off-season, rates drop dramatically.

Along the beach near Montauk, you'll find simple family-style resort motels, more moderately priced. Rates listed below are for double rooms, but many places also offer family packages. Meanwhile, historic inns and B&Bs are plentiful throughout the region. Most of the resort motels are closed in winter; most of the inns and B&Bs are open year-round.

A good online regional site is the Hamptons Web Home Page at www.hamptonsweb.com.

BEACH PARKING

Although all South Fork beaches are open to the public, parking can be a major problem. Many village and town beaches require parking permits, which usually cost nonresidents over $100 (good for the entire summer). However, some excellent public beaches have daily parking fees; the best of these are Atlantic Beach in Amagansett, the Main Beach in East Hampton, and the beach at Hither Hills State Park in Montauk. Many hotels and motels also offer low-cost day-parking passes to their guests; be sure to inquire when you book.

Parking illegally is not a good idea; rules are strictly enforced, and you will be ticketed with a heavy fine or towed away. Most parking rules apply during the summer only.

LONG ISLAND

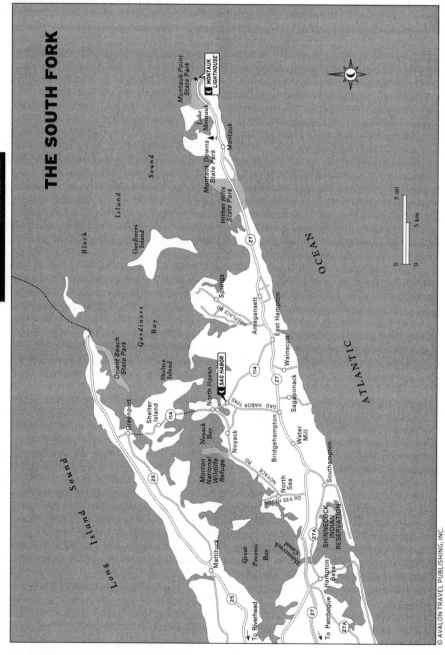

THE SOUTH FORK

MONTAUK LIGHTHOUSE

Montauk Point State Park

Lake Montauk

Montauk

Montauk Downs State Park

Hither Hills State Park

Block Island Sound

Gardiners Island

Gardiners Bay

Springs

FIREPLACE RD

Amagansett

East Hampton

27

Wainscott

Orient Beach State Park

Shelter Island

North Haven

SAG HABOR

114

27

Sagaponack

SAG HABOR TPKE

Greenport

Shelter Island

114

Noyack Bay

Morton National Wildlife Refuge

Noyack

NOYACK RD

Bridgehampton

Water Mill

25

Long Island Sound

Mattituck

North Sea

NORTH SEA RD

Southampton

OCEAN

ATLANTIC

Great Peconic Bay

Shinnecock Canal

SHINNECOCK INDIAN RESERVATION

27A

25

Hampton Bays

To Riverhead

27

To Patchogue

27A

5 mi

5 km

0

0

NIGHTLIFE

The South Fork is noted for its nightlife, which runs the gamut from casual bars to discos. In general, things get going as late out here as they do in major urban centers—say 11 P.M.—and don't shut down until 2 A.M. or even 4 A.M. on weekends.

SOUTHAMPTON

The oldest of the Hamptons' villages is Southampton, a pristine and deceptively simple-looking town attracting a high quotient of socialites and the nouveaux riche. The downtown is just a few blocks long, but it's lined with leafy trees, posh boutiques, and expensive cars—Jaguars are especially well represented. All around town are winding wooded lanes dotted with splashy second homes, most of which are protected from prying eyes by tall privacy hedges.

Settled in 1640, Southampton was first called Conscience Point; its name was changed to honor the Earl of Southampton. The town centers on the intersection of Main Street and Job's Lane. Walking maps and brochures can be picked up at the **Southampton Chamber of Commerce** (76 Main St., 631/283-0402, www.southamptonchamber.com, 10 A.M.–4 P.M. Mon.–Fri., 11 A.M.–3 P.M. Sat.–Sun.).

Historical Buildings

The oldest building in Southampton is also the oldest wooden frame house in the state. It's the 1648 **Old Halsey House** (S. Main St., a half mile from the Job's Ln. and Main St. intersection, 631/283-2494, noon–5 P.M. Fri.–Sat. and 1–5 P.M. Sun. July–Oct., adults $3, seniors $2, children $1), a tiny gray cottage sitting primly behind a fence, oblivious to the modern world. Built by one of the town's original settlers, the homestead is still in excellent condition and is furnished with 17th- and 18th-century antiques.

Not far away is the **Southampton Historical Museum** (17 Meeting House Ln. [an extension of Job's Ln.], 631/283-2494 or 631/283-1612, 11 A.M.–5 P.M. Tues.–Sat. and 1–5 P.M. Sun. May–Dec., noon–4 P.M. Thurs.–Sat. Jan.–Apr., adults $4, seniors $3, children $2),

which centers around a snug Greek Revival home built by a whaling captain in 1843. Inside the home are period furnishings, a Shinnecock Indian exhibit, and Revolutionary War artifacts. Out back cluster a compact collection of historical buildings, including a one-room schoolhouse, blacksmith's shop, carpenter's shop, and cobbler.

Parrish Art Museum

Founded in 1898 by a wealthy summer resident, the Parrish Art Museum (25 Job's Lane, 631/283-2118, 11 A.M.–5 P.M. Mon.–Sat., 1–5 P.M. Sun., closed Tues.–Wed. off-season, adults $5, seniors and students $3, children under 12 free) houses a notable collection of 19th- and 20th-century American art. William Merritt Chase and Fairfield Porter, both of whom spent much time in the area, are especially well represented. Out back, find an arboretum and a sculpture garden shaded by rare trees. In summer, the museum presents many lectures, concerts, films, and other special events.

Beaches

Southampton's main public beach is **Cooper Neck Beach,** at the end of Cooper Neck Lane, where parking fees hover around $25. No parking permit is required at the often uncrowded **Old Town Beach,** at the end of Old Town Road. There are only about 30 parking spaces, however, and no facilities.

Shinnecock Reservation

Just west of town, the Shinnecock Reservation is home to about 400 Native Americans and the **Shinnecock Nation Cultural Center and Museum** (Montauk Hwy. at West Gate Rd., 631/287-4923, www.shinnecock-museum.org, 11 A.M.–4 P.M. Wed.–Sun., adults $5, seniors $4, children under 12 free). Opened in 2001, the museum showcases historic birchbark canoes and farm implements, beadwork, basketry, weavings, photographs, and an informative video.

Visitors are also welcome to attend the annual **Shinnecock Pow Wow,** held on Labor

LONG ISLAND

Day weekend. This major event attracts Native Americans from all over the country. Traditional dances, foods, and arts and crafts are featured.

Accommodations

Nestled in the heart of the village is the Tudor-style **⊂ Southampton Inn** (91 Hill St., at First Neck Ln., 631/283-6500, www.south-amptoninn.com, $239–489 d July–Aug., $129–489 d Sept.–June), offering 90 spacious rooms done up in easy-on-the-eye earth tones and pastels, some accented with African motifs. All rooms have cable TV, phones with data-ports, and ceramic-tiled bathrooms, and some have separate seating areas. The inn offers free shuttle-bus service to nearby Coopers Beach, a heated outdoor swimming pool, tennis courts, five acres of grounds on which crafts fairs and other special events are staged, and a cozy courtyard patio where breakfast is served in fair weather. Voted "The Best Inn in Southampton" by *Dan's Paper,* the resort is especially popular among families and wedding parties.

Also an excellent choice is the historic, 70-room **Southampton Village Latch Inn** (101 Hill St., 631/283-2160, www.villagelatch.com). Now owned by a local group of artists, the inn was once an annex to the then-famous Irving Hotel, Long Island's oldest established hostelry, since burned down. Tall hedges frame the mansion's green-shuttered front, while outside are a swimming pool and tennis courts. Exotic crafts such as Burmese puppets and African masks hang on the walls. Many rooms have refrigerators and some have private patios (summer weekend rates start at $350 d, with a three-night minimum, weekdays at $250 d; about one-third less in the off-season).

Food

The **Golden Pear** (99 Main St., 631/283-8900), a gourmet café, offers homemade baked goods, sandwiches, and pasta. It's an especially good place for brunch or lunch, but also serves dinner; average main dish $10. For takeout, try the **Village Gourmet & Cheese Shop** (11 Main St., 631/283-6949).

More serious meals can be had at **⊂ Le Chef Bistro** (75 Job's Ln., 631/283-8581), a bustling French restaurant with a lively bar to one side, dining to the other. A surprisingly reasonable prix fixe $25 dinner menu includes a half-dozen tasty appetizers (crab cakes, lobster bisque) and an equal number of equally tasty entrées (nut-encrusted flounder, grilled tuna, veal chops).

The **Red Bar Brasserie** (210 Hampton Rd., 631/283-0704) serves creative American fare in a stylish, white-tablecloth setting. At night, the restaurant's bar is crowded with beautiful people. The newly revamped **James on Main** (75 Main St., 631/283-7575) features a large spiffy bar area up front and a restaurant in back. On the menu is innovative American fare; average entrée $25.

Refined, imaginative Thai cuisine is the specialty of the congenial **⊂ Q, A Thai Bistro** (129 Noyac Rd., 631/204-0007), where dishes range from green-curry salmon to drunken noodles with basil and red pepper. Located about 10 miles north of the village, the upscale restaurant offers a laid-back bar to one side, dining to the other, and outdoor porch dining in good weather; average entrée $22.

WATER MILL AND BRIDGEHAMPTON

A few miles east of Southampton is the small village of Water Mill, named for the big gristmill near the town center. The village's first gristmill was built in 1644: this one dates to 1800 and now operates as the **Water Mill Museum** (41 Mill Rd., off Rte. 27, 631/726-4625, 11 A.M.–5 P.M. Thurs.–Mon. June–Sept., adults $3, seniors $2.50). During the summer, the mill still grinds corn and wheat with its all-wooden gears, shafts, and wheel. Also at the museum are various arts-oriented exhibits and events.

A few miles east of Water Mill is Bridgehampton, named for a small bridge that was built over Sagg Pond in 1686. During the 1800s, Bridgehampton was known for helping distressed ships at sea. The first headquarters of the Life Saving Service of Long Island was founded here in 1878; it merged with the Coast Guard in 1915.

Today, Bridgehampton is another picture-perfect town. Big red-brick buildings line its Main Street, along with a number of antiques shops.

Food

Sit indoors or outdoors at **Bobby Van's** (2393 Main St., 631/537-0590), a place to see and be seen—once frequented by the literati, now by celebs. On the menu is classic steakhouse fare; average entrée $25–35.

EAST HAMPTON

At the center of the Hamptons lies East Hampton, an Old Money stronghold now better known for its famed artists and writers, actors and directors, publishers and media moguls. East Hampton has been a mecca for successful "creative types" since the 1870s, when artists William Merritt Chase, Childe Hassam, and others summered here.

In the late 1970s, the now-defunct *Saturday Evening Post* ran a contest asking readers to vote for the most beautiful town in America. East Hampton won, and it's not hard to see why. Even more than Southampton, East Hampton is an idyllic New England village that seems to have stepped out of time. Everywhere are perfect Colonial homes, emerald-green lawns, and white picket fences. Nothing seems quite real, but who cares? What could possibly go wrong in a world such as this?

A pond, a village green, and the Old Burying Ground split Main Street at the western end, while at the eastern end, in isolated splendor on a plush lawn, stands the weathered Hook Windmill. Between these two landmarks lie most of the town's shops, restaurants, and historic sites, all of which can be explored on foot. To catch a glimpse of the area's many posh summer homes, take a drive along Ocean Avenue or Lily Pond Lane.

The **East Hampton Chamber of Commerce** (4 Main St., 631/324-0362, www.easthamptonchamber.com, 10 A.M.–4 P.M. Mon.–Sat. June–Sept., call for off-season hours) is well stocked with brochures and maps. The **East Hampton Historical Society** (101 Main St., 631/324-6850, www.easthamptonhistory.org) sponsors downtown and cemetery **walking tours** in summer and fall. Many are led by guides dressed in Colonial garb.

Historic James Lane

At the western end of the village are the Town Pond—once a watering hole for East Hampton's cattle—and the snug **Home Sweet Home** (14 James Ln., 631/324-0713, 10 A.M.–4 P.M. Mon.–Sat. and 2–4 P.M. Sun. May–Sept., adults $4, children $2), a nicely restored 1650 saltbox that was the boyhood home of John Howard Payne, composer of the song "Home Sweet Home." Inside the house is a good collection of English ceramics and early American furniture, while out back are a windmill and garden.

Next door to Payne's old residence is a complex of restored weathered buildings known as the **Mulford Farm** (10 James Ln., 631/324-6850, 11 A.M.–4 P.M. Thurs.–May June–Oct., free admission). Owned by the same family from 1712 to 1944, the four-acre homestead includes a farmhouse, barn, garden, and various outbuildings. In summer, costumed guides lead tours.

Among the many Mulfords who once lived on the homestead was a stubborn Colonial whaler named Samuel. Samuel didn't like anyone telling him what to do, so when a New York governor levied a tax on the whale trade, Samuel headed to London to complain to the king. No one would let him into the palace, but one day, after his pocket was picked while he was waiting outside, Samuel had a brainstorm. Returning to his inn, he sewed several fishhooks into his pockets and went back to the palace. Soon he heard a curse from a would-be thief and called over a guard, who marched the pickpocket off to jail. The event was written up in the papers, Mulford got his audience with the king, and the whale tax was lifted.

Historic Main Street

Just east of James Lane stands **Clinton**

Academy (151 Main St., 631/324-6850, 11 A.M.–3 P.M. Sat.–Sun. June–Oct., free admission), a large wood-and-brick building dating back to the late 1700s. Once housing the first prep school in the state and one of the first coed schools in the country, the academy is now a historical museum. Out back is a wildflower garden.

Next to the Clinton Academy is the **Town House** (same phone and hours). an elfin, one-room schoolhouse with a potbellied stove. The building also once served as the town hall.

At the other end of Main Street reigns the 1806 **Hook Windmill** (631/324-0713, 10 A.M.–4 P.M. Mon.–Sat. and 2–4 P.M. Sun. July–Aug., adults $2, children under 12 $1), the best surviving example of the many windmills that once dotted the South Fork (11 still stand but most are not open to the public). It was built by Nathaniel Dominy V, an innovative designer who included several then-unheard-of labor-saving devices—including a grain elevator—in his remarkably efficient mill.

© CHRISTIANE BIRD

Hook Windmill stands at the eastern end of East Hampton's Main Street.

Guild Hall

Across the street from Clinton Academy is Guild Hall (158 Main St., 631/324-0806, www.guildhall.org, 11 A.M.–5 P.M. Mon.–Sat. and noon–5 P.M. Sun. June–Aug., 11 A.M.–5 P.M. Thurs.–Sat. and noon–5 P.M. Sun. Sept.–May, adults $5, seniors $4, students $3.50), one of the premier art institutions on Long Island. Inside its three large galleries are temporary exhibits featuring top contemporary artists such as Jackson Pollock, Willem de Kooning, and Larry Rivers. Also part of Guild Hall is **John Drew Theatre,** which presents dance, theater, music events, and literary readings by some of the famed authors who summer in the Hamptons. Every August, the **Clothesline Art Sale** presents work by both established and emerging artists.

Beaches

In summer, the gorgeous **Main Beach** at the end of Ocean Avenue comes equipped with bathhouses, lifeguards, concession stands, and a large crowd; parking is $20 a day. All the other beaches in East Hampton are usually less crowded, but require a parking permit. Among them are the family-oriented **Georgica Beach** at the end of Apaquogue Road, and **Two Mile Hollow** at the end of Two Mile Hollow Road. Georgica, surrounded by ritzy estates, has showers and restrooms; Two Mile Hollow is in the middle of a nature sanctuary and has no facilities.

Accommodations

Among the more moderately priced inns in this expensive town is the **Bassett House Inn** (128 Montauk Hwy., 631/324-6127, www.bassethouseinn.com, $175–275 d), a large white wooden hostelry with black shutters. Built in the 1830s, with several add-ons over the years, it offers 12 guest rooms, all outfitted with antiques. Some of the cheaper rooms share baths; some of the more expensive ones have fireplaces, and one has a whirlpool.

The cozy, old-fashioned, and very lovely ◖ **Maidstone Arms** (207 Main St., 631/324-5006, www.maidstonearms.com, $290–240 d) overlooks the village green. Outside is a breezy patio and porch, while inside, unusual antiques decorate the 16 rooms and three cottages. Also on site is the Old-World **Maidstone Arms Restaurant** (631/324-5494), serving innovative American fare; average entrée $28.

Among the oldest of hostelries on the South Fork is **Hedges Inn** (74 James Ln., 631/324-7100, www.Hedgesinn.com, $275–375 d in summer, $175–300 d off-season). Built by one of the town's founding families, with sections dating back to the mid-1700s, the inn features 11 nicely restored rooms, some overlooking Town Pond. On the ground floor is the romantic **James Lane Cafe;** average entrée $27.

Another historic spot, surrounded by a pristine white-picket fence, is **Huntting Inn** (94 Main St., 631/324-0410, www.Hunttinginn.com, $275–375 d in summer, $200–250 d off-season, includes breakfast), which dates back to the Revolutionary War. All 19 rooms have been thoroughly modernized but still contain plenty of antiques, while downstairs is a long airy verandah. Adjoining the inn is the **Palm Restaurant** (631/324-0411, www.thepalm.com), a branch of the ritzy New York steakhouse; average entrée $32.

Food

Great deli sandwiches can be had at **Dreesen's Excelsior Market** (33 Newtown Ln., 631/324-0465), a family-owned business established in 1920. For a simple lunch or dinner, **Nicole's** (100 Montauk Hwy., 631/324-3939) is an easy-going pub that features seafood pie and 10 kinds of draft beer.

⟨ Bostwick's Seafood Grill & Oyster Bar (39 Gann Rd., 631/324-1111) is a casual, festive place specializing in fresh seafood. The dining area overlooks the ocean and is a good place to watch the sun set; average entrée $18.

Not surprisingly, East Hampton also has its share of posh eateries where getting a reservation is no mean feat. One long-time hot spot is the airy and elegant **Della Femina** (99 N. Main St., 631/329-6666), serving innovative American and Italian fare; average entrée $30. Another choice spot for people-watching is **Nick**

& Toni's (136 N. Main St., 631/324-3550), offering Mediterranean cuisine in a sophisticated yet relaxed setting; average entrée $30.

⟨ SAG HARBOR

Driving north from East Hampton along Route 114, through lush and fertile farm country, you'll soon come to the old whaling port of Sag Harbor. During its heyday, Sag Harbor was a bustling and bawdy commercial town, and some of that lively atmosphere—so different from the elegance of the Hamptons—still lingers.

Sag Harbor is a good town to explore on foot. Lower Main Street is filled with shops and restaurants, while upper Main and the side streets hold dozens of 19th-century homes and huge old trees. At the foot of Main Street is the weather-beaten 1,000-foot Long Wharf, which offers close-up views of the harbor.

Plentiful parking is available near the waterfront, especially between Main and Meadow Streets. Traffic usually doesn't get quite as congested here as it does in the Hamptons, but it can still be daunting.

History

The Algonquins once lived in a village called Wegwagonock at the foot of the Sag Harbor hill. The village was known for producing wampum, which was exported throughout New England, New York, and New Jersey. Many pieces of shell can still be found in the area.

The first white settlers arrived in the harbor around 1730 and quickly turned it into a seaport. In 1753, the town's first wharf was built, and in 1760, its first whaling ships set out. The colonists had learned about whaling from the Algonquins, who taught them how to drive whales onto the beach and use the blubber for food and oil.

In 1797, Sag Harbor became the first official port of entry in New York State. By 1839, it boasted a 31-boat whaling fleet, making it the world's third-largest whaling port. In town were over 80 thriving businesses, including coopers, boat builders, tool makers, and rope makers, as well as taverns and brothels. Lower

LONG ISLAND

LONG ISLAND

Main Street was lined with rum-sellers; upper Main with the fashionable homes of ship captains, a number of them African American. Whaling was the first truly integrated industry in America, and you'll see far more black residents in Sag Harbor than in the rest of the Hamptons combined.

Sag Harbor's high spirits did not go overlooked by writers. The port appears in Herman Melville's *Moby Dick* and in the works of James Fenimore Cooper. Cooper, married to the daughter of a local, lived in Sag Harbor from 1819 to 1823, and wrote part of his first novel, *Precaution,* while working as an agent for a whaling company.

Sag Harbor's heyday was short-lived, however. Whaling began to decline in the mid-1800s, as petroleum products began replacing oil. By 1849, the town had only two whalers left. The last voyage of a Sag Harbor whaler took place in 1871, and in 1913, the town was decommissioned as a port. Sag Harbor then went into a sleepy hibernation until the tourism boom of the 1980s began.

Sag Harbor Whaling and Historical Museum

One of the finest buildings in town is the elegant Sag Harbor Whaling Museum (200 Main St., at Garden St., 631/725-0770, www.sagharborwhalingmuseum.org, 10 A.M.–5 P.M. Mon.–Sat. and 1–5 P.M. Sun. May–Oct., noon–4 P.M. Sat.–Sun. Oct.–Dec., adults $4, seniors $3, children 6–13 $2), its entrance marked with tall Corinthian columns and the gleaming jawbones of a right whale. The mansion was built in 1845 by architect Minard Lafever for whaling-ship owner Benjamin Huntting.

Inside is a hodgepodge of jumbled exhibits—some absolutely fascinating, others looking suspiciously like junk—which makes exploring the museum a lot of fun. On display you'll find everything from wooden boats and tools used by whalers to ostrich eggs and the needlework of a Miss Fannie Tunison, an 1800s Sag Harbor resident who was paralyzed except for her lips and tongue.

Custom House

Around the corner from the Whaling Museum is the former home of 18th-century customs inspector Henry Packer Dering (Garden St., 631/725-0250 or 631/692-4664, 10 A.M.–5 P.M. Sat.–Sun. June and Sept.–Oct., 10 A.M.–5 P.M. daily July–Aug., adults $3, seniors and children under 12 $2). Dering's job was to record all the goods entering the harbor and collect entry taxes. He used his front room as an office; the room is equipped with wooden window shields that Dering shut whenever he wanted to count money.

Other Historic Sites

All along Main Street near the Custom House stand impressive **sea captains' houses,** while nearby is the **Old Whalers' Church** (Union and Church Sts., 631/725-0894). Designed in 1844 by Minard Lafever, the church is built in an unusual Egyptian Revival style, and has a soaring interior where concerts are frequently presented.

Shopping

Most of Sag Harbor's shops and boutiques are located along Main Street. The **Sag Harbor Variety Store** (45 Main St., 631/725-9706) is an old-fashioned five-and-dime with two cigar-store Indians out front and lots of odds and ends for sale inside.

Wildlife Refuge

About four miles west of Sag Harbor is 187-acre **Elizabeth Morton National Wildlife Refuge** (Noyack Rd., 631/286-0485, $4 parking). The refuge overlooks Peconic and Noyack Bays, and features sandy and rocky beaches, wooded bluffs, ponds, and nature trails. It's also a nesting stop for the endangered piping plover. The refuge is open daily sunrise-sunset, but much of the beach is closed April–mid-August.

Accommodations

On the edge of downtown is the **Sag Harbor Inn** (W. Water St., 631/725-2949, www.sagharborinn.com, $210–395 d in summer, $90–295 d

© CHRISTIANE BIRD

boating on Sag Harbor

off-season, includes breakfast), a modern, two-story hotel with about 40 clean, spacious rooms, many with balconies overlooking the harbor. Similar in style is the (**Baron's Cove Inn** (31 W. Water St., 631/725-2100, www.baronscove.com, $190–480 d in summer, $80–280 d off-season), an upscale resort motel with its own marina. All the rooms here have kitchenettes, and some have private balconies. On site is a pool and roof-top sun deck.

In the heart of the village stands its classiest hostelry, the 1846 (**American Hotel** (25 Main St., 631/725-3535, www.theamericanhotel.com, $210–335 d May–Oct., $155–250 d Nov.–Apr.), which dates back to the town's whaling era. Built of red brick with a white porch out front, the hotel is a member of the Historic Hotels of America. Upstairs are eight guest rooms done up in Victorian antiques; downstairs is an acclaimed restaurant (see below).

Food

Lively **La Super Rica** (Main and Bay Sts., 631/725-3388) specializes in Mexican dishes

made with healthy ingredients, and giant-sized margaritas. Not surprisingly, it's a favorite with twenty-somethings; average entrée $13.

For great views of the yacht basin while dining, check out the (**Dockside Bar & Grill** (26 Bay St., 631/725-7100), serving lots of seafood, along with other American favorites, in a cavernous former American Legion Hall with an enormous patio; average entrée $16. Also offering great views is **B. Smith's** (Long Wharf at Bay Street, 631/725-5858), owned by Barbara Smith, former model and expert on African American cuisine. Specialties here include hickory ribs, roast chicken, and fresh fish, all served with Long Island wines; average entrée $20.

A Sag Harbor institution since 1972, **Il Capuccino Ristorante** (30 Madison St., 631/725-2747) serves Northern Italian fare in a rambling yet cozy wooden building filled with red-checked tablecloths and Chianti bottles; average entrée $18.

The classic spot for dining in Sag Harbor is the red-brick **American Hotel** (25 Main St.,

631/725-3535), which despite its name has a European feel. The restaurant has won numerous awards for its 46-page wine list; the cuisine is French-American; average entrée $28.

Information and Services
In summer, the Sag Harbor Chamber of Commerce (55 Main St., 631/725-0011, www.sagharborchamber.com) runs a **visitors information center** in the old windmill at the entrance to Long Wharf (9 A.M.–5 P.M. daily July–Aug.). The Society for the Preservation of Long Island Antiquities (631/692-4664, www.splia.org) publishes a succinct **walking-tour map** of historic Sag Harbor sites inside their brochure on the Custom House (see below).

AMAGANSETT
Small, picturesque Amagansett takes its name from the Algonquin word for "place of good waters." Indians traveling between East Hampton and Montauk often stopped here for fresh water; a monument and plaque on Bluff Road mark the spot.

Miss Amelia's Cottage
At the intersection of Montauk Highway and Windmill Lane stands a snug Colonial home (631/267-3020, 10 A.M.–4 P.M. Fri.–Sun. late June–Sept., adults $3, children $1). Miss Mary Amelia Schellinger lived here between 1841 and 1930, and a look inside her house—still furnished with her belongings—gives visitors a good sense of what life on the South Fork was like back then. Behind the cottage is the **Roy K. Lester Carriage Museum,** which contains about 30 restored carriages, including a surrey with a fringe on top.

East Hampton Marine Museum
On the outskirts of town is the long, creaky East Hampton Town Marine Museum (Bluff Rd., 631/267-6544 or 631/324-6850, 10 A.M.–5 P.M. daily July–Sept., adults $4, seniors and children under 13 $2), filled with artifacts relating to whaling, fishing, and the sea. On the first floor are boats and more boats, along with

an exhibit on shipwrecks; upstairs are exhibits on shellfish harvesting, scalloping, ice-fishing, harpooning, and whaling. The museum also offers great views of the dunes and Atlantic. To reach the museum from Montauk Highway, turn south onto Atlantic Avenue. Watch for Bluff Road and turn right.

Beaches
At the end of **Atlantic Avenue** is a wide and wonderful public beach (631/324-2417). Equipped with lifeguards and a large concession stand, the beach was once known as "asparagus beach" because it attracted bunches of singles who stood together watching everyone else. Now it attracts a more mixed crowd. Parking is $10 during the week; on the weekends, a permit is required.

Accommodations
The **Mill-Garth Country Inn** (23 Windmill Ln., 631/267-3757, $225–350 d in summer, $165–230 d off-season, breakfast included), parts of which date back to 1840, is a romantic and eclectic B&B composed of cozy cottages and studio rooms clustered around small patios. Lush vegetation and wicker furniture are everywhere, and the beach is about a half mile away.

Food
Amagansett's most popular restaurant, in business for over 30 years, is the **Lobster Roll** (1980 Montauk Hwy., between Amagansett and Montauk, 631/267-3740). Also known as "Lunch" because of the huge sign it sports out front, the place is a modern roadside diner serving fresh, no-frills seafood; average main dish $12. Popular with the locals is **Gordon's** (Main St., 631/267-3010), an elegant, low-key spot known for its fresh seafood and wine list; average entrée $19.

Nightlife
The oldest and most beloved of nightspots on the South Fork is **Stephen Talkhouse** (161 Main St., 631/267-3117), where first-rate musicians—everyone from Bob Dylan to Billy

© CHRISTIANE BIRD

In Amagansett, no-frills seafood diner The Lobster Roll is also known simply as "Lunch."

LONG ISLAND

Joel—have played for decades. The place was established in 1932 and has a nice laid-back feel, with worn wooden tables and a friendly wait staff. A limited menu is available.

SPRINGS

At first, there doesn't seem to be any reason to visit this out-of-the-way spot, located at the intersection of Fireplace Road and Old Stone Highway, north of Amagansett. The place has no downtown, and no real stores or parking lots.

But Springs—a village of winding roads overhung with dark scrub pines—actually carries quite a cache. Painters Jackson Pollock and Lee Krasner, husband and wife, bought a house here in 1945, and soon thereafter, numerous other artists followed suit. Today the village continues to be recognized as a vital artistic center.

Springs is also home to a tightly knit community of farmers and fisherfolk. Long isolated from the rest of the world, the community developed its own dialect—complete with the vowel pronunciations of post-Elizabethan

England—still spoken by some of the older villagers today.

Art Sites

The unassuming 19th-century farmhouse where Pollock and Krasner lived is now open to the public. Known today as the **Pollock-Krasner House and Study Center** (830 Fireplace Rd., 631/324-4929, by appointment only 11 A.M.–4 P.M. Thurs.–Sat. June–Aug., adults $5, children under 12 free), it houses the artists' collection of Victorian furniture, books, and jazz records. Out back is a creaky barn—complete with a paint-spattered floor—where Pollock created many of his greatest works. Also on site is a collection of photographs documenting the lives of the two painters.

On Accabonac Road, not far from Pollock's old residence, is **Green River Cemetery,** which has recently become one of the Hamptons' odder tourist attractions. Pollock, who died in a car accident in 1956, is buried in the cemetery, beneath a boulder marked with an engraving of his signature. Since his death, numerous other personages—including artist Stuart Davis, poet Frank O'Hara, and art critic Harold Rosenberg—have also chosen to be buried in Green River, also beneath engravings of their signatures. As a result, carloads of visitors often drop by to show their respects, sometimes leaving tributes such as paintbrushes behind.

All this doesn't make the locals very happy. The cemetery is small, and the villagers worry that there won't be room left for them when their time comes. Some of the outsiders buried here—such as Davis—never even lived in Springs. The cemetery, surrounded by a white fence, is located on Accabonac Road, just south of Old Stone Highway.

Wildlife Refuge

The **Merrill Lake Sanctuary** (off Fireplace Rd., near Hog Creek Rd., 631/329-7689, free admission), run by the Nature Conservancy, is an easily accessible salt marsh especially good for bird-watching. A trail leads through the refuge. Ospreys nest here in late June and early July.

MONTAUK

I stand on some mighty eagle's beak,
Eastward the sea absorbing, viewing,
(Nothing but sea and sky)

The tossing waves, the foam, the ships
in the distance

The wild unrest, the snowy, curling caps–
that inbound urge and urge of waves,

Seeking the shore forever.

-Walt Whitman, "Montauk Point"

From Amagansett to Montauk is a drive of only about 10 miles, but the landscape changes dramatically along the way. Near Amagansett, the South Fork still feels like a well-tended region of small towns and farms; near Montauk, the terrain becomes windswept, barren, and wild. Despite all the tourists who flock here in summer, Montauk basically remains an isolated fishing village surrounded by dunes and sandy beach. Commercial deep-sea fishing is big business here.

Montauk proper centers on a circular green with a weathered gazebo. On one side of the green, known as the Village Plaza, is **White's** (631/668-2994), a creaky old variety store where you can buy everything from postcards and sunglasses to small appliances and 14-carat-gold jewelry.

The **Montauk Chamber of Commerce** (Main St., at the Village Plaza, 631/668-2428, www.montaukchamber.com, 10 A.M.–5 P.M. Mon.–Fri., 10 A.M.–2 P.M. Sat.–Sun.) is well stocked with brochures and maps. Parking is usually available in the lots along Main Street or on side streets.

North of Montauk proper is **Montauk Harbor,** always teeming with fishing and pleasure craft. The drive to the Harbor passes cornflower-blue Lake Montauk, while the harbor itself is home to a number of restaurants. Every June, the harbor hosts the festive **Blessing of the Fleet,** in which hundreds of boats receive prayers for a safe season.

Montauk comes as a welcome respite after the heady, moneyed land of the Hamptons. Though it, too, now has its share of trendy hot spots, Montauk's main attraction remains the sea and shore.

History

Some 15,000 years ago, Montauk—Algonquin for "hilly land" or "island country"—was an island unto itself, separate from Long Island. Not until relatively recently in its geologic history did it become connected to the mainland.

The earliest white settlers arrived in the area in the mid-1600s, but didn't settle in Montauk for another 150 years. Instead they used the spit of land as a summer pasture for their sheep and cattle, thus making Montauk the country's oldest cattle ranch.

To house the keepers of their cattle, as well the hunters who came to Montauk for its abundant game, the English built three houses. The First House was destroyed by fire, but the **Second House** and **Third House,** originally built in 1746 and 1747, respectively, still stand and function as small historical museums.

In 1898, Theodore Roosevelt and his Rough

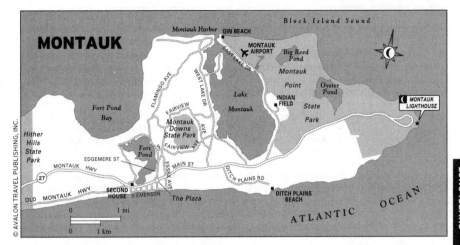

© AVALON TRAVEL PUBLISHING, INC.

Riders, along with close to 30,000 other men who had fought in the Spanish-American War, used Montauk as a quarantine station. Many of the soldiers had contracted infectious diseases during the war, and they recuperated on Montauk. During World War I, the area was home to a naval aviation base built to house dirigibles and hydroplanes; during World War II, it was home to a torpedo-testing range.

In 1926, developer Carl Graham Fisher bought up most of Montauk in hopes of turning it into a sort of "Miami Beach of the North." Fisher built the village center and office tower that still stand today, along with a Tudor-style luxury hotel called Montauk Manor (now condos) at the top of North Fairview Avenue. Unfortunately, Fisher went bankrupt in the Crash of 1929 and his office tower stood vacant for over 50 years. Not until the 1980s did Montauk boom into a popular vacation spot.

Second House Museum

The oldest building in Montauk is the Second House Museum (Second House Rd., off Montauk Hwy. [Rte. 27] west of the village, 631/668-5340, 10 A.M.–4 P.M. Thurs.–Tues. July–Oct., 10 A.M.–4 P.M. Sat.–Sun. June, adults $2, children $1), a dark and long-ceilinged affair, first built in 1746 and rebuilt in

1797. Inside you'll find period furniture and small, casual exhibits on Montauk history.

One of the most interesting displays concerns Samson Occom, a Monhegan Indian born in Connecticut. Occom came to Montauk in 1744 after converting to Christianity. He married a Montauk woman and became a noted preacher, as well as the author of several hymns still sung today. Together with two white ministers, Occum went to England in the 1760s to raise money for indigent Indians. The earl of Dartmouth was so impressed with Occum's powerful preaching that he donated £10,000 to the cause. Back in America, however, the white ministers took over administration of the funds—which they used to found Dartmouth College in 1769. Occum withdrew from village life, a disillusioned, discouraged man.

Third House

The Third House, in **Theodore Roosevelt County Park** (off Rte. 27 east of the village center, 631/852-7878, 10 A.M.–5 P.M. Wed.–Sun. June–Sept., free admission) is a big, rambling affair several times the size of the Second House. Set in the middle of what is now **Theodore Roosevelt County Park,** it was used by Teddy Roosevelt and his Rough Riders in 1898, and currently functions as the park headquarters. In the house is a small

THE MONTAUK CATTLE DRIVE

For over 250 years, from 1661–1926, cattle and sheep were driven onto Montauk in the spring and off again in the fall. Most were owned by farmers in East Hampton village or Amagansett, but some may have come from as far as Patchogue, a good two days' ride away. Depending on the year, anywhere from 1,000–3,000 cattle were pastured on Montauk. The farmers kept their animals apart with ear marks, which they registered with the town office.

The cattle's first stop was the green at the west end of East Hampton, where they were "baited," or fed; hence the street name, Baiting Hollow Road. They were then funneled through Amagansett's wide main street and onto the isthmus.

A Mrs. Elizabeth Cartwright, born in the mid-1800s, once recounted the excitement of those so-called Cattle Days for the *East Hampton Star:* "The family was astir long before daylight; East Hampton street was noisy with cattle lowing, men and boys on horseback, one herd after another going slowly by. … It was a busy time on Montauk the day before, preparing batches of bread, milkpans of pork and beans, dripping pans of roast veal, home-cured ham, pickles, coffee and pie, for sixty or more men."

exhibit on Roosevelt and his troops, along with early Montauk artifacts.

Indian Field

At the end of Pocahontas Lane, off East Lake Drive, is Indian Field, a burial ground. The last piece of land owned by the Montauks on Long Island, Indian Field today sits surrounded by modern homes, but still retains a peaceful feel. According to ancient custom, the Indians were buried here in a sitting position, in a circle relative to one another. Each grave is marked with a rough fieldstone.

The cemetery's largest and only engraved stone belongs to Stephen Pharaoh, better known as Stephen Talkhouse, who died in 1879. A whaler, Civil War soldier, and the last of the Montauk sachems, Talkhouse was also a famous walker who charged 25 cents to carry a letter from Montauk to East Hampton. Talkhouse's long legs enabled him to make the 35-mile round-trip journey in a day.

Beaches and Parks

About three miles west of Montauk is **Hither Hills State Park** (Old Montauk Hwy., 631/668-2554, dawn-dusk daily, parking $8 May–Sept.). Home to the only official public beach in Montauk where you can park without a permit, Hither Hills has a bathhouse, general store, picnic area, and campground

(see below). The park is also laced with hiking trails leading into isolated dunes, far from humankind. The dunes offer wonderful views of ocean and bay.

An unofficial public beach borders the village's center. Just park in the village, walk south down South Essex Street at the end of town, and you're there. Don't expect any facilities, however.

North of Montauk is **Montauk Downs State Park** (50 S. Fairview Ave., 631/668-3781, daily Apr.–Dec.), offering tennis courts, a swimming pool, and a golf course, all of which are open to the public.

Six miles east of Montauk, at the tip of the South Fork, is **Montauk Point State Park** (Montauk Hwy., 631/668-3781, $6–8 parking), a lonely and windy spot overlooking the sea. Throughout the park are hiking and biking trails.

◖ Montauk Lighthouse

Within Montauk Point State Park, but not officially a part of it, is the still-operating Montauk Lighthouse (631/668-2544, www.montauklighthouse.com, 10:30 A.M.–5:30 P.M. daily June–Sept., call for off-season hours, adults $6, seniors $5, children 6–11 $3, children under 41 inches tall not admitted to tower), one of the most popular visitor attractions on Long Island. The striped black-and-white structure was commissioned by George Washington in 1792 and has been protecting vessels traveling the transatlantic trade route ever since. At one time, the lighthouse burned whale oil. Today it's automated and no longer requires a keeper. The Coast Guard still runs the technical end of the lighthouse but leases the building to the Montauk Historical Society, which operates it as a museum. On display are the keeper's quarters, lots of lighthouse memorabilia, and an extensive collection of lenses. Visitors can also climb up into the tower for a grand view of the ocean.

Recreation

The nation's oldest cattle ranch, established in 1658, is **Deep Hollow Ranch** (Montauk Hwy. three miles east of village center, 631/668-2744, www.deephollowranch.com). Today a center for horseback riding, the ranch offers guided trail rides through 4,000 acres of parklands, pastures, and beach, along with pony rides, family barbecues, and riding lessons. Rates for the standard 1.5-hour beach and trail ride is $65.

Sportfishing is one of Montauk's major attractions. "Party boats" take out large groups of anglers daily (www.montauksportfishing.com).

Montauk Lighthouse

To sign on, call **Lazybones in Montauk** (631/668-5671), **Viking Fishing Fleet** (631/668-5700, www.vikingfleet.com), or **Marlin V** (631/668-2818). The Viking Fleet also offers **whale-watching** cruises departing from the Montauk Harbor in July and August.

Camping and Resort Motels

About 165 very popular campsites are available at (**Hither Hills State Park** (Old Montauk Hwy., 631/668-2554). Reservations are a must; the sites can be reserved by the week only. For reservations, call 800/456-CAMP.

Among the many resort motels in and near Montauk is the clean and friendly **Atlantic Terrace** (21 Surfside Pl., 631/668-2050, $175–249 d in summer, $95–155 d off-season), conveniently located right on the ocean and three blocks from downtown. One half mile west of the village is **Breakers at the Ocean** (Old Montauk Hwy., 631/668-2525, $160 d in summer, $95 d off-season), which offers motel rooms, studios, and cottages, all of which face the beach. The **Royal Atlantic Beach Resort** (126 S. Edgemere St., at Montauk Hwy., 631/668-5103, $185–235 d in summer, $95–125 d off-season) offers a variety of accommodations as well, including studios, one-bedroom suites, and "two-story luxury beach houses"; all have kitchenettes and private terraces.

Inns, Condos

The easygoing **Shepherd's Neck Inn** (90 Second House Rd., 631/668-2105, www.shepherds-neckinn.com, $120–280 d in summer, $90–130 d off-season) is a long, white, half-timbered building that looks like a modern Swiss chalet. Out back are five lush acres, a swimming pool, tennis courts, and putting green; inside is a restaurant specializing in fresh seafood.

On the edge of Montauk village, by the beach, is the modern, gray-shingled (**Surf Club** (S. Essex St. and Surfside Ave., 631/668-3800, www.duneresorts.com), a condominium resort that also rents spiffy one- and two-bedroom duplexes. The condos are built around an attractive pool ($315–545/unit in summer; about a third less off-season).

© CHRISTIANE BIRD

Now over 60 years old, Montauk's grande dame is 【 **Gurney's Inn Resort & Spa** (290 Old Montauk Hwy., 631/668-2345, www.gurneys-inn.com). The inn is perched on a bluff overlooking the ocean and has a rustic, old-fashioned feel. Heavy wooden furniture fills the main lodge, while along the beach are new and very spacious guest rooms filled with amenities. Gurney's also features a state-of-the-art spa and a full-service restaurant serving continental fare ($290–465 d in summer, including a full breakfast and dinner; $190–345 d off-season; special packages and spa packages are available).

Food and Drink

John's Pancake House (Main St. in the village center, 631/668-2383) serves an especially good breakfast, featuring pancakes, waffles, and crepes. The **Naturally Good Foods & Cafe** (S. Etna and S. Essex Sts., 631/668-9030) is a small natural-foods store that also serves breakfast and lunch.

The 【 **Lakeside** (183 Edgemere St., 631/668-3455) is a new restaurant and club. From the outside it looks like a creaky wooden house, but inside there's a sleek lounge. Out back is a huge patio lined with picnic tables and a bar overlooking the lake. On the menu are burgers, clam chowder, and the like; at night, the dance party begins.

Sitting high above the ocean, offering great views from its porch and patio, is the **Surfside Inn** (685 Montauk Hwy., 631/668-5958). Known for its friendly bar, complete with a fireplace, the Surfside specializes in seafood and continental fare; average main dish $20.

In business for over 30 years, **Shagwong** (774 Main St., 631/668-3050) caters to Montauk's large Irish population—and anyone else looking for local flavor. On the menu is plenty of good seafood (average entrée $18), but the place is equally well known for its lively nightlife.

Now over 50 years old is bustling 【 **Gosman's Dock** (500 West Lake Dr. at the Harbor, 631/668-5330). A Montauk institution, this enormous dockside restaurant has three dining rooms, all of which overlook the harbor, and serves consistently fresh fare; average entrée $18.

【 **Dave's Grill** (468 Flamingo Rd., 631/668-9190) is a classy, intimate diner specializing in grilled fish. During the summer, there's often a long wait, but it's worth it; average entrée $22.

Getting There

The two-lane Montauk Highway is the only road that runs all the way from Southampton to Montauk. During the summer and on weekends, it often gets unbearably congested, but there is no alternative route.

Sports and Recreation

BIKING

Since much of the terrain on Long Island is relatively flat, bicycling is a popular activity, especially on the North and South Forks. Bike-rental companies are located in many of the villages. Alternatively, you can take your bike on the Long Island Railroad if you have a permit ($5, downloadable from the LIRR's website, www.lirr.org). The Long Island Convention and Visitors Bureau outlines about two

dozen suggested bike routes on their website, www.funonli.com.

HIKING

The **Long Island Greenbelt Trail,** maintained by the Long Island Greenbelt Conference (631/360-0753, www.hike-li.com), runs the 34-mile width of Long Island, from Heckscher State Park on the South Shore to Sunken Meadow State Park on the North Shore. The trail follows the Connetquot and Nissequogue River valleys through wetlands, pine barrens, and forest. Other suggested hikes are outlined by the Long Island Convention and Visitors Bureau on their website, www.funonli.com.

WATER SPORTS

Sailboats, windsurfing boards, and **canoes** for exploring the area's ponds can be rented in many villages. Inquire at the local chambers of commerce.

Getting There and Around

The major west-east thoroughfares transversing Long Island are Routes 25 and 25A to the north; the Long Island Expressway (LIE), or I-495, mid-island; and the Sunrise Highway/Route 27 and the older Montauk Highway (Routes 27A and 80) to the south. The Southern State Parkway also traverses the South Shore, but ends mid-island, at Heckscher State Park.

Keep in mind that traffic on Long Island can be horrific. Avoid the Long Island Expressway during rush hour and on summer Friday afternoons, when thousands of Manhattanites head for the Hamptons.

Many Long Island communities, including those on the North and South Forks, can be reached from Manhattan via the **Long Island**

Rail Road (718/217-LIRR or 516/822-5477). Fares are reasonable and taxis are usually available at the other end.

The **Sunrise Express** (631/477-1200 or 800/527-7709) offers bus service between Manhattan and various North Fork villages. The **Hampton Jitney** (631/283-4600 or 800/936-0440, or 800/327-0732) services the Hamptons.

Ferries operate between Connecticut and Long Island. The **Cross Sound Ferry** (631/323-2525 or 860/443-5281, www.longislandferry.com) travels between New London and Orient Point. The **Bridgeport/Point Jefferson Ferry** (631/473-0286) lands you in Port Jefferson, an easy hour's drive to the west of the North Fork.

LONG ISLAND

Information and Services

For general information on Long Island, contact the **Long Island Convention and Visitors Bureau and Sports Commission** (330 Motor Pkwy., Suite 203, Hauppauge 11788, 631/951-3440 or 877/FUN-ON-LI, www.funonli.com). They operate four visitor information centers on the eastbound side of the Long Island Expressway (I-495) between Exits 51 and 52 in Deer Park; on the eastbound side of the Southern State Parkway between Exits 13 and 14 at Valley Stream; in

the Tanger Outlet Center, Tanger Drive, Riverhead, and at MacArthur Airport. All are open daily 9 A.M.–5 P.M. June–September; the Tanger Outlet and MacArthur Airport locations are also open year-round.

Long Island's **Pages of Pages** (www .fordyce.org) lists links to a wide variety of Long Island sites.

For more information on any of the state parks or campgrounds mentioned below, visit www.nysparks.com.

THE HUDSON VALLEY

As hard as it is to believe, to the immediate north of honking, teeming, steaming New York City lies some of the most splendid scenery in the Northeast. The visual feast begins at the edge of the Bronx, where for a 21-mile stretch the blue-gray Palisade cliffs drop precipitously into the Hudson River—never mind all the traffic and crowded towns nearby. Farther north and to the west sprawl the scrappy Ramapo Mountains, while to the east you'll glimpse the long, dark, silent reservoirs of New York City's water system. Midway up the Valley begin the Hudson Highlands, an extension of the Appalachian Mountains made up of steep cliffs, craggy bluffs, and brooding blue-black peaks. Lush, loamy farmland, heavy with fruits and vegetables, characterizes the regions to the east, west, and north of the Highlands.

Along with its seductive landscape, the Hudson Valley lays claim to dozens of major historic sites, ranging from Revolutionary War battlefields to grand river estates. The region also offers first-rate cultural institutions, off-beat museums, gourmet restaurants, luxurious hostelries, and glorious state parks.

Albany, the state capital, guards the northern end of the Hudson Valley. The Catskill Mountains lie to its northeast.

ORIENTATION

As with other New Yorkers, the people of the Hudson Valley don't think by region, they think by county, and everything they tell you will be phrased accordingly. Hyde Park is not in the Hudson Valley, it's in Dutchess County; to get to West Point from Nyack, you don't just

HIGHLIGHTS

◖ **Sunnyside:** Writer Washington Irving once resided in this house-museum, "as full of angles and corners as an old cocked hat." It's a charming, fairytale-like place, complete with costumed guides, a landscaped garden, and a pond with a bevy of swans (page 228).

◖ **Playland:** The dreamy art deco refuge, complete with original green-and-cream buildings, was built in 1928 as the nation's first amusement park (page 238).

◖ **Harriman and Bear Mountain State Parks:** Together the adjoining state parks cover more than 50,000 mountainous acres. Harriman is much less developed than often-crowded Bear, but both are great for hiking and scenic views (page 243).

◖ **West Point:** The nation's oldest and best-known military academy offers spectacular views of the Hudson River and a fine military history museum (page 245).

◖ **Storm King Art Center:** The breathtakingly beautiful hilltop park is filled with stunning sculpture by the likes of Henry Moore and Alexander Calder (page 250).

◖ **Dia:Beacon:** The region's major new art museum, housed in a former printing plant, contains the permanent collection of the innovative Dia Art Foundation, of New York City (page 260).

◖ **FDR's Home, Library, and Museum:** Franklin D. Roosevelt's former home and adjoining library and museum offer excellent insight into the man and his times (page 264).

◖ **Downtown Rhinebeck:** The picturesque historic village is home to many antiques shops, good hostelries and restaurants (page 267).

◖ **Olana State Historic Site:** Perched high on a hill is this eccentric Persian-style castle, built by landscape artist Frederic Church and filled with much of his artwork (page 275).

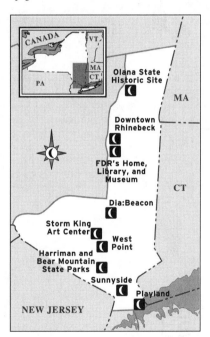

THE HUDSON VALLEY

LOOK FOR ◖ TO FIND RECOMMENDED SIGHTS, ACTIVITIES, DINING, AND LODGING.

THE HUDSON VALLEY

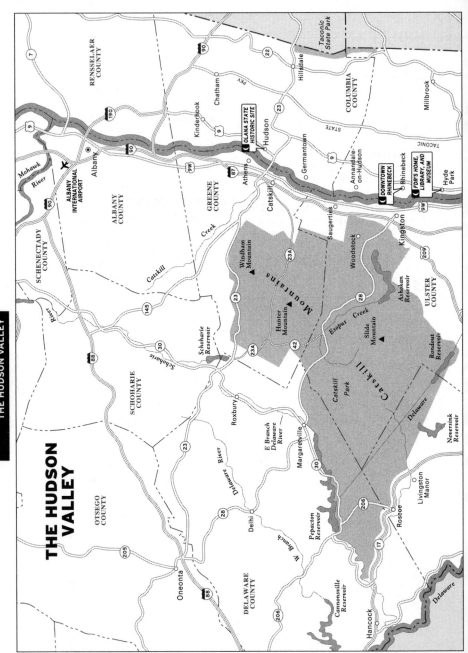

THE HUDSON VALLEY

RENSSELAER COUNTY

Taconic State Park

COLUMBIA COUNTY

Millbrook

Chatham

Kinderhook

Hillsdale

Hudson

Germantown

OLANA STATE HISTORIC SITE

Annandale-on-Hudson

DOWNTOWN RHINEBECK

Rhinebeck

FDR'S HOME, LIBRARY, AND MUSEUM

Hyde Park

Mohawk River

ALBANY INTERNATIONAL AIRPORT

Albany

Athens

Catskill

Saugerties

Kingston

ALBANY COUNTY

GREENE COUNTY

Woodstock

SCHENECTADY COUNTY

Catskill Creek

Windham Mountain

Mountains

Ashokan Reservoir

ULSTER COUNTY

Catskill

Hunter Mountain

Esopus Creek

Slide Mountain

Rondout Reservoir

River

SCHOHARIE COUNTY

Schoharie Reservoir

Schoharie

Catskill Park

Catskill

Delaware

Neversink Reservoir

Roxbury

E Branch Delaware River

Margaretville

Delaware

OTSEGO COUNTY

Delaware River

Livingston Manor

Delhi

Pepacton Reservoir

W Branch

Roscoe

Oneonta

DELAWARE COUNTY

Cannonsville Reservoir

Hancock

Delaware

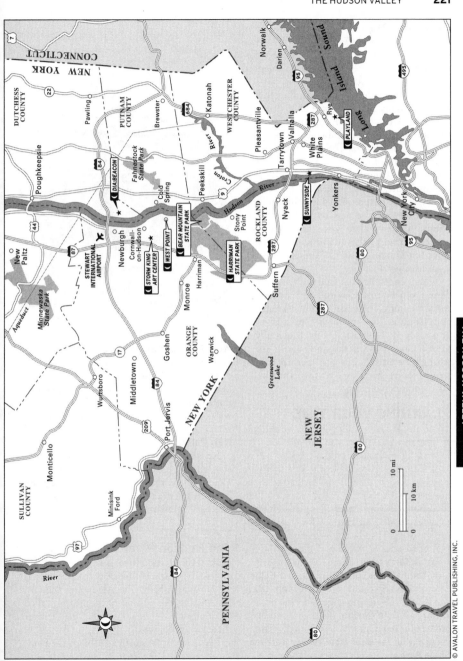

THE HUDSON VALLEY

© AVALON TRAVEL PUBLISHING, INC.

travel north on Route 9W, you cross over from Rockland County to Orange County. Anyone would think you were traveling between foreign countries, and each county does indeed have its own distinct character.

Depending on how you count, the Hudson Valley encompasses all or part of 10 different counties: Westchester, Rockland, Putnam, Orange, Dutchess, Columbia, Ulster, Greene, Albany, and Rensselaer. Since much of Ulster and most of Greene lie in the Catskills, however, and most of Albany and Rensselaer in Central New York, they are not included in this chapter. Keep in mind though, that Ulster and Greene Counties—home to Kingston, New Paltz, Woodstock, and Saugerties—are just a short drive across the Hudson from Dutchess and Columbia Counties, respectively.

Westchester and Rockland are the counties closest to New York City and are, not surprisingly, the most suburban. Dutchess and Orange Counties have the most to offer in terms of developed visitor attractions. Much of Columbia County is still farmland and is astonishingly beautiful. Putnam County is best known for its charming river towns and many lakes and reservoirs.

PLANNING YOUR TIME

To do the Hudson Valley justice would take at least two weeks, but you can also see a lot over a long weekend or on day trips from New York City. Easily accessible, the area sights are closely spaced; to drive from Manhattan to the northern reaches of the Valley takes less than three hours. If you're pressed for time, it's best to avoid crossing the Hudson River, as accessing the bridges can be time-consuming.

A good one- or two-day trip from the Big Apple is **Tarrytown,** home to four major historic homes, including Sunnyside and Kykuit. Another day trip could take in **Beacon,** where you'll find the cutting-edge Dia:Beacon museum, and **Cold Spring,** an attractive village on the Hudson. Outdoor lovers might want to take a day hike in **Bear Mountain or Harriman State Park** and stop in **Nyack** on the way back.

Kykuit, the Rockefeller Estate

West Point and **Storm King** make up another good day- or two-day outing.

A three- or four-day trip could take in one of the above sites, and two days in **Hyde Park,** home to the Roosevelt and Vanderbilt estates, with an overnight in or near **Rhinebeck.** Or, spend those extra two days in **Kingston** and **New Paltz.**

Six days could take in two or three of the sites above before traveling on to Columbia County. Here, visit the historic city of **Hudson,** home to a Persian-style castle (Olana) and the American Museum of Firefighting.

THE LAND
The Hudson River

Most of the Hudson River isn't a river at all but an estuary, or arm of the sea; ocean tides run as far north as Albany. The Algonquin Indians, recognizing this natural phenomenon, called the Hudson "Muhheahkantuck," or "the river that flows both ways."

Navigable as far north as Albany, the Hudson begins at Lake Tear in the Clouds atop

Mt. Marcy in the Adirondacks. Only 315 miles long from its source to New York Harbor, it varies in width from two feet to 3.5 miles, and in depth from a few inches to 216 feet. The Hudson's widest point is at Haverstraw Bay; its deepest is between Newburgh and West Point.

When European settlers first arrived in New York, they found the banks of the Hudson—like all the Northeast—lined with primeval forest. The trees were of gargantuan size, with foliage so dense there was virtually no undergrowth. By the mid 1800s, most of those trees were gone, cleared away for agriculture. Then came the Industrial Revolution, and cities, towns, and factories sprang up all along the river, bringing with them increasingly toxic levels of pollution. By the early 1970s, the Hudson had become, in the words of one local newspaper, a "flowing cesspool that was the shame of the Empire State."

Today, thanks largely to the Clean Water Act of 1972, the Hudson is a much cleaner place. Towns no longer spew untreated sewage into its waters, and factories have significantly reduced their chemical discharge. Much work remains to be done, but the Hudson is now regarded as a "recovering" river with an "improving" environmental condition.

Geology

The New York Metropolitan Region, which includes most of the Hudson Valley, is one of the world's most geologically diverse areas. Over the past millions of years, as geologist Christopher J. Schuberth writes in the *New York Walk Book,* it has been subjected to "an unprecedented barrage of one dynamic geologic process after another," including "submergence beneath marginal seas; sedimentation and crustal subsidence; volcanism; mountain-building; metamorphism and plutonism; more mountain-building; long-term and deep erosion. ..."

Ahem! What all this amounts to, in layperson's terms, is an extremely varied terrain that can be divided into five distinct geological subregions: (1) the flat Atlantic Coastal Plain, once submerged beneath the Atlantic (Rockland County); (2) the New England Upland, which includes both relatively flat terrain and the imposing peaks of Bear Mountain and Storm King (Westchester, Orange, Putnam, and Rockland Counties); (3) the Newark Basin, made up largely of red sandstone and the igneous bluestone of the Palisade cliffs (Rockland County); (4) the Folded Appalachians, composed of horizontal layers from ancient seas (Orange, Dutchess, and Columbia Counties); and (5) the Appalachian Plateau, a broad terrain of conglomerate, sandstone, and shale (Ulster and Greene Counties).

What this also amounts to is a surprising number of mountains in a region that is otherwise flat. Through the center of the Valley, in an area known as the Hudson Highlands, run the Appalachians. On the Rockland-Orange border are the Ramapos. West of the Ramapos is Schunemunk Mountain. In Columbia County are the Taconics. On the western edge of the Valley, and covered in the Catskills chapter, are the Shawangunks and Catskills.

HISTORY
Early History

Before the arrival of Europeans, the banks of the Hudson River were inhabited by the Algonquins, a group of linguistically related tribes who once controlled most of the Atlantic seaboard from Maine to the Carolinas. On the west bank, just north of Manhattan, lived the Lenapes, which included the Munsees and the Tappans, while on the east bank lived the Manhattans and the Wappingers. Further north, between today's Albany and Lake Champlain, lived the strongest of all the Algonquin tribes, the Mohicans.

A handsome and peaceful people, the Algonquins survived through hunting, fishing, and agriculture. They built canoes out of single large trees, and planted fields of corn and pumpkin. Too easygoing and loosely organized to be victorious in war, the Algonquins lived in fear of their fierce neighbors to the north, the Mohawks.

European Settlement

The first European to set eyes on the Hudson was Giovanni da Verrazano, who explored the coast of North America for France in 1524. But it was Henry Hudson, looking for a route to the Orient in 1609, who sailed the river as far north as Albany and put it on the Western map.

Most of Hudson Valley's early European settlers were poor tenants recruited by the Dutch patroons, or shareholders of the Dutch West India Company. The patroons had received huge tracts of land in exchange for establishing settlements of 50 people or more, and they lured tenants to the New World with promises of wealth and an easier life. But with one major exception—the ruthlessly run Rensselaerswyck, near Albany—the system was a dismal failure.

The English took over the Dutch colony in 1664, and soon replaced the patroon system with a similar system of their own. "Manor lords" built great estates along the Hudson and brought tenants north to work them.

During the Revolutionary War, the Hudson Valley played a prominent role. Major battles were fought near White Plains, Stony Point, Bear Mountain, and Saratoga farther north. Benedict Arnold's plot to betray West Point was foiled by the capture of the British spy, Maj. John Andre, at Tarrytown. General Washington declared the Continental Army's victory over the British from his headquarters in Newburgh in 1781, and it was here, too, that he first received what he later called an "offer of a crown." He turned the suggestion down "with abhorrence," paving the way for the establishment of today's democratic system.

Prosperity

After the war, the fertile valley began to develop into a thriving agricultural community, shipping many of its products south to New York City. This prosperity grew even greater after 1825, when the building of the Erie Canal opened up the nation's first trade route to the west. The canal helped turn New York City, and by extension the Hudson Valley, into the most important metropolitan region in the new republic.

As New Yorkers grew more wealthy, more great estates were built along the Hudson, especially in the region between Yonkers and Peekskill. The newly rich wished to prove to their more established counterparts in Europe that they, too, were a sophisticated and cultured bunch who enjoyed living in baronial style.

The coming of the railroad in the mid-1800s allowed the middle and working classes to move up the Hudson as well. For the first time, it was no longer necessary for people to live within streetcar distance of their jobs—they could commute. Small villages sprang up along the railroad lines; the suburban era was born.

At the same time, the railroad brought with it dozens of riverfront factories manufacturing everything from shoes to ball bearings, textiles to elevators. The factories attracted large numbers of Italian, Irish, and Eastern European immigrants, many of whose descendants still live in the Valley today.

Modern Times

In the mid-1900s, the Valley's luck began to change. Factories closed down due to changes in industrial demands. Small farms went bankrupt due to increasing operating costs and competition from large farms. Urban renewal knocked the guts out of some once-thriving cities. The woes of modern society—pollution, poverty, crime—spread.

Somehow, though, the Hudson Valley took it all in stride, and today the region remains one of the most interesting in the state. Small farmers live next door to commuters and second-home owners; recent immigrants from the Caribbean or Central America share counties, if not villages, with high-powered New York City executives. Some of the river towns remain scruffy and forlorn, but others have been nicely restored.

Westchester County

Westchester County is considerably more complex than it seems at first sight. While partly a bland land of posh suburbs and glitzy corporate headquarters, it also holds much Revolutionary War history, grand estates, a stretch of the Hudson River, and a large number of parks.

Most of Westchester County south of I-287 is densely suburban. This is where you'll find such wealthy communities as Scarsdale and Rye, the gritty cities of Yonkers and Mt. Vernon, and a growing number of ethnic communities.

North of I-287, Westchester begins to take on a whole different feel. Well-tended suburbs gradually give ground to trees, reservoirs, and lakes. By mid-county, you'll find bona fide historic villages, complete with New England–style greens, and by the time you reach the county's far northeast, you're in a rural land of winding back roads, horse farms, and old-moneyed estates. Northern Westchester has remained relatively undeveloped because it's largely owned by New York City, which began building reservoirs here in the mid-1800s.

And then there are the towns and villages along the Hudson River, which have a character all their own. Commuter towns since the late 1800s, many center on a railroad station and one main street. Meanwhile, on their outskirts—carefully hidden from prying eyes—stand dozens of grand, turn-of-the-century estates, only a few of which are open to the public.

Orientation

First-time visitors will probably want to concentrate on the Hudson River towns and villages. To explore them by car, follow Route 9, or Broadway, which is an extension of Manhattan's Broadway. To reach Route 9 from Manhattan, take the West Side Highway (Route 9A) north and watch for signs.

YONKERS

Yonkers, on the Hudson just north of New York City, takes its name from *younker* (young nobleman) Adriaen Van Der Donck, who first

acquired it from the Dutch West India Company in the early 1600s. With a population of over 200,000, Yonkers is actually the fourth-largest city in New York State, but it functions primarily as a sort of scruffy extension of its much larger neighbor to the south.

Originally a Lenape Indian village, Yonkers became an important manufacturing center in the second half of the 19th century. Among its chief products were textiles, carpets, patent medicines, insulated wire and cable, and elevators. Yonkers inventor Elisha G. Otis introduced the world's first "perpendicular stairway" in 1853.

Hudson River Museum

Yonkers' biggest visitor attraction is the Hudson River Museum (511 Warburton Ave., off Rte. 9 at the north end of town, 914/963-4550, www.hrm.org, noon–5 P.M. Wed.–Sun., 5–8 P.M. Fri., adults $5, seniors and children 5–16 $3), partially housed in an impressive

WEIRD, WONDERFUL, OFF-THE-BEATEN PATH HUDSON VALLEY

Museum of the Early American Circus, Somers: Housed in the former Elephant Hotel, built by the man who imported the first elephant to the United States in 1796.

Hambletonian's Grave, Chester: Most pacers and trotters racing today trace their lineage back to Hambletonian, who sired 1,331 foals in 24 years.

Wing's Castle, Millbrook: An idiosyncratic "castle" built out of everything from antique barn doors to toilet bowl floats to carousel animals.

Old Rhinebeck Aerodrome, Rhinebeck: Where Sir Percy Good Fellow fights the Evil Black Baron for the heart of Trudy Truelove.

THE HUDSON VALLEY

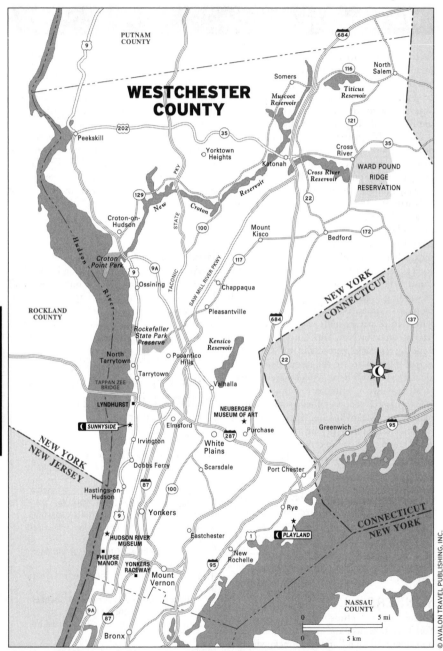

PUTNAM COUNTY

WESTCHESTER COUNTY

Somers

North Salem

Muscoot Reservoir

Titicus Reservoir

Peekskill

Yorktown Heights

Katonah

Cross River

WARD POUND RIDGE RESERVATION

Cross River Reservoir

Croton-on-Hudson

New Croton Reservoir

Mount Kisco

Bedford

Croton Point Park

Ossining

Chappaqua

Pleasantville

NEW YORK
CONNECTICUT

ROCKLAND COUNTY

Rockefeller State Park Preserve

Kensico Reservoir

North Tarrytown

Pocantico Hills

TAPPAN ZEE BRIDGE

Tarrytown

Valhalla

LYNDHURST

NEUBERGER MUSEUM OF ART

SUNNYSIDE

Elmsford

Purchase

Greenwich

Irvington

White Plains

Dobbs Ferry

Scarsdale

Port Chester

NEW YORK
NEW JERSEY

Hastings-on-Hudson

Yonkers

Rye

CONNECTICUT
NEW YORK

HUDSON RIVER MUSEUM

PHILIPSE MANOR

YONKERS RACEWAY

Eastchester

PLAYLAND

Mount Vernon

New Rochelle

NASSAU COUNTY

Bronx

0   5 mi

0   5 km

© AVALON TRAVEL PUBLISHING, INC.

stone mansion overlooking the Hudson. Built by financier John Bond Trevor in 1876, Glenview Mansion is still outfitted with its original Victorian furnishings and art. Next door is a large, modern museum wing that presents first-rate exhibits on everything from regional flora and fauna to Hudson River history. Also at the museum are the exuberant Red Grooms Bookstore—an "environmental sculpture" designed by the artist—and the Andrus Planetarium, equipped with a Zeiss star machine (shows cost adults $5, seniors and children $3). The museum's café is a good spot for lunch.

Philipse Manor Hall State Historic Site

A few miles south of the Hudson River Museum, next door to a well-worn park, is the grand Philipse Manor Hall (29 Warburton Ave., at Dock St., 914/965-4027, www.philipsmanorfriends.org, noon–5 P.M. Mon.–Sat. and 11 A.M.–4 P.M. Sat.–Sun. Apr.–Oct., noon–4 P.M. Sat.–Sat. Nov.–Mar., adults $4, seniors and students $3, children 5–12 $1). The manor was originally built in the 1680s for Dutchman Frederick Philipse, who came to New York to work as a carpenter for Gov. Peter Stuyvesant. Through his own skills and a strategic marriage, Philipse later rose to become one of the most powerful men in the Hudson Valley. By the end of his life, he owned an estate that covered virtually all of today's Westchester County.

A prominent Loyalist, Philipse was one of the 200-plus Colonial New Yorkers who signed the Declaration of Dependence, swearing allegiance to King George III shortly after those 56 other Americans signed the Declaration of Independence. Documents and artifacts from that era are on display, along with an excellent collection of American portraits by Gilbert Stuart and the like.

Yonkers Raceway

At Yonkers Raceway (810 Central Ave., at Yonkers Ave., 914/968-4200, post time 7:40 P.M. Mon.–Sat.), nighttime harness racing can be seen year-round. The current track dates back to 1958, but the first Yonkers track was built in 1898 and was long known as the "poor man's racecourse." In fact, one of its earliest owners, chain-store magnate James Butler, liked to pretend that he was poor. He once declined to play golf with John D. Rockefeller, Sr.—calling it a rich man's game—and rode around town in a rickety, out-of-date automobile.

THREE RIVER TOWNS
Hastings-on-Hudson

Heading north from Yonkers on Route 9, you'll soon come to the tidy residential community of Hastings-on-Hudson. Like Yonkers, Hastings began to grow after the construction of the Hudson River Railroad in 1849. Famed newspaperman Horace Greeley was one of the town's earliest resident commuters, while one of his neighbors was Johannus Stalton, an eccentric button maker who may have been the model for Washington Irving's Rip Van Winkle.

Another prominent Hastings resident was Hudson River School painter Jasper Francis Cropsey, whose former home is open to the public. Located on the slopes of a steep hill overlooking the Hudson, the yellow Gothic-style **Cropsey Home and Studio** (49 Washington Ave., 914/478-1372, weekdays by appointment only) contains about 100 of his luminous works, hung here and there throughout the house. Especially wonderful is the artist's former studio, an enormous wood-paneled room the walls of which are packed from floor to ceiling with canvases of all shapes and sizes.

Dobbs Ferry

Route 9 continues north to Dobbs Ferry, another commuter community, this one named after Jeremiah Dobbs who in 1698 hollowed out a log to ferry passengers back and forth across the Hudson River. During the Revolutionary War, Benedict Arnold meant to betray West Point to Major Andre in Dobbs Ferry, but Andre was captured in Tarrytown before Arnold could get to him. Later, in the late 1800s and early 1900s, many Italians, imported into the country to build the great Hudson estates

THE HUDSON VALLEY

and the Croton Reservoir System, settled in Dobbs Ferry because it reminded them of the hill towns from which they had come. Due partly to these Italian immigrants, and partly to its long history, Dobbs Ferry has an interesting variety of architectural styles.

Irvington

Beyond Dobbs Ferry is the fashionable suburb of Irvington, where sections of Route 9 are lined with imposing stone walls. Named for Washington Irving, who once lived next door in Tarrytown, Irvington has been home to a number of famous people, including artist Albert Bierstadt and businesswoman Madame C. J. Walker.

Walker, the country's first African American female millionaire, was the daughter of former slaves who made her fortune by selling hair and beauty products. She began her career in 1905 in St. Louis, selling a patented hair-straightener door to door. By 1910, she had earned enough money to open up the Madame C. J. Walker factory and laboratories in Indianapolis, Indiana. A woman of many interests and talents, Walker also founded a beauty school, established a center for black intellectuals, organized numerous social-welfare clubs, and was a leader in community affairs.

Walker's former home, an ornate brick mansion called **Villa Lewaro,** is located on North Broadway (Route 9) just north of Fargo Lane. Designed in 1917 by the first black architect of New York State, Ventner Woodson Tandy, the 34-room home is still privately owned but can be glimpsed from the road. In Walker's day, the Italian Renaissance mansion boasted a Gold Room—its ceilings trimmed with gold leaf—and a $25,000 organ that chimed on the quarter-hour and piped music throughout the house.

TARRYTOWN AND SLEEPY HOLLOW

Among the most popular visitor destinations in Westchester are Tarrytown and Sleepy Hollow, the latter formerly known as North Tarrytown. Despite being busy commuter villages, the towns are also home to four major historic sites and a handful of smaller ones. Washington Irving once quipped that the name Tarrytown came from the early Dutch farmers' tendency to linger too long at the village tavern. But most historians agree that "tarry" is a corruption of *tarwe,* the Dutch word for wheat.

Tarrytown is located at one of the Hudson River's widest points, the Tappan Zee. *Zee* means sea in Dutch, and the Tappan were an Algonquin tribe. Across the Tappan Zee runs the exquisite Tappan Zee Bridge, its graceful silver lines glinting in the sun.

Many of the historic sites in Tarrytown and Sleepy Hollow are operated by **Historic Hudson Valley** (914/631-8200 or 800/448-4007, www.hudsonvalley.org), an educational institution founded by John D. Rockefeller. The organization began back in 1937 when the 17th-century Philipsburg Manor was in danger of being torn down; Rockefeller bought it just in time. Today, Historic Hudson Valley operates six historic sites in the Hudson Valley region.

NY Waterway (800/533-3779) offers one-day **boat tours** from Manhattan to the Sunnyside, Philipsburg Manor, and Kykuit historic sites.

(Sunnyside

One of Tarrytown's earliest commuters was Washington Irving. In 1835 he moved into an old village farmhouse, now called Sunnyside (89 W. Sunnyside Ln., off Rte. 9 at the southern end of Tarrytown, 914/591-8763 or 800/448-4007, 10 A.M.–4 or 5 P.M. Wed.–Mon. Apr.–Dec., adults $10, seniors $9, students 5–17 $6), where he felt he could find the quiet he needed for his work, yet still be within easy reach of New York City. Almost immediately upon moving into his new abode, Irving began remodeling it, adding gables, dormers, and towers until the place was, as he described it, "as full of angles and corners as an old cocked hat."

Today the 17-room, wisteria-draped Sunnyside is open to the public. It's a charming, fairytale-like place, complete with costumed

Washington Irving's Sunnyside is covered by wisteria, planted by Irving himself.

guides, a landscaped garden, and a pond with a bevy of swans. Much of Irving's furniture, including his desk and woodstove, is still in the house, along with many of his books. Just below Sunnyside runs the Hudson River Railroad, which Irving allowed to be built through his property on the condition that it stop to pick him up whenever he wanted.

Lyndhurst

Less than a mile north of Sunnyside is Lyndhurst (635 S. Broadway [Rte. 9], 914/631-4481, www.lyndhurst.org, 10 A.M.–5 P.M. Tues.–Sun. May–Oct., 10 A.M.–4 P.M. Sat.–Sun. Nov.–Apr., adults $10, seniors $9, students 12–17 $4), a magnificent Gothic Revival mansion designed by Alexander Jackson Davis in 1838. Originally built for William Paulding, a former New York City mayor, Lyndhurst was later owned by the unscrupulous financier Jay Gould. Among Gould's many questionable acts were his attempt to corner the gold market, which resulted in the disastrous panic of Black Friday, September 24, 1869, and his engineer-

ing of a deal that ruined his former business associate, Cyrus W. Field. Not surprisingly, none of this history is discussed at the site.

Covered with gables and chimneys, turrets and towers, Lyndhurst from the outside is a magical place. Inside, however, it feels heavy and dark. Much of the Goulds' heavy furnishings and art collection is still in place.

Surrounding the mansion are 67 acres, complete with formal gardens, a children's playhouse, a bowling alley, nature paths, and spectacular views of the Hudson. Don't miss the romantic ruins of an enormous greenhouse, the 14 rooms of which once housed a renowned orchid collection.

Tarrytown Village Sights

North of Lyndhurst is the compact but often congested village of Tarrytown, where on September 23, 1780, the town's residents captured Maj. John Andre, a British spy who had conspired with Benedict Arnold to betray West Point. A Captors Monument in Patriots' Park commemorates the event.

Tarrytown today is an eclectic mix of corporate executives and blue-collar workers, neighborhood taverns and antique shops. Most of the latter are located along Main Street, a sleepy, old-fashioned thoroughfare that slopes gently down to the river.

Old Dutch Church and Burying Ground

Continuing north a few miles, you'll come to Sleepy Hollow and the Old Dutch Church (540 N. Broadway [Rte. 9], at Pierson St., 914/631-1123, www.sleepyhollowcemetary.org). Dating back to 1685, it's believed to be the oldest church in continuous use in New York State, but except for its thick walls, little of the structure is original.

Surrounding the church is a romantic Dutch cemetery that early settlers believed was haunted by a headless Hessian ghost. That local

GREAT RIVER ESTATES

WESTCHESTER COUNTY

Philipse Manor Hall, Yonkers: The oldest of the Hudson River estates, originally built for Dutchman Frederick Philipse in the 1680s. The grounds are no more, but the house is nicely restored.

Sunnyside, Tarrytown: Writer Washington Irving's former abode, a fairytale-like place "as full of angles and corners as an old cocked hat."

Lyndhurst, Tarrytown: Financier Jay Gould's magnificent Gothic Revival estate, designed by the great Alexander Jackson Davis in 1838.

Philipsburg Manor, Tarrytown: A carefully reconstructed 17th- and 18th-century manor house complete with costumed guides and a working gristmill. Especially good for kids.

Kykuit, Tarrytown: The former Rockefeller estate, famed for its magnificent grounds and collection of modern art.

Van Cortlandt Manor, Croton-on-Hudson: A lovely 18th-century stone-and-clapboard house that's half-English, half-Dutch. Not as well known as the Tarrytown mansions and therefore a good place to visit on summer weekends.

PUTNAM COUNTY

Boscobel, Garrison: An elegant, early-19th-century mansion that features an extraordinary collection of decorative arts from the Federal period.

DUTCHESS COUNTY

Locust Grove, Poughkeepsie: A romantic octagonal villa that was once the summer home of artist-scientist-philosopher Samuel Morse, inventor of the telegraph. One of the smaller estates.

Roosevelt Estates, Hyde Park: Perhaps the most interesting of the Hudson River estates. Springwood, FDR's former home, is a deeply personal place; adjoining it is a first-rate library-museum. Nearby is Eleanor Roosevelt's equally personal Val-Kill.

Vanderbilt Mansion, Hyde Park: The most extravagant of the Hudson River estates, built in a posh beaux arts–style by McKim, Mead & White. Go here to drool over lavish furnishings, gold-leaf ceilings, Flemish tapestries, and the like.

Staatsburg State Historic Site, Staatsburg: A vast, 65-room mansion on a hill. Edith Wharton based the Trenor estate in *The House of Mirth* on the place.

Wilderstein, Rhinebeck: A playful all-wooden Queen Anne mansion set on grounds designed by Calvert Vaux. One of the smaller estates.

Montgomery Place, Annandale-on-Hudson: Perhaps the loveliest of the river estates, with every line, every inch, perfectly in place. Built in 1802, remodeled in the 1860s by Alexander Jackson Davis.

COLUMBIA COUNTY

Clermont, Germantown: A grand mansion, with an especially fine front lawn lined with black locust trees.

Olana, Hudson: An eccentric Persian-style castle, perched high on a hill. Built by Hudson River School painter Frederic Church in 1870.

tale later became the inspiration for Washington Irving's *The Legend of Sleepy Hollow;* Irving took many of his characters' names from the cemetery's tombstones.

Adjacent to the old Dutch cemetery is the newer **Sleepy Hollow Cemetery** (430 N. Broadway), a scenic and peaceful place where Washington Irving, Andrew Carnegie, William Rockefeller, and other early movers and shakers are buried.

Philipsburg Manor

Across the street from the Old Dutch Church is Philipsburg Manor (381 N. Broadway [Rte. 9], 914/631-3992 or 800/448-4007, 10 A.M.–4 or 5 P.M. Wed.–Mon. Apr.–Dec., adults $10, seniors $9, students 5–17 $6), a carefully reconstructed 17th- and 18th-century manor house, complete with a working gristmill and small farm. Once owned by Frederick Philipse of Yonkers, the estate is now often jammed with tour buses and groups of schoolkids; of all the Historic Hudson Valley properties, this one is the best for families. Costumed guides describe life in Colonial times as visitors pass through the main stone house, gristmill, Dutch barn, and other buildings.

Kykuit

Just northeast of Sleepy Hollow is the elite little village of Pocantico Hills, home to Kykuit (KYE-cut) (914/631-9491 or 800/448-4007, escorted tours offered Apr.–Oct.). Only opened to the public in 1994, Kykuit—Dutch for lookout—was built in 1908 by John D. Rockefeller, Sr. The house served as the weekend home for three generations of the Rockefeller family.

Compared to many of the estates along the Hudson, the beaux arts Kykuit is a relatively modest affair, done up in 18th- and 19th-century antiques. In fact, the house tour doesn't become especially interesting until it descends to Nelson Rockefeller's astonishing subterranean art gallery, filled with more than 100 works by such modern masters as Picasso, Motherwell, Warhol, and Léger.

Even more wonderful are Kykuit's 87 acres of meticulously landscaped grounds, offering glorious views of the Hudson and Palisades. The gardens—complete with boxwood hedges, romantic arbors, and linden allées—are whimsically dotted with yet more modern-art masterpieces, including sculptures by Gaston Lachaise, Aristide Maillol, and Alexander Calder.

The Kykuit tours leave from Philipsburg Manor (381 N. Broadway [Rte. 9] 10 A.M.–5 P.M. Wed.–Mon. Apr.–Oct). Five different kinds of tours are offered and reservations for most are not required; same-day tickets are given out on a first-come, first-served basis starting at 9 A.M. Depending on the tour chosen, tickets cost $19–36 adults, $18–36 students under 17. The tours are not appropriate for children under 10.

Union Church of Pocantico Hills

A sleeper of an attraction is the serene Union Church of Pocantico Hills (555 Bedford Rd. [Rte. 448], 914/631-8200 or 800/448-4007, 11 A.M.–5 P.M. Mon. and Wed.–Sat. and 2–5 P.M. Sun. Apr.–Dec., admission $5) in the center of Pocantico Hills. Inside are nine stunning stained-glass windows by Marc Chagall and a luminous rose window by Henri Matisse. The Chagall windows depict biblical scenes. The Matisse window—a leafy swirl of green, yellow, and blue—was the final work completed by the artist before his death.

Rockefeller State Park Preserve

Once part of the Rockefeller estate, this well-kept 750-acre preserve (off Rte. 117 near Rte. 9, Mount Pleasant, 914/631-1470, 8 A.M.–dusk, parking $7) is filled with meadows and woodlands, a small lake, and over 14 miles of mostly level carriage and walking paths. Maps are available at the entrance.

Entertainment

Built in 1885, the **Tarrytown Music Hall** (13 Main St., 914/631-3390) is the oldest live theater in Westchester County. A National Historic Landmark, it is best known for its jazz concerts. Theater and art films are also presented.

THE HUDSON VALLEY

COURTESY OF HISTORIC HUDSON VALLEY

Kykuit gardens

Accommodations

One of the most romantic hideaways in Westchester County is the **(Castle on the Hudson** (400 Benedict Ave., 914/631-1980 or 800/616-4487, www.castleonthehudson.com, $305 d and up). Perched on a hill overlooking the Hudson, this authentic castle with its 75-foot-high main tower was built near the turn of the 20th century by the son of a Civil War general. Now a luxury establishment that's a member of the Small Luxury Hotels of the World and National Trust Historic Hotels networks, it offers 24 deluxe guest rooms and six luxury suites, some with working fireplaces. On the premises is the acclaimed Equus restaurant (see *Food*, below).

Also scoring high in the romance department is the **(Tarrytown House Estate & Conference Center** (E. Sunnyside Ln., 914/591-8200 or 800/553-8118, www.tarrytownhousehotel.com, $119–219 d). It's housed in two pristine 19th-century estates; one a Greek Revival mansion once owned by B&O Railroad executive Thomas King, the other a sprawling "castle" that belonged to tobacco heiress Mary Duke Biddle. Together, the estates boast lavish gardens, a well-equipped health club, a bowling alley, and a billiard room. Individual travelers may feel a bit out of place here, as most of the guests are conference attendees, but the reasonable rates more than offset the slight discomfort.

The **Tarrytown Courtyard** (475 White Plains Rd., 914/631-1122, $129–169 d), operated by Marriott, offers 140 rooms surrounding a pleasant pool and scenic courtyard. A café is on the premises.

Food

Horsefeathers (94 N. Broadway, 914/631-6606) is a cozy local institution, serving up home-style lunches and dinners ranging from simple sandwiches to filet mignon; average dinner entrée $16. The **Santa Fe** (5 Main St., 914/332-4452) is a small but very popular spot specializing in make-your-own tacos, quesadillas, and—especially—fajitas (including shark); entrées are $9–16.

THE HUDSON VALLEY

Serving both Portuguese and Brazilian fare is casual ◖ **Caravela** (53 N. Broadway, 914/631-1863). Brazilian music plays softly in the background while broiled sardines, shrimp mango, charbroiled codfish, seafood stew, and other tasty dishes are served (entrées cost $16–25).

The ultra-romantic **Equus Restaurant** (914/631-3646) at the Castle at Tarrytown (see *Accommodations,* above) is spread out over several elegant rooms and an enclosed terrace that offers great views of the Hudson. On the menu is innovative French cuisine; the prix fixe lunch costs $38, the prix fixe dinner, $71.

Blue Hill at Stone Barns (630 Bedford Rd., Pocantico Hills, 914/366-9600) is a branch of Manhattan's Blue Hill, known for its seasonal cuisine, low-key elegance, and high prices. This northern outpost, similarly inclined, is housed in a beautifully restored old barn. All around is the **Stone Barns Center for Food and Agriculture** (914/366-6200, www.stonebarnscenter.org), a nonprofit education center and 80-acre farm.

OSSINING

The next large village north of Sleepy Hollow is Ossining. The village was known as Sing Sing until 1901, when the villagers grew tired of hearing jokes about their hometown's largest employer, the state prison.

Sing Sing prison—original inspiration for the colloquial phrase, "to send up the river"— was built in Ossining between 1825 and 1828 by a group of prisoners transported south from Auburn State Prison in the Finger Lakes region. The shackled prisoners toiled in the village's marble quarries to build their new home, and lived under what was then known as the "Auburn system"—silent group labor by day, solitary confinement by night.

When the prison was finished, things got even worse. Sing Sing became known as the "House of Fear," largely because of its tyrannical warden who often complained that he couldn't find keepers who were ruthless enough. The inmates were punished for laughing, talking, or making any sort of noise. Flog-

ging and torture were routine. Reform didn't come until much later in the century. Even so, between 1891 and 1963, 614 people were put to death at Sing Sing, including Julius and Ethel Rosenberg in 1953.

Exhibits on Ossining's prison history are on display at the **Ossining Visitor Center** in the Joseph G. Caputo Community Center (95 Broadway [Rte. 9], 914/941-3189, near Rte. 133, 9 A.M.–6 P.M. Mon.–Fri., free admission). Here you'll find a replica of the electric chair and one of the cells from 1825, homemade weapons confiscated from the prisoners, an example of a current cell, and an excellent film.

Not far from the center are the blackened ruins of the original prison destroyed in the early 1940s, and the massive walls of today's Sing Sing, which continues to operate as a maximum-security prison housing more than 2,000 prisoners. The prison is just barely visible from **Lewis Engle Waterfront Park,** on the Hudson at Westerly Road, where you can sometimes hear the eerie sounds of bells, clanking doors, and voices coming from within the prison walls.

Ossining is also a good place to get a good view of the 1840 **Croton Aqueduct.** Its two tiers of arches run right through the town center near the intersection of Routes 9 and 133.

Teatown Lake Reservation

A few miles northeast of Ossining, peaceful 650-acre Teatown Lake Reservation (1600 Spring Valley Rd., off Rte. 9, 914/762-2912, www.teatown.org, dawn–dusk daily) holds a shimmering blue lake, hiking trails, an interpretive museum in two Colonial buildings (9 A.M.–5 P.M. Tues.–Sat., 1–5 P.M. Sun.), and wildflowers-galore in the spring, summer, and fall. Most of the 200 species of flowers grow on an isolated two-acre island in the middle of the park, accessible only a few times a week by tour ($4 per person; reservations required).

CROTON-ON-HUDSON

Originally settled in the 1800s by the Irish and Italian stonemasons and laborers who

THE HUDSON VALLEY

were building the Croton Reservoir, Croton-on-Hudson is still a small and homey, working- and middle-class village. Its one fashionable period came around the time of World War I, when writer Max Eastman, poet Edna St. Vincent Millay, radical John Reed, and other Greenwich Village artists and intellectuals— looking to escape city life—acquired land in the hills overlooking the town. This bohemian influx caused great excitement among the locals, who were appalled by the sight of women wearing shorts and smoking cigarettes.

Van Cortlandt Manor

The 18th-century Van Cortlandt Manor (S. Riverside Ave., off Rte. 9, 914/271-8981 or 800/448-4007, 10 A.M.–5 P.M. Wed.–Mon.

Apr.–Dec., adults $10, seniors $9, students 5– 17 $6) is another splendid estate owned by Historic Hudson Valley (see *Tarrytown and Sleepy Hollow*, above). Oloff Van Cortlandt arrived in this county in 1638, and his son, Stephanus Van Cortlandt, became the first native-born mayor of New York City. The Van Cortlandt family once owned 87,000 acres of land stretching from Croton all the way east to Connecticut. They were staunch supporters of the Revolution, and among their many famous guests were Generals Washington and Lafayette.

The deed to the Van Cortlandts' property still hangs in the house, along with original family portraits. Also on display are period furnishings and a working kitchen where guides concoct Colonial recipes. Outside, a long,

---

THE CROTON RESERVOIR SYSTEM

One of the most important events in New York City history occurred in June 1842, when the first water from the artificially constructed Lake Croton in Ossining flowed south along 32 miles of aqueduct into a giant reservoir at 42nd Street and 5th Avenue, Manhattan. Hundreds of church bells and a 38-gun salute rang out as the reservoir filled up with 150 million gallons of water. Then, and arguably still now, the Croton reservoir system (greatly augmented today with Catskill waters) provided New York with the best water system in the world; its creation allowed the city to escape the devastating 19th-century plagues of cholera and fire.

Although Lake Croton – made by damming the Croton River – was big, it wasn't big enough. In 1892, a new dam was begun just outside Ossining. Hundreds of homes were relocated and thousands of Italian stonemasons imported to construct what would become, 17 years later, the second-largest piece of hand-hewn masonry in the world. At 297 feet high and 2,168 feet long, the dam is said to have used as much stone as was used to build the Great Pyramid in Egypt.

HIKING THE OLD CROTON AQUEDUCT

Westchester's portion of the Old Croton Aqueduct, shut down in 1955, is now a 26-mile-long linear state park popular with hikers and cross-country skiers. Throughout the park, the walkway is wide, level, and grassy, and half-ruined stone ventilation shafts jut up at one-mile intervals.

The trail begins on the east side of the New Croton Dam (closed to visitors) in Croton-on-Hudson, where it passes through a wooded area of pine, oak, and hemlock. In spring, the area is rife with dogwood and mountain laurel.

If you pick up the trail farther south, between Tarrytown and the Hudson River Museum in north Yonkers, you'll pass a number of historic churches and 19th-century estates, and get great views of the Hudson. One easy access point is located just opposite the Hudson River Museum.

For a guide to hiking along the old aqueduct, contact **Friends of the Old Croton Aqueduct** (15 Walnut St., Dobbs Ferry, NY 10522; 914/693-4117). The guide includes historical information; cost is $5.75.

COURTESY OF HISTORIC HUDSON VALLEY

The principal rooms of the Van Cortlandt Manor are on the upper level.

brick-paved walk flanked with flower beds leads to a restored 18th-century inn.

A good spot for lunch is **Justin Thyme** (171 Grand St., 914/271-0022), offering everything from sandwiches to dinner entrées. To one side is a pub area with a copper-topped bar; to the other, the main dining room.

NORTHEASTERN WESTCHESTER
Katonah

About 10 miles east of the Hudson River, where Route 35 meets I-684, is the well-heeled, picturesque village of Katonah. On broad, tree-lined Bedford Street alone are 55 historic homes, all part of an area that's on the National Register of Historic Places.

And therein lies a tale. The homes were moved here between 1895 and 1897 when the original village of Katonah, located a half mile away, was flooded to create Cross River Reservoir. That event is known locally as "the Inundation."

Katonah Avenue, running parallel to Bedford, is also lined with Victorian-era buildings that were moved from the old village. Among them are the creaky, old-fashioned **Charles Department Store** (113 Katonah Ave., 914/232-5200), still operated by descendants of the original owners.

Museum Mile

Route 22 just outside Katonah is known as Museum Mile because of the three major cultural institutions found there. Most famous among them is the **Caramoor Center for Music and the Arts** (149 Girdle Ridge Rd., off Rte. 22, 914/232-5035, www.caramoor.org). An overgrown and romantic estate built in the 1930s by financier Walter Tower Rosen, Caramoor presents a highly acclaimed outdoor **music festival** (box office 914/232-1252, tickets $10–85) every summer, featuring many top names in classical music and opera and a few top names in jazz.

Originally built by Rosen to house his outstanding art collection, the Caramoor house museum (1–4 P.M. Wed.–Sun. May–Oct., adults $9, children under 16 free) is also well worth visiting. The fascinating main house was created by combining entire rooms from historic European buildings and surrounding them with a Mediterranean-style shell. One of the bedrooms comes from a 1678 French chateau; the exquisite music room was originally part of a 16th-century Italian villa. Meanwhile, all around the house are sunbaked courtyards and deserted gardens strewn with weathering statuary.

Down the street from Caramoor is **John Jay Homestead** (400 Rte. 22, 914/232-5651, 10 A.M.–4 P.M. Wed.–Sat. and noon–4 P.M. Sun. Apr.–Oct., call for winter hours, adults $4, seniors and children under 12 $2). Jay was president of the Continental Congress, first chief justice of the U.S. Supreme Court, and co-author of both the Federalist Papers and the Treaty of Paris (which ended the American Revolution). He retired here after leaving public office in 1801. The large wooden house with purple shutters and an inviting veranda is filled with period antiques and memorabilia. Surrounding the house are landscaped gardens and a 900-acre farm.

Just north of John Jay's former home is the small but exceedingly lovely **Katonah Museum of Art** (Rte. 22 at Jay St., 914/232-9555, www.katonah-museum.org, 1–5 P.M. Tues.–Fri. and Sun., 10 A.M.–5 P.M. Sat., with extended hours in summer, free admission). Designed by Edward Larrabee Barnes, the museum features unusual temporary exhibits by major contemporary artists such as Milton Avery and Mark Rothko.

Somers

The main reason to visit tiny Somers, located about five miles north of Katonah, is the oddball **Museum of the Early American Circus and the Somers Historical Society** (intersection of Rts. 100 and 202, 914/277-4977, 2–4 P.M. Thurs., 1–4 P.M. second and fourth Sun. of each month, admission by donation), housed on the top floor of the former Elephant Hotel. This once-elegant hostelry, now used for town offices, was built in 1825 by one Hachaliah Bailey, "the father of the American circus." Bailey made his fortune by importing the first elephant to the United States in 1796. For years he traveled up and down the East Coast showcasing his prized possession, who he called Old Bet. He later expanded his business to include other exotic animals. Hachaliah's younger distant relative, James A. Bailey, perhaps inspired by the older man's example, later became one of the founders of the famed Barnum & Bailey Circus.

The walls of the somewhat musty museum, run by the Somers Historical Society, are covered with early circus posters and broadsides, while the main exhibit is a miniature of a three-ring circus. In the display cases are Old Bet's trappings—an elephant prod, a chain—and a hodgepodge of memorabilia from dozens of other circuses.

On the way to Somers, you'll pass the vast **Muscoot Reservoir** and the **Muscoot Farm** (Rte. 100, just south of Rte. 35, 914/232-7118, 10 A.M.–4 P.M. daily, with extended hours in summer, free admission), an interpretive 1920s farm run by the county. Primarily of interest to kids, the 777-acre farm includes a dairy barn, horse barn, duck pond, pig pen, and nature trails.

North Salem

In the northeast corner of Westchester county lies North Salem, a rustic but moneyed one-stoplight burg surrounded by horse farms, wooded hills, and Titicus Reservoir. The village also boasts the Golden's Bridge Hounds, the only hunt club left in Westchester. During the hunting season, the club's 70-odd members ride to the hounds on nearby golf courses as often as three times a week.

On a hill overlooking North Salem is the unusual **Hammond Museum and Japanese Stroll Garden** (28 Deveau Rd., off June Rd., a quarter-mile north of Rte. 116, 914/669-5033, www.hammondmuseum.org, noon–4 P.M. Wed.–Sat. May–Sept., adults $5, seniors $4, and children under 12 free). Established by Natalie Hays Hammond in 1957, the place bills itself as a "cross-cultural center" for Eastern and Western arts. Inside the museum are changing exhibits on such subjects as antique Japanese fans and watercolors, while outside are meticulously designed Japanese gardens.

Hammond was the daughter of John Hays Hammond, the mining engineer who discovered and developed the long-lost King Solomon Mines in South Africa. She traveled the world as a child, became engaged eight times but never married, and worked as a Broadway set and costume designer, author, miniaturist, and needlepoint artist.

The museum's romantic, outdoor **◖ Silk Tree Cafe** (914/669-6777, open Wed.–Sat. May–Sept.) is an excellent place for lunch. On the menu are imaginative salads, sandwiches, and the like. Reservations are recommended; average dish $9.

Cross River

A few miles east of Katonah is 4,700-acre **Ward Pound Ridge Reservation** (Rts. 35 and 121, 914/864-7317, 8 A.M.–dusk daily, parking $8 May–Sept.), the largest park in Westchester County. Laced with 35 miles of good, fairly rugged hiking trails, the park also features two rivers for fishing and a small **Trailside Nature Museum** (10 A.M.–4 P.M. Wed.–Sun.). Year-round camping under lean-tos is available.

Shoppers might like to stop at nearby **Yellow Monkey Village** (Rte. 35 just east of Rte. 121, 914/763-5848, Tues.–Sun.), an attractive collection of shops housed in reproduction 18th-century buildings. The shops sell everything from Portuguese pottery to silk flowers.

Bedford

A few miles south of Katonah, where Route 22 meets Routes 121 and 172, is Bedford, another picture-perfect village. Here, pristine white 19th-century homes cluster around a village green, along with a carpenter-Gothic Presbyterian church and the nicely restored 1787 Court House—the oldest public building in Westchester County.

On a plaque in front of the Court House is printed a walking tour of the village. Take the tour and you'll pass the 1681 Old Burying Ground, a general store, post office, and library that date back to the early 1800s. On Court Road just off the green is a row of shops selling antiques, clothing, and gifts.

Chappaqua

About eight miles south of Katonah is one of Westchester's more unusual lodgings, the 12-bedroom **◖ Crabtree's Kittle House** (11 Kittle Rd., off Rte. 117, 914/666-8044, www.kittlehouse.com, $127 s, 147 d, with continental breakfast). Now over 200 years old, the building has been a carriage house, roadhouse, girls' school, guest house for the Mount Kisco Little Theater, restaurant, and inn. Henry Fonda and Tallulah Bankhead were among the actors who once overnighted here.

Attached to the inn is a restaurant serving lunch Monday–Friday, brunch on Sunday, and dinner daily. The eclectic menu includes a mix of innovative Italian, French, Asian, and American dishes, and live jazz is often offered on the weekends. Dinner entrées are $18–32.

SOUTHEASTERN WESTCHESTER
Purchase

Despite its bland appearance, the wealthy community of Purchase is home to two remarkable cultural sites. The **Neuberger Museum** (735 Anderson Hill Rd., 914/251-6100, www.neuberger.org, 10 A.M.–4 P.M. Tues.–Fri., 11 A.M.–5 P.M. Sat.–Sun., adults $5, seniors and students $3, children under 12 free), on the campus of the State University of New York, is a first-rate art museum with an outstanding collection of modern works by such masters as Georgia O'Keeffe, Jackson Pollock, Henry Moore, Frank Stella, Mark Rothko, Edward Hopper, and—especially—Milton Avery. Avery was the favorite painter of the museum's founder, Roy Neuberger, and 20 of his canvases are on display.

Just down the street from the Neuberger are the **Donald M. Kendall Sculpture Gardens at PepsiCo** (700 Anderson Hill Rd., 914/253-2000, 9 A.M.–dusk daily, free admission). Here at the corporate headquarters of the Pepsi-Cola company is an impressive outdoor sculpture garden filled with works by Alexander Calder, Jean Dubuffet, George Segal, Claes Oldenburg, and many others. Over 40 works are on display, scattered over carefully landscaped grounds complete with dramatic fountains. A path winds through the area, and a map is available at the entrance.

To reach either the museum or the gardens from I-684, take the State University of New York exit and follow the signs.

Playland

A sprawling suburban town located on Long Island Sound, Rye dates back to the 1660s when it was a notable stopping place on the old Post Road between New York and Boston. Then, as now, the town centered around Purchase Street, which today is lined with trees and sleepy antiques shops.

At the southern end of Rye is the wonderful Playland (end of Playland Pkwy., 914/813-7000, www.ryeplayland.org). Built in 1928 as the nation's first amusement park, this dreamy art deco refuge still boasts its original green-and-cream buildings and a number of original rides, including the Carousel, the Derby Racer, the Old Mill boat ride, and the wooden Dragon Coaster. Also in the park are about 40 other rides, a crescent-shaped beach with a weathered boardwalk, an Olympic-size pool, and a lake where rowboats can be rented.

Most of the rides at Playland are open May–Labor Day; hours vary, but midsummer hours are noon–11 P.M. Tuesday–Sunday. Admission is free, but parking is $5–7. Major rides cost $2.50–5, kiddie rides cost $2.50. To reach Playland from downtown Rye, head east on Playland Parkway. From I-95, take Exit 19.

Rockland County

Rockland County is named for the great outcroppings of rock that tower over the Hudson River at the northern end of the county. At only 176 square miles, Rockland is one of the smallest counties in the state. Just 33 miles northwest of New York City, it holds a predictable share of nondescript suburbs, congested highways, and glass-sheathed corporate headquarters. But a closer look reveals a rich tapestry of historic river towns and Revolutionary War sites. Due largely to the preservation efforts of its concerned citizenry, Rockland is also about 30 percent green. Two of Hudson Valley's biggest state parks—Bear Mountain and Harriman—straddle the Rockland/Orange County border here.

NYACK

First inhabited by the Nyack Indians, Nyack was settled by Dutch farmers in the mid-1600s and became home to thriving shipping, boatbuilding, and shoe- and cigar-manufactur-

ing industries in the 1800s. The village fell into decline after the Depression, but in the 1970s was reborn as an antiques and arts-and-crafts center. Today, most of Nyack's quaint Victorian downtown has been restored, while homes of the rich and famous perch on the steep wooded hills surrounding the village. Famous residents here have included Edward Hopper, Ben Hecht, Carson McCullers, Helen Hayes, Jonathan Demme, Ellen Burstyn, Harvey Keitel, and Toni Morrison.

To reach Nyack from New York City, take the Palisades Parkway north to Exit 4 and follow Route 9W north. To reach Nyack from Westchester County, take I-287 to Exit 10 and follow signs.

Edward Hopper House Art Center

The birthplace and home of painter Edward Hopper (1882–1967) is a two-story clapboard house in downtown Nyack (82 N. Broadway, 845/358-0774, www.edwardhopperhouse-

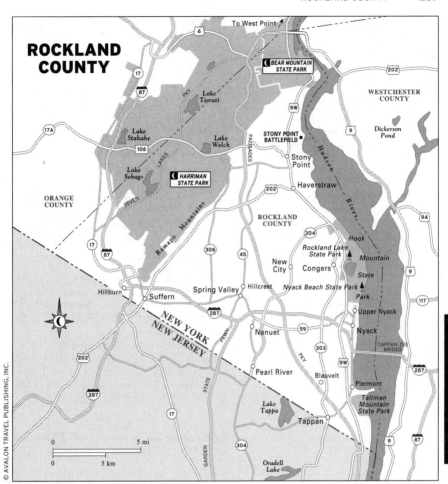

THE HUDSON VALLEY

© AVALON TRAVEL PUBLISHING, INC.

artcenter.org, 1–5 P.M. Thurs.–Sun., admission by donation). The son of a prosperous dry-goods merchant, Hopper grew up in Nyack and held title to the house until his death, even though he left the village in 1910 to live in New York City. Hopper is buried in Nyack's Oak Hill Cemetery.

The rooms of the Hopper House are wonderfully evocative—filled with a clean white light reminiscent of the artist's work. Unfortunately, only a small section of one room is devoted to Hopper's art. Most of the house is a gallery showcasing the work of local artists, while out back is a picturesque garden where summer jazz concerts are presented.

Pretty Penny

Continuing up North Broadway to the district known as Upper Nyack, you'll pass a number of grand Victorian estates. Helen Hayes once lived with her husband, playwright Charles MacArthur, at 233 North Broadway, a white house with a widow's walk that she called "Pretty Penny."

In 1939, during the Depression, Hayes and MacArthur commissioned a portrait of their house from a resentful Edward Hopper. Hopper took the work because he needed it, but he disdained working on commission. Recalled Hayes in 1981, "As a performer I just shriveled under the heat of this disapproval. I backed into a corner and there I stayed in the dark, lost... really, I was utterly unnerved by this man."

Today, Hopper's remarkable portrait, *Pretty Penny*, hangs in the Smith College Museum of Art.

Parks and Recreation

The riverfront **Memorial Park,** off Main Street in the village center, offers great views of the Hudson. Two miles farther north is **Nyack Beach State Park** (off N. Broadway, 845/268-3020, dawn–dusk daily, parking $6 June–Oct.), a riverfront stretch offering hiking, fishing, and more great views.

At the steep northern end of North Broadway reigns **Hook Mountain State Park** (845/268-3020, dawn–dusk daily, parking $6 June–Oct.), offering bird's-eye views of the Hudson, along with hiking and biking trails. Once a favorite campground among Native Americans, the park is said to be haunted by the Guardian of the Mountain, a medicine man who appears every September during the full moon to chant the ancient harvest festival. A hawk watch is held in the park in the spring and fall.

Entertainment

The 700-seat **Helen Hayes Performing Arts Center** (123 Main St., 845/358-6333) presents first-rate theater, concerts, lectures, and dance. At lively, rollicking **O'Donoghue's** (66 Main St., 845/358-0180), you're bound to hear many a tale; live Irish bands perform on Monday night.

Shopping

Most of the village's shops are found along Main Street (Rte. 59) and South Broadway. Among them are **Hand of the Craftsman** (5 S. Broadway, 845/358-3366), offering kaleidoscopes, kaleidoscopes, kaleidoscopes; and the **Pickwick Book Store** (8 S. Broadway, 845/358-9126), selling new and old books and art postcards.

Nyack also hosts many street fairs and festivals. Three of the biggest, all featuring about 200 vendors, are the **Art, Craft & Antiques Dealers' Fairs** (845/353-6981), usually held on the third Sundays of May, July, and October.

Accommodations

Several motels are located on the outskirts of town. Among them are the **Super 8 Nyack** (47 Rte. 59 at Waldron Rd., 845/353-3880, $72–99 d) and the **Nyack Motor Lodge** (110 Rte. 303 at Rt. 59, 845/358-4100, $70–85 d).

Food

Simple, casual **Strawberry Place** (72 S. Broadway, 845/358-9511) is a local favorite that's especially good for breakfast. **Temptations** (80 Main St., 845/353-3355) is the place to go for ice cream and desserts.

The newly redecorated **King & I** (91–93 Main St., 845/353-4208) is known for its fresh and authentic Thai food; average entrée $14. Local favorite **Heather's Open Cucina** (12 N. Broadway, 845/358-8686) is a lively Italian restaurant serving imaginative contemporary fare; average entrée $16. Asian-fusion cuisine is the order of the day at sleek, stylish ◖ **Wasabi** (110 Main St., 845/358-7977); average entrée $16.

For dinner in a historic setting, try the ◖ **Hudson House of Nyack** (134 Main St., 845/353-1355), housed in an old town hall with pressed tin walls and ceilings. On the menu is eclectic American cuisine and lots of homemade desserts. Patio dining is featured in summer; average entrée $18.

Information

In summer, when Nyack is overrun with tourists, a Nyack Chamber of Commerce **information booth** (845/353-2221), operates daily at the corner of Main Street and

Broadway. The booth is also open weekends in spring and fall.

PIERMONT

Just south of Nyack is the village of Piermont, which in its heyday was a bustling commercial center at the terminus of the Erie Railroad. Today it's a quieter, less touristy version of Nyack. Woody Allen filmed much of *The Purple Rose of Cairo* here in the early 1980s.

Most of the village's shops and art galleries are located on or just off Piermont Avenue. Among them are **Boondocks** (490 Piermont Ave., 845/365-2221), an "environmental marketplace" selling rainforest kits and the like, and **Piermont Flywheel Gallery** (220 Ash St., 845/365-6411), which features the work of its 24 co-owners, all artists and sculptors.

In the center of town is **Piermont Pier,** which extends out into the river about a mile. Built by Chinese immigrants to allow the railroad easier access to Hudson River ships, the pier today is delightfully overgrown with cottonwoods, poplars, and goldenrod. From along its length you'll have unobstructed views of the Tappan Zee bridge and **Piermont Marsh,** a 950-acre wetland and bird sanctuary.

If you're interested in actually visiting Piermont Marsh, enter **Tallman Mountain State Park** (off Rte. 9W, 845/359-0544, dawn–dusk daily, parking $6 June–Sept.) just south of the pier and follow the bike path to the shore. The preserve, covered with wildflowers in the spring, is one of the most important fish-breeding areas along the Hudson and an excellent bird-watching spot.

Food

A number of restaurants are located along Piermont Avenue. Classiest among them is **Xaviar's at Piermont** (506 Piermont Ave., 845/359-7007), a highly acclaimed fine dining establishment serving contemporary American fare; prix fixe lunch, $40; prix fixe dinner, $60; chef's tasting menu, $80. Next door is a less-expensive sister restaurant, the informal yet sophisticated **◖ Freelance Cafe and Wine Bar**

(506 Piermont Ave., 845/365-3250), serving an eclectic cuisine with Asian, French, and Italian influences; average entrée $20.

For a simpler meal, head over to **Pasta Amore** (200 Ash St., 845/365-1911), where you'll find a wide variety of Northern Italian dishes, as well as glorious views of the Hudson; average entrée $15.

Nightlife

One of the Hudson Valley's oldest and best-loved music clubs is the **Turning Point** (468 Piermont Ave., 845/359-1089, www.turningpointcafe.com, tickets $12–25). Low-ceilinged and filled with dark wood, the club presents mostly folk and folk-rock, along with some jazz and blues. The club also serves a moderately priced lunch and dinner; average dinner entrée $15.

TAPPAN

To the west of Piermont is the historic town of Tappan, the first town in New York State to establish an official historic district. Its Main Street is flanked with many nicely restored 18th- and 19th-century buildings, and in the town center is a village green that once held public stocks and a whipping post.

Revolutionary War Sites

Tappan is associated with both the beginning and the end of the planned betrayal of West Point by Benedict Arnold and British major John Andre during the Revolutionary War. It was in the DeWint House on Livingston Avenue that Washington entrusted West Point to Arnold, and it was in the Mabie House on Main Street that Andre—after his capture in Tarrytown—was imprisoned before being hanged.

Both buildings are still standing and open to the public. The DeWint House, also known as **Washington's Headquarters** (20 Livingston Ave., 845/359-1359, 10 A.M.–4 P.M. daily, free admission) is now a bona fide museum holding Washington memorabilia, artifacts regarding Masonic history, and information about the

Andre trial. Washington was headquartered here in 1780 and 1783, and was a Mason for 47 years. On the day of Andre's execution, Washington closed the shutters to his room.

The Mabie House is now better known as the **Old '76 House** (110 Main St., 845/359-5476) and is a dark, low-ceilinged establishment that has functioned as a tavern and restaurant since 1800 (see *Food*, below). Andre's former bedroom is now a dining room.

Also connected with Andre is the **Andre Monument** (Old Tappan Rd. at Andre Hill Rd.). Here, a large crowd of spectators, held back by 500 infantrymen, watched Andre's execution on October 2, 1780. Only upon seeing the hangman's noose did Andre realize that his request to be shot as a soldier, rather than hung as a spy, was not to be granted. Impatient with his slow-moving hangman—a sympathetic fellow prisoner—Andre placed the noose around his own neck and the handkerchief around his own eyes. "All I request of you gentlemen," he said before the final signal was given, "is that

you bear witness to the world that I die like a brave man."

Food

The **Old '76 House** (110 Main St., 845/359-5476), complete with exposed beams, Dutch tiles, and fireplaces, specializes in traditional American fare for lunch and dinner. A jazz vocalist or pianist often perform on the weekend; average dinner entrée $20.

THE RAMAPO MOUNTAINS

Near the western edge of Rockland County rise the craggy foothills of the Ramapo Mountains. At nearly 600 million years old, the Precambrian Ramapos—which spill over into New Jersey—are one of the oldest land masses in North America. At one time, their slopes—now eroded and dotted with erratics left during the Ice Age—constituted a mountain system as grand as the Rockies.

In New York, most of the Ramapos fall within two very popular state parks—Harri-

The Old '76 House has been a tavern and restaurant for more than a century.

man and Bear Mountain. The parks were created largely through the efforts of Mrs. E. H. Harriman, widow of the railroad tycoon Edward Harriman and mother of the late statesman W. Averell Harriman. When the state proposed building a prison at Bear Mountain in 1908, Mrs. Harriman offered to give the Palisades Interstate Park Commission 10,000 acres in return for dropping the project. The proposal was accepted and since then the parks have been significantly enlarged through other gifts and purchases.

◖ Harriman and Bear Mountain State Parks

Straddling Rockland and Orange Counties is Harriman State Park (off Rte. 17 or Palisades Pkwy. [Exits 17 or 18], 8:30 A.M.–dusk daily, parking $6–8 June–Sept. and weekends year-round), a 46,000-acre preserve that is considerably less developed than its better-known neighbor to the north, Bear Mountain State Park. Through the heart of Harriman runs **Seven Lakes Drive,** which hugs the shores of only a small portion of the many bodies of water to be found in this preserve. Two of the most spectacular of these are crystal-clear **Lake Tiorati** and **Lake Sebago.** Ironically, their Native American names—bestowed upon them by white men eager to create a romantic atmosphere—are not local, but rather names that come from Western tribes. Both

THE RAMAPOUGH PEOPLE

In the foothills of the Ramapo Mountains live the Ramapough people, who trace their mixed ancestry to Munsee Indians, early freed blacks and escaped slaves, and the Dutch. Most of the 3,000 or so Ramapoughs live in or near **Hillburn,** a small town just south of Harriman State Park, and in Ringwood and Mahwah, New Jersey.

The first permanent residents of the Ramapos were the Munsees, a subgroup of the Algonquins who moved into the area after being displaced from the lowlands by the Europeans around 1700. The Munsees were joined by early settlers – both black and white – around 1750. Many of the settlers came to the area to escape discrimination or the law, or to achieve a level of independence impossible in more settled communities.

Living on the fringes of developing America, the Ramapoughs survived by hunting, subsistence farming, and selling crafts, fruits, and berries door to door. Treated as outcasts throughout much of the 19th and 20th centuries, they were the subject of much local gossip and lore. Many disparagingly called them the "Jackson Whites" and "Jackson Blacks" in reference to a trader who allegedly furnished hundreds of white and black prostitutes for

His Majesty's troops in Manhattan during the Revolution. After the war, so the story goes, the prostitutes were driven out of New York City and into the Ramapos.

Only since World War II and the influx of new residents have local attitudes regarding the Ramapoughs started to change. In fact, during the past few decades, several civic groups composed of both the mountain people and their neighbors have been actively working to improve community relations.

Since 1980, too, the Ramapough people have been petitioning the federal government to acknowledge them as a legitimate American Indian tribe. So far, that recognition – which would bring many benefits, including housing and health care – has been withheld. The government says that the Ramapoughs have not conclusively proven their Indian heritage. However, the group has been recognized by the State of New Jersey, New York State, and numerous other Indian tribes. And with or without federal recognition, the Ramapoughs continue to practice many of their Indian traditions. They divide themselves into three clans – the Turtle, Deer, and Fox – elect a chief and council, and carry tribal identity cards.

of the large, artificially constructed lakes have swimming beaches.

About 200 miles of **marked trails** loop through Harriman and its neighbor, Bear Mountain. Basic information on some of these trails can be picked up at the headquarters of the Palisades Interstate Park Commission (Bear Mt., Rte. 9W, 845/786-2701). For more detailed information and maps, stop at the superb **Park Visitor Information Center** (between Exits 16 and 17 on the Palisades Pkwy., 845/786-5003) or contact the **New York-New Jersey Trail Conference** (201/512-9348, www.nynjtc.com). The park also offers an excellent, 200-site **campground;** call 800/456-CAMP for reservations.

Just south of the park, on a mountaintop near Hillburn, is ◖ **Mount Fuji** (Rte. 17, 845/357-4270), a big, glitzy Japanese steakhouse offering stunning views of the valley below; entrées range from $19–37. On the western border of the park are the Clove Furnace Historic Site, Tuxedo Park, and Sterling Forest (see *Orange and Putnam Counties,* below).

When New Yorkers think about getting out of the city for a day-hike, they think about Bear Mountain (Palisades Pkwy. [Exit 19] and Rte. 9W, 845/786-2701, 8:30 A.M.–dusk daily, parking $6–8 June–Sept. and weekends year-round)—one of the most popular recreational areas in the region. Abutting Harriman to the north, the park offers dramatic views of the Hudson River and—on the clearest of days—the New York City skyscrapers. Because Bear Mountain can get very crowded on weekends, it's best to come during the week. This is also no place for the outdoors purist; almost every inch of the 5,000-acre park has been trodden over many times.

To hike to the top of Bear Mountain and back takes three to four hours. For those who prefer to drive to the summit, **Perkins Memorial Drive** (open March–Oct.) offers stunning overlooks and historic markers that tell of the Revolutionary War battles that took

place here. Legend has it that Hessian Lake was named for the many dead Hessian soldiers whose bodies were weighted and dumped into the lake after the battle of Fort Clinton. The fort's ruins are nearby.

Though overrun with crowds on summer weekends, the rustic ◖ **Bear Mountain Inn** (Rte. 9W, 845/786-2731, www.bearmountain-inn.com, $99 d) is a charming spot, now over 80 years old. The inn's 61 rooms are divided among the Main Inn, four small stone lodges, and the Overlook, a hotel near Hessian Lake. Come on a weekday in fall and you'll have the place to yourself.

Also in the inn are a cafeteria and a restaurant serving standard American fare (average entrée $14). Other attractions include the **Trailside Museum and Wildlife Center** (9 A.M.–5 P.M. daily), ball fields, a swimming pool, and an ice-skating rink.

To reach Bear Mountain from the south, take Palisades Parkway or Route 9W. From Harriman State Park, head northeast on Seven Lakes Drive.

STONY POINT

South of Bear Mountain is **Stony Point Battlefield** (Park Rd., off Rte. 9W, 845/786-2521, 10 A.M.–5 P.M. Wed.–Sat. and 1–5 P.M. Sun. Apr.–Oct., weekend parking $7), where the British army that was threatening West Point was based in the summer of 1779. Stony Point was captured by the Americans in a daring midnight raid led by Gen. "Mad" Anthony Wayne. A tour of the battlefield takes visitors through a small interpretive museum, past the ruins of the British fortifications, and past the oldest lighthouse on the Hudson River. All around is beautiful countryside.

Stony Point is also home to ◖ **Annie's Restaurant** (149 Rte. 9W, 845/942-1011). Since 1952, motorists have been coming to this drive-in, which serves its fast food in paper plates shaped like Chevy convertibles. The eatery is said to attract lots of bikers and soap-opera stars. Bruce Springsteen is also a fan.

Orange and Putnam Counties

Eastern Orange County is one of the most popular tourist destinations in the Hudson Valley, and it shows. You'll see more signs directing you toward visitor attractions here than in most of the region, and more tourist-oriented shops. Most visitors head first to the justifiably popular West Point, perched on cliffs overlooking the Hudson, and then to the important Revolutionary War sites near Newburgh or the spectacular Storm King Art Center—surely one of the most beautiful outdoor sculpture parks in the world. Afterward, though, many get trapped in the Central Valley region, where commercialized establishments act as magnets to dollars, checkbooks, charge cards, and loose change.

In contrast, much of central and western Orange County is still largely rural farm country. In the laid-back county seat of Goshen is a unique museum dedicated to trotters, pacers, and harness racing. Near Pine Island is the "black dirt" or "drowned lands" farming region dotted with produce stands and pick-your-own farms. At the southeastern end of the county, straddling the Rockland border, are the adjoining Bear Mountain and Harriman State Parks.

Putnam County, directly across the Hudson River from Orange, is full of quiet small towns, lakes, and reservoirs. Along its riverbank are the Victorian village of Cold Spring and a splendid Federal-style mansion called Boscobel. Much of Putnam County (two thirds, to be exact), like northeastern Westchester County, is part of New York City's watershed system, which has helped to preserve its rural character.

◖ WEST POINT

The Hudson Valley between Dunderberg Mountain to the south and Storm King Mountain to the north is known as the **Hudson Highlands.** Along this 15-mile stretch, the Hudson River, narrowing and deepening, cuts through the Appalachian Mountain Range, creating a spectacular rocky gorge.

About halfway up this stretch, where the river takes a sharp turn, is a rocky outcropping known as West Point. With its strategic views of both sides of the river, it's easy to see why it was such an important stronghold during the Revolutionary War.

On West Point today sits the country's oldest and best-known **U.S. Military Academy** (www.usma.edu), authorized by Congress in 1802. About 4,400 cadets are enrolled here each year. Graduates have included Generals Grant, Lee, Pershing, MacArthur, and Eisenhower; misfits have included James Whistler and Edgar Allan Poe.

Near the Thayer Gate entrance to the Gothic, fortresslike academy is a giant **visitors center** (Rte. 218, 845/938-2638, 9 A.M.–4:45 P.M. daily). The center stocks brochures and maps, holds a large gift shop, and screens a short movie about the cadets' lives.

Next door to the visitors center is the **West Point Museum** (Rte. 218, 845/938-2203, 10:30 A.M.–4:15 P.M. daily, free admission), filled with a wide and fascinating array of exhibits on military history. Here you'll find everything from a Stone Age axe to weapons used in Vietnam and the Gulf War; dioramas of famous battles fought between the 16th and 20th centuries; the letter that Einstein wrote to President Roosevelt urging him to begin research on the uses of plutonium; and a pistol that once belonged to Adolf Hitler. One philosophical panel, simply entitled "Reflections," includes quotes by famous military leaders throughout history—from Thucydides to Eisenhower.

Since the September 11 attacks, the academy can only be visited via escorted tours (adults $8, children 5–12 $5), which leave from the visitors center throughout the day, except during special events such as football games. Tour highlights include the **Cadet Chapel,** lined with lovely stained-glass windows donated by graduated classes; the **Plain,** where the cadets march out in formation at precisely 12:20 P.M. every day; and **Trophy**

THE HUDSON VALLEY

THE HUDSON VALLEY

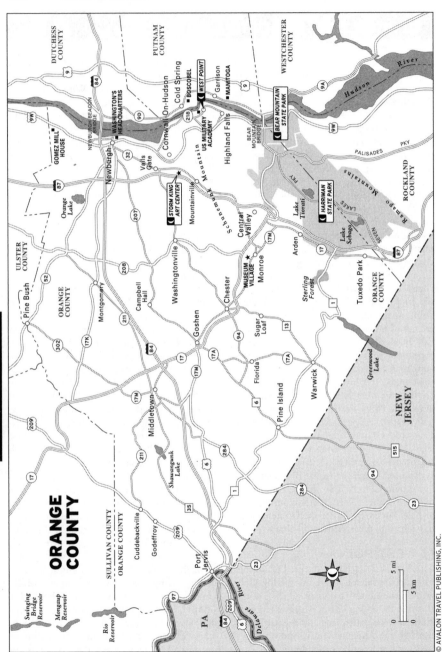

ORANGE COUNTY

© AVALON TRAVEL PUBLISHING, INC.

Point, where you'll find unforgettable views of the blue-gray Hudson. Also at the point are links of the "Great Chain" that the patriots once stretched across the river here to prevent the passage of British ships.

Constitution Island

One of the more unusual spots at West Point is Constitution Island (845/446-8676, www.constitutionisland.org, Wed.–Thurs. afternoons June–Oct., adults $10, seniors and students $9, children 3–6 $3), accessible only by boat, which leaves from West Point's South dock; reservations required. Strategically important during the Revolution, the island later became the home of Susan and Anna Warner, two 19th-century writers who taught Bible classes at West Point. Susan was the author of the popular 1850 novel *The Wide, Wide World;* Anna was best known for writing the words to the hymn "Jesus Loves Me."

The sisters lived in the **Warner House,** a 17-room Victorian mansion built on the island by their father in 1836. One wall of the mansion dates back to Revolutionary War days, and the whole house is furnished more or less as it was when the sisters lived here.

Recreation

Hudson Highland Cruises (845/534-7245, www.hudsonhighlandcruises.com) offers cruises of the Hudson that leave from West Point's South Dock and West Haverstraw May–October.

Accommodations and Food

On the academy grounds just inside Thayer Gate off Route 218 stands the big, gray, castlelike ◖ **Thayer Hotel** (674 Thayer Rd., 845/446-4731 or 800/247-5047, www.theth-ayerhotel.com, $180–230 d), where the rooms are outfitted in the style of late-19th-century Americana. Some rooms overlook the Hudson, others the West Point campus, while the lobby and restaurant are outfitted with marble floors and iron chandeliers. Outside is a pleasant terrace with more great views of the Hudson. The hotel's upscale restaurant serves traditional American and Continental cuisine; average dinner entrée $22.

THE HUDSON VALLEY

inside the Warner House on Constitution Island

COURTESY OF ORANGE COUNTY TOURISM

CORNWALL-ON-HUDSON

From West Point north to the tidy village of Cornwall-on-Hudson runs the **Storm King Highway** (Route 218), a twisting, narrow roadway that hugs the cliffs of the Hudson River gorge, offering stunning views of the landscape below. It's a particularly fine drive in fall, when the hills are ablaze with maroon, bright red, orange, and yellow.

Museum of the Hudson Highlands

Cornwall's Museum of the Hudson Highlands (The Boulevard, off Payson Rd., 845/534-7781, www.museumhudsonhighlands.org, noon–5 P.M. Thurs.–Sun., admission $2), founded by a group of teenagers in 1959, is one of the oldest environmental museums in the country. The high schoolers began what was then thought of as a temporary display in a room in the Town Hall, where they exhibited specimens of plants, animals, and rocks.

Today, the museum is considerably larger but still retains a hands-on, down-to-earth feel. In the natural-history wing are re-created regional habitats filled with live turtles, reptiles, ferrets, and the like. In an adjacent gallery hang the works of local artists.

The museum also owns Kenridge Farm, once a 174-acre horse farm, now an environmental-education center. Open to the public are the farm's interpretive nature trails (open dawn–dusk), a historic sheep trail, meadows, wooded areas, and a gallery (noon–4 P.M. Sat.–Sun.).

Accommodations and Food

The luxurious **⟨** **Cromwell Manor Inn** (174 Angola Rd., 845/534-7136, www.cromwell-manor.com, $165–370 d) is an elegant 1820s B&B with 12 guest rooms, some equipped with working fireplaces, Jacuzzis, or steam rooms. Listed in the National Register of Historic Places, the manor is situated on a seven-acre estate surrounded by mountains and has its own formal gardens and croquet courts.

A Cornwall institution since 1985, **⟨** **Painter's** (266 Hudson St., 845/534-2109) offers an eclectic array of sandwiches and burgers, salads and pasta, along with some Italian,

Japanese, and Mexican specialties. The walls are hung with works by local artists; average dinner entrée $12. Upstairs are seven B&B guestrooms ($80–120 d).

NEWBURGH AND VICINITY

North of Cornwall-on-Hudson, Route 9W leads to the small city of Newburgh. Once a thriving whaling port and later an important factory town manufacturing everything from lawn mowers to handbags, Newburgh spent much of the late 20th century in a very sorry state. Many of its buildings were boarded up, and residents joked that the place was so untouchable they couldn't even get the county legislature to build a toxic dump here. More recently, however, Newburgh has benefited from a downtown renewal plan, and boasts a revitalized waterfront, Newburgh Landing, that is flush with restaurants, bars, and shops. Come on a summer's evening and you'll find lots of strollers here.

Washington's Headquarters State Historic Site

At the far edge of downtown, on bluffs overlooking the Hudson, is Washington's Headquarters (84 Liberty St., at Washington St., 845/562-1195, 10 A.M.–5 P.M. Wed.–Sat. and 1–5 P.M. Sun. Apr.–Oct., adults $4, seniors $3, children 5–11 $1), where the general spent the last six months of the war while his officers and troops waited farther south. It was from this headquarters—originally a farmhouse built by the Hasbrouck family—that Washington issued a victorious order for a "cessation of hostilities," bringing about an end to the Revolutionary War on April 19, 1783.

Now run by the National Park Service, Washington's Headquarters has been restored to reflect his stay, and the place has a very personal feel. Its small, whitewashed rooms are simply furnished with cots, firearms, and facsimiles of Washington's account books, along with the desk he once used. The general remained in the house for about a year after the war ended, waiting for the British to leave New York. During much of that time, he was

COURTESY OF ORANGE COUNTY TOURISM

Washington's Headquarters

restless and bored, and resentful of the public demands upon his time.

Surrounding the house are a wide lawn and high stone wall. At the entrance is an excellent visitors center, while near the bluffs is the 53-foot Tower of Victory, built to commemorate the 100th anniversary of the war's end.

Crawford House

History buffs might also want to visit the 1830 David Crawford House (189 Montgomery St., 845/561-2585, www.newburghhistorical-society.com, 1–4 P.M. June–Oct., donations welcomed), just a few blocks away from Washington's Headquarters. The home of the Historical Society of Newburgh, the house is filled with period antiques, Hudson Valley paintings, and an intriguing series of photo exhibits that document Newburgh's more prosperous days.

New Windsor Cantonment

Several other Revolutionary War sites are located within a few miles of Washington's Headquarters. Most interesting among them is the New Windsor Cantonment (Temple Hill Rd. [Rte. 300], New Windsor, 845/561-1765, 10 A.M.–5 P.M. Wed.–Sat., 1–5 P.M. Sun. Apr.–Oct., adults $4, seniors $3, children 5–11 $1), where the general's 7,000 troops, accompanied by some 500 women and children, waited out the last months of the war. Here they lived in log huts during a long, hard winter—a situation that almost led to rebellion.

Today's cantonment re-creates the lives of the Continental Army's soldiers and camp followers. Inside the visitors center are two floors of exhibits and a slide show. Outside, a military drill including the firing of muskets and cannons is staged every afternoon.

Gomez Mill House

Four miles north of Newburgh is the 1714 Mill House (Mill House Rd., off Rte. 9W, Marlboro, 914/236-3126, www.gomez.org, 10 A.M.–4 P.M. Wed.–Sun. Apr.–Oct., adults $7.50, seniors $5, and students $2)—the oldest extant house of a Jewish family in the nation. Continuously occupied for more than

275 years, the Mill House has been home to fur traders, merchants, Revolutionary War soldiers, farmers, artisans, and statesmen.

The house was originally built by Louis Moses Gomez, who bought 6,000 acres along the Hudson after fleeing the Spanish Inquisition. Several Indian paths converged on his property, and Native Americans once gathered near his home to hold ceremonial rites. In the early 20th century, Dard Hunter, a renowned craftsperson and papermaker, lived in the house.

Recreation

Hudson River Adventures (845/220-2120, www.prideofthehudson.com) offers narrated two-hour river cruises leaving from Newburgh Landing, May–October.

Food

Commodore's (482 Broadway, 845/561-3960) is an old-fashioned ice-cream parlor that's also a good spot for a simple lunch. The place is famous for its handmade chocolates.

Yobo's (1297 Union Ave., 845/564-3848) serves a wide variety of dishes from China, Korea, Indonesia, and other Asian countries in a artificially constructed atmosphere of babbling brooks and waterfalls; average entrée $15.

One of the area's most popular Italian restaurants is **Il Cena'Colo** (228 S. Plank Rd., 845/564-4494), which serves Tuscan-style and Northern Italian fare. Among the tasty specials are oyster stew, fried baby artichokes, and gnocchi with venison sauce; average entrée $20.

In downtown Marlboro, near the Gomez Mill House just north of the Orange-Ulster County border, is the lively **Raccoon Saloon** (1330 Western Ave. [Rte. 9W], 845/236-7872). On the menu is an enormous selection of tasty burgers and beers, along with homemade ketchup and ice cream.

MOUNTAINVILLE
Storm King Art Center

One of Hudson Valley's most astonishing sights is Storm King Art Center (Old Pleasant Hill Rd., off Rte. 32 a few miles south of Vails Gate, 845/534-3115, www.stormking.org, 11 A.M.–5:30 P.M. Wed.–Sun. Apr.–Nov., adults $10, seniors and students $9, children 5–17 $7), a breathtakingly beautiful sculpture park built on a hilltop. About 120 permanent works and many more temporary ones are scattered over jade-green lawns and wheat-blond fields, while in the distance

THE BATTLE FOR STORM KING MOUNTAIN

An important chapter in the history of the environmental movement was played out in the 1960s over Storm King Mountain, a magnificent blue-black peak that architectural historian Vincent Scully once called a "dome of living granite, swelling with animal power."

The chapter began in 1963 when Consolidated Edison Co. of New York filed for a license to build a hydroelectric plant at the mountain's base. It was to be the largest hydroelectric plant in the world, generating 2,000 kilowatts of power. A 40-foot-wide tunnel would have to be blasted through the heart of Storm King, a 300-foot-deep cut made across its face, 200 acres of forest appropriated, and a 15-story powerhouse built. Once completed, the plant would need six billion gallons of water a day to operate.

When the plan was made public, citizens were outraged. Not only would the plant destroy the area's natural beauty, but it would also seriously harm recreational and commercial fishing as far south as Long Island. An environmental group called the Scenic Hudson Preservation Conference quickly mobilized the protests and brought the case to court.

Much to the industrialists' surprise, in December 1965, the U.S. Court of Appeals ruled for the people against Con Ed. That historic decision marked the first time that ordinary citizens successfully brought suit against a commercial developer. The case has since been cited as precedent in dozens of other environmental cases.

are the dusk blue Shawangunks. Nearly every major post-WWII sculptor is represented here—Alexander Calder, Henry Moore, Louise Nevelson, Isamu Noguchi, and Richard Serra among them. A map of the 400-acre park and its sculptures is available at the gate. In the park's center stands an imperial Norman-style building that was originally the home of lawyer Vermont Hatch. The stone mansion now houses temporary exhibits and a café that's open weekends.

Accommodations
Offering excellent views of Storm King Mountain is the **Storm King Lodge** (100 Pleasant Hill Rd., 845/534-9421, www.stormkinglodge.com, $150–175 d). Housed in a converted carriage house, centered on an expansive common room with a stone hearth, the lodge offers four cozy guest rooms, two of which have private fireplaces.

SOUTHERN ORANGE COUNTY
Central Valley
Just north of the junction of I-87 and Route 17 is the town of Central Valley and **Woodbury Common Premium Outlets** (498 Red Apple Ct., off Rte. 32, Exit 16 off I-87, 845/928-4000 or 845/928-6840, open daily), which attracts about 10 million shoppers a year. The complex houses over 200 shops, including Calvin Klein, Donna Karan, Gucci, Giorgio Armani, and Jones New York. Also here is an Orange County **visitor information booth** (845/928-6840, 10 A.M.–7 P.M. daily).

About 1.5 miles north of Woodbury Common is **Gasho of Japan** (365 Rte. 32, 845/928-2277), a big touristy spot that nonetheless serves tasty Japanese food, cooked at your table. The restaurant is housed in a centuries-old Japanese farmhouse that was transported here from Japan; average entrée $18.

Route 17 South
South of Central Valley, Route 17 runs along the western edge of Harriman State Park. In an earlier incarnation, Harriman was mining country, and its mountains are still pocked with mine shafts and foundries. A small museum documenting the area's mining history now stands at the **Clove Furnace Historic Site** (Clove Furnace Rd., off Rte. 17, Arden, 845/351-4696, 8 A.M.–noon and 1–5 P.M. Mon.–Fri., free admission).

Just behind the museum is the romantic, ivy-covered Arden House, which served as the residential estate of the Harriman family until 1972. Local lore has it that Edward Harriman built his mansion on this mountain site because he'd been shunned by the exclusive nearby community of Tuxedo Park, and wanted his wife to be able to look down on it daily.

Continuing south on Route 17, you'll come to Route 17A. Travel west on the road about two miles to reach the dark, quiet woods of **Sterling Forest State Park** (open dawn–dusk). The park is best known for the popular **New York Renaissance Festival** (914/351-5174 after June 1, www.renfair.com, adults $19, children 5–12 $9) that is presented weekends August–September. During the festival, which attracts about 175,000 visitors annually, knights in shining armor joust on horseback, minstrels strum love songs, a human chess game is played, and Shakespearean plays are staged. A special Short Line bus leaves for the festival from Manhattan (212/736-4700 or 800/631-8405).

Farther south on Route 17, you'll catch a glimpse of **Tuxedo Park.** Watch for a high stone wall and gatehouse on the right. The residential community was designed in the 1880s as a millionaires' refuge and is filled with turreted mansions. Etiquette maven Emily Post lived here for many years, and it was in Tuxedo Park that the formal dinner jacket of the same name was first introduced.

Monroe
West of Central Valley is Monroe, home to one of the largest museums in America devoted to everyday folk arts. **Museum Village** (1010 Rte. 17M [Exit 129 off Rte. 17], 845/782-8247, www.museumvillage.org, 11 A.M.–4 P.M. Wed.–Sun. July–Aug., call for spring and fall hours, adults $10, seniors $6,

children 4–15 $5) is a reconstructed settlement composed of about 35 historic buildings moved here from elsewhere. Self-guided tours take visitors past costumed guides who pound out horseshoes, churn butter, operate a printing press, and otherwise engage in activities of the preindustrial age. The village also hosts many special events, including square dancing, magic shows, and the largest **Civil War encampment** in the Northeast, reenacted every Labor Day weekend.

Also in Monroe is the **Ananda Ashram** (Sapphire Rd., 845/782-5575, www.anandaashram.org), a 100-acre retreat-resort run by the Yoga Society of New York. On the grounds are nature trails, a lake, and an outdoor pool. The basic rate for dormitory-style accommodations is $55–60 per night; included are three meals, *satsangs*, lectures, cultural programs, and one yoga or tai chi class a day. Semiprivate rooms are also available, or you can opt to visit the ashram as a day visitor for a small fee (about $10).

Sugar Loaf Village

Back in the 18th century, this village at the base of Sugar Loaf Mountain was filled with artisans who sold their handmade goods to local farmers. By 1900, however, the Industrial Revolution had all but put an end to this tradition.

Enter the 1960s and a sudden explosion of interest in crafts. A few local residents decided to revive their heritage and today, Sugar Loaf Village (845/469-9181) bustles with dozens of shops selling everything from rag dolls to woodcarvings. Some of the shops are sophisticated galleries; others are dishearteningly commercial.

Most of the shops are open 10 A.M.–5 P.M. Wednesday–Sunday. To reach Sugar Loaf Village from Monroe, take Route 17 west to Route 13 (Exit 127) and travel south a few miles. A good stop for lunch is the **Barnsider Tavern** (King's Hwy., 845/469-9810), offering burgers, salads, and simple entrées in a taproom setting.

GOSHEN

Named after the biblical land known for its fertile soil, Goshen was once a major dairy center. The first milk shipped into New York City came from this area, and Goshen butter was famous. The town has been the Orange County seat since 1798.

Historic Buildings

Numerous historic buildings line the village's

COWBOY OF THE RAMAPOS

As befits an ancient mountain range, the Ramapos have their share of legend and lore. Most pervasive is the story of the "Cowboy of the Ramapos," Claudius Smith. Around the time of the Revolution, Smith led a group of outlaws who stole horses and cattle from local farmers to sell to the British. Smith was also said to have tortured old men and women out of their life savings, and to have ambushed supply trains en route to Gen. Washington. After each raid, Smith and his outlaws hid out in caves in the Ramapos, where the authorities had little chance of tracking them down.

Known for his irrepressible high spirits, Smith seemed invincible until October 1777, when he murdered patriot Nathaniel Strong at his family homestead. That brutal act caused Gov. George Clinton to put a $1,200 bounty on Smith's head, and the outlaw was subsequently captured and hanged in Goshen, Orange County, on January 22, 1779.

New York's eminent folklorist Harold W. Thompson writes of Smith's last day in *New York State Folktales, Legends, and Ballads*: "Dressed in a handsome suit of broadcloth with silver buttons, the tall outlaw had made his last graceful bows to former neighbors when he was addressed by an elderly person who elbowed his way to the scaffold. 'Mr. Smith, Mr. Smith,' he called, 'where shall I find those deeds and other papers that you–er–*had* from me?' Smith turned his gaze. ...'Mr. Young,' he said, 'this is no time to talk about papers. Meet me in the next world, and I'll tell you about them.'"

Legend also has it that Smith's abnormally large skull is encased in the cornerstone of the Old Courthouse in Goshen.

© CHRISTIANE BIRD

harness racers in Goshen, "the Cradle of the Trotter"

sleepy streets. Most interesting among them is the yellow-brick 1841 **Orange County Courthouse** (101 Main St.). Local legend has it that the abnormally large skull of outlaw Claudius Smith is encased in the courthouse's cornerstone.

Also of interest is **St. James Episcopal Church** (Church St. at Park Pl.). Designed by Richard Upjohn in 1803, the church features windows made in the Tiffany studios and an altar designed by Cass Gilbert.

Harness Racing Museum and Hall of Fame

Goshen, the "Cradle of the Trotter," was once home to the most important harness-racing track in the country. "In July and August," stated one guidebook of the 1930s, "the nearby roads are daily congested with horse lovers; it is hard to find rooms in the town."

Those days are now long gone, but their history lives on in the Harness Racing Museum and Hall of Fame (240 Main St., 845/294-6330, www.harnessmuseum.com, 10 A.M.–5 or 6 P.M. daily, adults $7.50, seniors $6.50, children 6–15 $3.50), a large and sophisticated affair with exhibits on virtually every aspect of harness racing. Recently renovated, the museum houses state-of-the-art interactive exhibits such as a three-dimensional simulator that makes you feel as if you're driving a sulky and a booth where you can judge and call a race. Theaters tell the history of the sport, and changing art exhibits are on display.

Just behind the museum is the **Historic Track,** the only sports facility in the United States that's a National Historic Landmark. The track, which dates back to the 1830s, is now used primarily for training purposes, but the Grand Circuit races are still held here once a year on Fourth of July weekend.

Hambletonian's Grave

Almost all trotters and pacers racing today trace their lineage back to Hambletonian, a colt born in Sugar Loaf on May 5, 1849. Though "extremely ugly" and never a racehorse himself, Hambletonian sired 1,331 foals in 24 years, many of whom went on to become racing champions. In fact, Hambletonian's sons' bloodlines were so strong that they eventually eliminated all other horse families. Hambletonian's grave is located six miles east of Goshen in Chester, on Hambletonian Avenue off Route 94.

Food

Catherine's (153 W. Main St., 845/294-8707), housed in a historic 1869 building, is a congenial spot for lunch or dinner, or a nightcap, and serves especially good pasta; average dinner entrée $13.

THE DROWNED LANDS

County Route 6, not to be confused with U.S. Route 6, heads southwest out of Goshen into the fertile "black dirt" region. Over 10,000 acres are under cultivation here, and although a variety of produce is grown, onions—New York's most successful vegetable crop—are particularly popular. The region's unofficial capital is the village of Pine Island.

"Black dirt" is actually a highly organic soil, scientifically known by the unscientific name of "muck," that was deposited about 10,000 years ago by glacial lakes. Orange County has the second-largest concentration of muck in the United States, second only to the Everglades in Florida. The Orange County muck was inaccessible until about 100 years ago when impoverished Polish, German, and Italian immigrants drained the swamps for farmland.

Scattered throughout the region are farm stands and more farm stands. Just east of the black-dirt region in Warwick, the **Peach Grove Inn** (205 Rte. 17A, 845/986-7411, www.peachgroveinn.net, $130–150 d) offers rooms in a restored 1850 Greek Revival home that sits on the site of a former peach grove. The owner, an antiques dealer for years, has decorated the premises with handsome Victorian furniture, while all the rooms feature tall canopy beds topped with fluffy eiderdowns.

GARRISON

If you head south from West Point, rather than north to Newburgh, on Routes 218 and 9W, you'll come to the small and graceful **Bear Mountain Bridge,** once the world's longest suspension bridge. The bridge offers great views of the Bear Mountain Gorge as it heads across the Hudson to **Putnam County** and Route 9D. About four miles north on Route 9D is the village of Garrison.

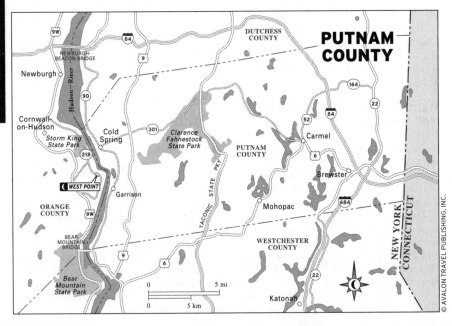

Take the turnoff to **Garrison Landing,** and you'll find yourself in a small parklike area by the riverfront. Nearby is a 19th-century gazebo used in the filming of *Hello Dolly,* an old stone railroad station, and the **Garrison Art Center** (845/424-3960, www.garrisonartcenter.org, noon–5 P.M. daily, free admission). The center presents exhibits and special events such as arts-and-crafts fairs and auctions.

Boscobel Restoration

Just north of Garrison proper is an elegant, early-19th-century mansion known as Boscobel, or "beautiful wood" (1601 Rte. 9D, 845/265-3638, www.boscobel.org, 9:30 A.M.–4 or 5 P.M. Wed.–Mon., last tour 45 minutes before closing, closed Jan.–Feb., adults $10, seniors $9, children 6–14 $7). Standing high on bluffs overlooking the Hudson, the historic house features an extraordinary collection of decorative arts from the Federal period.

Much of the collection was assembled by the home's extravagant original owner, States Morris Dyckman, who wanted Boscobel to have the finest of everything. He even told his more frugal wife that the house would be their "last sacrifice to Folly." The house is filled with china, silver, and New York–made furniture, along with more idiosyncratic treasures like a hand-carved staircase and a rocking horse from 1800. Outside are gardens bursting with orchids and roses, as well as an orangery and herb garden.

Incredibly, Boscobel was almost destroyed by a wrecker's ball in the 1950s. Only at the last moment were enough funds raised to purchase the house and transport it piece by piece to its current location.

Constitution Marsh

Boscobel looks out over Constitution Marsh Sanctuary (Indian Brook Rd., off Rte. 9D, 845/265-2601, 9 A.M.–dusk Tues.–Sun. year-round), a 207-acre tidal marsh managed by the National Audubon Society. An interpretive nature trail and boardwalk run through the preserve, while at river's edge is a visitors

THE HUDSON VALLEY

© CHRISTIANE BIRD

The 19th-century mansion, Boscobel, now peacefully overlooks the Hudson River just north of Garrison.

center (9 A.M.–5 P.M. Tues.–Sun. May–Oct., free admission). The sanctuary is rich with birds—194 species have been spotted—and wildflowers.

In the preserve are canals created by farmers who hoped to use the marshlands to grow rice. Once a day at high tide, from May through early October, the Audubon Society runs guided canoe trips through these canals. The trips are free but are enormously popular, and reservations must be made weeks in advance.

Manitoga

South of Garrison off Route 9D—watch closely for signs—is the idiosyncratic Manitoga (845/424-3812, www.russelwrightcenter.org). Created by industrial designer Russel Wright over a period of about three decades beginning in 1947, Manitoga is designed, as the artist put it, to "bring to American culture an intimacy with nature." Throughout the center run three hiking trails that Wright carefully manipulated to their best natural effect. Some parts are reminiscent of a Japanese garden; others are considerably wilder.

At Manitoga's center is Wright's glass-walled home, **Dragon Rock,** built on the edge of a small quarry. Wright rerouted a waterfall to turn the quarry into a sleepy pond.

The trails at Manitoga are open daily during daylight hours (suggested donation $5). House tours (adults $15, seniors $13, children under 13 $5) are offered April–October at 11 A.M. weekdays, 11 A.M. and 1:30 P.M. weekends.

Graymoor

Due east of Manitoga is Graymoor (off Rte. 9, 845/424-3671, grounds open 9 A.M.–dusk daily), a monastery of the Franciscan Friars of the Atonement. Built by the Episcopal Church in 1898, the monastery is perched high on a hill with magnificent views of the Hudson Valley. On the grounds are shrines, chapels, and Stations of the Cross. To reach Graymoor from Manitoga, located just a few miles away, take Route 9D north to Route 403 south to Route 9 south.

COLD SPRING

Legend has it that the quaint village of Cold Spring was first named by George Washington after he took a sip of the local waters. The village didn't flourish, however, until the 1800s when the federal government created an iron foundry here. Around the same time, tourists traveling by steamboat first discovered the glories of the Hudson Valley. Cold Spring, with the granite dome of Storm King Mountain looming across the way, was a favorite overnight stop.

Today, much of Cold Spring still dates back to its Victorian heyday. Throughout the area are a number of old inns, while along Main Street are restored 19th-century buildings housing dozens of attractive antique and gift shops. **Walking tours** of the village are frequently offered on Sunday afternoon by the Putnam County Historical Society and Foundry School Museum.

At the foot of Main Street is the Hudson River, but you can't get there without first detouring south, under the Metro-North train tracks (a sign marks the way). Once at the shore, you'll find the **Riverfront Bandstand and Dock,** the latter jutting out into the river and offering outstanding views.

Foundry School Museum

Originally a school for children of the Irish immigrants employed by Cold Spring's foundry, this small 1820 building is now a local history museum (63 Chestnut St., 845/265-4010, 10 A.M.–4 P.M. Tues.–Thurs. and 2–5 P.M. Sat.–Sun. Mar.–Dec., suggested donation $5). Run by the Putnam County Historical Society, the museum houses a re-created foundry room, school room, country store, and country kitchen, along with a dugout canoe, horse-drawn sleigh, and historic photographs.

Chuang Yen Monastery

Take a detour east from Cold Springs on Route 301 to view the largest indoor statue of the Buddha in the Western Hemisphere at the largest monastery in the eastern United

States (2020 Rte. 301, Carmel, 845/225-1819, www.baus.org/baus, 9 A.M.–5 P.M. daily, free admission). Standing 37 feet tall, the Buddha sits surrounded by 10,000 small Buddha figurines in the Great Buddha Hall. Gravel walkways lead to several smaller halls, a lovely lake, and the Woo-Ju Library, which holds a large collection of books on Tibetan religion.

Accommodations

Smack on the banks of the Hudson, with close-up views of Storm King Mountain, is the boxy **Hudson House Inn** (2 Main St., 845/265-9355, www.hudsonhouseinn.com, $185–250 d, with continental breakfast), the second-oldest continuously operating inn in New York. Built in 1832 to house steamboat passengers, the inn features 12 renovated guest rooms nicely furnished with antiques. On site is an airy indoor-outdoor restaurant serving lunch and dinner (see *Food,* below).

The charming **(Pig Hill Inn** (73 Main St., 914/265-9247, www.pighillinn.com, $120–220 d) is housed in a brick Georgian townhouse with antiques for sale. Six of the nine guest rooms have a fireplace or wood stove, and four have private baths. Out back is a terraced garden.

Food

The friendly **Cold Spring Depot** (1 Depot Sq., 845/265-2305) is a casual joint housed in an old railroad station; average dish $7. The **Foundry Cafe** (55 Main St., 845/265-4504) specializes in naturally healthy foods and regional American cooking. On the menu are lots of soups, home-baked goods, and grain dishes; next door is a gourmet health-food store.

On the shores of the Hudson River you'll find the historic **(Hudson House Restaurant** (845/265-9355; see *Accommodations,* above), serving fresh seafood and regional American cuisine. In summer, an outdoor dining area opens up, and many tables have great views of the river; average entrée $18.

One of the village's most upscale spots is the **Plumbush Inn** (Rte. 9D south of the village center, 845/265-3904), housed in an 1867 building. Here you'll dine by candlelight in a lush Victorian dining room complete with working fireplaces and dark wood paneling. The restaurant serves prix fixe dinners from $35.

EASTERN PUTNAM COUNTY
Clarence Fahnestock Memorial State Park

Fahnestock State Park (off Rte. 301, east of Taconic State Pkwy., Carmel, 845/225-7207, dawn–dusk daily, parking at the beach $8) spreads out over 12,000 acres of Putnam Valley. It's crisscrossed with a number of hiking trails, including the Appalachian Trail, and offers lakes (boat rentals available), swimming beaches, fishing ponds, and an extensive performing-arts program. An 86-site campground is open May–October; for reservations, call 800/456-CAMP.

Southeast Museum

This idiosyncratic museum (67 Main St., Brewster, 845/279-7500, www.southeastmuseum.org, 10 A.M.–4 P.M. Tues.–Sat., closed Jan.–Mar., suggested donation $5) is full of oddities. Housed in the 1896 Old Town Hall, it contains a large collection of minerals from local mines, early artifacts from the Harlem Railroad Line, and an assortment of early memorabilia from the Borden condensed-milk factory. Gail Brewster began producing condensed milk here in the 1850s; he hit upon the idea while sailing home from England, when he longed for a glass of fresh milk. The town's other famous resident was Rex Stout, creator of the orchid-loving detective Nero Wolfe and his sidekick Archie Goldwin.

Food

One of the few old-fashioned drive-ins left in the region is the ever-popular **Red Rooster Diner** (Rte. 22, two miles northeast of Brewster, 845/279-8046), always crowded with families and enthused kids. On the grounds, you'll find a miniature golf course.

THE HUDSON VALLEY

Dutchess County

Named for England's Duchess of York, who was later crowned Queen Mary, Dutchess County lies in the center of the Hudson Valley and feels much like its hub. Most of the grand riverfront estates for which the area is famous are located here, as are Vassar and Bard Colleges, the historic town of Rhinebeck, the Culinary Institute of America, and a plethora of country villages, pick-your-own farms, public gardens, and excellent restaurants and lodgings. More than two million people visit Dutchess County every year.

The historic museum-estates are all in a 20-mile riverfront stretch between Hyde Park in the center of the county and Clermont just over the border to the north. In 1990, this stretch was declared a National Historic Landmark District—the second largest such district in the United States. It contains some 2,000 buildings, only a handful of which are open to the public. These include Franklin Delano Roosevelt's home (Springwood), the Vanderbilt Mansion, Mills Mansion, Wilderstein, Montgomery Place, and Clermont.

Of these, FDR's estate is by far the most personal and popular, and can be combined with a visit to Val-Kill, Eleanor Roosevelt's retreat. Between the two homes and the nearby FDR Library and museum, you'll come away with a good sense of both the Roosevelts and the times in which they lived. Of the other museum-estates, the Vanderbilt Mansion is the most lavish, Montgomery Place the most beautiful, Mills Mansion the most cavernous, Clermont the most elegant, and Wilderstein the smallest and least known.

South of Hyde Park are the river cities of Beacon and Poughkeepsie. Both have fallen on hard times, yet have interesting historic and cultural sites to offer; Beacon is also home to a mammoth new Dia Art Foundation museum. A few miles east of Route 9, the expansive rural countryside is dotted with small villages, wineries, produce stands, and horse farms. The entire Hudson Valley is a major horse-breeding area, with about half of its 100 horse farms located in Dutchess County.

BEACON

Once a bustling manufacturing town best known for its brick and hat factories, Beacon, like many towns along the Hudson, fell on hard times in the 20th century. Many of its 19th-century buildings were boarded up or covered with dust; the town was used as the setting for the 1995 movie *Nobody's Fool,* starring a down-and-out Paul Newman. In the last few years, however, revitalizing change has come to town, thanks largely to Dia:Beacon, a major contemporary arts museum which opened here in 2003, bringing gentrification in its wake. During its first year of operation, Dia:Beacon attracted almost 100,000 visitors—twice as many as projected. Main Street now boasts artsy clothing boutiques, bistros, and antique shops, while second-home owners have jacked up real estate prices.

Mount Beacon towers over the city and has played an important role in the town's history. During the Revolutionary War, the colonists set signal fires on the summit to warn their compatriots of British troop movements. During the early 1900s, a casino serviced by a funicular sat atop the mountain—the tracks are still visible today.

Two Historic Houses

At the **Mount Gulian Historic Site** (145 Sterling St., 845/831-8172, 1–5 P.M. Wed.–Fri. and Sun. Apr.–Oct., 1–5 P.M. Wed. and Sun. Nov.–Mar., adults $5, children $3), you'll learn about the Dutch, Native American, and African American culture of the Revolutionary War–era Hudson Valley. Costumed guides conduct tours.

Though it's open by appointment only, the 1708 **Madam Brett Homestead** (50 Van Nydeck Ave., 845/831-6533), built by

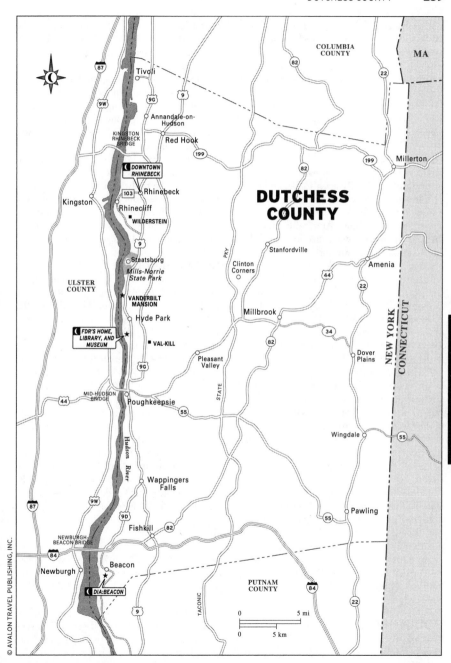

DUTCHESS COUNTY

COLUMBIA COUNTY

MA

Tivoli

Annandale-on-Hudson

Red Hook

Millerton

KINGSTON RHINEBECK BRIDGE

DOWNTOWN RHINEBECK

Rhinebeck

Kingston

Rhinecliff

WILDERSTEIN

Stanfordville

Clinton Corners

Amenia

Staatsburg

Mills-Norrie State Park

ULSTER COUNTY

VANDERBILT MANSION

Hyde Park

Millbrook

FDR'S HOME, LIBRARY, AND MUSEUM

VAL-KILL

Dover Plains

Pleasant Valley

MID-HUDSON BRIDGE

Poughkeepsie

Hudson River

Wingdale

Wappingers Falls

Pawling

NEWBURGH-BEACON BRIDGE

Fishkill

Newburgh

Beacon

DIA:BEACON

PUTNAM COUNTY

TACONIC

STATE

PKY

NEW YORK

CONNECTICUT

THE HUDSON VALLEY

0   5 mi

0   5 km

© AVALON TRAVEL PUBLISHING, INC.

Catheryna and Robert Brett, has an interesting history. After the death of her husband by drowning, Mme. Brett succeeded in establishing the region's first thriving business venture—the Frankfort Storehouse and Mill. The locals used to joke, "All roads lead to Mme. Brett's mill." During the Revolutionary War, Catheryna's granddaughter entertained Generals Washington and Lafayette here.

◖ Dia:Beacon

Housed in a 240,000-square-foot former printing plant, Dia:Beacon (3 Beekman St., 845/440-0100, www.diabeacon.org, 11 A.M.–6 P.M. Thurs.–Mon. May–Oct., 11 A.M.–4 P.M. Fri.–Mon. Nov.–Apr., admission $10) displays the permanent collection of the Dia Art Foundation, an innovative arts institution based in New York City. Among the highlights on display are Andy Warhol's 1979 *Shadows,* composed of 102 paintings; Richard Serra's monumental Torqued Ellipses series; a large-scale sculpture by Walter De Maria, a series of fluorescent light works by Dan Flavin, and Agnes Martin's 1999 suite of paintings *Innocent Love,* created specifically for Dia:Beacon.

Redesigned from a factory into a museum by artist Robert Irvin, Dia:Beacon sits on 34 landscaped acres peppered with flowering fruit trees. The museum is within walking distance of the Metro-North train station, and on weekends, the Beacon Shuttle trolley bus provides transportation to various stops in town.

Food

"The meeting and eating spot of Beacon" is **Quinn's** (330 Main St., 845/831-8065), an old-fashioned town café with a big American flag outside and great homemade bread, meat loaf, potato soup, and rice pudding inside. Housed in an 1880s former bank building is **The Piggy Bank** (448 Main St., 845/838-0028), serving Southern barbeque; the former vault is now a wine cellar.

POUGHKEEPSIE

The seat of Dutchess County, Poughkeepsie was founded in 1683 and was designated the state capital in 1777. From the mid-1800s through the mid-1900s, the town was a major industrial center, serving as home base for IBM after World War II. But the late 20th century was not kind to Poughkeepsie. First, many of the factories closed down. Then urban renewal ravaged the city, replacing 19th-century brick buildings with stingy, low-slung edifices. Finally, in the 1990s, IBM laid off thousands upon thousands of employees.

Today, however, Poughkeepsie (Wappinger Indian for "reed-covered lodge by the little water place") is in the midst of a radical upgrade. A $40 million waterfront project, which promises to revitalize the entire city, is under construction. Included in the project are a convention center, restaurants, shops, and a marina.

Downtown Culture

Near the river and railroad station, where Union and Academy Streets intersect Main and Mill, are two bustling, restored **historic districts** filled with shops, pubs, and restaurants. Just up the hill from the restored historic district near the railroad station is the **Cunneen-Hackett Cultural Center** (9 and 12 Vassar St., 845/471-1221). The center occupies two handsome 1880s Italianate buildings built by the nephews of Matthew Vassar, the Poughkeepsie brewer who founded Vassar College. No. 9 now houses a small art gallery; No. 12 is home to another gallery and an exquisite Victorian auditorium—complete with gold-cushioned seats and stained-glass windows—where plays, concerts, and films are frequently presented. The center's galleries are free and are open 9 A.M.–5 P.M. Mon.–Fri.

The *Clearwater*

Poughkeepsie is home to the sloop *Clearwater* (112 Market St., 845/454-7673, www.clearwater.org), which often docks downtown at the Main Street pier. Built by a handful of river-loving volunteers, *Clearwater* has been sailing the Hudson since 1969, bringing with it a message of environmental urgency. The vessel has been instrumental in helping to clean up the Hudson, and is the impetus behind the popular, three-day **Clearwater Great Hudson River Festival,** held in the region every June.

Locust Grove, the Samuel Morse Historic Site

Immediately south of downtown is Locust Grove (370 South Rd. [Rte. 9], 845/454-4500, www.morsehistoricsite.org, 10 A.M.–5 P.M. May–Nov., last tour at 3 P.M., adults $7, seniors $5, children under 12 $3), a romantic octagonal villa that was once the summer home of artist-scientist-philosopher Samuel Morse, inventor of the telegraph. Morse bought his home in 1847 when he was already a widower in his fifties. With the help of renowned landscape architect Alexander Jackson Davis, he transformed it into a Tuscan-styled estate with a four-story tower, skylit billiard room, and extensive gardens.

Relatively new to the estate is a big visitors center, complete with an orientation video, a collection of telegraph equipment and other Morse inventions, and an art gallery showcasing paintings by Morse, John James Audubon, and other of the inventor's contemporaries.

Vassar College and Art Gallery

At the southeastern edge of town is Vassar College, founded as a women's college in 1861 by the brewer Matthew Vassar, at the instigation of his friend Samuel Morse. Considered a risky experiment at the time, Vassar today—now coeducational—is recognized as one of the best colleges in the country.

Surrounding much of the campus are towering stone walls with arched gates. Inside is the 1865 Main Building—reputedly designed in such a way that it could be converted into a brewery should the educational experiment fail—and a Norman-style chapel with five Tiffany windows. One of the windows depicts Elena Lucrezia Cornaro Piscopia, the first woman to receive a doctorate (from the University of Padua in 1678).

Near the main gate stands the Frances Lehman Loeb Art Center (124 Raymond Ave., off Rte. 44/55, 845/437-5632, http://fllac.vassar.edu, 10 A.M.–5 P.M. Tues.–Sat., 1–5 P.M.

Sun., free admission), designed by Cesar Pelli. Vassar was the first college in the country to have its own art gallery, and today owns more than 12,500 works ranging in origin from ancient Egypt to modern-day New York. Especially strong are the collections of Hudson River landscape paintings, Old Master prints by Dürer and Rembrandt, and contemporary European and American art.

Springside

Also connected with Matthew Vassar is the "ornamental farm" he used as a summer home. Now a National Historic Landmark, Springside (181 Academy St., just west of Rte. 9, 845/454-2060, dawn–dusk daily, free admission) is the only remaining domestic commission of Andrew Jackson Downing, the brilliant 19th-century landscape architect.

Due to neglect and vandalism, all but one of the small buildings that once dotted Springside are gone, but the grounds have been restored. Gentle rolling hills and rounded shrubbery contrast with rocky outcroppings and gnarled tree trunks. Maps are available at the entrance.

Entertainment

The county's premier performing-arts venue is the **Bardavon 1869 Opera House** (35 Market St., 845/473-2072, www.bardavon.org). One of the oldest theaters in the country, it presents everything from top-caliber opera to serious drama. Two small but interesting professional theater groups connected with Vassar College are the **New Day Repertory Co.** (845/485-7399) and the **Powerhouse Theatre** (845/437-7235).

For live music, stop into **The Chance** (6 Crannel St., 845/471-1966), where nationally known artists playing everything from country to R&B perform. The weekend editions of the *Poughkeepsie Journal* contain good entertainment listings.

Accommodations

One of the nicest places to stay in Poughkeepsie is the classy [**Inn at the Falls** (50 Red Oaks Mill Rd., 845/462-5770, www.innatthefalls.com, $130–205 d, with breakfast), which overlooks Wappingers Creek on the outskirts of town. The rooms are handsomely outfitted in contemporary European and country styles.

Downtown you'll find the attractive, upscale **Poughkeepsie Grand Hotel and Conference Center** (40 Civic Center Plaza, 845/485-5300, www.pokgrand.com, $99–149 d, with full American breakfast), one of the few hostelries in the immediate area to offer a health club.

Food

For tasty baked goods and sandwiches in the historic district, try the **Cafe Aurora** (145 Mill St., 845/454-1900).

For terrific views of the Hudson, stop into the **Brass Anchor** (31 River Point Rd., just north of the bridge, 845/452-3232), equipped with outdoor tables in warm weather. On the menu is American Continental fare, with lots of seafood specials and vegetarian dishes (dinner entrées $18–30); you can also come just for a drink.

A favorite among locals and out-of-towners alike is the tiny **C Busy Bee Café** (138 South Ave., at Reade Pl., 845/452-6800), a bistro offering contemporary American fare prepared from fresh regional ingredients; average entree $15. The **Haymaker** (718 Dutchess Tnpk., 845/486-9454), specializing in regional American cuisine; average entrée $15. For Cajun-Creole fare, try **Spanky's** (85 Main St., 845/485-2294), a lively and casual downtown spot. On the menu is everything from gumbos to jambalayas; average entrée $14.

MILLBROOK AND VICINITY

About 12 miles northeast of Poughkeepsie on Route 44 is sleepy yet moneyed Millbrook, surrounded by large estates and horse farms. Though it seems hard to believe today, in this village of pricey antique stores and gift shops, Timothy Leary once ran his League for Spiritual Discovery out of the old Danheim estate on Franklin Avenue. The estate, located about a mile from the village green, is recognizable by its large stone gatehouse built in Bavarian style. Others who've made Millbrook their home in more recent years are Mary Tyler Moore, Daryl Hall, Liam Neeson, and Natasha Richardson.

Innisfree Garden

Landscaped around a small glacial lake just outside Millbrook is a serene 200-acre sanctuary (362 Tyrell Rd., one mile off Rte. 44 west of Millbrook, 845/677-8000, www.innisfreegarden.org, 10 A.M.–4 P.M. Wed.–Fri. and 11 A.M.–5 P.M. Sat.–Sun. May–Oct., admission $4 on weekdays, $5 on weekends, children under 6 free). Founded by painter Walter Beck and his wife Marion, and designed according to Eastern principles, the so-called "cup garden" is actually a series of many little gardens, each arranged to draw attention to one especially beautiful object at its center. One of the small gardens focuses on a lotus pool, another on a group of "purple smoke trees," a third on a hillside cave. On a spit of land jutting out into the lake are the Dragon, the Turtle, and the Owl—three large rocks standing sentinel over the preserve.

Despite the garden's careful design, it has a wild and natural feel. Spreading out over a series of small hills and dales, dappled by sunlight, it features many isolated spots where visitors can dreamily linger.

Insitute of Ecosystem Studies

A few miles west of Millbrook is a 1,900-acre preserve that's home to both the **Flagler Cary Arboretum** (Rte. 44A, just off Rte. 44, 845/677-5359, 9 A.M.–4 P.M. Mon.–Sat. and 1–4 P.M. Sun., with extended hours to 6 P.M. daily May–Sept., free admission) and the Institute of Ecosystem Studies (www.ecostudies.org). The arboretum is open to the public, as is much of the institute's grounds, where ecological research is being conducted. Both are connected to the prestigious New York Botanical Garden in New York City.

Visitors to the arboretum must stop first at the Gifford House Visitor and Education Center to pick up a visitor permit, information, and maps. Directly behind the center are the perennial gardens, filled with over 1,000 species of plants. Among these gardens is a daffodil bed with 12 kinds of daffodils, a poisonous plants bed, and a garden specifically planted to attract butterflies. Surrounding the gardens are short hiking trails that lead past meadows, fern glens, and pine and hemlock forests.

Wing's Castle

One of the oddest sites in the Hudson Valley is the whimsical Wing's Castle (717 Bangall Rd., off Rte. 44 northeast of Millbrook, 845/677-9085, noon–4:30 P.M. Wed.–Sun. June–Dec., adults $7, children $5), set atop a rolling, lime-green hill with a panoramic view of the Hudson Valley. Built by Peter and Toni Wing and family, the castle is a 30-odd-year-old work-in-progress, lovingly put together out of everything from antique barn doors to toilet-bowl floats. Much of its stone came from abandoned railroad bridges.

It all began in the late 1960s when Peter, just back from Vietnam, and his wife Toni needed a place to live. They owned a piece of land, but had only $1,100 between them. The solution? They'd build the place themselves, out of salvaged materials; never mind the fact that they had no construction experience whatsoever.

Everyone told them it couldn't be done, but today the castle stands, quirky and proud. Each part is designed in a different style—Asian, Tibetan, Germanic, French—and it all works beautifully, with bits of colored fiberglass winking in the walls and a water-filled moat leading to an inviting hot tub. Inside is a hodgepodge collection of military artifacts, carousel animals, Native American arts, and the Wings' personal possessions.

Area Wineries

Spread out over 50 acres just below Wing's Castle is **Millbrook Vineyards** (26 Wing Rd., at the Shunpike [Rte. 57], 845/677-8383 or 800/662-9463, www.millbrookwine.com, noon–5 P.M. daily). Millbrook is especially known for its chardonnay, but it also produces a pinot noir, merlot, and other wines.

About 10 miles northeast of Millbrook is the award-winning **Cascade Mountain Winery and Restaurant** (835 Cascade Mountain Rd., Amenia, 845/373-9021, www.cascademt.com, 11 A.M.–5 P.M. Wed.–Sun.). The chalet-style restaurant is open for lunch Wednesday–Sunday; average lunch entrée $9; closed January–February. To reach the winery, take Route 44 east to Cascade Mountain Rd.

Accommodations

Camping is available at 40-site **Wilcox Memorial Park** (Rte. 199, off the Taconic Pkwy., Stanfordville, 845/758-6100).

The refreshingly down-to-earth **A Cat in Your Lap** (Rts. 82 and 343, 845/677-3051) is a B&B housed in a gracious 1840s farmhouse and a converted barn ($85 d in the main house; $120 d for the studios in the barn).

About 10 miles south of Millbrook, find the **Old Drovers Inn** (196 E. Duncan Rd., Dover Plains, 845/832-9311, www.olddroversinn.com), named after the cattle drovers who once roared through here on their way to New York City. Now a member of the exclusive Relais & Chateaux group, the inn dates back to the 18th century, and features all the amenities, including working fireplaces in three of its four guest rooms and plenty of antiques. The inn is as known for its fine dining as it is for its accommodations; the menu features innovative American/Continental cuisine ($170–250 d midweek with breakfast; $330–450 d weekends, with breakfast and dinner; average entrée $26).

Food

The vintage, stainless-steel **Millbrook Diner** (3266 Franklin Ave., village center, 845/677-5319) serves dependable diner fare and especially good breakfasts. Foremost among the area's more serious eateries is **Allyn's Restaurant and Cafe** (42–58 Rte. 44 midway between Millbrook and Amenia, 845/677-5888), which always offers a few regional specialties along with more general innovative American fare on its huge menu; average entrée $22. Next door is a moderately priced café decorated with a long mural of Millbrook; average entrée $14. Tables are set out on the lawn in warm weather.

THE HUDSON VALLEY

HYDE PARK AND VICINITY

The most popular visitor destination in Dutchess County is Hyde Park, once home to Franklin Delano Roosevelt, Eleanor Roosevelt, and a branch of the Vanderbilt family. Despite its blue-blood ancestry, the sprawling village is a downscale affair filled with aging shopping malls, tour buses, traffic jams, and motels named after the village's famous former residents.

Henry A. Wallace Visitor, Education, and Conference Center

Opened to the public in late 2003, the Wallace center at the Franklin D. Roosevelt Presidential Library and Museum (4079 Albany Post Rd. [Rt. 9], 800/FDR-Visit, www.nps.gov/hofr, 9 A.M.–5 P.M. daily) is now the best first stop for visitors to Hyde Park. The center provides a good, comprehensive orientation to the Roosevelt and Vanderbilt sites, run by the National Park Service, through exhibits and an introductory film. Visitors can buy tickets and get directions here; a large café and museum shop is also on site.

FDR's Home, Library, and Museum

Franklin Delano Roosevelt was born and grew up in Springwood (4079 Albany Post Rd. [Rte. 9], 845/229-9115 or 800/FDR-VISIT, www.nps.gov/hofr, 9 A.M.–5 P.M. daily, adults $14, children under 17 free), a low-lying Georgian-style mansion along the Hudson. Later, he and his wife Eleanor raised their five children here, while Franklin rose through the political ranks. In 1928, he was elected governor of New York; in 1932, president of the United States.

Now a National Historic Site, FDR's home has been restored to look much like it did during his presidential days, and has a very intimate feel. In the living room are the leash and blanket of his dog Fala; in the "snuggery" are furnishings once belonging to his domineering mother, Sara Delano Roosevelt; in his office are the books and magazines he was reading during his last visit here in March 1945. At the

eastern end of the estate is **Top Cottage** (open Thurs.–Mon.), where Roosevelt entertained his closest friends.

Of at least equal interest is the next-door Franklin D. Roosevelt Library and Museum (800/FDR-VISIT), which houses a superb series of exhibits on the family and their times. Here you'll find everything from FDR's christening dress and early political speeches to Eleanor's diary entries describing the enormous pain she felt upon learning of her husband's extramarital affairs.

Tickets to the FDR sites often sell out on fall weekends; to make a reservation, call 800/967-2283.

Val-Kill

By 1924, Eleanor Roosevelt had had enough of both her husband's political cronies and her mother-in-law. She built a weekend retreat for herself two miles east of the family estate, and moved there permanently after FDR's death in 1945.

Surrounded by fields and woodlands, the Eleanor Roosevelt National Historic Site, a.k.a. Val-Kill (Rte. 9G, off Rte. 9, 845/229-9115, www.nps.gov/elro, 9 A.M.–5 P.M. daily June–Sept., 9 A.M.–5 P.M. Thurs.–Mon. Nov.–May, adults $8, children under 17 free) is a simple and rustic place that, compared to Springwood, attracts relatively few visitors. The former First Lady's tastes were delightfully unassuming; she used regular china, set up card tables for extra guests at Christmas, and hung family photographs helter-skelter over the cottage's rough-hewn walls. Nonetheless, it was in this simple setting that Mrs. Roosevelt drafted the U.N. Declaration of Human Rights and entertained important world leaders such as Nikita Khrushchev, Haile Selassie, Adlai Stevenson, and John F. Kennedy. A photograph of a 40-something JFK and a 70-something Eleanor is prominently displayed in the living room.

Vanderbilt Mansion

Two miles north of the relatively modest Roosevelt homes is the ultra-extravagant Vanderbilt Mansion National Historic Site (Rte. 9,

COURTESY OF THE DUTCHESS COUNTY TOURISM

Vanderbilt Mansion

845/229-9115, www.nps.gov/vama, 9 A.M.–5 P.M. daily, adults $8, children under 17 free), built in a posh beaux arts style complete with lavish furnishings, gold-leaf ceilings, Flemish tapestries, and hand-painted lampshades. Built between 1896 and 1898 by Frederick and Louise Vanderbilt, the mansion—designed by McKim, Mead & White—cost what was then a whopping $2.5 million. Nonetheless, it was the smallest of the Vanderbilt estates and was used only in spring and fall.

Next door to the mansion are extensive formal gardens and a coach house (not open to the public) in which the Vanderbilts housed six limousines that were always at their guests' disposal. From the gardens are glorious views of the Hudson, with the smoky Shawangunk Mountains rising behind.

Hugging the riverbank between the Vanderbilt Mansion and the Roosevelt homes is the **Hyde Park Trail,** an 8.5-mile system of easy hiking trails, well marked by white-and-green signs. Maps of the trails can be picked up at the Wallace Center.

Staatsburgh State Historic Site

In Staatsburg, about five miles north of the Vanderbilt mansion, reigns the Staatsburgh State Historic Site (Old Post Rd., off Rte. 9, 845/889-8851, 10 A.M.–5 P.M. Tues.–Sat. and noon–5 P.M. Sun. Apr.–Sept., call for off-season hours, adults $5, seniors $4, children 5–12 $1). Also known as **Mills Mansion,** the vast 65-room hilltop hideout is in a continual process of being restored. Guides take visitors through a series of cavernous rooms—some plush with Louis XIV, XV, and XVI furnishings, others filled with craftspeople busy at restoration work. The most beautiful room is the long dining room, flanked with Flemish tapestries and large windows overlooking the Hudson.

Parts of Mills Mansion date back to 1825, but most of the house was built in 1896 by McKim, Mead & White. Once owned by financier Ogden Mills, the mansion was frequented by Edith Wharton, who used it as the model for the Trenor estate, Bellomont, in *The House of Mirth.*

Surrounding Mills Mansion is **Mills-Norrie State Park** (845/889-4646, dawn–dusk daily), a 1,000-acre preserve with a marina, campground, small environmental museum, and two nine-hole golf courses. Scenic hiking trails run along the west side of the park, overlooking the Hudson. The 55-site campground is open May–October; for reservations, call 800/456-CAMP.

Culinary Institute of America

A half mile south of Hyde Park proper is the Culinary Institute of America, or CIA (1946 Campus Dr., off Rte. 9, 845/452-9600, www.ciachef.edu), the nation's most prestigious cooking school, founded in 1946. Housed in a former Jesuit seminary overlooking the Hudson, the institute trains about 1,850 students at a time, in a 21-month program that includes courses in everything from pork butchering to purchasing. Between classes, the students hurry about campus dressed in traditional white chefs' tunics and white-and-gray checked pants.

The CIA is open daily and visitors are welcome to stroll the grounds, browse the well-stocked **Craig Claiborne Bookstore,** take a tour (call for details; cost is $5), or eat in one of the five first-rate, student-staffed restaurants (see *Food*, below), all but one open by reservation only.

Accommodations

Directly across from the Vanderbilt Mansion is the attractive **Journey Inn Bed & Breakfast** (1 Sherwood Pl., off Rte. 9, 845/229-8972, www.journeyinn.com, $105–185 d), filled with antiques and memorabilia from the owners' international travels. The inn offers six comfortable air-conditioned guest rooms, each done up to reflect a different destination, including Kyoto, Mombassa, and Tuscany.

Hyde Park has an abundance of decent budget motels, many of which cater to families and tour groups. Among them is the family-owned, 24-room **Roosevelt Inn** (4360 Albany Post Rd. [Rte. 9], 845/229-2443, $70–95 d), where you can choose between rooms with queen, king, double, or twin beds.

Culinary Institute of America

COURTESY OF THE DUTCHESS COUNTY TOURISM

Food

Hyde Park's best restaurants are in the Culinary Institute of America (1946 Campus Dr., off Rte. 9, 845/471-6608, www.ciachef.edu), where reservations are essential. Each of the four restaurants has its own distinct style. The most casual is **St. Andrew's Cafe,** which offers everything from wood-fired pizza to beef tenderloin; average dinner, $35. The most elegant is the award-winning **Escoffier Restaurant,** offering classic French cuisine; average dinner, $50–60. In between are **Caterina de Medici,** featuring contemporary and traditional Italian specialties (average dinner $30–45); and the **American Bounty Restaurant,** dedicated to regional American dishes (average dinner $45–50). Jackets and reservations are required in all rooms.

The one CIA restaurant that does *not* require a reservation is the **Apple Pie Bakery Café,** open 9 A.M.–5 P.M. Monday–Friday. On the menu find sandwiches, salads, soups, and desserts.

RHINEBECK

Continuing north along Route 9, you'll come to the picturesque village of Rhinebeck, the shady streets of which are lined with restored Victorian buildings. Rhinebeck was first settled in 1686 by Dutch immigrants and has been home to five illustrious Hudson Valley families—the Beekmans, Livingstons, Astors, Montgomerys, and Schuylers.

◖ Downtown Rhinebeck

In the center of town is the **Beekman Arms** (6387 Mill St., 845/876-7077). Built in 1766, it's said to be the oldest inn in continuous operation in America. Everyone from George Washington and Aaron Burr to William Jennings Bryan and FDR once ate or slept at the Beekman. Even if you're not planning to do so yourself, the place is worth a look-see. Inside are low ceilings, heavy beams, wide floorboards, walk-in fireplaces, and benches dating back to the Revolutionary War.

Next door to the Beekman Arms is a tiny **U.S. post office,** a WPA project built in 1939

as a replica of the first home built in Rhinebeck. Inside are artifacts from the original building along with murals depicting the town's history.

Across the street from the post office stands the **Dutch Reformed Church,** designed by Robert Upjohn in 1808. Next to the church is a picturesque graveyard with tombstones that date back to the 1700s.

Rhinebeck today is known for its antique stores, restaurants, and galleries, many of which are located along Route 9 or Market Street. One popular site is the **Beekman Arms Antique Market** (Beekman Square at the Beekman Arms, 845/876-3477), which houses 30 vendors.

Tucked in between the newer stores are two creaky village institutions: the **Rhinebeck Department Store** (1 E. Market St., 845/876-5500) and **A.L. Stickles Five and Dime** (13 E. Market St., 845/876-3206). Both are veritable time capsules from the 1940s.

The Rhinebeck Chamber of Commerce (845/876-4778, www.rhinebeckchamber.com) operates a **Visitor Information Booth** (Mill St., 10 A.M.–4 P.M. Mon.–Sat., noon–4 P.M. some Sun.) diagonally across from the Beekman Arms. The chamber also runs a lodging hotline (845/876-8626).

Old Rhinebeck Aerodrome

Most summer Sundays at the storybook Old Rhinebeck Aerodrome (42 Stone Church Rd., off Rte. 9 about three miles north of Rhinebeck, 845/758-8610, www.oldrhinebeck.org), Sir Percy Good Fellow climbs into his biplane to fight the Evil Black Baron for the heart of Trudy Truelove. Cheering the adversaries on as the rotary engines roar and the castor oil burns are the excitable Madame Fifi, the dashing Pierre Loop-da-Loop, and a crowd of early-21st-century citizens who have donned WWI-era hats and scarves, dresses, and coats at the gate.

Appearances to the contrary, this charming aerodrome—holding a hodgepodge of hand-painted signs and rickety hangars—is a serious place. On its grounds are about 75 historic airplanes dating back to the early 1900s. Among them are a 1911 Curtiss D, a 1929 Sopwith Camel, and a 1908 Voison whose double canvas wings, light as gossamer, resemble those of a giant dragonfly. Summer Saturdays feature an air show reenacting historic flights.

The aerodrome is open as a museum 10 A.M.–5 P.M. daily June–October (adults $6, children $2). The air shows take place 2–4 P.M. Saturday–Sunday June–October (adults $15, seniors $10, children $5; includes museum admission). After the shows, flights in a 1929 open-cockpit biplane are offered ($45 for a 15-minute ride).

Wilderstein

This playful all-wooden Queen Anne mansion (330 Morton Rd., off Rte. 9 south of Rhinebeck, 845/876-4818, www.wilderstein.org, noon–4 P.M. Thurs.–Sun. May–Oct., adults $6, students under 17 free) sits in the middle of a 19th-century estate designed by Calvert Vaux, one of the two men who designed Central Park. Inside the 1852 house—adorned with dormers, gables, and a magnificent, five-story tower—are lavish interiors by J. B. Tiffany. Outside are 40 acres of meadows and woods, drives and trails offering great views of the Hudson.

Wilderstein means "wild man's stone" and was named after an Indian petroglyph found on the property. Guest speakers and complimentary teas are occasionally featured.

Entertainment and Events

Upstate Films (6415 Montgomery St. [Rte. 9], 845/876-2515), is a revival movie theater screening foreign, independent, and documentary films, along with the classics. The **Center for the Performing Arts at Rhinebeck** (661 Rte. 308/E. Market St., 845/876-3080) offers theater, children's shows, concerts, jazz under the stars, and other events throughout the year.

Rhinebeck's **Dutchess County Fairgrounds** (Rte. 9 north of the village, 845/876-4001) hosts a number of events throughout the year. Among them are an **Antiques Fair** in May, **crafts fairs** in June and October, and the six-day **Dutchess County Fair** in late July or early August. The latter is the largest county fair in the state, second in size only to the New York State Fair held in Syracuse.

Accommodations

The famed **Beekman Arms** (6387 Mill St., 845/876-7077, www.beekmandelamater-inn.com) is an inn that has expanded in recent years to include a cluster of about 10 small buildings. Rooms in the historic main building have plenty of atmosphere but are small ($140–150 d); those in the handsome, American Gothic ◖ **Delamater Inn,** designed by Alexander Jackson Davis, are the most splendid and popular ($100–250 d). Also at Delamater are six guesthouses perfect for families. Rooms in the other buildings cost $100–300 d.

B&B fans will find many good choices in the area. In the heart of the town is the Gothic Victorian **Gables at Rhinebeck** (6358 Mill St., 845/876-7577, www.gablesbnb.com, $150–225 d). Once owned by two eccentric sisters who shared the house with a huge doll collection, the home now offers three recently renovated guest rooms and an inviting porch. A complimentary afternoon tea with lemonade and scones is served.

On the outskirts of town, surrounded by fields and woodlands, is the delightful ◖ **Whistle Wood Farm** (52 Pells Rd., off Rte. 308, 845/876-6838, www.whistlewood.com, $120–325 d). Both a working horse farm and a friendly B&B, the Whistle Wood boasts a Jacuzzi, decks overlooking the corral and fields of wildflowers, and plenty of in-room amenities. Stay in the main house or in the Carriage House, divided into two suites.

Motels in town include the tiny, eight-room **Rhinebeck Motel** (117 Rte. 9, 845/876-5900, $77–92 d) and the family-owned **Rhinebeck Village Inn** (6 Rte. 9, 845/876-7000, $80–98 d). Both are clean and friendly.

Food

A good place for burgers and fries, sandwiches and salads is **Foster's Coach House Tavern**

(22 Montgomery St., 845/876-8052). Housed in an actual former coach house, Foster's is filled with wacky horse paraphernalia, including horseshoes, a horse carriage that's now a telephone booth, and mock horse stalls; average main dish $9.

The **China Rose** (1 Shatzell Ave., two miles west of Rt. 9, 845/876-7442) is an upscale Chinese restaurant known for its use of fresh ingredients and its peaceful outdoor patio overlooking the Hudson (average entrée $15). Lively, noisy **Gigi Trattoria** (6422 Montgomery St., 845/876-1007), housed in what was once an automobile showroom, bills itself as "Hudson Valley Mediterranean." On the menu are flatbread pizzas and lots of pasta dishes; average main dish $15.

Traphagen at the Beekman Arms (6387 Mill St., 845/876-1766) is partially in the historic inn and partially housed in a new greenhouse room filled with plants and flowers. The restaurant serves solid American fare with an emphasis on regional foods; average entrée $21.

◖ **Le Petit Bistro** (8 E. Market St., 845/876-7400, a classy yet casual bistro and bar with worn pine floors. On the menu is tasty French cuisine prepared with fresh local ingredients; average entrée $18.

NORTH OF RHINEBECK

About a mile west of Rhinebeck is County Road 103, or the old **River Road**, a short scenic drive that'll take you past grand estates and luscious river vistas. Just north of Rhinebeck on River Road is **Ferncliff**, once the estate of William Astor, now a nursing home. Farther north, at the intersection of Route 199, is **Rokeby**, a working family farm originally built in 1811 by Revolutionary War general John Armstrong and his wife.

Red Hook

Five miles north of Rhinebeck is Red Hook, a small, low-key village filled with a surprising number of restaurants, inns/B&Bs, and historic buildings. Among the latter are **Elmendorph Inn**, which dates back to the mid-1700s, and the **Octagonal House**, which now houses the Red Hook Library.

A good spot for breakfast, lunch, or a simple dinner is the wonderful old **Village Diner** (39 N. Broadway, 845/758-6232). Built in 1927, the art deco eatery is still family-owned and operated. Try the homemade doughnuts, soups, and/or egg creams.

Anchoring the village is the handsome Federal-style **Red Hook Inn** (7460 S. Broadway, 845/758-8445, $150–250 d), sporting a wide front porch. Inside are five spacious guestrooms and a suite, a restaurant serving fresh regional fare (average entrée $16), and a cozy tavern complete with a fireplace and mahogany bar.

Within walking distance of downtown is the striking, blue **Grand Dutchess Bed and Breakfast** (7571 Old Post Rd., 845/758-5818, www.granddutchess.com, $135–175 d), a Victorian Italianate mansion offering six light-filled guest rooms. All have private bath and air conditioning, and antiques are everywhere.

The Hudson Valley region in general has been a supplier of cut flowers since Victorian times, and Dutchess County in particular was once the violet and anemone capital of the world. One of the oldest nurseries still around is **F. W. Battenfeld's & Sons** (845/758-8018), on Rte. 199 just outside Red Hook. The best time to visit is Oct.–May, when the anemones are in bloom. Also of note near Red Hook is the large, family-owned **Greig Farm** (Pitcher Ln., just west of Rte. 9, 845/758-1234), where you can pick your own apples, pumpkins, peaches, and berries.

Annandale-on-Hudson

Three miles west of Red Hook, in Annandale-on-Hudson, is **Montgomery Place** (River Rd., off 9G, 845/758-5461 or 800/448-4007, www.hudsonvalley.org, house closed for renovations, grounds open 10 A.M.–5 P.M. Sat.–Sun. May–Oct., free admission). One of the loveliest mansions along the Hudson, this quiet, 1802 Federal-style gem was remodeled in the 1860s by the famed Alexander Jackson Davis, and every line of the classical structure, every inch of the romantic grounds seems perfectly in its place. From the mansion's circular, columned portico are stunning views of the Hudson and the Catskills beyond.

THE HUDSON VALLEY

Bard's new performing arts center, designed by Frank Gehry

© PETER AARON

For almost 200 years, Montgomery Place was home to the prominent Livingston family. Members of the family continued to live in the house until the 1980s, and it is still almost entirely furnished with their treasures.

Surrounding Montgomery Place are landscaped grounds laced with walking trails. Just outside the estate's gates are its still-thriving **Montgomery Place Orchards** (845/758-6338), where you can pick your own fruits and berries June–October.

Abutting Montgomery Place is **Bard College** (Rte. 9G at Annandale Road, 845/758-6822, www.bard.edu), an idyllic 540-acre campus peppered with gardens and wooded groves. Once owned by Columbia University in New York City, Bard is now an independent institution known for its creative arts programs. Cutting-edge exhibits are showcased in the **Center for Curatorial Studies** (845/758-7598, 1–5 P.M. Wed.–Sun., free admission). Concerts and the critically acclaimed Bard Music Festival (which each year studies a different composer) are presented in the dramatic,

brushed-stainless-steel **Richard B. Fisher Center for Performing Arts** (845/758-7900), designed by architect Frank Gehry and acoustical designer Yasuhisa Toyota. Tours of the center, whose swooping lines reflect the surrounding landscape, are offered at 11 A.M., 1 P.M., and 2 P.M. most days of the year.

Tivoli

If you continue north of Annandale-on-Hudson on Route 9G to Route 78 and head west, you'll come to the hamlet of Tivoli. Henry Hudson is thought to have anchored offshore here in 1609, and nearby Crugers Island may once have been an important meeting ground for the local Wappinger and upstate Iroquois Indians.

Today, Tivoli is a popular hang for Bard College students and professors; hence its many restaurants and bars. Among the most popular is the boisterous **Ⓒ Santa Fe** (52 Broadway, 845/757-4100), offering authentic Southwestern and Mexican food. In summer, a small outdoor dining area opens upstairs; average entrée $14. Also a favorite, serving tasty, high-quality sushi, tempura, and noodles in a more relaxed setting, is **Osaka** (74 Broadway, 845/757-5055); average entrée $14.

At the **Black Swan Pub** (66 Broadway, 845/757-3777), you can hear live rock, folk, or bluegrass music most nights of the week. On tap are about a dozen beers, while out back is a patio adorned with twinkling lights.

Columbia County

Though it lacks the drama of the mountainous Hudson Highlands, Columbia may be the most beautiful of the Hudson Valley counties. Rolling, forested hills give way to fields of silvery grain dotted with maroon silos and barns, which in turn give way to historic hamlets centered on village greens and white-steepled churches. Columbia, still highly dependent on agriculture, is also one of the least developed and visited of the Hudson Valley counties.

Columbia's only city, and its county seat, is Hudson, once a major whaling port. Originally settled by a group of seafaring Quakers from Nantucket and Martha's Vineyard, Hudson today is an architectural treasure trove in the process of being restored, as well as an antiques center and popular get-away for Manhattanites. On its outskirts are two unusual attractions: Olana, a Persian-styled castle built by the painter Frederic Church; and the largest fire-fighting museum in the United States, filled with hundreds of surprisingly beautiful artifacts.

South of Hudson are Clermont—the furthest north of the grand Hudson Valley estates—and two glorious parks, Lake Taghkanic State Park and Taconic State Park. To the northeast are the picturesque villages of Kinderhook, the Chathams, and New Lebanon.

Almost every road in Columbia County is a scenic drive, but byways particularly worth exploring include Route 9H north of Hudson, and Routes 82 and 22 in the southern and western parts of the county. The five-mile stretch of Route 11 between Routes 23 and 27 near Taghkanic was declared a **National Beautiful Highway** in the late 1960s.

SOUTHERN COLUMBIA COUNTY
Clermont State Historic Site

Just north of the Dutchess County border is Clermont (Woods Rd., off Rte. 9G, Germantown, 518/537-4240, www.friendsofclermont.org, 11 A.M.–5 P.M. Tues.–Sun. Apr.–Oct., 11 A.M.–4 P.M. Sat.–Sun. Nov.–Mar., adults $5, seniors and students $4, children 5–12 $1; $5 vehicle user fee Sat.–Sun. Apr.–Oct.), a grand historic estate that was once home to seven generations of the Livingston family. The Georgian manse sits on the edge of a wide lawn lined with enormous black locust trees. Views from the estate are superb; down below is the Hudson River, and in the distance are the high Catskill Mountains peaks that inspired the estate's name. *Clermont* is French for "clear mountain."

The 35-room mansion holds many of the Livingstons' heirlooms, including period furniture and family portraits by Gilbert Stuart and others. Robert R. Livingston (1746–1813) was arguably the most famous of the clan. He administered the first oath of office to George Washington, helped draft the Declaration of Independence, and served as minister to France under Thomas Jefferson.

The landscaped grounds include a Lilac Walk (in bloom in May), formal gardens, and many acres of fields, forests, and wetlands laced with carriage paths and hiking trails. On the front lawn near the river is a plaque honoring inventor Robert Fulton whose steamboat, the *Clermont,* first traveled up the Hudson from New York City to Albany in August 1807.

THE HUDSON VALLEY

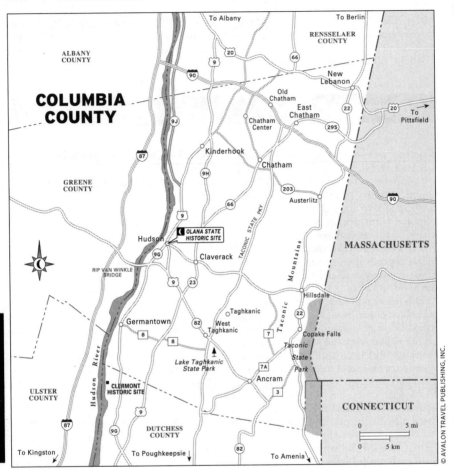

Lake Taghkanic State Park and Vicinity

To the east of Clermont, amid rolling hills, is a pristine state park (1582 Rte. 82, just east of Taconic State Pkwy., Ancram, 518/851-3631, daily sunrise–sunset, parking $8 May–Sept.) centering on cool, blue Lake Taghkanic, a 1,569-acre body of water ringed with bathing beaches and boat launches. Hiking trails climb small peaks to offer splendid views of the valley below. Also in the park are a top-rated campground with 60 campsites, picnic areas, a boat-rental shop, ball field, and fitness trail. The campground is open May–October; for reservations, call 800/456-CAMP.

Not far from Lake Taghkanic State Park is the classic **(West Taghkanic Diner** (Rte. 82 at the Taconic State Pkwy., 518/851-7117), where the red, neon-lit profile of a Native American chief greets motorists as they pull up.

A farm in Ancramdale has long been home to the peerless four-day **Grey Fox Bluegrass Festival** (988/946-8495. www.greyfoxblue-grass.com), which comes to town in mid-July. The festival will take place in 2006 as usual, but its site in future years is unclear, as the farm is for sale.

Taconic State Park

Not to be confused with Lake Taghkanic State Park is the much larger Taconic State Park (253 Rte. 344, off Rte. 22, Copake Falls. 518/329-3993, daily 8 A.M.–sunset, parking $8 May–Sept.), another lovely preserve. It's on the New York–Massachusetts border amid the Taconic Mountains, a small range that extends northward into Vermont. In the 5,000-acre park are two separate recreation areas—Rudd Pond and Copake Falls—featuring hiking trails, bathing beaches, 112 campsites, boat rentals, picnic areas, and playgrounds.

The park's greatest attraction is Bash-Bish Glen, where Bash-Bish Brook cascades down a striking series of waterfalls. A craggy outcropping known as Eagle Cliff stands at the top of the cataract; local legend has it that several Indians once fell to their deaths over its edge. Among them was a woman named Bash Bish, after whom the brook was named. Her spirit is said to still inhabit the area. Also nearby is an ice-cold, 40-foot-deep quarry pool.

The camping facilities are open May–Oct.; for reservations, call 800/456-CAMP.

Copake Falls

On the edge of Taconic State Park is the serene little hamlet of Copake Falls, centered around a handful of historic wooden buildings and a small traffic circle with a historic four-faced clock. One of the county's most popular weekend events, attracting everyone from farmers to second-home owners, is the **Copake Country Auction,** held on Saturday nights. Watch for advertisements in the *Independent,* a Columbia County paper that comes out on Monday and Thursday.

Hillsdale

Winter brings skiers to Hillsdale's **Catamount Ski & Snowboarding Area** (Breezy Hill Rd., off Rte. 23, 518/325-3200). The small ski resort offers 32 slopes and trails, three terrain parks, and seven lifts, along with a laid-back atmosphere that makes it especially good for families.

The comfortable **Swiss Hutte** (Breezy Hill Rd., off Rte. 23, 518/325-3333, www.swisshutte.com, $150–220 d) sits in the middle of the Catamount ski area, overlooking the slopes. On site is a cozy wood-paneled bar and separate dining room that serve Swiss-American fare; bar dishes $5–18, restaurant entrées $20–28.

The creaky, near-legendary **Rodgers Book Barn** (Rodman Rd., off West End Rd., off Rte. 23, 518/325-3610, noon–6 P.M. Thurs.–Mon., reduced hours in winter) is filled with books, books, and more books—over 50,000 titles, all secondhand. They're housed in a two-story barn with lots of nooks and crannies.

The **Falcon Ridge Folk Festival** (Long Hill Farm, Rte. 23, 860/364-0366, www.falconridgefolk.com) comes to Hillsdale every late July, though it may soon be moving to a new site. On tap are top folk performers from around the country.

For good regional American cuisine or wood-fired pizza, try the circa-1811 **Hillsdale House** (Rte. 23 in the village center, 518/325-7111); average entrée $14. **Aubergine** (Rts. 22 and 23, 518/325-3412), housed in a 1783 brick Colonial home, serves French-American fare that changes according to the season. Open for dinner only; average entrée $26.

HUDSON

Hudson is one of the most interesting towns along its namesake river. The town is part gentrified second-home-owner territory, part 19th-century boomtown now down on its luck. Handsome antique stores and sophisticated Manhattanites live side-by-side with weathered Victorian buildings and proud descendants of African American whalers, struggling to make ends meet.

History

The Dutch began arriving in Hudson in the 17th century. But the town wasn't really settled until the 1780s, when a group of seafaring New Englanders—seeking a harbor safe from British attack—discovered the area's deep waters and steep bluffs. They purchased the land in 1783 and by the following spring, several families had arrived and built homes.

THE HUDSON VALLEY

Many of the new settlers were Quakers who made a pact to either remain in Hudson permanently or sell their property to others "at first cost, without interest." They carefully designed their new city to be a shipping center, complete with straight main streets, a shipyard, wharves, and warehouses. In 1785, Hudson received the third city charter granted in New York State, and by 1790, 25 schooners—most in the whaling business—were registered in the city. Forty-one liquor licenses had been granted, and a red-light district flourished. In 1797, Hudson missed becoming the capital of New York State by one vote.

By the mid 1800s, however, the whaling industry had all but disappeared, and Hudson began a transformation into a small industrial city. The coming of the railroads in the late 1840s enabled the area's existing gristmills, tanneries, and breweries to flourish, and new knitting mills, brick yards and car-wheel works to be built. Business boomed until the early 1900s, when industrial demands changed and Hudson began a slow decline that hit rock bottom in the 1960s and '70s. The city was rediscovered in the 1980s, largely by second-home owners, and has since been significantly gentrified.

Warren Street

The heart of downtown Hudson and the gentrification process is Warren Street, lined with one historic building after another. Along the 100 block alone are a Greek Revival mansion with a "widow's walk" that once belonged to a whaling captain (No. 32), a Federal-style brick house with "eyebrow" windows (No. 102), a Queen Anne clapboard house with attractive trim (No. 114), and a rare Adam-style house with an ornamental marble frieze (No. 116).

The 1811 **Robert Jenkins House** (113 Warren St., 518/828-9764, 1–3 P.M. Sun.–Mon. July–Aug., or by appointment, adults $3, seniors $2, children under 12 free) houses a small local history museum. Exhibits include paintings by several lesser-known Hudson River School artists, the jawbone of a whale, General Grant's "personal table," and other curious odds and ends.

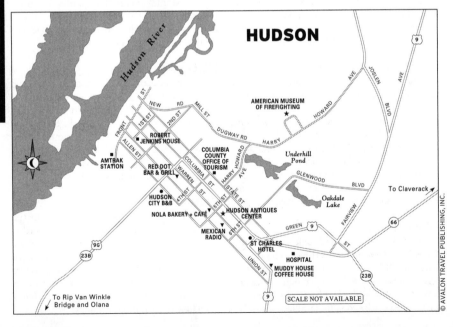

© AVALON TRAVEL PUBLISHING, INC.

© CHRISTIANE BIRD

Hudson's Warren Street is a walkable exhibit of varied historic architecture.

Antiques and Art

In recent years, Warren Street has become a mecca for antiques lovers; dozens of stores of varying quality are located here, most between 5th and 7th Streets. Among them are the **Hudson Antiques Center** (536 Warren St., 518/828-9920), housing about 20 dealers; **Theron Ware** (548 Warren St., 518/828-9744), specializing in classic Americana and ornate European antiques; and **Ornamentum** (506½ Warren St., 518/671-6770), part jewelry store and part art gallery. The two-story **Carrie Haddad Gallery** (622 Warren St., 518/822-9744) exhibits paintings, photographs, and sculpture by both established and up-and-coming artists.

◖ Olana State Historic Site

Perched high on a hill just south of Hudson is Olana (off Rte. 9G, just south of the Rip Van Winkle Bridge, 518/828-0135, www.olana.org, 10 A.M.–5 P.M. Tues.–Sun. Apr.–Nov., call for off-season hours, adults $7, seniors $5, children 5–12 $2; $5 vehicle user fee Sat.–Sun. Apr.–

Oct.), an eccentric, Persian-style castle built in 1870 by landscape artist Frederic Church, with the help of architect Calvert Vaux. Church was then at the height of his career and had just returned from a trip to the Middle East, a land with which he had fallen in love.

A tour of Olana begins in the formal greeting room, which is hung with a dozen paintings, including one by Church's teacher and the founder of the Hudson River School, Thomas Cole. Here, a guide explains that one of the largest contributions the Hudson River School made to America was its portrayal of the wilderness as something approachable and worth preserving; before, it had been regarded as hostile and dangerous. One of Church's most famous paintings, of Niagara Falls, was used to spearhead a movement to save the falls from destruction.

Throughout the castle, painted in deep blues, reds, and yellows, are romantic arched doorways, wide-open windows, stenciled Persian lettering, and plush Persian rugs. Every room is filled with unique objects carefully picked out by the artist, who one critic said had the "best taste of his time." Each room also houses a number of Church's majestic, luminous canvases, while the dining room is an amazing picture gallery hung floor to ceiling with hundreds of canvases from the 16th to 18th centuries.

American Museum of Firefighting

This delightful spit-and-polish hall (125 Harry Howard Ave., off Rte. 9 just north of Rte. 23B, 518/828-7695 or 800/479-7695, 9 A.M.–4:30 P.M. daily, free admission) boasts the nation's largest collection of fire-fighting equipment and related paraphernalia, including dozens of exquisite old horse-drawn fire carriages, many equipped with fairy-tale finery. Several carriages sport engraved lanterns and velvet-covered seats. One even has silver-and gold-plated hubcaps.

Part of the museum's charm is its location on the grounds of New York's retirement home for volunteer firemen. You'll see the retirees hanging out on the porch as you drive up, and you'll meet them as you tour the museum. From them you'll learn that 80 percent of New York State's firefighters are still volunteers, a fact that poses a serious problem as the demands of firefighting are not compatible with busy modern-day lives.

Accommodations

The green-and-cream Victorian ❰ **Hudson City B&B** (326 Allen St., 518/822-8044, www.hudsoncitybnb.com, $119–199 d) was built by Joshua Waterman, a former Hudson mayor, in the 1860s. Outside, find a wide veranda lined with wicker chairs. Inside, find a parlor with a fireplace and six guestrooms filled with antiques.

Built in the late 1800s, the red-brick **St. Charles Hotel** (16–18 Park Pl., 518/822-9900, www.stcharleshotel.com, $89–119 d, with continental breakfast) offers somewhat worn but adequate rooms with cable TV and Internet hook-up. Downstairs is the Rip Van Winkle taproom and the Maharani Restaurant, serving Indian cuisine.

HUDSON'S STREET OF SIN

As sleepy as the small town of Hudson seems today, it once had a nationwide reputation for vice. For a century or so before 1950, a dozen or more houses of ill repute lined Diamond Street (now known as Columbia Street). Alongside them stood illegal horserooms, gambling parlors, floating craps games, and hole-in-the-wall taverns and bars.

No one knows exactly when the illicit businesses began, but by 1840, local citizens were complaining about the "riotous gatherings" on Diamond Street. During Prohibition, the street was a favorite haunt of gangster Legs Diamond and friends, while in the 1940s, it was so popular that out-of-towners arriving by the carloads had a hard time finding parking spots. "Columbia Street was famous as a well-managed, sensual shopping center where even the most discriminating could find what they wanted," writes Bruce Edward Hall in *Diamond Street: The Story of the Little Town with the Big Red Light District* (Black Dome Press, 1994). "American servicemen at bases around the globe found their familiarity with [Hudson] a common bond."

Many of the most popular bordellos on Columbia Street lay between 3rd and 4th Streets—a stretch known as "The Block." During the 1930s, for example, Madam Mae Healy was at No. 328, Dottie Pierson at No.342, and Daisy Rawley at No.358. Evelyn White's brothel at No. 320 boasted walls lined with velvet, while the Mansion House at No. 332 was a three-storied extravaganza with an enormous bar and bartenders named "Burger Baby" and "Woofing Sam."

Columbia Street was padlocked for good in the 1950s, and today the once-teeming thoroughfare is just a nondescript section of the truck route. Few driving by suspect its notorious past.

About 10 miles south of downtown Hudson is the inviting **(Inn at Blue Stores** (2323 Rte. 9, 518/537-4277, www.innatbluestores.com, $125–225 d), a Spanish-style B&B outfitted with tile roofs and stucco walls. Situated on a farm, the inn includes a pool and veranda. All rooms have king-size beds; two have private baths.

Food

A good place for breakfast is the **Nola Bakery & Cafe** (Warren and North Fifth St.). The **Muddy House Coffee House** (742 Warren St., 518/828-0555) crowded with overstuffed furniture, offers a wide variety of coffees and teas, along with smoothies and desserts.

At the sleek and trendy **(Red Dot Bar & Grill** (321 Warren St., 518/828-3657), you can order everything from burgers and exotic salads to grilled lamb chops and soft shell crabs in season; average dinner entrée $16. Sister restaurant to a Manhattan eatery of the same day, **Mexican Radio** (537 Warren St., 518/828-7770) offers high-end Mexican fare in a room filled with Mexican art; average entrée $16.

KINDERHOOK

The charming village of Kinderhook, or "children's corner," was first settled by the Dutch—a fact reflected in the town's neat tree-lined streets, historic wooden buildings, and laid-back atmosphere. The village's most famous native son was Martin Van Buren, and signs directing visitors to the former president's birth site, home, and gravesite are everywhere. It is to Van Buren, nicknamed "Old Kinderhook," that we owe the expression "O.K."

To reach Kinderhook from Hudson, take Route 9 north about 10 miles.

Martin Van Buren National Historic Site

Martin Van Buren, a tavern owner's son who rose to hold the highest office in the land, spent the last 21 years of his life in this large yellow house surrounded by linden trees (1013 Old Post Rd., off Rte. 9H south of the village, 518/758-9689, www.nps.gov/mava,

9 A.M.–4:30 P.M. daily May–Oct., 9 A.M.–4:30 P.M. Sat.–Sun., Nov.–Apr., adults $4, children under 17 free, ground free). Before Van Buren bought the property in 1839, Washington Irving had often visited here, sometimes even tutoring the former residents' children.

A visit to Lindenwald, as the house is known, begins with a short film on the "Little Magician" (Van Buren was only five feet six inches), who avidly supported Jeffersonian democracy, served as vice-president under Andrew Jackson, and established the country's independent treasury. In his day, Van Buren was regarded as a cool and competent diplomat who operated most effectively behind the scenes, "row[ing] to his object with muffled oars."

In the sitting room, all done up in elegant gold and light blue, is a fine collection of musical instruments. In the banquet room is a magnificent French wallpaper mural depicting the landscape of the hunt. The room is kept dark at all times to preserve the mural, which can only be viewed by flashlight.

Luykas Van Alen House

Also off Route 9H, just north of Lindenwald, is the Luykas Van Alen House (518/758-9265, 11 A.M.–5 P.M. Thurs.–Sat. and 1–5 P.M. Sun. June–Sept., adults $3, seniors $2, children under 12 free), a 1737 Dutch farmhouse complete with a steeply pitched roof, wide chimneys, Delft tile, and sturdy furnishings. If the place looks familiar, it's because it was used in Martin Scorsese's film *The Age of Innocence,* based on the Edith Wharton novel.

In front of the farmhouse is a dark and peaceful pond that's home to several swans, while to one side is the one-roomed **Ichabod Crane School House.** Washington Irving apparently based his famous character on a schoolteacher from Kinderhook; the building has been restored to look as it did in the 1920s.

Downtown Historic Sites

By the village green is the 1820 **James Vanderpoel House** (16 Broad St., 518/758-9265, 11 A.M.–5 P.M. Thurs.–Sat. and 1–5 P.M.

Sun. June–Sept., adults $3, seniors $2, children under 12 free). Vanderpoel—a contemporary of Martin Van Buren—was a prominent attorney, state assemblyman, and judge. The house is an excellent example of Federal-style architecture and contains an interesting collection of period furnishings and paintings by early area artists.

Nearby is the **Columbia County Museum** (5 Albany Ave., 518/758-9265, 10 A.M.–4 P.M. Mon.–Fri. and 1–5 P.M. Sat. May–Oct., 10 A.M.–4 P.M. Mon., Wed. and Fri. Dec.–Apr., free admission), housed in what was once a Masonic temple. Changing exhibits focus on the history and culture of the county.

Shopping

At one end of the Kinderhook green is the well-stocked **Blackwood and Brouwer Booksellers Ltd.** (7 Hudson St., 518/758-1232), home to summer story hours, author breakfasts, readings, and book-signings. At the other end is the creaky, old-fashioned **Fisher's O.K. Rock Shop** (2 Chatham St., 518/758-7657), selling minerals, fossils, jewelry, and gifts made from polished rock.

Kinderhook also has its share of antique shops. One of the biggest is the **Kinderhook Antiques Center** (518/758-7939), housed in an old dairy barn on Route 9H several miles south of the green.

Accommodations

Housed in a classic 1900s home surrounded by flowering gardens and an inviting side porch is the **Kinderhook B&B** (67 Broad St., 518/758-1850, $109–139). The four air-conditioned guest rooms—two in the main house, two in a guest cottage—are smartly outfitted with country antiques, high featherbeds, and private baths.

Food

The idiosyncratic, log cabin **Carolina House** (59 Broad St., 518/758-1669) is a local favorite that attracts diners from miles around. On the menu is such hearty Southern fare as baby-back ribs, Southern-fried chicken, catfish, crab cakes, biscuits, and pecan pie; average entrée $15.

THE CHATHAMS

To the east of Kinderhook, in a countryside of rolling hills and horse farms, are the Chathams—the Village of Chatham, Chatham Center, East Chatham, North Chatham, and Old Chatham. Old Chatham, settled in 1758, is little more than a crossroads; the Village of Chatham is the Chathams' commercial hub. During the late 1800s, over 100 trains a day passed through here on their way to Albany or Boston. The streets are still lined with Italianate brick storefronts dating back to that era. In the village center you'll find the **Chatham Bakery and Coffee Shoppe** (1 Church St., 518/392-3411), a family-run institution known for its baked goods and burgers served on homemade bread.

Near East Chatham is **Librarium Second Hand Books** (Black Bridge Rd. [Rte. 295], 518/392-5209, 11 A.M.–4 P.M. most days in summer, Sat.–Sun. in winter), a homey book barn with over 35,000 used titles.

Shaker Museum and Library

Outside Old Chatham is the Shaker Museum and Library (88 Shaker Museum Rd., off County Rd. 13, 518/794-9100, www.shakermuseumandlibrary.org, 10 A.M.–5 P.M. daily June–Oct., adults $8, seniors $6, children 8–17 $4), dedicated to the history and culture of the Protestant sectarians who emigrated from England to the United States in the 1770s. Named for their tendency to dance and sway during worship, the Shakers were known for their industry, thrift, and celibate lifestyle. They constructed everything they needed with a great deal of thought and care, and to this day, Shaker-designed items are highly valued for their simplicity and grace.

The museum houses the country's largest collection of Shaker handiwork. Spread out over several buildings are many fine examples of the oval boxes and baskets, clean-lined cabinets and chairs, and ingenious crafts and tools for which the sect is famous. It is to the Shakers that we owe the invention of the flat broom, clothespin, circular saw, screw propeller, turbine water wheel, cut nails, and water-repellent fabric.

THE SHAKERS

HISTORY

The Shaker religious movement began in England in 1758, under the leadership of a woman who would later be known as Mother Ann Lee. Lee was originally a Quaker, but instead of worshipping quietly as did her fellow congregants, she would fall into a religious ecstasy, whirling and trembling and "shaking" off evil.

In 1762, Lee married and had four children, all of whom died in infancy following difficult births. Lee saw this as a judgment from God and began to avoid all sexual relations with her husband. Shortly thereafter, she had a conversion – "My soul broke forth to God," she said – and ventured forth to spread the word. Central to her preachings was the philosophy that men and women should live apart from one another.

Before long, Lee was thrown in jail for her radical ideas, and there she had a vision that told her to go to America. In the spring of 1774, she and eight followers (including her husband, from whom she had already separated) set sail, to eventually settle in Watervliet, near Albany.

The Shakers slowly gained converts, and by 1794 they had established 11 communities throughout New York and New England. At their peak in the 1850s, the sect had about 6,000 members from Maine to Kentucky. One of their settlements, Sabbathday Lake, Maine, is still a living, working Shaker community open to the public in summer (207/926-4597). "Are you worried about dying out?" one of their members was asked recently. "Nay! Not unless God and Christ and Eternal verities are failing," was the answer.

BELIEFS AND LIFESTYLE

Among the basic tenets of Shakerism are celibacy, separation from the world, communal sharing of goods, confessions of sins, equality of the sexes, and pacifism. Children come into the community through the conversion of their parents, or through adoption.

During their heyday, the Shakers were organized into "families" of about 50 members who lived in a home with separate doorways, stairs, and sleeping quarters for the sexes. The "brothers" and "sisters" would only come together for daily meditation, meals, which would be eaten in silence, Sunday worship services, and occasional "union meetings." During the latter, the brothers and sisters would sit facing each other a few feet apart, and converse or sing.

The children lived separately from the adults in a Girls' House and Boys' House. School was held for the girls during the summer and for the boys in winter.

Each family had its own gardens, crops, livestock, and workshops. The sisters did the cooking, cleaning, washing, spinning, weaving, and gardening, while the brothers tended to the heavier farmwork and manufactured products such as chairs, brooms, and oval boxes to sell to the outside world. The Shakers also raised a wide variety of medicinal herbs which they marketed through pharmaceutical companies.

While the Shakers shunned the material culture of modern society, they were not opposed to new ideas, and were frequently ahead of their time in farming and sanitation practices. Many had running water and electricity long before their more worldly neighbors. As early as 1910, many were buying automobiles – to be used, of course, for Shaker business, not personal pleasure.

HANCOCK SHAKER VILLAGE

In Massachusetts, not far from Columbia County, is the most interesting Shaker site in the area, the Hancock Shaker Village (Rts. 20 and 41, five miles west of Pittsfield, Mass., 413/443-0188, www.hancockshakervillage.org, 9:30 A.M.-5 P.M. daily May-Oct., 10 A.M. - 3 P.M. daily Apr.-Nov.). This superbly restored living-history museum comprises 20 buildings set on 1,200 acres. Craftspeople are at work during the day and candlelight dinners are served on Saturday evenings. The village's finest building is its Round Barn, erected in 1826, which permitted one man working in the center of the building to feed and water the cattle with a minimum of motion.

Dinners must be reserved well in advance.

Note: A plan is now underway to move the Shaker Museum and Library to Mount Lebanon Village (see below), where 80 percent of the museum's collection originated. Before that move is made, several of the village's buildings must first be repaired, renovated, or enlarged; no timetable for the merger has been set. Visit the museum's website for an update.

Events

The **Columbia County Fair** (518/828-3375) comes to the Chatham fairgrounds (junction of Rtes. 66 and 203) over Labor Day weekend. It's the nation's oldest continuously running county fair.

Camping and Accommodations

Camping is available in nearby Austerlitz at the 200-site **Woodland Hills Campground** (86 Fog Hill Rd., 518/392-3557). Between Chatham and Chatham Center, budget travelers will find the **Chatham Travel Lodge** (Rte. 295 and Taconic State Pkwy., 518/392-4066, $65–95 d).

The **Inn at Silver Maple Farm** (1871 Rte. 295, East Chatham, 518/781-3600, www.silvermaplefarm.com, $90–230 d) is an 1830s dairy farm turned lovely B&B. Complete with pine floors, exposed beams, and hand-painted murals, the hostelry sits surrounded by fields and woods. The rooms are airy and comfortable, while a deck offers scenic views of the Berkshire Mountains.

NEW LEBANON
Mount Lebanon Shaker Village

A community of Shakers once lived to the east of Old Chatham in the Mount Lebanon Shaker Village (Shaker Rd., off Rte. 20, 518/794-9500, 10 A.M.–5 P.M. Fri.–Sun. June–Oct., adults $5, seniors $4.50, children 6–12 $2, families $10). Twenty-four original village buildings still stand. For years, many were leased to a prep school that occupied this site since the 1930s, but others have been restored and are open to the public.

Near the entrance to the village, in the former wash house, is a visitors center where you can watch a short slide show and view exhibits on the community's early leaders. Down the road are a granary, now being used as a gift house and workshop for reproduction furniture; a plant nursery and herb garden; and the brethren's workshop, which once housed a seed shop, printer's shop, and shoemaking shop.

Stock Car Racing

On summer Saturday nights, the bleachers are always filled with families and fans at the **Lebanon Valley Speedway** (1746 Rte. 20, just west of West Lebanon, 518/794-9606, www.lebanonvalley.com). Racing season runs April–October.

Sports and Recreation

Serious hikers will want to contact the **New York-New Jersey Trail Conference** (156 Ramapo Valley Rd., Mahwah, NJ 07430, 201/512-9348, www.nynjtc.com). The conference publishes *Harriman Trails* and "East Hudson Trails" (a map set), among many other things, and operates the excellent **Park Visitor Center** off the Palisades Interstate Parkway (see *Harriman and Bear Mountain State Parks* under *Rockland County,* above).

Two excellent books cover hiking in the region. One is the classic *New York Walk Book,* published by the New York-New Jersey Trail Conference. Another is *Fifty Hikes in the Hudson Valley* by Peter Kick, Barbara McMartin, and James M. Long (Backcountry Press).

The Hudson Valley region also offers a wide variety of other outdoor activities, including **fishing, hot-air ballooning, horseback riding, canoeing, biking,** and **golf.** For more information, inquire at local tourism offices.

For more information on any of the New York State parks, visit www.nysparks.com.

Getting There and Around

The easiest way to explore the Hudson Valley is by car. However, many towns along the east bank of the Hudson River and some in Westchester's Harlem Valley and Orange County are serviced by **Metro-North Commuter Railroad** (212/532-4900 or 800/638-7646), which leaves Grand Central Station in Manhattan. Taxis are usually available at the villages' railroad stations. **Amtrak** (800/872-7245) provides rail service between New York City and Rhinecliff, Hudson, and points further north.

If traveling up the Hudson River valley by train, be sure to sit on the left-hand side of the car. The railroad hugs the eastern shoreline and offers spectacular views.

Adirondack-Pine Hill Trailways (212/967-2900 or 800/225-6815) and **Shortline Bus** (212/736-4700 or 800/631-8405) offer daily bus service between the Port Authority Bus Terminal in Manhattan and many Hudson Valley communities.

Travelers can opt to fly into either New York City or the Albany County Airport. Among the major airlines flying into Albany are **American** (800/433-7300), **Delta** (800/221-1212), **Northwest** (800/225-2525), and **United** (800/241-6522).

Information and Services

For general information on the region, contact **Hudson Valley Travel & Tourism,** P.O. Box 284, Salt Point, NY 12578, 800/232-4782, www.travelhudsonvalley.org.

Hudson Valley (845/485-7844, www.hudsonvalleymagazine.com) is a glossy monthly with informative articles; available at area newsstands.

Each county has its own tourist information office, as listed below. Most are open 9 A.M.–5 P.M. Monday–Friday.

Westchester County Visitors Bureau (222 Mamaroneck Ave., White Plains 10605, 914/995-8500 or 800/833-9282, www.westchestertourism.com)

Rockland County Tourism (18 New Hempstead Rd., New City 10956, 845/708-7300 or 800/295-5723, www.rockland.org)

Orange County Division of Tourism (124 Main St., Goshen 10924, 845/291-2136 or 800/762-8687, www.orangetourism.org)

Putnam County Visitors Bureau (110 Old Rte. 6, Carmel 10512, 845/225-0381, www.visitputnam.org)

Dutchess County Tourism Promotion Agency (3 Neptune Rd., Poughkeepsie 12610, 845/463-4000 or 800/445-3131, www.dutchesstourism.com)

Columbia County Tourism (401 State St., Hudson 12534, 518/828-3375 or 800/724-1846, www.columbiacountyny.org)

THE CATSKILLS

For an overview map of the Catskills, see *The Hudson Valley* chapter map.

The dense, dark, smoke-blue Catskill Mountains, crowded together to the west of the Hudson, are a strangely enigmatic place. They're not particularly high or particularly grand—the tallest peak is only about 4,200 feet—and they're certainly not remote. Yet the Catskills possess an oddly evocative wildness and solitude. Stepping into them is like stepping into an ancient woodcut, carved to illustrate a dark fairy tale. No wonder Rip Van Winkle met a mysterious "company of odd-looking personages playing at ninepins"

here, and drank of their large flagons to fall into a 20-year sleep.

The Catskills have had a remarkable influence on the American imagination. They were the first American landscape to be romanticized in literature and art; author Washington Irving and later the Hudson River School painters discovered the region's beauty and brought it to the public eye in their works. By the mid-1800s, the primeval Catskills—filled with both impenetrable shadows and luminous shafts of light—had come to symbolize the New World wilderness.

A popular vacation destination from the mid-1800s well into the mid-1900s, the Catskills fell

COURTESY OF ORANGE COUNTY TOURISM

HIGHLIGHTS

◖ **Huguenot Street:** "The oldest street in America with its original buildings" was built by French Huguenot Protestants in the late 1600s to early 1700s (page 288).

◖ **Minnewaska State Park:** Located high in the Shawangunk Mountains, the park is filled with panoramic views, glacial lakes, and hiking trails (page 292).

◖ **Historic Stockade Area:** The eight-block historic district, originally settled by the Dutch, is now an attractive, vibrant urban center (page 295).

◖ **Opus 40:** The unusual environmental sculpture, created by artist Harvey Fite, covers six acres of an abandoned bluestone quarry (page 297).

◖ **Downtown Woodstock:** The famed arts colony cum tourist center is filled with small shops and galleries. The legendary 1969 Woodstock Music Festival took place in Bethel, 60 miles away (page 300).

◖ **Escarpment Trail:** The historic hiking trail runs along the edge of a cliff. Hike all 24 miles or just stroll a few hundred yards to the edge (page 306).

◖ **Catskill Fly Fishing Center:** The state-of-the-art museum and cultural center is situated in one of the world's best trout-fishing regions (page 317).

◖ **Andes:** The especially pretty, lively, and historic village, reached by a scenic road, is located high in the Catskills (page 325).

LOOK FOR ◖ TO FIND RECOMMENDED SIGHTS, ACTIVITIES, DINING, AND LODGING.

THE CATSKILLS

into decline in the late 1900s. It became worn-out and shabby in many parts, with forlorn houses, abandoned farms, and out-dated resorts clinging tenuously to the roadsides.

Today, the Catskills are in the midst of a rebirth. Due largely to an influx of second-home owners and ex-urbanites, upscale restaurants, shops, and B&Bs pepper the region. Evolving as well is a greater appreciation of the area's diversity. The Catskills are not just about mountains and resorts. Small museums and historic attractions can be found everywhere, along with creaky general stores, country auctions, a strong arts scene, excellent canoeing and day-hiking, and some of the best trout fishing in the world.

PLANNING YOUR TIME

All of the Catskills' 10 highest peaks are situated in northern Ulster and Greene Counties, so you'll want to spend at least two or three days here, taking scenic drives along **Routes 28, 23, and 23A,** visiting such mountain villages as **Woodstock** and **Saugerties,** and hiking along the **Escarpment Trail.** Ulster County is also home to the historic towns of **Kingston, New Paltz,** and **Hurley,** and to the **Shawangunk Mountains,** dotted with glacier lakes, which will take another three days or so to explore. Alternatively, spend those additional days in lovely, all-but-unspoiled Delaware County, home to more scenic drives and the attractive villages of **Margaretville, Andes,** and **Roxbury;** and in western Sullivan County, home to the trout-fishing capitals of **Roscoe** and **Livingston Manor,** and to the idyllic **Upper Delaware River.** Make a side trip to **Bethel,** where the legendary 1969 Woodstock Music Festival took place. In the best scenarios of all, spend 10 days to two weeks in the region and you'll have time to visit many of the most interesting sites.

THE LAND
Mountains

Geologically speaking, the Catskill Mountains are not mountains at all but an uplifted section of the Allegheny Plateau that was once the floor of a shallow sea. During the Middle- and Late-Devonian and Carboniferous periods, that seabed—made up largely of shales and sandstones—was heaved upward to an elevation of 5,000–6,000 feet, forming the Catskills. Since then, the plateau has eroded, leaving peaks that range 3,000–4,200 feet in height; one unusual characteristic of the Catskills is their near uniform elevation, seldom found in true mountain ranges. Also unlike other ranges, here you'll see little bare rock, and few flat ledges or exposed cliffs.

Marking the eastern edge of the Catskills is a steep, clifflike escarpment known as the Great Wall of Manitou. To the west, the slopes are gentler, and eventually taper off altogether.

A second, much smaller mountain range, the Shawangunks, lies at the southwestern edge of Ulster County. Formed during the Silurian Age and therefore much older than the Catskills, the Shawangunks are composed primarily of limestone and quartz conglomerate. Thick, jointed strata form cliffs several hundred feet high, making the Shawangunks a favorite among rock-climbers.

Waterways

Two major river systems drain most of the Catskills: the Hudson-Mohawk and the Delaware. Principal tributaries of the first include the Schoharie River, Catskill Creek, Kaaterskill Creek, and the Esopus. The headwaters of the Delaware River begin in Delaware County; principal tributaries include Beaver Kill, Willowemoc Creek, and Mongaup Creek.

Since 1828, when the Delaware & Hudson Canal was built, the Catskills have also been known for their artificially constructed waterways. Today, two main reservoir and aqueduct systems network through the region. The older Catskill Reservoir System, begun in 1909, includes Ashokan Reservoir, Schoharie Reservoir, and the Catskill Aqueduct. Powered by gravity, the mostly surface-level aqueduct passes 1,400 feet beneath the Hudson River to flow into Kensico Reservoir in Westchester County. There the water is chlorinated and sent another 17 miles downstream to Yonkers, where it's distributed to Manhattan and Brooklyn.

The Delaware Reservoir and Aqueduct System was built in the 1930s, when it became painfully apparent that the Catskill System was no longer large enough to satisfy New York City's ever-increasing water needs. The system is composed of the 18.5-mile-long Pepacton Reservoir; the smaller Rondout, Neversink, and Cannonsville Reservoirs; and the Delaware Aqueduct.

Flora and Fauna

Before the Catskills were decimated by the

tanning and logging industries in the 1800s, they were covered with hemlock, beech, chestnut, and sugar maple. Today, like much of the Northeast, the Catskills forests are predominantly oak and hickory, although some hemlock, beech, and sugar maple have returned in second growth.

The largest mammals inhabiting the Catskills are the white-tailed deer, red fox, porcupine, opossum, woodchuck, and occasional black bear. Southern Sullivan County supports the largest winter population of bald eagles in the northeastern United States. About 200 bald eagles flying south from New England and Canada spend their winters on reservoirs here.

HISTORY
Early History
Prehistoric humans may have occupied the area near the town of Catskill as early as 10,000 B.C., but the region's recorded history doesn't begin until about A.D. 1300. At that point, the Lenape Indians were living along the Delaware River in today's southern Sullivan County, and the Esopus Indians had settled along Esopus Creek near Kingston. Few Native Americans actually lived up in the mountains, but many used the heights as hunting grounds.

The Hardenbergh Tract
The area's first European residents were Dutch and French Huguenots, who settled in eastern Ulster County near the Hudson River in the mid-1600s. There they established the early villages of Kingston, Hurley, and New Paltz.

The English followed close behind, but in 1708, a patent of almost two million acres, covering most of the Catskill region, was granted to one Johannis Hardenbergh by the English governor Lord Cornbury. Not surprisingly, many colonists passed by the Catskills to settle farther west where they could own their own land.

The Hardenbergh Tract was eventually sold to other large landholding families, but they, too, continued to collect rents. In 1844–45, the tenant-farmers' long-smoldering resentments

finally broke out in the Anti-Rent Wars. Tenants dressed as Indians resisted rent collectors, and riots ensued. Martial law was declared. Only in 1852, with the election of a new governor and state legislators, were pardons issued and the feudal land system declared illegal.

Commercial Development
Canals, turnpikes, and railroads began penetrating the Catskills in the early- to mid-1800s, and the area soon developed a solid agricultural and industrial base. Products such as maple syrup, hops, vegetables, milk, and honey were produced to ship south to New York City, while sawmills and small factories sprang up along the Hudson.

It was the tanning industry, however, that soon dominated and all but destroyed the Catskills. Before the automobile age, leather for saddles and harnesses was in great demand. To cure the hides required tannin, best obtained from the bark of hemlock trees. Because an enormous amount of bark was needed to extract a small amount of tannin, it made economic sense to bring the hides to the hemlocks. Vast tanneries filled with clanking machinery and stinking vats set up shop all over the mountains, while sweat-drenched horses pulled wagons loaded with hides up the mountainsides. Millions of trees were cut down only for their bark and then left behind to rot. As soon as one area's hemlock supply was exhausted, the tanneries moved on to another, until virtually the entire hemlock forest was gone. The tanneries then turned to the oak trees.

Catskill Preserve
Finally, in the 1880s, New York State woke up. Citizens concerned with the depletion of both the Catskills and the Adirondacks banded together to fight for the creation of a forest preserve. Most people supported a preserve either for aesthetic reasons or because they were avid hunters or anglers. The business community, on the other hand, feared that the denuded slopes would cause New York Harbor to fill with silt and the Erie Canal to dry up. Largely

DEFINING THE CATSKILLS

The Dutch-derived word "Catskills," probably named for the wildcats who once roamed the region (*kaat* for cat, *kill* for stream), means different things to different people at different times. The most obvious definition would seem to be the one that refers to the Catskill Mountains. But these are primarily located only in northern Ulster and Greene Counties, and most people use the word Catskills to refer to a far bigger region.

A second definition refers to Catskill State Park, which encompasses about 900 square miles and includes both private lands and the state-owned Catskill Forest Preserve, established in 1894 to protect the area's remaining forests. The park extends over parts of all four counties, but is again primarily located in northern Ulster and Greene Counties. Since Catskill State Park, unlike most state parks, does encompass both public and private lands, don't come here expecting to find an isolated preserve like the Grand Canyon – you'll be disappointed.

A broader, more general definition of the Catskills, and the one used by most travel guides, including this one, encompasses both the state park and its surrounding foothills and resorts. This area is three to four times the size of the park alone, and includes some sections that have nothing to do with either mountains or forests.

Yet a fourth definition of the Catskills refers only to Sullivan County's so-called "Borscht Belt," a string of Jewish megaresorts where many famous comedians and entertainers got their starts. Many of these resorts (none of which, by the way, are located in the mountains) have shut down in recent years. Yet they still represent "the Catskills" for many older vacationers.

Resorts

Starting in the late 1820s, artists Thomas Cole, Asher Durant, and others of the Hudson River School began painting the Catskills landscape. Their work was unlike anything the American public had ever seen, and it created an overnight sensation. Before long, everyone wanted to visit the mountains.

Although stagecoach inns and boardinghouses had existed in the Catskills in the late 1700s and early 1800s, the first real resort was the Catskill Mountain House. Built in 1823, it was America's first great mountain resort.

Erected high atop the Great Wall of Manitou, near Kaaterskill Falls in Greene County, the early Mountain House had only 10 rooms and attracted mostly hunters, anglers, and the Hudson River School artists. But the resort quickly expanded as word of its magnificent view spread; by 1845 it had 50 rooms, and by the 1880s more than 300. Thirteen mammoth Corinthian columns marched across its facade, while to the rear were wings upon wings. The hotel could be seen for miles around—"a small white cloud in the midst of the heavens," as one guest put it—and everyone who was anyone came to stay. Among them were Ulysses Grant, Jenny Lind, Mark Twain, Henry James, and Oscar Wilde.

Dozens upon dozens of other hostelries soon opened in the area. Some were luxurious affairs, as grand as the Mountain House; others were just rustic lodges. By the mid-1800s, six trains a day were leaving New York City for the Catskills, bringing an estimated 300,000 guests annually.

The popularity of the Catskills began to decline in the 1920s; the advent of the automobile had given Americans a much wider choice of vacation destinations. As the traditional resorts began to shut down, however, Sullivan County was discovered by Jewish immigrants living in New York City. In the decades that followed, dozens of inexpensive boardinghouses and luxurious megaresorts went up, and an elaborate entertainment circuit flourished, featuring comedians, singers, and big bands. Among the most famous of these resorts were Flagler's, Grossinger's, and the Concord.

due to the influence of the latter group, the state legislature passed the Forest Preserve Act in 1885, and made it an amendment to the state constitution in 1894. From then on, the lands of both the Adirondacks and the Catskills were "to be forever kept as wild forest lands."

Ulster County

Ulster is a county with a split personality. To the south are towns and farmland that sit squarely in the Hudson Valley. To the north and northwest are the Catskills. In the valley, the land is neat, the residents flush. But in the Catskills, all is poorer and much more wild.

Southern Ulster is notable for its many pre-Revolutionary stone houses, built by early Dutch and French Huguenot settlers. Most of these houses have been nicely restored; the largest clusters are in New Paltz and Hurley. Also in the south are the stunning white escarpments of the Shawangunk (SHON-gum) Mountains, a range formed some 100 million years before the Catskills. Perched atop the Shawangunks are the famed Mohonk Mountain House—a 19th-century resort—and Minnewaska State Park, which harbors several glacial lakes.

Midway up the county on the Hudson is Kingston, a large and interesting town with an attractive historic district. North of Kingston are the legendary villages of Woodstock and Saugerties, still inhabited largely by artists and artisans. Northwest of Kingston begins Catskill Forest Preserve, where you'll find the enormous Ashokan Reservoir, marvelous scenic drives, excellent hiking trails, and the Catskills' highest peak—Slide Mountain.

The eastern half of Ulster County is well populated, thanks largely to the presence of the New York State Thruway (I-87). In the mountainous west, however, towns shrink into hamlets and highways into two-lane roads.

In summer, an Ulster County Tourism **visitor information center** operates off the New York State Thruway (I-87) at Exit 19, Kingston (845/340-3766).

NEW PALTZ

Between the Hudson River and the Shawangunk Mountains lies the small town of New Paltz. New Paltz was founded in 1677 by a group of French Huguenot Protestants who came to the New World seeking religious freedom.

The Huguenots first settled just north of New Paltz, in Kingston and Hurley. But in June 1663, the area's Esopus Indians raided the two small settlements, kidnapping 45 women and children.

That September, a Huguenot search party found and freed the hostages. While embracing his family, one member of the party—Louis DuBois—noticed the fertile land around him. He returned in 1677 with 11 others to buy and patent a 33,000-acre tract of land, and the next year, the 12 families settled along what is now known as Huguenot Street.

The new town was governed by a kind of corporation called the Duzine, referring to the 12 partners. That arrangement continued until well after the Revolution, by special permission of the New York State legislature. The system apparently worked well; one later commentator wrote, "So fine and

---

WEIRD, WONDERFUL, OFF-THE-BEATEN PATH CATSKILLS

Opus 40, Woodstock: An environmental sculpture covering six acres of an abandoned bluestone quarry; created by artist Harvey Fite.

Ukrainian Churches, Lexington and Glen Spey: Two grand Byzantine sanctuaries built of rich brown woods, entirely without nails, in the middle of nowhere.

Mahayana Buddhist Temple and Monastery, Cairo: Red-and-gold temples, pavilions, bridges, and pagodas in a woodsy setting.

The village of East Durham: Shamrocks, leprechauns, Irish pubs, and Irish sweaters; nicknamed Ireland's 33rd County.

Siddha Yoga Dham, South Fallsburg: An ashram and the headquarters of a powerful Eastern spiritual movement, surrounded by brightly colored statues of Hindu gods.

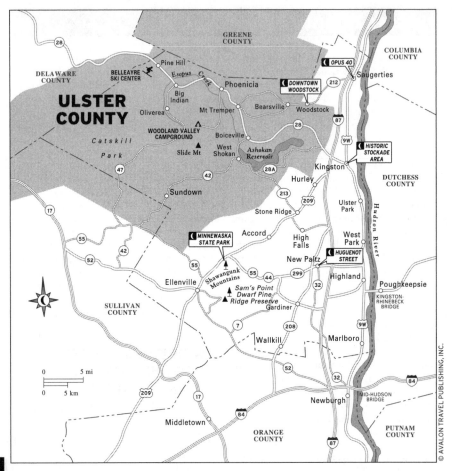

THE CATSKILLS

free from animosity and greed has been the life of the people of New Paltz that previous to 1873 no lawyer ever found a permanent residence here."

Today, the center of New Paltz lies just east of historic Huguenot Street, along Chestnut and Main Streets. Here, you'll find a clutch of attractive stores and restaurants. New Paltz is also home to a State University of New York (SUNY) branch that offers an especially strong arts department, which helps account for the town's strong cultural scene.

To reach New Paltz from I-87, take Exit 18 and head west on Route 299, which becomes Main Street. For more information on the area, visit the **New Paltz Chamber of Commerce** (124 Main St., 845/255-0243, www.new-paltzchamber.org, 9 A.M.–5 P.M. Mon.–Fri., 10 A.M.–3 P.M. Sat.–Sun).

◖ Huguenot Street

"The oldest street in America with its original buildings" is now a National Historic Landmark. Along its cool and shady time-ripened blocks stand six stone houses built in the early 1700s, as well as a reconstructed 1717 French church and cemetery, a 1799 house, a library, and museum.

All official walking tours of the street begin at the **1705 DuBois Fort Information Center** on Huguenot Street between Broadhead Avenue and North Front Street. A small museum there documents the street's history. Houses on the tours include the Abraham Hasbrouck House—once the village's social center—and the Bevier-Elting House. The most interesting house is the **Jean Hasbrouck House,** which contains much original woodwork and a beautiful "jambless" fireplace. Downstairs are rooms that once served as a tavern and general store, while upstairs are period furnishings, including a "senility cradle" used for the old and infirm.

Huguenot Street is run by the **Huguenot Historical Society** (18 Broadhead Ave., 845/255-1889 [tours] or 845/255-1660 [office], www.hhs-newpaltz.net), which includes among its members many descendants of the original families. The society offers walking tours of the street 10 A.M.–5 P.M. Tuesday–Sunday May–October, with the last tours leaving at 4 P.M. The standard tour lasts 90 minutes (adults $10, seniors $9, children 6–17 $5, families $24); an abbreviated tour lasts 55 minutes (adults $7, seniors $6, children 6–17 $3, families $17). During the **Colonial Street Festival,** held on Huguenot Street the second Saturday of August, all the houses are open and various Colonial-era skills, such as quilting and musket firing, are demonstrated.

Locust Lawn

Four miles south of New Paltz are yet more historic sites administered by the Huguenot Historical Society. Most important among them is Locust Lawn (400 Rte. 32, Gardiner),

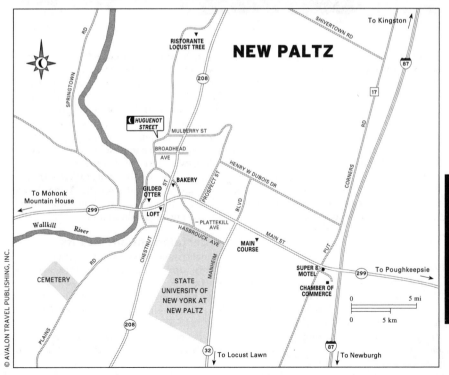

© AVALON TRAVEL PUBLISHING, INC.

THE CATSKILLS

© 2005 HUGUENOT HISTORICAL SOCIETY

Jean Hasbrouck House

an elegant Federal-style mansion built by Revolutionary War hero Col. Josiah Hasbrouck in 1814. After the war, the colonel became one of the wealthiest men in Ulster County. He filled his home with fine period furniture, magnificent china, and paintings by the likes of Ammi Phillips and John Vanderlyn.

Nearby is the considerably more rustic **Terwilliger House,** built in 1738. A wonderful example of Huguenot and Dutch architecture combined, the stone-and-wood cottage features a wide central hallway, long sloping roof, and creaky front porch.

To arrange a tour of either site, call the Huguenot Historical Society (845/255-1660).

Wineries

Wine enthusiasts might want to visit **Adair Vineyards** (75 Allhusen Rd., 845/255-1377, noon–5 P.M. Fri.–Sun. May–Nov.), which centers on a 200-year-old National Historic Landmark dairy barn. The tasting room is in the old hayloft.

Or, head east to **Route 9W,** which hugs the shores of the Hudson River. Many small wineries are located along the route between West Park and Marlboro. Most famous among them is **Benmarl Winery** (156 Highland Ave., Marlboro, 845/236-4265, www.benmarl.com, noon–5 P.M. Thurs.–Mon.). First planted as a vineyard in the late 16th century, it sits on a hilltop with great views of the river. The winery produces award-winning varietals, including chardonnays and cabernets. An on-site art gallery showcases the work of owner Mark Miller, a magazine illustrator.

Entertainment and Events

Concerts and plays are often on tap at the **State University of New York at New Paltz** (Rte. 32, just south of New Paltz, one mile west of I-87, 845/257-2121); many are staged at the university's **Parker Theatre** (845/257-3880).

Though now primarily a casual restaurant, **P&G's** (91 Main St., 845/255-6161) began as

THE CATSKILLS

a dancehall in the 1900s and still presents live local bands on the weekends.

The **Ulster County Fair** is held on the Ulster County Fairgrounds (Libertyville Rd., off Rte. 299) in early August. The fairgrounds also host the **Woodstock-New Paltz Arts & Crafts Fairs** on Memorial Day and Labor Day weekends. Call 845/340-3566 for more information.

Accommodations

The most popular resort in New Paltz is the Mohonk Mountain House, about five miles northwest of downtown, in the Shawangunks (see below). East of town in Highland is the family-oriented **Rocking Horse Ranch** (600 Rte. 44/55, 845/691-2927 or 800/647-2624, www.rhranch.com), a family-owned resort and dude ranch. The Rocking Horse sits beside a lake and features indoor and outdoor pools, saunas, tennis courts, activities for kids, nighttime entertainment, and trail rides. In winter, the ranch offers cross-country skiing, ice-skating, snowshoeing, and sleigh rides. A two-night high-season package costs $425 per adult/double, which includes use of all facilities, instruction, entertainment, day care for kids, breakfast and dinner; each child is an additional $185–195.

In Wallkill, between Walden and New Paltz on Rte. 208, is the 1740 **Audrey's Farmhouse** (2188 Brunswick Rd., 845/895-3440, www.audreysfarmhouse.com, $100–179 d). The B&B offers five comfortable guest rooms with featherbeds, a swimming pool, library, and splendid views of the Shawangunks. Well-behaved dogs are welcome.

Convenient to downtown New Paltz is the two-story, 65-room **Super 8 Motel** (7 Terwilliger Lane, at Main St., 845/255-8865, $79–99 d). A restaurant is on site.

Food

With its outdoor café and homemade treats, the **Bakery** (13A N. Front St., 845/255-8840) is a good spot for breakfast or a simple lunch. Situated in a small shopping mall is the **Main Course** (232 Main St., 845/255-2600), serving healthy contemporary American fare, including lots of vegetarian dishes and gourmet salads; average entrée $13.

The popular ◖ **Loft** (46 Main St., 845/255-1426), complete with skylights, cooks up innovative American fare ranging from pastas to grilled Gulf shrimp to duck breast topped with an orange sauce; average entrée $15.

The Gilded Otter (3 Main St., 845/256-1700) is the place to go for live music, local brews, good pub grub, and views of the fabulous Shawangunks; average main dish $12.

Serious diners might want to check out the **Ristorante Locust Tree** (215 Huguenot St., 845/255-7888), housed in a cozy 18th-century stone house with fireplaces and hard-carved woodwork. The candlelit restaurant specializes in upscale European-Italian fare, and its menu changes daily. Jackets are required; entrées $18–28, tasting menus $50–70.

THE SHAWANGUNKS

Just west of New Paltz rise the Shawangunk Mountains, a tilted ridge of translucent quartz conglomerate cemented into sedimentary rock. One-tenth the age of the earth, the Shawangunks are often mistakenly assumed to be an extension of the Catskills, but are a distinct, separate range.

Climbing the Gunks

The Shawangunks' steep escarpments make them a favorite haunt of rock climbers. The oldest rock-climbing guide service and school in the Shawangunks is **High Angle Adventures** (178 Hardenburgh Rd., Ulster Park, 845/658-9811, www.highangle.com). Beginners are welcome; group size is limited to three.

Mohonk Mountain House and Preserve

High in the heart of the Shawangunks is the Mohonk Mountain House (1000 Mountain Rest Rd., off Rte. 299, 845/255-1000 or 800/772-6646, www.mohonk.com, $389–735 d, includes three meals and afternoon tea), an enormous castlelike affair on the edge of a deep-blue glacial lake. Built by Quaker twins Albert and Alfred Smiley in 1870, Mohonk is the last of the magnificent resort hotels that once lined the Hudson.

In its heyday, the Mountain House hosted a long line of distinguished guests, including Presidents Hayes, Taft, and Wilson. Albert Smiley was deeply concerned about the welfare of the American Indian, and from 1883 to 1916, numerous important Friends of the Indian conferences were held here.

From a distance, Mohonk is an ultra-romantic place, bursting with gables and chimneys, turrets and towers. Up close, however, the romance dims. The lodgelike interior is packed to the rafters with people, people, people. A beehive of activities is scheduled throughout the day, and you can't even set foot on the grounds without first having your credentials checked.

Nonetheless, Mohonk is well worth a visit. Reserve a spot for a prix fixe meal—breakfast ($25), lunch ($40), or dinner ($41–44)—by calling 845/256-2056, or hike the adjacent 5,600-acre preserve (845/255-0919; www.mohonkpreserve.org). Twenty-eight miles of trails and 22 miles of carriage roads crisscross the preserve. Hikers must purchase day passes (adults $8, children under 12 free). The passes do not permit access to the Mountain House or its facilities.

◖ Minnewaska State Park

If the idea of spending $8 per person to hike the Mohonk Mountain House preserve sounds a bit steep, head farther west through fertile farmland to Minnewaska State Park (off Rt. 44/55, 845/255-0752, 9 A.M.–dusk daily). Also located high in the Shawangunks, the park is filled with panoramic views, hiking trails, paved carriage roads, waterfalls, and lakes—all available for a $7 parking fee in summer and on weekends, free on weekdays the rest of the year.

Near the center of the park is deep-blue **Lake Minnewaska**—Iroquois for floating waters—surrounded by white sandstone cliffs. The lake was created during the Ice Age when a glacier sliding by pulled out a hunk of soft sandstone.

On Lake Minnewaska is a sandy beach area where swimming is permitted, but if you like your bathing more secluded, hike the three-mile trail to **Lake Awosting.** This mile-long lake can only be reached on foot and is an idyllic spot surrounded by dark, piney woods.

To reach the park from New Paltz, take Route 299 west to Route 44/55 and turn right, up the mountain. After visiting the park, you might want to stop into the old-fashioned, family-owned **Mountain Brauhaus** (Rts. 299 and 44/55, Gardiner, 845/255-9766) for a frothy mug of German beer and a plate of *rouladen* or *kassler rippchen.* The roadhouse sits at the base of the Shawangunks, and offers spectacular views; average dinner entrée $14, closed Monday–Tuesday.

Just minutes away from Minnewaska State Park is the deservedly popular ◖ **Minnewaska Lodge** (3116 Rte. 44/55, Gardiner, 845/255-1110, www.minnewaskalodge.com, $135–319 d). Catering to outdoors enthusiasts, the 26-room hostelry features rooms with cathedral ceilings and decks overlooking the Gunks, along with Mission-style furniture, oversized picture windows, and a wood-burning stove. Works by local artists hang on the walls.

Ellenville

Southwest of Minnewaska State Park, where Rte. 209 meets Rte. 52, is the village of Ellenville. Located at the western base of the Shawangunks, Ellenville has traditionally been known for its Jewish boardinghouses and megaresorts. Most of these are gone now, but still in town are many fine Colonial and Greek Revival buildings, and a few remaining kosher shops and restaurants. Among them is **Cohen's Bakery** (89 Center St., 845/647-7620), famed locally for first-rate raisin-pumpernickel bread.

The Ellenville area also has a reputation for good hang-gliding. **Mountain Wings Hang Gliding Center** (150 Canal St., 845/647-3377, www.flightschool.net) rents equipment and offers introductory one-day hang-gliding courses.

Sam's Point Dwarf Pine Ridge Preserve

For years, Ellenville's biggest visitor attraction was Ice Caves Mountain, a sort of natural-history theme park perched on a mountaintop just outside town. The park, which had a wonderful 1950s feel, was centered on the caves, which were created 330 million years ago as cold-trapping fissures and still contain ice year-round. But as of 1997, alas, the caves were closed due to safety concerns, and the mountain is now a preserve managed by the Nature Conservancy (Sam's Point Rd., off Rte. 52 south of Ellenville, 845/647-7988, parking $5).

Truth be told, however, the mysterious caves weren't ever all that exciting. Much more interesting was—and is—the mile-long hike around "bottomless" Lake Maratanza. The lake sits so high atop the mountain that it seems as if it will surely slop over, and great views are all around. The highest lookout here and in all the Shawangunks is 2,255-foot Sam's Point, named after one Sam Gonsales. As the story goes, Gonsales jumped from the outcropping to escape from Indians, all the while knowing that a thick clump of hemlocks 40 feet below would break his fall. The ploy worked, and he lived to tell the tale.

NORTH ON ROUTE 209

Today's 209 closely parallels Old Route 209, reputedly the oldest highway in America. Originally known as the Old Mine Road, the old route ran between the copper mines near Pahaquarry, New Jersey, and Kingston on the Hudson, and was built sometime in the early 1600s. Many old homes and markers commemorating Indian raids are situated along Old Route 209, which runs concurrently with today's route in many places.

Accord

Heading north on Route 209 out of Minnewaska State Park, you'll soon come to the small village of Accord. Shortly after the Revolution, this then-unnamed hamlet was in need of a post office. A resident wrote to the post office department in Washington, D.C., suggesting that the settlement be called Discord because the townspeople couldn't agree on a name. The department did authorize an office, but optimistically changed the name. Railroad buffs will want to take a look at the **Accord Train Station** (Rte. 209 in the village center), an attractive maroon depot built in 1902 for the Ontario & Western Railroad.

High Falls and Vicinity

About six miles north of Accord (take Rte. 209 north to Rte. 213 east) is High Falls, where the **D&H Canal Museum** (Mohonk Rd. off Rte. 213, 845/687-9311, www.canalmuseum.org, 11 A.M.–5 P.M. Thurs.–Sat. and Mon. and 1–5 P.M. Sun. June–Sept., call for off-season hours, adults $3, children $1) tells the story of the Delaware and Hudson Canal. Built in the 1820s, the canal was originally used to ship coal from the mines of Pennsylvania to the factories of New York. Later it was used to ship cement made in the High Falls area to New York City. In the museum are dioramas of the canal; working models of locks; and maps, photos, and artifacts.

Overlooking Lock 16 is the 🅲 **DePuy Canal House** (Rte. 213, 845/687-7700, www.depuy-canalhouse.net), built in 1797 by Simeon DePuy. Once an inn, the two-story building is now a renowned four-star restaurant serving innovative American cuisine in an intimate setting complete with fireplaces, steep staircases, and wide floorboards. Multicourse prix fixe meals are a popular choice here; $65 for five courses, $80 for seven. The Canal House also features a handful of cozy guestrooms in its Locktender Cottage ($100–225 d).

For a simpler meal, try the **Egg's Nest** (Rte. 213, at Bruceville Rd., 845/687-7255), an eccentric spot offering tasty sandwiches and soups (average main dish $7) or the artsy **Northern Spy Cafe** (Rte. 213, 845/687-7295), which serves everything from burgers to Thai chicken with ginger (entrées $8–19).

Stone Ridge

Bed-and-breakfast fans have two excellent choices in Stone Ridge. **Bakers'** (24 Old King's

Hwy., 845/687-9795, www.bakersbandb.com, $98–138 d) occupies a 1780 stone farmhouse furnished with period antiques and a fireplace. All six guest rooms have private baths, and breakfast is served on a deck overlooking the Shawangunks.

The **Inn at Stone Ridge/Hasbrouck House** (Rte. 209 just outside the village, 845/687-0736, www.inatstoneridge.com, $195–425 d) is an elegant 18th-century Colonial mansion. It offers 10 guest rooms, an antique billiard room, 40 acres of gardens and woods, and a lake.

Hurley

Off Route 209 on the outskirts of Kingston lies a small village of 24 meticulously restored stone cottages similar to those found in New Paltz. Almost all are private homes open to the public only on **Hurley Stone House Day** (the second Saturday in July), but they're still interesting to view from afar.

Hurley dates back to 1651, when French Huguenots built wooden homes along Esopus Creek. The settlers didn't treat the local Eso-pus Indians as well as they might have, and in 1663, the Indians retaliated by burning down the Huguenot settlement. Six years later, the settlers rebuilt—this time in stone.

Self-guided walking tours of Hurley can be picked up at the post office at the town's entrance, or at the Hurley Library or Elmendorf House, both on Main Street. A plaque with a town map also stands by the library.

The **Elmendorf House,** built in the late 1600s, is believed to be the oldest house in Hurley. Known as the Half-Moon Tavern in Revolutionary days, it now houses a small museum run by the Hurley Heritage Society (52 Main St., 845/338-1661, www.hurleyheritag-esociety.org, 10 A.M.–4 P.M. Sat. and 1–4 P.M. Sun. May–Oct.).

Also on Main Street is the **Polly Crispell Cottage,** equipped with a "witch catcher," or set of iron spikes set into the chimney. Just west of Main Street is the **Hardenberg House,** where abolitionist and evangelist Sojourner Truth, born a slave in Ulster County, spent her first 11 years.

a stone house in Hurley, built by the Dutch in the late 1600s

© CHRISTIANE BIRD

THE CATSKILLS

KINGSTON

The small city of Kingston centers on a peaceful, tree-lined historic district known as the Stockade. A few miles away, down by the Hudson, is the city's equally pleasant harbor, Rondout Landing. There you'll find more nicely restored buildings, along with historic vessels and tour boats.

Kingston was first settled by the Dutch in 1652, making it the third oldest settlement—after Albany and New York City—in the state. In 1777, the town served as state capital; in the early 1800s, it was known for its boat-building and cement industries. Remnants of these can still be seen at Rondout Landing. The landing is also the endpoint of the Delaware & Hudson Canal. Built in 1828 to help transport coal from Pennsylvania to the Hudson River, the canal turned Kingston from a sleepy port into a major commercial center.

Visitors centers are located in the Stockade (308 Clinton Ave., 845/331-9506, www.ci.kingston.ny.us) and at Rondout Landing (20 Broadway, 845/331-7517). Summer hours are 11 A.M.–5 P.M. daily; call for off-season hours. Kingston is one of New York's 17 State Heritage Areas, which are loosely delineated historic parks linked by a common theme; in Kingston, the theme is transportation.

To reach Kingston from the New York State Thruway, take Exit 19. From Hurley, continue north on Route 209.

◀ Historic Stockade Area

In 1658, hostilities broke out between the new Dutch settlers and the Esopus Indians, prompting Governor Peter Stuyvesant to come up from Manhattan to oversee the building of a stockade. The settlers moved their homes inside the 13-foot-high stockade walls, and no Esopus were allowed in after dark.

By 1700, the stockade itself was gone, but the site continued to function as the village center. Over the next 200 years, many of Kingston's most important buildings were erected here. Today the eight-block district is lined with shady trees, inviting shops and restaurants, and historic sites.

The district centers on the **Old Dutch Church,** Main and Wall Streets, designed in 1852 by Minard Lafever. Renaissance Revival in style, the church features a vaulted ceiling reminiscent of Christopher Wren.

Nearby stands the 1818 **Ulster County Courthouse** (285 Wall St.). A plaque out front honors Sojourner Truth, who was born a slave in Ulster County in 1797 (see *Hurley,* above). In this courthouse on November 26, 1883, Truth won a lawsuit that saved her son from slavery in Alabama. It was the first such case ever won by a black parent.

The ivy-covered **Senate House State Historic Site** (296 Fair St., off Clinton St., 845/338-2786, 10 A.M.–5 P.M. Mon. and Wed.–Sat., and Sun. 1–5 P.M. Apr.–Oct., adults $4, seniors $3, children 5–12 $1) was the meeting place of the first New York State Senate. Inside the former Dutch home, viewable only by guided tour, is the parlor where the 24-member Senate met in 1777 to ratify the first New York State Constitution. Connected to the house is a museum with exhibits on Kingston's history and a collection of paintings by John Vanderlyn, one of America's first landscape painters. Vanderlyn painted the enormous *Landing of Columbus* that hangs in the Capitol rotunda in Washington, DC. Nonetheless, he lived most of his life in penury and died of starvation in his Kingston apartment.

A printed guide to the walking tour of the Stockade can be picked up at the visitors centers (see above). Many of the area's shops and restaurants are located along Wall, John, and North Front Streets.

Rondout Landing

To reach the harbor area from the Stockade, take Broadway downtown and descend a long, gentle hill. Once a bustling area of boatyards and factories, the landing is now a sleepy semicircle of historic buildings in various stages of restoration.

At the far end of the landing is the **Hudson River Maritime Museum** (1 Rondout Landing, 845/338-0071, 11 A.M.–4 P.M. Fri.–Mon. May–Oct., adults $5, seniors and children

5–12 $4), which features temporary exhibits on various aspects of Hudson River life. Exhibits in the past have covered such themes as sunken ships, WWII ships, and tourism in the Catskills. Out back are historic vessels; next door is a wooden-boat restoration shop.

From the Maritime Museum, you can take a boat ride to **Rondout Lighthouse.** The largest of the Hudson River lighthouses, the building sits alone on an artificially constructed island and has been restored to look as it did in the 1950s. Tickets for the lighthouse tour are $15 adults, $12 children under 13, and include $3 off same-day admission to the Maritime or Trolley Museum.

The **Trolley Museum** (89 E. Strand St., 845/331-3399, noon–5 P.M. Sat.–Sun. June–Oct., adults $4, seniors and children $3) is across from the Maritime Museum. Here you'll find a collection of antique trolleys, as well as kids excitedly waiting to take a trolley ride around Rondout Creek.

Recreation
Paralleling Route 28 west of Kingston is the Esopus River, long known for its **trout fishing.** Access points are marked with brown-and-yellow signs.

Kingston's Rondout Landing is home port to **Hudson River Cruises** (845/340-4700, www.hudsonrivercruises.com), which offers some of the best cruises on the Hudson. Among their offerings are sightseeing, music, and dinner cruises aboard the roomy *Rip Van Winkle*. The cruises run May–October and operate daily during the height of the summer.

Entertainment
On the National Register of Historic Places is the 1927 **Ulster Performing Arts Center** (601 Broadway, 845/339-6088, www.upac.org), a former vaudeville theater. The largest theater between Manhattan and Albany, the center presents everything from Broadway shows to rock concerts to children's theater.

Backstage Studio Productions (323 Wall St., Stockade District, 845/338-8700) presents everything from live music to performance art.

The experimental **Gallery at Deep Listening Space** (75 Broadway, Rondout Landing, 845/338-5984) is both a gallery and a performance space.

To find out more about Kingston's vibrant art scene, contact the **Arts Society of Kingston** (845/338-0331, www.askforarts.org) or the **Ulster County Arts Council** (845/339-9935).

Camping and Accommodations
Near town is **Hidden Valley Lake** (290 Whiteport Rd., off Rte. 32, 845/338-4616). The 50-site campground is open year-round and offers both campsites and cabins.

Kingston's upscale **Holiday Inn** (503 Washington Ave., 845/338-0400 or 800/HOLIDAY, www.hikingston.com, $129–259 d) offers over 200 nicely decorated rooms and a large indoor recreation center with indoor-outdoor pools, fitness center, sauna, and video games. Near Rondout Landing is the secluded, turn-of-the-century **Rondout B&B** (88 W. Chester St., 845/331-8144, www.rondoutbandb.com, $95–125 d), surrounded by large porches and filled with local artwork.

Food
Deising's (109–117 N. Front St., Stockade District, 845/338-7503) is an excellent bakery and coffee shop known for its tasty soups and sandwiches. The lively **Armadillo Bar & Grill** (97 Abeel St., 845/339-1550) specializes in Southwestern and New World cuisine, along with the best frozen margaritas in town; average dinner entrée $13. Tiny **El Coqui Latin Jazz Cafe** (21 Broadway, Rondout Landing, 845/340-1106) is the place to go for Puerto Rican food and music.

For more sophisticated dining, try **23 Broadway** (23 Broadway, Rondout Landing, 845/339-2322). Run by graduates of Hyde Park's Culinary Institute, this renovated 19th-century storefront with its long sultry bar offers an eclectic international menu; average entrée $21. **Le Canard Enchaine** (276 Fair St., Stockade District, 845/339-2003) is a relaxed French bistro serving traditional favorites. Live jazz is featured on Saturday night; average entrée $20.

SAUGERTIES

About 15 miles north of Kingston, where Route 212 meets Route 9W, is Saugerties, filled with turn-of-the-century brick buildings. Saugerties was once a river port known for its packet-trade and racing steamers. Most famous among them was the *Mary Powell,* the fastest ship on the Hudson between 1861 and 1885.

[Opus 40

Between Saugerties and Woodstock is one of the most unusual spots in Ulster County, an environmental sculpture known as Opus 40 (7480 Fite Rd., 845/246-3400, www.opus40.org, noon–5 P.M. Fri.–Sun. June–Oct., adults $6, students and seniors $5, children 6–12 $3). Created by artist Harvey Fite over a period of 37 years, Opus 40 covers more than six acres of an abandoned bluestone quarry. Its pools and fountains, sculptures and walkways, all center on a towering blue-gray monolith reminiscent of the mysterious Stonehenge. Behind rises the dark crest of Overlook Mountain.

Fite, a professor at Bard College, created his monumental work using traditional quarrier's tools. Adjacent to the site is the **Quarryman's Museum,** itself a work of art. The museum is filled with hammers and screws, chains and wagon wheels—everything arranged according to size and shape. A seven-minute video on the site is featured.

To reach Opus 40 from Saugerties, take Route 212 west to Sickles Road, turn left, and watch *very* carefully for Fite Road on the right.

Shopping

Downtown Saugerties is full of antique shops, most of which are located along Main and Partition Streets. Some are serious affairs, others sell what looks suspiciously like junk. One of the largest emporiums is the **Saugerties Antique Center & Annex** (220 Main St., 845/246-8234), which houses about 25 dealers. A guide to the town's antique stores can be picked up in many shops.

A BOOKWORM'S PARADISE

Ulster County boasts a high number of unusual bookstores, ranging from creaky used-book emporiums to modern independent shops. Looking for that out-of-print 19th-century novel, unusual art book, or obscure tome about New York State? Chances are good you'll find it here.

In Kingston reigns one of the region's best-known shops, **Alternative Books** (35 N. Front St., 845/331-5439), which has long been a lively gathering place for local artists and writers. The shop's stock of over 20,000 used books includes a large poetry selection, modern first editions, journals, and art books. Also in Kingston is **Three Geese in Flight Books** (275 Fair St., 845/338-2358), perhaps the only store in the country specializing in Celtic mythology and Arthurian legend; and **Pages Past** (Pearl and Wall Sts., 845/339-6484), known for its selection of used general interest, regional, and children's books.

Not far away in Ashokan sprawls **Editions** (Rte. 28, 845/657-7000), a used-book emporium with an eight-foot-high chart at the front listing all the store's categories. In the 10 quiet rooms here, filled with lots of nooks and crannies perfect for hiding out, you'll find over 60,000 titles.

Two good modern independent bookshops are New Paltz's **Ariel Books** (3 Plattekill Ave., 845/255-8041) and Woodstock's **Golden Notebook** (25-29 Tinker St., 845/679-8000). Also in New Paltz is **Barner Books** (3 Church St., 845/255-2635, barnerbook@aol.com), a barn of a used-book shop where newly arrived volumes sit piled up in boxes. Barner Books also conducts a brisk Internet business, ferreting out obscure titles for clients from all over the world. Not far from Woodstock is **Hope Farm Press & Bookshop** (252 Main St., Saugerties, 845/246-3522), specializing in history, genealogy, and New York State.

© CHRISTIANE BIRD

Opus 40 covers more than six acres of an abandoned bluestone quarry.

Entertainment and Events

In summer, well-known jazz, folk, and classical players are occasionally featured at **Opus 40,** which *Rolling Stone* once called, "the best outdoor concert venue in the Northeast." In September, Saugerties celebrates everyone's favorite odorous herb with the **Hudson Valley Garlic Festival** (845/340-3566).

Camping and Accommodations

The largest campground in Saugerties is the **Rip Van Winkle** (14 Robinson St., off Blue Mountain Rd., 845/246-8334), offering 170 sites. The **Saugerties-Woodstock KOA** (7227 Rte. 212, 845/246-4089) offers 100 sites and camping cabins.

One of the most unusual B&Bs in upstate New York is the **⟨ Saugerties Lighthouse B&B** (168 Lighthouse Dr., 845/247-0656, $135–160 d), where guests can watch boats pass by on the Hudson from their second-story rooms. From the parking lot, it's a 10-minute walk to the lighthouse.

Food

Receiving raves from the locals is the **⟨ New World Home Cooking Co.** (1411 Rte. 212, 845/246-0900), a "funky world cuisine cafe" offering a variety of dishes with Asian, Creole, Cajun, and Caribbean influences; average entrée $15.

The chic yet casual **⟨ Cafe Tamayo** (89 Partition St., 845/246-9371) is housed in an attractive 1864 brick building complete with ceiling fans, an old-style bar, and a patio. On the menu is contemporary American fare; average entrée $18.

WOODSTOCK AND VICINITY

The famed arts colony of Woodstock is still a picturesque and unusual spot, inhabited by an idiosyncratic bunch of artists and craftspeople, individualists and ne'er-do-wells. But the place is often so overrun with tourists that it's hard to tell.

Woodstock the town dates back to the 1700s, but Woodstock the arts colony dates back to 1902, when a wealthy Englishman, free thinker, and lover of the arts named Ralph Radcliffe Whitehead came here to set up an arts-and-crafts community. A student of John Ruskin who railed against the evils of the Industrial Revolution, Whitehead envisioned his colony as living apart from the modern world, surrounded by scenic splendor, and supporting itself with its arts and crafts.

With two partners, Whitehead bought 1,300 acres and built a small village, Byrdcliffe, just above Woodstock. A few years later one of his followers, poet Hervey White, became fed up with Whitehead's authoritarian demands and started up a second arts community, Maverick, on the south side of town. Then, in 1906, the Art Students League of New York City arrived, opening a summer school in Woodstock's downtown. The village thronged with ever-increasing numbers of painters, potters, weavers, poets, dancers, musicians, novelists, hangers-on, and tourists eager to "see the artists."

In the late 1940s, folk singers Pete Seeger, Joan Baez, and Peter, Paul & Mary discovered Woodstock, and in the 1960s, Bob Dylan

THE CATSKILLS

ETHNIC RETREATS

Ever since the 1930s, '40s, and '50s, the Catskills – and especially Sullivan County have been renowned for their enormous Jewish resorts. Many famous entertainers, including Milton Berle and Henny Youngman, have helped spread images of the Jewish Catskills all over the world.

Yet the Catskills have long been home to a wide variety of other ethnic groups as well. Germans, Italians, Eastern Europeans, Irish, Greeks, Armenians, African Americans, Spanish Americans, Russians, Koreans, Chinese – all have had, or continue to have, resorts in the Catskills.

"What's especially interesting," says Linda Norris, former director of the Delaware County Historical Association Museum, "is that everyone says they come to the Catskills because it reminds them of home."

The first immigrants to vacation in the Catskills in large numbers were Jews from Germany and Eastern Europe. Arriving during the 1880s, long before the Sullivan County resorts were built, the immigrants flocked to boardinghouses in northern Ulster and Greene Counties. Not always welcome at traditional resorts – one ad for the Hotel Lawrence read, "No Bar. No consumptives or Hebrews" – the Jews soon developed hostelries of their own. One of the first all-Jewish resort towns was Fleischmanns, named after its founder, the yeast magnate from Cincinnati.

In the early 1900s, the Jews were joined by Irish and German Catholics – all looking to escape the stifling heat of New York City. Then came the Italians, the Spanish Americans, and the Armenians. By the time of the Depression, people were joking not only about the Catskills' "Borscht Belt," but also about its "Bocce Belt," "Cuchifrito Circuit," and "Yogurt Belt." And still, the region's diversity continued to grow – by the 1940s, a good two dozen ethnic groups had established resorts here.

The Spanish Americans tended to congregate near Plattekill, the Germans near Roundtop, the Ukrainians near East Jewett, the Poles near Ellenville and New Kingston, the Irish near East Durham, the Greeks near Windham, the African Americans near Otisville, and the Italians near Hunter, Tannersville, and Cairo. Today, most of these towns – almost all of which are located in Greene County – have only a few vestiges of their ethnic heritage left, usually in the form of a resort, church, and restaurant or two.

One major exception is East Durham, where dozens of Irish-run resorts and bars crowd the main street, and the Irish brogue lilts over everything. East Durham had all but died by the late 1970s, when cheap airline flights to Ireland lured vacationers abroad. But the town has recently come to life again, thanks to a new wave of Irish immigrants.

Plattekill, once the resort of choice of wealthy Spanish Americans, now caters to large numbers of Puerto Ricans and others from the Caribbean and Central America. Interestingly, the Puerto Ricans first came to the Catskills as entertainers playing the mambo for sophisticated crowds. Now they're back on their own terms, having purchased a number of resorts and dance halls that are favorite destinations for social clubs coming up from New York, Beacon, and Newburgh.

African Americans have never vacationed in the Catskills in great numbers, but several black resorts were established in southwestern Ulster County in the early- to mid-1900s. One of the most famous of these was the Peg Leg Bates Country Club in Kerhonkson, founded by the entertainer in 1951 largely because although he often entertained in the Catskills, no hotel would allow him to stay overnight. Still in operation today, the Peg Leg Bates Country Club is now run by a Jamaican-American couple.

Not surprisingly, given current immigration trends, the latest ethnic groups to discover the Catskills are the Koreans, Chinese, and Russians. The Russians favor the bungalows of Sullivan County; the Chinese have taken over several former Italian resorts in Greene County; and the Koreans now own several former Jewish resorts near Monticello and Liberty. One Korean businessman has even purchased Grossinger's, once the quintessential Jewish Catskills resort.

moved in, buying a farm on an isolated mountaintop. The town's first recording studio was built, and a series of small concerts, the Woodstock Soundoffs, was staged. The Soundoffs were the immediate forerunner of the legendary 1969 Woodstock Music Festival that took place in Bethel, 60 miles away (see *Sullivan County,* below). The concert organizers wanted to hold the event closer to home, but Woodstock had no open space large enough, and last-minute ordinances imposed by nervous officials prevented the concert from taking place in Saugerties as originally planned.

◖ Downtown Woodstock

For all its renown, Woodstock remains a small village, with a population of about 6,000. Its main thoroughfare is **Tinker Street,** which according to legend is named after a tinker's wagon that sank into the mud here one fine spring day.

Where Tinker Street meets Rock City and Mill House Roads is the **village green,** often filled with teenagers wearing the tie-dyed T-shirts and long granny dresses of their parents' generation. Nearby is the Millstream, immortalized in Tell Taylor's classic song, "Down By the Old Millstream."

Dozens of small shops, galleries, and restaurants crowd the streets of Woodstock. Among the oldest is the **Woodstock Artists Association** (28 Tinker St., 845/679-2940, www.woodstockart.org, noon–5 P.M. Thurs.–Mon.), which has exhibited the works of area artists since 1920. Among the newest is the first-rate **Center for Photography at Woodstock** (59 Tinker St., 845/679-9957, www.cpw.org, noon–5 P.M. Wed.–Sun.), housed in what was once the Espresso Café, where Bob Dylan, Janis Joplin, and other '60s-era icons performed. The **Golden Notebook** (29 Tinker St., 845/679-8000) is a good bookstore.

From May to December, visitor information can be picked up at the **Woodstock Chamber of Commerce** (10 Rock City Rd., near the village green, 845/679-6234, www.woodstock-chamber.com, 11 A.M.–6 P.M. Fri.–Sun.). For hotline information on lodging and dining, call 845/679-6234.

Overlook Mountain

Looming behind Woodstock is Overlook Mountain, the summit of which offers splendid views of the valley and river below. To reach the mountain from town, take Rock City Road to Meads Mountain Road; the trailhead is opposite **Karma Triyana Dharmachakra** (845/679-5906, www.kagyu.org), a Tibetan Buddhist monastery. In its shrine room (open 1:30–3:30 P.M. Sat.–Sun.) is a 13-foot-high statue of the Buddha, which was used by Martin Scorsese in his film *Kundun,* about the life of the Dalai Lama.

The two-mile walk to the top of the mountain follows an old roadbed, is of easy-to-moderate difficulty, and takes about an hour. Along the way you'll pass the ruins of the Overlook Mountain House, once a popular resort that was anchored to the mountain by strong cables to keep it from being blown away. Plaques tell of the resort's fascinating history.

Entertainment

The **Colony Café** (22 Rock City Rd., 845/679-5342) presents local, regional, and national performers most nights of the week. The café serves beer, wine, coffees, and desserts.

Now housed in the 1902 Byrdcliffe art colony is the **Woodstock Guild** (34 Tinker St., 845/679-2079, www.woodstockguild.org), an arts center featuring performance art, theater, and film. Since 2000, Woodstock has been home to the **Woodstock Film Festival** (www.woodstockfilmfestival.com).

The **Maverick Concerts** (845/679-8217, www.maverickconcerts.org) are a famed musical event, founded in 1916 by poet Hervey White. The oldest chamber-music series in the country, the concerts are staged in a hand-hewn auditorium (Maverick Rd., off Rt. 375) that seats only 400, but the music can also be heard from the surrounding hillsides. The series runs late July through early September.

In Bearsville is the **Bearsville Theater Complex** (Rte. 212, 845/679-5555), which includes two restaurants (see below), several off-site studios secluded in the woods, and a 250-seat theater that presents original drama throughout the summer. The complex was originally planned and financed by the late Albert Grossman, former manager of Bob Dylan and Janet Joplin.

To find out what's going on in the area, check the *Woodstock Times* or the *Catskill Mountain News*. Or listen to Woodstock's independent radio station, WDST, FM 100.1.

Accommodations

Downtown you'll find the attractive ❰ **Woodstock Inn on the Millstream** (38 Tannery Brook Rd., 845/679-8211, www.woodstock-inn-ny.com, $109–215 d with breakfast, two-night minimum on summer weekends), an upscale motel with both standard rooms and efficiency units. A swimming hole is nearby. Also downtown, the mustard yellow **Twin Gables** (73 Tinker St., 845/679-9479, www.twingableswoodstockny.com, $69–115 d) has functioned as a homey, affordable guesthouse since the 1940s. Some of the nine guest rooms share baths.

Built as the home of Woodstock artist Jo Cantine, the elegant, hide-away **Woodstock Country Inn** (27 Cooper Lake Rd., 845/679-9380, www.woodstockcountryinn.com, $145–265 d) offers four guest rooms filled with light and antiques. There is also an outdoor pool and great mountain views.

Food

One of Woodstock's oldest restaurants is the hole-in-the-wall **Joshua's** (51 Tinker St., 845/679-5533), serving simple but tasty Middle Eastern fare. One of the town's newest eateries is the **Red Onion** (1654 Rte. 212). Housed in a 1830s farmhouse on the outskirts of town, the restaurant serves an eclectic international fare; average dinner entrée $17.

Overlooking a golf course is the **Blue Mountain Bistro** (1633 Glasco Tnpk., at Rte.

212, 845/679-8519), serving French Mediterranean cuisine. In summer, there's dining on a deck overlooking a stream and live jazz on Saturday nights. Open for dinner only; average entrée $18.

On the road to nearby Bearsville, you'll find the brightly colored **Gypsy Wolf Cantina** (Rte. 212, 845/679-9563), a lively Mexican café serving great margaritas; average entrée $14. In the Bearsville Theater Complex in Bearsville is the streamside ❰ **Bear Cafe** (off Rte. 212, 845/679-5555), housed in a modern barn-like building with a big, comfortable bar. On the menu is imaginative American fare ranging from blackened chicken to grilled fish; average dinner entrée $18. Next door to the Bear Cafe is **Little Bear** (845/679-8899), offering tasty Chinese food.

WEST ON ROUTE 28

Route 28 heads out of Kingston into the heart of **Catskill State Park and Catskill Forest Preserve.** Just past Boiceville, the land turns wooded, wild, and wonderful, with mountains rising to the left and right. Five of the Catskills' highest peaks are located in Ulster County.

Near the entrance to the park begins the 12-mile-long **Ashokan Reservoir.** Built between 1909 and 1919, despite fierce local opposition, the reservoir displaced eight communities, 2,600 graves, 64 miles of road, and 11 miles of railroad. Around the reservoir runs Route 28A, a marvelous **scenic drive** that skirts Ashokan Dam, fountains, and a picnic area. Peaks rising to 3,000 feet surround the western end.

To either side of Route 28 are small, wistful villages that were once major resort destinations but now aren't much more than clutches of well-worn buildings, huddled together against the modern world. The original Route 28 once ran through their centers; the modern route bypasses them completely.

Boiceville

On the outskirts of Boiceville is ❰ **Onteora, the Mountain House** (96 Piney Point Rd.,

THE CATSKILLS

845/657-6233, www.onteora.com, $185–265 d), a noteworthy B&B. Onteora sits high on a mountaintop overlooking Catskill Park. Once the posh retreat of mayonnaise mogul Richard Hellman, the home features huge picture windows, cathedral ceilings, and a massive stone fireplace. The B&B offers seven guest rooms, all with private baths and most with magnificent views.

The very popular **Bread Alone Bakery & Cafe** (Rte. 28, 845/657-3328) offers much more than just great fresh bread baked in a wood-fired oven. Also on the menu are homemade soups, sandwiches, pastries, and coffees.

Mount Tremper

One of the odder attractions in the Catskills is **Emerson Place** (5340 Rte. 28, 845/688-5800, 10 A.M.–6 P.M. Thurs.–Mon., adults $7.50, children under 12 free), where you'll find the world's largest kaleidoscope, housed in a former grain silo painted with blue sky, white clouds, and a pair of honey-colored eyes. Inside the 60-foot-tall tower, visitors provided with headrests stare straight up into a myriad of images that are multiplied by 254 facets covering about 45 feet. Shows on American history are presented.

Also in the complex are shops selling kaleidoscopes, furniture, clothing, books, and gifts; the **Catamount Cafe,** serving "international farmhouse cuisine" in a setting overlooking the Esopus River (average entrée $15); and the luxurious **Lodge at Emerson Place** (845/688-2828, $190–300 d), furnished in an upscale log-cabin-style decor.

◖ **La Duchesse Anne Inn** (1564 Wittenberg Rd., 845/688-5329, www.laduchesseanne.com, $90–150 d), built in 1850 as a Norwegian guesthouse, is both an inviting B&B and a popular French restaurant run by a French-born owner. Perched on a small hill surrounded by woodlands, the inn offers about a dozen guest rooms, many of which share bathrooms, and a wide, lovely veranda. The romantic dining room serves classic French favorites such as assorted pâtés, escargot, and scallops Provençal, and offers a French and American wine list (average entrée $21).

Another classic French restaurant in the area is the luminous **Catskill Rose** (5355 Rte. 212, 845/688-7100), its front door framed with pink neon. To one side is an art deco bar glowing blue, to another a clutch of dining tables. Dishes are prepared by a husband-and-wife team; average entrée $17.

A good area campground is the **Kenneth L. Wilson Campground** (859 Wittenberg Rd., one mile off Rte. 28, 845/679-7020). Reservations should be made well in advance; call 800/456-CAMP.

Phoenicia

One of the largest and most prosperous of the villages along Route 28 is Phoenicia, known for its trout fishing, kayaking, and tubing—all done on nearby Esopus Creek. From May to September, floating down the creek on huge black inner tubes is one of the county's most popular "sports." Many of the tube-rental shops are located at the entrance to Phoenicia. Among the largest and most prominent is **Town Tinker** (10 Bridge St., 845/688-5553).

Besides outfitter shops, Phoenicia's Main Street holds turn-of-the-century wooden homes, wide porches, creaky gift shops, general stores, and **Upstate Art** (60 Main St., 845/688-9881), a six-room upstairs gallery that showcases the works of regional artists. Housed in the old railroad station at the town's east end is the **Empire State Railway Museum** (Main St., 845/688-7501, www.esrm.com, 11 A.M.–4 P.M. Sat.–Sun. June–Oct., adults $3, seniors $2, children $1), which documents the history of the five different railroads that serviced the Catskills between the late 1860s and the 1940s.

Between the railroad museum and nearby Mt. Pleasant runs the **Catskill Mountain Railroad** (845/688-7400, www.catskillmtrailroad.com, 11 A.M.–5 P.M. Sat.–Sun. June–Sept., adults $8, children 4–12 $5). The scenic rides hug the banks of Esopus Creek.

Brio's (Main St., 845/688-5370) is a good, dependable luncheonette. And "everyone goes" to ◖ **Sweet Sue's** (49 Main St., 845/688-7852), especially for brunch. On the menu are over a dozen pancake dishes.

Woodland Valley Recreation

Off Route 28 one mile west of Phoenicia, Woodland Valley Road turns off to the left and leads through Woodland Valley, one of the deepest and most romantic valleys in the Catskills. Four miles in, the road comes to a parking lot at **Woodland Valley State Campground** (1319 Woodland Valley Rd., 845/688-7647), where reservations should be made well in advance (call 800/456-CAMP).

Also here is a well-marked trail that takes hikers to the top of Wittenberg Mountain. The 3.4-mile, 2,800-foot ascent takes about three hours. It's steep near the beginning and again near the top, but only of moderate difficulty most of the way. The spectacular view from the summit—one of the best in the Catskills—encompasses almost all of Ashokan Reservoir.

From Wittenberg Mountain, a short, narrow trail leads via a connecting ridge to Cornell Mountain, which offers good views of Slide Mountain, the highest peak in the Catskills. The hike from Wittenberg to Cornell takes about 30 minutes.

Big Indian

Farther west on Route 28 lies the hamlet of Big Indian, named after a seven-foot-tall Indian named Winnisook. Legend has it that young Gertrude, a farmer's daughter, fell in love with Winnisook but was forced by her father to marry a man named Joe Bundy. Lovelorn, she ran away, found Winnisook, and lived happily with him and his people for seven years.

Then one day, Joe Bundy, out looking for cattle raiders, came across Winnisook and shot him. Before dying, Winnisook took refuge in a hollow tree where he was discovered, still standing, by Gertrude. She had him buried nearby and lived by the tree for the rest of her life.

In Big Indian begins Route 47, a scenic drive among the finest in Ulster County. Take it up a steep hill, past several gorgeous mountain vistas, to Oliverea, a small resort village (see below). The road then descends five miles to Winnisook Lake and then

another nine miles through an expansive valley with more great views. From there, you can either retrace your steps or continue on to Route 42, which circles back up through Sundown and West Shokan—ringed all around by mountains—to Route 28. The entire circuit is about 60 miles.

Oliverea

High on the slopes of Oliverea is the Indian-run **Mountain Gate Lodge** (212 McKinley Hollow Rd., 845/254-6000, www.mountain-gatelodge.com, $66–99 d). The upscale motel offers an outdoor pool, flower gardens, and the **Mountain Gate Indian Restaurant,** where smells of curry waft out of the door; average entrée $13. Also on the premises is the new **Shangri-La Spa,** an Indian health retreat specializing in centuries-old Ayurveda health and beauty treatments. The lodge is surrounded by woodlands, and good hiking is nearby.

Pine Hill and Highmount

One of the most economical places to stay in all the Catskills is the friendly **Belleayre Hostel and Cabins** (15 Hostel Dr., off Main St., Pineville, 845/254-4200, www.belleayre-hostel.com). The establishment offers a bunkhouse with two bunk rooms ($20/person) and dining hall, three private rooms ($50/night), and a handful of cottages ($75–90/night) and log cabins ($150–200/night). Hostelers should bring their own linens and towels.

Anchoring the small village is the old-fashioned **Pine Hill Arms Hotel** (Main St., 845/254-4012), which features a beautiful old bar, a restaurant serving an especially good breakfast, and live music on some weekends.

Good downhill skiing can be found at New York State–owned **Belleayre Mountain Ski Area** (Belleayre Rd., off Rte. 28, Highmount, 845/254-5600 or 800/431-4555, www.belleayre.com). On the upper mountain are 16 trails for intermediate or expert skiers; on the lower mountain are beginner and intermediate slopes. The vertical drop is 1,404 feet. During the off-season, you can hike or take a chairlift to the summit.

THE CATSKILLS

Greene County

Many of the Catskills' highest peaks and longest waterfalls are in Greene County, making it an especially pretty region to explore. It was in Greene County, after all, near the village of Palenville, that Rip Van Winkle supposedly fell into his deep, 20-year slumber, waking to find his fowling-piece rusted, his trusty dog Wolf gone, Dame Van Winkle departed to another world, and his son full-grown into a carbon copy of his younger self.

At the eastern edge of the county, along the Hudson, are Catskill, the county seat, and Coxsackie, home of the preeminent Bronck Museum. Most of the county's points of interest are farther west, however, in the mountains. There you'll find scenic drives, good day-hikes, and numerous quirky sites—two Ukrainian churches built without nails, a Buddhist temple, an all-Irish village.

The downside of Greene County is that some areas are highly commercialized and tawdry looking, especially in the off-season. Tourism is big business here, with about 640,000 tourists—including a half-million skiers—visiting each year. Full-time residents number only about 45,000.

Routes 23 and 23A are the most important east-west routes in the region and offer two of the most scenic drives, through the heart of the Catskills' high peaks. The Greene County Promotion Department (518/943-3223 or 800/355-CATS) operates a **Visitor Information Center** off the New York State Thruway/I-87, Exit 21, in Catskill (9 A.M.–4 P.M. daily, with extended hours in summer). After-hours, travelers can consult an information kiosk.

CATSKILL AND VICINITY

Catskill, the Greene County seat, sits on the sloping banks of the Hudson at the mouth of Catskill Creek. The natural harbor here helped the town grow steadily after its founding in the late 1600s. By the early 1900s, Catskill was the prosperous home of small knitting factories, brickyards, and distilleries.

During Prohibition, the town was known for its "retailers of liquid damnation." Catskill applejack was brewed in the hills surrounding town and buried in jugs whenever the law came around. The lucrative moonshine trade coupled with the inaccessible hills made Catskill a favorite haunt of New York City gangsters Legs Diamond and Vincent Coll. Diamond was once tried in the **Greene County Courthouse,** an imposing neoclassical building that still stands at the corner of Main and Bridge Streets.

Today, the town feels well worn around the edges, but retains a distinct charm. Besides the courthouse, **Main Street** showcases one big wooden building after another, many housing friendly old-fashioned businesses. **Catskill Gallery** (398 Main St., 518/943-3400, 10 A.M.–4 P.M. Tues.–Sat.), run by the Greene County Council on the Arts, presents exhibits, concerts, readings, and plays throughout the year. Running parallel to Main Street is **Spring Street,** a treasure trove of Victorian homes.

Thomas Cole House

The father of the Hudson River School, Thomas Cole lived in Catskill much of his adult life. Born in England in 1801, Cole came to New York City in 1818. He taught himself to paint landscapes, and in 1825 took his first sketching trip up the Hudson. The works he produced on that trip won him instant recognition.

Cole's former home, Cedar Grove (218 Spring St., 518/943-7465, www.thomascole.org, 10 A.M.–4 P.M. Fri.–Sun. May–Oct., adults $5, children under 12 free) is a big yellow-and-white affair with a wide veranda overlooking the Hudson. The house features exhibits on Cole and his family, other Hudson River artists such as Frederic Church, and the Catskills. Also on display are a few small works by Cole, and memorabilia such as his paint box and Bible. Out back is Cole's old studio, housed in what were once slave quarters.

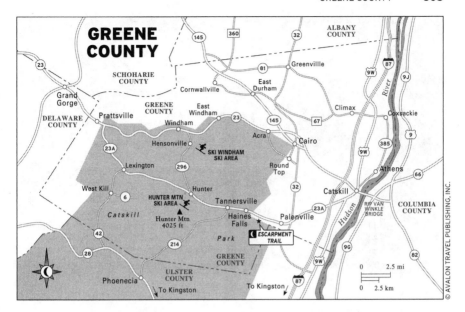

GREENE
COUNTY

SCHOHARIE
COUNTY

Cornwallville

Greenville

East
Durham

Climax

Coxsackie

Grand
Gorge

DELAWARE
COUNTY

Prattsville

GREENE
COUNTY

East
Windham

Windham

Acra

Cairo

Athens

Hensonville

SKI WINDHAM
SKI AREA

Round
Top

Lexington

Catskill

Rip Van
Winkle
Bridge

COLUMBIA
COUNTY

West Kill

Hunter

Tannersville

Catskill

HUNTER MTN
SKI AREA

Hunter Mtn
4025 ft

Haines
Falls

Palenville

Park

ESCARPMENT
TRAIL

Phoenecia

ULSTER
COUNTY

GREENE
COUNTY

To Kingston

To Kingston

Albany County

Hudson River

© AVALON TRAVEL PUBLISHING, INC.

0   2.5 mi
0   2.5 km

Athens

About four miles north of Catskill on Route 385 is the attractive village of Athens, first settled by the Dutch in 1686. At one time or another, the town has been a center for brick-making, shipbuilding, ice-harvesting, and mushroom-growing (grown in the abandoned icehouses, after the advent of refrigeration).

Today Athens feels like a smaller and sleepier version of Catskill. Its streets, too, are lined with big old wooden buildings, many of them from the Victorian age, and the village hovers on an economic edge between neglect and gentrification. Route 385 south of Athens parallels the Hudson at water level, offering splendid views of the river and the 1874 Hudson-Athens lighthouse (518/828-5294, tours offered in summer).

Downtown, smack on the shores of the Hudson, is the Victorian **Stewart House** (2 N. Water St., 518/945-1357, www.stewart-house.com). Downstairs is a formal dining room and more casual bar/bistro area where contemporary American and French fare is served (average dinner entrée $17; average

bistro fare $11). Upstairs are five guestrooms ($100–125 d).

Catskill Game Farm

Heading west out of Catskill on Route 23A, you'll soon bump into Route 32, where you'll find the widely promoted Catskill Game Farm (400 Game Farm Rd., 518/678-9595, www.catskillgamefarm.com, 9 A.M.–5 P.M. daily May–Oct., adults $17.95, children 4–11 $12.95). A much more sophisticated operation than its name implies, the "farm" is really a shaded, well-kept zoo housing over 2,000 animals, including lions, tigers, elephants, giraffes, and bears. Nearby is a huge petting area where visitors can wander among grown llamas and deer or go to the nursery and feed baby lambs and piglets by bottle. Also in the park are amusement rides and a small train.

WEST ON ROUTE 23A

Some of the most dramatic scenery in the Catskills lies west of Route 32 on Route 23A. For about four miles, between Palenville and Haines Falls, the road winds steeply up nearly

THE CATSKILLS

The Catskill Game Farm houses over 2,000 animals.

1,500 feet, past craggy cliffs and rocky streams, forested walls and outstanding views. The incline continues at a gentler angle between Haines Falls and Hunter, then levels out to run along Schoharie Creek.

Not to be missed is the view from the Catskill Mountain House site, just east of Haines Falls. The site can be reached by hiking the Escarpment Trail or by driving into North-South Lakes Campground and walking a short distance to the edge of the Great Wall of Manitou. From here, the whole world seems to lie at your feet. Straight ahead, in the distance, are the gray-blue Taconic and Berkshire Mountains; below is the Hudson, shrunk to a slim silver line.

The view is perhaps best described in James Fenimore Cooper's *The Pioneers,* one of his Natty Bumppo tales: "'What see you when you get there?' asked Edwards. 'Creation!' said Natty,… 'all creation, lad.'"

Kaaterskill Falls

Off Route 23A about three miles west of Palenville are Kaaterskill Falls, marked with a sign and roadside parking lot. At 260 feet (compared to Niagara's 167 feet), these are the highest waterfalls in the state. During the Romantic Age, everyone from Thomas Cole and Asher Durand to James Fenimore Cooper and William Cullen Bryant were inspired by this long glittering torrent. The falls were portrayed in countless paintings, illustrations, and poems until they became an icon for the American wilderness. Near the top of the falls once stood the Catskill Mountain House, the nation's first mountain resort.

To reach the lower basin of Kaaterskill Falls, follow the trail on the north side of Route 23A. The hike, which begins at Bastion Falls, takes less than an hour round-trip, and although there are steep spots, the trail is mostly level.

Escarpment Trail

One of the most unusual hikes in the Catskills is the Escarpment Trail, which stretches 24 miles between Route 23A in Haines Falls and Route 23 in East Windham without crossing a single highway. Parts of the trail have been used for more than 150 years, as initials and dates carved along its ledges attest.

To access the popular section of the Escarpment Trail that leads past the former site of the Catskill Mountain House, continue about two miles past the Kaaterskill Falls parking area and take the first right onto County Road 18, following signs to North-South Lakes Campground. At the end of this four-mile road, just before the campground, turn right onto Scutt Road, where you'll find a parking area and a blue-marked trail.

Follow the trail through a forested area, past Spruce Creek and a four-way intersection, toward Layman Monument and Sunset Rock. Soon after the intersection, the trail skirts along the top of the Great Wall of Manitou. The terrain here is fairly level and all along the way are overlooks offering magnificent views. Near the Layman Monument you can see Kaaterskill Clove ("clove" comes from the Dutch word for gorge), with Hunter Mountain behind.

About a mile and a half past Inspiration Point is a red-marked cutoff trail leading to the site of the former Catskill Mountain House. Take this shorter trail, or continue on the more scenic blue trail past Split and Boulder Rocks. Either way, in 20–30 minutes you'll reach the large open ledge upon which the famed resort once stood. An informative plaque marks the spot.

To hike from the parking lot to the Catskill Mountain House site takes about an hour and a half. From there, you can return the way you came or take the service road back to the parking lot.

North-South Lakes

If you're short on time, or would rather not hike, you can reach the former Catskill Mountain House site directly by entering the 219-site North-South Lakes Campground (County Rd. 18, Haines Falls, 518/589-5058, parking $6–8, closed late Oct.–mid May) and driving to the end of the service road. The short trail that leads to the site is located at the far end of the parking lot.

The North-South Lakes are the focus of a popular state park, where you'll find two long, pristine lakes ringed by deciduous trees that erupt with fiery color in fall, a sandy beach, bathhouses, and hiking trails. Rowboats can be rented, and fishing is good. For campground reservations, call 800/456-CAMP.

According to legend, North and South Lakes are the two eyes of a great reclining giant, Onteora; nearby Lake Creek is his tears. South Lake, formerly known as Sylvan Lake, was one of Thomas Cole's favorite subjects. He painted his well-known "Lake With Dead Trees" and "Catskill Lake" here.

Tannersville

Part scruffy mountain village, part cheery tourist town, Tannersville—named for its once-extensive tanning industry—is now home to a few shops and cafés, several inns and B&Bs, and a large number of tattoo parlors. In the village center, you'll find **Maggie's Krooked Cafe** (3066 Main St., 518/589-6101), offering home-cooked specialties such as pancakes and fried shrimp in beer batter (open for lunch and dinner only). **Last Chance Antique and Cheese Cafe** (602 Main St., 518/589-6424) is a combination store/café featuring overstuffed sandwiches, homemade soups, cheeses, and chocolates.

The popular **Eggery Inn** (288 Platte Clove Rd./County Rd. 16, off Rte. 23A, 518/589-5363, www.eggeryinn.com, $119–149 d with breakfast) has accommodated guests since 1900. The inn features a wood-burning Franklin stove, heavy oak bar, wraparound porch, and great views of the Catskills. Another favorite lodging option is the nearby **Redcoat's Country Inn & Restaurant** (50 Dale Ln. off Elka Park Rd., Elka Park, 518/589-9858, www.redcoatsonline.com, $99–139 d with breakfast), an English-style inn housed in an attractive 1850s farmhouse. Attached is a cozy restaurant serving Continental fare; open for dinner on weekends only, entrées $12–28.

Hunter

Known first for its tannery and then for its

chair factory, Hunter is now a small ski town. Behind it rises the trail-carved wall of Hunter Mountain Ski Area, while along Main Street stand lodges and restaurants, many done up in ersatz Swiss motif. During the off-season, many of these establishments seem shut down and the village takes on a neglected feel.

Housed in an inviting red barn in the center of town is the **Catskill Mountain Foundation** (7967 Main St., www.catskillmtn.org, 518/263-4908), a nonprofit group dedicated to the arts. The foundation runs a performing arts center in the red barn, as well as the **CMF Theater, Bookstore, and Gallery** in two renovated buildings across the street (518/263-5157, 11 A.M.–5 P.M. daily, with extended hours on weekends).

In summer, anglers can be found **trout fishing** in Schoharie Creek along Route 23A, while hikers take to the slopes of Hunter Mountain (see below). Four miles south of town is the 24-site **Devil's Tombstone Campground** (Rte. 214, 845/688-7160; for camping reservations, call 800/456-CAMP).

The charming [**Fairlawn Inn** (7872 Main St., 518/263-5025, www.fairlawninn.com, $95–100 d) is a three-story Victorian hostelry with nine attractive guestrooms, many with brass or four-poster beds, along with cable TV and in-room Internet access. Stained-glass windows, parquet floors, 19th-century antiques, wraparound porches, and a stunning central staircase add to the ambiance.

The modern [**Scribner Hollow Lodge** (Main St./Rte. 23A, just east of Hunter Mountain, 518/263-4211 or 800/395-4683, www.scribnerhollow.com, $110–260 per person d, with breakfast and dinner) is a full-service lodge with an outdoor pool, an unusual indoor grotto, saunas, and fireplaces. Each of the 37 rooms is furnished differently, and artwork is everywhere. Adjoining the lobby is **Prospect Restaurant,** offering American regional cuisine prepared with fresh local ingredients, along with scenic vistas; average entrée $24.

Near the base of Hunter Mountain is the chalet-style **Hunter Mountain Inn** (7433 Main St., 518/263-3777, www.hunterinn.com),

whose bar is a favorite haunt of the après ski crowd; live music is often featured on the weekends. The inn holds 27 standard double rooms and 14 suites, which feature cathedral ceilings and whirlpool tubs.

Hunter Mountain Ski Area

Hunter Mountain Ski Area (off Rte. 23A in the heart of the village, 518/263-4223, www.huntermtn.com) is the Catskills' best-known ski center and one of its biggest businesses. In winter, boisterous New York City folk flock here by the thousands to ski its crowded slopes. The three-mountain complex offers 49 trails, 15 lifts and tows, and 100 percent snowmaking capability.

In summer, the **Hunter Mountain Festivals** are staged here. Regular events include the German Festival, Oktoberfest, and the International Celtic Festival, during which dozens of sturdy men in kilts march down the mountainside.

On summer and fall weekends, the **Hunter Mountain Sky Ride** travels to the mountain's summit (10 A.M.–5 P.M. Sat.–Sun. July–Oct., $6 per person). Open year-round is the resort's small **Ski Museum** (10 A.M.–5 P.M., free admission), which documents the history of the sport.

Lexington

Continuing west on Route 23A, you'll pass through the nondescript hamlets of South Jewett and Jewett Center before coming to the startlingly beautiful **St. John the Baptist Ukrainian Catholic Church** (Rte. 23A just east of Lexington, 518/263-3862). The church was built in 1962 in memory of the Ukrainians killed by the Communists in World War II. The entire edifice—with its rich brown cedar shingles, onion domes, and steeply pitched roofs—was constructed without nails in the traditional Ukrainian manner. The interior features a stunning hand-carved altar, along with woodcarvings and icons. On Saturday evenings in July and August, classical chamber-music concerts are presented in the adjacent *Grazhda,* or community center.

Hiking

A number of good, well-marked hiking trails lace the area around Hunter Mountain. Many start at the back of the mountain on Old Spruceton Road. To get there, continue west on Route 23A past the Ukrainian church and turn left onto Route 42 south. Continue to the hamlet of Westkill, turn east onto County Road 6, and follow it six miles through pastoral Spruceton Valley. At the end, after the road has become dirt, are two parking lots with trailheads.

The main trail leading to Hunter's summit is of moderate difficulty, covers 7.2 miles round-trip, and takes about six to seven hours. Along the way is a mile-long spur leading to **Colonel's Chair,** a northern protuberance of the mountain supposedly resembling a giant armchair. The chair was named after Col. William Edwards, an early tanner who made his fortune decimating the area's hemlock forest, and then unceremoniously pulled out. It was Edwards who first put Hunter, then known as Edwardsville, on the map.

One of the easiest hikes in the Catskills, leading to Diamond Notch Falls, also begins at the parking lots. The gently inclining trail is about a mile long and runs alongside West Kill Creek. Wildflowers and birds are abundant.

For more information on hiking Hunter Mountain, stop in at the main Hunter Mountain ski lodge.

PRATTSVILLE

On Route 23, just west of the Route 23A intersection, is the tidy village of Prattsville—one of the first planned communities in New York State. Prattsville began in 1824 when a man named Col. Zadock Pratt came to what was then known as Schoharie Kill to establish "the largest tannery in the world." Pratt not only succeeded in establishing his tannery—which over 20 years tanned more than a million hides and cleared over 10,000 acres of hemlock—but also built an elaborate village.

First, the "Colonel" widened Main Street and built 100 handsome Greek Revival houses and stores along it. Then he lined the street with 1,000 elm, maple, and hickory trees, and laid slate sidewalks. Next, he built four textile factories, three gristmills, five schools, three churches, and several hotels. On his 53rd birthday, in 1843, he opened his own bank and had currency printed with his image on it.

For all of this, Pratt—who once said that he had come to "live with the people, not on them"—became a folk hero in his own time, and is still spoken of with a great deal of affection. Many of his buildings and trees still stand.

Zadock Pratt Museum

Pratt's former home has been turned into a museum (Main St., 518/299-3395, www.prattmuseum.com, 1–4:30 P.M. Thurs.–Mon. June–Oct., adults $3, children 12 and under $1). Inside you'll find everything from pictures of his wives (he had five, including two pairs of sisters) to documents from the years he spent as a U.S. Congressman (he never missed a single session).

Pratt Rock

In addition to his many accomplishments, Pratt was also an eccentric who liked to play practical jokes, compete in contests of strength and skill (at age 36, he beat all challengers in the running broad jump), and judge a man's character by the look of his hands. Evidence of Pratt's eccentricity can be found at the entrance to the village, where he had a small park with rock sculptures built into the mountainside. The sculptures, painted white, tell the story of Pratt's life through symbols—a horse, a hemlock tree, the bust of his son who died in the Civil War.

Also in the park is a half-completed stone coffin. Pratt wanted to be buried in the park as well, but the rock proved too hard and he was buried conventionally, in the Prattsville Cemetery.

EAST ALONG ROUTE 23
Ashland

Heading back east along Route 23, you'll pass a wide and wonderful waterfall on the right

THE CATSKILLS

© CHRISTIANE BIRD

Pratt Rock

known as **Red Falls.** At its base is a deep, dark swimming hole. From the waterfall, Route 23 winds through the hamlet of Ashland. The area is popular with anglers who try their luck in **Batavia Kill.**

On a woodsy back road several miles off Route 23 is the secluded 1870 **Ashland Farmhouse** (W. Settlement Rd., 518/734-3358, $75–90 d). The B&B boasts its own stocked trout pond, grassy fields, hot tub, wood-burning stove, and four comfortable guest rooms.

Windham

Route 23 continues past Ashland to the bustling ski-resort village of Windham. More upscale than Hunter, Windham is filled with Greek Revival buildings, ski lodges, and restaurants.

Ski Windham (off South St., one mile from Rte. 23, 518/734-4300 or 800/754-9463, www.skiwindham.com) is considerably smaller than Hunter Mountain, but it's also less hectic. The resort offers 33 trails, a 3,050-foot summit, and 97 percent snowmaking capability.

Windham Fine Arts (5380 Main St., 518/734-6850, noon–5 P.M. Fri.–Mon.), housed in a historical Federal-style building, showcases local and regional artists. Exhibits change every five or six weeks.

For a hearty breakfast or lunch, or a glass of Guinness, try **Jimmy O'Connor's Windham Mountain Inn** (South St., 518/734-4270), a lively Irish pub. The homey **Michael's** (Main St., 518/734-9862) serves breakfast all day, along with sandwiches, homemade soups, and Greek specialties. German-Swiss cuisine is served at the cozy **Chalet Fondue Restaurant** (Rte. 296, 518/734-4650), decorated in traditional German style with fireplaces, giant wine casks, and carved woodwork.

In a rural setting on the outskirts of town is the **Albergo Allegria B&B** (43 Rte. 296, off Rte. 23, a half mile east of Windham, 518/734-5560, www.AlbergoUSA.com, $79–299 d), a charming Victorian manor house that feels more like an inn than a B&B. Upstairs are 16 guest rooms all nicely done up in period antiques, while downstairs is a comfortable lounge with overstuffed couches and a fireplace. All of the rooms have cable TV and phones.

Campers can pitch their tents at **White Birches** (Nauvoo Rd., off Rte. 23, 518/734-3266), a well-kept campground offering 100 campsites and hiking, swimming, and fishing in a spring-fed lake year-round.

East to Cairo

Between East Windham and Cairo (KAY-ro), Route 23 turns from scenic to spectacular as it traverses the big wide slopes of Windham High Peak, Burnt Knob, and Acra Point. The expansive Helderberg Valley opens up below, while in the distance are the Green Mountains of Vermont and the White Mountains of New Hampshire.

A scenic overlook is located midway, or you can stop for a meal or a drink at the **(Point Lookout Inn and Victorian Rose Restaurant** (Rte. 23, East Windham, 518/734-3381, www.pointlookoutinn.com), about two miles east of the overlook. The modern, casual hostelry overlooking five states serves everything from salads and sandwiches to pasta and steaks (average dinner entrée $16). Fourteen simple, nicely appointed lodge rooms are available ($80–165 d), while on the grounds are hot tubs and nature trails.

At Acra, you can continue east directly into Cairo, or loop south through the community of **Round Top,** once known for its German resorts—one or two of which are still in operation. The hamlet's foremost accommodation, however, is the wonderful old **(Winter Clove Inn** (2965 Winter Clove Rd., off Rte. 32, 518/622-3267, www.winterclove.com, $95 a day per person including all meals, or $75 a day with breakfast only), a big white colonial sitting on a hillside. Owned by the same family since 1830, the Winter Clove has its own swimming pools, tennis courts, nine-hole golf course, hiking trails, and bowling alley. Outside is a big, wide porch lined with wicker rocking chairs; inside are 50 spacious rooms filled with flowered wallpaper and antiques.

Buddhist Temple

Just beyond the scrappy town of Cairo, off Route 23B, is Ira Vail Road and signs that will lead you to the Mahayana Buddhist Temple and Monastery (518/622-3619, 7 A.M.–7 P.M. daily). The retreat of the Eastern States Buddhist

© CHRISTIANE BIRD

THE CATSKILLS

The Mahayana Buddhist Temple is a retreat of the Eastern States Buddhist Temple of America.

Temple of America, based in New York City, the red-and-gold enclave sits in a peaceful woodsy area at the end of a dirt road. Not far from the red-gated entrance are the serene Lake of Fortune and Longevity and the Pagoda of Jade Buddha. To one side are the Grand Buddha Hall and several smaller temples.

A plaque at the Grand Hall tells the story of the Yings, who immigrated to the United States from China in 1955, only to find no organized Buddhist temple in New York. Seven years later they founded the first, at 64 Mott Street in New York City's Chinatown, and soon thereafter built the Mahayana retreat.

Inside the Grand Hall is an altar laden with three golden Buddhas, fruit, and flowers. Two monks in orange robes sit against one wall. The retreat actively welcomes visitors, as the many unobtrusive donation boxes attest.

Don't leave the Mahayana retreat without visiting the fascinating Five Hundred Arhats Hall. Here, 500 golden Buddhas, each one different from the next, sit in a darkened room lit only with small spotlights.

EAST DURHAM AND VICINITY

On Route 145, about five miles northwest of Cairo, is the remarkable village of East Durham. At first, nothing seems too out of the ordinary in this scenic spot surrounding by rolling hills, but then you start to notice one shamrock after another, one green building after another, one Irish name after another. O'Sullivan, Kelly, McGrath, McGuire, O'Connor, McLaughlin, Ryan, O'Shea. Ethnic resorts may be dying out elsewhere in the Catskills, but someone forgot to tell East Durham.

Variously nicknamed Ireland's 33rd County, the Irish Catskills, or the Irish Alps, East Durham and environs have been an Irish resort since the late 1800s, when immigrants living in New York City escaped the summer heat by coming up here to the hills that reminded them of home. With the advent of cheap flights to Ireland in the 1970s, much of this tourist trade died down. But it's recently skyrocketed again thanks to a new wave of Irish immigrants to New York.

Irish American Heritage Museum

In the center of town is the Irish American Heritage Museum (2267 Rte. 145, 518/634-7497, noon–4 P.M. Wed.–Sun., June–Sept., adults $4, seniors and children $2.50), housed in a 1850s farmhouse with lots of airy gallery space. Established in 1990, the museum documents the history of the Irish in the United States through changing exhibits on such subjects as Irish immigration and Irish music. Also on tap are frequent concerts, lectures, and readings.

Guaranteed Irish

Another unique stop in the village center is Guaranteed Irish (2220 Rte. 145, 518/634-2392, open daily Apr.–Dec., weekends only Jan.–Mar.), "the largest Irish import store in the United States." Inside this sprawling building you'll find everything from Irish sweaters and china leprechauns to an excellent selection of Irish music and literature. Most everyone who shops here seems to have at least a touch of Irish brogue, so even if you don't intend to buy, it's great fun just to listen.

Entertainment and Events

The **Michael Quill Irish Cultural & Sports Centre** (Rte. 145 in the village center, 518/634-2286) presents theater, music, dance, and sporting events.

Irish music can also be heard at many of the casual, fly-by-night pubs along Route 145, or the more formal lounges situated in the village's resorts. Two resorts with extensive concert schedules are the **Fern Cliff House** (Rte. 67A, off Rte. 145, 518/634-7424) and **Gavin's Golden Hill Resort** (Golden Hill Rd., off Rte. 145, 518/634-2582). The **Shamrock House** (Rte. 145 in the village center, 518/634-2897, www.shamrockhouse.com), owned by the Kellegher family since 1938, is a well-kept motel with a restaurant, pub, and live Irish music on weekends ($110–140 d with breakfast and dinner).

The popular **East Durham Irish Festival** (518/634-2286), featuring Irish bands, bagpipes, and dancers, takes place over Memorial Day weekend.

GREENVILLE TO COXSACKIE
Greenville

About five miles northeast of East Durham is the picture-perfect, New England–style village of Greenville, centered around the **◖ Greenville Arms 1889 Inn** (South St., at Rte. 32, 888/665-0044, www.greenvillearms.com, $115–195 d, with breakfast and afternoon tea). Built as a private residence by William Vanderbilt in 1889, the retreat now features 15 guest rooms, all furnished with fine antiques. Out back are the swimming pool and flower gardens.

Bronck Museum

One of the most important museums in the Catskills is the Bronck Museum (Pieter Bronck Rd., off Rte. 9W four miles south of Coxsackie, 518/731-6490, noon–4 P.M. Wed.–Fri. and 10 A.M.–4 P.M. Sat. and noon–4 P.M. Sun.

June–Oct., adults $4, students ages 12–15 $2, children 5–11 $1.50), run by the Greene County Historical Society (www.gchistory.org). This complex of Dutch Colonial dwellings and 19th-century barns was operated as a working farm by eight generations of the Bronck family. The oldest building, a 1663 stone house, contains an Indian lookout loft. Next door is the 1738 Brick House, now used to display household items, glass, silver, and a collection of paintings by artists such as Frederic Church, Thomas Cole, and Ammi Phillips.

Outside you'll find three barns, each representing a different era. The squat Dutch barn is equipped with heavy, blackened beams; the 13-sided Liberty barn is built around a central pole; and the Victorian-house barn is filled with period carriages and wagons.

To reach the museum from I-87, take Exit 21B and head south.

Sullivan County

None of the Catskill Mountains and only a sliver of the Catskill Preserve lies in Sullivan County, and yet for many, for many years, Sullivan County *was* the Catskills. That's largely because in the decades following World War II, the county became known for its mega-resorts, many catering to a Jewish clientele. Most of these luxury retreats boasted their own private golf courses, lakes, riding stables, ice rinks, ski slopes, and health clubs, and offered three gargantuan meals daily, along with live entertainment nightly. The resorts made Sullivan County into the cradle of the Catskill comedian—the heart of the so-called "Borscht Belt." Henny Youngman, Moss Hart, Jerry Lewis, Joan Rivers, Milton Berle, and Mel Brooks all cut their teeth in Sullivan County.

Those days are now long gone, and Sullivan County has yet to recover. Those few megaresorts that remain, such as the Concord, have restyled themselves into golf resorts or convention centers, while much of the county remains severely depressed. Proposals to build

casinos—and thus, supporters say, save the region—have been constantly defeated in the state legislature. As in the rest of the Catskills, however, serious change finally appears to be underway. Thanks to second home-owners, ex-urbanites, and suburban sprawl, Sullivan County is now one of the fastest growing counties in New York State.

The northern and southern sections of Sullivan County are very different in feel from the once-resort-based east. To the north are the dense, quiet woods of the Catskill Preserve and some of the world's best trout fishing. The two most famous streams are the Beaverkill and the Willowemoc.

To the south is the often strangely overlooked Upper Delaware Scenic and Recreational River, offering great scenic vistas, canoeing, and tubing. The Delaware is a Class I river with "few or no obstructions" and attracts many canoeists, kayakers, and inner-tubers, as well as fisherfolk.

In July and August, and on spring and fall

THE CATSKILLS

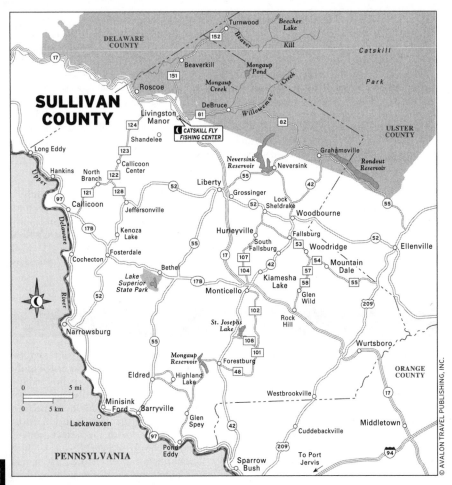

THE CATSKILLS

weekends, the Sullivan County Visitors Association (845/794-3000, ext. 5010, or 800/882-CATS) maintains a **visitor information booth** in Rock Hill, at Exit 109 off Route 17.

WURTSBORO AND VICINITY

Heading into the heart of Sullivan County is Route 17, also known as the **Quickway**. Once the main artery leading from New York City to the Borscht Belt—a distance of only 90 miles—Route 17 is dotted with scrappy billboards in various stages of neglect. Here and there are outlet shops and roadside food stops, while in the distance rise layers upon layers of mountainous green.

Just over the Orange-Sullivan County border is the village of Wurtsboro, centering on a wide main street flanked with lumbering wooden buildings and American flags. Wurtsboro today is best known for **Wurtsboro Airport** (Rte. 209, north of town, 845/888-2791, 8:30 A.M.–5 P.M. daily), the oldest soaring center in the United States (established in 1927). Demonstration rides over the Shawangunks last 15–20 minutes and cost about $40 per person.

Also in Wurtsboro is **Canal Towne Emporium** (Sullivan and Hudson Sts., 845/888-2100, 10 A.M.–5 P.M. daily). Billing itself as a country store from the 1840s, Canal Towne has won awards for historic preservation. But it's still basically an upscale tourist shop, selling candles, cards, toys, and handcrafted items.

For homemade baked goods, soups, and daily specials made with herbs and vegetables grown in their garden, stop in at the **Potager** (116 Sullivan St., 845/888-4086). The simple café is housed in a century-old church that also sells antique cupboards and garden accessories.

MONTICELLO

About 12 miles west of Wurtsboro on Route 17 is Monticello, the county seat and unofficial capital of the Borscht Belt. The town does boast a few historic buildings—most notably the **Sullivan County Courthouse**—but is mostly unsightly tourist-oriented sprawl.

At the western end of town is **Monticello Raceway** (Exit 104 off Rte. 17B, 845/794-4100, www.monticelloraceway.com), where you'll find one of the fastest harness-racing tracks in the country. Inside gleam 1,800 video-gaming machines and a food court. Live nighttime entertainment is regularly featured.

TO WOODBOURNE AND HURLEYVILLE
Kiamesha Lake

At one time, the mighty **Concord** (Concord Rd., 845/794-4000, www.concordresort.com) was one of the Catskills' most famous megaresorts, boasting 1,200 rooms, 3,000 acres, three golf courses, 40 tennis courts, indoor and outdoor pools, a health club, horseback riding trails, big-name entertainment, and a full activities program for all ages. More recently, however, the Concord has morphed into a golf resort (two-night packages start at $320 per person, including three days of golf).

The Fallsburgs

Fallsburg and South Fallsburg are surrounded by both beautiful countryside and disheartening poverty. Boarded-up buildings pockmark the landscape, and the unemployed linger on village street corners. There's a sense of glory gone by, and a sense of waiting.

More interesting than what's *in* the towns is what's outside them. The region is a spiritual mecca for a diversity of religious sects. On the back roads surrounding the Fallsburgs are many Hasidic bungalows, and the Hasidim are often out walking, their black frock coats and long dresses flapping in the wind. Just outside South Fallsburg is the ashram of the **Siddha Yoga Dham of America Foundation (SYDA)** (845/434-2000), a low-slung complex of whitewashed buildings hidden behind a high wall. With tens of thousands of followers around the world, SYDA is one of the most popular Eastern spiritual movements.

On a typical summer weekend, the South Fallsburg ashram attracts hundreds of visitors. Most come to attend a two-day "Intensive"— a sort of spiritual initiation seminar—or to stop into the bookstore. And today's devotees are no longer the spaced-out flower children of the '60s generation; instead, most are young professionals and/or serious students of Eastern meditation. Among the many celebrities who've been attracted to SYDA over the years are Jerry Brown, John Denver, Diana Ross, Isabella Rossellini, Don Johnson, and Melanie Griffith.

For the casual visitor, the South Fallsburg ashram is an intriguing place. Outside are the grounds, dotted with Hindu gods; inside are meeting rooms, their air thick with overpoweringly sweet incense. A few very American-looking men and women dressed in orange robes and saris stroll about, while blown-up photographs of the Foundation's beatific guru, Chidvilasananda, are everywhere. As a day visitor, you may be questioned at the gate, but generally speaking, outsiders are welcome to look around.

To reach the site from Main Street (Route 42) in South Fallsburg, take the road by the movie theater and bear immediately left at the fork onto Laurel Avenue. Continue 2.5 miles to a flashing red light and turn left onto Brickman Road. The ashram is located about 200 feet down on the right, and the bookstore is a few hundred yards beyond that.

Hurleyville

In tiny Hurleyville, on Route 104 between Monticello and Route 52, are a number of antique shops and the **Sullivan County Museum, Art, and Cultural Center** (265 Main St., 845/434-8044, www.sullivancountyhistory.org, 10 A.M.–4:30 P.M. Wed.–Sat., 1–4:30 P.M. Sun., suggested admission $2). Among the exhibits is one explaining the tanning process, and another containing a large collection of vintage clothing, including lavender, blue, brown, and even black wedding dresses. It wasn't until the turn of the century that white became de rigueur.

Also in the center is the **Frederick A. Cook Society Room.** Born in Sullivan County, Cook was a physician, anthropologist, and explorer who—according to his admirers—got to the North Pole before its generally recognized discoverer, Adm. Robert Peary.

LIBERTY

Continuing north on Route 17 another 12 miles, you'll come to Liberty, the second unofficial capital of the Borscht Belt. Though the town has little to offer in the way of tourist attractions, lining North Main Street are pretty historic buildings, including the Gothic Revival Town Hall and a Greek Revival Methodist church. **Ferndale Marketplace Antiques** (52 Ferndale Rd., Exit 101 off Rte. 17, 845/295-8701) is a four-story emporium packed with everything from furniture to jewelry.

NORTHERN SULLIVAN COUNTY

The northernmost sliver of Sullivan County belongs to the Catskill Forest Preserve, and you can see the difference from the rest of the county immediately. Though still far from mountainous, the land here is much more woodsy and wild, laced with narrow winding roads, lakes, and reservoirs.

Neversink

Heading east out of Liberty on Route 55, you'll come to the hamlet of Neversink, primarily a debarkation point for anglers trying their luck on scenic, 1,472-acre **Neversink Reservoir.**

DeBruce

West of the reservoir is the hamlet of DeBruce, dotted with a number of big abandoned homes that must once have been very fine. DeBruce sits on the banks of Willowemoc Creek, where fisherfolk often cast their lines. Along DeBruce Road just east of the hamlet is the **Willowemoc Covered Bridge,** which was built in Livingston Manor in 1860 and cut in half in 1913 to be moved to its present site. Off Mongaup Road several miles north of the hamlet is the **New York State Catskill Fish Hatchery** (402 Fish Hatchery Rd., 845/439-4328, 8:30 A.M.–4:30 P.M. Mon.–Fri. and 8:30>A.M.–noon Sat.–Sun. June–Oct., free admission). This is a serious industrial operation that raises more than one million trout annually for distribution throughout New York State. The tanks aren't always full, however, so you might want to call ahead.

Accommodations in DeBruce are provided by the spacious, turn-of-the-century (**DeBruce Country Inn** (982 DeBruce Rd., 845/439-3900, www.debrucecountryinn.com, $100–125 per person per night, includes breakfast and dinner). The inn is within the Catskill Forest Preserve on the banks of the Willowemoc, and each of its 14 rooms and two suites is decorated differently. The adjoining restaurant, **Ianine's,** is an airy and attractive spot specializing in healthy American-European fare. The inn is closed December–March.

Camping is available at the 160-site **Mongaup Pond Campground** (Mongaup Pond Rd., three miles north of DeBruce, 845/439-4233), which offers swimming, boat rentals, and hiking. Call 800/456-CAMP for reservations.

Livingston Manor

For years, Livingston Manor, on the banks of

a covered bridge near Livingston Manor

the Willowemoc, was a rustic sportsman's retreat primarily known for its superb trout fishing. The village center consisted of little more than a bridge, a few shops, and a roadside park, where a plaque quoted the Fisherman's Prayer: "God grant that I may live to fish until my dying day, And when it comes to my last cast I then most humbly pray, When in the Lord's safe landing net I'm peacefully asleep, Then in His mercy I be judged good enough to keep."

Livingston Manor is still renowned for its fishing, but since the early 2000s, it's been metamorphosing into a mini mini-Manhattan, complete with a bookstore, Japanese art gallery, and upscale shops and restaurants. Much of the change is due to a wealthy Wall Street investor, Andy Krieger, who bought a home here and then decided to revamp Main Street. Krieger also hopes to build an $80 million spa, resort and luxury housing community on the outside of town.

Meanwhile, back on a more rustic level, take Lewbeach Road (Rte. 151) five miles north of Livingston Manor to reach the 1860 **Livingston Manor Covered Bridge,** built in

a rare lattice-truss style. Nearby is the 80-site **Covered Bridge Campsite** (68 Conklin Hill Rd., 845/439-5093).

Beaverkill and Lewbeach

Continuing further up Lewbeach Road, you'll enter Catskill Park and soon come to the hamlets of Beaverkill and Lewbeach. In Beaverkill is the state-run **Beaverkill Campground** (792 Berrybrook Rd., off Beaverkill Rd., 845/439-4281), situated on the banks of the Beaverkill River, another world-famous trout-fishing stream. The 97-site campground on 62 wooded acres also offers river swimming. For reservations, call 800/456-CAMP.

Operating in Lewbeach is the **Wulff School of Fly Fishing** (845/439-4060 or 800/328-3638), which offers weekend trout-fishing and fly-casting workshops May–June. Run by Joan Wulff, a champion fisherwoman and author, the school is set on 100 acres and includes a private stretch of the Beaverkill River.

◖ Catskill Fly Fishing Center

Appropriately situated about midway between

Livingston Manor and Roscoe (a.k.a. Trout Town U.S.A.) is the state-of-the-art Catskill Fly Fishing Center (1031 Old Rte. 17, 845/439-4810, www.cffcm.org, 8 A.M.–4 P.M. daily Apr.–Oct., 10 A.M.–1 P.M. Tues.–Fri. and Sat. 10 A.M.–4 P.M. Nov.–Mar., adults $3, children $1). Started up by a group of local fisherfolk in 1981 and considerably expanded in 1994, the center does an excellent job of documenting the history of fly-fishing in the United States.

On display in the museum are hundreds of meticulously crafted flies, along with rods, reels (some dating back to 1850), historic photos, and other artifacts. To the uninitiated, that might sound ho-hum, but don't pass judgment until you've seen the bumble puppy, midge, quill gordon, wet spider, cow dung, red ant, silver doctor, picket pin, spectral spider... Fly-tying is a bona fide folk art, and each fly is an intricate affair, individually designed and named. At one time, flies were made out of feathers and furs; today, the material is usually synthetic.

Also at the center are fly-tying demonstrations, lectures, and fly-tying classes for beginners. Out front runs the Willowemoc, usually lined with hip-booted fisherfolk casting their lines.

Roscoe

Trout Town U.S.A. is considerably larger and more sophisticated than Livingston Manor, but its raison d'etre is the same. It was at **Junction Pool,** just west of Roscoe where the Willowemoc and Beaverkill meet, that American fly-fishing was first developed.

Downtown Roscoe's attractive wooden buildings house everything from restaurants to sports stores. At the western end of town is the **Roscoe O&W Railway Museum** (7 Railroad Ave., 607/498-5500, 11 A.M.–3 P.M. Sat.–Sun. June–Oct.), housed in a red caboose that also serves as a visitor information center.

A number of expert fly-tiers still live and work in Roscoe. Among them is Mary Dette, whose parents started an early fly-tying business back in 1928. Among anglers, the Dette name is known around the world.

Most days, Mary Dette can be found sitting in the front room of her big white house, tying flies. Most of the flies she ties are the traditional kind, made of natural materials. She says she makes too many different kinds to count. Once she gets down to the actual tying—as opposed to the assembling and cutting of materials—each fly only takes her about five minutes. Since the flies sell for only $3 or $4 each, she has to be quick.

Lots of amateur tiers, some from as far away as Italy and France, stop by Dette's house to watch her work. If you're interested in doing the same, inquire at the Catskill Fly Fishing Center.

The **◖ Reynolds House Inn** (Old Rte. 17 in the village center, 607/498-4422, www.reynoldshouseinn.com, $70–110 d) was built by the present owner's great, great "Uncle Billy" as a tourist home in 1902. Today, the place features seven airy guest rooms nicely done up in period furniture, a cozy piano parlor, and a commodious wraparound porch. Out back is a modern motel extension.

Restaurants in town include the enormous **◖ Roscoe Diner** (Old Rte. 17 at the entrance to the village, 607/498-4405), a local favorite serving breakfast, lunch, and dinner until midnight.

WESTERN SULLIVAN COUNTY
Jeffersonville

Where Route 128 meets Route 52 is Jeffersonville, an attractive village of boxy Victorian buildings and wide shady streets. Originally founded by German immigrants, Jeffersonville is now home to many artists and craftspeople. Several arts-oriented shops are located along Main Street.

The gracious **◖ Griffin House** (27 Maple Ave., 845/482-3371, www.griffin-house.com, $190–210 d) was built in 1895 by 10 master carpenters working in American chestnut. Exquisite woodwork is everywhere, along with fine antiques, plush rugs, and floor-length lace curtains. At **Ted's Restaurant** (Main St., 845/482-4242), a local favorite, you can order both excellent Turkish cuisine and standard American fare; average main dish $9.

Kenoza Lake

Route 52 continues further south through green rolling hills to Kenoza Lake and **Stone Arch Bridge Historic Park,** a quiet retreat centering on a three-arched bridge. The only bridge of its kind in the United States, the structure was built in 1872 by two Swiss-German stonemasons working with hand-cut local stone. Plaques in the park tell the story of the bridge and of a murder that took place here in 1882. A local farmer, believing that his brother-in-law had put a hex on him, convinced his son that in order for the curse to be lifted, the man had to be killed. The son complied with his father's wishes and dumped the body near the bridge. The case gained great notoriety in its day and is one of the few hex murders on record; the brother-in-law's ghost is said to still haunt the park.

Bethel

From Route 52, head east on Route 17B, through mile after mile of scenic farm country. Just when the land is at its prettiest, you've come to Bethel, where the famed Woodstock Music Festival took place on Max Yasgur's farm in 1969 (see *Woodstock and Vicinity* under *Ulster County,* above).

The former Yasgur farm is off Hurd Road. Signs off Route 17B point the way to an enormous lime-green field sloping down to borders of dark green trees. A horizontal stone marker near the road reads: "This is the original site of the Woodstock Music and Arts Fair held on Aug. 15, 16, 17, 1969." The marker was erected by the farm's former owners, the Gelish family, and goes on to list the festival's many "onsite performers": Richie Havens, Arlo Guthrie, Joan Baez, Joe Cocker, Ravi Shankar, Santana, Janis Joplin. …

In 1996, the Woodstock site was purchased by Alan Gerry, a Sullivan Country native and cable-TV mogul who added the landscaped grounds that now surround the marker and the nearby **Bethel Woods Center for the Arts.** Scheduled to open on July 1, 2006, with a performance by the New York Philharmonic, the $65-million center will include a 4,800-seat

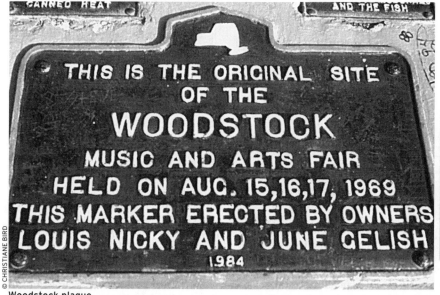

Woodstock plaque

THE CATSKILLS

© CHRISTIANE BIRD

covered pavilion, outdoor stage area, theater, inn, interpretive center, and permanent farmer's market. Featured will be an ambitious line-up of performers ranging from the New York Philharmonic to ballet troupes, jazz, and pop-music stars.

Not far from the new arts center is the exquisite **Lake Superior State Park** (Dr. Duggan Rd., off Rte. 17B, 845/794-3000, ext. 5002, 9 A.M.–dusk, parking $7 in summer), an all-but-untouched recreation area open for swimming, picnicking, boating, and fishing. Boats are available for rent.

ALONG THE DELAWARE

The drive along the wide, gentle Delaware River, which runs across the southern and western borders of Sullivan County up into Delaware County, is one of the prettiest sights in the region. About 73 miles in length, this portion of the Delaware is known as the **Upper Delaware Scenic and Recreational River,** as opposed to the lower, much-less-scenic Delaware, which runs between Port Jervis and Delaware Bay.

Meandering South from Monticello

The most interesting way to get to Route 97, which parallels the Delaware, is to take Route 102 out of Monticello. About eight miles down the woodsy back road, you'll come to County Road 108, which leads to the secluded **Inn at Lake Joseph** (400 St. Joseph Rd., 845/791-9506, www.lakejoseph.com, $170–385 d, including breakfast and lunch). Once owned by the Roman Catholic Church and used as a retreat for Cardinals Spellman and Hayes, the Queen Anne–style Victorian mansion sits on the shores of a 250-acre lake. Inside are 10 posh bedrooms with canopy beds and Persian rugs; outside are opportunities for swimming, boating, tennis, hiking, and cross-country skiing.

Route 102 continues south, passing the dark **Stephen Crane Pond** on the right. The author of *The Red Badge of Courage* lived with his brother Edmund during several summers in the early 1890s and may have written one of

WATCHING BALD EAGLES

After being nearly extinct for years, the bald eagle has returned to the United States, with the largest groups of eagles in the northeast to be found wintering around the Upper Delaware River. The eagles migrate here primarily from Canada and are attracted by the area's large amount of open fresh water. Here, our feathered friends can eat their fill of fresh fish and then relax on large tracts of undisturbed land, including about 12,000 state-owned acres managed strictly for the eagles.

The peak season for viewing the national bird is January through March, when several hundred usually winter in the area. For more information about the eagles and the best way to view them, contact the nonprofit **Eagle Institute** (P.O. Box 182, Barryville, NY 12719; 845/557-6162, www.eagleinstitute.org). During the winter, as many as 15 institute-trained volunteers are on site, guiding group tours, helping individual birders, and monitoring the eagles' activity. The Sullivan County Visitors Association also has maps, eagle-viewing sites, and tips on eagle etiquette on its website, www.scva.net. The trip to the Upper Delaware directly from New York City takes about two hours.

his lesser-known novels, *The Third Violet,* here. The Crane cottage is no longer standing, but a plaque marks the spot.

Forestburgh to Glen Spey

About a mile beyond Crane Pond is a T-intersection, where County Road 48 leads west into Forestburgh. Here, the **Forestburgh Playhouse** (39 Forestburgh Rd./County Rd. 43, just past the Route 42 intersection, 845/794-1194), offers summer-stock theater and musicals throughout the summer and early fall. The theater is housed in a historic barn.

Continuing west from Forestburgh, County Road 43 takes a bend just past the hamlet of Fowlerville. Here gleams **Mongaup Reservoir,** where hundreds of bald eagles spend the winter. The best way to find out about where and how to see the birds is to contact the **Eagle Institute** (845/557-6162, www.eagleinstitute.org).

Continuing south toward the Delaware River, the next junction is at Glen Spey. Just south of the hamlet on County Road 41 stands the gorgeous, mottled-brown **St. Volodymr Ukrainian Church,** built entirely without nails. Even bigger than the Ukrainian church in Lexington (see *Greene County*), the Byzantine, onion-domed St. Volodymr looks as if it belongs in a Russian fairy tale. Also not far away, on the right side of County Road 41, are the equally incongruous golden domes of St. Peter and Paul Church.

West to Barryville

Heading west on Route 97 from Pond Eddy, you'll pass one lovely river vista after another. On both banks are lush, rolling hills, covered with low-growing forest. The river provides

feeding grounds for muskrat, mink, raccoon, beaver, white-tailed deer, and the occasional black bear. The river's most common birds are turkey vultures, hawks, and owls, but bald eagles, ospreys, and great blue herons also inhabit the area.

Canoe outfitters in Barryville are numerous. Oldest among them is **Kittatinny Canoes** (Rte. 97, 800/FLOAT-KC, www.kittatinny.com); it also rents rafts, inner tubes, and kayaks. Younger operations include **Cedar Rapids Kayak & Canoe Outfitters** (Rte. 97, 914/557-6158) and **Indian Head Canoes** (Rte. 97, 800/874-BOAT, www.indianheadcanoes.com). **Campgrounds** are connected with many of the canoe outfitters.

Eldred and Vicinity

Detouring north about five miles from Barryville on Route 55, you'll come to **Eldred Preserve** (1040 Rte. 55, 845/557-8316, www.eldredpreserve.com). Spread over 3,000 acres, the preserve includes woodlands, wetlands, ponds, and lakes. Nature trails run

© CHRISTIANE BIRD

Near Glen Spey, St. Volodymr Ukrainian Church is built entirely without nails.

THE CATSKILLS

through the park, and boats can be rented. Eldred attracts large numbers of hunters and anglers, so you won't be surprised to also find a tackle shop, sporting-clay range, and trout pools. You must pay for the fish you catch, unless you fish in the catch-and-release pools.

Overlooking the preserve is **Eldred Preserve Motel and Restaurant** (1040 Rte. 55, 845/557-8316 or 800/557-FISH), which offers 20 rooms ($85–95 d), trout and bass fishing, boat rentals, tennis courts, and nature trails. A restaurant specializing in variations on a theme of trout is on the premises (average entrée $16), as is a coffee shop. The restaurant will clean and cook the fish you catch.

Minisink Ford

Back on Route 97, about four miles west of Barryville, is the 57-acre **Minisink Battleground Park** (Rte. 97, 845/794-3000, ext. 5002, dawn–dusk daily May–Oct., free admission). The Battle of Minisink, the Upper Delaware's only major Revolutionary War skirmish, was fought on these heights on July 22, 1779. It began after an alliance of Iroquois Indians and Tories under the leadership of Mohawk Chieftain Joseph Brant burned the settlement of Minisink. A hastily assembled Colonial militia unit struck back, and many on both sides were killed in what was one of the bloodiest battles of the war.

Opposite Minisink Battleground Park is **Roebling's Aqueduct,** now a lonely highway toll bridge and the oldest extant wire suspension bridge in the United States. Built in 1848 by John Roebling, of Brooklyn Bridge fame, the aqueduct was originally designed to carry canal boats traveling the Delaware and Hudson Canal over the Delaware River.

Zane Grey Museum

Roebling's bridge leads across the river to Lackawaxen, Pennsylvania, and the Zane Grey Museum (Scenic Drive, a half mile from the bridge, 570/685-4871; call for hours and admission fees), also run by the Upper Delaware National Park Service. The museum was once home to the Father of the Western Novel,

whose best-known work, *Riders of the Purple Sage,* is still considered one of the finest Western novels ever written.

As a young aspiring writer who had trained to be a dentist, Grey left his practice in 1905 to move to Lackawaxen. Here he met his future wife, Lina Elise Roth, who encouraged him to pursue a full-time writing career and provided him with financial backing until he published his first book in 1910.

Today's museum is filled with Grey memorabilia, including fishing trophies and mementos from his trips west. Grey first discovered his subject matter during a journey to the Grand Canyon in 1907.

Narrowsburg

Narrowsburg is a delightful river town whose curving, narrow Main Street is crowded with well-kept wooden buildings dating back to the early 1900s. Here you'll find the newspaper offices of the *River Reporter,* antique shops, and the grand old 1894 Arlington Hotel (37 Main St.).

Listed on the National Register of Historic Places, the Arlington no longer functions as a hotel, but is home to the **Delaware Valley Arts Alliance** (845/252-7576) and the **National Park Service Center** (845/252-3947, 9 A.M.–4:30 P.M. Sat.–Sun. June–Sept.). The Arts Alliance operates a small art gallery (10 A.M.–4 P.M. Tues.–Sat.). The National Park Center is stocked with brochures and includes an excellent bookstore; when the center is closed, brochures can be found by the door.

The creaky 1840 **Narrowsburg Inn** (176 N. Bridge St., 845/252-3998, www.narrowsburginn.com) is one block from the river. The oldest inn in the county, and the third oldest in the state, it's a bit worn around the edges, but nonetheless offers seven adequate rooms with shared baths at reasonable rates ($65–75 d), along with a suite with a private bath ($115–135). Also on site is a newly renovated restaurant and lounge that's popular with the locals.

Tiny **Dave's Big Eddy Diner** (40 Main St., 845/252-3817) is a popular place for breakfast or lunch.

THE CATSKILLS

Fort Delaware Museum of Colonial History

A replica of the small Connecticut Yankee settlement that stood on this site in the mid-1700s, the Fort Delaware Museum (Rte. 97 north of Narrowsburg, 845/252-6660 or 845/794-3000, ext. 3066, 10 A.M.–5 P.M. Wed.–Sun. July–Sept., 10 A.M.–5 P.M. Sat.–Sun. in June, adults $4, children 6–16 $2.25) is surrounded by thick stockade walls built of logs. Inside are three sturdy settler's cabins, an armory, meetinghouse, and blacksmith shop. Costumed guides demonstrate such arts as candle-making, weaving, and cannon-firing.

North to Delaware County

North of Narrowsburg, the idyllic countryside continues as Route 97 passes through the villages of Cochecton and Callicoon, Hankins, and Long Eddy. Cochecton, or "place of red stone hills," was once an important Indian settlement.

Callicoon features a number of attractive restaurants. The **Callicoon Depot** (Main St., 845/887-5324) is a good spot for lunch. Considerably more upscale is the **1906 Restaurant** (41 Lower Main St., 845/887-1906), which serves regional American fare and much game, including buffalo and ostrich; average entrée $18. Upstairs is a cabaret offering live music on the weekends. Also in Callicoon is the indoor **Callicoon Flea Market** (Main St., 845/887-5411, Fri.–Mon. May–Sept.).

The Upper Delaware Scenic and Recreational River ends just upriver near Hancock in Delaware County.

Delaware County

On the western slopes of the Catskills lies Delaware County, a seductive land of small peaks and valleys, picturesque villages and dairy farms. The third-largest county in New York State, Delaware is about the size of Rhode Island, and has a gentle, settled quality that's unlike the rest of the Catskills. Though traditionally the region's least "discovered" county, Delaware has recently been attracting more and more tourists and second-home owners. At the same time, its dairy industry—long the economic mainstay of the community—has dwindled precipitously, with the number of family-run farms shrinking from about 1,200 in 1970 to less than 300 today.

Both the East and West Branches of the Delaware River begin in the northeastern part of the county—the West Branch in Stamford, the East Branch in Grand Gorge—and traverse the county before joining forces at Hancock. Delaware County boasts more than 750 miles of streams and rivers in all, along with about 11,000 acres of reservoirs. The eastern half of the county holds most of the county's historical points of interest, as well as two especially pretty villages: Margaretville and Roxbury.

Among the most popular events in Delaware County are auctions. Some are weekly affairs, others special events, and most advertise in the local paper, *The Reporter*. Look for popular auctions in Fleischmanns, Bovina, and Hamden.

FLEISCHMANNS

Just over the Ulster-Delaware border off Route 28 is the long main street that comprises most of the village of Fleischmanns. Once a major resort town lined with "stores and establishments for refreshment and amusement," as one guidebook put it, Fleischmanns today feels weary and run-down, though not without charm. Worn turn-of-the-20th-century wooden buildings are everywhere.

One of the first Jewish enclaves in the Catskills, Fleischmanns was named after Cincinnati yeast-and-distilling magnate Charles F. Fleischmann, who bought 60 acres here in 1883. He and his relatives then proceeded

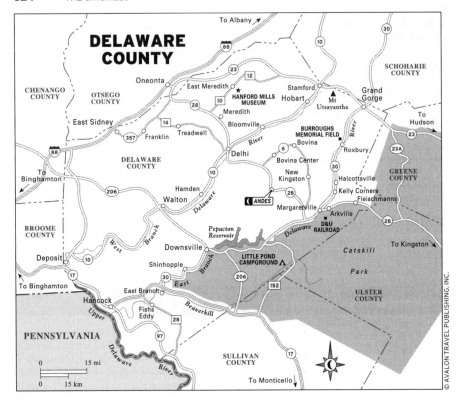

DELAWARE COUNTY

To Albany

SCHOHARIE COUNTY

CHENANGO COUNTY

OTSEGO COUNTY

Oneonta East Meredith Stamford Grand Gorge

★ HANFORD MILLS MUSEUM Hobart Mt Utsayantha

East Sidney Meredith Bloomville BURROUGHS MEMORIAL FIELD Bovina Roxbury

DELAWARE COUNTY

Franklin Treadwell Delhi Bovina Center Halcottsville Kelly Corners Fleischmanns

To Binghamton Hamden New Kingston GREENE COUNTY

Walton Margaretville ANDES Arkville D&U RAILROAD

BROOME COUNTY Pepacton Reservoir Catskill

Deposit Downsville LITTLE POND CAMPGROUND Park

To Binghamton Shinhopple ULSTER COUNTY

East Branch Hancock Fishs Eddy

PENNSYLVANIA To Kingston To Monticello

0   15 mi
0   15 km

© AVALON TRAVEL PUBLISHING, INC.

to build a luxurious summer settlement, filling their homes with costly furniture, rugs, and works of art. A local band was hired to perform at the railroad station whenever the Fleischmanns arrived (via their private railroad cars) and famous professional ballplayers were hired to play on the Fleischmanns' private baseball diamond.

For more on the town's history, stop in at the **Museum of Memories** (Main St., behind the Skene Memorial Library; open weekends in summer).

Auction House

Taking place most Saturday nights at 7 P.M. is the popular **Roberts' Auction** (820 Main St., 845/254-4490), selling everything from antiques to junk. Signs on the walls read Think Before Buying, No Refunds, and Pay Out

Back, as auctioneer Eddie Roberts barks out orders to one and all.

Accommodations and Food

Two-time winner of the Catskill Service Award, the **River Run B&B** (882 Main St., 845/254-4884, www.catskill.net/riverrun, $75–165 d) was originally built as a summer retreat for a wealthy businessman. Now, it offers eight comfortable guest rooms, four with private baths and all named for a Catskill River. A good motel in town is the **Northland Motel & Restaurant** (Depot St., 845/254-5125, $76 d).

La Cabana (Main St., 845/254-4966) is a popular Mexican restaurant—so popular that when it burned down in 2003, the townspeople raised money to help the owners rebuild. Open on the weekends and for dinner only; average entrée $11.

ARKVILLE
Delaware & Ulster Railroad
A few miles west of Fleischmanns in the village of Arkville is the Delaware & Ulster Railroad (Rte. 28, 845/586-DURR, www.durr.org). Excursions onboard this vintage steam-powered line, earlier known as the Ulster & Delaware, takes passengers to the nearby hamlets of Halcottsville or Roxbury and back, past lots of scenic countryside.

At one time, the U&D—nicknamed the "up and down" because of all the hills it had to climb—was a major transportation route into the Catskills. The journey north brought trainloads of tourists; the journey south took milk down to Kingston where it was shipped to New York City.

Today's sightseeing train operates every weekend June–October, and Wednesday–Friday July–Labor Day. Trains depart weekends at 11 A.M., 1 P.M., and 3 P.M.; weekdays at 11 A.M. and 2 P.M. (adults $7–10, children 3–11 $5–6).

Erpf House
Several nonprofit cultural organizations are headquartered in this big white building on a hill (43355 Rte. 28, 845/586-2611, www.catskillcenter.org, 9 A.M.–5 P.M. Mon.–Fri., noon–5 P.M. Sun.). Most of the center is devoted to offices, but the downstairs **Erpf Gallery** features local artwork and a display on environmental concerns. This is also a good place to pick up information on cultural events taking place throughout Delaware County.

MARGARETVILLE AND VICINITY
Heading west out of Arkville on Route 28, you'll soon come to the compact village of Margaretville, nestled into a valley between Pakatan Mountain to the south and Kettle Hill to the north. For a great view, take Walnut Street up the hill to Margaretville Mountain Road.

Along Main Street are attractive shops and restaurants, and The Commons, a mini-mall where you'll find a Margaretville Chamber of Commerce **information booth** (open summer weekends, 800/586-3303, www.marga-

retville.org). Housed in a 1920s theater is the **Margaretville Antique Center** (845/586-2424), crammed with artifacts of all kinds.

West of Margaretville is Route 30, which skirts around long, skinny **Pepacton Reservoir** all the way to Downsville. When the waters are low enough, you can still see some of the roads and bridges that once belonged to the now-flooded towns of Arena, Pepacton, Shavertown, and Union Grove.

Accommodations
Located on what was once a cauliflower farm, the **Margaretville Mountain Inn** (Margaretville Mountain Rd., one-half mile north of the village center, 845/586-3933, www.margaretvilleinn.com, $75–105 d, with breakfast) is a restored Victorian boardinghouse with great views of the valley below. Each of the six guest rooms is furnished differently, with many period antiques, and out front is an inviting porch with wicker chairs.

The **Hanah Country Inn and Resort** (576 W. Hubbell Hill Rd., 854/586-2100 or 800/752-6494, www.hanahcountryclub.com, $150–275 d), caters mostly to golf enthusiasts, but all are welcome. Features include standard hotel-style rooms, a health club, tennis courts, and a restaurant.

Food
The **Inn Between** (Rte. 28 just east of the village, 845/586-4265) is a restaurant and café serving breakfast, lunch, and dinner. Outside is a deck; average dinner entrée $13. For more serious dining, try **Binnekill Square** in the mini-mall of the same name (Main St., 845/586-4884). The Square specializes in American and Swiss cuisine, and offers a deck overlooking a small stream; average entrée $16. At the snug **Café on Main** (Main St., 845/586-2343), the menu changes frequently; French and continental fare prepared with fresh local produce is usually featured. Open for dinner only.

ANDES
Route 28 continues past Margaretville about eight miles to the mountain-high village of

Andes (www.andesny.com). Along the way, it passes through some lovely mountainous countryside, shaded with heavy growth.

In Andes occurred the climax of the 1845 Anti-Rent War, which brought about the end of the feudal land system in New York. That year, when a Sheriff Osman Steele attempted to evict a farmer for unpaid rent, the farmer's neighbors turned on the lawman and fatally shot him. Martial law was declared, and two men were sentenced to be hanged. However, the succeeding governor issued pardons, and in 1852, the state legislature declared the feudal land system illegal.

This history is on display at the **Hunting Tavern Museum** (Main St., 845/676-3747, call for hours), once a working tavern owned by Ephraim Hunting. Sheriff Steele reportedly downed his last drink here, proclaiming "Lead cannot penetrate Steele," shortly before he was shot and killed.

In the heart of the village stand a number of historic wooden buildings, including the striking red-and-white **Andes Fire Hall** and the venerable **Andes Hotel** (Main St., 845/676-4408,

www.andeshotel.com, $60 d). Run by the same family for decades, the hotel is now under new ownership. The rooms are simple but comfortable and a revamped restaurant serves "contemporary American fare with French influences." The Andes' laid-back bar is a favorite hangout.

After decades of hard times, Andes, like many parts of the Catskills, is now in the midst of a small renaissance. In recent years, new antique shops and galleries have sprouted up, most along Main Street. In the works are plans to convert the old railroad station into a visitors' center and museum.

Route 6

Narrow, meandering Route 6 detours off Route 28 north of Margaretville through the hamlets of **New Kingston, Bovina,** and **Bovina Center.** All along the way are steeply pitched hills and valleys, sprawling dairy farms, and a great mountain vista. In Bovina is **Russell's** (Main St., 607/832-4242), a country store that's been in the same family for generations. April–November, the popular **McIntosh Auction** (607/832-4829) takes place in the

backroad barns near Bovina

Bovina Creamery (Main St.) every Saturday at 6:30 P.M. It's a good idea to arrive early, as seats go fast.

NORTH ON ROUTE 30
Halcottsville

Several miles northeast of Margaretville on Route 30 is the splendid golden-brown **Round Barn** (845/586-3326), surrounded by an overgrown field. The reconstructed 1899 barn is the site of a farmers market, held on Saturdays throughout the summer. Just past the barn on the left is Lake Wawaka, often filled with ducks and geese, and the hamlet of Halcottsville.

Roxbury

Continue another six miles farther north on Route 30, and you'll come to the elegant town of Roxbury, built around a long Main Street flanked with stately white homes and big shady trees. Much of the town's moneyed ambience is due to the Gould family.

Future financier Jay Gould was born the son of a struggling farmer on the outskirts of Roxbury in 1836. At age 16, he began working in the village store, carefully saving his money until he had enough to invest in a small tannery, on which he made a handsome profit. From there, Gould turned to railroading. By 1880—thanks to some heavy-duty scheming—he controlled one-tenth of the country's rail systems. In 1869, he tried to corner the gold market, causing a disastrous stock-market crash.

Gould had many idiosyncrasies, such as taking his personal cow with him whenever he traveled. He returned to Roxbury frequently throughout his lifetime. After his death in 1892, his daughter Helen served as the town philanthropist. Many of the Gould family retainers and servants also retired to Roxbury.

One of the town's landmarks is the 1892 **Jay Gould Memorial Reformed Church** (53738 Main St., open Sunday mornings only), an impressive gray stone building with Tiffany windows, built by Jay Gould's children. Behind it is a compact park with stone picnic tables.

Also downtown is the **Walt Meade Gallery**

and Hilt Kelly Hall (5025 Vega Mountain Rd., 607/326-7908, www.roxburyartsgroup.org), run by the Roxbury Arts Group. The hall hosts music, dance and theater performances, and holds a small gallery (9 A.M.–4 P.M. Mon.–Fri., 1–4 P.M. Sat., free admission) showcasing the work of Catskill artists.

Taste Bud's Country Store and Restaurant (53535 Main St., 607/326-3663) is a classic, old-fashioned soda fountain that also serves breakfast, lunch, and a popular Sunday brunch. **The Roxbury** (2258 Rte. 41, 607/326-7200, www.theroxburymotel.com, $95 d) may be the only motel in the country, and certainly in the state, where guests are greeted with champagne and wine at check-in. Colorful room accents give the motel a stylish kick.

John Burroughs Memorial State Historic Site

Roxbury's other famous native son—a man about as different in temperament from Gould as it's possible to get—is writer and naturalist John Burroughs. Born in 1837, one year after Gould, Burroughs was as well known in his day as his contemporary and kindred spirit Henry David Thoreau. The author of 27 books that sold over 1.5 million copies, Burroughs was also a good friend of Walt Whitman, Teddy Roosevelt, John Muir, Henry Ford, and Thomas Edison.

During the last years of his life, Burroughs lived in Woodchuck Lodge, a simple frame house on the outskirts of Roxbury, overlooking wide fields and the blue Catskill hills. By the roadside is a series of plaques outlining Burrough's life and work, while nearby is his grave and Boyhood Rock, upon which he used to sit and dream.

To reach Burroughs Memorial Field, take Route 30 north out of Roxbury about two miles to Hardscrabble Road and watch for signs. The field is open daily dawn–dusk; the lodge is closed to visitors.

Grand Gorge

Beyond Roxbury, Route 30 continues north to Grand Gorge where the East Branch of

THE CATSKILLS

the Delaware begins. Here, the road squeezes through a scenic pass between high rugged hills before heading out of Delaware County into Schoharie County.

WEST ON ROUTE 10

Eight miles northwest of Grand Gorge, Route 23 intersects Route 10, which follows the valley of the West Branch of the Delaware. Legend has it that a lumber camp once operating in the valley boasted an excellent but temperamental and strong-willed cook. When her cat was killed by one of the lumberjacks, she not only knocked the man out cold, but also punished the whole crew by serving them her pet cooked in a meat pie.

Stamford

Route 10 enters the county at Stamford, filled with grand white homes and former boardinghouses. Stamford was also once home to one of the most luxurious resorts in the Catskills, the Hotel Habana, which catered exclusively to wealthy Cubans and South Americans.

During the summer, an imaginative array of music concerts are held in the historic Rexmere Hotel, now known as the **Frank W. Cyr Center** (159 W. Main St., 607/652-1200). Sponsored by the Friends of Music of Stamford, New York (www.friendsmusic.org), the concerts have ranged from a birthday tribute to Chopin to klezmer music. Local art exhibits are usually on display in the old hotel (8 A.M.– 5 P.M. Mon.–Fri.).

Just outside Stamford is **Mount Utsayantha,** named after a beautiful Mohawk princess who fell in love with a Sioux brave. Indian taboo barred the intertribal marriage, and Utsayantha jumped into a lake and drowned. Her grief-stricken father had her buried on the mountaintop, where a marker is said to still stand. Mountain Avenue, off Route 23 east of town, leads to the top of Utsayantha; the way is twisting and steep. At the summit, find an old fire tower and spectacular views. A hiking trail also leads to the top.

DELHI

The seat of Delaware County, Delhi (DEL-high) is an attractive place, built around a historic courthouse square lined with Greek- and Gothic Revival buildings. The square was once featured on the cover of the *Saturday Evening Post*. On Wednesdays from Memorial Day to October, a farmers market now operates here.

Delhi received its name back in the 1780s, when some of its more facetious residents suggested that their settlement be named after its most prominent citizen, state legislator Ebenezer Foote. Foote's nickname was the Great Mogul; Delhi was named for Delhi, India, the capital of the real Great Mogul.

Delaware County Historical Association Museum

This museum (46549 Rte. 10, two miles north of Delhi center, 607/746-3849, 11 A.M.–4 P.M. Tues.–Sun., June–Oct., adults $4, children $1.50) is divided into two parts. One is a gallery hall featuring changing exhibits on such imaginative topics as ethnic resorts, family farms, and the Anti-Rent wars. The other is a complex of nicely restored historic buildings.

At the center of the complex is the 1797 **Gideon Frisbee Homestead,** a Federal-style residence that at one time or another served as a tavern, inn, post office, and community meeting house. Each room is furnished to reflect a different era, from Colonial days to the early 1900s, thereby showing how technology has changed the way we live.

Other historic buildings on site include the 1860 Amos Wood Gunshop, filled with antique guns, and the turn-of-the-century Husted Hollow Schoolhouse. The museum also holds a gift shop selling regional handicrafts and books.

Taxidermy

It's hardly for everyone, but taxidermy is a flourishing art in Delaware County; several award-winning taxidermists live in the Delhi area. Inside their shops you'll find mounts of fish and animals, some available for purchase, as well as pelts and leather goods. Among the shops are **Borow's Taxidermy** (Rte. 28 three miles northwest of Delhi, 607/746-2560) and **Perkins Taxidermy** (Arbor Hill Rd., off Rte. 28 south of Delhi, 607/746-3205).

Food

A good spot for lunch or a simple dinner is **Angelos Family Restaurant** (82 Main St., 607/746-7171). On the menu are many Greek specialties such as spinach pie and moussaka, along with sandwiches, salads, and pasta dishes.

EAST MEREDITH
Hanford Mills

Heading north out of Delhi on narrow, twisting Elk Creek Road (off Main Street), you'll pass through more wooded countryside before coming to the second major museum in Delaware County, Hanford Mills (County Rds. 10 and 12, 607/278-5744 or 800/295-4992, www.hanfordmills.org, 10 A.M.–5 P.M. daily May–Oct., adults $6, seniors $5, children under 12 $3). Sitting beside a pond, Hanford is a group of weathered red buildings that once provided area residents with everything from tools to feed. Within its confines are a sawmill, gristmill, feed mill, woodworking shop, and hardware store. Between 1898 and 1927, the complex even generated the region's first electricity.

Today, Hanford Mills has been meticulously restored to look much as it did around 1900. The toasty aroma of freshly cut wood fills the air as interpreters demonstrate everything from an enormous circular saw and early generator to a machine that cuts broom handles. Over 20 vintage machines are demonstrated in all, while in the center of things churns a massive waterwheel surrounded by whirring gears and belts.

West Kortright Centre

Down the street from Hanford Mills is the West Kortright Centre (Turnpike Rd., 607/278-5454, www.wkc.org), an oasis for the arts. Housed in a handsome 1850s Greek Revival church originally built by Scotch-Irish immigrants, the center is filled with rich stained-glass windows, polished wooden pews, and unusual kerosene chandeliers. May–November, the center sponsors special events ranging from jazz concerts to chicken barbecues to gallery exhibits. Many of its performers are well known; names from the past have included Dakota Staton, Kenny Neal, and Ping Chong. Call for art gallery hours.

To reach the center from Hanford Mills, take Elk Creek Road south to Turnpike Road and turn left.

WESTERN DELAWARE COUNTY
Hamden and Walton

Route 10 west of Delhi leads through hilly dairy country to the hamlet of Hamden, where a creaky **covered bridge** just north of Route 10 is usually lined with fly fishermen. Beyond Hamden is the town of Walton, where the popular **Delaware County Fair** (607/746-2281) takes place on the Walton Fairgrounds in August.

The unusual **Octagon Farm Bed and Breakfast** (34055 Rte. 10, Walton, 607/865-7416, $80–120 d) is housed in a historic brick octagon house built in 1855; nearby is a working farm and the Octagonal Farm Market. The B&B holds four guestrooms with shared baths.

Downsville and Vicinity

Five miles southeast of Walton off Route 206 lies **Bear Spring Mountain State Park** (607/865-6989, parking $8), holding a lake, beach, bathhouses, boat rentals, hiking trails, and 41 campsites. Call 800/456-CAMP for camping reservations.

Beyond the park is the rustic village of Downsville, at the western end of Pepacton Reservoir, near the dam. Here you'll find another **covered bridge,** this one a 174-foot span built in 1854. Canoes for paddling the East Branch of the Delaware can be rented at **Al's Sport Store** (Rte. 206 in the village, 607/363-7740), which also offers pick-up service.

The **Victorian Rose B&B** (Main St.,

607/363-7838, $85 d) is a lovely Victorian home offering four guest rooms tastefully furnished with antiques. Breakfast, an afternoon tea, and evening refreshments are included in the room rates.

Open for lunch and dinner, the **C Schoolhouse Inn and Restaurant** (Upper Main St., 607/363-7814) serves standard American fare in an old schoolhouse with original tin ceilings and oak floors. The former first-grade classroom is now a popular bar; average dinner entrée $13.

Nearby Shinhopple is home to the **Peaceful Valley Bluegrass Festival** (Rte. 30, 607/746-2281), which takes place in mid-July. This is one of the top bluegrass festivals in the Northeast. It draws about 7,000 fans, many of whom camp at **Peaceful Valley Campground** (Rte.

30, 607/363-2211), which also offers canoe rentals and paddler shuttle service.

Deposit

At the far western edge of Delaware County along the West Branch of the Delaware is Deposit, a small village once known as an early lumbering town and later as a resort. Many fine old homes still line the streets. Housed in an 1868 Italianate bank is the **Deposit Community Historical Society Museum** (Second St., 607/467-4422, call for hours).

At August's **Lumberjack Festival** (Riverside Park, 607/746-2281), you'll see all sorts of unusual events, including a beard-growing contest, cherry-picking contest, and open lumberjack competitions.

Sports and Recreation

FISHING

Fishing in the Catskills is legendary. World-famous trout streams—including the Beaverkill, Willowemoc, Esopus, and Schoharie—are located here, along with six reservoirs and the Hudson River. Guides to Catskill fishing can be picked up at tourist centers. Fishing licenses are mandatory for everyone over age 16 and can be obtained in sporting-goods stores, bait shops, and town offices.

For a daily report on fishing conditions along the Beaverkill and Willowemoc April–July, call 607/498-5350.

HIKING AND OTHER OUTDOOR ACTIVITIES

More than 200 miles of hiking trails, leading to the summits of over 20 peaks, weave through Catskill Forest Preserve. Surprisingly, unlike the over-hiked Adirondack trails, most of these are underused.

The trails are maintained by the **Department of Environmental Conservation**

(625 Broadway, Albany, NY 12233, www.dec .state.ny.us), whose excellent website offers extensive information about the preserve. Free maps and other publications can be ordered through the site, but serious hikers will want to supplement these with maps from the **New York–New Jersey Trail Conference** (201/512-9348, www.nynjtc.com). The conference publishes the excellent "Catskill Trails" five-map set and "Shawangunk Trails" four-map set.

A few popular day hikes are outlined above. For more detailed information and other suggestions, pick up a copy of *Fifty Hikes in the Hudson Valley* by Kick, McMartin, and Long. The book covers the Catskills and is available in area bookstores or by contacting Countryman Press (800/245-4151).

For more information about recreation along the Delaware River, contact the **National Park Service Center** (41 Main St., Narrowsburg, 845/252-3947 or 845/252-7100 [recorded report on river conditions]).

Getting There and Around

The only real way to explore the Catskills is by car. But public transportation can get you into the area if you don't have your own vehicle.

Adirondack-Pine Hill Trailways (212/967-2900 or 800/225-6815) offers regular bus service to sections of Ulster, Greene, and Delaware Counties. Sullivan County is served by **Shortline** (212/736-4700 or 800/631-8405).

Traveling up the east bank of the Hudson just across from the Catskills are **Metro-North Commuter Railroad** (212/532-4900 or 800/638-7646) and **Amtrak** (800/872-7245). Metro-North travels between New York City and Poughkeepsie. Amtrak makes stops in Poughkeepsie, Rhinebeck, and Hudson.

The closest large airport is the Albany County Airport, about an hour north of the Catskills. Major airlines flying into Albany include **American** (800/433-7300), **Delta** (800/221-1212), **Northwest** (800/225-2525), and **United** (800/241-6522).

Information and Services

For general information, contact the **Catskill Association for Tourism Services** (Box 400, Catskill 12414, 800/355-CATS, www.catskillregiontoday.com).

Each county has its own tourist information center, as listed below. Most are open 9 A.M.–5 P.M. Monday–Friday, and some have weekend hours in summer and fall.

Ulster County Tourism (10 Westbrook Lane, Kingston 12401, 845/340-3566 or 800/342-5826, www.ulstertourism.info)

Greene County Tourism (Rte. 23B, Catskill 12414, 518/943-3223 or 800/355-CATS, www.greenetourism.com)

Sullivan County Visitors Association (100 North St., Monticello 12701, 845/794-3000, ext. 5010, or 800/882-CATS, www.scva.net)

Delaware County Chamber of Commerce (114 Main St., Delhi 13753, 607/746-2281, www.delawarecounty.org)

CENTRAL NEW YORK

Central New York is a jumbled mix of dying industrial cities, wooded hillsides, and wide pastoral vistas blanketed with farmers' fields. The land here is a gently rolling plateau, laced with enormous rivers—the Hudson, the Mohawk, the Susquehanna, and the Chenango. The Mohawk is named after the Mohawk Indians, an Iroquois tribe.

Sophisticated Albany, the state capital, sits near the eastern edge of the region, just south of the confluence of the Hudson and Mohawk. The oldest city in New York, Albany offers an especially interesting collection of architectural sites, as well as the fine New York State Museum and Albany Institute of History and Art. North of Albany lie Troy and Schenectady, a pair of faded, relic-strewn industrial towns evocative of the not-so-distant past.

Through Albany and the adjoining Mohawk River Valley runs Route 20, America's longest highway. Once known as the Great Western Turnpike, from the 1780s to the 1820s Route 20 was *the* major gateway to the West. Land-hungry settlers on their way to the Great Lakes Basin and elsewhere passed through here in droves.

With the completion of the Erie Canal in 1825, the Mohawk River Valley took on even greater importance. Hundreds of factories producing everything from velocipedes to baby food sprang up along its banks, employing thousands of Southern and Eastern European immigrants. The valley became the

COURTESY OF ALBANY COUNTY CONVENTION AND VISITORS BUREAU

HIGHLIGHTS

New York State Museum: The oldest and largest state museum in the country is packed with life-sized dioramas and historical artifacts documenting all aspects of New York history (page 338).

New York State Capitol Building: The centerpiece of the stunning castle-like edifice is its stone staircase, hand-carved with 300 tiny faces, each different from the next (page 338).

The Stockade District: First settled by the Dutch in 1661, the district contains architectural landmarks of many styles and periods (page 350).

National Baseball Hall of Fame and Museum: The homage to America's favorite pastime is packed to the busting point with exhibits covering every aspect of the sport (page 357).

Fenimore Art Museum: Run by the New York State Historical Association, the museum holds the state's premier collection of fine art, folk art, and Native American art (page 360).

Sharon Springs: A Victorian-era town once known for its sulfur springs and grand old hotels, is now poised between neglect and gentrification (page 365).

Howe Caverns: Deep inside one of New York's oldest visitor attractions is an extensive labyrinth of cathedral-like caves filled with shimmering stalactites, stalagmites, and flowstones (page 365).

Iroquois Indian Museum: Designed in the shape of a longhouse, the fine, state-of-the-art museum pays as much attention to the Iroquois' present as it does to their past (page 366).

Munson-Williams-Proctor Institute: The Philip Johnson–designed building contains more than 5,000 works of art by the likes of Picasso, Dali, Pollock, Moore, and Burchfield. A highlight is Thomas Cole's *Voyage of Life* (page 368).

Cazenovia: The historic village sitting on the edge of a quiet lake by the same name holds three grand inns and the Lorenzo State Historic Site (page 376).

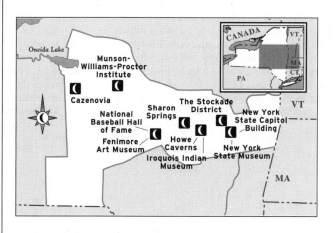

LOOK FOR **(** TO FIND RECOMMENDED SIGHTS, ACTIVITIES, DINING, AND LODGING.

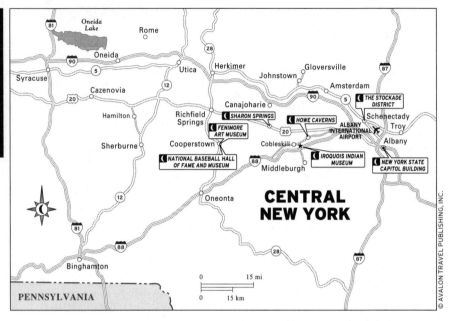

© AVALON TRAVEL PUBLISHING, INC.

most densely populated area upstate. Today, the valley is relatively sparsely populated but is still home to a few working factories, along with historic villages, Revolutionary War sites, and Erie Canal artifacts.

South of the Mohawk Valley lie Schoharie, Otsego, Madison, and Chenango Counties, sleepy lands of fertile farms, one-stoplight villages, lakes, and forests. In the center lies Cooperstown, site of the National Baseball Hall of Fame and former home to James Fenimore Cooper. Cooper set many of his novels in Central New York, accounting for the area's nickname, Leatherstocking Country. The term refers to the leather leggings worn by early Yankee settlers.

PLANNING YOUR TIME

Most travelers will probably want to spend about three days in the **Cooperstown** area, home to three world-class museums, luxurious inns and B&Bs, good restaurants, and much scenic beauty. American history buffs could then spend another day or two in **Albany,** founded by the Dutch in the early 1600s, and filled with architectural gems from many different periods of New York history, along with cultural attractions. Lovers of the off-beat could hopscotch through the region instead, stopping in such villages as **Sharon Springs** (once a grand spa resort), **Chittenango** (birthplace of L. Frank Baum, author of *The Wizard of Oz*), and **Oneida** (once home to the utopian Oneida Community).

Albany

From a distance, Albany may look like just another average, midsize city clustered around a handful of high-rise office buildings, but beneath its apparently calm surface you'll find a surprisingly complex soul. Albany, as William Kennedy writes in *O Albany!*, is "as various as the American psyche itself, of which it was truly a crucible."

The oldest city in New York and one of the oldest in the nation, Albany is located at the head of the navigable portion of the Hudson River. Henry Hudson arrived in 1609, and by the mid-1600s the Dutch settlement of Fort Orange was a flourishing trading post.

Albany was an early home to writers Bret Harte, Herman Melville, and Henry James, whose grandfather William founded the family dynasty here. President Chester A. Arthur is buried here; Presidents Martin Van Buren, Millard Fillmore, Grover Cleveland, Theodore Roosevelt, and Franklin Roosevelt all got their starts in the city, along with a number of less-upstanding citizens. Most notorious of these was gangster Jack "Legs" Diamond, murdered in 1931 in a rooming house at 67 Dove Street. Albany is also home to a large branch of the State University of New York (SUNY).

As the state capital, Albany is dominated by the government. Come here at lunchtime when the legislature is in session and you'll see thousands of workers hurrying out for a sandwich and a few moments of sun. Though everyone seems harmless enough, this is a city notorious for political wheeling and dealing. When asked to explain Albany, one assemblywoman said, "Read Swift."

HISTORY
Early Dutch Rule

In 1630 Dutchman Kiliaen Van Rensselaer bought 700,000 acres of land with Fort Orange at its center, establishing the patroonship of Rensselaerswyck. Under this Dutch system, a patroon was granted a sort of mini-kingdom in return for settling at least 50 people upon his land. Van Rensselaer brought over hundreds of settlers, and Rensselaerswyck soon grew into the most successful patroonship in the New World.

Dutch rule ended in 1664, but Albany retained its Dutch character for the next 130 years. Banker Gorham A. Worth, visiting Albany in 1790, stated the town was "indeed Dutch, in all its moods and tenses; thoroughly and inveterately Dutch. ... The people were Dutch, the horses were Dutch, and even the dogs were Dutch."

The Boom Years

Around 1800 Albany began developing into a major transportation hub. The world's first successful steamboat run—Robert Fulton's *Clermont* in 1807—ended in Albany, and soon boats were chugging into the harbor daily.

The Erie Canal was completed in 1825, linking the Great Lakes to the Atlantic, and the city's population doubled in five years. Shortly thereafter came the railroads, as Albany blossomed into upstate New York's prime financial center and a major link between East and West. Cattleyards established in West Albany handled up to two million animals a year.

Large groups of Irish immigrants settled in Albany while building the Erie Canal, and thousands more Irish and Germans arrived with the coming of the Industrial Revolution. Soon factories manufacturing everything from checkers and dominoes to textiles and woolens lined the Hudson.

The 20th Century

Albany's prosperity continued through the first half of the 20th century. In the late 1930s, nearly 150 passenger trains and 90 freight trains passed through the city daily, and the port handled cargoes of 250 ocean-going vessels a year.

During this same period, Albany was prominent in national politics. Theodore Roosevelt,

Alfred Smith, and Franklin Roosevelt all ran for the U.S. presidency after serving as New York State governors.

Albany fell on hard times in the 1950s when, like many other Northeastern cities, its manufacturing base began to decline and its downtown population moved to the suburbs. The city seemed well on its way to becoming a windswept slum, when in 1962 Gov. Nelson Rockefeller proposed building "the most spectacularly beautiful seat of government in the world"—the Nelson A. Rockefeller Empire State Plaza.

Legend has it Rockefeller conceived of the plaza during a visit from Princess Beatrix of the Netherlands in 1959: It humiliated him to drive royalty through the moldering capital. The plaza eventually cost at least $1 billion—an extraordinary sum for the time—and displaced 3,600 households, many of them poor. All this caused much controversy at the time, but the plaza has been largely responsible for the rejuvenation of Albany's downtown.

ORIENTATION

Albany is an easy city to navigate. Traffic is generally light, with several major interstates

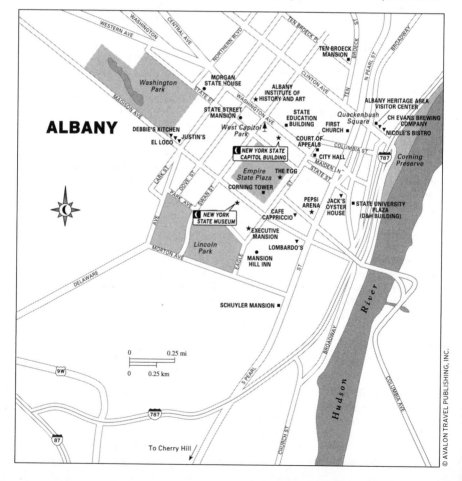

providing easy routes around the region. Most visitor sights are located in or near downtown, which hugs the west bank of the Hudson. The recently constructed Hudson River Way is a pedestrian bridge connecting downtown Albany to the Albany Riverfront Park and Corning Preserve.

Albany is centered on the Empire State Plaza and State Capitol Building, which sit perched side by side on a hill. From here, the downtown slopes eastward to the river.

Information and Services

The best place to pick up information is at the **Albany Heritage Area Visitor Center** (25 Quackenbush Sq., at Broadway and Clinton Ave., 518/434-0405 or 800/258-3582, 9 A.M.–9 P.M. Mon.–Fri. and 10 A.M.–4 P.M. Sat.–Sun.). In the same complex is the **Albany County Convention & Visitors Bureau** (518/434-1217 or 800/258-3582, www.albany.org, 9 A.M.–5 P.M. Mon.–Fri.).

Tours

The **Albany Heritage Area Visitor Center** (25 Quackenbush Sq., 518/434-0405, www.albany.org) offers a variety of guided tours April–October, along with free walking-tour maps of downtown. The new **Albany Aqua Ducks** (518/462-3825) offer combination land-water tours aboard the state's only amphibious vehicles; the tours leave from the Visitor Center and reservations are required.

One of Albany's foremost attractions is its architecture. A few highlights are mentioned below; for a thorough, self-guided architectural tour, pick up a copy of *Albany Architecture,* edited by Diana S. Waite (Mount Ida Press, 518/426-5935). The book outlines eight architectural tours and is available in most Albany bookstores.

SIGHTS
Empire State Plaza

Dominating downtown Albany is the Empire State Plaza (between Eagle and Swan Sts., Madison Ave. and State St.), the extravagant brainchild of Nelson Rockefeller. An enormous marble platform sitting atop a hill, the plaza covers 98.5 acres and includes 11 buildings, among them the Legislative Building, Justice Building, and the Empire Center at the Egg—a round, whimsical performing-arts center. Through the middle of the plaza knifes a long reflecting pool surrounded by modern sculpture.

Visitors to the plaza can relax by the reflecting pool (which becomes a public skating rink in winter), ascend to the 42nd-floor **observation deck** (open 9 A.M.–2:30 P.M. daily, free admission) in the Corning Tower, and tour the plaza's fine art collection of 92 modern sculptures and paintings by the likes of Alexander Calder and David Smith. Maps are available at the **Visitors Assistance Office** (Concourse level, north end of the Plaza, 518/474-2418), which also offers tours of the Plaza at 11 A.M. and 1 P.M. Monday–Friday.

WEIRD, WONDERFUL, OFF-THE-BEATEN PATH CENTRAL NEW YORK

The Big Dog, Albany: A 25-foot-high, four-ton statue of Nipper sits atop the former Victor Company factory.

Uncle Sam's Grave, Troy: The inspiration for the cartoon-figure symbol of the United States was a meatpacker named Sam Wilson.

Herkimer Diamond Mines, Herkimer: Hunt for "diamonds" in the former bed of the Devonian Sea.

Petrified Creatures Museum, Richfield Springs: Dig for ancient fossils in the former bed of the Devonian Sea.

The yellow brick road, Chittenango: Built to honor L. Frank Baum, author of *The Wizard of Oz.*

The Mansion House, Oneida: Once home to the Perfectionists, a long-lived Utopian society founded by John Humphrey Noyes.

New York State Museum

On Madison Avenue at the southern end of the Empire State Plaza is the oldest and largest state museum (518/474-5877, 9:30 A.M.–5 P.M. daily, free admission) in the country. Spread out over a maze of high-ceilinged rooms, it's packed with life-size dioramas, sound and video shows, historical artifacts, and scientific specimens of all types.

The museum is divided into three major exhibit areas: New York Metropolis, Adirondack Wilderness, and Upstate New York Native American Peoples. The Adirondack Wilderness exhibit is especially impressive. Here, in a vast darkened room, you hear the sounds of running water and birdsong before turning the corner to enter a "prehistoric wilderness." Other exhibits re-create a logging operation, canoeing expedition, blast furnace, and black-bear habitat. In the New York Metropolis section is an exhibit on the September 11 terrorist attack on the World Trade Center.

New York State Capitol Building

On State Street at the northern end of the Empire State Plaza stands the stunning State Capitol Building. Begun in 1867, the castle-like edifice required 32 years and $25 million to complete—indeed, it was never entirely finished, as the original plans called for a dome and central rotunda. A clutch of architects, including Thomas Fuller, Henry Hobson Richardson, and Frederick Law Olmsted participated in the design, which explains its riotous hodgepodge of architectural styles.

Capitol tours lead visitors past the gold-leaf walls of the Senate Chamber and the marble columns of the Assembly Chamber before culminating at the "Million Dollar Staircase." Here 300 tiny faces carved by mostly Italian stonecutters smile, glare, or stare at passersby. Seventy-seven of the faces are of such famous men as Abraham Lincoln and Walt Whitman, but most are anonymous, and each is different from the next.

The free tours are offered Monday–Friday at 10 A.M., noon, 2 P.M., and 3 P.M.; and Saturday–Sunday at 11 A.M., 1 P.M., and 3 P.M. Reservations

are recommended; call 518/474-2418. Free self-guided audio tours are also available. Be prepared to pass security clearance and present an ID.

Albany Institute of History & Art

One of the oldest museums in the United States, founded in 1791, the Albany Institute (125 Albany Ave., 518/463-4478, www.albany-institute.org, 10 A.M.–5 P.M. Wed.–Sat., noon–5 P.M. Sun., adults $7, seniors and students $5, children 6–12 $3) is housed in an elegant beaux arts building and contains some wonderful gems, including many paintings by artists of the Hudson River School. Early works of American portraiture are in the museum's collection, along with Dutch ceramics, Albany-made silver, and New York–made furniture. Changing exhibits on the Hudson Valley and Capital District are also featured.

Albany Heritage Area Visitor Center

A good place to learn about Albany's history and culture is in this large, refurbished water pumping station (25 Quackenbush Sq., at Broadway and Clinton Ave., 518/434-0405, 10 A.M.–4 P.M. daily, free admission), which contains informative exhibits on everything from the city's ethnic heritage to its industrial past. Find here, for example, the tale of the modern (celluloid) billiard ball, invented in Albany in 1868.

Albany is part of the New York State Heritage Areas program, which includes loosely delineated historic parks linked by a common theme. The Albany theme is business and capital. Also in the center is the **Henry Hudson Planetarium,** featuring a changing schedule of programs throughout the year.

Albany Center Galleries

One of Albany's foremost art galleries, the Albany Center Galleries (161 Washington Ave., in the Albany Public Library, 518/462-4775, www.albanycentergalleries.org, noon–5 P.M. Tues.–Sat.) has been the site of more than 100 major exhibitions since its opening in 1977. Numerous special events are also presented here.

COURTESY OF HISTORIC HUDSON VALLEY

The Albany Institute of History & Art is one of the oldest museums in the United States.

Albany Riverfront Park and Corning Preserve

From downtown Albany, walk across the **Hudson River Way,** a pedestrian bridge, to reach these two Hudson River parks. In them you'll find walking/biking trails, picnic tables, exercise stations, and panoramic views of the Hudson, often busy with fishing boats, college crew teams, private yachts heading to and from the Erie Canal, and, at times, the Half Moon, an exact replica of the ship Henry Hudson used to reach Albany in 1609. During the summer, an 800-seat amphitheater presents free concerts. At the Corning Preserve's north end is a restaurant on a barge.

The entrance to the Hudson River Way is off Broadway not far from the visitors center; note the lampposts, each of which tells about a different episode in Albany history.

New York State Executive Mansion

One block south of the Empire State Plaza is the governor's mansion (138 Eagle St.), open to the public by reserved tour only. An impressive Italianate building with a wraparound porch, the mansion dates to 1856, when it was constructed as a private residence. The state purchased the property in 1877, and each successive governor has put his stamp on it: Theodore Roosevelt built a gym, FDR sunk a pool, animal-lover Al Smith installed a zoo.

To arrange a tour of the mansion, call visitor services, Empire State Plaza (518/473-7521). Tours are offered on Thursday afternoons only, September–June; closed July–August.

Schuyler Mansion

Perched on a hill that once offered a great view of the Hudson is this gracious 1761 Georgian mansion (32 Catherine St. at Elizabeth, 518/434-0834, 10 A.M.–5 P.M. Wed.–Sun. Apr.–Oct., adults $4, seniors $3, children 5–12 $1). Now a State Historic Site, the home was built by Philip Schuyler, a leading Albany citizen who served as a general during the Revolutionary War. Daniel Webster once honored Schuyler as "second only to

A SHORT WALKING TOUR OF DOWNTOWN ALBANY

From the Albany Visitors Center at Quackenbush Square, walk two blocks to the corner of Clinton Avenue and North Pearl Street to view the sleek **Palace Theatre,** designed by noted movie palace architect John Eberson in 1929. A jewel of the RKO chain, built at a cost of $3 million, the Palace has housed the Albany Symphony Orchestra since 1931.

Cross Clinton Avenue to Clinton Square; the young Herman Melville lived in **No. 3 Clinton Square** when his first satirical sketches were published in the local *Albany Microscope.*

Next to the square, at North Pearl and Orange Streets, stands the graceful **First Church of Albany,** designed by famed Albany architect Philip Hooker in 1798. The church features the oldest pulpit and weathercock in America, as well as Tiffany stained-glass windows.

Two blocks south, at 79 North Pearl Street, stands the former **Kenmore Hotel,** now an office building. Designed in 1878 by Edward Ogden, the hotel was originally owned by Adam Blake, a wealthy African American who began his career as a waiter. The city's finest hotel for many years, the Kenmore hosted all the big bands of the 1920s, including Duke Ellington's and Benny Goodman's, and was a favorite hangout of gangster Legs Diamond.

Heading west up **Columbia Street,** you'll pass a row of fine residences built between 1820 and the early 1900s. On the hill at Columbia and Lodge stands the handsome **Albany County Courthouse,** built in 1916.

Continue past the county courthouse and turn left on Eagle Street to reach the **New York State Court of Appeals.** Designed by Henry Rector in 1831, the structure features a fine domed rotunda and an even finer oak-paneled courtroom. Across the street is **Academy Park,** once home to Albany Academy, where Herman Melville and Henry James, Sr. attended school.

One block further south on Eagle Street is **City Hall,** Henry Hobson Richardson's stunning 1882 Romanesque work. The tower was built to store the city archives, and features a 60-bell carillon.

City Hall provides a good view of the State Capitol and the 1912 **State Education Building.** The south side of the latter structure features 36 striking Corinthian columns—the longest colonnade in the United States.

Another block south of City Hall is **State Street,** an unusually wide thoroughfare dating back to Albany's days as a walled stockade. Most of the fort's churches and public buildings then stood in the middle of this street; today, it's lined with 17 banks in four blocks.

Walk down the State Street hill past the banks and **St. Peter's Episcopal Church** to Broadway. To your right stands the former **Delaware & Hudson Building and Albany Evening Journal Building,** a magnificent 660-foot-long structure with a lavish central tower. Designed in 1914 in the Flemish Gothic style, the building is considered architect Marcus Reynold's masterpiece. It now houses the administrative offices of the State University of New York.

Left of the State Street–Broadway intersection, at the corner of Maiden Lane, is yet another splendid building – the art deco **U.S. Post Office,** built in the 1930s. A frieze along the top recounts the story of the U.S. mail delivery system; inside you'll find a long ceiling mural covered with maps of the continents.

At the corner of Broadway and Columbia Street stands the former **Union Station.** Built in 1900, the station was once an important transportation hub linking the New York Central to the Boston and Albany Railroad.

Washington in the services he performed for his country," but he was relieved of his duties and court-martialed for ordering the evacuation of Fort Ticonderoga. A probable victim of political infighting, Schuyler was eventually acquitted, though he resigned his post.

The Schuyler mansion hosted all the major players of the day—Benjamin Franklin, Benedict Arnold, George Washington, Aaron Burr—and served as a prison for Gen. Burgoyne following the British surrender at Saratoga. Schuyler's daughter, Elizabeth, married Alexander Hamilton here.

Historic Cherry Hill

To the south of downtown Albany stands the homey, Colonial-era Cherry Hill (523 S. Pearl St., at 1st Ave., 518/434-4791, www.historic-cherryhill.org, 10 A.M.–4 P.M. Tues.–Sat. and 1–4 P.M. Sun. July–Sept., last tour at 3 P.M., call for spring and fall hours, adults $4, seniors

$3, students $2, children 6–17 $1). Built in 1787 by Philip and Mary Van Rensselaer, the house was home to five generations of the Van Rensselaer and Rankin families; the last member died in 1963.

The frugal Van Rensselaers had a hard time throwing anything away, so inside you'll find an odd assortment of furnishings from all five generations. Among the highlights are early Dutch tiles, a striking sleigh bed, turn-of-the-20th-century swimming trunks, postcards from the 1920s, and an early Castro convertible. The kitchen is equipped with both a Colonial-era wall oven and a freestanding gas stove.

Lark Street

Two blocks west of the Empire State Plaza is 19th-century Lark Street. The bohemian hub of Albany, Lark Street is lined with an eclectic array of small shops, ethnic restaurants, and

Historic Cherry Hill, a Georgian-style home built in 1787 by Philip Van Rensselaer

nightclubs. Most are located in the eight blocks between Madison and Washington Avenues.

Lark Street sits on the edge of Center Square, a prosperous residential neighborhood notable for its fine architecture. Some of the best examples stand along State Street between Lark Street and the Empire State Plaza. In these two short blocks you'll find one opulent 19th-century home after another, many designed by Albany architects Charles Nichols, Albert Fuller, and Ernest Hoffman.

Washington Park and State Street

Continue another block west of Lark Street to Washington Park, a lush green oasis designed by Frederick Law Olmsted and Calvert Vaux in the 1870s. Carved throughout its 81 acres are curved roads, wooded glades, open meadows, ornate gardens, and skinny Washington Lake. On its shores stands the Lake House, an extravagant terra-cotta affair with pink terrazzo floors and wrought-iron chandeliers.

The opulence of State Street continues along the north side of the park. Highlights include No. 397, designed by Henry Hobson Richardson, and No. 441, the work of William Ross Proctor.

Ten Broeck Mansion

On the north side of Albany, in a neighborhood known as Arbor Hill, stands an imperial Federal-style home (9 Ten Broeck Pl. between Ten Broeck and N. Swan Sts., 518/436-9826, 10 A.M.–4 P.M. Thurs.–Fri. and 1–4 P.M. Sat.–Sun. May–Dec., adults $5, seniors and students $4, children 5–12 $3), built for Abraham Ten Broeck and his wife Elizabeth Van Rensselaer in 1797–98. Ten Broeck served as a general in the Continental Army and later as state senator, judge, and mayor of Albany.

Now owned by the Albany County Historical Association, the mansion contains a fine collection of period furniture, and showcases changing historic exhibits. In the basement hides a snug wine cellar that wasn't rediscovered until the 1970s. Its rare contents were sold for a whopping $42,000, and the proceeds used to restore the house.

THE BLACK WIDOW OF CHERRY HILL

The story of the Cherry Hill murder began in August 1826 when Jesse Strang, a man who'd feigned his own murder to abandon his family and flee to Albany, met Elsie Lansing Whipple at Bates' Tavern. Elsie, a relative of the Van Rensselaers, was 24 at the time, and unhappily married to engineer John Whipple. She'd already tried to poison her husband twice, to no effect.

Jesse was hired as a handyman at Cherry Hill, home of the Whipples. He and Elsie plunged into a secret love affair, passing notes in the halls and making love in the hayloft.

On May 27, Jesse bought a rifle, climbed into a shed next door to the mansion, and fatally shot John Whipple through the window. Elsie was downstairs placidly smoking a pipe.

Soon after the murder, Jesse's suspicious behavior led to his arrest. He confessed, but blamed Elsie for putting him up to it. Both were tried, but only Jesse was found guilty. Writes Louis C. Jones in *The Murder at Cherry Hill* (Cherry Hill Publications): "The Albany Establishment had closed ranks, however distasteful it may have been to do so, and saved one of their number from the disgrace of a public hanging."

Jesse was hanged on August 24, 1827–the last criminal in Albany publicly hanged. Between 30,000 and 40,000 people watched the gruesome event.

Afterward, Elsie moved to New York City, where she remarried. Her second husband died under mysterious circumstances; she then moved back upstate, and disappeared somewhere in the area of Onondaga.

"Nipper"

All along Broadway in northern Albany hulk old factory buildings dating back to the city's era of industrial activity. A highlight is the former **RTA Building** (991 Broadway, at Loudonville Rd.). RTA was a distributor of RCA electrical appliances and on the building's roof sits a 25-foot-high, four-ton statue of Nipper, the canine symbol of the RCA-owned Victor Company. Nipper's head is cocked to the side and he wears a quizzical expression, as if to ask, what am I still doing here? The statue was built in Chicago about 1858 and shipped in five sections on railroad flat cars.

Shaker Settlement

On the western outskirts of Albany near the airport is America's first Shaker settlement, established in 1776 (875 Watervliet Rd. [Rt. 155], off Albany-Shaker Rd. [Rte. 151], 518/456-7890, 9:30 A.M.–4 P.M. Tues.–Sat., free admission). A religious sect founded in England in 1758, the Shakers later established 24 American communities from Maine to Florida (see sidebar on the Shakers in *The Hudson Valley* chapter).

In Albany eight sturdy, clean-lined Shaker buildings still stand, grouped around a crossroads. Seven are used by a geriatric nursing home, giving the place an off-limits feel. But the splendid 1848 Meeting House has been converted into a visitors center where you'll find a small exhibit area, gift shop offering Shaker crafts, and the large hall where the Shakers once held their meetings. The bleachers in back were set aside for the "World's People"—nonbelievers—who often came to the meetings to watch and listen to the Shakers' music. Today the hall is used for Shaker-related concerts, workshops, and crafts shows.

Free walking-tour maps are available in the gift shop. Nearby is the cemetery where the sect's founder, Mother Ann Lee, and 444 others are buried.

ENTERTAINMENT

The city's best entertainment sources are the Thursday and Sunday editions of the *Times-Union* (518/454-5694) and *Metroland* (518/463-2500), a free alternative weekly.

Performing Arts

The Egg (Empire State Plaza, Madison Ave. and Swan St., 518/473-1845), named for its shape, is the capital's premier arts venue. It houses an 880-seat main theater and a 500-seat recital hall; both present a wide range of music, theater, and dance.

The **Capital Repertory Theatre** (111 N. Pearl St., 518/445-7469) presents classical, contemporary, and world-premier works October–June. The company performs in the 258-seat Market Theater, formerly a grocery store.

Recently restored and updated, the 1931 **Palace Theatre** (19 Clinton Ave., 518/465-4663), which seats 2,800, was once an opulent movie palace. Today, it's home to the Albany Symphony Orchestra, and host to touring concert acts, Broadway shows, and movies.

The tiny **Albany Civic Theater** (235 2nd Ave., 518/462-1297), occupying a converted turn-of-the-century firehouse, presents four theater productions every year. Each runs but three weeks and tickets sell out fast.

The **Pepsi Arena** (51 South Pearl St., 518/487-2000) is a multi-purpose facility with adaptable seating arrangements that can accommodate crowds ranging in size from 6,000 to 17,500. Concerts, family shows, sporting events, and trade shows are presented.

Comedy Works (141 State St., 518/689-0490) features nationally recognized comedy acts Thursday–Saturday; dinner is available before the show.

Film

Spectrum Eight Theaters (290 Delaware Ave., 518/449-8995) presents art, foreign, commercial, and independent films.

Clubs and Nightlife

Popular **Jillian's** (59 North Pearl St, 518/432-1997) is a three-story dance club inside an entertainment complex. On **Lark Street,** long Albany's center for nightlife, you'll find a good blues club, the **Lionheart Blues Cafe** (258 Lark St., 518/436-9530), and **Justin's** (301 Lark St., 518/436-7008), a popular restaurant and singles bar with weekend jazz.

The intimate **Valentine's** (17 New Scotland Ave., 518/432-6572) is a top club for local rock. The **Lark Tavern** (453 Madison

Ave., 518/463-9779) hosts local rock, reggae, and "psycho-country" bands.

Another good blues spot is **Pauly's Hotel** (337 Central Ave., 518/426-0828), which bills itself as Albany's oldest tavern. For a drink in a friendly neighborhood bar, step into **McCaffrey's** (332 S. Allen St., at New Scotland Ave., 518/435-9537), a long, creaky, hole-in-the-wall that dates back to 1901.

EVENTS

Albany celebrates its Dutch heritage with the **Tulip Festival** and **Pinksterfest** (518/434-1217), held concurrently on the second weekend of May. Pinksterfest commemorates the day Fort Orange's African American slaves were freed by the Dutch.

Throughout the summer, **free concerts** and other special events are staged at the Empire State Plaza (518/474-2418). The **Park Playhouse** (518/434-2035) presents free plays and other events at the Lake House in Washington Park in July and August.

The fairgrounds in the nearby village of Altamont host some of the region's top special events. Among them are the **Old Songs Festival of Traditional Music and Dance** in June, the 100-year-old **Altamont Fair** in August, and the **Capital District Scottish Games** in early September. Call 518/434-1217 or visit www.albany.org for more information.

RECREATION

The **Hudson-Mohawk Bikeway** follows the Mohawk and Hudson Rivers for about 60 miles, from Albany north to Rotterdam Junction and east to St. Johnsville. Maps are available at the Albany Heritage Visitors Center. In Albany you can access the trail from the Corning Preserve.

Dutch Apple Cruises (137 Broadway, 518/463-0220) and **Capt. JP** (518/270-1901) offer sightseeing, lunch, brunch, and dinner cruises along the Hudson April–October.

ACCOMMODATIONS

One of the best—and for many years, only— places to stay in the heart of downtown is the **Mansion Hill Inn** (115 Philip St., 518/465-2038, www.mansionhill.com, $165–195 d, with breakfast), a friendly hostelry consisting of several historic buildings built around a picturesque courtyard, and an excellent restaurant (see Food, below). All the rooms are completely modernized, with queen-size beds, cable TV, and full private baths.

Also a good choice is the elegant, 19th-century **Morgan State House** (393 State St., 518/462-6780, www.statehouse.com, $160–260 d) on Washington Park. The B&B's signature is its feather mattresses and down comforters.

In the Center Square district stands the neoclassical **State Street Mansion** (518/462-6780, www.statestreetmansion.com, $105–175 d). This 1881 townhouse offers a half dozen elegant guest rooms, all with private bath.

Near the airport is Albany's foremost hotel, the **Desmond Hotel and Conference Center** (660 Albany-Shaker Rd., 518/869-8100, www.desmondhotels.com, $145–185 d), a charming hotel-inn filled with period furnishings, artwork, and rich dark-wood paneling. Many rooms feature balconies or private patios; two heated indoor pools, a health club, and several restaurants are on-site.

FOOD
Historic Albany

Just north of downtown reigns the yellow-and-maroon **Miss Albany Diner** (893 Broadway, 518/465-9148), which dates back to 1941. Once known as Lil's Diner, it was renamed after the filming of William Kennedy's novel *Ironweed* here in 1986.

A classic downtown Albany restaurant, frequented by legislators, is **Jack's Oyster House** (42 State St., 518/465-8854). Specializing in seafood, it is said to be the oldest eatery in Albany. Run by the same family for generations, it features white tablecloths, tiled floors, and big pane-glass windows. Reservations are highly recommended; average entrée $16.

Lark Street

Along this lively street are many small restaurants serving both lunch and dinner. For

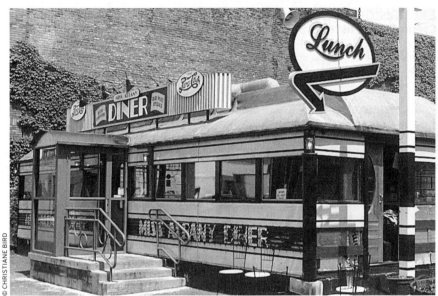

© CHRISTIANE BIRD

The Miss Albany Diner dates from 1941.

imaginative and contemporary American fare, try **Justin's** (301 Lark St., 518/436-7008), a lively and inviting basement spot partially housed in a historic building. Jazz is often featured on the weekends; average entrée $14. **Debbie's Kitchen** (456 Madison Ave., near Lark, 518/463-3829) is famed locally for its overstuffed sandwiches; average price $8.

Laid-back **☾ El Loco** (465 Madison Ave., at Lark, 518/436-1855) has been voted the city's best Mexican restaurant many years running. On the menu are traditional, Tex-Mex, and vegetarian dishes, and a wide selection of Mexican beers; average entrée $11.

Elsewhere Downtown

The **C.H. Evans Brewing Company at the Albany Pump Station** (19 Quackenbush Square, 518/447-9000) is a popular microbrewery and full-service restaurant with a 120-year family heritage. It's located in the building that once housed the original pumping station for Albany Water Works.

A few blocks south of the Empire Plaza is the cozy 1861 **☾ Mansion Hill Inn** (115 Philip St., 518/465-2038; see *Accommodations,* above) which serves innovative new American-style fare ranging from pasta to trout and leg of lamb. The restaurant is usually open for dinner only; average dinner entrée $18.

The modern, upscale **Cafe Capriccio** (49 Grand St., 518/465-0439) is a local favorite specializing in Northern Italian fare; average entrée $16. For a more old-fashioned Italian dining experience, try the classic **Lombardo's** (121 Madison Ave., 518/462-9180), frequented by politicians. It offers wall murals, tile floors, and traditional Italian dishes; average entrée $16.

Many regard **Nicole's Bistro at the Quackenbush House** (25 Quackenbush Sq., Broadway and Clinton Ave., 518/465-1111) to be the best restaurant in Albany. Located in the city's oldest residence, dating back to the 1700s, it serves fine French cuisine in a cozy brick setting lined with black-and-white photographs. The prix fixe dinners start at a reasonable $20, and the menu changes nightly; entrées cost $19–26.

EXCURSIONS FROM ALBANY
Crailo State Historic Site

Directly across the Hudson from Albany in Rensselaer is the 1704 Crailo mansion (9 Riverside Ave., 518/463-8738, 11 A.M.–5 P.M. Wed.–Sun. Apr.–Oct., adults $3, seniors $2, children 5–12 $1). Home to the Van Rensselaer family until the mid-1800s, the house is now a museum focusing on the history of Dutch culture in the Hudson River Valley. Exhibits range from archaeological artifacts to a restored cellar kitchen. Surrounding the house is a riverside park where summertime concerts are held.

John Boyd Thatcher State Park

For terrific views of the Hudson and Mohawk Valleys and the Adirondacks, head 18 miles west of Albany to Thatcher State Park (Rte. 157 off Rte. 85, 518/872-1237, 8 A.M.–dusk, parking $6–8). Here you'll also find the unusual **Indian Ladder Geologic Trail,** a half-mile-long ledge that is one of the richest fossil-bearing formations in the world. The park is open daily year-round, but the geologic trail is only open May–November, weather permitting.

Rensselaerville

About 25 miles southwest of Albany is the charming one-street village of Rensselaerville, originally settled in the late 1700s by Connecticut families who arrived via Long Island. On the National Register of Historic Places, the village is filled with restored post-Colonial and Greek Empire homes, many built by Ephraim Russ (1784–1853), a talented carpenter-architect who once lived in the village.

On Main Street, you'll find lots of shops selling the handiwork of Valley craftspeople, including jewelers, fiber artists, glass-blowers, and ceramists. Rensselaerville is also home to the **Rensselaerville Institute** (Rte. 85, 518/797-3783), which houses a small gallery (9 A.M.–5 P.M. Mon.–Fri.) and presents concerts during the summer.

Accommodations

About 15 minutes east of Albany is the ◖ **Gregory House Bed and Breakfast, Country Inn and Restaurant** (3016 Rte. 43, Averill Park, 518/674-3774, www.gregoryhouse.com, $115–125 d), a gracious 150-year-old homestead and modern inn with 12 nicely appointed guest rooms. On site are an outdoor pool, a popular Italian restaurant called La Perla, and a pub room serving coffees, desserts, appetizers, and drinks.

Troy

At times, Troy feels like a Victorian ghost town. Enormous abandoned stores with big plate-glass windows and faded gold lettering occupy downtown, while nearby residential neighborhoods feature elegant town- and row houses in various states of repair. The sidewalks are all but empty and traffic ridiculously light. No wonder they filmed *The Age of Innocence, The Bostonians,* and *Ironweed* here.

At other times, Troy just feels like a nice place to live, especially in recent years, since its waterfront has been revitalized and various neighborhoods have been gentrified, in part by artists fleeing New York City's skyrocketing rents. People are friendly, rents low, and there's plenty of room to move about. The city sits on the east bank of the Hudson River, about 15 minutes north of Albany, and is home to three colleges (Rensselaer Polytechnic Institute, Russell Sage College, Hudson Valley Community College) and a prestigious private girls' school (the Emma Willard School).

History

From the mid-1800s through the early 1900s, Troy was a major industrial city that led the world in the manufacture of stoves and horseshoes, bells and brushes, and, especially, collars and shirts. A housewife tired of washing her husband's shirts invented the detachable

CENTRAL NEW YORK

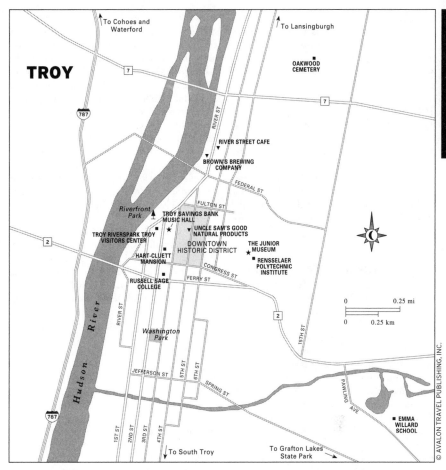

TROY

To Cohoes and Waterford

To Lansingburgh

OAKWOOD CEMETERY

RIVER STREET CAFE

BROWN'S BREWING COMPANY

FEDERAL ST

FULTON ST

Riverfront Park

TROY SAVINGS BANK MUSIC HALL

UNCLE SAM'S GOOD NATURAL PRODUCTS

TROY RIVERSPARK TROY VISITORS CENTER

DOWNTOWN HISTORIC DISTRICT

THE JUNIOR MUSEUM

HART-CLUETT MANSION

RENSSELAER POLYTECHNIC INSTITUTE

CONGRESS ST

RUSSELL SAGE COLLEGE

FERRY ST

0   0.25 mi

0   0.25 km

Washington Park

JEFFERSON ST

SPRING ST

PAWLING AVE

EMMA WILLARD SCHOOL

1ST ST 2ND ST 3RD ST 4TH ST 5TH ST 6TH ST

Hudson River

RIVER ST

15TH ST

© AVALON TRAVEL PUBLISHING, INC.

To South Troy

To Grafton Lakes State Park

collar here in 1825; Collar City, as Troy came to be known, once boasted 26 firms manufacturing over three million collars a year. Many of the factories were located along the Hudson just north of the city—their abandoned shells still stand today.

Always grittier and more industrialized than Albany, 19th-century Troy featured two distinct populations: the wealthy industrialists who built the lavish downtown, and the workers, many immigrants from Ireland, Germany, Italy, Poland, and French-speaking Canada. South Troy still harbors large Italian and Polish populations, while North Troy has historically been largely German. In more recent years, a large Latino population has taken root.

Troy's industrial fortunes were already beginning to decline by 1900, due to transportation shifts and the rise of Pittsburgh's steel mills, but it wasn't until after World War II that the city really fell on hard times. The population dropped from a high of 76,000 to 54,000 today. Somehow, however, Troy managed to escape the scourge of urban renewal, and so retains its Victorian heart—making it a fun city to explore on a lazy summer afternoon.

Orientation

Troy is a small and compact city with numbered streets running north-south and named streets running east-west. Most of the sights below are located in the downtown area and are easily accessed on foot.

Tours

Hudson-Mohawk Industrial Gateway (1 E. Industrial Pkwy., foot of Polk St., 518/274-5267) offers unusual tours that delve into the city's industrial and architectural past. The company's offices, which include a small museum, are housed in the Burden Iron Works Building, which once featured a 60-foot-high waterwheel and produced most of the horseshoes used in America.

SIGHTS

Troy RiverSpark Visitor Center

For a good introduction to Troy, stop by this first-rate center (251 River St., edge of Riverside Park, 518/270-8667, www.troyvisitorcenter.org, 11 A.M.–5 P.M. Tues.–Sat. May–Sept., call for off-season hours, free admission), where you'll find everything from an informative film to an electronic map that generates printed information. Most exhibits focus on the region's labor and industrial history, and include all sorts of interesting factual tidbits. Here you'll learn that the first all-woman labor union was formed in Troy (in 1864), and that the first person to seriously study the geological sciences was lawyer Amos Eaton, who began his scientific career while serving a life sentence for forgery (luckily for science, he was pardoned after four years).

RiverSpark is one of New York's State Heritage Areas—loosely delineated historic parks linked by a common theme. The theme in this park, which includes both Troy and five smaller communities nearby, is labor and industry; pick up a free driving-tour guide at the center.

River Street Historic District

At the northern end of River Street, the **Arts Center of the Capitol Region** (265 River St., 518/273-0552, www.artscenteronline.org,

9 A.M.–7 P.M. Mon.–Thurs., 9 A.M.–4 P.M. Fri.–Sat., noon–4 P.M. Sun.) houses a gallery with temporary exhibits ranging from contemporary art to folk arts. A bit further south, below the RiverSpark Visitor Center, is an attractive row of 19th-century storefronts furnished with period signs and awnings for the 1992 filming of Martin Scorsese's *The Age of Innocence.* Troy townspeople liked the effect so much they decided to retain the signs and awnings, though some of the stores remain empty.

Near where 1st Street intersects with River Street is Troy's former **Banker's Row.** Most of the buildings here feature ornate, locally manufactured cast-iron storefronts.

Hart-Cluett Mansion

The **Rensselaer County Historical Society** is partially housed in the elegant 1827 Hart-Cluett townhouse (59 2nd St., 518/272-7232, noon–5 P.M. Tues.–Sat., closed in Jan., adults $4, seniors and students $3, children 6–12 $2). Names after the prominent Troy families who once lived here, the mansion is filled with 19th-century furnishings by such well-known cabinetmakers as Phyfe, Galusha, and Moore.

Downtown Historic District

The heart of downtown Troy is located between 3rd and 5th, Fulton and Congress Streets. Strolling among the many 19th-century storefronts here, it's easy to imagine you're in the Victorian age—a man in a top hat or woman in hoop skirt could emerge at any moment.

One of the district's most impressive buildings is the **Frear Building,** at Fulton and 3rd Streets. Built around a courtyard topped with a skylight, the edifice was once home to Frear's Troy Cash Bazaar, a dry-goods company that conducted a $1-million-a-year mail-order business years before Sears Roebuck was born. Though the building now houses offices, the words Troy Cash Bazaar are still visible near the rooftop.

The Junior Museum

Children will enjoy this cheery hideaway (105 Eighth St., 518/235-2120, www.juniormuseum.org, 11 A.M.–4 P.M. Wed.–Fri., 10 A.M.–5 P.M. Sat.–Sun., admission $5, children under two free) filled with hands-on exhibits, live reptiles and fish, a children's art gallery, and a planetarium. Explore a log cabin and Iroquois longhouse, view temporary exhibits, and attend special events.

Uncle Sam's Grave

One of Troy's odder claims to fame is the fact it was once home to Uncle Sam, a meatpacker whose full name was Sam Wilson. During the War of 1812, Wilson's firm was contracted to send meat to the troops. Shipped barrels were marked U.S., for United States, but Wilson's workers joked the initials stood for their boss, whom they'd nicknamed Uncle Sam. Later, when these workers enlisted in the army, the joke spread through the ranks, and soon the words Uncle Sam and United States became synonymous. The first cartoon figures, dressed in stars and stripes, appeared around 1830; the beard was added during the Civil War.

Sam Wilson himself lived a quiet life, dying in 1854 at the age of 88. He is buried in the **Oakwood Cemetery** (518/272-7520, 9 A.M.–4:30 P.M. daily), a hilly, tree-shaded retreat with great views of the city. Emma Willard and other prominent Trojans are also buried here. To reach the cemetery, take 2nd Street north to 101st Street, turn right, and watch for signs to the cemetery and grave.

ENTERTAINMENT

Just east of RiverSpark stands the imposing 1871 **Troy Saving Bank** (32 2nd St.), renowned for its acoustically perfect concert hall. The bank originally built the hall as a gift for its shareholders. World-class musicians such as Isaac Stern and Yo-Yo Ma have recorded here, and free noontime concerts are presented September–June on second Tuesdays. For more information, contact the box office (7 State St., 518/273-0038, www.troymusichall.org).

Thanks largely to its sizable student population, Troy possesses an active nightlife. **Valenti's Pub** (729 Pawling Ave., 518/283-6766) is a good spot for local rock-and-roll.

Housed in a 19th-century warehouse, the atmospheric **Revolution Hall** (425 River St., 518/273-2337) presents jazz, blues, rock, and folk acts. To find out about other clubs, check *Metroland* (518/463-2500), a free alternative weekly.

A popular local hangout in South Troy is the **South End Tavern** (757 Burden Ave., 518/272-9661), a former speakeasy that once had separate entrances for men and women.

RECREATION

The **Capt. J. P. Cruise Line** (278 River St., 518/270-1901) offers sightseeing, dinner, and music cruises aboard a re-created Mississippi paddleboat May–October.

FOOD

Uncle Sam's Good Natural Products (77 4th St., 518/271-7299) is a simple vegetarian deli where you can pick up a good salad or tofu burger; average main dish $6. Along the Hudson in Riverfront Park is **Brown's Brewing Company** (417–419 River St., 518/273-2337), which brews its own beer and soft drinks and serves a variety of American fare; average entrée $12. Also in Riverfront Park is the high-ceilinged, brick-walled **◖ River Street Cafe** (429 River St., 518/273-2740), serving an eclectic array of international dishes ranging from Vietnamese specialties to Norwegian salmon. It's open for dinner only; average entrée $17.

EXCURSIONS FROM TROY
Elsewhere in RiverSpark

From Troy, the 28-mile RiverSpark Heritage Trail winds past five communities and more than 40 significant industrial sites. Free trail maps are available in the RiverSpark Visitor Center.

In **Waterford,** the oldest incorporated village in the United States (1794), you'll find industrialists' mansions and the so-called **"Waterford Flight."** The village is located at the confluence of the Hudson and Mohawk Rivers, and the flight is a series of five lift locks that raise and lower boats 170 feet from one river to the other.

Cohoes is a former company town still

dominated by the old factory buildings of Harmony Mills, at one time the single largest producer of cotton cloth in America. The town centers on the 80-foot waterfalls that powered the mills and endless rows of interconnected red brick and stone buildings. Most are abandoned but are in excellent condition and so handsome, it's hard to believe they once housed dirty, clanking machinery.

Grafton Lakes State Park

About 12 miles southeast of Troy lies an idyllic, 2,357-acre outdoor recreation area (Rte. 2, 518/279-1155, dawn–dusk daily, parking $6–8), centered on four ponds and the Martin-Dunham Reservoir. Long Pond features a large sandy beach with a lifeguard in summer, a bathhouse, and rowboat rentals; hiking trails encircle several of the lakes.

Schenectady

The third city in the Albany-Troy-Schenectady triumvirate, poor Schenectady is not in the best of health. Since the late 1930s, its population has shrunk from about 96,000 to 65,000. One of the town's primary employers, the American Locomotive Company, went out of business in 1968; another, the General Electric Company, has shrunk from a high of 43,000 employees to a mere 8,000. The "City that Lights and Hauls the World" lights and hauls no more, and although a new urban-development program was begun in 2000, it will be some time before its effects are felt.

Today Schenectady is best visited for its history. The oldest European settlement in the Mohawk Valley, the city boasts one of the largest and best collections of 18th-century buildings in New York—the historic Stockade. The visitor walking along this district's quiet, crooked streets, heavy with trees, will be transported back to a gentler age.

Orientation

Schenectady spreads out like a fan from a bend in the Mohawk River. Major arteries are Nott, Union, and State (Route 5) Streets. I-890 runs along the west side of the city.

SIGHTS
Schenectady Museum and Suits-Bueche Planetarium

Like Albany and Troy, Schenectady is one of New York State's Heritage Areas—loosely designated historic parks linked by a common theme. The theme in Schenectady, as in Troy, is labor and industry, chronicled in this museum (15 Nott Terrace Heights, off Nott Terrace, 518/382-7890, www.schenectady-museum.org, 10 A.M.–4:30 P.M. Tues.–Fri., noon–5 P.M. Sat.–Sun., adults $5, seniors $4, children 4–12 $3).

Exhibits focus on early settlement, General Electric, and the American Locomotive Company. In 1935 General Electric produced more than one-half the world's electricity; at the peak of World War II American Locomotive employed 11,000 workers and produced the first M-7 "tank killer" in 19 days. The museum is also known for its science exhibits and 30-foot-high planetarium (shows Sat.–Sun., $1.50 per person).

◖ The Stockade District

Along the banks of the Mohawk River, in the triangle formed by State and North College Streets, lies the Stockade (www.historicstockade.com), one of the nation's oldest continuously occupied neighborhoods. Settled in 1661 by Dutch merchants and fur traders, the outpost flourished until 1690, when a party of French-Canadians and their Indian allies burnt it to the ground, massacring most of the inhabitants and marching the rest off to Quebec.

Native Mohawks encouraged the Dutch to rebuild, and two years later the Stockade was

CENTRAL NEW YORK

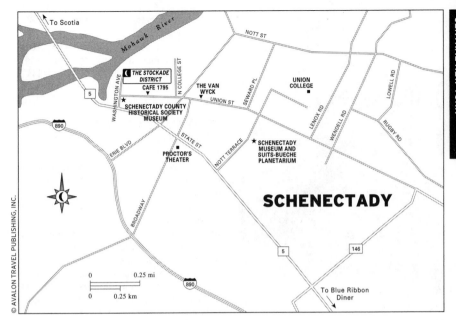

© AVALON TRAVEL PUBLISHING, INC.

flourishing once again. During the next two centuries all of Schenectady's most important families settled here, and today the residential district is a wonderful spot, filled with architectural landmarks of all styles and periods. The oldest are churches and graveyards dating back to the 1690s; the newest are homes built in the 1930s.

Plaques pinpointing some of the Stockade's more interesting sites are located throughout the district. Maps are available in the Schenectady County Historical Society Museum, located on the southern edge of the Stockade.

Schenectady County Historical Society Museum

On display in this friendly, three-story museum (32 Washington Ave., 518/374-0263, www.schist.org, 1–5 P.M. Mon.–Fri., 10 A.M.–4 P.M. Sat., adults $2, children under 12 $1) is everything from antique dolls and guns to period costumes and furniture. Highlights include an elaborate dollhouse that once belonged to the family of Governor Yates, and the

notebooks and letters of GE's electrical genius, Dr. Charles Steinmetz.

Union College

The first planned college campus in America, Union College was designed in 1814 by classical landscape architect Joseph Jacques Ramee. Filled with broad lawns and giant elms, Union admitted only men until 1970.

At the center of the campus is the high-Gothic **Nott Memorial,** the only 16-sided building in the Northern Hemisphere. Nearby are **Jackson's Gardens,** beautifully landscaped formal gardens first planted in the early 1800s by mathematics professor Isaac Jackson.

Union College (518/388-6000, www.union.edu) is located between Lenox Road, Seward Place, Union Avenue, and Nott and Union Streets. Parking is available in the lots at Nott Street and Seward Place.

ENTERTAINMENT

If possible, try to catch a show at the historic **Proctor's Theater** (432 State St.,

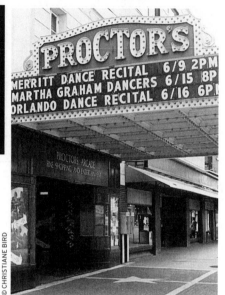

© CHRISTIANE BIRD

The 1925 Proctor's Theater was once a vaudeville venue.

musicals, concerts, operas, dance troupes, and classic movies.

On the edge of the Stockade is an excellent jazz and blues club, **The Van Wyck** (247 Union St., off Erie Blvd., 518/381-1111). Downstairs is an atmospheric bar; upstairs, the performance space.

ACCOMMODATIONS AND FOOD

In the Stockade find **Café 1795** (35 N. Ferry St., 518/372-4141), selling gourmet sandwiches and salads, as well as simple entrées. Located on the site of the 17th-century Old Public Market, Café 1795 sits on an attractive patio with a handful of picnic tables. For heaping platters of diner fare, try the modern **Blue Ribbon Diner** (1801 State St., 518/393-2600), especially known for its cheesecake.

Overlooking the Mohawk across from Schenectady is the **❰ Glen Sanders Mansion** (1 Glen Ave., Scotia, 518/374-7262), an upscale inn housed in a historic stone home with original Dutch floors and doors. The inn's formal, white-tablecloth restaurant serves Mediterranean-style fare (average dinner entrée $17), while a downstairs pub has a more casual take on the same. Ten standard guest rooms offer double queen-size beds; 10 suites offer king-size beds and sitting areas, some with fireplaces.

518/382-1083), an architectural gem built in 1925. Once a vaudeville palace, it features an ornate auditorium complete with 2,700 seats and a 1931 Golub Mighty Wurlitzer Organ. On its events calendar are Broadway

The Mohawk River Valley

To the west of Albany lies the mighty Mohawk, flanked by river flatlands, aging industrial towns, and rolling hills. The river valley was first settled over 10,000 years ago by the Mohawk; the first European settlers, Dutch and German Palatines, arrived in the 1720s. During the Revolutionary War, the valley's loyalties were deeply divided between its many resident Tories and their allies the Mohawks, and the Colonial rebels.

The most scenic road through the valley is Route 5, supplemented by Route 5 S across the

river to the south. Numerous bridges connect the two routes.

AMSTERDAM

Amsterdam lies about 18 miles west of Schenectady on Route 5. By far the largest town (pop. 21,000) between Schenectady and Utica, Amsterdam was once the center of a thriving carpet industry, and still manufactures clothing, toys, and electronic equipment.

Downtown you'll find the **Guy Park State Historic Site,** built in 1766 by Sir William

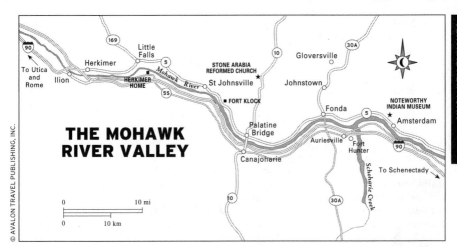

Johnson, British Superintendent of Indian Affairs, for his daughter Mary and her husband Guy Johnson. The site now houses the offices of the **Montgomery County Chamber of Commerce** (Guy Park, 366 West Main St., www.montgomerycountyny.com, 518/842-8200 or 800/743-7337, 8:30 A.M.–4:30 P.M. Mon.–Fri.).

School-age kids might enjoy a stop at the **Walter Elwood Museum** (300 Guy Park Ave., 518/843-5151, 8:30 A.M.–3:30 P.M. Mon.–Fri., free admission), housing youth-oriented exhibits on the Iroquois and Mohawk Valley history. The museum is housed in a 1902 schoolhouse.

The Noteworthy Indian Museum

Housed in a snug historic building, this museum (Prospect and Church Sts., 518/843-4761, 11 A.M.–5 P.M. Tues.–Fri. and 11 A.M.–4 P.M. Sat. July–Aug., donations welcomed) tells the story of Native Americans in the Mohawk Valley from 12,000 years ago to the present. On display are over 60,000 artifacts ranging from clay pots and stone tools to beadwork and baskets. Poetry and paintings by contemporary artists are also featured. Most of the museum's artifacts were collected by one man, Tom Constantino.

Food

Just north of Amsterdam is the **Happi Daze Charcoal Pit** (4479 Rte. 30, 518/843-8265), a vintage drive-in dating back to the 1950s. The car hops are long-gone, but foot-long hot dogs, burgers, and shakes are still on the menu.

FORT HUNTER

A few miles beyond Amsterdam on the southern shores of the Mohawk is the **Schoharie Crossing State Historic Site** (129 Schoharie St. [Rte. 5 S], 518/829-7516, dawn–dusk, free admission), where the Erie Canal once crossed Schoharie Creek. The seven arches of the aqueduct that carried the canal across the creek were an engineering marvel in their day—they still stand, along with other historic canal structures. A small visitors center (10 A.M.–5 P.M. Wed.–Sat. and 1–5 P.M. Sun. May–Oct.) provides historical background; nearby is a three-mile hiking trail.

AURIESVILLE

A few miles farther west on Route 5 S is an unexpected sight—the **National Shrine of Our Lady of Martyrs** (Rte. 5 S, at Noeltner Rd., 518/853-3033, www.martyrshrine.org, 10 A.M.–4 P.M. Mon.–Sat. and 9:30 A.M.–5 P.M. Sun. May–Oct.), spread over a shaded, parklike area seemingly located in the middle of nowhere. Welcome Pilgrims reads the sign over the entrance arch.

Auriesville was the birthplace of the Blessed

Kateri Tekakwitha, born in 1656 to a Christian Algonquin mother and a Mohawk chief. Orphaned at the age of three and baptized at 20, Tekakwitha was the first laywoman in North America honored as "Blessed," and is said to have performed many miracles.

The shrine is also dedicated to Father Isaac Joques and seven other Jesuit priests who were killed by the Mohawks in the 1640s. In 1930 the Catholic Church canonized the eight martyrs as the first saints of North America.

On an ordinary weekday, the National Shrine attracts but a handful of worshippers and curious visitors who stroll past a rustic open-air chapel, the Stations of the Cross, numerous statues, and the circular Coliseum Church. On Sunday, however, busloads of people fill the giant parking lot to attend masses and the priest-led Rosary, Stations, Eucharistic Procession, which winds past the Stations of the Cross beginning at 2:30 P.M.

FONDA

To learn more about Kateri Tekakwitha, take the bridge over the Mohawk to Fonda and the **Kateri Tekakwitha Memorial Shrine** (Rte. 5, 518/853-3646). Tekakwitha was baptized here in 1676, and it was here where she was later persecuted by her tribe for her Christian beliefs.

At the shrine is a snug wooden church with a peaked roof, built in the tradition of the Iroquois longhouse, and the **Mohawk-Caughnawaga Museum** (10 A.M.–4 P.M. daily May–Oct., free admission), holding a sizable collection of Iroquois artifacts and modern art. Behind both buildings is a vast lawn, peppered with the Stations of the Cross, a woodsy grove, and the only completely excavated Native American village in the United States. The excavation sounds more interesting than it actually is; there's not much to see here except a few stones.

The entire site is administered by the Franciscan friars, and a brother dressed in brown robes and sandals is usually on hand to answer questions.

Kanatsiohareke

In 1993, a traditional Mohawk community known as Kanatsiohareke was established on a 400-acre-site that had once held Mohawk villages. Today, the Mohawk living here farm the land much the way their ancestors did and work to keep their people's language and traditions alive.

In the heart of the community is the **Mohawk Indian Craft Shop** (4934 Rte. 5, 518/673-2534), selling handmade crafts, books, and clothing. Next door is the **Mohawk Indian Bed & Breakfast** (4934 Rte. 5, 518/673-5092), offering four comfortable guest rooms decorated with Native American paintings and crafts.

JOHNSTOWN

If you detour north of Fonda on Route 30A, you'll come to the small town of Johnstown, founded in 1762 by Sir William Johnson, the British Superintendent of Indian Affairs. Sir Johnson had an unusually close relationship with the Iroquois; he was a good friend of Joseph Brandt, one of the most respected Mohawks of his day, and the husband of Molly Brant, Joseph's older sister, with whom he sired eight children. A contemporary once said of Molly, "She seldom imposed herself into the picture, but no one was in her presence without being aware of her."

Johnson's former home, the **Johnson Hall State Historic Site** (Hall Ave., 518/762-8712, 11 A.M.–5 P.M. Wed.–Sun. May–Oct., adults $4, seniors $3, children 6–12 $1) is now a meticulously restored museum, filled with Colonial artifacts and exhibits on the French and Indian War. An inviting park, perfect for picnicking, surrounds the house.

GLOVERSVILLE

Industrial-history devotees will want to continue north on Route 30A to Gloversville, a sprawling and largely depressed town named for its number one industry—gloves. Together with Johnstown, Gloversville was once the glove-making capital of the world; a number of small factories here still produce them, and glove outlet stores still operate in the area.

The best place to learn about the glove industry is the **Fulton County Historical**

Society & Museum (237 Kingsboro Ave., 518/725-2203, noon–4 P.M. Tues.–Sat. Apr.–June and Sept.–Now., 10 A.M.–4 P.M. Tues.–Sat. July–Aug., donations appreciated), housed in a creaky mansion on the edge of town. In 1800, there were over 170 glove manufacturers in the Gloversville area, most employing women who worked at home. After the invention of the sewing machine, nearly every kitchen contained a Singer upon which women worked when not caring for their children or cooking meals.

CANAJOHARIE

Back on Route 5 S on the south side of the Mohawk just west of Fonda is Canajoharie, Iroquois for "The Pot That Washes Itself." The name comes from the large geological pothole in Canajoharie Gorge, just south of the village, where water from a nearby waterfall churns and churns and churns. Both the pothole and the waterfall are now part of **Canajoharie Wintergreen Park and Gorge** (Wintergreen Park Rd., 518/673-5512, 9 A.M.–9:30 P.M. May–Sept.).

The town's biggest visitor attraction is the **Canajoharie Library and Art Gallery** (2 Erie Blvd., 518/673-2314, www.clag.org), billed as the "finest private gallery of any municipality of its size." This claim may be hard to prove but the gallery does house an outstanding collection of 19th- and early-20th-century American paintings by the likes of Albert Bierstadt, Thomas Eakins, Gilbert Stuart, Winslow Homer, Andrew Wyeth, and Edward Hopper. In April 2005, the gallery shut down for a major expansion and renovation; it is scheduled to reopen in summer 2006.

ST. JOHNSVILLE

West of Palatine Bridge is St. Johnsville, formerly a mill town producing felt shoes and underwear. Find here several handsome stone houses, including **Fort Klock** (Rte. 5, 518/568-7779, 9 A.M.–5 P.M. Tues.–Sun. June–Oct., adults $1, children under 10 50 cents), a fortified homestead and fur-trading post built by the Klock family in 1750. Although restored,

the limestone house has never been altered from its original construction. Behind it stand an early 19th-century schoolhouse, blacksmith's shop, Dutch barn, and cheese house, all moved here from nearby.

LITTLE FALLS

Formerly awash in bicycle, velocipede, and tissue-paper factories, this former Erie Canal mill town now features an appealing restored waterfront lined with shops, restaurants, and flowers. Little Falls is also home to **Lock 17**, which at 40 feet is one of highest lift locks in the world. Tankers and pleasure craft still pass through daily.

On Route 169 three miles southeast of Little Falls, across the Mohawk, stands the **Herkimer Home State Historic Site** (315/823-0398, 10 A.M.–5 P.M. Wed.–Sat. and 1–5 P.M. Sun. May–Oct., adults $3, seniors and students $2, children 5–11 $1). Once one of the grandest homes in the Mohawk Valley, the red-brick house was built by Gen. Nicholas Herkimer, who led the Colonial militia in the bloody Battle of Oriskany. Today costumed guides conduct guided tours, and you can attend such special events as a Colonial maple-sugaring bee.

Food and Accommodations

Along the historic waterfront is the inviting **Canal Side Inn** (395 S. Ann St., 315/823-1170, www.canalside.com), serving classic French cuisine, including several fish dishes and daily specials (average entrée $17, dinner only). The inn also has several rooms for rent.

The 1889 **Gansevoort House** (42 W. Gansevoort St., 315/823-1833, $75–90 d) is a cozy B&B equipped with fireplaces, a music room, wraparound porch, and book shop. There are three rooms in the main house and a family suite in the carriage house.

HERKIMER AND ENVIRONS

The seat of Herkimer County, Herkimer sprawls over a broad flat area at the mouth of West Canada Creek, a major Mohawk tributary. Once an important industrial and

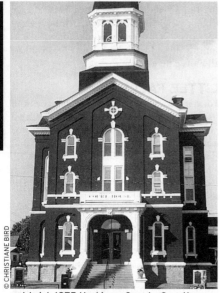

© CHRISTIANE BIRD

red-brick 1875 Herkimer County Courthouse

which Theodore Dreiser based his famous novel, *An American Tragedy.*

Across the street from the courthouse looms the former Herkimer County Jail, where Gillette once awaited trial, and the **Herkimer County Historical Society Museum** (400 N. Main St., 315/866-6413, 10 A.M.–4 P.M. Mon.–Fri. year-round, 10 A.M.–3 P.M. Sat. July–Aug., free admission). Museum exhibits focus on county history, dollhouses, and miniatures.

Herkimer Diamond Mines

Travel seven miles north of Herkimer on Route 28 and you'll come across a parched brown patch of earth where you can hunt for "diamonds" (4626 Rte. 28, 315/891-7355, www.herkimerdiamond.com, 9 A.M.–5 P.M. daily Apr.–Oct., adults $8, children 5–12 $7). Actually brilliant quartz crystals, these 18-faceted rocks began forming a half-billion years ago when the area lay beneath the Devonian Sea. Water seeped into the pores of the rock beneath the sea's surface, evaporating millions of years later and leaving silica behind.

Visitors to the "mines" are equipped with hammers to break open the rocks, and the "diamonds" are easy to find. Also on-site is an extensive gift shop with a museum upstairs.

Across from the Herkimer Diamond Mines is a **KOA** campground (Rte. 28, 315/891-7355) offering campsites and cabins April–November.

shipping center, the town is cut in two by a fat, ugly swatch of railroad tracks.

Along Main Street stand many striking historic buildings, the finest being the red-brick 1875 **Herkimer County Courthouse** topped with a black-and-white wooden cupola. The courthouse was the site of the sensational Gillette murder trial of 1906, on

Otsego County

One of the region's most prosperous counties, thanks largely to touristic Cooperstown, Otsego County is mostly back roads, tiny villages, and wooded hills and valleys. Two small lakes—Canadarago and Otsego—sit to the north, while to the south lies the county's only city, Oneonta, population about 14,000.

COOPERSTOWN

Home to the National Baseball Hall of Fame and Museum, Cooperstown likes to think of itself as the most famous small town in America. It centers on a friendly, old-fashioned Main Street, and boasts a population of just 2,300. To the north are the still waters of Otsego Lake; to the south, east, and west, the rolling, forested hills of Leatherstocking Country.

Cooperstown was first settled in 1790 by William Cooper, father of James Fenimore, America's first internationally recognized author. The fiercely ambitious Cooper Sr. obtained the land through unscrupulous means during the confusion following the Revolutionary War, then immediately set about establishing himself as a grand gentleman. Within a decade he'd built the largest private home west of Albany, won widespread respect for his skill as a land developer, and established Cooperstown as the Otsego County seat. Later he became a county judge and a representative to the U.S. Congress.

James Fenimore Cooper wrote about Cooperstown in his novel *The Pioneers,* and set many of his Natty Bumppo tales on the shores of "The Glimmerglass"—Otsego Lake. After travels at sea and abroad, he settled down in his hometown and took over where his father had left off, playing lord of the manor. Cooper was buried in the town's Christ Church Cemetery in 1851.

In the late 1800s Cooperstown became home to the Clark family, who'd made a fortune in Singer Sewing Machines. Edward Clark, the family patriarch, built a miniature castle called Kingfisher Tower on Otsego Lake in 1876. In the late 1930s and '40s one of his descendants, Stephen C. Clark, established the town's three famous museums—the National Baseball Hall of Fame, the Farmers' Museum, and the Fenimore Art Museum.

On a summer's day Cooperstown's population swells by the thousands. Tourists wearing baseball caps and T-shirts are everywhere, and parking can be a major problem. The best approach then is to park in one of the park-and-ride lots on Routes 80 and 28 and ride the free trolley into town. During the off-season, street parking is generally available.

SIGHTS
◖ National Baseball Hall of Fame and Museum

Newly reopened after an extensive $20-million renovation, this homage to America's favorite pastime (25 Main St., 607/547-7200 or 888/425-5633, www.baseballhalloffame.org, 9 A.M.–9 P.M. daily June–Sept., 9 A.M.–5 P.M. Oct.–May, adults $14.50, seniors $9, children 7–12 $5) is loaded with state-of-the-art displays covering every aspect of the sport, from famous ballparks and women's baseball to the World Series and the Negro League. Here you'll find loads of history, along with such memorabilia as Jackie Robinson's warm-up jacket, Hank Aaron's locker, Willie Mays's glove, Yogi Berra's catcher's mitt, and that rarest of all baseball cards, the Honus Wagner 1909 T-206 tobacco card, recalled at the request of the nonsmoking ballplayer.

Occupying three floors and 60,000 square feet, the museum begins with a cavernous Hall of Fame honoring the greats. A ramp to one side leads to exhibits on such subjects as "Scribes and Mikemen" and "Baseball at the Movies," while stairs lead to the second and third floors, where the heart of the collection is housed. One room honors Babe Ruth; another, the game in the 19th century, a third, "Today's Game." Separate exhibit cases are devoted to such major players as Hank Aaron, Jackie

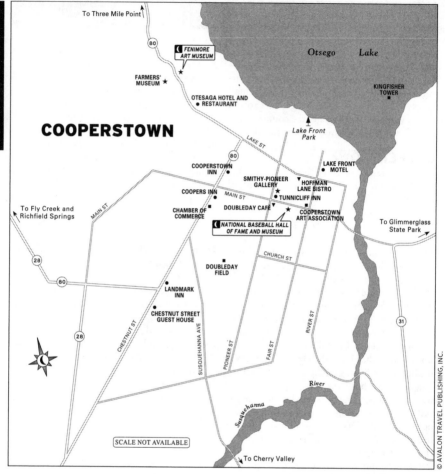

Robinson, and Ty Cobb. A 13-minute multimedia show, "The Baseball Experience," is presented throughout the day, while film and audio clips pepper the exhibits. Daily trivia games and educational programs are also featured. Combinaton tickets with the Farmers' Museum and Fenimore Art Museum are available.

Doubleday Field

Down Main Street from the Hall of Fame lies the oldest baseball diamond in the world, the site of the first official game in 1839. Originally built for 8,000 spectators and later expanded to accommodate 10,000, the field is now available for rent and is very popular among local groups, meaning that a game is often in progress. Doubleday Field (607/547-2270) is open daily year-round.

Lake Front Park

Two blocks north of the Baseball Hall of Fame lies Otsego Lake, created during the last great Ice Age. Like many glacial lakes, Otsego is cool and deep, with steep banks and overhanging trees. Fed by springs, it is the source of the Susquehanna River, which flows south to Chesapeake Bay and the Atlantic Ocean.

Along the edge of the lake is Lake Front Park, a pleasant spot frequented by families. To one side is a statue called *Indian Hunter;* to the other, **Council Rock.** Once a meeting place for various Indian tribes, the rock was employed by Cooper in *The Deerslayer* as a rendezvous point for Deerslayer and his friend Chingachgook. "The rock was not large. . . ," wrote Cooper, "The incessant washing of the water for centuries had so rounded its summit, that it resembled a large beehive." Today, a flight of stone steps leads down to a terrace overlooking the rock.

From the park you can see the 65-foot-high, 1907 **Kingfisher Tower,** designed in the style of a European castle by architect Henry Hardenbergh, who also designed the Plaza Hotel in New York City. The tower is off-limits to the public.

Elsewhere Downtown

The galleries of the **Cooperstown Art Association** (22 Main St., 607/547-9777, 11 A.M.–4 P.M. Mon.–Sat., 1–4 P.M. Sun., free admission) lie diagonally across from the Baseball Hall of Fame. Founded in 1928, the association showcases a variety of works ranging from contemporary to traditional.

Flanking **Pioneer Street,** which intersects Main Street by the flagpole, are some of the oldest buildings in the village. Foremost among them is the dark, low-ceilinged **Smithy-Pioneer Gallery** (55 Pioneer St., 607/547-8671, 10 A.M.–5 P.M. Tues.–Sat. and noon–5 P.M. Sun. June–Sept., free admission), part of which was built about 1786 by William Cooper. Originally a storehouse, the building was later converted into a blacksmith's shop and now contains both historic artifacts and an art gallery.

Cooper's Town

Although the old Cooper family mansion was torn down long ago, Cooperstown still contains about 20 buildings that date back to

HALLS OF FAME AND GLORY

From baseball players to boxers, dancers to feminists, jockeys to fly-fisherfolk – it seems like everywhere you go in New York State, there's a Hall of Fame honoring the best of class, both famous and obscure. At the top of the list are such known institutions as the National Baseball Hall of Fame and Museum in Cooperstown, the National Soccer Hall of Fame in Oneonta, the National Women's Hall of Fame in Seneca Falls, and the National Museum of Racing and Hall of Fame in Saratoga Springs, not to mention the Catskill Fly Fishing Museum and Hall of Fame in Livingston Manor, the National Museum of Dance and Hall of Fame in Saratoga Springs, and the International Boxing Hall of Fame in Canastota.

But that doesn't end there. Lovers of the off-beat might want to check out the **National Toy Hall of Fame** located inside the Strong Museum in Rochester (1 Manhattan Sq., 585/263-2700) or the **American Maple Museum and Hall of Fame** in Croghan (Main St., 315/346-1107). The **North American Fiddlers Hall of Fame and Museum** (1121 Comins Rd., Osceola, 315/599-7009) was created in 1976 by the New York State Old Tyme Fiddlers Association to honor "every fiddler who has ever made hearts light and happy with the fiddle's lilting music."

Said to be the oldest Hall of Fame in the country is the **Hall of Fame for Great Americans** at the Bronx Community College of the City of New York (University Ave. at W. 181st St., Bronx, 718/289-5161). Designed by Stanford White, the hall is actually a sweeping, semi-circular, indoor-outdoor colonnade, lined with bronze busts of 98 famous men and (a few) women. Perched above the Harlem and Hudson Rivers, the neoclassical complex also offers stunning views.

According to state's tourism division, New York currently boasts 20 halls of fame. For a complete list, call 800/CALL-NYS.

James Fenimore's time. Most closely associated with Cooper is **Christ Church** on Fair Street, consecrated in 1810 on land donated by his father. In Cooper's fiction the church appears as "New St. Paul's"; the Cooper family plot is located in the cemetery behind the church.

For more Cooper-related sites, pick up a copy of *Cooper's Otsego County* by Hugh Cooke MacDougall (New York State Historical Society).

Farmers' Museum

Just outside downtown Cooperstown is the second of its famous museums (Lake Rd. [Rte. 80], 607/547-1400, www.farmersmuseum.org, 10 A.M.–5 P.M. daily June–Sept., 10 A.M.–4 P.M. Tues.–Sun. Apr.–May and Oct.–Nov., adults $11, seniors $9.50, children 7–12 $5), composed of a dozen meticulously restored pre–Civil War buildings. Run by the New York State Historical Association, this is not just another living history museum, but rather, a sort of granddaddy of them all; founded in 1943, it was the first open-air museum in New York State and one of the first in the country.

The museum is spread along one looping street, lined with a general store, blacksmith's shop, printing office, doctor's office, and druggist's shop. In the Main Barn near the entrance hang imaginative exhibits on early rural life; everywhere roam skillful guides in period dress, some demonstrating such arts as broom-making and open-hearth cooking. Sheep graze in the village common, fat cows wander a nearby hill.

One of the museum's odder exhibits is the 2,900-pound Cardiff Giant. Supposedly unearthed in nearby Cardiff in 1869 by the hitherto unassuming William Newell, the sleeping stone man with the mysterious smile soon drew visitors from all over the country. One Harvard professor claimed the Giant dated back to Phoenician times; Oliver Wendell Holmes drilled a hole behind his left ear to see if the brain was petrified. Only after Newell had raked in some tens of thousands of dollars was the statue proven to be a hoax.

Combination tickets with the Baseball Hall of Fame and Fenimore Art Museum are available.

Fenimore Art Museum

Directly across the street from the Farmers' Museum is the third of Cooperstown's museum triumvirate (Lake Rd. [Rte. 80], 607/547-1400, www.fenimoreartmuseum.org, 10 A.M.–5 P.M. daily June–Sept., 10 A.M.–4 P.M. Tues.–Sat. Apr.–May and Oct.–Nov., adults $11, seniors $9.50, children 7–12 $5). Also run by the New York State Historical Association, the Fenimore house holds the state's premier collection of folk art, fine art, and Native American art. Highlights include Thomas Cole's *Last of the Mohicans,* Gilbert Stuart's *Joseph Brandt,* a version of Edward Hicks' *Peaceable Kingdom,* and an eclectic collection of weathervanes, trade signs, cigar-store Indians, and decoys.

One wing of the museum houses the Eugene and Clare Thaw Collection of American Indian Art. Perhaps the most important privately owned collection of its kind, the collection includes about 700 works spanning 2,500 years of native North American culture. Among the many stunning items on display are a flowing Blackfoot headdress, a Lakota painted horsehide, and a brilliant blue Heiltsuk moon mask.

On-site is a first-rate book store. Combination tickets with the National Baseball Hall of Fame and Farmer's Museum are available.

Glimmerglass State Park

At the northern end of Otsego Lake shimmers this peaceful oasis of green (East Lake Rd., 607/547-8662, 8 A.M.–dusk, parking $6–8), perched on rolling hills. Features include a swimming beach, plenty of hiking and biking trails, a playground, and a 39-site campground. The park is accessible off County Road 31; for campground reservations, call 800/456-CAMP.

In the heart of the park stands a grand, neoclassical mansion known as **Hyde Hall** (607/547-5098, www.hydehall.org, 10 A.M.– 5 P.M. Thurs.–Tues. June–Oct., adults $7, seniors $6, children 5–12 $4). Once home to the Clarke family, the building had fallen into serious disrepair but is now being restored.

Breweries

Two breweries offering guided tours are in the Cooperstown area. Located on a farmstead is **Brewery Ommegang** (656 County Road 33, 607/544-1800, noon–5 P.M. daily, adults $4, children free), the only brewery in the United States that brews all Belgian-style beers. The **Cooperstown Brewing Company** (River St., Milford, 607/286-9330, 10 A.M.–6 P.M. Mon.–Sat., noon–5 P.M. Sun., adults $3, children free) creates products such as Nine Man Ale, Old Slugger, and Strike-Out Stout.

ENTERTAINMENT

An acclaimed opera festival takes place every July–August at the **Glimmerglass Opera,** Route 80, a partially open-air theater by Otsego Lake. The box office is downtown (18 Chestnut St., 607/547-2255, www.glimmerglass.org). Chamber-music concerts, lectures, and plays take place regularly in **Hyde Hall** (607/547-5098).

The basement **Taproom at the Tunnicliff Inn** (34–36 Pioneer St., 607/547-9860) is a favorite local late-night hangout. The tables are carved with the initials of Cooperstown pilgrims, and beers on tap start at just $1.50.

For an elegant evening out, step into the Templeton Lounge of the **Otesaga** (60 Lake St., 607/547-9931). Live music and dancing are often offered, starting at 9 P.M.

SHOPPING

Numerous shops selling everything from baseball memorabilia to clothing occupy Cooperstown and the surrounding area. The chamber of commerce publishes several helpful brochures.

A few miles south of Cooperstown is the **Fly Creek Cider Mill** (288 Goose St., off Route 28/80, 607/547-9692, www.flycreekcider.com, 9 A.M.–6 P.M. daily), where apples are pressed in a wooden, 19th-century cider mill. The mill is powered by water and all original equipment

is used. Also on site is an extensive gift shop and a snack bar selling lots of tasty homemade treats, including donuts, pies, chili, and, of course, fresh cider. Out back is a duck pond and play area that will delight young kids.

Among the region's more unusual stores is **Wood Bull Antiques** (3920 Rte. 28, 607/286-9021), in a large barn eight miles south of Cooperstown. According to the owners, the merchandise has been gathered from over 20 years of attic rummaging and close to 3,000 auctions.

SPORTS AND RECREATION

To catch a live game, baseball fans might want to head south on Route 28 to Oneonta to watch the Class A Oneonta Tigers.

You'll find good swimming at the public beaches on Otsego Lake at Glimmerglass State Park, off County Road 31; Three Mile Point, off Route 80; and Fairy Springs, off County Road 31.

ACCOMMODATIONS
Camping and Motels

In addition to the campground at Glimmerglass State Park, camping options include the **Cooperstown Beaver Valley Campground** (Rte. 28 S, 607/293-7324), boasting three beaver ponds and a petting zoo; and the **Cooperstown Shadow Brook Campground** (East Lake Rd., 607/264-8431). Both feature about 100 sites.

Cooperstown has a number of good, clean motels to choose from. In the heart of the village, overlooking Otsego Lake, is the 45-room **Lake Front Motel** (10 Fair St., 607/547-9511, www.lakefrontmotelandrestaurant.com, $115–190 d in summer, $65–150 d off-season). An on-site restaurant serves breakfast, lunch, and dinner; a deck overlooks the lake.

On the lake seven miles north of Cooperstown is the **Lake 'N Pines Motel** (7102 Rte. 80, 607/547-2790, $130–160 d in summer, $55–85 off-season). Here guests can choose between motel rooms and cottages. On site are indoor and outdoor pools, and a small beach equipped with paddle boats.

Hotels and Inns

The 1902 【 **Otesaga Hotel and Restaurant** (60 Lake St., 607/547-9931, www.otesaga.com, $320–550 d with full breakfast and dinner) is a delicious grande dame of a hotel that's affiliated with Historic Hotels of America. Out front tower stately white columns; out back stretches a long, long, circular porch with rocking chairs overlooking the lake. Facilities include a romantic ballroom with a 20-foot-high coffered ceiling, a main dining room, the appealing **Hawkeye Bar & Grill,** tennis courts, and the first-rate Leatherstocking Golf Course. All 135 rooms are outfitted with period furnishings.

The Otesaga also operates the luxurious **Coopers Inn** (Main and Chestnut Sts., 607/547-9931, $205 d in summer, $110–160 off-season; breakfast included), built circa 1820. Reigning over its own little park in the heart of the downtown, the inn offers 20 handsomely decorated rooms and the use of all Otesaga facilities.

Meanwhile, the 【 **Inn at Cooperstown** (16 Chestnut St., 607/547-5756, www.inn-atcooperstown.com, $187 d in summer, $99–167 off-season, breakfast included) is all that an inn should be—big, creaky, lined with a wide porch, and shaded with magnificent trees. All 17 guest rooms feature private baths and queen or double beds.

Cooperstown's oldest inn, now somewhat worn but still atmospheric, is the 1802 **Tunnicliff Inn** (34–36 Pioneer St., 607/547-9611, $160–190 d in summer, $60–140 d off-season). Here, you'll find 17 guest rooms, a restaurant, and a historic bar.

Bed-and-Breakfasts

Among the many inviting B&Bs in Cooperstown is the stately 【 **Landmark Inn** (64 Chestnut St., 607/547-7225, www.land-markinncooperstown.com, $200–295 d July–Aug., $115–210 d off-season), in a 1856 Italianate mansion. Beautifully restored, the inn offers a plush parlor complete with fireplace, hardwood floors polished to a high gleam, a game room, various cozy sitting areas, and nine spacious guest rooms equipped with feather duvet beds, refrigerators, air-conditioning, Cable TV, and antiques. Internet access is also available. One of the inn's especially nice touches is its sumptuous homemade breakfasts, served in your room or in the dining room.

Just down the street is the **Chestnut Street Guest House** (79 Chestnut St., 607/547-5624, www.chestnut79.com, $95–125 d). This comfortable spot offers four attractive rooms, one completely outfitted in baseball memorabilia.

FOOD

The high-ceilinged 【 **Doubleday Cafe** (93 Main St., 607/547-5468) has a friendly small-town feel, with a counter bar to one side and lots of tables and chairs in back. The menu has a nice variety of sandwiches, salads, and simple entrée s. Most dishes are priced under $10.

The **Hawkeye Bar & Grill** in the Otesaga Hotel (60 Lake St., 607/547-9931, average lunch entrée $9) is especially good for lunch in summer, when lakeside patio seating opens up. On the menu are overstuffed sandwiches and simple entrées. A more elaborate dinner menu is also served.

Less than two blocks from the Baseball Hall of Fame is the cozy, two-level **Hoffman Lane Bistro** (2 Hoffman Ln., 607/547-7055, average entrée $15). This local favorite serves everything from linguine with meatballs to sesame-seared tuna steaks. Downstairs is a square-shaped bar and one snug dining area, while upstairs is another.

Another local favorite is 【 **Nicolleta's Italian Café** (96 Main St., 607/547-7499, average entrée $16), housed in an airy, high-ceilinged, former storefront. They serve lots of tasty pasta dishes made from fresh local ingredients, along with such classics as veal picatta and salmon filet.

A variety of international dishes are offered at the lovely lakeside 【 **Blue Mingo Grill** (Sam Smith's Boatyard, Rte. 80, 607/547-7496, open in summer only, average dinner entrée $19). Lunch dishes include salads, grilled fish, and pizzas, while the dinner menu changes weekly and can include anything from Thai dishes to fresh lobster.

CHERRY VALLEY

About 12 miles north of Cooperstown is the village of Cherry Valley, named for the wild cherries thriving in the surrounding countryside. Though now an unusually peaceful spot, Cherry Valley has endured a turbulent history.

During the Revolutionary War, Cherry Valley was the site of a massacre perpetrated by 500 Tories and Mohawks under the command of Capt. Walter Butler and Chief Joseph Brandt. Thirty-two residents were killed and 70 taken prisoner, and the village burned to the ground.

After the war all but one of the prisoners returned to the valley to rebuild the town, soon the largest settlement southwest of the Mohawk. In 1800, the Great Western Turnpike—now Route 20—arrived, and by 1815 there were 15 taverns in the village and 62 more in the 52 miles between it and Albany. Sometimes as many as 40 wagons heading west spent the night in the village square, and Cherry Valley boasted its own marble works, iron foundries, tanneries, and distilleries.

Then came the Erie Canal in 1825, followed by the New York Central Railroad. Both diverted traffic away from the town, and by the early 1900s Cherry Valley was again a sleepy little village.

In the 1960s and '70s Cherry Valley was known for its thriving arts community. Allen Ginsberg once occupied a farm on the outskirts of town, and even today, in the fond words of one resident, the village attracts "the weirdos of the county."

Cherry Valley Museum

Much of the village's history is on view at this creaky, two-story museum (49 Main St., 607/264-3303, www.cherryvalleymuseum.org, 10 A.M.–5 P.M. daily May–Oct., adults $3, seniors $2.50, children under 12 free), where artifacts range from inkwells and children's clothes to Civil War uniforms and an 1885 fire engine. A video tells the story of the massacre, and free walking/driving tour brochures to the village are available.

Food

Housed in a 200-year-old home is the chef-owned and -operated **Rose & Kettle** (4 Lancaster St., 607/264-3078, dinner and Sunday brunch only, average entrée $17). On the menu, which changes frequently, is contemporary European-American fare, made with fresh local ingredients. Call for exact days of operation and reservations.

RICHFIELD SPRINGS

Travel a few miles west of Cherry Valley on Route 20 and you'll come to Richfield Springs, formerly known for its sulfur springs and grand old hotels. Evidence of these bygone days can still be seen in the bright white gazebo in the center of town and in the aging Victorian buildings along the main streets. The once-famous sulfur waters still flow from the fountain in **Spring Park** on Main Street.

Petrified Creatures Museum of Natural History

In the quirky Petrified Creatures Museum (Rte. 20, 315/858-2868, 10 A.M.–6 P.M. Thurs.–Mon. May–Sept. and 10 A.M.–6 P.M. Tues.–Wed. July–Aug., adults $8, children 5–11 $4), you'll see life-size dinosaurs painted purple, red, and green; listen to narrations about prehistoric life; and, best of all, dig for fossils. Like much of central New York State, the museum is located on land once covered by the Devonian Sea and sits on the edge of a "fossil pit." When the sea retreated, small creatures were left behind in the pits' primordial ooze; that ooze turned to limestone and the creatures to fossils. Forty-six different species have been found here, and fossils are so plentiful visitors are guaranteed to find at least one.

Established in 1934, the Petrified Creatures Museum is the oldest museum in central New York State. Hammers and chisels for fossil hunting are provided.

Holy Trinity Russian Orthodox Monastery

About six miles north of Richfield Springs off Route 167 is a most surprising sight—the Holy

© CHRISTIANE BIRD

Jordanville's Holy Trinity Russian Orthodox Monastery

Trinity Russian Orthodox Monastery (Robinson Rd., Jordanville, 315/858-0940). Established here shortly after the 1917 Russian Revolution, this is the largest Eastern Orthodox monastery on the continent.

Approaching from the south, you'll pass through a quiet region of farms and woodlands before suddenly spotting the magnificent grouping of golden domes and spires on your left. Inside the main chapel is a dizzying collection of icons, shimmering in dim light, while out back are gardens and a graveyard. Monks in long brown robes stroll the grounds.

Visitors are welcome at the monastery, but if you'd like to see the chapel's interior, make reservations in advance.

ONEONTA

Snuggled into hills at the southernmost end of Otsego County is the small city of Oneonta. Iroquois for Stony Place, Oneonta is home to Hartwick College, a branch of the State University of New York, and the **National Soccer Hall of Fame** (18 Stadium Circle, off Brown St., off Rte. 205 [Exit 13 from I-88], 607/432-3351, www.soccerhall.org, 9 A.M.–7 P.M. daily June–Aug., 9 A.M.–7 P.M. daily Sept.–May, adults $9, seniors $8, children under 12 $6.50). The museum traces the history of soccer in the United States from its 1860 beginnings to the present. Housed in a large complex on a 61-acre campus, the hall begins with a Hall of Fame atrium and then goes on to two floors of exhibits. Historic photos, trophies, uniforms, and other memorabilia are on display, while out back are four well-used soccer fields.

Sports and Recreation

Baseball: The Class A **Oneonta Tigers,** a farm team for Detroit, play ball at the old-time Damaschke Field (Neawha Park, 607/432-6326) June–Labor Day. The games draw large crowds, primarily tourists visiting Cooperstown.

Recreation: About seven miles north of the city is bucolic **Gilbert Lake State Park** (Cty. Rd. 12 off Rte. 205, Laurens, 607/432-2114, $6–8 parking), offering swimming, hiking, boating, and camping.

Information and Services

The **Cooperstown Chamber of Commerce** (31 Chestnut St., off Main St., 607/547-9983, www.cooperstownchamber.com) is open July–August, daily 9 A.M.–6 P.M.; June and September–October, daily 10 A.M.–5 P.M.; call for off-season hours. A visitor information kiosk is located on Main Street near the flagpole.

Schoharie County

To the east of Cooperstown and southwest of Albany sits Schoharie County, a quiet haven of agricultural land centered around the fertile Schoharie Valley. During the Revolutionary period, the valley was a breadbasket for the colonies, producing much of its wheat; at the turn of the century, the valley's hop fields were among the richest in the world. Today the Schoharie Valley is known for its enormous truck farms producing wheat and corn, fruit and vegetables.

(SHARON SPRINGS

Heading into Schoharie County on Route 20 from Cherry Valley, you'll come to Sharon Springs, once known for its sulfur springs and grand old hotels. Most of the latter are located along Route 10, a delicious array of rambling old Victorians that until recently were in various states of abandonment. Now, however, Sharon Springs is being rediscovered—partly by its own residents, who have opened new shops and other establishments along Main Street.

At the heart of Sharon Springs is the 1847 **American Hotel** (192 Main St.), which re-opened for business in 2001 after a four-year restoration. Also watch out for the striking white-and-turquoise **Imperial Baths** (248 Main St., 518/284-2285, www.adlerhotel-spa.com, 8 A.M.–4 P.M.) Sun.–Fri. June–Sept.), housed in the 1927 **Adler Hotel,** a National Historic Landmark.

Across the street from the Imperial Baths is the **Sharon Historical Museum and Schoolhouse** (Main St., 518/284-2350 or 518/284-2839, 1–4 P.M. daily July–Aug., free admission), filled with historic photos, tintypes, and documents dating back to the 1850s. As the photos show, the surviving baths are nothing compared to the "water temples" that once filled the town. The museum is partially housed in an 1863 one-room schoolhouse.

Food and Accommodations

Complete with enormous white pillars and porches, the **(C American Hotel** (192 Main St., 518/284-2105, www.americanhotelny.com, $150 d, with full breakfast) offers nine comfortable guestrooms and a popular 65-seat restaurant. On the menu, which changes daily, is American fare ranging from filet mignon to grilled fish; average entrée $20.

The family-run **Clausen Farms B&B Inn** (106 Clausen Ridge Rd., off Rte. 20, 518/284-2527, www.reu.comclausen, $80–120 d) is a grand old Victorian homestead listed on the National Historic Register. The inn offers 11 guest rooms, four (all with private baths) in the main house and seven (all with adjoining baths) in the Victorian gentleman's guesthouse, complete with a dramatic tower and large porch. Also on site are 80 acres laced with trails, a swimming pool, restored bowling lane, 12 resident llamas, and—best of all—90-mile views of the Mohawk Valley.

(HOWE CAVERNS

The oldest tourist attraction in central New York is Howe Caverns (Caverns Rd., off Rte. 7 or Exit 22 off I-87, 518/296-8900, www.howe-caverns.com, 9 A.M.–6 P.M. daily, adults $18, seniors $15, children 7–12 $9), an extensive labyrinth of cathedral-like caves filled with shimmering stalactites, stalagmites, and flowstones. Through the caverns' center runs a small river, while at the far end laps a mysterious, quarter-mile-long lake.

Howe Caverns was discovered in 1842 by farmer Lester Howe. Finding a dark opening in a ledge, Howe tied a long rope to a sturdy tree and lowered himself inside. Each day he penetrated a bit deeper, until he'd explored nearly 1.5 miles of caves.

Word of Howe's discovery quickly spread, and before long he was conducting tours. Visitors paid 50 cents for a torturous eight-hour scramble underground. Later Howe lit the passageways with gas, and in 1854 his daughter was married in one of the caves—a tradition that continues to this day. Over

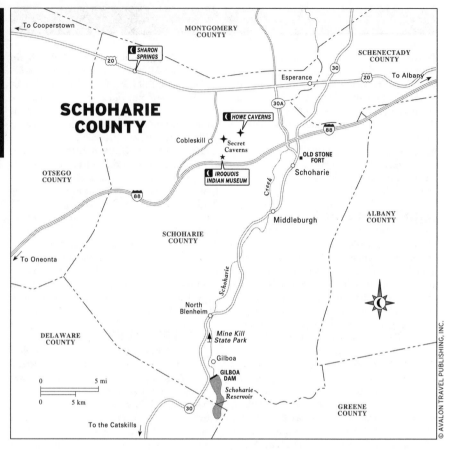

© AVALON TRAVEL PUBLISHING, INC.

350 weddings have to date taken place in the caverns.

A modern-day visit to the caves begins with an elevator ride descending down into the earth 156 feet. Tours proceed along paved walkways, where guides point out unusual rock formations lit by colored lights; then everybody climbs aboard for a boat ride on the lake. Temperatures below are always a steady 52°F.

CAVERNS CREEK GRISTMILL
Less than a mile from Howe Caverns is a handsome gristmill (Caverns Rd., 518/296-8448, www.cavernscreekgristmill.com, 11 A.M.– 7 P.M. daily June–Sept., adults $4, children

2–12 $3), a working 1816 National Historic Landmark equipped with a 12-foot-high waterwheel and 1,400-pound millstone. The mill grinds wheat into flour for use in pancake mixes; the nation's first packaged pancake mix was concocted here in 1890.

(IROQUOIS INDIAN MUSEUM
The newest addition to Caverns Road is the fine Iroquois Indian Museum (Caverns Rd., 518/296-8949, www.iroquoismuseum.org, 10 A.M.–5 P.M. Tues.–Sat. and noon–5 P.M. Sun. Apr.–Dec., also open Mon. July–Aug., closed Jan.–Mar., adults $7, seniors and students 13–17 $5.50, children 5–12 $4). Unlike most Native

American exhibits, this museum pays as much attention to the present as it does to the past, through its remarkable collection of contemporary Native American art. You'll see artifacts such as ancient pottery and arrow points here, to be sure, but chances are what you'll remember best are the museum's exquisite watercolors, oils, clay figures, stone carvings, and baskets.

Largely run by the Iroquois and learned scholars, the museum features many special programs, including dance and crafts demonstrations, storytelling hours, and nature walks. Downstairs is a children's museum where young ones can play musical instruments or craft beaded bracelets; upstairs is an excellent bookstore.

SECRET CAVERNS

Much less commercialized than Howe Caverns, the Secret Caverns (Caverns Rd., 518/296-8558, www.secretcaverns.com, 9 A.M.–6 P.M. daily June–Sept., 10 A.M.–4:30 P.M. daily May and Oct., adults $14, children 6–11 $6) provide an interesting contrast. Everything here has been left as natural as possible, allowing visitors to absorb the sights of this wondrous underworld without the distractions of megaphones, boat rides, and large tour groups. Even the descent is via natural means—stone steps rather than an elevator.

Like Howe Caverns, the Secret Caverns are filled with iridescent stalactites and stalagmites, illuminated along well-lit walkways under soaring ceilings. At the far end of the caves is a thundering 100-foot waterfall; everything else is eerily quiet.

Accommodations and Food

On Howe Caverns property are the well-kept, 21-room **Howe Caverns Motel** (Caverns Rd., 518/296-8950, $100–150 d in summer, $85–125 d off season, breakfast included, kids stay free), which was once air-conditioned by cool breezes from the caves. A casual restaurant serving lunch and early dinner fare is attached to the motel.

SCHOHARIE

The quaint historic village of Schoharie is best known for its **Old Stone Fort** (N. Main St.,

518/295-7192, 10 A.M.–5 P.M. Tues.–Sat. and noon–5 P.M. Sun. May–Oct., also open Mon. July–Aug., adults $5, seniors $4.50, students 5–18 $1.50). The largest British raid in the area occurred here on October 17, 1780, when Col. John Johnson and Chief Joseph Brant entered the valley and set fire to everything in sight. The valley was devastated, but the attackers failed to take stout Old Stone Fort.

Today, the restored fort serves as the centerpiece of the village. On display are war artifacts from the Revolution through World War II and period furnishings from historic Schoharie homes. Out back find a restored carriage shed, schoolhouse, two Colonial homes, and several barns.

Food

Built in 1800, and remodeled in 1874, the **Schoharie Pharmacy & Soda Fountain** (Main St., 518/295-7300) boasts an antique soda fountain where you can order over 20 flavors of ice-cream sodas. For lunch or dinner in a historic setting, step into the 1870 **Parrott House** (Main St., 518/295-7111); average dinner entrée $12.

In nearby Cobleskill, the 1802 **Bull's Head Inn** (2 Park Pl., 518/234-3591) offers open-hearth cooking, steaks, sandwiches, pasta, and over 70 kinds of beer. Live jazz and blues are often presented on the weekends; average dinner entrée $13.

Petrified Forest

Heading south of Schoharie on Route 30 will bring you to the Gilboa Dam and Schoharie Reservoir, part of the Catskill Reservoir system. Near the dam is Route 990v, leading to a small but amazing petrified forest consisting of stone stumps from now-extinct seed-bearing fern trees. Among the oldest types of trees known to humankind, these plants grew on the shores of New York's Devonian Sea about 365 million years ago. The stumps were uncovered by the New York Board of Water Supply in the 1920s.

Continue another half mile on Route 990v to reach a scenic overlook with great views of the reservoir.

Oneida County

Compared to the other counties in Leatherstocking Country, Oneida County is positively crowded. Two large cities—Utica and Rome—are located here. The Mohawk River runs through the county as far west as Rome, while at its western edge lies whale-shaped Oneida Lake.

The Oneida County Convention and Visitors Bureau (315/724-7221 or 800/426-3132, www.oneidacountycvb.com) runs a **visitor information center** at Exit 31 off the New York State Thruway (I-90) in Utica (9 A.M.–5 P.M. Mon.–Fri.).

UTICA

Near the western end of the Mohawk River Valley lies Utica. Once an important industrial city best known for its knitting mills, Utica lost much of its manufacturing base over the past few decades and now feels oddly arrested in time. Everywhere stand handsome but underutilized public buildings and abandoned red-brick factories.

Located at what was once for many miles the only ford across the Mohawk River, Utica was first settled by whites in the mid-1700s. In 1825 the Erie Canal brought prosperity to the town, along with new industries and immigrants. The first woolen mills opened in 1847, the first cotton mills in 1848, and the first firearm factories in the 1860s. Thousands of Irish and German immigrants began arriving in the mid-1800s; thousands of Poles and Italians came around the turn of the 20th century, and Utica still harbors a large Italian community. More recent arrivals have included refugees from Bosnia, Belarus, and Vietnam, and their presence is starting to bring new life to the city.

The heart of old Utica, where Main, Genesee, and Whitesboro Streets meet, is **Baggs Square,** named for Moses Baggs, who built a log tavern here in 1798. The square is lined with impressive turn-of-the-century buildings, as is Genesee Street itself, a main drag running virtually the entire length of the city. Three

blocks south of Baggs Square is Bleecker Street, where Frank Woolworth opened his first five-and-dime in 1879; it was a failure.

◖ Munson-Williams-Proctor Institute

This fine institute (310 Genesee St., 315/797-0000, www.mwpi.edu, 10 A.M.–5 P.M. Tues.–Sat., 1–5 P.M. Sun., free admission), housed in a streamlined Philip Johnson building filled with air and light, is part art museum, part art school, and part performing-arts center. The museum's collection contains more than 5,000 works of art by the likes of Picasso, Dali, Pollock, Moore, and Burchfield. An institute highlight is the "Voyage of Life" series painted by Hudson River School artist Thomas Cole, depicting man's passage through the four stages of life—childhood, youth, manhood, and old age.

Next door to the art museum stands the **Fountain Elms,** an Italianate villa once home to the Proctor and Munson families. Now a museum, the mansion is still outfitted with its original furnishings, which include several enormous gilt-bronze chandeliers and two "slipper chairs" designed to help the ladies put on their high-button shoes.

Saranac Brewery

Makers of Saranac beer, among others, the F. X. Matt Brewing Company (Court and Varick Sts., 315/732-0022, www.saranac.com, 1–4 P.M. Mon.–Sat. and Sun. 1–3 P.M. June–Aug., call for off-season hours, adults $3, children 6–12 $1) was founded in 1888 by F. X. Matt and is now run by his grandson. When operating at full capacity, the plant can produce 2.4 million bottles of beer a day, most distributed within 200 miles of Utica.

Visitors to F. X. Matt are met by guides in costume dress who conduct one-hour tours through the plant. Stops include the brewhouse, where two enormous copper kettles hold 18,000 gallons of beer each; the temperature-

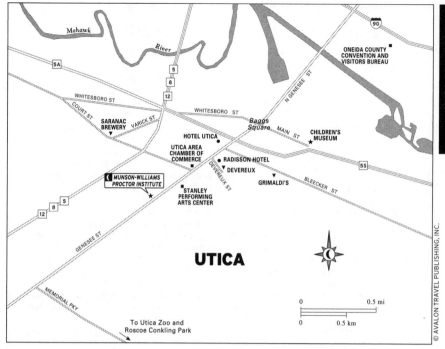

UTICA

0   0.5 mi
0   0.5 km

To Utica Zoo and
Roscoe Conkling Park

© AVALON TRAVEL PUBLISHING, INC.

controlled tanks, where the beer is fermented; and the bottling department, where the bottles are washed, filled, capped, and labeled. Visitors are then transported via trolley to a restored 1888 tavern where they're offered a mug of draft or root beer, compliments of the house.

Utica Zoo

This popular zoo (99 Steele Hill Rd., at Memorial Pkwy., 315/738-0472, www.uticazoo.org, 10 A.M.–5 P.M. daily, adults $5, children 2–12 $3, free admission in winter) is located at the southern end of the city, next door to **Roscoe Conkling Park,** designed by Frederick Law Olmsted. Residing here are about 300 species of mammals, birds, and reptiles, including the endangered Siberian tiger, golden lion tamarin, red panda, and bald eagle. The Children's Zoo holds barnyard animals and a petting area. Sea lion shows are presented every day but Tuesday, at noon and 3 P.M.

Children's Museum

Billed as the finest children's museum between New York City and Toronto, this lively institute (311 Main St. at Railroad St., 315/724-6129, www.museum4kids.net, 10 A.M.–4 P.M. Mon.–Tues. and Thurs.–Sat., $6 admission, kids under 1 free) holds a wide variety of imaginative exhibits and hands-on displays. Here, children can visit a Native American longhouse, examine dinosaur life of the Mesozoic era, find out what's under the "skin" of a new car, and experiment with laser light. Herd younger children to the Dino Den and play area.

Entertainment

The city's premier performance venue is the **Stanley Performing Arts Center** (259 Genesee St., 315/724-4000), originally built as a 2,945-seat movie theater in a "Mexican Baroque-style." Now on the National Register of

THE ERIE CANAL: PAST AND PRESENT

The Erie Canal was the making of New York City and New York State. With its completion in 1825 came an explosion of trade between the East and the Midwest. Shipping rates between Buffalo and New York City dropped 80-90 percent; by 1834, the canal's tolls had more than paid for the entire cost of its $7.7 million construction.

Pre-Erie Canal, New York City was the nation's fifth largest seaport, behind Boston, Baltimore, Philadelphia, and New Orleans. Fifteen years post-Erie Canal, New York was America's busiest port, moving tonnages greater than those of Boston, Baltimore, and New Orleans combined.

With the exception of Binghamton and Elmira, every major city in New York falls along the trade route established by the Erie Canal. And, even today, approximately 75 percent of the state's population still lives along the corridors created by the canals and the Hudson River.

BUILDING THE CANAL

One of the first to envision the Erie Canal was a Geneva miller named Jesse Hawley. While languishing in debtor's prison in the early 1800s,

Hawley wrote 14 newspaper essays promoting a cross-state canal. When President Jefferson first heard of the plan, he said, "It is a splendid project and may be executed a century hence... but it is little short of madness to think of it at this day." However, the essays came to the attention of politician DeWitt Clinton, who was swept into the governor's office in 1817 on a pro-canal platform.

Work on the canal began that very year. An engineering marvel of its day, the canal was built almost entirely by shovel and pick-ax, by men who had no engineering experience whatsoever. Over 25 percent of the canal builders were recent Irish immigrants earning 80 cents an hour. They started in Rome, where a light soil ensured rapid progress, and in 1819, the first 15-mile-long section opened up between Rome and Utica. It would take another six years, however, before the canal was completed, and many lost faith along the way. The project became known as "Clinton's Ditch" and "Clinton's Folly."

The work was grueling and often dangerous. Close to 1,000 men died of malaria while running the canal through the Montezuma Swamp. Others died while constructing a flight of locks

Historic Places, the center presents an interesting mix of classical music, opera, and theater. The **Munson-Williams-Proctor Institute** (310 Genesee St., 315/797-0000) features occasional jazz and blues artists, as well as classic movies.

Accommodations

The grand 1912 **(Hotel Utica** (102 Lafayette St., 315/724-7829, $125–140 d) boasts a delicious period lobby complete with high ceilings, faux-marble columns, crystal chandeliers, and antique birdcages. Rooms are airy and attractive; downstairs is the upscale 1912 Restaurant.

Also downtown, find the sleek **Radisson Hotel** (200 Genesee St., 315/797-8010, $139

d). This modern establishment is equipped with a pool, restaurant, and cocktail lounge with live entertainment on the weekends.

Food

A number of Italian restaurants and pastry shops are located along Bleecker Street. Among them is **(Grimaldi's** (428 Bleecker St., 315/732-7011), a cheery eatery that's one of the oldest and biggest restaurants in town; average dinner entrée $15.

The landmark **(Devereux** (37 Devereux St., 315/735-8628) offers hearty soups and overstuffed deli sandwiches, with live music on weekends; average sandwich $7.

through the Niagara Escarpment – a solid wall of rock rising 565 feet above sea level.

Finally finished in 1825, the canal measured 363 miles long, 40 feet wide, and four feet deep. Alongside it ran a towpath for the mules and drivers who pulled the barges along before the advent of steam power.

The astonishing success of the Erie Canal sparked a canal-building craze, and between 1823 and 1828, several important lateral canals were opened up, including the Champlain, Oswego, and Cayuga-Seneca. The canals were enlarged three times over the years to accommodate larger boats. The completion of the enormous St. Lawrence Seaway in the 1950s, however, rendered New York's canal system all but obsolete.

EXPLORING THE CANALS TODAY

Today, less than 100 commercial barges a year ply the waters between Buffalo and Albany. The New York State Canal System primarily serves as a low-key, relatively unknown tourist attraction for boaters, bikers, and day trippers. It offers great potential to become much more than that, but as of yet, most of the canal system remains undeveloped. Its main attractions are

its backside glimpses into an older, more industrialized America and its pastoral countryside.

Various boat companies operate excursions, or you can rent your own canoe or canal boat. Daily tour boats include the *Dutch Apple* in Albany (518/463-0220) and **Lockport Lock and Erie Canal Cruises** in Lockport (716/433-6155). Three-day cruises are offered out of the Syracuse area by **Mid-Lakes Navigation** (315/685-8500 or 800/545-4318), a company that also rents canal boats. Canoes and kayaks are available for rent at the **Boat House** in Schenectady (518/393-5711).

The canal system also offers excellent biking. Among the most popular routes are the 60-mile Mohawk-Hudson Bikeway, which runs along both those rivers west and north of Albany; the 32-mile Old Erie Canal State Park Bikeway, which runs east of Syracuse; and the 60-mile Barge Canal Recreationway, which travels through Monroe and Orleans Counties in western New York.

For more information on cruising or biking along the canal system, contact the **New York State Canal Corporation** (P.O. Box 189, Albany 12201, 518/436-2799 or 800/4-CANAL4, www .canal.state.ny.us).

ORISKANY BATTLEFIELD

Off Route 69 between Utica and Rome is the Oriskany Battlefield (315/768-7224, 9 A.M.–5 P.M. Wed.–Sat. and Sun. 1–4:45 P.M. May–Oct., adults $3, children $1), the site of the bloodiest battle of the American Revolution. The battle took place during the siege of Fort Stanwix when 900 Continental troops, coming west to reinforce the fort, were ambushed by the British. Hundreds of soldiers on both sides were killed and the American general Herkimer fatally wounded. Subsequently the British general St. Leger, fearing yet more Colonial militiamen were about to arrive, abandoned the siege of Fort Stanwix and withdrew

to Canada. Two months later, surrounded and cut off, British general Burgoyne surrendered his army at Saratoga—the turning point of the war.

At the battlefield site is a small museum and 100-foot commemorative monument. National Park Service rangers offer guided tours.

ROME

Rome must be the flattest city in all New York. Sitting athwart the basin of the upper Mohawk River, the city feels like a tiny windswept nub surrounded by a vast antediluvian plain. The fact that much of the downtown was destroyed during urban renewal doesn't help matters

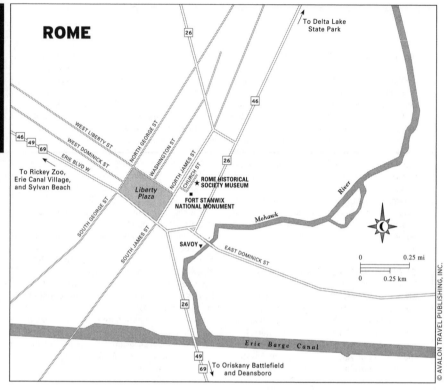

© AVALON TRAVEL PUBLISHING, INC.

much either. Most of the city feels empty, depressed, forgotten.

Before white people arrived, Rome was an important Native American site known as De-O-Wain-Sta, or "The Lifting or Setting Down of Boat." The site marked the one-mile canoe portage between the upper end of the Mohawk River and Wood Creek, which linked the Great Lakes to the Atlantic Ocean. The English realized the strategic importance of the place and in 1758 built Fort Stanwix.

The Americans took over Fort Stanwix in 1776, and in 1777 successfully withstood a three-week siege waged by British general St. Leger. After the war, the settlement was renamed Rome in tribute to the "heroic defence of the Republic made here."

The digging of the Erie Canal began in

Rome on July 4, 1817, and by mid-century the town was a bustling transportation center. Railroads followed the canals; then came the Rome Brass and Copper Company, attracting large numbers of Italian and Polish immigrants. By the 1930s Rome was processing one-tenth of all the copper mined in the United States. Today, copper is still processed in Rome, though in much-diminished amounts.

Fort Stanwix National Monument

Dominating downtown Rome is its primary tourist attraction, the reconstructed Fort Stanwix (112 E. Park St., 315/336-2090, 9 A.M.–5 P.M. daily Apr.–Dec., extended hours in summer, free admission). Built on a large parcel of land razed during urban renewal, the monument opened in 1976 to the tune of $7 million. It is said to be one of the most accurate reconstructed log-and-earth fortifications in the world.

Run by the National Park Service, the fort includes two long barracks, a guardhouse, officers' quarters, and various casemates, sentry boxes, and gun platforms. Surrounding the place is an ultra-neat wall built of pointy blond logs; at the entrance is a drawbridge. Costumed guides interpret military life; a small museum exhibits artifacts.

Rome Historical Society Museum

Just north of Fort Stanwix is a large, rambling, rather musty but fascinating museum (200 Church St., 315/336-5870, 10 A.M.–5 P.M. Tues.–Fri. year-round, 10 A.M.–3 P.M. summer Sat., free admission), where you can learn more about the city's history. Exhibits cover the Colonial period to Rome's recent industrial past; on-site is a well-stocked gift shop, where you can pick up free walking tours of downtown. Most of Rome's finest buildings, erected in the 1800s, are located along nearby North Washington Street.

Erie Canal Village

After touring Fort Stanwix, visitors usually head west a few miles on Erie Boulevard (Route 46/49 W) to Erie Canal Village (Rts.

46/49W, 315/337-3999, www.eriecanalvillage.net, 10 A.M.–5 P.M. Wed.–Sat., noon–5 P.M. Sun. June–Sept., adults $15, seniors and students $12, children 5–12 $10). Built along the banks of the canal, on what was once a German neighborhood, the village re-creates the early *canawlers'*—or canal workers'—lives through a cluster of 19th-century buildings and mule-drawn packet boat rides.

In the village you'll find the 1858 Canal Store, packed with boat horns, tow ropes, and other essential provisions, and the 1869 Skull House, a gorgeous Italianate home built by wealthy cattleman Jacob Skull. The 1862 Verona Cheese Factory once churned out 60-pound rounds of cheddar cheese, while the 1862 Bennett's Tavern still serves cold draft or root beer, pretzels, and pickled eggs. Guides in period dress drive mules pulling the packet boat *Independence* along a 1.5-mile stretch of canal; rides last 45 minutes.

Food

Not far from Fort Stanwix is East Dominick Street, once a veritable cornucopia of Italian restaurants. These are dying out now, but the street still features a few good pizza parlors and the family-owned **Savoy** (255 E. Dominick St., 315/339-3166), specializing in pasta and seafood; average entrée $12.

Madison County

Rural Madison County is in the dead center of the state. Among its more unusual towns are Oneida, once home to the Utopian Oneida Community; and Chittenango, the birthplace of L. Frank Baum, author of *The Wizard of Oz*. Near the eastern edge of the county is Cazenovia, an attractive, tourist-oriented village overlooking Cazenovia Lake.

ONEIDA

Perversely located in Madison rather than Oneida County is the town of Oneida, a gra-

cious place filled with wide, shady streets and prosperous homes. Oneida was established in the mid-1800s when a Mr. Sands Higinbotham, who lived on the site, struck a deal with the railroad whereby it received free right of way across his property on the condition every passenger train stop for 10 minutes. The wily Higinbotham then built a refreshment stand and restaurant, and Oneida was born.

Along Route 46 just north of the city, and technically located in Oneida County, is the 35-acre Oneida Nation Territory. The Oneida are

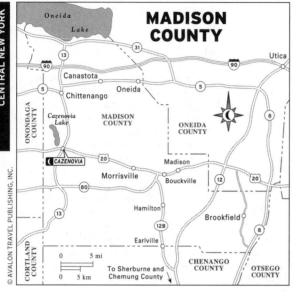

Tours are given by descendants of the Oneida Community who still live in the Mansion House. Most are single men and women in their 70s who impart short anecdotes as they guide visitors through the Big Hall, Outer Library, Upper Sitting Room, Nursery Kitchen, Lounge, Dining Room, and History Room. A portrait of a stern-looking John Humphrey Noyes, the community's founder, hangs in one hallway; the History Room contains evocative photographs, letters, and ledgers. Everything is in mint condition.

Tours of the house are offered Wednesday–Saturday at 10 A.M. and 2 P.M., Sundays at 2 P.M. ($5 per person). To reach the house from downtown, take Route 5 east to Sherrill Road to Kenwood Avenue.

an Iroquois tribe that has lived in upstate New York since before the arrival of the whites.

Cottage Lawn Museum

The best place to learn about Oneida's history is at Higinbotham's former home (435 Main St., 315/363-4136, 9 A.M.–4 P.M. Mon.–Fri year-round, 9 A.M.–4 P.M. Sat. July–Aug., $2 admission), now a museum operated by the Madison County Historical Society. Designed by Alexander Jackson Davis, the handsome Gothic Revival mansion showcases period furnishings, Erie Canal artifacts, and locally produced ceramics, glassware, and textiles.

The Mansion House

The Oneida Community, a Utopian society that flourished in the mid-1800s, once occupied this large, red-brick Mansion House (170 Kenwood Ave., 315/363-0745, www.oneida-community.org) on the edge of town. Built around a central tower, the house is surrounded by a wide jade-green lawn and towering elms. Inside are over 300 rooms, many converted into apartments and guest rooms.

Shako:Wi Cultural Center

On Route 46 a few miles south of the city is an Oneida cultural center (5 Territory Rd. [Rte. 46], 315/829-8801, www.oneida-nation.net/shakowi, 9 A.M.–5 P.M. daily, free admission), housing classrooms, a gift shop, and the Oneida Nation Museum. The museum features archaeological artifacts, photographic essays, silverwork by Oneida artist Richard Chrisjohn, and the collection of the late Bill Rockwell, Sr. Rockwell was one of the Oneida Nation's last traditional chiefs, and his collection includes traditional dress, beadwork, and woodwork.

Turning Stone Resort & Casino

Off Route 365 about five miles northeast of the city is the big, glitzy Turning Stone Resort & Casino (Rte. 365, Verona, [Exit 33 off I-90], 315/361-7711, www.turning-stone.com, open 24 hours/day), the first legal casino in New York State, opened in 1993 and now one of upstate's biggest tourist attractions (a second

THE UTOPIAN ONEIDA COMMUNITY

Founded in 1848 by John Humphrey Noyes, the Oneida Community – a.k.a. the Perfectionists – believed that the second coming of Christ occurred in the year A.D. 70, meaning that the human race had been freed from sin, and personal perfection was possible. Men and women should work together to achieve that perfection, and relinquish all personal property. Marital vows should be abandoned in favor of "complex" marriages that allowed for several sexual partners.

When the Perfectionists first arrived in Oneida, they eked out a meager living by farming. However, they soon turned to more lucrative pursuits, such as selling canned fruits and vegetables, steel traps and chains, and finally the famed flatware still produced by Oneida, Ltd., today. All community members, men and women, shared equally in the work, taking turns at both menial and managerial tasks.

When not working, they improved their minds by reading the Bible and books about science, religion, and history.

In existence from 1848 to 1881, the Oneida Community was one of the longest-lived Utopian societies. At its zenith, it claimed about 300 members. In 1879, however, outside criticism – which had always been present – grew especially hostile, forcing Noyes to move to Canada. Here, he ruled from afar for about a year, but finally in 1881 the community disbanded. Property was distributed equally among all members, including the children, and the business incorporated.

Today, many descendants of the Oneida Community still live in Oneida; note the many mailboxes marked Noyes. A few live in the Mansion House, which was once home to the entire community, and is now open to the public for guided tours, meals, and lodging.

casino opened on the St. Regis Mohawk Reservation in Akwesasne, near Canada, in 1999). Owned and operated by the Oneida Indian Nation of New York, the Turning Stone offers blackjack, craps, roulette, big six, baccarat, red dog, mini baccarat, acey deucey, pai gow poker, and 2,400 cashless slot machines. One traditional element is missing, however—liquor. The Oneida decided alcohol had done enough damage to their people over the years.

Connected to the casino is an enormous bingo hall seating about 1,100. Games are played throughout the day, with doors opening at 10 A.M. Also on site are four **hotels,** three championship-caliber **golf courses,** a **spa,** upscale boutiques, entertainment halls, and some of the fanciest **restaurants** in the region.

CANASTOTA

Continuing west on Route 5 from Oneida, you'll come to the village of Canastota, notable for its well-preserved canal buildings along the old Erie Canal. One has been turned into the **Canal Town Museum** (122 N. Canal St., 315/697-3451,

10 A.M.–4 P.M. Mon.–Fri. and 10 A.M.–1 P.M. Sat. June–Aug., 11 A.M.–3 P.M. Tues.–Fri. Apr.–May and Sept.–Oct., free admission), which succinctly explains canal history.

Canastota's other claim to fame is the **International Boxing Hall of Fame Museum** (1 Hall of Fame Dr., [Exit 34 off I-90], 315/697-7095, www.ibhof.com, 9 A.M.–5 P.M. Mon.–Fri., 10 A.M.–4 P.M. Sat.–Sun., adults $5, seniors $4, youths 9–15 $3), founded in Canastota in 1984 largely because two major boxing champs—Carmen Basilio and Billy Backus—hailed from here. Most of the museum is housed in one large room. To one side are the robes of boxing greats and the fist casts of dozens of champs; to another, the Wall of Fame, inscribed with the names of all inductees. The famous purple trunks of Joe Louis are on display, along with Rocky Marciano's gloves and Mike Tyson's mouthpieces.

CHITTENANGO

A few miles west of Canastota is Chittenango, an old-fashioned village filled with boxy wooden homes and sturdy brick storefronts. Author L. Frank Baum was born here on May 15, 1856, the son of a maker of "fine barrels and butter firkins."

Chittenango honors its most famous native son with a pale **yellow brick road** that runs along the sidewalks of Genesee Street. Auntie Em's, the Emerald City Grill, The Wizard's Printer read various signs. Oz souvenirs, including T-shirts, postcards, and baseball cards, are for sale in the **Chittenango Pharmacy** (219 Genesee St., 315/687-7801) and the L. Frank Baum-Oz Museum.

L. Frank Baum-Oz Museum

Housed in a storefront next to the Emerald City Grill is a small museum (227 Genesee St., 315/687-3423, noon–3 P.M. Mon.–Sat. July–Aug., noon–2 P.M. Wed.–Sat. Sept.–June, free admission) dedicated to Baum and *The Wizard of Oz*. On display are first-editions of Baum's books, some of his personal effects, memorabilia from *The Wizard of Oz* movie, Oz plates, and lots of photos and posters. Oz souvenirs for sale range from books and tee shirts to decorative tins and mugs.

Chittenango Falls State Park

On Route 13 about four miles south of downtown are Chittenango Falls (315/655-9620, open daily Apr.–Oct., $6–8 parking), cascading for some 167 feet down, over, and under steplike rock ledges. Wider than most waterfalls, with streams that spread out like fans, the Chittenango Falls are among the most beautiful in the state. The park also offers hiking and nature trails, good fishing sites, and a 22-site campground. For camping reservations, call 800/456-CAMP.

Food

Oz lovers will want to dine in ◖ **Auntie Em's Restaurant** (262 Genesee St., 315/687-5704), all decked out in blue-checked curtains, *Wizard of Oz* posters, music scores from the 1939 movie, and little tin men hanging from the ceiling. The family-style eatery specializes in Auntie Em's homemade fare and is open for breakfast, lunch, and dinner. Another good choice for Oz fans is the **Emerald City Grill** (225 Genesee St., 315/687-7453), serving up some of the best burgers in the region.

Events

The **Ozfest** (315/687-3903) celebrates Baum's birthday with a parade, music, mimes, a crafts show, and an annual spaghetti dinner with Munchkins from the 1939 movie. The Munchkins are all in their seventies and eighties now, but a handful have arrived for this one-of-a-kind feast every year since 1988. The festival takes place on the weekend nearest May 15, Baum's birthday.

◖ CAZENOVIA

Continuing south on Route 13, you'll come to Cazenovia, a favorite weekend getaway for Syracusans. Composed primarily of three country inns, Cazenovia sits on the edge of Cazenovia Lake, a four-mile swath of deep blue rimmed with fine homes. The American Indians called the lake *Hod-way-gen-hen,* or Lake Where the Yellow Perch Swim.

Two of Cazenovia's inns, the Brae Loch and the Lincklaen House, occupy the heart of the village, surrounded by quaint, tourist-oriented shops. The third, the 1890 Brewster, is on a secluded drive by the lake.

Cazenovia was settled in 1793 by John Lincklaen, land agent for the Holland Land Company, which once controlled 3.3 million acres in western New York. In one of the greatest real estate promotions in U.S. history, the company sold plots of this land to settlers heading west on the Great Western Highway (Route 20). The main Holland Land Company office was actually located much farther west, in the town of Batavia, but Lincklaen opened a branch office here in hopes of catching settlers early. He named the town after the company's general agent in Philadelphia, Theophile Cazenove.

Lorenzo State Historic Site

"Situation suberb, fine land" were John Lincklaen's words when he first viewed Cazenovia;

within a few years, he'd built himself an elegant Federal-style mansion (17 Rippleton Rd. [Rte. 13], south of Rte. 20, 315/655-3200, 10 A.M.– 4:30 P.M. Tues.–Sun. May–Oct., adults $3, seniors $2, children under 12 $1). An educated man with an especially strong interest in the Italian Renaissance, Lincklaen named his new home Lorenzo in honor of the Medici.

Now a house museum open to the public, Lorenzo features an especially fine carriage house filled with dozens of horse-drawn vehicles. During the summer, carriage races are staged, just as they were back in the 19th century.

Accommodations and Food

If you'd like to stay overnight, the Scottish **Brae Loch** (5 Albany St., 315/655-3431, www.braelochinn.com, $120–155 d, continental breakfast included) offers 12 rooms nicely outfitted with antiques from the British isles. All of the rooms have private baths, heat and air-conditioning, cable TV, and Internet access). On site is a restaurant serving American cuisine with Scottish and French influences; average dinner entrée $18.

The 1835 **❰ Lincklaen House** (79 Albany St., 315/655-3461, www.lincklaenhouse.com, $125–195 d), once a stagecoach stop and long an inn of note, features 18 rooms, each unique and furnished with Colonial-era antiques. The inn offers three menus—a tavern menu, casual fine dining menu, and fine dining menu—to suit all tastes and budgets.

The **❰ Brewster Inn** (Ledyard Ave., 315/655-9232, www.thebrewsterinn.com, $120–215 d), once the summer home of a wealthy financier, offers rooms in both its main house and carriage house. All are richly appointed with mahogany woodwork, antique furnishings, and Oriental rugs. The inn's casually elegant Terrace Bar offers great views of the lake; on the menu is classic American cuisine; average dinner entrée $22.

MADISON TO BOUCKVILLE

In Cazenovia you'll again bump into Route 20, America's longest highway. Head east on the old route a few miles—through hilly, bu-

colic farmland—and between Bouckville and Madison you'll find an extraordinary number of antiques shops. Over 100 dealers here comprise the largest grouping in the state. A guide to the shops, which specialize in everything from toys to furniture, is available in area tourist offices.

HAMILTON

From Route 20 just west of Bouckville, take Route 12B south through more fertile farmland to the town of Hamilton, home of **Colgate University.** The university (Broad St. and Kendrick Ave., 315/228-1000) clusters around a peaceful quadrangle flanked by rectangular buildings built in early Georgian and neo-Gothic styles.

EARLVILLE

On Route 12B a few miles south of Hamilton is tiny, tree-lined Earlville, once a wealthy village on the Chenango Canal. In the center of the village is the 1892 **Earlville Opera House** (16 E. Main St., 315/691-3550, www.earlvilleoperahouse.com), a rare, second-story theater. During the summer a wide variety of first-rate opera, theater, vaudeville, folk, jazz, and blues events are staged in this National Historic Landmark, which also houses a small art gallery. Call for events and tour information.

Surrounding the opera house are a number of shops and restaurants, often crowded with Colgate students and professors. For a welcome pint on a hot summer afternoon, step into the laid-back **Huff-Brau Tavern** (4 W. Main St., 315/691-3300).

Nearby Recreation

Just south of Earlville in Chenango County is the 571-acre **Rogers Environmental Education Center** (2721 Rte. 80 W, Sherburne, 607/674-4017, 8:30 A.M.–4:45 P.M. Mon.–Fri. and 1–4:45 P.M. Sat. year-round, 1–4:45 P.M. summer Sun., free admission). In the main building are exhibits on local flora and fauna, including 350 mounted birds, while outside, five hiking trails wind around an observation tower. Trails are open 24 hours a day.

Binghamton and Vicinity

At the confluence of the Chenango and Susquehanna Rivers lies the flat, half-empty city of Binghamton, population 53,000. To its west, over the Chenango, lie Johnson City and Endicott; collectively, the area is known as the Triple Cities, or "Home of the Square Deal." And therein lies a tale.

Though not much more than a small town until the time of the Civil War, Binghamton exploded into a major metropolis with the coming of the Industrial Revolution. Dozens of factories sprang up along its rivers, employing thousands of immigrants, most from southern and eastern Europe.

Binghamton's first major industry was cigar making. Then in 1889, the first large-scale shoe factory was established in the city; by 1905, that one factory had expanded to 22. All were run by Endicott-Johnson, arguably the country's first paternalistic corporation.

Endicott-Johnson was responsible for building Binghamton's two sister cities. It also built the cities' parks, provided employee health benefits, instituted what may have been the nation's first eight-hour workday, and sponsored frequent company picnics and ball games. In return, E-J, as it was affectionately known, received fierce employee loyalty. Statues of George F. Johnson, the company's founder, stand everywhere.

In its heyday E-J employed more than 20,000 people. By 1966 that number had fallen to 10,154. Today all that's left is one small workboot division.

Until recently, the vacuum created by a shrinking Endicott-Johnson was filled by a growing IBM. With IBM's downsizing around the turn of the 21st century, however, the Triple Cities are once again experiencing high unemployment.

A major branch of the State University of New York is located here.

Visitor Information

The Broome County Convention and Visitors Bureau **information center** (49 Court St., in the Metro Center, 2nd Fl., 607/772-8860 or 800/836-6740, www.binghamtoncvb.com, 8:30 A.M.–5 P.M. Mon.–Fri.) is stocked with an enormous number of brochures covering the entire region.

SIGHTS
Downtown

Binghamton centers around **Courthouse Square,** located along Court Street between State and Exchange Streets. Here stand the neoclassical 1898 Broome County Courthouse, a Civil War Monument, and the beaux arts 1898 Old City Hall. This magnificent building with its elegant staircase and marble floors is now the **Clarion Collection Grand Royale Hotel.** The polished brown desk in the lobby was once staffed by a police sergeant.

Along Riverside Drive at the southern tip

the 1898 Broome County Courthouse, on Binghamton's Courthouse Square

© CHRISTIANE BIRD

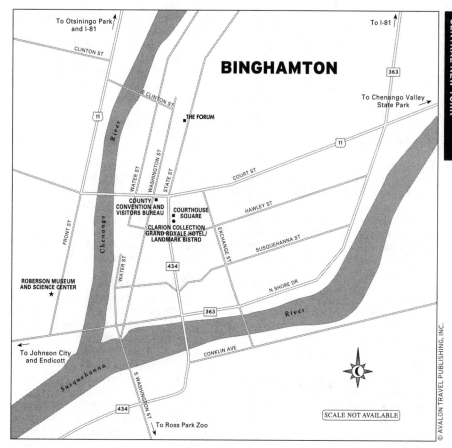

To Otsiningo Park
and I-81

CLINTON ST

BINGHAMTON

To I-81

363

E CLINTON ST

11

To Chenango Valley
State Park

THE FORUM

River

11

COURT ST

WATER ST

WASHINGTON ST

STATE ST

Chenango

COUNTY
CONVENTION AND
VISITORS BUREAU

COURTHOUSE
SQUARE

HAWLEY ST

FRONT ST

CLARION COLLECTION
GRAND ROYALE HOTEL/
LANDMARK BISTRO

EXCHANGE ST

SUSQUEHANNA ST

WATER ST

434

ROBERSON MUSEUM
AND SCIENCE CENTER
★

N SHORE DR

363

River

To Johnson City
and Endicott

Susquehanna

S WASHINGTON ST

CONKLIN AVE

SCALE NOT AVAILABLE

434

To Ross Park Zoo

© AVALON TRAVEL PUBLISHING, INC.

of downtown is the confluence of the Susquehanna and Chenango Rivers, a ferocious brown cauldron of churning waters. The best way to get there is by car.

Roberson Museum and Science Center

Housed in both an elegant 1910 mansion and a modern building, this enjoyable complex (30 Front St., 607/772-0660, www.roberson.org, 10:30 A.M.–4:30 P.M. Tues.–Sat., noon–4:30 P.M. Sun., adults $6; seniors, students, and children 4–12 $4) contains art and history galleries, period rooms, a planetarium, a 300-seat theater, and a gift shop. Exhibits range from a room devoted to native son Edwin Link, who developed the Link Flight Simulator, to displays on the region's folk art and varied ethnic heritage. There's also a science wing, a children's center with plenty of hands-on exhibits, and the **Binghamton Heritage Area Visitor Center.** The center publishes free walking- and driving-tour maps.

Clinton Street

If you drive north of the Roberson on Front Street about five long blocks, turn left, and head down Clinton about a mile, you'll come across a spread-out string of antique stores. One of the oldest and best known among them is the **Mad Hatter** (284 Clinton St., 607/729-6036).

Also on Clinton St. are three **gold dome churches:** Sts. Cyril and Methodius at No. 148, St. Michael's at No. 280, and the Holy Spirit Byzantine at No. 360. These sanctuaries are a testament to the region's strong Eastern European heritage.

The Carousels

In each of the Triple Cities' six major parks is an elaborate wood-carved carousel, donated to the public by Endicott-Johnson founder George F. Johnson. The carousels, crowded with animals, operate at no charge for the price of "one piece of litter." As a young boy, Johnson didn't have the nickel fare needed for a carousel ride, and so promised himself that when he grew up and grew rich no one would ever be denied a ride.

All six carousels were manufactured in the early 1900s by the Allan Herschell Companies of North Tonawanda, NY. They're all designed in the "country fair" style and feature original Wurlitzer Band Organs.

The six carousels are located in Ross Park (Morgan Rd.) and Recreation Park (Beethoven St.) in Binghamton; George W. Johnson Park (Oak Hill Ave.) and West Endicott Park (Page Ave.) in Endicott; C. Fred Johnson Park (C.F.J. Blvd.) in Johnson City; and Highland Park (Hooper Rd.) in Endwell. Hours of operation vary.

Ross Park Zoo

The fifth-oldest zoo in the country, Ross Park (60 Morgan Rd., 607/724-5461, www.rossparkzoo.com, 10 A.M.–5 P.M. daily Apr.–Oct., adults $4.50, seniors and children 3–12 $3) is home to a wide variety of exotic creatures, including white tigers, snow leopards, spectacled bears, black swans, Siberian lynxes, Patagonian cavies, Japanese snow monkeys, and Rocky Mountain sheep. One of the zoo's finest exhibits is its 2.5-acre Wolf Woods where timber wolves and endangered red wolves roam free.

The zoo is located in Ross Park (607/724-5461), where you'll also find the **Ross Park Carousel** and **Carousel Museum** (same hours as zoo, free admission), holding a handful of historic exhibits.

Rod Serling Exhibit

Though born in Syracuse, *Twilight Zone* creator Rod Serling grew up in Binghamton, and a small exhibit honoring his memory can be found in the Forum, a performing-arts center (236 Washington St., 607/778-2480, 8 A.M.–4 P.M. Mon.–Fri.). The exhibit features quotes from Serling's childhood friends, pictures from his *Twilight Zone* days, and a 1960s-era TV set. Though the tribute is disappointingly meager, die-hard fans may want to stop by.

ENTERTAINMENT

The city's top performance centers are the **Forum Theatre** (236 Washington St., 607/772-2480) and the **Anderson Center for the Performing Arts** (State University of New York, Rte. 434 [Vestal Pkwy.], Vestal, 607/777-ARTS). The first presents a mix of classical music, opera, and theater; the second hosts everything from R&B to experimental theater.

About 35 miles north of the city is the intimate **Night Eagle Cafe** (15 LaFayette Pl., 607/843-7378), overlooking the park in the village of Oxford. The café hosts an eclectic array of music and cultural events, but focuses on singer-songwriters.

EVENTS

The July **Otsiningo Pow Wow,** held on the site of an 18th-century Otsiningo Indian settlement, features dances, crafts, food, music, and storytelling. Come to the August **Spiedie Fest & Balloon Rally** for hot-air balloons and that local culinary treat, the spiedie sandwich. At the September **Apple Festival** you can sample 70-foot-long strudels and innumerable home-baked pies. For more information, call the Broome County Chamber of Commerce, 607/772-8860.

ACCOMMODATIONS

The **🄲 Clarion Collection Grand Royale Hotel** (80 State St., 607/722-0000, $85–198 d, breakfast included) is housed in Birmingham's grand former City Hall. The 1897 building has been divided into about 60 guest rooms of varying shapes, sizes, and price ranges, all with modern amenities. On site is the classy **Landmark Bistro** (607/722-9242), serving breakfast, lunch, and dinner; average dinner entrée $15.

FOOD

Binghamton's culinary claim to fame is the spiedie, a sandwich made of marinated chunks of lean meat on a skewer served on Italian bread. The tastiest and most authentic spiedies are available in the hole-in-wall **Sharkey's** (56 Glenwood Ave., 607/729-9201) or at one of the **Lupo's** delis scattered around town.

A good spot for lunch or dinner is the cheery **🄲 Copper Cricket** (266 Main St., 607/729-5620), offering dining on a closed-in front porch and a different menu daily; average dinner entrée $14. **Theo's** (14 Main St., Johnson City, 607/797-0088) serves tasty soul food; average main dish $9.

Worth driving out of the way for is Sunday brunch at the **🄲 Silo** (Moran Rd., off Rte. 206 E, Greene, 607/656-4377), housed in its namesake; the restaurant also serves a good dinner (average entrée $14). Though located in a sterile shopping mall, some of the best Thai food in the area is available at the **P.S. Restaurant** (100 Rano Blvd., Giant Plaza, Vestal, 607/770-0056); average entrée $14.

Sports and Recreation

The elbow-shaped **Hudson-Mohawk Bikeway** follows the Mohawk and Hudson Rivers for about 60 miles, from Rotterdam Junction north of Albany to St. Johnsville east of Albany. The bikeway, which is paved and popular among hikers as well as bikers, is part of the Canalway Trail System. For a free map, contact **Cycling the Erie Canal** (518/434-1583, www.nypca.org/canaltour).

For more information on any of the **New York State Parks,** visit www.nysparks.com.

Getting There and Around

The **Albany County Airport** is the oldest municipal airport in the United States, serviced by American Airlines (800/433-7300), Continental (800/525-0280), Delta (800/221-1212), Northwest (800/225-2525), United (800/241-6522), and USAirways (800/428-4322).

Amtrak (800/872-7245) provides train service to Albany-Rensselaer, Amsterdam, Utica, and Rome. **Adirondack-Pine Hill Trailways** (518/436-9651) and **Greyhound Bus Lines** (800/231-2222) service the Capital District. Greyhound also provides bus service to Leatherstocking Country.

The only practical way to tour the region is by car.

Information and Services

For general information on the Capital District (Albany, Troy, and Schenectady), contact the **Albany County Convention and Visitors Bureau** (25 Quackenbush Sq., Albany 12207, 518/434-1217 or 800/258-3582, www.albany.org). For general information on Cooperstown and environs, contact **Cooperstown/Otsego County Tourism** (242 Main St., Oneonta 13820, 607/643-0059 or 800/843-3394, www.visitcooperstown.com).

Each county and major towns also have their own visitor information office, as listed below. Most are open 9 A.M.–5 P.M. Monday–Friday.

Rensselaer County Chamber of Commerce (31 2nd St., Troy 12180, 518/274-7020, www.renscochamber.com)

Schenectady Chamber of Commerce (306 State St., Schenectady 12305, 518/372-5656 or 800/962-8007, www.schenectadychamber.org)

Montgomery County Chamber of Commerce (Box 309, Amsterdam 12010, 518/843-8200 or 800/743-7337, www.montgomerycountyny.com)

Herkimer County Chamber of Commerce (28 W. Main St., Mohawk 13407, 315/866-7820 or 877/984-4636, www.herkimercountychamber.com)

Cooperstown Chamber of Commerce (31 Chestnut St., Cooperstown 13326, 607/547-9983, www.cooperstownchamber.org).

Schoharie County Chamber of Coomerce (315 Main St., Schoharie, 12157, 518/295-7032 or 800/418-4748, www.schohariechamber.com)

Oneida County Convention and Visitors Bureau (Box 551, Utica 13503, 315/724-7221 or 800/426-3132, www.oneidacountycvb.com)

Rome Area Chamber of Commerce (139 W. Donimick St., Rome 13440, 315/337-1700, www.romechamber.com)

Madison County Tourism (Rte. 20, near South St., Morrisville 13408, 315/684-7320 or 800/684-7320, www.madisontourism.com)

Broome County Convention and Visitors Bureau (49 Court St., 2nd Fl., Binghamton 13903 607/772-8860 or 800/836-6740, www.binghamtoncvb.com)

THE NORTH COUNTRY

I am glad I shall never be young without wild country to be young in. Of what avail are forty freedoms without a blank spot on the map?

-Aldo Leopold, 1945

Just exactly what or where the North Country is depends on who you ask. For some, it is everything that falls within Adirondack Park. For others, it is the country north of the Adirondacks, along the St. Lawrence River, bordering Canada. For still others, it is all 14 counties that lie above the Mohawk River.

Close to one-third of New York State is a big, blank space on the map. Most of it is contained within Adirondack Park, a six-million-acre refuge that is an unusual mixture of public and private lands. Forty-three percent of the park is Forest Preserve that belongs to the people of New York. Fifty-seven percent is privately owned by industries and individuals, and devoted primarily to forestry, agriculture, and recreation. Within Adirondack Park live about 130,000 people in 105 towns and villages, most of which have populations of less than 1,000.

Parts of Adirondack Park are a vast and silent forest, filled with thousands of gleaming lakes and ponds, hundreds of rugged smoke-blue peaks, and endless miles of rushing rivers and streams. Other parts bustle with resort villages, scruffy industrial towns, and crowded recreational areas. During the region's short summers, vacationers flock here by the thousands to canoe, fish, camp, and hike. During its endless harsh winters, year-round residents

COURTESY OF LAKE PLACID/ESSEX COUNTY VISITORS BUREAU

HIGHLIGHTS

◖ National Museum of Racing and Hall of Fame: Learn more about the "sport of kings" in this one-of-a-kind, state-of-the-art museum and adjoining Hall of Fame in the charming Victorian town of Saratoga Springs (page 392).

◖ Hyde Collection: Housed in a 1912 mansion styled as a Renaissance villa is an important collection of Old Masters, including works by Rembrandt, El Greco, and Degas (page 404).

◖ Fort Ticonderoga: The French, British, and Americans all once held control of this now-meticulously restored fort holding everything from stables to a lock of Washington's hair (page 412).

◖ Essex: The loveliest village along surprisingly undeveloped Lake Champlain is filled with trim white buildings that date back to before the Civil War (page 415).

◖ Hiking from Adirondak Loj: Run by the nonprofit Adirondack Mountain Club, the lodge holds a first-rate information center about hiking in the Adirondacks. Many trails into Adirondack country begin here (page 423).

◖ Adirondack Museum: By far the most important museum in the region, the compact complex covers virtually every aspect of Adirondack life—and overlooks stunning Blue Mountain Lake (page 434).

◖ Sackets Harbor: Built on a bluff overlooking Lake Ontario, the village is peppered with handsome limestone buildings and a battlefield that dates back to the War of 1812 (page 443).

◖ Boldt Castle: On one of the Thousand Islands, the huge, abandoned castle was built by hotel magnate George Boldt for his beloved wife, who died before it was completed (page 450).

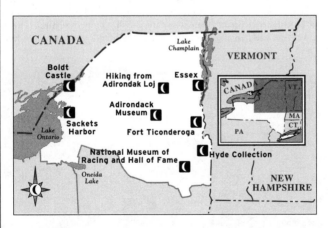

LOOK FOR ◖ TO FIND RECOMMENDED SIGHTS, ACTIVITIES, DINING, AND LODGING.

eke out livings through factory work, trapping, and logging.

Marking the southeastern entrance to the Adirondacks is Saratoga Springs, a small urban jewel known for its superb horse racing and mineral springs. North of the Adirondacks lie the Thousand Islands, an evocative place-name for the insular flecks scattered up the St. Lawrence River. Most of the Thousand Islands are as unpopulated as the Adirondacks, home to many more trees than people.

PLANNING YOUR TIME

A minimum of four or five days is necessary to explore some of the highlights of the Adirondacks, though one to two weeks would allow for more leisure and flexibility, especially if you want to do some hiking or canoeing. A good base of operations is **Lake Placid** or **Saranac Lake**—from these two scenic village/towns, located amidst the **High Peaks,** it's an easy drive to various attractions and good hiking trails. Alternatively, you might want to base yourself in the charming Victorian town of **Saratoga Springs,** and take overnight trips to the **Lake George** and **Lake Champlain** regions. Take an extra three days to explore the **Thousand Islands region** if you possibly can—or travel there directly. The region is unique to the state.

Travelers who stick only to the Adirondacks' roads and villages will get a one-sided sense of the place. The roads offer superb views, to be sure, but roads also make it easy to underestimate the park's vast and haunting wildness. The only way to truly experience the Adirondacks is by canoe or foot.

With the exception of major towns such as Saratoga Springs and Lake Placid, and ski resort areas, much of the North Country closes down during the off-season, which begins in mid-fall and runs through mid- to late-spring. If you're traveling during that period, be sure to call ahead to make sure attractions, restaurants, and hotels are open.

With the exception of major towns such as Saratoga Springs and Lake Placid, and ski resort areas, much of the North Country closes down during the off-season, which begins in mid-fall and runs through mid-to-late spring. If traveling during that period, be sure to call ahead to make sure attractions, restaurants, and hotels are open.

THE ADIRONDACKS
The Land

Contrary to popular perception, the Adirondacks are not an extension of the Appalachian Mountains, but rather are part of the vast Canadian Shield. Nearly twice as old as the Appalachians, the Adirondacks are composed of Precambrian igneous and metamorphic rock thrust upward about 10 million years ago. Atop the summits is a bluish erosion-resistant bedrock that, at 1.2 million years old, is among the oldest exposed bedrock in the world.

Also contrary to popular perception, much of the Adirondacks is not mountainous. Most of the area lies between 1,000 and 2,000 feet above sea level, with the western and southern sections composed of gentle hills strewn with lakes, ponds, and streams. Most of the highest summits—known as the High Peaks—are in the northeastern section, around Lake Placid. Forty-two of the 46 High Peaks are over 4,000 feet; Mt. Marcy, at 5,344 feet, is the highest.

Throughout the Adirondacks run 1,200 miles of rivers fed by an estimated 30,000 miles of brooks and streams. Most significant among them are the Hudson—whose highest source is Lake Tear of the Clouds on Mt. Marcy—Raquette, Ausable, Sacandaga, Beaver, Oswegatchie, St. Regis, and Moose. The park also contains about 2,800 lakes and ponds, the largest of which are Lake George and Lake Champlain. Between Lake Champlain and the mountains runs the long and fertile Champlain Valley.

Flora and Fauna

The Adirondack forest supports over 70 different species of trees, most of which are in the spruce and fir, or beech, birch, and maple families. White pines grow at the park's lowest elevations in the Champlain Valley, while spruce grows above 2,500 feet. In between thrive spruce swamps and hardwood forests.

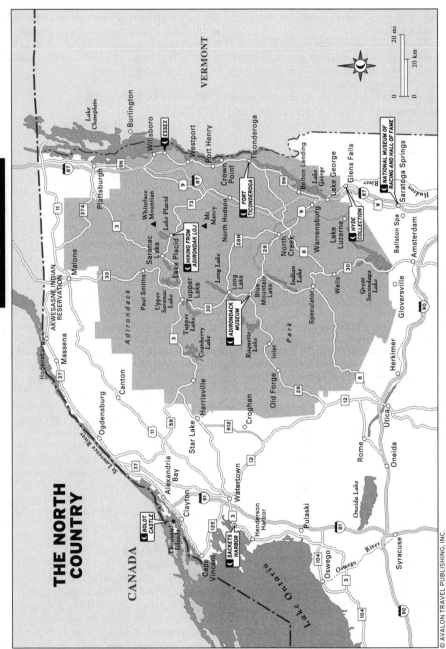

THE NORTH COUNTRY

VERMONT

CANADA

Lake Ontario

Lake Champlain

St. Lawrence River

Adirondack Park

AKWESASNE INDIAN RESERVATION

Burlington

Willsboro

ESSEX

Westport

Port Henry

Ticonderoga

Crown Point

FORT TICONDEROGA

Plattsburgh

Whiteface Mountain

Lake Placid

Saranac Lake

Mt Marcy

HIKING FROM ADIRONDAK LOJ

North Hudson

Bolton Landing

Lake George

Glens Falls

Saratoga Springs

NATIONAL MUSEUM OF RACING AND HALL OF FAME

Ballston Spa

Amsterdam

HYDE COLLECTION

Lake Luzerne

Warrensburg

North Creek

Paul Smiths

Upper Saranac Lake

Tupper Lake

Long Lake

Blue Mountain Lake

Indian Lake

Speculator

Wells

Great Sacandaga Lake

Gloversville

Malone

Cranberry Lake

Raquette Lake

ADIRONDACK MUSEUM

Inlet

Old Forge

Herkimer

Utica

Canton

Harrisville

Croghan

Hogansburg

Massena

Ogdensburg

Star Lake

Watertown

Rome

Oneida

Oneida Lake

Syracuse

Alexandria Bay

Clayton

Cape Vincent

SACKETS HARBOR

Henderson Harbor

Pulaski

Oswego

Oswego River

BOLDT CASTLE

Thousand Islands

Hudson River

20 mi

20 km

© AVALON TRAVEL PUBLISHING, INC.

THE NORTH COUNTRY

Woodland wildflowers such as dewdrops and lily-of-the-valley flourish in the lower Adirondacks, while on the peaks grow bright specks of alpine flora, mosses, lichens, and other hardy plants. Several good guides to the park's flora and fauna are published by the Adirondack Mountain Club.

As for mammals, the Adirondacks are home to 55 species, including raccoon, porcupine, weasel, mink, otter, bobcat, fox, coyote, white-tailed deer, and black bear. The elusive moose and lynx have recently been reintroduced into the forest.

Birdlife in the park ranges from the very small (chickadees and nuthatches) to the very large (grouse and osprey). At least 218 species have been spotted, including hawks, kingbirds, peregrine falcons, and bald eagles. One of the most characteristic sounds of the Adirondacks is the haunting call of the loon.

In Adirondack waters swim 86 species of fish, including trout, salmon, northern pike, and small- and large-mouth bass. The region also supports 35 species of reptiles and amphibians. Pesky blackflies thrive in the mountains late May–June, and mosquitoes are plentiful throughout the summer.

Early History

Once the hunting grounds of the Iroquois and Algonquin, the Adirondacks were largely overlooked by early white settlers. Military outposts went up along the shores of Lakes George and Champlain in the mid-1700s, but the rest of the region remained the haunt of hunters and trappers until well into the 1800s. Even logging proceeded slowly in the mountains, due to the difficulty of reaching the trees and getting them to market.

It wasn't until 1837 that New York State finally commissioned a natural-history survey of the wilderness. Led by geologist and botanist Prof. Ebenezer Emmons, the party ventured into the High Peaks region and climbed Mt. Marcy. Accompanying Emmons was artist Charles Cromwell Ingham, whose paintings of the Adirondacks astonished the general public. Few realized that so great a wilderness remained in the Northeast.

By the 1840s, lumbermen had penetrated deep into the forest, and by the 1850s, New York was producing more lumber than any other state. Vacationers and enthusiasts were also beginning to discover the region. Most famous among them were the members of the Philosophers' Camp. Organized by William Stillman of Cambridge, Massachusetts, the camp included such eminent men as Ralph Waldo Emerson and Louis Agassiz, who came to hike, fish, canoe, botanize, talk, and write.

After the Civil War, the Adirondacks began attracting many more vacationers, due largely to the 1869 publication of William H. H. Murray's *Adventures in the Wilderness*. Murray, a minister from Boston, both vividly described the wilderness and—more importantly—told readers how to get there. Within weeks after his book came out, the rush to the Adirondacks was on.

At first, vacationers stayed in the region's few large and rustic hotels, but soon it became fashionable to build private summer camps. In 1879, William West Durant created an architectural camp style that combined the features of a log cabin with those of a Swiss chalet. Wealthy families such as the Vanderbilts and Rockefellers embraced the style and built luxurious "great camps" that resembled self-contained villages. Many of these great camps still stand.

Verplanck Colvin and Adirondack Park

In 1872, years after explorers had discovered the sources of the Nile and various rivers out West, a young surveyor named Verplanck Colvin finally traced the Hudson River to its mysterious source. Starting in the Champlain Valley, he and his party hiked from peak to peak until reaching Mt. Marcy and what is now known as Lake Tear of the Clouds. "Far above the chilly water of Lake Avalanche," Colvin later reported to the state legislature, "at an elevation of 4,293 feet, is *Summit Water*, a minute unpretending tear of the clouds as it were—a lonely pool, shivering in the breezes of the mountains, and sending its limpid surplus through Feldspar Brook to the Opalescent River, the well-spring of the Hudson."

THE NORTH COUNTRY

From that expedition on until 1900, Colvin surveyed the entire Adirondack region. Often financing his own expeditions, he sent back frequent reports to the state legislature, passionately arguing for the creation of a park to preserve the forest and its watershed.

Few listened at first, but as the century wore on, downstate New Yorkers began to worry about their water supply, and businesses about the build-up of silt in New York Harbor. Protecting the forests would help solve both problems and create a giant "pleasuring-grounds for the people." Largely because of the businessmen's influence, the idea took hold, and in 1885, the state passed an unprecedented bill establishing a 681,374-acre Adirondack Forest Preserve. This law, strengthened in 1892 and again in 1894, even went so far as to dictate that the preserve remain "forever wild," a phrase that has created considerable controversy ever since.

Modern Times

During the past 100 years, numerous land purchases by the state have increased the Adirondack Forest Preserve from its original 681,374 acres to its present 2.6 million acres. The park's Blue Line—a term derived from the color ink used in 1884 to delineate the park's boundaries on a map—now encompasses nearly six million acres, as opposed to its early 2.8 million acres.

With this growth has come conflict, exacerbated by increased tourism and a boom in second homes. The conflict has pitted conservationists concerned about the park's ecological future against those advocating varying forms of economic development.

The conflict reached one early crisis point in the late 1960s, when the building of the Northway (I-87) opened up the region to yet more visitors. And so in 1968, Gov. Nelson Rockefeller appointed a state commission to study the future of the park. Among the commission's proposals was the establishment of an Adirondack Park Agency (APA) to encourage wise land-use planning.

Duly established in 1971, the APA has since instituted zoning laws for both the park's state *and* private lands. This has infuriated many residents, who feel that the state has no right to tell them what they can or cannot do with private property. Many also feel that the zoning laws, along with the original "forever wild" clause, are inhibiting economic growth in an area already suffering from out-migration and severe unemployment.

For the conservationists, of course, there is no real debate. In a world of ever-decreasing blank spots on the map, the park must be preserved.

It is a conflict unlikely to be resolved for decades to come.

WILDERNESS GRIDLOCK AT ADIRONDACK PARK

The biggest ecological problem facing Adirondack Park today is not pollution, erosion, or even acid rain. It is overuse. More than 120,000 hikers enter the High Peaks region annually, and on a fine summer day, as many as 200 people can be found atop Mount Marcy. Trees around Marcy Dam and Lake Colden bear the scars of ax marks, and the destruction of saplings by backpackers has caused certain campsites to be cordoned off.

Adirondack Park personnel urge hikers to shy away from the most famous summits – including Mount Marcy, Ampersand, and Whiteface – and tackle some of the lesser-known ones instead. Hiking outside the High Peaks region is especially recommended, as many other sections of the park also offer challenging peaks, yet attract only a handful of hikers. Hamilton County, just south of the High Peaks, has several stunning, under-hiked mountains, including Owls Head Mountain near Long Lake and Snowy Mountain near Indian Lake. Other less strenuous hikes can be found in the Northwest Lakes region.

Saratoga Springs and Environs

Dukes and kooks, counts and no-accounts, stars and czars have added to the legend of Saratoga, where it isn't enough to stay the 30 days. Staying the 30 nights is the true test of stamina.
 –Joe Hirsch, *Daily Racing Form*

For 11 months out of the year, Saratoga Springs is a charming Victorian town known for its first-rate arts scene, grand romantic architecture, sophisticated shops and restaurants, and therapeutic mineral springs. But on the 12th month, the town turns itself upside down with the buyers and sellers of dreams. From dawn until dusk, and then from dusk until dawn, gossiping socialites mix with shrewd business-people mix with innocent tourists mix with breeders and trainers and grooms. And all for the love of the horse.

The Saratoga Race Course, built in 1864, is the oldest racetrack in America, and it has long represented the very best of what racing has to offer. Louisville may have its Kentucky Derby, Baltimore its Preakness, but it is to Saratoga that the serious cognoscenti come, every summer, for six weeks of exclusive racing. Attendance at the sprawling, Victorian-era grandstand—complete with striped awnings, clapboard siding, and gilded cupolas—averages about 25,000 a day, or the equivalent of Saratoga's population year-round.

During nonracing season, too, Saratoga is an unusual place. The arts thrive at the Saratoga Performing Arts Center, Skidmore College, and Yaddo, a renowned artists' retreat; and harness racing takes place January–November at the Saratoga Raceway. The town also supports several fine museums, the regal Saratoga Spa State Park, and a plethora of good hotels and B&Bs. Surrounding Saratoga is lush, rolling countryside offering more cultural, historical, and scenic attractions. Best known among them is the Saratoga National Historic Park,

where the 1777 battles that turned the course of the Revolutionary War were fought.

HISTORY
Early History

Saratoga Springs owes its existence to its mineral springs, first discovered by the Mohawk in the 14th century. In 1771, the Mohawk brought their ill friend Sir William Johnson to the "Medicine Spring of the Great Spirit." The waters helped ease the British Indian agent's suffering, and introduced the mineral springs to the white world.

In 1802, pioneer Gideon Putnam arrived in the area, bought the land around the present Congress Park, and built the three-story Union Hall. Other pioneers and hotels followed, and by the 1840s, the resort was known as a hot spot where high society met to partake of the waters and dally with games of chance.

Saratoga didn't really take off, however, until the 1860s, when prizefighter, gambler, and general roustabout John Morrisey built the Saratoga Race Course. The track was a near-instant success and was soon joined by elaborate gambling casinos and posh block-long hotels. Here fluttering socialites danced with hard-nosed gamblers beneath crystal chandeliers.

Saratoga regulars included prominent horsemen such as William R. Travers, financiers such as J. Pierpont Morgan, actresses such as Lillian Russell, and high rollers such as Diamond Jim Brady, who sometimes wore as many as 2,548 diamonds with his evening outfits. Ace reporter Nellie Bly of the New York *World* sent stories downstate about "Our Wickedest Summer Resort."

Modern Times

By the early 1900s, the wickedness seemed to be all but over. A reform movement closed down the casinos, some of the springs dried up

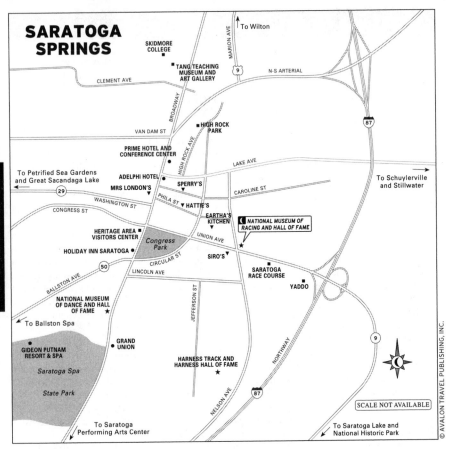

SARATOGA SPRINGS

SKIDMORE COLLEGE

TANG TEACHING MUSEUM AND ART GALLERY

CLEMENT AVE

To Wilton

MARION AVE

N-S ARTERIAL

9

87

VAN DAM ST

BROADWAY

HIGH ROCK PARK

PRIME HOTEL AND CONFERENCE CENTER

HIGH ROCK AVE

LAKE AVE

To Petrified Sea Gardens and Great Sacandaga Lake

ADELPHI HOTEL
MRS LONDON'S

29

WASHINGTON ST

CONGRESS ST

SPERRY'S

PHILA ST

HATTIE'S

CAROLINE ST

To Schuylerville and Stillwater

EARTHA'S KITCHEN

HERITAGE AREA VISITORS CENTER

HOLIDAY INN SARATOGA

Congress Park

UNION AVE

NATIONAL MUSEUM OF RACING AND HALL OF FAME

CIRCULAR ST

SIRO'S

50

LINCOLN AVE

SARATOGA RACE COURSE

YADDO

BALLSTON AVE

JEFFERSON ST

NATIONAL MUSEUM OF DANCE AND HALL OF FAME

To Ballston Spa

GRAND UNION

GIDEON PUTNAM RESORT & SPA

Saratoga Spa

State Park

HARNESS TRACK AND HARNESS HALL OF FAME

NORTHWAY

9

87

NELSON AVE

SCALE NOT AVAILABLE

To Saratoga Performing Arts Center

To Saratoga Lake and National Historic Park

© AVALON TRAVEL PUBLISHING, INC.

due to excessive commercial pumping, and the fashionable crowd moved on.

Enter New York State, which in 1909 established a state reservation to preserve the largest cluster of springs. Within the next 25 years, the state transformed the reservation into Saratoga Spa State Park, building a hotel and two magnificent bathhouses. Saratoga's golden era of the spa began, with people coming from all over to take the cure—drinking mineral waters, taking baths, and exercising. The casinos, in full swing again, were this time under the control of gangsters such as Lucky Luciano and Dutch Schultz.

Saratoga suffered another decline after World War II as the public's interest in spa

therapy declined and the casinos were shut down again, this time for good. Only the race course mustered on, with races held every August without fail.

Then in the 1960s, Saratoga's many charms were discovered by a new generation. Old Victorian buildings were snatched up and renovated, and a new wave of socialites and vacationers moved in.

ORIENTATION

Saratoga Springs is a small and compact city (population 25,000) centered on Broadway. The track lies to the east of downtown, off Union Avenue, while Saratoga Spa State Park is to the south, off South Broadway (Route 9). The Northway (I-87) passes within a few miles of the city.

All of the sites along Broadway lie within easy walking distance of each other. The track and the state park are each about a mile from downtown. Park downtown in the large free lots between Broadway and Circular Street.

The Saratoga County Chamber of Commerce (28 Clinton St., 518/584-3255) operates an **information booth** on Broadway near the entrance to Congress 9 A.M.–5 P.M. daily June–September; extended hours during racing season.

SIGHTS
Heritage Area Visitors Center
A good place to start a tour of Saratoga is at this center (297 Broadway, at Congress St., 518/587-3241, www.saratoga.org/visitorcenter, 9 A.M.–4 P.M. daily May–Oct., 9 A.M.–4 P.M. Mon.–Sat. Nov.–Apr., free admission), housed in Drink Hall, where mineral waters were once sold. Back then, different waters were recommended for different times of the day: Hathorn in the morning, Coesa before dinner, and Geyser in the evening.

Today, the beaux arts hall with its barrel-vaulted ceiling is filled with history exhibits and racks bursting with tourism brochures. Saratoga is one of New York State's Heritage Areas—loosely designated historic districts linked by a common theme. The theme in Saratoga is the natural environment. Free walking-tour maps pinpointing the area's springs can be picked up here.

Congress Park
Across from the visitors center lies Congress Park (Broadway and Congress Sts., 518/587-3241), a small jewel of a retreat filled with jade-green lawns, graveled walkways, and flowering plants. In the center of things reigns the Italianate red-brick **Canfield Casino,** now home to the Museum of the Historical Society of Saratoga Springs.

One of the oldest parks in the country, Congress Park dates back to 1792 when Nicholas

Gilman, a member of the first U.S. Congress, "discovered" and named Congress Spring. Then along came Gideon Putnam, who in 1806 bought the swampland next to the spring, siphoned off some of its waters, and built Saratoga's first mineral-water bathhouse. In 1876, Frederick Law Olmsted completely redesigned the park, replacing the old structures with high Victorian Gothic buildings. Tours of the park are offered in summer.

Canfield Casino
Lavish Canfield Casino (Congress Park, 518/584-6920, www.saratogahistory.org, 10 A.M.–4 P.M. Mon.–Sat. and 1–4 P.M. Sun. June–Sept., 10 A.M.–4 P.M. Wed.–Sat. and 1–4 P.M. Sun. Oct.–May, adults $5, seniors $4, students $3, children under 12 free) was built by John Morrissey in 1870 as an adjunct to his new racetrack. One writer of the day described the place as having "gorgeously furnished toilet rooms, faro parlors and drawing rooms."

In 1894, Richard Canfield purchased the

WEIRD, WONDERFUL, OFF-THE-BEATEN PATH NORTH COUNTRY

Grant Cottage, Wilton: One of the oddest and most moving of house museums, located in the middle of a correctional facility.

New Skete Monastery, Cambridge: A hilltop retreat known for its homemade cheesecake, smoked meats, and German shepherds.

Pember Museum of Natural History, Granville: Hundreds upon hundreds of specimens, all but bursting out of their display cases.

Camp Santanoni, Newcomb: A deserted great camp accessible only by hiking five miles in and five miles back out.

Thousand Islands Park, Wellesley Island: Hundreds of wooden Victorian homes painted in luscious ice-cream pastels.

© CHRISTIANE BIRD

THE NORTH COUNTRY

the 1870 Canfield Casino

building and embellished it with more ostentatious touches, including stained-glass windows. Fabulous sums were won and lost in the casino's gaming rooms, and many "Monte Carlo suicides" were said to have been committed. Before the casino was shut down in 1907, Canfield purportedly netted the then-enormous profit of $2.5 million.

Today, the casino houses the **Museum of the Historical Society of Saratoga Springs.** Downstairs temporary exhibits focus on the history and culture of Saratoga. Upstairs are period rooms and an oddball collection of artifacts including Egyptian spears, bullets from the Battles of Saratoga, and old gaming tables.

Broadway
North of Congress Park begin the bustling blocks of downtown Broadway, lined with shops and restaurants that spill out onto the sidewalks in summer. Leafy trees spread their boughs, and inviting park benches beckon here and there.

At one time, Broadway was flanked with one

grand hotel after another, some sporting balconies that stretched hundreds of feet. Today, only the 1877 **Adelphi,** No. 365, remains. Inside you'll find a romantic period lobby while out back is an expansive garden that's a good place for afternoon tea or a late-night drink.

Other buildings worth noting along Broadway include the 1916 Classic Revival **Adirondack Trust,** No. 473, adorned with Adirondack symbols and bronze Tiffany doors; and the 1910 beaux arts **post office,** No. 475. At Lake Avenue, across from the post office, is the 1871 Italian palazzo **city hall,** the birthplace of the American Banking Association and the American Bar Association.

Tang Teaching Museum and Art Gallery at Skidmore College
Relatively new to Saratoga's art scene is this dynamic arts center (815 N. Broadway, 518/580-8080, www.skidmore.edu/tang, 11 A.M.–5 P.M. Tues.–Fri., noon–5 P.M. Sat.–Sun), hosting both contemporary art exhibits and cultural events. Donated to Skidmore College in 2000 by Chinese-born American businessman Oscar Tang, whose daughter and wife are both Skidmore alumni, the museum is dedicated to "fostering interdisciplinary thinking." The permanent collection includes works in a wide range of media, while temporary exhibits focus on everything from pop art to site-specific installations.

Union Avenue
After Broadway, Union Avenue is Saratoga's other main drag. A wide boulevard leading east to the Saratoga Race Course, the avenue features some of the grandest Victorian architecture in town. Several of the buildings now operate as posh B&Bs that charge outrageous prices during the racing season; others hold offices, apartments, and condominiums. During the summer, Union Avenue, like the racecourse itself, is planted with thousands of white, purple, and pink impatiens.

◖ National Museum of Racing and Hall of Fame
Even nonracing fans will want to step into

© CHRISTIANE BIRD

Historic grand Victorian houses line Union Avenue, which leads east to the Saratoga Race Course.

this one-of-a-kind museum (191 Union Ave., 518/584-0400, www.racingmuseum.org, 10 A.M.–4 P.M. Mon.–Sat., noon–4 P.M. Sun., with extended hours during racing season, adults $7, seniors and students $5, children under 5 free), filled with intriguing exhibitions on the history and mechanics of thoroughbred racing. Exhibits on the horse explain how all thoroughbreds trace their origins back to one of three Arabian progenitors, and how at a full gallop, a horse takes in five gallons of air a second. Exhibits on racing champs tell the stories of Man o' War and Secretariat, Seattle Slew and Affirmed. Exhibits on Saratoga tell of the resort's gambling heyday, when it was frequented by Diamond Jim Brady, Lillian Russell, Lillie Langtry, and Florenz Ziegfeld.

In summer, the museum offers tours of the training track Wednesday–Sunday at 8:30 A.M. ($10 per person).

Saratoga Race Course

The nation's oldest thoroughbred track (267 Union Ave., near East Ave., 518/584-6200, www.nyra.com/saratoga) comes to life every late July through early September. Most U.S. tracks present one weekly stakes race, featuring top-of-the-line horses; Saratoga has one every day. The meet's highlight is the Travers Stakes held on the fifth Saturday; other big events are the Whitney, the Alabama, and the prestigious Fasig-Tipton yearling sales.

Saratoga, filled with striped tents and bright flowers, remains one of the world's best tracks in which to get a close-up view of the horse-racing world. The thoroughbreds are walked through the crowd before being saddled in the paddock, and jockeys stop to talk and sign autographs between races.

Breakfast at the track is a Saratoga tradition. Between 7 and 9:30 A.M., visitors can dine on steak and eggs in the clubhouse or munch donuts in the grandstand while watching the horses go through their morning workouts. Afterward, tours of the backstretch are available.

Yaddo

Just east of the racetrack lies this artists'

RACING-SEASON TIPS

Track Basics: The six-week meet runs from late July to early September; Tuesday is dark. The track opens at 11 A.M. weekdays, 10:30 A.M. weekends, and post time is 1 P.M. General admission is $2, clubhouse admission is $5. No "abbreviated attire" is allowed in the clubhouse.

For general information during the meet, call the Saratoga Race Course at 518/584-6200. For advance ticket sales, contact the **New York Racing Association** (718/641-4700, www.nyra.com).

Parking and Traffic: The New York Racing Association maintains large parking lots across from the track. Parking is also available in many private lots surrounding the track. If you're not planning to go to the track, avoid Union Avenue between noon and 1 P.M., and again around 5:30 P.M.

Seating: Most of the 6,688 reserved seats in the grandstand and clubhouse are sold by mail in January. However, about 1,000 grandstand seats go on sale ($4 each) every race day at the track's Union Avenue entrance. On weekdays, tickets are often available up until post time, but on weekends, they're gone by 10 or 11 A.M.

Many fans bring lawn chairs, blankets, and coolers to the shady grounds behind the track, which are equipped with short-circuit TVs. Others watch the races on their feet, then retreat to benches near the betting windows.

How to Bet: Easy-to-follow instructions are printed inside the daily program, the *Post Parade*, available at the gate for $1.50. The minimum bet is $1.

After the Races: The most popular racetrack hangout is **Siro's** (168 Lincoln Ave., 518/584-4030), adjacent to the track on the south side. A long bar is set up beneath a striped canvas tent, and live bands play until about 8:30 P.M.; the party then moves inside.

Polo Matches: Throughout August, world-class polo matches (518/584-8108, www.saratogapolo.com) take place on Tuesday, Friday, and Sunday at the Saratoga Polo Field at Bloomfield and Denton Road. Most of the games begin at 6 P.M.

Accommodations: Most hotels and B&Bs double their prices during racing season, and many of the most popular places are booked solid many months in advance. Even if you arrive at the last minute, however, you will find something. The chamber of commerce maintains an updated list of available rooms.

retreat (312 Union Ave., between the racecourse and I-87, 518/584-0746, 8 A.M.–dusk daily), housed in a Victorian Gothic mansion that was once home to Spencer and Katrina Trask. Spencer Trask was a New York financier and philanthropist, Katrina a poet.

Artists come to Yaddo to get away from the noisy outside world and work in uninterrupted peace. About 4,000 writers, composers, and visual artists have worked here since the program began in 1926, including Flannery O'Connor, Saul Bellow, Leonard Bernstein, Langston Hughes, John Cheever, and Aaron Copland.

Though the house is off-limits to the general public, the landscaped grounds are not. Visitors are welcome to stroll through an Italian garden planted with over 100 varieties of roses, and a rock garden strewn with flowering perennials. Wistful marble statues stand here and there.

Harness Track and Harness Hall of Fame

South of the main track stretches the half-mile-long Saratoga Raceway, a foremost trotting track. Opened in 1941, the track features evening racing January–November with a short break in April. Some of the track's top races take place during the thoroughbred meet.

In the old horseman's building is the Saratoga Harness Hall of Fame (352 Jefferson St., off Nelson Ave., 518/587-4210, 10 A.M.–4 P.M. Thurs.–Sat. June–Sept., call for off-season hours, free admission). On display are antique horseshoes, racing silks, high-wheel sulkies, and other memorabilia. One exhibit honors Lady Suffolk, the "Old Grey Mare" of folksong fame who raced in Saratoga in 1847, 16 years before thoroughbred racing began.

National Museum of Dance and Hall of Fame

South Broadway leads out of downtown past the only museum in the country devoted exclusively to professional American dance (99 S. Broadway [Rte. 9], 518/584-2225, www.dancemuseum.org, 10 A.M.–5 P.M. Tues.–Sun. June–Oct., adults $6.50, seniors and students $5, children under 12 $3)—including ballet, modern dance, vaudeville, and tap. Housed in a low-slung building, the museum spreads out over four spacious halls filled with blown-up photographs and plaques. Temporary exhibits hang near the entrance, while TV monitors screening famous performances are featured throughout. Overall, however, the museum is a surprisingly static affair that will appeal primarily to dance aficionados.

Saratoga Spa State Park

More European than American in feel, Saratoga Spa State Park (off S. Broadway [Rte. 9] just south of downtown, 518/584-2000, parking $6) spreads out over 2,200 pristine acres, every one of which is meticulously planned. At one end is the Avenue of the Pines, flanked with towering green-black trees. At the other, Loop Road leads past a half-dozen mineral springs, all of which have a different taste, depending on their mineral content. In between are tennis courts, swimming pools, mineral baths, two golf courses, the Spa Little Theater, the Saratoga Performing Arts Center, and the Gideon Putnam Hotel, a grand Georgian affair built in the 1930s.

Though no longer the drawing card they once were, the heart of the park remains its mineral baths. Near the Gideon Putnam are the **Roosevelt Baths** (518/226-4790, www.gideonputnam.com, 9 A.M.–7 P.M. daily, treatments $18–110). Newly renovated, the place includes a fitness center and private rooms and tubs, where clients relax in bubbling golden-brown waters, indulge in algae body wraps, and succumb to muscle-relief treatments.

Near the park's center lies the regal **Victoria Pool** (adults $6, children $3), embellished with colored tiles, romantic archways, and a small café. Even on the hottest days, the pool remains delightfully empty, partly because the park also boasts a second, larger pool—the **Peerless Pool** (adults $3, children 5–12 $1.50), adjoined with diving and wading pools.

Petrified Sea Gardens

A sleeper of a Saratoga visitor attraction, the gardens (Petrified Gardens Rd., off Rte. 29

SARATOGA'S MINERAL SPRINGS

Saratoga's springs gurgle up from ancient seas trapped in limestone layers that are sealed by a solid layer of shale. Through these layers runs a geological fault line which cracks the shale, allowing the water to escape to the surface. The limestone enriches the water with minerals, and carbon dioxide adds natural carbonation.

Most of the springs bubble up in Congress Park, High Rock Park, and the Saratoga Spa State Park. Some are marked by pavilions, others by fountains, and each has its own distinct taste. A complete guide to the springs and their supposed therapeutic values can be picked up at the Heritage Area Visitor Center.

Two bottling companies continue to operate within the city: the world-famous **Saratoga Spring Water Company,** and the **Excelsior Springs Water Company.** The Saratoga Spring Company has been located on Geyser Road at the Route 50 entrance to Saratoga Spa State Park since 1872. Take the time to see its lovely Victorian gazebo, built in the late 1800s.

Saratoga Spa State Park still offers mineral baths at its recently renovated **Roosevelt Baths** (518/226-4790). The privately run **Crystal Spa** (92 S. Broadway, 518/584-2556) offers mineral baths as well.

three miles west of downtown, 518/584-7102, www.petrifiedseagardens.org, 11 A.M.–5 P.M. daily June–Sept., 11 A.M.–5 P.M. Sat.–Sun. May and Oct.–Nov., adults $3.50, seniors and students $2.50, children $1.75) feature a 500-million-year-old stromatolite reef clearly etched with fossils. Once at the bottom of the Cambrian Sea, the reef is strewn with wavy, pizza-size shapes that were made by crypto-zoan colonies, odd-shaped glacial crevices, and potholes. Trails lead through the woods past petrified trees and mysterious erratics, or boulders left behind by receding glaciers. Also on-site are a re-created Native American medicine wheel, a homespun rock and mineral museum, and the "Iroquois Pine," a 295-year-old white pine reputedly the tallest white pine in the Northern Hemisphere.

ACCOMMODATIONS
Motels
One of the best deals in town is the eight-room **Saratoga Lake Motel** (Rte. 9P, 518/584-7438, www.saratogalakemotel.com, 45–70 d May–July and Sept., $85–90 d in racing season), overlooking Saratoga Lake. A cottage is also available for rent.

The **(Grand Union** (92 S. Broadway, 518/584-9000, www.grandunionmotel.com, $53–174 d, $155–240 d in racing season) features 64 well-kept rooms with king-sized beds, a large pool area, and easy access to the adjoining Crystal Spa, which offers everything from facials to mineral baths.

Hotels
Good package rates are sometimes offered by the 150-room **Holiday Inn Saratoga** (232 Broadway, 518/584-4550, www.holiday-inn.com/saratoga, $110–160 d, $275–375 d in racing season). Ditto for the sleek 240-room **Prime Hotel & Conference Center** (534 Broadway, 518/584-4000, $130–200 d, $280–300 d in racing season).

The most romantic hostelry in town is the Victorian-era **(Adelphi Hotel** (365 Broadway, 518/587-4688, www.adelphihotel.com, $120–265 d, $200–450 d in racing season),

one of the loveliest buildings in downtown Saratoga. Featured are an opulent lobby and 35 attractive guest rooms filled with antiques. Many of the rooms are on the small side.

In the middle of well-manicured Saratoga Spa State Park is the Georgian Revival **Gideon Putnam Resort & Spa** (off S. Broadway, 518/584-3000, www.gideonputnam.com, $130–280 d, $310–550 d in racing season). The renovated hotel is a grand affair, offering 120 guestrooms and suites, a lobby ringed with historic paintings, a fine-dining restaurant, and bar.

Bed-and-Breakfasts
Downtown Saratoga has a plethora of Victorian-era B&Bs. One of the most spectacular is the Italianate **Batcheller Mansion Inn** (20 Circular St., 518/584-7012, www.batchellermansioninn.com, $150–295 d, $265–400 d in racing season), which offers nine spacious guest rooms. Equally unique is the 1901 Queen Anne **Union Gables** (55 Union Ave., 518/584-1558, www.uniongables.com, $140–230 d, $360–400 d in racing season), all but surrounded by a wonderful wide porch. Each of the 10 guest rooms has a private bath and small refrigerator. The **Westchester House B&B** (102 Lincoln Ave., 518/587-7613, www.westchesterhousebandb.com, $115–225 d, $240–445 d in racing season) dates back to 1886, when it was the "Family home of Almeron King, Master Carpenter." All of the rooms are filled with antiques.

On the shores of Saratoga Lake is the inviting **(Harren-Brook Inn** 286 Rte. 9P, 518/583-4009, www.harrenbrookinn.com, $125–195 d, $175–250 d in racing season) run by two former schoolteachers with a good knowledge of the area. The nine guest rooms appear nicely appointed, while up front beckons a cozy sitting room, breezy porch, and small private beach. All of the rooms have private baths and queen-sized beds; some have separate sitting rooms).

Numerous other B&Bs are located in and around Saratoga (see *Excursions from Saratoga,* below). For a complete list, contact the chamber of commerce.

FOOD
Bakeries and Diners

Mrs. London's (464 Broadway, 518/581-1652) offers a mouth-watering selection of desserts, baked goods, and gourmet coffees. The big and bustling **Saratoga Diner** (153 S. Broadway, 518/584-9833), formerly known as the Spa City Diner, is the kind of comforting eatery that offers an extensive menu 24 hours a day. The family-owned **Shirley's Restaurant** (74 West Ave., 518/584-4532) is a good spot for breakfast, lunch, and homemade pies.

American

◖ **Hattie's** (45 Phila St., 518/584-4790) has been a Saratoga institution since 1938. This is the place to go for tasty fried chicken, barbecued ribs, catfish, and sweet potato pie; average entrée $10.

Also an institution is the casual **Olde Bryan Inn** (123 Maple Ave., 518/587-2990), housed in a rustic 1832 stone house. On the menu is everything from chili to seafood kebab, and up front is a big, comfortable bar; average entrée $14.

Lillian's (408 Broadway, 518/587-7766) is outfitted with woodwork, brass, Tiffany-style lamps, and stained glass. The dependable menu includes lots of standard steak, chicken, and fish dishes, along with lighter fare; average entrée $14. Down the street is the Holmesian **Professor Moriarty's** (430 Broadway, 518/587-5981), a classy bar/restaurant serving "plots" (appetizers), "crimes" (entrées), and "verdicts" (desserts); average entrée $15.

◖ **Sperry's** (30½ Caroline St., 518/584-9618), a favorite haunt of horsemen and -women during the racing season, is an upscale bistro filled with memorabilia dating back to Saratoga's days as a fashionable spa. Specialties include fresh fish, jambalaya, and homemade pasta; average entrée $18. **43 Phila Bistro** (43 Phila St., 518/584-2720) serves sophisticated American-style bistro fare. On the menu is everything from Jamaican jerk chicken to dry-aged steak; average entrée $20.

The small and casually elegant ◖ **Eartha's Kitchen** (60 Court St., 518/583-0602) features an innovative menu that changes frequently but always includes a grilled dish or two and much fish; average entrée $19.

Continental and French

Only open during racing season, ◖ **Siro's** (168 Lincoln Ave., 518/584-4030) boasts the best after-track bar scene, as well as the most exclusive restaurant in town. Featured are both innovative and traditional continental dishes; entrées range $25–38; reservations are essential.

An especially good time to visit the **Gideon Putnam Hotel** (Saratoga Spa State Park, off S. Broadway, 518/584-3000) is Sunday brunch. Expect an enormous buffet for about $18.

About four miles south of Saratoga is the excellent **Chez Sophie Bistro** (2853 Rte. 9, Malta, 518/583-3538). Housed in an elegant old diner that's been completely remodeled, it serves an interesting selection of fish, chicken, meat, and duck dishes, but with entrées averaging $30, is overpriced.

Italian, Mexican, and Indian

Good eats are to be had at three smaller restaurants, all of which offer entrées priced under $12. For fajitas, tostadas, and burritos, along with regional Mexican specialties on the weekends, try the **Mexican Connection** (41 Nelson Ave., 518/584-4466). In operation since 1979, the Connection was the first Mexican restaurant to open in the Saratoga-Albany region. For curries, *biryanis,* and many vegetarian dishes, try **Little India** (423 Broadway, 518/583-4151). For wood-fired pizza, pastas, creative salads, and Elvis memorabilia, try **Bruno's** (237 Union Ave., 518/583-3333), across from the main track.

ENTERTAINMENT
Performing Arts

The **Saratoga Performing Arts Center** (SPAC) (Saratoga Spa State Park, off S. Broadway (Rte. 9), 518/587-3330, www.spac.org) is an outdoor amphitheater with 5,000 seats below cover and more seats available on the surrounding lawns. The preeminent performing-arts center of the North Country, SPAC presents the New York City Opera in June, the New York City Ballet in July, the Philadelphia Orchestra in August, and well-known rock, pop, and jazz stars throughout the summer. Picnicking before the concerts is a Saratoga tradition.

The **Baroque Festival** (165 Wilton Rd., Greenfield Center, 518/893-7527) takes place in July in an exquisite private music hall that seats only 110. Featured is baroque music played on period instruments, among them a handcrafted harpsichord played by director Robert Conant.

Clubs and Nightlife

Thanks largely to the presence of Skidmore College and the racetrack, Saratoga has a lively nighttime scene. **Caroline Street** is especially known for its many clubs and bars, most catering to twentysomethings.

9 Maple Ave. (9 Maple Ave., 518/583-CLUB) is the place to go for serious jazz. **Desperate Annie's** (12–14 Caroline St., 518/587-2455), a.k.a. DA's, is a popular college and local hangout, complete with pool table.

Caffé Lena (45–47 Phila St., 518/583-0022, www.caffelena.com) is the oldest continuously run coffeehouse in America, founded in 1960 by Lena Spencer. Bob Dylan played here on his first tour of the East; Don McLean first played "American Pie" on the café's small stage. Lena is gone now, but her legacy continues through the café's lineup of top acoustic acts—Odetta, Jimmie Dale Gilmore, Tom Paxton, and others. Coffees and desserts are served.

The big and boisterous **Parting Glass** (40–42 Lake Ave., 518/583-1916) presents first-rate Irish bands. On the menu are 170 beers and Guinness on tap, along with a wide selection of pub grub.

Lively **bar scenes** can be found at many restaurants, including Siro's, Sperry's, Professor Moriarty's, and the Olde Bryan Inn, all mentioned above. Behind the lobby of the **Adelphi Hotel** (365 Broadway, 518/587-4688) lies a candlelit garden where drinks are served beneath the stars.

SHOPPING

Many **clothing boutiques** and **gift shops** pepper Broadway. Housed in the old Saratoga National Bank building is the **Lyrical Ballad Bookstore** (7 Phila St., 518/584-8779), a packed-to-the-rafters antiquarian shop that stocks about 30,000 books. The rarest volumes are stored in the bank's old safe-deposit vaults. The **Regent Street Antique Center** (153 Regent St., 518/584-0107) houses about 20 dealers.

EXCURSIONS FROM SARATOGA
Stillwater

The battles that turned the course of the American Revolution were fought about 12 miles southeast of Saratoga. The former battlefield is now part of **Saratoga National Historic Park** (648 Rte. 32, at Rte. 4, 518/664-9821, 9 A.M.–dusk Apr.–Nov., weather permitting, $5 per car, $3 per hiker or biker).

In October 1777, British general Burgoyne and his forces marched south from Canada to take control of the Hudson River. They planned to meet up with Col. Leger and his forces in Albany, and continue on to New York City to join up with Gen. Howe. Instead, just outside Saratoga, Gen. Burgoyne came upon the American forces, 9,000 strong. Led by Gen. Horatio Gates and Gen. Benedict Arnold, the Americans defeated the British in two fierce battles.

A tour of the park begins at the visitors center (9 A.M.–5 P.M. daily Apr.–Nov.), where you can watch an informative film. Beyond the center begins a nine-mile self-guided driving tour past strategic points equipped with audio recordings, plaques, and maps. Only a few bunkers remain, but the countryside is exceptionally lovely, especially in the late afternoon when the mists roll in from the nearby Hudson River.

Schuylerville

Continue north of the battlefield on Route 4 for about eight miles to reach Schuylerville, lined with worn white buildings and empty storefronts. Just south of the Route 32 intersection stands the **General Philip Schuyler House** (Rte. 4, 518/664-9821, 9:30 A.M.–4:30 P.M. Thurs.–Sun. June–Sept., free admission). Also part of the Saratoga National Historic Battlefield, the house once belonged to the Schuyler family, who ran a self-sufficient estate here that employed about 200 people. The house was burnt by Burgoyne during the Battles of Saratoga but was rebuilt that same year.

Take Route 32 west of the Schuyler House about a half mile to reach the **Saratoga Monument** (9:30 A.M.–4:30 P.M. Thurs.–Sun. June–Sept., weekends in fall, free admission), a beautifully restored gray obelisk on a hill. The third part of Saratoga National Historic Park, the monument features four niches honoring the battles' American leaders—Gen. Philip Schuyler, Gen. Horatio Gates, Col. Daniel Morgan, and Gen. Benedict Arnold. Statues stand in the first three niches, but the fourth stands deliberately empty.

Ballston Spa

Before the Civil War, Ballston Spa outranked Saratoga as a fashionable resort and watering hole. After the war, however, the racetrack and casinos drew the crowds away, and Ballston Spa turned to knitting mills and tanneries. Today little evidence of any of these industries remains except at the **Brookside Saratoga County History Center** (6 Charlton St., at Front St., 518/885-4000, www.brooksidemuseum.org, 10 A.M.–4 P.M. Tues.–Fri, noon–4 P.M. Sat., adults $2, children 5–18 $1). Housed in what was once a resort hotel, the Brookside showcases exhibits on the town's 19th-century spas, 20th-century amusement parks, early African American settlers, and dairy farming.

Also in Ballston Spa is the eclectic **National Bottle Museum** (76 Milton Ave. [Rte. 50], 518/885-7589, 10 A.M.–4 P.M. daily June–Sept., 10 A.M.–4 P.M. Mon.–Fri. Oct.–May, admission by donation). On display are hundreds of antique and handmade bottles, most without signage; a video on antique bottles is featured.

Wilton

One of the oddest and most moving of house museums in all of New York State is **Grant Cottage** (off Ballard Rd., Wilton, 518/587-8277 or 518/584-2000, 10 A.M.–4 P.M. Wed.–Sun. June–Labor Day, 10 A.M.–4 P.M. Sat.–Sun. Sept.–Oct., adults $4, seniors $3, children 6–16 $2), perched on the hilltop in the middle of Mt. McGregor Correctional Facility. To get to the cottage, you must stop at a guard booth and enter a walled minimum-security complex topped with shiny barbed wire.

President Ulysses S. Grant came to Mt. McGregor in June of 1885 and spent the last six weeks of his life here, completing his memoirs. Afflicted with throat cancer, he was working frantically against time, trying to finish his book so that his family would have something to live on after he was gone. Grant had become bankrupt paying back the moneys he had urged his friends to invest in his son's company; the company went belly-up after his son's partner absconded with the funds.

In 1885, Mt. McGregor was home to the popular Hotel Balmoral, owned by Grant's friend Duncan McGregor. McGregor lent Grant his cottage both out of the goodness of his heart and because, as a shrewd businessman, he knew that if Grant died in the cottage, it would become a popular tourist attraction.

Die Grant did, and to this day, the house remains exactly as it was when he and his family left it. In one room are Grant's toothbrush, his nightshirts, and a half-empty bottle of medicinal cocaine and spring water. In another are the notes that Grant scribbled in pencil after he could no longer talk, and a bedspread stained with the wreaths brought by mourners.

Before his death, Grant—often sleeping as few as two hours a night—did succeed in finishing his memoirs. They are considered to be among the finest ever written by an American general and earned the family handsome royalties.

To reach the cottage from Saratoga, take Route 9 north eight miles to Ballard Road and turn left.

Bed-and-Breakfasts

About seven miles from Saratoga stands the 1786 **Wayside Inn** (104 Wilton Rd., Greenfield, 518/893-7249, www.waysidein.com, $85–115 d, $135–175 d in racing season), a rambling, low-ceilinged affair with wide floorboards and broad beams. The five guest rooms are comfortably fitted; next door is a laid-back performing-arts and conference center.

In Schuylerville, the wood-frame, Federal-style **Dovegate Inn** (184 Broad St., 518/695-3699, www.dovegateinn.com, $85–120 d,

$150–175 d in racing season) is a welcoming B&B offering three spacious guestrooms with private baths, a small restaurant, and a gift shop.

About five miles south of Ballston Spa is the **Olde Stone House Inn** (Round Lake, 518/899-5048, www.oldestonehouseinn.com, $85–150 d, $150–180 d in racing season), an elegant 1820 cobblestone home with four guest rooms (two with shared bath) and extensive grounds. In the U.S., cobblestone houses are all but unique to New York.

Washington County

Between Saratoga and Vermont, the Adirondack Mountains and the Green Mountains, lies a sliver of a county reaching north to Lake Champlain. Though often overlooked by travelers in the region, the countryside here is exceptionally lovely and quite different from elsewhere in the state. The hills are smaller, greener, and closer together; the villages, more genteel and picturesque. So it comes as no surprise to learn that this is **Grandma Moses Country.** The self-taught folk artist grew up near Eagle Bridge in southern Washington County, and painted the scenes she found around her. Her legacy is acknowledged by the many artists who live in the area, and by the vibrant arts scene flourishing along the New York–Vermont border.

CAMBRIDGE

About 25 miles east of Saratoga Springs, Cambridge is the official birthplace of pie à la mode. The historic moment occurred one evening in the mid-1890s when a Prof. Charles Watson Townsend, dining at the Hotel Cambridge, ordered ice cream with apple pie; a neighbor eating at the next table dubbed the concoction "pie à la mode." The professor ordered it by its new name during a subsequent visit to Delmonico's in New York City. The waiter had never heard of it and called for the manager, who declared in consternation, "Delmonico's

never intends that any other restaurant shall get ahead of it. ... Forthwith, pie à la mode will be featured on the menu every day." A *New York Sun* newspaperman, overhearing the conversation, reported it the next day, and before long, pie à la mode was a standard on menus across the country.

The renovated **Cambridge Hotel** (4 W. Main St., 518/677-5626) still stands in the middle of town, where it is open for lunch, dinner, and as accommodations for overnight guests (see *Accommodations*). Elsewhere along the nicely restored, turn-of-the-century Main Street lie several art galleries, natural-foods stores, and **Hubbard Hall** (25 E. Main St., 518/677-2495). Originally a rural opera house, the 1878 hall now houses an arts and clothing shop on the ground floor, and a restored theater up above. A wide range of music, dance, and theater events take place throughout the year, including the popular **Music from Salem** classical series held on Fridays in summer.

New Skete Monastery

On a thickly wooded hilltop between Cambridge and Vermont stands the Eastern Orthodox New Skete Monastery. Home to a handful of brothers, the monastery centers around a rough-hewn wooden chapel filled with icons painted by the monks. Nearby presides a more elaborate church.

WARREN COUNTY

Lake Champlain

WASHINGTON COUNTY

VERMONT

SARATOGA COUNTY

Lake George

Whitehall

WASHINGTON COUNTY

THE HYDE COLLECTION

Glens Falls

Hudson Falls

Fort Edward

Granville

Hartford

Hebron Nature Preserve

Salem

SARATOGA COUNTY

Cambridge

RENSSELAER COUNTY

Eagle Bridge

Hudson River

0   5 mi

0   5 km

© AVALON TRAVEL PUBLISHING, INC.

THE NORTH COUNTRY

3928, www.newskete.com, 9 A.M.–noon and 1–4 P.M.Tues.–Wed., 10 A.M.–4 P.M. Thurs.–Sat., 2–4 P.M. Sun.), stocked with the monks' homemade cheesecake, smoked meats, and various dog-related items. The main church is open during Sunday-morning services only. The nuns of New Skete run a similar gift and bake shop five miles away (343 Ash Grove Rd., off Chestnut Hill Rd., 518/677-3810).

Accommodations and Food

The pride of Cambridge is the 1874 **C Cambridge Hotel** (4 W. Main St., 518/677-5623, www.cambridgehotel.com, $135–175 d in summer, about a third less off season), renovated through the effort of dozens of area citizens. Downstairs you'll find a large, airy, Victoriana dining room that's open for lunch and dinner (dinner entrées $12–21). Upstairs are 16 modernized guest rooms, all equipped with private baths, air conditioning, and cable TV.

EAGLE BRIDGE

The **homestead of Grandma Moses** (1860–1961) is still owned by her descendants, who operate the **Mount Nebo Gallery** (60 Grandma Moses Rd., off Rte. 22 south of Cambridge, 518/686-4334, 9 A.M.–4 P.M. Mon.–Fri., 10 A.M.–5 P.M. Sat., noon–5 P.M. Sun.) next door to their farmhouse. For sale inside are paintings, prints, posters, calendars, and greeting cards by Moses' great-grandson Will Moses. Also a self-taught artist, Will carries on in his great-grandmother's tradition, painting farm and village scenes of a bygone era.

To view the largest public collection of paintings by Grandma Moses, as well as the one-room schoolhouse that she once attended, continue south on Route 22 to Route 7, then head east across the state line to the **Bennington Museum** (W. Main St., 802/447-1571, 10 A.M.–5 P.M. daily, adults $8, seniors and students $6, under 12 free) in Bennington, Vermont. The museum is about 18 miles from Eagle Bridge.

GRANVILLE

This sturdy town of red-brick buildings was settled first by Quakers from Vermont in 1781.

The New Skete community's secular claim to fame, however, is—dogs. The monks began breeding and training German shepherds shortly after moving here in the 1960s, when it became apparent that they could not support themselves by farming. The business took off, especially after 1978, when one of the brothers wrote a best-selling, award-winning book, *How to Be Your Dog's Best Friend* (Little, Brown).

Though the kennels are off-limits to the public, you can stop into the chapel and a gift shop (New Skete Rd., off Chestnut Hill Rd. [Rte. 67] east of Cambridge, 518/677-

Later, in the mid-1800s, it was famed for its colored slate quarries—producing maroon, green, and blue slate—worked primarily by people of Welsh descent. Granville today still sports slate roofs, slate chimneys, slate patios, slate sidewalks, and even slate business signs.

Pember Museum of Natural History

Housed in a striking Victorian mansion, the Pember Museum (33 W. Main St. [Rte. 149], 518/642-1515, www.pembermuseum.com, 1–5 P.M. Tues.–Fri., 10 A.M.–3 P.M. Sun., adults $2.50, children $1) is a surprisingly Old World place filled with elegant glass and wood exhibit cases. Preserved inside are hundreds upon hundreds of birds, insects, reptiles, and mammals, all collected by amateur naturalist Franklin Pember in the late 1800s.

Some of these species, such as the passenger pigeon and Carolina parakeet, are now extinct. Others, such as the South American possum and red kangaroo, come with their offspring in tow. Larger specimens, such as the Alaskan brown bear and brown pelican, almost burst out of their cases. Walk down the aisles here and you'll feel as if you're surrounded by a magical, about-to-awaken menagerie.

Slate Valley Museum

To learn more about Granville's slate history, step into this renovated 19th-century Dutch barn (17 Water St., off Main St., 518/642-1417, www.slatevalleymuseum.com, 1–5 P.M. Tues.–Fri., 10 A.M.–4 P.M. Sat., adults $2, children under 12 free). Inside, memorabilia, tools, machinery, photography, and artwork date back to the days when Granville was known as the "Colored Slate Capital of the World." During the town's heyday around the turn of the 20th century, 64 slate companies employing 3,000 men were located here.

At the heart of the collection is a powerful 25-foot mural depicting 13 men at work in a slate quarry. The mural was painted in 1939 by Woodstock artist Martha Levy for the federal Works Progress Administration.

WHITEHALL

At the head of Lake Champlain at the county's northern end lies Whitehall, the birthplace of the U.S. Navy. The first American fleet was built here in 1776 under the supervision of Benedict Arnold.

Along the eastern edge of modern-day Whitehall runs a trim historic Main Street listed on the National Register of Historic Places. Nearby are pleasant waterfront parks and the **Skenesborough Museum** (off Rte. 4, 518/499-1155, 10 A.M.–4 P.M. Mon.–Sat. and noon–4 P.M. Sun. June–Sept.), housing models of the first U.S. Navy ships, along with canal and railroad exhibits. The museum also runs the **Heritage Area Visitors Center,** which is stocked with free walking-tour maps.

Lake George and Southeastern Adirondacks

Christened Lac du St. Sacrement in 1609 by Father Jogues, its European discoverer, Lake George lies in a deep fault valley the ends of which are blocked by glacial debris. Thirty-two magnificent miles long, the dark, spring-fed lake surrounds 225 islands. At the lake's southern end sprawls the busy tourist village of Lake George, but otherwise, much of the shoreline is crowded with dense pine.

As part of a strategic water route connecting Canada with New York City, Lake George played an important role in both the French and Indian War and the American Revolution. Between 1690 and 1760, the French and British fought four major battles along the shores of Lake George and nearby Lake Champlain. Fort Ticonderoga, at the foot of Lake George overlooking Lake Champlain, and Fort William Henry, at the head of Lake George, date back to that period. During the Revolutionary

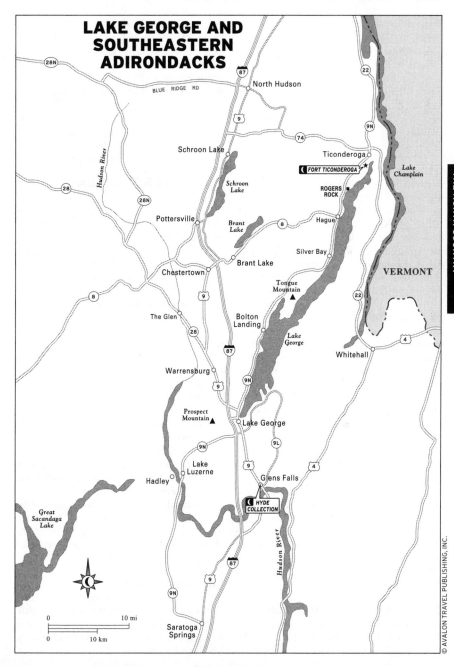

LAKE GEORGE AND SOUTHEASTERN ADIRONDACKS

THE NORTH COUNTRY

© AVALON TRAVEL PUBLISHING, INC.

War, the taking of Fort Ticonderoga from the British in 1775 marked the Americans' first major military victory.

Surrounding Lake George are the forested foothills of the Adirondacks, the summits of which offer glorious views of the lake below and the higher peaks farther north. To the west gleam a smattering of smaller lakes, including Lake Luzerne, Schroon Lake, and Brandt Lake.

GLENS FALLS

Between Saratoga Springs and Lake George lies Glens Falls, a town of wide, empty downtown streets, peppered with handsome brick buildings. Nearby flows the Hudson River and a 60-foot-high waterfall that was responsible for turning the town into an early industrial center. An Adirondacks **information booth** (518/792-2730) is located in Glens Falls between Exits 17 and 18 off I-87 northbound.

(Hyde Collection

The main reason to stop in Glens Falls is to tour the first-class Hyde Collection (161 Warren St., east of the Rte. 9 intersection, 518/792-1761, www.hydeartmuseum.org, 10 A.M.–5 P.M. Tues.–Sat., noon–5 P.M. Sun., free admission), housed in a 1912 mansion styled as a Renaissance villa. Step inside this long, low-slung building, and you'll find yourself surrounded by palm trees, balconies, tile floors, fine antiques, and an important collection of Old Masters. Among them are works by Rembrandt, Rubens, El Greco, Botticelli, Tintoretto, Degas, Cézanne, van Gogh, and Picasso. American artists also are well represented, including Eakins, Homer, and Whistler.

The Hyde Collection was amassed by Louis Fiske and Charlotte Pruyn Hyde in the first half of the 20th century. Mrs. Hyde turned the family mansion into a museum in 1952, following her husband's death.

Chapman Historical Museum

Also worth a stop, especially for photography buffs, is the Chapman Museum (348 Glen St. [Rte. 9], at Bacon, 518/793-2826, www.chap-manmuseum.org, 10 A.M.–5 P.M. Tues.–Sat., adults $2, seniors and students $1, under 12 free), run by the Glens Falls–Queensbury Historical Association. Housed in an 1867 Victorian mansion, complete with several period rooms, the museum showcases an outstanding collection of photographs by Seneca Ray Stoddard. An artist, writer, cartographer, and surveyor, Stoddard wrote numerous early guidebooks to the Adirondacks and captured the region's majesty through countless photographs.

LAKE GEORGE VILLAGE

Everything at Lake George, from the House of Frankenstein wax museum to the Million Dollar Beach, seems to date back to the 1950s. Mom-and-pop motels, miniature golf courses, the Great Escape amusement park, the Magic Forest with its giant Uncle Sam statue looming out front—all cajole you back in time. Look at the place with one eye and it's a kitschy Americana theme park, with great appeal for kids. Look at it with another and it's a greedy tourist trap, sadly out of place in its majestic setting in the Adirondack foothills.

Lake George is basically a one-street town, with the majority of its souvenir shops and restaurants laid out along Canada Street (Route 9). Intersecting Canada Street at the lakefront, Beach Road leads to Fort William Henry and the **Million Dollar Beach,** which is much, *much* smaller and tamer than its name implies. Along the way are docks where boats and water-sports equipment can be rented. A small beach is also located in **Shepard Park,** at Canada and Montcalm Streets.

During the summer, Lake George village is packed with tourists—most of them families. After Labor Day, the place shuts down abruptly, to remain shuttered until Memorial Day of the following year.

Lake Excursions

Brave the hordes of tourists and take a cruise on Lake George. Though the boats are highly commercialized affairs, they do take you out into deep, dark blue waters framed with moody forests and peaks.

Affiliated with the Shoreline Restaurant (see *Food*, below), **Shoreline Cruises** (2 Kurosaka Ln., 518/668-4644, www.lakeshorecruises.com) offers day and evening cruises onboard five different-sized boats, May–October. **Lake George Steamboat Cruises** (Steel Pier, Beach Rd., 518/668-5777, www.lakegeorgesteamboat.com) offers sightseeing, dinner, and entertainment cruises onboard three large reproduction steamships May–October.

Fort William Henry Museum

Across from the Lake George Steamboat Company dock stands a facsimile reconstruction of Fort William Henry (Beach Rd., 518/668-5471, www.fortwilliamhenry.com, 10 A.M.–6 P.M. daily Apr.–Oct., adults $12, children 5–11 $7.25). Featured are some French and Indian War artifacts, audiovisual presentations, life-size dioramas, and demonstrations of cannon and musket firings.

The original fort was built in 1756 by British general William Johnson, the man responsible for naming the lake—after King George III. In 1757, the fort was attacked by 1,600 French soldiers and 3,000 Native Americans under the command of Gen. Montcalm. After a long siege, Montcalm arranged for a peaceful surrender. The Native Americans, however,

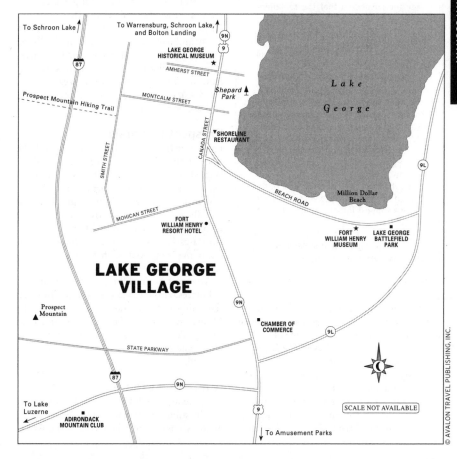

To Schroon Lake

To Warrensburg, Schroon Lake, and Bolton Landing

LAKE GEORGE HISTORICAL MUSEUM

AMHERST STREET

Prospect Mountain Hiking Trail

MONTCALM STREET

Shepard Park

SMITH STREET

CANADA STREET

SHORELINE RESTAURANT

Lake George

MOHICAN STREET

FORT WILLIAM HENRY RESORT HOTEL

BEACH ROAD

Million Dollar Beach

FORT WILLIAM HENRY MUSEUM

LAKE GEORGE BATTLEFIELD PARK

LAKE GEORGE VILLAGE

Prospect Mountain

STATE PARKWAY

CHAMBER OF COMMERCE

To Lake Luzerne

ADIRONDACK MOUNTAIN CLUB

To Amusement Parks

SCALE NOT AVAILABLE

© AVALON TRAVEL PUBLISHING, INC.

THE SUNKEN TREASURE OF LAKE GEORGE

Beneath the waters of Lake George lie approximately 75 bateaux (flat-bottomed boats) that date back to the French and Indian War. The boats were part of a 260-vessel fleet deliberately scuttled by the British and the American colonists in 1758 to protect the craft from the French and Native Americans. The British returned to the lake in 1759 and raised close to 200 of the ships.

No one suspected that the remaining bateaux still existed until two teenage divers discovered them in 1960. That same year, three of the boats were raised from the lake, and one was put on exhibit at the Adirondack Museum in Blue Mountain Lake.

Beginning in 1987, a team of divers – now known as Bateaux Below, Inc. – began a survey of the seven sunken boats at the southern end of the lake. These boats were listed on the National Register of Historic Places in 1992 and are now a Shipwreck Preserve, open to divers Memorial Day–September.

In 1990, yet another ship was discovered—a 52-foot radeau (seven-sided battleship) named the *Land Tortoise*. Also part of the scuttled fleet, this fragile vessel is North America's oldest intact warship. It is off-limits to divers.

For a brochure on the Shipwreck Preserve, call the **Department of Environmental Conservation** at 518/402-9428.

ignored the agreement and attacked without warning, butchering the many men, women, and children who had taken refuge in the fort. James Fenimore Cooper based *The Last of the Mohicans* on the incident.

Though interesting enough as far as it goes, the fort does not present much that's original. You might want to save your money for the considerably more authentic Fort Ticonderoga, located at the northern end of Lake George.

Lake George Battlefield Park

In a small, hilly park behind the fort you'll find the largely unexcavated ruins of the original Fort William Henry, along with plaques explaining various aspects of the 1757 battle. Picnic tables throughout the park offer good views of the lake.

Lake George Historical Museum

Housed in the Old Court House (Canada and Amherst Sts., 518/668-5044, 11 A.M.–4 P.M. Fri.–Sat. and Tues., and 3–8 P.M. Wed.–Thurs. July–Aug., call for off-season hours, free admission) are three floors of exhibits on the history of Lake George. Of particular interest are the 1845 jail cells in the basement, an exhibit on lake shipwrecks, photos from the steamboat era, and an elaborate, doll-size wooden church carved by convicted murderer George Ouellet in 1881. After finishing his church, Ouellet sold it for a sizeable sum, hired a new lawyer to appeal his conviction, and was acquitted.

Prospect Mountain

For a terrific view of Lake George and the southeastern Adirondacks, drive up the Prospect Mountain State Parkway (518/668-5198, 9 A.M.–5 P.M. daily June–Oct., $6 per vehicle), which intersects with Route 9 just south of the village. The 5.5-mile drive leading up the 2,030-foot mountain offers 100-mile views of five states. Park your car near the top and board one of the "viewmobiles" that travel to the very crest of the mountain.

An easy 1.6-mile hiking trail, marked with red blazes, also leads to the summit. To reach the trailhead from Lake George village, take Montcalm Street to Smith Street and turn south. The trail begins midway down the block, and follows the roadbed of an old cable railroad.

Amusement Parks

Lake George wouldn't be Lake George without its amusement parks. Five miles south of the village reigns the largest—the **Great**

Escape & Splashdown Kingdom (1172 Rte. 9, 518/792-3500, adults $36, children under 48 inches $20, children under age 2 free), offering over 125 rides, shows, and attractions, including Steamin' Demon Loop Rollercoaster and Black Cobra.

Three miles south of the village, **Magic Forest** (Rte. 9, 518/668-2448, adults $15, children $12) offers 20 rides for children and five for adults. Lots of animals are on the premises; during the daily "Diving Horse Act," a horse walks off a plank into a pool.

One mile south of the village, **Water Slide World** (Rte. 9, at Rte. 91, 518/668-4407, adults $27, children under 11 $24, seniors and toddlers $11) includes a wave pool, water slides, bumper boats, and hot tubs.

All three parks open in June and close after Labor Day.

Adirondack Mountain Club (ADK)

Also to the south of Lake George village, near the intersection of Route 9 and Route 9N, is an **information center** run by the Adirondack Mountain Club (814 Goggins Rd., off Rte. 9N west of I-87, 518/668-4447 or 800/395-8080, 8:30 A.M.–5 P.M. Mon.–Sat.), a nonprofit organization dedicated to broadening the public's appreciation of the Adirondack wilderness. Stop here for information on hiking trails and camping areas. Various guidebooks for sale describe day-hikes, canoe routes, and backpacking trips, and experts are on hand to answer questions. To reach the center directly from I-87, take Exit 21.

Hiking Buck Mountain

On the southeastern shore of Lake George is Buck Mountain. A well-marked, 3.3-mile hiking trail leads to the summit and great views of Lake George, Lake Champlain, the Adirondacks, and Vermont's Green Mountains. To reach the trailhead, head east from the village to Route 9L. Turn left and continue for about seven miles until you see a turn for Pilot Knob and Kaatskill Bay. Follow this road about 3.5 miles to the trailhead, marked with a large sign

and parking lot. The easy-to-moderate round-trip hike takes about four hours.

Camping and Accommodations

To make reservations at the 68-site **Lake George Battleground State Campground** (off Beach Rd., 518/668-3348) or the 251-site **Hearthstone Point** (Rte. 9N north of the village, 518/668-5193), call 800/456-CAMP.

Dozens of small, moderately priced motels are located along Rts. 9 and 9N. One of the friendliest and most reliable among them is the clean, family-run **Admiral Motel** (401 Canada St., 518/668-2097, www.admiralmotel.com, $95–115 d in summer; $65–75 off-season) complete with a heated outdoor pool).

If you'd like to stay near the village but away from the madness, choose a hostelry on the lake's quiet east shore. A good option here is the classy **Dunham's Bay Lodge** (Rte. 9L, 518/656-9242, www.dunhamsbay.com, $200 d).

The modern, well-kept ◖ **Fort William Henry Resort Hotel and Conference Center** (50 Canada St., 518/668-3081, www.fortwilliamhenry.com, $180–500 d in summer; about one-third less off-season) features two pools, three restaurants, a concierge in season, and a wide variety of spacious rooms and suites configured to accommodate families of all sizes.

Food

Fast food and sandwich shops are located all along Canada Street and Beach Road. Among them is **Garrison Koom Café** (Beach Rd., 518/668-5281), serving burgers, sandwiches, and simple entrées.

For more serious dining, try the airy, multilevel ◖ **Shoreline Restaurant** (4 Kurosaka Ln., 518/668-2875), nicely situated overlooking a small marina. Menu selections range from fresh fish to chicken teriyaki. Sit out back on the deck and enjoy live entertainment in summer; average entrée $19. Also overlooking the water is the big, boisterous **Boardwalk** (foot of Amherst St., 518/668-5324), offering burgers and sandwiches at lunch, considerably more elaborate entrées at dinner (average price $18).

LAKE LUZERNE

Take Route 9N out of Lake George village to reach Lake Luzerne, a quieter resort community about 10 miles away. Lake Luzerne traditionally has been known for its dude ranches, which is why you'll notice signs pointing to Big Hat Country along the way. Though the dude-ranch business is not what it was once, the country's oldest weekly rodeo still takes place weekend nights in summer at **Painted Pony Ranch** (703 Howe Rd., off Rte. 9N, 518/696-2421).

The trim village of Lake Luzerne, bounded by two rivers, consists of a few small streets crowded with Victorian homes. At the eastern end flows the Hudson River, where bubbling Rockwell Falls rushes downstream through a small park. At the western end, the Sacandaga River attracts white-water rafters and canoeists. Rental equipment and guided white-water raft trips down the Sacandaga's Class II and III waters are offered by the **Adirondack River Outfitters Adventures** (518/696-5101) in Lake Luzerne, and by **Wild Waters Outdoor Center** (518/494-4984) in nearby Warrensburg.

Hiking Hadley Mountain

Although Hadley Mountain is only 2,700 feet high, it affords magnificent views from its summit. To the north loom the High Peaks, to the south are the Catskills and Great Sacandaga Lake, and to the east Lake George and the Green Mountains. The Adirondack Mountain Club considers the four-mile round-trip hike to the summit easy to moderate in difficulty. The hike should take about three hours.

To reach the trailhead, take Route 9N north of Lake Luzerne to Hadley and head north on Stony Creek Road. Continue three miles to Hadley Hill Road and turn left. Proceed slightly over four miles to Tower Road, turn right, and continue another 1.5 miles to the trailhead on the left, marked with a sign.

Camping and Accommodations

To make reservations at the 174-site **Luzerne State Campground** (Rte. 9N south of the village, 518/696-2031), call 800/456-CAMP.

© CHRISTIANE BIRD

The Sacandaga River is popular with white-water rafters and canoeists.

The gracious **Lamplight Inn B&B** (2129 Lake Ave., 518/696-5294, www.lamplight-inn.com, $175–250 d in summer) is an award-winning 1890 hostelry featuring 10 bedrooms, fireplaces, 12-foot ceilings, and a wraparound porch. An addition offers five modern rooms equipped with Jacuzzis.

Between Lake George and Lake Luzerne, the **Roaring Brook Ranch and Tennis Resort** (Luzerne Rd. [Rte. 9], 518/668-5767, www.roaringbrookranchresort.com) still operates as one of the oldest and best dude ranches in the area. Spread out over 500 acres, the well-kept resort includes 142 simple but comfortable rooms, 30-odd horses, five lighted tennis courts, three swimming pools, and saunas and fitness rooms (summer rates $101–129 per person double occupancy, including riding, use of all facilities, breakfast, and dinner; family rates available).

Events

The free **Lake Luzerne Chamber Music Festival** (518/696-2771), featuring members of the Philadelphia Orchestra, takes place on summer Monday nights at the Luzerne Music Center (Lake Tour Rd., off Rte. 9N).

BOLTON LANDING

Back along the shores of Lake George about 10 miles north of Lake George village sits Bolton Landing, another congested tourist town. During the summer the village traffic is bumper to bumper.

For many visitors, Bolton Landing's main attractions are its gift shops, most along Main Street. The **Bolton Historical Museum** (Lakeshore Dr. [Rte. 9N], 518/644-9960, 11 A.M.–4 P.M. Tues.–Sun. July–Aug.), housed in a former Catholic church, includes a collection of photographs by Seneca Ray Stoddard and an exhibit on sculptor David Smith, who once lived in the area

Isolated on its own private island at one end of the village reigns the storybook **Sagamore Resort** (110 Sagamore Rd., 518/644-9400). Originally built in 1883 and now listed on the National Register of Historic Places, the columned, gabled hotel remains a luxurious year-round resort. Features include four excellent restaurants, a full-service spa, tennis courts, playground, nearby golf course, and a sandy beach with great views of Lake George. Cruises of the lake are offered by the *Morgan,* a sleek wooden boat (sightseeing cruise free for guests, $10 for nonguests, dinner cruises cost $55 per person).

Marcella Sembrich Opera Museum

From 1921 to 1935, Marcella Sembrich, a soprano who sang with the Metropolitan Opera, summered in Bolton Landing. In those days, the village was a favorite resort of opera stars, and Sembrich brought several students with her each year. Today, the diva's former studio (4800 Lakeshore Dr., 518/644-9839, www.operamuseum.com, 10 A.M.–12:30 P.M. daily June–Sept., adults $2, under 12 free) still houses her sizeable collection of music, along with her costumes, furniture, and other memorabilia.

Accommodations and Food

Across the street from the Sembrich estate is the **Hilltop Cottage B&B** (Lakeshore Dr., 518/644-2492, www.hilltopcottage.com, $80 d), whose owners are responsible for creating and maintaining the museum. Sembrich's students stayed in the cottage back in the days when she was teaching here. Today, the B&B offers two guestrooms with private baths.

The █ **Sagamore Resort** (110 Sagamore Rd., 518/644-9400, www.thesagamore.com) offers 100 luxurious rooms and suites in the historic main hotel ($180–305 d off-season; $410–625 d in summer) and 240 private lodges ($149–385 d off-season; $269–659 d in summer). On site are a variety of restaurants. **Mr. Brown's Pub** serves sandwiches and salads ($9–18). **Club Grille** serves hamburgers and basic fare at lunch, top-of-the-line steaks and other grilled items at dinner (entrées $18–32). The **Sagamore Dining Room** specializes in innovative American cuisine served upscale-buffet style. Call 518/743-6110 for reservations.

The casual **Algonquin Restaurant** (Lakeshore Dr., 518/644-9442), built over the water, is a local favorite for both lunch and dinner. On the menu is everything from burgers to fresh fish; average entrée $16.

NORTHERN LAKE GEORGE

Route 9N continues north of Bolton Landing into much wilder countryside. At last the tourist centers are left behind as you veer away from the lakeshore, past the Tongue Mountain Range, and then return to it once again, passing the isolated resort communities of Sabbath Day Point, Silver Bay, and Hague.

Scenic **Route 8** heads west out of Hague to Brant Lake, about 10 miles away. En route, lookouts offer great views of the High Peaks; in the fall, the surrounding Dixon Forest turns vivid hues of red, yellow, and orange. Mohawk legend describes this as the land of Broken Wing, a crippled brave who saved his village and is remembered every autumn by the turning of the leaves.

About two miles north of Hague on Route 9N are the **Indian Kettles,** shallow glacial potholes 1–3 feet in diameter. The white man's legend has it that Native Americans once used the potholes for cooking.

Rogers Rock State Park

Just north of the Indian Kettles, Rogers Rock State Park (Rte. 9N, 518/585-6746, $6–8 parking) offers a 321-site campground, beach, and bathhouse, along with a 2.5-mile hiking trail that leads up 500 feet to Rogers Slide. At first, the trail winds mostly uphill and northerly, but then it flattens out to run along a ledge and open expanse. Keeping to the right at a fork just past the ledge will bring you to cliffs overlooking Lake George. For campground reservations, call 800/456-CAMP.

Camping and Accommodations

Forty-eight of the islands dotting Lake George are available for camping, though accessible only by boat. For more information, contact the local Department of Environmental Conservation office (518/623-1200) or visit the DEC's website (www.dec.state.ny.us) and type in "Lake George islands."

One of the last of the old lakeside hotels that once flourished in this region is the **Northern Lake George Resort** (Rte. 9N, Silver Bay, 518/543-6528, www.northernlakegeorge.com, $77–110 d). Built in 1896, when it was known as the Hotel Uncas, the hostelry has been altered over the years but still features an old-fashioned rustic lobby complete with stone fireplace and high ceilings. Also on-site are lakeside villas and motel rooms.

SCHROON LAKE AND VICINITY

West of Lake George lies Schroon Lake, a quiet resort community with a laid-back Main Street and good-size public beach. During the summer, one-hour narrated cruises of the lake are offered by **Schroon Lake Boat Tours** (518/532-7675). The area is also home to the **Seagle Music Colony** (Charley Hill Rd., 518/532-7875, www.seaglecolony.com), a music retreat founded by concert baritone Oscar Seagle in 1915. The

colony stages opera concerts and musical theater July–early August.

Pottersville

At the lake's southern end lies Pottersville and the **Natural Stone Bridge and Caves** (535 Stone Bridge Rd., off Rte. 9, 518/494-2283, 9 A.M.–7 P.M. daily June–Oct., adults $10, children 6–12 $5). Formed by the Ausable River, this geological park holds odd-shaped rock formations, waterfalls, and potholes large enough to park a truck in.

Chesterton

One of the finest restaurants in the area, specializing in innovative American dishes, is the rambling Civil War–era (**Friend's Lake Inn** (Friends Lake Rd., 518/494-4751, www.friendslake.com), about seven miles south of Schroon Lake in historic Chestertown. The wine list alone runs about 25 pages long (full menu offered at dinner only, average entrée $23; bar and light lunch menu also offered in summer), while upstairs and out back are 17 lovely guest rooms, all equipped with queen-size beds and private baths. Many of the rooms also have Jacuzzis and two have fireplaces ($295–345 d, including breakfast and dinner; B&B rates (breakfast only) $255–305).

Hiking Pharaoh Mountain

To the east of Schroon Lake rises Pharaoh Mountain, surrounded by the Pharaoh Lake Wilderness Area. The splendid views from the mountaintop—covered with open rock—take in nearby ponds and craggy hills, as well as the more distant High Peaks. The nine-mile round-trip hike is of moderate difficulty and takes 4–5 hours.

To reach the trailhead, head north of Schroon Lake on Route 9 about two miles. Turn right onto Alder Meadow Road and continue 2.2 miles to a fork. Bear left on Crane Pond Road and travel 1.4 miles to a parking lot. Continue on the road on foot 1.9 miles to Crane Pond, where the trailhead begins at the end of another parking lot (parking is not permitted here).

Detour to North Hudson

On the edge of the High Peaks region about seven miles north of Schroon Lake village lies North Hudson, a tiny mountain hamlet surrounded by ponds and wilderness; year-round population is under 200. The place is well worth a detour for the magnificent views along the way.

Blue Ridge Road (Route 2) heads west out of North Hudson to skirt the southern edge of the High Peaks. The route runs alongside the Branch, which flows between Elk Lake and Schroon River; about three miles from the village cascade the lovely **Blue Ridge waterfalls.**

Accommodations

Situated on a grassy knoll, the friendly

Schroon Lake Bed and Breakfast (Rte. 9, 518/532-7042, www.schroonbb.com, $115–150) offers five comfortable guest rooms furnished with antiques, along with a breezy front porch providing good views of the lake and Adirondacks.

Tucked into the mountains north of North Hudson is the ultra-secluded 🌙 **Elk Lake Lodge** (Elk Lake Rd., off Blue Ridge Rd., 518/532-7616, www.elklakelodge.com, $110–150 per person, double occupancy, includes all meals). One of the finest rustic lodges in the Adirondacks, the hostelry is situated on its own private lake surrounded by a 12,000-acre preserve. The 1906 main lodge offers six rooms with private baths, as does the more modern Emerson Lodge. On the lakefront are eight cottages.

THE NORTH COUNTRY

Champlain Valley

In 1609, 11 years before the Pilgrims landed in Massachusetts, French explorer Samuel de Champlain "discovered" the long, thin, sparkling blue lake that now bears his name. Shortly after his arrival he killed two Iroquois with a single blast of his arquebus, thereby establishing the tenor of European–Native American relationships for centuries to come.

One hundred and ten miles long and 400 feet deep in spots, Lake Champlain is the largest freshwater lake in the United States after the Great Lakes. Encompassing 490 square miles, it stretches from New York north into Canada and east into Vermont. Even bigger than the lake itself is the basin in which it sits. On the New York side, that basin extends as far west as the Adirondack Mountains and as far south as Hudson Falls. About 25 percent of Adirondack Park lies within the Champlain Valley.

Compared to Lake George, the shores of Lake Champlain appear sparsely forested and surprisingly undeveloped. The countryside becomes especially magnificent north of Port

Henry, where the raw jagged High Peaks of the Adirondacks rise to one side, the moody rounder peaks of Vermont's Green Mountains to the other.

Throughout the 19th and much of the 20th centuries, Lake Champlain supported numerous iron-ore and manufacturing plants, most of them along the shore. Many of these have closed in recent years, which helps account for the region's current high unemployment rate.

Away from the shore, the valley opens into rich farmland. Red barns, silver silos, and a patchwork of green fields spread out over one gentle slope after another. Dairy farming is especially big business here.

Visitor Services

Near the Lake Champlain Bridge connecting New York with Vermont stands the **Lake Champlain Visitors Center** (814 Bridge Rd., off Rtes. 9 and 22, 888/THE-LAKE, www.lakechamplainregion.com, 9 A.M.–4 P.M. Mon.–Fri.). Inside you'll find a multitude of brochures and several exhibits.

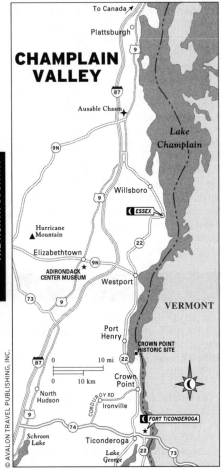

TICONDEROGA

Sandwiched in the two miles between Lake George and Lake Champlain lies Ticonderoga—the town and the fort. The town sits at the foot of Lake George; the fort overlooks Lake Champlain.

The Town

Sprawling, scruffy Ticonderoga centers around a historic downtown containing several interesting buildings. Among them is the **Heritage Museum** (Montcalm St. at Bicentennial Park,

518/585-2696, July–Sept., call for hours), which houses displays on the area's industrial history. Traditionally, Ticonderoga has been known for its pencil and papermaking plants. The first commercial pencils—bearing the name Ticonderoga—were produced in the area in 1840; still operating in town is International Paper.

◖ Fort Ticonderoga

One of the Adirondacks' most popular visitor attractions, Fort Ticonderoga (Fort Rd. [Rte. 74], 518/585-2821, 9 A.M.–5 P.M. daily May–Oct., call for off-season hours, adults $12, seniors and students $10, children 7–11 $6) sits within a shade-filled park. Originally built by the French in 1755, the fort bore the nickname "Key to a Continent." Strategically located along the Canada–New York waterway, Ticonderoga was attacked six times during the French and Indian and Revolutionary Wars. Three times it successfully held, and three times it fell. France, Great Britain, and the Americans all once held control.

Inside the fort are meticulously restored barracks, kitchens, stables, cannons, and artifacts pertaining to both wars. Among the more unusual items on display are a lock of George Washington's hair, a pocket watch once owned by Ethan Allen, and a rum horn given to Gen. Schuyler by Paul Revere. Throughout the summer, numerous special events are staged daily, including parades, cannon firings, and fife-and-drum musters.

Fort Ticonderoga Ferry

Continue east past the fort on Route 74 to reach a public boat ramp and dock for the sleepy Fort Ticonderoga Ferry (802/897-7999), in operation in one form or another since the mid-1700s. May–October, the flatbed ferry crosses whenever there's traffic to Shoreham, Vermont. The low-key journey only takes a few minutes ($8 per car with up to four passengers one-way, $12 round-trip; $2 per bicycle and rider; $1 per biped).

CROWN POINT

About eight miles north of Ticonderoga is the village of Crown Point, not to be confused with the Crown Point Historic Site a few miles farther north. The village of Crown Point was once known for its iron industry, while at the Historic Site are the ruins of two forts.

Ironville

Hard though it is to believe today, the quiet, near-deserted area just west of Crown Point was once a major industrial center filled with dirty clanking machinery. A rich bed of iron ore was discovered here in the early 1800s, and throughout that century, the region teemed with mines, forges, and railroads. The high-quality ore attracted the U.S. Navy, intent on securing iron to build its first iron-clad warship, the Civil War–era *Monitor*.

Crown Point's industrial activity centered on the company town of Ironville, now a village so small it's all but disappeared. In its heyday, Ironville boasted a company store, company housing, and company script. Today, it's an exceptionally lovely hamlet with a strong New England feel.

Behind a white picket fence in Ironville's center presides the **Penfield Homestead Museum** (708 Creek Rd., 518/597-3804, www.penfield-museum.org, 11 A.M.–4 P.M. Thurs.–Sun. June–Oct., adults $4, children $2). This 1828 Federal-style building was once home to industrialist Allen Penfield, the first man to use electricity for industrial purposes (in 1831). Exhibits tell the story of Penfield's inventions and the area's industrial past. A collection of ancient machinery slumbers out back.

To reach Ironville from Ticonderoga, take Route 74 to Corduroy Road. From Crown Point, take Route 47 west, which becomes Ironville Road and then Corduroy Road.

Crown Point State Historic Site

North of Crown Point, a pudgy spit of land juts into Lake Champlain. Flat and windswept, with sweeping views of the north, the point once provided an ideal lookout spot. The French built Fort St. Frederic here in 1734, only to be conquered by the British in 1759, who in turn built Fort Crown Point.

The ruins of both forts still stand, near a visitors center (739 Bridge Rd., off Rts. 9N and 22 near the Champlain Bridge, 518/597-3666, 9 A.M.–5 P.M. Wed.–Mon. May–Oct., adults $3, seniors and students $2, children under 12

Crown Point Historic Site is home to ruins of both French and British 18th-century forts.

$1) that provides historical background. Much of the area has not been fully excavated, but it has a lonely and haunting appeal.

PORT HENRY

On the mainland just north of the Crown Point Historic Site sprawls Port Henry, a large town of red-brick buildings spread over several steep hills. Like Crown Point, Port Henry was once known for its iron industry, which peaked here during World War II. West of town hulks a giant 18-million-ton mountain of ore tailings that's visible for miles around.

Welcome to the Home of the Champ reads the sign at the town's entrance, while nearby stands a cheerful green serpent with a zigzagging tail. The **Champ** is a legendary monster who lives in the depths of Lake Champlain. Stories about him have circulated among the Iroquois for hundreds of years and among whites since 1609, when Samuel de Champlain reported seeing a 20-foot-long creature in the lake. Since then there have been over 300 reported sightings of the Champ, many of which have occurred near Port Henry.

Although there is no concrete proof that the Champ exists, the legislatures of both New York and Vermont have passed resolutions encouraging scientific inquiry into the depths of the lake.

WESTPORT

Lying on a natural terrace above a deep bay, the tidy Victorian village of Westport has been a favorite stopping-off place since steamship days, when families traveling north on Lake Champlain debarked here to catch stagecoaches for points farther west. Later, Westport became a destination in its own right, as evidenced by the elegant homes along Route 22. Today, Westport remains one of the few villages in the Adirondacks that's accessible by rail; Amtrak travels through here on its way between New York and Montreal.

Westport is known for its historic inns and the **Depot Theater** (Rte. 9, 518/962-4449), which presents professional summer stock in a restored 19th-century railway station. Along

the lakeshore is a busy marina where boats can be rented, and a public beach. Bordering Main Street are a variety of shops, including the **Westport Trading Company** (6521 Main St., 518/962-4801), which sells the work of more than 100 area artists and artisans.

Accommodations

The clapboard **Westport Hotel** (6691 Main St. [Rte. 9N], 518/962-4501, www.thewestporthotel.com, $35–50 with shared bath, $85 with private bath) dates back to 1876, the same year the railroad came to town. Inside are 10 guest rooms nicely outfitted in antiques; outside is an inviting wraparound porch.

The stately 1875 **Inn on the Library Lawn** (1234 Stevenson Rd., 518/962-8666, www.the-innonthelibrarylawn.com, $69–125 d, with breakfast), situated across the street from the town library, features 10 spacious guest rooms with period furnishings. Downstairs is a sitting room with a fireplace, upstairs is a library, and outside is a deck.

The fine Dutch Colonial **All Tucked Inn** (6455 Main St., 518/962-4400, www.all-tuckedinn.com, $75–130 d), set back on a lawn behind a white picket fence, offers nine guest rooms and a glass-enclosed porch that overlooks the lake. Three of the rooms have fireplaces.

Food

For casual dining at the marina, try the **Galley** (foot of Washington St., 518/962-4899). On the menu is eclectic international fare; live bands play on summer weekend nights (average entrée $12). The **Westport Hotel** (6691 Main St., 518/962-4501) runs a cozy restaurant spread over several small rooms; dinner entrées range $11–22.

ELIZABETHTOWN

About 10 miles west of Westport and Lake Champlain on Route 9N lies Elizabethtown, the Essex County seat. Settled in 1791 by pioneers from Vermont, Elizabethtown was at first known for its lumber mills and later for its resort hotels.

In the town's center on Court Street (Rte. 9N) is the **Essex County Court House,** where the body of abolitionist John Brown lay in state on the way to burial in nearby North Elba (see Lake Placid). His wife and other members of the funeral entourage spent the night at the town's Deer's Head Inn while four young men from the village stood guard over the body. Today, the courthouse features a mural of Brown speaking in his own defense at his 1859 trial in West Virginia. Another mural depicts Samuel de Champlain firing his arquebus at the Iroquois.

Adirondack History Center
Housed in a big old schoolhouse on the edge of town, the laid-back Adirondack History Center (Court St. [Rte. 9], 518/873-6466, www .adkhistorycenter.org, 9 A.M.–5 P.M. Mon.–Sat. and 1–5 P.M. Sun. June–Oct., adults $3.50, seniors $2.50, youths 6–16 $1.50) corrals an enormous hodgepodge of exhibits. A re-created log-cabin kitchen and artifacts from an iron mine take up one floor; on another is an exhibit on the Iroquois and displays pertaining to the lumbering industry. A light-and-sound show offers some perspective on the French and Indian War, while Adirondack guideboats, early farm implements, antique bobsleds, and a roomful of dolls tell their stories of everyday life.

◖ ESSEX
The loveliest village along the Lake Champlain shore is Essex. Filled with trim white buildings that date back to before the Civil War, the entire village is on the National Register of Historic Places. To the west rise the Adirondack's dramatic High Peaks; to the east sparkle the blue waters of the lake, offset by the dusk-blue mountains of Vermont.

Founded in 1765, Essex was one of the earliest European settlements on Lake Champlain. The community was completely destroyed during the American Revolution but soon rose again to become a prosperous shipbuilding center and lake port. By 1850, Essex was one of the largest and busiest towns on the lake, with a population of 2,351.

Then came the Civil War, the opening of the West, and the building of the railroads, all of which drew commerce away from Lake Champlain. Essex's economy suffered and its population dwindled. There was little money for building; standing structures had to do. And so it remains today.

Essex centers on two parallel streets, Main and Elm, both just two blocks long. Excellent examples of Federal, Greek Revival, and Victorian architecture abound, while along the waterfront stretches a park and small marina.

Lake Champlain Ferries (802/864-9804, www.ferries.com) dock at the northern end of the village, crossing between Essex and Charlotte, Vermont. The ride takes 20 minutes one-way ($8.25 for a car and driver one-way, round-trip $15; round-trip rates for walk-on traffic, adults $3.50, children 6–12 $1).

Accommodations
At the heart of Essex sits the 180-year-old ◖ **Essex Inn** (16 Main St., 518/963-8821, www.theessexinn.com, $85–145 d, with full breakfast, some rooms share baths), a long and thin hostelry with an even longer and thinner two-tiered front porch. Breakfast and dinner are served outside in warm weather (average dinner entrée $14), while inside are nine guest rooms. The inn also contains a courtyard, clothing shop, and arts gallery; pick up free walking-tour brochures here.

NORTH TO AUSABLE CHASM
Continuing north of Essex on Route 22, you'll hug the lakeshore for a few glorious miles before heading inland to **Willsboro,** on the Bouquet River. Willsboro is a favorite spot among anglers thanks to its fish ladder at the Willsboro Dam. The ladder, off Route 22, allows landlocked salmon to ascend the river to spawning grounds farther upstream; you can watch the action from a viewing window.

Continue another 13 miles north and you'll bump into Ausable Chasm (off Rte. 9, 518/834-7454, www.ausablechasm.com, 9:30 A.M.–4:30 P.M. daily June–Oct., adults $16, seniors and teens $14, children 5–11 $9).

After the serene back roads and peaceful vistas of Lake Champlain, this place comes as a shock. Ausable Chasm is one of the oldest tourist attractions in the United States, opened in 1870; count on dozens of tour buses crowding its parking lot.

Carved out by the Ausable River over the past 500 million years, the Ausable Chasm's massive stone gorge stretches out over a mile and a half. Twenty to 50 feet wide, and 100–200 feet deep, it is filled with odd rock formations, caves, rapids, and waterfalls. A three-quarter-mile trail leads through the gorge to Table Rock, where visitors can opt to take rafts the rest of the way ($8 per person).

PLATTSBURGH

The small industrial city of Plattsburgh (pop. 21,255) played an important role in both the American Revolution and the War of 1812. In 1776, the British won the Battle of Lake Champlain off Plattsburgh's shores. In 1814, the American Commodore Thomas MacDonough defeated a British fleet from Canada here by using an intricate system of anchors and winches that enabled him to swivel his vessels completely around.

Historic Plattsburgh centers on **RiverWalk Park,** which runs along the banks of the Saranac River downtown. The park begins at Bridge Street and extends to the Champlain Monument at Cumberland Avenue. Addresses worth noting along the way include the 1830 **Trinity Episcopal Church** at Trinity Place; the 1917 **City Hall,** City Hall Place, designed by John Russell Pope; and the **Champlain Monument** itself, a gift to the city from France in 1909, commemorating the tercentenary of Samuel de Champlain's voyage.

Visitor Services

The Plattsburgh–North Country Chamber of Commerce runs a **visitor information center** (800/487-6867) off I-87 heading south between Exits 41 and 40.

Kent-Delord Museum House

Across from the Champlain Monument stands the city's foremost visitor attraction, the Kent-Delord House (17 Cumberland Ave., 518/561-1035, noon–3 P.M. Tues.–Sat., adults $5, children under 12 $3). Built in 1797 and enlarged in 1811, the gracious house was commandeered by the British during the War of 1812. Home to three generations of the Delord family, the house contains nine period rooms and an interesting collection of portraits. Of special interest is an exhibit on Fanny Delord Hall, a self-taught healer who in the late 1800s patented and marketed her own home remedy, Fanoline, "a healing, antiseptic and curative ointment, in cases of Eczema, Fever-sores, Catarrh, Salt-rheum, Piles, Sore Nipples, Burns, Blisters, Scratches, Corns, Sore Eyes, Chapped Hands and Lips."

Clinton County Historical Museum

To learn about Plattsburgh's history, visit the county museum (48 Court St., at Oak, 518/561-0340, noon–4 P.M. Tues.–Fri., adults $4, seniors $3, children under 12 $2), housed in a trim

Ausable Chasm

COURTESY OF LAKE PLACID/ESSEX COUNTY VISITORS BUREAU

THE NORTH COUNTRY

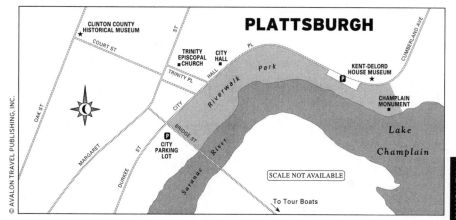

THE NORTH COUNTRY

© AVALON TRAVEL PUBLISHING, INC.

1805 building two blocks from RiverWalk. On permanent display are a diorama on the battles of Lake Champlain, an exhibit on underwater archaeological discoveries, and historic maps. Temporary exhibits highlight such North Country activities as crafts and lumbering.

Recreation

The **Spirit of Plattsburgh** (2 Dock St., 518/566-7447, www.soea.com) offers sightseeing, lunch, dinner, and entertainment cruises of the lake onboard a 500-passenger ship May–October.

High Peaks and Northern Adirondacks

The term "High Peaks" generally refers to the heart of the Adirondacks, where 46 of the region's highest peaks can be found. Just west of the Champlain Valley, the High Peaks are loosely bounded by Elizabethtown to the east, Wilmington to the north, the Franklin County line to the west, and Newcomb to the south. At the center lies Lake Placid.

Many hikers come to the High Peaks region intent on climbing all 46 of its highest summits and thereby becoming a "46er." The tradition dates back to the early 1920s, when two young brothers, George and Robert Marshall, climbed to the top of Whiteface Mountain with their guide Herb Clark. Upon reaching the summit, they made a pact to climb all the peaks in the park measuring 4,000 feet or more in height. Later, it turned out that some of the peaks on their list were under 4,000

feet, but no matter, a pattern had been set. Today, hikers come from all over the country to carry on the tradition.

WEST ON ROUTES 9N AND 86

Heading into the High Peaks region from Ausable Chasm on Route 9N, you'll pass through **Au Sable Forks**, once home to illustrator Rockwell Kent; and tiny **Jay,** beautifully situated on the East Branch of the Ausable River. In Jay are several old-fashioned country stores and the **Jay Craft Center** (Rte. 9N, 518/946-7824), housing a pottery studio and a gift shop. A few miles south in **Upper Jay** are attractive **antiques shops.**

From Jay, take Route 86 west to reach **Wilmington,** a small ski town huddled at the base of towering Whiteface Mountain. Adirondack Hospitality Since 1822, reads a sign.

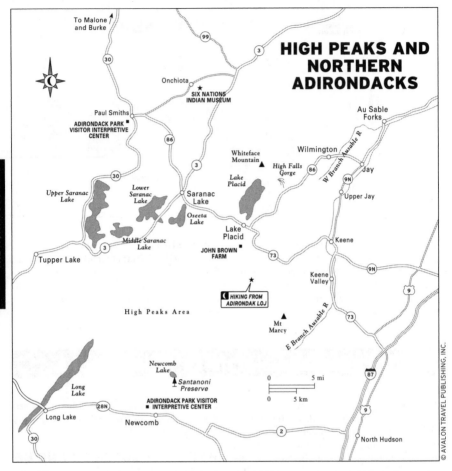

HIGH PEAKS AND NORTHERN ADIRONDACKS

To Malone and Burke

Onchiota
★ SIX NATIONS INDIAN MUSEUM

Paul Smiths
■ ADIRONDACK PARK VISITOR INTERPRETIVE CENTER

Au Sable Forks

Whiteface Mountain ▲
High Falls Gorge

Wilmington

Jay

W Branch Ausable R.

Lake Placid

Upper Jay

Upper Saranac Lake
Lower Saranac Lake
Saranac Lake

Oseeta Lake

Lake Placid

Keene

Middle Saranac Lake

Tupper Lake

JOHN BROWN FARM ■

Keene Valley

High Peaks Area

★ ◖ HIKING FROM ADIRONDAK LOJ

Mt Marcy ▲

E Branch Ausable R.

Newcomb Lake
▲ Santanoni Preserve

ADIRONDACK PARK VISITOR ■ INTERPRETIVE CENTER

Long Lake

Long Lake

Newcomb

North Hudson

0   5 mi
0   5 km

© AVALON TRAVEL PUBLISHING, INC.

Whiteface Mountain

The largest ski resort in New York, the state-owned Whiteface Mountain (off Rte. 86, 518/946-2223, www.whiteface.com) boasts 65 trails, nine chairlifts, and the highest vertical drop in the Northeast—3,216 feet. The mountain attracts expert skiers, but intermediate and novice trails are also plentiful.

During the summer, the mountain's peaks are accessible via the **Whiteface Mountain Cloudsplitter Gondola Ride** (9 A.M.–4 P.M. June–Oct., adults $14, seniors and children 5–12 $9) and the **Whiteface Mountain Memorial Highway** ($9 per car and driver, $4 each additional passenger). The chairlift leads to Little Whiteface Peak (3,676 feet), while the highway leads to Whiteface Summit (4,867 feet). Both afford superb views of the High Peaks to the south, Lake Champlain and the Green Mountains to the east, the St. Lawrence River and Canada to the north, and the Saranac Lake Valley to the west. Of the Adirondack's 46 High Peaks, only Whiteface is accessible by car.

Santa's Workshop

Near the entrance to the Whiteface Mountain Memorial Highway stands a cheery red-and-white cottage surrounded by flowers (Rte. 431, off Rte. 86, 518/946-2211, www.north-poleny.com, 9:30 A.M.–4:30 P.M. daily June–Sept., call for fall hours). Inside is a post office/gift shop where visitors can send letters postmarked the "North Pole," or buy T-shirts reading "I believe in Santa Claus." Out back, a cozy, kid-oriented theme park (same hours, adults $18, children 3–17 $16) includes amusement-park rides, Santa's reindeer, and Santa's elves. Special events such as a Santa Claus Parade are presented daily.

Accommodations and Food

Best known for its restaurant, the **❰ Hungry Trout Motor Inn** (Rte. 86, Wilmington, 518/946-2217, www.hungrytrout.com, $69–179 d) also offers 22 upscale motel rooms, all with picture windows, along with a pool and playground. The inn's restaurant, overlooking the churning white waters of the Ausable River, specializes in its namesake prepared a myriad of tasty ways, along with continental fare; average entrée $19.

Stop into the **Country Bear** (Rte. 86, Wilmington, 518/946-2691) for a satisfying breakfast or lunch.

WEST ON ROUTES 9N AND 73

Route 9N leads northwest from Elizabethtown to **Keene,** the "Town of High Peaks." Completely surrounded by jagged mountaintops, Keene centers on one main street lined with white frame houses, white picket fences, and tourist-oriented shops. Most noticeable among them is **North Country Taxidermy** (Main St. [Rte. 73], 518/576-4318), sporting stuffed bears and wolves out front. The shop stocks a wide array of gifts, including antlers—sold out of big bins—stuffed birds, mounted heads, leather goods, and bearskin rugs.

Route 73 climbs west out of Keene to Lake Placid. For much of the way, the route follows the riverbed of the wide Cascade Brook. En

THE NORTH COUNTRY

quaint Adirondack shops in the heart of the High Peaks, Maine Street, Keene

route you'll pass two sparkling lakes ringed with trees.

Hiking Hurricane Mountain

On the north side of Route 9N, 6.8 miles west of Elizabethtown and 1.6 miles past Hurricane Road, a small parking area and sign point the way to Hurricane Mountain. The red-marked trail passes through a pretty coniferous forest before heading up a ridge to the rocky summit pass. At the top await superb views of the Jay Range, the Green Mountains, Mt. Marcy, and Whiteface Mountain. The Adirondack Mountain Club lists the moderate-to-difficult hike as 5.3 miles round-trip, averaging about 4.5 hours.

Outfitters and Guides

Adirondack Alpine Adventures (518/576-9881, www.alpineadventures.biz) offers rock- and ice-climbing guide service and instruction, as well as backcountry ski trips.

Accommodations

The historic (**Bark Eater Inn** (Alstead Hill Rd., Keene, 518/576-2221, www.barkeater.com, $89–148 d, with breakfast) centers on a sprawling, two-story farmhouse complete with stone fireplaces, wide floorboards, and seven guest rooms with shared baths. Two snug annexes offer four more rooms, these with private baths, while a new log cabin reigns as the honeymoon suite ($245 d). Surrounding the inn are miles of woodland perfect for horseback riding, hiking, and cross-country skiing. The inn keeps a string of 50 horses and offers guided horse-back-riding trips at no extra charge.

Housed in a lovely Italianate building is the **Keene Valley Lodge** (Rte. 73, Keene Valley, 518/576-2003, www.keenevalleylodge.com, $75–175 d, with breakfast), a B&B that offers a variety of rooms, some of which share baths, some of which are suites. Guest rooms are furnished with antiques, while downstairs is a lounge with a fireplace and wraparound porch.

Food

A Keene Valley landmark, the **Noon Mark Diner** (Main St. [Rte. 73], 518/576-4499) is the place to go for homemade pies of every fruit and mix of fruits imaginable, as well as homemade donuts, soups, and bread, and chili, burgers, and simple dinners.

NORTHWEST ON ROUTE 28N

Scenic Route 28N heads out of North Creek in the southeastern Adirondacks to skirt the southern edge of the High Peaks region. Along the way you'll pass one splendid lake and mountain vista after another; the ride is especially magnificent in the fall.

Adirondack Park Visitor Interpretive Centers

In the hamlet of Newcomb is the smaller of the Adirondack Park Agency's two visitors centers (Rte. 28N, 518/582-2000, 9 A.M.–5 P.M. daily, free admission); the larger one is in Paul Smiths. Both offer an excellent introduction to the park, with exhibits ranging from the region's logging history to local flora and fauna. Print out free information about trailhead locations and canoe routes at one of the computerized touch-screen stations, or follow one of the interpretive trails outside. In Newcomb, the trails lead out onto a peninsula in Rich Lake, past beaver ponds and old-growth hemlocks.

Hiking to Camp Santanoni

On the shores of Newcomb Lake stands deserted Camp Santanoni, one of the old great camps, this one built in 1892 by Albany industrialist Robert Pruyn. Surrounded by the 12,000-acre Santanoni Preserve, the eerily empty camp built of massive logs includes a central lodge, boathouse, studio, and guest cottages. None of the deteriorating buildings are open to the public, and the only way in is to hike five miles along Santanoni Road.

The road is located on the north side of Route 28N, about a mile east of the Adirondack Park Visitor Center. Near the camp's gatehouse is a parking area, while beyond stretch fields etched with stone fences. About a mile and a half in is a deserted farmstead that once provided the great camp with its provisions.

A yellow-marked trail runs north of the

great camp along Newcomb Lake. Here you'll find several remote campsites with their own private beaches.

For more information, inquire at the Park Visitor Center or the Newcomb Town Offices (Rte. 28N, 518/582-3211).

LAKE PLACID

Twenty-five years ago, Lake Placid was a quiet mountain village best known to avid hikers and skiers and to those who had attended the 1932 Winter Olympics. All that changed in a heartbeat with the coming of the 1980 Winter Games, which put the place on the map.

Today, almost everyone who visits the Adirondacks visits Lake Placid, which centers on one long and sometimes very congested Main Street running alongside the lake. The village draws almost as many visitors because of its upscale shops and restaurants as it does for its lonely, mountainous countryside. Even the former Olympic sites, now managed by the Olympic Regional Development Authority, have become popular tourist attractions.

One of the more confusing things about Lake Placid is that it's not located on Lake Placid, but on Mirror Lake. Lake Placid, a much larger body of water, lies to the immediate north of the village.

Olympic Center

At the entrance to the village stands the elongated Olympic Center (2634 Main St., 518/523-1655, www.orda.org), built for the 1932 Winter Olympics and renovated for the 1980 games. The center still houses four Olympic **ice-skating arenas,** one of which is sometimes open for public skating, along with the **Lake Placid/ Essex County Visitors Bureau** (518/523-2445 or 800/447-5224, www.lakeplacid.com, 9 A.M.–5 P.M. daily, closed some Sun.) and the **1932 and 1980 Lake Placid Winter Olympic Museum** (10 A.M.–5 P.M. daily, adults $4, seniors $3, children 7–12 $2).

Around Mirror Lake

Main Street heads north of the Olympic Arena past about 100 shops, some of them one-of-a-kind, others—The Gap, Geoffrey Beene—ubiquitous chains. **With Pipe and Book** (2495 Main St., 518/523-9096), a village institution, sells used books, rare books, pipes, and tobacco.

At the end of Main Street lies Saranac Avenue, home to two top North Country shops. The **Adirondack North Country Craft Center** in the Lake Placid Center for the Arts (2114 Saranac Ave., 518/523-2062) represents about 250 upstate artists and artisans working in both traditional and contemporary styles.

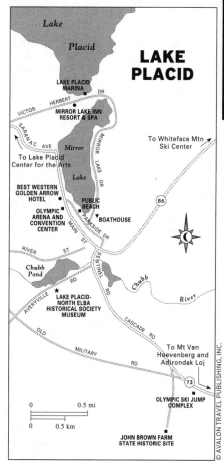

© AVALON TRAVEL PUBLISHING, INC.

The **Adirondack Store** (2024 Saranac Ave., 518/523-2646) sells everything from hand-knit sweaters to Winslow Homer prints.

A small **public beach** (Parkside Dr., off Main St.) is situated south of the Olympic Center. Just beyond the northern end of Mirror Lake lies Lake Placid and the **Lake Placid Marina** (Mirror Lake Dr., 518/523-9704), where one-hour lake cruises depart May–October.

Lake Placid-North Elba Historical Society Museum

Now occupying the old Lake Placid railroad station, this eclectic local history museum (Station St.—an extension of Averyville Rd.—off Rte. 73, 518/523-1608, noon–4 P.M. Tues.–Wed. and 9 A.M.–4 P.M. Thurs.–Sun. June–Sept., free admission) houses everything from antique sporting equipment to mementos of conductor Victor Herbert, who once summered on the lake. Especially interesting are the exhibits on the experimental colony for former slaves founded in 1849 by abolitionist John Brown.

Hiking to Wanika Falls

Also on Averyville Road, 1.2 miles past the intersection with Old Military Road, is a blue-marked trail that leads to Wanika Falls. The day-long hike takes about seven hours over 13.4 miles, but the terrain is easy, and the waterfalls make the trip worthwhile. According to the Adirondack Mountain Club, the route leads through some of the finest forest in the region before ascending an old road leading to the Chubb River and the cascading falls, several hundred feet high. The trail is part of the much longer Northville–Placid Trail laid out by the Adirondack Mountain Club in 1922 and 1923.

Olympic Ski Jump Complex

If you approached Lake Placid from the east on Route 73, the first thing you undoubtedly noticed were the stark towers of the Olympic ski jumps (off Rte. 73, 518/523-2202, www.orda.org, 9 A.M.–4 P.M. daily May–Oct. and Dec.–Mar., adults $8, children 6–12 $5),

THE LEGEND OF WHITEFACE

There once was a young brave who wanted to win the hand of a beautiful Iroquois princess. The princess asked him to prove his love by bringing her the skin of the Great White Stag who roamed the region's highest peak.

Armed with two magic arrows an old chief had given him, the brave went to the mountain. For weeks, he hunted for the stag in vain. At last, late one evening, he found him standing in the mist at the top of the mountain. The brave deftly shot his two arrows. One pierced the stag's neck, the second his haunch; but when the brave rushed forward to claim his trophy, he couldn't reach him—the mountainside was too steep. The stag remained pinned to a ledge by the magic arrows, just out of reach.

When the brave awoke the next morning, the stag had disappeared, but the rock where he had hung had turned white. From then on, the Iroquois called the mountain Whiteface.

looming out of the landscape like giant misshapen thumbs. The site still serves as a training center and is open year-round, thanks to plastic mats, water ramps, and snow-making machines.

Upon entering the complex, stop first at the **freestyle aerial facility,** where—with any luck—you'll see athletes practicing their maneuvers by sailing over pools, off water-filled ramps. Next, visit the main lodge to view a photo exhibit on the history of ski-jumping, and catch the chairlift to the 90-meter jump. If training is taking place here, you can watch from an observation deck. If not, take the glass-enclosed elevator to the top of the 120-meter jump for great views of the High Peaks.

Verizon Sports Complex at Mount Van Hoevenberg

South of the ski-jumping complex rises Mount

Van Hoevenberg, the site of the Olympic bobsled and luge runs (off Rte. 73, 518/523-4436, www.orda.org, 9 A.M.–4 P.M. daily). The bobsled run measures 1,400 meters long with 16 curves. The luge run is 1,000 meters long with 15 curves. Passenger rides on the bobsleds are offered year-round ($40 per person).

Also on Mount Van Hoevenberg, the excellent **Cross-Country Center** offers a 31-mile system of trails. In winter, the trails are groomed frequently and open to cross-country skiers of all levels. In summer, the trails are used by mountain bikers and horseback riders. Skis and bikes can be rented on-site, and guided horseback rides are available.

John Brown Farm State Historic Site

In 1849, abolitionist Gerrit Smith, later joined by John Brown, established a farming community (2 John Brown Rd., off Rte. 73, 518/523-3900, 10 A.M.–5 P.M. Wed.–Sun. May–Oct., adults $2, children $1) for free blacks and escaped slaves in the Adirondacks. Each new farmer was given 40 acres to till, but since few came prepared to cope with the region's harsh climate, most left within a few years. Brown himself lived on the farm for several more years, in a trim cabin that has been nicely restored, and erected his own gravestone.

Brown was executed in Charlestown, Virginia, on December 2, 1859, following his seizure of the U.S. Arsenal at Harper's Ferry. His body was shipped north to New York City, where his coffin was exchanged for a new one so that he would not be buried in Southern property. At each stop along the way upstate, his entourage was greeted with sympathetic crowds and tolling bells.

Hiking Mount Marcy

Mount Marcy, elevation 5,344 feet, is the highest mountain in the Adirondacks, and the one that draws the most hikers each year. More than 20,000 people make the seven-mile trek annually, and on a busy July weekend, as many as 200 people crowd at the summit. Things have certainly changed since that day

in 1872, when Verplanck Colvin first hiked the mountain and discovered Lake Tear of the Clouds. "But how wild and desolate this spot!" he wrote. "It is possible that not even an Indian ever stood upon these shores. There is no mark of ax, no barked tree, nor blackened remnants of fire; not a severed twig or a human footprint. ..."

Because of problems with over-use, park personnel urge hikers to shy away from Mount Marcy and tackle lesser-known peaks instead. If, however, hike Mount Marcy you must, one main trail begins at the Adirondak Loj (see below). Known as the Van Hoevenberg Trail, it is marked in blue. Along the way you'll pass the Marcy Dam, Phelps Brooks, and Indian Falls. From the summit of Mt. Marcy, a 1.1-mile trail leads to Lake Tear of the Clouds, the source of the Hudson River.

Hiking from Adirondak Loj

High in the mountains on the shores of Heart Lake is **Adirondak Loj** (Adirondak Loj Rd., off Rte. 73, 518/523-3441, www.adk.org), the retreat of the Adirondack Mountain Club (ADK). Built in the 1920s, the classic lodge centers on a common room equipped with rocking chairs, a large fireplace, and a moose head. The lodge offers accommodations for 46 people (ranging in type from private rooms to 18-person dormitories), along with a campground, cabins, and the **High Peaks Information Center** (8 A.M.–5 P.M. Mon.–Fri., 8 A.M.–8 P.M. Sat.–Sun. May–Nov., call for off-season hours), selling camping supplies, maps, and outdoor guidebooks. In summer, the lodge sponsors numerous seminars and workshops; in winter, skis and snowshoes can be rented here. Several trailheads begin at the Loj.

The Loj is eight miles south of Lake Placid. Rates for private rooms start at $110 d; rates for bunk beds start at $34 per person. Breakfast, served family style, is included in the room rates; dinners and trail lunches can be arranged. You don't have to be an ADK member to stay here, but you must make reservations well in advance.

Motels and Hotels

Just outside Lake Placid village is the 61-room **Econo Lodge** (Cascade Rd., 518/523-2817, $79–129 d), a good, dependable choice for budget travelers.

In the upscale motel category find the (**Best Western-Golden Arrow Hotel** (150 Main St., 518/523-3353, $89–210 d), offering excellent-value accommodations. On the lake, the completely non-smoking hotel has its own small beach equipped with boats (free for guests), heated indoor pool, sauna, restaurant, lounge, and nightclub. Most of the rooms have balconies.

Another good, moderately priced choice is the big, modern **Adirondack Inn** (2625 Main St. [Rte. 86], 518/523-2424, www.adirondack-inn.com, $89–179 d). It offers 50 nicely appointed rooms, indoor and outdoor pools, and a small lakefront beach.

Luxury Inns and Lodges

At the end of the village reigns the posh (**Mirror Lake Inn Resort and Spa** (5 Mirror Lake Dr., 518/523-2544, www.mirrorlakeinn.com, $240–350 d for rooms and $420–660 d for suites in summer, about a third less off-season), a grand Colonial-style structure that was rebuilt after a 1988 fire. Also on-site at this AAA Four Diamond resort are the Averil Conwell Dining Room, a bar, cozy lounges, a spa, tennis courts, indoor and outdoor pools, and a private beach.

On the shores of Lake Placid lies secluded **Lake Placid Lodge** (Whiteface Inn Rd., 518/523-2700, www.thelakeplacidinn.com, $400–900 d), an authentic great camp complete with a stone fireplace and moose head. Now a member of the exclusive Relais & Chateaux group, the lodge boasts 17 very attractive guest rooms, 17 cabins, and a breezy porch overlooking the lake.

Food

For tasty scones and other baked goods, step into **Bluesberry Bakery** (26 Main St., 518/523-4539). For mouth-watering barbecue served inside or out, stop at **Tail o' the Pup**

(Rte. 86, 518/891-5092), a classic roadside eatery located halfway between Lake Placid and Saranac Lake.

The **Lake Placid Pub and Brewery** (14 Mirror Lake Drive, 518/523-3813) is a popular spot, offering hearty pub food upstairs, a boisterous Irish bar below. At **Nicola's On Main and Grill 211** (2470 Main St., 518/523-4430) you'll find two restaurants in one. Nicola's is an upscale Italian restaurant serving pasta, fresh fish, veal, and pizza baked in a wood-fired oven. Grill 211 is a New York City–style steakhouse with wooden floors, tin ceilings, and wooden booths. Entrées range $13–25.

On the lake across from the village is the (**Boathouse** (89 Lake Placid Club Dr., 518/523-4822), a large and comfortable blond-wood eatery with an outdoor deck and great views of the lake. The menu ranges from salads and burgers to fresh fish and steak; average entrée $17.

One of the region's top restaurants, the elegant, candle-lit **Averil Conwell Dining Room** (Mirror Lake Inn, 5 Mirror Lake Dr., 518/523-2544) specializes in an innovative fare that ranges from fresh pastas and seafood to steak and grilled duck (average entrée $26). Also on site is the (**Cottage** (5 Mirror Lake Dr., 518/523-2544), a sort of upscale pub built directly on the lake, where the menu is simpler but just as good (average entrée $16). A wide selection of wines and microbrews is available here.

Entertainment and Events

The **Lake Placid Center for the Arts** (2114 Saranac Ave., 518/523-2512) presents music, dance, theater, film, and special events throughout the year. The 18-piece **Lake Placid Sinfonietta** (518/523-2051) performs free concerts in the Mirror Lake bandshell Wednesday evenings, July–August.

Figure-skating, hockey games, and speed-skating events take place in the **Olympic Center Ice Arena** (2634 Main St., 518/523-1655) throughout the year. The **Lake Placid Horse Show** and **I Love New York Horse Show** (518/523-2445) are held in July.

Outfitters, Guides, and Recreation

Canoes and other boats can be rented at **Jones Outfitters** (2733 Main St., 518/523-3468) and **Captain Marney's** (3 Victor Herbert Dr., 518/523-9746). **Bear Cub Adventure Tours** (30 Bear Cub Rd., 518/523-4339) offers guided canoeing, fishing, backpacking, and hiking trips. For a scenic flight over the High Peaks, contact **Adirondack Flying Service** (Airport Rd., off Cascade Rd., 518/523-2473, www.flyanywhere.com).

SARANAC LAKE

After the heavy tourist traffic of Lake Placid, Saranac Lake village comes as a relief. Saranac Lake, an unpretentious place with a busy downtown, caters to residents, not tourists.

Although classified as a village, Saranac Lake is a sizeable town (pop. 5,830), with stores, banks, churches, and supermarkets. Like Lake Placid, it is not located on the shores of its namesake, but on smaller Lake Flower, the body of water that you see downtown. The Saranac Lakes—Lower, Middle, and Upper—are farther west. Upper Saranac Lake is famous for its rustic Adirondack architecture, best glimpsed by boat.

Settled in 1819 by Jacob Smith Moody, Saranac Lake soon established itself as a center for Adirondack guides. All of Moody's sons became guides, and their Uncle Martin once guided everyone from President Grover Cleveland to Ralph Waldo Emerson.

In 1876, a Dr. Livingston Trudeau, suffering from tuberculosis, came to Saranac Lake to die. Instead, the fresh mountain air restored him, and in 1884 he opened the first outdoor sanatorium for the treatment of tuberculosis. By the early 1900s, the Trudeau Sanatorium was famed worldwide, with thousands flocking to "The City of the Sick" to take the cure.

The Trudeau Sanatorium closed in 1954, after antibiotics were developed, but its legacy lives on in the Trudeau Institute, a scientific research institute, and in "Doonesbury" cartoonist Garry Trudeau. Garry is the great-grandson of Dr. Livingston Trudeau.

Saranac Lake centers on Main Street and Lake Flower. Lively **Hotel Saranac**—a regional landmark run by students from Paul Smith's College—provides a good base from which to explore the area. A pleasant **public beach** is located on Lake Colby, just north of downtown.

Robert Louis Stevenson Memorial Cottage and Museum

Among the pioneer "lungers" who came to Saranac Lake to take the cure was Robert Louis Stevenson. In 1887, fresh from the success of his just-published *Dr. Jekyll and Mr. Hyde*, the author rented a cozy cottage (11 Stevenson Ln., 518/891-1462, 9:30 A.M.–noon and 1–4:30 P.M. Tues.–Sun. July–Oct., adults $5, children under 12 free) on a hill within easy reach of Dr. Trudeau. While living here, Stevenson wrote some of his best essays and started his long tale, *The Master of Ballantrae.* "I was walking on the veranda of a small house outside the hamlet of Saranac. It was winter, the night was very dark, the air clean and cold and sweet with the purity of forests. For the making of a story, here were fine conditions," reads the quote by the door.

THE NORTH COUNTRY

NORTH COUNTRY CRAFTS

Rustic furniture, birchbark baskets, plaid woolen jackets, quilts, woodcarved decoys, bulky sweaters, balsam pillows, boats. ...

Handcrafted items have always been part of the North Country scene. Over the past few decades, however, as the nation's love affair with mass-production has waned, there's been a true renaissance in the North Country arts. Hundreds of artists and artisans working in both traditional and more contemporary styles can be found throughout the region. Most use local natural resources such as wood, pine cones, balsam fir needles, and locally raised wool to create their wares.

The region's long winters have contributed much to the strong folk-art tradition. Confined to their homes for "11 months of snow, one of bad sledding," as some old-timers put it, people naturally turned to working with their hands. From the Mohawk came the art of basketmaking, from the French Canadians, woodcarving.

Perhaps most emblematic of the Adiron-dacks crafts is the traditional Adirondack guideboat, a specialized rowboat light enough to carry between lakes and rivers. Around the turn of the century, as many as 50 men were producing the handmade boats; each boat took about 300 hours to build and sold for around $50. Today, a handmade traditional guideboat costs about $7,000.

Most emblematic of Thousand Islands crafts is the decoy. Duck hunting has been popular in the region since the 1800s, when a market hunter could easily harvest 50-100 birds a day. Sleeping in tents the entire duck season, the hunters often turned to carving decoys at night, in between slugs of whiskey.

To find crafts shops and artisans' studios in the North Country today, contact the **Adirondack North Country Association** (28 St. Bernard St., Saranac Lake 12983; 518/891-6200). The nonprofit organization publishes a free "Craft Trails" map, available in many tourism offices, hotels, and B&Bs.

COURTESY OF LAKE PLACID/ESSEX COUNTY VISITORS BUREAU

Many antiques stores and crafts centers offer browsing delights.

In the cottage today is a large collection of Stevenson memorabilia, including his ice skates, playing cards, letters to Henry James, autographed first editions, and the velvet jacket that he always wore while writing. On the mantelpiece are Stevenson's cigarette burns, which he left wherever he went.

Outfitters, Guides, and Recreation

For lovers of the outdoors, Saranac Lake is ideally situated between the High Peaks and the Northwest Lakes, which offer some of the best canoeing in the Northeast.

The large and friendly **St. Regis Canoe Outfitters** (73 Dorsey St., 518/891-1838, www.canoeoutfitters.com) is both a sprawling retail shop and the place to go to set up a canoeing or kayaking trip. St. Regis rents boats and camping gear, provides instruction and trip-planning advice, and offers guided trips and shuttle services. Trips can be arranged for as short as one morning or as long as two weeks or more.

Both **Adirondack Foothills** (518/359-8194, www.adkfoothills.com) and **McDonnell's Adirondack Challenges** (518/891-1176, www.macscanoe.com) offer customized hiking, camping, canoeing, and fishing trips. **XTC Ranch** (Forest Home Rd., Lake Clear, 518/891-5684) offers horseback riding and wagon and sleigh rides.

Accommodations and Food

(Hotel Saranac of Paul Smith's College (100 Main St., 518/891-2200, www.hotelsaranac.com, $60–120 d) is a full-service, snug brick hostelry built in 1927. Contained within are 88 small but comfortable rooms, and a lobby that's a replica of the foyer in the Danvanzati Palace in Florence, Italy. The hotel is run by eager-to-please students studying hotel management at nearby Paul Smith's College.

The hotel's restaurant, **A. P. Smiths',** is also run by students. On the menu is contemporary American fare; average dinner entrée $14. In back, you'll find **Boathouse Lounge,** which serves lighter fare.

It might seem rather surprising to find a good Mexican restaurant in the heart of the Adirondacks, but nonetheless, here is the bright and cheery **Casa del Sol** (154 Lake Flower Ave. [Rte. 86], 518/891-0977). In summer, dine on the outdoor patio; average entrée $12.

Morgan's 11 (33 Broadway, 518/897-1111, is the place to go for wood-fired pizza and pasta, or for a drink at a friendly local bar. An outdoor patio overlooks the Saranac River.

Entertainment and Nightlife

The **Pendragon Theatre** (148 River St., 518/891-1854) presents professional regional theater November–January and June–September. On the docket are both classic and contemporary works.

A number of popular bars, many hosting local bands on the weekends, hug Main Street near the Hotel Saranac and along Broadway north of Main. Among them are the teeming indoor-outdoor **Water Hole** (43 Main St., 518/891-9502) and **Schue's Adirondack Bar and Grille** (65 Broadway, 518/891-4630), offering pub grub, a bar laminated with maps of the region's canoe routes, and an outdoor patio. The **Boathouse Lounge** in the Hotel Saranac (100 Main St., 518/891-2200) is a cozy, low-ceilinged bar/lounge that gets quite crowded on Saturday nights.

PAUL SMITHS

About 10 miles northwest of Saranac Lake lies the hamlet of Paul Smiths, named after Appollos (Paul) Smith, a famed Adirondack guide who established one of the Adirondack's first hotels here in 1859. Charles Dickens once said of Smith, "he has no bad habits, and is, withal, the best rifle shot, paddler, and compounder of forest stews in the whole region." When Smith died in 1912, his funeral was the largest ever held in northern New York, drawing more than 700 people.

The original Paul Smiths hotel has closed, but its spirit lives on through **Paul Smith's College,** Rts. 86 and 30, founded by the hotelier's son in the 1930s. The school is known for its degrees in hotel management and the culinary arts.

Adirondack Park Visitor Interpretive Center

For an excellent introduction to the Adirondacks, step into this large and informative center (Rte. 30, 518/327-3000, 9 A.M.–5 P.M. daily, free admission), one of two run by the Adirondack Park Agency (the second, smaller center is in Newcomb). Inside you'll find exhibits on everything from logging camps and Trudeau's Sanatorium to the region's problems with over-use and acid rain. Three different slide shows run continuously throughout the day, while information about trailhead locations and canoe routes is available on computerized touch-screen stations that provide free printouts. Out back are a butterfly house and interpretive trails leading through a 60-acre marsh.

White Pine Camp

After years of deterioration, the great camp that served as President Calvin Coolidge's summer White House in 1926 reopened to the public in 1995 (White Pine Rd., a half mile east of the Rt. 86/30 intersection, www.whitepinecamp.com, 518/327-3030). Built in 1907, the camp overlooks Osgood Pond and contains about 20 asymmetrical buildings complete with soaring rooflines, unusual angles, and skylights. In the main cabin, exhibits explain the site's history and architecture, while among the surrounding outbuildings are a tennis house, indoor bowling alleys, and a Japanese teahouse. There are also six renovated guest cottages that are available for rent by the week.

Tours of the camp are offered at 10 A.M. and 1:30 P.M. on Saturdays July–Labor Day (adults $9, seniors $8, kids 5–15 $5). Reservations are necessary; call Adirondack Architectural Heritage at 518/834-9328.

ONCHIOTA

"Leaving 67 of the friendliest people in the Adirondacks (plus a couple of soreheads)" reads the sign at the northern end of Onchiota. Just who exactly those soreheads are, no one seems quite sure, but to meet the first variety, stop into the one-of-a-kind **Six Nations Indian Museum** (Buck Pond Campsite Rd., 518/891-2299, 10 A.M.–5 P.M. Tues.–Sun. July–Sept., adults $4, children $2).

From the outside, the museum looks much like an ordinary house. But move inside and you'll find yourself surrounded by a kaleidoscopic array of pictographs, paintings, basketwork, beadwork, quillwork, pottery, canoes, masks, drums, and lacrosse sticks—all very, very neatly arranged to cover virtually every square inch of wall and peaked wooden ceiling. The museum is the creation of one man, Ray Fadden, a Mohawk who drew most of the elaborate pictographs himself. The works tell traditional Iroquois tales.

Fadden, who spent much of his life as a schoolteacher, began fighting for the preservation of Iroquois culture as early as the 1940s. Back then hardly anyone listened, but Fadden never faltered and eventually was instrumental in the founding of numerous Iroquois heritage programs. Many of his former students are now major leaders in the Mohawk Nation.

The museum is now run by Fadden's son and daughter-in-law. Visitors are warmly greeted at the door and conducted on personalized tours. To reach Onchiota from Paul Smiths, take Route 86 east to County Roads 31 or 30 north (not to be confused with state Route 30, which leads to Malone). The museum is in the hamlet's center and is easy to find.

BURKE

Fans of Laura Ingalls Wilder might want to head north of Paul Smiths about 35 miles to the **Almanzo Wilder Homestead** (Burke Rd., off Rte. 11, 518/483-1207, www.almanzowilderfarm.com, 11 A.M.–4 P.M. Wed.–Sat. and 1–4 P.M. Sun. June–Sept., adults $6, children 6–15 $3), located in farm country east of Malone. Wilder's husband, Almanzo Wilder, grew up here, and the author based her book *Farmer Boy* on his childhood.

The trim, airy house has been carefully restored to reflect the book. Downstairs is the parlor where "Almanzo didn't mean to throw the blacking brush," and upstairs is his "soft, cold feather bed." In the kitchen are kerosene lamps, tallow candles, and a butter churn—all similar to the ones used by Almanzo—while out back is the red barn where he did his chores.

Wilder, who met her husband in South Dakota, never visited the Wilder homestead, but according to family members, the house was "as described in the book." In the entrance hall are photocopies of the sketches that Almanzo drew for Wilder, along with several of her letters.

Northwest Lakes

The northwestern section of the Adirondacks is a sparsely populated area often overlooked by vacationers. Much of the land here is quite flat and covered with hundreds of lakes and ponds, along with endless unbroken forest. Though the region is primarily a canoer's paradise, it also has much to offer in the way of easy-to-moderate hikes.

ST. REGIS CANOE AREA

To the immediate west of Paul Smiths begins the St. Regis Canoe Area, a 20,000-acre region encompassing 58 lakes and ponds. Standing alone at the area's northern edge, and offering wide-angled views of the watery terrain, looms St. Regis Mountain.

St. Regis Canoe Outfitters, one of the area's largest outfitters, based in Saranac Lake (see above), maintains an outpost (518/891-8040) in the canoe area at Lake Clear. To reach the outpost and several good boat-launch sites, take Route 86 north from Saranac Lake to Route 186. Turn left and follow Route 186 west to its end and junction with Route 30. Continue straight ahead, past the junction, for 5.5 miles, crossing the Saranac Inn Golf Club. Just beyond the course, at a paved four-way intersection, turn right on Floodwood Road. Continue straight ahead 4.1 miles to the base.

Camping, Accommodations and Food

Off Route 30 between the St. Regis Canoe Area and Tupper Lake village lie the secluded 355-site **Fish Creek Pond Campground** (518/891-4560) and 290-site **Rollins Pond Campground** (518/891-3239). For reservations at either, call 800/456-CAMP.

Tucked into the woods near a fish hatchery is **Sunday Pond B&B** (Rte. 30, Saranac Inn, 518/891-1531, www.sundaypond.com, $75 d), a simple, Adirondack-style lodge with three guest rooms and a sleeping loft that's good for families. All rooms have private baths.

Just west of the St. Regis Canoe Area is the classic **Lodge at Lake Clear** (Rtes. 30 and 186, 518/891-1489, www.lodgeonlakeclear.com, $149–259 d), where you can choose among four guest rooms filled with Adirondackiana, two housekeeping chalets, and two suites complete with Jacuzzis. The snug lodge is renowned locally for its restaurant, **Hohmeyer's,** which serves German and Adirondack specialties. The menu changes nightly, but entrées such as Wiener schnitzel or sauerbraten are always featured. Downstairs in the main lodge is a German **Bierkeller.**

The region's most exclusive hostelry is **The Point** (Upper Saranac Lake, 518/891-5674 or 800/255-3530, www.thepointresort.com), an ultra-luxurious great camp once owned by the Rockefellers. Now open to the public, the 11-guestroom Point features the absolute utmost in hedonistic delights—all for a mere daily rate of $1,250–2,500 d, which includes gourmet meals, wine and other beverages, and recreational activities.

TUPPER LAKE

Once a major industrial center known for its lumbering, papermaking, and woodworking plants, Tupper Lake still harbors its share of smokestacks, especially along the lakefront.

THE NORTH COUNTRY

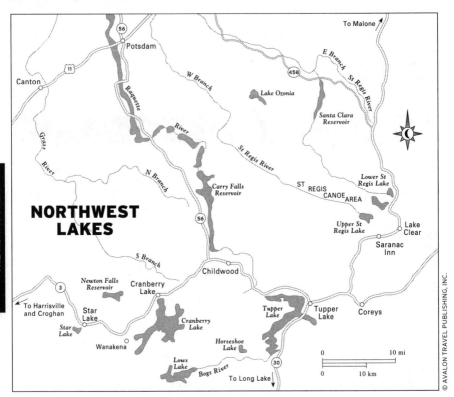

© AVALON TRAVEL PUBLISHING, INC.

Meanwhile, the downtown remains small, tightly knit, and compact, made up of early-20th-century brick buildings. Many of the street names bear evidence of the town's French-American heritage.

Historic Beth Joseph Synagogue

The oldest synagogue in the Adirondacks, Beth Joseph (Lake St., 518/359-7229, 11 A.M.–3 P.M. Tues.–Fri. July–Aug.; Fri. Sabbath services at 7 P.M. July–Aug.) is an architectural gem built in 1905 by Russian Jewish immigrants who had originally come to the region as peddlers. At its peak in the mid-1920s, the synagogue served about 35 families but was closed in 1959 due to a dwindling congregation. Now on the State Registry of Historic Buildings, the synagogue functions as a small museum. All fixtures and furnishings are original, and the vestibule houses an exhibit on the town's early Jewish community. Downstairs is a small art gallery.

Outfitters and Guides

Raquette River Outfitters (1754 Rte. 30, 518/359-3228, www.raquetteriveroutfitters.com) rents canoes, provides car shuttles, and offers guided canoe trips. **Cold River Ranch** (Rte. 3, Coreys, 518/359-7559) offers trail rides and overnight horse-pack trips.

Accommodations and Food

Hidden in an idyllic woodsy setting six miles east of the village is **❰ The Wawbeek** (553 Panther Mountain Rd., off Rte. 30, 518/359-2656, www.wawbeek.com, $175–495 d). Once a private boy's camp, the Wawbeek centers on the regal Mountain House Lodge. Next door is a restaurant where regional American dishes are served (average entrée $21). Also on-site are a modern guest annex, log-cabin cottages, tennis courts, and a private beach.

CRANBERRY LAKE

Eleven miles square, with 55 miles of shoreline, Cranberry Lake remains one of the largest remote areas in New York State. Mostly state-owned, the lake has been virtually bypassed by civilization. Along Route 3 at the eastern end of Cranberry Lake sits a hamlet of the same name. To the west of the hamlet is a boat-launching site, and to the east, the public **Cranberry Lake Campground.** Campers who prefer to rough it can row out to one of the 46 primitive tent sites designated with yellow markers along the lake's shoreline.

One of the area's most popular canoe trips begins at Inlet, off Route 3 southwest of the lake, and continues 16 miles along the **Oswegatchie River** to the lake itself. An easy hiking trail up **Bear Mountain** on the east side of the lake begins at the Cranberry Lake Campground. The hike is 3.6 miles round-trip, takes about two hours, and offers good views of the lake.

Services, Food, and Accommodations

The creaky, stuffed-to-the-rafters **Emporium** (Rte. 3, 315/848-2140) can equip you with everything from groceries and bait to maps and canoes.

To reserve one of the 173 sites at the **Cranberry Lake Campground** (Long Pine Rd., off Rte. 3, 315/848-2315), call 800/456-CAMP. If you'd prefer a motel, try the simple but comfortable **Cranberry Lake Lodge** (7209 Rte. 3, 315/848-3301, www.cranberrylakelodge.com, $39–59 d), offering 23 rooms and a family-style restaurant (average main dish $8).

WEST ON ROUTE 3

From Cranberry Lake, Route 3 heads west through flat, woodsy, isolated countryside. Just over the St. Lawrence–Lewis County border, about 35 miles from Cranberry Lake, lies **Harrisville,** built on the banks of the Oswegatchie River.

If you head north of Harrisville on Route 812 about 50 miles, you'll come to the Thousand Islands. If you continue south about 14 miles along Route 812 toward Croghan, you'll come to the hamlet of Indian River and an astonishing outdoor **sculpture park.** Created by the late Veronica Terrillion, a folk artist, the park is alive with over 400 brightly painted statues of animals, people, and religious figures. Near the driveway poise zebras, leopards, and a giraffe; in a small, lily-filled pond floats a boat transporting the figures of Terrillion's family.

Visitors are welcome to stop and take pictures of the park from the road, but please keep in mind that this is private property.

THE NORTH COUNTRY

Central Adirondacks

Nestled into the center of Adirondack Park are more still blue lakes, encircled by densely packed forests and small- to moderate-size peaks. The climate here is not as harsh as it is farther north, and the landscape has a more human-size feel. Some sections of the Central Adirondacks, such as Indian Lake, attract only a handful of visitors; others, such as Old Forge, are disturbingly overrun.

LONG LAKE

Heading south from Tupper Lake on Route 30, you'll come to Long Lake, a 14-mile stretch of water that is really just an engorged section of the Raquette River. At the intersection of Routes 30 and 28N presides the village of Long Lake, dominated by the creaky, rectangular **Adirondack Hotel,** an 1870s hostelry with wide verandas. Just across the Long Lake bridge from the hotel is a **public beach** and boat launch.

One of the region's most popular **canoe trips** begins at the Long Lake launch and heads north along the Raquette River through the High Peaks region. Past the High Peaks, paddlers can choose to either continue on the Raquette River to Tupper Lake or portage to Upper Saranac Lake. Either way, the trip covers about 40 miles and takes about four days.

Hiking Owls Head Mountain

At the southern end of Long Lake ascends the double-peaked Owls Head. The well-marked, 3.5-mile trail leading to the top is of moderate difficulty and takes about four hours to hike round-trip. Along the way you'll pass streams, valleys, a fire tower, Lake Eaton—a good place for a swim—and good views of the High Peaks.

To reach the trailhead, take Route 30 one mile north of Long Lake village to Endion Road and watch for signs.

© CHRISTIANE BIRD

Seaplanes offer sightseeing excursions on Long Lake.

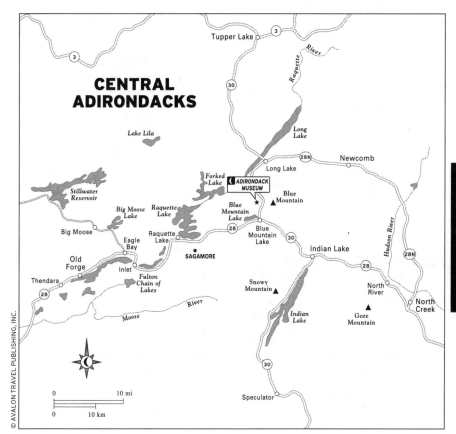

Camping and Accommodations

Two miles north of the village is the 137-site **Lake Eaton Campground** (Rte. 30, 518/624-2641). Five miles west of Long Lake is the 80-site **Forked Lake Campground** (North Point Rd., off Rte. 30, 518/624-6646). For reservations at either, call 800/456-CAMP.

On the shores of the lake is the fourth-generation, family-run (**Long View Lodge** (Deerland Rd., Rtes. 28 and 30, 518/624-2862, www.longviewlodge.com, $75–95 d, with breakfast), a comfortable, low-key place with 17 guest rooms, two cottages, and a private beach equipped with canoes and other boats.

Though now better known for its restau-

rants than for its guest rooms, the **Adirondack Hotel** (Rte. 30, 518/624-4700, www.adirondackhotel.com, $80–95 d in summer, $60–75 d off season, some rooms share baths) still accommodates overnight visitors. The rooms are spartan but clean.

Food

The **Long Lake Diner** (Rte. 30, 518/624-3941) serves breakfast and lunch, along with a bar menu later in the day. The (**Adirondack Hotel** (Rte. 30, 518/624-4700) holds a popular café that's open for breakfast, lunch, and a light dinner, and a more formal dining room that serves full-course dinners. In the lobby stands an enormous stuffed bear, and to one side is an inviting tap room (average dinner entrée $16).

Recreation
Boats and canoes can be rented at **Long Lake Marina** (Rte. 30, 518/624-2266), in the village center. To take a scenic seaplane flight, contact **Helms Aero Service** (Rte. 30, 518/624-3931).

Shopping
You can't miss **Hoss's Country Corner** (Lake St., 518/624-2481), a big, square emporium built in the classic Adirondack style. Inside you'll find everything from groceries and clothing to handicrafts and a good selection of regional books.

BLUE MOUNTAIN LAKE
One of the loveliest lakes in all the Adirondacks is dark, spring-fed Blue Mountain Lake. Situated 1,800 feet above sea level, the isolated lake is sprinkled with small islands and flanked by towering Blue Mountain, a moody peak that the Iroquois once called "Hill of Storms." The lake, one of a chain of three, is stocked with bass, whitefish, and trout.

At the southern edge of the lake, along Routes 28 and 30, clusters the village of Blue Mountain Lake. Though home to only about 230 permanent residents, the village is a major cultural center, thanks to the presence of the renowned Adirondack Museum and the much smaller Adirondack Lakes Center for the Arts. A postage-stamp-size **public beach** is situated in the heart of the village, and several crafts galleries are located along Route 30. Among them is **Blue Mountain Designs** (Rte. 30, 518/352-7361), now over 25 years old.

A popular **canoe trip** starts at Blue Mountain Lake and heads west through Eagle and Utowana Lakes to the 0.4-mile Bassett Carry. At the end of the portage flows the Marion River, which leads to Raquette Lake, which in turn leads to the Fulton Chain of Lakes. Depending on how far you paddle, the trip can take anywhere from one to five days. A lean-to is situated on the north shore of Utowana Lake about a half mile above the dam.

☾ Adirondack Museum
High on a slope overlooking Blue Mountain Lake presides the Adirondack Museum (Rte. 30, 518/352-7311, www.adkmuseum.org, 10 A.M.–5 P.M. daily June–Oct., adults $14, seniors $13, children 7–16 $7), a compact complex of 22 buildings that covers virtually every aspect of Adirondack life. By far the most important museum in the region, the complex has been described by the *New York Times* as "the best of its kind in the world."

Featured in the museum's two main buildings are first-rate exhibits on Adirondack history, natural science, culture, and art. Dioramas simulate scenes such as a logging camp, an early Adirondack hotel, and a hermit's cabin, while nearby are displays on fishing, trapping, and surveying. In one room is a Victorian hearse equipped with wheels for summer and runners for winter; in another, over 800 wooden miniatures carved by one man.

Smaller buildings focus on specific themes. The Boat Building is packed with dozens of sleek wooden vessels; the Transportation Building, with 50 horse-drawn vehicles and a private railroad car. At the Photo Belt, visitors watch historic photographs slide by on a moving belt.

Adirondack Lakes Center for the Arts
This inviting center (Rte. 28, 518/352-7715, 10 A.M.–4 P.M. Mon.–Fri. year-round, 10 A.M.–4 P.M. Sat. July–Aug., gallery admission free, evening events $4–16) presents both visual and performing arts. Exhibits in the past have covered everything from traditional quilts to contemporary pottery, while concerts have ranged from the Tokyo String Quartet to Aztec Two-Step. The center also holds a gift shop selling regional arts and crafts.

Hiking Blue Mountain
One of the best ways to get a good view of Blue Mountain Lake is to hike up brooding

Blue Mountain, elevation 3,759 feet. Though quite steep in parts, the four-mile round-trip hike is of moderate difficulty overall and takes about three hours. At the summit gleams the restored 1917 Blue Mountain Fire Tower, staffed with a ranger/guide on summer weekends. The trailhead and a well-marked hiking trail begin off Route 30, a half mile north of the Adirondack Museum.

Outfitters and Recreation

Boats and canoes can be rented at the friendly, family-run **Blue Mountain Lake Boat Livery** (Rte. 28, 518/352-7351). Docked outside are two classic wooden launches that take visitors to isolated parts of Blue Mountain Lake and two smaller neighboring lakes. Filled with interesting historical information, the low-key **sightseeing tours** operate daily June–September (adults $15, seniors $13, students and children over three $11; reservations recommended).

Blue Mountain Outfitters (Rte. 30, 518/352-7306) rents canoes and kayaks, sells outdoor gear, and offers guided canoe trips.

INDIAN LAKE

Southeast of Blue Mountain Lake lounges long, skinny Indian Lake, named after Sabael Benedict, an Abenaki and the area's first settler. A hamlet of the same name clusters around the intersection of Routes 28 and 30 at the lake's northern end, while to the east stretches the Siamese Ponds Wilderness Area.

Siamese Ponds Wilderness Area

Covering an area of 112,000 acres, the Siamese Ponds region is roughly bounded by Route 28 to the north, Route 30 to the west and south, and Route 8 to the east. Often overlooked by vacationers, the area encompasses gentle mountains, dense forests, crystal-clear ponds, and rushing streams. In certain sections, you can hike all day without encountering another person.

Thirty-three miles of marked hiking trails—and many more unmarked ones—run through the wilderness. Major trailheads are located at the end of Big Brook Road (off Route 30 a half mile south of Indian Lake

THE NORTHVILLE-PLACID TRAIL

Laid out by the Adirondack Mountain Club in 1922, the Northville-Placid Trail is a favorite among serious hikers and backpackers. Traversing over 133 miles of forest, it runs from Northville on Great Sacandaga Lake in the southern Adirondacks to Lake Placid in the High Peaks. It takes about 19 days to complete, and some sections are quite rugged and minimally maintained. Usage is low to moderate from Northville to Blue Mountain Lake, and heavy from Blue Mountain Lake to Lake Placid.

For a free brochure with basic information on the trail, contact the Department of Environmental Conservation. For maps and more detailed information, contact the Adirondack Mountain Club.

village); at Thirteenth Lake and the end of Old Farm Clearing Road (take Rte. 28 east to Thirteenth Lake Rd.); and on Route 8 about four miles west of Bakers Mills.

Hiking Chimney Mountain

One of the trails at the end of Big Brook Road leads up Chimney Mountain, named after its unusual central bulwark of layered gneiss, granite, and marble. The mountain is also known for its many crevices and caves. These should be explored by expert spelunkers only, but you might want to bring along a flashlight to shine down into the depths.

The round-trip hike up and down Chimney Mountain covers three miles, takes two and a half hours, and is quite rugged in spots. From up top are good views of Kings Flow, Round Pond, and the High Peaks.

Hiking Snowy Mountain

The tallest of the southern Adirondacks, Snowy Mountain (elevation 3,899 feet) offers a long and challenging climb best suited for hikers in good condition. The hike to the summit—which offers excellent views of the surrounding lakes—is about seven miles round-trip and takes about five hours. Steep sections are located near the trailhead and again near the top, while in between are rolling terrain and a sparkling brook that follows the trail for close to a mile. A complete description of the hike is outlined in Barbara McMartin's *Fifty Hikes in the Adirondacks.*

To reach the trailhead, take Route 30 south of the hamlet of Indian Lake 6.5 miles. Watch for a sign marking the trail on the right and a paved parking area on the left.

Rafting Trips

White-water rafting trips down the nearby Hudson River Gorge and Moose River are offered by the **Adventure Sports Rafting Co.** (Main St., 518/648-5812) and the **Adirondack Rafting Co.** (Rtes. 27 and 30, 518/523-1635).

NORTH CREEK

Off Route 28 midway between Indian Lake and Warrensburg in the southeastern Adirondacks lies North Creek, a small town wedged between mountains and the **Hudson River Gorge.** Towering over North Creek to the south is Gore Mountain; to the north flows the Hudson River and a 16-mile stretch of white-water that's considered the finest rafting run in the east.

The Hudson River Gorge begins east of Indian Lake, just beyond the confluence of the Indian and Hudson Rivers. During the spring, when the water runs high, the gorge should be tackled only by experts; the river offers near continuous Class III and IV rapids, and a number of deaths have occurred here over the years.

Gore Mountain

The second-largest ski resort in New York, state-owned Gore Mountain (Peaceful Valley Rd., off Rte. 28, 518/251-2411, www.goremountain.com) particularly attracts intermediate skiers. Featured are 44 trails, a vertical drop of 2,100 feet, and eight ski lifts, including the state's only gondola ride and a quad-chairlift. From July 4th to Columbus Day, the gondola ride (adults $9, seniors and kids under 12 $7) operates to the summit, offering bird's-eye views of the countryside.

Barton Garnet Mines

On the back side of Gore Mountain lies Barton Mines (Barton Mines Rd., North River, just north of North Creek, off Rte. 28, 518/251-2706, 9:30 A.M.–5 P.M. Mon.–Sat. and 11 A.M.–5 P.M. Sun. July–Aug., Sat.–Sun. Sept.–Oct., adults $10, seniors $9, children $7), a sprawling operation that produces 90 percent of the world's industrial garnet; garnets are also New York State's stone. During the summer, visitors can tour the open-pit mines with guides who explain the area's geology and history.

Outfitters and Guides

One of the oldest rafting outfitters in the state, the **Hudson River Rafting Company** (1 Main St., 518/251-3215, www.hudsonriverrafting.com) offers guided trips down the Hudson River Gorge and along the Moose, Black, and Sacandaga Rivers.

Accommodations and Food

The **◖ Copperfield Inn** (307 Main St., 518/251-2500, www.copperfieldinn.com, $200–285 d) is an upscale motor lodge where you'll find 24 spacious rooms with plenty of amenities, a heated pool, health club, hot tub, and tennis courts. Also on the premises is **Trappers Tavern,** serving casual meals like pizza and chili, and **Gardens,** a spiffy restaurant serving contemporary American dishes such as grilled tuna and rack of lamb (average entrée $16).

RAQUETTE LAKE

Heading west of Blue Mountain Lake on Route 28 instead of east, you'll come to Raquette Lake. It was here that W. W. Durant built Camp Pine Knot, the first Adirondack great camp, in 1877. Durant combined elements of the Adirondack log cabin and the Swiss chalet, a style that continues to predominate in the Adirondacks. Camp Pine Knot still stands near the lake, along with four other great camps—Camp Echo, Bluff Point, North Point, and

© CHRISTIANE BIRD

the main lodge at Great Camp Sagamore

Sagamore. Only Sagamore is open to the public, but you can glimpse the other four by touring Raquette Lake by boat.

Alvah Dunning (1816–1902), a famed early guide, once lived at Raquette Lake. Dunning killed his first moose at the age of 11 and guided his first party at the age of 12. Forced to leave Piseco Lake after he outraged his neighbors by brutally beating his wife, Dunning spent much of his life railing against civilization and city people, "them city dudes with velvet suits and pop guns, that can't hit a deer when they see it and don't want it if they do hit it."

At the southwestern edge of Raquette Lake lies a hamlet of the same name, equipped with three marinas and little else. At the lake's southeastern edge stretches the **Golden Beach State Park** (Rte. 28, 315/354-4230, $10–14 parking), offering a swimming beach, hiking trails, boat rentals, 205-site campground, and good fishing spots.

Great Camp Sagamore

A self-contained rustic village hidden deep in the woods, Sagamore (Sagamore Rd., off Rte. 28, 315/354-5311, www.sagamore.org, tours at 10 A.M. and 1 P.M. daily late June–Aug., adults $12, children $6; call for fall hours) was built by W. W. Durant in 1897 and sold to Alfred G. Vanderbilt, Sr. in 1901. Considered the prototypical great camp, Sagamore centers on a seemingly indestructible main lodge built of huge dark logs, while outbuildings house a dining hall, guest cottages, boathouse, horse barn, icehouse, and bowling alley.

One of Sagamore's most interesting buildings is the casino playhouse, the walls of which are covered with animal "trophies" killed by generations of Vanderbilts. The camp was once known as the "headquarters of the gaming crowd," and the Vanderbilts entertained lavishly, inviting up everyone from Gary Cooper and Gene Tierney to Lord Mountbatten and Madame Chiang Kai-Shek.

Now a National Historic Site owned by the Sagamore Institute, Sagamore hosts weekend and week-long learning vacations focusing on such subjects as woodcarving, storytelling, and folk music. You can also book a simple "Outdoor Weekend" with no classes. Summer weekend packages start at $280 per person.

Outfitters and Recreation

Boats, canoes, and water-sports equipment can be rented at **Bird's Boat Livery** (Rte. 28, 315/354-4441). Bird's also offers a **mail boat cruise** around the lake at 10:15 A.M. Mon.–Sat. July–Aug.

The **Raquette Lake Navigation Co.** (off Rte. 28 in the village, 315/354-5532, www.raquettelakenavigation.com) features lunch, dinner, sightseeing, and moonlight cruises aboard the *W. W. Durant,* June–October.

Shopping

Inside the sprawling **Raquette Lake Supply Co.** (Main St., 315/354-4301), owned by the same family since the late 1800s, you'll find everything from a post office and launderette to groceries and fishing supplies.

OLD FORGE AND THE FULTON CHAIN

After the relative solitude of Blue Mountain Lake, Indian Lake, and even Raquette Lake, Old Forge and much of the Fulton Chain come as a disheartening shock. The roads and hamlets here are surprisingly built up, and tourists slurping down ice-cream cones seem to be everywhere.

Nestled in the western foothills of the Adirondacks, the Fulton Chain is a series of eight lakes, flanked by long ridges. None of the ridges reach higher than 600 feet, but they feature steep, glaciated cliffs that drop dramatically down into the lakes. Excellent bird's-eye views can be had by hiking up Bald Mountain or by taking a ride up the McCauley Mountain chairlift.

Heading west from Raquette Lake on Route 28, you'll come first to Eighth and Seventh Lakes—the most pristine of the Fulton Chain—and to the attractive hamlet of **Inlet.** About two miles beyond Inlet is Big Moose Public Road (County Road 1), a wooded back lane that leads north four miles to Big Moose Lake. So far, so good. But then, about 10 miles beyond Inlet lies Old Forge, dominated by endless souvenir shops, motels, and the Enchanted Forest/Water Safari theme park.

One of the Adirondacks' most famed and popular **canoe trips** begins in Old Forge and proceeds north through the Fulton Chain to Raquette Lake, Long Lake, and the Raquette River. Canoeists can then head to either Saranac or Tupper Lakes. The entire route is about 100 miles long, involves about nine miles of portage, and takes about six days. To canoe just the 18-mile-long Fulton Chain, from Old Forge to the Eighth Lake Campground, takes a full day and involves 1.7 miles of portage.

Detour to Big Moose Lake

Located off the beaten tourist track, Big Moose Lake is worth a detour, especially for fans of Theodore Dreiser's *An American Tragedy.* Dreiser based his classic on an actual tragedy; it was in the lake's South Bay that Chester Gillette drowned Grace Brown. Bear left on Big Moose Road upon reaching the lake, and you'll come to the old railroad station (now Big Moose Station restaurant) where Gillette and Brown alighted. Bear right and you'll reach the former site of the Hotel Glennmore, where the couple registered and rented their boat. The hotel is gone now, but several outbuildings remain.

Writes Dreiser: "The quiet, glassy, iridescent surface of this lake… seemed, not so much like water as oil—like molten glass that, of enormous bulk and weight, resting upon the substantial earth so very far below… Everywhere pines—tall and spearlike. And above them the humped backs of the dark and distant Adirondacks beyond."

Old Forge Arts Center

The oldest multiarts center in the Adirondacks, founded in the early 1950s, the Arts Center (Rte. 28, Old Forge, 315/369-6411, www.artscenteroldforge.org, 10 A.M.–4 P.M. Mon.–Sat., noon–4 P.M. Sun., free gallery admission, events $5–12) occupies a former boat-storage barn. The main gallery focuses on changing art and photography exhibits, while in the Adirondack room are selected works—such as quilts and baskets—from the permanent collection.

THE AMERICAN TRAGEDY THAT BECAME *AN AMERICAN TRAGEDY*

On July 11, 1906, a young man named Chester Gillette overturned a rowboat in the middle of Big Moose Lake, drowning – accidentally or deliberately? – his pregnant girlfriend Grace Brown. The case caught the attention of the entire nation, and became the basis for Theodore Dreiser's novel *An American Tragedy*. Dreiser stuck surprisingly close to the facts of the case. Like Gillette, his protagonist, Clyde Griffiths, grew up in a religious family that roamed the West; he traveled east to work in his uncle's skirt factory and was desperate to achieve the American Dream – no matter what it took.

Gillette was arrested the day after the drowning and incarcerated in the Herkimer County jail. Visitors lined up around the block to tour past his cell, and reporters flocked there from all over the country. Among those covering the case was ex-lawman Bat Masterson, who had become a sportswriter for the *New York Morning Telegraph*. Masterson was one of the few to question whether Gillette could receive a fair trial in Herkimer County – a charge that infuriated local officials.

Several buildings connected with the Gillette case still stand. In Cortland, south of Syracuse, is the rooming house where Chester lived while working at his uncle's factory. In Herkimer, in the Mohawk River Valley, stand the courthouse and jail in which he was tried and incarcerated. And the railroad station through which the couple passed just hours before the fateful event remains in Big Moose Lake.

Chester Gillette was found guilty of first-degree murder and was electrocuted at Auburn State Prison on March 30, 1907.

Film, concert, and lecture series are presented throughout the summer, along with crafts workshops, children's programs, and nature hikes.

Hiking Bald Mountain

Four and a half miles east of Old Forge rises Bald Mountain, which offers superb views of the Fulton Chain for surprisingly little effort. From the well-marked parking lot at the foot of the mountain, the trail climbs only 400 feet in less than a mile: "If the climb were not too short to call a hike, or if you were not apt to meet hordes of other hikers, it could be one of the most satisfying treks in the Adirondacks," writes hiking guru Barbara Martin in *Fifty Hikes in the Adirondacks*.

To reach the trailhead, take Route 28 to Rondaxe Road and watch for signs.

Outfitters and Guides

In Old Forge, boats and canoes can be rented at **Rivett's Boat Livery** (on the waterfront, 315/369-3123). **Adirondack River Outfitters** (315/369-3536) conducts guided rafting trips down the Hudson, Moose, Black, and Sacandaga Rivers. **Tickner's Moose River Canoe Trips** (315/369-6286) offers guided canoe and kayak trips, along with instruction, rentals, and sales.

Accommodations

The expansive **◖ Big Moose Inn** (Big Moose Rd., Big Moose Lake, 315/357-2042, www.bigmooseinn.com, $59–188 d, some rooms share baths) sits by itself on the lakeshore, surrounded by pine. Inside you'll find 16 guest rooms, a central fireplace, restaurant, bar, and a comfortable lounge. Outside is a small beach equipped with canoes and other boats.

The low-slung **Van Auken's Inne** (Forge St., Thendara, 315/369-3033, www.vanaukensinne.com, $79–99 d), with its long, two-tiered porch, contains 12 renovated guest rooms with private baths. Some open out onto a breezy second-story balcony, while on the ground floor are a comfortable lobby, tap room, and restaurant, all filled with antiques.

Food

Big Moose Station (Big Moose Rd., Big Moose Lake, Eagle Bay, 315/357-3525), in the old Adirondack Railroad station, serves American cuisine made of fresh local ingredients. Open for dinner only; average entrée $17.

Housed in its namesake, complete with soaring ceilings, exposed beams, and a waterwheel, is the historic **Old Mill Restaurant** (Rte. 28, 315/369-3662) in Old Forge. On the menu are a multitude of traditional American favorites, including steak, pork chops, and shrimp and chicken dishes; average entrée $15.

In Thendara, the 1893 **Van Auken's Inne** (Forge St., off Rte. 28, 315/369-3033) serves contemporary American and continental fare.

On the lunch menu are salads and sandwiches, while the dinner menu includes everything from grilled veal chops to fresh fish; average dinner entrée $16.

Shopping

Old Forge Hardware (Rte. 28, Old Forge, 315/369-6100) bills itself as the "Adirondacks' Most General Store." Inside, you'll find everything you could possibly need, from snowshoes and bird feeders to cookbooks and paperweights. **Moose River Trading Company** (Rte. 28, Thendara, 315/369-6091) stocks classic Adirondack gear.

The Thousand Islands

Along the St. Lawrence River, at the northwest end of the state, stretches an area known as the Thousand Islands. In point of fact, there are 1,864 islands here, ranging in size from a few square feet to 22 miles long. Some support nothing more than a lone tree; one is home to Boldt Castle, a haunting Gothic presence near Alexandria Bay that is the region's premier visitor attraction.

Though the term "Thousand Islands" is often used to describe the large area reaching from Oswego in the south to Akwesasne in the north to Adirondack Park in the east, the islands themselves are clustered only in the center, between Cape Vincent and Alexandria Bay. Much of the rest of the region supports farms or endless unbroken acres of low-growing forest, rivers, and lakes. Several small industrialized cities flourish as well, the largest of which is Watertown. Outside Watertown bustles Fort Drum, a 107,000-acre military training facility.

For the visitor, most of the Thousand Islands' attractions lie along the Seaway Trail, which hugs the shores of the St. Lawrence and Lake Ontario. From the trail, views of the river and its bypassing boat traffic are outstanding. Enormous tankers and cargo vessels slide by,

on their way between the Atlantic Ocean and the Great Lakes. The 1959 completion of the St. Lawrence Seaway—a series of connecting channels and locks—turned the river into the longest navigable inland passage in the world. It stretches over 2,300 miles.

Because the Thousand Islands lie between the United States and Canada, the region attracts as many Canadian as American visitors. The Thousand Islands International Bridge (an extension of I-81) crosses over the St. Lawrence River near Alexandria Bay; the Prescott-Ogdensburg Bridge connects the two cities, and the Seaway International Bridge spans the river near Massena.

History

Prior to the arrival of the whites, the Thousand Islands were inhabited by the Iroquois, who called the region *Manitonna,* or Garden of the Great Spirit. According to Iroquois legend, the islands were created by accident by the Great Spirit, who had promised all the tribes on earth a paradise if only they would stop quarrelling. The tribes promised and the Great Spirit delivered, only to have to retrieve his garden when the mortals broke their word. But as the Great Spirit was about to return to

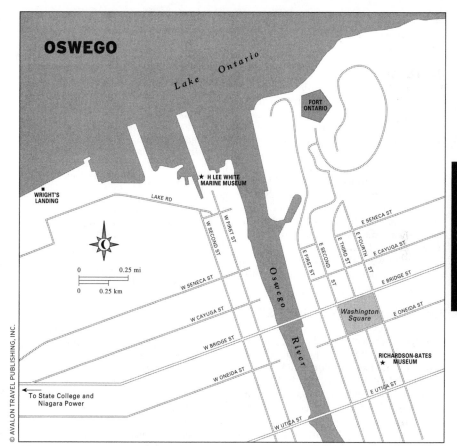

THE NORTH COUNTRY

© AVALON TRAVEL PUBLISHING, INC.

the sky, the garden slipped out of his grasp and crashed into the St. Lawrence River, breaking into a thousand pieces.

The first white man to enter the region was Jacques Cartier, who sailed down the St. Lawrence in 1635 and allegedly exclaimed, *"Les milles isles!"* The region maintained a close connection with France throughout the 1700s and early 1800s, when refugees fleeing France after Napoleon's reign settled near Cape Vincent. Among them were Napoleon's brother and sister, Joseph and Caroline Bonaparte.

The region also bore the brunt of much of the War of 1812. Fought between the United States and Britain, with the Americans hoping to drive the English out of North America once and for all, the war went largely unsupported by area residents. Many earned their livelihood by trading with England and Canada, and dubbed the three years' worth of battles "Mr. Madison's War." Handsome stone fortifications still stand in Sackets Harbor and Oswego, where major battles were fought, and historic War of 1812 plaques line the Seaway Trail.

The wealthy discovered the beauty of the Thousand Islands in the 1870s and soon built magnificent summer homes on private islands. Grand hotels went up on the shore as well, and huge steamboats plied the waters. All this opulence ended with the Depression, but evidence of it remains.

OSWEGO

At the southwestern end of the region, just north of the Finger Lakes, lies the small city of Oswego (population 19,195). Straddling the mouth of the Oswego River, overlooking Lake Ontario, Oswego operated as an important fort and trading post throughout the 1700s. During the American Revolution, Oswego served as a haven for Loyalists fleeing the Mohawk Valley, and remained in British hands until 1796. Named the first freshwater port in the United States in 1799, Oswego protected the supply route to the naval base at nearby Sackets Harbor during the War of 1812.

Today, Oswego continues to function as a Great Lakes port and is a major sportfishing center.

Fort Ontario State Historic Site

Presiding over Lake Ontario is Fort Ontario (1 E. 4th St., 315/343-4711, 10 A.M.–4:30 P.M. Tues.–Sat. and 1–4:30 P.M. Sun. May–Oct., adults $4, children under 12 $2). Originally built by the British in 1755, the site was attacked and rebuilt four times, with the present-day fort constructed between 1839 and 1844.

During World War II, Fort Ontario served as a sort of emergency refugee center/internment camp for victims of the Nazi Holocaust. The only one of its kind for European refugees in the country, the center invited 874 Jews and 73 Catholics to relocate here, but upon arrival, the refugees were placed in a fenced-in compound and told not to leave. The shocked refugees were interned for a total of 18 months.

Today, Fort Ontario has been restored to its 1867–72 appearance. Costumed guides interpret the lives of the men and civilians who once lived here.

H. Lee White Marine Museum

Oswego's most delightful tourist attraction is the White Marine Museum (foot of W. 1st

THE SEAWAY TRAIL

The Seaway Trail is a 454-mile scenic highway that parallels New York's northern coastline along the St. Lawrence River, Lake Ontario, the Niagara River, and Lake Erie. Marked by green-and-white route markers, as well as brown-and-white War of 1812 signs, it forms the longest national recreational trail in the United States.

In the Thousand Islands region, the Seaway Trail runs from Oswego in the south to Akwesasne in the north along Routes 104, 3, 180, 12 E, and 37. More parks and beaches are located along this section of the trail than anywhere else in New York State. In total, the Thousand Islands region boasts 45 New York and Canadian state parks; two of the largest are Wellesley Island and Robert Moses.

Seaway Trail, Inc. (W. Main and Ray Sts., Sackets Harbor, 315/646-1000 or 800/SEAWAY-T, www.seawaytrail.com) publishes a free annual magazine, available in most regional tourism offices, and helpful touring guides. Among them are *Seaway Trail Bicycling*, which outlines some of the region's excellent bike routes, and *Seaway Trail Lighthouses*.

St., 315/342-0480, www.hleewhitemarinemuseum.com, 1–5 P.M. daily May–Dec., 10 A.M.–5 P.M. daily July–Aug., $3.50, children 5–12 $2), a sprawling, hodgepodge affair filled with everything from archaeological artifacts to mounted fish. One exhibit focuses on Lake Ontario shipwrecks, another on the city's once-thriving shipbuilding industry, a third on the legendary "monsters" of the lake, a fourth on the region's strong abolitionist history. Most everything in the museum has been donated, which gives it a folksy appeal. Outside, a World War II tugboat and a derrick barge invite exploration.

Richardson-Bates Museum

Built in the late 1860s, the Richardson-Bates house (135 E. 3rd St., 315/343-1342, 10 A.M.–5 P.M. Tues.–Fri., 1–5 P.M. Sat., adults $4, seniors and children over 12 $2) is a regal

Italianate mansion still equipped with 95 percent of its original furnishings. The five plush period rooms downstairs are arranged according to photographs taken around 1890, while upstairs, succinct exhibits explain the history of Oswego County. The museum is run by the Oswego County Historical Society.

Camping and Accommodations

On the lakeshore about 15 miles northeast of Oswego lies **Selkirk Shores State Park** (Rte. 3, 315/298-5737), equipped with a beach, hiking trails, and 148-site campground. For reservations, call 800/456-CAMP. Good motels in the area include a 44-room **Days Inn** (Rte. 104 E, 315/343-3136, $79–99 d) and the 94-room **Best Western Captain's Quarters** (26 E. 1st St., 315/342-4040, $90–125 d).

Food

The ever popular **Rudy's** (Washington Blvd. on the lakeshore, 315/343-2671), a quarter-mile west of the State University of New York (SUNY) College at Oswego, specializes in fish and chips, and fried scallops and clams.

EN ROUTE TO SACKETS HARBOR

The **Seaway Trail** (Route 104 to Route 3) heads north out of Oswego to Selkirk Shores State Park and the mouth of the Salmon River. Take a two-mile detour east on Route 13 along the river to reach the Salmon Capital of **Pulaski.** Almost everything here caters to anglers: Salmon Acres Motel, Portly Angler Lodge, Fish Inn Post, and Angler Parking—read the signs.

Continue another five miles east on Route 13 to reach Altmar and the **New York State Salmon River Fish Hatchery** (Rte. 22, 315/298-5051, 9 A.M.–4 P.M. daily March–Nov., free admission). Over 4.5 million fish are raised here each year, including chinook and coho salmon, and brown, rainbow, and steelhead trout.

From the mouth of the Salmon River, the Seaway Trail continues north along the shores of Lake Ontario. It bypasses several more parks and then bumps into deep blue **Henderson Harbor,** a perfectly shaped semicircle ringed with historic homes, vacation cottages, marinas, and ship-shape small boats.

About a mile southeast of Henderson Harbor is the hamlet of **Henderson,** where Confederate general Stonewall Jackson came for medical treatment for a stomach ailment before the Civil War. Part of his cure was to walk between the hamlet and the harbor daily.

◖ SACKETS HARBOR

About 45 miles north of Oswego, or eight miles west of Watertown, lies picturesque Sackets Harbor. Built on a bluff overlooking Lake Ontario, Sackets Harbor is peppered with handsome limestone buildings that date back to the early 1800s. Though now primarily a resort village, Sackets Harbor remains for the most part undiscovered, which helps account for its charm.

During the War of 1812, Sackets Harbor dominated American naval and military activity. A large fleet was constructed in its shipyard and thousands of soldiers were housed in the barracks built on its shores. Heavy fighting between the British and American troops took place on the bluffs.

The former shipyard and adjoining battlefield is now Sackets Harbor's foremost visitor attraction. It is located at the end of a short Main Street that's lined with cheery shops, cafés, and historic buildings; more historic buildings flank quiet, tree-shaded Broad Street.

A mile or two east of the village center stand the former barracks, now known as **Madison Barracks** (85 Worth Rd., 315/646-3374), a converted complex holding apartments, restaurants, and a small inn. Visitors are welcome to explore barracks' bucolic grounds, encompassing a parade ground, polo lawn, stone tower, officers' row, and military burial ground. Pick up walking-tour brochures in the management office just inside the main gate.

Sackets Harbor Battlefield State Historic Site

Hard though it is to believe today, the silent and all-but-deserted Sackets Harbor Battlefield

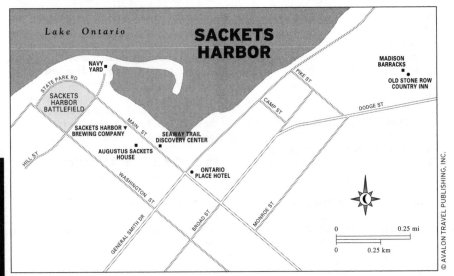

(foot of Main and Washington Sts., 315/646-3634, 10 A.M.–5 P.M. Mon.–Sat. and 1–5 P.M. Sun. June–Aug., 10 A.M.–5 P.M. Fri.–Sat. and 1–5 P.M. Sun. Sept.–Oct., adults $3, senior $2, children 6–12 $1) was once the site of intense fighting between American and British troops. Monuments and plaques commemorating the events are strewn here and there, but for the most part, the battlefield remains an idyllic park, set atop a lush green bluff with glorious lake views. The **Battle of Sackets Harbor** is reenacted here every July.

Adjoining the battlefield is the partially restored Navy Yard, enclosed by a white picket fence. Built in the 1850s to replace the thriving shipyard once situated here, the yard contains a restored commandant's house and a museum showcasing exhibits on the War of 1812.

Augustus Sackets House

Housed in this handsome 1803 residence (301 W. Main St.) are the **Sackets Harbor Chamber of Commerce** (315/646-1700, www.sacketsharborny.com, 10 A.M.–5 P.M. Mon.–Fri.) and the **Sackets Harbor Visitors Center** (315/646-2321, 10 A.M.–4 P.M. daily June.–Oct., free admission). The latter contains three rooms of

exhibits and a good introductory video on the area. Sackets Harbor is one of New York State's Heritage Areas—loosely designated historic districts linked by a common theme. The theme in Sackets Harbor is defense.

Seaway Trail Discovery Center

One block away from the visitors center is the Seaway Trail Discovery Center (401 Main St., at Ray St., 315/646-1000, www.seawaytrail.com, 10 A.M.–5 P.M. daily May–Oct., 10 A.M.–5 P.M. Tues.–Sat. Nov.–Apr., adults $4, military and seniors $3, children $2). Here you'll find nine rooms of exhibits and lots of free literature on the historic trail.

Accommodations

At the Madison Barracks (85 Worth Rd., www.madisonbarracks.com), the attractive **(Old Stone Row Country Inn** (123 Bartlett Rd., 315/646-3374, $60–150 d) offers eight modern guest rooms complete with kitchenettes. In the heart of the village, the three-story **Ontario Place Hotel** (103 General Smith Dr., 315/646-8000, www.ontarioplacehotel.com, $80–175 d) offers 28 spacious rooms and 10 suites equipped with Jacuzzis.

Food

In a refurbished railroad station in the heart of the village, find the **Sackets Harbor Brewing Company** (212 Main St., 315/646-BREW), maker of the War of 1812, Railroad Red, and Grant's Golden ales. On the dining room menu, find everything from fresh fish to pot pies (main dishes $11–23); a pub menu is also available. In the Madison Barracks (85 Worth Rd.), **Kathy's Barracks Inn** (42 Madison Barracks, 315/646-2376) offers a wide-ranging lunch and dinner menu (gourmet sandwiches, pasta, steak) and patio dining with great views of the lake; open seasonally, average entrée $14. Recently moved from the Barracks to the downtown is **Sackets Cantina** (212 W. Main St., 315/646-3333), offering the only Mexican cuisine and tequila bar in the region.

CAPE VINCENT

Situated on a windswept spit of land at the mouth of the St. Lawrence River is Cape Vincent, "home of the gamey black bass" ("gamey" as in "feisty"). Cape Vincent doesn't really have much to offer in the way of visitor attractions but is a pretty village to drive through, with historic homes along Broadway.

The area's first settlers were French, a fact celebrated every July on **French Heritage Day.** On Real Street once stood the "Cup and Saucer House," built in 1818 by Napoleon's chief of police, Count Real, in the hopes that the emperor could be rescued from the island of St. Helena. The building burned to the ground in 1867.

Sights

In the heart of the village, the **Cape Vincent Historical Museum** (174 James St., 315/654-3094 or 315/654-3640, 10 A.M.–4 P.M. Mon.–Sat. and noon–4 P.M. Sun. July–Aug., free admission) showcases historical artifacts and a delightful collection of tiny figures created out of scrap metal by local farmer Richard Merchant. Not far from the museum is the **NYS DEC Research Station and Aquarium** (541 Broadway, 315/654-2147, 9 A.M.–5 P.M. daily May–Oct., free admission), housing several hundred local fish.

THE NORTH COUNTRY

COURTESY OF 1000 ISLANDS INTERNATIONAL TOURISM COUNCIL

aerial view of historic Sackets Harbor on eastern Lake Ontario

Worth driving out to is the 1854 **Tibbetts Point Lighthouse,** several miles west of the village on the very tip of the cape. The lighthouse is not open for touring—it's now a youth hostel—but the drive along the shore road (Route 6) is outstanding.

Horne's Ferry

Cape Vincent is the only community left in New York State with a ferry to Canada crossing the St. Lawrence River. The ferry (315/783-0638) operates hourly May–October ($10 for car and driver); crossing time is 10 minutes.

Accommodations

The **Tibbetts Point Lighthouse** (33439 County Rte. 6, 315/654-3450) is a Hosteling International–American Youth Hostel offering 31 dormitory-style beds in single-sex rooms; family rooms also are available ($14/night for HI-AYH members, $17/night for nonmembers).

The boxy, brick **Roxy's Motel** (Broadway and Market St., 315/654-2456, $50 d) has operated continuously since 1894. Downstairs, an old-fashioned restaurant and bar sport mounted fish and aging photographs of anglers with their catch; upstairs are 10 simple but adequate guest rooms.

CLAYTON

One of the most interesting villages along the St. Lawrence, Clayton spreads along the riverfront, with lots of park benches ideal for watching the swift current slide by. The village contains four museums and the Thousand Islands Inn, where Thousand Islands salad dressing was invented. All along Riverside Drive stand sturdy brick storefronts, built in the late 1800s, while at the corner of Riverside Drive and Merrick Street reigns the **Simon Johnston House,** a clapboard Italianate home with a widow's walk and decorative eaves.

Settled in 1822, Clayton soon developed into a major shipbuilding center and steamboat port. The St. Lawrence skiff, known for its sleekness and beauty, was first constructed here by Xavier Colon in 1868, and the 900-passenger *St. Lawrence,* the largest steamboat ever made, was built in the 1890s. During World War I, the Clayton shipyards produced submarine chasers and pontoon boats.

Tibbetts Point Lighthouse, Cape Vincent, one of the oldest lighthouses on the Great Lakes.

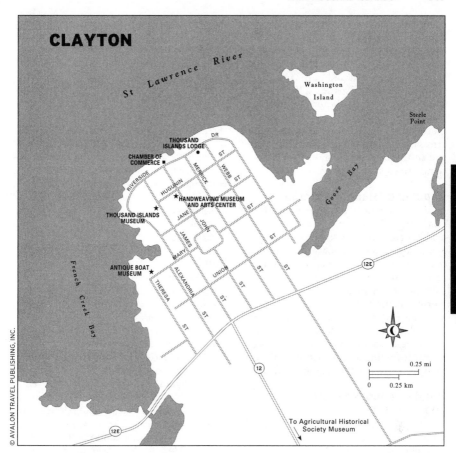

CLAYTON

St Lawrence River

Washington Island

Steele Point

DR

THOUSAND ISLANDS LODGE

CHAMBER OF COMMERCE

RIVERSIDE

HUGUNIN

MERRICK

WEBB

ST

ST

ST

HANDWEAVING MUSEUM AND ARTS CENTER

JANE

JOHN

ST

THOUSAND ISLANDS MUSEUM

JAMES

MARY

ST

ANTIQUE BOAT MUSEUM

THERESA

ALEXANDRIA

UNION

ST

ST

ST

ST

ST

ST

French Creek Bay

Goose Bay

12E

12E

12

0   0.25 mi

0   0.25 km

To Agricultural Historical Society Museum

THE NORTH COUNTRY

Tourists began frequenting Clayton in the late 1800s. Most came to fish and boat, and they stayed in huge wooden hotels—since burned down—along the waterfront. During Clayton's heyday, five express trains arrived here daily from New York City, and one hotel was equipped with a direct line to the New York Stock Exchange. Some vacationers even came during the winter, to ice-fish and watch the horse races run on the frozen St. Lawrence River.

Walking tour maps of the town are available at the **Clayton Chamber of Commerce** (517 Riverside Dr., 315/686-3771 or 800/252-9806, www.1000islands-clayton.com, 9 A.M.–5 P.M. daily July–Sept., 9 A.M.–4 P.M. Mon.–Fri. Oct.–June).

Antique Boat Museum

Appropriately enough, Clayton has the finest collection of antique wooden boats in America. Among them are canoes, sailboats, launches, raceboats, runabouts, and, of course, the famed St. Lawrence skiff.

The gleaming boats, most built of highly polished woods and brass, are housed in a former lumberyard (750 Mary St., 315/686-4104, www.abm.org, 9 A.M.–5 P.M. daily May–Oct., adults $12, seniors $11, students $10, children 5–17 $6) on the edge of town. There are over 150 vessels in all, spread out over eight buildings, along with a boatbuilding shop, almost 300 inboard and outboard motors, and 12,000 nautical artifacts. The museum also contains extensive historical exhibits, including one on Clayton's rum-running days. During Prohibition, men smuggled liquor across the river from Canada on sleds, skates, and small boats honeycombed with hidden compartments.

Thousand Islands Museum

Inside this eclectic local history museum (312 James St., 315/686-5794, www.thousandislandsmuseum.org, 10 A.M.–4 P.M. daily June–Sept., admission by donation), you'll find the "Muskie Hall of Fame," devoted to the region's most prized fish, and an enormous collection of hand-carved decoys, a popular North Country folk art. According to the exhibit, one riverman claims to have carved over 1,000 decoys, another about 5,000. Also on site are re-created turn-of-the-century storefronts, including a general store, millinery shop, law office, and old country kitchen.

Handweaving Museum and Arts Center

Hand-woven North American textiles are the specialty of this small and low-key museum (314 John St., 315/686-4123, www.hm-ac.org, 9 A.M.–4 P.M. Mon.–Fri. year-round, 9 A.M.–4 P.M. Sat.–Sun. in summer, admission by donation). Exhibits range from 18th-century lace collars and handkerchiefs to modern shawls and scarves. Adjoining the museum are classrooms where workshops are offered; visitors are welcome to enroll if space is available.

Houseboat Rentals

Vacationing onboard houseboats is a popular activity in the Thousand Islands, and numerous houseboat-rental companies once lined the St. Lawrence. Many still exist on the Canadian side, but insurance costs have forced most U.S. companies to close. The one exception is

Remar Houseboat Rental (510 Theresa St., 315/686-3579). No experience is necessary, and instruction is provided. Reservations should be made well in advance.

Camping and Accommodations

Campsites are available at 174-site **Cedar Point State Park** (Rte. 12 E, 315/654-2522) and at three island campgrounds accessible only by boat. For reservations, call 800/456-CAMP.

The 1897 **【 Thousand Islands Inn** (355 Riverside Dr., 315/686-3030, $65–95 d) is the last of the great old hotels that once lined Clayton. Significantly smaller than it was in its heyday, it offers 14 modernized guest rooms, some overlooking the river. Downstairs is a restaurant (see below).

Food

The **Harbor Inn** (625 Mary St., 315/686-2293) serves a tasty diner-style breakfast (including homemade donuts) and lunch; in the evening, it becomes more formal, offering lots of seafood and scallop dishes; average dinner entrée $15. The **Koffee Kove** (220 James St., 315/686-2472) is known for its chili and homemade breads.

The **Riverside Cafe** (506 Riverside Dr., 315/686-2940) is one of the few restaurants in town that overlooks the water. On the menu is American and Greek fare; average entrée $14. The chef-owned **Clipper Inn** (126 State St., 315/686-3842) is a local favorite, serving lots of seafood in an upscale yet casual setting.

In the **Thousands Islands Inn** (355 Riverside Dr., 315/686-3030), you'll find a comfortable, old-fashioned restaurant serving everything from fish to pasta; average entrée $14. For sale are bottles of "Original Thousand Islands Salad Dressing," created here in the early 1900s by one Sophia LaLonde.

Events

One of the region's most popular events, sponsored by the Antique Boat Museum, is the resplendent **Antique Boat Show,** held every August for over 30 years. The **Decoy and Wildlife Art Show,** attracting over 200 exhib-

THE PECULIAR STORIES OF THE THOUSAND ISLANDS

The 1,864 islands of the Thousand Islands laze in the deep blue St. Lawrence River like a "drunken doodle made by an addled cartographer," as one observer once said. Each and every one tells a story.

The largest of the islands is Wolfe Island. The smallest is Tom Thumb. The only artificial island, Longue View Island, was formed by filling in the area between two shoals. As the story goes, Longue View was created by a doting husband who wanted to build a summer home for his wife. When he couldn't find a single island that suited her, he had one built, and then added a luxurious mansion atop it. His wife then ran off with another man.

Devil's Oven on Devil's Island was the 1838 refuge of Canadian patriot Bill Johnston. After an abortive attempt to wrest Canada from the British empire, Johnston hid out in the cave for nearly a year before surrendering to the authorities. He was later pardoned and appointed a lighthouse keeper.

The Price is Right Island was given away in 1964 by Bill Cullen on *The Price is Right* TV game show. Deer Island is owned by the Skull and Bones Society of Yale University. Abbie Hoffman lived incognito – under the name Barry Freed – on Wellesley Island after jumping bail in 1974 on cocaine charges.

Florence Island, Arthur Godfrey's isle, was given to him as a gift by the Thousand Islands Bridge Authority in return for free advertising. Godfrey sang the song "Florence on the St. Lawrence."

Grindstone Island was the site of the last existing one-room schoolhouse in New York State, in use up until 1989. Ash Island has its own private railroad line running from the boathouse to the main house on the cliff.

George Pullman of Pullman Car fame once owned Pullman Island and played frequent host to President Ulysses S. Grant. Calumet Island was once the property of Charles Emery, president of the American Tobacco Company. Picton Island was owned by M. Heineman, originator of Buster Brown Shoes, and Oppawaka Island by J. H. Heinz of Heinz 57 fame.

itors, is held in the Clayton Arena mid-July. For either event, call 315/686-3771.

ALEXANDRIA BAY

About 10 miles northeast of Clayton is Alexandria Bay, a busy tourist village that could be called the Lake George of the North. Here you'll find all sorts of '50s-era attractions, including miniature golf courses, junior speedways, kitschy souvenir shops, and mom-and-pop motels.

But for all its summertime hustle and bustle, Alexandria Bay has a permanent population of just 1,355 and a laid-back, down-home charm. The village centers on a snug waterfront, where a few narrow streets are crowded with tiny shops and restaurants. Teenagers strut their stuff in front of an amusement arcade, while twentysomethings exchange glances outside a boisterous bar. A white-haired woman wearing a pink apron, saddle shoes, and green socks sits on her stoop, watching the foot traffic go by.

Like Clayton, Alexandria Bay was a popular tourist resort and steamboat stop throughout the late 1800s and early 1900s. Millionaires built second homes on the islands across from the village, while hotels went up along the shore.

Evidence of those days can be found at the **Cornwall Brothers' Store** (foot of Market St., 315/482-4586, 10 A.M.–6 P.M. Mon.–Sat. May–Oct.). Originally owned by the town's founder, Azariah Walton, the building is now part museum, part re-created general store. Up front choose from a nice selection of penny candy, vintage postcards, handicrafts, and books; in back are historic photographs and artifacts.

From both ends of the village extend weathered piers at which excursion boats dock.

Alexandria Bay is the main port for touring the Thousand Islands. For more information on the area, stop into the **Alexandria Bay Chamber of Commerce** (7 Market St., 315/482-9531 or 800/541-2110, www.alexbay.org, 9 A.M.–5 P.M. daily, with extended hours in July–Aug.).

◖ Boldt Castle

Looming over Heart Island, across from Alexandria Bay, is a gloomy, 127-room replica of a Rhineland castle (315/482-2501, www.boldtcastle.com, 10 A.M.–6 P.M. daily May–Oct., with extended hours July–Aug., adults $5.25, children 6–12 $3, plus the cost of the boat ride over). The castle was built by George Boldt, who came to the United States from Prussia in the 1860s. The son of poor parents, Boldt had tremendous industry and skill, and eventually became the most successful hotel magnate in the country. Both the Waldorf-Astoria in New York City and the Bellevue-Stratford in Philadelphia were his.

Boldt was deeply in love with his wife, Louise, and built the castle around the turn of the 20th century as a symbol of his love for her. The castle was to be their summer home, and he employed the finest craftspeople, instructing them to embellish the building with hearts wherever they could. Boldt even had the island reshaped into the form of a heart.

Then in 1904, when the castle was 80 percent complete, Louise passed away. Boldt sent a telegram to the construction crew to stop work immediately, and never set foot on the island again. The castle was abandoned and allowed to deteriorate.

Finally, in 1977, the Thousand Islands Bridge Authority bought Boldt Castle, partially rehabilitated it, and introduced it to the tourist trade. Today, hundreds of visitors traipse through it daily, but all the activity in the world can't erase the castle's haunted and wildly romantic feel. All around are broken moldings, half-finished walls, and cold, echoing hallways. In the former ballroom, exhibits explain the castle's history.

A shuttle boat operates from the castle to the **Boldt Yacht House** (adults $3, children 6–12 $2), perched on a separate island nearby. Completed before Louise's death, the boathouse contains three original spit-and-polish boats and restored living quarters furnished with handsome antiques.

Excursion Boats

The only way to reach Boldt Island, as well as the other 1,800-plus islands in the St. Lawrence River, is by boat. And several boat companies offer tours.

Largest among them is **Uncle Sam's Boat Tours** (315/482-2611, www.usboattours.com), whose huge replica paddleboats dock at the eastern end of James Street. Uncle Sam's features an hourly shuttle service to Boldt Castle (adults $7, children 4–12 $4.50) that allows visitors to stay as long as they like, as well as various sightseeing and dining cruises.

Empire Boat Tours (4 Church St., 315/482-TOUR, www.empireboat.com) also travels to Boldt Island (adults $6, children $3) and offer various sightseeing and dining cruises.

If you'd prefer to rent your own motorboat

boating toward Boldt Castle

COURTESY OF 1000 ISLANDS INTERNATIONAL TOURISM COUNCIL

THE NORTH COUNTRY

or pontoon boat, stop in at **O'Briens U-Drive** (51 Walton St., 315/482-9548). Rentals are available by the hour, day, or week, and river maps and trip-planning advice are provided.

Wellesley Island State Park

To reach Wellesley Island and Wellesley Island State Park (315/482-2722, Exit 51 off I-81, $6–8 parking) you must travel over the **Thousand Islands International Bridge,** a slim suspension expanse that seems to lead straight up into the sky. Built in 1938, the bridge extends over five spans and stretches seven miles.

At the end of the first span lies the 2,636-acre state park, featuring hiking trails, swimming beaches, a campground, nine-hole golf course, playground, and great views of the river. Covering 600 acres of the park is the **Minna Anthony Common Nature Center** (44927 Cross Island Rd., 315/482-2479, 8 A.M.–4:30 P.M. daily, extended hours in summer, free admission), which includes both a museum and a wildlife sanctuary laced with trails. In the museum are live fish and reptiles, mounted birds, and an observation beehive.

Thousand Islands Park

South of the state park, at the very tip of Wellesley Island, lies Thousand Islands Park (www.1000islandpark.com), a quiet community filled with hundreds of wooden Victorian homes painted in luscious ice-cream pastels. Ornate carvings, shingled roofs, porches, turrets, and gables abound.

On the National Register of Historic Places, the park is largely privately owned but visitors are welcome. The community has its own movie theater, post office, library, and playground.

On the way to and from Thousand Islands Park, you'll pass by the smaller, scruffier community of **Fineview,** once home to a man who went by the name Barry Freed. During the late 1970s, Freed began a still-active—and quite effective—environmental organization called Save the River. Then, in 1980, locals were astounded to discover that Barry Freed was actually activist Abbie Hoffman, on the lam from the FBI since 1974. Hoffman arranged a deal with the authorities and moved back into the national arena, only to commit suicide in 1989.

Camping and Accommodations

Campsites are available at the 80-site **Grass Point State Park** (Rte. 12 E, 315/686-4472) and the 429-site **Wellesley Island State Park** (Wellesley Island, 315/482-2722). For reservations, call 800/456-CAMP.

Capt. Thomson's (1 James St., 315/482-9961, www.captthomsons.com, $79–139 d) contains 68 standard rooms, some equipped with balconies overlooking the river. Featuring views of the river and Boldt Castle is the luxurious **◖ Riveredge Resort Hotel** (17 Holland St., 315/482-9917, www.riveredge.com, $140–298 d). The hotels' rooms and suites are spacious and well-appointed; on-site are a health spa, indoor and outdoor pools, and two restaurants.

The sleek **Bonnie Castle** (Holland St., 315/482-4511 or 800/955-4511, www.bonniecastle.com, $150–250 d) is the region's largest resort, equipped with 128 rooms and suites, a conference center, private beach, swimming pools, tennis courts, nightclub, miniature golf courses, and restaurants.

Food

Numerous casual restaurants stand along James and Market Streets downtown. Among them is the lively **Dockside Pub** (17 Market St., 315/482-9849), serving sandwiches, soups, and pizza in a setting near the water.

The historic **Admiral's Inn** (20 James St., 315/482-2781) features a comfortable bar to one side, several cheery dining rooms to the other. Sandwiches and salads are offered at lunch, while dinner entrées include prime rib and fresh seafood; average entrée $14.

The best restaurant in town is the **Jacques Cartier Dining Room** in the Riveredge Resort Hotel (see *Accommodations,* above). On the menu is creative American and French cuisine; the dining room offers fine views of Boldt Castle; average entrée $18.

OGDENSBURG

The oldest settlement in northern New York, established in 1749, Ogdensburg is a busy port and industrial town at the juncture of the Oswegatchie and St. Lawrence Rivers. Along the St. Lawrence downtown runs the **Greenbelt Riverfront Park** (Riverside Dr.), dotted with historical plaques that detail the War of 1812 Battle of Ogdensburg. A few blocks south of the park is the town's foremost visitor attraction—the Frederic Remington Art Museum.

Frederic Remington Art Museum

Artist Frederic Remington (1861–1909), best known for his paintings and bronzes of the American West, was born in the northernmost reaches of New York State. In his youth he made a total of 18 trips out West, collecting information and taking photographs that he would later use in his studio in New Rochelle, NY, to create his masterpieces. Remington never lived in Ogdensburg, but was born and is buried in nearby Canton. His wife moved to Ogdensburg after his death.

Housed in an imposing 1810 mansion, the Remington Art Museum (303 Washington St., at State, 315/393-2425, www.frederickemington.org, 10 A.M.–5 P.M. Mon.–Sat. and 1–5 P.M. Sun. May–Oct., 11 A.M.–5 P.M. Tues.–Sat. Nov.–Apr., adults $8, students and seniors $7, children under 5 free) contains the largest single Remington collection in the United States. On display are scores of oil paintings, watercolors, drawings, illustrations, and bronzes, including many small and relatively unknown gems. One room is filled with watercolors depicting the Adirondacks, another with a reproduction of Remington's studio. The most valuable Remingtons are kept in a locked gallery that is only open during guided tours, scheduled regularly throughout the day.

CANTON

About 20 miles east of Ogdensburg lies Canton, Remington's birthplace. Settled by Vermonters in the early 1800s, Canton today is a busy small town (pop. 11,120), best known as the home of St. Lawrence University.

Traditional Arts in Upstate New York

Detour to Canton for the small but unusual Traditional Arts gallery (2 W. Main St., 315/386-4289, 10 A.M.–4 P.M. Tues.–Sat., closed Sat. in Aug., admission by donation), which focuses on the folk arts of the North Country. Exhibits in the past have highlighted such subjects as St. Lawrence River fishing arts, Mohawk tourist arts, quilts and quilting bees, and Old Order Amish crafts. Thoughtfully laid out displays offer plenty of background information and photographs.

The gallery is also a good place to find out about folk-arts events. Storytelling still thrives in the North Country, and there are occasional traditional-music concerts and dance fests. One of the region's biggest traditional celebrations is the Festival of North Country Folklife, held in nearby Massena.

Silas Wright Museum

Now run by the St. Lawrence County Historical Association, this columned Greek Revival mansion (3 E. Main St., 315/386-8133, noon–4 P.M. Tues.–Sat., free admission) once belonged to U.S. senator and New York governor Silas Wright. Regarded as an honest and intelligent man, Wright was so respected by his neighbors that he won his first election to the state senate in 1823 by 199 votes to one; legend has it that he himself cast the one dissenting vote. The first floor of the house has been restored to its 1830–50 period appearance, while upstairs are local history exhibits. St. Lawrence County is one of the largest and least populated counties east of the Mississippi.

MASSENA

The main reason to make a stop in the small industrial city of Massena is to get a good look at the giant **St. Lawrence Seaway,** which connects the Atlantic Ocean with the Great Lakes. A joint project of the United States and Canada, the Seaway can accommodate ships up to 730 feet long and 76 feet wide. The public-works project was formally dedicated on June 26, 1959 by Queen Elizabeth II and President Eisenhower.

Dwight D. Eisenhower Lock

Atop the long, spare Eisenhower Lock (Barnhart Island Rd., off Rte. 37, 315/764-3200) is a viewing deck from which you can watch ships being raised or lowered 42 feet as they pass through the Seaway. The process takes about 10 minutes and displaces 22 million gallons of water. Ships pass through regularly, except in the winter when the St. Lawrence freezes over, but the viewing deck is only open June–September. Below the lock a small interpretive center (315/769-2049, 9 A.M.–9 P.M. daily June–Sept.) offers exhibits and a short film.

Robert Moses State Park and Campground

Adjoining the Power Project, Robert Moses State Park (315/769-8663) includes a swimming beach, bathhouse, boat rentals, picnic tables, playground, and great views of the river. The park also offers a 168-site campground; for reservations, call 800/456-CAMP.

The **Festival of North Country Folklife** (315/769-3525) takes place in the park every August. Featured are traditional music concerts, dancing, and storytelling, along with crafts and ethnic foods.

AKWESASNE

At the confluence of the St. Regis and St. Lawrence Rivers lies the St. Regis Indian Reservation, or *Akwesasne,* Where the Ruffed Grouse Drums. You'll see signs along Route 37: This Is Indian Land; Private Property; No FBI, IRS, Or Other Agencies. Gas stations selling tax-free gasoline, and mock tepees selling souvenirs strew the roadsides.

Akwesasne is home to about 6,000 Mohawk. The reservation straddles the St. Lawrence Seaway and the United States/Canadian border, and includes several islands.

In Hogansburg, about 10 miles east of Massena, is the large and well laid out **Akwesasne Museum** (Rte. 37, 518/358-2240 or 518/358-2461, 8:30 A.M.–4:30 P.M. Mon.–Fri. July–Aug.; noon–5:30 P.M. Mon. and Fri., 8:30 A.M.–8:30 P.M. Tues.–Thurs., and 11 A.M.–3 P.M. Sat. Sept.–June, adults $2, children 5–16 $1), housed in a big brown building that's also home to the Akwesasne Cultural Center and Library. The museum covers an entire floor and contains an outstanding collection of medicine masks, wampum belts, lacrosse sticks, carved cradle boards, water drums, Bibles written in the Mohawk language, beadwork, quillwork, modern artwork, historical photographs, and basketry.

Especially striking are the photography and basket exhibits. The photographs date back to the 1920s and depict a prosperous, pre-Depression Mohawk community bustling with shiny cars, sturdy baby prams, women in white dresses, and men in hats. The basket exhibit contains everything from a wedding basket, which looks just like a cake, to a thimble basket.

East of the museum is the **Akwesasne Mohawk Casino** (837 Rte. 37, 518/358-2222, www.mohawkcasino.com, 24 hours/day). Opened in spring 1999, the casino offers blackjack, craps, and roulette tables, and hundreds of video lottery terminals.

Sports and Recreation

HIKING AND CANOEING

With 2,000 miles of hiking trails, and canoe routes stretching 100 miles or more, the Adirondacks is an outdoor lovers' paradise. Free, basic information on hiking trails, canoe routes, and tips for using the state's lands can be obtained by contacting the **Department of Environmental Conservation** (DEC) (625 Broadway, Albany, NY 12233, 518/402-9428, www.dec.state.ny.us).

Some of the DEC's brochures include enough information to actually embark on a hike or canoe trip, but many do not. The best source for more detailed information and maps—essential in many areas—is the **Adirondack Mountain Club** (814 Goggins Rd., Lake George, NY 12845, 518/668-4447, www.adk.org). The ADK maintains visitor information centers at Lake George and Lake Placid and runs the Adirondak Loj, a rustic lodge and campground at Lake Placid.

Two of the best hiking guides for visitors new to the Adirondack region are the ADK's *An Adirondack Sampler: Day Hikes for All Seasons,* by Bruce Wadsworth; and *Fifty Hikes in the Adirondacks,* by Barbara McMartin (Backcountry Publications). Wadsworth's book focuses primarily on hikes for beginners, while McMartin's describes hikes of varying difficulty.

A number of day-hikes and canoe trips are sketched out above. These short descriptions should be supplemented with more detailed information from the ADK or other hiking-canoeing guides.

FISHING

Among the many fish that swim the Adirondack waters are landlocked salmon, brook trout, lake trout, northern pike, pickerel, and small- and large-mouth bass. Meanwhile, the St. Lawrence River in the Thousand Islands offers some of the world's best bass and muskie

fishing. The largest muskellunge ever caught in the region weighed over 69 pounds.

Fishing licenses are mandatory for everyone over age 16 and can be obtained in sporting-goods stores, bait shops, and town offices. The DEC maintains fishing hotlines with information on good fishing spots: In the southeastern Adirondacks, call 518/623-3682; for the High Peaks and northwestern lakes, call 518/891-5413; for the Thousand Islands, call 800/248-4FUN.

NORTH COUNTRY GUIDES AND OUTFITTERS

The guide is a firmly entrenched Adirondack institution. Traditionally thought of as a crusty, plaid-jacketed man wise in the ways of the woods, he's been around since the mid-19th century, when naive city folk coming up to explore the wilderness needed someone to help them find their way around and stay alive.

The Adirondack Guides' Association was formed in 1891 to help establish a uniform pay scale, and today hundreds of guides operate throughout the region. They're not as necessary as they once were, thanks to well-marked trails and detailed maps, but they can still guide you to out-of-the-way spots. Many also offer guided group trips, and rent or sell outdoor gear.

A number of guide companies and outfitters are listed by location above. For a more complete list, contact the **New York State Outdoor Guides Association** (1936 Saranac Ave., Lake Placid, NY 12946, 866/4-NYSOGA, www.nysoga.com).

CAMPING AND ACCOMMODATIONS

The DEC maintains 42 campgrounds and 500 island-based campsites within Adirondack Park. Some are listed above, but for a complete list, contact the DEC through their website, www.dec.state.ny.us. Campground reservations, highly recommended on summer weekends, can be made by calling 800/456-CAMP.

Several B&B registries operate exclusively in the North Country. Among them are the **Adirondack B&B Association** (www.adirondackbb.com), **B&B Adirondack Collection** (P.O. Box 814, Elizabethtown, NY 12932, 581/946-8323, www.adirondackinns.com), and **Adirondack B&B Reservation Service** (www.adirondackbedbreafkast.com.).

Getting There and Around

No major airports service the North Country. Most visitors fly to New York City, Albany, Syracuse, or Montreal, and then drive. **USAirways** (800/428-4322) flies into Watertown in the Thousand Islands area.

Amtrak (800/872-7245) operates daily between New York and Montreal, with stops in Saratoga Springs, Glens Falls, Fort Ticonderoga, Port Henry, Westport, and Plattsburgh. The scenery along the way is spectacular.

Among bus companies, **Adirondack-Pine Hill Trailways** (800/225-6815) is the only one that provides service throughout the Adirondacks. **Greyhound** (800/231-2222) travels to Saratoga Springs, Glens Falls, Plattsburgh, and the Thousand Islands.

By far the best ways to explore the North Country are by car, canoe, and foot. The **Adirondack North Country Association** (ANCA, 22 St. Bernard St., Saranac Lake, 518/891-6200, www.adirondack.org) publishes a good map that outlines scenic and historic driving routes; copies can be picked up for free in most tourism offices.

Information and Services

For general information on the Adirondacks, contact the **Adirondack Regional Tourism Council** (Box 2149, Plattsburgh 12901, 518/846-8016 or 800/487-6867, www.adk.com). For general information on the Thousand Islands, contact the **Thousand Islands International Tourism Council** (43373 Collins Landing Rd., Alexandria Bay 13607, 315/482-2520 or 800/847-5263, www.visit1000islands.com).

Adirondack Life (518/946-2191) is a glossy monthly covering a wide variety of Adirondack topics; available at area newsstands.

For more information on the Saratoga area, contact the **Saratoga County Chamber of Commerce** (28 Clinton St., Saratoga 12866, 518/584-3255).

For more information on Lake George and the southeastern Adirondacks, contact the **Lake George Regional Chamber of Commerce** (2176 U.S. 9, Lake George 12845, 518/668-5755 or 800/705-0059, www.lakegeorgechamber.com).

For more information on the Lake Champlain Valley and High Peaks region, contact the **Lake Placid/Essex County Visitors Bureau** (2634 Main St., Lake Placid 12946, 518/523-2445 or 800/447-5224, www.lakeplacid.com).

Other useful area information centers include:

Warren County Department of Tourism (Municipal Center, 1340 Rte. 9, Lake George 12845, www.visitlakegeorge.com)

Plattsburgh-North Country-Lake Champlain Regional Visitors Center (7061 Rte. 9, Plattsburgh, 518/563-1000, www.north-countrychamber.com)

Hamilton County Tourism (White Birch Lake, Indian Lake 12842, 518/648-5239 or 800/648-5239, www.hamiltoncounty.com)

Franklin County Tourism (10 Elm St., Malone 12953, 518/483-9470 800/709-4895, www.adirondacklakes.com)

Town of Webb/Old Forge Tourism Department (Main St., Old Forge 13420, 315/369-6983, www.oldforgeny.com)

Oswego County Department of Promotion and Tourism (46 E. Bridge St., Oswego 13126, 315/349-8322 or 800/248-4386, www.oswegocounty.com)

St. Lawrence County Chamber of Commerce (101 Main St., Canton 13617, 315/386-4000 or 877/228-7810, www.north-country guide.com)

THE FINGER LAKES

According to Iroquois legend, the Finger Lakes were created when the Great Spirit reached out to bless the land and left imprints of his hands behind. Six of his fingers became the major Finger Lakes—Skaneateles, Owasco, Cayuga, Seneca, Keuka, and Canandaigua. The other four became the Little Finger Lakes—Honeoye, Canadice, Hemlock, and Conesus.

Geologists tell it differently. They say the long, skinny parallel lakes formed from the steady progressive grinding of at least two Ice Age glaciers. As the glaciers receded, the lake-valleys filled with rivers that were backed by dams of glacial debris.

The Finger Lakes are a singular place. Depending on the weather, the water varies in hue from a deep sapphire blue to a moody gray, while all around lie fertile farmlands heavy with fruit trees, buckwheat, and—especially—vineyards.

Along the lakes' southern edges, deep craggy gorges are sliced through the middle by silvery waterfalls. To the north preside hundreds of drumlins, or gentle glacier-created hills.

But scenic beauty tells only part of the Finger Lakes story. Despite its somnolent air, the region has an important industrial, civil rights, and religious history. In Auburn stand the homes of abolitionists Harriet Tubman and William Seward; Seneca Falls hosted the first Women's Rights Convention; and in Palmyra is the Sacred Grove where Joseph Smith, founder of the Mormon religion, is said to have first seen the Angel Moroni.

The region also holds a number of interesting small cities. Syracuse, the eastern gateway

COURTESY OF FINGER LAKES WINE COUNTRY TOURISM MARKETING ASSOCIATION

HIGHLIGHTS

◖ Skaneateles Village: The highest and most beautiful of the Finger Lakes is anchored by a picturesque village of the same name, filled with shops and restaurants (page 468).

◖ Seward House: Filled with original artifacts, the former home of the ardent abolitionist William Seward is one of the most interesting house-museums in the state (page 471).

◖ Women's Rights National Historic Park: The site of the first women's rights convention, organized by Elizabeth Cady Stanton and friends, met in the mill town of Seneca Falls in 1848. The park is complete with an informative visitors center and historic sites (page 476).

◖ Herbert F. Johnson Museum of Art: Housed in a striking I.M. Pei–designed building, the museum holds a strong collection of Asian and contemporary art (page 484).

◖ Mark Twain's Study: Modeled after a Mississippi steamboat pilot house, the standalone octagonal study holds the writer's typewriter and other belongings (page 492).

◖ Corning Museum of Glass: The state's third-most-popular tourist destination (after New York City and Niagara Falls) houses a remarkable collection of glass objects spanning over 3,000 centuries (page 495).

◖ Sonnenberg Gardens and Mansion: The former summer home of banker Frederick Ferris Thompson is encircled by one of the most magnificent Victorian-era gardens in America (page 503).

◖ Letchworth State Park: The 17-mile-long "Grand Canyon of the East," Letchworth Gorge is flanked by dark gray cliffs rising about 600 feet (page 510).

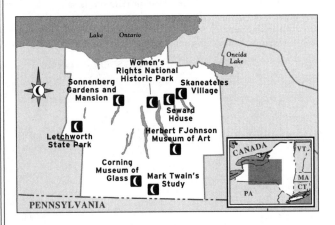

LOOK FOR ◖ TO FIND RECOMMENDED SIGHTS, ACTIVITIES, DINING, AND LODGING.

to the Finger Lakes, was once an Erie Canal boomtown. Ithaca, home to Cornell University, is surrounded by awesome steep gorges and waterfalls. Rochester, the birthplace of Eastman Kodak, is a cultural capital, filled with first-rate museums and theaters.

PLANNING YOUR TIME

The Finger Lakes is one of the largest regions in New York state, and to tour it all would take a good 10 days to two weeks. But it's also possible to see a substantial amount in three or four days, as traffic throughout the region is light and many of the most interesting sites are grouped together.

Most travelers will probably want to start their tour in **Skaneateles,** the prettiest of the Finger Lakes, which can easily be explored in an afternoon. Just down the road is **Auburn,** home to the fascinating house-museums of abolitionists William Seward and Harriet Tubman, and beyond that lies **Seneca Falls,** a must stop for anyone interested in women's history.

Outdoor lovers might want to focus on the southern side of the Finger Lakes region. Here, you'll find **Ithaca,** a university town surrounded by dramatic gorges and great hiking trails; the **Finger Lakes National Forest;** and, at the far western edge of the region, **Letchworth State Park,** home to the "Grand Canyon of the East."

Wine lovers should focus on **Hammondsport** and **Keuka Lake,** which have an especially large number of vineyards, as well as lovely scenic vistas. Culture buffs will want to spend two or three days in **Rochester.**

If you're traveling in July, be sure to find out the date of the **Hill Cumorah Pageant,** the Mormon celebration that commemorates the day when Joseph Smith received the Book of Mormon from the Angel Moroni. The largest, oldest, and most state-of-the-art outdoor drama in the United States, the pageant is well worth traveling out of your way to attend.

HISTORY
The People of the Longhouse

When French explorers first arrived in the Finger Lakes area in the early 1600s, they found it occupied by a confederacy of five Indian nations. The French called the Indians "Iroquois"; the Indians called themselves "Haudenosaunee," or "People of the Longhouse."

The Mohawk Nation (Keepers of the Eastern Door) lived to the east of what is considered the Finger Lakes region, along Schoharie Creek and the Mohawk River Valley. The Seneca (Keepers of the Western Door) lived to the west, along the Genesee River. In the middle were the Onondaga (Keepers of the Council Fire), and it was on their territory the chiefs of the Five Nations met to establish policy and settle disputes. The two other "little brother" nations were the Cayuga, who resided between the Onondaga and the Seneca, and the Oneida, who lived between the Onondaga and the Mohawk. A sixth nation, the Tuscarora, joined the Iroquois confederacy in 1722.

During the Revolutionary War, all of the Iroquois except the Oneida sided with the British, as they had during the French and Indian War. Together with the Tories, they terrorized the pioneer villages and threatened the food supply of the Continental Army. In 1779, an angered General Washington sent Maj. Gen. John Sullivan into the region, ordering him to "lay waste all the settlements around so that the country may not only be overrun but destroyed." Sullivan punctiliously carried out his orders, annihilating 41 Iroquois settlements and burning countless fields and orchards. By the time he was done, the Iroquois nation was in ruins. Thousands fled to Canada; others were resettled onto reservations in 1784.

The Military Tract

After the Revolution, many of Sullivan's soldiers, impressed by the rich farmland they had seen, returned to the Finger Lakes, where they were given land in the "Military Tract" in lieu of payment. The tract, stretching roughly from Chittenango west to Geneva and from Ithaca north to Lake Ontario, covered some two million acres or one-sixteenth of present-day New York. The tract was divided into townships named by a surveyor with a love of the classics,

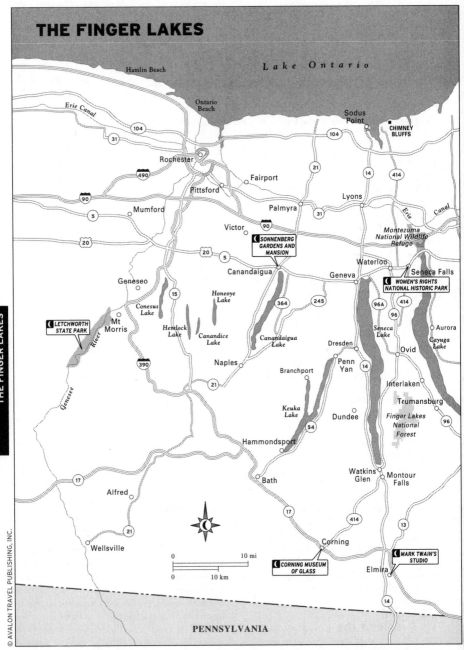

THE FINGER LAKES

Lake Ontario

Hamlin Beach

Ontario Beach

Erie Canal

Sodus Point

■ CHIMNEY BLUFFS

104

31

104

Rochester

Fairport

21

14

414

490

Pittsford

Lyons

Palmyra

Erie Canal

90

Mumford

5

Victor

90

31

Montezuma National Wildlife Refuge

20

☾ SONNENBERG GARDENS AND MANSION

Waterloo

20

5

Canandaigua

Geneva

☾ WOMEN'S RIGHTS NATIONAL HISTORIC PARK

Seneca Falls

Geneseo

15

Honeoye Lake

96A

414

96

Aurora

☾ LETCHWORTH STATE PARK

Conesus Lake

364

245

Seneca Lake

Cayuga Lake

Mt Morris

Hemlock Lake

Canandice Lake

Canandaigua Lake

Dresden

Ovid

Genesee River

390

Naples

Branchport

Penn Yan

14

Interlaken

Keuka Lake

Trumansburg

Dundee

Finger Lakes National Forest

96

21

Hammondsport

Watkins Glen

Montour Falls

17

Alfred

Bath

17

414

13

21

Corning

☾ CORNING MUSEUM OF GLASS

☾ MARK TWAIN'S STUDIO

Wellsville

0   10 mi

0   10 km

Elmira

14

PENNSYLVANIA

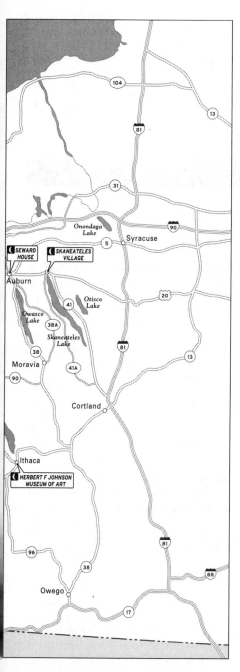

hence the many Greek and Latin names remaining today: Ithaca, Ovid, Cato, Fabius, Manlius, Cicero, Dryden, Ulysses, Hector…

The region developed rapidly. Other settlers from New England and Pennsylvania arrived by the thousands, and by the early 1800s the woodlands of the Iroquois had become a busy agricultural region. Many communities sprang up on the sites of old Iroquois villages; many highways followed old Indian trails.

Prosperity and Reform

By 1825 the Erie Canal was completed, and the development of the Finger Lakes skyrocketed. Inland ports grew up all along the canal, and for 20 years, the area's rich farmland served as the breadbasket of the nation. When the Midwest took over that role, the Finger Lakes' farmers focused on fruit and dairy farming, shipping many of their goods east to New York City.

At the same time, the ports developed into major industrial centers. Extensive water power helped fuel the Industrial Revolution, and by the mid-1800s, factories manufacturing everything from woolens to glass flourished throughout the Finger Lakes. Syracuse, Auburn, Seneca Falls, Elmira, and Rochester were among the largest manufacturing centers.

Along with increasing prosperity came increasing social unrest. Upstate New York in the late 1820s, '30s, and '40s was rocked by one fiery religious movement after another. Sects and cults sprang up all over the region until it became known as the "burned-over district." Among the best-known movements were the Perfectionists, led by John Humphrey Noyes in Oneida to the east; the Mormons, founded by Joseph Smith in Palmyra; and the Spiritualists, led by the Fox sisters near Rochester. The religious fervor not only converted tens of thousands of citizens but also stimulated reform movements. Upstate became a hotbed for humanitarian causes, most notably the abolitionist and women's rights movements. Frederick Douglass and Susan B. Anthony worked in Rochester, Elizabeth Cady Stanton in Seneca Falls, Gerrit Smith in Peterboro and Skaneateles, and William Seward and later Harriet Tubman in Auburn. The first Women's Rights Convention convened in Seneca Falls in 1848, and one of the most dramatic rescues of a fugitive slave took place in Syracuse in 1851.

Modern Times

By the early 1900s, the dust settled. The Erie Canal declined in importance, thanks largely to the advent of the railroad; newer and larger factories opened up elsewhere, and the religious and reform movements lost fervor. The region's major cities remained important commercial centers, to be sure, but the rest of the land eased back into the sleepy agricultural state it is today.

Syracuse

The main streets of Syracuse are oddly wide and flat, fat gray rubber bands stretched out to their sides. It begs the question: who would lay out a city with so much empty space? The answer is simple. One street was once the Erie Canal (Erie Boulevard); another, the Genesee Valley Turnpike (Genesee Street).

Like many towns in central New York, Syracuse boomed with the opening of the Erie Canal. But long before the canal, settlers were attracted to the area by its many valuable salt springs. As early as 1797, the state took over the springs in order to obtain tax revenues on salt, then worth so much it was referred to as "white gold."

With the opening of the Erie Canal, the salt industry developed rapidly, reaching a high point of eight million bushels a year during the Civil War. Other Syracuse industries flourished as well, including foundries and machine shops. The Irish, who had arrived to dig the canal, remained to work the factories and were soon joined by large numbers of German immigrants.

After the Civil War, other industries took over: among them, typewriters, ceramics, and Franklin cars, equipped with air-cooled engines. The Irish and Germans were joined by Italians, Poles, Russians, Ukrainians, and African Americans.

Today, Syracuse still supports a wide variety of peoples and industries, including the Niagara Mohawk Power Corporation, Bristol-Myers Squibb, and Syracuse University. The fourth-largest city in the state (pop. about 165,000), Syracuse also has its share of urban ills.

Orientation

The heart of Syracuse is Clinton Square, where Erie Boulevard and Genesee Street meet. The main business district lies just south of the square and is dominated by Salina and Montgomery Streets. Syracuse University sits on a hill to the southeast, while to the northwest is Onondaga Lake. South of the city, the sovereign 7,300-acre Onondaga Reservation houses about 750 Native Americans. The Iroquois Confederacy's Grand Council of Chiefs still meets here every year, as it has for centuries.

I-90 runs east-west north of downtown. I-81 runs north-south through the center of the city. Street parking is generally available. Sights downtown are within easy walking distance of each other.

DOWNTOWN SIGHTS
Heritage Area Visitor Center and Erie Canal Museum

This long, low-slung 1850s building (318 Erie Blvd., at Montgomery St., 315/471-0593, www.eriecanalmuseum.org, 10 A.M.–5 P.M. Mon.–Sat., 10 A.M.–3 P.M. Sun., free admission) was once an Erie Canal weigh station for boats. Today, it's home to a visitors center, historical exhibits, a theater where a good introductory film on the city is screened, and a 65-foot-long reconstructed canal boat. In the boat remain the original personal effects of some early passengers, including one heart-

THE FINGER LAKES

© AVALON TRAVEL PUBLISHING, INC.

breaking letter from an Irishwoman who had just buried her husband at sea.

Syracuse is one of New York's Heritage Areas—loosely delineated historic districts linked by a common theme. The Syracuse theme is transportation, and business and capital. Free walking-tour brochures can be picked up here.

West on Erie Boulevard

Heading west two blocks from the visitors center, you'll reach the heart of the city, **Clinton Square.** The former intersection of the Erie Canal and Genesee Valley Turnpike, the square in days past teemed with farmers' wagons, ped-dlers' carts, canal boats, hawkers, musicians, and organ grinders. Today, many free outdoor events are held here.

In the mid-1800s, Clinton Square evolved from a marketplace into a financial center. The four bank buildings along Salina Street—all on the National Register of Historic Places—hark back to those days. The four-sided, 100-foot clock tower on the 1867 Gridley Building was originally lit by gas jets.

At the western end of Clinton Square, near Clinton Street, stands the **Jerry Rescue Monument.** The monument commemorates William "Jerry" McHenry, born into slavery in North Carolina about 1812. Jerry successfully

© CHRISTIANE BIRD

Clinton Square, the heart of Syracuse

escaped to Syracuse, where he got a job in a cooper's shop making salt barrels. There he was discovered and arrested by federal marshals in 1851. A vigilante abolitionist group headed by Gerrit Smith and Dr. Samuel J. May attacked the police station and rescued Jerry, who fled to Canada a few days later. That rescue, which challenged the Fugitive Slave Act of 1850, was one of the early precipitating events leading up to the Civil War.

One block further west on Erie Boulevard at Franklin Street reigns the stunning **Niagara Mohawk Power Corporation** building. Completed in 1932, the steel-and-black structure is a superb example of art deco architecture. The edifice is especially worth seeing at night, when lit by colored lights.

Armory Square District
Head south on Franklin Street three blocks, and you'll find yourself in the redbrick Armory Square District, Syracuse's answer to Greenwich Village. At one end hulks the old Syracuse Armory, while all around are shops, cafés, and restaurants. The district centers on the junction of Franklin and Walton Streets.

Rubenstein Museum of Science and Technology
The old Syracuse Armory now houses the MOST, a.k.a. the Rubenstein Museum of Science and Technology (500 S. Franklin St., at W. Jefferson St., 315/425-9068, www.most.org, 11 A.M.–5 P.M. Wed.–Sun., adults $4, seniors and children 2–11 $3.50). The MOST moved into this location in 1992, finishing renovations in 1996.

The armory's former Riding Hall now holds exhibits on the earth, the human body, and the environment; the former Drill Hall showcases a 225-seat IMAX theater (tickets $8). Especially popular with kids are the old 1863 stables, now packed with hands-on exhibits, and the Silverman Planetarium.

Landmark Theatre
Just 1.5 blocks east of the MOST stands the 2,922-seat Landmark Theater (362 S. Salina St., at E. Jefferson St., 315/475-7979, www.landmarktheatre.org, 10 A.M.–5 P.M. Mon.–Fri., tours by appointment), designed in 1928 by Thomas Lamb, a preeminent movie-palace architect. The building's relatively sedate exterior does little to prepare you for its riotous interior—an ornate Indo-Persian fantasy bestrewn with gold carvings. Nearly destroyed by a wrecking ball in the 1970s, the Landmark is now a beloved local institution.

Onondaga Historical Association Museum
One of the best county museums in the state, this fine institution (321 Montgomery St., between E. Jefferson and Fayette Sts., 315/428-1864, www.cnyhistory.org, noon–4 P.M. Wed.–Fri., 11 A.M.–4 P.M. Sat., free admission) covers virtually every aspect of Central New York's history, from the Onondaga Nation and early African American settlers to the Erie Canal and the salt industry. One display explores the 50 breweries that once operated in

Syracuse; another, the city's natural history. A plethora of historic maps, photographs, paintings, and artifacts are displayed.

Everson Museum of Art

Housed in a sleek 1968 building designed by I. M. Pei, the Everson (401 Harrison St., at State St., 315/474-6064, www.everson.org, is open noon–5 P.M. Tues.–Fri. and Sun., 10 A.M.–5 P.M. Sat., free admission) contains one of the world's largest collections of ceramics. The museum also displays small but fine collections of 18th-century American portraits, African and Latin American folk art, and contemporary photography. Temporary exhibits usually focus on one major American artist such as Winslow Homer, Ansel Adams, or Helen Frankenthaler.

ELSEWHERE IN THE CITY
Rosamond Gifford Zoo at Burnet Park

The 36-acre Rosamond Gifford Zoo (500 Burnet Park Dr., off S. Wilbur Ave., 315/435-8511, www.syracusezoo.org, 10 A.M.–4:30 P.M. daily, adults $6; seniors, students, and children 3–15 $4.50) on the west side of town houses close to 1,000 animals and birds living in re-created natural habitats. The various inhabitants enjoy an arctic tundra, a tropical rain forest, an arid desert, and a region called the Wild North, where bears, red pandas, and bison roam free.

Tipperary Hill

Also west of downtown, at the juncture of West Fayette and West Genesee Streets, is the "Gateway to Tipperary Hill." Syracuse's oldest Irish neighborhood, Tipperary Hill is known for its **upside-down traffic light** at the intersection of Tompkins and Lowell Streets—the only one in the country. When the stoplight was first installed, right-side-up, its lenses were immediately destroyed by irate citizens who did not want British red placed above Irish green. The city's fathers, realizing this was one battle they could never win, reversed the lenses to accommodate the neighborhood.

In the heart of today's Tipperary Hill, now only about half Irish, stands the **Cashel House**

(224 Tompkins St., 315/472-4438), packed with goods imported from Ireland. Across the street, **Coleman's Authentic Irish Pub** boasts both human- and leprechaun-size doors, along with Irish pub grub.

Salt Museum

To the north, in the suburb of Liverpool, lies lozenge-shaped Onondaga Lake, whose rich salt deposits first attracted settlers to the area. Unfortunately, the lake is now seriously polluted, but to one side stands a homespun museum (Onondaga Lake Pkwy. [Rte. 370], 315/453-6715 or 315/453-6767, May–Sept. daily noon–6 P.M., free admission) equipped with an original "boiling block." Brine was once turned into salt here through boiling and solar evaporation. On display are battered antique iron kettles, wooden barrels, and other equipment, along with a fascinating collection of historic photographs.

The museum and lake belong to **Onondaga Lake Park,** which also offers bicycle rentals, a tram ride, a playground, and Ste. Marie Among the Iroquois—a second museum on the other side of the parkway.

Ste. Marie Among the Iroquois

Much more elaborate than the Salt Museum, Ste. Marie Among the Iroquois (Onondaga

---

WEIRD, WONDERFUL, OFF-THE-BEATEN PATH FINGER LAKES

Tipperary Hill, Syracuse: Home to the only upside-down traffic light in the country.

Wilder Brain Collection, Cornell University, Ithaca: The eight surviving stars of a human brain collection that once numbered over 1,600.

Wine & Grape Museum of Greyton H. Taylor, Hammondsport: An eccentric collection assembled by a local rebel turned hero.

Caboose Motel, Avoca: Spend the night in one of five red cabooses, salvaged from a railroad yard.

Lake Pkwy. [Rte. 370], 315/453-6767, May–Oct., interpretive guides on site noon–5 P.M. Sat.–Sun., self-guided tours Mon.–Fri., adults $2, seniors $1.50, children $1) re-creates the 17th-century world of the French Jesuits and Iroquois who once lived on the shores of Onondaga Lake. The exhibit begins indoors with displays on the Onondaga, then explores the meeting between the two cultures through artifacts, art, and historical documents.

Outdoors in a re-created French fort, costumed guides forge horseshoes, bake bread, and hollow out canoes. The French only lived in the area for 20 months. The Onondaga welcomed their presence, but the Mohawk did not, and in March 1658 the French withdrew. Their legacy lives on in the large community of Catholic Onondagas residing in Syracuse today.

Owned by the county, the Ste. Marie museum was shut down in 2002, due to a lack of funding, but concerned citizens, who hated to see the beautiful site fall into ruin, started it up again. Today, Ste. Marie is largely volunteer-run.

SPORTS AND RECREATION

Mid-Lakes Navigation (315/685-8500 or 800/545-4318, www.midlakesnav.com) offers excursion and dinner cruises on the Erie Canal. The boats leave from Dutchman's Landing off Route 370 north of Liverpool. The company also offers three-day cruises and has boats available for weekly rental.

Take in a Syracuse University football, basketball, or lacrosse game at the 50,000-seat **Carrier Dome** (900 Irving Ave., 315/443-4634).

ENTERTAINMENT AND EVENTS
Performing Arts

One of the more unusual arts organizations in town is the **Open Hand Theater** (518 Prospect Ave., 315/476-0466, www.openhand-theater.org), featuring giant puppets from around the world. Connected to the theater is an **International Mask and Puppet Museum,** complete with hands-on activities (Mon.–Fri. by appointment).

The **Syracuse Symphony Orchestra,** John H. Mulroy Civic Center (411 Montgomery St., 315/424-8222) performs classical and popular music concerts October–May. The **Landmark Theatre** (362 S. Salina St., 315/475-7979) hosts concerts, plays, dance troupes, and classic movies throughout the year.

Clubs and Nightlife

The best source for what's going on where is the *Syracuse New Times* (315/422-7011), a free alternative newsweekly available throughout the city. Many bars and clubs are located in the **Armory Square District** (for details, visit www.armorysquare.com).

One of the liveliest music clubs in town is **Dinosaur Bar-B-Cue** (246 W. Willow St., 315/476-4937), a friendly hole-in-the-wall filled with dinosaurs and blues paraphernalia, bikers and businesspeople. Live blues is presented most nights.

A good club in which to hear local bands is **Shifty's** (1401 Burnet Ave., 315/474-0048). On weekends, traditional Irish music fills the **Limerick Pub** (134 Walton St., 315/475-1819).

EVENTS

The **Syracuse Jazz Fest** is the largest free jazz festival in the Northeast. The celebration runs for seven days in mid-June, and features a wide variety of jazz events, artists, and styles. In July, the city hosts a smaller but growing **Blues Festival.** In July and August, the Syracuse Pops and the Syracuse Orchestra play **free concerts** in the city's parks. Call 315/470-1910 for more information.

One of the state's grandest parties is the **New York State Fair** (New York State Fairgrounds, 581 State Fair Blvd., Exit 7 off I-690, www.nystate-fair.org, 315/487-7711), featuring agricultural and livestock competitions, music and entertainment, amusement rides and games of chance, business and industrial exhibits, and talent competitions. The fair runs for 12 days, ending on Labor Day, and attracts about 850,000 people.

In November, the **Festival of Nations** (315/470-1910) celebrates the traditions, song, and dance of 35 Native American groups.

ACCOMMODATIONS

In a lovely residential neighborhood just east of downtown stands the **Dickerson House on James** (1504 James St., 315/423-4777, www.dickersonhouse.com, $99–350 d). This stately English Tudor B&B offers five attractive guest rooms filled with antiques, a small garden out back, and a guest kitchen generously stocked with snacks, beer, and wine.

In Fayetteville, 10 miles southeast of Syracuse, find the comfortable **Craftsman Inn** (7300 E. Genesee St., 315/637-8000, www.craftsmaninn.com, $99–180 d), where all 90-odd rooms and suites are furnished in Arts and Crafts style.

Not far from Syracuse University stands **The Marx Hotel and Conference Center** (701 E. Genesee St., 315/479-7000, www.marxsyracuse.com, $99–120 d). Now affiliated with Radisson Hotels, the renovated hostelry offers 285 rooms, an indoor pool, and two popular restaurants. Redfield's is a two-story American bistro with al fresco dining in summer; the Library Lounge, a more intimate spot serving lighter fare.

FOOD

In the Armory Square District, try **Pastabilities** (311 S. Franklin St., 315/474-1153) for home-cooked Italian fare; average entrée $11. Significantly more upscale is **Pascale Wine Bar & Restaurant** (204 W. Fayette St., 315/471-3040), a historic townhouse serving imaginative French-American cuisine and Finger Lakes wines; average entrée $17. The **Lemon Grass Grille and 238 Bistro** (238 W. Jefferson St., 315/475-1111) specializes in Pacific Rim cuisine; average entrée $15.

Dinosaur Bar-B-Cue (246 W. Willow St., 315/476-4937), awhirl with murals of frolicking dinosaurs, serves straightforward barbecue dishes for lunch and dinner.

The Mission Restaurant (304 E. Onondaga St., 315/475-7344) is built to look like a tiny church, complete with a steeple and stained-glass windows. On the menu is Mexican and Caribbean fare, along with great margaritas; average entrée $14.

In Tipperary Hill, **Coleman's Authentic Irish Pub** (100 S. Lowell Ave., 315/476-1933) is a neighborhood institution featuring menus written in both Gaelic and English, and lots of hearty Irish fare. For Old World German food in a simple setting, try **Weber's Grill** (820 Danforth St., 315/472-0480), also a Syracuse institution, located north of downtown.

EXCURSIONS FROM SYRACUSE
Beaver Lake Nature Center

This serene 560-acre nature preserve (8477 East Mud Lake Rd., off Rte. 370, Baldwinsville, 315/638-2519, 7 A.M.–dusk daily, free admission, $2 parking) northwest of Syracuse offers 10 miles of well-marked trails and boardwalks, along with a 200-acre lake that's a favorite resting spot for migrating duck and geese. A visitors center displays exhibits on local flora and fauna.

Highland Forest

Onondaga County's largest and oldest park is the 2,700-acre Highland Forest (off Rte. 80, 315/683-5550, dawn–dusk daily, free admission), in Fabius, about a 30-minute drive southeast of Syracuse. Spread out atop Arab Hill, the park offers great views of the surrounding countryside.

Adirondack-like in appearance, the forest is laced with four hiking trails ranging in length from less than a mile to eight miles. One-hour guided trail rides on horseback are offered April–November; hay and sleigh rides, on fall and winter weekends.

Green Lakes State Park

About 10 miles due east of Syracuse, the 2,000-acre Green Lakes State Park (7900 Green Lakes Rd., off Rte. 290, Fayetteville, 315/637-6111, dawn–dusk daily, $6–8 parking) contains two aquamarine glacial lakes. Facilities include a swimming beach, hiking and biking trails, playground, campground, and 18-hole golf course. Boats can also be rented. For campground reservations, call 800/456-CAMP.

THE FINGER LAKES

Skaneateles Lake Area

The farthest east of the Finger Lakes, deep blue Skaneateles (Scan-ee-AT-i-less) is also the highest (867 feet above sea level) and most beautiful. Fifteen miles long and 1–2 miles wide, the lake is surrounded by gentle rolling hills to the south and more majestic, near-mountainous ones to the north. Iroquois for "long lake," Skaneateles is spring fed, crystal clean, and clear. In the summer, its waters are specked with sailboats; in the winter, ice fishers build igloos.

The only real village on the lake is Skaneateles. Elsewhere along the shoreline preside handsome summer homes placed judicious distances apart.

SKANEATELES

Skaneateles the village spreads out along one long main street (Route 20) at the north end of the lake. Graceful 19th-century homes, white-columned public buildings, and trim brick storefronts are everywhere. Skaneateles has been a favorite retreat among wealthy Syracusans for generations.

The first Europeans in Skaneateles were Moravian missionaries who visited an Onondaga village here in 1750. From 1843 to 1845, the village was the short-lived site of a Utopian community that advertised in the newspapers for followers and advocated communal property, nonviolence, easy divorce, and vegetarianism. Prior to the Civil War, Skaneateles served as the headquarters for abolitionist Gerrit Smith and was an important stop on the Underground Railroad.

◖ Skaneateles Village

In the center of the village is **Clift Park,** a waterfront refuge with a gazebo and wide-angled views of the lake. Docked at the end of a small pier are the two classic wooden boats of the **Mid-Lakes Navigation Co.** (315/685-8500 or 800/545-4318, www.midlakesnav.com). May–September, the spit-and-polish vessels offer sightseeing, lunch, and dinner cruises. These same craft also deliver the mail on Skaneateles Lake—a 100-plus-year-old tradition.

Across from the park stands the hospitable **Sherwood Inn,** a rambling, Colonial blue building that was once a stagecoach stop. The inn was established in 1807 by one Isaac Sherwood, a 300-pound man who began his career by delivering the mail on foot between Utica and Canandaigua, and ended it as the "stagecoach king."

Just down the street is **Krebs** (53 W. Genesee St.), a Finger Lakes institution dating back to 1899. For many years, Krebs reigned as the best restaurant in New York outside Manhattan, and diners flocked here from all over the state. At its peak in 1920, Krebs served 3,000 meals a day.

The Creamery

To learn about the lake's history, step into this small local museum (28 Hannum St., 315/685-1360, 1–4 P.M. Fri. year-round, 1–4 P.M. Thurs.–Sat. May–Sept., free admission) housed in the former Skaneateles Creamery building. From 1899 to 1949, area farmers brought their milk here to be turned into buttermilk, cream, and butter. Displays include scale models of the boats that once sailed the lake, exhibits on dairy farming, and information about the teasel, a thistle-like plant once used in woolen mills to raise a cloth's nap. For 120 years, Skaneateles was the teasel-growing capital of the United States. The Creamery is run by the **Skaneateles Historical Society,** which also offers walking tours of the village.

Scenic Drives

For spectacular views of the lake, drive down either Route 41 to the east or Route 41A to the west. Route 41A veers away from the shoreline at the southern end and leads to **New Hope Mills** (315/497-0783, 9 A.M.–5 P.M. Mon.–Fri. and 10 A.M.–2 P.M. Sat. May–Dec.), an 1823 flour mill where grain is still ground with granite and burr stones operated by a 26-foot overshot waterwheel. Unbleached flours and grains are for sale.

Events

Weekly **sailboat races** take place throughout the summer, while free **band concerts** are held on Friday evenings in Clift Park. **Polo games** are played on Sunday afternoons in July and August at the Skaneateles Polo Club (West Lake and Andrews Rds.). Since 1980, the **Skaneateles Festival** (www.skanfest.org) has been bringing top chamber-music artists to town in August. The town's largest event is the **antique and classic boat show** in early July.

Accommodations

The upscale yet casual 🄲 **Sherwood Inn** (26 W. Genesee St., 315/685-3405, www.thesherwoodinn.com) includes a very popular restaurant serving traditional American fare (average entrée $15), a tavern with frequent live entertainment, and 24 attractive guest rooms, all decorated with antiques. Contributing to the inn's relaxed atmosphere are a big screened-in porch with wonderful views of the lake, an outdoor patio for summer dining, lots of fresh flowers, and a snug lounge ($95–195 d).

Near the heart of downtown is **The Gray House** (47 Jordan St., 315/685-0131, $89–150 d), a welcoming B&B housed in a spacious Victorian home, complete with four guest rooms, a large parlor, two breezy porches, and gardens.

A half mile east of downtown is the **Bird's Nest Motel** (1601 E. Genesee St., 315/685-5641, $55–99 d), with a pond, pool, nature trails, and simple but comfortable rooms and suites.

On the outskirts of Skaneateles is the ultra-luxurious **Mirbeau Inn and Spa** (851 W. Genesee St., 315/685-5006 or 877/MIRBEAU, www.mirbeau.com, $185–385 d). An elegant, European-style inn complete with wall frescoes, waterfalls, soft lighting, and 34 spacious guest rooms, the Mirbeau offers a wide variety of spa treatments. The inn is also known for its serene restaurant, serving creative American cuisine that uses fresh local ingredients. The menu often changes daily; four- and five-course prix fixe dinners cost $49–54.

Food

One of the oldest restaurants in the Finger Lakes (Franklin Roosevelt and Charles Lindbergh once ate here), 🄲 **Krebs** (53 W. Genesee St., 315/685-5714, open May–Oct. for dinner only), is most famous for its seven-course continental dinners ($44 per person), but also serves lighter fare. Three basic entrés are served—chicken, lobster, and prime rib—along with homemade soups and baked goods. Out back is a formal garden while upstairs is a low-ceilinged tavern where locals congregate.

The laid-back 🄲 **Doug's Fish Fry** (8 Jordan St., 315/685-3288) is a local favorite, renowned for its chowder, fried scallops, gumbo, and fish sandwiches. Tasty pancakes, soups, sandwiches, and burgers are served at **Johnny Angel's Heavenly Hamburgers** (22 Jordan St., 315/685-0100).

Rosalie's Cucina (841 W. Genesee St., 315/685-2200) offers first-rate Italian fare, ranging from pizza and pasta to grilled lobster tails, in an adobe taverna; average entrée $17. For fresh Japanese food in a peaceful setting, step into **Kabuki** (12 W. Genesee St., 315/685-7234); dinner entrés $8–20.

The **Sherwood Inn** and **Mirbeau** are also excellent dining choices (see *Accommodations,* above).

CORTLAND

About 12 miles from the southern tip of Skaneateles Lake sprawls the city of Cortland (pop. 19,800). Set in the midst of fertile farm country, Cortland was once a small industrial center, best known for its wire cloth, lingerie, and corset factories. Along Main Street between Tompkins Street and Clinton Avenue is a **National Historic District** of handsome homes and commercial buildings.

Cortland also claims literary fame. It was here that Chester Gillette, the real-life counterpart to the character Clyde Griffiths in Theodore Dreiser's *An American Tragedy,* met Grace Brown. Writes Dreiser of Griffiths' arrival in his new hometown: "He found himself ambling on and on until suddenly he was… in touch with a wide and tree-shaded thoroughfare of residences, the houses of which, each and every one, appeared to possess more room space, lawn space, general ease and repose and dignity even than any with which he had ever been in contact. ..." Gillette once worked in his uncle's Gillette Skirt Factory on the north side of town, and lived in the still-standing double house at No. 17 East Main Street.

Historic Sights

Perhaps one of the houses spotted by Gillette-Griffiths in his ramble was the castlelike **1890 House Museum** (37 Tompkins St. [Rte. 13], 607/756-7551, 1–4 P.M. Tues.–Sun. Apr.–Jan., adults $3.50, seniors and students $2.50, children under 12 free), built by wire manufacturer Chester F. Wickwire. Now an informal museum, the house holds 30 rooms filled with parquet floors, stained-glass windows, ornate stenciling, and hand-carved woodwork. Above the top floor, a tower provides excellent views of the town. Walking-tour maps of Cortland's Historic District can be picked up here.

Cortland Country Music Park

Part RV camp, part country-music mecca, this 18-acre site (1804 Truxton Rd. [Rte. 13], one mile north of the I-88 intersection, 607/753-0377, www.cortlandcountrymusicpark.com) bills itself as the "great Nashville of the North-east." During the summer, four or five concerts by such top performers as Roy Acuff and Kenny Rogers are staged, along with two-steppin' dance classes, square dances, and jamborees. The park offers live music by regional bands weekends year-round, and special events including horseshoe tournaments, the Old Timers Show, and the Festival of Bands.

Largely built by volunteer fans, the music park was started up in 1975. Centered on a low-slung Opry barn, it is equipped with one of the largest dance floors in the Northeast, an outdoor stage, and a Hall of Fame Museum (open only during events). In the museum, you'll find everything from a black-sequined dress formerly owned by Tammy Wynette to white boots once worn by Roy Acuff.

Shopping

It's worth traveling about eight miles south of Cortland to visit the **Book Barn of the Finger Lakes** (198 North Rd., Dryden, 607/844-9365, 10 A.M.–5:30 P.M. Mon.–Sat., noon–5 P.M. Sun.). The sprawling 1850s barn houses nearly 98,000 used, rare, and scholarly books. It is run by Vladimer Dragan, who buys and sells all his books in person, even making house calls to estates and libraries. The bookstore is located off Route 13 opposite the Tompkins-Cortland Community College.

Owasco Lake Area

The smallest of the major Finger Lakes, Owasco is 12 miles long and 1.5 miles wide at its widest point. Iroquois for "the crossing," it lies 720 feet above sea level. For great views of Owasco, take Route 38 south, hugging the western shore, or Route 38A south, which travels high above the lake to the east. A few miles down, Route 38A bumps into Rockefeller Road, a shoreline route lined with 150-year-old camps and houses.

At the northern end of Owasco sits the city of Auburn, population 31,200. At the south-ern end are the village of Moravia, birthplace of President Millard Fillmore, the Fillmore Glen State Park, and miles of farm country.

AUBURN

For a small industrial city, Auburn has been home to an unusually high number of remarkable men and women. Among them are Logan, or Tahgahjute, the Iroquois orator; Harriet Tubman, the African American leader; William H. Seward, the visionary statesman; Thomas Mott Osborne, the pioneer of prison reform; and

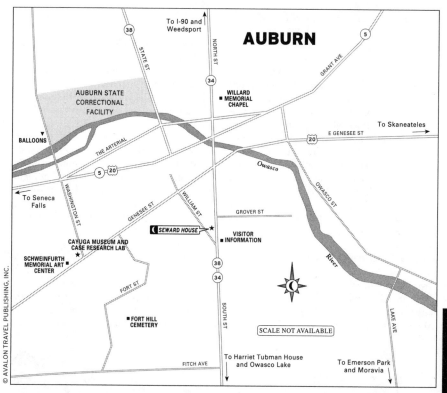

© AVALON TRAVEL PUBLISHING, INC.

Theodore W. Case, the inventor of sound film. Tributes to all can be found in the city.

Before the invasion of the whites, Auburn was a Cayuga Indian village established at the junction of two trails. Revolutionary War veteran Col. John Hardenbergh arrived in 1793 and built the area's first gristmill. By 1810, the budding village boasted 90 dwellings, 17 mills, and an incorporated library containing 200 books.

The opening of the Auburn State Prison in 1817 and the Auburn Theological Seminary in 1821 greatly stimulated growth, and by the mid-1800s, Auburn was thriving. It even entertained hopes of becoming the state capital. The impressive public buildings on Capitol Street and lavish private homes on State Street date back to those heady days.

❰ Seward House

One of the most interesting house museums in New York is this stately 1816 Federal-style home shaded by leafy trees (33 South St., 315/252-1283, www.sewardhouse.org, 10 A.M.–4 P.M. Tues.–Sat. and 1–4 P.M. Sun. July–Oct., 1–4 P.M. Tues.–Sat. Oct.–June, closed Jan., adults $5, seniors $4, students $2, under 12 free). The house belonged to William H. Seward, ardent abolitionist, New York governor, and U.S. senator, best remembered for purchasing Alaska from the Russians in 1857. Seward also served as Lincoln's secretary of state and was almost assassinated by a co-conspirator of John Wilkes Booth at the same time as the president.

Amazingly, almost everything in the Seward house is original. Inside you'll find not only

Seward's furniture, but his grocery bills, top hats, pipe collection, snuff-box collection, 10,000 books, political campaign buttons, tea from the Boston Tea Party, personal letters from Abraham Lincoln, and calling cards of former visitors Horace Greeley, Frederick Douglass, Millard Fillmore, and Daniel Webster.

Seward first moved to Auburn for the love of Miss Frances Miller, whose father, Judge Elijah Miller, built the house. As a newly minted lawyer, Seward got a job in the judge's law firm, and proposed to his daughter. The ornery judge allowed the liaison on one condition: Seward could never take his daughter away from him. Seward agreed and, despite his enormous worldly success, lived under his father-in-law's thumb for the next 27 years.

Harriet Tubman Home

On the outskirts of Auburn, next door to the AME Zion Church, stands a brick house and adjacent white clapboard house wrapped with a long front porch (180 South St., 315/252-2081, 10 A.M.–4 P.M. Tues.–Fri. and 10 A.M.–3 P.M.

Sat. Feb.–Oct., last tour one hour before closing, adults $4.50, seniors $3, children $1.50). Harriet Tubman, known as the "Moses of her people," settled here after the Civil War, largely because her close friend and fellow abolitionist William Seward lived nearby.

Born a slave in Maryland in 1820 or 1821, Tubman escaped in 1849, fleeing first to Philadelphia and then to Canada. Yet as long as others remained in captivity, her freedom meant little to her. During the next dozen years, she risked 19 trips south, rescuing more than 300 slaves. She mostly traveled alone and at night. Her motto: "Keep going; children, if you are tired, keep going; if you are scared, keep going; if you are hungry, keep going; if you want to taste freedom, keep going."

A visit to the Tubman property begins in a small museum exhibiting displays on famous African American women and a video on Tubman's life. Afterward, a member of the AME Zion Church takes visitors on a tour of the clapboard house where Tubman tended to the elderly and where a few of her belongings—

Harriet Tubman tended to the elderly in a home near the AME Zion Church.

including her bed and Bible—are on display. Tubman herself lived in the brick house, which is not open to the public.

Fort Hill Cemetery

Harriet Tubman, William Seward, and numerous other Auburn notables are buried in the Fort Hill Cemetery (19 Fort St., 315/253-8132, 9 A.M.–4 P.M. Mon.–Fri.), on a hill to the west side of State Street. Native Americans used the site as burial grounds as early as A.D. 1100.

A large stone fortress-gate marks the cemetery entrance, while inside towers the 56-foot-high **Logan Monument.** Erected upon a mound believed to be an ancient Native American altar, the monument pays homage to Logan, or Tahgahjute, the famed Cayuga orator born near Auburn in 1727. Logan befriended the European settlers until 1774, when a group of marauding Englishmen massacred his entire family in the Ohio Valley. In retaliation, he scalped more than 30 white men. Later that same year in Virginia, at a conference with the British, he gave one of the most moving speeches in early American history. "Logan never felt fear," he said. "He will not turn his heel to save his life. Who is there to mourn for Logan? Not one."

Cayuga Museum and Case Research Lab

Housed in a musty Greek Revival mansion, the Cayuga Museum (203 Genesee St., 315/253-8051, 10 A.M.–5 P.M. Sat.–Sun. and noon–5 P.M. Tues.–Fri. Feb.–Dec., free admission) is devoted to local history. Exhibits cover early Native American culture, the Civil War, the Auburn Correctional Facility, Millard Fillmore, and women's rights.

Behind the museum mansion stands a simple, low-slung building known as the Case Research Lab. Here, in 1923, Theodore W. Case and E. I. Sponable invented the first commercially successful sound film, ushering in the movie era. Displays include the first sound camera and projector, original lab equipment, and Case's correspondence with Thomas Edison and Lee De Forest, a self-

promoter who claimed *he* was the inventor of sound film.

Schweinfurth Memorial Art Center

Behind the Cayuga Museum, a modest art center (205 Genesee St., 315/255-1553, 10 A.M.–5 P.M. Tues.–Sat., 1–5 P.M. Sun., closed Jan., admission by donation) features temporary exhibits by contemporary and classic artists. Shows feature everything from fine art and photography to folk art and architecture. Each winter the museum hosts a popular quilt show.

Willard Memorial Chapel

The only complete Tiffany chapel known to exist, the Willard Memorial (17 Nelson St., 315/252-0339, 10 A.M.–4 P.M. Tues.–Fri and summer Sat. mornings, suggested donation $3) glows with the muted, bejeweled light of 15 windows handcrafted by the Tiffany Glass and Decorating Company. Louis C. Tiffany also designed the chapel's handsome oak furniture inlaid with mosaics, leaded-glass chandeliers, and gold-stenciled pulpit.

A visit to the chapel begins with a video on the chapel's history and the now-defunct Auburn Theological Seminary of which it was once a part. In July and August, free organ recitals and concerts are played in the chapel.

Auburn State Correctional Facility

Near the center of the city, along the arterial between State and Washington Streets, looms one of the area's foremost employers: the Auburn State Correctional Facility. Established in 1816, New York's oldest prison has had a long and grim history.

Auburn was the first facility to institute solitary cells: 3.5 by 7 by 7 feet, the smallest possible area in which a human could both lie down and stand up. Auburn also devised the shower bath punishment, in which prisoners endured cold water poured over them. Under the "silent system," prisoners were marched lock-step to fields and contract shops and forced to work all day without saying a word, then marched back again. Guards brandishing whips made sure no one spoke.

Despite, or perhaps because of, all this, visitors flocked from all over the country to tour the prison in the early years. Admission cost 12.5 cents until 1822, when the fee doubled to 25 cents to stem the over-enthusiastic tide.

In 1890 at Auburn the first person in the world to be put to death—a murderer from Buffalo—met his fate in an electric chair. Others executed at Auburn before executions shifted in 1916 to Sing Sing included Leon Czolgosz, the assassin of President McKinley; and Chester Gillette, upon whose life Theodore Dreiser's *An American Tragedy* is based.

In 1913 state prisoner commissioner Thomas Mott Osborne brought relief to Auburn inmates. After serving undercover for a week, Osborne introduced the ideas of prisoner self-government and education. Riots in 1929 resulted in still more improvements and by the 1950s, the Auburn prison had been rebuilt. Today it continues to function as a walled, maximum-security facility.

Accommodations and Food

One mile south of Auburn you'll find the **Springside Inn** (41 W. Lake Rd. [Rte. 38], 315/252-7247, www.springsideinn.com), a striking red Victorian with big white porches. The inn is best known for its restaurant, which is a local favorite for special occasions; on the menu are such traditional American dishes as shrimp Newburg, Long Island Duck, steak, and lobster (dinner and Sunday brunch only;

entrées cost $9–20). Upstairs are a half-dozen renovated guest rooms furnished with antiques ($100–200 d).

Balloons (65 Washington St., across from the state prison, 315/252-9761) is a friendly spot with an art deco decor, serving heaping platters of Italian food since 1934.

MORAVIA

Well off the beaten track, this small village boasts a number of handsome 19th-century buildings and the 1820s **St. Matthew's Episcopal Church** (14 Church St., 315/497-1171). The sanctuary's interior is covered with elaborate oak carvings designed and executed in Oberammergau, Germany.

Fillmore Glen State Park

Just south of the village lies the 857-acre Fillmore Glen State Park (Rte. 38, 315/497-0130, dawn–dusk daily, $6–8 parking), centered on a deep and rugged ravine with five spectacular waterfalls. At the foot of the main falls is a geometric rock formation known as the Cowpens, and a popular swimming hole. Nearby await hiking trails, a campground, and a playground. For campground reservations, call 800/456-CAMP.

The park also contains a replica of the tiny log cabin in which President Millard Fillmore was born. His actual birthplace lies about five miles east of the park. Fillmore grew up dirt poor and went to work at an early age; he later described his upbringing as "completely shut out from the enterprises of civilization and advancement."

Cayuga Lake Area

The longest of the Finger Lakes, Cayuga stretches out for 38 moody miles, 381 feet above sea level. It varies in depth from a few feet to 435 feet, and supports a wide variety of marinelife. In shallow waters swim carp and large-mouth bass; in deeper ones, northern pike and lake trout.

Iroquois for "boat landing," Cayuga was named after the Iroquois nation that originally lived along and farmed its shores. The Cayugas were called Gue-u-gweh-o-no, or people of the muckland, exemplified by the once-enormous Montezuma Marsh at the northern end of the lake.

Today, just south of the marsh, sits Seneca Falls, the small industrial town where the first Women's Rights Convention met in 1848. Anchoring the southern end of the lake is Ithaca, a friendly cultural center that's home to Cornell University, Ithaca College, and craggy gorges with waterfalls higher than Niagara. Along the lake's western shores are a half-dozen wineries; on the eastern shores, the historic village of Aurora.

SENECA FALLS

Seneca Falls owes its early development to a series of waterfalls dropping over 50 feet. The first gristmill was built here in 1795, and by the 1840s, the town supported dozens of water-powered factories. Many employed women worked 14-hour days for wages they had to turn over to their husbands. In 1840s America, women were not allowed to own money or property or to even serve as legal guardians of their own children.

Elizabeth Cady Stanton and her abolitionist husband Henry Stanton moved to Seneca Falls from Boston in 1847, a time when Seneca Falls was a major transportation hub and the Finger Lakes, a center for the abolitionist movement. Often home alone, caring for her children, Stanton felt isolated and overwhelmed by housework. She also noticed the worse plight of her poorer neighbors: "Alas! alas!," she wrote in her autobiography *Eighty Years and More,* "Who can measure the mountains of sorrow and suffering endured in unwelcome motherhood in the abodes of ignorance, poverty, and vice. ..."

On July 13, 1848, Stanton shared her discontent with four friends; then and there the group decided to convene a discussion on the status of women. They set a date for six days thence and published announcements in the local papers. About 300 people—men and women—showed up, a Declaration of Sentiments was issued, and the women deemed the convention a success. They were little prepared for the nationwide storm of outrage and ridicule that followed. Their lives, the town of Seneca Falls, and the nation would never be the same.

Orientation

Seneca Falls centers around Fall Street (Rtes. 5 and 20). Running parallel is the Seneca River and the Cayuga-Seneca Canal, which links Cayuga and Seneca Lakes. At the eastern end of town is the artificially constructed Van Cleef Lake.

Heritage Area Visitors Center

For a good general introduction to Seneca Falls, stop into this center (115 Fall St., 315/568-6894, 10 A.M.–4 P.M. Mon.–Sat., noon–4 P.M. Sun., free admission). The exhibits cover virtually every aspect of the town's history, from its Iroquois beginnings and early factory days to its women's history and ethnic heritage.

Seneca Falls is one of New York State's Heritage Areas—loosely designated historic districts linked by a common theme. The Seneca Falls theme is reform movements, but the center pays at least equal attention to the town's industrial past. Seneca Falls once held world fame for its knitting mills and pump factories, several of which still operate.

Don't leave the center without learning about the destruction of the city's once invaluable waterfalls. The falls were eliminated in 1915 to create the Cayuga-Seneca Canal and,

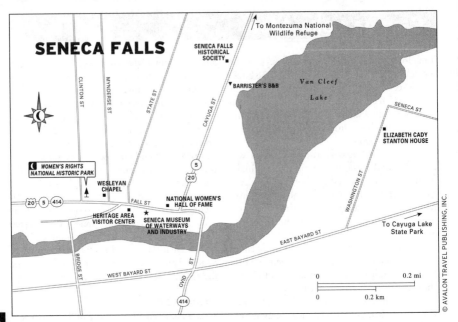

THE FINGER LAKES

by extension, Van Cleef Lake. The flooding destroyed more than 150 buildings, and today, many foundations are still visible beneath the lake's clear waters.

Women's Rights National Historic Park

Down the street from the visitors center stand the ruins of the **Wesleyan Chapel** (126 Fall St.), where the historic 1848 convention took place. Alas, all that remains of the church today are two fragile brick walls and a piece of roof. The nearby 140-foot-long wall and fountain bears the Declaration of Sentiments: "We hold these truths to be self-evident; that all men and women are created equal. ..."

Across the street from the chapel, in the spacious, two-story **Women's Rights Visitor Center** (136 Fall St., 315/568-2991, 9 A.M.– 5 P.M. daily, adults $3, under 17 free), you'll find exhibits on the convention, its leaders, and the times in which they lived. Other sections focus on such women's issues as em-

ployment, marriage, fashion, and sports. The exhibits are overly wordy, but there's lots of information here, along with free handouts and a good bookstore.

Elizabeth Cady Stanton House

Also part of the Women's Rights National Historic Park, the Stanton house (32 Washington St.) is about a mile from the visitors center on the other side of Van Cleef Lake. Stanton lived here with her husband and seven children from 1846 to 1862. During much of that time, she wrote extensively about women's rights.

Among the many reformers who frequented the Stanton home was Amelia Bloomer, the woman who popularized the pantaloons that bear her name. Though a resident of Seneca Falls, Bloomer did not sign the Declaration of Sentiments, believing it to be too radical.

Today, the airy Stanton home has been meticulously restored. Few furnishings remain, but everything is authentic, including the bronze cast of Stanton's hand clasping that of Susan B. Anthony's. Stanton met Anthony soon after the 1848 convention, and the women worked closely together throughout their lives.

House tours are offered daily June–September ($1 per person). Visitors must sign up for the tours at the visitors center.

Mary Baker Eddy Museum

One block down from the Women's Rights National Historical Park stands a small museum dedicated to the life of Mary Baker Eddy (118 Fall St., 315/568-6488, www.marybakereddy.com, call for hours, free admission). Interactive displays document the life of this 19th-century woman who challenged conventional thinking in theology, science, and medicine.

Seneca Museum of Waterways and Industry

Housed in a historic building, this museum (89 Fall St., 315/568-1510, www.senecamuseum.org, 11 A.M.–5 P.M. Tues.–Sat. and 1–5 P.M. Sun. June–Aug., free admission) is filled with exhibits on the history of the village and its surrounding waterways. A colorful 35-foot mural lines one wall, while elsewhere are antique fire engines, pumps, looms, and printing presses. One exhibit shows how the Erie Canal was built, another is a working lock model.

National Women's Hall of Fame

The Women's Hall of Fame (76 Fall St., 315/568-8060, www.greatwomen.org, 10 A.M.–5 P.M. Mon.–Sat. and noon–4 P.M. Sun. May–Oct., 11 A.M.–4 P.M. Wed.–Sat. Nov.–Apr., adults $3, seniors and students $1.50, children under 6 free) bills itself as "the only national membership organization devoted exclusively to the accomplishments of American women." Blown-up photos and plaques pay homage to everyone from painter Mary Cassatt to anthropologist Margaret Mead.

Seneca Falls Historical Society

Formerly known as the Mynderse/Partridge/Becker House, this museum (55 Cayuga St., 315/568-8412, 8:30 A.M.–4 P.M. Mon.–Fri. year-round, noon–4 P.M. Sat.–Sun. in summer, adults $3, seniors and students $1.50, families $7) is housed in a notable Queen Anne home, set back from the street behind an iron fence. Inside, 23 elegant rooms feature period furnishings, elaborate woodwork, and an extensive costume collection. A rare collection of 19th-century circus toys is strewn through the children's playroom.

Montezuma National Wildlife Refuge

Five miles east of Seneca Falls is the Montezuma Wildlife Refuge (3395 Rtes. 5 and 20E [Exit 40 or 41 off I-90], 315/568-5987, dawn–dusk daily Apr.–Nov., free admission), a haven for migrating and nesting birds. Spread out over 6,300 acres of swamplands, marshlands, and fields, the refuge includes a visitors center, nature trail, driving trail, and two observation towers. Nearly 315 species of birds have been spotted in the refuge since it was established in 1937. Migrating waterfowl arrive by the tens of thousands in mid-April and early October. Late May to early June is a good time to spot warblers; in mid-September, the refuge fills with shorebirds and wading birds.

Before the turn of the century, Montezuma Marsh was many times its current size, stretching about 12 miles long and up to eight miles wide. The Erie Canal and Cayuga Lake dam projects greatly reduced its size.

Cayuga Lake State Park

Three miles east of Seneca Falls lies the 190-acre Cayuga Lake State Park (off Rte. 89, 315/568-5163, dawn–dusk daily, $6–8 for parking), offering a swimming beach, a bathhouse, hiking trails, a playground, and a 287-site campground. In the late 1700s, the park was part of a Cayuga Indian reservation, and in the late 1800s it was a resort area serviced by a train from Seneca Falls. The state park was established here in 1928. To reserve a campsite, call 800/456-CAMP.

THE FINGER LAKES

Accommodations

Several lovely B&Bs are in the heart of Seneca Falls. The 1855 **Hubbell House** (42 Cayuga St., 315/568-9690, www.hubbellhousebb.com, $105–135 d), built in "Gothic cottage" style, overlooks Van Cleef Lake. Downstairs are a large double parlor, library, and dining room; upstairs are four guest rooms furnished with antiques.

The 1825 **Van Cleef Homestead B&B** (86 Cayuga St., 315/568-2275, www.flare.net/van-cleef, $90–110 d) was built by Seneca Falls' first permanent resident, Lawrence Van Cleef. It's a Federal-style home offering three comfortable, air-conditioned guest rooms and a swimming pool.

The large, historic **(Barristers Bed and Breakfast** (56 Cayuga St., 800/914-6145, www.sleepbarristers.com, $110–155 d), built by master craftsmen in the 1800s, features five spacious guest rooms furnished with antiques, a large front porch, cozy common room, and stone patio with a fire pit, perfect for sitting around on cool evenings. Guest amenities include a refreshment center.

Food

There's something for everyone at the **Pump House** (16 Rumsey St., 315/568-9109, main dishes $6–14), which offers a wide variety of healthy dishes, including veggie and tuna wraps, steaks, pasta, and seafood.

Events

The **Convention Days Celebration** (800/732-1848), commemorating the first Women's Rights Convention, takes place on the weekend closest to July 19–20. Featured are concerts, dances, speeches, historical tours, food, kids' events, and a re-enactment of the signing of the Declaration of Sentiments.

WATERLOO

A few miles west of Seneca Falls on Routes 5 and 20 is Waterloo, a surprisingly busy

THE VINEYARDS OF THE FINGER LAKES

The hills of the Finger Lakes, covered with vineyards, glow pale green in spring, dust green in summer, red-brown-purple in fall. Ideal grape-growing conditions came about tens of thousands of years ago when the retreating glaciers deposited a layer of topsoil on shale beds above the lakes. The lakes in turn create a microclimate that moderates the region's temperatures.

In 1829 near Hammondsport, a Reverend Bostwick planted a few grapevines to make sacramental wine. His successful efforts were duly noted by his neighbors, and soon vineyards ringed the village. In 1860, 13 Hammondsport businesspeople banded together to form the country's first commercial winery – the Pleasant Valley Wine Company – and dozens of other entrepreneurs soon followed suit.

For many years, the Finger Lakes vineyards produced only native American Concord, Delaware, and Niagara grapes, used in the production of ho-hum sweet and table wines. About 25 years ago, however, several viticulturists began experimenting with the more complex European Vinifera grape, and today, excellent chardonnays, Rieslings, seyval blancs, and sparkling wines are made throughout the region.

The Finger Lakes currently boasts close to 50 wineries, ranging in size from giant commercial Widmer's (in Naples) to small, family-run McGregor's (in Dundee). Most hug the shores of Cayuga, Seneca, or Keuka Lakes, and each lake has its own wine-growing association that publishes free maps and brochures, available throughout the region.

Most wineries are open May–October, 10 A.M.–5 P.M. Monday–Saturday and noon–5 P.M. Sunday, with more limited hours off-season. Tastings are usually free, but sometimes cost $1-2.

Some of the region's best wineries are described by geographic location throughout this chapter. For a complete list, contact the **New York Wine and Grape Foundation** (315/536-7442, www.newyorkwines.org).

village filled with aging red-brick buildings and shady trees. As a plaque along Main Street attests, Waterloo claims to be the birthplace of Memorial Day. Originally known as Declaration Day, the event apparently first took place here on May 5, 1866, in honor of the Civil War dead. Flags flew at half-mast, businesses closed, and a solemn parade marched down Main Street. In 1966, the U.S. Congress and President Johnson officially recognized Waterloo as the birthplace of Memorial Day.

In the middle of town reigns the **Terwilliger Museum** (31 E. Main St., 315/539-0533, 1–4 P.M. Tues.–Fri.). Here you'll find a reconstructed Native American longhouse and village store, along with antique pianos, carriages, fire equipment, and a 1914 Waterloo mural.

AURORA

Halfway down Cayuga's expansive eastern shore is picture-perfect Aurora, its houses laid out like beads on a string. Most date back to the mid-1800s; the entire village is on the National Register of Historic Places.

Called Deawendote, or Village of Constant Dawn, by the Cayuga, Aurora attracted its first white settlers in the late 1780s. Henry Wells founded Wells College here in 1868, and the school—a premier liberal arts college for women that only went coed in 2005—remains a focal point of Main Street.

Also in Aurora is **MacKenzie-Childs** (3260 N. Main St. [Rte. 90], 315/364-7123, 9:30 A.M.–6 P.M. daily, call for studio tour information), a classy home-furnishings-design studio best known for its whimsical terra-cotta pottery. The studio employs about 100 craftspeople, who design everything from glassware to lamps, and is housed on a 19th-century estate with great views of the lake.

Accommodations and Food

In the center of Aurora presides the lovely 1833 **Aurora Inn** (391 Main St. (Rte. 90), www.aurorainn.com, $125–350 d). Owned by Wells College, the red-brick inn with its wide white balconies and well-groomed gardens was re-

cently restored. Inside, find 10 luxurious guestrooms furnished with antiques and oriental rugs, a waterside restaurant with views of the lake, and a cozy tavern with a fireplace and mahogany bar. On the menu is classic American cuisine; average entrée $20.

Entertainment

The charming, turn-of-the-century **Morgan Opera House** (Rte. 90 at Cherry Ave., 315/364-5437) offers musical and dramatic events May–September.

ROMULUS

Midway down the west side of the lake lies Romulus, known for its vineyards and wineries. Two of the best, only five miles apart, are the **Swedish Hill Vineyard** (4565 Rte. 414, 315/549-8326, www.swedishhill.com) and the **Knapp Winery, Vineyards, and Restaurant** (2770 County Rd. 128, 607/869-9271, www.knappwine.com). Swedish Hill, a very large operation, produces about 30,000 cases of 25 different kinds of wines a year; Knapp is much smaller, but its wines are among the region's finest. Both wineries are open Apr.–Dec., Mon.–Sat. 10 A.M.–5 P.M. and Sun. noon–5 P.M.; call for off-season hours.

The breezy **Knapp Winery Restaurant** (607/869-9481) serves lunch daily April–October and dinner on summer weekends; call for hours. Local produce is emphasized (average lunch entrée $8, average dinner entrée $18).

OVID

Heading south of Romulus on Route 96, you'll come to the hamlet of Ovid, astride a small ridge surrounded by farmland. In the heart of the village stand three red-brick Greek Revival buildings known as the **Three Bears** because of how they diminish progressively in size. The "Papa Bear" was once the county courthouse; "Mama Bear," the village library; and "Baby Bear," the county jail. Today, the buildings house county offices.

Camping and Accommodations

Off Route 89 overlooking Cayuga Lake is

THE FINGER LAKES

Sned-Acres Campground (6590 Cayuga Lake Rd., 607/869-9787), a good place for families, as it's equipped with a playground and miniature golf course.

Nearby lies the **Driftwood Inn** (Rte. 89, Sheldrake-on-Cayuga, 607/532-4324, $85–135 d), offering four guest rooms in the main house, two efficiency units, and two housekeeping cottages. Out front is a 260-foot-long waterfront equipped with small boats and views of the lake.

The **Tillinghast Manor B&B** (7246 S. Main St., 607/869-3584, $75–85 d) is a palatial Victorian mansion with a square central tower, an inviting porch, and a large circular drive. Inside is a grand walnut staircase and five spacious guest rooms with king-size beds.

TRUMANSBURG

About 10 miles north of Ithaca thunder **Taughannock Falls,** a skinny but dazzling 215-foot-long stream of water flanked on either side by towering stone walls. Just 10,000 years ago, the falls cascaded straight down into Cayuga Lake, but erosion has moved them almost a mile inland. Thirty feet higher than Niagara, Taughannock Falls are the highest straight falls east of the Rockies.

The falls are situated within the 783-acre **Taughannock Falls State Park** (Rte. 89, 607/387-6739, dawn–dusk daily, $6–8 for parking), which also offers lake swimming, fishing, boating, hiking, cabins, and a 76-site campground. Children will enjoy the park's imaginative playground, equipped with wooden towers and platforms. For campground reservations, call 800/456-CAMP.

Accommodations and Food

The friendly **Taughannock Farms Inn** (2030 Gorge Rd., 607/387-7711, www.t-farms.com) is a large, rambling Victorian country inn overlooking the lake. Long a favorite among Finger Lakes residents, it includes both a relaxed restaurant serving traditional American cuisine (dinner only, entrées range $21–42) and 20 comfortable guest rooms, five of which are located in the main house, the rest in guest cottages ($70–235 d).

Entertainment and Events

One of the top music clubs in the region is the **Rongovian Embassy to the U.S.A.** (Rte. 96, 607/387-3334, www.rong.com), a big, comfortable, laid-back joint with live jazz, rock, reggae, country, or blues most nights of the week. Tasty Mexican food is served.

In July and August, free jazz, Latin, folk, and rock concerts take place weekly in Taughannock Falls State Park.

Ithaca

At the southern tip of Cayuga Lake lies Ithaca, a small, progressive university town whose population of about 30,000 nearly doubles in size whenever its two colleges—Cornell University and Ithaca College—are in session. This is the kind of laid-back place where everyone wears Birkenstocks and reads Proust in outdoor cafés.

Ithaca was originally a Cayuga settlement that was destroyed during General Sullivan's ruthless 1779 campaign. The first white settlers arrived in 1788, but the town didn't really begin to grow until the opening of Cornell University in 1868.

For several years beginning in 1914, Ithaca was a center for the motion picture business. The Wharton Studios based itself here; *Exploits of Elaine,* starring Lionel Barrymore and Pearl White, and *Patria,* starring Irene Castle, were both filmed in Ithaca. The region's unpredictable weather proved less than ideal for moviemaking, however, and in 1920 the industry moved west.

Ithaca also claims to be the birthplace of

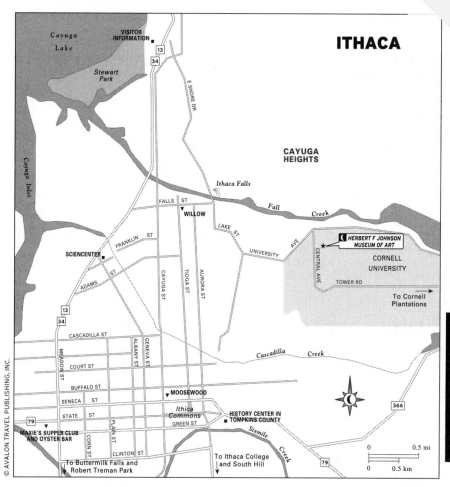

the sundae, supposedly first concocted here in 1891. "As the story goes," writes Arch Merrill in *Slim Fingers Beckon,* "an Ithaca preacher came into C. C. Platt's drugstore, weary and sweating after the Sunday morning service. He asked the druggist to fix a dish of ice cream and pour some syrup on it… and thus another American institution was born."

Orientation

Idyllically situated at the edge of Cayuga Lake, Ithaca is all but surrounded by steep hills and gorges. Three powerful waterfalls plunge right through the heart of the city.

The downtown is small, low-slung, and compact. In its flat center lies **Ithaca Commons,** a pedestrian mall spread out along State Street. Perched on a steep hill to the east is Cornell University. The roller-coaster streets surrounding Cornell are known as **Collegetown.** On another hill to the south sits Ithaca College.

The best way to explore Ithaca and environs is by foot and car. Street parking is generally

but there are also three downtown garages.

SIGHTS
Ithaca Commons

The pedestrian-only Commons runs along State Street between Aurora and Cayuga Streets and along Tioga Street between Seneca and State. Somewhat European in feel, it's filled with fountains, trees, flowers, and benches, and is flanked with shops and restaurants. At the western end is **Clinton House** (116 N. Cayuga St.), a historic hotel now housing various arts organizations and the Ticket Center.

Most of the buildings along the Commons were built between the 1860s and the 1930s. Note the handsome Italianate building at **No. 158 East State Street,** and the art deco storefront at **No. 152 East State Street.** Just beyond the Commons, at **No.**

101 West State Street, glows a 1947 neon sign of a cocky chanticleer.

The **Sagan Planet Walk** was built in memory of astronomer Carl Sagan. It starts at the "sun" on the Commons and continues on to visit nine "planets" along a three-quarter-mile route leading to the ScienCenter Museum. Visitors who get their "Passport to the Solar System" stamped along the way earn a free visit to the museum.

DeWitt Mall

One block north of the Commons, at the corner of Seneca and Cayuga Streets, is the DeWitt Mall. This former school building now contains about 20 shops, galleries, and restaurants, including the famed **Moosewood Restaurant** (see Food, below). Among the galleries are the **Sola Art Gallery** (607/272-6552, 10:30 A.M.–5:30 P.M. Mon.–Sat.), which

---

BUYING AND SELLING WITH "ITHACA HOURS"

In Ithaca, they make their own money – a scrip called Ithaca Hours. The bills, which come in five denominations, are about the same size as U.S. dollars and are worth $10 an hour – the average wage in Tompkins County. They are used in a sort of barter system to exchange services. For example, a carpenter builds a cabinet for a neighbor for which he receives 10 bills. He sticks these in his wallet to use the next time he needs a participating member's expertise or the services of one of the 500 Ithaca businesses that accept Ithaca Hours.

In 1991 Ithaca resident Paul Glover developed Ithaca Hours. Lying in bed after a back injury, he envisioned a way to both improve the local economy and strengthen community ties. "The system expands the local money supply by making it easier for us to hire each other," he says. "It also makes it easier to start up new businesses – we extend loans without interest – and support local arts organizations."

In the beginning, about 90 people, including accountants, carpenters, and tutors, agreed to use the scrip as pay for their services. Today,

that number has grown to several thousand residents and over 500 businesses, including fancy restaurants, a bowling alley, a medical center, and a used-car dealership. Glover publishes a newsletter online to keep subscribers up to date on who accepts the taxable scrip. He estimates that the equivalent of several million dollars in traditional money has exchanged hands so far.

Word of the program's success has spread around the world. Glover has mailed his Hometown Money Starter Kit to over 2,000 communities worldwide and has seen it adopted by groups in Argentina and Japan. He has been visited by Madame Mitterand of France and a top official from the People's Republic of China, and once sent a kit to Dr. Stephen Nzta, then a candidate for the presidency in Zaire. Glover is currently working with dozens of other communities to help them develop their own versions of Ithaca Hours.

To order a Hometown Money Starter Kit, send $25 to Hour Town (P.O. Box 365, Ithaca, NY 14851; 607/272-4330, www.ithacahours.com).

specializes in graphic arts, and the **Upstairs Gallery** (607/272-8614, 11 A.M.–3 P.M. Tues.– Sat.), exhibiting the work of area artists, many affiliated with Cornell or Ithaca College.

Historic DeWitt Park

The oldest buildings in the city are located on or near DeWitt Park, a peaceful retreat at East Buffalo and North Cayuga Streets one block north of DeWitt Mall. Many buildings in this National Historic District date back to the early 1800s.

On the park's north side stands the 1817 **Old Courthouse,** thought to be the oldest Gothic Revival building in the state; and the **First Presbyterian Church,** designed by James Renwick, the architect of St. Patrick's Cathedral in New York City. On the east side is the Romanesque **First Baptist Church,** built in 1890.

Other Downtown Galleries

The eight-room **Asia House Gallery and Museum** (118 S. Meadow St., 607/272-8850) specializes in the traditional fine arts, decorative arts, and antique folk arts of Asia. **Handwork** (102 W. State St., 607/273-9400) showcases the work of 25 local craftspeople.

History Center in Tompkins County

Inside this large, renovated building you'll find a fine historical museum (401 E. State St., at Seneca and Green Sts., 607/273-8284, 11 A.M.–5 P.M. Tues., Thurs., and Sat., free admission) run by the DeWitt Historical Society. The society owns an impressive collection of over 20,000 objects, 3,000 books, and 100,000 photographs.

Permanent displays show the city's beginnings, its industries, and its surprising film history. Temporary exhibits focus on such subjects as folk arts, alternative medicine, Italian immigrants, and Finnish-American saunas.

The ScienCenter

The recently renovated, hands-on ScienCenter (601 1st St., at Franklin St., 607/272-0600, www.sciencenter.org, 10 A.M.–5 P.M. Tues.– Sat, noon–5 P.M. Sun., adults $6, children

3–17 $4) primarily appeals to young ones, but adults can learn something here as well. Walk into a camera for a zoom-lens view of how it works. Draw your own picture on a "harmonograph." Measure the electrical current running through your body. Or, play outdoor mini-golf on the Galaxy Golf Course. Pre-schoolers will want to explore the Curiosity Corner, while older kids will probably head to the animal room or space exhibits.

The ScienCenter was largely created by volunteers, many of them Cornell scientists and engineers, which helps account for its homey yet high-tech feel. Out back is an imaginative wooden playground filled with games that teach kids about physical principles such as gravity and heat.

Ithaca Falls

At the corner of Falls and Lake Streets thunder Ithaca Falls, the last and greatest of the six waterfalls along the mile-long Fall Creek gorge. These "pulpit falls" are closely spaced rapids created by layers of resistant rock. To reach the site from Ithaca Commons—about a 20-minute walk—head north along Cayuga Street to Falls Street and turn right. To one side is a small grassy park and a wooded path that leads to a popular fishing hole.

Cornell University

High on a hill overlooking downtown Ithaca presides Cornell University, built around a long, lush green lined with ivy-covered buildings. The views from here are especially fine at twilight, when Cayuga's waters glow with the setting sun and the gorges begin a slow fade into black.

Cornell was founded in 1865 by Ezra Cornell and Andrew D. White, who vowed to establish an "institution where any person can find instruction in any study." In so doing, they challenged a number of long-standing mores. Their university was one of the first to be nonsectarian; to offer instruction to all qualified applicants, regardless of sex, race, or class; and to feature courses in everything from agriculture to the classics.

Traffic and information booths are located at each entrance to the central campus. Except in a few metered areas, parking is by permit only; purchase a permit at the traffic booths. Visitors to the Herbert F. Johnson Museum can park in metered spaces out front. To tour the campus, contact the **Information and Referral Center** (Day Hall, Tower Rd. and East Ave., 607/254-INFO, www.cornell.edu).

Herbert F. Johnson Museum of Art

At the northern end of the Cornell campus reigns the Johnson Museum of Art (University Ave., 607/255-6464, www.museum.cornell.edu, 10 A.M.–5 P.M. Tues.–Sun., free admission), housed in a striking modern building designed by I. M. Pei. The museum features especially strong collections of Asian and contemporary art but is also a teaching museum, containing a little bit of almost everything.

The Asian collection is situated on the fifth floor, where big picture windows open out onto 360-degree views of Cayuga Lake and the surrounding countryside. Among the many exquisite objects on display are funerary urns from the T'ang dynasty, silk paintings from 19th-century Japan, and bronze Buddhas from 15th-century Thailand.

Wilder Brain Collection

Those interested in the odd and macabre will want to step into Cornell's Uris Hall, East Avenue and Tower Road, and ride an elevator up to the second floor. In a small case to the rear of the building are the eight surviving stars of the Burt Green Wilder brain collection, which once numbered about 1,600 floating specimens.

Wilder was Cornell's first zoologist. He began assembling his collection in the late 1800s in the hopes of proving the size and shape of a person's brain were related to his or her race, sex, intelligence, and personality. Alas, his studies only disproved his theories, and in 1911 he rocked the scientific world by declaring that there was no difference between the brains of black and white men.

The pickled collection includes the extraor-dinarily large brain of criminal Edward Howard Ruloff, who was hanged in Binghamton on May 18, 1871. Ruloff allegedly killed his wife and daughter and was convicted of killing three men. He was also highly intelligent, and had published several scholarly papers despite his lack of formal education.

Burt Green Wilder's brain is also in the collection. Considerably smaller than Ruloff's, it sits yellowing in viscous formaldehyde. The creator has joined his creation.

Cornell University Plantations

Just north of the Cornell campus, a 2,800-acre oasis of green (1 Plantations Rd., off Rte. 366, 607/255-3020, open daily, free admission) encompasses an arboretum, specialty gardens devoted to everything from wildflowers to poisonous plants, and nature trails winding through the Fall Creek gorge. Pick up maps in the gift shop.

Sapsucker Woods Bird Sanctuary

At the eastern edge of the city lies a world-class center for the study, appreciation, and conservation of birds. Not everything is open to the public, but key attractions include 4.2 miles of trails through the Sapsucker Woods Sanctuary and the Stuart Observatory, which overlooks a waterfowl pond and bird-feeding garden.

The 220-acre Sapsucker Woods were named by bird artist Louis Agassiz Fuertes in 1901 after he spotted a pair of yellow-bellied sapsuckers—unusual for the region—nesting in the area. Sapsuckers continue to breed here each year. Near the woods you'll find a **visitors center** (159 Sapsucker Woods Rd., 607/254-BIRD, www.birds.cornell.edu, 8 A.M.–5 P.M. Mon.–Thurs., 8 A.M.–4 P.M. Fri., 10 A.M.–4 P.M. Sat.) where you can pick up maps and view paintings by Agassiz Fuertes.

Buttermilk Falls State Park

Just south of downtown is Buttermilk Falls (Rte. 13, 607/273-5761, daily dawn–dusk May–Nov., $6–8 parking), plummeting more than 500 feet past 10 waterfalls, churning rapids, sculptured pools, and raggedy cliffs.

Alongside the falls runs a trail leading up to spirelike Pinnacle Rock and Treman Lake. At the base of the falls are a natural swimming hole, ball fields, and a campground. For campground reservations, call 800/456-CAMP.

Robert H. Treman State Park

Five miles south of Ithaca lies Treman Park (off Rte. 13, 607/273-3440, dawn–dusk daily Apr.–Nov., $6–8 parking)—1,025 acres of wild and rugged beauty. Near the entrance is Enfield Glen, a forested gorge traversed by a stone pathway and steps. The steps lead to 115-foot-high Lucifer Falls and a vista stretching 1.5 miles down into a deep glen threaded by the Gorge Trail. A three-story 1839 gristmill, a natural swimming pool, and a campground are also on the grounds. For campground reservations, call 800/456-CAMP.

SPORTS AND RECREATION

Circle Greenway is a 10-mile walk that leads to many of Ithaca's foremost natural and urban attractions, including gorges, the waterfront, Cornell, and the Commons. A free map can be picked up at the Ithaca/Tompkins County Convention and Visitors Bureau.

Cayuga Lake Cruises (702 W. Buffalo St., 607/256-0898) offers dinner, lunch, brunch, and cocktail cruises aboard the M/V *Manhattan*. **Tiohero Tours** (607/697-0166 or 866/846-4376, www.Tioherotours.com) offers narrated tours of the lake that depart from the Farmers Market pier at 11 A.M. and 1 P.M.

ACCOMMODATIONS

As the teaching hotel of Cornell's School of Hotel Administration, the **Statler Hotel** (11 East Ave., Cornell University Campus, 607/257-2500 or 800/541-2501, www.statler-hotel.cornell.edu, $115–165 d) is Ithaca's hotel of choice for visiting parents, academics, and travelers. The hotel features 150 guest rooms and two restaurants; guests have access to most of Cornell's facilities, including the gym, pool, tennis courts, and golf course.

The delightful **Buttermilk Falls B&B**

(110 E. Buttermilk Falls Rd., off Rte. 13 S, 607/272-6767, www.buttermilkfallsbedandbreakfast.com, $95–265 d) is located at the foot of its namesake on the edge of town. The brick B&B dates back to 1820 and features five spacious, antique-filled guest rooms, one cottage suite, and very knowledgeable hosts. Some rooms share baths.

The **Log Country Inn B&B** (607/589-4771, 4 LaRue Rd., at S. Danby Rd., www.logtv.com/inn, $70–200 d) may sound rustic but it features soaring cathedral ceilings, fireplaces, a sauna, and a dozen guestrooms, some with Jacuzzis. Next door is a 7,000-acre forest perfect for hiking and cross-country skiing. Some rooms share baths.

For more bed-and-breakfast suggestions, contact the Tompkins County Convention & Visitors Bureau or **Bed & Breakfast of Greater Ithaca** (800/806-4406, www.bbithaca.com). You can also check room availability by visiting the visitors bureau's website www.VisitIthaca.com.

FOOD

A number of casual eateries are located along Ithaca Commons. The 100 block of Aurora Street just off the Commons has one restaurant after another.

Famed worldwide for its best-selling cookbooks and natural foods, the cooperatively owned **C Moosewood** (215 N. Cayuga St., DeWitt Mall, 607/273-9610) is a simple, casual place, crowded with rustic wooden tables. An outdoor dining area opens in the summer; average dinner entrée $11.

The upscale **Willow** (202 E. Falls St., 607/272-0656) is a local favorite, serving contemporary American fare; average entrée $18. Also serving contemporary American cuisine, as well as seafood, is the **Boatyard Grill** (525 Taughannock Blvd., 607/256-6228), overlooking the waterfront; average entrée $17.

Just a Taste Wine and Tapas Restaurant & Bar (16 N. Aurora St., 607/277-WINE) serves 50 wines by the glass and an international menu. Outside is a lovely garden; average tapa $8. **Madeline's Restaurant and**

Bar (North Aurora and East State Sts., on the Commons, 607/277-2253) offers excellent Asian cuisine from a variety of countries; average entrée $14. For the best Thai food in town, step into **The Thai Cuisine** (501 S. Meadow St., 607/273-2031); average entrée $12. Hot spot **Maxie's Supper Club and Oyster Bar** (635 W. State St., 607/272-4136), all done up in purples and reds, offers both spicy Cajun cuisine and stick-to-your-ribs Southern soul food. Everything's homemade at this family-run affair; average entrée $14.

ENTERTAINMENT
Performing Arts
Cornell's **Schwartz Center for Theatre Arts** (430 College Ave., 607/254-ARTS) stages 6–12 plays September–May, along with the Cornell Dance Series and numerous guest performances. Professional regional theater is staged by the acclaimed **Hangar Theatre** (Rte. 89, Cass Park, 607/273-8588) June–August. The **Kitchen Theater** (607/272-0403) presents contemporary theater in the historic Clinton House.

Among the groups performing regularly in the city is the **Cayuga Chamber Orchestra** (116 N. Cayuga St., 607/273-8981), the official orchestra of Ithaca. The **Ithaca Ballet** (607/277-1967) performs both classical and contemporary works.

Nightlife
Good club listings can be found in the *Ithaca Times* (607/277-7000), a free alternative news weekly. One of the best music clubs in the area is the **Rongovian Embassy** in nearby Trumansburg (see above). The **ABC Cafe** (308 Stewart Ave., 607/277-4770) features folk, a weekly open mike, and jazz on Sunday.

INFORMATION AND SERVICES
The **Ithaca/Tompkins County Convention & Visitors Bureau** (904 East Shore Dr., near Stewart Park, Ithaca 14850, 607/272-1313 or 800/284-8422, www.visitithaca.com) is open 9 A.M.–6 P.M. Monday–Friday, 10 A.M.–4 P.M. Saturday, and 10 A.M.–4 P.M. Sunday mid-May–October, and 9 A.M.–5 P.M. Monday–Friday and 10 A.M.–5 P.M. Saturday November–mid-May.

In the Clinton House (116 N. Cayuga St., Ithaca Commons) is the **Ticket Center** (607/273-4497), which sells tickets for various arts organizations.

DETOUR TO OWEGO
Route 96B runs south of Ithaca to hook up with Route 96, an old stagecoach road that leads to Owego. Along the way you'll pass through farm country, much of it worn down and depressed.

Located on the Susquehanna River, five miles from the Pennsylvania border, Owego centers around a four-towered 1872 courthouse. Along the river runs Front Street, where historic brick buildings house snug shops and restaurants.

The town's most famous early citizens were Gen. Robert, who wrote Robert's Rules of Order in 1872, and Belva Lockwood, the first woman to run for the presidency—in 1884. To learn more about them, visit the **Tioga County Historical Society Museum** (110 Front St., 607/687-2460, 10 A.M.–4 P.M. Tues.–Sat., free admission), which also houses Native American artifacts, folk arts, and pioneer crafts.

Also in town is the vintage **Tioga Scenic Railroad,** composed of early-1900s open-air cars that travel between Owego and Newark Valley in summer. The trains leave from the original **Owego Depot** (25 Delphine St., 607/687-6786, www.tiogascenicrailroad.com, 8 A.M.–4 P.M. Mon.–Fri. year-round and Sat.–Sun. in summer, call for train schedule and ticket prices), a striking two-story wooden building containing railroad memorabilia and a large model-train layout.

Seneca Lake

At 36 miles long and 618 feet deep, Seneca Lake is one of the deepest bodies of water in the United States. It seldom freezes over and is renowned for its superb lake-trout fishing. Given to sudden, capricious gusts of wind, it's the most mysterious of the Finger Lakes.

Ever since the days of the Native Americans, area residents have reported strange, dull rumblings coming from Seneca's depths. The sounds are usually heard at dusk in the late summer or early fall and are most distinct midway down the lake. The Native Americans believed that the rumblings were the voice of an angry god; early settlers considered them omens of disaster; science attributes them to the popping of natural gas released from rock rifts at the bottom of the lake.

Whatever the cause, the dull rumbles—a sound much like gunfire—may have had some portent, for during World War II, a huge munitions depot and naval station was built along Seneca's eastern shore. The naval station is now long gone, but the 11,000-acre **Seneca Arms Depot** remains. Officially, it functions to "maintain and demilitarize ammunition," but the herd of snow-white deer that roam the grounds can't help but make you wonder. The deer can best be seen from Route 96A at dawn and dusk.

At the northern end of Seneca Lake lies Geneva, a historic town whose South Main Street has been called "the most beautiful street in America." At the southern end is Watkins Glen, a rugged, 700-foot-deep gorge that's been turned into a natural theme park.

GENEVA

One of the larger towns in the region, Geneva is home to about 15,000 residents. Though overall a nondescript place, through its center runs the elegant South Main Street, lined with leafy trees, stately homes, and Hobart and William Smith Colleges.

Geneva was once a major Seneca settlement known as Kanadesaga. During the French and Indian War, the British erected a fort here from which they and the Seneca conducted murderous raids—only to be massacred themselves during the 1779 Sullivan campaign.

Soon after the Revolution, settlers began to arrive. A visionary land agent laid out the town along a broad Main Street and a public green. This gave the place an air of dignity which, during the 1800s, attracted an usually large number of retired ministers and spinsters. Geneva soon earned the nickname "The Saints' Retreat and Old Maids' Paradise."

In 1847, the Medical College of Geneva College (now Hobart) received an application of admission from one Elizabeth Blackwell of Philadelphia. The students and deans, assuming it to be a joke, laughingly voted to admit her. A few weeks later, to everyone's amazement, Ms. Blackwell arrived, and in 1849, she graduated—the first woman ever granted a medical diploma in America.

Prouty-Chew Museum

The only South Main Street mansion open to the public is the Prouty-Chew (543 S. Main St., 315/789-5151, 9:30 A.M.–4:30 P.M. Tues.–Fri., 1:30–4:30 P.M. Sat., free admission). Built in the Federal style in 1829 by a Geneva attorney, the house was enlarged several times in the 1850s and 1870s, which accounts for its eclectic look. Now home to the Geneva Historical Society, the museum showcases changing exhibits on local history and art.

Rose Hill Mansion

Three miles east of downtown lies Geneva's foremost visitor attraction—the fine 1839 Rose Hill Mansion (Rte. 96A, 315/789-3848, 10 A.M.–4 P.M. Mon.–Sat. and 1–5 P.M. Sun. May–Oct., adults $3, seniors and youths 10–18 $2), built in the Greek Revival style with six Ionic columns out front. The mansion was once home to Robert Swan, an innovative farmer who installed the country's first large-scale drainage system. Tours of the house take visitors past a fine collection of Empire-style furnishings. Next door is the former carriage house; out front, an emerald green lawn slopes down to Seneca Lake.

Accommodations and Food

For dockside dining, try **Crow's Nest on Seneca Lake** (415 Boody's Hill Rd., off Rte. 96A near Rose Hill Mansion, 315/781-0600). On the menu are sandwiches and salads, seafood and beef; average dinner entrée $14.

The extravagant, Romanesque **Belhurst Castle** (4069 Rte. 14 S, 315/781-0201, www.belhurst.com, $110–325 d, with breakfast) took 50 workers toiling six days a week four years to complete. Finished in 1889, it features everything from turrets to stained-glass windows. Inside is an upscale restaurant serving continental fare for both lunch and dinner (average lunch entrée $9, average dinner entrée $24), and about a dozen modernized guest rooms that vary greatly in size and price. Out front are formal gardens and a lakefront beach. Also operated by Belhurst Castle is the lovely Georgian **Whitesprings Manor** and the brand new **Vinifera Inn;** the same contact information and rates apply.

The luxurious, all-suite **Geneva-on-the-Lake** (1001 Lochland Rd., 315/789-7190 or 800/3-GENEVA, www.genevaonthelake.com, $210–550 d, with continental breakfast) is especially popular among honeymooners. The property centers on a 1911 mansion built in the style of a 16th-century Italian villa. Each suite differs from the next, and outside extend 10 acres of formal gardens. The dining room, open to the public for lunch and dinner, serves continental fare using fresh local produce (average dinner entrée $25).

DETOUR TO SODUS POINT AND ENVIRONS

Worth a 30-mile detour north of Geneva on Route 14 is Sodus Point, which overlooks Lake Ontario. The village boasts gorgeous views, an inviting public beach, and the handsome 1870 **Old Sodus Point Lighthouse and Maritime Museum** (7606 N. Ontario St.,

315/483-4936, 10 a.m.–5 p.m. Tues.–Sun. May–Oct., free admission).

The real reason to venture up here, however, are the **Chimney Bluffs.** Located on the eastern side of Sodus Bay, the bluffs rise 150 feet above the lake like some giant confectionery delight. All pinnacles, spires, and peaks, they're part of a glacier-created drumlin that has been eroded, carved, and shaped by water, wind, and snow. Atop some of the pinnacles sit lone trees; below them extends a stony beach.

Dozens of other drumlins (minus the pinnacles and peaks) can be found throughout this part of the Lake Ontario region. The only other places to view drumlins in North America are the areas bordering Lake Superior in Minnesota.

The Chimney Bluffs and its beach form part of the undeveloped Chimney Bluffs State Park. The park can be reached by taking Route 414 north to the end of Lake Bluff Road.

Alasa Farms

On your way to and from Sodus Point, you'll pass through serious farm country, heavy with rich black soil. Near the lake thrive apples, cherries, and peaches. Farther inland grow corn, wheat, potatoes, onion, and lettuce.

Off Route 14 just south of Sodus Point lies Alasa Farms (6450 Shaker Rd., Alton, 315/483-6321, open June–Oct. by appointment). Once a 1,400-acre Shaker religious community, the site passed into private hands in the 1800s. Throughout the 1920s and 1930s, the farm raised everything from shorthorn cattle and hackney ponies to timberland and orchards, and today, it's still a 700-acre working farm. Visitors can opt for either a self-guided farm tour or an escorted tour of the Shaker Dwelling House.

Events

One of the region's foremost events is the **Sterling Renaissance Festival** (315/947-5783), held in Sterling, near Fair Haven, about 25 miles west of Sodus Point. For seven weekends in July and August, the fest celebrates the

Middle Ages with music, jousting, outdoor theater, crafts, and food.

SOUTH ON ROUTES 96A AND 414

From Rose Hill Mansion in Geneva, Route 96A heads south along the eastern shore of Seneca Lake. About 10 miles down is the 1,852-acre **Sampson State Park** (315/585-6392, $6–8 parking), once a naval training station where thousands of soldiers trained during World War II. Today, the park is equipped with a marina, swimming beach, bathhouses, picnic area, playground, and 245-site campground. To reserve a campsite, call 800/456-CAMP.

South of Willard, Route 96A veers inland to Ovid (see *Cayuga Lake Area,* above), where it hooks up with Route 414. Continue south on Route 414 to more small villages and a cluster of vineyards and wineries.

Wineries

Around the village of Lodi you'll find several wineries. Among them is the **Lamoreaux Landing Wine Cellars** (9224 Rte. 414, 607/582-6011, www.lamoreauxwine.com, 10 A.M.–5 P.M. Mon.–Sat., noon–5 P.M. Sun.) housed in a Greek revival building with great views of the lake. Lamoreaux produced everything from chardonnay to pinot noir.

A few more miles down the road sprawls the highly commercialized **Wagner Vineyards** (9322 Rte. 414, 607/582-6450, www.wagnervineyards.com, 10 A.M.–5 P.M. Mon.–Sat., noon–5 P.M. Sun.), centered on a weathered octagonal building overlooking the lake. Established in 1979, Wagner produces over 75,000 gallons a year. On the premises is a microbrewery and **Ginny Lee Cafe** (607/582-6574), open for lunch and Sunday brunch only.

Finger Lakes National Forest

Between the southern ends of Seneca and Cayuga Lakes stands Finger Lakes National Forest (Logan Rd., off Rte. 414, south of Hector, 607/546-4470). The only real forest in the region, it supports evergreens, oaks, and maples, along with white-tailed deer, wild turkey,

and grouse. Twelve miles long and five miles wide, the forest is laced with 25 miles of easy-to-moderate hiking trails. Near the entrance you'll find a **visitors center** (5218 Rte. 414, 607/546-4470, 8 A.M.–4:30 P.M. Mon.–Fri.) where you can pick up maps; maps are also stacked in the vestibule on weekends. A small campground is available on a first-come, first-served basis for a small fee, and free camping is also allowed throughout the park.

SOUTH ON ROUTE 14

From Geneva, Route 14 heads south along the western shore of Seneca Lake past two excellent wineries. **Fox Run Vineyards** (670 Rte. 14, Penn Yan, 315/536-4616, www.foxrunvineyards.com), is housed in an 1860s dairy barn with sweeping views of the lake. The **Anthony Road Wine Company** (1225 Anthony Rd., Penn Yan, 315/536-2182, www.anthonyroadwine.com) is not particularly scenic but produces a good seyval and Riesling. Both are open 10 A.M.–5 P.M. Monday–Saturday and noon–5 P.M. Sunday.

Dundee Wineries

More good wineries cluster near the lake's southern end. Among them is the **Hermann J. Wiemer Vineyard** (3962 Rte. 14, Dundee, 607/243-7971, www.wiemer.com), run by a foremost viticulturalist. Born on the Mosel River in Germany, Wiemer is known for his Rieslings.

A few miles farther south is **Glenora Wine Cellars** (5435 Rte. 14, Dundee, 607/243-5511, www.glenora.com). Established in 1977, Glenora produces over 150,000 gallons a year and is best known for sparkling wines. The winery offers panoramic lake views and presents **jazz concerts** in summer.

Also on site is the large, modern, and very comfortable **Inn at Glenora Wine Cellars** (5435 Rte. 14, 607/243-9500, www.glenora.com, $140–235 d), which features big picture windows overlooking the vineyards and spacious guestrooms complete with private balconies or patios. Connected with the inn is an equally spacious restaurant and outdoor

THE FINGER LAKES

dining patio that serves tasty "regional fusion" specialties; average entrée $17.

WATKINS GLEN AND VICINITY

At the southern tip of Seneca Lake lies Watkins Glen, named for the astonishing gorge that rips right through its center. Near the entrance to the glen, now a state park, stand family-style eateries and lots of souvenir shops.

Back in the 1950s and '60s, the main street of Watkins Glen and the steep roads surrounding it were the speedway of the American Grand Prix. During the races, as many as 75,000 spectators descended on the village,

whose year-round population was—and is—under 3,000. Today, world-class auto races take place at the Watkins Glen International Race Track, four miles south of Watkins Glen.

Watkins Glen State Park

Created some 12,000 years ago during the last Ice Age, Watkins Glen (off Rte. 14/414, 607/535-4511, 8 A.M.–dusk daily May–Nov., parking $6–8) is a wild and raggedy gorge flanked by high cliffs and strange, sculpted rock formations. Through its center rushes Glen Creek, dropping some 700 feet in two miles over rapids, cascades, and 19 waterfalls.

Alongside the gorge runs the 1.5-mile Gorge

THE NATIVE AMERICAN CONFEDERACY OF SIX NATIONS

Before the arrival of whites, Algonquin and Iroquois tribes lived freely in New York. The Algonquin resided in the south and along the Hudson River Valley, while the Iroquois spread out across the north.

The Iroquois were actually a confederacy of five tribes – the Mohawk, the Oneida, the Onondaga, the Cayuga, and the Seneca – who had banded together around 1450 to end intertribal warfare. A sixth nation, the Tuscarora, joined the Confederacy in 1722.

The Iroquois survived through hunting, fishing, and the planting of the "Three Sisters" – corn, beans, and squash. Records were kept through storytelling and the weaving of elaborate wampum belts. Each of the Iroquois tribes was divided into matrilineal clans that took their names from birds and animals. The clans lived in longhouses comprised of 50-60 families, and all clan members were considered part of one family. Women selected the clan chiefs.

The men responsible for founding the Confederacy were a Huron now known as "The Peacemaker" and Hiawatha, an Onondaga chief. The two traveled from tribe to tribe for months, convincing their people to lay down their arms and embrace the Great Law of

Peace. The Law gave equal voice to each of the tribes, guaranteed freedom of speech, set up a system for the impeachment of corrupt chiefs, and outlined an amendment procedure.

Sound familiar? It's because the Great Law served as one of the models for the U.S. Constitution. No firm textual evidence exists, but several framers of the Constitution met frequently with the Iroquois after the Revolution, and Benjamin Franklin in particular expressed a wish to use their system as a model. In 1988, Congress passed a resolution acknowledging this Native American contribution to the U.S. Constitution.

Today, approximately 40,000 Native Americans still live in New York State. About 35 percent reside on reservations, while the rest live in large urban areas, most notably Brooklyn. That metropolis has traditionally drawn an especially large number of Mohawk because of their sure-footed skill as high-rise steelworkers.

Eight Iroquois communities are located upstate, ranging in size from the 30,469-acre Allegany Reservation (Seneca) to the 5,700-acre Tuscarora Reservation. The state's only casinos are on Oneida territory about 20 miles east of Syracuse and in Mohawk territory near the Canada border.

COURTESY OF FINGER LAKES WINE COUNTRY TOURISM MARKETING ASSOCIATION

Indy car at Watkins Glen International Race Track

Trail, made up of 832 stone steps, stone paths, and numerous bridges. The trail leads past tunnels, caves, and a natural stone bridge, all carved out of the sedimentary rock by Glen Creek. If you hike the trail on a fine summer's day, you'll have lots of company, but the gorge inspires awe nonetheless.

The park also offers campgrounds; for reservations, call 800/456-CAMP.

Montour Falls

Route 14 leads south of Watkins Glen through narrow winding Pine Valley to Montour Falls, a small industrial community surrounded by seven glens. In the middle of town, flanked by buildings, is **Chequagua Falls,** plunging downward 165 feet into a deep pool. The falls are illuminated at night and near the top is a pedestrian bridge.

Along Genesee and Main Streets you'll find a handsome **National Historic District** composed of 24 brick buildings dating back to the 1850s. Among them is Memorial Library with Tiffany windows and the Greek Revival Village Hall.

Sports and Recreation

World-class auto racing takes place June–Sept. at the **Watkins Glen International Race Track** (2790 County Rd. 16, off Rte. 14/414 S, 607/535-2481). Ticket prices depend on the race.

May–October, 50-minute cruises of Seneca Lake are offered every hour on the hour by **Captain Bill's Seneca Lake Cruises** (1 N. Franklin St., 607/535-4541). Captain Bill also runs dinner cruises.

Accommodations

One of the more idiosyncratic hostelries in the area is the **Seneca Lodge** (Rte. 329, off Rte. 14/414 at the south entrance to Watkins Glen State Park, 607/535-2014, $63–73 d). A favorite haunt of bow hunters, the lodge centers on a restaurant and bar whose back wall, bristled with arrows, looks like the hide of a porcupine. As the tradition goes, the first bow hunter to shoot a deer each season shoots an arrow into the wall.

More conventional digs can be found at

the **Villager** (106 E. 4th St., 607/535-7159, www.wgvillagermotel.com), which offers motel, hotel, and B&B-style rooms that vary in price, with the motel rooms the cheapest ($65–95 d) and the B&B rooms, the most expensive ($115–145). On site is a heated swimming pool.

Food

Chef's Diner (Rte. 14, 607/535-9975) is a classic American eatery, now in its sixth decade. Come here for tasty pancakes or grilled-cheese sandwiches. **Seneca Harbor Station** (foot of Franklin St., 607/535-6101) is a seafood restaurant with great views of the lake. Out back is a large deck from which to watch the sun set; average entrée $18.

Just west of the village you'll find **Castel Grisch Estate** (3380 County Rd. 28, off Rte. 409, 607/535-9614), a winery with a German-style restaurant. It's open for lunch and dinner Friday–Sunday. Outside is a deck with lake views; main dishes are $8–16.

Events

During the **Grand Prix Festival** in early September, the 1948 American Grand Prix, complete with vintage cars, is reenacted in the streets of Watkins Glen.

Elmira

Elmira sits on both sides of the Chemung River, a few miles north of the Pennsylvania border. Some parts of the city are quite historic, with handsome stone and red-brick buildings; other parts are crumbling, windswept, and seriously depressed.

Once the site of a Seneca village, Elmira was first settled by whites in the 1780s. By the 1840s, the town was known for its lumbering and woolen mills, and by the 1860s, for its metal industries and iron furnaces. Elmira also served as a major transportation center, sitting at the crossroads of the Erie Railroad, the Chemung River, and the Chemung and Junction Canals.

During the Civil War, the Union Army set up barracks in Elmira. In 1864, one of those barracks was turned into a prison camp for Confederate soldiers. The prison was poorly built and desperately overcrowded; thousands of prisoners died within a year.

Samuel Clemens, a.k.a. Mark Twain, spent more than 20 summers in Elmira. His wife, Olivia Langdon, grew up in the area and Twain wrote many of his masterpieces—including *Tom Sawyer* and *The Adventures of Huckleberry Finn*—while staying at the Langdon family farm. Mark Twain's Study has since been moved onto the campus of Elmira College, which was one of the earliest colleges for women, founded in 1855.

Outside the city lies the National Soaring Center. Elmira has been known as the Soaring Capital of America ever since 1930, when the first National Soaring Contest took place here.

Orientation

Most of Elmira is north of the Chemung River. Exiting off Route 17 onto Route 352W (Church St.) will take you into the heart of the city. Route 14N runs past Elmira College and Woodlawn Cemetery (off West Woodlawn Ave.).

In July and August, the Chemung County Chamber of Commerce (607/734-5137 or 800/627-5892) offers hour-long **trolley tours** of Elmira's historical attractions; call for details.

DOWNTOWN SIGHTS
ⓒ Mark Twain's Study

The story of Mark Twain and Olivia Langdon began in 1867 when Twain fell in love with her after viewing her portrait, shown to him by a friend as they were crossing the Atlantic. Upon arrival back in the United States, Twain immediately set up a meeting with Olivia. At first,

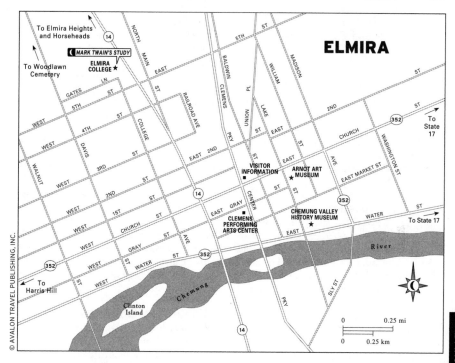

she was not at all impressed. He was a rough-and-tumble self-made man; she was a refined young woman of good family.

But Twain was stubborn. For the next two years, he visited Elmira regularly, and eventually won over the entire Langdon family. In fact, near the end of his courtship, Olivia—who was sickly and delicate—was only allowed to visit with him for five minutes a day because she became so excited.

Twain's former study (Park Pl., Elmira College Campus, 607/735-1941, www.elmira.edu, 9 A.M.–5 P.M. Mon.–Sat. June–Labor Day, or by appointment, free admission), modeled after a Mississippi steamboat pilot house, was built for him by his sister-in-law. Though it now looks rather forlorn, sitting by itself near a crossroads, Twain once described it as "the loveliest study you ever saw. It is octagonal in shape with a peaked roof, each space filled with a spacious window and it sits perched in com-plete isolation on the very top of an elevation that commands leagues of valleys and city and retreating ranges of blue hill."

Inside, the study is simple and functional. A Remington Rand sits on a desk, a trunk inscribed with the name "Clemens" rests on the floor. Twain was one of the first writers to submit a typed manuscript to a publisher.

Woodlawn Cemetery

Samuel Clemens is buried in the Langdon family plot, along with his wife, his father-in-law, and his son-in-law Ossip Gabrilowitsch, a noted Russian-born pianist. A 12-foot-high monument commemorates the two famous men.

Adjacent to the main cemetery is the **Woodlawn National Cemetery,** containing the graves of the 2,963 Confederate soldiers who died in the Elmira prison. Surrounding the Confederate graves are the graves of 322 Union soldiers.

The main cemetery (1200 Walnut St., 607/732-0151) and the national cemetery (1825 Davis St., 607/732-5411) are both open daily dawn–dusk.

Elmira Correctional Facility

Just north of the cemetery, at Davis Street and Bancroft Road, stands the grim Elmira Correctional Facility. The facility is built on the site of the Civil War prison camp and was originally a reformatory for first offenders between the ages of 16 and 30. Today, it houses a more general prison population.

Arnot Art Museum

In this restored 1833 neoclassical mansion (235 Lake St., at W. Gray, 607/734-3697, www.arnotartmuseum.org, 10 A.M.–5 P.M. Tues.–Sat., 1–5 P.M. Sun., adults $5, seniors and students $4.50, children 6–12 $2.50) hangs a fine collection of 17th- to 19th-century European and 19th- to 20th-century American paintings. At the heart of the collection are works acquired by Matthias Arnot in the late 1800s. Among them are paintings by Breughel, Daubigny, Rousseau, and Millet, hung floor to ceiling in the old salon style.

Behind the mansion, a handsome modern wing houses both temporary exhibitions and rotating selections from the museum's Asian, Egyptian, and pre-Columbian collections.

Chemung Valley History Museum

To learn more about Elmira'a past, stop into this local history museum (415 E. Water St., at Lake St., 607/734-4167, www.chemungvalleymuseum.org, 10 A.M.–5 P.M. Tues.–Sat., free admission). Featured are exhibits on the Seneca, Mark Twain in Elmira, and the Civil War prison camp.

NEARBY SIGHTS
Harris Hill Soaring Center and National Soaring Museum

A few miles west of Elmira rises Harris Hill, an idyllic, woodsy spot surrounded by other hills and valleys that produce good updrafts. The Harris Hill Soaring Center (102 Soaring Hill Dr., off Rte. 352, 607/734-0641 or 607/796-2988, www.harrishillsoaring.org) has been attracting gliding and soaring aficionados since the 1910s.

Visitors to Harris Hill can take a sailplane ride aboard one of the delicate vessels parked in the airfield's hangar. All the pilots are FAA certified, and the rides take about 20 minutes, soaring from air current to air current high above the countryside. Sailplane rides are offered daily June–Labor Day, and weekends April–May and September–October. Cost is $70 per person.

Just down from the airfield sits the National Soaring Museum (51 Soaring Hill Dr., 607/734-3128, www.soaringmuseum.org, 10 A.M.–5 P.M. daily, adults $6.50, seniors $5.50, youth 5–17 $4), which chronicles the history of Harris Hill and flying in America. Of special interest are the museum's 12 antique gliders and sailplanes, and the simulated cockpit.

National Warplane Museum

Run primarily by enthusiastic senior-citizen volunteers, this indoor-outdoor museum (17 Aviation Dr., Elmira-Corning Airport [Exit 51 off Rte. 17], 617/739-8200, www.warplane.org, 9 A.M.–5 P.M. Mon.–Sat., 11 A.M.–5 P.M. Sun., adults $7, seniors $5.50, students 6–17 $4, families $18) is dedicated to the restoration and maintenance of flying-condition WWII and Korean War aircraft. The planes are spread out like hulking insects all around a small visitors center and hangar where someone is always busy repairing something. A highlight of the museum's collection is the "Fuddy Duddy"—a B-17 Flying Fortress used during World War II.

One of the best times to visit the museum is during its Wings of Eagles Airshow, held the third weekend in August. Throughout the rest of the year, volunteers are always on hand to conduct personalized tours.

CAMPING AND ACCOMMODATIONS

A few miles south of Elmira lies the **Newtown Battlefield Reservation** (Lowman Rd. off

Rte. 17, 607/732-6067) where Gen. John Sullivan won a decisive battle over a large force of Iroquois and Tories on August 19, 1779. Situated on a hilltop with wide-angled views of the Chemung Valley, the former battlefield is now a county park with hiking trails, a picnic area, and campgrounds.

Several miles north of downtown find the

◖ **Lindenwald Haus** (1526 Grand Central Ave., 607/733-8753, $74–115), a romantic Italianate mansion built in 1875. Surrounded by five acres, the inn features 18 spacious guest rooms, long creaky hallways, and an airy living room that stretches most of the length of the house. Rocking chairs and braided rugs are everywhere. Some rooms share baths.

Corning

Strange though it seems, Corning and its famed glass center is the third-most-popular tourist destination in New York State. This is undoubtedly largely due to a first-rate promotion and marketing campaign, and to Corning's strategic location more or less midway between New York City (the state's No. 1 destination) and Niagara Falls (No. 2). However, the Corning Museum of Glass *is* an impressive place, especially since its major 1999 expansion, and well worth braving the herds of tour buses to visit. You don't have to worry about long lines, either. Crowd control is down to a science here.

Corning, current population 11,000, became a one-industry town not long after 1868, when the Flint Glass Company of Brooklyn relocated here. The company chose Corning largely because of its strategic position on the Chemung River and Chemung Canal, which would allow for the easy delivery of raw materials.

In 1875, the company began to produce specialized types of glass, such as railway signal lenses and thermometer tubing. In 1880, the lightbulb division was developed in response to Edison's invention, and by the early 1930s, Corning was manufacturing 1,250,000 bulbs a day. In 1915, the company's research and development department invented Pyrex. In the early 1970s, a fiber optics division was established.

Today, about 6,000 Chemung County residents still work for Corning, Inc. Many others are involved in the tourism industry, servicing visitors who come to town to visit the Corning Museum of Glass.

◖ Corning Museum of Glass

The state-of-the-art Glass Museum (1 Museum Way, Exit 46 off I-86, 607/937-5371 or 800/732-6845, www.cmog.org, 9 A.M.–5 P.M. daily, with extended hours in summer, adults $12, seniors and students $10.80, children under 17 free) sits surrounded by sleek corporate buildings on the north side of town. Its undulating walls are made of a blue-gray glass, while its modern entrance is built of four giant panes of glass.

The museum is divided into several sections, including the relatively new Glass Innovation Center, which tells of scientific advances in glassmaking, and the Glass Sculpture Gallery, the largest of its kind in the world. The heart of the institution, however, remains its main museum building, which showcases more than 10,000 glass objects at a time, many dramatically displayed in darkened rooms with spotlights. The oldest objects date back to 1400 B.C., the newest to the 1990s. Among the many highlights are an iridescent vase from 10th-century Iran, an 11-foot-high Tiffany window, and a table-long glass boat cut by Baccarat in 1900.

At the Hot Glass Show, visitors can observe the art of glassblowing up close. At the Steuben Factory, skilled craftspeople are at work. This is the only place in the world where Steuben glass is made.

THE FINGER LAKES

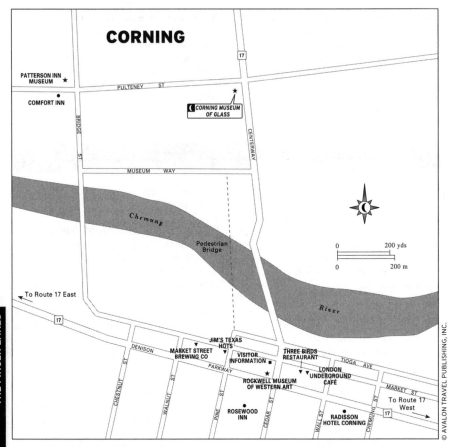

Historic Market Street

After visiting the Glass Museum, most visitors stroll down a wide walkway that leads to Corning's historic downtown. This 19th-century district—once just another dying downtown—was extensively restored following Hurricane Agnes in 1972, when the street was all but destroyed by the flooding of the Chemung River.

Today, Market Street is brick sidewalks, locust trees, and one bustling shop or restaurant after another. At one end are contemporary glass studios with artisans at work: **Vitrix Hot Glass Studio** (77 W. Market St.,

607/936-8707) and **Noslo Glass Studio** (89 W. Market St., 607/962-7886).

Rockwell Museum of Western Art

Near the eastern end of Market St. presides the Rockwell Museum (111 Cedar St., 607/937-5386, www.rockwellmuseum.org, 9 A.M.–5 P.M. daily, with extended hours in summer, adults $6.50 adults, seniors and students $5.50, children under 17 free, families $20), which has nothing to do with Norman Rockwell and everything to do with Western art. Collected by Corning denizen Robert F. Rockwell, this is said to be the most comprehensive assemblage of Western art in the East.

The museum occupies the restored Old City Hall and is nicely arranged around three themes—the Indian, the Landscape, and the Cowboy. Works by Frederic Remington, Charles M. Russell, and Albert Bierstadt hang from the walls, and Navajo rugs drape the stairwell. Exhibit cases contain Native American art and artifacts.

After the crowds of the Corning Glass Center, the Rockwell Museum comes as a quiet relief. Rockwell was a passionate collector who once used the walls of his father's department store to exhibit his artwork, and the museum has an engaging, personal feel.

Benjamin Patterson Inn Museum Complex

A half mile north of Market Street is a complex of restored historic buildings (59 W. Pulteney St., 607/937-5281, 10 A.M.–4 P.M. Mon.–Fri. Mar.–Dec., adults $3, students 6–18 $1) peopled by guides in costume dress. Buildings include the Benjamin Patterson Inn, complete with a women's parlor, tap room, and ballroom; the De Monstoy Cabin, furnished as it would have been by early settlers; and a 1860s barn equipped with antique farm implements.

Accommodations

Across from the Patterson Inn Museum stands a 62-room **Comfort Inn** (66 W. Pulteney St., 607/962-1515, $85–112 d). Within walking distance of Market Street and the Glass Museum is the more upscale **Radisson Hotel Corning** (125 Denison Pkwy. E., 607/962-5000, $99–148 d). The hotel offers 177 rooms and suites, two restaurants, a heated indoor pool, and a fitness center.

Also located near the downtown is one of the area's most popular B&Bs, the handsome 1855 ◖ **Rosewood Inn** (134 E. 1st St., 607/962-3253, www.rosewoodinn.com, $99–185 d). The five guest rooms and two suites are outfitted with antiques and have private baths. Downstairs is an elegant parlor with a fireplace, where afternoon tea is served.

THE FINGER LAKES

COURTESY OF FINGER LAKES WINE COUNTRY TOURISM MARKETING ASSOCIATION

Rockwell Museum of Western Art

Food

Visit **Jim's Texas Hots** (8 W. Market St., 607/936-1820) for ice cream and hot dogs, Texas-style. The airy, three-level **London Underground Cafe** (69 E. Market St., 607/962-2345) serves gourmet salads and sandwiches, light entrés, and desserts.

The **Market Street Brewing Co.** (63–65 W. Market St., 607/936-BEER) offers something for everyone, including rooftop and biergarten dining, dishes ranging from salads to steaks, a kids' menu, and, of course, fresh brews on tap; average entrée $15. The casually elegant **Three Birds Restaurant** (73 E. Market St., 607/936-8862) serves "progressive American fare" made with fresh local ingredients, and hosts a popular martini bar; average entrée $17; open for dinner only.

Keuka Lake

Gentle, Y-shaped Keuka Lake is the only one of the Finger Lakes with an irregular outline. The name means canoe landing in Iroquois, and the lake sports over 70 miles of curving lakeshore, scalloped with coves and bays.

At the southern head of Keuka Lake lies Hammondsport, site of the nation's first winery, established in 1860. The small-town Penn Yan occupies the lake's northern tip. Several Mennonite communities are scattered throughout the Keuka Lake region. Driving south between Penn Yan and Dundee along Routes 14A or 11, or north of Penn Yan along Routes 14A, 374, and 27, you're bound to pass a horse-and-buggy or two clip-clopping down the road. Handwritten signs advertising Mennonite quilts, furniture, or produce for sale sometimes appear by the roadside, while more permanent shops are located near Penn Yan and Dundee.

HAMMONDSPORT

Nestled between steep, verdant hills and Keuka Lake, Hammondsport is a fetching Victorian village with a lively tourist trade. At its center lies the Village Square, anchored by a big, white Presbyterian Church. Shops and restaurants line Sheather Street, the main drag. Along the lakeshore are a sleepy park and two public beaches; the beach at the foot of Sheather Street is said to be the best. However, local viticulture draws the most visitors. Tumbling down the surrounding hillsides are vineyard after vineyard, all supplying grapes for the area's nine wineries.

Glenn Hammond Curtiss, the pioneer aviator, was born in Hammondsport in 1878. Though not as well known as the Wright brothers, Curtiss made the world's first preannounced flight on July 4, 1908, when he piloted his "June Bug" airplane over 5,090 feet just outside Hammondsport. Curtiss developed the U.S. Navy's first amphibian airplane, opened the first flying school in America, and

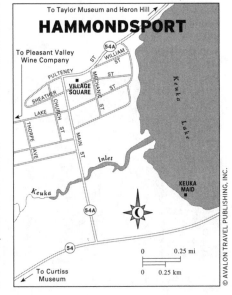

established the Curtiss Aeroplane Company—all in Hammondsport. During World War I, the Curtiss company manufactured the popular Curtiss Jenny airplane, which later became a favorite of barnstormers.

Pleasant Valley Wine Company Visitor Center

Even if the thought of touring wineries bores you to tears, you might want to stop into this center (8260 Pleasant Valley Rd. [County Rd. 88], 607/569-6111, 10 A.M.–5 P.M. daily Apr.–Dec.; 10 A.M.–4 P.M. Tues.–Sat. Jan.–Mar., free admission), one of the largest tourist attractions in the region. The Pleasant Valley Wine Company is the oldest continuous maker of wine in the United States, founded by a group of Hammondsport businessmen in 1860.

The visitors center holds historic exhibits and an informative film, screened inside a 35,000-gallon former wine tank. A nearby working model train replicates the old Bath-Hammondsport Railroad, and a tasting bar offers products for sampling. Everything's very commercialized and the wine is mediocre, but the place is interesting nonetheless. Winery tours are offered throughout the day.

Bully Hill

One of the odder tales in the chronicles of viticulture is that of the battle waged over the name Taylor. Walter S. Taylor, a grandson of the founder of the Taylor Wine Co., was kicked out of the company in 1970 after publicly attacking its "incompetence, greed, and jealousy." Subsequently, he and his father Greyton began their own winery high on Bully Hill.

In 1977, Coca-Cola bought the Taylor Wine Co. and sued Walter for using his family name on his own labels. The case went to court and Walter lost, only to become a local hero. "They have my name and heritage but they didn't get my goat!" he proclaimed and flamboyantly struck out the Taylor name on all his labels. "Branded For Life, by a man that shall remain nameless without Heritage" reads the bylines in his brochures.

The **Wine and Grape Museum of Greyton H. Taylor** (8843 Taylor Memorial Dr., off Rte. 54A, 607/868-4814, 10 A.M.–5 P.M. Mon.–Sat.

THE FINGER LAKES

AMONG THE MENNONITES

A surprisingly large number of Mennonite and Amish Mennonite communities are scattered throughout the Finger Lakes and Western New York. Some were established generations ago, but many others were set up over the past decade or two by people originally from Pennsylvania and Ohio, attracted to New York by its many recently abandoned family farms.

The Mennonite religion is a Protestant sect, founded by Dutch reformer Menno Simons in Switzerland in the 1500s. The Amish are the Mennonites' most conservative branch, established in Pennsylvania in the 18th century. Both groups shun modern society and technology, but the Amish are the most severe.

Throughout the region, you'll see traffic signs alerting you to horse and buggies, and you'll spot occasional plaques advertising handmade quilts, furniture, or baskets for sale.

An especially large Amish population lives in Cattaraugus County in Western New York, while many Mennonites live in Yates, Schuyler, and Ontario Counties in the Finger Lakes. Local residents estimate that the Mennonite population in these last three counties – centered around Keuka Lake – has more than tripled in the past 15 years, to over 1,000.

Why the Amish and Mennonites have success as farmers when others have failed is a topic for debate. Many believe that it has to do with the "plain people's" smaller-size farms and low labor costs. In Mennonite communities, everyone in the family, from young children to great-grandparents, contributes to the operation of the farm.

The Amish and Mennonites dislike having their pictures taken. Please respect their wishes.

and Sun. noon–5 P.M. May–Oct., free admission) tells little of this story. Instead, it focuses on antique wine-making equipment and the delicate, lyrical Bully Hill labels, all drawn by "Walter St. Bully." Adjacent to the museum are the **Bully Hill Vineyards,** open for tastings. Also on site is the Bully Hill Restaurant, offering great views of the lake (see *Food*, below).

Other Wineries

One of the region's top wineries is **Dr. Frank's Vinifera Wine Cellars** (9749 Middle Rd., 607/868-4884, www.DrFrankWines.com). Dr. Frank, an immigrant from Ukraine who arrived in Hammondsport in 1962, was one of the first in the region to grow the European Vinifera grape. Today, his cellars, run by his son, are best known for their chardonnays and Rieslings.

A few miles beyond Bully Hill is the **Heron Hill Winery** (9301 Rte. 76, 607/868-4241, www.heronhill.com) offering chardonnays and Rieslings and more superb views of the lake. Established in 1977, the 45-acre vineyard produces about 30,000 gallons of wine a year.

Both wineries are open 10 A.M.–5 P.M. Monday–Saturday and Sunday noon–5 P.M. May–October.

Glenn H. Curtiss Museum

The cavernous hangars of the former Curtiss Aeroplane Company now contain a sprawling museum (8419 Rte. 54, 607/569-2160, www.linkny.com/curtissmuseum, 9 A.M.–5 P.M. Mon.–Sat. and 11 A.M.–5 P.M. Sun. May–Oct., call for off-season hours, adults $7, seniors $5, students 7–18 $4) devoted to both Curtiss and the early history of aviation. About a dozen spiffy antique airplanes crowd the main hall, along with antique bicycles, motorcycles, propellers, and engines. Curtiss' first interest was the bicycle. One of his earliest planes, the Curtiss Pusher, looks just like a bike with double wings and wires attached.

A highlight of the museum is a replica of the famous "June Bug" airplane, built by volunteers in the mid-1970s. A Curtiss Jenny and delicate Curtiss Robin—resembling a giant grasshopper—stand nearby.

COURTESY OF FINGER LAKES WINE COUNTRY TOURISM MARKETING ASSOCIATION

a bicycle on display at the Glenn H. Curtiss Museum

Recreation

The **Keuka Maid Dinner Boat** (607/569-2628, www.keukamaid.com), a 500-passenger vessel, offers lunch, brunch, and dinner tours May–October. The boat docks in the village off Route 54A; reservations are recommended.

Accommodations

A good choice for bargain hunters is the 17-room **Hammondsport Motel** (William St., 607/569-2600, $65–70 d), which sits on the edge of the village by the lake. The 30-room **Vinehurst Inn** (Rte. 54, 607/569-2300, $70 d) features unusually spacious motel rooms with high ceilings.

In the heart of the village is the 1861 **Park Inn** (Village Square, 607/569-9387, $70–80 d). The inn offers four small suites upstairs and a popular tavern downstairs.

About 15 miles away in the village of Avoca is the storybook **◖ Caboose Motel** (8620 Rte. 415, off Rte. 390, 607/566-2216). Here, you can sleep in snug, restored 1916 train cabooses outfitted with all the modern conveniences and kept in trim shape ($75–80 d), or in more conventional motel rooms ($50 d).

Food

In addition to its mouth-watering ice-cream treats, the cozy **Crooked Lake Ice Cream Parlor** (on the Village Square, 607/569-2751) serves a good breakfast and lunch. The Victorian **Park Inn Tavern** (Village Square, 607/569-9387), open daily until midnight, serves lunch, dinner, and drinks; average dinner entrée $13.

The **◖ Bully Hill Restaurant** at Bully Hill Vineyards (8834 Greyton H. Taylor Memorial Dr., 607/868-3490) offers salads, vegetarian pizzas, grilled chicken, and the like, all prepared with the freshest of ingredients. Open for lunch, and for dinner on the weekends; average lunch entrée $9.

Along the shores of Keuka Lake two miles north of Hammondsport, you'll find **Snug Harbor Restaurant** (144 W. Lake Rd., 607/868-3488), parts of which date back to 1890. Dockside dining is featured in summer.

On the menu is contemporary American fare; entrées cost $15–23.

A bit further north is the **Waterfront Restaurant** (648 W. Lake Rd., Pulteney, 607/868-3455), where at least half the diners arrive by boat. Clambakes are featured throughout the summer, along with live entertainment. Seafood, pasta, and grilled meats are on the menu; average entrée $15.

NORTH ON ROUTE 54A

Route 54A heads north of Hammondsport into steep, vineyard-covered hills with great views of the lake. The route hugs the shoreline as far north as Branchport, then veers east to Penn Yan, located at the northern tip of the lake's longer prong.

Just east of Branchport is **Keuka Lake State Park** (3370 Pepper Rd., 315/536-3666, $6–8 parking) featuring a swimming beach, bathhouse, hiking trails, campground, and good fishing sites. To reserve a campsite, call 800/456-CAMP.

Next you'll hit **Bluff Point,** a headland from which you can see both arms of the lake as well as, some say, seven counties and 10 lakes on a clear day. In the center of Bluff Point stands the **Garrett Memorial Chapel,** a lovely Gothic-style sanctuary built in memory of Charles Garrett, the son of a wealthy winemaker, who died of tuberculosis in his twenties. From Bluff Point south, between Keuka's arms, runs the eight-mile-long **Skyline Drive.**

PENN YAN

Named for its early Pennsylvanian and Yankee settlers, Penn Yan is an attractive small town (pop. 5,500), the seat of Yates County. Its downtown centers on historic Main Street, where you'll find **Belknap Hill Books** (106 Main St., 315/536-1186), packed with more than 20,000 out-of-print, used, and rare books.

On a windowless wall of **Birkett Mills** (1 Main St.) are mounted half of an enormous griddle and the words: "The annual Buckwheat Harvest Festival. Size of big griddle used to make world record pancake, Sept. 27, 1987.

28 feet, 1 inch." Birkett is the world's largest producer of buckwheat products and maintains a small retail shop in its offices (163 Main St., 315/536-3311).

Oliver House Museum

This local history museum (200 Main St., 315/536-7318, 9:30 A.M.–4 P.M. Mon.–Fri., summer Sat. 10 A.M.–2 P.M., free admission), housed in a handsome brick building, is run by the Yates County Genealogical and Historical Society. One especially interesting exhibit pertains to Jemima Wilkinson, the 18th-century religious leader from Rhode Island who called herself the "Publick Universal Friend."

While in her early 20s, Wilkinson awoke from a severe fever one day to announce that she had been dead, her carnal existence had ended, and she was now reanimated by a Divine Spirit. Her mission was to be neither man nor woman but the Publick Universal Friend, brought back to life to save sinners from damnation.

An exceptionally beautiful woman, with brilliant black eyes and hair, Wilkinson preached celibacy and loyalty to her sect above all else. Despite her illiteracy and a strong accent difficult to understand, she gathered converts from all over New England, some of them quite wealthy. After being thrown out of several communities, she and her followers settled down in 1788 in the Finger Lakes, about eight miles west of Penn Yan. There, in a white clapboard house, Wilkinson held religious meetings attired in a silk purple robe, fine white dress, and man's shirt so that she appeared androgynous.

As more settlers came into the region, and Wilkinson's beauty began to fade, she lost much of her hold over her followers. After her death, the sect disintegrated, but the original Jemima Wilkinson House, now privately owned, still stands on Friend Road in Branchport.

Recreation

Auctions take place Saturday at 7 P.M. at **Hayes Auction Barn** (1644 Rte. 14A, 315/536-8818). The *Viking Spirit* **Cruise Ship** (680 East Lake Rd., 315/536-7061, www.vikingresort.com) offers daily cruises May–October.

Accommodations

Overlooking the lake just west of town stands the simple but adequate 17-room **Colonial Motel** (175 W. Lake Rd., 315/536-3056, $75–95 d). Also near the downtown is the considerably more stylish **Fox Inn** (158 Main St., 315/536-3101 or 800/901-7997, www.foxinnbandb.com, $120–150 d), a 1820s Greek Revival home with five cozy guest rooms and formal gardens out back.

Situated on an 18-acre estate with great views of both Keuka and Seneca Lakes presides **Merritt Hill Manor** (2756 Coates Rd., 315/536-7682, www.merritthillmanor.com, $80–150). The 1822 country manor offers five guest rooms, a breezy porch, and a fireplace-equipped living room.

Food

Diner aficionados will want to stop into the squat, classic **Penn Yan Diner** (131 E. Elm St., off Main St., 315/536-6004), which dates back to 1925. **Millers' Essenhaus** (1300 Rte. 14A, Benton Center, 315/531-8260) is a Mennonite restaurant serving such homemade specialties as barbecue sandwiches, split pea soup, and whoopie and shoofly pies.

Shopping

Midway between Penn Yan and Dundee sprawls the **Windmill Farm and Market** (Rte. 14A, 315/536-3032, www.thewindmill.com), the oldest and biggest of several indoor/outdoor farm-and-crafts markets operating in the Finger Lakes. Every Saturday, May–December, 8 A.M.–4:30 P.M., about 250 local vendors set up shop in a large fairgrounds area off Route 14A. For sale are produce, flowers, furniture, crafts, wine, antiques, and homemade food. Many Mennonite families operate booths here.

In Dundee, you'll find **Martin's Kitchen** (4898 John Green Rd., 607/243-8197) selling homemade pickles, pickled watermelon rinds, jams, apple butter, and other Mennonite specialties.

Events

The **Yates County Fair** takes over the Penn Yan fairgrounds in mid-July. On the Fourth of July and the Saturday before Labor Day, the shores of Keuka Lake glow with magical **Rings of Fire,** as in the days of the Seneca. The Seneca lit bonfires to celebrate the harvest; today highway flares celebrate the holidays. For information about any of these events, call the Yates County Chamber of Commerce (315/536-3111).

Canandaigua Lake Area

The farthest west of the major Finger Lakes, Canandaigua is also the most commercialized. Rochester (pop. 235,000) is less than 30 miles away, and the lake has served as the city's summer playground since the late 1800s. At the northern end of the lake lies the historic city of Canandaigua, now largely a resort town. At the southern end rests the trim village of Naples.

Canandaigua is Iroquois for "The Chosen Place," and according to legend, the Seneca people were born at the south end of the lake, on South Hill. As the legend goes, the Creator caused the ground to open here, allowing the Seneca to climb out. All went well until a giant serpent coiled itself around the base of the hill. Driven by an insatiable hunger, the snake picked off the Seneca one by one until at last a young warrior slew him with a magic arrow. The dying serpent writhed down the hill, disgorging the heads of its victims as he went; large rounded stones resembling human skulls have been found in the area. South Hill is now part of the Hi Tor Wildlife Management Area.

Also connected with the Seneca is tiny Squaw Island, located in the northern end of the lake. The Seneca people relate that many women and children escaped slaughter by hiding out here during General Sullivan's 1779 campaign.

CANANDAIGUA

The sprawling city of Canandaigua has a wide and expansive feel. Through its center runs busy Main Street, a four-lane thoroughfare lined with leafy trees and imposing Greek Re-vival buildings set back from the street. At the foot of Main extends the lake and City Pier. Tourist-oriented businesses dominate.

Following the Revolution, two New Englanders, Oliver Phelps and Nathaniel Gorham, purchased what is now Canandaigua, along with the rest of western New York, from the Native Americans. The first white settlers arrived in 1789, and shortly thereafter, the first land office in the United States was established near present-day Main Street.

On November 11, 1794, the Seneca chiefs and Gen. Timothy Pickering met in Canandaigua to sign what was later known as the Pickering Treaty. A document of enormous significance, the treaty granted whites the right to settle the Great Lakes Basin. An original copy of the treaty can be found in the Ontario County Historical Society Museum.

C Sonnenberg Gardens and Mansion

In the heart of the bustling downtown sits a serene 50-acre garden estate (151 Charlotte St., 585/394-4922, www.sonnenberg.org, 9:30 A.M.–5:30 P.M. daily June-Oct., adults $10, seniors $9, students $5, children under 12 free), composed of nine formal gardens, an arboretum, a *long* turn-of-the-20th-century greenhouse, and a massive 1887 stone mansion. The Smithsonian Institution credited the place "one of the most magnificent late-Victorian gardens ever created in America."

Sonnenberg (German for "Sunny Hill") was once the summer home of Mary Clark and Frederick Ferris Thompson. Mr. Thompson, whose father helped to establish the Chase

THE FINGER LAKES

© AVALON TRAVEL PUBLISHING, INC.

Bank, was co-founder of the First National City Bank of New York City.

The estate's nine gardens were created by Mrs. Thompson as a memorial after her husband's death in 1899. A classic Rose Garden features over 4,000 rose bushes, and the Japanese Garden took seven workers six months to create. The secluded Sub Rosa Garden contains statues of Zeus, Diana, and Apollo. The Blue & White Garden contains only blue and white flowers.

Visitors to Sonnenberg can wander freely—even the mansion is self-guided-though guided walking tours are also offered June–September. Near the entrance is an inviting café, housed in one of the greenhouses, and the huge, commercial **Finger Lakes Wine Center** (585/394-9016, 11 A.M.–4 P.M. daily, May–Oct.), selling regional wines.

Granger Homestead and Carriage Museum

This 1816 Federal-style mansion (295 N. Main St., 585/394-1472, www.grangerhomestead.org, 1–5 P.M. Tues.–Sun. May–Oct., adults $5, seniors $4, students $1) once housed Gideon Granger, U.S. postmaster general under Presidents Jefferson and Madison. The home—"unrivalled in all the nation," Granger once boasted—is especially notable for its elaborate carved moldings and mantelpieces, and for its fine original furnishings.

Dark, towering trees surround the house. Out back is a carriage museum, packed with about 50 spit-and-polish coaches, sporting carriages, sleighs, commercial wagons, and an undertaker's hearse.

Ontario County Historical Society Museum

To learn more about the history of Canandaigua, step into this local museum (55 N. Main St., 585/394-4975, 10 A.M.–4 P.M. Mon.–Sat., admission $2), situated in a handsome brick building. On display is the original Six Nations' copy of the Pickering Treaty with the signatures of the Iroquois leaders Red Jacket, Cornplanter, Handsome Lake, Farmer's Brother, Little Beard, and Fish Carrier. Each signed with an X. The museum also features "life masks" of Abraham Lincoln (plaster-of-Paris masks taken from a mold of his face), a small children's discovery area, and temporary exhibits.

Ontario County Courthouse

Dominating downtown Canandaigua, and indeed much of the surrounding countryside, is the bulbous dome of the Ontario County Courthouse (27 N. Main St., at Gorham, 585/396-4200, 8:30 A.M.–5 P.M. Mon.–Fri.). Hung in the two courtrooms of this 1858 Greek Revival structure is a marvelous collection of portraits. Among them are likenesses of Red Jacket and Susan B. Anthony, who was tried here in 1873 for voting in the national election in Rochester. She was found guilty and fined $100. A boulder on the courthouse grounds commemorates the Pickering Treaty, signed here in 1794.

Recreation

The *Canandaigua Lady* (205 Lakeshore Dr., 585/396-7350) is a 150-passenger paddlewheel boat offering lunch, dinner, and moonlight cruises May–October. **Captain Gray's Boat Tours** (5 Main St., 585/394-5270) features one-hour narrated tours of the lake daily

July–August, weekends May–October; the boat leaves from behind the Canandaigua Inn on the Lake.

Seven miles northwest of Canandaigua lies **Finger Lakes Gaming & Race Track** (Rtes. 332 and 96, Exit 44 off I-90, 585/924-3232). Thoroughbred racing takes place Friday–Tuesday April–November. Also on site are 1,000 video-gaming machines.

Accommodations

On the waterfront stands the **Canandaigua Inn on the Lake** (770 S. Main St., 585/394-7800 or 800/228-2801, www.visitinnonthelake.com, $150–275 d), a full-service hotel and conference center. Among its features are 147 nicely appointed guest rooms, many with patios or balconies; a pristine outdoor pool; saunas; and the airy, inviting Nicole's restaurant (see *Food*, below).

The Canandaigua region is home to many luxury B&Bs. One of the best is the snug, Colonial **C Acorn Inn** (4508 Rte. 64 S, Bristol

THE FINGER LAKES TRAIL

Through the heart of the Finger Lakes runs a 557-mile main trail extending from the Pennsylvania-New York border in Allegany State Park to the Long Path in the Catskill Forest Preserve. Six branch trails and two loop trails that extend an additional 278 miles intersect the main trail. Most of the trailheads are marked with the yellow-and-green Finger Lakes Trail logo, and camping facilities are available along most sections.

The **Finger Lakes Trail Conference** publishes 45 maps that cover the entire trail system, along with several guidebooks. The individual maps cost about $1 each; a complete set is about $20. For a list of the maps and publications available, contact the Finger Lakes Trail Conference (6111 Visitor Center Rd., Mt. Morris, NY 14510, 585/658-9320, www.fingerlakestrail.org).

THE FINGER LAKES

Center, 585/229-2834, www.acorninnbb.com, $165–240 d). Once a stagecoach stop, the inn now pampers guests with comfy canopy beds, luxurious private baths, an outdoor hot tub, and multicourse breakfasts.

Not too far away is the plush 1810 **Morgan-Samuels B&B Inn** (2920 Smith Rd., 585/394-9232, www.morgansamuelsinn.com, $175–275 d), which offers six guest rooms, eight fireplaces, tennis courts, and gourmet breakfasts by candlelight. High on a bluff overlooking Deep Run Cove stands the peaceful turn-of-the-century **Thendara Inn** (4356 E. Lake Rd., 585/394-4868, $170–250 d), containing four spacious guest rooms furnished with antiques and a good restaurant (see *Food*, below).

Entertainment

During the summer, the Rochester Philharmonic Orchestra performs every weekend at the **Finger Lakes Performing Arts Center** (Rte. 364 and Lincoln Hill Rd., 585/325-7760), an outdoor amphitheater. Rock, jazz, and pop-music concerts are sometimes presented as well.

Food

Koozina's (699 S. Main St., 585/396-0360) is a lively spot specializing in wood-fired pizza and pasta dishes; average entrée $9.

◖ Nicole's at the Inn on the Lake (770 S. Main St., 585/394-7800) offers great views of the lake and contemporary American fare. It's open for breakfast, lunch, and dinner; average dinner entrée $18.

The Victorian **Thendara Inn** (4356 E. Lake Rd., 585/394-4868) serves American cuisine in three period dining rooms with panoramic views of the lake; in summer, an outdoor patio is opened up (average entrée $18; open for dinner only). Also at the inn is the more casual **Boathouse,** serving lighter fare for both lunch and dinner.

VICTOR

About 10 miles northwest of Canandaigua sprawls the village of Victor, worth visiting because of the **Ganondagan State Historic Site**

(1488 Victor-Bloomfield Rd., 585/742-1690, www.ganandagan.org, 9 A.M.–5 P.M. Tues.–Sun. May–Oct., adults $3, children $2). During the 17th century, atop this grassy lime-green knoll, stood an important Seneca village and palisaded granary. The village was home to about 4,500 people; the granary stored hundreds of thousands of bushels of corn. All was destroyed in 1687 by a French army led by the governor of Canada. The French wished to eliminate the Seneca as competitors in the fur trade.

A visit to Ganondagan, which means "Town of Peace," begins with an interesting video that tells the story of the Seneca Nation and that of Jikohnsaseh, or Mother of Nations. Together with "The Peacemaker" and Hiawatha, Jikohnsaseh was instrumental in forging the Five Nations Confederacy; it was she who proposed that the Onondangan chief, who at first refused to join the confederacy, be appointed chairman of the Chiefs' Council. Jikohnsaseh once lived in the vicinity of Ganondagan and is believed to be buried nearby. No one searches for her grave, however, as a sign of respect.

Outside the visitors center begin three trails that lead over gentle terrain past informative plaques. The Trail of Peace relates important moments in Seneca history. The Earth of Our Mother Trail identifies plants important to the Seneca. The Granary Trail re-creates the day in 1687 Ganondagan was destroyed, through journal entries from the French forces.

To reach the site, from Rte. 332 heading north, turn left onto County Road 41 to Victor-Bloomfield Road. Trails stay open year-round 8 A.M.–sunset.

PALMYRA

About 15 miles due north of Canandaigua is Palmyra, an old Erie Canal town where Joseph Smith allegedly received, from the angel Moroni, a set of gold tablets inscribed with the Book of Mormon. The Hill Cumorah Pageant, the largest outdoor pageant in the United States, celebrates that event every July.

Downtown Palmyra is small and compact, lined with sturdy brick buildings. At each corner of the intersection of Main Street and

Route 21 stand four soaring churches—a fact that once made it into *Ripley's Believe It or Not.* Just west of downtown is a graceful stone **Erie Canal Aqueduct,** off Route 31.

In downtown Palmyra are three small museums run by Historic Palmyra. On the outskirts of town are the Hill Cumorah Visitor Center and Joseph Smith Farm, run by the Mormon Church.

Historic Palmyra

The **Alling Coverlet Museum** (122 Williams St., off Main, 315/597-6737 or 315/597-6981) houses the largest collection of handwoven coverlets in the United States. Often referred to as the American tapestry, coverlets are ornate bed coverings made out of wool, cotton, or linen.

The nearby **Palmyra Historical Museum** (132 Market St., 315/597-6981) occupies the former St. James Hotel. Exhibits here include 19th-century furniture, Erie Canal art and artifacts, children's toys, and lots of stern Victorian portraits.

Finally, the **William Phelps General Store** (140 Market St., 315/597-6981) was operated by the Phelps family from the 1860s until the 1940s. The museum recreates the general store of the 1890s.

All three museums are open 1–4 P.M. Tuesday–Saturday June–September. Admission is free.

Hill Cumorah Visitor Center

A good place to learn about the Mormon religion is this modern center (603 Rte. 21, 315/597-5851, www.hillcumorah.com, 9 A.M.–5 P.M. Mon.–Sat., 1–5 P.M. Sun., with extended hours in summer, free admission), four miles south of the downtown. Most visitors are well-scrubbed Mormons straight from the heartland, but nonbelievers are welcome and are left more or less in peace to peruse the exhibits. A film provides a good introduction to Mormon history and beliefs, and exhibits tout the growth of the religion. There are currently about nine million Mormons worldwide, though only 1,500 live in upstate New York.

Behind the center stands Hill Cumorah,

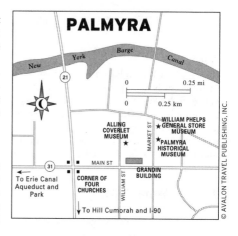

© AVALON TRAVEL PUBLISHING, INC.

the drumlin where Joseph Smith is said to have found the gold tablets on September 22, 1827. It took him years to translate the tablets, and after he was done, he reburied them. Atop Hill Cumorah today is a gold statue of the angel Moroni.

Joseph Smith Farm and Sacred Grove

Born in Vermont in 1805, Joseph Smith first came to Palmyra with his family in 1815. The Smiths were farmers, and Joseph—described by one contemporary as a "quiet, low-speaking, unlaughing" boy—lived in this simple, white clapboard house (29 Stafford Rd., 315/597-4383 or 315/597-5851, 9 A.M.–5 P.M. Mon.–Sat., 1–5 P.M. Sun., free admission) until he was 22. He received his first vision in the Sacred Grove behind the house when he was only 14.

SOUTH ON ROUTES 364 AND 245

Heading south down Canandaigua's eastern shore, you'll pass through a series of picturesque valleys. At the southern end of the lake, the route skirts around South Hill and the **High Tor Wildlife Management Area** (585/226-2466). Hiking trails traverse the preserve, which is also one of the few places left in New York where you can still spot bluebirds—the state bird. The main entrance to

THE FINGER LAKES

the area is off Route 245 between Middlesex and Naples.

NAPLES

Just south of Canandaigua Lake, surrounded by hills, lies Naples, population 2,500. A tidy village with a brisk tourist trade, Naples centers around a historic **Old Town Square.** Naples is one of the best places in the Finger Lakes to sample a sweet regional specialty—**grape pie.** The pies, made with dark grapes, are only available during the harvest season in fall.

Widmer Wine Cellars

One mile due north of the Old Town Square is Widmer's (1 Lake Niagara Ln., off Rte. 21, 585/374-6311, www.widmerwine.com, noon–4:00 P.M. daily May–Dec., free admission)—one of the largest, oldest, and most commercialized wineries in the region. Tours start in a cool stone cellar filled with enormous oak vats, and end in a busy bottling plant that processes 300,000 cases of wine a year.

Widmer's has been producing Manischewitz, a kosher wine, since 1986. The wine is made in a separate winery equipped with all-stainless-steel vats. Rabbis come down from Rochester to oversee the process.

Cumming Nature Center

About eight miles northwest of the village lies the 900-acre Cumming Nature Center (6472 Gulick Rd., 585/374-6160, 9 A.M.–4:30 P.M. Sat.–Sun., admission $3), owned by the Rochester Museum and Science Center. A veritable outdoor museum, the preserve holds six miles of themed trails leading through forests and wetlands. The Conservation Trail illustrates theories of forest management; the Pioneer Trail, complete with a reconstructed homestead, teaches about the early settlers' lives. The Beaver Trail focuses on the principles of ecology, and the Iroquois Trail focuses on Native American life. Near the entrance is a visitors center.

Gannett Hill

Scenic Route 21 heads due north out of Naples

THE MASSIVE HILL CUMORAH PAGEANT

The largest and oldest outdoor drama in America is the Hill Cumorah Pageant, staged just outside Palmyra every July since 1937. Likened by one critic to a "George Lucas techno-dazzler with the scope of a Cecil B. DeMille epic," the pageant tells the story of the Book of Mormon. The show includes a 37-foot-high erupting volcano, a 56-foot-long ship that's struck by lightning, and medieval battle scenes complete with swords and lances. The nativity scene is lit with a 5,000K carbon arc light – so bright that it required FAA clearance. A digital sound recording of the Mormon Tabernacle Choir provides the music. The pageant's cast numbers about 600 and the audience about 54,000 over a seven-night period.

The pageant is free and open to the general public. Many non-Mormons as well as Mormons attend, and although some proselytizing goes on, it's very low key. "Welcome to the Hill Cumorah Pageant, America's Witness for Christ" reads a sign over the entranceway; young people in medieval costume move excitedly through the crowd. They're eager to know where you're from and if you've ever attended before, but after handing out literature, they move on to greet other arriving guests.

The pageant doesn't begin until nightfall, but it's best to arrive by early evening to claim a seat and watch the pre-show activity. For more information, contact Hill Cumorah Pageant (315/597-5851, www.hillcumorah.com).

© CHRISTIANE BIRD

Mormon founder Joseph Smith lived in this Palmyra house and had his first vision in the Sacred Grove behind the house.

THE FINGER LAKES

to the highest point in Ontario County—Gannett Hill, 2,256 feet above sea level. Now part of Ontario County Park, the hill offers bird's-eye views of the surrounding countryside.

Food

Bob and Ruth's (204 Main St., Old Town Square, 585/374-5122) is a village institution containing both a casual dining area and the more formal Vineyard Room. Specialties range from rotisserie chicken to Angus beef (average entrée $17). In summer, an outdoor patio opens up.

The historic 1895 **Naples Hotel Restaurant** (111 S. Main St., 585/374-5630) specializes in traditional American fare; on Saturdays, live music is often presented in the hotel's rathskeller downstairs (average entrée $14). Five rooms are also available here for overnight guests ($75–125 d).

The Little Finger Lakes and Beyond

LITTLE FINGER LAKES

West of the six major Finger Lakes extend what are known as the little Finger Lakes: Honeoye (pronounced Honey-oy), Canadice, Hemlock, and Conesus. Honeoye sports a village of the same name at its northern end, and Conesus—closest to Rochester—is crowded with summer homes. Canadice and Hemlock serve as reservoirs for Rochester and remain largely undeveloped. Set in deep, wooded valleys with no towns nearby, these are also the highest of the Finger Lakes—1,100 and 905 feet respectively.

At the southwestern end of Honeoye lies the largely undeveloped **Harriet Hollister Spenser State Park** (Canadice Hill Rd. [Rte. 37], 585/335-8111). Set on Canadice Hill, the park offers great views of the lake and—on a clear day—the Rochester skyline.

◖ LETTCHWORTH STATE PARK

Along the Genesee River at the far western edge of the Finger Lakes plunges one of the most magnificent sights in the state: the 17-mile-long **Letchworth Gorge,** now part of a state park (off Rtes. 36 and 19A, Castile, 585/493-3600, 6 A.M.–11 P.M. daily, $6–8 for parking). Dubbed the "Grand Canyon of the East," the gorge is flanked by dark gray cliffs rising nearly 600 feet. All around grows a dense, thicketed forest; through the center of things sparkle three thundering waterfalls.

Much of the Letchworth Gorge was purchased by industrialist William P. Letchworth in 1859. A conservationist and humanitarian, Letchworth bought the gorge both for his own personal use and to save the falls from becoming Rochester's hydroelectric plant. Before his death in 1910, he deeded the gorge to the people of New York to be used as a permanent park.

One main road runs through the park alongside the gorge, affording scenic views. At the southern end stand the Glen Iris Inn, a favorite luncheon spot, and the Letchworth Museum. Recreational facilities include 20 hiking trails ranging from one-half to seven miles in length, two swimming pools, 82 cabins, and a 270-site campground.

The park can be entered from Mt. Morris (off Rte. 36), Portageville (off Rtes. 19A or 436), or Castile (off Rte. 19A); the Portageville entrances are closed in winter. For camping reservations, call 800/456-CAMP.

GLEN IRIS INN

The creaky, yellow-and-white ◖ **Glen Iris Inn** (585/493-2622, www.glenirisinn.com, $80–85 d) sits in a large flat field overlooking the 107-foot Mid Falls. Once the home of William Letchworth, the Victorian mansion is now a modernized inn with 15 simple but comfortable guest rooms, a library with a good collection of regional books, and a gift shop. The inn's bustling restaurant, flanked by picture windows, specializes in gourmet salads, seafood, and veal; open for breakfast, lunch, and dinner; average dinner entrée $18.

LETCHWORTH MUSEUM

Across from the Glen Iris is a rambling museum (585/493-2760, 10 A.M.–5 P.M. daily May–Oct.) haphazardly packed with exhibits on the Seneca, William Letchworth, and the gorge's natural history. Note especially the exhibits relating to Mary Jemison, the "white woman of the Genesee."

The daughter of Irish immigrants, Jemison was taken prisoner by the Seneca at the age of 15 and lived the rest of her life among them. She married first a Delaware warrior and then, following his death, a Seneca chief; she bore seven children, and became a Seneca leader in her own right. Under the Big Tree Treaty of 1797, she was granted close to 18,000 acres along the Genesee River. Eventually, however, Jemison was moved to the Buffalo Creek Reservation with the rest of her people, where she died at the age of 91.

Letchworth moved Jemison's remains to the gorge in 1910 when her grave was in danger of being destroyed, and today, the **Mary Jemison Grave** stands on a hill behind the museum. Also on the hill is the **Council House** in which the last Iroquois council on the Genesee River was held on October 1, 1872. In attendance were the grandchildren of Red Jacket, Joseph Brant, and Mary Jemison; and William Letchworth and Millard Fillmore.

Rochester

Straddling the Genesee River gorge just south of Lake Ontario, presides Rochester (pop. 220,000). New York's third-largest city, Rochester has traditionally been known for its behemoth high-tech industries—Eastman Kodak, Xerox, Bausch & Lomb. Many major educational and cultural institutions are based here as well, including the Eastman School of Music, Rochester Philharmonic, Strong Museum, and International Museum of Photography at the George Eastman House.

For much of the 20th century, Rochester was famed for its prosperity—thanks in large part to Eastman Kodak. But in more recent decades, the city has been forced to reinvent itself. As Eastman Kodak and other major employers have downsized to shadows of their former selves, laying off thousands upon thousands of workers, the city has lost its identity as a paternalistic company town to become one made up of many small firms. Rochester today is home to dozens of thriving but relatively unknown computer software, telecommunications, and medical equipment companies, and its population has learned to take nothing for granted. The areas around Rochester remain extremely prosperous, while its downtown suffers from common urban woes.

Rochester is a Midwestern city, with lots of solid brick buildings surrounded by a flat landscape. It was first established in 1803, but didn't really begin to grow until 1825 when the Erie Canal came to town. As America's first boomtown, Rochester's population increased 13-fold between 1825 and 1845.

Famous Rochesterians have included abolitionist Frederick Douglass, women's rights leader Susan B. Anthony, industrialist George Eastman, and musicians Cab Calloway, Mitch Miller, and Chuck Mangione. Native son Garth Fagan continues to live and headquarter his world-renowned dance troupe in the city.

Orientation

Downtown Rochester is encircled by I-490, and is sometimes called the Inner Loop. Main Street runs east-west through the center of the downtown; Clinton Avenue runs north-south. Just west of South Street is the Genesee River.

Major thoroughfares fanning out from I-490 include East Avenue, Park Avenue, Monroe Avenue (Route 31), and Mt. Hope Avenue (Route 15). I-90 runs just south of the city. Lake Ontario lies about eight miles north of the downtown.

The best way to explore Rochester is by car. You'll find several parking garages downtown, on or just off Main Street. Elsewhere in the city, street parking is generally available. Downtown sights are within walking distance of each other and the major museums in southeast Rochester.

HISTORY
Early History

When the first white settlers arrived in the Rochester area in the late 1700s, they found a rattlesnake-infested swamp and three tremendous Genesee River waterfalls. The settlers deemed braving the dangers of the swamp

THE FINGER LAKES

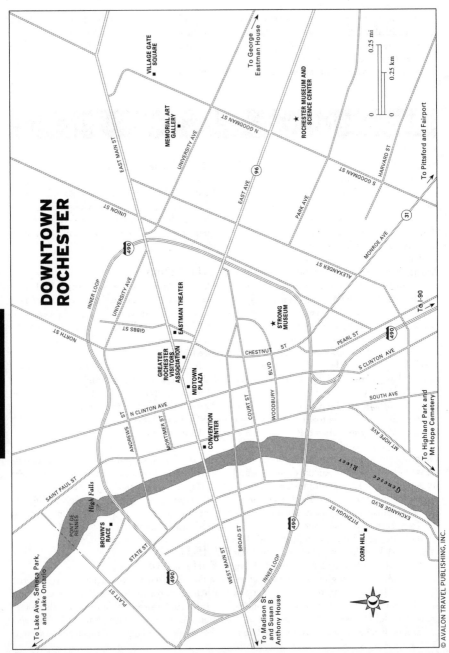

DOWNTOWN ROCHESTER

VILLAGE GATE SQUARE

MEMORIAL ART GALLERY

To George Eastman House

ROCHESTER MUSEUM AND SCIENCE CENTER

N GOODMAN ST

UNIVERSITY AVE

EAST MAIN ST

EAST AVE

PARK AVE

S GOODMAN ST

HARVARD ST

To Pittsford and Fairport

96

UNION ST

MONROE AVE

31

490

INNER LOOP

UNIVERSITY AVE

NORTH ST

ALEXANDER ST

EASTMAN THEATER

GIBBS ST

GREATER ROCHESTER VISITORS ASSOCIATION

MIDTOWN PLAZA

STRONG MUSEUM

CHESTNUT ST

PEARL ST

To I-90

490

S CLINTON AVE

WOODBURY BLVD

COURT ST

CLINTON AVE

N CLINTON AVE

SOUTH AVE

CONVENTION CENTER

ANDREWS ST

MORTIMER ST

MT HOPE AVE

To Highland Park and Mt Hope Cemetery

SAINT PAUL ST

Genesee River

EXCHANGE BLVD

High Falls

PONT DE RENNES

BROWN'S RACE

STATE ST

WEST MAIN ST

BROAD ST

FITZHUGH ST

490

INNER LOOP

CORN HILL

To Lake Ave, Seneca Park, and Lake Ontario

PLATT ST

To Madison St and Susan B Anthony House

0   0.25 mi

0   0.25 km

© AVALON TRAVEL PUBLISHING, INC.

worth the rewards of the falls, and soon grist-mills were operating all along the river banks. After the opening of the Erie Canal, the mills became so prosperous Rochester was dubbed the Flour Capital. When the grain industry moved westward, Rochester turned to other businesses, including horticulture, and re-named itself the Flower City.

During the mid-1800s, Rochester was a hotbed of social activism and radical thought. Frederick Douglass, the escaped slave and abolitionist, settled in Rochester in 1847 and published his newspaper, the *Northern Star,* here for 17 years. One of his close associates was Susan B. Anthony, who was arrested in 1872 for daring to vote in a national election.

Kodak and the 20th Century
In 1881, a quiet young bank clerk named George Eastman patented and produced the world's first rollable film—an invention that would change Rochester forever. By the turn of the century, Eastman Kodak was Rochester's largest employer, and Eastman a generous phi-

lanthropist. During his lifetime, he gave away over $100 million—about $1 billion in today's economy—mainly to schools, parks, the University of Rochester, and local hospitals. "I want to make Rochester the best city in which to live and work," he once said, and as far as many Rochesterians were concerned, he succeeded.

Like many other Northeastern cities, Rochester fell on hard times in the 1960s. Factories closed, citizens fled the downtown, and racial tensions exploded in the riots of 1964. For the most part, however, things were never as bad in Rochester as they were elsewhere in the country. Eastman Kodak was still there, along with two new high-tech companies—Xerox and Bausch & Lomb.

Today, Eastman Kodak is still there. Although the company has downsized considerably from the 60,200 people it employed in its 1982 heyday, it is still the city's largest employer.

DOWNTOWN
At first, Rochester's downtown seems much like any other. Encircled by I-490, it centers

Rochester skyline

on Main Street, flanked with a mix of historic buildings and modern glass-sheathed skyscrapers. At the corner of Main and Clinton Avenue sprawls the 1962 **Midtown Plaza,** the oldest downtown shopping mall in the country; at the corner of Main and South Avenue stand the **Rochester Riverside Convention Center.** The graceful **Eastman Theatre,** with its rounded facade, is tucked onto Gibbs Street near Main, while the stunning art deco **Times Square Building** towers one block off Main at the intersection of Exchange Boulevard and Broad Street.

But walk a few blocks north of Main Street to Brown's Race, and you'll see why this is no ordinary downtown. An enormous gaping gorge rips right through the heart of the city.

Brown's Race and the Center at High Falls

Brown's Race sits at the edge of wide, semi-circular High Falls—96 feet high. Cupping the falls to both sides, but especially to the east, are jagged brown walls streaked with dull red. A **pedestrian bridge** crosses the river just south of the falls.

Brown's Race is made up of four interconnected brick buildings that once contained water-powered mills. The word "race" refers to the diverted raceways that once harnessed the power of the falls. Brown's Race was extensively renovated in the early 1990s and now features shops, restaurants, and one of New York's **Heritage Area Visitor Centers** (60 Brown's Race, at Platt St. and the Genesee River, 585/325-2030, www.centerathighfalls.org, 10 A.M.–4 P.M. Tues.–Fri., noon–5 P.M. Sat.–Sun., free admission)—loosely delineated historic districts united by a common theme. The theme in Rochester is the natural environment, but the center's many exhibits cover virtually every aspect of the city's history.

At dusk May–September, the center presents a free laser light show projected onto a 500-foot section of the gorge. The show tells the story of a Seneca spirit said to inhabit the river, and the tale of Sam Patch, a daredevil who lost his life going over the falls in 1829.

Strong Museum

Up until the late 1990s, the Strong (1 Manhattan Square, at Chestnut and Woodbury Blvd., 585/263-2700, www.strongmuseum.org, 10 A.M.–5 P.M. Mon.–Sat., noon–5 P.M. Sun., adults $7, seniors $6, children 2–17 $5) was one of the most unusual museums in New York State, specializing in everyday American history and folk art. In it, you could find over a half million objects ranging from antique toys, dollhouses, and advertising memorabilia to weathervanes, political campaign buttons, and quilts.

Those objects are still there, but they've been relegated to the back rooms, as today's Strong has been reconstructed into the second-largest children's museum in the country. The main exhibits now are: Sesame Street, Time Lab (with lots of hands-on history games), a kid-sized supermarket, and a 1918 carousel. The museum is undoubtedly more popular today than it was in its earlier incarnation—and a must-stop for families—but much has been lost in the transformation.

Before her death in 1969, the museum's founder, Margaret Woodbury Strong, the daughter of wealthy parents, had amassed more than 300,000 objects, some of which she began collecting as a child. Often, during her family's many trips abroad, she was given a large shopping bag at the start of each day and told she could shop until she filled it.

Strong's many passions included fans, parasols, Asian artifacts and art, dolls, dollhouses, miniatures, toys, marbles, canes, paperweights, glass, pottery, samplers, figurines, kitchen equipment, and costumes. Her doll collection, numbering 27,000, is especially impressive.

SOUTHEAST ROCHESTER

The genteel southeastern quadrant of Rochester boasts three major museums, two minor ones, the University of Rochester, Mt. Hope Cemetery, and Highland Park. Through its center runs expansive **East Avenue,** peppered with stately mansions, gardens, and churches. Parallel to East Avenue runs **Park Avenue,** known for its classy boutiques, restaurants, and outdoor cafés. South of Park lies **Monroe Avenue,** a major commercial artery that's also one of the city's more eclectic neighborhoods.

Memorial Art Gallery

Connected with the University of Rochester, the Memorial Art Gallery (500 University Ave., between Prince and Goodman Sts., 585/473-7720, http://mag.rochester.edu, 10 A.M.–4 P.M. Wed.–Fri., 10 A.M.–5 P.M. Sat., noon–5 P.M. Sun., adults $7, seniors and students $5, children 6–18 $2) is a small gem, containing a little bit of everything, from pre-Columbian sculpture and ancient Chinese ceramics to American folk art and late-20th-century painting. The gallery owns more than 9,500 objects in all, spanning 5,000 years; a dozen or so temporary exhibitions are staged each year. In the center of the gallery is an enclosed, skylit sculpture garden filled with works by Henry Moore and Albert Paley, a known Rochesterian.

Woodside Mansion

One of the city's smaller museums, this 1839 Greek Revival–style home (485 East Ave., 585/271-2705, noon–4 P.M. Mon.–Fri., adults $3, seniors and students $2, children $1) now serves as the headquarters for the Rochester Historical Society. Lots of fine architectural touches complement the inside, including a spiral staircase. Paintings, costumes, period furniture, toys, and historic photos are on display.

Rochester Museum and Science Center

Like many other top science museums, the Rochester Museum and Science Center (RMSC) (657 East Ave., 585/271-4320 or 585/741-1880, www.rmsc.org, 10 A.M.–5 P.M. Mon.–Sat., noon–5 P.M. Sun., adults $8, seniors and students $7, children 3–18 $6) houses plenty of fossils, dioramas, exhibits on flora and fauna, and prehistoric beasts. What makes the place really unusual, however, is **"At the Western Door,"** a powerful exhibit on the Seneca Nation.

The exhibit examines Seneca life from pre-European contact in the 1550s to the present. Separate sections, brimming with artifacts, focus on such subjects as the fur trade, the Iroquois Confederacy, the Sullivan campaign, and the sad history of broken treaties. As late as 1960, the Allegheny Senecas lost one-third of their reservation when it was flooded to create Kinzua Dam.

Also at the museum is the state-of-the-art **Strasenburgh Planetarium.** The sky shows cost $4–8.

George Eastman House

Just east of the RMSC is the grand 50-room Georgian mansion (900 East Ave., 585/271-3361, www.eastmanhouse.org, 10 A.M.–5 P.M. Tues.–Sat., 1–5 P.M. Sun., adults $8, seniors $6, students $5, kids 5–12 $3) where Eastman Kodak founder George Eastman lived alone with his mother for much of his life. The house contains all the finest furnishings of its day, including Persian rugs, oil paintings, and carved mahogany furniture polished to a high gleam, but what makes the place interesting is Eastman himself.

Born in 1854, Eastman left school at age 13 to help support his family. He worked first as a messenger boy earning $3 a week, then as an accountant. He began taking photographs at age 23 while on vacation and began searching for an easier way to develop negatives. He spent three years experimenting in his mother's kitchen. By 1880, George had invented a dry plate coating machine—the genesis of the Eastman Kodak Company.

Eastman's passions included music, fresh flowers, wild game hunting, and philanthropy. One year, he gave a free camera to every child in America who was turning 13. Then, at age 78, suffering from an irreversible spinal disease, he committed suicide in his bedroom. His suicide note read: "To my friends; My work is done—why wait?"

Adjoining the mansion is the **International Museum of Photography,** a modern museum holding a fascinating collection of antique cameras and photographic equipment, along with two theaters and four galleries. First-rate

THE FINGER LAKES

COURTESY OF GREATER ROCHESTER VISITORS ASSOCIATION

George Eastman House and the International Museum of Photography

exhibits by artists such as Ansel Adams and Henri Cartier-Bresson are presented.

Stone-Tolan House Museum

Continuing to the far eastern end of East Avenue, you'll come to the oldest structure in Rochester, the 1792 Stone-Tolan House (2370 East Ave., near Clover St., 585/546-7029, www.landmarksociety.org, noon–3 P.M. Fri.–Sat. Mar.–Dec., adults $3, children $1). A handsome, rustic building with wide floorboards, large fireplaces, and an orchard out back, the house was once both the Stone family home and a popular tavern. It is now owned by the Landmark Society of Western New York.

Highland Park

In 1888, Frederick Law Olmsted designed Highland Park (585/256-4950, 24 hours/day), a planned arboretum bounded by Mt. Hope, Highland, and Elm Avenues, and Goodman Street. One of the city's biggest celebrations, the Lilac Festival, takes place here every May, when the park's 1,200 lilac bushes bloom.

But lilacs are just the beginning. From early spring through late fall, Highland offers a riotous delight of fragrant Japanese maples, sweet-smelling magnolias, dazzling spring bulbs, delicate wildflowers, and 700 varieties of rhododendrons, azaleas, and mountain laurel.

In the center of the park reigns the 1911 **Lamberton Conservatory** (180 Reservoir Ave.). Under the main dome grows a tropical forest, while other rooms contain orchid collections, banana trees, cacti, and house plants. Across from the conservatory is the 1898 **Frederick Douglass statue,** the first public statue erected to honor an African American.

Mount Hope Cemetery

From the corner of Mt. Hope and Elmwood Avenues extends the extravagant Mt. Hope Cemetery (entrance at 1133 Mt. Hope Ave.), a landscaped oasis of green strewn with knobby hills, ancient trees, marble tombs, and elaborate mausoleums. One of the oldest cemeteries in the country, established in 1838, Mt. Hope contains the graves of every Rochesterian who was anyone, including Frederick Douglass and Susan B. Anthony.

A 1874 neo-Romanesque gatehouse marks the cemetery entrance, while just inside are a Gothic chapel and a white Moorish gazebo. The Douglass grave is off East Avenue near the northern end of the cemetery; the Anthony grave is off Indian Trail Avenue at the far northern end.

Maps to the cemetery are available at the Rochester Convention and Visitors Bureau. Friends of Mt. Hope Cemetery (585/461-3494, www.fomh.org) offers guided walking tours on Saturday, spring–fall.

Monroe Avenue

This haven for students, artists, performers, and activists packs an eclectic array of neighborhood stores, "alternative" shops right out of the '60s, and ethnic restaurants. Most of the activity is centered between I-490 and Goodman Street.

ELSEWHERE IN THE CITY
Susan B. Anthony House

In a quiet, somewhat run-down neighborhood west of downtown stands the narrow red-brick home that once belonged to women's rights advocate Susan B. Anthony (17 Madison St., off W. Main St., 585/235-6124, www.susanbanthonyhouse.org, 11 A.M.–5 P.M. Tues.–Sun. June–Aug., 11 A.M.–4 P.M. Sept.–May, adults $6, seniors $5, students and children $3). Simply furnished in the style of the late 1800s, the house contains much Anthony memorabilia, including her typewriters, clothes, letters, photos, and stuffed Victorian furniture.

Anthony, born in Massachusetts in 1820, lived in this house from 1866 until her death in 1906. It was here she was arrested for voting in 1872, and here that she met and planned with fellow reformers Elizabeth Cady Stanton and Frederick Douglass. Together with Elizabeth Cady Stanton and Matilda Gage, Anthony wrote her *History of Woman Suffrage* in the third-floor attic, a wonderful hideaway now once again strewn with her books and papers.

Seneca Park and Zoo

North of the downtown, along the Genesee River, runs the long, skinny Seneca Park and Zoo (2222 St. Paul St., a quarter mile north of Rte. 104, 585/266-6846, www.senecazoo.org, 10 A.M.–5 P.M. daily, adults $7, seniors $6, children ages 3–11 $4, reduced rates in winter). About 500 animals from nearly 200 species live in the zoo, including polar bears, a Siberian tiger, and reindeer. Don't miss the aviary, where brightly colored tropical birds fly about free. Younger kids will enjoy the barnyard petting area.

Ontario Beach Park

When in downtown Rochester, it's easy to forget that Lake Ontario is less than 15 minutes away. But indeed, north of the city along Lake Avenue, you'll soon find a land of wide open spaces, beaches, and parks.

Just before reaching the lake, you'll pass the 1822 **Charlotte-Genesee Lighthouse** (70 Lighthouse St., at Lake Ave. and Latta Rd., 585/621-6179, 1–5 P.M. Sat.–Sun. May–Oct., adults $2, children under 12 free), now a small museum with exhibits tracing the history of lighthouses and lake transportation. Originally, the lighthouse stood on the lakeshore, but sand deposits have moved it inland.

On the shores of Lake Ontario runs the Ontario Beach Park (Lake and Beach Aves., 585/256-4950), a half-mile-long beach with an aging art-deco bathhouse and weathered fishing pier illuminated on summer nights. Around the turn of the century, the park was the "Coney Island of the West," attracting tens of thousands of Rochesterians to its elephant shows, water slides, and beachfront hotels. Harking back to those heady days is the park's still-operating 1905 **Dentzel menagerie carousel,** one of the oldest carousels in the United States. Stop by the locally famous **Abbotts Custard,** at the park's entrance, for sweet, creamy ice cream.

Seabreeze Amusement Park

From Ontario Beach Park, travel east about five miles along Lake Shore Boulevard to reach the Seabreeze Amusement Park (4600 Culver Rd., 585/323-1900, www.seabreeze.com, noon–10 P.M. daily June–Aug., weekends in May). First established in 1879, the park now has 75 rides and attractions, including the Raging Rivers Water Park and the Jack Rabbit Roller Coaster. The 1920 Jack Rabbit is one of the few surviving all-wooden coasters.

General admission with two ride tickets is $9; an unlimited Ride & Slide pass is adults $19.95, children under 18 $15.95.

RECREATION

The 49-passenger *Sam Patch* (250 Exchange Blvd., at the Genesee River, 585/262-5661, www.sampatch.org), a replica packet boat, offers sightseeing, lunch, and dinner cruises May–October.

ENTERTAINMENT
Classical Music

The renowned **Rochester Philharmonic Orchestra** (585/454-5000) performs at the Eastman Theatre October–May. One of the world's premier music schools, the **Eastman School of Music** (26 Gibbs St., 585/274-1100) stages over 700 performances annually by students, faculty, and guest artists. The **Hochstein Music School Auditorium** (50 N. Plymouth Ave., 585/454-4596) hosts the Rochester Chamber Orchestra, the Borinquen Dance Theatre, and classical music concerts.

Theater

Rochester's only resident professional theater, the **GeVa Theatre** (75 Woodbury Blvd., at Clinton, 585/232-GEVA) stages nine productions annually. It's housed in a historic brick-and-limestone building that was once the Naval Armory. The **Downstairs Cabaret Theatre** (585/325-4370) produces popular comedies and musicals.

The **Rochester Broadway Theatre League** (585/325-7760) presents touring Broadway shows and concerts, while the **Rochester Contemporary** (137 East Ave., 585/461-2222) is the place to go for performance art and avant-garde theater.

Music and Nightlife

The best music listings are published by *City Newspaper* (585/244-3329), a free alternative weekly. One of the biggest and most active music clubs in the city is the **Water Street Music Hall** (204 N. Water St., 585/325-5600). Regional and national acts play blues, rock, funk, and industrial.

The **Milestones Music Room** (50 East Ave., 585/325-6490) brings in regional and occasionally national acts playing acoustic, blues, alternative, rock, and pop. The **California Brew Haus** (402 W. Ridge Rd., 585/621-1480) presents a good dose of Southern rock.

ACCOMMODATIONS
Downtown

Several large glass-sheathed hotels are located downtown. Though they cater mostly to business travelers, they often offer reasonably priced packages, especially on the weekends.

Connected to the Rochester Riverside Convention Center is the 15-story, 467-room **Clarion Riverside** (120 E. Main St., 585/546-6400, $79–149 d). Across the street is the 26-story, 330-room **Hyatt Regency** (125 E. Main St., 585/546-1234, $139–199 d). The **Crowne Plaza Rochester** (70 State St., 585/546-3450, $129–149 d) is a 364-room luxury hotel on the Genesee River, complete with a large pool and fitness center.

Southeast Rochester

In the museum district you'll find the quiet and comfortable **East Avenue Inn** (384 East Ave., 585/325-5010, $74–89 d), a motel that offers some of the lowest prices downtown. Nearby is the **Strathallan** (550 East Ave., 585/461-5010, www.strathallan.com, $109–179 d), a recently renovated all-suite hotel with a spiffy solarium, health club, and rooftop bar. All of the 156 rooms are equipped with refrigerator and microwave, making it a good choice for families.

One of the loveliest bed-and-breakfasts in Rochester is the **Dartmouth House** (215 Dartmouth St., 585/271-7872, www.dartmouth-house.com, $125–150 d), a spacious English

Tudor home with a fireplace, window seats, very knowledgeable hosts, and three luxurious guest rooms equipped with private baths and phones. The B&B is within easy walking distance of the museums and many cafés and shops.

Another good B&B choice is the Victorian **428 Mt. Vernon** (428 Mt. Vernon Ave., 585/271-0792 or 800/836-3159, www.428mtvernon.com, $125 d), located near the entrance to Highland Park. The seven antique-filled guest rooms are spacious and comfortable.

Pittsford

In Pittsford, to the immediate southeast of the city, is the modern **Brookwood Inn** (800 Pittsford-Victor Rd., 585/248-9000, $99–149 d). On its premises are 108 large guest rooms, a heated indoor pool, fitness facilities, and a sauna. It's spacious and friendly, clean and comfortable.

Also in Pittsford is **Oliver Loud's Inn** (1474 Marsh Rd., 585/248-5200, $120–140 s or d), a restored 1812 stagecoach inn on the canal, next to the renowned Richardson's Canal House (see Food, below). Room rates include a continental breakfast and a picnic basket.

FOOD
Downtown

For a quick and casual breakfast or lunch, visit the **food court** at the Midtown Plaza (Main St. and Clinton Ave., 585/454-2070). At Brown's Race, you'll find the **Triphammer Grill** (585/262-2700), featuring lots of grilled fare, including steaks, seafood, and poultry, along with vegetarian dishes; average dinner entrée $15.

In the heart of downtown, **Dinosaur Bar-B-Q** (99 Court St., 585/325-7090) offers great ribs and Cajun and Cuban food, along with live blues on the weekends; average main dish $10. Romantic **Tapas 177** (177 St. Paul St., 585/262-2090) is a very popular spot, serving an eclectic menu by candlelight, a wide variety of martinis, and live music on the weekends; average entrée $16.

Nestled into the East End entertainment district is the popular new **2 Vine** (24 Winthrop St., 585/454-6020), serving lots of fresh seafood that's flown in daily, fresh local produce, and homemade pastries; it was voted "Best Restaurant" in a *City Newspaper* survey. Average entrée $18.

Southeast Rochester

For a simple salad or tofu burger, step into the no-frills **Aladdin's Natural Eatery** (646 Monroe Ave., 585/442-5000). On Clinton Avenue, parallel to Monroe, is the **Highland Park Diner** (960 S. Clinton Ave., 585/461-5040), a classic 1948 art deco Orleans diner.

Back on Monroe Avenue, you'll find the **Olive Tree** (165 Monroe Ave., 585/454-3510), serving an imaginative "nouvelle Greek cuisine." Housed in a renovated 1864 brick storefront, the eatery uses fresh local ingredients and also serves Greek wines and beer; average entrée $16. Not far away is another good ethnic spot, the **Raj Mahal** (324 Monroe Ave., 585/546-2315), known for its tandoori and vegetarian dishes and fresh breads. Chefs prepare dishes behind a glass window while guests look on; average entrée $14.

Pittsford

One of Rochester's landmark restaurants is **Richardson's Canal House** (1474 Marsh Rd., Pittsford, 585/248-5000), a restored 1818 Erie Canal tavern with its own secluded garden. Elegant and highly acclaimed, the restaurant serves French country and American regional fare by candlelight; average entrée $25.

EXCURSIONS FROM ROCHESTER
Hamlin Beach State Park

Off the Lake Ontario State Parkway about 20 miles west of Ontario State Park, the 1,223-acre Hamlin Beach State Park (585/964-2121, $6–8 parking) offers swimming beaches, hiking trails, nature trails, bike paths, a playground, and concession stands. One of the area's largest campgrounds is also located here. To reserve a campsite, call 800/456-CAMP.

THE FINGER LAKES

Genesee Country Village and Museum

Twenty miles southwest of Rochester, the world-class Genesee Country Village and Museum (1410 Flint Hill Rd., off Rte. 36, Mumford, 585/538-6822, www.gcv.org, 10 A.M.–4 P.M. Tues.–Sun. May–Oct., with extended hours July–Aug., adults $12.95, students and seniors $9.95, children ages 4–16 $7.50) consists of 57 meticulously restored 19th-century buildings laid out around a village square. Among them are an early land office, two-story log cabin, fly-tier's shop, octagonal house, Greek Revival mansion, Italianate mansion, bookshop, small-scale farm, blacksmith's shop, doctor's office, and pharmacy. Gravel walkways lead between the buildings; guides in period dress cook, spin, weave, and demonstrate other folk arts of the pre-industrial age.

Near the entrance are a Carriage Museum and a Gallery of Sporting Art, featuring works by such artists as Audubon and Remington. To the north is a 175-acre Nature Center, networked with three miles of hiking and nature trails.

Getting There and Around

The **Syracuse Hancock International Airport** and the **Greater Rochester International Airport** are serviced by Jet Blue (800/JET-BLUE), American Airlines (800/433-7300), Continental (800/525-0280), Delta (800/221-1212), United (800/241-6522), and USAirways (800/428-4322). USAirways also services the **Tompkins County Airport** (Ithaca) and the **Elmira-Corning Regional Airport.** A taxi ride from any of these airports to their respective downtowns costs $14–20.

Amtrak (800/872-7245) travels to Syracuse and Rochester. **Greyhound** (800/231-2222) and **New York State Trailways** (800/295-5555) provide bus service throughout the region.

By far the best way to explore the Finger Lakes is by car.

Information and Services

The **Greater Rochester Visitors Association** (45 East Ave., Suite 400, Rochester 14604, 585/546-3070 or 800/677-7282, www.visitrochester.com) is open year-round 8:30 A.M.–5 P.M. Monday–Friday and 10 A.M.–3 P.M. Sunday; also 9 A.M.–5 P.M. summer Saturdays. The association also operates a booth on the first floor of the Greater Rochester International Airport and runs an **Events Line** (585/546-6810). You can pick up maps and brochures at the Heritage Area Visitor Center at Brown's Race as well.

Walking tours are offered periodically by the **Landmark Society of Western New York** (585/546-7029, www.landmarksociety.org).

The **Finger Lakes Tourism Alliance** (309 Lake St., Penn Yan 14527, 315/536-7488 or 800/548-4386, www.fingerlakes.org) is a good central information source for the entire region.

Contact the **Finger Lakes Wine Country Tourism Marketing Association** (1 W. Market St., Corning 14830, 607/936-0706 or 800/813-2958, www.fingerlakeswinecountry.com) for information about the grape-growing regions around Keuka, Seneca, and

Cayuga Lakes. Each of the lakes also has a "wine trail" website: www.keukawinetrail.com, www.senecawinetrail.com, and www.cayugawinetrail.com.

Several B&B registries operate in the Finger Lakes. Among them are the **Finger Lakes B&B Association** (877/422-6327, www.flbba.org), the **B&B Network of Central New York** (315/498-6560 or 800/333-1604, www.cnylodging.com), and the **B&B Association of Greater Ithaca** (607/589-6073 or 800/806-4406, www.bbithaca.com).

Many counties, cities, and towns also have their own visitor information centers, listed below. Most are open 9 A.M.–5 P.M. Monday–Friday.

Greater Syracuse/Onondaga County Convention and Visitors Bureau (572 S. Salina St., Syracuse 13202, 315/470-1910 or 800/234-4797, www.visitsyracuse.org)

Schuyler County Chamber of Commerce (100 Franklin St., Watkins Glen 14891, 607/535-4300 or 800/607-4552, www.schuylerny.com)

Skaneateles Chamber of Commerce (11 Jordan St., Skaneateles 13152, 315/685-0552, www.skaneateles.com)

Cayuga County Chamber of Commerce (94 Frances St., Auburn 13021, 315/253-6047, www.cayugacountychamber.com)

Seneca County Tourism (1 DiPronio Dr., Waterloo 13165, 315/539-1759 or 800/732-1848, www.visitsenecany.net)

Ithaca/Tompkins County Convention and Visitors Bureau (904 East Shore Dr., Ithaca 14850, 607/272-1313 or 800/284-8422, www.visitithaca.com)

Geneva Area Chamber of Commerce (35 Lakeside Dr., Geneva, 315/789-1776, www.genevany.com)

Chemung County Chamber of Commerce (400 E. Church St., Elmira 14901, 607/734-5137 or 800/627-5892, www.chemungchamber.org)

Corning Area Chamber of Commerce (1 W. Market St., Corning 14830, 607/936-4686, www.corningny.com)

Yates County Chamber of Commerce (2375 Rte. 14A, Penn Yan 14527, 315/536-3111, www.yatesny.com)

Canandaigua Chamber of Commerce (113 S. Main St., Canandaigua 14424, 585/394-4400, www.canandaigua.com)

Greater Rochester Visitors Association (45 East Ave., Suite 400, Rochester 14604, 585/546-3070 or 800/677-7282, www.visitrochester.com)

THE FINGER LAKES

WESTERN NEW YORK

Western New York, reaching so far west that it almost borders Ohio, has a distinctively Midwestern feel. Like the heartland, the region wasn't settled until the early 1800s, and so lacks eastern New York's Colonial history and even the Finger Lakes' post-Revolutionary War past. Most of the region's cities started as frontier boomtowns, and much of the countryside supports farmland.

Western New York's two largest cities are Buffalo and Niagara Falls, situated about 20 miles apart along the Niagara River, across from Canada. At Buffalo's southwestern edge lies Lake Erie, while north of Niagara Falls presides Lake Ontario, a favorite haunt of serious fisherfolk.

Buffalo is New York's second largest city. Seriously depressed following the decline of its steel industry in the 1970s, it still faces many economic difficulties, but has also rejuvenated itself to a surprising extent, with a renovated waterfront and theater district.

Niagara Falls has long been regarded as one of the world's great natural wonders. As far back as 1678, missionary Father Louis Hennepin wrote, "Betwixt the Lake Ontario and Erie, there is a vast and prodigious Cadence of Water. ... The Universe does not afford its Parallel. ... The Waters which fall from this horrible Precipice do foam and boyl after the most hideous manner imaginable, making an outrageous Noise, more terrible than that of Thunder."

To the east of Buffalo extends especially fertile farm country. To the south begin the dark, rolling foothills of the Allegheny Mountains. To the southwest lies Chautauqua Lake, a popular resort

© CHRISTIANE BIRD

HIGHLIGHTS

(Allentown: The nation's second-largest historic district is chock-a-block with Victorian buildings and home to the Anchor Bar, where Buffalo chicken wings were invented (page 529).

(Albright-Knox Art Gallery: Known around the world for its superb collection of contemporary art, the museum was the first in the U.S. to purchase works by Picasso and Matisse (page 530).

(Niagara Reservation State Park: The famed waterfalls straddling the U.S.-Canada border may be a cliché, but they incite wonder nonetheless (page 538).

(Artpark: Spread over 20 acres, this is the only national park in the U.S. devoted to the visual and performing arts (page 544).

(Seneca-Iroquois National Museum: This first-class museum covers the history of the Seneca Nation from prehistory to the present day (page 557).

(Allegany State Park: The largest and wildest state park in New York is situated in the dark, rolling foothills of the Allegheny Mountains (page 558).

(Griffis Sculpture Park: Whimsical, 20-foot-high humanoid figures, created by Buffalo artist Larry Griffis, perch on a hill with sweeping views of the valley below (page 559).

(Chautauqua Institution: The 856-acre education center for families and adults features dozens of fine Victorian buildings and a lake-side setting (page 563).

LOOK FOR **(** TO FIND RECOMMENDED SIGHTS, ACTIVITIES, DINING, AND LODGING.

area that's also home to the famed Chautauqua Institute—a sort of cultural camp for adults.

PLANNING YOUR TIME

Most visitors will probably want to concentrate on **Buffalo** and **Niagara Falls,** perhaps spending two or three days in Buffalo—home to several top-notch cultural institutions and an amazing array of architectural landmarks—and taking an overnight excursion to the falls. Travelers interested in exploring an especially scenic part of lesser-known New York should also spend a couple of days in **Allegany and Cattaraugus Counties,** the state's southwestern-most provinces. Here you'll find the dark, rolling foothills of the Allegheny Mountains, the magnificent Allegany State Park, the excellent Seneca-Iroquois National Museum, and lots of scenic back roads and antique shops.

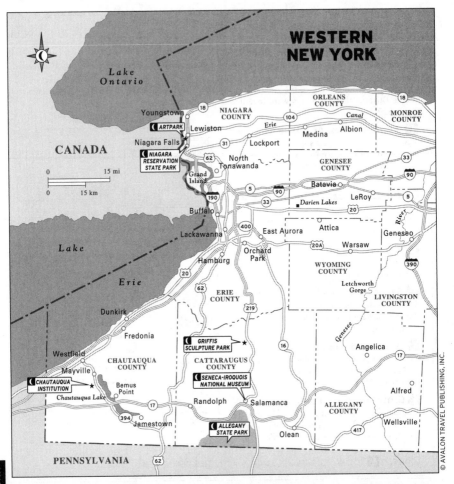

WESTERN NEW YORK

Lake Ontario

Youngstown

ARTPARK

Lewiston

CANADA

Niagara Falls

NIAGARA RESERVATION STATE PARK

Grand Island

North Tonawanda

Buffalo

Lackawanna

Lake Erie

Hamburg

Orchard Park

East Aurora

NIAGARA COUNTY

ORLEANS COUNTY

MONROE COUNTY

Canal Erie

Medina   Albion

Lockport

GENESEE COUNTY

Batavia

Darien Lakes

LeRoy

Attica

Warsaw

WYOMING COUNTY

Geneseo

Letchworth Gorge

LIVINGSTON COUNTY

Dunkirk

Fredonia

Westfield

Mayville

CHAUTAUQUA INSTITUTION

Chautauqua Lake

Bemus Point

Jamestown

GRIFFIS SCULPTURE PARK

CHAUTAUQUA COUNTY

CATTARAUGUS COUNTY

SENECA-IROQUOIS NATIONAL MUSEUM

Randolph   Salamanca

ALLEGANY STATE PARK

Olean

Angelica

Alfred

ALLEGANY COUNTY

Wellsville

PENNSYLVANIA

© AVALON TRAVEL PUBLISHING, INC.

0   15 mi
0   15 km

Buffalo

If ever there was a city of rabid sports fanatics, Buffalo is it. What other metropolis would build its two largest sports stadiums—Dunn Tire Park and the HSBC Arena—in the heart of downtown, not far from government offices?

If ever there was a city of strong ethnic persuasions, Buffalo is it. What other midsize city—Buffalo's population is only about 310,500—can boast the largest St. Patrick's Day Parade west of Manhattan (population eight million) and the largest Pulaski Day Parade east of Chicago (population three million)?

If ever there was a city of broad, tree-lined streets, expansive Victorian homes, and striking architectural landmarks, Buffalo is it. There aren't many places that have received the architectural stamp of approval from both *The New Yorker* critic Brendan Gill and architectural historian John D. Randall. Randall states that Buffalo has a wider range of American and European architectural forms than any other city in the world.

Visiting Buffalo is like visiting an overgrown small town. People talk to strangers here and point to recent civic improvements with enormous, and quite justified, pride. Nonetheless, the city has its share of urban problems, including a population exodus to more prosperous areas and rising crime rates.

HISTORY
Early History
Once the domain of the Iroquois, the Buffalo area was visited sporadically by French explorers in the 18th century. The French called the Niagara River *beau fleuve,* or beautiful river, which the English allegedly bastardized into "buffalo."

The city was laid out in 1803–04 by Joseph Ellicott, a land agent for the Holland Land Company. He modeled his plans after those of Washington, D.C., which his brother Maj. Andrew Ellicott had helped Pierre L'Enfant lay out. Niagara Square, like the White House, serves as a focal point from which major streets radiate.

Buffalo was incorporated in 1816 but didn't thrive until the Erie Canal was completed in 1825. The town stood at the transportation break between the Great Lakes and the canal, and soon warehouses sprang up all along the lakefront. Thousands of immigrants, most from Ireland and Germany, arrived.

Mrs. Frances Trollope, visiting the city in 1828, wrote: "All the buildings have the appearance of having been run up in a hurry, though everything has an air of great pretension; there are porticos, columns, domes and colonnades but all in wood."

The Rise of Industry
Buffalo's first iron foundry went up in 1826, and its first steam engine plant in 1829. By 1845, the city also boasted a stove factory, nail factory, cabinet factory, bell foundry, and numerous other plants producing such products as mirrors, picture frames, and bathtubs.

In the mid- to late 1800s, the rapid development of the railroads turned Buffalo into a major grain and livestock market. Eleven main railroad lines served five passenger and

BLIZZARD-BLITZED BUFFALO
Buffalo has earned a reputation as the Blizzard Capital of the United States. This isn't entirely fair. There are snowier places – northern Michigan, for example – and most of Buffalo's snow falls south of the city proper, in the region's ski belt. Still, the Queen City of the Lakes does see more than its share of white stuff. Writes native son Verlyn Klinkenborg in *The Last Fine Time:*

Snow begins as a rumor in Buffalo, New York. ... The first flake appears and vanishes like a virtual particle in the mind of a physicist. ... But suddenly, without seeming to begin, the sky is full of real particles falling so slowly that they appear to stand, wavering, in air. ...

By ten o'clock at night, the Niagara Frontier is shut tight. ... The airport closed at seven o'clock. Transport has ground to a halt. The only thing open is the Niagara River, and that is not navigable in this season. Even indoors, you can hear the hush over Buffalo. You can feel the way the heavy snowfall changes a room, the way it redefines the interior, making the walls seem closer together, the roof heavier, the insulation thicker, as if the house had been built of logs and chinked with sphagnum moss, as if you might wake up in the morning and find the windswept tracks of lynx and snowshoe rabbit running down the middle of the street, as if the street itself were a frozen lake ringed by a forest of dark hemlock and spruce.

WESTERN NEW YORK

WESTERN NEW YORK

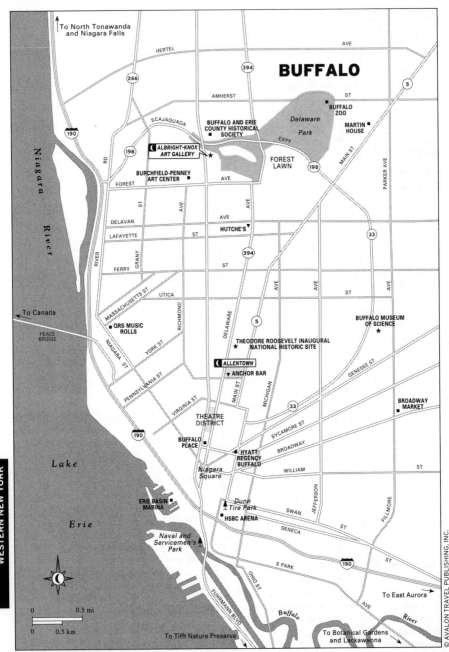

To North Tonawanda
and Niagara Falls

HERTEL   AVE

BUFFALO

AMHERST   ST

SCAJAQUADA

BUFFALO AND ERIE
COUNTY HISTORICAL
SOCIETY

Delaware
Park

BUFFALO
ZOO

MARTIN
HOUSE

ALBRIGHT-KNOX
ART GALLERY

BURCHFIELD-PENNEY
ART CENTER

FOREST
LAWN

EXPY

AVE

FOREST   ST

DELAVAN

LAFAYETTE   ST

HUTCHE'S

AVE   AVE

FERRY   ST

UTICA

Niagara   River

To Canada

PEACE
BRIDGE

MASSACHUSETTS ST

QRS MUSIC
ROLLS

YORK ST

RICHMOND   ST

GRANT   ST

DELAWARE

BUFFALO MUSEUM
OF SCIENCE

THEODORE ROOSEVELT INAUGURAL
NATIONAL HISTORIC SITE

ALLENTOWN

ANCHOR BAR

GENESEE ST

NIAGARA ST

PENNSYLVANIA ST

VIRGINIA ST

THEATRE
DISTRICT

BUFFALO
PLACE

MICHIGAN

BROADWAY
MARKET

HYATT
REGENCY
BUFFALO

SYCAMORE ST

BROADWAY

Niagara
Square

WILLIAM   ST

JEFFERSON   ST

FILLMORE   ST

Lake

ERIE BASIN
MARINA

Dunn
Tire Park

HSBC ARENA

SWAN

SENECA

Erie

Naval and
Servicemen's
Park

S PARK

To East Aurora

0   0.5 mi

0   0.5 km

FUHRMANN BLVD

OHIO ST

AVE

To Tifft Nature Preserve

Buffalo   *River*

To Botanical Gardens
and Lackawanna

266

394

5

198

190

198

33

394

5

5

33

190

190

© AVALON TRAVEL PUBLISHING, INC.

14 freight terminals, with 300 passenger and 3,000 freight trains passing through daily. Today, Buffalo is still a major railroad center, handling more than 25,000 trains a year.

One of the railways, completed in 1873, connected Buffalo with the anthracite coal fields of Pennsylvania. That coal, together with Lake Superior iron ore and the newly developed Bessemer process, allowed for the large-scale production of steel. More immigrants, this time from Poland and Italy, poured in; the newly rich built lavish mansions along Delaware Avenue.

The Modern Era

By 1900, Buffalo was ready to show off its wealth and sophistication to the world. What better way to do so than to host the 1901 Pan-American Exposition? The exposition covered 350 acres, attracted eight million visitors, and featured everything from columned temples to the latest scientific inventions. The glamorous event was tragically marred, however, by the assassination of President William McKinley, who was shot at the expo on September 6, 1901 by anarchist Leon Czolgosz.

Following the exposition, Buffalo continued to prosper. Blast furnaces went up along the Buffalo River, huge grain elevators along the harbor. But the McKinley assassination seemed to have robbed the city of its earlier self-assurance. Trade routes shifted and Buffalo failed to fulfill its one-time promise to become a truly great city.

Buffalo reached its industrial zenith shortly after World War II. Relative prosperity continued, however, until the early 1970s, when newer, more efficient steel plants abroad caused a major shakedown of the steel industry. Buffalo's steel plants closed, the region's economy declined, and its population ebbed.

Enter the 1980s. Smaller manufacturing, finance, and advanced technology companies opened—and flourished. Then, in 1989, the U.S.-Canada Free Trade Agreement was signed and Buffalo became a center for American companies looking to expand into Canada. Today, Buffalo owes much of its economic base to that agreement.

ORIENTATION

Buffalo lies along the eastern shores of Lake Erie at the source of the wide Niagara River. Through the city's southern part runs the considerably narrower Buffalo River.

Downtown Buffalo centers on Niagara Square and Buffalo Place, a pedestrian-only thoroughfare along Main Street. The **MetroRail** (716/855-7211) runs along Main Street from the Buffalo River to the University at Buffalo South Campus. The system is above ground and free along Buffalo Place (Main St. south of Tupper St.); below ground, the fare is $1.50. Tickets may be purchased from vending machines at all stations.

Most downtown sites are within walking distance of each other. The downtown area has many parking lots. Elsewhere, street parking is usually available.

DOWNTOWN SIGHTS
Niagara Square

A good place to begin touring Buffalo is Niagara Square, which centers on the **McKinley Monument,** designed by architects Carrere and Hastings. The monument honors President William McKinley, who was assassinated in Buffalo while attending the 1901 Pan-American Exposition.

Dominating Niagara Square is the monumental art deco **Buffalo City Hall,** erected in 1929. The hall's front entrance is lined with eight Corinthian columns three stories high, while inside are vast, vaulted ceilings covered with sculpted figures and paintings depicting local history. An **observation deck** (716/851-4200, 9 A.M.–4 P.M. Mon.–Fri., free admission) on the 28th floor provides great views.

On Franklin Street just south of Niagara Square stands the 1870s **Old County Hall,** where President Grover Cleveland got his start, first as a lawyer and then as mayor of Buffalo. Designed in the high Victorian Gothic style, the building contains a lavish lobby done up in marble and bronze.

Church Street Architecture

Another block south, at the corner of Franklin

WEIRD, WONDERFUL, OFF-THE-BEATEN PATH WESTERN NEW YORK

Anchor Bar, Buffalo: Where Buffalo chicken wings were invented.

The grain elevators of Buffalo Harbor: Giant, silolike structures made of poured concrete—mute, monolithic, mysterious.

Pedaling History Bicycle Museum, Orchard Park, Buffalo: The only all-bicycle museum in America.

Herschell Carousel Factory Museum, North Tonawanda: The plant that once produced hundreds of beloved wooden carousels.

Le Roy House, Le Roy: Includes an exhibit on Jell-O, invented in Le Roy in the early 1900s.

The roque court, Angelica: One of only two places in the country where roque – a game similar to croquet – is still played.

Griffis Sculpture Park, Ashford Hollow: Towering humanoid sculptures frolic atop a hill. Created by artist Larry Griffis.

Lily Dale Assembly, Cassadaga: A spiritualist community; services, lectures, and sessions with clairvoyants.

and Church, stands the **Guaranty Building,** also known as the Prudential Building. Designed by Louis H. Sullivan in 1894, the 12-story terra-cotta skyscraper is covered with elaborate ornamentation repeated on the elevators and mosaic ceilings indoors.

One block farther east, at the corner of Church and Pearl Streets, reigns **St. Paul's Episcopal Cathedral.** Designed by Richard Upjohn in the 1880s, the brown sandstone church features a front central tower topped with a tall, delicate spire.

Main Street and Buffalo Place

In the late 1970s, downtown Main Street—semi-abandoned for years thanks to urban flight—was transformed into a pedestrian

thoroughfare named Buffalo Place. A sleek, above-ground section of the Metro Rail was built through its center, and slowly business began returning to the downtown.

Entering Buffalo Place from Church Street, you'll spot the **Ellicott Square Building** (295 Main St.) on the southeast corner. When completed in 1896, this block-wide edifice was the world's largest commercial office building.

On the northwest corner of Main and Church stands the **Main Place Mall,** housing standard shops and a food court. Two long blocks north, at Huron Street, is the **M&T Bank Gold Dome Building,** whose rotunda features some of the finest murals in Buffalo. On the north side is a scene depicting the city's harbor in the 1940s; the east side shows the Seneca, headed by Red Jacket.

Theater District

One block north of the Hyatt begins the restored Theater District, a 20-block area extending west as far as Delaware Avenue and north to Tupper Street. A half-dozen theaters and cabarets operate here, along with restaurants, galleries, and shops (see *Entertainment* and *Food*, below). Along Chippewa Street is the **Chippewa District,** known for its nightclubs.

Buffalo has an impressive theater history, which began in the mid-1800s, thanks to the traffic along the Erie Canal. Dozens of theaters catering to travelers sprang up almost overnight, and by the turn of the 20th century, Buffalo was one of the country's foremost drama centers. Actress Katherine Cornell, songwriter Harold Arlen, and choreographer Michael Bennett are among the many who've come out of Buffalo's performing arts scene.

The centerpiece of the district is **Shea's Performing Arts Center** (646 Main St., 716/847-1410, www.sheas.org), an opulent 1926 movie palace filled with marble and gilt. Saved at the last moment from the wrecker's ball in 1975, Shea's is now fully restored.

Galleries

Across the street from the Shea Center is the CEPA Gallery (617 Main St., 716/856-2717, www.cepagallery.com, 10 A.M.–5 P.M. Mon.–Fri., noon–5 P.M. Sat.), a first-rate exhibit space that focuses on photography, video, and film. Short for **C**enter for **E**xploratory and **P**erceptual **A**rt, CEPA is also a gathering spot for regional artists and a good place to go to find out about other arts events in town. Buffalo has a thriving alternative-arts scene, with as many as a dozen small galleries—which tend to come and go—operating at any one time.

Another gallery with a long track record is the renowned **HallWalls Contemporary Arts Center** (341 Delaware Ave., 716/854-1694, www.hallwalls.org, 11 A.M.–6 P.M. Tues.–Fri., 1–4 P.M. Sat.). Recently relocated into the former Asbury Delaware Church building, now owned by Righteous Bay Records/Ani Defranco, HallWalls has been showcasing cutting-edge alternative art for over 20 years.

To find out more about what's happening in the city arts-wise, pick up a copy of *ArtVoice* (716/881-6604), a free biweekly publication.

Buffalo/Erie County Naval and Military Park

At the southern end of downtown, along Lake Erie, extends a six-acre maritime park dedicated to all branches of the armed forces (1 Naval Park Cove, foot of Pearl and Main Sts., 716/847-1773, www.buffalonavalpark.org, 10 A.M.–5 P.M. daily Apr.–Oct., 10 A.M.–4 P.M. Sat.–Sun. Nov., adults $8, seniors and students 6–16 $5). Most of the exhibits, however, have to do with the U.S. Navy; three decommissioned ships are berthed here.

Largest among them is the USS *Little Rock,* a 610-foot-long guided missile cruiser outfitted much the way it was in the 1960s when 1,400 men lived onboard. Next door slumbers the USS *Croaker,* a compact submarine that sank 11 Japanese vessels during World War II. Also seeing action in World War II was USS *The Sullivans,* a destroyer named after five brothers from Waterloo, Iowa, who died in 1942 when a Japanese torpedo sank their ship. Shamrocks on the destroyer's smokestacks pay tribute to the brothers' Irish heritage.

Erie Basin Marina

Along Marina Drive north of the Naval Park is the Erie Basin Marina, where hundreds of pleasure boats dock. One side of the marina features a pleasant park, while to the other several restaurants overlook Lake Erie. At the end of the dock is an observation tower (8 A.M.–10 P.M. daily May–Oct.).

◖ ALLENTOWN

Northwest of the Theatre District lies Allentown, the nation's second-largest historic district. The streets here are lined with one Victorian structure after another, with all styles represented. Many now house restaurants, art galleries, boutiques, and antique shops.

Allentown is roughly bounded by Main Street to the east, Edward Street to the south, North Street to the north, and Cottage and Pennsylvania Streets to the west. Through its center runs Allen Street and Virginia Street.

Among the district's foremost architectural treasures are the typically middle-class **Tifft Houses** (Allen St. between Park and Irving Pl.); the extravagant **Williams-Butler Mansion,** now housing the Jacobs Executive Development Center (672 Delaware Ave.); and the **Wilcox Mansion** (now the Roosevelt Inaugural Site). Samuel Clemens, a.k.a. Mark Twain, once lived at 472 Delaware Avenue, and F. Scott Fitzgerald spent part of his childhood at 29 Irving Place.

Theodore Roosevelt Inaugural National Historic Site

Theodore Roosevelt was formally inaugurated in the stately Wilcox Mansion (641 Delaware Ave., between North and Allen Sts., 716/884-0095, 9 A.M.–5 P.M. Mon.–Fri., noon–5 P.M. Sat.–Sun., adults $5, seniors and students $3, children 6–14 $1) in 1901 after the assassination of President McKinley. "It is a dreadful thing to come into the Presidency this way," wrote the pragmatic Roosevelt shortly after the event, "but it would be far worse to be morbid about it. Here is the task, and I have got to do it to the best of my ability; and that is all there is about it."

Once owned by a prominent lawyer named

Ansley Wilcox, the 1838 house is now run by the National Park Service. The library where Roosevelt was sworn in has been fully restored; among the items on display elsewhere in the house is the handkerchief that assassin Leon Czolgosz used to cover his handgun.

NORTH OF DOWNTOWN

Many of Buffalo's museums cluster together about four or five miles north of downtown, near Delaware Park. To get there take Delaware Avenue, a wide thoroughfare lined with mansions, most once owned by wealthy families and now home to law firms and the like.

Follow Delaware Avenue to Gates Circle and turn left on Chapin Parkway to reach Lincoln Parkway and Delaware Park. At the intersection of Chapin and Lincoln Parkway is the **William R. Heath House** (72 Soldier's Pl.), one of five houses in the city designed by Frank Lloyd Wright.

◖ Albright-Knox Art Gallery

The centerpiece of Buffalo's art scene, this airy, low-slung museum (1285 Elmwood Ave., near Scajaquada Expressway, 716/882-8700, www.albrightknox.org, 10 A.M.–5 P.M. Wed.–Sun., 5 –10 P.M. Fri., adults $10, students 13–18 and seniors $8) is known around the world for its superb collection of contemporary art. The Albright-Knox was the first museum in the United States to purchase works by Picasso and Matisse, and the first anywhere to present a major exhibition of photography, in 1910.

All the major American and European artists of the past 50 years are well represented, including van Gogh, Gauguin, Pollock, Miró, and Mondrian. The museum also presents 10 first-rate temporary exhibits each year and houses a solid general collection that spans the history of art. The Gallery Shop includes an extensive selection of art books, and the Garden Restaurant serves gourmet sandwiches and salads.

Buffalo/Erie County Historical Society

Overlooking a small lake across from the Albright-Knox sits the only remaining permanent building (25 Nottingham Court, at Elmwood Ave., 716/873-9644, 10 A.M.–5 P.M. Tues.–Sat., noon–5 P.M. Sun., adults $4, seniors and students $4, children 7–12 $2.50) from the 1901 Pan-American Exposition. Inspired by the Parthenon, the lovely structure once housed the New York State pavilion and is now home to the Buffalo and Erie County Historical Society Museum.

The museum features two unusual permanent exhibits. "Bflo. Made!" showcases virtually every product ever produced in the Buffalo region, from Pierce-Arrow cars and General Mills cereal to pacemakers and kazoos. "The People of Erie County" focuses on the area's vibrant ethnic history, from the Poles of the east side to the Irish of south Buffalo.

Burchfield-Penney Art Center

Also near the Albright-Knox is Buffalo State College, with jade green lawns and sturdy red-brick buildings. Signs point the way to Rockwell Hall and the third-floor Burchfield-Penney Art Center (1300 Elmwood Ave., 716/878-6011, 10 A.M.–5 P.M. Tues.–Sat., 1–5 P.M. Sun., free admission).

Buffalo/Erie County Historical Society

COURTESY OF BUFFALO/NIAGARA CONVENTION AND VISITORS BUREAU

Spread out over a few galleries, the center is a low-key affair dedicated primarily to Charles E. Burchfield, one of the finest watercolorists of the 20th century. Originally from Iowa, Burchfield spent most of his life living and teaching in Buffalo. He was fascinated by the Buffalo streets and by patterns of fire and sound, which he depicted in a mystical, expressionist style.

The center owns the world's largest collection of Burchfield works, exhibited on a rotating basis. Works by other contemporary Western New York artists are also exhibited.

Art lovers might also be interested in visiting the **Charles Bruchfield Nature & Art Center** (2201 Union Rd., 716/677-4843) in nearby West Seneca, where Burchfield once lived. The center offers an exhibition area, nature trails, a meditation garden, and a sculpture garden.

Delaware Park

Buffalo State College, the Albright-Knox, and the Buffalo and Erie County Historical Society all sit on the western edge of Delaware Park, a glorious, 350-acre expanse of green designed and laid out by Frederick Law Olmsted in the 1870s. Olmsted, who also designed Central Park in New York City, created an extensive park system throughout Buffalo that also includes Front, Martin Luther King, Jr., Cazenovia, and South Parks.

Near Lincoln Parkway on the park's west side lies Hoyt Lake and the regal **Delaware Park Casino** (716/882-5920). Originally built as a boathouse and restaurant for the Pan-Am Expo, the building now houses a concessions stand that's open April–October, and an office where paddleboats can be rented.

Buffalo Zoological Gardens

In the heart of Delaware Park flourishes the city's most popular tourist attraction—the Buffalo Zoo (300 Parkside Ave., 716/837-3900, www.buffalozoo.org, 10 A.M.–4 or 5 P.M. daily, adults $8.50, seniors and children 2–14 $5). One of the oldest zoos in the country, founded around the turn of the century, the park is home to over 1,300 inhabitants. Among them

are a rare white tiger, a one-horned Indian rhino, reticulated giraffes, and lowland gorillas. Highlights include "Habicat," where lions and tigers roam free; a tropical rain forest; an Asian forest; one of the largest reptile collections in the country; and—this is Buffalo, after all—a large herd of bison.

Martin House

To the east of Delaware Park stands the 1904 Darwin D. Martin House (175 Jewett Pkwy., at Summit), one of Frank Lloyd Wright's most important works. The long, horizontal building with its wide porches and few enclosed spaces is characteristic of the architect's early Prairie style.

Tours of the home and the nearby Barton House (also designed by Wright), are offered Tuesday–Thursday and Saturday–Sunday. Call 716/856-3858 for exact hours. Tour price is adults $10, students $8.

Forest Lawn Cemetery

Abutting Delaware Park to the south extends expansive Forest Lawn Cemetery (1411 Delaware Ave., 716/885-1600, www.forestlawn.com, 8:30 A.M.–5 P.M.), the final resting place of Buffalo trappers, farmers, tradespeople, and statesmen since 1850. Near the entrance cluster small Iroquois graves and a tall monument honoring the famed Seneca orator Red Jacket, or "Sa-Co-Ye-Wat-Ha"—"he who keeps them awake." An all-too-prophetic quote on the memorial reads, "When I am gone and my warnings are no longer heeded, the craft and avarice of the white man will prevail. My heart fails me when I think of my people, so soon to be scattered and forgotten."

Beyond the Red Jacket memorial, the cemetery spreads out over low hills networked with roadways. By the shores of the deep blue Mirror Lake stands the unusual Blocher monument, featuring life-size marble figures behind glass. President Millard Fillmore is also buried in Forest Lawn.

Free maps of the cemetery are available in the cemetery office, open Monday–Saturday 9 A.M.–4 P.M.

Buffalo Museum of Science

On the east side of Buffalo presides the four-story Buffalo Museum of Science (1020 Humboldt Pkwy., at Utica Street, 716/896-5200, 10 A.M.–5 P.M. Wed.–Sat., noon–5 P.M. Sun., adults $7; seniors $6, students and children 3–17 $5), including exhibits on anthropology, astronomy, botany, geology, meteorology, and zoology. Children will love the hands-on exhibits in the Discovery Room, not to mention an exhibit called Dinosaurs and Co.

Broadway Market

Though no longer the dynamic marketplace it once was, this Old World landmark (999 Broadway, near Fillmore, 716/893-0705, 8 A.M.–5 P.M. Mon.–Sat.), founded in 1888 in the heart of Buffalo's Polish neighborhood, still sells fresh ethnic foods. Over 40 vendors hawk everything from homemade soups and potato dumplings to chickens' and pigs' heads.

QRS Music Rolls

Established in 1900, QRS (1026 Niagara St., 716/885-4600, www.qrsmusic.com) is the world's oldest and largest manufacturer of player piano rolls. In the 1920s, the company sold as many as 10 million rolls a year; today, that number is down to two to three hundred thousand, but thanks to enthusiastic hobbyists, is holding steady.

Tours (10 A.M. and 2 P.M. Mon.–Fri., adults $3, children $2) of the low-key QRS factory begin with a short audiovisual presentation and then proceed to the factory floor. En route you'll learn that it once took an arranger eight hours to cut a master roll for a three-minute song, and that staff artist J. Lawrence Cook once wrote over 20,000 different arrangements. Today, no surprise, the songs are all cut by computer.

SOUTH OF DOWNTOWN
Buffalo and Erie County Botanical Gardens

In Frederick Law Olmsted's South Park reigns a pristine white conservatory (2655 South Park Ave., at McKinley Pkwy., 716/827-1584, www.buffalogardens.com, 10 A.M.–5 P.M. Tues.–Sun., adults $4, seniors and students $3, children under 14 free), all domes, semicircular windows, and sheets of glass. Designed by the famed greenhouse architectural firm of Lord and Burnham in the 1890s, the conservatory is actually 12 small connected greenhouses. Each specializes in a different plant variety—bromeliads, orchids, cacti, fruit trees. In the center of things soars a pale-green glass dome crowded with palms. Outside flourish acres of shrubs and flowering plants.

Steel Plant Museum

Just south of the botanical gardens begins the suburb of Lackawanna. As hard as it is to believe today, this quiet neighborhood was once home to Bethlehem Steel, then the world's largest steel plant. During its heyday, the company employed more than 20,000 workers producing 6.5 million ingot tons annually. The 1,300-acre plant was located a few miles west of the Basilica, along Ridge Road near Lake Erie and Route 5.

Most of the plant is gone now, so to get a sense of the past you have to stop into the Lackawanna Public Library. On its lower level is a small museum (560 Ridge Rd., 716/823-0630, www.steelplantmuseum.org, 1–9 P.M. Mon. and Wed., 9 A.M.–5 P.M. Tues. and Thurs.–Sat., free admission) honoring the area's former steel industry through historic photos, exhibits, and memorabilia.

Tifft Nature Preserve

Near the city's harbor lies 264-acre Tifft Nature Preserve (1200 Fuhrmann Blvd. [Rte. 5 S], 716/825-6397 or 716/896-5200, dawn–dusk daily), administered by the Buffalo Museum of Science. Contained within are a 75-acre cattail marsh, a lake, several ponds, and five miles of easy hiking trails. Near the entrance a visitors center exhibits displays on local flora and fauna (9 A.M.–4 P.M. Wed.–Sat. May–Oct., 10 A.M.–4 P.M. Thurs.–Sat. Nov.–Apr.).

Grain Elevators

Walter Gropius, founder of the Bauhaus movement, once compared them to the monuments of ancient Egypt. Le Corbusier called them the "magnificent first fruits of a new age."

All along the Buffalo River rise the giant grain elevators whose smooth facades inspired these architects of the early 20th century. First developed by Buffalo resident Joseph Dart in 1842, grain elevators helped turn the city into a major grain port. The elevators' innovative system of buckets and belts put Buffalo 20 years ahead of other ports that were still using manual laborers.

The earliest grain elevators were built of wood, but frequent fires soon led first to steel or tile construction, then to concrete. In the early 1900s, a cylindrical concrete design became standard across the country.

Buffalo's grain elevators, some still in use, are best viewed from the waterfront. Barring that, drive along Ohio Street, South Park Avenue, or Louisiana Street north of the Tifft Preserve near the mouth of the Buffalo River. The elevators rise up—mute, monolithic.

SPORTS AND RECREATION
Spectator Sports
The **Buffalo Bisons** (716/846-2000), a AAA team for the Cleveland Indians, play downtown at Dunn Tire Park (275 Washington St., Apr.–Sept.) Tickets are generally available.

The National Football League **Buffalo Bills** play at Ralph Wilson Stadium (1 Bills Dr., Orchard Park, 716/648-1800, www.buffalobills.com, Sept.–Jan.). Tickets are available for most games, especially if you order a few weeks in advance.

The National Hockey League **Buffalo Sabres** play downtown at the HSBC Arena (foot of Main St., 716/855-4100, www.sabres.com, Sept.–Apr.). Tickets are generally available.

Cruises
The **Miss Buffalo Cruise Boats** (716/856-6696) offer sightseeing tours of the Buffalo harbor, Lake Erie, and the Niagara River. The boats leave from the Erie Basin Marina June–September.

ENTERTAINMENT
Performing Arts
The renowned **Buffalo Philharmonic**

Orchestra (716/885-5000) performs in the Kleinhans Music Hall (Symphony Circle, 716/883-3560). The hall, one of the nation's best for acoustics, was designed by Eliel and Eero Saarinen.

Shea's Performing Arts Center (646 Main St., 716/847-1410, www.sheas.org) is a historic 1926 theater resembling a European opera house. Shows range from Broadway productions to opera and dance.

Theater
In the Theatre District, the 637-seat **Studio Arena Theatre** (710 Main St., 716/856-5650), Buffalo's professional regional theater for over 25 years, presents both classic and contemporary drama.

More intimate Theatre District venues include the 100-seat **Alleyway Theatre** (1 Curtain Up Alley, 716/852-2600) and the **Buffalo Ensemble Theatre at the New Phoenix** (95 N. Johnson Park, 716/855-2225), which specializes in theatrical revivals and the classics.

Just west of the Theatre District is the **Ujima Theatre Company** (545 Elmwood Ave., 716/883-0380), dedicated to the works of African Americans and Third World artists. The nonprofit **African American Cultural Center** (350 Masten Ave., near Utica St., 716/884-2013) presents drama and other events in its Paul Robeson Theatre.

On D'Youville Square to the northwest of downtown reigns the **Kavinoky Theatre** (320 Porter Ave., 716/881-7668), a beautifully restored 250-seat Victorian theater.

Clubs and Nightlife
The best sources for information about Buffalo's music and nightlife are the Friday edition of the *Buffalo News* (716/849-3434) and *ArtVoice* (716/881-6604), a free biweekly arts publication. An ever-shifting array of nightclubs operate in the **Chippewa District,** along Chippewa Street downtown. Lively, upscale bars can be found on **Elmwood Avenue** near Buffalo State College.

One of the oldest and best-known clubs in the city is laid-back **Nietszche's** (248 Allen

St., 716/886-8539), offering rock, country, reggae, blues, and folk. The **Continental** (212 Franklin St., 716/855-3938) is the place to go for heavy metal. The **Anchor Bar** restaurant in Allentown (see *Food*, below) presents jazz on a regular basis.

A must stop for jazz fans is the **Colored Musicians Club** (145 Broadway, 716/855-9383), a laid-back joint that was once the union local for black musicians. Folk music can be heard at tiny **Metzger's Pub** (4135 Seneca St., 716/674-9897).

EVENTS

Buffalo loves a festival. In mid-May, there's the **Hellenic Festival,** featuring Greek food, dance, and music. In early June the **Allentown Art Festival** highlights work by over 400 artists and artisans. In mid-June the **Juneteenth Festival** takes place in Martin Luther King, Jr. Park.

The **Friendship Festival** in early July commemorates two centuries of peace between the United States and Canada with fireworks, food, and musical acts. One of the nation's largest outdoor food fests is the **Taste of Buffalo** in mid-July. Two popular heritage fests are the **Italian Heritage and Food Festival** in July and **Polish-American Arts Festival** in August.

For more information on these events, contact the Buffalo Convention and Visitors Bureau (716/852-2356, www.visitbuffaloniagara.com).

ACCOMMODATIONS

A good downtown motel is the 61-room **Best Western Inn on the Avenue** (510 Delaware Ave., 716/886-8333, $99–139 d, includes breakfast and parking). A good place for families is the 168-room **Holiday Inn Buffalo Downtown,** featuring a heated pool (620 Delaware Ave., 716/886-2121, $109–129 d).

Buffalo's finest hostelry is the 394-room **C Hyatt Regency Buffalo** (2 Fountain Plaza, at Main and Huron Sts., 716/856-1234, $119–209 d), housed in a lovely historic building equipped with a three-story glass atrium,

indoor pool, and three restaurants. The 468-room **Adams Mark Buffalo** (120 Church St., 716/845-5100, $119–199 d) offers a marble-floored lobby with a waterfall, rooms overlooking Lake Erie, and a big health club. The lowest rates at both hotels are usually available on the weekends.

To the east of downtown, in the suburb of Clarence (known for its many antiques stores) is the acclaimed **C Asa Ransom House** (10529 Main St., 716/759-2315, www.asaransom.com). The 1853 inn features nine spacious guest rooms ($105–225 d, with breakfast) and an excellent restaurant serving American fare (average entrée $18; open for dinner Sun. and Tues.–Thurs. only).

FOOD

Thanks to its diverse population, Buffalo offers many inexpensive ethnic restaurants. A good guide to these spots is *The Cheap Gourmets' Dining Guide to the Niagara Frontier,* by Doug and Polly Smith, available in area bookstores.

The city is also the birthplace of two oddball food specialties. One is Buffalo chicken wings—spicy wings served mild, moderate, or hot, with celery sticks and blue-cheese dressing—invented at the Anchor Bar (see *Allentown*, below). The other is beef-on-'weck sandwiches—thinly sliced roast beef piled high on fresh kimmelweck rolls sprinkled with pretzel salt and caraway seeds.

Downtown

Near Niagara Square stands **Chef's** (291 Seneca St., 716/856-9187), a Buffalo landmark specializing in Southern Italian fare; average entrée $14. A good place for a quick and simple lunch is the **Greenhouse Food Court** (Main Place Mall, 350 Main St., 716/855-1900).

Favorite restaurants in the Theatre District include the **Bijou Grille** (643 Main St., 716/847-1512), a California-style bistro (average entrée $14), and **Hemingway's** (492 Pearl St., 716/852-1937), a good place for a sandwich or burger (average main dish $9). For fine French fare, try **Rue Franklin** (341 Franklin St., 716/852-4416), Buffalo's oldest—and some say best—French restaurant, housed in an elegant brick townhouse (average entrée $22; dinner only).

Allentown

A famed Buffalo institution, the **⦗** **Anchor Bar** (1047 Main St., 716/886-8920) is the friendly Italian restaurant where Buffalo chicken wings were invented in 1964 by Teressa Bellissimo, mother of the late owner Dominic Bellissimo. Live jazz is often featured on weekends; average entrée $12.

Though not as well known, another Allentown institution is the Greek-American **Towne Restaurant** (186 Allen St., 716/884-5128). The eatery has been open 23 hours a day (closed 6–7 A.M. for cleaning) for the past 30-plus years; it's famed locally for its chicken souvlaki.

North of Downtown

Dozens of trendy eateries operate along Elmwood Avenue north of downtown. Among them is **Toro** (492 Elmwood Ave., 716/886-9452), the place to go for tasty *tapas* (average tapa $7). **Ambrosia's Greek** (467 Elmwood, 716/881-2196) serves savory Greek fare in a casual setting (average entrée $15).

Frequent winner of the local People's Choice award is **⦗** **Hutch's** (1375 Delaware Ave., near Gates Circle, 716/885-0074), a casual, bustling southwestern/Cajun bistro serving everything from rib-eye steak rubbed with garlic to grilled tuna; average entrée $15. Not far away is **The Hourglass** (981 Kenmore Ave., 716/877-8788), another Buffalo institution, this one offering continental cuisine, homemade desserts, and an extensive wine list; average entrée $22.

Heading toward the airport, you'll pass extravagant **Salvatore's Italian Gardens** (6461 Transit Rd., Cheektowaga, 716/683-7990), a sprawling, over-the-top Italian eatery painted in vibrant pastels (average entrée $19).

SOUTHERN EXCURSIONS
Orchard Park

Off a suburban street about 12 miles south-

west of downtown Buffalo is **Pedaling History Bicycle Museum** (3943 North Buffalo Rd. [Rte. 240/277], 716/662-3853, www.pedalinghistory.com, 11 A.M.–5 P.M. Mon.–Sat., 1:30 P.M.–5 P.M. Sun., adults $6, seniors $5.40, children 7–15 $3.75), America's only all-bicycle museum and one of the few in the world. Over 200 bicycles are on display, including fat-tired streamliners, crude and heavy "bone shakers," impossibly high unicycles, courting tandems, and a floating marine cycle. First-rate historical exhibits explain how the bicycle was invented, and how the citizens of Victorian-era Boston once complained about the new craze, saying they could no longer control their horses for all the "racing bicyclists attired in black tights and long mustaches."

East Aurora

Along Route 20A a few miles east of Orchard Park lies East Aurora (www.eastaurorany.com), an idyllic village surrounded by hilly dairy country. East Aurora was once home to President Millard Fillmore, and to Elbert Hubbard, a former soap salesman turned charismatic leader of the Arts and Crafts movement. "Conformists die, but heretics live forever," Hubbard was fond of saying. "Weep not peeling other people's onions."

Hubbard was the founder of an idealistic crafts community, the Roycrofters, whose **Roycroft Campus** still stands at the corner of Main and Grove Streets. Now a National Historic Landmark District, the 14-building complex still houses a number of artisans' workshops, along with gift shops, offices, a small museum, and the Roycroft Inn.

At the heart of the campus, **Roycroft Shops** (31 S. Grove St., 716/655-0571) sells arts and crafts of Roycroft design. Out back is **Roycroft Potters** (37 S. Grove St., 716/652-7422). Down the street is the **Elbert Hubbard-Roycroft Museum** (363 Oakwood Ave., 716/652-4735, 2–4 P.M. Wed. and Sat.–Sun. June–Oct.), which documents the community's history. Nearby is the **Roycroft Inn** (see *Camping, Accommodations and Food,* below).

Another must-stop is **Vidler's 5 & 10**

© CHRISTIANE BIRD

In East Aurora, Vidler's carries a little bit of just about everything.

(690–694 Main St., 716/652-0481, www.vidlers5and10.com, 9 A.M.–5:30 P.M. Mon.–Sat., noon–4 P.M. Sun.). Out front flaps a spiffy red-and-white awning; inside are creaky wooden floors and display cases from the '20s selling old-fashioned *stuff,* including penny candy, wooden animals, marbles, magic cards, Buster Brown socks, mousetraps, lace, and ribbon. Almost everything costs under $1.

Two blocks off Main Street is the **Toy Town Museum** (636 Girard Ave., 716/687-5151, www.toytownusa.com, 10 A.M.–4 P.M. Wed.–Sat., free admission), a fascinating place for both children and adults. The museum documents the history of toys in the 20th century, along with children's games, stuffed animals, marionettes, music, and books. On display are one-of-a-kind toys, special exhibits, and the Fisher-Price Toy Collection. The toy company has been based in East Aurora since 1930.

Just off Main is the 1826 **Millard and Abigail Fillmore House** (24 Shearer Ave., 716/652-8875, 2–4 P.M. Wed. and Sat.–Sun.

June–Oct., suggested donation $3), built by the future U.S. president with his own hands in 1826. Fillmore was then a young lawyer fresh off the farm.

Hamburg

Along Route 62, 15 minutes south of Buffalo, lies old-fashioned Hamburg—"the town that friendship built." This is supposedly where the hamburger was born, at the 1885 Erie County Fair. Vendor Frank Mensches had run out of the pork sausage he needed to make his specialty, a pork sausage sandwich. Hurrying to the local market, he picked up chopped meat instead, formed it into patties, and cooked it on his stove. The result was an instant success.

The Erie County Fair still takes place at Hamburg's Fairgrounds (716/649-1280) in August.

Eden

As the self-proclaimed "Garden Spot of New York State," Eden, just south of Hamburg on Route 62, is a pristine small town surrounded by farm country. Downtown stands the **Original American Kazoo Company: Museum, Gift Shop, Factory** (8703 S. Main St., near 1st St., 716/992-3960, www.kazooco.com, 10 A.M.–5 P.M. Tues.–Sat., noon–5 P.M. Sun.).

Established in 1916, the Original is now the only metal kazoo factory in the world. The company paid $5,000 for its first kazoo patent and still manufactures kazoos the way it always has, using die presses and sheet metal.

On display is a wooden kazoo, similar to its African prototype, and liquor-bottle-shaped kazoos made to celebrate the end of Prohibition. The record for the most kazoos ever played at one time was set in Rochester on January 2, 1986, when 54,500 kazoo-ists performed.

Camping, Accommodations, and Food

To the southwest of East Aurora is **Colden Lakes** (9504 Heath Rd., Colden, 716/941-5530), offering 120 campsites. To the southeast is **Sleepy Hollow Lake** (13081 Siehl Rd., Akron, 585/542-4336), offering 200 campsites.

The handsome 1905 **(Roycroft Inn** (40 S. Grove St., East Aurora, 716/652-5552, www.roycroftinn.com, $120–230 d) is a one-of-a-kind place, filled with all original or reproduction Roycroft furnishings—mostly heavy, beautifully designed pieces in oak. All 29 suites have at least one sleeping area, a sitting area, and a whirlpool tub, while the common rooms feature fireplaces, rich wood paneling, and Roycraft lamps. The inn's restaurant serves innovative American cuisine with a continental touch; average dinner entrée $19.

Just outside East Aurora sprawls the **Old Orchard** (2095 Blakely Rd., off Rte. 16, 716/652-4664), a historic farmhouse and former hunting lodge dating back to 1901. Featured are large stone fireplaces and American/continental fare; average entrée $16.

Near Rich Stadium in Orchard Park, find **Eckl's Beef & Weck Restaurant** (4936 Ellicott Rd., 716/662-2262), a good spot to sample the local culinary invention; average dinner entrée $13.

BETWEEN BUFFALO AND NIAGARA FALLS

One way to reach Niagara Falls from Buffalo is to take Niagara Street north to River Road and the Robert Moses Parkway. The routes hug the shore of the Niagara River and, though highly industrialized in spots, offer an interesting back-side look at the region.

Grand Island

Just north of Buffalo begins Grand Island, the country's largest freshwater island. About five square miles larger than Manhattan, Grand Island was once seriously considered as a possible site for the United Nations. Earlier, in 1825, Maj. Mordecai Manual Noah founded Ararat on Grand Island as a refuge for persecuted Jews from Europe. He got as far as erecting a cornerstone for his new city, but the plan eventually failed due to lack of support.

Now primarily a suburban community, Grand Island hosts **Martin's Fantasy Island,** an 80-acre theme park with thrill rides, live entertainment, and a petting zoo (2400 Grand Island Blvd., 716/773-7591, www.martinsfantasyisland.com, 11:30 A.M.–8:30 P.M. daily June–Sept., adults $21, seniors $13, children under 48 inches tall $17).

Herschell Carousel Factory Museum

In the sprawling industrial city of North Tonawanda, directly across the river from Grand Island, stands the old Herschell Carousel Factory (180 Thompson St., off River Rd., 716/693-1885, www.carouselmuseum.org, 11 A.M.–5 P.M. daily July–Aug., 1–5 P.M. Wed.–Sun. Apr.–June and Sept.–Dec., adults $5, seniors $4, children 2–12 $2.50). In its heyday in the 1920s and '30s, the plant produced over 50 carousels a year. Until 1928, all featured animals were carved entirely of wood; after 1928, the magical creatures were half-wood and half-aluminum.

Now both an informal museum and a workshop, the old factory contains a major exhibit on Allan Herschell, an expert woodcarver who was once the best-known carousel maker in the United States. Also on display are hand-carved animals dating back to the early 1900s, new carved animals in various states of completion, and historical exhibits. Out back spins a working 1916 carousel that adults as well as kids are invited to ride.

Camping and Food

Within easy reach of both Buffalo and Niagara Falls is the 587-site **Niagara Falls KOA** (2570 Grand Island Blvd., 716/773-7583).

The whimsical **(Old Man River** (375 Niagara St., Tonawanda, 716/693-5558) sports a whale on its roof and washing machine fountains; on the menu is everything from Sahlen's hot dogs, a Buffalo specialty, to sweet potato french fries. Almost as quirky, and serving a similar menu, is **Mississippi Mudds** (313 Niagara St., Tonawanda, 716/694-0787).

INFORMATION

The **Buffalo Visitor Center** (617 Main St., in the Market Arcade, 716/852-2356), run by the Buffalo Niagara Convention and Visitors Bureau (716/852-0511 or 800/BUFFALO, www.buffaloniagara.com), is open Mon.–Fri. 10 A.M.–4 P.M. The city also has an **Events Hotline** (716/854-4FUN).

Tours of the city's extraordinary archi-tecture are offered by the **Preservation Coalition of Erie County** (716/885-3897, www.perservationcoalition.org) and the **Campaign for Buffalo's Architecture, History, and Culture** (716/884-3138, http://cfb.bfn.org).

Niagara Falls

The name Niagara Falls refers to both the city and the waterfalls. The city is a nondescript place, surrounded by endless industrial plants and humming electrical wires, but the falls… ah, well, the falls.

Oscar Wilde once called Niagara Falls "the second biggest disappointment in a young bride's life," but he must have been showing off that day, for despite the tourists, hoopla, and clichés, the falls are a sight to be seen. Stand in front of that white wall of water and you'll catch your breath. Guaranteed.

Located along the Niagara River between the United States and Canada, Niagara Falls are actually three falls in one: the American and Bridal Veil Falls on the New York side, and the even more spectacular Horseshoe Falls on the Ontario side. The thundering water is on its way from four of the Great Lakes—Superior, Michigan, Huron, and Erie—to the fifth, Ontario.

The falls began forming about 12,000 years ago at the end of the Ice Age. As the last glaciers melted away, huge torrents of water channeled along what is now the Niagara River, over the Niagara Escarpment. The water began eating away at the escarpment and the falls slowly moved upstream. Today, the falls cascade seven miles from their original location; carved out along as their path descends is the seven-mile canyon known as Niagara Gorge.

Five miles below the falls squats massive Robert Moses Niagara Power Plant, providing electricity for much of the Northeast. The world's first commercial-scale, alternating-current generator opened here in 1895. The alternating-current technology made it practical to transmit power over long distances for the first time.

Orientation

The city of Niagara Falls centers around its compact downtown dominated by the Seneca Niagara Casino (310 4th St.). The falls and their accompanying attractions are located on the western edge of the city in Niagara Reservation State Park. The park's major sights are within easy walking distance of each other; the same holds true downtown.

Across the river from the city of Niagara Falls, New York, is the city of Niagara Falls, Ontario. The two are connected by the Rainbow Bridge, off Robert Moses Parkway.

Tours

Gray Line of Niagara Falls (716/694-3600) offers daily tours of both sides of Niagara. **Bedore Tours** (716/285-7550) is a smaller company also offering tours. **Rainbow Air** (454 Main St., 716/284-2800) features helicopter tours over the falls.

◖ NIAGARA RESERVATION STATE PARK

In the mid-1800s the land surrounding Niagara Falls was privately owned and cluttered with factories and shacks. Visitors wishing to see the waterfalls had to pay owners a fee just to peek through a hole in a fence. Even so, the falls was a notorious tourist trap. Reported one traveler of the day, "I know of no place where one is so constantly pestered, where hackmen so incessantly worry you when you want to be

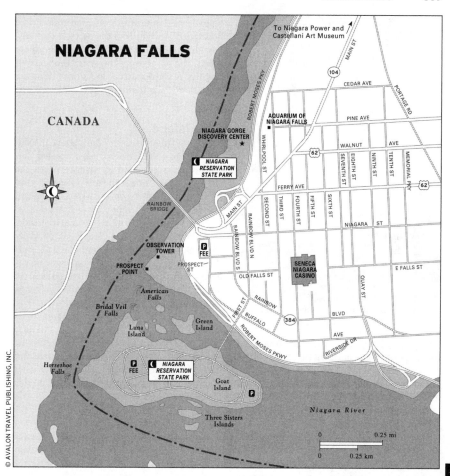

at peace, where you are so dogged over every inch of ground you tread."

Enter artist Frederick Church, landscape architect Frederick Law Olmsted, and the "Free Niagara" movement, established around 1870. For 15 long years, the movement's proponents lobbied heavily to establish a park at the falls. The political opposition was enormous, but finally, in 1885, Gov. David Hill signed an appropriations bill that marked the beginning not only of Niagara Park but also of the entire New York State Park System.

Today, Niagara Reservation State Park (off Robert Moses Pkwy., 716/278-1770, www.niagarafallsstatepark.com, parking $8–10) is the oldest state park in the country. Designed by Olmsted, it receives about 12 million visitors a year.

There are two main entrances to the park. One is at Prospect Point, the other at Goat Island.

Prospect Point

The best place to view the falls on the New

a breathtaking 30-minute seasonal boat ride up close to one of the wonders of the world

York side is Prospect Point. The point sits at the edge of the American Falls' 1,000-foot brink, where you can look straight down into the foamy, turbulent waters. Rainbows often form in the cataract's mist.

Behind Prospect Point presides the **Visitor Center** (716/278-1796, 8 A.M.–6 P.M. daily, with extended hours in summer, free admission), which offers a good introduction to the falls, the park's attractions, and the entire surrounding area. Departing from behind the center are Viewmobiles (adults $2, children 6–12 $1), which travel throughout the park April–October, weather permitting, stopping at all points of interest. Beyond the center stands the **Observation Tower** ($1 per person), featuring dramatic views from glass-enclosed elevators that rise 200 feet.

The tower's elevators also travel down to the foot of the Falls, where the *Maid of the Mist* boats dock (716/284-8897, www.maidofthemist.com, 9 A.M.–6 P.M. daily May–Oct., adults $11.50, children 6–12 $6.75). Visitors are provided with voluminous yellow slickers before

being herded onto sturdy wooden vessels. The boats head straight into the bases of the falls, passing almost close enough to touch. Spray stings, the boats rock, and water thunders all around. A tourist attraction since 1846, the *Maid of the Mist* is still the best way to experience the falls.

Goat Island

Upstream from Prospect Point, above the waterfalls, sits quiet Goat Island, a wooded flatland often overlooked by visitors. With the Bridal Veil and American Falls on one side and the Horseshoe Falls on the other, the island provides a very different view of the cataracts.

From Goat Island's western end descends the **Cave of the Winds Trip** (716/278-1730, daily May–Oct., weather permitting, adults $8, children 6–12 $7), another excursion involving voluminous yellow slickers. This time, guides lead groups of visitors along soggy wooden walkways down to the base of Bridal Veil Falls.

Goat Island is flanked by several smaller islands, including the **Three Sisters Islands,** surrounded on all sides by swift, whitecapped waters. Step out onto these specks of land, and you'll feel as if you're part of the river itself and about to be swept over the curved edge of the falls.

Niagara Gorge Discovery Center

Perched on the edge of Niagara Gorge, at the northern end of the park, is a museum (716/278-1780, 9 A.M.–5 P.M. daily, with extended hours in summer, adults $3, children 6–12 $1.50) dedicated to the geological history of the falls. Highlights include a multimedia show on the gorge's formation, and fossil and mineral exhibits. A footpath leads from the museum down deep into the gorge; explore on your own or take one of the guided walking tours, of varying length and difficulty, led by the park's naturalists (716/745-7848).

NIAGARA FALLS ONTARIO, CANADA

Niagara's most spectacular cataract is Horseshoe Falls, best viewed from **Queen Victoria**

Park (905/356-2241) on the Canadian side. Though slightly shorter than American Falls—176 feet as opposed to 184—Horseshoe Falls boasts a much wider brink (2,200 feet) and handles about 90 percent of the river's volume of flow.

Queen Victoria Park can be reached via **Rainbow Bridge,** near Prospect Point. Proof of citizenship such as a driver's license or birth certificate is required to cross the border. Once on the other side, a People Mover bus operates between all points of interest.

Considerably more built up than the American side, the Canadian side is also both more stylish and more commercial. Queen Victoria Park is beautifully landscaped, while along nearby Clinton Hill stands one kitsch museum after another: **Tussaud's Wax Works, Ripley's Believe It or Not, Guinness Museum of World Records.** A good restaurant offering buffet-style dining and superb views revolves atop the **Skylon Tower** (5200 Robinson Rd., 905/356-2651).

A high point of a visit to the Canadian side is the **Journey Behind the Falls** (905/354-1551, 9 A.M.–11 P.M. June–Sept., 9 A.M.–5 P.M. Oct.–May, adults $10 plus tax Canadian, children 6–12 $6 plus tax Canadian). Out come the big yellow slickers again, followed by a walk *behind* Horseshoe Falls.

For more information, contact the **Niagara Falls, Canada Visitors and Convention Bureau** (5433 Victoria Ave., 905/356-6061 or 800/56-FALLS, 9 A.M.–5 P.M. Mon.–Fri.).

DOWNTOWN SIGHTS
Seneca Niagara Casino

Dominating downtown is the Seneca Niagara Casino (310 4th St., 716/299-1100, www.seneca.com, 24 hours a day). Opened in the summer of 2002, the casino holds about 2,600 slot machines and 90 games tables, along with a 425-seat theater where pop stars and comedians perform, a nightclub, and several restaurants.

Aquarium of Niagara Falls

Directly across from the northern end of Niagara State Park is a first-rate aquarium (701 Whirlpool St., at Niagara Falls Blvd., 716/285-3575, www.aquariumofniagara.org, 9 A.M.–5 P.M. daily, with extended hours in summer, adults $7.50, children 4–12 $5.50), housing over 2,000 marine animals. Atlantic bottle-nose dolphins, California sea lions, Peruvian penguins, electric eels, and shark galore—including blacktip reef shark, lemon shark, nurse shark, and leopard shark—all call the aquarium home. Freshwater fish from the Great Lakes and exotic fish of the coral reefs also fin their way through the waters. Various animal feedings are scheduled daily. An observation deck provides good views of the gorge.

Tourist Museums

In back of one of the town's souvenir shops, find the so-called **Daredevil Museum** (303 Rainbow Blvd., 716/282-4046, 9 A.M.–10 P.M. daily, free admission), actually a small, informal exhibit area. Here you'll learn about 63-year-old Annie Taylor, a schoolteacher who rode over Horseshoe Falls in a wooden barrel in 1901 and lived to tell the tale, and about the aerialists who challenged the Niagara Gorge on tightropes. **Niagara's Wax Museum of History** (303 Prospect St., 716/285-1271, 10 A.M.–8 P.M. daily, adults $6, children $4) tells similar stories through life-size wax figures.

Accommodations

The cheapest beds in town are offered by **Hosteling International Niagara Falls** (1101 Ferry Ave., 716/282-3700). Seven dormitory rooms are equipped with four, six, or eight beds ($17/night for members, $20/night for nonmembers), and two private rooms have beds for three ($22/night for members, $25/night for nonmembers). Also on site are laundry and kitchen facilities.

Within easy walking distance of the falls is the **Quality Hotel and Suites** (240 Rainbow Blvd., 716/282-1212, $99–259 d) with 217 upscale motel rooms and an indoor pool. A good downtown B&B is the Victorian **Rainbow House B&B** (423 Rainbow Blvd. S, 716/282-1135, $80–125 d July–Aug., $60–90 off-season), offering four guest rooms furnished with antiques—and an on-site wedding chapel. A Honeymoon Suite has a porch with a swing.

Housed in what was once the landmark Niagara Hotel, built in 1924, is the 194-room **Fallsview Travelodge** (201 Rainbow Blvd., 716/285-9321, $74–124 d July–Aug., $64–79 d off-season), centered on a grand, columned lobby. Though now somewhat worn, the hotel is still a good value. Some of the rooms have heart-shaped whirlpool tubs.

The modern, attractive **(Holiday Inn Select** (3rd and Old Falls Sts., 716/285-3361, $139–179 d July–Aug., $89–129 off-season) offers 400 spacious guest rooms, as well as indoor/outdoor pools and several restaurants.

Overlooking the upper falls perches the Tudor-style **(Red Coach Inn** (2 Buffalo Ave., 716/282-1459, $139–339 d in summer, $89–249 d off-season), notable for its leaded windows and working stone fireplaces. Best known as a restaurant (see Food, below), the inn also offers one- and two-bedroom suites, some of which have views of the river.

Food

Offering great views of the falls is the **(Top of the Falls Restaurant** (Terrapin Point, Goat Island, 716/278-0348). On the menu is contemporary American cuisine, including lots of fish and pasta dishes, as well as sandwiches, salads, and pizza at lunch; average dinner entrée $17.

Directly across from the Rainbow Bridge is the **Misty Dog Grill** (716/285-0702), where you can order veggie dogs, turkey dogs, Sinatra ("your way") dogs... you get the idea. Wedged between Niagara Park and the Rainbow Centre Mall is a **Hard Rock Cafe** (333 Prospect Ave., 716/282-0007), offering classic American food and a souvenir shop.

At the cozy, Tudor-style **(Red Coach Inn** (2 Buffalo Ave., 716/282-1459), outfitted with heavy wooden tables and chairs, waiters dress in old English attire. The food ranges from omelettes to steak (average dinner entrée $16), and an outdoor patio is open in warm weather.

Six miles north of the falls find **John's**

Flaming Hearth (1965 Military Rd., 716/297-1414), a local institution famed for its charcoal-broiled steak; average entrée $18.

NORTH OF NIAGARA FALLS

Heading north of Niagara Falls on Robert Moses Parkway, you'll pass **Whirlpool State Park**, offering great views of a giant, swirling whirlpool, and **Devil's Hole State Park,** situated along the Niagara River's lower rapids. Both parks (716/278-1770) feature hiking trails.

Niagara Power Project's Power Vista

North of the parks reigns the immense Niagara Power Project (5777 Lewiston Rd., 716/285-3211, 9 A.M.–5 P.M. daily, free admission), one of the largest hydroelectric plants in the world. During the tourist season, about half of the Niagara River's water power (or 100,000 of 202,000 cubic feet) is diverted away from the falls for the production of electricity here and in Canada; at other times, that ratio rises to 75 percent.

The plant's visitors center does an excellent job explaining the principles of hydroelectric power through hands-on exhibits and computer games. Also on site are exhibits on Niagara Falls, past and present. Ascend to the observation deck for outstanding views of the Niagara Gorge.

Castellani Art Museum

Off Lewiston Road directly across from the Devil's Hole State Park runs University Drive, which leads to Niagara University and the Castellani Art Museum (Senior Dr., off University Dr., 716/286-8200, www.niagara.edu/cam, 11 A.M.–5 P.M. Tues.–Sat., 1–5 P.M. Sun., free admission). Dedicated in 1990, the airy edifice houses over 3,000 artworks ranging from the Hudson River School to modern sculpture. Contemporary artists (David Hockney, Charles Burchfield, Alexander Calder, Willem de Kooning, Cindy Sherman, Nam June Paik) are especially well represented. The museum's strong Folk Arts Program sponsors temporary

THE UNDERGROUND RAILROAD AT THE NIAGARA FRONTIER

Throughout the early to mid-1800s, the Niagara frontier served as the last stop on the Underground Railroad for slaves funneled north through New York City and Philadelphia. Though few records were kept, it is estimated that as many as 30,000 people may have passed through here on their way to Canada.

Seven "Stations," or sculptures, honoring those who helped the escaping slaves are displayed throughout the region. Conceived by artist Houston Conwill in 1988, the project was largely sponsored by the Castellani Art Museum in Niagara Falls.

Each of Conwill's sculptures is a tall, thin, bronze-and-copper "house" standing about six feet tall. At the top is an "attic" embossed with maps of the Underground Railroad and African symbols. At the base is a "cellar" with a door opening into a hiding place. On the door are notes taken from the cryptic correspondence once passed between stationmasters.

Information about the Stations of the Underground Railroad is available at the Castellani Art Museum, Niagara University (716/286-8200). The Buffalo Niagara Convention and Visitors Bureau (716/852-0511 or 888/228-3369) also publishes a free driving-tour guide to underground railroad sites throughout the region. Four especially interesting sites are:

1) The **St. John's A.M.E. Church** (917 Garden Ave., Niagara Falls). St. John's was one of the first African American churches founded in Niagara County. From its hillside site, the fugitive slaves could see the beckoning lights of Canada and freedom.

2) The **Parliament Oak School** (325 King St., Niagara-on-the-Lake, Canada). It was in this unassuming building that Canada's Act of 1793 was signed, guaranteeing freedom to slaves and their descendants. A quote from Harriet Tubman reads: "When I found I had crossed, there was such a glory over everything. I felt as if I was in Heaven. I am free and they shall be free. I shall bring them here."

3) The **First Presbyterian Church** (505 Cayuga St., Lewiston). Abolitionist Josiah Tryon attended this white stucco church, built in the 1820s, and is buried in the graveyard next door. As the story goes, Josiah's wealthy brother Thomas Tryon had built a mansion along the Niagara River gorge north of Lewiston. The house was so isolated, however, that Thomas's wife refused to move into it, and Thomas allowed Josiah to hide fugitive slaves in his cellar.

4) The **Thomas Root Home** (3106 Upper Mountain Rd., Pekin). Located midway between Niagara Falls and Lockport, the former Root home contains a trapdoor leading to a 5-by-10-foot cellar. Here "volumes bound in black," as the coded messages once read, spent the night before being driven to the border, hidden beneath piles of vegetables. The house is now privately owned, but the station is set amidst a small row of pine trees accessible to the public.

exhibits on such subjects as Polish-American Easter traditions, African American gospel traditions, and Halloween.

Lewiston

Continue north of the power project about four miles to Lewiston, a historic 19th-century village. Proudly ensconced in one of the many National Historic Landmarks here is a McDonald's restaurant (460 Center St.). For more information on the history of the village, stop into **Historic Lewiston** (476 Center St., 716/754-9500).

One of the region's oldest and best bakeries is [**DiCamillo's** (535 Center St., 716/754-2218), established in 1920. The **Apple Granny** (433 Center St., 716/754-2028) is a good spot for lunch, dinner, or a snack. For a more upscale meal, try the **Clarkson House** (810 Center St., 716/754-4544), housed in an 1818 landmark. On the menu is lobster, steak, and open-hearth cooking (average main dish $16).

■ Artpark

At the southern edge of Lewiston reposes the 200-acre Earl W. Brydges Artpark (150 S. 4th St., 716/754-9000, www.artpark.net, 8 A.M.–dusk daily, $6–8 parking), the only state park in the United States devoted to the visual and performing arts. During the summer, all sorts of events are staged, including storytelling, acrobatics, and theater and dance workshops (free–$7). Other park features include hiking trails; a 2,300-seat **Artpark Theater,** bringing in national acts; and a burial mound dating back over 2,000 years, to when the area was inhabited by the Hopewell Indians. Thirty feet long by 20 feet wide, the mound is listed on the National Register of Historic Places.

Old Fort Niagara

Even if you have no interest in military history, it's worth continuing a few miles further north to Youngstown and Old Fort Niagara (off Robert Moses Pkwy., 716/745-7611, www.oldfortniagara.org, 9 A.M.–4:30 P.M. daily, with extended hours in summer, adults $8, children 6–12 $5). Strategically located at the mouth of the Niagara River, where it controlled access to the Great Lakes, the fort is a strikingly handsome place with commanding views of Lake Ontario.

Fort Niagara was originally established by the French in 1726 and was occupied by American soldiers as late as the early 1900s. Its oldest standing structure is the 1726 French Castle, a rectangular stone edifice equipped with a bakery, guardhouse, living quarters, and chapel. Nearby plunges a well purportedly haunted by a headless ghost searching for its missing body part.

During the summer, the fort stages frequent daily events such as military musters and fife-and-drum drills. Surrounding the fort is **Fort Niagara State Park** (716/745-7273), offering easy hiking trails, playgrounds, and swimming pools.

Along Lake Ontario

East of Youngstown, the county spreads out past orchards and farmland, small harbors and

good fishing spots. **Route 18** hugs the shoreline as it passes through the townships of Wilson, Newfane, and Somerset, all filled with unusual cobblestone homes. To visit the Cobblestone Museum in Childs, continue on Route 18 to Ontario County and head south on Route 98. **Route 104** east of Lewiston offers an equally scenic route, and an even greater allotment of cobblestone homes, and fruit farms.

EAST OF NIAGARA FALLS
Lockport

Head 25 minutes east of Niagara Falls via Route 31/270 to the Erie Canal town of Lockport, hometown of volleyball. As the story goes, the townspeople used a basketball for the game at first, but broken fingers soon led to the development of a lighter ball. Also said to be a Lockport invention is the fire hydrant— developed by a man whose factory later burned to the ground.

Two-hour cruises of the Erie Canal, highlighted by a trip through Locks 34 and 35, are offered by **Lockport Locks & Erie Canal Tours** (210 Market St., off Main St., 716/693-3260, May–Oct., adults $14.50, children 5–12 $10). Nearby, the **Lockport Canal Museum** (80 Richmond Ave., at Locks 34 and 35, 716/635-6250, 9 A.M.–5 P.M. daily May–Oct.) documents the area's canal history, with photos from 1812 to the present. Down the street, the **Lockport Cave and Underground Boat Ride** (21 Main St., 716/438-0174, 11 A.M.–5 P.M. daily June–Sept., adults $8.50, children $6.50) takes visitors through five flights of locks, industrial ruins, and a 2,430-foot-long tunnel that was blasted out of solid rock in the late 1850s.

Camping and Accommodations

Several small campgrounds and a long, long line of motels extend to the immediate east of downtown Niagara Falls along Niagara Falls Boulevard. Among the campgrounds are the 80-site **Niagara Falls Campground** (2405 Niagara Falls Blvd., 716/731-3434). Among the motels is a 70-room **Quality Inn** (7708 Niagara Falls Blvd., 716/283-0621, $79–139 d July–Aug., $50–75 off-season).

Orleans County

East of Niagara County lies Orleans County, one of the flattest and quietest areas in the state. Agriculture is the number one industry here, and enormous truck farms raising fruits and vegetables spread out all along the highways and byways. Route 104, which cuts through the center of the county, is peppered with **pick-your-own farms.**

Albion, the county capital, and Medina, the main commercial center, are small historic villages along the Erie Canal. To the north lie Lake Ontario and Point Breeze, a harbor known for its world-class salmon fishing. Orleans County is also the best place in the state to learn about cobblestone architecture, a building style that is all but unique to New York.

MEDINA

The main attraction in Medina is its wide, old-fashioned Main Street, flanked by mid-19th-century buildings. Many were built of local red sandstone and still house thriving small businesses such as bakeries, variety stores, and clothing shops.

Along East Central Street just east of Main reigns **St. John's Episcopal Church,** once listed in Ripley's *Believe It or Not* as "the church in the middle of the street." At the north end of Main find the Erie Canal, and a boat basin in which the canal boats once turned around.

Medina hosts the mellifluous **New York State Duck Calling Championship and Wildlife Festival** (585/798-4287) every September. The event attracts hunters from all over the region.

ALBION

Farther east along the Erie Canal lies quiet Albion, centered around a 34-building **Historic Courthouse District** (Rte. 98 off Rte. 31). The handsome 1858 **Orleans County Courthouse,**

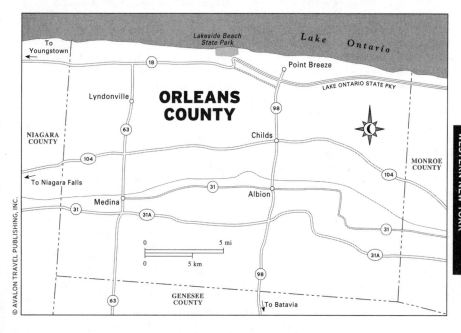

COBBLESTONE HOUSES

All across Western New York stand handsome houses built of smooth rounded stones small enough to hold in one hand. An ancient form of construction that dates back to Roman times, cobblestone masonry can be found in parts of England, Italy, and France. Of the approximately 1,000 cobblestone houses in North America, however, 800 are in Western and Central New York.

Cobblestone masonry in New York began after the construction of the Erie Canal. Masons from Ireland and England who had worked on the canal settled in the area, where they found abundant building materials on hand.

There are two kinds of cobblestone houses: those made of rough ice-laid cobbles, and those made of polished water-laid cobbles. The ice-laid variety can be found in the drumlin areas between Rochester and Syracuse. The water-laid variety – built of stones tumbled in the waters of Lake Ontario – are located west of Rochester.

Most of the cobblestone houses were built in a Greek Revival style between 1825 and 1860.

1834 cobblestone house

Some featured meticulous patterns, such as herringbone or striped designs. Each mason had his own secret techniques and formula for mortar. By the late 1860s, however, cobblestone houses had become too expensive for the industrial age and the art died out.

A good concentration of cobblestone houses stands along Route 104 (Ridge Rd.) in Orleans and Monroe Counties. The Cobblestone Society, established to help preserve the houses, maintains a small Cobblestone Museum in Childs.

Greek Revival in style, sports a silver dome visible for miles around and an old-fashioned courtroom crowded with polished wooden pews.

Another interesting stop is the elongated 1904 **Pullman Memorial Universalist Church** (E. Park St. and Rte. 98). The old English Gothic edifice was built by the manufacturer of railroad sleeping cars, George M. Pullman, who grew up in Albion before moving to Chicago and becoming a millionaire.

CHILDS
Cobblestone Museum

The Cobblestone Museum (14393 Rte. 104, at Route 98, 585/589-9013, 11 A.M.–5 P.M. Tues.–Sat. and 1–5 P.M. Sun. June–Sept., adults $3, children 6–12 $2) is housed in the basement of one of the oldest (1834) and best preserved of New York's 25 cobblestone churches. Simple exhibits explain the mason-

ry's history and technique, while upstairs is an intimate sanctuary lined with wood. Next door stand two more cobblestone buildings—an 1849 schoolhouse and an 1840 house filled with Victorian-era furnishings. Also on-site are reconstructed blacksmith and print shops.

Food

Across from the museum is one of the county's best restaurants, **Tillman's Village Inn** (Rts. 98 and 104, 585/589-9151). A former stagecoach stop, built in 1824, the inn serves various sandwiches and salads for lunch, and meat and fish entrées for dinner.

Continue about five miles north of Childs to reach **Brown's Berry Patch** (14264 Rte. 18, 8 A.M.–8 P.M. daily Apr.–Oct., 585/682-5569). A barn-size country store run by the same family since 1804, Brown's sells everything from raspberries and green beans to sandwiches and ice cream; out back you can pick your own berries and other fruits in season.

POINT BREEZE

On the shores of Lake Ontario, directly north of Childs, lies Point Breeze Harbor, centered around a busy marina. The **County Marine Park** (Rte. 98) is a good spot to have a picnic.

For easy hiking and biking, head a few miles west of Point Breeze to **Lakeside Beach State Park** (Lake Ontario State Pkwy., 585/682-5246). To reserve a spot in the park's 274-site campground, call 800/456-CAMP.

Genesee County

More flat, prosperous farmland fills the 500 square miles of Genesee County, located just south of Orleans County, midway between Buffalo and Rochester. According to the 1990 census, Genesee produces over $80 million of agricultural products each year. Dairy farming is the main occupation, with truck farming following close behind. Encircling the village of Elba stretches a rich, black muckland that yields the nation's second largest onion crop.

Genesee County's only city is Batavia, established in 1801 at the crossing of two Native American trails. To the county's northwest lies the Iroquois National Wildlife Center; to the southwest, Darien Lake, the state's largest "entertainment complex." Le Roy, a small town east of Batavia, is where Jell-O was invented.

BATAVIA

Once a lively industrial and trading center, Batavia received a near-fatal blow in the 1960s thanks to urban renewal. Dozens of downtown brick storefronts were razed and replaced by a soulless mall. The townspeople still haven't forgiven those involved, and the mall remains a target of local resentment.

Batavia does have a few historic buildings left, most notably the striking Holland Land Office Museum and Richmond Memorial Library on Main Street, and the gracious homes along Ellicott Avenue.

The author John Gardner grew up in Batavia, and set his novel *Sunlight Dialogues* here. Those familiar with the city can recognize many of the streets and people he describes in the book.

In summer, the Genesee County Chamber of Commerce operates a **visitor information booth** outside the Holland Land Office Museum (10 A.M.–5 P.M. daily).

Holland Land Office Museum

In the early 1800s, Western New York was divided into several enormous land tracts by investors eager to sell parcels to pioneers. The largest of these companies—surveying 3.3 million acres—was the Holland Land Company, composed of bankers from Amsterdam, Holland.

The business of selling the company's land was conducted in Batavia. Surveyor Joseph Ellicott built the company's first log-cabin office here in 1801 and a permanent stone office in 1815. Land sold for about $2 an acre.

Today, the Holland Land Company building (131 W. Main St., 585/343-4727, www.hollandoffice.com, 10 A.M.–4 P.M. Tues.–Sat., free admission) is a National Historic Landmark exhibiting prehistoric mastodon bones, Native American artifacts, and pioneer artifacts.

Old Batavia Cemetery

Along Harvester Avenue, off Main Street, lies the Old Batavia Cemetery, final resting place of Joseph Ellicott and other early pioneers. Of particular interest is the **Morgan Monument,** erected in 1880 by the National Christian Association Opposed to All Secret Societies.

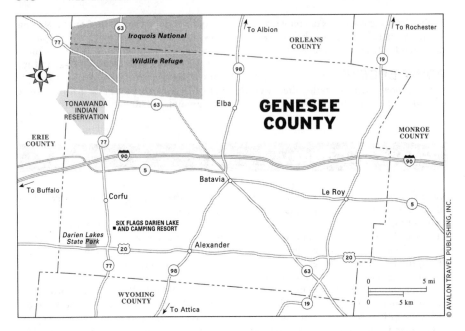

© AVALON TRAVEL PUBLISHING, INC.

The monument honors William Morgan, who mysteriously disappeared one night in 1826 after threatening to reveal the secret laws and rituals of the Free Masons. His disappearance led to a great public outcry against secret societies and to the establishment of the Anti-Masonic Party. Anti-Masonry was the first third-party movement in the United States, and although short-lived, it helped launch the careers of William Lloyd Garrison and William Seward. The inscription on the monument—built with over 2,000 contributions from 26 states—describes Morgan as "a martyr to the freedom of writing, publishing and speaking the truth."

Batavia Downs

North of the city find the oldest parimutuel harness track in the United States. Established in 1940, Batavia Downs (8315 Park Rd., 585/343-3750) offers evening racing August–November. To reach the track from I-90, take Exit 48.

Food and Treats

Miss Batavia (566 E. Main St., 585/343-9786) is a classic old-time diner serving homemade fare. **Oliver's Candies** (211 W. Main St., 585/343-5888) has been selling homemade chocolates and nut crunches since 1932.

LE ROY

Several miles east of Batavia lies Le Roy, a surprisingly elegant, if somewhat run-down, town of fine old stone churches and Victorian homes. Through the center of things runs tree-lined Main Street.

Le Roy is best known as the birthplace of Jell-O, invented by a local carpenter named Pearl Bixby Wait in 1897. Wait lacked the means to market his product, however, and in 1899 he sold the formula to businessman Orota Woodward for $450. By 1906, Woodward had a $7 million enterprise on his hands; Wait was still working as a carpenter. Jell-O was later purchased by General Mills, but the plant continued operating in Le Roy until 1964.

Le Roy House and Jell-O Gallery Museum

Built in 1817 as a land office, the massive stone Le Roy House (23 E. Main St., 585/768-7433, www.jellomuseum.com, 10 A.M.–4 P.M. Mon.–Fri. and 1–4 P.M. Sun. May–Oct., donations welcomed) now serves as a local history museum featuring several period rooms, an exhibit on area pottery, and a gallery filled with memorabilia commemorating the wiggly dessert. On display are old packages, cookbooks, and advertisements dating back to the early 1900s. "Jell-O The Dainty Dessert" reads one ad from 1907; "When I'm eating Jell-O I wish I were a whale" reads another from 1952.

The museum also contains exhibits on Ingham University, an early school for women, in operation in Le Roy between 1837 and 1892. The university was founded by two sisters, Marietta and Emily Ingham, with money they had inherited from their mother.

Food

The **D&R Depot** (63 Lake St. [Rte. 19], 585/768-6270), housed in its 1901 namesake, serves all-homemade American fare; average main dish $9. The 1820s **Creekside Inn** (1 Main St., 585/768-9771), a Le Roy landmark, overlooks Oatka Creek; on the menu find American and continental dishes; average main dish $14. Between Batavia and Le Roy stands the **Red Osier Landmark** (Rte. 5, Stafford, 585/343-6972), a steak and seafood restaurant acclaimed for its prime rib, carved tableside (average main dish $16; dinner only).

IROQUOIS NATIONAL WILDLIFE REFUGE

Once covered by a vast glacial lake, the Iroquois Refuge (1101 Casey Rd., off Rte. 63, Alabama, 585/948-5445, dawn–dusk daily) is now a 10,818-acre preserve of marshland, wooded swamp, wet meadows, pasture, and cropland. Tens of thousands of Canada geese and ducks stop over here during their spring migration, while others nest in the marshes throughout the summer. Muskrat, opossum, beaver, mink, fox, and white-tailed deer also abound.

Near the entrance, a visitors center (7:30 A.M.–4 P.M. Mon.–Fri. year-round, with weekend hours in migration season, free admission) displays exhibits on local flora and fauna. Three nature trails run through the refuge, and four overlooks provide for wildlife observation.

DARIEN LAKES

In the county's southwest corner find 1,846-acre **Darien Lakes State Park** (10289 Harlow Rd., at Sumner Road, Darien Center, 585/547-9242), a quiet, wooded oasis centered around a large, lovely lake. The lake offers good fishing and a swimming beach, while nearby are 19 miles of hiking trails and a 150-site campground; for reservations, call 800/456-CAMP.

Kitty-corner to the park bustles the much noisier **Six Flags Darien Lake and Camping Resort** (Rte. 77 and Sumner Rd., 585/599-4641, 10:30 A.M.–10 P.M. daily July–Sept., weekends in spring and fall, all-day admission adults $34, seniors and children under 48 inches $20). Established in 1964 as a 164-acre campground, the park has since become an enormous entertainment complex. Featured are over 100 rides, shows, and attractions, including one of the world's top-10 wooden roller coasters and the nation's second-largest Ferris wheel. Other attractions include a water park, kids' amusement park, 2,000-site campground, hotel accommodations, and the Darien Lake Performing Arts Center, presenting nationally known rock and pop stars.

Wyoming County

In Wyoming County, the flat farmland of Genesee County turns into a gentle sea of broad, rolling hills. Tucked into almost every valley are trim maroon barns topped with silvery silos, while all around graze cows. Especially scenic roads, bordered with patchwork fields, are **Routes 78 and 39.**

The county's key villages are Warsaw, Perry, Attica, and Arcade, all of which contain a number of striking architectural landmarks; most were built in the late 1800s and early 1900s.

Along the southeastern edge of the county lies the famed **Letchworth Gorge,** also known as the Grand Canyon of the East. The park can be accessed from the villages of Castile and Portageville.

WYOMING VILLAGE

Wyoming village may be small, but it boasts over 70 buildings listed on the National Register of Historic Places. Equally unusual is the fact that its downtown is still lit with original gas streetlights.

Though first established in 1802, Wyoming didn't flourish until 1817, when Silas Newell founded Middlebury Academy here. The first institution of higher learning west of the Genesee River, the academy was a near overnight success, with as many as 200 students attending at one time. Most were the sons of wealthy Rochester and Buffalo businesspeople.

In the late 1800s, the village's cultural status was further enhanced by the presence of Mrs. Lydia Avery Coonley Ward. A devotee of the arts, Ward summered at Hillside, the family mansion on the edge of town, and brought many artists, intellectuals, and other leaders to visit. Among them were Susan B. Anthony, John Muir, and the Roosevelts.

Wyoming centers around a tidy **village green.** To one side presides the Greek Revival **Middlebury Academy** (22 S. Academy St., no phone, open summer afternoons), now housing a small local history museum. Down the

street stands a stately Edwardian **village hall,** donated to the town by Mrs. Ward.

About three miles south of Wyoming sprawls **The New Farm** (Rte. 19, 585/237-2652, 10 A.M.–5 P.M. Sat.–Sun. Apr.–Dec.), an indoor/outdoor farmers' market selling everything from fresh produce to handmade quilts.

Accommodations

Mrs. Lydia Ward's old family mansion is now the delightful **C Hillside Inn** (890 E. Bethany Rd., between Rtes. 19 and 20, 585/495-6800, www.hillsideinn.com, $125–225 d, with breakfast), an elegant yet homey Classic Revival mansion. Set amidst 48 acres of woodland, the inn offers 10 very spacious guest rooms, an enormous front porch, fireplaces, whirlpools, and a restaurant serving innovative American fare for lunch and dinner (average dinner entrée $15).

WARSAW

Just south of Wyoming lies the stately town of Warsaw, the county seat. Set in the deep narrow valley of Oatka Creek, Warsaw owes much of its fine architecture to the salt boom of 1878–1894. During those years, Warsaw was the nation's largest producer of table salt.

Striking architectural landmarks stand along West Buffalo, Liberty, Court, Park, and Main Streets. Buildings especially worth viewing include the large Queen Anne **Humphrey Mansion** (230 W. Buffalo St.), built in 1884 by one of the city's first bankers; and the simple white **Trinity Episcopal Church** (W. Buffalo St., downtown), designed by architect Richard Upjohn in 1853.

ATTICA

West of Wyoming lies Attica, best known today as the home of the Attica Correctional Facility. Built in 1931 along Route 98 on the outskirts of town, the prison is surrounded by high massive walls, visible for miles.

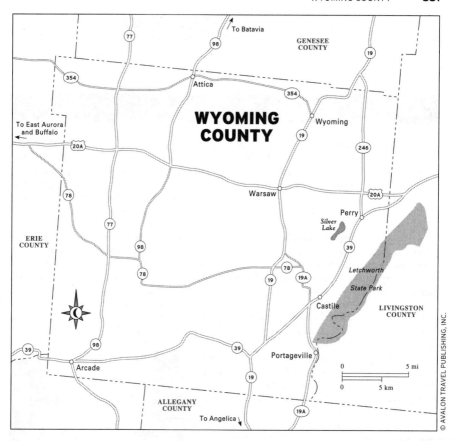

Once a flourishing mill and railroad center, Attica is filled with mid-Victorian architecture, especially of the Second Empire style. Good examples stand downtown along Main and Market Streets. The **Attica Historical Museum** (130 Main St., 585/591-2161, 1–4 P.M. Wed. and Sat., free admission) contains Victorian fashions and furnishings, and railroad memorabilia.

Every August, the **Attica Rodeo** (585/493-3190) comes to town. Rodeo circuit cowboys rate it one of the top rodeos in the east.

ARCADE

Tucked into the far southwestern corner of the county sits Arcade. Surrounded by fertile dairy country, Arcade was a major shipping center for cheese and other agricultural goods throughout the late 1800s and early 1900s. Rambling Victorian homes still stand along West Main Street.

Today, Arcade's main attraction is the orange-and-black **Arcade & Attica Steam Railroad,** whose vintage cars date back to 1915. Ninety-minute rides take passengers into the rural countryside, past fields and grazing cows, to the Curriers Station Stop. Entertainers keep things lively en route, while at Curriers is a small railroad museum.

The train leaves from the **Arcade & Attica Railroad Station** (278 Main St., 585/492-3100, www.anarr.com), a turn-of-the-

WESTERN NEW YORK

20th-century depot with a double-pitched hipped roof. Excursions depart at noon and 2 P.M. Saturday–Sunday June–October, with an extended schedule July–August (adults $12, seniors $10, children 3–11 $7).

Allegany County

Allegany County is one of the least-known and most under-appreciated counties in New York State. Bordering Pennsylvania, in the foothills of the Allegheny Mountains, it has a reputation for being hicker than hick. And yet the countryside here is remarkably beautiful. One dark rolling hill leads into another, while up above climb towering cumulus clouds. Storms break out violently and unexpectedly, only to disappear again a half-hour later.

Allegany County is blanketed with 23 state forests, covering some 46,000 acres. It harbors the largest population of white-tailed deer and wild turkey in the state, along with a few black bears and much trout and bass. Hunting and fishing are big business here.

Allegany County has no cities and very little in the way of tourist "attractions." Instead, there are lots of scenic back roads and villages to explore, along with good hiking trails. The county is also known for its antiques. Small shops pepper the back roads, and auctions usually take place several times a week. Watch the *Wellsville Daily Reporter, Olean Times Herald,* and especially the *Pennysaver* for announcements.

Driving through the countryside, you'll spot an occasional wildcat oil drill, its rusted head bobbing up and down. The first oil drill in the nation was set up in Allegany County in 1867, and by the mid 1930s, the county was producing about 5.4 million barrels a year. Today, Allegany's remaining oil field—part of the much greater field that centers in Pennsylvania—is all but impossible to access, but this is a poor county and dreams die hard.

ANGELICA

At the county's center is the unusual village of Angelica. Founded in 1800 by Philip Church,

a nephew of Alexander Hamilton, it's laid out around a large circular park lined with imposing churches and public buildings, most dating back to the 1800s. Intersecting the circle to either side extends wide, shady Main Street, flanked by roomy Victorian homes in various states of repair.

To one side of the park lies a small clay court where the ancient game of roque takes place on summer nights. Played on a hard surface and similar to croquet, roque originated in France centuries ago. At one time, it was popular throughout this part of the state, but today roque is only played in Angelica and in one other town in the United

a church in Angelica

© CHRISTIANE BIRD

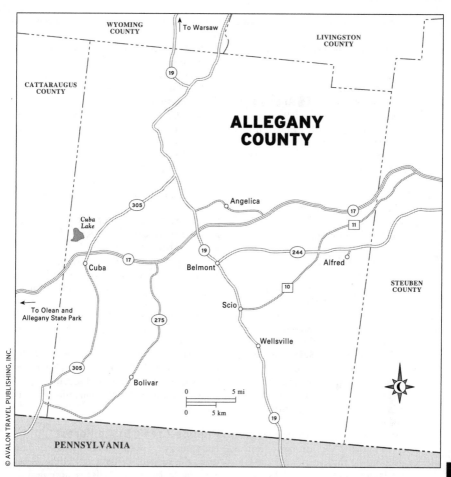

To Warsaw

WYOMING
COUNTY

LIVINGSTON
COUNTY

CATTARAUGUS
COUNTY

19

Cuba
Lake

305

Angelica

17

11

17

19

244

Alfred

Cuba

Belmont

10

STEUBEN
COUNTY

To Olean and
Allegany State Park

275

Scio

Wellsville

0   5 mi

0   5 km

305

Bolivar

19

PENNSYLVANIA

© AVALON TRAVEL PUBLISHING, INC.

States—in Texas. Games in Angelica usually begin at dusk, and many of the players are old men, who take the game *very* seriously. Local legend even has it that once a player had a heart attack on the court, only to be pushed out of the way by his obsessed colleagues, who insisted that the game go on until the ambulance arrived.

Back in the 1800s, Angelica was a bustling railroad village and the county seat. Both enterprises moved out around the turn of the century, leaving Angelica to become a sleepy grande dame with a population under 1,000.

Along Main Street stand a half-dozen or so antiques stores.

Allen Lake State Forest

Continue north of Angelica about five miles to reach the 2,420-acre Allen Lake State Forest, sitting atop a high, flat hill. In the forest's center is Allen Lake, encircled by four intersecting roads. The lake is a good spot for a picnic, or you can hike the roads, which offer great views. Hiking around the entire lake takes about 2.5 hours.

To reach the forest from Angelica, take Peavy Road north off County Road 16. Proceed about five miles to Vincent Hill Road and turn left, into the forest. Vincent Hill Road turns into Muckle Road, which leads to Allen Lake and a parking lot.

Accommodations

In the center of town is the **⟨ Angelica Inn B&B** (64 W. Main St., 585/466-3295, www.an-gelica-inn.com, $79–119 d). Painted in pale greens and purples, the inn offers seven attractive guest rooms and suites, three equipped with fireplaces, and one with a veranda and Jacuzzi.

Events

One of the oldest county fairs in the state is the **Allegheny County Fair** (845/268-0220), held on the Angelica Fairgrounds in late July.

SOUTH ON ROUTE 19

Route 19 meanders south of Angelica past the Southern Tier Expressway (Rte. 17) to Belmont, the county seat. Although there's not much to see here, you might want to check out the **Alleghany County Museum** (7 Court St., 585/268-9222, 9 A.M.–5 P.M. Mon.–Fri.). South of Belmont is tiny **Scio,** home to an antiques store or two, and Wellsville, a small industrial town that was once the hub of the county's oil industry. A large refinery operated here until 1957, but nowadays all that's left are a few wildcat drill sites.

Wellsville centers around an expansive Main Street frozen in the 1950s. Just down from an old art deco movie theater presides the family-run **Wellsville Texas Hots** (132 N. Main St., 585/593-1400), a 1921 eatery marked with a green-striped awning and neon sign. Inside echoes a high-ceilinged hall lined with well-worn booths that still have call-buttons for summoning the waitstaff. The specialty of the house is, of course, Texas hots (hot dogs)—"famous for many, many miles."

ALFRED

Near the eastern edge of the county lies Alfred, a small village tucked into dark, wooded hills. Many of the buildings here are painted a surprising bright white, with orange terra-cotta roofs reminiscent of the Mediterranean. The roofs are due to the rich clay soils surrounding the village, and to the presence of Alfred University, known for its College of Ceramics. Established here in 1900, the college has educated over one-third of all the ceramic engineers in the United States, along with an infinite number of fine artists.

Alfred University sits on a wooded hillside at the edge of the village, along Route 244. Of special interest to visitors are its International Museum of Ceramic Art. The village itself is a small cluster of shops and businesses, most oriented to the university's needs. The area immediately surrounding Alfred is known as Alfred Station.

Schein-Joseph International Museum of Ceramic Art at Alfred University

Currently housed in an arts center on campus, this small museum (Binns-Merrill Bldg., 607/871-2421, www.ceramicsmuseum.al-fred.edu, 10 A.M.–4 P.M. Wed.–Fri., free admission) exhibits ceramics from the university's collection of over 8,000 pieces. Many of the pieces were produced in the Alfred area, but other national and international styles are also well represented. The museum's current exhibit space only covers 3,000 square feet, but a new $1-million, 20,000-square-foot facility is in the works.

Phillips Creek State Forest

Four miles west of Alfred along Route 244 extends the rugged, 2,708-acre Phillips Creek State Forest, laced with trails that are especially popular among cross-country skiers. The trail-heads are located off a well-marked parking lot on Route 244.

A good choice for hikers is the Blue Trail, which makes an 8.6-mile loop through some of the thickest parts of the forest. The varied terrain includes gullies, creeks, and steep hills with excellent views. The hike takes about four hours.

Food and Shopping

The **Collegiate** (7 N. Main St., 607/587-9293) is a village institution, serving breakfast all day, along with lunch and dinner.

The **Canacadea Country Store** (599 Rte. 244, Alfred Station, 607/587-8634), housed in an 1860s building with a tile roof, sells old-time toys, old-fashioned candy, baskets, and terra-cotta and porcelain pottery. Along Route 244 are various small shops and studios selling the works of area potters.

CUBA

Near the western edge of the county lies Cuba, a low-key local resort that, thanks to Cuba Lake, is especially popular among fisherfolk. Built in 1858 as part of the Genesee Valley Canal System, Cuba Lake was known for years as the world's largest manufactured body of water.

Cuba centers around historic Genesee, Main, and South Streets. At 53 Genesee St. stands the **Cuba Cheese Shoppe** (585/968-3949), selling a large selection of New York–made cheeses, cheesecakes, and gourmet foods. Cuba has been known for its locally made cheese since the late 1800s.

Along South Street between Grove Street and Stevens Avenue lies a Victorian-era **historic district.** At the south end of South Street, past the railroad tracks, reigns an unusual **Block Barn**—a long, rectangular, silver-gray structure with a multileveled red roof.

Cuba Lake itself is north of the downtown, off Route 305. Adjoining the lake is the Seneca Oil Spring, where white men first saw petroleum in North America in 1627. The Seneca had already known about the oil and for generations, harvested it by spreading blankets on the surface of the water. The blankets absorbed the oil, which the Seneca then wrung out and used for medicinal purposes. Now part of the mile-square Oil Spring Reservation, Seneca Oil Spring is still owned by the Seneca Nation.

BOLIVAR

To learn more about the county's early oil history, head south to Bolivar and the **Pioneer Oil Museum of New York** (Main St., 585/928-1433, call for hours, donations welcomed). Inside you'll find historic photos, maps, and documents, along with tools and some heavy equipment used in the old days.

Cattaraugus County

The dark, rolling hills of Allegany County continue on into Cattaraugus County, home to magnificent Allegany State Park. Cattaraugus also has its share of meandering back roads, lost-in-time villages, and good hiking trails, but it is considerably more developed than Allegany County. Two small cities—Olean and Salamanca—and a popular ski resort (Ellicottville) are located here.

Abutting Allegany State Park to the north is the 30,469-acre Allegany Indian Reservation, the largest Native American reservation in the state. On the northern edge of the county, and spilling over into Erie and Chautauqua Counties, is the 21,680-acre Cattaraugus Indian Reservation. Both are home to the Seneca Nation.

In and around the villages of Randolph, Conewango, and Leon, as well as Cherry Creek in Chautauqua County, lives one of the oldest and most established Amish communities upstate; the Amish first arrived in the county from Ohio in 1949.

OLEAN

Alongside the broad main drag of downtown Olean runs an even broader swatch of scruffy railroad yards. The yards date back to the days when Olean was an important junction of the Erie and Pennsylvania Railroads, and a receiving depot for local oil refineries. The name "Olean" comes from the Latin *oleum,* meaning oil.

Though no longer an oil town, Olean today is the county's largest manufacturing and shopping center. Several antique shops are located on Union Street. History buffs may want to stop into the **Fannie Bartlett House and Olean Point Museum** (302 Laurens St., 716/376-5642, 1–5 P.M. Wed.–Sun.).

WESTERN NEW YORK

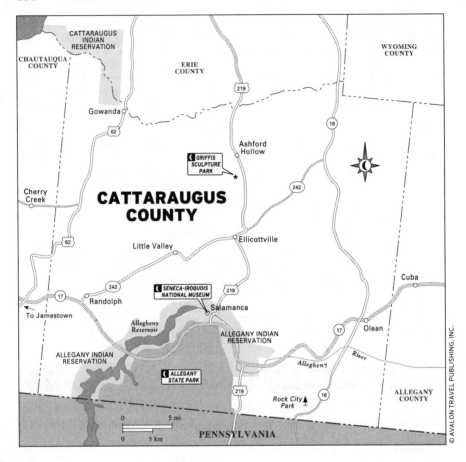

© AVALON TRAVEL PUBLISHING, INC.

Along Route 417 a few miles west of downtown is **St. Bonaventure University,** a Franciscan institution chartered in 1875. In the middle of the trim, landscaped campus find the **Friedsam Memorial Library** (716/375-2323, 8 A.M.–8 P.M. Mon.–Thurs., 10 A.M.–5 P.M. Fri., 10 A.M.–4 P.M. Sat.), housing paintings by Rembrandt, Rubens, and Bellini, along with Chinese porcelain, rare books, and contemporary art.

Rock City Park

This enormous outcropping of quartz conglomerate (505 Rte. 16 S, 716/372-7790, 9 A.M.–6 P.M. daily May–Oct., adults $4.50,

children 6–12 $2.50), formed some 320 million years ago, has attracted tourists since 1890. Once the bottom of a prehistoric ocean, it now sits on a hilltop, offering 35-mile views of the Allegheny Mountains. Water and wind have sculpted many sections into odd shapes—the Tepee Rock, Monkey Face, the Half Sphinx.

Accommodations and Food

Partially housed in the town's former 1889 public library is the striking **◖ Old Library Restaurant and B&B** (116–120 S. Union St., 716/372-2226, www.oldlibraryrestaurant.com, $75–125 d). The B&B side boasts original

© CHRISTIANE BIRD

Rock City, formed some 320 million years ago

woodwork, parquet floors, and stained glass windows, along with eight guest rooms outfitted with antiques. Next door is the restaurant, serving a large variety of mostly American and Italian dishes (average dinner entrée $16).

SALAMANCA

In the heart of the thin, arc-shaped Allegany Indian Reservation lies Salamanca, the only city in the nation situated on a Native American reservation. The Seneca lease the land to the United States on a long-term basis; the current lease, signed in 1990, is due to expire in 2031, with an option to renew for another 40 years.

A few Seneca-run convenience store/gas stations flank the city's main thoroughfare, Broad Street, along with the very fine Seneca-Iroquois National Museum and the high-stakes **Seneca Bingo Parlor** (768 Broad St., 716/945-4080). At one end of town is the new **Seneca Allegany Casino** (777 Seneca Allegany Blvd., 877/553-9500, www.senecaallegganycoasion,com, open 24 hours/day), offering about 1,700 slot machines, gaming tables, two

snack bars, and a buffet restaurant. Otherwise, however, Salamanca looks like any other well-worn hinterlands town. South of the city extends the 65,000-acre Allegany State Park, the crowning jewel of southwestern New York.

◖ Seneca-Iroquois National Museum

This thoughtful, well-laid-out museum (794-814 Broad St., 716/945-1738, www.senecamuseum.org, 9 A.M.–5 P.M. Mon.–Fri. year-round, 9 A.M.–5 P.M. Sat. and noon–5 P.M. Sun. Apr.–Nov., closed Jan., adults $5, seniors and students $3.50, children 7–13 $3) covers the history of the Seneca Nation from prehistory to the present day. The exhibits cover a wide variety of subjects, from the Seneca's use of medicinal plants to contemporary Native American art. In one section is a life-size bark longhouse; in another, an explanation of the Iroquois clan system; in a third, a small theater where an informative slide show is presented.

Some of the most beautiful items in the museum are the white-and-purple wampum belts that the Iroquois wove to record significant events, laws, and treaties. "Great nations, like great men, should keep their words," reads a quote over the display. One wampum belt records the Treaty of 1794 negotiated between the Iroquois Confederacy and Timothy Pickering on behalf of George Washington. This treaty was broken as recently as 1964, when a section of the Allegany Reservation was confiscated to build the Kinzua Dam and Reservoir. The tribe still retains ownership of the land under the reservoir, but 130 Seneca were relocated against their will.

Salamanca Rail Museum

At the eastern end of town stands a fully restored 1912 passenger depot (170 Main St., 716/945-3133, 10 A.M.–5 P.M. Tues.–Sat. and noon–5 P.M. Sun. Apr.–Dec., also summer Mon., free admission) housing exhibits on the Buffalo, Rochester, and Pittsburgh Railway. The high-ceilinged waiting room is still lined with rich red oak wainscoting, while to one side is a "Ladies Retiring Room" and an

WESTERN NEW YORK

old-fashioned ticket office complete with telegraph keys. The exhibits tell the story of how the railroad built the city of Salamanca.

[ALLEGANY STATE PARK

The largest and wildest state park in New York, the Allegany (2373 State Park Rd., Exit 17 or 18 off Rte. 17, 716/354-9121, $6–8 parking) stretches over mysterious, heavily wooded hills laced with 90 miles of hiking, biking, and horseback-riding trails. In the park's center lie two cobalt-blue lakes offering fishing, boating, and swimming in-season. Camping, nature hikes, and kids' programs are featured year-round; bikes and rowboats can be rented. To reserve a campsite, call 800/456-CAMP.

The park's hiking trails range in difficulty from the easy 2.5-mile Three Sisters Hiking Trail in the Quaker Lake area to the rugged North Country Trail, which covers 18 miles before entering the Allegheny National Forest at the Pennsylvania border. An interesting moderate hike is the four-mile Bear Caves–Mt. Seneca Trail which passes by three small caves.

Camping
Overlooking the Allegheny Reservoir about eight miles west of the park is **High Banks Campground** (Rte. 394, Steamburg, 716/354-4855), owned and operated by the Seneca. Cabins and campsites are available and fees go toward tribal social-service programs.

Events
The mid-July **Keeper of the Western Door Pow Wow** (716/945-2034) features traditional Native American arts, crafts, food, and dance.

ELLICOTTVILLE
After the quiet backcountry of much of Western New York, Ellicottville comes as a surprise. This is a bona fide resort village that's especially popular during the ski season, thanks to the **Holiday Valley Resort** (Rte. 219 south of the village, 716/699-2345, www.holidayvalley.com). The mountain can't really compare with those of the Adirondacks, but it's a mecca

for skiers living in the flatlands of Buffalo, Cleveland, and Toronto. During the summer, Holiday Valley offers an 18-hole golf course, tennis courts, mountain biking, a spa, and a three-pool swimming complex.

In downtown Ellicottville stand historic brick buildings housing upscale shops, restaurants, and bars. At the tree-shaded town square, find an imposing town hall and a turn-of-the-century gazebo. At the village's northern end, adjacent to the Cornell Cooperative Extension, lies the peaceful **Nannen Arboretum** (28 Parkside Dr., off Rte. 219, 716/699-2377, dawn–dusk, free admission), planted with more than 250 species of rare trees and shrubs.

Accommodations
The handsome brick [**New Ellicottville Inn** (4–10 Washington St., 716/699-2373, www.ellicottvilleinn.com, $99–159 d in summer, $125–155 d in winter) is a deservedly popular place to stay. Upstairs are 23 nicely appointed and immaculately clean guest rooms furnished with rustic antiques. Downstairs is a comfortable restaurant serving traditional American fare (average entrée $16) and a lively bar/lounge.

The **Ilex Inn B&B** (6416 E. Washington St., 716/699-2002, www.ilexinn.com, $85–125 d in summer; $125–195 d in winter) is a renovated Victorian farmhouse. Inside the main house are six modernized guest rooms, while out back is a small cottage ($115–225 d) and a heated swimming pool.

Food
The casual **Balloons** (30 Monroe St., 716/699-4162) features Tex-Mex food and country-and-western line dancing on the weekends; average main dish $10. The historic **Gin Mill** (24 Washington St., 716/699-2530), housed in its namesake, serves an especially good lunch (average entrée $9).

Dina's (15 Washington St., 315/699-5330), nicely laid out in an 1840 building, serves an eclectic mix of American, Italian, and Mexican fare; average entrée $15. The [**Ellicottville Brewing Company** (28A Monroe St., 716/699-

2537) is a trendy hotspot serving microbrews and English specialties such as shepherd's pie and fish and chips. Outside is a German-style beer garden.

Events

During the summer, the Buffalo Philharmonic performs at Holiday Valley, and **free concerts** are presented at the village gazebo. The village's top chefs strut their stuff during the **Taste of Ellicottville** (716/699-5046) in mid-August.

🄲 GRIFFIS SCULPTURE PARK

Head 10 miles north of Ellicottville to reach the magical Griffis Sculpture Park (6902 Mill Valley Rd., off Rte. 219, Ashford Hollow, 716/667-2808, 9 A.M.–dusk daily May–Oct., adults $5, seniors and students $3), perched on a hilltop with sweeping views of the valley below. Created by Buffalo artist Larry Griffis, the upper park is filled with whimsical 20-foot-high humanoid sculptures built of iron and steel. Some have middles as round and hollow as donuts, others are all lean, angular lines.

Surrounding the creatures is a pale-green meadow, busy with rabbits and butterflies, while just below lies a still pond encircled with smaller sculptures of birds and wildlife. Roads and paths lead down through the woods to larger ponds and a second, less-interesting sculpture area showcasing the works of about 20 other artists.

RANDOLPH AND AMISH FARM COUNTRY

Bustling Randolph sits on an ancient city of the Mound Builders, a prehistoric people who lived in upstate New York before the Iroquois. The town's main streets are flanked with handsome historic buildings.

From Randolph, Route 241 heads north into Conawango Valley and Amish farm country. Trim white homes complete with birdhouses, small gardens, and laundry lines abut the roads, while all around are rolling fields planted with corn and wheat. Black buggies sit in driveways,

children dressed in somber blues and blacks play in a schoolyard, bonneted women in long dresses hang the morning wash out to dry.

Many of the Amish sell quilts, baskets, handmade furniture, birdhouses, baked goods, and maple syrup out of their front doors. Hand-printed signs advertising these wares are sometimes posted out front, while maps indicating the informal shops—which change frequently—are printed up each year (available at the Cattaraugus County Department of Tourism). Shops can usually be found on Route 241 between Randolph and Conewango; on Pope Hill Road and North East Road off Route 241; along Route 62 between Conewango and Leon; along County Road 6 between Leon and Cherry Creek, and on West Road off County Road 6.

The occasional prosperous-looking Amish farm aside, this is poor country out here. Many family farms have been abandoned in recent years, and the villages are sad affairs, with shuttered shops and homes in disrepair.

Camping, Accommodations, and Food

JJ's Pope Haven Campground (Rte. 241 and Pope Rd., Randolph, 716/358-4900), surrounded by Amish farmland, offers a playground, stocked pond, and swimming beach. For a casual breakfast, lunch, or dinner, stop into the **R&M Restaurant** (265 Main St., Randolph, 716/358-5141), open 24/7.

In the northwestern corner of Cattaraugus County is the Cattaraugus Indian reservation, where you'll find the **Tee Pee** (14396 Four Mile Level Rd., 716/532-2168, $50 d), a modern, four–guest room B&B run by a Seneca Indian couple. In addition to accommodations, the hosts offer tours of the reservation and of Amish country.

Events

Featured at the mid-September **Fall Festival,** a major event held on the **Cattaraugus Indian Reservation** (Rte. 438, 716/938-9111), are traditional Iroquois arts, crafts, foods, and dancing.

Chautauqua County

Chautauqua County has been a popular regional resort since the late 1800s, and it shows. Considerably more built up than most of Western New York, Chautauqua is a mix of old-fashioned resort villages, commercialized tourist attractions, homespun agricultural communities, and still-scenic back roads.

Chautauqua County centers on Chautauqua Lake, a 22-mile-long glacier lake 1,400 feet above sea level. Around the turn of the century, the lake was encircled with enormous hotels, while on its waters chugged a busy steamboat trade. Most famous of all the lake's attractions was and is the Chautauqua Institution, a National Historic Landmark that has been offering "learning vacations" since 1874.

The word Chautauqua is said to be Iroquois for "two moccasins fastened together," an apt

WESTERN NEW YORK

description of the long, thin lake, indented in the middle. The Iroquois and later the French portaged their canoes between Chautauqua Lake and Lake Erie, located eight miles to the north. The old portage trail is now known as Portage Road, or Route 394.

Running along the shore of Lake Erie is the so-called **Grape Belt,** a five-mile-wide swatch of clay soil that's particularly well suited for growing grapes. In 1896, a Dr. Thomas Branwell Welch invented a way to preserve unfermented grape juice here, and Chautauqua proclaimed itself the "Grape Juice Capital" of the world. Welch's was headquartered in Westfield for years, and wineries prosper along the back roads.

JAMESTOWN

At the southeastern end of Chautauqua Lake lies Jamestown, a hilly city of red-brick industrial buildings, lavish Victorian homes, neat working-class neighborhoods, and a steadily declining number of abandoned storefronts. Once a leading furniture manufacturing center, Jamestown fell on hard times in the late 1900s, but is now in the midst of a comeback, thanks largely to several high-tech medical companies that have recently relocated here.

Founded by James Prendergast in 1811, Jamestown's earliest settlers included a number of skilled woodworkers who made furniture for the pioneers in the area. In the 1850s, Swedish cabinetmakers, attracted by the fledgling industry, began to arrive, and by the late 1800s, Jamestown was predominantly Swedish. The Swedes were joined by the Italians in the 1890s, and today, most of the city is still of Swedish or Italian descent.

Two famous Jamestown natives are naturalist Roger Tory Peterson and comedienne Lucille Ball. The band 10,000 Maniacs also hails from Jamestown.

Fenton History Center

Perched on a hilltop overlooking the compact downtown is an Italianate mansion (67 Washington St., 716/664-6256, www.fentonhistorycenter.org, 10 A.M.–4 P.M. Mon.–Sat., adults

$5, children 3–12 $4) built by Reuben Eaton Fenton, governor of New York from 1865 to 1869. Now home to the Fenton Historical Society, the house contains an interesting series of exhibits on Jamestown, Chautauqua Lake, and Lucille Ball.

The daughter of an electrical telephone lineman and a concert pianist, Lucille Ball was born in Jamestown in 1911. Her family encouraged her theatrical interests and at age 15, she took a bus to New York City and landed a job in the chorus of a Broadway musical. She was fired shortly thereafter, perhaps because of her age, and during the next seven years suffered one disappointment after another. Her first big break didn't come until 1940, when she met Desi Arnaz during the filming of *Too Many Girls.*

Near the Ball exhibit are period rooms furnished as they would have been in Fenton's time, and rooms devoted to Jamestown's Swedish and Italian communities. The exhibits on Chautauqua Lake showcase photographs from the resort's Victorian heyday, as well as artifacts relating to ice-harvesting and shipbuilding—two formerly prosperous industries along the lake.

Lucy-Desi Museum

More exhibits on the town's favorite daughter are housed in this museum (212 Pine St., 716/484-0800, www.lucy-desi.com, 10 A.M.–5:30 P.M. Mon.–Sat. and 1–5 P.M. Sun. May–Oct., weekends only Nov.–Apr., adults $6, seniors $5, youth children $4). One panel features taped interviews with two of Lucy's childhood friends; another, an actor reading from Desi's autobiography. Excerpts from the Lucy-Desi radio shows are played and a two-hour video of their TV shows runs continuously throughout the day. In addition, tapes of every single *I Love Lucy* episode are available for the watching, along with CD-ROMs of Lucy's scrapbook. About 2,000 items from Miss Ball's estate are showcased in all, including costumes, gowns, photographs, scripts, and awards. While here, be sure to pick up a list of Lucy landmarks around town.

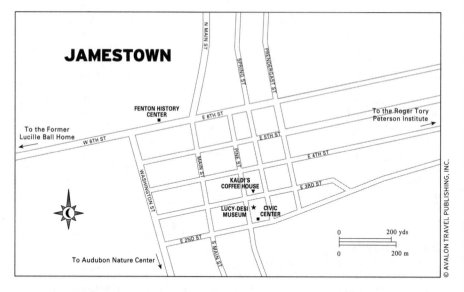

Lucille Ball Landmarks

Another small exhibit devoted to Lucille Ball is housed in the **Reg Lenna Civic Center Theater** (116 E. 3rd St., 716/664-2465), which contains a stunning blue-and-white-domed ceiling, flanked by the muses. Lucy frequented the theater throughout her youth, often in the company of her grandfather, who was the first to urge her to perform. On display in the lobby are the comedienne's old dancing boots, top hat, favorite hair products (she was not a real redhead), and the like. The theater, which is housed in the same building as the Lucy-Desi Museum, is only open during performances, or by appointment.

Around the corner from the theater stands the **Lucille Ball Little Theatre** (18 E. 2nd St., 716/483-1095), where Lucy made her show business debut, and **Jones Bakery** (209 Pine St., 716/484-1988), where she purchased her favorite Swedish rye. Even after finding fame and fortune, Ball continued to have the bread shipped to her in Hollywood, and it's still for sale in the family-run shop.

Ball's childhood home is in the suburbs at 59 West 8th Street, off Dunham Avenue, Celeron. The small, neat, private home is now painted a pale green with white trim. "Lucy Lane" reads the street sign on the corner.

Roger Tory Peterson Institute

Off a cobblestone street at the edge of the city presides the Roger Tory Peterson Institute (311 Curtis St., 716/665-2473, www.rtpi.org, 10 A.M.–4 P.M. Tues.–Sat., 1–5 P.M. Sun., adults $4, students $3), a striking modern building of fieldstone and wood, surrounded by 27 acres. Primarily a national center used to teach children about nature, the institute also houses an art gallery that showcases wildlife-art exhibits, a library, and gift shop. Artwork by Peterson and other naturalists is often featured.

Jamestown Audubon Nature Center

In a valley formed by retreating glaciers lies a 600-acre wildlife sanctuary crisscrossed with five miles of trails. The trails lead past forest, marshes, swamps, and ponds that are favorite stops for migrating birds. An especially large variety of plants grow in the sanctuary; over 400 species have been catalogued.

At the entrance to the park stands the Roger Tory Peterson Nature Building (1600 Riverside

Rd., 716/569-2345, 10 A.M.–4:30 P.M. Mon.–Sat., 1–4:30 P.M. Sun., free admission), where you can pick up guide booklets to the nature trails. Also in the center are exhibits by Roger Tory Peterson, a children's discovery center with hands-on displays, and 200 mounted birds, some of which are now extinct.

To reach the nature center from Jamestown, take Route 60 south to Route 62 south. Proceed three miles to Riverside Road and turn left.

Food

At **Kaldi's Coffee House** (106 E. Third St., 716/484-8904), you can order a Mrs. Grundy sandwich, named after Lucy and Ethel's road-trip companion, as well as other foods with names inspired by the Lucy show. The coffee's good here, too. Romantic **MacDuff's** (317 Pine St., 716/664-9414) is an upscale spot housed in an 1873 townhouse; average entrée $17.

In the heart of the city, find a 149-room **Holiday Inn** (150 W. 4th St., 716/664-3400, $89–109 d). On the outskirts is a 101-room **Comfort Inn** (2800 N. Main St., 716/664-5920, $79–109 d).

Events

Lucy-Desi Days (716/484-0800) featuring young comics, a film fest, and other special events, takes place over Memorial Day weekend. Then, during the first week of August, there's **Lucy's Birthday Celebration.**

AROUND CHAUTAUQUA LAKE

From Jamestown, Route 430 heads north along the eastern shore of Chautauqua Lake, through one resort community after another. At the northern tip of the lake lies Mayville, the county seat, and Route 394, which circles back south along the lake's western shore. The Southern Tier Expressway (Route 17) crosses Chautauqua Lake just south of Bemus Point and Stow.

Bemus Point

Strung along the very edge of the waterfront is tiny Bemus Point, an old-fashioned resort vil-

lage sprinkled with gift shops and restaurants. Through the heart of things runs Lakeshore Drive, crowded with piers and boats on one side, cottages and vacationers lolling about on lounge chairs on the other.

Lakeshore Drive ends at the **Casino,** a recently remodeled building where special events are sometimes held during the summer. Out front docks the small, flat **Bemus Point-Stow Ferry,** which crosses Chautauqua Lake whenever there's a passenger. The ride takes about five minutes each way.

Anchoring Bemus Point is the creaky old **Hotel Lenhart** (20–22 Lakeside Dr.), a big, mustard-colored building with a long, long line of rockers out front. Though now somewhat worn around the edges, the 1881 hostelry is a classic, owned by the same family for three generations.

Long Point State Park

Just north of Bemus Point, find this busy 300-acre state park and beach (4459 Rte. 430, 716/386-2722, 9 A.M.–dusk daily, parking $5), a draw for swimmers, boaters, and picnickers. Lifeguards are on duty during the summer.

Midway Park

Immediately north of Long Point begins Midway Park (4859 Rte. 430, 716/386-3165, 1 P.M.–sunset June–Sept.), a family amusement park equipped with go-karts, bumper boats, miniature golf, an antique carousel, a roller rink, and an arcade. Along the shore are a swimming beach and paddleboat area. Admission, parking, and swimming are free; rides and attractions, individually priced.

Mayville

Historic Mayville is a pretty place, centered on the 1880s **Chautauqua County Courthouse** on Main Street. Overlooking the lake is peaceful Lakeside Park, equipped with piers at which small pleasure craft dock.

◖ Chautauqua Institution

South of Mayville reigns the famed 856-acre Chautauqua Institution (off Rte. 394,

716/357-6200 or 716/357-6250 [box office], www.chautauqua-inst.org), a self-contained Victorian village-cum-learning camp for families and adults. Most vacationers live on the premises for a week or two at a time and take courses—often taught by renowned scholars—in everything from philosophy to film. Day visitors are welcome to tour the grounds, use the beaches, and attend many of the lectures, concerts, and other events (day passes $7–15 Mon.–Sat., free admission Sun., evening passes $25–37).

Chautauqua is a peculiarly American institution, founded as a vacation school for Sunday school teachers in 1872. The idea of self-improvement in a pastoral setting caught on immediately, and soon mini- and traveling chautauquas advertising "pure, wholesome entertainment" found audiences all over the country. The Chautauqua movement, as it became known, pioneered many developments in adult education, including correspondence courses and the "great books" curricula.

These roots remain evident in Chautauqua today. The institution is a truly magnificent place, filled with palatial Victorian buildings and four wide white-sand beaches, but it retains a prim and proper Sunday school feel. Alcohol is not served in any of the institution's restaurants.

One of Chautauqua's highlights is the very fine 1881 Athenaeum Hotel, once the largest wood-frame building in the country. The hotel was wired for electricity by Thomas Alva Edison, and his table still stands by one dining-room window. A shy man, Edison often escaped out the window to avoid admirers.

Open late June–August, the institute offers a variety of accommodations and vacation packages; call for a brochure or check out their website. Tours are offered daily at 2 and 4 P.M.

Panama Rocks Scenic Park
Detour eight miles southwest of Chautauqua Lake to reach the well-kept Panama Rocks Scenic Park (1 Rock Hill Rd., off Rte. 474, 716/782-2845, www.panamarocks.com, 10 A.M.–5 P.M. daily May–Oct., adults $6,

seniors $4, children 6–12 $3). The park is similar to Rock City in Cattaraugus County, but is set in a forest rather than on a hilltop. Spread out over a half mile of quartz conglomerate, the park is laced with deep crevices, dark caves, 60-foot-high cliffs, and hiking trails. Native Americans and outlaws may have used the caves for shelter.

Camping and Accommodations
A few miles north of Bemus Point find the 120-site **Wildwood Acres Campground** (Brown Rd., off Rte. 430, 716/386-7037). Between Chautauqua and Stow, the 400-site **Camp Chautauqua** (Rte. 394, 716/789-3435) offers an indoor swimming pool, restaurant, tennis courts, dock sites, and petting farm.

South of Mayville, on the shores of Chautauqua is **Webb's Year-Round Resort** (115 W. Lake Rd. [Rte. 394 S], 716/753-2161, www.webbsworld.com, $89–159 d), a big, modern, family-oriented hostelry with its own marina, miniature golf course, and fudge factory. The resort also holds 52 upscale motel rooms, a five-room Captain's Table restaurant, and a deck overlooking the lake.

At the **Hotel Lenhart** (20–22 Lakeside Dr., 716/386-2715, www.hotellenhart.com, $105–175 d in summer, includes breakfast and dinner, $55–125 d without meals), the guest rooms are spartan but comfortable; many of the less-expensive rooms share baths. Downstairs find an old-fashioned parlor and dining room serving traditional American fare.

Food
Most popular among Bemus Point eateries is lively **Italian Fisherman** (61 Lakeside Dr., 716/386-7000). During the summer, its dining deck over the lake is always packed. Live music is often featured on weekends; average entrée $15.

If you'd like to eat at the **[Athenaeum Hotel** (716/357-4444) at the Chautauqua Institution, reservations are a must. The menu is prix-fixe at $16 for breakfast, $23 for lunch, $36 for dinner. Dinner includes two desserts.

ALONG LAKE ERIE

Westfield

Head north of Chautauqua Lake on Route 394 to reach Westfield, a town of solid brick storefronts and antiques shops. There are close to a dozen along Main Street (Rte. 20) alone.

Downtown presides the **McClurg Museum** (Rte. 394 and Main St., 716/326-2977, 10 A.M.–5 P.M. Tues.–Sat., adults $2, children under 12 $1), an 1818 mansion that's now home to the Chautauqua County Historical Society. Inside are restored period rooms, Native American artifacts, and an exhibit on Grace Bedell. Grace was an 11-year-old Westfield girl who wrote to Abraham Lincoln during his 1860 campaign to suggest that he "would look a lot better" if he grew whiskers. Surprisingly, Lincoln followed her advice, and asked to meet her when his train stopped in Westfield the following year.

Continue north on Route 394 to reach the beginning of the **Seaway Trail,** which starts at the Pennsylvania border, and Barcelona Harbor. Here you'll find a marina and the 1829 **Barcelona Lighthouse.** Originally powered by natural gas, the graceful stone tower is now privately owned and off-limits to the public.

East to Dunkirk

The busy New York State Thruway (I-90), Route 5, and Route 20 all head east of Westfield to Dunkirk. Running closest to the shore is Route 5, also known as the Seaway Trail, which bypasses **Lake Erie State Park** (5905 Lake Rd., Brockton, 716/792-9214, dawn–dusk daily, parking $8 in summer). Situated on a bluff overlooking the lake, the park offers hiking trails, a campground, and great views. For campground reservations, call 800/456-CAMP.

Dunkirk itself is a low-key industrial city named after Dunkerque, France, whose harbor Dunkirk's own is said to resemble. The main visitor attraction is the **Historic Dunkirk Lighthouse and Veteran's Park Museum** (1 Lighthouse Point Dr., off Rte. 15, 716/366-5050, www.dunkirklighthouse.com, 10 A.M.–4 P.M. Mon.–Tues. and Thurs.–Sat. July–Aug., 10 A.M.–2 P.M. Mon.–Tues. and Thurs.–Sat. Apr.–June and Sept.–Dec., adults $5, children 4–12 $2), a well-kept site run almost entirely by volunteers. Guided tours (last tour at 2:30 P.M. in summer, 1 P.M. in spring and fall) take visitors through the old keeper's quarters, furnished as they were in the 1940s, and up into the 1875 tower. Also on the grounds is a museum dedicated to the armed forces.

Fredonia

Just south of Dunkirk lies Fredonia, a pretty, historic town of red-brick buildings and tree-lined streets. The nation's first gas tank was sunk here in 1821, making it possible to light the entire village with gas lamps when the Marquis de Lafayette passed through on his 1825 tour.

Wineries

The region around Westfield, Dunkirk, and Fredonia is conducive to growing grapes, and a half-dozen wineries can be found on or just off Route 20 between the towns. Among them are the **Johnson Estate Winery** (Rte. 20 west of Westfield, 716/326-2191); **Woodbury Winery** (S. Roberts Rd., off Rte. 20 east of Dunkirk, 716/679-WINE), and **Merritt Estate Winery** (2264 King Rd., off Rte. 20 near Silver Creek, 716/965-4800). All offer tastings and tours, and are open 10 A.M.–5 P.M. Monday–Saturday, 1–5 P.M. Sunday.

Westfield was once the headquarters of Welch's Grape Juice and calls itself the grape-juice capital of the world.

Accommodations

One of the area's best-known hostelries is the handsome 1821 **William Seward Inn** (6645 S. Portage Rd. [Rte. 394], Mayville, 716/326-4151, www.williamsewardinn.com. $80–195 d, with breakfast). Featured are 12 antiques-filled guest rooms of varying sizes, some with Jacuzzis.

Also an excellent choice is the 1868 Greek Revival **White Inn** (52 E. Main St., Fredonia, 716/672-2103, www.whiteinn.com, $79–189 d, with breakfast), the region's oldest continuously operated hotel. Extensively renovated over the years, the inn offers 12 standard-sized rooms and 11 suites. Downstairs is a good restaurant.

Food

A fine place for lunch, dinner, or a cool drink on a hot day is the upscale **K Dockside Cafe & Bar** (30 Lake Shore Dr. E, Dunkirk, 716/366-8350), housed in the Ramada Inn, on the shores of Lake Erie, near the Dunkirk Lighthouse (average dinner entrée $15; seasonal).

One of the region's best restaurants is housed in the elegant **White Inn.** A charter member of the Duncan Hines Family of Fine Restaurants, the restaurant specializes in innovative American and continental fare; average entrée $19. The **William Seward Inn** is also known for its gourmet dining; four-course prix-fixe dinners cost $45.

CASSADAGA

One of the more surprising offerings of Chautauqua County is the **Lily Dale Assembly** (5 Melrose Park, off Rte. 60, Cassadaga, 716/595-8721 or 716/595-8722, open June–Aug.), a spiritual-development, natural-healing community that attracts mediums from all over the country. Throughout the summer, the assembly offers daily services, lectures, laying-on of hands, and sessions with clairvoyants.

Located on the forested shores of deep blue Lake Cassadaga, Lily Dale unofficially dates back to 1879 with the arrival of the Fox sisters of Rochester. The sisters had been communicating with the spirit world since 1849, when they awoke to sounds of a fight and a heavy body being dragged down the stairs. No humans appeared to be making the noises, and the sisters ascribed them to the spirit of a peddler who had been murdered in the house four years before.

Lily Dale centers around an 1883 auditorium where speakers and clairvoyants lecture and lead services daily. Events take place at the Healing Temple, Forest Temple, and Inspiration Stump.

Overlooking the lake stands the **Maplewood Hotel** (716/595-2505), a creaky, no-frills Victorian hostelry. Walk onto the wide front porch and you're apt to hear groups of believers humming or worshipping together. "No readings, healing, circles or seances in this area please," reads a sign in the parlor.

Lily Dale attracts both day and overnight visitors. Day visitors (passes $5–10) are welcome to attend most of the daily lectures and to explore the grounds. Private readings ($35–60) can be arranged on the spot, but it's best to call ahead; many of the most popular mediums are booked weeks in advance.

Sports and Recreation

The southern half of Western New York is covered with state forests, through which run all-but-undiscovered hiking trails. Some are part of the Finger Lakes Trail network; most are not. A first-rate guide to hiking the area is *Fifty Hikes in Western New York* by William P. Ehling (Backcountry Publications).

For more information on the Finger Lakes Trail, contact the **Finger Lakes Trail**

Conference (6111 Visitor Center Rd., Mt. Morris, NY 14510, 716/288-7191, www.fingerlakestrail.org). The conference publishes 45 sectional maps, all priced around $1.

Fishing is big business in this part of the country, especially along Lake Ontario, which the state stocks with more than three million salmon and trout each year. For more information, contact the visitor information centers listed below.

Getting There and Around

Airlines that serve the **Greater Buffalo International Airport** include American Airlines (800/433-7300), Continental (800/525-0280), Delta (800/221-1212), JetBlue (800/JET-BLUE), Northwest (800/225-2525), United (800/241-6522), and USAirways (800/428-4322). USAirways also serves the **Jamestown Airport.**

A taxi ride from the airport to downtown Buffalo costs about $20; from the airport to Niagara Falls a taxi costs about $40. **ITA Buffalo Shuttle** (716/633-8294 or 716/633-8318) provides service between the airport and Buffalo ($14) or Niagara Falls ($22). **Metro Bus and Rails** (716/855-7211) provides local bus service.

Amtrak (800/872-7245), **Greyhound** (800/231-2222), and **New York Trailways** (800/295-5555) all serve both Buffalo and Niagara Falls. Many smaller towns are serviced by Greyhound, **Coach USA** (716/372-5500), or **Chautauqua Area Regional Transit** (716/665-6466).

By far the best way to explore the region is by car.

Information and Services

For information about Buffalo, Niagara Falls, and the northern counties of Western New York, contact the **Buffalo Niagara Convention and Visitors Bureau** (617 Main St., Buffalo 14203, 716/852-0511 or 800/BUFFALO, www.visitbuffaloniagara.com). For information on Allegany, Cattaraugus, and Chautauqua Counties, contact the county or town tourism offices listed below.

Orleans County Tourism Office (14016 Rte. 31 W, Albion 14411, 585/589-3198 or 800/724-0314, www.orleansny.com)

Genesee County Chamber of Commerce (210 E. Main St., Batavia 14020, 585/343-7440 or 800/622-2686, www.geneseeny.com)

Wyoming County Tourist Promotion Agency (30 N. Main St., Castile 14427, 585/493-3190 or 800/839-3919, www.wyomingcountyny.com)

Allegany County Tourism (Room 208, County Office Bldg., 7 Court St., Belmont 14813, 585/268-9229 or 800/836-1869, www.alleganyco.com)

Cattaraugus County Department of Economic Development, Planning, and Tourism (303 Court St., Little Valley 14755, 716/938-9111 or 800/331-0543, www.enchantedmountains.info)

Ellicottville Chamber of Commerce (9 W. Washington St., Ellicottville 14731, 716/699-5046, www.ellicotvilleny.com)

Salamanca Area Chamber of Commerce (26 Main St., Salamanca 14779, 716/945-2034)

Chautauqua County Visitors Bureau (Chautauqua Institution, Main Gate, off Rte. 394, Chautauqua 14722, 716/357-4569 or 800/242-4569, www.tourchautauqua.com)

WESTERN NEW YORK

BACKGROUND

The Land

Geography has shaped the development of New York State more than any other single factor. Though bordered on the north, south, and east by mountains, lakes, and rivers, the state's central position between the Atlantic and the Great Lakes, along with its flat western terrain, made it a major thoroughfare for early settlers heading west. Highways were established through the Mohawk River basin and Finger Lakes in the late 1700s, followed in 1825 by the Erie Canal. The canal was largely responsible for New York's rise to prominence, and by 1900, four out of five New Yorkers were living along either the Hudson River or the Erie Canal.

Though New York ranks only 30th among the states in terms of area, it is one of the largest states east of the Mississippi and is extremely diverse geographically. Mountains, plateaus, lowlands, forests, swamps, lakes, rivers, gorges, and beaches all make up the state, which was formed mainly during the last Ice Age, when a continental ice sheet up to two miles thick covered almost all of New York. Today, most of the state is comprised of farmland, abandoned farmland, or semi-wilderness. Eighty-five percent of New York's population may be urban, but 85 percent of its land is rural.

COURTESY OF ORANGE COUNTY TOURISM

New York is bounded to the north by the St. Lawrence River and Lake Ontario, to the east by Lake Champlain and the Taconic Mountains, to the southeast by the Atlantic Ocean, to the south by the Delaware River and Allegheny Plateau, and to the west by Lake Erie and the Niagara River. The state's highest point is Mt. Marcy (5,344 feet) in the Adirondack region; its lowest is the Atlantic coastline.

The Hudson River, which originates at Lake Tear of the Clouds atop Mt. Marcy, flows north-south through the eastern end of the state. Running east-west through the center of the state is the Mohawk River, which arises in Oneida County, near Rome. Other important rivers include the Genesee and Oswego, which flow northward into Lake Ontario; and the Delaware, Susquehanna, and Allegheny, which drain the state's southern and western portions.

CLIMATE

Late spring, early summer, and early fall are the best times to visit New York City and much of upstate. Temperatures then generally hover in the 70s, and you're more likely to wake up to one of the state's precious cloudless days. Midsummers in New York City and much of upstate tend to be hot and humid; winters are overcast, wet, and cold. In contrast, summer is the best time to visit the more highly elevated regions of the Catskills and Adirondacks.

Average July temperatures range from 77°F in New York City to 64°F in the Adirondacks; average January temperatures range from 33°F on Long Island to 14°F in the Adirondacks. The coldest winters occur in the central Adirondacks and St. Lawrence River Valley, where temperatures often drop below -10°F.

Annual precipitation is 32–45 inches annually, with the Catskills, Long Island, and Tug Hill receiving the most. The typical cloudiness throughout the state results in few completely clear days; New York City averages about 100 inches, Syracuse and Buffalo 72 inches, and Albany 73 inches.

Flora and Fauna

Over half of New York State is blanketed with forests, in which grow over 150 kinds of trees. Among them are a few southern species such as the tulip tree and sweetgum, and far more northern species such as beech, sugar maple, red maple, hickory, ash, cherry, birch, various oaks, white pine, spruce, balsam fir, and hemlock. In the Adirondacks and Catskills, evergreens predominate, while elsewhere in the state, hardwoods are more numerous.

Among the state's most common wildflowers are buttercups, violets, daisies, black-eyed Susans, devil's paintbrush, wild roses, and Queen Anne's lace. Bright specks of alpine flora can be found high on the Adirondack peaks, while woodland flora such as dewdrops and Jack-in-the-pulpits flourish in the forests. Hundreds of species of shrubs, herbs, grasses, ferns, mosses, and lichens also abound throughout the state.

Birdlife in New York runs the gamut from pigeons and common house sparrows—first introduced in North America from Europe in Brooklyn in 1850—to grouse and osprey. Raptors, including bald eagles and peregrine falcons, are making a comeback, while during the migrating season, hundreds of thousands of wild ducks and geese pass through the state.

In New York's fresh waters swim more than 90 species of fish, including perch, trout, salmon, walleye, northern pike, and small- and large-mouth bass. Saltwater fish such as bluefish and flounder inhabit the waters off New York City and Long Island, also known for its oysters and clams.

As for mammals, the smaller varieties predominate. Among them are raccoon, skunk, porcupine, weasel, fox, woodchuck, squirrel, and opossum. The most common larger species is the white-tailed deer, but beaver, black bear, and wildcats can be found in remote areas. Recently reintroduced into the Adirondacks are the elusive moose and lynx.

Environmental Issues

As elsewhere in the East, New York's great outdoors has been badly affected by environmental contamination. The Adirondacks and Catskills suffer from acid rain, the Great Lakes from chemical pollution. Oil spills intermittently blight New York's Atlantic coast, thanks to oil refineries in nearby New Jersey, and solid-waste management is a problem in some areas around New York City.

On a brighter note, most of New York's rivers flow significantly cleaner today than they did 30 years ago. Back then, the Hudson, St. Lawrence, and Niagara Rivers were heavily polluted with PCBs, petrochemicals, and pesticides. The Clean Water Act of 1972, along with other state laws, has helped to greatly reduce this pollution. Much work remains to be done, but a solid start has been made.

History

EARLY PEOPLES

When the Europeans first arrived in what is now New York State, they found it inhabited by two major tribes. The Algonquins lived near the Atlantic coast and along the Hudson River Valley, while upstate dwelled the five tribes of the Iroquois—the Mohawk, Oneida, Onondaga, Cayuga, and Seneca. New York then was a land of great abundance, filled with verdant forests and meadows, ice-blue rivers, lakes and streams, plump fish and game.

Around 1570, the Iroquois tribes banded together to form the Iroquois League, an advanced confederacy with social laws and government institutions designed to promote peace among its members. Fifty sachems, chosen from the village chiefs, governed the confederacy, and each nation had one vote. In 1722, a sixth nation, the Tuscarora, joined the Iroquois League.

Within a century after the arrival of whites, the Algonquin population was decimated, due largely to virulent European diseases such as measles and smallpox. The Iroquois, however, thrived during initial contact. First the Dutch, and then the French and British, enlisted their help in the profitable fur trade, and cultivated their friendship through gifts and the selling of firearms. During the French and Indian War, the alliance of the Iroquois with the British against the French was instrumental in allowing England to gain control over North America.

The Iroquois did not fare so well during the American Revolution. Once again allying themselves with the British, they became the object of a ruthless 1779 campaign waged by American generals Clinton and Sullivan. By the time the campaign was over, the Iroquois nation was in ruins. Thousands fled to Canada; others were resettled onto reservations.

EUROPEAN SETTLEMENT

In 1524, first white man, Giovanni da Verrazano arrived in what is now New York State by sailing into New York Harbor. However, due to a sudden "violent contrary wind [that] blew in from the sea and forced us to return to our ship," Verrazano never set foot on New York.

In 1609, Samuel de Champlain sailed south from Canada to explore the lake that now bears his name. That same year, Englishman Henry Hudson made the first of two voyages aimed at finding a northwest passage to the Orient. Backed by the Dutch West India Company, he sailed into New York harbor and ventured halfway up the Hudson River before abandoning his quest and returning home.

The following year, he returned as captain of a British ship. This time he sailed into Hudson Bay, where the ship became icebound. Starving and doubting their captain's navigational abilities, the crew mutinied. They cast Hudson, his son, and several others adrift in a small boat, never to be seen again.

Though unsuccessful in his search for a northwest passage, Hudson was instrumental in drawing Europeans to the New World. His reports described the area's abundant natural resources—including a wealth of beaver and

NEW YORK "FIRSTS"

First school in America (NYC, 1663)
First uniformed police force (NYC, 1693)
First algebra book (NYC, 1730)
First state constitution (April 20, 1777)
First commercial manufacture of ice cream (NYC, 1786)
First dental drill invented (1790)
First turnpike (Albany to Schenectady, 1797)
First insurance company (NYC, 1804)
First steamboat (NYC–Albany, 1807)
Natural gas first used to illuminate village (Fredonia, 1824)
First engineering college (Troy, 1824)
First railroad (Albany–Schenectady, 1831)
First telegraph (1831)
First streetcar (NYC, 1832)
First powered knitting machine operated (Cohoes, 1832)
First photograph taken in United States (NYC, 1839)
First grain elevator (Buffalo, 1840)
First cheese factory (Rome, 1851)
First artificial insemination (NYC, 1866)
First veterinary school (Cornell University, Ithaca, 1868)
First advertising agency (N. W. Ayer and Son, 1869)
First state-designated forest preserve (May 15, 1885)
Birthplace of tennis in United States (Staten Island, 1874)
First practical typewriter manufactured (by Remington, 1874)
First mass-circulation magazine in United States (*McClure's*, 1881)
First tuxedo coat (Tuxedo Park, 1886)

First chartered golf course in United States (Shinnecock Hills Country Club, 1891)
First hydroelectric power plant (1894)
First motion picture (April 23, 1896)
First cancer laboratory (Buffalo, 1898)
First motorcycle (Buffalo, 1900)
First billion-dollar corporation (U.S. Steel, 1901)
First film-pack camera (Rochester, 1903)
First subway operated (NYC, 1904)
First airplane sold commercially (Hammondsport, 1909)
Birthplace of the NAACP (1910)
First Boy Scouts of America troop (Troy, 1911)
First radio station (WABC-FM, October 7, 1921)
First potato chips (Saratoga Springs, 1925)
First artificial heart invented (NYC, 1935)
First television network (NYC and Schenectady, 1940)
First atomic reactor in medical therapy (Brookhaven, 1951)
First sugar-free soft drink (College Point, 1952)
First solar-powered battery (NYC, 1954)
World's first nuclear plant to produce electricity (GE, near Schenectady, 1955)
First solid-state electronic computer (Ilion, 1958)
First Council for the Arts (created by Governor Rockefeller, 1960)
First statewide minimum-wage law (1960)
First bank automatic teller (NYC, 1969)
First corporation to have more than three million stockholders (AT&T, NYC, 1972)

–Mario Cuomo, *The New York Idea*

mink—and in 1624, a group of Dutch merchants established Fort Orange, New York's first European settlement. Situated at present-day Albany, the fort served primarily as an outpost for the fur trade.

One year later, the Dutch established a similar outpost, Fort Amsterdam, at the foot of Manhattan Island. In 1626, Peter Minuit was appointed the colony's first governor. Almost immediately, he purchased Manhattan Island from the Algonquins for trinkets worth about $24. The Algonquins considered it a good deal at the time. Having a different sense of ownership than did the Dutch, they thought they were selling only the right to use land, not the land itself.

Unlike the dour religious colonizers of New England, the Dutch traders proved to be a fun-loving bunch who had to be constantly reminded by their governors not to play tennis when they should be working and not to drink on Sunday when they should be listening to sermons. Both men and women smoked, and as one observer of the day noted, "All drink here from the moment they are able to lick a spoon."

The last and most flamboyant of New Amsterdam's Dutch governors was Peter Stuyvesant, in power from 1647 to 1664. Nicknamed "Old Peg Leg," due to a leg lost in battle, Stuyvesant was an arrogant, quick-tempered man with a puritanical streak. He ordered the taverns closed on Sundays and tried to prevent a group of Portuguese Jews from settling in the colony—an action for which he was swiftly reprimanded by his bosses back in Amsterdam.

For all his failings, however, Stuyvesant was responsible for turning New Amsterdam into a semblance of a town. He straightened the streets, repaired the fences, and established a night watch. And he was one of the few Dutch colonists who wanted to fight off the English. The rest of the colony didn't much care; the English, who had by this time established a strong presence in New England, had promised the New Amsterdam residents that if they surrendered, their lives would go on as before. That was just fine with the Dutch merchants. As long as they were making money, it made no difference to them who governed the colony.

ENTER AND EXIT THE BRITISH

The British took over New Amsterdam in 1664, renaming the colony New York after the Duke of York, later crowned King James II. The Dutch system of government was replaced with the British one, but for most of the colonists, life did go on as before. The colony remained predominantly Dutch until the end of the century and continued to prosper and grow, with New York City reaching a population of 25,000 in 1750. In the New World, only Philadelphia was bigger.

For the colonists of African heritage, however, life under British rule became increasingly difficult. The slave trade was encouraged and a slave market was set up on Wall Street. Some black families who had owned land under the Dutch had their property confiscated; others lost it after passage of a 1712 law prohibiting blacks from inheriting land.

The land-use system in upstate New York also continued much as it had before. The Dutch had used the patroon system, whereby an individual was given a large tract of land in return for bringing over at least 50 settlers to work that land. The English established a similar landlord-tenant arrangement whereby a few men were given enormous manor estates, which they then rented out in parcels to poor farmers. In some parts of the Hudson Valley and Catskills, remnants of this feudal-like system remained in effect until the 1840s.

By the time of the Revolutionary War, New York City had reached a population of 25,000. Albany and Kingston were thriving as river ports, and several smaller settlements, including Saratoga and Fort Stanwix, had been established as far north as Lake Champlain and as far west as Rome. Manor estates lined the Hudson River, and Long Island was peppered with productive farm communities.

When rumblings of revolution began, New York took a pro-Tory stance at first. Merchants and manor landlords intent on making money wanted nothing to do with war. "What is the reason that New York must continue to embarrass the Continent?" queried John Adams at one point. As tensions escalated, however, New

Yorkers changed their position and, after 1753, supported the Revolution wholeheartedly.

No state bore the brunt of the war more than New York. The earliest battles were fought in New York City—which remained in British hands throughout the war—and many of the later ones took place upstate. The Americans were badly defeated by the British at Oriskany, near Rome, in 1777. The British were unexpectedly defeated by the Americans at Saratoga, also in 1777. Benedict Arnold plotted to betray the Continental Army at West Point in 1780. General Washington declared victory over the British in Newburgh in 1781.

In 1789, Washington was inaugurated as the first president of the United States in Federal Hall on Wall Street, New York City. The city served as the nation's capital until 1790, when the federal government transferred to Philadelphia.

RISE TO POWER

After the war, New York made a rapid recovery. Upstate, settlers poured into the Mohawk River Valley and the Finger Lakes region. Many of the new settlers were Yankees, tired of eking out marginal livings on rocky New England soils. Attracted to New York's fertile farmland, they brought with them their strong work ethic, Protestant religion, and austere architectural styles, many examples of which still stand.

Settlers also poured into New York City. Between 1790 and 1830, the city gradually transformed itself from one of many important Colonial centers into the largest and wealthiest metropolis in the new republic.

The factors leading to New York's ascendancy were many, but probably the most important was the opening of the Erie Canal in 1825. The hand-dug canal—stretching from the Hudson River to Lake Erie—established a water route to the West, thereby reducing the cost of transporting goods by a whopping 90 percent. Hundreds of thousands of small boats were soon plying the new route, carrying cargo to New York City for transfer onto oceangoing vessels. By 1834, the canal's tolls had more than paid for the entire cost of its $7.7 million construction. New York Harbor became one of the world's busiest ports, with grain elevators and warehouses sprouting up all along the docks.

The Erie Canal was the making of New York. It transformed New York City from one of many important colonial centers into the largest metropolis in the New World, and gave rise to virtually every other major city in the state, including Syracuse, Rochester, and Buffalo.

About the same time, New York established the country's first regularly scheduled transatlantic shipping service. Previously, ships had sailed only when their holds were full. This innovation gave the metropolis a competitive edge for decades to come.

Manhattan's famous grid street system was established in 1811. All of the island that had not yet been settled was scored into 12 major avenues—each 100 feet wide—and 155 consecutively numbered streets. Most of the streets were 60 feet wide, but those that intersected the already established Broadway when it crossed an avenue were 100 feet wide. Later, when the subway system was built, stops were placed along many of the wider streets.

In 1842, New York opened the Croton Aqueduct Water System, then the world's largest water system. The $12 million project dammed the Croton River, 40 miles upstate, and brought water into the city through a series of reservoirs and aqueducts. New York thus became one of the first cities in the world to supply all its citizens—even the poorest—with clean fresh water. As a result, outbreaks of cholera and other epidemic diseases were drastically reduced. Today, New York still has one of the world's best water systems.

SLAVERY AND CIVIL WAR

Slavery had been a fact of life in New York since 1626, when 11 African slaves were brought to New Amsterdam and forced to work as servants and craftspeople. Before the Revolution, New York had the largest number of slaves of any colony north of Maryland. Later, as a state conducting lucrative business with the cotton-growing South, New York often turned its back on the cruelties of the "curious institution." In fact,

New York was one of the last of the Northern states to abolish slavery, only doing so in 1827.

Despite this dismal beginning, New York played a critical role in the antislavery movement before and during the Civil War. Many of the country's most ardent abolitionists—including William Seward, Frederick Douglass, Gerrit Smith, and Martin Van Buren—lived upstate, and the Finger Lakes region was regarded as a hotbed of antislavery sentiment. Gerrit Smith and John Brown established a farm for escaped slaves near Lake Placid in 1849, and Underground Railroad stations dotted the state, especially along the Niagara frontier. When escaped slave William "Jerry" McHenry was arrested by federal marshals in Syracuse in 1851, he was promptly rescued by vigilante abolitionists. That rescue, which challenged the Fugitive Slave Act of 1850, was one of the early precipitating events leading up to the Civil War.

The pre–Civil War years also witnessed the influx of the first of the great waves of immigrants that swept into New York City between the mid-1800s and the 1920s. From 1840 to 1855, over three million Irish and Germans arrived. Many of the Irish were escaping the potato famines; many of the Germans, the failed Revolution of 1848.

When the Civil War began, New York officially supported the Union. But the citizenry remained divided. The city's newest immigrants resented having to fight to free slaves, who might then come north and compete for jobs. In 1863, this deep-rooted discontent led to the Draft Riots, in which 2,000 people were injured or killed.

About 500,000 New Yorkers served in the war, and about 50,000 were killed. The state also contributed much in the way of supplies and weapons.

After the war, the infamous William Marcy "Boss" Tweed rose to power in New York City. A tough street fighter, Tweed was America's first "political boss." He never held mayoral office, but he controlled the city from behind the scenes, through the Democratic machine known as Tammany Hall. During Tweed's corrupt reign, from 1866 to 1871, he and his henchmen pocketed as much as $200 million from padded or fraudulent city expenditures and tax improprieties. Eventually indicted, Tweed died in a Ludlow Street jail not far from his birthplace.

THE LATE 1800S

The Civil War put a temporary dent in New York's economy, but by the 1880s, it was back in full force. Corporations all over the state doubled, tripled, or even quadrupled in size, with a corresponding explosion of activity in commerce, transportation, banking, and, especially, manufacturing fields.

New York City was in its full glory. In 1892, 1,265 millionaires lived either in the city or its suburbs. In 1895, the city housed nearly 300 companies worth over one million dollars—more than the next six largest cities combined. In 1898, New York annexed Brooklyn, Queens, Staten Island, and the Bronx, thereby increasing its area from 23 to 301 square miles.

The rich and the powerful flocked to New York City from all over the country, and the social elite were soon defined as the "Four Hundred"—the maximum number of guests who could squeeze into Mrs. Astor's Fifth Avenue ballroom. Investment bankers such as J. P. Morgan and August Belmont became household names, as did leaders of commerce and industry such as John D. Rockefeller, Andrew Carnegie, and F. W. Woolworth.

New York City became the nation's cultural capital as well. Theaters sprang up along Broadway, and the Metropolitan Museum of Art and the Metropolitan Opera opened their doors in 1880 and 1890, respectively. Walt Whitman sang the city's praises in poems such as "Leaves of Grass" and "Crossing Brooklyn Ferry," and Henry James and Edith Wharton reported on the lives of the upper crust in *Washington Square* and *The Age of Innocence*.

But the years surrounding the turn of the century also had a darker side. Between 1880 and 1919, a new wave of more than 17 million immigrants—this time mainly from Southern and Eastern Europe—swept into New York City. Many settled in the Lower East Side, where they worked miserable, low-paying jobs in the garment industry. Overcrowding became a serious problem; by 1900, more than two-thirds of the city's residents were crowded into some 80,000 tenements in Manhattan and Brooklyn. The Lower East Side had a population density of 209,000 people per square mile, equal to that of today's Bombay.

Immigrants who settled upstate to work the region's many burgeoning factories suffered as well. Often illiterate and unable to speak fluent English, they were subject to exploitation, poor health and housing conditions, pollution, and increasing crime.

The larger the cities grew, the greater became the need for improved transportation. Horsecars gave way to streetcars, and by 1900, nearly every city upstate had a streetcar system.

In 1904, Manhattan opened its first subway, long after London (1863) and shortly after Boston (1897). But New York's subway system would soon be distinguished for both its enormous size and its technological innovations. Within a year after opening, New York's subway—then just a single line running up Park Avenue, across 42nd Street, and up Broadway—was carrying over 600,000 passengers per day. By 1937, the city boasted over 700 miles of track handling 4.2 million passengers per day. Today, the subway system still has about 700 miles of track, but it handles only about 3.5 million passengers a day.

REFORM, DEPRESSION, AND WAR

At the beginning of the 20th century, New York was the most powerful state in the United States. Two-thirds of the nation's leading corporations were headquartered in New York City, and the state as a whole produced one-sixth of the gross national product. Ex–New York governor Theodore Roosevelt had just succeeded President William McKinley—assassinated in Buffalo in 1898—to the White House.

The Progressive Era in politics had begun—to peak about a decade later, following the 1911 Triangle Shirtwaist factory fire that took the lives of 146 workers in Greenwich Village.

Many progressive reforms were propelled through the state legislature by Democrat Al Smith, who later became one of New York's greatest governors. A self-educated man, born poor on the Lower East Side, Smith helped create dozens of monumental labor, safety, education, and housing bills.

After World War I, the United States emerged as a world power, and nowhere was this newfound status more evident than in dazzling New York City. Business and manufacturing flourished. The Jazz Age arrived and the liquor flowed. F. Scott Fitzgerald came to town, and Jimmy Walker was elected mayor. A dandified gentleman with a taste for the good life, Walker spent most of his time visiting nightclubs, sporting halls, and showgirls. Thanks to his late-night carousing, he rarely appeared at City Hall before 3 P.M., if at all. "No civilized man," he once said, "goes to bed the same day he wakes up."

The strict new federal immigration laws of 1921 and 1924 slowed the influx of foreigners into New York to a trickle, but Harlem boomed as black Southerners fleeing poverty took refuge in the city. In 1910, Manhattan was home to about 60,000 blacks; by 1930, that number had tripled. Harlem became the center for African American culture, with the Harlem Renaissance attracting writers and intellectuals such as Langston Hughes and W. E. B. DuBois, and jazz clubs and theaters attracting the likes of Duke Ellington and Chick Webb.

The Great Depression of 1929 hit New York State especially hard. By 1932 industrial production upstate had fallen by one-third, bread lines filled city blocks, and New York City banks shut down and reopened as soup kitchens. Scores of shantytowns called "Hoovervilles" dotted Central Park and other city parks upstate.

Enter Franklin Delano Roosevelt. In 1930, as governor of New York, he devised a five-point program to help the state cope with the economic disaster. In 1932, elected president of the United States, he applied and expanded his New York program into the national New Deal. New Yorkers went back to work on public works projects ranging from transportation to housing. Many were projects envisioned and developed by Robert Moses, the autocratic "master builder" largely responsible for the shape of modern-day New York.

However, like the rest of the nation, New York's greatest boon to post-Depression recovery was World War II. Overnight the state's factories and shipyards thrived anew, producing arms, uniforms, and other items for the war effort.

During the war, Columbia University at 116th Street and Broadway was the site of a nuclear experiment conducted by Dr. Robert Oppenheimer. Code-named the "Manhattan Project," the experiment led to the creation of the world's first atomic bomb, dropped on Japan in August 1945.

POST-WAR DECLINE AND NYC'S RECOVERY

Despite the prosperity brought to New York by World War II, the state reached its economic peak relative to the rest of the country around 1940. Thereafter, certain trends already in effect began to undermine both New York and the entire Northeast. These trends would not become visible for many years, but they were there, slowly eating away.

In 1880, 16 percent of all U.S. production workers lived in the New York Metropolitan Region. By 1900, that figure had fallen to 14 percent, and by 1990, it had fallen to four percent. Between 1956 and 1985, the New York City region lost over 600,000 industrial jobs, while upstate lost hundreds of thousands more. Some companies left the region due to demographic shifts toward the South and West, others due to technological changes that allowed them to decentralize. Still others fled from the rising cost of doing business in New York.

In 1959 Nelson A. Rockefeller was elected governor of New York. An ambitious man with grand visions, Rockefeller greatly expanded the state university system and built Albany's impressive, futuristic Empire State Plaza. By the time Rockefeller left office in 1973, however, the state budget had grown 400 percent from its 1959 level and the state debt had increased 14 times over.

During this same period, New York's once-thriving port also declined. The advent of container ships—which require large dockside cranes for loading—spelled its death. New York's old shipyards simply did not have the space needed to maneuver the cranes.

With these economic shifts came considerable social unrest. Urban race riots and antiwar demonstrations rocked the state. In 1969 the Woodstock Music and Arts Festival drew young people from all over the country to a dairy farm in the Catskills. In 1971 a deadly uprising at Attica prison left 43 inmates and guards dead. Between 1950 and 1970, over one million families left New York City in the "Great White Flight."

On the up side, New York City's cultural scene was thriving. The Guggenheim Museum opened in 1959, followed by Lincoln Center in the mid-'60s. Broadway was producing one great hit after another, including *My Fair Lady* and *West Side Story.* "Culture had become a commodity," wrote historian Harold Syrett, "and New Yorkers were its largest producers. Most other Americans had to be content with being consumers."

Things finally came to a head in New York City in 1975. Cultural attractions aside, the city was all but bankrupt. Banks shut off credit, and the city, in desperation, turned to the federal government for help. The famous *Daily News* headline "Ford to City: Drop Dead" caustically summed up Washington's stony response.

The city was temporarily rescued by the Municipal Assistance Corporation, put together by financier Felix Rohatyn and Gov. Hugh Carey to issue city bonds and thereby borrow money. Washington was impressed enough by this effort to finally extend the city a short-term loan of $2.5 billion.

The city's recovery was further aided in 1978 by the election of Mayor Ed Koch. A one-time liberal from the Bronx via Greenwich Village, Koch helped set the city back on track through budget cuts and austerity programs. Brash, shrewd, and outspoken, Koch managed to play the city's various interest groups off one another to the general public's advantage, winning the respect of many New Yorkers in the process. Much of the '80s construction boom, which included Trump Tower and the World Financial Center, was attributed to his efforts. Unfortunately, so was the city's steadily increasing homeless population.

Upstate, however, the economic picture remained gloomy. More jobs were lost throughout the '70s and again in the early '90s as companies moved from the Northeast to the South and West. Many New Yorkers blamed these industrial losses on the state's steep tax rate—among the highest in the nation—but the truth was, and is, that no amount of tax cuts can make New York the state it once was. The emergence of the Pacific Rim, the shift in the nation's demographics, and the rise of a global economy have irrevocably altered New York's economic position.

THE 21ST CENTURY

At the end of the 1990s, while much of upstate languished, New York City was riding the crest of the bull stock market. Dozens of new businesses, restaurants, bars, and shops were opening up daily, on even the most depressed of blocks. Rents were skyrocketing, while the streets teemed with well-dressed twentysomethings earning salaries their grandparents never even dreamed of.

In addition, New York was—and is—benefiting from the energy and spirit of yet another enormous influx of immigrants. Many had been steadily arriving since the easing of immigration quotas in 1965; others have come since the end of the Cold War, or following political upheaval in their home countries. Some 90,000 documented immigrants enter the city each year; one out of every three New Yorkers is foreign born.

Then came the recession, and the September 11 terrorist attack on the World Trade Center that killed about 2,700 innocent people in a morning that will be forever seared into New York's sense of itself. In a few short moments, the city was plunged into death, devastation, and unspeakable horror.

But even as New Yorkers reeled with grief and fear, they also rose to meet the crisis. In one of the city's finest hours, thousands of citizens quickly pulled themselves together to volunteer their time, donate their money, and keep each others' spirits up, while Mayor Rudy Giuliani became a hero nationwide for his strong leadership. The attacks unified the city—rich and poor, black and white—in a way never before seen in modern times.

Giuliani was unable to run for mayor again in 2001 due to term-limits law and the new Republican Mayor Michael Bloomberg was elected. A billionaire businessman, who many accused of winning the election because of his seemingly limitless coffers, Bloomberg quickly set about dealing with the aftermath of the attacks and reaching out to some of the minority groups that Giuliani shunned. Today, despite painful memories and a still-struggling upstate, New York City is thriving once again.

Upstate Vs. Downstate

How does one encapsulate in one history both upstate and metropolitan New York? Like a massive geological fault, the rivalry between these two sections has ruptured state unity for centuries.
    -David Maldwyn Ellis,
    New York State and City

The antagonism between upstate—a vague term that refers to everything outside New York City—and downstate began as far back as the early 1700s, when upstate farmers and New York City merchants disagreed over taxes and trade regulations. A few decades later, the American Revolution split the regions further when the British captured New York City and held on to it for seven years.

And that was only the beginning. After 1800, the conflict between city and state not only continued but also grew more complex. The more

New York City evolved into an economic and cultural capital, the less regard it seemed to have for the rest of the state. Upstaters, then largely Protestant and native-born, began to eye the metropolis, then largely Catholic and foreign-born, with increasing distrust.

By the late 1800s, the animosity between the two regions had become firmly entrenched. One upstate delegate to the 1894 constitutional convention called New York City "a sewer of ignorance and corruption flowing in... from foreign lands." George Templeton Strong of New York City observed in 1905 that "the feeling between this city and the hayseeds that make a livin' by plunderin' it is every bit as bitter as the feelin' between the North and South before the war."

Much of this animosity has its roots in politics. New York City, predominantly Democratic since 1800, runs counter to upstate New York, which has voted Republican since 1856. Nationally, city dwellers tend to vote Democratic, but upstate New York cities usually cast significantly lower Democratic votes than do most other cities.

Certain recurring issues have divided New York City and State time and again. Among them are representation in the state legislature, allocation of state tax revenues, and state control of the city's finances. The first issue was resolved finally by the Supreme Court in 1964, but the last two—along with countless other, more hidden, agendas—continue to sharply divide the state.

New York City residents claim, with much justification, that they pay far more in taxes than they receive in state aid. Upstate residents claim, also with much justification, that the city's intellectual elites treat them as backcountry fools. Severely aggravating the situation are the regions' markedly different populations. New York City is home to over 80 percent of the state's African Americans and Jews, and to over 90 percent of its Spanish speakers and Asians. Upstate New York is predominantly white.

Government

New York's government is led by an exceptionally strong governor with power over hundreds of appointments, and a legislature comprised of a 61-member Senate and 150-member Assembly. Members of both houses are elected for two-year terms, and each house has standing committees concerned with public policy issues. The governor also appoints nonlegislative commissions to investigate such problems as education aid and welfare administration.

The state's finances are overseen by an independently elected state comptroller.

On a local level, New York is divided into 62 counties that are further subdivided into towns. The towns, which function as townships do elsewhere, contain cities and villages, most governed by a mayor and a council. Larger cities such as New York also have a second legislative body, usually called the Board of Estimate.

ESSENTIALS
Getting There

BY AIR

Most major U.S. airlines and many foreign carriers offer regularly scheduled flights into New York City's La Guardia, John F. Kennedy (JFK), or Newark International airports. Several major U.S. airlines also offer flights to other cities in the state, including Albany, Rochester, and Buffalo. For more details, consult the regional chapters.

Bargain air fares for international travelers are often available. Most are APEX (advance purchase excursion) fares requiring advance purchase, with minimum and maximum stays.

BY TRAIN

Amtrak (800/872-7245) offers service between New York City's Pennsylvania Station and Niagara Falls, with stops in Croton-Harmon, Poughkeepsie, Rhinecliff, Hudson, Albany-Rensselaer, Schenectady, Amsterdam, Utica, Rome, Syracuse, Rochester, and Buffalo. Amtrak also travels between New York City and Montreal, Canada, making stops in Croton-Harmon, Poughkeepsie, Rhinecliff, Hudson, Albany-Rensselaer, Schenectady, Saratoga Springs, Fort Edward-Glens Falls, Whitehall, Ticonderoga, Port Henry, Westport, Port Kent, Plattsburgh, and Rouses Point.

COURTESY OF ORANGE COUNTY TOURISM

Metro-North (212/532-4900 or 800/638-7646), a commuter railroad, offers service between New York City's Grand Central Station and the Hudson Valley region, while the **Long Island Rail Road** (718/217-LIRR or 516/822-LIRR, www.lirr.org) offers service between New York City's Penn Station and Long Island.

BY BUS

Greyhound (800/231-2222, www.greyhound.com) offers regular bus service to major cities and popular tourist destinations throughout the state. **Adirondack-Pine Hill Trailways** (800/225-6815) and **New York Trailways** (800/295-5555) also service major cities, as well as a variety of rural areas; two branches of the same company, their website is www.trailways.com.

Getting Around

Though New York City is best explored by foot, subway, bus, and taxi, upstate New York is best traversed by car. Outside the downstate metropolitan region, public transportation is limited and infrequent.

I-87 is the principal highway running north-south from New York City to Canada. I-90 is the main highway running east-west, from Buffalo to Albany and Massachusetts.

The statewide speed limit for open highway driving is 65 miles per hour. Speed limits for cities, towns, villages, and smaller roads are considerably slower. It is against the law to drive without using seatbelts in the driver's and front passenger's seats. Unless otherwise stated, a right turn on red is permitted almost everywhere except New York City.

If renting a car, try to do so outside Manhattan. Rates are considerably lower at the airports, in the boroughs, and elsewhere in the state. Major car-rental companies operating in New York State include **Avis** (800/331-1212), **Budget** (800/527-0700), **Hertz** (800/654-3131), and **National** (800/328-4567).

Accommodations

CAMPING

Excellent campgrounds are located in most of New York's 200-plus state parks. For $15–25 a night, campers are provided with a tent site, table, fire ring, running water, flush toilets, and hot showers; RV hookups are extra. Some of the campgrounds also offer cabins or lean-tos. Only a handful remain open through the winter.

Some of New York's state-run and private campgrounds are described elsewhere in this book; for a complete list, contact the NYS Division of Tourism (518/474-4116 or 800/CALL-NYS, www.iloveny.com). Make reservations for all state-operated campsites and cabins by calling 800/456-CAMP.

YOUTH HOSTELS AND YMCA'S

The **Hosteling International-American Youth Hostels** organization offers clean and friendly accommodations for people of all ages. A hostel usually consists of dormitory rooms, kitchen, common room, and sometimes several private rooms available for families. Hosteling International–AYH facilities are located in New York City, Buffalo, New Paltz, Syracuse, Niagara Falls, and Cape Vincent. Overnight rates are $15–25 per person.

You must be a member to stay at many AYH hostels. Annual membership fees are adults $28, seniors $18, and youths under 18 free. Membership cards are usually sold on-site or through the AYH national office (8401 Colesville Rd., Suite 600, Silver Springs, MD 20910, 301/495-1240, www.hiayh.org). Reservations at all AYH hostels should be made well in advance.

The **Young Men's Christian Association** offers inexpensive, but not necessarily especially clean, accommodations in New York City, Syracuse, Buffalo, Tarrytown, and other urban areas throughout the state. For information on New York's YMCAs, which are co-ed, contact the YMCA of Greater New York (212/630-9600).

MOTELS AND HOTELS

Motels offering anywhere from 6 to 200 rooms abound throughout New York State. Some are independent operations, others belong to nationwide chains, and they provide an especially good choice for families or anyone looking for affordable accommodations. Among the motel chains operating in New York are **Days Inn of America** (800/325-2525), **Motel 6** (800/466-8356), **Super 8 Motels** (800/800-8000), **Red Roof Inns** (800/733-7663), and **Econo Lodge** (800/553-2666). All will send a free listing of locations and prices upon request.

Choice Hotels (866/446-6900) can help you locate a Quality Inn, Comfort Inn, or Sleep Inn in various locations upstate.

An extraordinary number of hotels, from flea-ridden to ultra-deluxe, are located in New York City. Other large cities, such as Rochester and Buffalo, also offer a good choice of hotels.

BED-AND-BREAKFASTS

B&Bs are a popular lodging option in New York State, especially in the Hudson Valley, Cooperstown, Saratoga Springs, Rochester, Ithaca, and eastern Long Island regions. Many are quite expensive, and cater more to city folk looking for pampering than to budget travelers.

Numerous individual B&Bs, and local registries or reservation services, are described elsewhere in this book. Two B&B associations that operate throughout the state are **Empire State B&B Association** (www.esbba.com), which covers all regions, including New York City, and **American Country Collection of Bed and Breakfasts** (1353 Union St., Schenectady 12308, 518/370-4948 or 800/810-4948, www.bandbreservations.com), which covers the Hudson Valley, Catskills, Adirondacks, and Central New York regions only.

Visas and Officialdom

Most foreign visitors entering the United States are required to carry a current passport, a visitor's visa, and proof they intend to leave (a return airplane ticket is usually enough). It's also wise to carry proof of citizenship, such as a driver's license or birth certificate. Canadian citizens entering New York from Canada need only carry proof of residence.

Since 9/11, obtaining a U.S. visa has become more difficult and the process more lengthy. Apply early to avoid disappointment. Tourist visas are valid for up to six months; special visas are required to work or study in the United States.

To extend your visa for a maximum of six months, contact the nearest Immigration and Naturalization Service office. To replace a passport lost while in the United States, contact your country's nearest embassy; many consulates are located in New York City.

Visitors to the United States do not need inoculations unless they are coming from an area known to be suffering from an epidemic such as cholera or yellow fever. Visitors with medical conditions requiring treatment with narcotics or the use of drug paraphernalia such as syringes must carry a valid, signed physician's prescription.

Tips for Travelers

The **Council on International Educational Exchange** (7 Custom House Street, 3rd Floor, Portland, ME 04101, 207/553-7600 or 800-40-STUDY, www.ciee.org) provides information on low-cost travel and work-study programs in the United States, including New York State. The CIEE also sells the International Student Identity Card, good for travel and entertainment discounts.

Help for disabled travelers is available through the **Society for Accessible Travel and Hospitality** (212/447-7284, www.sath.org), a nationwide, nonprofit membership organization that collects data on travel facilities around the country.

Disabled residents of New York State should apply for the **Access Pass,** which provides free entry to most state parks and recreation areas. For an application, contact New York State Parks (Empire State Plaza, Albany, NY 12238, 518/474-2324, www.nysparks.com).

The **Golden Age Program** provides New York State residents age 62 or older with free entry to state parks and recreation areas any weekday, excluding holidays. Simply present your current driver's license or Non-Driver's Identification Card at the entrance gate.

Similarly, the National Park Service issues Golden Age Passports to people 62 years or older for national historic sites and parks. For more information, visit the National Park Service website (www.nps.gov).

Anyone over age 50 is eligible to join the AARP (601 E St. NW, Washington, D.C. 20049, 202/434-2277 or 888/OUR-AARP, www.aarp.org), which provides its members with hotel, airfare, car-rental, and sightseeing discounts. **Elderhostel** (11 Avenue de Lafayette, Boston, MA 02110, 617/426-7788 or 877/426-8056, www.elderhostel.org) offers educational tour packages in New York City and State for travelers age 60 and older.

Health and Safety

EMERGENCIES AND MEDICAL CARE
Call 911 for any emergency throughout New York State.

Twenty-four-hour healthcare services are available in clinics and hospital emergency rooms throughout much of the state. To make sure service will be readily provided, carry proof of healthcare coverage.

CITY SAFETY
Though drastically reduced in New York City in recent years, crime continues to be an issue in the Big Apple and other New York cities. Wherever you go, stay alert and use common sense. Carry only small amounts of cash; ignore hustlers and con artists; keep a tight hold on your purse and camera; label and lock your

luggage; lock your car; and avoid lonely and unlit stretches, especially after dark.

OUTDOOR SAFETY
Before heading into the forests and semi-wilderness areas of New York State, be sure you know where you're going and what you're doing. Check with park officials and other knowledgeable outdoorspeople about trail conditions, weather, water sources, and fire danger. Be sure your equipment is functioning properly, and don't head out alone. If you're an outdoors novice, accompany someone with more experience.

Basic accoutrements for most day hikes include a small knapsack, hat, sunscreen, lip balm, compass, whistle, insect repellent, multipurpose knife, good hiking boots, layered clothing, food, and an ample water supply. For longer or more demanding hikes, bring a butane lighter or waterproof matches, nylon rope, first-aid kit, "space blanket," extra socks and shoelaces, and a waterproof poncho or large plastic bag.

LYME DISEASE

Anyone who spends much time outdoors in New York should be aware of the symptoms of Lyme disease. The bacterium that causes the disease is carried by the deer tick, which is found in brush, meadows, forests, and even lawns. In early stages, the disease is easily treatable with antibiotics, but if left unattended, it can lead to serious neurological, heart, and joint problems.

Many—*but not all*—of those infected develop a red circular rash around the bite location within three days to one month. The rash usually begins with a small red dot that expands to a diameter of one to five inches. The expanded rash may feature a bright red border and a hard, pale center.

The rash is usually accompanied by flu-like symptoms. These include fatigue, nausea, vomiting, diarrhea, pain in the muscles and joints, stiff neck, swollen lymph glands, headaches, fevers, chills, sore throat, dry cough, dizziness, sensitivity to the sun, and chest, ear, and/or back pain.

Lyme disease was first identified in Old Lyme, Connecticut, in 1975, and quickly spread throughout New England. It's now one of the fastest growing communicable diseases in New York. If you suspect that you have Lyme disease, contact your doctor immediately.

Prevention: Wear light-colored clothing to make it easier to spot ticks, and long pants and long-sleeved shirts to discourage them. Tuck pants cuffs into socks, and use an insect repellent with a 25–30 percent DEET content around clothing openings and on exposed skin.

Use gloves and tweezers to remove ticks; grasp the tick's head parts as close to your skin as possible and apply slow steady traction. Wash both your hands and the bitten area afterward. Do not attempt to remove ticks by burning them or coating them with anything like nail polish remover or petroleum jelly. If you remove a tick before it has been attached for more than 24 hours, you greatly reduce your risk of infection.

Ticks do not jump, but usually crawl upward until they find exposed skin. Among their favorite dining spots are the back of the neck, the scalp, armpits, the groin area, and the backs of knees. Not all bites result in illness.

If you plan to spend much time outdoors in New York State, you may wish to ask your doctor about the newly developed inoculation for Lyme disease.

Information and Services

BUSINESS HOURS AND MONEY

Standard business hours in New York are Monday–Friday 9 A.M.–5 P.M. Banks are usually open Monday–Friday 9 A.M.–3 P.M., with some branches open Saturday 9 A.M.–1 P.M. Many banks offer 24-hour automated teller service.

Most shops are open Monday–Saturday from 9 or 10 A.M. to 5 or 6 P.M. In New York City, Sunday afternoon and evening hours are also common, and many grocery stores and delis remain open 24/7. The state sales tax is 8.25 percent.

With the exception of some inexpensive motels, restaurants, and shops, credit cards are accepted almost everywhere in the state, and are mandatory for renting cars and most sports equipment. The safest way to bring cash is to carry traveler's checks. American Express traveler's checks are the most widely accepted.

MEASUREMENTS, MAIL, AREA CODES

Like the rest of the United States, New York still eschews the metric system. See the U.S.-Metric Conversion Chart in the back of this book. New York lies within the eastern standard time zone. Daylight saving time, which sets the clocks one hour ahead, goes into effect from the first Sunday in April to the last Sunday in October.

Normal post office hours are Monday–Friday 8:30 A.M.–5 P.M., and Saturday 8:30 A.M.–noon. Some post offices are also open late one night a week.

New York State uses an ever-proliferating number of area codes. To obtain a number from directory services, dial 411.

MAPS AND TOURIST INFORMATION

The best source for general information on New York State is the **New York State Division of Tourism** (P.O. Box 2603, Albany 12220, 800/CALL-NYS or 518/474-4116, www.iloveny.com). It publishes a free, 200-page *I Love New York* guide that's updated annually, as well as a wide variety of brochures on specific regions. For an updated calendar of events staged throughout the state, including New York City, call 800/CALL-NYS.

For a free basic guide to New York's 160-odd state parks, including hiking and camping information, contact **New York State Parks** (Empire State Plaza, Albany, NY 12238, 518/474-0456, www.nysparks.com).

Most regions, cities, and towns also staff their own tourism offices and/or visitors centers. Addresses are listed by location elsewhere in this book.

Excellent maps of New York State are published by the **Automobile Association of America.** The AAA maps are available free to members at any local AAA office. For more information about AAA membership and services in New York, contact the American Automobile Association (1415 Kellum Pl., Garden City, NY 11530, 516/746-7730 or 212/586-1166, www.aaany.com).

Rand-McNally and Hagstrom publish excellent street maps of Manhattan and the other New York City boroughs; these are available at most bookstores and many newsstands. The DeLorme Mapping Company publishes two excellent oversize map books: **New York State Atlas & Gazetteer** and **Upstate New York City Street Maps.**

RESOURCES
Suggested Reading

NEW YORK CITY

New York, city of writers, has been the subject of or setting for innumerable essays, biographies, memoirs, histories, guidebooks, poems, and novels. Here are but a few:

Specialty Guides

Federal Writers' Project. *The WPA Guide to New York City.* New York, NY: New Press, 1995. First published in 1939 and since reissued, the classic guidebook remains remarkably on target. It provides long and evocative descriptions of everything from Ebbetts Field to the then-new Empire State Building.

Frank, Gerry. *Gerry Frank's Where to Find It, Buy It, Eat It in New York.* Portland, OR: Gerry's Frankly Speaking, 2003. A monumental, nearly 600-page, reference manual on where to find everything from bridal gowns to massage therapists.

White, Norval, and Elliot Willensky, eds. *AIA Guide to New York City.* Three Rivers, MI: Three Rivers Press, 2000. The most important and entertaining book on New York architecture, organized as a series of walking tours. An urban classic, with over 2,000 photos and 100 maps.

Nonfiction

Caro, Robert A. *The Power Broker: Robert Moses and the Fall of New York.* New York, NY: Vintage, 1975. Much more than a biography, this Pulitzer Prize–winning tome tells the fascinating and often scandalous story behind the shaping of 20th-century New York. Though over 1,000 pages, the book is a compelling page-turner.

Johnson, James Weldon. *Black Manhattan.* New York, NY: Da Capo Press, 1991. First published in 1930, this classic work paints one of the earliest portraits of the lives of African Americans in New York City. Much more than a history, the book also illuminates the Harlem Renaissance, of which Johnson was a part.

Kazin, Alfred. *A Walker in the City.* New York, NY: Harvest/HBJ, 1969. This is the perambulatory memoir of a distinguished literary critic who grew up in immigrant Brownsville. Kazin's sojourns into other neighborhoods and boroughs exposed him to new worlds.

Magnum Photographers, with introduction by David Halberstam. *New York September 11.* New York, NY: powerHouse Books, 2001. A moving tribute to the city, its emergency workers, the World Trade Center, and the victims of the terrorist attack.

Mitchell, Joseph. *Up in the Old Hotel.* New York, NY: Vintage, 1993. A reprint of four classics penned by the deadpan *New Yorker* chronicler of city life. "McSorley's Wonderful Salon," "Old Mr. Flood," "The Bottom of the Harbor," and "Joe Gould's Secret" are included.

Sante, Luc. *Low Life.* New York, NY: Farrar, Straus, and Giroux, 2003. A highly original and literate book that delves into the under-belly—opium dens, brothels, sweatshops—of old New York.

Fiction

Auster, Paul. *The New York Trilogy: City of Glass, Ghosts, the Locked Room.* New York, NY: Penguin Books, 1994. Dark humor, suspense, mind games, and film noir in a modern classic about New York City.

Capote, Truman. *Breakfast at Tiffany's.* New York, NY: Vintage, 1993. The moving story of a glamorous madcap adrift on the Upper East Side in the 1950s.

Ellison, Ralph. *Invisible Man.* New York, NY: Vintage, 1995. The classic 1952 novel follows a nameless protagonist from his home in the Deep South to the basements of Harlem. A masterpiece of African American literature that chronicles the effects of bigotry on victims and perpetrators alike.

Finney, Jack. *Time and Again.* New York, NY: Simon & Schuster, 1970. A cult classic that time-travels back and forth between the present and the 1880s, when New York was little more than an overgrown small town.

Hijuelos, Oscar. *The Mambo Kings Play Songs of Love.* New York, NY: Perennial Classics, 2000. A rich and deeply resonant novel that re-creates the world of immigrant Cuban musicians living in New York post–World War II.

James, Henry. *Washington Square.* New York, NY: Modern Library, 2000. One of James's shorter and more accessible novels, *Washington Square* is an engrossing tale of the manners and mores of upper-crust 19th-century New York.

McInerney, Jay. *Bright Lights, Big City.* New York, NY: Vintage Contemporaries, 1984. A young man immerses himself in the excesses of 1980s New York—the clubs, the drugs, the after-hour hot spots—until brought to an abrupt reckoning.

Paley, Grace. *Enormous Changes at the Last Minute.* New York, NY: Farrar, Straus and Giroux, 1985. Quirky, funny, sad, combative, vulnerable Paley, who grew up in immigrant New York in the '20s and '30s, captures the soul of New York in one of her best collections of stories.

Parker, Dorothy. *The Portable Dorothy Parker.* New York, NY: Penguin Books, 1991. Poems, stories, articles, and reviews by that most quotable of *New Yorker* writers.

Wharton, Edith. *The Age of Innocence.* New York, NY: Modern Library, 1999. The first book written by a woman to win the Pulitzer Prize is a subtle, elegant portrait of desire and betrayal in moneyed Old New York. Among Wharton's other books set in the city are *The House of Mirth, A Backward Glance,* and *Old New York.*

Poetry

Among the many poets who have written extensively on New York City are Djuna Barnes, Hart Crane, Allen Ginsberg, Langston Hughes, Frank O'Hara and Walt Whitman.

NEW YORK STATE

A number of excellent regional presses, publishing everything from history to fiction, are located upstate. Foremost among them are the **Black Dome Press** (RR1, Box 422, Hensonville 12439; 518/734-6357, www.black-domepress.com) and **Purple Mountain Press** (P.O. Box E-3, Fleischmanns 12430; 845/254-4062, www.catskill.net/purple/), both in the Catskills; and **Heart of the Lakes Publishing** (P.O. Box 299, Interlaken 14847; 607/532-4997, www.hlpbooks.com) in the Finger Lakes. Their books are generally available in local bookstores.

Outdoor Guides

McMartin, Barbara. *50 Hikes in the Adirondacks.* Woodstock, VT: Countryman Press, 2003. The doyenne of New York's outdoor writers and an authority on the Adirondacks outlines the region's top trails. Detailed maps are included.

New York–New Jersey Trail Conference, Inc. *New York Walk Book*. Mahwah, NJ: New York-New Jersey Trail Conference, 2001. This updated "hiker's Bible" reflects the many changes that have occurred in the region since the book was first published in 1923. Some of the old trails are gone, of course, but a surprising number of new areas have also opened up, thanks largely to the public acquisition of land. The book also features excellent sections on the history, geology, flora, and fauna of the regions immediately surrounding New York City.

Wadsworth, Bruce. *An Adirondack Sampler: Day Hikes for All Seasons*. Lake George, NY: Adirondack Mountain Club, 1988. An excellent guide for beginning hikers and those new to the Adirondacks. Fifty hikes are recommended.

Fiction and Memoir

Banks, Russell. *The Sweet Hereafter*. New York, NY: Perennial, 1992. A horrific school-bus accident in Sam Dent, NY, results in the deaths of 14 children. Banks writes compassionately of how the small town responds and somehow moves beyond grief to redemption.

Dobyns, Stephen. *Saratoga Haunting*. New York, NY: Viking Press, 1993. Low-key detective Charlie Bradshaw, operating in the summer horse-racing capital of America, reopens two cases he thought he had solved 20 years earlier. The seventh of poet Dobyns's Charlie Bradshaw books; all are set in Saratoga.

Dreiser, Theodore. *An American Tragedy*. New York, NY: Signet Classics, 2000. The classic book on the dark side of the American Dream, set largely in the Adirondacks and Central New York.

Fitzgerald, F. Scott. *The Great Gatsby*. New York, NY: Scribner, 1995. One of the finest works of 20th-century literature takes place largely on the north shore of Long Island.

Gardner, John. *The Sunlight Dialogues*. New York, NY: Random House, 1972. A grand and complex portrait of America in the '60s, set in the small, agricultural town of Batavia, New York.

Irving, Washington. *Rip Van Winkle and the Legend of Sleepy Hollow*. Tarrytown, NY: Sleepy Hollow Press, 1980. The first American literary writer of note tells the tales of the Headless Horseman galloping through Sleepy Hollow and Rip Van Winkle awakening from his 20-year sleep.

Kennedy, William. *Billy Phelan's Greatest Game*. New York, NY: Penguin Books, 1982. The second, and arguably best, of Kennedy's triumvirate of novels set in underworld Albany chronicles the fall and redemption of a small-time hustler. The other two books in the cycle are *Legs* and *Ironweed*.

Oates, Joyce Carol. *Bellefleur*. New York, NY: Plume Books, 1991. The complex and opulent tale of six generations of Bellefleurs, a wealthy and notorious family who live in a region much like the Adirondacks. Other Oates novels set upstate are *A Bloodsmoor Romance* and *Mysteries of Winterthurn*.

Wilson, Edmund. *Upstate: Records and Recollections of Northern New York*. Syracuse, NY: Syracuse University Press, 1990. One of the rare books that examines the character of upstate New York, where Wilson and his family summered for generations. The first third of the book, covering various aspects of New York history, is especially astute; the rest is diary entries.

Zabor, Rafi. *The Bear Comes Home*. New York, NY: W.W. Norton, 1998. In this winner of the PEN–Faulkner Award, an intellectual sax-playing bear, well versed in literature, jazz and philosophy, fights to find his place in the world. A comic gem, with great insights into what it means to be an artist, set largely in New York City and Woodstock/Bearsville, New York.

Internet Resources

FIRST STOP

The Official New York State Tourism Website
www.iloveny.com

This official site is packed with information on all regions of the state. Recreational areas, accommodations listings, "travel ideas," road maps, and state facts—they're all here.

RECREATION AND THE OUTDOORS

New York State Office of Parks, Recreation and Historic Preservation
www.nysparks.com

Each state park and historic site has its own extensive page on this informative site. Search by region or by activity.

New York State Department of Environmental Conservation
www.dec.state.ny.us

This site should be the first stop for information on hiking, canoeing, camping, and other outdoor activities in the Adirondacks and Catskills. News articles on environmental issues and special events listings are also included.

Adirondack Mountain Club
www.adk.org

This can be your second stop for more detailed information on outdoor activities in the Adirondacks. All topics from camping and hiking to educational seminars are covered; books, maps, and gear can be ordered from the site.

America's Byways
www.byways.org

This is a U.S. Department of Transportation site that offers descriptions and maps of New York's most scenic back roads. Three byways are highlighted; a total of 14 routes are included.

NEW YORK CITY

NYC & Company
www.nycvisit.com

At the official website of New York City's convention and visitors bureau, you can book a hotel, learn about attractions and special events, check the weather, search out the perfect restaurant, and create your own itinerary. An excellent first stop for Big Apple visitors.

Citysearch: New York City Guide
www.citysearch.com or http://newyork.citysearch.com

Citysearch provides online information about entertainment, events, hotels, and attractions in New York City. Recommendations, reviews, and a "yellow pages" listing are included.

UPSTATE NEW YORK

Fun on Long Island
www.funonli.com

Run by the Long Island Convention and Visitors Bureau and Sports Commission, this site covers cultural attractions, recreation, golf courses, restaurants, shopping malls, and more. Information on hotels and special events is also included.

Hudson Valley Tourism
www.travelhudsonvalley.com

This official tourism site provides information on the ten counties that line the Hudson River, from Westchester County in the south to Albany County in the north. Category listings include accommodations, antiques, art, dining, the outdoors, and tours.

Travel the Hudson Valley
www.enjoyhv.com

Sponsored by the Poughkeepsie Journal, a newspaper published in Dutchess County, this site nonetheless covers the entire region. Here, you'll find interesting articles about the

Hudson Valley, along with information on attractions, lodging, shopping, dining, and nightspots.

Catskill Region Today
www.catskillregiontoday.com

This official tourism site covers the four counties of the Catskills. Category listings include the outdoors, historic sites, antique and craft shops, "spiritual journeys," lodging, and special events.

Welcome to Albany, N.Y.
www.albany.org

Visitors to Albany might want to check out this official tourism site. A link will take you to "hot deals," where you can find out about travel bargains throughout the state.

Saratoga County
Chamber of Commerce
www.saratoga.org

Here you'll find information on where to stay, where to eat, and where to play in the horse racing capital of New York, as well as a special kids section and calendar of special events.

Adirondacks Mountain Region
www.adk.com

To help plan your trip to the North Country, visit this site run by the Adirondacks Regional Tourism Council. A "trip planner" feature can assist you in setting up a personalized itinerary.

Thousand Islands International
Tourism Council
www.visit1000islands.com

Everything you wanted to know about the Thousand Islands, from where to stay or play golf to "1000 Things to Do." The "community profiles" section offers details about each town and its attractions.

Cooperstown, N.Y. Visitors Guide
www.visitcooperstown.com

Although this site concentrates on Cooperstown, home to the National Baseball Hall of Fame, it also does a good job of covering other parts of the region. Information on everything from hotels and restaurants to attractions and special events is included.

New York's Finger Lakes
www.fingerlakes.org

Visitors to the Finger Lakes will want to check out this site, run by the Finger Lakes Tourism Alliance. In addition to information on attractions, lodging, and restaurants, the site also recommends special-interest itineraries concentrating on subjects such as nature, art, and history.

The Greater Rochester
Visitors Association
www.visitrochester.com

Rochester hotel, airline, and auto rental reservations can all be made through this site, which is also packed with information on the city's attractions.

VisitIthaca.com
www.visitithaca.com

At this comprehensive site, run by the Ithaca/Tompkins County Convention and Visitors Bureau, you'll find information on lodging, dining, attractions, and recreation. Maps and driving directions are included.

Visit Buffalo Niagara
www.visitbuffaloniagara.com

Run by the Buffalo Niagara Convention and Visitors Bureau, this site covers attractions, hotels, restaurants, etc., in Western New York's two biggest cities. Information on regional driving tours and special packages is also included.

Index

CHILDREN'S ATTRACTIONS

SCENIC DRIVES

MAP SYMBOLS

═══════ Expressway	○ City/Town	✈ Airport
═══════ Primary Road	⊛ National Capital	▲ Mountain
═══════ Secondary Road	⬡ Highway Shield	🗞 Waterfall
--------- Unpaved Road	Ⓜ Metro Stop	⬗ Park
--------- Trail	★ Point of Interest	⯅ Church
▓▓▓▓▓▓ Pedestrian Walkway	• Accommodation	⬛ Gas Station
▪▪▪▪▪▪▪ Stairs	▾ Restaurant/Bar	✛ Unique Natural Feature
★ • ▾ ▪ Mexico City's Best	▪ Other Location	▰ Archaeological Site

CONVERSION TABLES

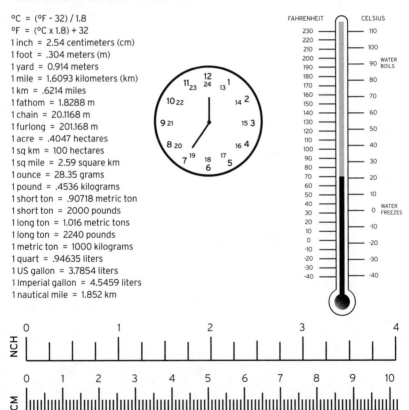

°C = (°F − 32) / 1.8
°F = (°C × 1.8) + 32
1 inch = 2.54 centimeters (cm)
1 foot = .304 meters (m)
1 yard = 0.914 meters
1 mile = 1.6093 kilometers (km)
1 km = .6214 miles
1 fathom = 1.8288 m
1 chain = 20.1168 m
1 furlong = 201.168 m
1 acre = .4047 hectares
1 sq km = 100 hectares
1 sq mile = 2.59 square km
1 ounce = 28.35 grams
1 pound = .4536 kilograms
1 short ton = .90718 metric ton
1 short ton = 2000 pounds
1 long ton = 1.016 metric tons
1 long ton = 2240 pounds
1 metric ton = 1000 kilograms
1 quart = .94635 liters
1 US gallon = 3.7854 liters
1 Imperial gallon = 4.5459 liters
1 nautical mile = 1.852 km

FAHRENHEIT CELSIUS
230 110
220
210 100
200
190 90 WATER BOILS
180 80
170
160 70
150
140 60
130
120 50
110 40
100
90 30
80
70 20
60
50 10
40
30 0 WATER FREEZES
20
10 -10
0
-10 -20
-20 -30
-30
-40 -40

www.moon.com

For helpful advice on planning a trip, visit www.moon.com for the **TRAVEL PLANNER** and get access to useful travel strategies and valuable information about great places to visit. When you travel with Moon, expect an experience that is uncommon and truly unique.

MOON NEW YORK STATE

Avalon Travel Publishing
An Imprint of
Avalon Publishing Group, Inc.

AVALON
publishing group incorporated

1400 65th Street, Suite 250
Emeryville, CA 94608, USA
www.moon.com

Editor: Elizabeth McCue
Series Manager: Kathryn Ettinger
Acquisitions Manager: Rebecca K. Browning
Copy Editor: Chris Hayhurst
Graphics Coordinator: Tabitha Lahr
Production Coordinator: Elizabeth Jang
Cover & Interior Designer: Gerilyn Attebery
Map Editor: Kevin Anglin
Cartographers: Kat Bennett, Chris Markiewicz,
   Suzanne Service, Mike Morgenfeld
Indexer: Judy Hunt

ISBN-10: 1-56691-796-4
ISBN-13: 978-1-56691-796-4
ISSN: 1542-6068

Printing History
1st Edition –1997
4th Edition – May 2006
5 4 3 2 1

Front cover photo: Adirondacks New York Blue Mountain Lake, © Andre Jenny/Alamy

Title page photo: Hawk's Nest, courtesy of Orange County Tourism

Page 4 photo: Tabitha Lahr

Page 5 photo: © Christiane Bird

Page 6 photo: courtesy of Finger Lakes Wine Country Tourism Marketing Association

Page 7 photo: Tabitha Lahr

Page 8 photo: courtesy of Finger Lakes Wine Country Tourism Marketing Association

Printed in Canada by Transcontinental

KEEPING CURRENT

If you have a favorite gem you'd like to see included in the next edition, or see anything that needs updating, clarification, or correction, please drop us a line. Send your comments via email to feedback@moon.com, or use the address above.